Math Expressions

Teacher Edition • Volume 1

Developed by
The Children's Math Worlds Research Project

PROJECT DIRECTOR AND AUTHOR
Dr. Karen C. Fuson

 This material is based upon work supported by the
National Science Foundation
under Grant Numbers
ESI-9816320, REC-9806020, and RED-935373.

Any opinions, findings, and conclusions, or recommendations expressed in this material
are those of the author and do not necessarily reflect the views of the National Science Foundation.

 HOUGHTON MIFFLIN HARCOURT

Teacher Reviewers

Kindergarten

Patricia Stroh Sugiyama
Wilmette, Illinois

Barbara Wahle
Evanston, Illinois

Grade 1

Sandra Budson
Newton, Massachusetts

Janet Pecci
Chicago, Illinois

Megan Rees
Chicago, Illinois

Grade 2

Molly Dunn
Danvers, Massachusetts

Agnes Lesnick
Hillside, Illinois

Rita Soto
Chicago, Illinois

Grade 3

Jane Curran
Honesdale, Pennsylvania

Sandra Tucker
Chicago, Illinois

Grade 4

Sara Stoneberg Llibre
Chicago, Illinois

Sheri Roedel
Chicago, Illinois

Grade 5

Todd Atler
Chicago, Illinois

Leah Barry
Norfolk, Massachusetts

Special Thanks

Special thanks to the many teachers, students, parents, principals, writers, researchers, and work-study students who participated in the Children's Math Worlds Research Project over the years.

Credits

© Kerstin Layer/Age Fotostock

Illustrative art: Robin Boyer/Deborah Wolfe, LTD; Dave Clegg, Geoff Smith, John Kurtz, Tim Johnson
Technical art: Nesbitt Graphics, Inc.
Photos: Nesbitt Graphics, Inc.; Page 93 © C Squared Studios/Photodisc/Getty Images; Page 455 © Nick Green/Jupiterimages

Introducing

Math
Expressions

Quick Practice
Helping Building Concepts
Community
Building Concepts
Student Leaders
Math Talk

1 2 3 4 5
6 7 8 9 10

60
6 0

3 + 3 =
3 + 3 = 6
3 + 4 =
3 + 4 = 7
3 + 5 = 8
3 + 6 =

A Fresh Approach to

Math Expressions is a comprehensive Kindergarten–Grade 5 mathematics curriculum that offers new ways to teach and learn mathematics. Combining the most powerful

Standards-Based Instruction

elements of standards-based instruction with the best of traditional approaches, *Math Expressions* uses objects, drawings, conceptual language, and real-world situations to help students build mathematical ideas that make sense to them.

Math Expressions implements state standards as well as the recommendations and findings from recent reports on math learning:

Curriculum Focal Points (NCTM, 2007)

Principles and Standards for School Mathematics (NCTM, 2000)

Adding It Up (National Research Council, 2001)

How Students Learn Mathematics in the Classroom (National Research Council, 2005)

Focused on Understanding

In **Math Expressions,** teachers create an inquiry environment and encourage constructive discussion. Students invent, question, and explore, but also learn

and Fluency

and practice important math strategies. Through daily Math Talk students explain their methods and, in turn, become more fluent in them.

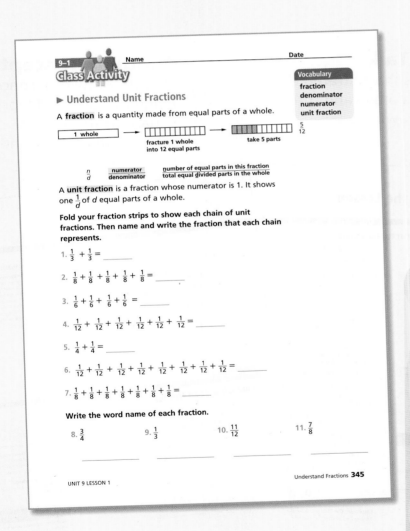

9–1

Class Activity

Name _____   Date _____

Vocabulary
fraction
denominator
numerator
unit fraction

► **Understand Unit Fractions**

A **fraction** is a quantity made from equal parts of a whole.

| 1 whole | → | fracture 1 whole into 12 equal parts | → | take 5 parts | $\frac{5}{12}$ |

$\frac{n}{d}$ numerator   number of equal parts in this fraction
denominator   total equal divided parts in the whole

A **unit fraction** is a fraction whose numerator is 1. It shows one $\frac{1}{d}$ of d equal parts of a whole.

Fold your fraction strips to show each chain of unit fractions. Then name and write the fraction that each chain represents.

1. $\frac{1}{3} + \frac{1}{3} =$ _____

2. $\frac{1}{8} + \frac{1}{8} + \frac{1}{8} + \frac{1}{8} + \frac{1}{8} =$ _____

3. $\frac{1}{6} + \frac{1}{6} + \frac{1}{6} + \frac{1}{6} =$ _____

4. $\frac{1}{12} + \frac{1}{12} + \frac{1}{12} + \frac{1}{12} + \frac{1}{12} + \frac{1}{12} =$ _____

5. $\frac{1}{4} + \frac{1}{4} =$ _____

6. $\frac{1}{12} + \frac{1}{12} + \frac{1}{12} + \frac{1}{12} + \frac{1}{12} + \frac{1}{12} + \frac{1}{12} + \frac{1}{12} =$ _____

7. $\frac{1}{8} + \frac{1}{8} + \frac{1}{8} + \frac{1}{8} + \frac{1}{8} + \frac{1}{8} + \frac{1}{8} =$ _____

Write the word name of each fraction.

8. $\frac{3}{4}$ 9. $\frac{1}{3}$ 10. $\frac{11}{12}$ 11. $\frac{7}{8}$

_____   _____   _____

UNIT 9 LESSON 1   Understand Fractions **345**

"As students are asked to communicate about the mathematics they are studying ... they gain insights into their thinking to others, students naturally reflect on their learning and organize and consolidate their thinking about mathematics."

- Principles and Standards for School Mathematics, National Council of Teachers of Mathematics (2000), p. 12

Math Expressions

Organized for

Math Expressions is organized around five crucial classroom structures that allow children to develop deep conceptual

Quick Practice
Routines involve whole-class responses or individual partner practice.

Math Talk
Students share strategies and solutions orally and through proof drawings.

Building Concepts
Objects, drawings, conceptual language, and real-world situations strengthen mathematical ideas and understanding.

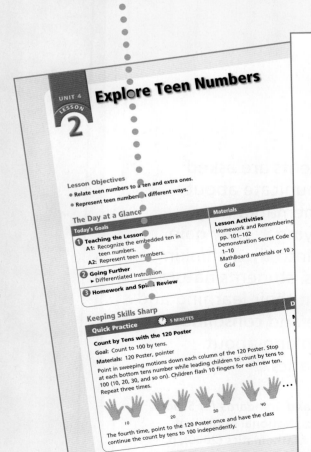

Classroom Success

understanding, and then practice, apply, and discuss
what they know with skill and confidence.

Helping Community

A classroom in which everyone is both
a teacher and a learner enhances
mathematical understanding,
competence, and confidence.

Student Leaders

Teachers facilitate students' growth by
helping them learn to lead practice and
discussion routines.

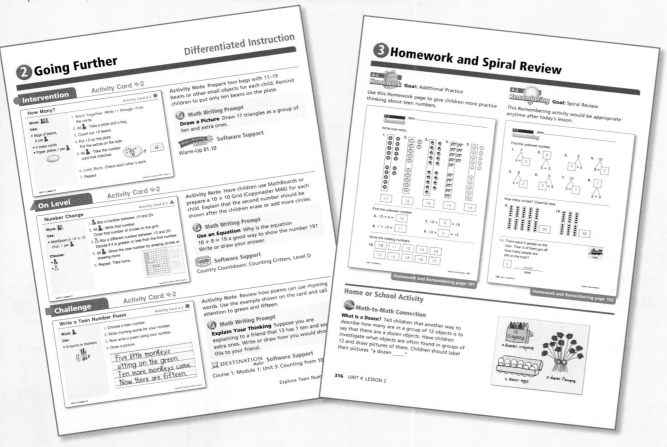

Differentiated for

Every **Math Expressions** lesson includes intervention, on level, and challenge differentiation to support classroom needs. Leveled Math Writing Prompts provide opportunities for in–depth thinking and analysis, and help prepare students for high-stakes tests.

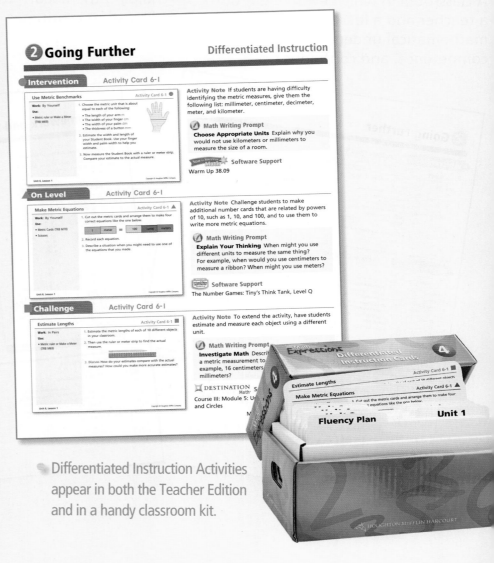

Differentiated Instruction Activities appear in both the Teacher Edition and in a handy classroom kit.

> "Activities and strategies should be developed and incorporated into instructional materials to assist teachers in helping all students become proficient in mathematics."
>
> - *Adding It Up: Helping Children Learn Mathematics*, National Research Council (2001), p. 421

All Learners

Support for English Language Learners is included in each lesson. A special Math Center Challenge Easel with activities, projects, and puzzlers helps the highest math achievers reach their potential.

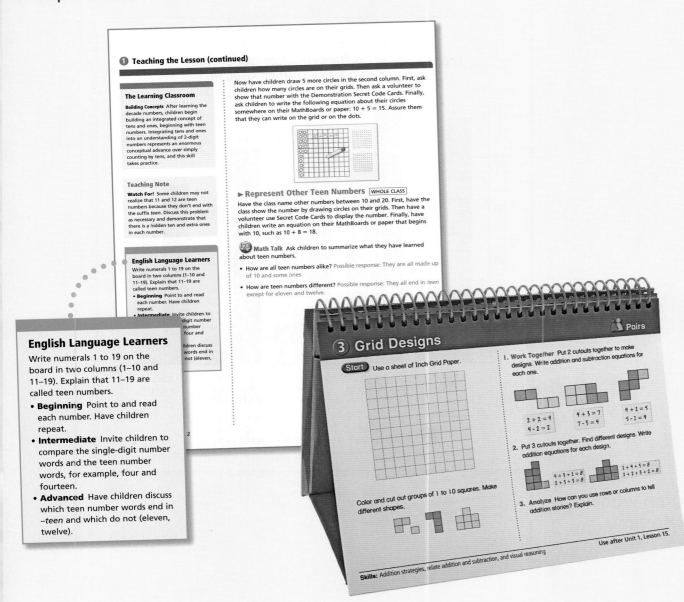

English Language Learners

Write numerals 1 to 19 on the board in two columns (1–10 and 11–19). Explain that 11–19 are called teen numbers.

- **Beginning** Point to and read each number. Have children repeat.
- **Intermediate** Invite children to compare the single-digit number words and the teen number words, for example, four and fourteen.
- **Advanced** Have children discuss which teen number words end in –*teen* and which do not (eleven, twelve).

Validated Through Ten

For twenty-five years, Dr. Karen Fuson, Professor Emeritus of Education and Psychology at Northwestern University, researched effective methods of teaching and learning mathematics.

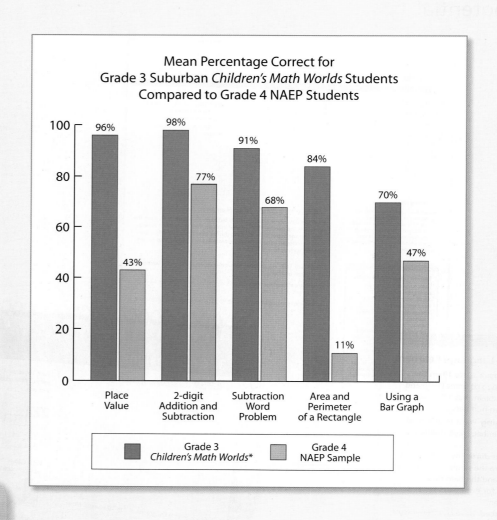

Mean Percentage Correct for
Grade 3 Suburban *Children's Math Worlds* Students
Compared to Grade 4 NAEP Students

"I have many children who cheer when it's math time."
- Grade 2 Teacher

Years of Research

During the last ten years, with the support of the National Science Foundation for the Children's Math Worlds research Project, Dr. Fuson began development of what is now the *Math Expressions* curriculum in real classrooms across the country.

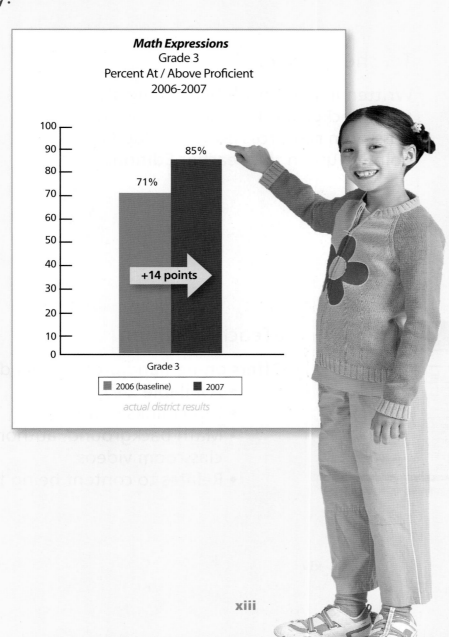

Math Expressions
Grade 3
Percent At / Above Proficient
2006-2007

71%

85%

+14 points

Grade 3

■ 2006 (baseline)   ■ 2007

actual district results

HOUGHTON MIFFLIN HARCOURT
Math Expressions

Powered by

Math Expressions is highly accessible by all teachers. To ensure the program gets off to the right start, our educational consultants are available to support districts implementing *Math Expressions.* Unique Teacher Edition support and professional development options are also provided.

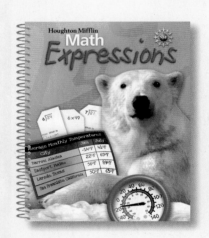

Teacher Edition

Written in a learn while teaching style, math background and learning in the classroom resources are embedded at point of use in the Teacher Edition.

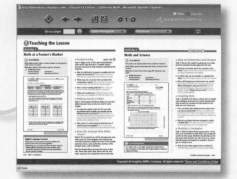

eTeacher Edition

Offers on-demand professional development

- Available 24/7
- Direct links in the eTE
- Math background, author talks, and classroom videos
- Relates to content being taught

Professional Development

Special in depth *Math Expressions* seminars
are also available.

- **Administrator Institute**
  For administrators with school-based
  curriculum responsibilities

- **Level I Institute**
  For teachers who are new to
  Math Expressions

- **Level II Institute**
  For teachers who have at least 6
  months' experience teaching
  Math Expressions

Components

New Hardcover Version Grades 3–5

	K	1	2	3	4	5
Core Components						
Teacher Edition	•	•	•	•	•	•
Student Activity Book*	•	•	•	•	•	•
Homework and Remembering	•	•	•	•	•	•
Assessment Guide	•	•	•	•	•	•
Teacher's Resource Book	•	•	•	•	•	•
MathBoards		•	•	•	•	•
Ready-Made Classroom Resources						
Individual Student Manipulatives Kit	•	•	•	•	•	•
Materials and Manipulatives Kit	•	•	•	•	•	•
Custom Manipulatives Kit	•	•	•	•	•	•
Math Center Challenge Easel	•	•	•	•	•	•
Differentiated Instruction Activities Kit	•	•	•	•	•	•
Literature Library	•	•	•	•	•	•
Anno's Counting Book Big Book	•					
Technology						
eTeacher Edition	•	•	•	•	•	•
eStudent Activity Book	•	•	•	•	•	•
Lesson Planner CD-ROM	•	•	•	•	•	•
ExamView Ways to Assess	•	•	•	•	•	•
Houghton Mifflin Harcourt Online Assessment System	•	•	•	•	•	•
MegaMath	•	•	•	•	•	•
Destination Math®	•	•	•	•	•	•
Soar to Success Math		•	•	•	•	•
Education Place	•	•	•	•	•	•

*Grades K–5 available as consumable workbook; Grades 3–5 available as Hardcover book with companion Activity Workbook.

Materials and Manipulatives for Grade 3

The essential materials needed for teaching *Math Expressions* are provided in the Student Activity Book and/or can be made from copymasters in the Teacher's Resource Book. However, many teachers prefer to use the more sturdy materials from the materials and manipulatives kits. This allows the students to take home the paper materials (from the Student Activity Book) or the cardstock materials (made from the copymasters) to facilitate the connection between home and school.

Material or Manipulative in Grade 3	Pages in Student Activity Book	Copymasters in Teacher's Resource Book
Demonstration Secret Code Cards*		M3–M18
Secret Code Cards*	8A–8D	M19–M22
Strategy Cards*	244A–244Z	M63–M88
120 Poster*		M60
Time Poster*		
Geometry and Measurement Poster*		
Class Multiplication Table Poster*		M50
Pointer		
Inch/Centimeter Ruler		M26
Play Coins (pennies, nickels, dimes, and quarters)		M40
Play Bills (1-dollar, 5-dollar, 10-dollar)		
2-Color Counters		
Connecting Cubes		
Number Cubes		
Base Ten Blocks		
Pattern Blocks		M27
3-D Shapes		
MathBoards		M1, M39

 * These materials were developed specifically for this program under the leadership of Dr. Karen C. Fuson, director of the Children's Math Worlds Research Project and author of *Math Expressions*.

Using Materials and Manipulatives for Each Unit

Material or Manipulative in Grade 3 Kit	Unit													
	1	2	3	4	5	6	7	8	9	10	11	12	13	14
Demonstration Secret Code Cards	●				●									
Secret Code Cards	●				●									
Strategy Cards							●		●					
120 Poster							●							
Time Poster										●				
Geometry and Measurement Poster														
Class Multiplication Table Poster							●		●					
Pointer	●	●	●	●	●	●	●	●	●	●	●	●	●	●
Inch/Centimeter Ruler		●		●				●					●	
Play Coins (pennies, nickels, dimes, and quarters)	●				●		●				●			
Play Bills (1-dollar, 5-dollar, 10-dollar)	●				●						●			
Two-Color Counters	●		●			●	●		●		●			●
Connecting Cubes					●		●		●		●	●		
Number Cubes	●		●		●				●			●		●
Base Ten Blocks	●				●		●					●	●	
Pattern Blocks		●		●		●					●			
3-D Shapes												●		
MathBoards	●	●	●	●	●		●	●	●		●		●	

All materials for each unit (including those not in the kits) are listed in the planning chart for that unit.

Introduction

History and Development

Math Expressions is a K–5 mathematics program, developed from the Children's Math Worlds (CMW) Research Project conducted by Dr. Karen Fuson, Professor Emeritus at Northwestern University. This project was funded in part by the National Science Foundation.

The Research Project

The project studied the ways children around the world understand mathematical concepts, approach problem solving, and learn to do computation; it included ten years of classroom research and incorporated the ideas of participating students and teachers into the developing curriculum.

The research focused on building conceptual supports that include special language, drawings, manipulatives, and classroom communication methods that facilitate mathematical competence.

Curriculum Design

Within the curriculum, a series of learning progressions reflect recent research regarding children's natural stages when mastering concepts such as addition, subtraction, multiplication, and problem solving. These learning stages help determine the order of concepts, the sequence of units, and the positioning of topics.

The curriculum is designed to help teachers apply the most effective conceptual supports so that each child progresses as rapidly as possible.

During the research, students showed increases in standardized test scores as well as in broader measures of student understanding. These results were found for a wide range of both urban and suburban students from a variety of socio-economic groups.

Philosophy

Math Expressions incorporates the best practices of both traditional and reform mathematics curricula. The program strikes a balance between promoting children's natural solution methods and introducing effective procedures.

Building on Children's Knowledge

Because research has demonstrated that premature instruction in formalized procedures can lead to mechanical, unthinking behavior, established procedures for solving problems are not introduced until students have developed a solid conceptual foundation. Children begin by using their own knowledge to solve problems and then are introduced to research-based accessible methods.

In order to promote children's natural solution methods, as well as to encourage students to become reflective and resourceful problem solvers, teachers need to develop a helping and explaining culture in their classrooms.

Student Interactions

Collaboration and peer helping deepen children's commitment to values such as responsibility and respect for others. *Math Expressions* offers opportunities for students to interact in pairs, small groups, whole-class activities, and special scenarios.

As students collaboratively investigate math situations, they develop communication skills, sharpen their mathematical reasoning, and enhance their social awareness. Integrating students' social and cultural worlds into their emerging math worlds helps them to find their own voices and to connect real-world experiences to math concepts.

Main Concept Streams

Math Expressions focuses on crucially important core concepts. These core topics are placed at grade levels that enable students to do well on standardized tests. The main related concept streams at all grade levels are number concepts and an algebraic approach to word problems.

Breaking apart numbers, or finding the embedded numbers, is a key concept running through the number concept units.

- Kindergartners and first-graders find the numbers embedded within single-digit numbers and find the tens and ones in multi-digit numbers.

- Second- and third-graders continue breaking apart multi-digit numbers into ones and groups of tens, hundreds, and thousands. This activity facilitates their understanding of multi-digit addition and subtraction as well as solving word problems.

- Second-, third-, and fourth-graders work on seeing the repeated groups within numbers, and this awareness helps them to master multiplication and division.

- Fourth- and fifth-graders approach fractions as sums of unit fractions using length models. This permits them to see and comprehend operations on fractions.

Students work with story problems early in kindergarten and continue throughout the other grades. They not only solve but also construct word problems. As a result, they become comfortable and flexible with mathematical language and can connect concepts and terminology with meaningful referents from their own lives. As part of this process, students learn to make math drawings that enable teachers to see student thinking and facilitate communication.

Concepts and skills in algebra, geometry, measurement, and graphing are woven in between these two main streams throughout the grades. In grades two through five, geometry and measurement mini-units follow each regular unit.

Program Features

Many special features and approaches contribute to the effectiveness of *Math Expressions.*

Quick Practice

The opening 5 minutes of each math period are dedicated to activities (often student-led) that allow students to practice newly acquired knowledge. These *consolidating activities* help students to become faster and more accurate with the concepts. Occasionally, *leading activities* prepare the ground for new concepts before they are introduced. Quick Practice activities are repeated so that they become familiar routines that students can do quickly and confidently.

Drawn Models

Special manipulatives are used at key points. However, students move toward math drawings as rapidly as possible.

These drawn models help students relate to the math situation, facilitate students' explanations of the steps they took to solve the problem, and help listeners comprehend these explanations.

The drawings also give teachers insight into students' mathematical thinking, and leave a durable record of student work.

Language Development

Math Expressions offers a wealth of learning activities that directly support language development. In addition to verbalizing procedures and explanations, students are encouraged to write their own problems and describe their problem-solving strategies in writing as soon as they are able.

Homework Assignments

To help students achieve a high level of mathematical performance, students complete homework assignments every night. Families are expected to identify a homework helper to be responsible for monitoring the student's homework completion and to help if necessary.

Remembering Activities

Remembering Activities provide practice with the important concepts covered in all the units to date. They are ideal for spare classroom moments when students need a quick refresher of what they have learned so far. These pages are also valuable as extra homework pages that promote cumulative review as an ongoing synthesis of concepts.

Student Leaders

Student Leaders lead Quick Practice activities and can help as needed during the solving phase of Solve and Discuss. Such experiences build independence and confidence.

Math Talk

A significant part of the collaborative classroom culture is the frequent exchange of mathematical ideas and problem-solving strategies, or Math Talk. There are multiple benefits of Math Talk:

- Describing one's methods to another person can clarify one's own thinking as well as clarify the matter for others.

- Another person's approach can supply a new perspective, and frequent exposure to different approaches tends to engender flexible thinking.

- In the collaborative Math Talk classroom, students can ask for and receive help, and errors can be identified, discussed, and corrected.

- Student math drawings accompany early explanations in all domains, so that all students can understand and participate in the discussion.

- Math Talk permits teachers to assess students' understanding on an ongoing basis. It encourages students to develop their language skills, both in math and in everyday English.

- Math Talk enables students to become active helpers and questioners, creating student-to-student talk that stimulates engagement and community.

The key supports for Math Talk are the various participant structures, or ways of organizing class members as they interact. The teacher always guides the activity to help students to work both as a community and also independently. Descriptions of the most common participant structures follow.

Math Talk Participant Structures

Solve and Discuss (Solve, Explain, Question, and Justify) at the Board

The teacher selects 4 to 5 students (or as many as space allows) to go to the classroom board and solve a problem, using any method they choose. Their classmates work on the same problem at their desks. Then the teacher picks 2 or 3 students to explain their methods. Students at their desks are encouraged to ask questions and to assist their classmates in understanding.

> Benefits: Board work reveals multiple methods of solving a problem, making comparisons possible and communicating to students that different methods are acceptable. The teacher can select methods to highlight in subsequent discussions. Spontaneous helping occurs frequently by students working next to each other at the board. Time is used efficiently because everyone in the class is working. In addition, errors can be identified in a supportive way and corrected and understood by students.

Student Pairs

Two students work together to solve a problem, to explain a solution method to each other, to role play within a mathematical situation (for example, buying and selling), to play a math game, or to help a partner having difficulties. They are called helping pairs when more advanced students are matched with students who are struggling. Pairs may be organized formally, or they may occur spontaneously as help is needed. Initially, it is useful to model pair activities, contrasting effective and ineffective helping.

> Benefits: Pair work supports students in learning from each other, particularly in applying and practicing concepts introduced

Math Talk (continued)

Student Pairs (continued)

applying and practicing concepts introduced in whole-class discussion. Helping pairs often foster learning by both students as the helper strives to adopt the perspective of the novice. Helping almost always enables the helper to understand more deeply.

Whole-Class Practice and Student Leaders

This structure can be either teacher-led or student-led. When students lead it, it is usually at the consolidation stage, when children understand the concept and are beginning to achieve speed and automaticity. It is an excellent way for students to work together and learn from each other.

> **Benefits:** Whole-class practice lets the less advanced students benefit from the knowledge of the more advanced students without having to ask for help directly. It also provides the teacher with a quick and easy means of assessing the progress of the class as a whole.

Scenarios

The main purpose of scenarios is to demonstrate mathematical relationships in a visual and memorable way. In scenario-based activities, a group of students is called to the front of the classroom to act out a particular situation. Scenarios are useful when a new concept is being introduced for the first time. They are especially valuable for demonstrating the physical reality that underlies such math concepts as embedded numbers (break-aparts) and regrouping.

> **Benefits:** Because of its active and dramatic nature, the scenario structure often fosters a sense of intense involvement among children. In addition, scenarios create meaningful contexts in which students can reason about numbers and relate math to their everyday lives.

Step-by-Step at the Board

This is a variation of the Solve and Discuss structure. Again, several children go to the board to solve a problem. This time, however, a different student performs each step of the problem, describing the step before everyone does it. Everyone else at the board and at their desks carries out that step. This approach is particularly useful in learning multi-digit addition, subtraction, multiplication, and division. It assists the least-advanced students the most, providing them with accessible, systematic methods.

> **Benefits:** This structure is especially effective when students are having trouble solving certain kinds of problems. The step-by-step structure allows students to grasp a method more easily than doing the whole method at once. It also helps students learn to verbalize their methods more clearly, as they can focus on describing just their own step.

Small Groups

Unstructured groups can form spontaneously if physical arrangements allow (for example, desks arranged in groups of four or children working at tables). Spontaneous helping between and among students as they work on problems individually can be encouraged.

For more structured projects, assign students to specific groups. It is usually a good idea to include a range of students and to have a strong reader in each group. Explain the problem or project and guide the groups as necessary. When students have finished, call a pair from each group to present and explain the results of their work or have the entire group present the results, with each member explaining one part of the solution or project. Having lower-performing students present first allows them to contribute, while higher-performing students expand on their efforts and give the fuller presentation.

> **Benefits:** Students learn different strategies from each other for approaching a problem or task. They are invested in their classmates' learning because the presentation will be on behalf of the whole group.

Volume 1 Contents

Basic Facts Fluency Plan Basic Additions and Subtractions

Big Idea Basic Addition and Subtraction Strategies

1 Basic Additions and Subtractions

ACTIVITIES: Review Addition Strategies • Review Subtraction Strategies

Unit 1 Place Value and Multi-Digit Addition and Subtraction

Big Idea Understand Place Value

ACTIVITIES: Represent Hundreds, Tens, and Ones • Practice Place Value Drawings for Hundreds, Tens, and Ones • Conceptualize and Represent 1,000

GOING FURTHER: Math Connection: Compare Numbers

 FAMILY LETTER

ACTIVITIES: Model Place Value with Secret Code Cards • Use Secret Code Cards • Draw Money Amounts

GOING FURTHER: Extension: Place Value through Ten Thousands

3 🌐 REAL WORLD Problem Solving

ACTIVITIES: Analyze Numbers • Solve Place Value Word Problems

ACTIVITIES: Scrambled Places • Place Value Word Problems • Extend Addition Strategies to Tens and Hundreds

✓ **Quick Quiz 1**

for Lessons 1, 2, 3, 4

Volume 1 Contents (Continued)

Unit 4   Figures, Angles, and Triangles

Unit 5   Use Addition and Subtraction

Overview 291A

Big Idea Complex Word Problems

Big Idea Pictographs, Bar Graphs, and Line Plots

Unit 6 Patterns

Unit 7 Multiplication and Division with 0–5, 9, and 10

Big Idea Meanings of Multiplication and Division

Big Idea Patterns and Strategies

Big Idea   Strategies for Products and Factors

Volume 2 Contents

MINI UNIT — Unit 8   Area and Perimeter

Big Idea   Area and Perimeter

Unit 9   Multiplication and Division with 6, 7, and 8 and Problem Solving

Big Idea   The Remaining Multiplications

Big Idea | Multiplication Comparisons and Square Numbers

Big Idea | Word Problems

🌐 REAL WORLD Problem Solving

Unit 10 Time

Unit 11 Exploring Fractions, Decimals, Probability, and Division with Remainders

Big Idea **Mixed Numbers and Division with Remainders**

REAL WORLD Problem Solving

MINI UNIT

Unit 12 Three-Dimensional Figures

Big Idea **Properties of Three-Dimensional Figures**

Unit 14 **Directions and Locations**

Big Idea **Name and Plot Points on Coordinate Grids**

 **Quick Quiz**
for Lessons 1, 2, 3

Extension Lessons

Pacing Guide

Unit 1 is designed as a review of topics from Grade 2 but extends multi-digit addition and subtraction to larger numbers. Unit 11 builds strong conceptual development and skill fluency at a level often seen in the curricula of other countries that rank high in math performance. In the first year many classes may not cover all of the content of the later unit(s). But as more students experience *Math Expressions* in the previous grade(s) and teachers become familiar with *Math Expressions*, movement through the earlier units is more rapid and

classes are able to do more of the later material in greater depth. Some lessons in every unit, but especially the geometry and measurement mini-units, can be omitted if they do not focus on important state or district goals.

Be sure to do the Quick Practice activities with student leaders that begin each lesson, as they provide needed practice on core grade-level skills as well as supporting the growth of students as they lead these activities.

Unit	First Year — Pacing Suggestions	Days	Later Years — Pacing Suggestions	Days
1	Elicit student ideas and build community. Develop place value and grouping concepts. Mastery can build throughout Units 3 and 5, so move along quickly.	25	Many ideas are review for students who had Grade 2 *Math Expressions.* Move as quickly as you can while eliciting student ideas and building community.	17
2	Be sure that students understand these ideas.	9	These are central Grade 3 ideas.	7
3	The multi-digit word problems will be challenging. Unit 5 will continue to develop understanding, so continue on without mastery.	16	The multi-digit word problems will be challenging. Unit 3 will continue to develop understanding, so continue on without mastery.	12
4	Be sure that students understand these ideas.	7	These are central Grade 3 ideas.	6
5	Two-step word problems are difficult for some. Continue on and build fluency in multi-digit addition and subtraction.	28	Continue to move more quickly as fluency in multi-digit addition and subtraction builds.	20
6	Teach only important district and state goals.	3	Teach only important district and state goals.	4
7	Spend time on patterns, word problem situations, and building fluency in multiplication and division. Most ideas will continue into Unit 9.	26	Move more quickly than in Year 1. In Unit 6, target word problems and basic multiplication and division fluency for individual students.	18
8	Area and perimeter are key Grade 3 topics.	6	Area and perimeter are key Grade 3 topics.	4
9	Fluency with 6s, 7s, and 8s can continue to build all year. Two-step word problems will remain difficult for some. All students should be mastering single-step (but not multi-step) word problems with all 4 operations.	26	Fluency with all numbers can build in Units 6 and 7 where basic multiplication and division are used, so go on. All students should be mastering single-step (but not multi-step) problems with all 4 operations.	21
10	Unit 10 extends the skills in telling time that students developed in Grade 2.	4	Do only important district and state goals.	4
11	Lessons 1 through 5 are a nice introduction. The ideas in this unit will be built in depth in Grade 4.	5	This unit provides experiences to support earlier ideas and will provide a strong basis for Grade 4 fractions.	20
12	Teach the important goals and content of the lessons.	2	This unit is good for building students' spatial visualization.	6
13	Concentrate on important district and state goals. Lessons 7 and 8 continue Unit 11 fraction ideas.	2	Concentrate on important district and state goals. Lessons 7 and 8 continue Unit 11 fraction ideas.	11
14	Maps and directions relate to other subject areas.	1	Explore coordinate graphing if these are part of your state goals.	4
All Units	**Total Days**	**160**	**Total Days**	**154**

Correlation to NCTM Curriculum Focal Points and Connections for Grade 3

Grade 3 Curriculum Focal Points	

1 *Number and Operations* and *Algebra*: Developing understandings of multiplication and division and strategies for basic multiplication facts and related division facts
Students understand the meanings of multiplication and division of whole numbers through the use of representations (e.g., equal-sized groups, arrays, area models, and equal "jumps" on number lines for multiplication, and successive subtraction, partitioning, and sharing for division). They use properties of addition and multiplication (e.g., commutativity, associativity, and the distributive property) to multiply whole numbers and apply increasingly sophisticated strategies based on these properties to solve multiplication and division problems involving basic facts. By comparing a variety of solution strategies, students relate multiplication and division as inverse operations.

1.1 understand multiplication of whole numbers through the use of equal-sized groups	U7 L1–3; U9 L3–5
1.2 understand multiplication of whole numbers through the use of arrays	U7 L3, L7, L8, L12, L13; U9 L3–5, L11, L14; Extension L2
1.3 understand multiplication of whole numbers through the use of area models	U7 L10, L12; U9 L1, L3, L4, L8, L11; Extension L4, L5, L7
1.4 understand multiplication of whole numbers through the use of equal "jumps" on number lines	U7 L1, L5; U7 L5
1.5 understand division of whole numbers through the use of successive subtraction	Extension L11
1.6 understand division of whole numbers through the use of sharing	U7 L4; U11 L20
1.7 use properties of multiplication (e.g., commutativity, associativity) to multiply whole numbers	U7 L3, L9, L12, L14
1.8 use the distributive property to multiply whole numbers	U7 L7; U9 L3, L5, L9; Extension L4–8
1.9 solve multiplication and division problems involving basic facts	U7 L5, L8, L11, L15, L16; U9 L2, L6, L7, L10–13; U11 L19; U13 L6, L11
1.10 relate multiplication and division as inverse operations	U7 L4–7, L9, L12–14; U9 L1, L3, L5; U11 L21; Extension L9

2 *Number and Operations*: Developing an understanding of fractions and fraction equivalence
Students develop an understanding of the meanings and uses of fractions to represent parts of a whole, parts of a set, or points or distances on a number line. They understand that the size of a fractional part is relative to the size of the whole, and they use fractions to represent numbers that are equal to, less than, or greater than 1. They solve problems that involve comparing and ordering fractions by using models, benchmark fractions, or common numerators or denominators. They understand and use models, including the number line, to identify equivalent fractions.

2.1 understand fractions as parts of a whole	U11 L1, L7, L10, L22
2.2 understand fractions as parts of a set	U11 L2, L3, L6, L8, L22
2.3 understand fractions as points or distances on a number line	U11 L16, L18

2.4 understand that the size of a fractional part is relative to the size of the whole	U11 L1, L17
2.5 use fractions to represent numbers that are equal to, less than, or greater than 1	U11 L1–5, L7, L9–16, L18; U13 L7
2.6 compare and order fractions by using models	U11 L15, L16
2.7 compare and order fractions by using benchmark fractions	U11 L16
2.8 compare and order fractions by using common numerators or denominators	U11 L15
2.9 use models, including the number line, to identify equivalent fractions	U11 L9–13

3 *Geometry:* Describing and analyzing properties of two-dimensional shapes

Students describe, analyze, compare, and classify two-dimensional shapes by their sides and angles and connect these attributes to definitions of shapes. Students investigate, describe, and reason about decomposing, combining, and transforming polygons to make other polygons. Through building, drawing, and analyzing two-dimensional shapes, students understand attributes and properties of two-dimensional space and the use of those attributes and properties in solving problems, including applications involving congruence and symmetry.

3.1 describe, analyze, compare, and classify two-dimensional shapes by their sides and angles	U2 L2–5; U4 L1, L3; U13 L11; U14 L3
3.2 connect attributes to definitions of shapes	U2 L2–5; U4 L1, L3; U12 L1, L3–5; U14 L3
3.3 decompose polygons to make other polygons	U2 L3, L4
3.4 combine polygons to make other polygons	U2 L3; U4 L1, L3; U11 L22
3.5 transform polygons to make other polygons	U6 L1
3.6 use attributes and properties to solve problems, including applications involving congruence and symmetry	U4 L1, L2; U5 L18; U11 L22

Connections to the Focal Points

**4 *Algebra:* ** Understanding properties of multiplication and the relationship between multiplication and division is a part of algebra readiness that develops at grade 3. The creation and analysis of patterns and relationships involving multiplication and division should occur at this grade level. Students build a foundation for later understanding of functional relationships by describing relationships in context with such statements as, "The number of legs is 4 times the number of chairs."

4.1 understand properties of multiplication	U7 L3, L7, L9, L12, L14; U9 L1, L3, L5; Extension L4–8
4.2 understand the relationship between multiplication and division	U7 L4–9, L12, L14; U9 L1, L3, L5; Extension L9
4.3 create and analyze patterns and relationships involving multiplication	U7 L1, L2, L5–9, L11, L12, L14; U9 L1, L3, L5, L8, L9

Correlation to NCTM Curriculum Focal Points and Connections for Grade 3 (cont.)

Connections to the Focal Points (cont.)	
4.4 create and analyze patterns and relationships involving division	U7 L5–7, L9, L12, L14; U9 L1, L3, L5
4.5 describe relationships in context	U7 L1, L2, L12; U9 L6, L7

5 Measurement: Students in grade 3 strengthen their understanding of fractions as they confront problems in linear measurement that call for more precision than the whole unit allowed them in their work in grade 2. They develop their facility in measuring with fractional parts of linear units. Students develop measurement concepts and skills through experiences in analyzing attributes and properties of two-dimensional objects. They form an understanding of perimeter as a measurable attribute and select appropriate units, strategies, and tools to solve problems involving perimeter.

5.1 measure with fractional parts of linear units	U13 L1, L2, L4, L11
5.2 develop measurement concepts and skills by analyzing attributes and properties of two-dimensional objects	U2 L1, L3–5; U4 L3, L4; U8 L1–3; U9 L14
5.3 understand perimeter as a measurable attribute	U2 L1, L3, L4; U8 L1–3; U13 L2
5.4 select appropriate units, strategies, and tools to solve problems involving perimeter	U2 L1, L3, L4; U8 L1–3; U13 L2

6 Data Analysis: Addition, subtraction, multiplication, and division of whole numbers come into play as students construct and analyze frequency tables, bar graphs, picture graphs, and line plots and use them to solve problems.

6.1 construct and analyze frequency tables and use them to solve problems	U5 L9, L10, L17, L18
6.2 construct and analyze bar graphs and use them to solve problems	U5 L15–L18; U9 L7, L14; U13 L11
6.3 construct and analyze picture graphs and use them to solve problems	U5 L17
6.4 construct and analyze line plots and use them to solve problems	U5 L17

7 Number and Operations: Building on their work in grade 2, students extend their understanding of place value to numbers up to 10,000 in various contexts. Students also apply this understanding to the task of representing numbers in different equivalent forms (e.g., expanded notation). They develop their understanding of numbers by building their facility with mental computation (addition and subtraction in special cases, such as 2,500 + 6,000 and 9,000 − 5,000), by using computational estimation, and by performing paper-and-pencil computations.

7.1 understand place value of numbers up to 10,000	U1 L1–4; U5 L1–3; Extension L1
7.2 represent numbers in different equivalent forms (e.g., expanded notation)	U1 L1–4; Extension L1
7.3 use mental math to add and subtract	U1 L8, L11, L13, L15; U5 L7
7.4 use estimation to add and subtract	U5 L1, L2, L7, L18
7.5 use paper-and-pencil to add and subtract	U1 L5–15; U3 L6–8; U5 L8–10; U13 L3

Measurement Standard	
Understand measurable attributes of objects and the units, systems, and processes of measurement	
• understand such attributes as length, area, weight, volume, and size of angle and select the appropriate type of unit for measuring each attribute;	Unit 2, Lesson 1–Lesson 4; Unit 4, Lesson 1; Lesson 2; Lesson 4; Unit 7, Lesson 10; Unit 8, Lesson 1–Lesson 3; Unit 9, Lesson 2; Lesson 4; Lesson 8; Unit 10, Lesson 1–Lesson 3; Unit 12, Lesson 5; Unit 13, Lesson 1; Lesson 3–Lesson 6; Lesson 9; Unit 14, Lesson 1; Lesson 3
• understand the need for measuring with standard units and become familiar with standard units in the customary and metric systems;	Unit 2, Lesson I; Unit 13, Lesson 1–Lesson 3; Lesson 5–Lesson 6; Lesson 9–Lesson 10; Unit 10, Lesson 1–Lesson 3
• carry out simple unit conversions, such as from centimeters to meters, within a system of measurement;	Unit 13, Lesson 2–Lesson 3; Lesson 5–Lesson 9
• understand that measurements are approximations and how differences in units affect precision;	Unit 2, Lesson 1; Unit 13, Lesson 1; Lesson 4
• explore what happens to measurements of a two-dimensional shape such as its perimeter and area when the shape is changed in some way.	Unit 2, Lesson 4; Unit 8, Lesson 1; Lesson 2
Apply appropriate techniques, tools, and formulas to determine measurements	
• develop strategies for estimating the perimeters, areas, and volumes of irregular shapes;	Unit 8, Lesson 1; Unit 12, Lesson 5
• select and apply appropriate standard units and tools to measure length, area, volume, weight, time, temperature, and the size of angles;	Unit 2, Lesson 1–Lesson 4; Unit 4, Lesson 2; Lesson 3; Unit 8, Lesson 1–Lesson 3; Unit 10, Lesson 1–Lesson 3; Unit 12, Lesson 5; Unit 13, Lesson 1–Lesson 5; Lesson 9–Lesson 10; Unit 14, Lesson 1–Lesson 3
• select and use benchmarks to estimate measurements;	Unit 13, Lesson 2–Lesson 3; Lesson 5; Lesson 9–Lesson 10
• develop, understand, and use formulas to find the area of rectangles and related triangles and parallelograms;	Unit 8, Lesson 2; Lesson 3
• develop strategies to determine the surface areas and volumes of rectangular solids.	Unit 12, Lesson 2

NCTM Standards and Expectations Correlation for Grade 3 (cont.)

Data Analysis and Probability Standard	
Formulate questions that can be addressed with data and collect, organize, and display relevant data to answer them	
• design investigations to address a question and consider how data-collection methods affect the nature of the data set;	Unit 5, Lesson 15; Lesson 17
• collect data using observations, surveys, and experiments;	Unit 5, Lesson 10; Lesson 15; Lesson 17
• represent data using tables and graphs such as line plots, bar graphs, and line graphs;	Unit 5, Lesson 8–Lesson 10; Lesson 15; Lesson 16; Lesson 17; Unit 7, Lesson 5
• recognize the differences in representing categorical and numerical data.	Unit 5, Lesson 17; Unit 11, Lesson 8
Select and use appropriate statistical methods to analyze data	
• describe the shape and important features of a set of data and compare related data sets, with an emphasis on how the data are distributed;	Unit 5, Lesson 10; Lesson 15; Lesson 17
• use measures of center, focusing on the median, and understand what each does and does not indicate about the data set;	Unit 5, Lesson 17
• compare different representations of the same data and evaluate how well each representation shows important aspects of the data.	Unit 5, Lesson 16–Lesson 17
Develop and evaluate inferences and predictions that are based on data	
• propose and justify conclusions and predictions that are based on data and design studies to further investigate the conclusions or predictions.	Unit 5, Lesson 15–Lesson 17; Unit 7, Lesson 5; Unit 9, Lesson 7; Unit 11, Lesson 3–Lesson 5; Lesson 7; Lesson 8
Understand and apply basic concepts of probability	
• describe events as likely or unlikely and discuss the degree of likelihood using such words as *certain, equally likely,* and *impossible*;	Unit 11, Lesson 8
• predict the probability of outcomes of simple experiments and test the predictions;	Unit 11, Lesson 8
• understand that the measure of the likelihood of an event can be represented by a number from 0 to 1.	Unit 11, Lesson 8

Problem Solving Standard	
• build new mathematical knowledge through problem solving;	Unit 1, Lesson 5; Lesson 10; Unit 3, Lesson 3–Lesson 4; Unit 5, Lesson 4–Lesson 6; Lesson 10; Lesson 13–Lesson 14; Lesson 17; Unit 7, Lesson 3–Lesson 4; Lesson 10; Lesson 12; Unit 9, Lesson 2; Lesson 6–Lesson 7; Lesson 10–Lesson 11; Lesson 14; Unit 11, Lesson 3; Lesson 6; Lesson 11; Lesson 14–Lesson 15; Lesson 17–Lesson 20; Unit 13, Lesson 5
• solve problems that arise in mathematics and in other contexts;	Unit 1, Lesson 3–Lesson 7; Lesson 10–Lesson 15; Unit 3, Lesson 1–Lesson 8; Unit 5, Lesson 4–Lesson 7; Lesson 9–Lesson 15; Unit 7, Lesson 1; Lesson 3–Lesson 6; Lesson 8; Lesson 10–Lesson 11; Unit 9, Lesson 2; Lesson 4; Lesson 6–Lesson 7; Lesson 10–Lesson 14; Unit 11, Lesson 3; Lesson 5–Lesson 6; Lesson 11–Lesson 13; Unit 13, Lesson 6–Lesson 7
• apply and adapt a variety of appropriate strategies to solve problems;	Unit 1, Lesson 3–Lesson 7; Lesson 10–Lesson 15; Unit 3, Lesson 1; Unit 5, Lesson 4–Lesson 7; Lesson 9–Lesson 15; Lesson 17; Unit 7, Lesson 1; Lesson 3–Lesson 4; Lesson 6; Lesson 8; Lesson 10–Lesson 12; Lesson 16; Unit 9, Lesson 4; Lesson 6–Lesson 7; Lesson 10–Lesson 14; Unit 11, Lesson 3; Lesson 5–Lesson 6; Lesson 11–Lesson 15; Lesson 17–Lesson 20
• monitor and reflect on the process of mathematical problem solving.	Unit 1, Lesson 3–Lesson 7; Lesson 10–Lesson 15; Unit 3, Lesson 1–Lesson 8; Unit 5, Lesson 4–Lesson 7; Lesson 9–Lesson 15; Unit 7, Lesson 3–Lesson 4; Lesson 6; Lesson 10–Lesson 11; Lesson 16; Unit 9, Lesson 3; Lesson 6; Lesson 7; Lesson 10–Lesson 14; Unit 11, Lesson 3; Lesson 5–Lesson 6; Lesson 11–Lesson 15; Lesson 17–Lesson 20; Unit 13, Lesson 5–Lesson 7

Reasoning and Proof Standard	
• recognize reasoning and proof as fundamental aspects of mathematics;	Unit 5, Lesson 1–Lesson 2; Lesson 9; Unit 9, Lesson 10
• make and investigate mathematical conjectures;	Unit 4, Lesson 1–Lesson 3; Unit 5, Lesson 1–Lesson 2; Unit 6, Lesson 2, Lesson 3; Lesson 5; Lesson 10; Unit 13, Lesson 5; Lesson 7
• develop and evaluate mathematical arguments and proofs;	Unit 5, Lesson 1–Lesson 2; Unit 6, Lesson 3; Lesson 5; Lesson 10; Unit 13, Lesson 5; Lesson 7
• select and use various types of reasoning and methods of proof.	Unit 3, Lesson 7; Unit 5, Lesson 1–Lesson 2; Lesson 9, Unit 6, Lesson 3; Lesson 4; Lesson 10–Lesson 11; Lesson 13–Lesson 14; Unit 9, Lesson 10; Unit 13, Lesson 5; Lesson 7

NCTM Standards and Expectations Correlation for Grade 3 (cont.)

Communication Standard	
• organize and consolidate their mathematical thinking through communication;	Unit 1, Lesson 3–Lesson 4; Unit 3, Lesson 1–Lesson 5; Unit 4, Lesson 4; Lesson 6; Lesson 12–Lesson 15; Unit 5, Lesson 3–Lesson 6; Lesson 8–Lesson 12; Lesson 15–Lesson 16; Unit 7, Lesson 11; Unit 9, Lesson 10; Unit 11, Lesson 15–Lesson 16; Unit 13, Lesson 1–Lesson 4; Lesson 9–Lesson 10
• communicate their mathematical thinking coherently and clearly to peers, teachers, and others;	Unit 1, Lesson 3–Lesson 4; Unit 3, Lesson 1–Lesson 5; Unit 4, Lesson 4; Lesson 6; Lesson 12–Lesson 15; Unit 5, Lesson 4–Lesson 6; Lesson 8–Lesson 9; Lesson 11–Lesson 12; Lesson 14; Lesson 16; Unit 7, Lesson 11; Lesson 13; Lesson 16; Unit 9, Lesson 6; Lesson 10; Unit 11, Lesson 15–Lesson 16; Unit 13, Lesson 1–Lesson 4; Lesson 9–Lesson 10
• analyze and evaluate the mathematical thinking and strategies of others;	Unit 1, Lesson 3–Lesson 4; Lesson 6; Lesson 12–Lesson 15; Unit 3, Lesson 1–Lesson 5; Unit 5, Lesson 4–Lesson 5; Lesson 8–Lesson 12; Lesson 14; Lesson 16; Unit 7, Lesson 11; Lesson 13; Lesson 16; Unit 9, Lesson 10; Unit 11, Lesson 16; Unit 13, Lesson 1–Lesson 4; Lesson 9–Lesson 10
• use the language of mathematics to express mathematical ideas precisely.	Unit 1, Lesson 3–Lesson 4; Lesson 6; Lesson 12–Lesson 15; Unit 2, Lesson 5; Unit 3, Lesson 1–Lesson 5; Unit 5, Lesson 3–Lesson 6; Lesson 8–Lesson 12; Lesson 16; Unit 7, Lesson 11; Lesson 16; Unit 9, Lesson 10; Unit 11, Lesson 15–Lesson 16; Unit 13, Lesson 1–Lesson 4; Lesson 9–Lesson 10

Connections Standard	
• recognize and use connections among mathematical ideas;	Unit 4, Lesson 1; Lesson 3; Lesson 4; Unit 5, Lesson 4; Lesson 10; Lesson 12; Lesson 14; Unit 7, Lesson 12–Lesson 13; Unit 8, Lesson 1–Lesson 3; Unit 9, Lesson 10; Lesson 14; Unit 10, Lesson 1–Lesson 3; Unit 12, Lesson 1–Lesson 5; Unit 14, Lesson 2
• understand how mathematical ideas interconnect and build on one another to produce a coherent whole;	Unit 5, Lesson 4; Lesson 10; Lesson 12; Lesson 14; Unit 7, Lesson 12–Lesson 13; Unit 9, Lesson 10; Lesson 14
• recognize and apply mathematics in contexts outside of mathematics.	Unit 1, Lesson 2–Lesson 3; Lesson 6–Lesson 15; Unit 3, Lesson 2–Lesson 8; Unit 5, Lesson 2–Lesson 11; Lesson 13–Lesson 16; Unit 7, Lesson 2; Lesson 4; Lesson 6; Lesson 8–Lesson 13; Lesson 15–Lesson 16; Unit 9, Lesson 2–Lesson 13; Unit 10, Lesson 1–Lesson 3; Unit 11, Lesson 2–Lesson 7; Lesson 9–Lesson 21; Unit 12, Lesson 2; Unit 13, Lesson 1–Lesson 10; Unit 14, Lesson 2

Representation Standard	
• create and use representations to organize, record, and communicate mathematical ideas;	Unit 1, Lesson 1–Lesson 4; Unit 2, Lesson 2; Lesson 4; Unit 3, Lesson 6–Lesson 8; Unit 4, Lesson 2; Unit 5, Lesson 4; Lesson 7; Lesson 10–Lesson 11; Lesson 14; Lesson 16; Unit 6, Lesson 1; Unit 7, Lesson 1–Lesson 5; Lesson 7–Lesson 8; Lesson 16; Unit 9, Lesson 1–Lesson 3; Lesson 5–Lesson 8; Lesson 11; Lesson 13; Unit 10, Lesson 2; Unit 11, Lesson 1–Lesson 7; Lesson 9–Lesson 17; Unit 12, Lesson 2–Lesson 4; Unit 13, Lesson 1–Lesson 4; Lesson 10; Unit 14, Lesson 1–Lesson 3
• select, apply, and translate among mathematical representations to solve problems;	Unit 1, Lesson 3–Lesson 5; Unit 3, Lesson 6–Lesson 8; Unit 5, Lesson 4; Lesson 7; Lesson 10–Lesson 11; Lesson 16; Unit 7, Lesson 1–Lesson 5; Lesson 7–Lesson 8; Lesson 16; Unit 9, Lesson 1; Lesson 3; Lesson 5–Lesson 8; Lesson 11; Unit 10, Lesson 2; Unit 11, Lesson 1–Lesson 7; Lesson 9–Lesson 17
• use representations to model and interpret physical, social, and mathematical phenomena.	Unit 3, Lesson 6–Lesson 8; Unit 5, Lesson 4; Lesson 7; Lesson 10–Lesson 11; Lesson 14; Unit 7, Lesson 1–Lesson 5; Lesson 7–Lesson 8; Lesson 16; Unit 9, Lesson 1–Lesson 3; Lesson 5–Lesson 8; Lesson 11; Unit 11, Lesson 1–Lesson 7; Lesson 9–Lesson 17; Unit 13, Lesson 1–Lesson 4; Lesson 10

Basic Facts Fluency Plan

As a Grade 3 teacher, you are aware that entering students vary widely in their knowledge of and fluency with addition and subtraction facts. It is important to ensure all students are fluent with addition and subtraction facts so that extra time is not needed in later lessons that build upon basic facts fluency.

Meeting the Needs of All Students

Before you begin Unit 1, use the Fluency Lesson to help you determine the fluency level of all students. The students will fall into three categories: those who have achieved fluency, those who need to learn strategies, and those who need practice.

Addition Checkup
Activity 1

Entering third graders should do well on the addition checkup, but if they do not, there are different ways to meet the needs of your students.

Teaching Addition Strategies
Activity 1

For those students who are struggling with basic addition facts, Activity 1 includes a comprehensive review of basic addition strategies that students have learned in earlier grades.

Counting on By Ones to Add

Students use their fingers, drawings, and mental math to find the answers.

Make a Ten to Add

Students add up to find the answer.

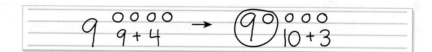

Practicing Addition Facts Have students create a Study Plan listing those basic addition facts that they need to practice.

Achieving Fluency For those students that know their addition facts but have not achieved fluency, an important strategy for addition, Make a Ten, is reviewed in Unit 1.

Unit 1

Use these lessons and activities for addition practice to help achieve fluency:
Lesson 4, Activity 3
Lesson 5, 6, 7, and 8, Quick Practice

Subtraction Checkup
Activity 2

Entering third graders should do well on the subtraction checkup, but if they do not, there are different ways to meet the needs of your students.

Teaching Subtraction Strategies
Activity 2

For those students who are struggling with subtraction facts, Activity 2 includes a comprehensive review of basic subtraction strategies that students have learned in earlier grades.

Counting on By Ones to Subtract

Students use their fingers, drawings and mental math to find the answers.

$$9 + 4 = 13$$
$$13 - 9 = 4$$

Make a Ten to Subtract

Students think of a related addition fact and then add up to find the answer.

$$10 + 3 = 13 \qquad 9 + 4 = 13$$
$$13 - 9 = 4$$

Practicing Subtraction Facts Have students create a Study Plan listing those basic subtraction facts that they need to practice.

Achieving Fluency For those students that know their subtraction facts but have not achieved fluency, an important strategy for subtraction, Make a Ten, is reviewed in Unit 1.

Unit 1
Use these lessons and activities for subtraction practice to help achieve fluency:
Lesson 10, 11, and 12

Basic Multiplication and Division Fluency
Units 7 and 9

Lessons involving concepts, strategies, and practice activities are included throughout Units 7 and 9. The lessons are designed to give students the opportunity to become fluent in multiplication and division by the end of the school year.

Basic Additions and Subtractions

Lesson Objectives

- Check Fluency with Additions and Subtractions
- Review Strategies for Additions
- Review Strategies for Subtractions

Vocabulary
Counting On strategy
Make a Ten Strategy

The Day at a Glance

Today's Goals	Materials	
1 **Teaching the Lesson** **A1:** Review strategies for adding 1-digit numbers **A2:** Review Subtraction Strategies **2** **Going Further** ▶ Differentiated Instruction **3** **Homework and Spiral Review**	**Lesson Activities** Student Activity Book pp. 1–2 or Student Hardcover Book pp. 1–2 and Activity Workbook pp. 1–2. Homework And Remembering pp. 1–2 Ten Frame (TRB M2) Two-color counters	**Going Further** Fluency Lesson Activity Cards Large Strip of paper with number line from 1–18 Index cards Number Cubes MathBoard materials Math Journals

123 *Use* **Math Talk** *today!*

Keeping Skills Sharp

Quick Practice ⏱ 5 MINUTES	Daily Routines
This section provides repetitive, short activities that either help students become faster and more accurate at a skill or help to prepare ground for new concepts.	**Strategy Problem** Tan has 4 more red cars than blue cars. He has 2 fewer blue cars than green cars. He has 10 green cars. How many red cars does he have? How many blue cars does he have? 12 red cars; 8 blue cars

1 Teaching the Lesson

Review Addition Strategies

 10 MINUTES

Goal: Review strategies for adding 1-digit numbers.

Materials: Student Activity Book or Hardcover Book p. 1 and Activity Workbook p. 1, Ten Frame (TRB M2), two-color counters

 NCTM Standards:
Number and Operations
Representation

Class Activity

Name _____ Date _____

▶ Check Up for Additions

Add.

1. 9 + 4 = <u>13</u>	2. 6 + 3 = <u>9</u>	3. 4 + 6 = <u>10</u>	4. 7 + 7 = <u>14</u>
5. 0 + 6 = <u>6</u>	6. 7 + 1 = <u>8</u>	7. 8 + 3 = <u>11</u>	8. 8 + 9 = <u>17</u>
9. 9 + 3 = <u>12</u>	10. 6 + 4 = <u>10</u>	11. 8 + 5 = <u>13</u>	12. 5 + 4 = <u>9</u>
13. 7 + 3 = <u>10</u>	14. 5 + 6 = <u>11</u>	15. 9 + 2 = <u>11</u>	16. 5 + 5 = <u>10</u>
17. 1 + 9 = <u>10</u>	18. 8 + 2 = <u>10</u>	19. 4 + 4 = <u>8</u>	20. 3 + 6 = <u>9</u>
21. 2 + 8 = <u>10</u>	22. 9 + 1 = <u>10</u>	23. 2 + 7 = <u>9</u>	24. 3 + 8 = <u>11</u>
25. 7 + 4 = <u>11</u>	26. 4 + 5 = <u>9</u>	27. 9 + 8 = <u>17</u>	28. 6 + 8 = <u>14</u>
29. 6 + 6 = <u>12</u>	30. 9 + 5 = <u>14</u>	31. 8 + 4 = <u>12</u>	32. 1 + 6 = <u>7</u>
33. 8 + 6 = <u>14</u>	34. 6 + 7 = <u>13</u>	35. 7 + 5 = <u>12</u>	36. 8 + 8 = <u>16</u>
37. 4 + 8 = <u>12</u>	38. 7 + 9 = <u>16</u>	39. 6 + 5 = <u>11</u>	40. 9 + 6 = <u>15</u>
41. 9 + 9 = <u>18</u>	42. 3 + 7 = <u>10</u>	43. 7 + 8 = <u>15</u>	44. 4 + 7 = <u>11</u>
45. 3 + 9 = <u>12</u>	46. 7 + 6 = <u>13</u>	47. 5 + 9 = <u>14</u>	48. 7 + 8 = <u>15</u>
49. 2 + 9 = <u>11</u>	50. 5 + 7 = <u>12</u>	51. 9 + 0 = <u>9</u>	52. 5 + 8 = <u>13</u>
53. 9 + 7 = <u>16</u>	54. 6 + 0 = <u>6</u>	55. 4 + 9 = <u>13</u>	56. 6 + 9 = <u>15</u>

FLUENCY LESSON   Basic Additions and Subtractions **1**

Student Activity Book page 1

▶ Check Up for Additions [WHOLE CLASS]

Tell students that today they will check to see if they recall basic additions.

● **Why is it important to know basic additions?** Possible answer: If you don't know basic additions, you will probably make errors when adding multi-digit numbers and when subtracting.

Give students time to complete Student Book page 1.

Have students check their answers as you read them. Tell students to put a check mark next to any basic addition they miss.

Next have students record any basic additions they missed, make a study plan to study the missed additions, and plan a time for **Student Pairs** to test each other on the missed additions.

▶ Discuss Addition Strategies WHOLE CLASS Math Talk

Review Student Book page 1. Ask students what strategies they used to add 9 + 4. Make sure to discuss the Counting On and Make a Ten strategies. Have volunteers demonstrate these strategies, or demonstrate them yourself.

Counting On by Ones Strategy

Mentally
- Say the first number to yourself: "9". Count on 4 more: "10, 11, 12, 13"

With Fingers
- Say the first number to yourself: "9". Count on, raising one finger for each number you say, until you have raised 4 fingers:

"10"　　　"11"　　　"12"　　　"13"

With a Drawing
- Write the number 9 (pretending you have already counted 9 dots) followed by four dots. Count on from the 9 to find the total.

$$9 \quad \overset{o}{10} \quad \overset{o}{11} \quad \overset{o}{12} \quad \overset{o}{13}$$

Make a Ten Strategy

- To add 9 + 4 by making a ten, take 1 from the 4 and add it to the 9 to make 10, then add the 3 that is left to get 13.

Mentally
- Start with 9. Add 1 to get 10. Add 3 more to get 13

Numerically
- $9 + 4 = 9 + 1 + 3 = 10 + 3 = 13$

With a Drawing
- Write 9 and draw 4 dots. Group the 9 with 1 of the dots to get a group of 10, plus 3 more.

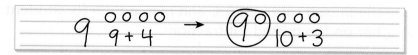

Review the remaining exercises on that page. If your students are not proficient with addition, have them find the answers by using the Counting On and Make a Ten strategies.

 Alternate Approach

Counters and Ten Frames When adding 1-digit numbers, students could also make a ten using two-color counters and a Ten Frame (TRB M2).

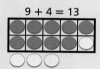

Invite students to explain how to fill the ten frame with the counters and how to count the counters that remain outside the frame.

$$9 + 1 = 10 \qquad 10 + 3 = 13$$

Review Subtraction Strategies

 10 MINUTES

Goal: Review subtraction strategies.

Materials: Student Activity Book or Hardcover Book p. 2 and Activity Workbook p. 2

 NCTM Standards:
Number and Operations
Representation

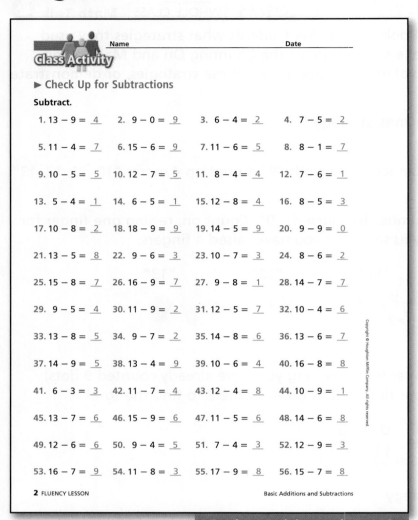

Name _____ **Date** _____

Class Activity

▶ Check Up for Subtractions

Subtract.

1. 13 − 9 = 4	2. 9 − 0 = 9	3. 6 − 4 = 2	4. 7 − 5 = 2
5. 11 − 4 = 7	6. 15 − 6 = 9	7. 11 − 6 = 5	8. 8 − 1 = 7
9. 10 − 5 = 5	10. 12 − 7 = 5	11. 8 − 4 = 4	12. 7 − 6 = 1
13. 5 − 4 = 1	14. 6 − 5 = 1	15. 12 − 8 = 4	16. 8 − 5 = 3
17. 10 − 8 = 2	18. 18 − 9 = 9	19. 14 − 5 = 9	20. 9 − 9 = 0
21. 13 − 5 = 8	22. 9 − 6 = 3	23. 10 − 7 = 3	24. 8 − 6 = 2
25. 15 − 8 = 7	26. 16 − 9 = 7	27. 9 − 8 = 1	28. 14 − 7 = 7
29. 9 − 5 = 4	30. 11 − 9 = 2	31. 12 − 5 = 7	32. 10 − 4 = 6
33. 13 − 8 = 5	34. 9 − 7 = 2	35. 14 − 8 = 6	36. 13 − 6 = 7
37. 14 − 9 = 5	38. 13 − 4 = 9	39. 10 − 6 = 4	40. 16 − 8 = 8
41. 6 − 3 = 3	42. 11 − 7 = 4	43. 12 − 4 = 8	44. 10 − 9 = 1
45. 13 − 7 = 6	46. 15 − 9 = 6	47. 11 − 5 = 6	48. 14 − 6 = 8
49. 12 − 6 = 6	50. 9 − 4 = 5	51. 7 − 4 = 3	52. 12 − 9 = 3
53. 16 − 7 = 9	54. 11 − 8 = 3	55. 17 − 9 = 8	56. 15 − 7 = 8

2 FLUENCY LESSON · · · · · · · · · · · · · · · Basic Additions and Subtractions

Student Activity Book page 2

▶ Check Up for Subtractions [WHOLE CLASS]

Tell students that next they will check to see if they recall basic subtractions.

Give students time to complete Student Book page 2.

Have students check their answers as you read them. Tell students to put a check mark next to any basic subtraction they miss.

Next have students record any basic subtractions they missed, make a study plan to study the missed subtractions, and plan a time for **Student Pairs** to test each other on the missed subtractions.

▶ Discuss Subtraction Strategies

Math Talk

WHOLE GROUP

Review the subtraction exercises on Student Book page 2. Ask students what strategies they used to find the answer to 13 − 9. Discuss the Counting On and Make a Ten strategies for subtraction described below.

Counting On by Ones to Subtract To subtract by counting on, think of the related addition and count on to the total.

- 13 − 9 = ? is 9 + ? = 13.
- Take away the first 9.

⊖⊖⊖⊖ ⊖⊖⊖⊖○ ○○○

- 9 + 4 = 13.

With Fingers
- Think: 9 + ? = 13. Say the first number to yourself: "9"
- Count on, raising one finger for each number you say, until you reach 13.

"10"   "11"   "12"   "13"

- You have raised 4 fingers, so 9 + 4 = 13, or equivalently 13 − 9 = 4.

With a Drawing
- Think: 9 + ? = 13
- Pretend you have already counted 9 dots. Write the number 9. Draw and count dots, one at a time, until you reach 13.

9 ○ ○ ○ ○
   10 11 12 13
  9 + 4 = 13
  13 − 9 = 4

- You have drawn 4 dots, so 9 + 4 = 13, or equivalently, 13 − 9 = 4.

Teaching Note

Subtraction Strategies In this activity, we review how to subtract using the counting on and make a ten strategies. Students experiencing difficulty with subtraction should learn one or both of these methods. With practice, these strategies will become efficient, reliable subtraction methods. Some children may be drawing "take away" pictures, and others may be counting down. Both are slow, and counting down often is inaccurate. Counting on is faster and more accurate for most children. In Unit 1 check what strategies students are using for column subtractions in the multidigit problems to see if any students need help counting on to be faster and more accurate.

Make a Ten to Subtract In order to subtract by making a ten, think of the related addition. Add to get to ten and then add to get to the total.

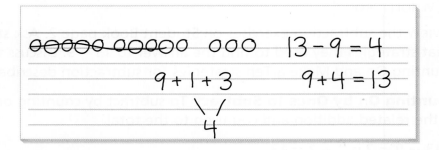

Mentally
- Think: 9 + ? = 13

- Start with 9. Add 1 to get 10 and then 3 more to get 13. You have added a total of 4, so 9 + 4 = 13, or equivalently, 13 − 9 = 4.

Numerically
(9 + 1) + 3 = 13

9 + (1 + 3) = 13; 9 + 4 = 13, or equivalently, 13 − 9 = 4

With a Drawing
- Think: 9 + ? = 13

- Draw 9 to represent 9 dots. Draw 1 more dot to get 10. Add 3 more to get 13. You have drawn 4 dots, so 9 + 4 = 13, or equivalently, 13 − 9 = 4.

Review the remaining subtraction exercises on page 2 as a class. If students are not proficient with subtraction, have them use the Counting On and Make a Ten strategies to subtract.

✔ Ongoing Assessment

▶ How many tens are in 300?

▶ Each basket can hold 10 apples. Describe what happens when 58 apples are put into the baskets.

▶ Explain how you can use an addition problem to help you solve 14 − 8.

② Going Further

Intervention — Activity Card Fluency Lesson

Leap Frog

Activity Card Fluency Lesson ●

Work: In small groups

Use:
- Large strip of paper with a 0–18 number line drawn on it, index cards (1 for each person in group)

1. Write the 5 basic additions and 5 basic subtractions that you think are the hardest on your index card. Pass your card to the student on your right.

$9 + 8 = \square$ $16 - 7 = \square$

2. Take turns using the number line to model an addition that the student with your card reads to you. Stand next to the greater number and hop along the line as the other students count on aloud to find the total.

0 1 2 3 4 5 6 7 8 9 10 11 12 13 14 15 16 17 18

3. Repeat for subtractions. Stand next to the number you are subtracting and hop to the number you are subtracting from, as the other students count aloud to find the answer.

Fluency Lesson

Copyright © Houghton Mifflin Company

Activity Note To reinforce understanding, point out the relationship between addition and subtraction as inverse operations.

🖉 **Math Writing Prompt**

You Decide Explain how to use a number line to count on to solve $9 + 7 = \square$.

Soar to Success Math ★ **Software Support**

Warm Up 10.17

On Level — Activity Card Fluency Lesson

Roll Equations

Activity Card Fluency Lesson ▲

Work: In pairs

Use:
- Number cubes (2–7 and 4–9)
- MathBoard materials

Decide:
Who will be Student 1 and who will be Student 2 for the first round.

1. **Student 1:** Roll both number cubes and write an addition equation and subtraction equation with an unknown number.

$2 + \square = 8$
$8 - \square = 2$

2. **Student 2:** Solve both equations by writing the unknown number.

3. Change roles and play again.

Fluency Lesson

Copyright © Houghton Mifflin Company

Activity Note This activity reinforces the inverse operation between addition and subtraction.

🖉 **Math Writing Prompt**

Investigate Math Carla had 16¢. After buying glitter, she had 7¢ left. How much did the glitter cost? Draw or explain how you solved the problem.

 MegaMath Grades K-6 **Software Support**

Numberopolis: Carnival Stories, Level H

Challenge — Activity Card Fluency Lesson

Magic Square

Activity Card Fluency Lesson ■

Work: In pairs

Use:
- Index card

1. Copy the Magic Square below onto an index card.

9	2	7
4	6	8
5	10	3

2. In a Magic Square, the numbers in each row, each column, and each diagonal have the same sum. What is the sum for this Magic Square? 18

3. **Think** How can you find the missing number in the first row? Add 2 + 7 and subtract the sum from 18.

4. **Work Together** Find the missing numbers.

Fluency Lesson

Copyright © Houghton Mifflin Company

Activity Note Finding the sum in the middle column will give the magic sum. Then finding missing numbers in the top and middle rows will make it possible to find the 2 numbers in the bottom row.

🖉 **Math Writing Prompt**

Find the Rule What is the next number in the pattern? 1, 5, 4, 8, 7, 11, 10, _____. Explain how you know.

 DESTINATION Math® **Software Support**

Course II: Module 2: Unit 1: Sums Less than 100

③ Homework and Spiral Review

Homework   **Goal:** Additional Practice

This Homework page provides practice in adding and subtracting basic facts.

Remembering   **Goal:** Spiral Review

This Remembering page would be appropriate anytime after today's lesson.

Name _____ Date _____

Homework

Write an equation for each situation. Then solve the problem.

Show your work.

1. Carol wrote 9 poems in her journal. Then, she wrote 7 more poems. How many poems did Carol write in her journal in all?

$9 + 7 = \square$; 16 poems

2. Jaipal had 14 pages left to read of his book. So far, he read 8 pages. How many pages does Jaipal have left to read?

$14 - 8 = \square$; 6 pages

3. Kele walked 6 blocks to the library. Then, he walked 6 blocks home. How many blocks did Kele walk in total?

$6 + 6 = \square$; 12 blocks

4. Julieta had 18 photos in all. She took 9 of these photos and her friend took the others. How many photos did her friend take?

$18 - 9 = \square$; 9 photos

5. Inez worked 7 hours on Monday. Then, she worked 5 hours on Tuesday. How many hours did Inez work altogether?

$7 + 5 = \square$; 12 hours

6. Dwight has 13 problems for math homework. He has finished 7 of the problems. How many more problems does Dwight have to finish?

$13 - 7 = \square$; 6 problems

FLUENCY LESSON   Basic Additions and Subtractions **1**

Name _____ Date _____

Remembering

Use the information in the bar graph to answer the questions.

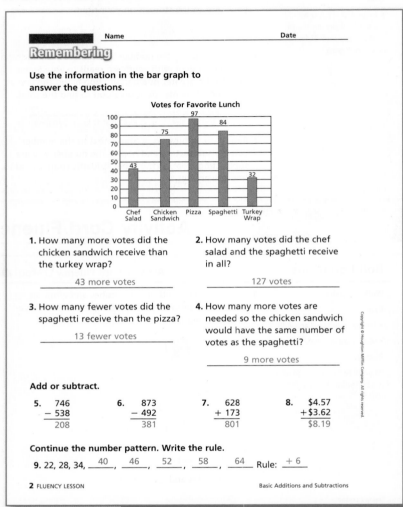

Votes for Favorite Lunch

1. How many more votes did the chicken sandwich receive than the turkey wrap?

43 more votes

2. How many votes did the chef salad and the spaghetti receive in all?

127 votes

3. How many fewer votes did the spaghetti receive than the pizza?

13 fewer votes

4. How many more votes are needed so the chicken sandwich would have the same number of votes as the spaghetti?

9 more votes

Add or subtract.

5.	**6.**	**7.**	**8.**
746	873	628	$4.57
− 538	− 492	+ 173	+$3.62
208	381	801	$8.19

Continue the number pattern. Write the rule.

9. 22, 28, 34, _40_, _46_, _52_, _58_, _64_   Rule: _+ 6_

2 FLUENCY LESSON   Basic Additions and Subtractions

Home and School Activity

 Science Connection

Rainfall Data Have students record the amount of rainfall each day for seven days to the nearest whole inch. Then have students write questions that can be answered using their data. Examples: Which day had the least amount of rainfall? Which day had the greatest amount of rainfall? What is the total rainfall for the seven days. Which two days had a total of 4 inches?

Day	Amount of Rainfall (Inches)
Sunday	1 inch
Monday	1 inch
Tuesday	0 inches
Wednesday	2 inches
Thursday	1 inch
Friday	3 inches
Saturday	6 inches

Place Value and Multi-Digit Addition and Subtraction

THE GOAL FOR UNIT 1 is to develop multi-digit addition and subtraction methods that are meaningful and easily used by students. Place-value activities build understanding of the base-ten numeration system and provide the foundation to understand grouping and ungrouping. Students will use drawings to show grouping and ungrouping, and then will describe and discuss the process.

Skills Trace

Grade 2	Grade 3	Grade 4
• Read, write, identify, and represent the place value of whole numbers through 999.	• Read, write, identify, and represent the place value of whole numbers through ten thousands. *(through hundred thousands, see Extension Lesson 1.)*	• Read, write, identify, and represent the place value of whole numbers through the millions.
• Add and subtract whole numbers to 999.	• Add and subtract whole numbers to 10,000. *(through hundred thousands, see Extension Lesson 1.)*	• Add and subtract whole numbers to the millions.
• Solve addition and subtraction story problems.	• Add and subtract money amounts.	• Add and subtract money amounts.
	• Write and solve related addition and subtraction word problems.	• Write and solve related addition and subtraction word problems.

Unit 1   Contents

 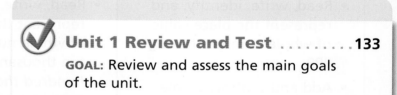

Unit 1   Assessment

✓ Unit Objectives Tested	Unit Test Items	Lessons
1.1 Read, write, identify, and represent the place value of whole numbers.	1–9, 20	1, 3, 4
1.2 Add and subtract whole numbers.	10–14	5, 6, 8, 10–12
1.3 Add and subtract money amounts.	15–17	7
1.4 Write a related subtraction word problem for an addition problem and vice versa.	18, 19	13

Assessment and Review Resources

Formal Assessment

Student Activity Book
- Unit Review and Test (pp. 43–44)

Assessment Guide
- Quick Quizzes (pp. A2, A3, A4)
- Test A–Open Response (pp. A5–A6)
- Test B-Multiple Choice (pp. A7–A9)
- Performance Assessment (pp. A10–A12)

Test Generator CD-ROM
- Open Response Test
- Multiple Choice Test
- Test Bank Items

Informal Assessment

Teacher Edition
- Ongoing Assessment (in every lesson)
- Quick Practice (in every lesson)
- Portfolio Suggestions (p. 135)

123 Math Talk
- ▸ The Learning Classroom (pp. 21, 22, 33, 91, 101, 108, 122)
- ▸ Math Talk in Action (pp. 25, 68, 74, 90, 94, 109, 111, 116, 122)
- ▸ Solve and Discuss (pp. 33, 39, 44–45, 48, 52, 67, 91, 92, 101, 106, 109, 116, 122, 124)
- ▸ Student Pairs (pp. 62, 73, 102, 112, 118, 123, 128)
- ▸ Small Groups (p. 32, 68)
- ▸ Scenarios (p. 73)
- ▸ Step-by-Step at the Board (pp. 56, 74, 82)
- ▸ In Activities (pp. 3, 5, 16, 21, 22, 40, 54, 60, 66, 78, 94, 122, 129)

Review Opportunities

Homework and Remembering
- Review of recently taught topics
- Spiral Review

Teacher Edition
- Unit Review and Test (pp. 133–136)

Test Generator CD-ROM
- Custom Review Sheets

Planning Unit 1

NCTM Curriculum Focal Points and Connections Key: **1.** Number and Operations and Algebra **2.** Number and Operations **3.** Geometry **4.** Algebra **5.** Measurement **6.** Data Analysis **7.** Number and Operations

Lesson NCTM Focal Points NCTM Standards	Resources	Materials for Lesson Activities	Materials for Going Further
1-1 **Make Place Value Drawings** NCTM Focal Points: 7.1, 7.2 NCTM Standards: 1, 10	TE pp. 9–18 SAB pp. 1–8 H&R pp. 3–4 AC 1-1 MCC 1	✓ MathBoard materials ✓ Base ten blocks Ten Frame (TRB M2) Dot Array (TRB M1)	✓ Base ten blocks ✓ Number cubes ✓ MathBoard materials Math Journals
1-2 **Build Numbers and Represent Money Amounts** NCTM Focal Points: 7.1, 7.2 NCTM Standards: 1, 10	TE pp. 19–28 SAB pp. 8A–8D; 9–10 H&R pp. 5-6 AC 1-2	✓ Demonstration Secret Code Cards ✓ Pointer ✓ Secret Code Cards Envelopes or small bags, Scissors ✓ MathBoard materials	Index cards ✓ Play Money ✓ MathBoard materials Math Journals
1-3 **Place Value in Word Problems** NCTM Focal Points: 7.1, 7.2 NCTM Standards: 1, 6, 8, 10	TE pp. 29–36 SAB pp. 11–12 H&R pp. 7–8 AC 1-3 MCC 2	✓ Demonstration Secret Code Cards ✓ Secret Code Cards ✓ MathBoard materials ✓ Base ten blocks	✓ MathBoard materials Sentence strips Index cards Math Journals
1-4 **Practice with Place Value** NCTM Focal Points: 7.1, 7.2 NCTM Standards: 1, 6, 8, 10	TE pp. 37–42 SAB pp. 13–14 H&R pp. 8, 9–10 AG Quick Quiz 1 AC 1-4	✓ Secret Code Cards ✓ MathBoard materials Ten Frame (TRB M2) ✓ Two-color counters	Place Value Strips (TRB M23) Scissors Index cards Math Journals
1-5 **Explore Multi-Digit Addition** NCTM Focal Point: 7.5 NCTM Standards: 1, 6, 10	TE pp. 43–50 SAB pp. 15–18 H&R pp. 11–12 AC 1-5	✓ MathBoard materials ✓ Secret Code Cards	✓ Base ten blocks ✓ MathBoard materials Index cards Game Cards (TRB M25) Math Journals
1-6 **Discuss Addition Methods** NCTM Focal Point: 7.5 NCTM Standards: 1, 6, 8	TE pp. 51–58 SAB pp. 19–20 H&R pp. 12, 13–14 AC 1-6 MCC 3	None	Spinner A (TRB M24) ✓ Secret Code Cards Paper clips ✓ Base ten blocks Game Cards (TRB 25) ✓ MathBoard materials Math Journals
1-7 **Addition with Dollars and Cents** NCTM Focal Point: 7.5 NCTM Standards: 1, 6, 8	TE pp. 59–64 SAB pp. 21–22 H&R pp. 15–16 AC 1-7	✓ MathBoard materials Grocery store ads	✓ Play Money Index cards Math Journals
1-8 **The Grouping Concept in Addition** NCTM Focal Points: 7.3, 7.5 NCTM Standards: 1, 6	TE pp. 65–70 SAB pp. 23–24 H&R pp. 17–18 AC 1-8	✓ MathBoard materials	Restaurant Menus ✓ MathBoard materials Game Cards (TRB M25), Index Cards ✓ Rulers Math Journals

Resources/Materials Key: TE: Teacher Edition   SAB: Student Activity Book   H&R: Homework and Remembering
AC: Activity Cards   MCC: Math Center Challenge   AG: Assessment Guide   ✓: Grade 3 kits   TRB: Teacher's Resource Book

NCTM Standards and Expectations Key: **1.** Number and Operations **2.** Algebra **3.** Geometry
4. Measurement **5.** Data Analysis and Probability **6.** Problem Solving **7.** Reasoning and Proof
8. Communication **9.** Connections **10.** Representation

Lesson NCTM Focal Points NCTM Standards	Resources	Materials for Lesson Activities	Materials for Going Further
1-9 **Practice Addition** NCTM Focal Point: 7.5 NCTM Standards: 1, 6	TE pp. 71–76 SAB pp. 25–26 H&R pp. 19–20 AC 1-9 AG Quick Quiz 2	None	Restaurant menus ✓ MathBoard materials ✓ Play money Math Journals
1-10 **Ungroup to Subtract** NCTM Focal Point: 7.5 NCTM Standards: 1, 2, 6	TE pp. 77–86 SAB pp. 27–28 H&R pp. 21–22 AC 1-10	✓ MathBoard materials	✓ Base ten blocks Game Cards (TRB M25) Math Journals
1-11 **Subtract Across Zeros** NCTM Focal Points: 7.3, 7.5 NCTM Standards: 1, 6	TE pp. 87–96 SAB pp. 29–32 H&R pp. 23–24 AC 1-11 MCC 4	✓ MathBoard materials	Play money Paper bags Math Journals
1-12 **Discuss Methods of Subtracting** NCTM Focal Point: 7.5 NCTM Standards: 1, 6, 8	TE pp. 97–104 SAB pp. 33–34 H&R pp. 25–26 AC 1-12	✓ MathBoard materials	✓ Base ten blocks ✓ MathBoard materials ✓ Number Cubes Math Journals
1-13 **Relate Addition and Subtraction** NCTM Focal Points: 7.3, 7.5 NCTM Standards: 1, 6, 8	TE pp. 105–114 SAB pp. 35–36 H&R pp. 27–28 AC 1-13	✓ Base ten blocks Chart paper ✓ MathBoard materials	Index cards Sticky notes Math Journals
1-14 **Subtraction Practice** NCTM Focal Point: 7.5 NCTM Standards: 1, 6, 8	TE pp.115–120 SAB pp. 37–38 H&R pp. 29–30 AC 1-14	Crayons, colored pencils, or markers	Chart paper, Index cards Game Cards (TRB M25) Math Journals
1-15 **Addition and Subtraction Practice** NCTM Focal Points: 7.3, 7.5 NCTM Standards: 1, 6, 8	TE pp. 121–126 SAB pp. 39–40 H&R pp. 31–32 AG Quick Quiz 3 AC 1-15	Toy store ads from Lesson 14 Index cards Paper bags	✓ MathBoard materials Calculators Index cards Paper bags Game Cards (TRB M25) Math Journals
1-16 **Use Mathematical Processes** NCTM Standards: 6, 7, 8, 9, 10	TE pp. 127–132 SAB pp. 41–42 H&R pp. 33–34 AC 1-16	Spinner (TRB 131) Scissors, Paper clips, Pencils ✓ Base ten blocks *Hannah's Collections*	✓ Number cubes Math Journals
✓ Unit Review and Test	TE pp. 133–136 SAB pp. 43–44 AG Unit 1 Tests		

Hardcover Student Book

- Together, the Hardcover Student Book and its companion Activity Workbook contain all of the pages in the consumable Student Activity Book.

Manipulatives and Materials

- Essential materials for teaching *Math Expressions* are available in the Grade 3 kits. These materials are indicated by a ✓ in these lists. At the front of this Teacher Edition is more information about kit contents, alternatives for the materials, and use of the materials.

Independent Learning Activities

Ready-Made Math Challenge Centers

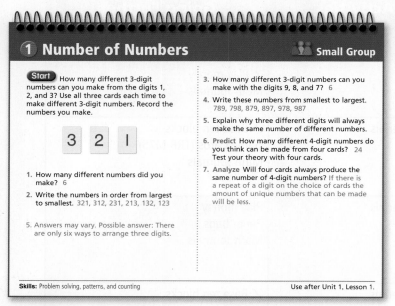

① Number of Numbers — Small Group

Start How many different 3-digit numbers can you make from the digits 1, 2, and 3? Use all three cards each time to make different 3-digit numbers. Record the numbers you make.

3 2 1

1. How many different numbers did you make? 6
2. Write the numbers in order from largest to smallest. 321, 312, 231, 213, 132, 123
5. Answers may vary. Possible answer: There are only six ways to arrange three digits.

3. How many different 3-digit numbers can you make with the digits 9, 8, and 7? 6
4. Write these numbers from smallest to largest. 789, 798, 879, 897, 978, 987
5. Explain why three different digits will always make the same number of different numbers.
6. **Predict** How many different 4-digit numbers do you think can be made from four cards? 24 Test your theory with four cards.
7. **Analyze** Will four cards always produce the same number of 4-digit numbers? If there is a repeat of a digit on the choice of cards the amount of unique numbers that can be made will be less.

Skills: Problem solving, patterns, and counting
Use after Unit 1, Lesson 1.

Grouping Small Group

Materials Number cards (optional)

Objective Students look for patterns when making all possible numbers with a given number of digits.

Connections Patterns and Problem Solving

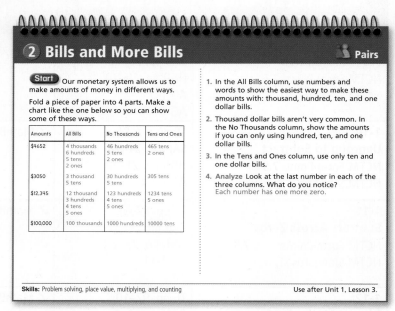

② Bills and More Bills — Pairs

Start Our monetary system allows us to make amounts of money in different ways.

Fold a piece of paper into 4 parts. Make a chart like the one below so you can show some of these ways.

Amounts	All Bills	No Thousands	Tens and Ones
$4652	4 thousands 6 hundreds 5 tens 2 ones	46 hundreds 5 tens 2 ones	465 tens 2 ones
$3050	3 thousand 5 tens	30 hundreds 5 tens	305 tens
$12,345	12 thousand 3 hundreds 4 tens 5 ones	123 hundreds 4 tens 5 ones	1234 tens 5 ones
$100,000	100 thousands	1000 hundreds	10000 tens

1. In the All Bills column, use numbers and words to show the easiest way to make these amounts with: thousand, hundred, ten, and one dollar bills.
2. Thousand dollar bills aren't very common. In the No Thousands column, show the amounts if you can only using hundred, ten, and one dollar bills.
3. In the Tens and Ones column, use only ten and one dollar bills.
4. **Analyze** Look at the last number in each of the three columns. What do you notice? Each number has one more zero.

Skills: Problem solving, place value, multiplying, and counting
Use after Unit 1, Lesson 3.

Grouping Pairs

Materials Paper money (optional)

Objective Students extend their knowledge of place value by representing amounts with different monetary combinations.

Connections Representing and Numeration

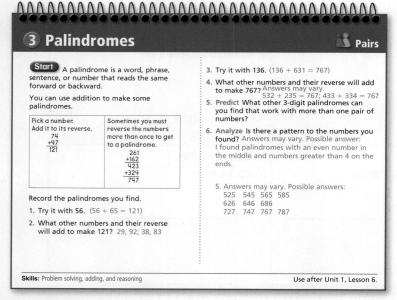

③ Palindromes — Pairs

Start A palindrome is a word, phrase, sentence, or number that reads the same forward or backward.

You can use addition to make some palindromes.

Pick a number. Add it to its reverse.	Sometimes you must reverse the numbers more than once to get to a palindrome.
74 +47 ——— 121	261 +162 ——— 423 +324 ——— 747

Record the palindromes you find.

1. Try it with 56. (56 + 65 = 121)
2. What other numbers and their reverse will add to make 121? 29, 92; 38, 83

3. Try it with 136. (136 + 631 = 767)
4. What other numbers and their reverse will add to make 767? Answers may vary. 532 + 235 = 767; 433 + 334 = 767
5. **Predict** What other 3-digit palindromes can you find that work with more than one pair of numbers?
6. **Analyze** Is there a pattern to the numbers you found? Answers may vary. Possible answer: I found palindromes with an even number in the middle and numbers greater than 4 on the ends.

5. Answers may vary. Possible answers:
525 545 565 585
626 646 686
727 747 767 787

Skills: Problem solving, adding, and reasoning
Use after Unit 1, Lesson 6.

Grouping Pairs

Materials None

Objective Students apply their knowledge of addition by finding palindromes and the numbers that make them.

Connections Problem Solving and Reasoning

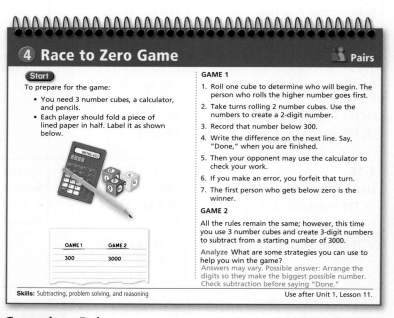

④ Race to Zero Game — Pairs

Start To prepare for the game:
- You need 3 number cubes, a calculator, and pencils.
- Each player should fold a piece of lined paper in half. Label it as shown below.

GAME 1	GAME 2
300	3000

GAME 1
1. Roll one cube to determine who will begin. The person who rolls the higher number goes first.
2. Take turns rolling 2 number cubes. Use the numbers to create a 2-digit number.
3. Record that number below 300.
4. Write the difference on the next line. Say, "Done," when you are finished.
5. Then your opponent may use the calculator to check your work.
6. If you make an error, you forfeit that turn.
7. The first person who gets below zero is the winner.

GAME 2

All the rules remain the same; however, this time you use 3 number cubes and create 3-digit numbers to subtract from a starting number of 3000.

Analyze What are some strategies you can use to help you win the game? Answers may vary. Possible answer: Arrange the digits so they make the biggest possible number. Check subtraction before saying "Done."

Skills: Subtracting, problem solving, and reasoning
Use after Unit 1, Lesson 11.

Grouping Pairs

Materials 3 number cubes, calculator

Objective Students play a subtraction game and record their work in a checkbook like fashion.

Connections Numeration and Subtraction

Ready-Made Math Resources

Technology — Tutorial, Practice, and Intervention

Use online, individualized intervention and support to bring students to proficiency.

Help students practice skills and apply concepts through exciting math adventures.

Extend and enrich students' understanding of skills and concepts through engaging, interactive lessons and activities.

Visit **Education Place**
www.eduplace.com

Visit **www.eduplace.com/mx2t/** and find family, teacher, and student materials, activities, games, and more.

Literature Links

How Much, How Many, How Far, How Heavy, How Long, How Tall Is 1000?

How Much, How Many, How Far, How Heavy, How Long, How Tall Is 1000?

This book by Helen Nolan can serve as a great introduction to the year of math study. It helps students understand just how many one thousand might be if you were to count a thousand French fries for example, or a pile of one thousand acorns.

Unit 1 Teaching Resources

Differentiated Instruction

Individualizing Instruction

Activities	Level	Frequency
Activities	• Intervention • On Level • Challenge	All 3 in every lesson.
	Level	Frequency
Math Writing Prompts	• Intervention • On Level • Challenge	All 3 in every lesson.
Math Challenges	For advanced students	
	4 in every unit	

Reaching All Learners

	Lessons	Pages
English Language Learners	1, 2, 3, 4, 5, 6, 7, 8, 9, 10, 11, 12, 13, 14, 15, 16	15, 24, 32, 39, 48, 53, 62, 67, 72, 78, 91, 102, 110, 118, 123, 129
	Lessons	Pages
Extra Help	1, 3, 6, 7, 8, 11, 12, 13, 14	14, 16, 31, 54, 61, 67, 94, 101, 109, 117

Strategies for English Language Learners

Present this problem to all students. Offer the different levels of support to meet student's levels of language proficiency.

Objective Review digits, numbers, and the concept of place value.

Problem Draw a 1 to 9 number line on the board. Say: **These are** *digits.* Write 15. Say: **This number has** *two digits.* Write 125. Ask: **How many digits does this number have?** (3).

Newcomer

• Give students number cards 1-9. Say: **Make a 2-digit number.**

• Have students use base-ten blocks to model the number.

Beginning

• Write 32 on the board. Say: **This number is 32. There are 3 tens and 2 ones.**

• Point to 3 groups of tens rods and 2 single blocks. Ask: **Are there 3 groups of ten?** yes **How many cubes are there in all?** 32

Intermediate

• Write 331 on the board. Point to each digit. Ask: **What place is this? What digit is this?**

• Have students use number cards to create 3 digit numbers and base-ten blocks to model them.

Advanced

• Write 218 on the board. Have students identify the digits and values and work in pairs to model 218 with base-ten blocks.

Connections

 Sport Connection
Lesson 14, page 120

 Social Studies Connections
Lesson 3, page 36
Lesson 7, page 64
Lesson 8, page 70
Lesson 11, page 96
Lesson 15, page 126

 Multicultural Connections
Lesson 2, page 28
Lesson 9, page 76

 Science Connections
Lesson 6, page 58
Lesson 10, page 86
Lesson 13, page 114

 Literature Connection
Lesson 12, page 104

 Math-to-Math Connection
Lesson 4, page 42

 Real-World Connection
Lesson 16, page 132

Math Background

Putting Research into Practice for Unit 1

From our Curriculum Research Project: Multi-Digit Addition and Subtraction Methods

We show three methods for multi-digit addition: the common algorithm **(New Groups Above),** plus two methods found to be effective during the research project, **New Groups Below** and **Show All Totals.** These methods are introduced to help students see and discuss core mathematical ideas about addition and subtraction.

New Groups Below Method

- Students record a regrouped digit on the line below the addition exercise, instead of above the addition exercise.

- Allows students to see the tens and ones, or hundreds and tens, more closely together than in the New Groups Above method.

Show All Totals Method

- Students add in each place, record the total for each place, then add these totals to find the sum.

Multi-Digit Subtraction Methods

To subtract multi-digit numbers, we teach students to ungroup all the places before they subtract. This approach reduces errors and helps develop conceptual understanding of multi-digit subtraction. Some students make the common error of consistently subtracting the smaller digit in a place-value column from the larger digit, even if the smaller digit is on top.

To help students remember to ungroup in subtraction, they

- Draw a "magnifying glass" around the top number to prepare for ungrouping.

- "Look inside" the magnifying glass to see which places need to be ungrouped.

Karen Fuson, Author
Math Expressions

From Current Research: Accessible Methods for Multi-Digit Addition

Method B [New Groups Below] is taught in China and has been invented by students in the United States. . . . [T]his method [where] the new 1 or regrouped 10 (or new hundred) is recorded on the line separating the problem from the answer . . . requires that children understand what to do when they get 10 or more in a given column. . . . Method C [Show All Totals], reflecting more closely many students' invented procedures, reduces the problem [of carrying] by writing the total for each kind of unit on a new line. The carrying-regrouping-trading is done as part of the adding of each kind of unit. Also, Method C can be done in either direction.

National Research Council. "Developing Proficiency with Whole Numbers." *Adding It Up: Helping Children Learn Mathematics.* Washington, D.C.: National Academy Press, 2001. p. 203.

Other Useful References: Addition and Subtraction

Number and Operations Standard for Grades 3–5. *Principles and Standards for School Mathematics.* Reston, VA: National Council of Teachers of Mathematics, 2000. pp. 148–155.

Van de Walle, John A., Elementary and Middle School Mathematics: Teaching Developmentally. 6th ed. Columbus: Longman, 2006. pp. 213–221.

Getting Ready to Teach Unit 1

In this unit, students build on place value concepts and develop methods for adding and subtracting multi-digit numbers. They begin to see addition and subtraction as inverse operations and apply their knowledge of these concepts and skills to problem solving.

Place Value Concepts

Secret Code Cards
Lessons 2, 3, 4, 5, 6, 7, 8, 9, 10, 11, 12, 13, 14, 15

Students explore place value by assembling Secret Code Cards to form **multi-digit** numbers. To make the number 1,983 students select the cards representing 1 thousand, 9 hundreds, 8 tens, and 3 ones and then assemble them, as shown:

Thousands Card   Hundreds Card   Tens Card   Ones Card

Assembled Cards

Each card has a small version of the number in the upper left corner. So even after the number 1,983 is assembled, students can see that the 1 represents 1,000, the 9 represents 900, and so on.

Place Value Drawings Secret Code Cards
Lessons 2, 3, and 4

The back of each Secret Code Card has a place-value drawing representation of the number shown on the front. This drawing helps students to further understand the value of each number by showing a pictorial representation of the base-ten form. Students can also easily compare the value of two numbers, or the value of different digits, visually.

Students can also use the place-value drawing sides of the Secret Code Cards to model numbers. Then students can determine what the related numeral is or find the value of the digits within the numeral, and then turn over the cards to check their answers.

Thousands Card   Hundreds Card   Tens Card   Ones Card

As you teach this unit, emphasize understanding of these terms:
- Counting On strategy
- Make a Ten strategy
- Make a Thousand strategy
- New Groups Above method
- New Groups Below method
- Proof Drawing
- place value drawing
- Show All Totals method

See Glossary on pp. T1–T17.

Place Value Drawings
Lessons 1, 2, 3, and 4

Students represent 3-digit numbers with drawings that show hundreds, tens, and ones. To start, students make drawings on the dot arrays on their MathBoards. They show ones by circling individual dots, tens by drawing lines through groups of ten dots, and hundreds by drawing squares around groups of 100 dots. *Math Expressions* uses the terms *ones, ten-sticks,* and *hundred-boxes* to describe the three representations.

Dot Drawing of 178

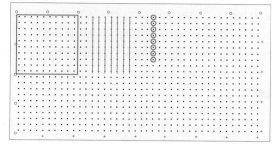

1 hundred-box   7 ten-sticks   8 ones

Proof Drawings
Lessons 5, 6, 7, 8, 9, 10, 11, 12, 13, and 14

Students soon move on to free-hand drawings, making squares for hundreds, lines for tens, and circles for ones. Students group ten-sticks and circles in subgroups of five to avoid errors and to make their drawings easier to read. Proof drawings are used to visually illustrate the grouping process in addition and the ungrouping process

Place Value Drawing of 178

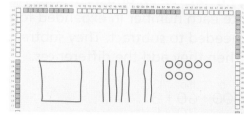

1 hundred-box   7 ten-sticks   8 ones

in subtraction. See Proof Drawing for All Methods below. Proof drawings are used to link each step of a proof drawing to each step of a numerical method. Students then begin to do only the numerical method but they can think of a drawing to self-correct. Occasionally, it is helpful for students to make a proof drawing to explain their numerical method to someone else and to keep the meanings attached to the numerical method.

Accessible Algorithms for Multi-Digit Addition and Subtraction

Addition: New Groups Below Method
Lessons 5, 6, 7, 8, and 9

Students record a regrouped digit on the line below the next left column beginning from the right.

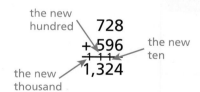

the new hundred ↘ 728
            +596   ↙ the new ten
the new ↙ 1,324
thousand

Addition: Show All Totals Method
Lessons 5, 6, 7, 8, 9, and 15

Students add in each place, record the total for each place, then add these totals to find the sum. This can also be done from the right.

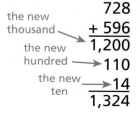

```
                    728
the new
thousand  ↘      + 596
the new        1,200
hundred  →      110
the new
ten    →       14
              1,324
```

Addition: New Groups Above Method
Lessons 5, 6, 7, 8, 9, and 15

Current Common Method The regrouped digit is recorded above the next left column.

```
 1 11
  728
+ 596
1,324
```

See pages 46–47 for steps in methods and how New Groups Below is easier for students than the New Groups Above.

Proof Drawing for All Methods
Lessons 5, 6, 7, 8, 9, and 15

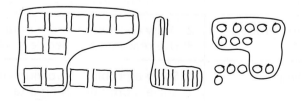

Subtraction: Ungroup First
Lessons 10, 11, 12, 13, 14, and 15
Students draw a "magnifying glass" around the top number to see which places need to be ungrouped. After ungrouping, they subtract in any direction. Students make proof drawings with hundred-boxes, ten-sticks, and ones to show ungrouping.

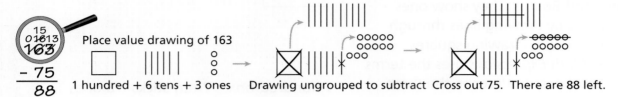

Place value drawing of 163

1 hundred + 6 tens + 3 ones   Drawing ungrouped to subtract   Cross out 75. There are 88 left.

Subtraction: Expanded Method
Lessons 10, 11, 12, 13, 14, and 15
Students write each number in expanded form. They ungroup as needed to subtract. They subtract in each place. Then they add the differences.

$$163 = \overset{0}{\cancel{100}} + \overset{150}{\cancel{60}} + \overset{13}{\cancel{3}}$$
$$-75 = \underline{ 70 + 5}$$
$$80 + 8 = 88$$

Subtraction: Alternating Steps Method
Lessons 10, 11, 12, 13, 14, and 15
Current Common Method Students ungroup tens, subtract ones, ungroup hundreds, subtract tens, and so on. See pages 80 to 84 for steps in methods, how both accessible methods can go right-to-left or left-to-right, and advantages of these methods.

Problem Solving

In *Math Expressions* a research-based, algebraic problem-solving approach that focuses on problem types is used: understand the situation, represent the situation with a math drawing or an equation, solve the problem, and see that the answer makes sense. In this unit, addition and subtraction skills are emphasized. In Unit 3, students work with different types of problems and how to represent them.

Use Mathematical Processes
Lesson 16
The NCTM process skills of problem solving, reasoning and proof, communication, connections, and representation are interwoven through all lessons throughout the year. The last lesson of this unit allows students to extend their use of mathematical processes to other situations.

NCTM Process Skill	Activity and Goal
Representation	1: Model problems with base-ten blocks. 2: Record data in a table. 4: Draw two numbers to show they have different values.
Communication	1: Act out word problems. 2: Play a game, compare and discuss results. 3: Explain how they solved a problem. 5: Explain how to solve a problem.
Connections	1: Math and Literature: Number Sense and Reading
Reasoning and Proof	2: Draw conclusions from data. 3: Use reasoning to decide if all possibilities are listed.
Problem Solving	1: Solve a problem involving addition and subtraction. 2: Solve a problem using a table. 3: Solve a problem involving money. 5: Solve a problem with multiple answers.

Make Place Value Drawings

Vocabulary

place value drawing
ten-stick
hundred-box
thousand-bar

Lesson Objectives

- Make and interpret place value drawings.
- Recognize that 1,000 is 10 hundreds.

The Day at a Glance

Today's Goals	Materials	
1 **Teaching the Lesson** **A1:** Create place value drawings for 2- and 3-digit numbers. **A2:** Interpret and make place value drawings for hundreds, tens, and ones. **A3:** Represent 1,000 with a place value drawing.	**Lesson Activities** Student Activity Book pp. 3–8 or Student Hardcover Book pp. 3–8 and Activity Workbook pp. 3–6 (includes Family Letter) Homework and Remembering pp. 3–4 Ten Frame (TRB M2) Dot Array (TRB M1) MathBoard materials (TRB M1) Base ten blocks	**Going Further** Activity Cards 1-1 MathBoard materials or Dot Paper Base ten blocks Number cubes Math Journals
2 **Going Further** ▶ Math Connection: Compare Numbers ▶ Differentiated Instruction		
3 **Homework and Spiral Review**		

123 Use **Math Talk** today!

Keeping Skills Sharp

Quick Practice	Daily Routines
This section provides repetitive, short activities that either help students become faster and more accurate at a skill or help to prepare ground for new concepts. Quick Practice for this unit will start in Lesson 2.	**Reasoning Problem** Aretha is taller than Sean. Sean is shorter than Hamid. Aretha is the tallest student. Order the students from shortest to tallest. Sean, Hamid, Aretha

① Teaching the Lesson

Represent Hundreds, Tens, and Ones

 20 MINUTES

Goal: Create place value drawings for 2- and 3-digit numbers.

Materials: MathBoard materials or Dot Array (TRB M1), base ten blocks

 NCTM Standards:
Number and Operations
Representation

 Class Management

If you do not have a Class MathBoard, you may wish to make a transparency of Dot Array (TRB M1) and display it on the overhead.

If you do not have student MathBoards, you may wish to put copies of Dot Array (TRB M1) in sheet protectors for students to use.

Teaching Note

Faster Ten-Sticks Point out the small circles along two edges of the dot array. Explain that there are 5 dots between each pair of circles. Students can use the circles as a guide to help them draw ten-sticks quickly.

 Class Management

Move as quickly as you can in this unit because it is written to refresh content that many students will know from the year before.

▶ **Place Value Drawings on the Dot Array** WHOLE CLASS

Ones Have students use the dot side of their MathBoards to make drawings of numbers. Make sure students hold their MathBoards as shown below. Each dot on the array represents 1. To show the number 6, circle 6 dots.

Circle 6 dots in a column on the Class MathBoard as students follow along. Point out to students that the small circles along the top and left edges will help them with their circling. There are 5 dots between each pair of circles.

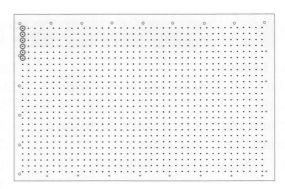

Ten-Stick Circle 4 more dots in the column so there are a total of 10.

● How many dots are circled now? 10

Draw a line through the 10 dots as shown below on the left.

● Use a shortcut to represent 10 by drawing a line through a group of 10 dots instead of circling 10 dots. Call the line a *ten-stick*.

Draw a ten-stick next to the column of 10 circles.

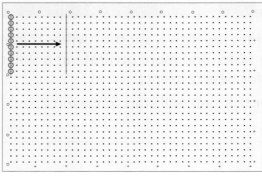

Ten-stick

On the Class MathBoard write: 76   *seventy-six*

Ask students to use ten-sticks and circles to show the number as a volunteer works at the Class MathBoard. Students should draw 7 ten-sticks and then circle 6 single dots as shown on the next page.

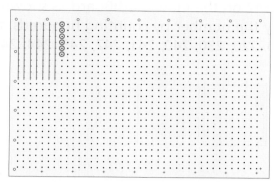

Dot Drawing of 76

● How can you check to make sure you have drawn 76 correctly without counting each individual dot? First count the tens: 10, 20, 30, 40, 50, 60, 70. Then count the ones: 71, 72, 73, 74, 75, 76.

Hundred-Box Write on the Class MathBoard:

123   *one hundred twenty-three*

Ask students to show 123 on their MathBoards as a volunteer shows it on the Class MathBoard. Most students will draw 12 ten-sticks and circle 3 individual dots. (Some students may draw a box or circle around 100 dots, and then draw 2 ten-sticks and circle 3 dots. This should be considered correct.)

● Let's count by tens and ones to make sure we have drawn 123 correctly: 10, 20, 30, 40, 50, 60, 70, 80, 90, 100, 110, 120, 121, 122, 123.

Have students draw a box around 10 of the ten-sticks.

● What amount does this box show? 100

Explain that just as a ten-stick is a quick way of drawing 10, a *hundred-box* is a quick way of drawing 100.

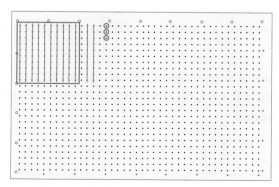

100 + 20 + 3
Dot Drawing of 123

Activity continued ▶

Alternate Approach

Base Ten Blocks In this lesson and in the lessons that follow, students could also show the numbers using base ten blocks. In the figure below, for instance, 1 thousands block, 3 hundreds blocks, 2 tens rods, and 7 ones cubes are used to represent 1,327.

The major difference between the base ten blocks and the *Math Expression* drawings is in the thousands (see pages 6 and 7). The 2-dimensional long thousands bar used to show 10 hundreds is clearer to some students than the thousands base ten block, because some students see only the 6 faces of the block and think there are 6 hundreds rather than 10 in one thousand.

The Learning Classroom

Building Concepts As a review during the lesson, ask students for the place value of each number. For example, point to each digit in the number 76 and ask for the value. 7 tens, 6 ones

Teaching Note

Language and Vocabulary When describing *ten-sticks*, some of your students may use the term *quick tens* which they used in the previous grade.

The Learning Classroom

Helping Community Create a classroom where students are not competing, but desire to collaborate and help one another. Communicate often that your goal as a class is that everyone understands the math you are studying. Tell students that this will require everyone working together to help each other.

Teaching Note

What to Expect from Students
Students may draw 5-groups in different ways. For example, here are four ways to show 10 ones with 5-groups. Similar arrangements may be used. Also when drawing ten-sticks, leave a space after the first 5 ten-sticks to show the 5-groups.

Emphasize that 100 can be thought of *either* as 10 tens (ten-sticks) *or* as 100 ones (dots). Students need to understand both of these representations to add and subtract multi-digit numbers. They will need to group 10 tens to get 1 hundred or ungroup 1 hundred to get 10 tens.

Draw the number 247 on the Class MathBoard as shown below. Ask students to identify the number by counting hundreds, then tens, then ones: 100, 200, 210, 220, 230, 240, 241, 242, 243, 244, 245, 246, 247.

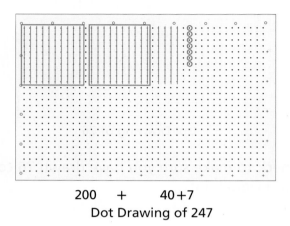

200   +   40+7
Dot Drawing of 247

▶ Place Value Drawings Without Dots WHOLE CLASS

Have students erase their MathBoards and turn them over.

● **How can you show 76 without dots?** Draw 7 sticks for 7 tens and 6 circles for 6 ones.

Help students make the drawing below, which shows a stick for each ten and a circle for each one. Explain that drawing "5-groups" makes counting easier because you can see at a glance that there are five without counting each item individually.

Place Value Drawing of 76

● **How can you represent a hundred without using the dots.** Draw a box.

Tell students to make a place value drawing for 123 on the blank part of their MathBoards. Ask for a volunteer to draw the place value drawing on the Class MathBoard.

Place Value Drawing of 123

Do more drawings as necessary for students to understand. You may wish to have students who are struggling work with a **Helping Partner**.

Practice Place Value Drawings for Hundreds, Tens, and Ones

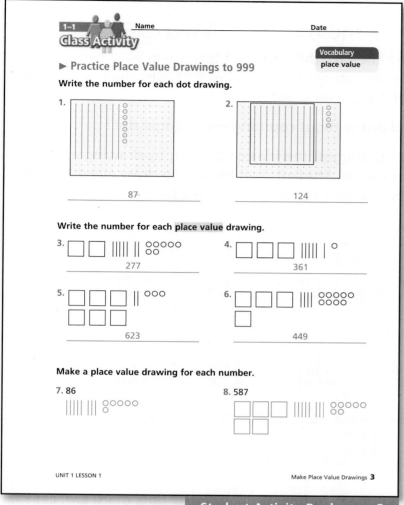

Student Activity Book page 3

 20 MINUTES

Goal: Interpret and make place value drawings for hundreds, tens, and ones.

Materials: Student Activity Book or Hardcover Book p. 3

 NCTM Standards:
Number and Operations
Representation

The Learning Classroom

Math Talk Make your classroom a place where all students listen to understand one another. Explain to students that this involves thinking about what a person is saying so that you can explain it yourself or help them explain it more clearly. By listening carefully, students will be able to ask a question or help the explainer.

▶ Practice Place Value Drawings to 999 INDIVIDUALS

Have students complete Student Book page 3. Exercises 1–8 provide practice with interpreting and making place value drawings. Encourage students to work independently, and then discuss the results as a class. Focus on place value by asking these questions:

● How much is a box worth? one hundred

● How much is a stick worth? ten

● How much is a circle worth? one

● How can you count to find the number shown in the drawing? First count the hundreds, then the tens, and then the ones.

Activity 3

Conceptualize and Represent 1,000

 20 MINUTES

Goal: Represent 1,000 with a place value drawing.

Materials: MathBoard materials, Student Activity Book or Hardcover Book p. 4

 NCTM Standards:
Number and Operations
Representation

Differentiated Instruction

Extra Help If students are not convinced these 5 × 20 boxes represent 100, have them draw horizontal ten-sticks.

Teaching Note

Homework Homework is crucial for learning in this program. Ask those students who did not complete the homework from the previous day to complete it and turn it in the following day. Establish a routine so that students know they are expected to complete their homework every day. Encourage students to see doing homework as a usual part of the daily routine.

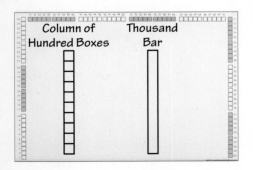

▶ Introduce the Thousand-Bar WHOLE CLASS

Have students erase their MathBoards and turn them back over so the dot array is face up. Ask students how many dots they think are on the entire board. Listen to several guesses.

● How can we find out without counting every single dot?

If no one brings it up, suggest the idea of starting by drawing as many hundred-boxes as possible. Students will be able to draw eight 10 × 10 hundred-boxes. The last two hundred-boxes will be 5 × 20.

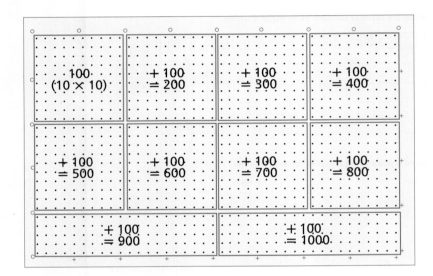

● Now, count by hundreds to find out how many dots there are. Let's count together. Point to each box as you count. 100, 200, 300, 400, 500, 600, 700, 800, 900, 1000.

Some students may get confused about what number comes after 900. They may say "10 hundred." Explain that "a thousand" is another name for "10 hundred." Write 1,000 in numerals and in words on the board.

Thousand-Bar Turn over the Class MathBoard and draw a column of 10 hundred boxes. Ask a volunteer to count by hundreds to find what number you have represented. 1,000

Next to the column of hundred-boxes, draw a column of the same height, without hundreds divisions. Explain that a *thousand-bar* is a fast way of drawing 1,000. Emphasize that a thousand-bar should be long and skinny so it doesn't get confused with a hundred-box. See sample to the left.

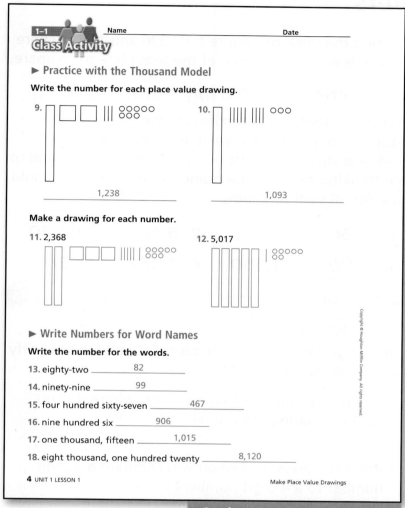

1-1 Class Activity

Name Date

▶ Practice with the Thousand Model

Write the number for each place value drawing.

9. 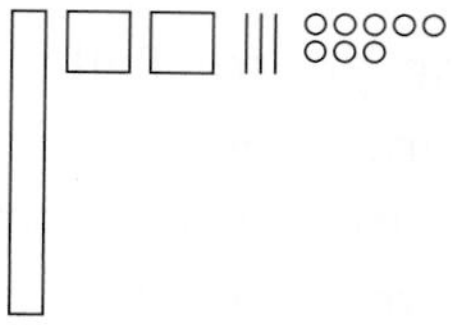

1,238

10. 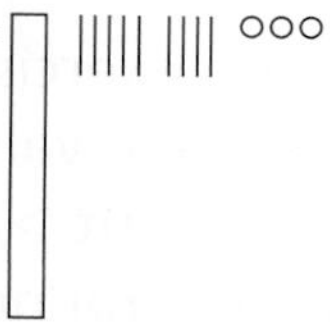

1,093

Make a drawing for each number.

11. 2,368

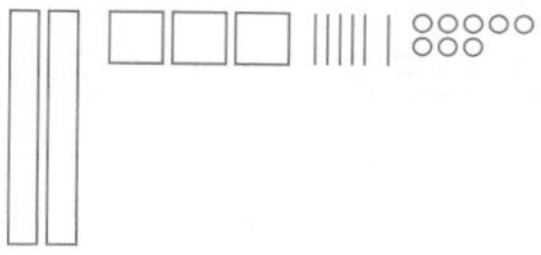

12. 5,017

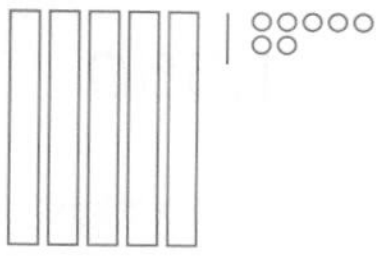

▶ Write Numbers for Word Names

Write the number for the words.

13. eighty-two 82

14. ninety-nine 99

15. four hundred sixty-seven 467

16. nine hundred six 906

17. one thousand, fifteen 1,015

18. eight thousand, one hundred twenty 8,120

4 UNIT 1 LESSON 1 Make Place Value Drawings

Student Activity Book page 4

▶ Practice with the Thousand Model WHOLE CLASS

As a class, work through exercises 9–12 on Student Book page 4.

▶ Write Numbers for Word Names INDIVIDUALS

Have students complete exercises 13–18 independently.

Exercises 13–18 provide practice for reading and writing numbers.

When students have finished, ask volunteers to write their answers on the board and read the answers aloud to check that they wrote them correctly. Be sure to correct any students who say the word "and" when reading a number. For example, 467 should not be read "four hundred and sixty seven." Explain that we will say "and" for the decimal point when we say decimal numbers later in the year so it is better to learn not to say it now.

Then, ask students:

- What word do you notice the volunteers saying at the comma in the number? thousand

Teaching Note

Watch For! Make sure students understand that a thousand-bar doesn't have to be the size of 10 hundred-boxes. Whenever they see or draw a long, skinny strip in a place value drawing, they will know that it is a thousand-bar and is equivalent to 10 hundreds.

English Language Learners

Help students understand the values of circles, ten sticks, and boxes. Model each one, and write its value on the board.

- **Beginning** Say: **This is a circle. It equals 1. Its value is 1.** Have students repeat. Continue with ten sticks and boxes.
- **Intermediate** Ask: **Does a circle equal 1 or 10?** 1 Say: **This is a ten stick. It equals ____.** 10 **A box equals ____.** 100
- **Advanced** Ask students the values for each drawing. Ask: **How many ten sticks do you draw for the number 30?** 3 ten sticks

Ongoing Assessment

Have students use dot drawings or place value drawings to explain how the number 251 is different from the number 521.

Going Further

Math Connection: Compare Numbers

Goal: Compare 4-digit numbers using the greater than and less than symbols.

Materials: MathBoard materials, base ten blocks

✓ **NCTM Standards:**
Number and Operations
Representation

 Class Management

These activities are intended to challenge students and to include mathematical topics required by state standards. Use these activities based on the individual needs of your students and/or according to specific state standards.

▶ **Compare Numbers Using Place Value**

WHOLE CLASS

Write the numbers 2,312 and 2,176 on the board. Ask a volunteer to make place value drawings for the numbers.

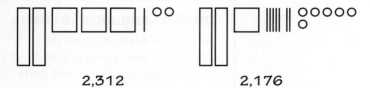

2,312   2,176

Ask students which of the numbers is greater and to explain why. Be sure that students use the drawings to explain that there are 2 more hundreds in 2,312 than in 2,176 so 2,312 is greater.

If necessary, help students explain that you look at the bigger place values farther left to decide, not the smaller places to the right.

● Describe whether you should put > or < after 2,312 and why. the greater than symbol because the bigger part of this symbol points to the greater number

Write the following on the board so students can see how to say a comparison and how to write a comparison using symbols.

2,312 is greater than 2,176.

2,312 > 2,176

Repeat the same procedure for 1,326 and 1,371, where students will need to look at the tens place to compare.

▶ **Practice Comparing Numbers** PAIRS

Write the following exercises on the board. Tell students to make place value drawings for exercises 1–4. Ask students to put >, <, or = in the circle and to be thinking of a general numerical method they could use for all such problems.

1. 8,056 ⊘> 8,037   2. 5,460 ⊘< 8,560

3. 1,429 ⊘< 1,550   4. 1,932 ⊘> 198

▶ **Discuss Patterns**   Math Talk 🔢

WHOLE CLASS

Discuss general patterns students found and exemplify with drawings as needed.

● When you compare two numbers, where do you start comparing the digits? At the left so you compare digits with the greatest place value.

● What is always true when you compare a 3-digit number to a 4-digit number? The 4-digit number is larger.

● If two 4-digit numbers have the same 4 digits, are the numbers equal? Explain. The numbers are equal if the same digits are in same places in both numbers.

Teaching Note

Math Connection This activity is designed to emphasize the connection between comparing numbers and place value. Students will use what they know about relative magnitude and place value to determine whether a number is less than, greater than, or equal to another number.

Differentiated Instruction

Extra Help Students can model each number in the pair with base ten blocks, then make the comparisons.

Differentiated Instruction

Race to 100

Activity Card 1-1 ●

Work: In pairs

Use:

- Base ten blocks (1 hundreds block, 20 tens rods, 20 ones cubes)
- 2 number cubes labeled 1–6

1. Take turns rolling number cubes and taking base ten blocks to play a game.

2. Roll two number cubes. Find the sum of the two numbers. Then take that number of ones cubes.

3. **Think** Can you trade 10 ones cubes for 1 ten rod? If so, make the trade.

The first person to trade 10 tens rods for 1 hundred block wins the game.

Unit 1, Lesson 1

Copyright © Houghton Mifflin Company

Activity Note Students may need to play several rounds before being able to make an exchange.

 **Math Writing Prompt**

Investigate Math Explain to a friend how the two 4s in the number 1,445 are different from each other.

Soar to Success Math ★ **Software Support**

Warm Up 1.11

Pass the Number

Activity Card 1-1 ▲

Work: In small groups

Use:

- MathBoard materials

1. Make a dot drawing of a three-digit number. Then pass your MathBoard to the student on your right.

2. Write the number in numerals for the drawing on the MathBoard you receive. Again, pass the MathBoard to the student on your right.

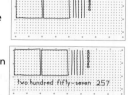

3. Write the number in words on the MathBoard you receive. Then pass the MathBoard to the student who made the drawing.

4. Check that the numerals and words are correct.

5. Repeat for another three-digit number.

Unit 1, Lesson 1

Copyright © Houghton Mifflin Company

Activity Note Be sure that students write a digit for each of the three place values in their number. Suggest that they count the number of hundreds, tens, and ones in the drawing.

 Math Writing Prompt

Explain Your Thinking Explain why you do *not* read the number 308 as "thirty-eight."

MegaMath Grades K-6 **Software Support**

Country Countdown: Block Busters, Level S

Number Riddles

Activity Card 1-1 ■

Work: On your own

Each riddle below has more than one answer. Find all the possible answers.

> I am a 3-digit number.
> The digit in my tens place is 5.
> The sum of all my digits is 7.
> What number could I be?

151 or 250

> I am a 4-digit number.
> The digit in my tens place is 5.
> The sum of all my digits is 8.
> What number could I be?

1,052, 1,151, 1,250, 2,051, 2,150, or 3,050

Unit 1, Lesson 1

Copyright © Houghton Mifflin Company

Activity Note For each riddle, students should list all possible digits that, when added to 5 tens, will equal the given sum. Then they can make an organized list of all possible combinations of digits.

 Math Writing Prompt

Bagging Marbles A toy factory made 1,800 marbles yesterday. How many bags can they fill with 10 marbles in each bag? Explain your answer.

 DESTINATION Math· **Software Support**

Course II: Module 1: Unit 1: Place Value: Hundreds, Tens, and Ones

Make Place Value Drawings   **17**

③ Homework and Spiral Review

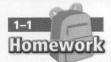

1-1 Homework **Goal:** Additional Practice

This Homework page gives students practice making and interpreting place value drawings.

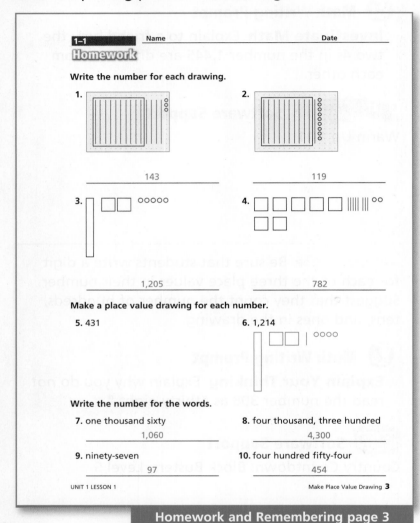

1-1 Homework Name ___ Date ___

Write the number for each drawing.

1. _143_

2. _119_

3. _1,205_

4. _782_

Make a place value drawing for each number.

5. 431

6. 1,214

Write the number for the words.

7. one thousand sixty _1,060_

8. four thousand, three hundred _4,300_

9. ninety-seven _97_

10. four hundred fifty-four _454_

UNIT 1 LESSON 1   Make Place Value Drawing **3**

Homework and Remembering page 3

1-1 Remembering **Goal:** Spiral Review

This Remembering page would be appropriate anytime after today's lesson.

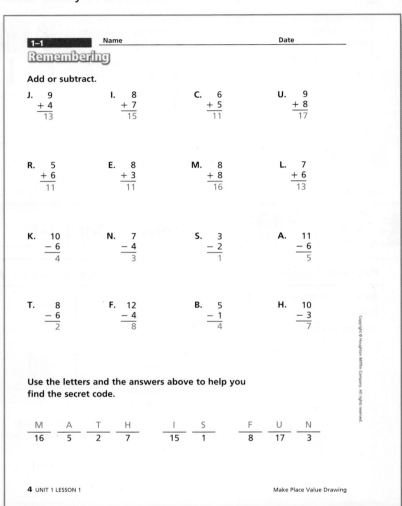

1-1 Remembering Name ___ Date ___

Add or subtract.

J. $9 + 4 = 13$ I. $8 + 7 = 15$ C. $6 + 5 = 11$ U. $9 + 8 = 17$

R. $5 + 6 = 11$ E. $8 + 3 = 11$ M. $8 + 8 = 16$ L. $7 + 6 = 13$

K. $10 - 6 = 4$ N. $7 - 4 = 3$ S. $3 - 2 = 1$ A. $11 - 6 = 5$

T. $8 - 6 = 2$ F. $12 - 4 = 8$ B. $5 - 1 = 4$ H. $10 - 3 = 7$

Use the letters and the answers above to help you find the secret code.

M	A	T	H		I	S		F	U	N
16	5	2	7		15	1		8	17	3

4 UNIT 1 LESSON 1   Make Place Value Drawing

Homework and Remembering page 4

Home and School Connection

Family Letter Have students take home the Family Letter on Student Activity Book pages 5–8 or Activity Workbook pages 3–6. A Spanish translation of this letter is on the following pages. This letter explains how the concept of place value is developed in *Math Expressions.* It gives parents and guardians a better understanding of the learning that goes on in math class and creates a bridge between school and home.

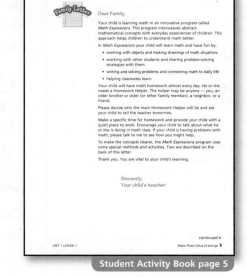

Student Activity Book page 5

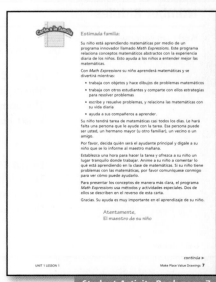

Student Activity Book page 7

▶ Money Drawings Without Dots INDIVIDUALS

Have students complete exercises 4–12 on Student Book page 9.
Discuss exercises that caused difficulty for students.

 Math Talk in Action

Ayame: In Exercise 6, how do the place values for the 1 and the 6 to the left of the decimal point differ if they both are dollars?

Emilio: The 1 on the left of the decimal point is in the ten dollars place. The 6 is in the one dollars place.

Ayame: How do you represent the ten and one dollars places?

Emilio: To represent the ten dollars place, you use the thousand-bar that equals 1,000 cents or $10. To represent the one dollars place, you use the hundred-box that equals 100 cents or $1.

Dao: In Exercise 7, how do you use the drawing to find the money value?

Farha: I look at and add the value of the bars from left to right. The thousand-bar equals $10. Each hundred-box equals $1. Each ten-stick equals 10 cents. Each individual dot equals 1 cent. So, 1 ten dollar + 3 one dollars + 1 dime + 6 cents.

Dao: And, that is the same as $10 + $3 + $0.10 + $0.06 = $13.16.

Yoon Ki: In exercises 11 and 12, how do you know where to put the 1 to the right of the decimal point?

Ben: The first place to the right of the decimal point is the dimes place. The second place to the right of the decimal is the pennies place.

Yoon Ki: So, Exercise 11 has 1 ten dollars + 1 cent and without dimes the amount is written as $10.01. Exercise 12 has 1 ten dollars + 1 dime and without cents the amount is written as $10.10.

 Ongoing Assessment

Ask students these questions.

▶ How are 7 + 4 and 70 + 4 different?

▶ In a money drawing, explain why a thousand-bar represents ten dollars.

▶ Compare adding 7 + 4 to adding 8 + 4. How are they the same? How are they different?

Extension: Place Value Through Ten Thousands

Goal: Identify the place value in numbers to 99,999.

Material: Student Activity Book or Hardcover Book p. 10.

✓ **NCTM Standards:**
Number and Operations
Representation

▶ Place Value to 99,999 WHOLE CLASS

Write 60,190 days on the board and explain that this is how long it takes Neptune to orbit the Sun. Draw a place value chart on the board and have students help you fill in the top row.

ten thousands	thousands	hundreds	tens	ones
6	0	1	9	0

Ask students if anyone knows how to say this number. Say, It is tricky because you don't say the name of the ten-thousands place.

Draw the bracket below the chart to show how you read those places.

ten thousands	thousands	hundreds	tens	ones
6	0	1	9	0

_____ _____ thousand _____ hundred _____ ty _____

sixty thousand, one hundred ninety

Then, ask students to suppose there are Secret Code Cards for numbers this large. Ask a volunteer to sketch the Secret Code Cards that they would use to build the number.

[60,000] + [100] + [90] = [60,190]

Summarize by writing the labels standard form, expanded form, and word form on the board and ask a volunteer to write the number in these ways next to the labels:

Standard form: 60,190
Expanded form: 60,000 + 100 + 90
Word form: Sixty thousand, one hundred ninety

Teaching Note

If your state curriculum requires place value through hundred thousands, see Extension Lesson 1.

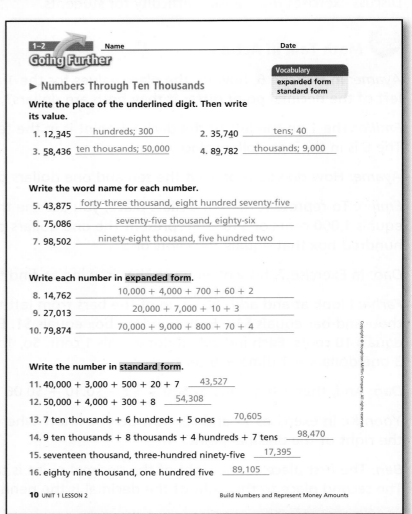

Student Activity Book page 10

▶ Numbers Through Ten Thousands
WHOLE CLASS

Ask a volunteer to think of a 5-digit number, say it in words, and write it on the board in standard form.

Example: 54,138

● What place is the digit 4 in? thousands

● What is the value of the digit 4? 4,000

● How would you write the number in expanded form? 50,000 + 4,000 + 100 + 30 + 8

Then, have students complete Student Activity Book page 10.

Differentiated Instruction

Mixed-up Money   Activity Card 1-2 ●

Work: In pairs

Use:

• 6 index cards

• Play Money (20 one-dollar bills, 20 dimes, and 20 pennies)

1. Choose any number from 1 to 9 and draw that number of hundred boxes on an index card.

2. Choose another number from 1 to 9 and draw that number of ten sticks on the second index card.

3. Choose another number from 1 to 9 and draw that number of circles on the third index card.

4. Mix up the cards and exchange with your partner. Place coins on each card equal to the amount shown. Then write the amount of money the set of cards represents. Check each other's work.

$5.29

Unit 1, Lesson 2   Copyright © Houghton Mifflin Company

Activity Note After the activity is completed, reinforce learning by asking students why each card must show a number less than 10.

 Math Writing Prompt

Explain Your Thinking Explain how you know that 7 + 5 is greater than 10.

 **Software Support**

Warm Up 3.16

Money Match   Activity Card 1-2 ▲

Work: In pairs

Use:

• 12 index cards

Decide:

Who will be Student 1 and who will be Student 2 for the first round.

1. **Work Together** Make six pairs of cards. Choose a different money amount for each pair. The first card shows the money amount and the second card shows the place value drawing of that amount.

2. Mix up the cards and turn them face down.

$3.29

3. **Student 1:** Turn two cards face up and try to find a matching pair to take off the table. If no match is made, turn the cards face down again.

4. **Student 2:** Take a turn and repeat the activity. Continue taking turns until all pairs are found.

Unit 1, Lesson 2   Copyright © Houghton Mifflin Company

Activity Note Reinforce learning by having partners justify each pair that they make.

 Math Writing Prompt

Investigate Math Explain why you can use a hundred-box to show both the number *one hundred* and the money amount *one dollar*.

 Software Support

Numberopolis: Lulu's Lunch Counter, Level S

Money Riddles   Activity Card 1-2 ■

Work: In pairs

Use:

• MathBoard materials

• Index cards

1. Choose a money amount over $10 and write it on an index card. On a second card, write a place value drawing riddle to describe the amount.

I am equal to one rectangle, two squares, and four circles. What amount am I?

$12.04

$12.04

2. Exchange only the riddle with your partner. Use your MathBoard to make the place value drawing and then try to name the amount. Write your answer to the riddle on the card. Check each other's work.

3. Repeat the activity three more times.

Unit 1, Lesson 2   Copyright © Houghton Mifflin Company

Activity Note Be sure that students understand that place value drawings should be described in terms of thousand-bars, hundred-boxes, ten-sticks, and circles.

 Math Writing Prompt

Create Your Own What amount of money do you think 10 thousand-bars represent? Create your own picture to show that amount.

 DESTINATION Math **Software Support**

Course II: Module 1: Unit 1: Place Value: Hundreds, Tens, and Ones

Build Numbers and Represent Money Amounts   **27**

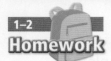

③ Homework and Spiral Review

Homework **Goal:** Additional Practice

This Homework page gives students an opportunity to practice making and interpreting drawings for money amounts.

Remembering **Goal:** Spiral Review

This Remembering page would be appropriate anytime after today's lesson.

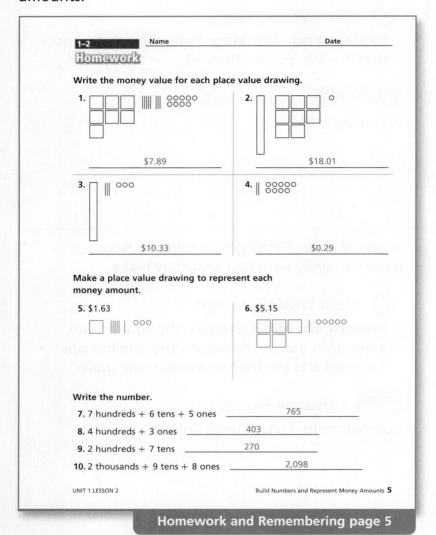

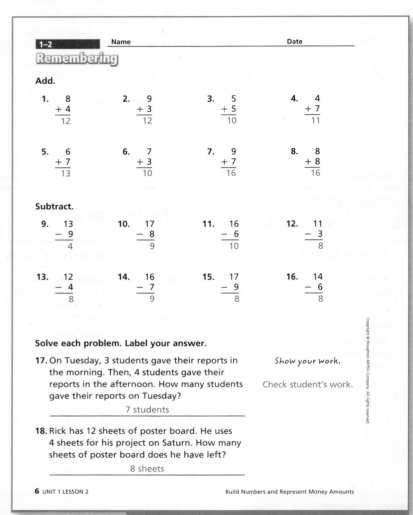

Home or School Activity

Multicultural Connection

International Coins Have students bring in real coins or pictures of coins from other countries to share with the class. Compare the design of the coins to one another and to U.S. coins.

Place Value in Word Problems

Lesson Objectives

- Group and ungroup multi-digit numbers.
- Solve word problems that require understanding of place value.

Vocabulary
place value drawing

The Day at a Glance

Today's Goals	Materials

1 Teaching the Lesson
A1: Represent multi-digit numbers as sums of thousands, hundreds, tens, and ones.
A2: Solve place value word problems.
 	
2 Going Further
▸ Differentiated Instruction
 	
3 Homework and Spiral Review
	Lesson Activities
	Student Activity Book pp. 11–12 or
	  Student Hardcover Book pp. 11–12
	Homework and Remembering
	  pp. 7–8
	Demonstration Secret Code Cards
	  (TRB M3–M18)
	Secret Code cards (TRB M19–M22
	  or from Lesson 2)
	MathBoard materials
	Base ten blocks
		Going Further
		Activity Cards 1-3
		MathBoard materials
		Sentence Strips
		Index Cards
		Math Journals

123 *Use* **Math Talk** *today!*

Keeping Skills Sharp

Quick Practice 5 MINUTES	Daily Routines
Goal: Read and form 3-digit numbers with Secret Code Cards. **Materials:** Demonstration Secret Code Cards (TRB M3–M18) **Read Place Value Drawings** Have a **Student Leader** form a 3-digit number with the place value drawings on the back of the Demonstration Secret Code Cards. After the class identifies the number, have the **Student Leader** demonstrate how to form the 3-digit number using the numerals on the cards. (See Unit 1 Lesson 2 Activity 1.)	**Homework Review** Have students discuss any errors made on the homework. Encourage students to help each other resolve these errors. **Create a Pattern** Have students choose a number between 10 and 20. Then, have students write a growing pattern that starts with the number chosen and write the rule they used.

500 90 3
5 9 3

Teaching the Lesson

Analyze Numbers

 20 MINUTES

Goal: Represent multi-digit numbers as sums of thousands, hundreds, tens, and ones.

Materials: Demonstration Secret Code Cards (TRB M3–M18), Secret Code Cards (TRB M19–M22 or from Lesson 2) (1 set per student)

✔ **NCTM Standards:**
Number and Operations
Representation

▶ **Build 4-digit Numbers** WHOLE CLASS

Have students use the Secret Code Cards they cut out in Lesson 2 for this activity. Use TRB M19–M22 to provide replacement sets if needed.

Write the number 1,237 on the board and ask students to build it with their Secret Code Cards. When they have finished, discuss the place value of each number.

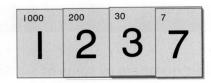

Have a volunteer make a place value drawing for 1,237 on the board.

Next, write the numbers below on the board.

1,659 1,302 1,847 1,263

Have students build the numbers, one at a time, with their Secret Code Cards. For each number, ask questions about place value, in mixed order. For example:

● What digit is in the tens place?

● What is the value of the digit in the tens place?

● What digit is in the thousands place?

● What is the value of the digit in the thousands place?

● What digit is in the ones place?

● What is the value of the digit in the ones place?

● What digit is in the hundreds place?

● What is the value of the digit in the hundreds place?

Write these equations on the board:

$$1{,}263 = 1{,}000 + 200 + 60 + 3$$

$$1{,}263 = 1 \text{ thousand} + 2 \text{ hundreds} + 6 \text{ tens} + 3 \text{ ones}$$

Point out that these are two ways to write the number in expanded form. Then, point to 1,263.

● One way to read this number is "one thousand, two hundred sixty-three." Does anyone know another way to read it?

If no one responds correctly, explain that some people read 1,263 as "twelve hundred sixty-three." Ask students to explain why this way of reading the number is also correct. Remind them that 1 thousand is equal to 10 hundreds. Because 1 thousand is 10 hundreds, 1,263 actually has 12 hundreds altogether.

Write the following beneath the equations that are already on the board:

$$1{,}263 = 12 \text{ hundreds} + 6 \text{ tens} + 3 \text{ ones}$$

Now, focus on the tens.

● What if we want to think of 1,263 as being made up of only tens and ones. How many tens are there in 1,263 altogether? 126

Have students explain how they found the answer. They should understand that 12 hundreds is the same as 120 tens. Combining 120 tens with the 6 tens shown in the tens place equals 126 tens. Write the following beneath the other equations:

$$1{,}263 = 126 \text{ tens} + 3 \text{ ones}$$

Finally, focus on the ones.

● Now, think of 1,263 as being made only of ones. How many ones are there altogether? 1,263

Write this last equation under the others.

$$1{,}263 = 1{,}263 \text{ ones}$$

Give students several numbers less than 2,000 to analyze in this way.

Discuss place value homework examples like these.

Have students discuss patterns they see and how they can use their knowledge of 9 + 5 = 14 to solve 9 tens + 5 tens is 14 tens or 140 and 9 hundreds + 5 hundreds is 14 hundreds or 1,400.

$$9 + 5 = \underline{\hspace{1cm}}$$
$$90 + 50 = \underline{\hspace{1cm}}$$
$$900 + 500 = \underline{\hspace{1cm}}$$

Teaching Note

Math Background Understanding how numbers can be grouped and ungrouped in different ways is important to developing and understanding methods for multi-digit addition and subtraction.

Differentiated Instruction

Extra Help If students are having difficulty visualizing the numbers in different groups of hundreds, tens, and ones, have them think of a thousand-bar as 10 hundred-boxes and a hundred-box as 10 ten-sticks. Then have students draw place value models to represent the numbers.

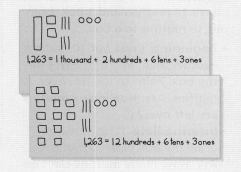

Teaching Note

Quick Practice Be sure to do the Quick Practice every day. It builds vital skills. In Unit 1 students practice mental addition and subtraction of tens and of hundreds, which helps with multidigit calculation.

Teaching the Lesson (continued)

Activity 2

Solve Place Value Word Problems

 25 MINUTES

Goal: Solve place value word problems.

Materials: MathBoard materials, Student Activity Book or Hardcover Book pp. 11–12, base ten blocks

 NCTM Standards:
Number and Operations
Problem Solving
Communication
Representation

English Language Learners

Model a simple word problem. Draw 12 muffins on the board. Say: **I have 12 muffins and 1 box. I can put 10 muffins in a box.**

- **Beginning** Cross out 10 muffins. Redraw them in a box. Say: **I fill the box.** Point to the left over muffins. Ask: **How many muffins are left over?** 2
- **Intermediate** Have students draw the box with 10 muffins. Ask: **How many muffins can't go in the box?** 2 Say: **2 muffins are left over.** Have students repeat.
- **Advanced** Draw a square around ten muffins. Ask: **How many muffins are left over?** 2 Have students describe how to solve a problem with 24 muffins and 2 boxes.

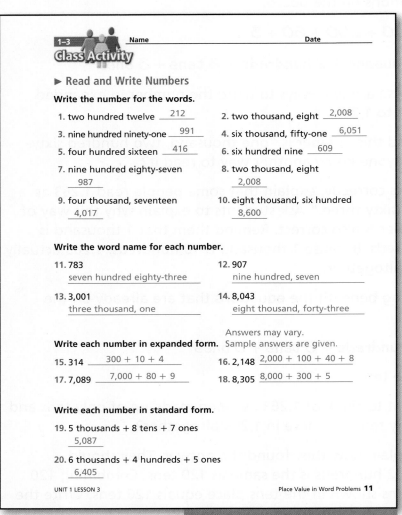

1–3 Class Activity

Name _____ Date _____

▶ **Read and Write Numbers**

Write the number for the words.

1. two hundred twelve ___212___
2. two thousand, eight ___2,008___
3. nine hundred ninety-one ___991___
4. six thousand, fifty-one ___6,051___
5. four hundred sixteen ___416___
6. six hundred nine ___609___
7. nine hundred eighty-seven ___987___
8. two thousand, eight ___2,008___
9. four thousand, seventeen ___4,017___
10. eight thousand, six hundred ___8,600___

Write the word name for each number.

11. 783 ___seven hundred eighty-three___
12. 907 ___nine hundred, seven___
13. 3,001 ___three thousand, one___
14. 8,043 ___eight thousand, forty-three___

Answers may vary.

Write each number in expanded form. Sample answers are given.

15. 314 ___300 + 10 + 4___
16. 2,148 ___2,000 + 100 + 40 + 8___
17. 7,089 ___7,000 + 80 + 9___
18. 8,305 ___8,000 + 300 + 5___

Write each number in standard form.

19. 5 thousands + 8 tens + 7 ones ___5,087___
20. 6 thousands + 4 hundreds + 5 ones ___6,405___

UNIT 1 LESSON 3   Place Value in Word Problems **11**

Student Activity Book page 11

▶ **Read and Write Numbers** [INDIVIDUALS]

Have students complete exercises 1–20 on Student Book page 11 to practice reading and writing numbers.

Have students work in **Small Groups** to check their answers.

1–3

Class Activity

Name _____   Date _____

▶ Solve and Discuss

Show your work.

Use a place value drawing to help you solve each problem. Label your answers.

21. Scott baked a batch of rolls. He gave a bag of 10 rolls to each of 7 friends. He kept 1 roll for himself. How many rolls did he bake in all?

    _____71 rolls_____

22. Sixty-two bags of hotdog buns were delivered to the school cafeteria. Each bag had 10 buns. How many buns were delivered?

    _____620 buns_____

> Mario and Rosa baked 89 corn muffins.
> They put the muffins in boxes of 10.

23. How many boxes did they fill?   24. How many muffins were left over?

    _____8 boxes_____   _____9 muffins_____

> Zoe's scout troop collected 743 cans of food to donate to a shelter. They put the cans in boxes of 10.

25. How many boxes did they fill?   26. How many cans were left over

    _____74 boxes_____   _____3 cans_____

27. Math Journal Write your own place value word problem. Make a drawing to show how to solve your problem. Check student's work.

12 UNIT 1 LESSON 3   Place Value in Word Problems

The Learning Classroom

Math Talk When using **Solve and Discuss,** choose presenters who used different solution strategies and have the class compare and contrast the strategies.

▶ Solve and Discuss [WHOLE CLASS]

Read aloud problem 21 on Student Book page 12.

123 Math Talk Use the **Solve and Discuss** structure for problem 5. Invite a few students to work at the board, while the other students work on their MathBoards. Ask students to solve using a place value drawing. Select two or three students to show their place value drawings and explain their thinking. Encourage other students to listen carefully and ask questions. Make sure students give the label, or unit, for their answer. If they forget, ask questions like the following:

● You said the answer is 71. 71 what? 71 rolls

✋ Alternate Approach

Base Ten Blocks Students could also solve place value word problems by using base ten blocks

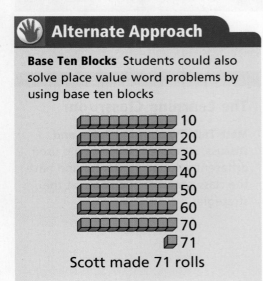

Scott made 71 rolls

The following is one possible solution for problem 21.

- Make a ten-stick for each bag of 10 rolls and a circle for the extra roll.

7 bags of 10 rolls   1 roll

- Count to find the total: 10, 20, 30, 40, 50, 60, 70, 71

- Scott made 71 rolls.

Continue using **Solve and Discuss** for problems 22–27 on Student Book page 12. Choose different students to work at the board for each problem. Then have students complete problem 11 and share their problems with the class. These problems are difficult for some students. Solving them is not a central unit goal.

The following is one possible solution for problem 22.

- Make a ten stick for each bag.

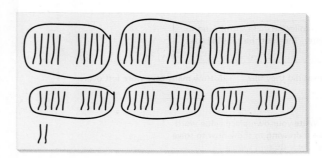

- Circle groups of 10 bags (100 buns).

- Count to find the total: 100, 200, 300, 400, 500, 600, 620

- 620 buns were delivered.

The following is one possible solution for problems 7 and 8.

- Make a ten stick for each box of muffins and a circle for the muffins left over.

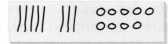

- Count the ten-sticks.

- 8 boxes were filled.

- 9 muffins were left over.

②Going Further

Intervention — Activity Card 1-3

Number Names — Activity Card 1-3

Work: On your own

Use:
• MathBoard materials

1. On your dot grid paper, copy the first drawing shown in the picture below. Then copy the label.

2. Write the number you have shown. Then copy the second drawing for the same number. Label the second drawing as shown.

3. Draw the four numbers below in two ways and write a label for each drawing.

   • **134** 1 hundred 3 tens 4 ones; 13 tens 4 ones
   • **571** 5 hundreds 7 tens 1 one; 57 tens 1 one
   • **289** 2 hundreds 8 tens 9 ones; 28 tens 9 ones
   • **642** 6 hundreds 4 tens 2 ones; 64 tens 2 ones

Unit 1, Lesson 3   Copyright © Houghton Mifflin Company

Activity Note Tell students that their second drawing should use only ten-sticks and circles.

📝 **Math Writing Prompt**

Write a Problem Write a place value word problem about groups of 10.

Soar to Success Math ★ **Software Support**

Warm Up 1.16

On Level — Activity Card 1-3

Scrambled Word Problems — Activity Card 1-3 ▲

Work: In pairs

Use:
• Sentence Strips

1. **Work Together** Copy the sentences below on strips.

   How many vases did Jen fill?

   Jen had 83 daisies.

   How many daisies were left over?

   Jen put 10 daisies in each vase.

2. Work with your partner to arrange the strips in the correct order and solve the problem. 8 vases filled; 3 daisies left over

3. **On Your Own** Write another place value word problem on sentence strips. Arrange the strips out of order.

4. Exchange sentence strips with your partner and repeat the activity.

Unit 1, Lesson 3   Copyright © Houghton Mifflin Company

Activity Note Encourage students to write problems with at least three simple sentences.

📝 **Math Writing Prompt**

Explain Your Thinking Explain how to use the Make a Hundred strategy to add 90 + 40.

MegaMath Grades K-6 **Software Support**

Numberopolis: Carnival Stories, Level P

Challenge — Activity Card 1-3

Write Place Value Problems — Activity Card 1-3 ■

Work: In pairs

Use:
• 12 Index cards

1. **On Your Own** Copy the three answers below, one on each of 3 cards.

   | 21 boxes and 7 cookies left over | 2 boxes and 17 cookies left over | 217 cookies |

2. Write a place value word problem for each answer on three other separate cards.

3. Exchange problems with your partner. Match each word problem with the correct answer.

4. **Work Together** Check your work.

Unit 1, Lesson 3   Copyright © Houghton Mifflin Company

Activity Note For problems involving remainders, suggest that students write about dividing a total amount into equal groups greater than the remainder.

📝 **Math Writing Prompt**

Investigate Math What pattern do you see in the value of the places in a number when you go from right to left?

✠ **DESTINATION Math** **Software Support**

Course II: Module 1: Unit 1: Place Value: Hundreds, Tens, and Ones

③ Homework and Spiral Review

1-3 Homework   Goal: Additional Practice

✓ Include students' completed Homework page as part of their portfolios.

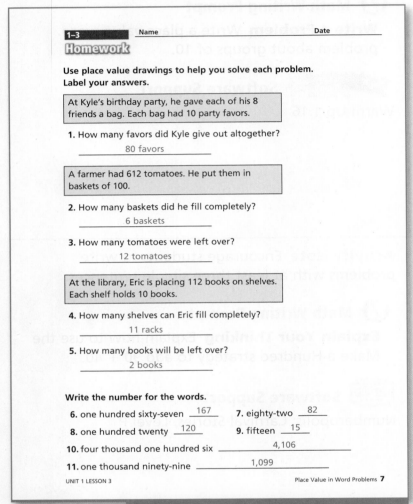

1-3 Homework   Name _____   Date _____

Use place value drawings to help you solve each problem. Label your answers.

> At Kyle's birthday party, he gave each of his 8 friends a bag. Each bag had 10 party favors.

1. How many favors did Kyle give out altogether?
80 favors

> A farmer had 612 tomatoes. He put them in baskets of 100.

2. How many baskets did he fill completely?
6 baskets

3. How many tomatoes were left over?
12 tomatoes

> At the library, Eric is placing 112 books on shelves. Each shelf holds 10 books.

4. How many shelves can Eric fill completely?
11 racks

5. How many books will be left over?
2 books

Write the number for the words.

6. one hundred sixty-seven 167   **7.** eighty-two 82

8. one hundred twenty 120   **9.** fifteen 15

10. four thousand one hundred six 4,106

11. one thousand ninety-nine 1,099

UNIT 1 LESSON 3   Place Value in Word Problems **7**

Homework and Remembering page 7

1-3 Remembering   Goal: Spiral Review

This Remembering page would be appropriate anytime after today's lesson.

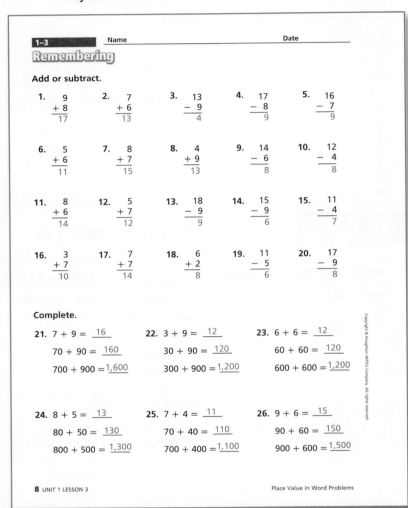

1-3 Remembering   Name _____   Date _____

Add or subtract.

1. $9 + 8 = 17$ **2.** $7 + 6 = 13$ **3.** $13 - 9 = 4$ **4.** $17 - 8 = 9$ **5.** $16 - 7 = 9$

6. $5 + 6 = 11$ **7.** $8 + 7 = 15$ **8.** $4 + 9 = 13$ **9.** $14 - 6 = 8$ **10.** $12 - 4 = 8$

11. $8 + 6 = 14$ **12.** $5 + 7 = 12$ **13.** $18 - 9 = 9$ **14.** $15 - 9 = 6$ **15.** $11 - 4 = 7$

16. $3 + 7 = 10$ **17.** $7 + 7 = 14$ **18.** $6 + 2 = 8$ **19.** $11 - 5 = 6$ **20.** $17 - 9 = 8$

Complete.

21. $7 + 9 = 16$
$70 + 90 = 160$
$700 + 900 = 1,600$

22. $3 + 9 = 12$
$30 + 90 = 120$
$300 + 900 = 1,200$

23. $6 + 6 = 12$
$60 + 60 = 120$
$600 + 600 = 1,200$

24. $8 + 5 = 13$
$80 + 50 = 130$
$800 + 500 = 1,300$

25. $7 + 4 = 11$
$70 + 40 = 110$
$700 + 400 = 1,100$

26. $9 + 6 = 15$
$90 + 60 = 150$
$900 + 600 = 1,500$

8 UNIT 1 LESSON 3   Place Value in Word Problems

Homework and Remembering page 8

Home or School Activity

Social Studies Connection

Timelines Have students find three events that happened between 1500 and today. They should write the year and event on sticky notes. Then, have students make a timeline by placing their sticky notes in the correct place on the poster board.

> DaVinci paints Mona Lisa
> 1503

> Thomas Jefferson elected President
> 1800

> Armstrong walks on Moon
> 1969

Practice with Place Value

REAL WORLD **Problem Solving**

Lesson Objectives

● Identify numbers from scrambled place value names.

● Solve place value word problems.

Vocabulary

Counting On strategy
Make a Ten strategy
place value

The Day at a Glance

Today's Goals	Materials

1 Teaching the Lesson
A1: Identify numbers expressed in scrambled order.
A2: Solve place value word problems.
A3: Extend the Counting On and Make a Ten strategies.
 	
2 Going Further
▸ Differentiated Instruction
 	
3 Homework and Spiral Review
	Lesson Activities
	Student Activity Book pp. 13–14 or
	  Student Hardcover Book pp. 13–14
	Remembering p. 8
	Homework and Remembering
	  pp. 9–10
	Secret Code Cards
	MathBoard materials
	Ten Frame (TRB M2)
	Two-color counters
	Quick Quiz 1 (Assessment Guide)
		Going Further
		Activity Cards 1-4
		Place Value Strips
		  (TRB M23)
		Scissors
		Index Cards
		Math Journals

123 *Use* **Math Talk** *today!*

Keeping Skills Sharp

Quick Practice   🕐 5 MINUTES

Goal: Read and form 3-digit numbers with Secret Code Cards.

Materials: Demonstration Secret Code Cards (TRB M3–M18)

Read Place Value Drawings Have a **Student Leader** form a 3-digit number with the place value drawings on the back of the Demonstration Secret Code Cards. After the class identifies the number, have the **Student Leader** demonstrate how to form the 3-digit number using the numerals on the cards. (See Unit 1 Lesson 2 Activity 1.)

Daily Routines

Homework Review Let students work together to check their work. Initially, pair less able students with more able students. Remind students to use what they know about helping others.

Function Machine A function machine adds 3 to each input. What is the output when the input is 3? 8? 12? 25? 6; 11; 15; 28

Teaching the Lesson

Scrambled Places

 15 MINUTES

Goal: Identify numbers expressed in scrambled order.

Materials: Secret Code Cards (TRB M19–M22 or from Lesson 2), Student Activity Book or Hardcover Book p. 13

✓ **NCTM Standards:**
Number and Operations
Representation

The Learning Classroom

Helping Community By discussing multiple methods for solving math problems, students become aware of other students' thinking. As students better understand other students' thinking, they become better **Helping Partners.** Instead of showing how they would solve problems using their methods, they are able to look at another student's work and help that student find errors using that student's method.

▶ Scrambled Place Value Names [WHOLE CLASS]

Write the expanded form of 1,653 on the board:

> **1 thousand + 6 hundreds + 5 tens + 3 ones**

Have students build the number using their Secret Code Cards. 1,653

Now, write 1,278 in scrambled form on the board:

> **7 tens + 1 thousand + 2 hundreds + 8 ones**

Have students build the number using their Secret Code Cards.

● What number did you build? 1,278

● How is this exercise different from the first one? The place values are given out of order.

Have students complete exercises 1–10 on Student Book page 13. Review and discuss their answers.

1–4	Name	Date

Class Activity

Vocabulary
place value

▶ Scrambled Place Value Names

Unscramble the place values and write the number.

1. 8 ones + 6 hundreds + 4 tens
   648
2. 9 hundreds + 7 tens + 1 one
   971
3. 5 ones + 0 tens + 7 hundreds
   705
4. 5 tens + 4 ones + 3 hundreds
   354
5. 2 tens + 2 hundreds + 2 ones
   222
6. 8 hundreds + 3 ones + 6 tens
   863

Unscramble the place values and write the number. Then, make a place value drawing for the number.

7. 6 hundreds + 9 ones + 3 tens
   639
8. 9 ones + 3 tens + 8 hundreds
   839

9. 8 ones + 3 hundreds + 4 tens
   348
10. 2 hundreds + 9 tens + 1 one
   291

UNIT 1 LESSON 4   Practice with Place Value **13**

Student Activity Book page 13

Activity 2

Place Value Word Problems

30 MINUTES

Goal: Solve place value word problems.

Materials: MathBoard materials, Student Activity Book or Hardcover Book p. 14

 NCTM Standards:
Numbers and Operations
Problem Solving
Communication
Representation

Student Activity Book page 14

1-4
Class Activity   Name _____ Date _____

▶ Solve and Discuss

Solve each problem. Label your answer.

11. The bookstore received 35 boxes of books. Each box held 10 books. How many books did the store receive?

_____ 350 books _____

Maya's family picked 376 apples and put them in baskets. Each basket holds 10 apples.

12. How many baskets did they fill?   13. How many apples were left over?
_____ 37 baskets _____   _____ 6 apples _____

Aidee had 672 buttons. She put them in bags with 100 buttons each.

14. How many bags did Aidee fill?   15. How many buttons were left over?
_____ 6 bags _____   _____ 72 buttons _____

When Joseph broke open his piggy bank, there were 543 pennies inside. He grouped the pennies into piles of 100.

16. How many piles of 100 did Joseph make?   17. How many extra pennies did he have?
_____ 5 piles _____   _____ 43 pennies _____

14 UNIT 1 LESSON 4   Practice with Place Value

▶ Solve and Discuss [WHOLE GROUP]

Direct students' attention to problems 11–17 on Student Book page 14.

 **Math Talk** Using the **Solve and Discuss** structure, have students solve problem 11. Allow students to use any method they choose. If students have difficulty, suggest they try making place value drawings.

● Draw a ten-stick for each box of books. Make a hundred box for each group of 10 ten-sticks. Count to find the total: 100, 200, 300, 310, 320, 330, 340, 350. There are 350 books in all.

Using **Solve and Discuss,** have students solve problems 12–16.

 Ongoing Assessment

Write this place value problem on the board.

> **Avi has 634 pennies.**

Ask students

▶ how many piles of 100 pennies can he make?

▶ How many extra pennies does he have?

English Language Learners

To prepare students for the next activity, model counting on by tens. Write 40 + 50 = on the board. Point to each number. Ask: **How many tens is this?** 4, 5 Say: **One finger is 1 ten. 4 fingers are_____.** 4 tens Hold up 4 fingers. Say: **Lets Count On by Tens.**

• **Beginning** Say: 1 ten, 2 tens... Ask: **Now how many tens are there?** 9 tens Say: **9 tens = _____.** 90

• **Intermediate** Raise 5 fingers as you count. Ask: **How many tens are there?** 9 tens **How much is 9 tens?** 90

• **Advanced** Say: Now count 5 more tens. **How many tens are there now?** 9 tens

Practice with Place Value   **39**

Activity 3

Extend Addition Strategies to Tens and Hundreds

 10 MINUTES

Goal: Extend the Counting On and Make a Ten strategies.

Materials: Remembering p. 8, Ten Frame (TRB M2), two-color counters

 NCTM Standards:
Number and Operations
Representation

Alternate Approach

Counters and Ten Frames When adding tens, students could also make a hundred using two-color counters and Ten Frame (TRB M2).

Invite students to describe how the frame could be used to add hundreds. Students should explain that each counter represents 10 and the frame represents 100.

80 + 50 = 130

80 + 20 = 100   100 + 30 = 130

Make a Thousand Strategy

Challenge another volunteer to solve the problem by making a new thousand.

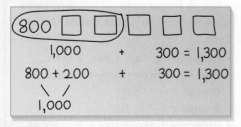
1,000   +   300 = 1,300

800 + 200   +   300 = 1,300

1,000

 **Quick Quiz**

See Assessment Guide for Unit 1 Quick Quiz 1.

▶ **Discuss Addition Strategies** WHOLE CLASS **Math Talk** 🔵123

Review exercises 24–26 on Remembering page 8 from Lesson 3. Ask what strategies students used to find the answer to exercise 24, 80 + 50. Make sure the strategies described below are discussed.

Counting On by Tens Strategy

Students can use their fingers as long as they realize each finger represents 10.

Mentally

● Say the first number to yourself: "80". Count on by tens, until you have counted 5 tens: "90, 100, 110, 120, 130." The answer is 130.

With a Drawing

Use Place Value

● Think: 8 tens + 5 tens.   ● Say: "8 tens"

● Count on, until you have counted 5 tens: "9 tens, 10 tens, 11 tens, 12 tens, 13 tens." The answer is 13 tens, or 130.

Make A Hundred Strategy

Students can also make a hundred to solve 80 + 50.

Numerically

● Start with 80. Take 20 from the 50 to get 100. Add the 30 that is left.

$$80 + 50 = 80 + 20 + 30 = 100 + 30 = 130$$

With a Drawing

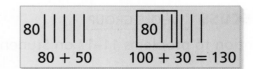

Use Place Value

● 8 tens + 5 tens = 8 tens + 2 tens + 3 tens

= 10 tens + 3 tens = 1 hundred + 3 tens = 130

Counting on by Hundreds Strategy

Write 800 + 500 = ? on the board. Ask a volunteer to count on by hundreds to find the answer.

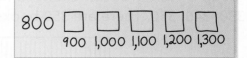

See side column for **Make a Thousand Strategy.**

Differentiated Instruction

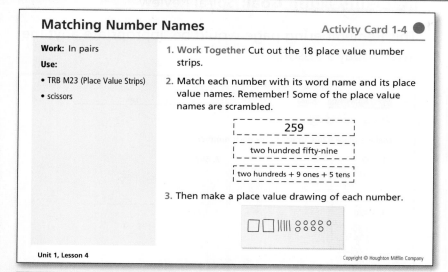

Matching Number Names   Activity Card 1-4 ●

Work: In pairs

Use:
- TRB M23 (Place Value Strips)
- scissors

1. **Work Together** Cut out the 18 place value number strips.

2. Match each number with its word name and its place value names. Remember! Some of the place value names are scrambled.

> 259
>
> two hundred fifty-nine
>
> two hundreds + 9 ones + 5 tens

3. Then make a place value drawing of each number.

Unit 1, Lesson 4   Copyright © Houghton Mifflin Company

Activity Note Suggest that students use the place value name of each number to help them create the place value drawing.

Math Writing Prompt

Compare and Contrast Compare 1,234 and 4,321. How are they alike? How are they different? Explain your thinking.

Soar to Success Math ★ **Software Support**

Warm Up 1.15

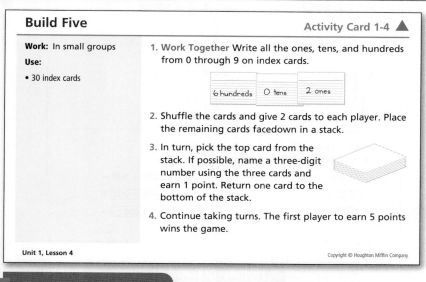

Build Five   Activity Card 1-4 ▲

Work: In small groups

Use:
- 30 index cards

1. **Work Together** Write all the ones, tens, and hundreds from 0 through 9 on index cards.

| 6 hundreds | 0 tens | 2 ones |

2. Shuffle the cards and give 2 cards to each player. Place the remaining cards facedown in a stack.

3. In turn, pick the top card from the stack. If possible, name a three-digit number using the three cards and earn 1 point. Return one card to the bottom of the stack.

4. Continue taking turns. The first player to earn 5 points wins the game.

Unit 1, Lesson 4   Copyright © Houghton Mifflin Company

Activity Note Students will need exactly one card from each place value to be able to name a three-digit number. Encourage students to use number sense in choosing which card to discard.

Math Writing Prompt

Investigate Math Describe a way to find the total number of paper clips needed so every student in a class has 10 paper clips.

MegaMath Grades K-6 **Software Support**

Country Countdown: Block Busters, Level S

Make an Organized List   Activity Card 1-4 ■

Work: In small groups

Use:
- Math Journals

1. **Work Together** Copy the organized list at the right to show all possible place value combinations of the number 138.

Hundreds	Tens	Ones
1	3	8
1	2	18
1	1	28
1	0	38
0	13	8
0	12	18
0	11	28
0	10	38
0	9	48
0	8	58
0	7	68
0	6	78
0	5	88
0	4	98
0	3	108
0	2	118
0	1	128
0	0	138

2. **Analyze** What patterns do you see in the list? Share your results with other groups.

3. Repeat the activity with the number 238.

Unit 1, Lesson 4   Copyright © Houghton Mifflin Company

Activity Note Suggest that students use the patterns they identified for the number 138 as they organize their place value list for the number 238.

Math Writing Prompt

Explain Your Thinking How many ways are there to scramble the place values in the number four hundred fifty-seven? Explain your answer.

DESTINATION Math® **Software Support**

Course II: Module 1: Unit 1: Place Value: Hundreds, Tens, and Ones

③ Homework and Spiral Review

Homework Goal: Additional Practice

✓ Include students' completed Homework page as part of their portfolios.

Remembering Goal: Spiral Review

This Remembering page would be appropriate anytime after today's lesson.

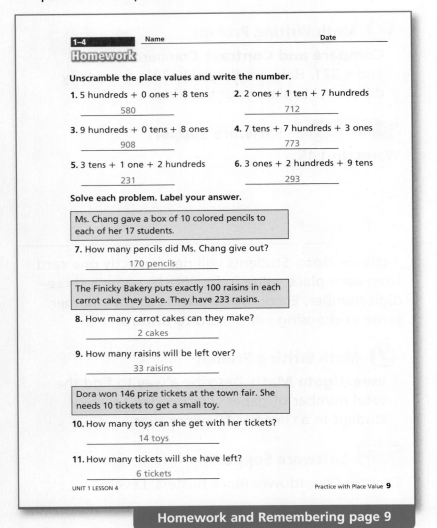

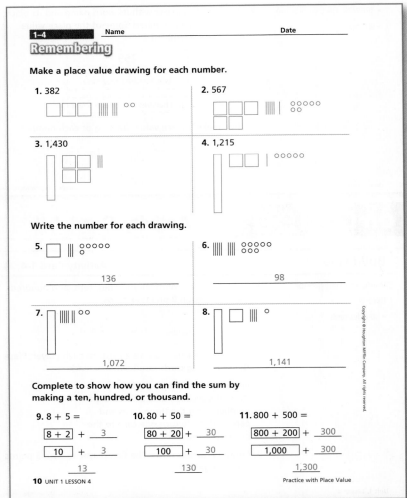

Home or School Activity

Math-to-Math Connection

Abacus Tell students that before place value charts were invented, people used an abacus to show numbers and perform computations. Have students find out how to show a number on an abacus.

To read the number on this abacus, count the beads moved to the center bar in each place value. The number 539,047 is shown on the Japanese abacus to the right.

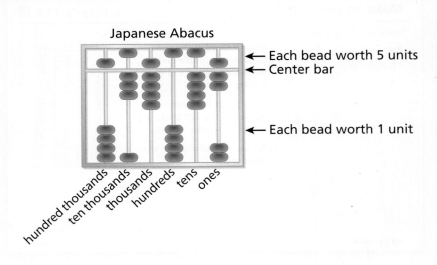

Japanese Abacus

← Each bead worth 5 units
← Center bar

← Each bead worth 1 unit

hundred thousands, ten thousands, thousands, hundreds, tens, ones

Discuss Addition Methods

REAL WORLD Problem Solving

Lesson Objectives

- Apply and discuss multi-digit addition methods.
- Discuss why it is necessary to align places before adding.

Vocabulary

Counting On strategy
Make a Ten strategy
expression
proof drawing

The Day at a Glance

Today's Goals	Materials
1 Teaching the Lesson **A1:** Solve multi-digit addition problems and discuss solution methods. **A2:** Discuss the importance of aligning place value columns before adding. **A3:** Extend Counting On and Make a Ten subtraction strategies. **2 Going Further** ▶ Extension: Sums to 10,000 ▶ Differentiated Instruction **3 Homework and Spiral Review**	**Lesson Activities** Student Activity Book pp. 19–20 or Student Hardcover Book pp. 19–20 Remembering p. 12 Homework and Remembering pp. 13–14 **Going Further** Activity Cards 1-6 MathBoard materials Secret Code Cards (TRB M19–M22) Spinner A (TRB M24) Paper clips Base ten blocks Game Cards (TRB M25) Math Journals

123 *Use Math Talk today!*

Keeping Skills Sharp

Quick Practice 🕐 5 MINUTES

Goal: Use the Make a Hundred strategy to add tens.

Materials: Demonstration Secret Code Cards (TRB M3–M18)

Add Tens Using the Demonstration Secret Code Cards, have a **Student Leader** hold up two tens cards. The leader gives students a few seconds to mentally add the numbers, and then says, "Add." The class says the addition equation aloud. The leader then chooses one student to explain the Make a Hundred strategy. Repeat for several pairs of cards.

⁶⁰ 6 0 **⁸⁰ 8 0**

Leader: Add.
Class: 60 plus 80 equals 140.
Student: 60 plus 40 equals 100, plus 40 more is 140.

Daily Routines

Homework Review Have students work at the board to show their solutions for problems 1 and 2. Have each student at the board explain his/her solution. Encourage the rest of the class to ask clarifying questions and make comments.

Elapsed Time Marta's day at school starts at 8:30 A.M. and ends at 2:30 P.M. How many hours is Marta in school?
6 hours

Teaching the Lesson

Solve Word Problems and Discuss Solutions

 25 MINUTES

Goal: Solve multi-digit addition problems and discuss solution methods.

Materials: Student Activity Book or Hardcover Book p. 19

✔ **NCTM Standards:**
Number and Operations
Problem Solving
Communication

The Learning Classroom

Math Drawings At this point, all students should include Proof Drawings with their numerical solutions. These drawings will provide conceptual support and facilitate students' explanations. After two or three days, you may decide to make drawings optional for students who are consistently accurate with addition and can explain their method, while continuing to require them from students who need more support.

Teaching Note

Language and Vocabulary When adding tens in the first problem, 359 + 245, some students may say they are adding 50 and 40 and 10 to get 100, rather than saying they are adding 5 tens and 4 tens and 1 ten to get 10 tens, or 1 hundred. Similarly, students may say they are adding 300 and 200 and 100 to get 600, rather than 3 hundreds and 2 hundreds and 1 hundred to get 6 hundreds. This language is correct and acceptable. If no students use this language, consider modeling it for them. Students should be comfortable with both kinds of place value language.

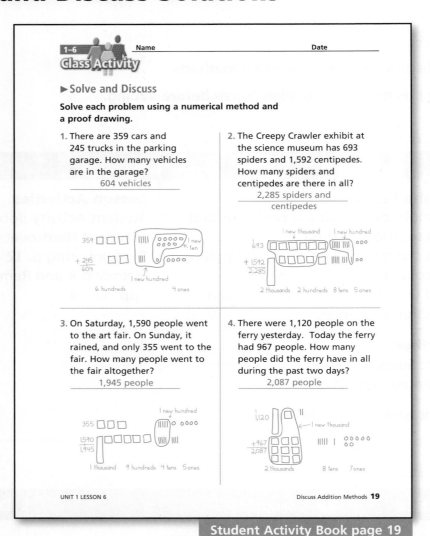

Student Activity Book page 19

▶ Solve and Discuss [WHOLE CLASS]

Math Talk Use the **Solve and Discuss** structure for problem 1. Invite three to six students to go to the classroom board and solve the problem relating each step of a proof drawing to each step of a numerical method while others work at their seats on MathBoards.

Ask students who used different addition methods to share their solutions. Encourage them to talk about grouping and make sure they are using correct language to talk about place value. Remind students to "wave tens or hundreds" if a presenter talks about tens and hundreds as if they were ones. Compare the solution methods that are presented.

Continue to use **Solve and Discuss** to complete problems 2–4.

Differentiated Instruction

Model Sums

Activity Card 1-6 ●

Work: In pairs

Use:
- TRB M24 (Spinner A)
- Paper clips
- Base ten blocks (1 thousand cube, 20 hundreds, 20 tens, 20 ones)

Decide:
Who will be Student 1 and who will be Student 2.

1. **On Your Own** Spin three times to create a 3-digit number. Record your number on paper. Then use base ten blocks to represent your number.

2. **Student 1:** Combine the blocks for both numbers. Trade ones for tens, tens for hundreds, and hundreds for thousands if possible.

3. **Student 2:** Write the two numbers in vertical form and find the sum.

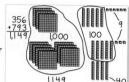 

4. **Work Together** Check your work.

Unit 1, Lesson 6

Copyright © Houghton Mifflin Company

Activity Note Students should work together to correct any inconsistency between their base ten blocks and the vertical addition exercise.

✎ Math Writing Prompt

Explain Your Thinking When adding two numbers in the hundreds, when do you need to make a thousand?

Soar to Success Math ★ **Software Support**

Warm Up 1.19

What's My Number?

Activity Card 1-6 ▲

Work: In pairs

1. **Work Together** Solve the riddles.

What's my number?
The number is less than 154 + 285.
The number is greater than 318 + 96.
The tens digit is even.
When the digits in the number are added, the total is 11. **425**

What's my number?
The number is greater than 117 + 113.
The number is less than 76 + 173.
The number is odd.
The ones digit is 4 more than the tens digit. **237**

2. **Analyze** What strategies did you use?

Unit 1, Lesson 6

Copyright © Houghton Mifflin Company

Activity Note Students can use number sense to identify possible digits for each place value.

✎ Math Writing Prompt

Apply Explain how to count on to solve this equation: $1,400 - 600 = \square$

MegaMath Grades K-8 **Software Support**

Country Countdown: Block Busters, Level V

The Greatest Sum

Activity Card 1-6 ■

Work: In pairs

Use:
- 2 copies of TRB M25 (Game Cards)

1. Shuffle the game cards and place them in a pile.

2. Each player chooses 8 cards from the pile and creates a 4-digit addition with the greatest possible sum.

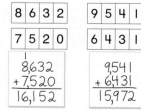

3. The greater sum wins 1 point. Repeat the activity until one player wins 5 points.

Unit 1, Lesson 6

Copyright © Houghton Mifflin Company

Activity Note Students can use number sense and place value to write each addend, working left to right and using the digits in order from greatest to least.

✎ Math Writing Prompt

Thousands Kim's father flew 596 miles and then flew another 4,256 miles. Kim said that her father flew over 9,000 miles. Is she correct? Explain why or why not.

✦ DESTINATION Math® **Software Support**

Course II: Module 2: Unit 1: Estimating and Finding Sums less than 1,000

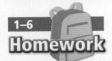

③ Homework and Spiral Review

Homework **Goal:** Additional Practice

This Homework page provides practice with solving addition word problems and with aligning place value columns before adding.

Remembering **Goal:** Spiral Review

This Remembering page would be appropriate anytime after today's lesson.

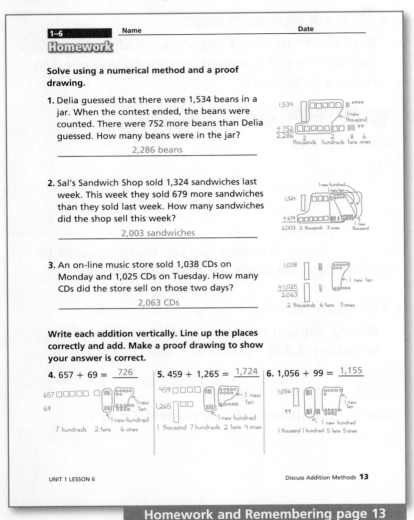

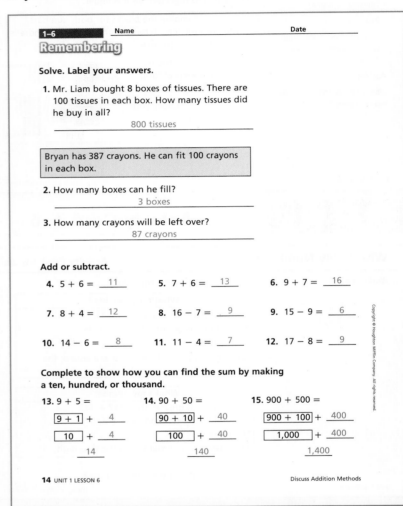

Homework and Remembering page 13

Homework and Remembering page 14

Home or School Activity

Science Connection

Breakfast Calories Provide students with the calorie chart shown at the right. Have students create a breakfast by choosing two to four of the items listed on the chart. Then have students find the total number of calories in the breakfast. Ask students to explain how they added.

Breakfast Food	Calories
Bagel	260
Banana	130
Cereal with lowfat milk	120
Hard boiled egg	76
Orange juice (8 oz.)	115
Whole wheat toast (two slices)	150
Yogurt (8 oz.)	240

Addition with Dollars and Cents

Vocabulary
proof drawing
Show All Totals method
New Groups Below method
New Groups Above method

Lesson Objective
● Add money amounts.

The Day at a Glance

Today's Goals	Materials

① Teaching the Lesson
A1: Review addition methods.
A2: Solve problems that involve adding money amounts and discuss solution methods.
A3: Find the total cost of items selected from a grocery store advertisement.

② Going Further
► Differentiated Instruction

③ Homework and Spiral Review

Lesson Activities
Student Activity Book pp. 21–22 or
    Student Hardcover Book pp. 21–22
Homework and Remembering
    pp. 15–16
MathBoard materials
Grocery store ads

Going Further
Activity Cards 1-7
Play money
Index cards
Math Journals

Use Math Talk today!

Keeping Skills Sharp

Quick Practice 5 MINUTES	Daily Routines

Goal: Use the Make a Hundred strategy to add tens.

Materials: Demonstration Secret Code Cards (TRB M3–M18)

Add Tens Using the Demonstration Secret Code Cards, have a **Student Leader** hold up two tens cards. The leader gives students a few seconds to mentally add the numbers, and then says, "Add." The class says the addition equation aloud. The leader then chooses one student to explain the Make a Hundred strategy. Repeat for several pairs of cards.

| 40 | 90 |
| 4 0 | 9 0 |

Leader: Add.
Class: 40 plus 90 equals 130.
Student: 90 plus 10 equals 100, plus 30 more is 130.

Homework Review Ask students to describe and share the proof drawings they used in their homework. Sometimes you will find that students with an incorrect answer completed the mathematics correctly, but did not use the given amounts.

Calendar Today is Tuesday. Jamil's game is Saturday. How many days until game day? 4 days

Teaching the Lesson

Review Addition Methods

 15 MINUTES

Goal: Review addition methods.

Materials: MathBoard materials

✓ **NCTM Standards:**
Number and Operations
Communication

▶ **Discuss Addition Methods** [WHOLE CLASS] **Math Talk**

Write 273 + 539 on the board. Ask for volunteers to solve using New Groups Below and Show All Totals at the board. Other students may solve using any method.

Discuss how each method used shows the new groups.

Adding Grocery Store Prices

 20 MINUTES

Goal: Solve problems that involve adding money amounts and discuss solution methods.

Materials: Student Activity Book or Hardcover Book p. 21

✓ **NCTM Standards:**
Number and Operations
Problem Solving
Communication

 Class Management

Looking Ahead Students will need Student Activity Book page 21 to complete the Homework page 15.

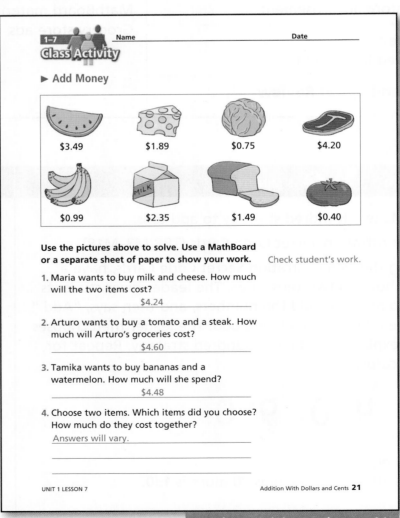

Student Activity Book page 21

▶ Add Money WHOLE CLASS

Read aloud the first problem on Student Book page 21. Ask these questions to encourage discussion.

- How much does the milk cost? $2.35
- How much does the cheese cost $1.89
- How can we find out how much they cost together? Add the two prices.

Write $2.35 + $1.89 vertically on the board, noting the alignment of places. Explain that hundred-boxes can be used to represent dollars, ten-sticks to represent dimes, and circles to represent pennies. Elicit solution strategies from students.

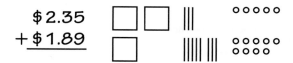

Encourage students to think about grouping 10 pennies to make a dime and 10 dimes to make a dollar. Work through a complete solution with proof drawings, using the New Groups Below method.

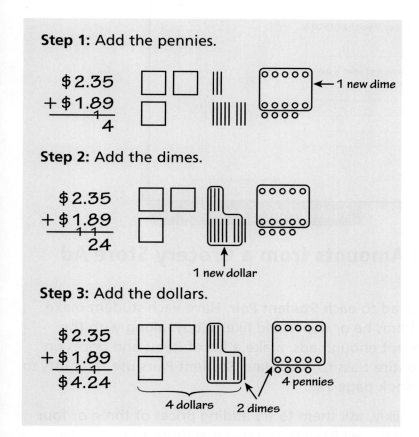

Step 1: Add the pennies.

← 1 new dime

Step 2: Add the dimes.

1 new dollar

Step 3: Add the dollars.

4 dollars   2 dimes   4 pennies

Have students work independently on problems 2–4.

Teaching Note

Watch For! Watch for students who fail to record their regrouping. Remind them to write a 1 in the proper column each time they make a new dime or a new dollar.

Differentiated Instruction

Extra Help Pair **Helping Partners** with students who are having difficulty with adding money. Remind students to use proof drawings to help them add money amounts. You might also want to work with a group of struggling students at the board so you can see their work easily. You may also wish to have students record their addition in grids like the one below.

Dollars	Dimes	Pennies
2	3	5
1	8	9
4	2	4

✋ Alternate Approach

Use Play Money Some students may benefit from using play money to check their computation. Provide students with play money. Review the value of each coin and bill before having students model the computation.

① Teaching the Lesson (continued)

Activity 3

Use a Real Grocery Store Ad

 20 MINUTES

Goal: Find the total cost of items selected from a grocery store advertisement.

Materials: Student Activity Book or Hardcover Book p. 22, grocery store ads

 NCTM Standards:
Number and Operations
Problem Solving

The Learning Classroom

Building Concepts Students generally learn more easily when they can relate a new idea to something in their own world.

English Language Learners

Use a grocery store ad to explain *most* and *least expensive*. Have students say the names and prices of some items.

- **Beginning** Point to an item. Say: **It's** *expensive/not expensive/ the most expensive/the least expensive.* Have students repeat.
- **Intermediate** Point to the most expensive item. Ask: **How much is this?** Say: **It costs the most. It's expensive. It's the most expensive.** Have students repeat. Continue with *least expensive.*
- **Advanced** Point to an expensive item. Ask: **Is this expensive? What is the most expensive? The least?**

✓ Ongoing Assessment

A carton of orange juice costs $2.49 and a box of cereal costs $4.37. How much do they cost together?

1–7 Class Activity | Name _____ | Date _____

▶ **Add Money Amounts from a Grocery Store Ad**

Use an ad from a grocery store. List the names and prices of five or six items you would like to buy. Then answer the questions below. Use a MathBoard or a separate sheet of paper to show your work.

_____   _____
_____   _____

5. How much would the two most expensive items on your list cost altogether?
   Answers will vary. Check student's answer.

6. How much would the two least expensive items cost in all?   Check student's work.
   Answers will vary.

7. What would be the total cost of your two favorite items?
   Answers will vary.

8. Which items would you buy if you had $5.00 to spend?
   Answers will vary.

9. Use the grocery ad to write and solve a word problem involving money.
   Answers will vary.

   _____
   _____
   _____

22 UNIT 1 LESSON 7   Addition With Dollars and Cents

Student Activity Book page 22

▶ Add Money Amounts from a Grocery Store Ad

PAIRS

Give a grocery store ad to each **Student Pair**. Have each student make a list of five or six items he or she would like to buy, along with the prices. (If there are not enough ads, make a list of items and prices on the board for the entire class to use.) Have **Student Pairs** use their lists to complete Student Book page 22.

If students finish quickly, ask them to try adding prices of three or four items; or tell them that they have only a given amount of money to spend and ask them to find combinations of items they can afford to buy.

② Going Further

Intervention — Activity Card 1–7

Model Addition

Activity Card 1-7 ●

Work: In pairs

Use:
• TRB M40 (Play Money: 10 one-dollar bills, 20 dimes, 20 pennies)

Decide:
Who will be Student 1 and who will be Student 2.

1. Use play money to show two money amounts between $1.00 and $5.00.

2. **Student 1:** Write and solve a vertical addition exercise using the two money amounts.

$$\begin{array}{r} \$2.43 \\ +\$3.18 \\ \hline \$5.61 \end{array}$$

3. **Student 2:** Combine the money for both amounts, trading pennies for a dime and dimes for a dollar when possible.

4. **Analyze** What do you notice about the sum and the combined amount of money? *The sum and the total amount of play money should match.*

Unit 1, Lesson 7

Copyright © Houghton Mifflin Company

Activity Note The calculated sum should match the play money representation after trading. So $5.61, for example, is shown as 5 dollars, 6 dimes, and 1 penny.

 **Math Writing Prompt**

Explain Your Thinking Explain how to add $1.59 + $2.64.

Soar to Success Math ★ Software Support

Warm Up 3.16

On Level — Activity Card 1–7

Playing Store

Activity Card 1-7 ▲

Work: In pairs

Use:
6 index cards, labeled as follows:
• Wind-up car, $3.59
• Whistle, $1.79
• Playing cards, $0.68
• Stuffed animal, $2.59
• Crayons, $4.62
• Stickers, $2.97

Decide:
Who will be Student 1 and who will be Student 2 for the first round.

1. **Student 1:** Pretend that you are a customer. Choose two items to purchase by taking two index cards. Give the cards to your partner.

2. **Student 2:** Pretend that you are the cashier. Find the total cost of the items on the cards that your partner gives you. Record your work.

$$\begin{array}{r} \$1.79 \\ +\$2.59 \\ \hline \$4.38 \end{array}$$

3. **Student 1:** Check your partner's work.

4. Switch roles and repeat the activity three more times.

Unit 1, Lesson 7

Copyright © Houghton Mifflin Company

Activity Note Either label the index cards prior to the activity or ask students to label them. If time permits, have students repeat the activity choosing 3 items.

 Math Writing Prompt

Compare and Contrast How is adding dollars, dimes, and pennies like adding hundreds, tens, and ones? How is it different?

MEGA MATH Grades K-6 Software Support

Numberopolis: Lulu's Lunch Counter, Level T

Challenge — Activity Card 1–7

Predict and Verify

Activity Card 1-7 ■

Work: In pairs

1. **Work Together** Predict, without adding, whether each pair of items will cost more or less than $5.00.
   • A baseball and a team flag. less
   • A poster and a cap. more
   • A cap and a horn. more
   • A postcard pack and a team flag. less

   Souvenirs at Baseball Stadium
   baseball.........$3.59
   team flag......$1.25
   poster...........$0.95
   cap................$4.29
   horn..............$0.79
   postcard pack....$2.59

2. Add to check each prediction.

3. **Analyze** Which prediction was the hardest to make? Which one was the easiest?

Unit 1, Lesson 7

Copyright © Houghton Mifflin Company

Activity Note One way students can predict the cost of pairs of items is by adding the dollars and then estimating whether the cents add up to more or less than $1.

 Math Writing Prompt

Making Predictions Explain how you can predict what the cost will be for three items that cost $3.79 each, if you do not need to find the exact total.

 DESTINATION Math® Software Support

Course II: Module 3: Unit 2: Money

 **Homework and Spiral Review**

3 Homework and Spiral Review

Homework **Goal:** Additional Practice

This Homework page gives students practice adding money amounts and aligning place value columns.

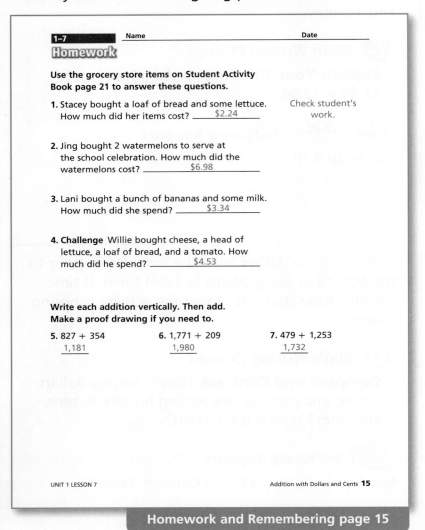

Homework and Remembering page 15

Remembering **Goal:** Spiral Review

This Remembering page would be appropriate anytime after today's lesson.

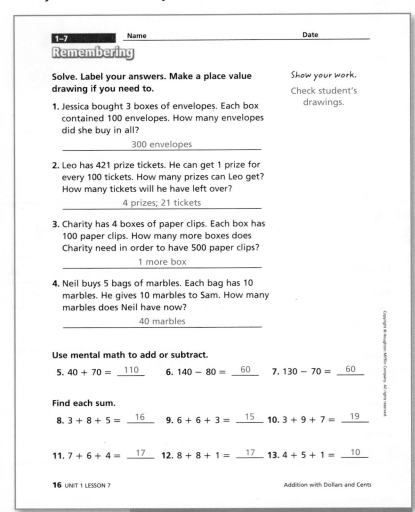

Homework and Remembering page 16

Home or School Activity

 Social Studies Connection

Design a Coin Tell students that the United States used to make many different kinds of coins and paper bills. For example, in the 1800s, coins worth 2¢ and 3¢ were minted. Until 1969, the United States Treasury distributed paper money for $500, $1,000.

Have students design a new coin or bill. Students can give the value of the new piece of money, then tell how many other coins or bills they would need to show an equivalent amount.

64 UNIT 1 LESSON 7

UNIT 1

LESSON

8

The Grouping Concept in Addition

REAL WORLD Problem Solving

Lesson Objectives

- Decide when and how to group in multi-digit addition.
- Practice adding money amounts.

Vocabulary

grouping
Make a Thousand strategy

The Day at a Glance

Today's Goals	Materials
1 Teaching the Lesson **A1:** Discuss when and how to group when adding. **A2:** Add prices of items on a menu. **2 Going Further** ▶ Problem Solving Strategy: Guess and Check ▶ Differentiated Instruction **3 Homework and Spiral Review**	**Lesson Activities** Student Activity Book p. 23 or Student Hardcover Book p. 23 Homework and Remembering pp. 17–18 MathBoard materials **Going Further** Student Activity Book p. 24 or Student Hardcover Book p. 24 Activity Cards 1-8 Restaurant menus MathBoard materials Index cards Game cards (TRB M25) Rulers Scissors Math Journals

123 Use Math Talk today!

Keeping Skills Sharp

Quick Practice ⏱ 5 MINUTES	Daily Routines
Goal: Add numbers in the hundreds using mental math. Use the Make a Thousand strategy to add numbers greater than a thousand. **Materials:** Demonstration Secret Code Cards (TRB M3–M18) **Add Hundreds** The **Student Leader** selects two hundreds cards, holds them up, and says, "Add." The class says the addition equation aloud. The leader then chooses one student to demonstrate the Make a Thousand strategy. This student adds either from the larger addend (easier) or the first addend. Repeat several times.	**Homework Review** Have students share the prices used to solve problems 1 through 4. Allow extra time for students to correct their incorrect answers. Have students with correct answers circulate and offer help. **Coins and Bills** Akio has 4 dollars, 3 quarters, and 2 nickels. How much money does he have? He spends $1.25. How much money does he have left? $4.85; $3.60

```
500        700
5 0 0      7 0 0
```

Leader: Add.
Class: 500 plus 700 equals 1,200.
Student: 700 plus 300 equals 1,000, plus 200 more is 1,200.

The Grouping Concept in Addition **65**

Teaching the Lesson

Deciding When to Group

 20 MINUTES

Goal: Discuss when and how to group when adding.

Materials: MathBoard materials

✔ **NCTM Standard:**
Number and Operations

The Learning Classroom

Building Concepts Students should not be required to make proof drawings once they have demonstrated that they have a solid understanding of place value and grouping and can explain their addition using place value language. Students who are struggling with these concepts should continue to make drawings until they are comfortable with these ideas.

 Ongoing Assessment

▶ Choose two items from the Lunchtime Diner menu on Student Book page 23 and add to find the total cost.

▶ **Group Ones, Tens, or Both** INDIVIDUALS

Write the four exercises below on the board. Have students copy the exercises and complete them on their MathBoards.

A.	467	B.	384
	+ 268		+ 263
	735		647

C.	765	D.	524
	+ 117		+ 263
	882		787

Students may use any method to solve these exercises. The New Groups Below method is shown here.

Math Talk When most students are finished, have a discussion about grouping.

● For which exercises did you need to group ones to make a new ten? A and C

● For which exercises did you need to group tens to make a new hundred? A and B

● Is there any exercise that didn't require any grouping? yes; exercise D

● How can you tell when you need to group? when the total number of ones or tens is more than 9

● What do you do when the total of the ones is greater than 9? Write 1 for the new ten in the tens column and then write the number of ones left over under the line in the ones column.

● What do you do when the total of the tens is greater than 9? Write 1 for the new hundred in the hundreds column and then write the number of tens left over under the line in the tens column.

Ask students to give word problem situations for exercise A. It is important to keep multi-digit calculation connected to real-world situations.

The Lunchtime Diner

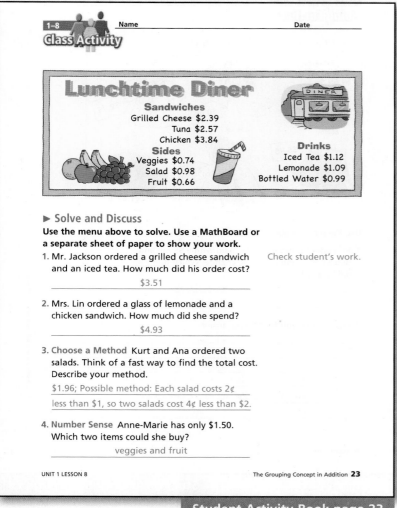

1-8 Class Activity

Name _____ Date _____

Lunchtime Diner

Sandwiches
Grilled Cheese $2.39
Tuna $2.57
Chicken $3.84

Sides
Veggies $0.74
Salad $0.98
Fruit $0.66

Drinks
Iced Tea $1.12
Lemonade $1.09
Bottled Water $0.99

▶ Solve and Discuss

Use the menu above to solve. Use a MathBoard or a separate sheet of paper to show your work.

1. Mr. Jackson ordered a grilled cheese sandwich and an iced tea. How much did his order cost?
   Check student's work.
   _____ $3.51 _____

2. Mrs. Lin ordered a glass of lemonade and a chicken sandwich. How much did she spend?
   _____ $4.93 _____

3. **Choose a Method** Kurt and Ana ordered two salads. Think of a fast way to find the total cost. Describe your method.
   $1.96; Possible method: Each salad costs 2¢
   less than $1, so two salads cost 4¢ less than $2.

4. **Number Sense** Anne-Marie has only $1.50. Which two items could she buy?
   _____ veggies and fruit _____

UNIT 1 LESSON 8   The Grouping Concept in Addition **23**

Student Activity Book page 23

▶ Solve and Discuss [WHOLE CLASS]   Math Talk

Have students turn to Student Book page 23 and briefly look at the menu for the Lunchtime Diner. Read aloud the first problem and give students a few minutes to solve it.

Use **Solve and Discuss** for the remaining problems. Suggest that before students add, they should think about whether they will need to trade pennies for a new dime or dimes for a new dollar. Try to choose students who used different methods to present, and encourage other students to ask questions if the explanations are unclear.

 35 MINUTES

Goal: Add prices of items on a menu.

Materials: Student Activity Book or Hardcover Book p. 23

 NCTM Standards:
Number and Operations
Problem Solving

Differentiated Instruction

Extra Help You might need to help some students understand money amounts written symbolically. Using play money, have students show the cost of two items; then, count the total amount and write that amount using dollar and cent notation.

English Language Learners

Make sure students understand the term *to group*. Write 163 + 918 on the board.

• **Beginning** Say: **3 plus 8 is 11.** Ask: **Is 11 more than 10?** yes **I have 10 ones. I make a new group of 10.** Ask: **How many ones are left?** 1

• **Intermediate** Ask: **What is 3 + 8?** 11 **Can I make a new group of 10 ones?** yes Continue with the other columns.

• **Advanced** Have students add each column and use short sentences to describe when to make a new group of ones or tens.

② Going Further

Problem Solving Strategy: Guess and Check

Goal: Use the Guess and Check strategy to solve a problem.

Materials: Student Activity Book or Hardcover Book p. 24

✓ **NCTM Standard:**
Problem Solving

▶ Use the Guess and Check Strategy

SMALL GROUPS

Introduce the Guess and Check strategy, with this analogy. You want to buy a pair of shoes but you don't know what size you wear. You make a guess and try a pair on and see if it fits. If it doesn't fit, you know whether you need a smaller or larger size. Then you use what you learned to try another pair. When solving math problems, sometimes we begin by guessing the answer and seeing if it works. If it doesn't work, we use what we've learned and try again.

Have **Small Groups** use the Guess and Check strategy to solve the problem on Student Book page 24. Have students explain their answer. See Math Talk in Action for a sample classroom dialogue.

 Math Talk in Action

Cora: How can I figure out which items José bought, if I don't know how much José spent?

Mario: Well you can figure out how much he spent because you know how much change he got back.

Cora: O.K., he got back 50 cents and he started with $7.00, so his clothing cost $6.50.

Mario: So now you can use the Guess and Check strategy to find the items that add up to $6.50. Rounding can also help you make your first two guesses.

Cora: Well, first of all I know that José didn't buy the jacket because that costs more money than he has, so I'll cross that off of my sheet. I'll guess that the socks and the shorts are what he bought because $5.00 and $1.00 is close to $6.00.

Mario: But he spent $6.50.

Cora: Yes, I know, but maybe the change will make the total add up to $6.50. $5.45 plus $.95 is only $6.40.

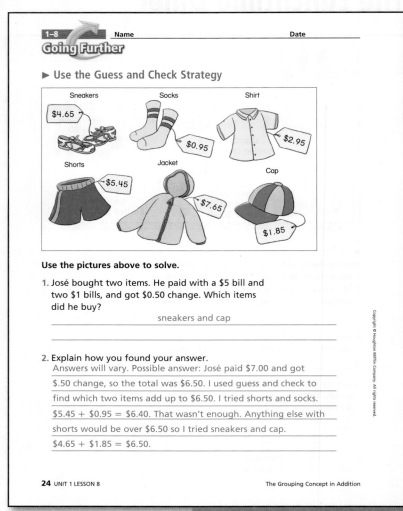

Student Activity Book page 24

Mario: You only were a dime off. Check your other clothing prices and see if there are other prices that are 10 cents higher than the socks or the shorts.

Cora: I didn't find any other prices that had a ten cents difference, so I'll just try two different combinations. Mario, why don't you try two also. That will work faster for us.

Mario: O.K. I'll try sneakers and T-shirt.

Cora: I'll try cap and sneakers.

Mario: I was way over. That would cost $7.60. I should have known not to pick those two pieces of clothing anyway because adding the numbers in the ten cents place wouldn't have totaled 50 cents after grouping.

Cora: I was right on. $4.65 plus $1.85 was $6.50.

68 UNIT 1 LESSON 8

Differentiated Instruction

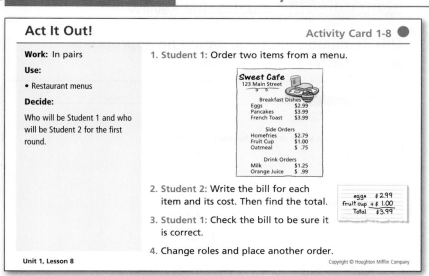

Act It Out!   Activity Card 1-8 ●

Work: In pairs

Use:
• Restaurant menus

Decide:
Who will be Student 1 and who will be Student 2 for the first round.

1. Student 1: Order two items from a menu.

2. Student 2: Write the bill for each item and its cost. Then find the total.

3. Student 1: Check the bill to be sure it is correct.

4. Change roles and place another order.

Unit 1, Lesson 8   Copyright © Houghton Mifflin Company

Activity Note Students can also use restaurant menus for this activity. Tell students to align the decimal points in the addends and the sum when they write the bill.

✎ **Math Writing Prompt**

Explain Your Thinking Explain to a friend how you know when to group the tens in an addition problem.

Soar to Success Math ★ **Software Support**

Warm Up 3.16

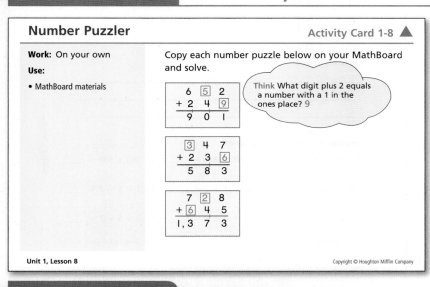

Number Puzzler   Activity Card 1-8 ▲

Work: On your own

Use:
• MathBoard materials

Copy each number puzzle below on your MathBoard and solve.

> Think What digit plus 2 equals a number with a 1 in the ones place? 9

Unit 1, Lesson 8   Copyright © Houghton Mifflin Company

Activity Note Students should use number sense and work from right to left to find each missing number.

✎ **Math Writing Prompt**

Choose a Method If you only had $5.00 to spend at the Lunchtime Diner, what's a quick way to make sure that you don't go over that amount?

HARCOURT MEGA MATH Grades K-6 **Software Support**

Numberopolis: Carnival Stories, Level O

Mix and Match   Activity Card 1-8 ■

Work: On your own

Use:
• TRB M25 (Game Cards)
• Index card
• Ruler
• Scissors

1. Write a plus sign on the index card. Then cut out 9 game cards, one for each of the digits 1–9.

2. Arrange the 9 game cards, the plus sign, and the ruler to show the sum of two 3-digit numbers.

3. Now make another 3-digit addition exercise with different addends and a different sum.

Possible answer

Unit 1, Lesson 8   Copyright © Houghton Mifflin Company

Activity Note There are more than two solutions. Encourage students to use number sense in choosing possible digits. For example, the digits in the hundreds place should have a sum less than 10.

✎ **Math Writing Prompt**

Investigate Math If you add a number in the hundreds and a number in the tens, will the total ever be a number in the thousands? Explain.

✸ **DESTINATION** Math **Software Support**

Course II: Module 2: Unit 1: Estimating and Finding Sums less than 1,000

③ Homework and Spiral Review

1-8
Homework **Goal:** Additional Practice

This Homework page gives students practice deciding when to group when solving addition problems.

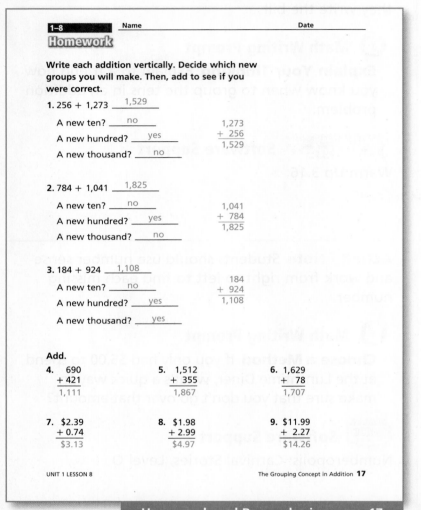

1-8 Name _____ Date _____
Homework

Write each addition vertically. Decide which new groups you will make. Then, add to see if you were correct.

1. 256 + 1,273 ___1,529___

   A new ten? ___no___   1,273
   A new hundred? ___yes___   + 256
   A new thousand? ___no___   1,529

2. 784 + 1,041 ___1,825___

   A new ten? ___no___   1,041
   A new hundred? ___yes___   + 784
   A new thousand? ___no___   1,825

3. 184 + 924 ___1,108___

   A new ten? ___no___   184
   A new hundred? ___yes___   + 924
   A new thousand? ___yes___   1,108

Add.

4.   690
  + 421
  1,111
	5. 1,512
	  + 355
	  1,867
		6. 1,629
		  + 78
		  1,707

7. $2.39
  + 0.74
  $3.13
	8. $1.98
	  + 2.99
	  $4.97
		9. $11.99
		  + 2.27
		  $14.26

UNIT 1 LESSON 8   The Grouping Concept in Addition **17**

Homework and Remembering page 17

1-8
Remembering **Goal:** Spiral Review

This Remembering page would be appropriate anytime after today's lesson.

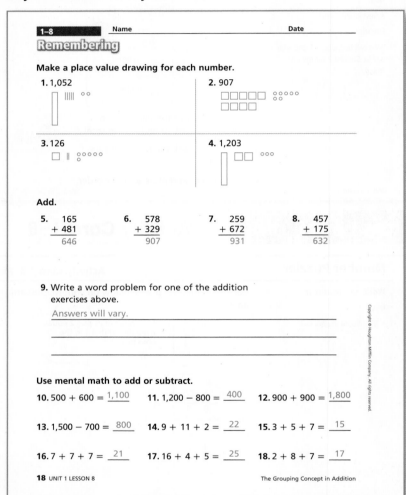

1-8 Name _____ Date _____
Remembering

Make a place value drawing for each number.

1. 1,052

2. 907

3. 126

4. 1,203

Add.

5.   165
 + 481
  646
	6. 578
	 + 329
	  907
		7. 259
		 + 672
		  931
			8. 457
			 + 175
			  632

9. Write a word problem for one of the addition exercises above.

   Answers will vary. _____

Use mental math to add or subtract.

10. 500 + 600 = ___1,100___   11. 1,200 − 800 = ___400___   12. 900 + 900 = ___1,800___

13. 1,500 − 700 = ___800___   14. 9 + 11 + 2 = ___22___   15. 3 + 5 + 7 = ___15___

16. 7 + 7 + 7 = ___21___   17. 16 + 4 + 5 = ___25___   18. 2 + 8 + 7 = ___17___

18 UNIT 1 LESSON 8   The Grouping Concept in Addition

Homework and Remembering page 18

Home or School Activity

Social Studies Connection

Number Code Explain to students that Egyptian numbers were called hieroglyphic numbers and were used thousands of years ago. The numbers were based on important symbols in the Egyptian culture. For example, the number 100 was a coil of rope, and the number 1,000 was a lotus flower.

Have students create their own set of numbers, a key to their code, and a few addition exercises for someone else to solve.

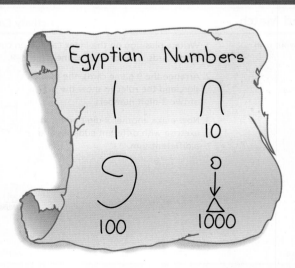

UNIT 1 LESSON 9

Practice Addition

REAL WORLD Problem Solving

Lesson Objectives

- Practice adding money amounts.
- Identify and explain errors in addition problems.

Vocabulary
grouping

The Day at a Glance

Today's Goals	Materials
1 Teaching the Lesson **A1:** Identify and correct addition errors. **A2:** Find the total cost of items on a menu. **2 Going Further** ▶ Extension: Add Money Amounts with Sums Greater than $20 ▶ Differentiated Instruction **3 Homework and Spiral Review**	**Lesson Activities** Student Activity Book p. 25 or Student Hardcover Book p. 25 Homework and Remembering pp. 19–20 Quick Quiz 2 (Assessment Guide) **Going Further** Student Activity Book p. 26 or Student Hardcover Book p. 26 Activity Cards 1-9 MathBoard materials Restaurant menus Play money Math Journals 123 *Use* **Math Talk** *today!*

Keeping Skills Sharp

Quick Practice ⏱ 5 MINUTES	Daily Routines
Goal: Use mental math to add numbers in the hundreds. **Materials:** Demonstration Secret Code Cards (TRB M3–M18) **Add Hundreds** Select students who have not been **Student Leaders** yet to lead this activity. All students should have a turn at being a **Student Leader** in order to develop their communication skills. From the Demonstration Secret Code Cards, have the **Student Leader** select and hold up two hundreds cards. The leader gives students a few seconds to mentally add the numbers, and then says, "Add." The class says the addition equation aloud. Repeat for several pairs of cards. (See Unit 1 Lesson 8.)	**Homework Review** As a class, discuss how students answered the questions in problems 1 through 3 without first completing the addition. Then, discuss the benefits to asking these questions prior to adding. **Write Numbers Different Ways** Write the number 134 on the board. Have students write this number in as many different ways as possible, such as an addition or subtraction expression. Possible answer: 100 + 30 + 4

① Teaching the Lesson

Activity 1

Identify Errors

 20 MINUTES

Goal: Identify and correct addition errors.

 NCTM Standard:
Number and Operations

Teaching Note

Be sure that students understand that this is a *Help the Teacher* activity. Encourage them to be alert just in case you make a mistake, and to point out your mistakes in a helpful way.

English Language Learners

Help students find the mistakes. Write the first example on the board. Say: **My answer is wrong.**

- **Beginner** Point to the ones column. Say: **4 plus 2 equals 6.** Ask: **Do I make a new ten?** no Point to the tens column. Ask: **Is this correct?** no Say: **I forgot to make a new hundred.**
- **Intermediate** Have students add the columns. Ask: **Do I make a new ten?** no **Do I make a new hundred?** yes **What did I forget?** to make a new hundred
- **Advanced** Have students solve the problem individually then work in pairs to find your mistake. Ask: **What did I forget to do?**

▶ **Identify Errors** WHOLE CLASS

Tell students you are going to solve some addition exercises on the board. Tell them that you might make errors, so they should watch carefully and help you catch mistakes. Ask students to explain each mistake and to suggest strategies for avoiding the errors you make.

Be sure to make each of the common errors you have seen your students make. Below are some examples that illustrate common errors.

Example:

$$\begin{array}{r} 744 \\ + 172 \\ \hline 816 \end{array}$$

Error: Forgot to make a new hundred.

Correct answer: 916

Example:

$$\begin{array}{r} \overset{2}{6}39 \\ + 183 \\ \hline 731 \end{array}$$

Error: Wrote the ones above the tens column and the new 1 ten in the ones column.

Correct answer: 822

Example:

$$\begin{array}{r} 477 \\ + 34\underset{1}{4} \\ \hline 811 \end{array}$$

Error: Forgot to make a new ten.

Correct answer: 821

Example:

$$\begin{array}{r} 329 \\ + 483 \\ \hline 702 \end{array}$$

Error: Forgot to make a new ten and a new hundred.

Correct answer: 812

Carmen's Café

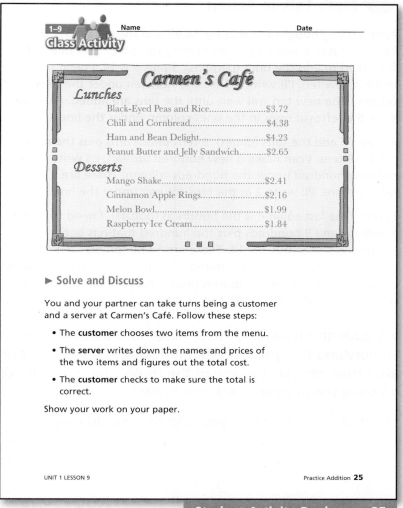

1–9
Class Activity
Name
Date

Carmen's Café

Lunches

Black-Eyed Peas and Rice	$3.72
Chili and Cornbread	$4.38
Ham and Bean Delight	$4.23
Peanut Butter and Jelly Sandwich	$2.65

Desserts

Mango Shake	$2.41
Cinnamon Apple Rings	$2.16
Melon Bowl	$1.99
Raspberry Ice Cream	$1.84

▶ Solve and Discuss

You and your partner can take turns being a customer and a server at Carmen's Café. Follow these steps:

• The **customer** chooses two items from the menu.

• The **server** writes down the names and prices of the two items and figures out the total cost.

• The **customer** checks to make sure the total is correct.

Show your work on your paper.

UNIT 1 LESSON 9   Practice Addition **25**

Student Activity Book page 25

▶ Solve and Discuss PAIRS   Math Talk

Have **Student Pairs** look at the menu for Carmen's Café on Student Book page 25. Read aloud the directions.

For this activity, one partner will be the customer and the other will be the server. Explain that after the customer chooses items from the menu, the server should use a separate sheet of paper to write down the names and prices of the two items, then add to find the total amount. You may want to hand out quarter sheets of paper for servers to take orders. The customer should check that the total is correct. Encourage students to think about whether they will need to trade pennies for a new dime or dimes for a new dollar.

Choose **Student Pairs** that used different methods to discuss how they found the total cost.

 30 MINUTES

Goal: Find the total cost of items on a menu.

Materials: Student Activity Book or Hardcover Book p. 25

 NCTM Standard:
Number and Operations

The Learning Classroom

Scenarios In this Act-It-Out scenario, students role-play being a customer and server to find the total cost of two items. This role playing in a real-life situation can foster a sense of involvement and create a meaningful context for adding money amounts.

 Ongoing Assessment

Ask students to explain what the error is in this example. Then they should find the correct answer.

$$\begin{array}{r} 478 \\ +\ 123 \\ \hline 591 \end{array}$$

 Class Management

Looking Ahead Students will need to use Student Book page 25 for homework.

 Quick Quiz

See Assessment Guide for Unit 1 Quick Quiz 2.

Going Further

Extension: Add Money Amounts with Sums Greater than $20

Goal: Find sums of money more than $10.00.

Materials: Student Activity Book or Hardcover Book p. 26

✔ **NCTM Standards:**
Number and Operations
Problem Solving

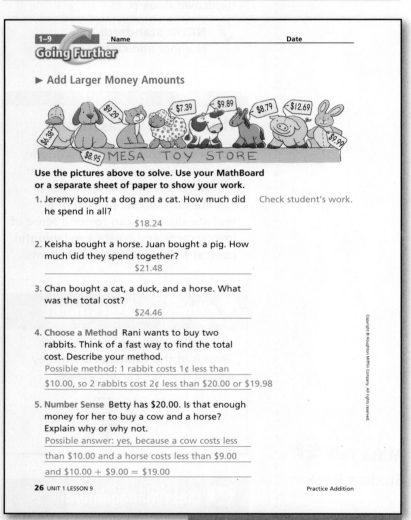

Student Activity Book page 26

► Add Larger Money Amounts

WHOLE CLASS

Have students look at the items for sale at Mesa Toys on Student Book page 26. Ask a student to read aloud problem 1. Use **Step-by-Step at the Board** and choose four students to come to the board to demonstrate how to solve the problem. As each student performs the addition, he or she describes the steps. The class performs the same steps at their seats.

 Math Talk in Action

Kyra: Jeremy bought the dog for $8.95 and the cat for $9.29. *There is a pause while Kyra writes the problem on the board.* I first need to add the ones (pennies). 5 plus 9 is 14. I need to make a new ten. I'll write a 1 for the new ten under the tens column. The new ten will wait until the tens are added. I'll write 4 for the leftover ones in the ones column under the line.

James: I'll add the tens (dimes). 9 tens plus 2 tens plus the new ten is 12 tens. I can make a new hundred (dollar). I'll write 1 for the new hundred under the hundreds column. There are 2 leftover tens. I'll write 2 in the tens column under the line.

Lucero: The last column is the hundreds (dollars). I need to add 8 hundreds and 9 hundreds plus the hundred that has been waiting. 8 plus 9 plus 1 is 18. There are 18 hundreds. That's the same as 1 thousand and 8 hundreds. I'll put the 8 in the hundreds place and the 1 in the thousands place. The total amount for the dog and the cat is 18 dollars and 24 cents.

As students discuss each step, make sure that students understand the grouping that is involved. Also point out that students may use any of the three addition methods to solve the problems. Ask the following questions:

● What happens when you add the tens (dimes)? Sample response: When I add the new ten (dime), 9 tens (dimes), and 2 tens (dimes), I get 1 new hundred (dollar) and 2 tens (dimes).

● Explain what happens when you add the hundreds. Sample response: I get 1 new thousand and 8 hundreds and that's the same as $18.00.

● Where do you place the 1 for the new thousand (ten dollars)? Sample response: It goes to the left of the 8.

Ask students to complete problems 2–5 independently. Then ask for volunteers to come to the board to show their work.

Differentiated Instruction

Intervention   Activity Card 1-9

Cash Only
Activity Card 1-9 ●

Work: In pairs

Use:
- Restaurant menus
- Play money

Decide:
Who will be Student 1 and who will be Student 2 for the first round.

1. **Student 1:** Choose two items from a menu.
2. **Student 2:** Add to find the total cost of the items.
3. **Student 1:** Use play money to show the cost of each item. Then show the total. Trade money to use the least number of coins possible in the total.
4. Check each other's work. Then change roles and choose two new items from the menu.

Unit 1, Lesson 9   Copyright © Houghton Mifflin Company

Activity Note Gather several restaurant menus for this activity. Matching the total shown in the calculated sum with the play money representation will tell students if they have made all possible trades with the coins and have calculated the sum correctly.

Math Writing Prompt

Explain Your Thinking Explain to a friend how you know when to group pennies as dimes and dimes as dollars.

Soar to Success Math ★ **Software Support**

Warm Up 3.14

On Level   Activity Card 1-9

Missing Numbers
Activity Card 1-9 ▲

Work: In pairs

Use:
- MathBoard materials

1. Copy each puzzle onto your MathBoard.

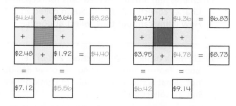

2. **Work Together** Use the Guess and Check Strategy to solve each puzzle.

Unit 1, Lesson 9   Copyright © Houghton Mifflin Company

Activity Note Students will need to use number sense and the Guess and Check strategy to find one missing number in the first puzzle and two in the second.

Math Writing Prompt

Summarize Explain how you know without adding that $6.59 and $4.29 will total more than $10.00.

MegaMath Grades K–6 **Software Support**

Country Countdown: Block Busters, Level N

Challenge   Activity Card 1-9

What's Next
Activity Card 1-9 ■

Work: In pairs

1. Copy each number pattern.
2. **Work Together** Find each rule and complete the addition pattern.
3. **On Your Own** Make two new addition patterns. Exchange with your partner to find the next three numbers in each pattern.
4. Check your work.

0, 1, 3, 6, 10, _15_, _21_, _28_,
add 1, add 2, add 3, etc.

$.75, $1.25, $1.75, _$2.25_, _$2.75_,
add $0.50.

1,500, 2,900, 4,200, _5,400_, _6,500_,
add 1,400, add 1,300, add 1,200, etc.

450, 575, 800, 1,125, _1,550_, _2,075_,
add 125, add 225, add 325, etc.

$7.37, $7.62, $7.97, _$8.42_, _$8.97_,
add $0.25, add $0.35, add $0.45, etc.

Unit 1, Lesson 9   Copyright © Houghton Mifflin Company

Activity Note The rule for addition patterns can vary in format. Some involve adding a single amount or sequence of amounts repeatedly. Others add amounts that increase by a constant amount.

Math Writing Prompt

Investigate Math Explain how to find the next number in the pattern $0.01, $0.06, $0.16, $0.17, $0.22, $0.32, $0.33, $0.38, $0.48, $0.49.

DESTINATION Math **Software Support**

Course II: Module 1: Unit 1: Comparing and Ordering

③ Homework and Spiral Review

Homework **Goal:** Additional Practice

This Homework page provides practice in solving addition problems involving money.

Remembering **Goal:** Spiral Review

This Remembering page would be appropriate anytime after today's lesson.

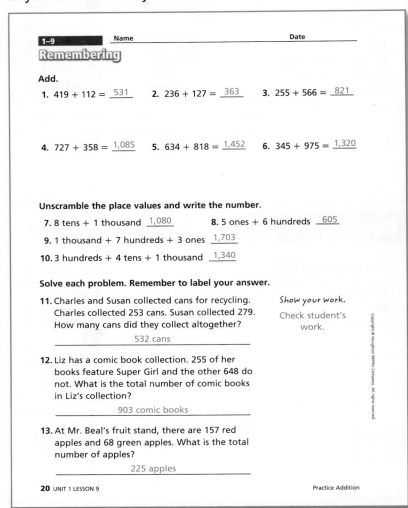

1–9 Name _____ Date _____
Homework

Use the menu from Carmen's Cafe on Student Book page 25 to solve each problem.

Check student's work.

1. Randy ordered a peanut butter and jelly sandwich and cinnamon apple rings. How much did he spend? _____ $4.81

2. Jamie and her dad went to lunch. He ordered the chili and cornbread. She ordered the black-eyed peas and rice. What was their bill? _$8.10_

3. Rafael ordered the ham and bean delight and a mango shake. What was the total cost?
_____ $6.64 _____

4. Teri ordered raspberry ice cream and a melon bowl. How much was her bill? _____ $3.83

5. Yao gave the saleswoman $3.88 for 2 melon bowls. Is $3.88 the correct amount? If not, explain the error Yao made.
Possible answer: Yao did not make a new ten when he added $1.99 and $1.99. The correct amount is $3.98.

UNIT 1 LESSON 9 | Practice Addition **19**

Homework and Remembering page 19

1–9 Name _____ Date _____
Remembering

Add.

1. 419 + 112 = _531_ 2. 236 + 127 = _363_ 3. 255 + 566 = _821_

4. 727 + 358 = _1,085_ 5. 634 + 818 = _1,452_ 6. 345 + 975 = _1,320_

Unscramble the place values and write the number.

7. 8 tens + 1 thousand _1,080_   8. 5 ones + 6 hundreds _605_

9. 1 thousand + 7 hundreds + 3 ones _1,703_

10. 3 hundreds + 4 tens + 1 thousand _1,340_

Solve each problem. Remember to label your answer.

11. Charles and Susan collected cans for recycling. Charles collected 253 cans. Susan collected 279. How many cans did they collect altogether?
_____ 532 cans _____

Show your work.
Check student's work.

12. Liz has a comic book collection. 255 of her books feature Super Girl and the other 648 do not. What is the total number of comic books in Liz's collection?
_____ 903 comic books _____

13. At Mr. Beal's fruit stand, there are 157 red apples and 68 green apples. What is the total number of apples?
_____ 225 apples _____

20 UNIT 1 LESSON 9 | Practice Addition

Homework and Remembering page 20

Home or School Activity

Multicultural Connection

Foods from Around the World Explain to students that countries and cultures have their own special foods. Ask students to share some of the special foods their families prepare and eat on holidays and at celebrations. Have students create a menu and then role play customers and servers ordering meals and finding total costs.

Chicken Curry	$4.95
Corn Kabobs	$1.75
Fruit Chaat	$1.15
Spinach Parathas	$2.25

Ungroup to Subtract

Lesson Objectives

- Explore methods for subtracting multi-digit numbers.
- Discuss a common subtraction error.

Vocabulary

ungroup

The Day at a Glance

Today's Goals	Materials	

1 **Teaching the Lesson**
  A1: Solve problems using subtraction methods.
  A2: Discuss ways to avoid a common subtraction error.
 	
2 **Going Further**
  ▶ Differentiated Instruction
 	
3 **Homework and Spiral Review**
	Lesson Activities
	Student Activity Book pp. 27–28 or
	  Student Hardcover Book pp. 27–28
	Homework and Remembering
	  pp. 21–22
	MathBoard materials
		Going Further
		Activity Cards 1-10
		Base ten blocks
		Game Cards
		Index cards
		Math Journals

123 *Use* **Math Talk** *today!*

Keeping Skills Sharp

Quick Practice ⏱ 5 MINUTES

Goal: Subtract larger numbers.

Materials: Demonstration Secret Code Cards (TRB M3–M18)

Subtract Tens Have a **Student Leader** select the 100 card and two tens cards. The leader assembles the cards to show a 3-digit number on the left and a number of tens on the right.

100	20		70
1	**2**	**0**	**7 0**

The leader says, "Subtract." The class says the subtraction equation aloud. Then, the leader selects a student to illustrate the Make a Hundred strategy (See page 55). Repeat several times.

It may help to have two **Student Leaders**. One leads the class while the other selects cards for the next exercise.

Daily Routines

Homework Review Ask students to place their homework at the corner of their desks. As you circulate during Quick Practice, check that students completed the assignment, and see whether any problem caused difficulty for many students.

Skip Count Have students skip count by 10s starting with 63.

63, 73, 83, 93, …

1 Teaching the Lesson

Share Different Subtraction Methods

 20 MINUTES

Goal: Solve problems using different subtraction methods.

Materials: Student Activity Book or Hardcover Book p. 27, MathBoard materials

 NCTM Standards:
Number and Operations
Algebra
Problem Solving

Teaching Note

What to Expect from Students
Some students may not be skilled with a particular subtraction method at this point. They will have many opportunities to develop subtraction understanding and skill over the next several lessons. Encourage students having difficulty to listen closely as other students present their methods and to ask questions when they do not understand.

English Language Learners

Review the term *ungroup*. Write 21 − 9 and make the place value drawings on the board. Say: **We can't take 9 away from 1.**

• **Beginner** Say: *We ungroup* 1 ten stick. Cross out 1 ten stick. Ask: **How many circles do I draw?** 10 **How many ones are there?** 11 Say: **Cross out 9 ones. We have 1 ten stick and 2 ones. The answer is ____.** 12

• **Intermediate** Ask: **What do we** *ungroup*? 1 ten stick **What do we draw?** 10 circles

• **Advanced** Have students use *First, Next, Then* to describe the steps to ungroup.

1–10
Class Activity

Name _____ Date _____

▶ Discuss Subtraction Methods

Solve this word problem.

> Mr. Kim had 134 jazz CDs. He sold 58 of them at his garage sale. How many jazz CDs does he have now?

1. Write a subtraction that you could do to answer this question.

    134 − 58

2. Make a place value drawing for 134. Take away 58. How many are left?

    76

3. Write a numerical solution method for what you did in the drawing. Possible answer:

    $\begin{array}{r} 0\ 12\ 14 \\ \cancel{1}\cancel{3}\cancel{4} \\ -\ 58 \\ \hline 76 \end{array}$

4. Describe how you ungrouped to subtract.
    Answers will vary.
    _____
    _____
    _____
    _____

UNIT 1 LESSON 10   Ungroup to Subtract **27**

Student Activity Book page 27

▶ Discuss Subtraction Methods

WHOLE CLASS   **Math Talk** 123

Ask a student to read aloud the word problem on Student Book page 27. Work with the class to make a place value drawing for exercise 1.

Have a student volunteer explain their place value drawing. Make sure students use correct place value language when explaining their subtraction.

As the student volunteer explains their drawing and subtraction, encourage the other students to ask questions so they understand how they can "get" more ones or more tens to subtract if they do not have enough.

Correct drawings should show a ten ungrouped to form 10 ones and the hundred ungrouped to show 10 tens. Students can ungroup from the left or from the right. Here are two ways students might show this.

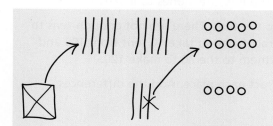

This student crossed out the hundred-box and 1 ten-stick and then redrew the tens and ones.

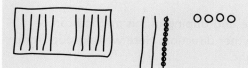

This student drew the 10 tens inside the hundred-box and drew the 10 ones on the ten-stick.

After ungrouping, students should cross out 5 tens and 8 ones. This leaves 7 tens and 6 ones, or 76. They can subtract from the left or from the right.

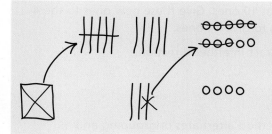

It is helpful to cross out within the ten. This helps support the Make a Ten method. Here 14 − 8 can be seen to be 2 (left in the 10) + 4 (over 10) = 6.

The student drew lines through the 5 tens and 8 ones.

The student drew the line through the 5 tens and circled the 8 ones before crossing them out.

Activity continued ▶

The Learning Classroom

Building Concepts Beginning in the next activity, students will link the steps in their drawings to steps in their numerical methods. This will make the numerical methods more meaningful. Linking each step in the drawing to each step in the numerical problem is the key to understanding. Students can stop making drawings when you are sure they understand and can explain their methods.

Teaching Note

Language and Vocabulary
Encourage students to use a variety of terms to describe ungrouping in subtraction. For example, they might talk about *trading* a ten for 10 ones, *borrowing* 10 ones from a ten, or *unpacking* a ten to get 10 ones. In *Math Expressions,* we use the word *grouping* when talking about addition and *ungrouping* when talking about subtraction. Regrouping can refer to either grouping or ungrouping. However, any language that is meaningful for students is acceptable.

❶ Teaching the Lesson (continued)

Teaching Note

Another Common Method: This method is widely used in other countries and so may be used by some of your students. The method is somewhat confusing because the way a small 1 written next to a digit is interpreted depends on whether it is in the top number or the bottom number. Allow your students to use this method if they understand it and can explain why it works.

$$\begin{array}{r} 134 \\ -\ 58 \end{array}$$

1. There are not enough ones to subtract from, so give 10 ones to the 4 ones to get 14 ones. To compensate, give 1 ten to the 5 tens in the bottom number. (In essence, you are adding 10 to both the top and bottom numbers, which does not affect the difference.) **Note:** The 1 next to the 5 is 1 ten, not 10 tens. So the ^{1}5 represents 6 tens, not ^{1}5 tens.

2. Subtract the ones.
$$\begin{array}{r} 13^14 \\ -\ ^158 \\ \hline 6 \end{array}$$

3. There are not enough tens to subtract from, so give 10 tens to the 3 tens to get 13 tens. To compensate, give 1 hundred to the 0 hundreds in the bottom number. (So, you have added 100 to both the top and bottom numbers, which does not affect the difference.)

4. Subtract the tens, keeping in mind that ^{1}5 represents 6 tens.

5. Subtract the hundreds. (The result is 0.)
$$\begin{array}{r} ^13^14 \\ -\ ^158 \\ \hline 76 \end{array}$$

Now have students use a numerical solution method to solve the word problem. Have student volunteers present their different solution methods.

Students who used *Math Expressions* in a previous grade may use the Expanded method or the Ungroup First method. Other students are likely to use the common U.S. method. These methods are shown below for your reference. Please *do not* "teach" any of these methods at this time. Allow students to show and explain the methods they are already using.

Expanded Method

Ungroup right to left

$$\begin{array}{r} 134 = \overset{0}{\cancel{100}} + \overset{120}{\cancel{30}} + \overset{14}{4} \\ -\ 58 \qquad -\quad 50 + 8 \\ \hline 70 + 6 = 76 \end{array}$$

Ungroup left to right

$$\begin{array}{r} 134 = \overset{0}{\cancel{100}} + \overset{120}{\underset{30}{\cancel{30}}} + \overset{14}{4} \\ -\ 58 \qquad -\quad 50 + 8 \\ \hline 70 + 6 = 76 \end{array}$$

1. Expand 134 as $100 + 30 + 4$ and 58 as $50 + 8$.

2. Start with the ones. There are not enough ones to subtract from, so take 10 ones from 30 and give them to the 4 ones to make 14.

3. Go to the tens. There are not enough tens to subtract from, so take 10 tens from 100 and give them to the 20 to make 120.

4. Subtract each place. Add the differences.

Ungroup First Method

Ungroup left to right

$$\begin{array}{r} 134 \\ -58 \end{array} \rightarrow \begin{array}{r} \overset{0\ 13}{1\cancel{3}4} \\ -58 \end{array} \rightarrow \begin{array}{r} \overset{12}{\overset{0\ \cancel{13}\ 14}{1\cancel{3}\cancel{4}}} \\ -58 \\ \hline 76 \end{array}$$

Ungroup right to left

$$\begin{array}{r} 134 \\ -58 \end{array} \rightarrow \begin{array}{r} \overset{2\ 14}{1\cancel{3}\cancel{4}} \\ -58 \end{array} \rightarrow \begin{array}{r} \overset{12}{\overset{0\ \cancel{2}\ 14}{1\cancel{3}\cancel{4}}} \\ -58 \\ \hline 76 \end{array}$$

Note: The ungrouping in this method can be done in either direction. Here we ungroup from left to right.

1. Starting with the hundreds, see if you can subtract at each place.

2. There are not enough tens, so ungroup 1 hundred to get 10 tens. Give these new tens to the 3 tens to get 13 tens.

3. There are not enough ones, so ungroup 1 ten to get 10 ones. Give these new ones to the 4 ones to give 14 ones.

4. Subtract in either direction.

Common U.S. Method

$$\begin{array}{r} 134 \\ -58 \end{array} \rightarrow \begin{array}{r} \overset{2}{1\,3^14} \\ -58 \end{array} \rightarrow \begin{array}{r} \overset{0\ ^12}{1\cancel{3}^14} \\ -58 \\ \hline 76 \end{array}$$

$$\begin{array}{r} \overset{2}{1\,3^14} \\ -58 \\ \hline 6 \end{array}$$

$$\begin{array}{r} \overset{2}{1\cancel{3}4} \\ -58 \\ \hline 136 \end{array} \quad \text{or} \quad \begin{array}{r} 134 \\ -58 \\ \hline 124 \end{array}$$

This method alternates ungrouping and subtracting:

1. Start with ones. There are not enough ones to subtract from, so ungroup 1 ten to get 10 ones. Give these new ones to the 4 ones to get 14 ones.

2. Subtract the ones.

3. Look at the tens. There are not enough tens, so ungroup 1 hundred to get 10 tens. Give these new tens to the 2 tens to get 12 tens.

4. Subtract the tens. There are no hundreds. With this alternating method, students in the middle step are more likely to make the common top from bottom error:

Avoid Subtracting the Wrong Way

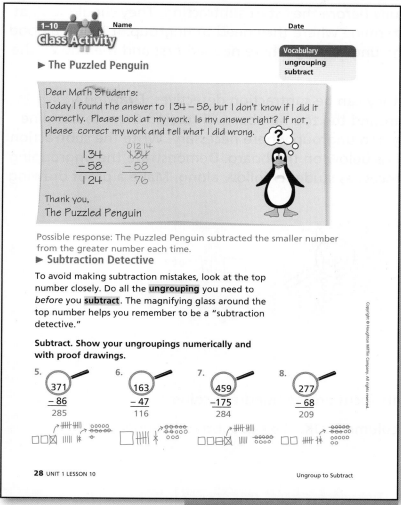

Student Activity Book page 28

35 MINUTES

Goal: Discuss ways to avoid common subtraction errors.

Materials: Student Activity Book or Hardcover Book p. 28, MathBoard materials

✓ **NCTM Standards:**
Number and Operations
Algebra
Problem Solving

Class Management

Depending on your class, you can work through some or all of the exercises together. The focus here is on understanding that the bottom number is *always* subtracted from the top number.

▶ The Puzzled Penguin WHOLE CLASS

Direct students' attention to the letter from the Puzzled Penguin on Student Book page 28. Ask them to look closely at the penguin's work and try to figure out what he did wrong. Then, do the subtraction correctly. Students should notice that he subtracted the top number from the bottom number in the tens and ones places.

Students should check that the bottom number is always subtracted from the top in their own work and the work of their classmates.

Activity continued ▶

The Learning Classroom

Math Talk Use the **Step-by-Step at the Board** structure with subtraction. Several Student Leaders solve and explain each step of a problem at the board. As an alternative, have different leaders describe what needs to be done as students work at their desks to carry out the direction. After students have had some time to record their responses, the leader records the direction on the board.

▶ **Subtraction Detective** WHOLE CLASS

Explain that students can avoid subtracting the wrong way by examining the problem carefully *before* they start subtracting. They should look at each place and determine where they need to ungroup. It is also a good idea to do all of the ungrouping where needed *first* and *then* do all the subtracting.

Tell students that they can be subtraction detectives. Drawing a magnifying glass around the top number will remind them to examine the number closely and ungroup where necessary. Write the subtraction and magnifying glass below on the board. Demonstrate the ungrouping and subtracting process as students follow along. Make a proof drawing as you work.

Step 1

First, have students focus on the hundreds column.

● The hundreds column is OK. We can subtract 0 hundreds from 1 hundred.

Step 2

Have students look at the tens column.

● Are there enough tens to subtract from? no

● How do we get more tens? Ungroup the 1 hundred to get 10 more tens.

● How can you show this in your drawing? Cross out the hundred-box and draw 10 ten-sticks.

● How many hundreds do you have after you ungroup the 1 hundred? none **How can you show this?** By crossing out the 1 in the hundreds column and writing 0.

● How many tens do you have? 13 **How can you show this?** By crossing out the 3 in the tens column and writing 13.

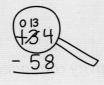

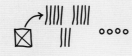

Step 3

Now look at the ones column.

- Are there enough ones to subtract from? no, 8 is more than 4

- How do we get more ones? Ungroup 1 ten to get 10 more ones.

- How can you show this in my drawing? Cross out a ten-stick and draw 10 circles.

- How many tens do you have after you ungroup 1 ten? 12
  How can you show this? By crossing out the 13 in the tens column and writing 12.

- How many ones do you have? 14
  How can you show this? By crossing out the 4 in the ones column and writing 14.

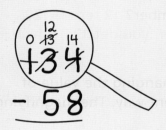 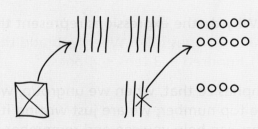

Step 4

- Is there anything left to ungroup? no

- What is the next step? Now that I have ungrouped everything, I can subtract.

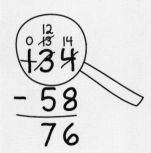 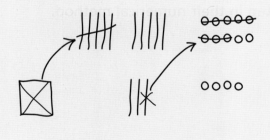

Activity continued ▶

Teaching Note

Watch For! As students make proof drawings for the subtraction, watch for those who make place value drawings for *both* the top number and the bottom number. Emphasize that they should start with a drawing for the top number and then find a way to "take away" the bottom number. Show an example with small numbers: 8 − 2.

- Do we draw 8 and draw 2? No, draw 8 and take away 2.

Suggest that students who have trouble remembering this, should draw a circle around the minus sign. The circle can remind them to draw the magnifying glass around the top number.

The Learning Classroom

Building Concepts Notice how taking the first objects from the ten shows the Make-a-Ten strategy:

14 − 8 is 2 + 4 = 6 ones

12 − 5 is 5 + 2 = 7 tens

Explain that, once everything is ungrouped, you can subtract the place value columns in any order. You might demonstrate by first subtracting from left to right, and then erasing your answer and subtracting from right to left.

Point out to students that, before ungrouping, the top number has 1 hundred, plus 3 tens, plus 4 ones. Write the following expression on the board:

$$\text{1 hundred} + \text{3 tens} + \text{4 ones}$$

● How many hundreds, tens, and ones does the top number have *after* ungrouping? 0 hundreds, 12 tens, 14 ones

Write the following expression under the first expression:

$$\text{0 hundreds} + \text{12 tens} + \text{14 ones}$$

● Why do the expressions represent the same number? 12 tens is 120 and 14 ones is 14. When you add these together, you get 134, which is 1 hundred + 3 tens + 4 ones.

Emphasize that, when we ungroup, we are not changing the value of the top number, we are just writing it in a different way. The magnifying glass can help you see and remember this.

Have students find the answer to exercise 5 on Student Book page 28 and then discuss the steps for subtracting as a class. Tell students that, if it is easier, they can make their proof drawing first and then use the picture to decide how to write the subtraction numerically.

Use the **Solve and Discuss** structure to solve the exercises 6–8. Have presenters show how each step in their proof drawing relates to each step in their numerical method.

 **Ongoing Assessment**

Write 364 − 187 on the board. Have students write the subtraction vertically, find the answer, and make a proof drawing.

Intervention   Activity Card 1–10

Modeling Subtraction   Activity Card 1-10 ●

Work: In pairs

Use:
• Base ten blocks

Decide:
Who will be Student 1 and who will be Student 2 for the first round.

1. Student 1: Use base ten blocks to model the subtraction 348 – 159.

2. Student 2: Describe each step as shown to the right.

3. Change roles and model the subtraction 235 – 88. 147

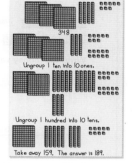

348

Ungroup 1 ten into 10 ones.

Ungroup 1 hundred into 10 tens.

Take away 159. The answer is 189.

Unit 1, Lesson 10   Copyright © Houghton Mifflin Company

Activity Note To reinforce understanding, have students explain why each ungrouping is needed.

🖊 **Math Writing Prompt**

Explain Your Thinking Explain what a "subtraction detective" does.

Soar to Success Math ★ **Software Support**

Warm Up 11.23

On Level   Activity Card 1–10

Plan Ahead to Ungroup   Activity Card 1-10 ▲

Work: On your own

Use:
• TRB M25 (Game Cards)

1. Shuffle the game cards and choose 6 without looking.

| 7 | 4 | 1 |
| 2 | 8 | 3 |

2. Use the cards to make two 3-digit numbers for a subtraction exercise. Arrange the digits so that you must ungroup before subtracting.

3. Copy the numbers on your paper and find the difference. 458

741
−283

4. Shuffle the cards again and repeat the activity.

Unit 1, Lesson 10   Copyright © Houghton Mifflin Company

Activity Note Have students check their work by adding. Then discuss any errors and how to avoid them.

 Math Writing Prompt

Write a Rule Write a rule about when to ungroup for subtracting.

 Software Support

Country Countdown: Block Busters, Level X

Challenge   Activity Card 1–10

How Old Are They?   Activity Card 1-10 ■

Work: On your own

1. Look at the table below. **Think** What subtraction exercise will tell you how many years ago the movie *Cinderella* was made? 2008 – 1950

Name of Movie	Year Made
Cinderella	1950
ET: The Extra-Terrestrial	1982
King Kong (original)	1933
The Sound of Music	1965
Star Wars	1977
The Wizard of Oz	1939

2. **Think** Will you need to ungroup before subtracting? Why or why not? yes, because you cannot subtract 5 tens from 0 tens.

3. Use the table to find out how many years ago each movie was made.

Unit 1, Lesson 10   Copyright © Houghton Mifflin Company

Activity Note Once students are finished, have a classmate check their work and correct any errors. Then discuss how to avoid the errors.

 Math Writing Prompt

Investigate Math Michelle knew that 134 – 58 was less than 100 without subtracting. Explain how Michelle may have known this.

 DESTINATION Math· **Software Support**

Course II: Module 2: Unit 1: Estimating and Finding Differences within 9,999

③ Homework and Spiral Review

Copyright © Houghton Mifflin Company. All rights reserved.

1–10
Homework **Goal:** Additional Practice

✓ Include students' completed Homework page as part of their portfolios.

1–10
Remembering **Goal:** Spiral Review

This Remembering page would be appropriate anytime after today's lesson.

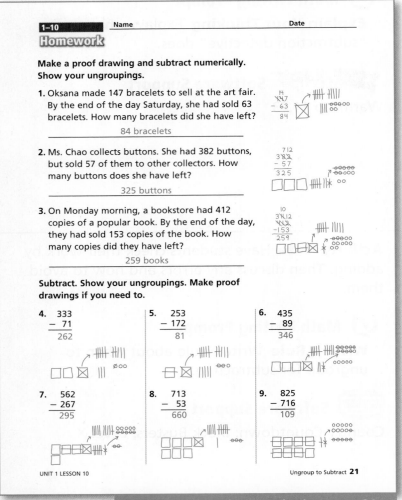

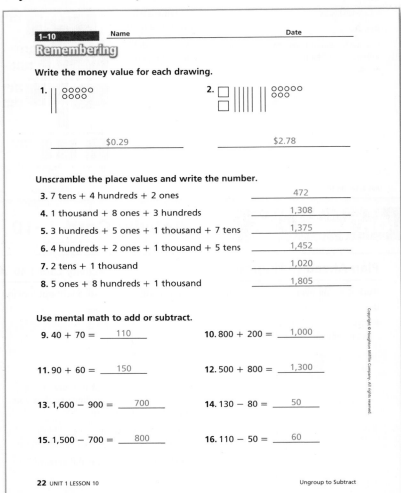

Homework and Remembering page 21

Homework and Remembering page 22

Home or School Activity

 Science Connection

Subtracting Sunny Days Have students gather statistics and create a chart about the average number of sunny days per year in some American cities. Then have them find the average number of days per year that are *not* sunny by subtracting the number of sunny days from 365 (days per year).

Name of City	Number of Sunny Days
Austin, TX	219 days
Seattle, WA	156 days
Chicago, IL	197 days
Orlando, FL	328 days
Philadelphia, PA	204 days

Subtract Across Zeros

Lesson Objectives

- Subtract with zeros in the top number.
- Solve subtraction problems involving money.

Vocabulary
ungrouping

The Day at a Glance

Today's Goals	Materials	

1 Teaching the Lesson
A1: Solve subtraction problems with zeros in the top number.
A2: Subtract from whole-dollar amounts.
A3: Practice subtraction with zeros in the top number.
A4: Decide when to ungroup.
	Lesson Activities
	Student Activity Book pp. 29–32 or
	  Student Hardcover Book pp. 29–32
	Homework and Remembering
	  pp. 23–24
	MathBoard materials
		Going Further
		Activity Cards 1-11
		Play money
		Paper bags
		Math Journals

2 Going Further ► Differentiated Instruction		
3 Homework and Spiral Review		123 *Use* **Math Talk** *today!*

Keeping Skills Sharp

Quick Practice ⏱ 5 MINUTES	Daily Routines
Goal: Subtract larger numbers. **Materials:** Demonstration Secret Code Cards (TRB M3–M18) **Subtract Tens** Have a **Student Leader** select the 100 card and two tens cards. The leader assembles the cards to show a 3-digit number on the left and a number of tens on the right. `100` `10` `1 1 0` `80` `8 0` The leader says, "Subtract." The class says the subtraction equation aloud. Then, the leader selects a student to explain the Make a Hundred strategy (See Unit 1 Lesson 6). Repeat several times. It may help to have two **Student Leaders**. One leads the class while the other selects cards for the next exercise.	**Homework Review** If students have difficulty with word problems, encourage them to write out the necessary step(s) to solving the problem before working on the mathematics and proof drawing. **Strategy Problem** Ji Sun bought two items. She paid with a $5 and a $1 bill, and got $0.25 change. If the store sells pens for $0.50 each, pencils for $0.55 each, a set of markers for $5.25, or a set of colored pencils for $5.50, which two items did she buy? 1 set of markers and 1 pen

1 Teaching the Lesson

Ungroup for Subtraction

 20 MINUTES

Goal: Solve subtraction problems with zeros in the top number.

Materials: Student Activity Book or Hardcover Book p. 29, MathBoard materials

✓ **NCTM Standards:**
Number and Operations
Problem Solving

Teaching Note

What to Expect from Students
Subtraction with zeros in the top number is especially challenging for students. *Math Expressions* has had success introducing this type of subtraction early on, rather than waiting until students have spent lots of time with other types of subtractions. Once students master the ungrouping required with top-number zeros, they can solve other multi-digit subtraction exercises with less difficulty.

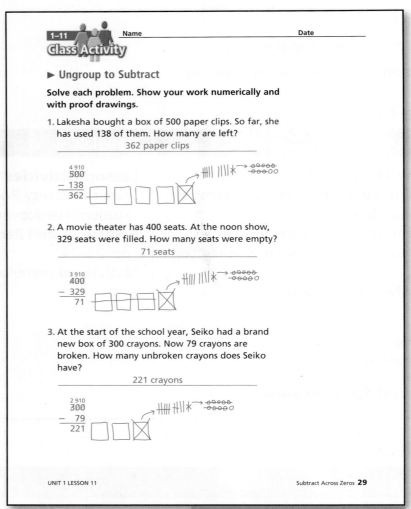

Student Activity Book page 29

▶ Ungroup to Subtract WHOLE CLASS

Read aloud problem 1 on Student Book page 29. Work through the problem with students, discussing each step of the solution.

● What do we need to do to solve the problem? Subtract 138 from 500.

Have students draw a magnifying glass to remember to look closely at the 500 and ungroup before subtracting.

● To make a proof drawing, what should you draw first? 5 hundred boxes

Have students focus on the hundreds column.

● Are there enough hundreds to subtract from? yes

Then move to the tens column:

● Are there enough tens to subtract from? no

● How can we get more tens? Ungroup one of the hundreds to get 10 tens.

● How do you show this in your proof drawing? Cross out 1 hundreds-box and draw 10 ten-sticks

● How do you show this with numbers? Cross out the 5 in the hundreds column and write 4. Cross out the 0 in the tens column and write 10.

● Now, how many hundreds and tens are there? 4 hundreds and 10 tens.

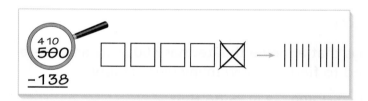

Now look at the ones column and ask if there are enough ones to subtract from. no Elicit responses from students on how to get more ones. Ungroup one of the tens to get 10 ones.

● How do you show this in your proof drawing? Cross out 1 ten-stick and draw 10 circles.

● How do you show this with numbers? Cross out the 10 in the tens column and write 9. Cross out the 0 in the ones column and write 10.

● How many tens and ones do you now have? 9 tens and 10 ones.

Students who start from the right will have to go clear over the hundreds place to get more ones. They will need to ungroup 1 hundred to get 10 tens so they can get 10 ones from 1 ten. They do not want to get 100 ones in the ones column.

Activity continued ▶

Teaching Note

What to Expect from Students
Students who are used to using the common subtraction method may be skeptical about the fact that, once everything is ungrouped, they can subtract the place value columns in any order. To demonstrate that you get the same answer either way, you might subtract in the order hundreds, tens, ones; erase your answer (just the answer, not the regrouping at the top); and then select a volunteer to subtract in the order ones, tens, hundreds.

Two Ways to Ungroup Zeros

1. Step-by-Step

$$\begin{array}{c} 9 \\ 4 \;\cancel{10}\,10 \\ \cancel{500} \end{array}$$

Know 100 = 90 + 10

2. Ungroup All at Once

$$\begin{array}{c} 4\;9\;10 \\ \cancel{500} \end{array}$$

Teaching Note

Watch For! Some students who try to "borrow" both more tens and more ones from the hundreds column, as illustrated below.

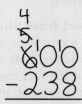

Encourage students who make this mistake to ungroup one place at a time and to think about the place-value of each number. Remind them that ungrouping 1 hundred gives 100 ones, not 10 ones. If they want to get 10 ones, they need to ungroup a ten, not a hundred.

Now that everything has been ungrouped, ask students what to do next. Subtract

● Does it matter which place value column you subtract first? no

● How do you show the subtraction in your proof drawing? Cross out 1 hundred, 3 tens, and 8 ones.

● Does your final drawing match your answer? yes

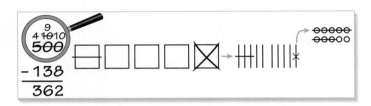

Use the **Solve and Discuss** structure for problems 2 and 3. As students work, walk around to monitor progress and provide help. Make note of the kinds of errors students are making. When you select presenters, include students who made common errors so these errors can be discussed and corrected.

 Math Talk in Action

Cameron: Problem 2 says that a movie theater has 400 seats and there were 329 filled. We need to find out how many were empty.

Justine: We have to subtract 400 – 329 to do that.

Cameron: Let's try this without a proof drawing.

Justine: Ok. There are 4 hundreds, 0 tens, and 0 ones in 400. I think that we have to ungroup something so that we can subtract 329.

Cameron: We can ungroup the 4 hundreds into 3 hundreds and 10 tens. I'll cross out the 4 in the hundreds column and write 3. I'll cross out the 0 in the tens column and write 10.

Justine: We've got 3 hundreds and 10 tens. We can't subtract the nine ones yet though because there aren't any ones to subtract from. Let's ungroup the 10 tens into 9 tens and 10 ones.

Cameron: Now we can subtract! 10 ones minus 9 ones is 1 one. 9 tens minus 2 tens is 7 tens.

Justine: And 3 hundreds minus 3 hundreds is 0 hundreds. We have 7 tens and 1 one left. The answer is 71!

Cameron: Don't forget that we have to answer the question. There are 71 empty seats.

Subtract from Whole-Dollar Amounts

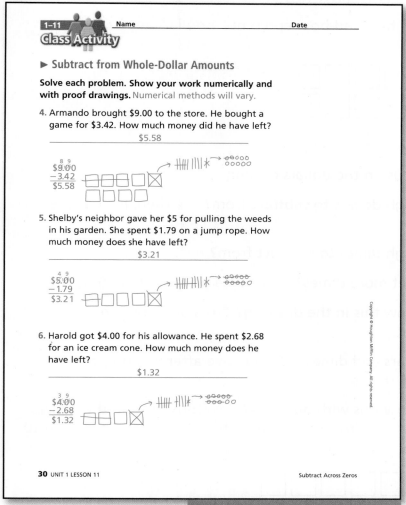

▶ Subtract from Whole-Dollar Amounts WHOLE CLASS

Read aloud problem 4 on Student Book page 30. Using the **Solve and Discuss** structure, have students complete the problem. If students have difficulty solving subtraction problems involving money, work together to set up and start solving the problem:

● What do we need to do to solve the problem? Subtract $3.42 from $9.00

● How do you line up the two numbers? Line up the decimal point, so dollars are lined up with dollars, dimes with dimes, and pennies with pennies.

 15 MINUTES

Goal: Subtract from whole-dollar amounts.

Materials: Student Activity Book or Hardcover Book p. 30, MathBoard materials

✔ **NCTM Standards:**
Number and Operations
Problem Solving

The Learning Classroom

Math Talk To continue to keep students in their seats engaged and to move this engagement to a deeper level, challenge them to listen carefully so that they might say the explainers' statements. Ask several students to *repeat* what has been explained by the student explainer in their own words.

English Language Learners

Review regrouping with money. Draw a dime and a penny on the board and ask: **How many cents is 1 penny?** 1 cent **How many cents is 1 dime?** 10 cents Write the values in ¢ on the board. Continue with the dollar and dimes.

● **Beginning** Say: **1 dime is equal to 1 group of 10 pennies.** Have students repeat. Draw an equal sign and 10 pennies next to the dime.

● **Intermediate** Say: **We group 10 pennies to make _____.** 10¢, 1 dime Draw an equal sign and 10 pennies next to the dime.

● **Advanced** Have students describe how to group pennies to make dimes and dimes to make dollars.

Activity continued ▶

Teaching the Lesson (continued)

Class Management

Suggested Groups You may want to divide the class into partners rather than using the **Solve and Discuss** structure with the entire class. Partners can work together to discuss how subtracting money amounts is similar to subtracting whole numbers. As partners work, check to be sure that each partner understands the method used to solve the subtraction problems.

Teaching Note

Math Drawings The proof drawings have two main functions: first, to help students understand the steps involved in calculating and relate these steps to their steps in numerical computations and second, to help the whole class understand all students' explanations of their work.

Because the drawings help to make computation or problem solving meaningful, students can and should stop making drawings as soon as they understand and can explain numerical computational methods using place-value language (for example, 5 tens plus 9 tens is 14 tens which is 1 hundred and 4 tens or 50 plus 90 is 140, not just 5 plus 9 is 14). At this point, for their own work and for homework, they do not need to make a proof drawing. However, if they are working at the board, students should make proof drawings so that their classmates can understand what they did (although toward the end of a unit, this is less necessary). And, throughout the year, it is useful to make a proof drawing once in a while so that the meaning stays attached to the numerical process.

Have students draw a magnifying glass to remember to do all of their ungrouping before subtracting.

- **What should you draw first?** 9 hundred-boxes
- **What does each hundred-box represent?** 1 dollar, or 100 pennies

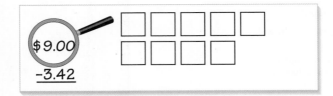

Have students focus on the dollars column.

- **Are there enough dollars to subtract from?** yes Then, look at the dimes column.
- **Are there enough dimes to subtract from?** no
- **How can you get more dimes?** Ungroup a dollar to get 10 new dimes.
- **How do you show this in the drawing?** Cross out a hundred-box and make 10 ten-sticks.
- **How many dollars and dimes will you have after you ungroup?** 8 dollars and 10 dimes
- **How do you show this with numbers?** Cross out the 9 in the dollars column and write 8. Cross out the 0 in the tens column and write 10.

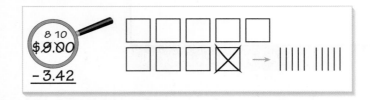

Have students finish subtracting. Then use the **Solve and Discuss** structure for problems 5 and 6. Explain in problem 5 that $5 can also be written as $5.00.

Activity 3

Practice Subtraction Across Zeros

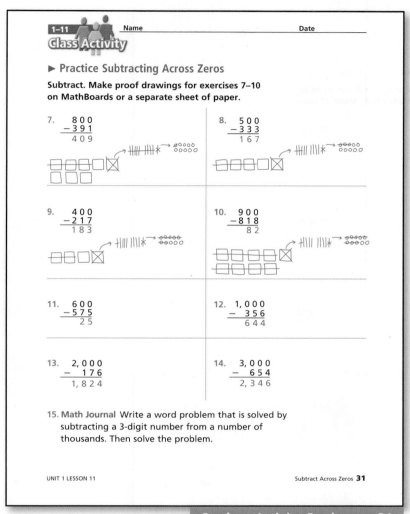

Student Activity Book page 31

▶ Practice Subtracting Across Zeros WHOLE CLASS

Ask students to suggest some word problems exercise 7 on Student Book page 31 might represent. Then have students complete the page.

Walk around, monitoring progress and noting common errors. Provide individual help for students who are struggling or pair these students with Student Helpers. If a large number of students are having difficulties, work through the first problem or two as a class.

When most students have completed Student Book page 31, discuss any difficulties for students and talk about the common errors you observed as you walked around the room. Students may have trouble subtracting from thousands in exercises 12–14. You might ask students to present solutions and proof drawings. See side column for a Sample Proof Drawing.

 20 MINUTES

Goal: Practice subtraction with zeros in the top number.

Materials: Student Activity Book or Hardcover Book p. 31, MathBoard materials

✔ **NCTM Standards:**
Number and Operations
Problem Solving

Teaching Note

Watch For! Some students may discover a shortcut that allows them to ungroup only once. For example, the problem below shows that we can ungroup 1 hundred all at once to get 9 tens and 10 ones.

Sample Proof Drawing:

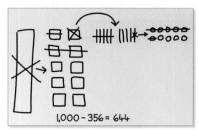

Decide When to Ungroup

 15 MINUTES

Goal: Decide whether to ungroup when solving a subtraction problem.

Materials: Student Activity Book or Hardcover Book p. 32, MathBoard materials

 NCTM Standards:
Number and Operations
Communication

Differentiated Instruction

Extra Help For students who have difficulty ungrouping 3- and 4-digit top numbers with zeros, have them practice ungrouping with 2-digit top numbers. For example, rewrite exercise 7. as 80 − 39, rather than 800 − 391. Once students are comfortable with ungrouping single top number zeros, then move them on to larger numbers.

Teaching Note

Subtraction with Larger Numbers If your district's goals require subtracting from numbers greater than 9,999, you might spend some time today having your students solve exercises such as: 10,912 - 6,265

The methods for solving such exercises are simple extensions of the methods for solving subtraction exercises involving smaller numbers. Students may need to make place-value drawings to help them visualize the subtraction. Have them create a symbol to represent ten-thousands in a place-value drawing.

1–11
Class Activity
Name _____ Date _____

► Practice Deciding When to Ungroup

Subtract. Make proof drawings if you need to on MathBoards or on a separate sheet of paper.

Check Students' drawings

16. 912 − 265

$$\begin{array}{r} 9\,1\,2 \\ -2\,6\,5 \\ \hline 6\,4\,7 \end{array}$$

17. 323 − 147

$$\begin{array}{r} 3\,2\,3 \\ -1\,4\,7 \\ \hline 1\,7\,6 \end{array}$$

18. 280 − 136

$$\begin{array}{r} 2\,8\,0 \\ -1\,3\,6 \\ \hline 1\,4\,4 \end{array}$$

19. 489 − 263

$$\begin{array}{r} 4\,8\,9 \\ -2\,6\,3 \\ \hline 2\,2\,6 \end{array}$$

20. 1,754 − 589

$$\begin{array}{r} 1,7\,5\,4 \\ -\ \ 5\,8\,9 \\ \hline 1,1\,6\,5 \end{array}$$

21. 2,567 − 956

$$\begin{array}{r} 2,5\,6\,7 \\ -\ \ 9\,5\,6 \\ \hline 1,6\,1\,1 \end{array}$$

22. 8,215 − 1,265

$$\begin{array}{r} 8,2\,1\,5 \\ -1,2\,6\,5 \\ \hline 6,9\,5\,0 \end{array}$$

23. 5,725 − 3,214

$$\begin{array}{r} 5,7\,2\,5 \\ -3,2\,1\,4 \\ \hline 2,5\,1\,1 \end{array}$$

32 UNIT 1 LESSON 11

Subtract Across Zeros

Student Activity Book page 32

► Practice Deciding When to Ungroup
WHOLE CLASS

Math Talk 123 Ask students a few general questions about ungrouping:

● When you need to subtract, how can you tell if you will need to ungroup? If the top number in any column is smaller than the bottom number, you will need to ungroup.

● What do you do if there are not enough tens to subtract from? Ungroup 1 hundred to make 10 new tens.

Direct students' attention to exercises 16–19 on Student Book page 32.

● Which of these involves ungrouping 1 hundred to make 10 more tens? 16 and 17

● What is different about exercise 19? You don't need to ungroup.

Then have students complete the page.

   Activity Card 1–11

Ungrouping Money   Activity Card 1-11 ●

Work: In pairs

Use:
- Play Money (pennies, dimes, and dollar bills)

Decide:

Who will be Student 1 and who will be Student 2 for the first round.

1. **Student 1:** Tell your partner how to use play money to model $3.00 – $1.48. Follow the example or choose your own method.

2. **Student 2:** Use the play money to model the subtraction and make the trades that your partner needs. Check each step as you work.

3. Change roles and model $5.00 – $2.61.

$3.00

Trade 1 dollar for 10 dimes

Trade 1 dime for 10 pennies

Subtract $1.48

Answer: $1.52

Unit 1, Lesson 11   Copyright © Houghton Mifflin Company

Activity Note Students may choose more than one method to model the subtraction exercises. The example given shows ungrouping from left to right.

 **Math Writing Prompt**

Explain Your Thinking Rico says that it is impossible to subtract from a zero in the top number, so the answer to 200 – 158 is 158. Explain the error in his thinking.

Soar to Success Math ★ Software Support

Warm Up 3.17

   Activity Card 1–11

What Is the Change?   Activity Card 1-11 ▲

Work: In pairs

Use:
- Slips of paper
- Paper bag

1. **Work Together** Write dollar amounts $2.00 through $7.00 on separate slips of paper. Put the slips of paper into the bag.

2. Take turns. Pull a slip of paper from the bag. Choose an item to buy from the list of arts and crafts supplies.

Arts and Crafts Supplies	
Water color paints	$4.65
Set of brushes	$3.84
Sketch paper	$5.79
Crayons	$2.58
Art chalk	$1.90

3. Your partner subtracts to find how much change you should receive or how much more money you need. Record the results.

4. Switch roles each time to make three more purchases.

Unit 1, Lesson 11   Copyright © Houghton Mifflin Company

Activity Note Be sure that students subtract the lesser money amount from the greater amount.

 Math Writing Prompt

Find the Error Chen used $6.00 to buy a game that cost $5.45. The store clerk gave Chen $1.55 in change. Is this the correct amount of change? Explain.

MEGA MATH Grades K-6 Software Support

Numberopolis: Lulu's Lunch Counter, Level Q

   Activity Card 1–11

Target Practice   Activity Card 1-11 ■

Work: In pairs

1. Copy each target onto a sheet of paper.

2. Use the digits around the outside of each target to write the missing three-digit numbers in the subtraction sentence.

3. **Think** What digits could work for the ones digit in each missing number? What digits could work for the tens digit in each missing number?

4. Use the digits around the outside of the second target to write the missing three-digit numbers in the second subtraction sentence.

$518 - 493 = 25$

$453 - 297 = 156$

Unit 1, Lesson 11   Copyright © Houghton Mifflin Company

Activity Note Working right to left, students should identify possible digits for each place value. As they proceed, the correct digits will become apparent.

 Math Writing Prompt

Mental Math Explain how to find the answer to $10.00 – $3.98 using mental math.

 DESTINATION Math® Software Support

Course II: Module 1: Unit 1: Comparing and Ordering

③ Homework and Spiral Review

1–11
Homework **Goal:** Additional Practice

✓ Include students' completed Homework page as part of their portfolios.

1–11
Remembering **Goal:** Spiral Review

This Remembering page would be appropriate anytime after today's lesson.

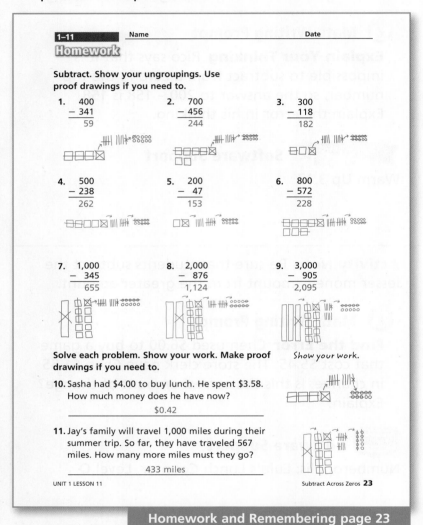

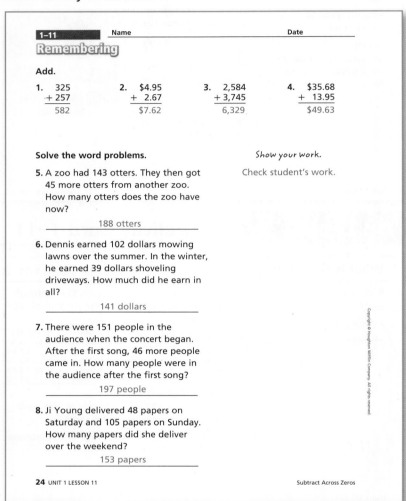

Homework and Remembering page 23

Homework and Remembering page 24

Home and School Activity

Social Studies Connection

Inventions Help students research and create a list of items that were invented years ago. Then, have them make a chart to show five inventions and the year in which they were developed in chronological order. Students can then subtract from the current year to find out how long the invention has been around.

For example, Thomas Edison patented the light bulb in 1879. If the current year is 2007, students will use 2007 – 1879 to discover that the light bulb has been around for 128 years.

Invention	Year
Paper	105
Pencil	1565
Telescope	1608
Ear Muffs	1873
Television	1927

Discuss Methods of Subtracting

REAL WORLD Problem Solving

Lesson Objectives

- Subtract using two different methods.
- Explain when and how to ungroup when subtracting multi-digit numbers.

Vocabulary
ungroup

The Day at a Glance

Today's Goals	Materials	
1 Teaching the Lesson **A1:** Compare two subtraction methods—ungrouping from the left and ungrouping from the right. **A2:** Choose items from a price list, find the total cost for the items, and determine how much money will be left from a given amount. **2 Going Further** ▶ Differentiated Instruction **3 Homework and Spiral Review**	**Lesson Activities** Student Activity Book pp. 33–34 or Student Hardcover Book pp. 33–34 Homework and Remembering pp. 25–26 MathBoard materials	**Going Further** Activity Cards 1-12 Base ten blocks MathBoard materials Number cubes Math Journals

123 *Use Math Talk today!*

Keeping Skills Sharp

Quick Practice 🕐 5 MINUTES	Daily Routines
Goal: Subtract tens from numbers that are greater than 100. **Materials:** Demonstration Secret Code Cards (TRB M3–M18) **Subtract Tens** Have one **Student Leader** select the 100 card and two tens cards. The first leader assembles the cards to show a 3-digit number on the left and a number of tens on the right.	**Homework Review** As a class, discuss the operation used to solve problems 10 and 11. Have students share reasons for selecting this operation. **Skip Count** Have students skip count by 25s from 25 to 1,000.

100	60		90
1	**6**	**0**	**9 0**

The second leader says, "Subtract." (See Unit 1 Lesson 10.)

Teaching the Lesson

Two Methods for Subtraction

 20 MINUTES

Goal: Compare two subtraction methods—ungrouping from the left and ungrouping from the right.

Materials: Student Activity Book or Hardcover Book p. 33, MathBoard Materials

✔ **NCTM Standards:**
Number and Operations
Communication
Problem Solving

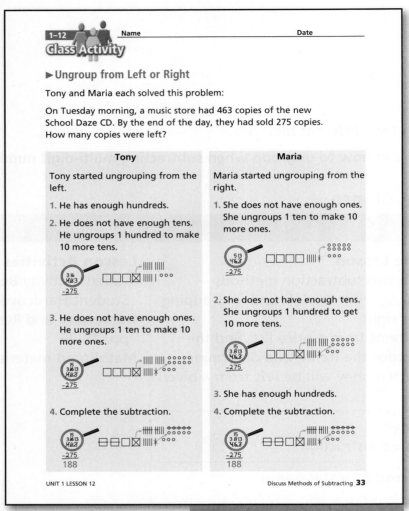

Student Activity Book page 33

▶ **Ungroup from Left or Right** WHOLE CLASS

Read aloud the word problem on Student Book page 33. Ask students how they would solve the problem. Subtract 275 from 463.

Tell students that Tony and Maria subtracted in different ways. Tony started on the left, with the hundreds place. Work through Tony's method as students follow along. Ask volunteers to explain what Tony did in each step and why he did it.

Next, tell students that Maria started from the right, with the ones place. Work through Maria's method, asking a volunteer to explain each step.

Ask students to compare the two methods, explaining what is different and what is the same.

Then, have students complete the subtraction.

Write 617 − 159 on the board in vertical form. Ask students to subtract by ungrouping from the right and then by ungrouping from the left on their MathBoards. Have some students work at the board. Have one student explain each method.

▶ A Special Case When Ungrouping from the Left

WHOLE CLASS

Write the following subtraction example and place value drawing on the board.

$$435 \quad \square\square \;|||\; \circ\circ\circ\circ\circ$$
$$-138 \quad \square\square$$

Tell students that you will subtract by ungrouping from the left.

● Are there enough hundreds to subtract? yes

● Are there enough tens to subtract? yes

● Are there enough ones to subtract? no. How can you get enough ones to subtract? Ungroup 1 ten to make 10 more ones.

Draw the ungrouping on the board. Then have a volunteer explain what happens when you subtract the ones. Write the result on the board.

$$\begin{array}{r} 2\ 15 \\ 4\cancel{3}\cancel{5} \\ -138 \\ \hline 7 \end{array} \quad \square\square \;||\cancel{|}\; \begin{array}{l} \circ\!\!\!\!\!\!\!\circ\circ\circ\circ\circ \\ \circ\!\!\!\!\!\!\!\circ\circ\circ\circ\circ \\ \circ\circ\circ\circ\circ \end{array}$$
$$\square\square$$

● Are there enough tens to subtract? no Why aren't there enough tens to subtract? because we ungrouped 1 ten

● How can you get enough tens to subtract? Go back and ungroup 1 hundred to make 10 more tens.

Activity continued ▶

The Learning Classroom

Building Concepts Students' understanding of each step that is taken in subtraction is reinforced through the process of starting at the left (hundreds), and going to the right without ungrouping, then going back to ungroup a hundred when this becomes necessary. Moreover, this process can give students added confidence in their ability to complete any addition or subtraction example. This is an opportunity for students to realize that if they pay attention to place value, they can create their own procedures for computation, and can go back and correct steps that they have already taken.

① Teaching the Lesson (continued)

Teaching Note

Watch For! To address common errors, such as failing to record ungrouping, solve a few problems yourself on the board, purposely making errors you have seen your students make. Ask students to observe and watch for mistakes. Students should identify the errors you make and offer suggestions for avoiding such errors.

Draw the ungrouping on the board. Have volunteers subtract the tens and the hundreds. Write the results on the board.

$$
\begin{array}{r}
\;\;12\;\;\;\\
3\,\overset{2}{\cancel{2}}\,15\\
435\\
-\,138\\
\hline
297
\end{array}
$$

Write the following examples on the board. Have volunteers come to the board and subtract starting at the left.

$$
\begin{array}{r}
865\\
-\,368\\
\hline
497
\end{array}
\qquad
\begin{array}{r}
453\\
-\,257\\
\hline
196
\end{array}
$$

Have students discuss how the examples are alike, and describe the patterns they see.

● When will you need to go back and ungroup a hundred in order to subtract tens? When there are the same number of tens in each number and there are not enough ones to subtract.

Andy's Arts and Crafts Store

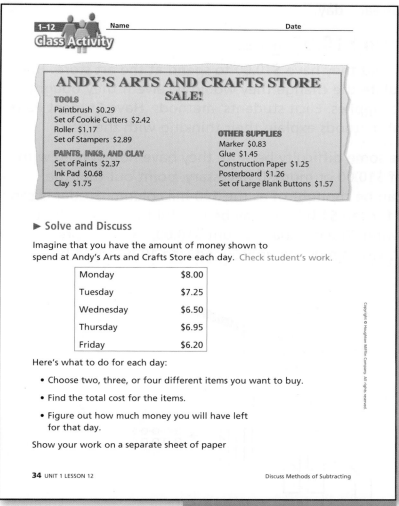

 20 MINUTES

Goal: Choose items from a price list, find the total cost for the items, and determine how much money will be left from a given amount

Materials: Student Activity Book or Hardcover Book p. 34

 NCTM Standards:
Number and Operations
Problem Solving
Communication

The Learning Classroom

Math Talk You can create math conversations by eliciting multiple strategies for solving problems. When you ask, "Did anyone do this problem differently?" your students will pay greater attention to the work on the board because they will be comparing and contrasting it with their own math strategies. The comparisons and contrasts that result can naturally springboard to significant math talk.

▶ Solve and Discuss [WHOLE CLASS]   Math Talk

Direct students' attention to the ad for Andy's Arts and Crafts Store on Student Book page 34.

Read aloud the directions for the activity. Then, ask a volunteer to choose three or four different items from the price list. Remind students that they only have a set amount of money each day. Have them begin with Monday's budget of $8.00. Using the **Solve and Discuss** structure, have students find the total price for the items.

Students may use different strategies for adding the prices. Some may add all of the prices at once. Some may add two prices, then add the total to the next price, and so on. If there are four prices, some students may add them in pairs and then add the two totals. Try to choose students who used different strategies to present their methods of solving.

Be sure that students understand how to figure out how much money they will have left over for the day. They should subtract the total

Differentiated Instruction

Extra Help Some students may have difficulty discovering a way to add more than two numbers. Suggest that students choose two of the prices, find the sum, and then add another price to the sum. If there is a fourth number, they can add this number to the second sum that they found.

Activity continued ▶

Discuss Methods of Subtracting **101**

① Teaching the Lesson (continued)

English Language Learners

Act out a grocery store check out scene with a student to make sure students understand the terms *change* and *cashier*.

• **Beginning** Pretend to buy a $1 item with a $5. Ask: **How much is this? How much did I give? How much do I get back?** Say: **This is my change.**

• **Intermediate** Say: **This is $1. I give the cashier $5. The cashier gives me____.** $4 **The cashier says ____.** Here's your change

• **Advanced** Ask: **If an item costs $1 and I pay with a $5 bill, how much does the cashier give me back? What is this called?**

✓ Ongoing Assessment

Ask students the following questions:

▶ Did you ungroup a dime to make ten pennies? Why?

▶ Why did you ungroup a dollar?

▶ How can you get more dollars to subtract?

amount for the art supplies they wish to buy from the amount of money they have listed for each day.

▶ Subtract from $10.00 PAIRS

Now, tell the class that they have $10.00 to spend at the art store. Have **Student Pairs** calculate the change they would receive if they bought $6.06 worth of art supplies. Elicit students' methods. Have **Student Pairs** who used different methods explain their thinking with the class.

Students may have some difficulty because they have not worked with money amounts of $10.00 or more. If necessary, point out that the leftmost column can be thought of as the $10-bill column. Students can trade one $10 bill for ten $1 bills. It may be helpful to have a volunteer make a proof drawing. The original amount $10.00, can be represented by a thousand bar, which must be ungrouped into 10 hundred-boxes, and so on.

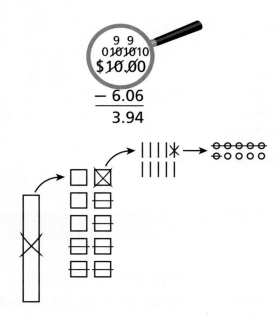

Have students who experience difficulty work with a **Helping Partner**.

② Going Further

Differentiated Instruction

Decide Before You Subtract

Activity Card 1-12 ●

Work: In pairs

Use:
- Base ten blocks (20 hundreds, 20 tens, 20 ones)
- MathBoard materials

1. Copy each subtraction exercise below on a MathBoard.

842	$2.77
−562	−$1.36
280	$1.41
500	963
−212	−269
288	694

2. Work with your partner. Use base ten blocks to find each answer. Record your work on your MathBoard as you use the blocks.

3. **Analyze** Did you need to ungroup for every subtraction? no, not for $2.77 − $1.36

Unit 1, Lesson 12   Copyright © Houghton Mifflin Company

Activity Note Students may choose to ungroup from left to right or from right to left. Partners should discuss when and why ungrouping is necessary.

 **Math Writing Prompt**

Choose a Method Write a rule about when to ungroup to subtract.

Soar to Success Math ★ Software Support

Warm Up 11.24

Race to Two Digits

Activity Card 1-12 ▲

Work: In small groups

Use:
- 3 number cubes (labeled 0–5, 1–6, 2–7)
- MathBoard materials

1. Copy the place value chart with the number 999 on your MathBoard. Write H for hundreds, T for tens, and O for ones.

H	T	O
9	9	9

2. Take turns to play a subtraction game. Roll the three number cubes to make a 3-digit number. Subtract the number from 999. Record your work in the chart.

H	T	O
9	9	9
−6	3	1
3	6	8
−2	7	5
	9	3

3. The next player rolls the number cubes again and subtracts the new number from the last result.

4. Continue until the difference is a 2-digit number.

Unit 1, Lesson 12   Copyright © Houghton Mifflin Company

Activity Note Students must arrange the digits they roll to make a number that is less than the previous difference, so that subtraction is possible.

 Math Writing Prompt

Think Critically Ben wrote this subtraction equation: 548 − 322 = 256. Explain the error that he made.

MEGA MATH Grades K-6 Software Support

Country Countdown: Block Busters, Level X

What's the Difference?

Activity Card 1-12 ■

Work: In pairs

Use:
- MathBoard materials

1. Copy these two sets of numbers on a MathBoard and draw the squares as shown.

115, 129, 141, 155

155	141	14 ←155 − 141 = 14
129	115	14 ←129 − 115 = 14
26	26	

155 − 129 = 26   141 − 115 = 26

122, 138, 210, 226

226	210	16 ← 226 − 210 = 16
138	122	16 ← 138 − 122 = 16
88	88	

226 − 138 = 88   210 − 122 = 88

2. Arrange one set of four numbers in each square, so the numbers in both rows of the square have the same difference and the numbers in both columns of the square also have the same difference.

3. **Think** How many possible subtraction sentences can be written with each set of numbers? 6

Unit 1, Lesson 12   Copyright © Houghton Mifflin Company

Activity Note Students should make a list of all possible subtraction sentences to help them choose the placement of the numbers in each square.

 Math Writing Prompt

Number Sense Will 572 − 352 equal more or less than 200? Explain how you know.

 DESTINATION Math· Software Support

Course II: Module 2: Unit 1: Estimating and Finding Differences within 1,000

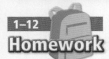

③ Homework and Spiral Review

Homework **Goal:** Additional Practice

This Homework page gives students practice in addition and subtraction.

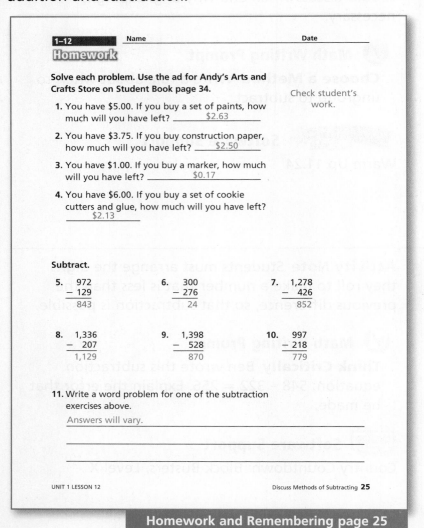

1-12
Homework

Name _____ Date _____

Solve each problem. Use the ad for Andy's Arts and Crafts Store on Student Book page 34.

Check student's work.

1. You have $5.00. If you buy a set of paints, how much will you have left? ____ $2.63

2. You have $3.75. If you buy construction paper, how much will you have left? ____ $2.50

3. You have $1.00. If you buy a marker, how much will you have left? ____ $0.17

4. You have $6.00. If you buy a set of cookie cutters and glue, how much will you have left? ____ $2.13

Subtract.

5. 972 − 129	6. 300 − 276	7. 1,278 − 426
843	24	852

8. 1,336 − 207	9. 1,398 − 528	10. 997 − 218
1,129	870	779

11. Write a word problem for one of the subtraction exercises above.
Answers will vary.
_____
_____

UNIT 1 LESSON 12   Discuss Methods of Subtracting **25**

Homework and Remembering page 25

Remembering **Goal:** Spiral Review

This Remembering page would be appropriate any time after today's lesson.

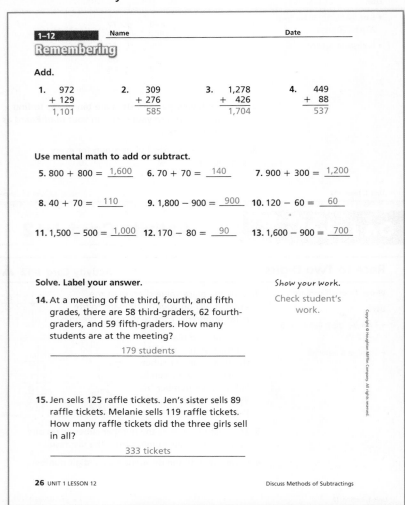

1-12
Remembering

Name _____ Date _____

Add.

1. 972 + 129	2. 309 + 276	3. 1,278 + 426	4. 449 + 88
1,101	585	1,704	537

Use mental math to add or subtract.

5. 800 + 800 = 1,600   6. 70 + 70 = 140   7. 900 + 300 = 1,200

8. 40 + 70 = 110   9. 1,800 − 900 = 900   10. 120 − 60 = 60

11. 1,500 − 500 = 1,000   12. 170 − 80 = 90   13. 1,600 − 900 = 700

Solve. Label your answer.

Show your work.

Check student's work.

14. At a meeting of the third, fourth, and fifth grades, there are 58 third-graders, 62 fourth-graders, and 59 fifth-graders. How many students are at the meeting?

_____ 179 students

15. Jen sells 125 raffle tickets. Jen's sister sells 89 raffle tickets. Melanie sells 119 raffle tickets. How many raffle tickets did the three girls sell in all?

_____ 333 tickets

26 UNIT 1 LESSON 12   Discuss Methods of Subtractings

Homework and Remembering page 26

Home or School Activity

 Literature Connection

Some Favorite Books Give students a copy of this reading list. Ask students how many more pages the book with the greatest number of pages has than the book with the least number of pages. Have students write and solve some other subtraction problems that compare the number of pages in the books.

The Hoboken Chicken Emergency	112 pages
Nate the Great	80 pages
I Was a Third Grade Science Project	96 pages
Charlotte's Web	192 pages
The Best School Year Ever	128 pages
Mr. Popper's Penguins	139 pages

Relate Addition and Subtraction

REAL WORLD Problem Solving

Lesson Objective

● Relate grouping in addition and ungrouping in subtraction.

The Day at a Glance

Today's Goals	Materials
1 Teaching the Lesson **A1:** Relate grouping in addition to ungrouping in subtraction and discuss that addition and subtraction undo one another. **A2:** Explore different ways of expressing the ideas of ungrouping and grouping. **2 Going Further** ▶ Differentiated Instruction **3 Homework and Spiral Review**	**Lesson Activities** Student Activity Book pp. 35–36 or Student Hardcover Book pp. 35–36 Homework and Remembering pp. 27–28 Base ten blocks Chart paper MathBoard materials **Going Further** Activity Cards 1-13 Index cards Sticky notes Math Journals

123 Use Math Talk today!

Keeping Skills Sharp

Quick Practice ⏰ 5 MINUTES	Daily Routines
Goal: Subtract hundreds. **Materials:** Demonstration Secret Code Cards (TRB M3–M18) **Subtract Hundreds** Have one **Student Leader** select the 1,000 card and the 200 card and assemble the cards to show a 4-digit number. Then, have the leader choose a hundred card and display it on the right.	**Homework Review** Review the prices used for problems 1 through 4. Then, have students write the subtraction on the board for problems 1, 3 and 4. Discuss and check as a class. **Place Value** Find 100 more than 1,555. Explain how you found your answer. 1,655; I added the 5 and 1 in the hundreds places of both addends. The other digits remain the same.

```
1000  200              700
 1   2  0  0         7   0  0
```

Have another **Student Leader** say, "Subtract." The class says the equation aloud. The leader selects a student to illustrate the Make a Thousand strategy (See page 55). Repeat, subtracting different hundreds from combinations between 1,100 and 1,900.

Teaching the Lesson

Activity 1

Relate Addition and Subtraction Methods

 30 MINUTES

Goal: Relate grouping in addition to ungrouping in subtraction.

Materials: Student Activity Book or Hardcover Book pp. 35–36, base ten blocks

✔ **NCTM Standards:**
Number and Operations
Problem Solving
Communication

✋ **Alternate Approach**

Base Ten Blocks Some students may find it interesting to use base ten blocks to model addition and subtraction problems.

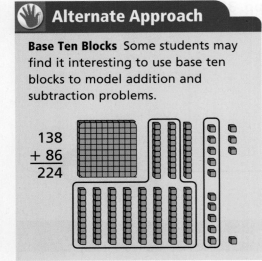

138
+ 86
224

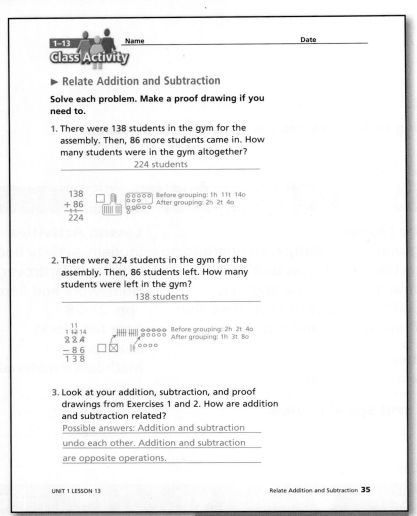

▶ Relate Addition and Subtraction WHOLE CLASS

Using the **Solve and Discuss** structure, have students solve problem 1 on Student Book page 35. Tell them to make a proof drawing, even if they don't need to. Choose a student who made a clear drawing to present the addition and proof drawing. Next to the drawing, record the number of hundreds, tens, and ones the drawing showed before grouping and after grouping. Remind students they can use the abbreviation H, T, and O for hundreds, tens, and ones to save time. Leave the drawing and labels on the board.

Read aloud problem 2. Ask students how they can figure out the answer without doing any work. Allow several students to share their ideas. Students should see that:

- In problem 1, they combined 138 students and 86 students to get a total of 224 students.

- In problem 2, they start with the total from problem 1, which is 224 students. Then they take away 86 students, so there must be 138 students left.

Math Mountains Review or introduce the idea of a Math Mountain. A Math Mountain shows the relationship between a *total* and two *partners* of the total; that is, two numbers that add to make the total. Make a Math Mountain for problem 1. You might tell students that they can visualize the total at the top breaking into two pieces, one of which rolls down one side and one of which rolls down the other side.

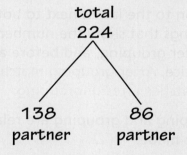

total
224

138   86
partner   partner

Explain to students that they can write an addition equation that shows that the two partners in the Math Mountain add to make the total. Write the following on the board:

138   +   86   =   224
partner   partner   total

Explain that they can also write a subtraction equation that shows that when one of the partners is taken away from the total, the result is the other partner. Write the following on the board:

224   −   86   =   138
partner   partner   partner

Point out that addition and subtraction undo each other.

Activity continued ▶

Teaching Note

Mental Math To make problems such as 999 + 347 easier, move 1 from 347 on the Math Mountain and add it to 999. Students can then use mental math to find the total.

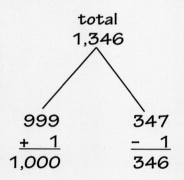

total
1,346

999   347
+ 1   − 1
1,000   346

Have students do exercises such as these using a Math Mountain to form a pair of partners that is easy to add using mental math.

1. 39 + 26 = 40 + 25 = 65

2. 58 + 37 = 60 + 35 = 95

3. 97 + 25 = 100 + 22 = 122

4. 199 + 24 = 200 + 23 = 223

5. 498 + 38 = 500 + 36 = 536

❶ Teaching the Lesson (continued)

Tell students that, even though they know the answer to problem 2, they will work through the subtraction and make a proof drawing to show how grouping in addition and ungrouping in subtraction are related. Ask students what subtraction you should write. Then, ask them how to start the proof drawing.

$$\begin{array}{r} 224 \\ -86 \end{array} \quad \square \ \square \ || \quad \circ\circ\circ\circ$$

Give students a few minutes to complete the subtraction and the proof drawing. Choose a student who made a clear drawing to present the subtraction and proof drawing. Next to the proof drawing, have the presenter record the number of hundreds, tens, and ones before and after ungrouping, eliciting what to record from students.

Have the presenter continue with the subtraction.

Before ungrouping: 2 h 2 t 4 o
After ungrouping: 1 h 11t 14 o

Direct students' attention to the labels next to both the addition and subtraction proof drawings that show the number of hundreds, tens, and ones before and after grouping, and before and after ungrouping. Ask them what they notice. After grouping matches before ungrouping and before grouping matches after ungrouping.

Talk about how ungrouping and grouping are related. Make sure the following key points are made:

● When adding, we sometimes need to *group* 10 ones to make a new ten or *group* 10 tens to make a new hundred.

● When subtracting, we sometimes need to *ungroup* a ten to make 10 new ones or *ungroup* a hundred to make 10 new tens.

● Grouping and ungrouping are opposites.

Have students complete exercise 3. Then, discuss their conclusions. Make sure these points are made:

● Addition and subtraction undo each other.

● Addition and subtraction are opposite operations.

Ask students how they can use addition to check the answer to a subtraction. Add the answer to the other partner. The sum should be the total.

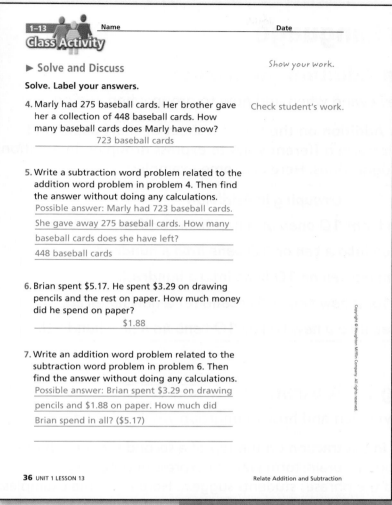

Student Activity Book page 36

► Solve and Discuss WHOLE CLASS   Math Talk

Problems 4–7 give students practice relating addition and subtraction. Have students solve these problems. Walk around the room to monitor progress and provide help. If students have trouble writing the subtraction word problem in problem 5, guide them by asking questions such as:

● When we subtract, we start with a total and take away one of the parts. What is the total in this situation? 723 baseball cards

● What are the parts? 275 baseball cards and 448 baseball cards

● Try to think of a problem where you start with the total and take away one of the two parts. How might your problem start? Possible answer: Marly had 723 cards.

● Now you need something about taking away one of the parts. What could you say next? Possible answer: Her brother took 448 of her cards.

● What question do you want to ask? Possible question: How many cards did Marly have left?

Using **Solve and Discuss,** have students present their answers.

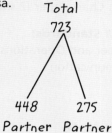
✓ Ongoing Assessment

Ask students to find the answer to the exercise:

Find 356 − 168. Check your answer by adding.

Relate Addition and Subtraction   **109**

Activity 2

Relate Grouping and Ungrouping Language

 20 MINUTES

Goal: Explore different ways of expressing the ideas of ungrouping and grouping.

Materials: Chart paper (2 sheets)

 NCTM Standards:
Number and Operations
Communication

Teaching Note

Language and Vocabulary Use this activity to introduce a number of new words that can be used to express grouping in addition and ungrouping in subtraction — pack, package, trade, regroup, unpack, borrow, and so on. After the words are on the chart paper, have students use the charts to act out what the words mean using base ten blocks.

English Language Learners

Model addition and subtraction strategies on the board to review *grouping* and *ungrouping*.

- **Beginning** Use a simple example to model each strategy step by step and have students repeat. Say: **First I... Next I... This is called...**
- **Intermediate** Ask: **What's the first step?** Encourage them to use the terms *grouping* and *ungrouping*.
- **Advanced** Demonstrate the strategies. Have students work in pairs to complete the problems. Help them describe the steps to each other. Ask: **Where did you group/ungroup/regroup____?**

▶ **Grouping in Addition** [WHOLE CLASS]

Begin by briefly reviewing when and how to group when adding.

Write **Grouping in Addition** on the top of a sheet of chart paper and have students brainstorm different ways to express grouping in addition. Record students' suggestions. Here are some examples:

Grouping in Addition
Make a new ten from 10 ones or a new hundred from 10 tens.
Package 10 ones into a ten or 10 tens into a hundred.
Pack 10 ones into a ten or 10 tens into a hundred.
Trade 10 ones for a new ten or 10 tens for a new hundred.
Regroup 10 ones into a new ten or 10 tens as a new hundred.

▶ **Ungrouping in Subtraction** [WHOLE CLASS]

Next, briefly review when and how to ungroup when subtracting.

Write **Ungrouping in Subtraction** on the top of a second sheet of chart paper and have students brainstorm ways to express ungrouping in subtraction. Record the phrases students suggest. Here are some examples:

Ungrouping in Subtraction
Unpack a ten to get 10 ones or a hundred to get 10 tens.
Open a ten to get 10 ones or a hundred to get 10 tens.
Break a ten into 10 ones or a hundred into 10 tens.
Trade a ten for 10 ones or a hundred for 10 tens.
Borrow 10 ones from a ten or 10 tens from a hundred.
Get 10 more ones from a ten or 10 more tens from a hundred.

Post both sheets of chart paper where everyone can see them.

Choose one of the addition exercises below and write it on the board.

Addition and Subtraction Exercises

159 + 267 426	576 − 358 218	382 + 295 677	892 − 712 180
493 + 377 870	932 − 485 447	549 + 214 763	712 − 428 284

Select a student to come to the board. Ask him or her to choose one of the sayings from the **Grouping in Addition** list. Ask the student to complete the addition, explaining the grouping using the chosen saying. Ask other students to listen and point out any mistakes. See sample dialogue in the Math Talk in Action at the bottom of the page.

Next, write one of the subtraction exercises on the board. Repeat the process above with a different student. This time have the student select an expression from the **Ungrouping in Subtraction** list.

Repeat this process a few more times, alternating addition and subtraction exercises. Have the student choose a different phrase each time.

 Math Talk in Action

Jason: We have to add 159 + 267. What should we do first?

Jonelle: We add 9 ones plus 7 ones. That gives us 16 ones.

Kurt: 16 ones is the same as 10 ones and 6 ones. We can trade the 10 ones for a new ten.

Jason: I'm going to write the new 10 above the tens column and I'm going to write the 6 ones under the line in the ones column.

Jonelle: Now we add the 5 tens plus the 6 tens to get 11 tens.

Kurt: Don't forget to add the new ten! 11 tens plus 1 more makes 12 tens.

Jonelle: Now we can trade 10 tens for a new hundred and we have 2 tens left.

Jason: That's right. I'll write the 1 for the new hundred above the hundreds column and the 2 in the tens column under the line.

Jonelle: 1 hundred plus 2 hundreds plus the new hundred make 4 hundreds. I'll write the 4 in the hundreds column under the line.

Kurt: So 159 + 267 equals 426.

② Going Further

Extension: Subtract Larger Numbers

Goal: Find differences involving numbers up to 10,000.

Materials: MathBoard materials

✓ **NCTM Standards:**
Number and Operations
Problem Solving
Communication

▶ Introduce Regrouping Thousands

WHOLE CLASS

Write 6,239 − 2,468 vertically on the board. Tell students to copy the subtraction on their MathBoards and make a proof drawing.

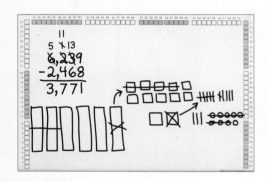

Give students a few minutes to complete the subtraction and proof drawing. Ask for two students to present their work. As they discuss their solutions, point out that they had to ungroup 1 thousand into 10 hundreds to find the answer.

▶ Subtract Larger Numbers PAIRS

Write the following word problems on the board.

A hippopotamus weighs 5,265 pounds. A giraffe weighs 3,418 pounds. How much heavier is the hippopotamus than the giraffe? 1,847 pounds

A great white shark weighs 7,684 pounds. A tiger shark weighs 1,990 pounds. How much heavier is the great white shark than the tiger shark? 5,694 pounds

A school district has 10,000 students. 2,385 were absent today. How many were at school? 7,615

123 Math Talk Have **Student Pairs** work together to complete the first problem. Give them a few minutes to complete the problem independently. Remind them to include a proof drawing.

Invite a **Student Pair** to the board to explain how they solved the problem.

As students discuss each step, make sure they understand the ungrouping that is involved.

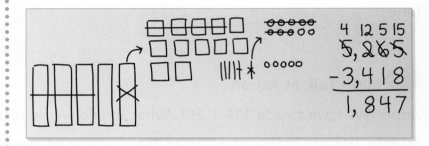

Have **Student Pairs** complete the two remaining problems.

Calculator You may wish to have **Student Pairs** check their work using a calculator.

Then have volunteers come to the board to explain their work.

Teaching Note

Watch For! Walk around the room and observe students as they subtract. Watch for students who do not understand when to ungroup, or who forget to record the ungrouping. Use questioning to help students decide when to ungroup and to record regrouping. For example:

▶ Can you subtract the hundreds? Why not?

▶ How can you get more hundreds to subtract?

▶ What happens to the number of thousands when you ungroup 1 thousand and make 10 hundreds? How can you record this?

Differentiated Instruction

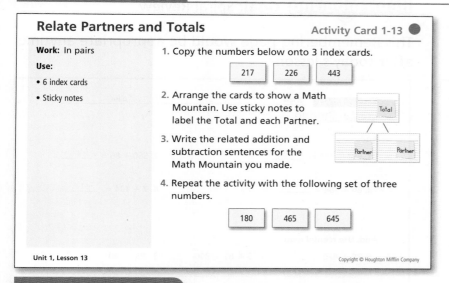

Relate Partners and Totals   Activity Card 1-13 ●

Work: In pairs

Use:
• 6 index cards
• Sticky notes

1. Copy the numbers below onto 3 index cards.

   217   226   443

2. Arrange the cards to show a Math Mountain. Use sticky notes to label the Total and each Partner.

3. Write the related addition and subtraction sentences for the Math Mountain you made.

4. Repeat the activity with the following set of three numbers.

   180   465   645

Unit 1, Lesson 13   Copyright © Houghton Mifflin Company

Activity Note Students must recognize that the total is the greatest number in each group. Reinforce understanding by having students suggest other partners for each total.

Math Writing Prompt

Make Connections How can you use addition to check subtraction? Use an example to explain your thinking.

Soar to Success Math **Software Support**

Warm Up 27.11

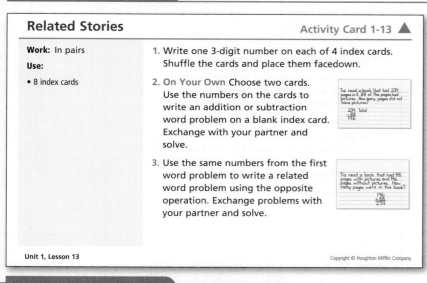

Related Stories   Activity Card 1-13 ▲

Work: In pairs

Use:
• 8 index cards

1. Write one 3-digit number on each of 4 index cards. Shuffle the cards and place them facedown.

2. **On Your Own** Choose two cards. Use the numbers on the cards to write an addition or subtraction word problem on a blank index card. Exchange with your partner and solve.

3. Use the same numbers from the first word problem to write a related word problem using the opposite operation. Exchange problems with your partner and solve.

Unit 1, Lesson 13   Copyright © Houghton Mifflin Company

Activity Note After students have completed writing and solving each problem, they should exchange their work with their partner to check their results.

Math Writing Prompt

Summarize Explain how a Math Mountain can be used to show both adding and subtracting.

MegaMath Grades K-8 **Software Support**

Numberopolis: Carnival Stories, Level R

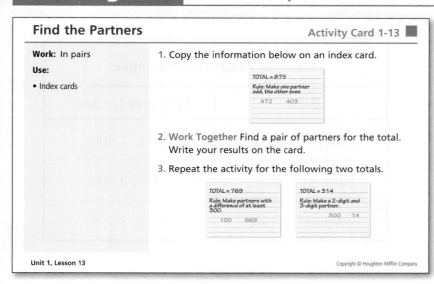

Find the Partners   Activity Card 1-13 ■

Work: In pairs

Use:
• Index cards

1. Copy the information below on an index card.

   TOTAL = 875
   Rule: Make one partner odd, the other even.
   472   403

2. **Work Together** Find a pair of partners for the total. Write your results on the card.

3. Repeat the activity for the following two totals.

   TOTAL = 769
   Rule: Make partners with a difference of at least 300.
   100   669

   TOTAL = 314
   Rule: Make a 2-digit and 3-digit partner.
   300   14

Unit 1, Lesson 13   Copyright © Houghton Mifflin Company

Activity Note After students have completed the activity, have them repeat the activity by finding a new set of partners for each rule.

Math Writing Prompt

What Are the Partners? The total is $7.71 and the rule for the partners is that they have a difference of at least $2.00. Explain how you can find three different pairs of partners.

DESTINATION Math **Software Support**

Course II: Module 2: Unit 1: Estimating and Finding Differences within 1,000

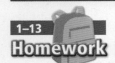

③ Homework and Spiral Review

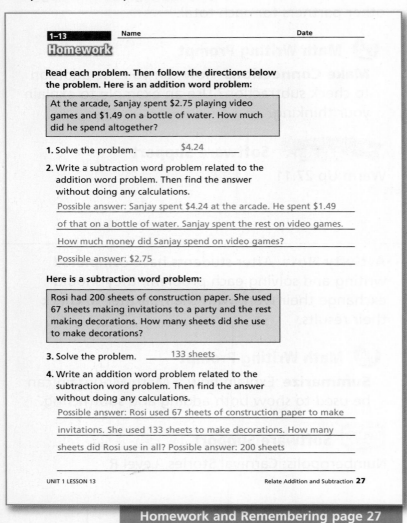

Homework **Goal:** Additional Practice

✓ Include students' completed Homework page as part of their portfolios.

1–13 | Name | Date

Homework

Read each problem. Then follow the directions below the problem. Here is an addition word problem:

> At the arcade, Sanjay spent $2.75 playing video games and $1.49 on a bottle of water. How much did he spend altogether?

1. Solve the problem. _____ $4.24

2. Write a subtraction word problem related to the addition word problem. Then find the answer without doing any calculations.

Possible answer: Sanjay spent $4.24 at the arcade. He spent $1.49

of that on a bottle of water. Sanjay spent the rest on video games.

How much money did Sanjay spend on video games?

Possible answer: $2.75

Here is a subtraction word problem:

> Rosi had 200 sheets of construction paper. She used 67 sheets making invitations to a party and the rest making decorations. How many sheets did she use to make decorations?

3. Solve the problem. _____ 133 sheets

4. Write an addition word problem related to the subtraction word problem. Then find the answer without doing any calculations.

Possible answer: Rosi used 67 sheets of construction paper to make

invitations. She used 133 sheets to make decorations. How many

sheets did Rosi use in all? Possible answer: 200 sheets

UNIT 1 LESSON 13 · Relate Addition and Subtraction **27**

Homework and Remembering page 27

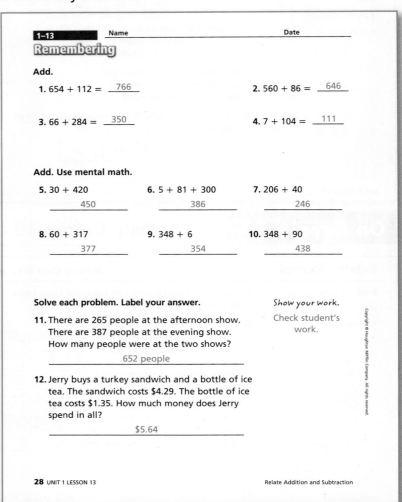

Remembering **Goal:** Spiral Review

This Remembering page would be appropriate anytime after today's lesson.

1–13 | Name | Date

Remembering

Add.

1. 654 + 112 = _766_   **2.** 560 + 86 = _646_

3. 66 + 284 = _350_   **4.** 7 + 104 = _111_

Add. Use mental math.

5. 30 + 420   **6.** 5 + 81 + 300   **7.** 206 + 40
    450   386   246

8. 60 + 317   **9.** 348 + 6   **10.** 348 + 90
    377   354   438

Solve each problem. Label your answer.

Show your work.
Check student's work.

11. There are 265 people at the afternoon show. There are 387 people at the evening show. How many people were at the two shows?
      652 people

12. Jerry buys a turkey sandwich and a bottle of ice tea. The sandwich costs $4.29. The bottle of ice tea costs $1.35. How much money does Jerry spend in all?
      $5.64

28 UNIT 1 LESSON 13 · Relate Addition and Subtraction

Homework and Remembering page 28

Home and School Activity

Science Connection

Migration Some birds live in Canada and in the United States during the summer. They travel south to Central and South America for the winter. This is called *migration*.

Display the migration distances table shown at the right. Explain that a Painted Bunting may fly anywhere from 300 to 3,000 miles when migrating. Have students write and solve addition and subtraction exercises based on the information in the table.

| One-Way Migration Distances ||
Bird	Distance (miles)
Lucy's Warbler	500 to 1,500
Painted Bunting	300 to 3,000
Wood Thrush	600 to 3,750

Subtraction Practice

Lesson Objective

● Practice and discuss subtraction methods.

Vocabulary
ungroup

The Day at a Glance

Today's Goals	Materials	
1 Teaching the Lesson **A1:** Solve and discuss subtraction word problems. **A2:** Create toy store ads and use them to practice addition and subtraction of money amounts. **2 Going Further** ► Differentiated Instruction **3 Homework and Spiral Review**	**Lesson Activities** Student Activity Book pp. 37–38 or Student Hardcover Book pp. 37–38 Homework and Remembering pp. 29–30 Crayons, colored pencils, or markers	**Going Further** Activity Cards 1-14 Index cards Game cards (TRB 25) Chart paper Math Journals

123 Use
Math Talk
today!

Keeping Skills Sharp

Quick Practice ⏱ 5 MINUTES

Goal: Subtract hundreds.

Materials: Demonstration Secret Code Cards (TRB M3–M18)

Subtract Hundreds Have one **Student Leader** select the 1,000 card and the 300 card and assemble the cards to show a 4-digit number. Then, have the leader choose a hundred card and display it on the right.

1000	300		600	
1	**3**	**0 0**	**6**	**0 0**

Have another **Student Leader** say, "Subtract." The class says the equation aloud. The leader selects a student to illustrate the Make a Thousand strategy (See page 55). Repeat, subtracting different hundreds from combinations between 1,100 and 1,900.

Daily Routines

Homework Review Ask several students to share the problems they wrote for the homework. Have the class ask clarifying questions about each problem. If necessary, model asking questions.

What's Wrong? Jerome subtracted 68 from 100 and got 168 for an answer. What did he do wrong? Possible answer: He used addition instead of subtraction.

1 Teaching the Lesson

Activity 1

Discuss Subtraction Methods

 20 MINUTES

Goal: Solve and discuss subtraction word problems.

Materials: Student Activity Book or Hardcover Book pp. 37–38

 NCTM Standards:
Number and Operations
Problem Solving
Communication

Class Management

If you would like to work with students needing extra help, use the **Solve and Discuss** structure for the first problem only. Then, work with the students experiencing difficulty at the board, while the remainder of the class completes the problems independently or in helping pairs.

 Math Talk in Action

Wilson: In Exercise 1, you subtracted 0 pennies from 6 pennies. We were to subtract $3.76 from $4.00, 6 pennies from 0 pennies.

Kai: But you cannot subtract 6 pennies from 0 pennies.

Wilson: You can ungroup one dime for ten pennies.

Kai: There were 0 dimes.

Wilson: I traded a $1 bill to make 10 dimes, leaving $3.00 and traded one dime for ten pennies leaving 9 dimes.

Kai: 6 pennies from 10 pennies is 4 pennies. 7 dimes from 9 dimes is 2 dimes. 3 from 3 dollars is 0 dollars. So the answer is 0 dollars, 2 dimes, and 4 pennies is $0.24.

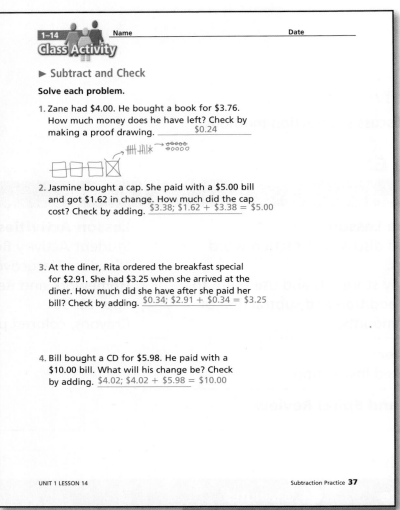

Student Activity Book page 37

▶ Subtract and Check WHOLE CLASS

Using the **Solve and Discuss** structure, have students solve the problems on Student Book page 37. As presenters explain their work, tell other students to watch for subtraction errors and to listen to the way the presenter uses place value language to describe the subtraction.

See side column for Math Talk in Action.

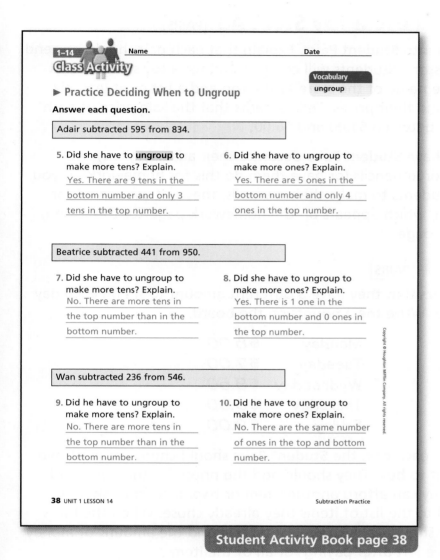

Student Activity Book page 38

The Student Activity Book page shown above contains:

1–14 Class Activity
Name _____ Date _____

Vocabulary
ungroup

► **Practice Deciding When to Ungroup**

Answer each question.

Adair subtracted 595 from 834.

5. Did she have to **ungroup** to make more tens? Explain.
Yes. There are 9 tens in the bottom number and only 3 tens in the top number.

6. Did she have to ungroup to make more ones? Explain.
Yes. There are 5 ones in the bottom number and only 4 ones in the top number.

Beatrice subtracted 441 from 950.

7. Did she have to ungroup to make more tens? Explain.
No. There are more tens in the top number than in the bottom number.

8. Did she have to ungroup to make more ones? Explain.
Yes. There is 1 one in the bottom number and 0 ones in the top number.

Wan subtracted 236 from 546.

9. Did he have to ungroup to make more tens? Explain.
No. There are more tens in the top number than in the bottom number.

10. Did he have to ungroup to make more ones? Explain.
No. There are the same number of ones in the top and bottom number.

38 UNIT 1 LESSON 14   Subtraction Practice

Differentiated Instruction

Extra Help To help students focus on the subtraction process in each place, have students write each problem in a place value grid. Then tell them to use any method to subtract. Ask students who subtracted right to left the following questions:

► Are there enough ones to subtract? Do you need to ungroup a ten to make more ones?

► Are there enough tens to subtract? Do you need to ungroup a hundred to make more tens?

Ask students who subtracted left to right the following questions.

► Are there enough tens to subtract? Do you need to ungroup a hundred to make more tens?

► Are there enough ones to subtract? Do you need to ungroup a ten to make more ones?

► Practice Deciding When to Ungroup | WHOLE CLASS |

Direct students' attention to questions 5 and 6 on Student Book page 38. Write the 834 − 595 on the board in vertical form. Ask a volunteer to answer questions 5 and 6. Student explanations should cover the following points:

● There are not enough tens to subtract 9 tens. So, students need to ungroup a hundred to make 10 tens.

● There are not enough ones to subtract 5 ones. So, students need to ungroup a ten to make 10 more ones.

Have students work independently to answer the rest of the questions. Invite volunteers to explain their answers. Have students who experience difficulty check their answers with a **Helping Partner**.

Activity 2

Create and Use an Ad

 35 MINUTES

Goal: Create toy store ads and use them to practice addition and subtraction of money amounts.

Materials: Crayons, colored pencils, or markers for each pair of students, Homework page 29

 NCTM Standards:
Number and Operations
Problem Solving

 Class Management

Looking Ahead Collect the toy store ads for use in Lesson 15.

English Language Learners

Show students a toy store ad to help them write their own. Write the names of different toys and their prices on the board.

• **Beginning** Say: This is a toy store advertisement. Ask: I have $5. What toy can I buy here? How much does it cost?
• **Intermediate** Have students suggest toys and prices. Make sure the prices are between $1 and $6.
• **Advanced** Have students work in pairs to write a list of toys and their prices. Have volunteers write a few examples from their list on the board to check spelling.

 Ongoing Assessment

Discuss one day's toy store purchases with student pairs. Have students explain how they determined the change they would receive. Make sure students explain how they knew whether or not to ungroup.

▶ **Create and Use a Toy Store Ad** PAIRS

Divide the class into **Student Pairs**. Explain that each pair should pretend they run a toy store. Students will create an ad for a toy sale. The ad should have the name of the store at the top and a list of at least six different toys and their prices. Tell students that the sale price of each item should be between $1.00 and $6.00.

If time allows, have **Student Pairs** decorate their ads using crayons, markers, or colored pencils (or have them do this for homework). If you do not want students to make their own ads, they can use the ad for Ted's Toy Town, which appears on the homework page for this lesson. See Homework page 29.

▶ **Use an Ad** PAIRS

Tell **Student Pairs** that they have a different amount to spend each day at the toy store. Write the amounts on the board.

Monday	$8.00
Tuesday	$7.00
Wednesday	$9.50
Thursday	$8.50
Friday	$9.00

Explain that for each day, the **Student Pairs** should choose at least two items they want to buy. They should add the prices for the items and figure out if they can afford another item or two. If so, they should add the item(s) to the list of items they already chose. When the list is complete, they should calculate the total cost and the amount of money they would have left after paying for all of the items.

As students work, walk around the room and provide help if needed.

Have pairs save their advertisements for use in the next lesson.

```
        K and L Toy Store
            Specials

   Puzzles    $2.25 each
   Block Set  $3.49
   Pony       $3.97
   Puppets    $2.89
   Marker Set $1.88
   Crayon Set $1.79
```

```
  Have $9.50 to spend
                  1 1
  marker set  $1.88
    puppet  +$2.89
                  1
                $4.77
    pony    +$3.97
                $8.74
              8  14
                 4 10
  Change  $9.50   Change is $.76
        - $8.74
          $0.76
```

②Going Further

Intervention   Activity Card 1-14

Compare Home Run Hitters   Activity Card 1-14 ●

Work: On your own

Use:
• Chart paper

1. Copy the table below on chart paper.

Some Famous Home Run Hitters	
Name	Home Runs
Hank Aaron	755
Hector Espino	484
Josh Gibson	962
Mickey Mantle	536
Sadaharu Oh	868
Babe Ruth	714

2. Josh Gibson is a famous baseball player who hit the most home runs ever recorded during a career. Choose four other players in the table.

3. How many *more* hits did Josh Gibson make than each of the four players you chose?

Unit 1, Lesson 14   Copyright © Houghton Mifflin Company

Activity Note Tell students that no one knows exactly how many home runs Josh Gibson hit because records were not kept early in his career. So the given number of home runs is an estimate.

 Math Writing Prompt

Do You Know? Explain how you know when to ungroup in a subtraction problem.

 **Software Support**

Warm Up 11.25

On Level   Activity Card 1-14

Less Is More   Activity Card 1-14 ▲

Work: In pairs

Use:
• 4 index cards, each labeled with one of the following numbers:

   500, 476, 319, 248

• TRB M25 (Game cards)

1. Mix the index cards and place them in a stack face down. Turn over the top index card in the stack.

   319

2. Mix up the Game Cards and give 4 to each player.

   4 8 2 7

3. Each player chooses two game cards to make a 2-digit number. Subtract the 2-digit number from the 3-digit number. The player with the smaller difference wins a point.

   319
   − 87
   232

4. Continue the activity. Turn over the top index card. Each player returns the game cards and chooses 4 new ones each time. The first player to win 5 points wins the game.

Unit 1, Lesson 14   Copyright © Houghton Mifflin Company

Activity Note Students should realize that choosing digits to make the greatest 2-digit number possible will give them the smallest possible difference.

 Math Writing Prompt

Summarize Explain how you would solve $5.45 − $1.79. You may add a proof drawing to help you.

 Software Support

Country Countdown: Block Busters, Level Q

Challenge   Activity Card 1-14

Magic Square   Activity Card 1-14 ■

Work: In pairs

Use:
• Index card

1. Copy the Magic Square onto an index card.

2. In a Magic Square, the numbers in each row, each column, and each diagonal have the same sum. What is the sum for this Magic Square? 621

Magic Square		
276	115	230
161	207	253
184	299	138

3. **Think** How can you find the missing number in the first row? Add the numbers 276 + 115 and subtract the sum from 621.

4. **Work Together** Find the missing numbers.

Unit 1, Lesson 14   Copyright © Houghton Mifflin Company

Activity Note Finding the missing numbers in the top and bottom rows will complete the third column.

 Math Writing Prompt

Looking Back Jerry took 162 pictures on his train trip to Florida and 128 pictures on the way back. Can he make two collages that each use 150 pictures? Explain.

DESTINATION Math® **Software Support**

Course II: Module 2: Unit 1: Estimating and Finding Differences within 1,000

③ Homework and Spiral Review

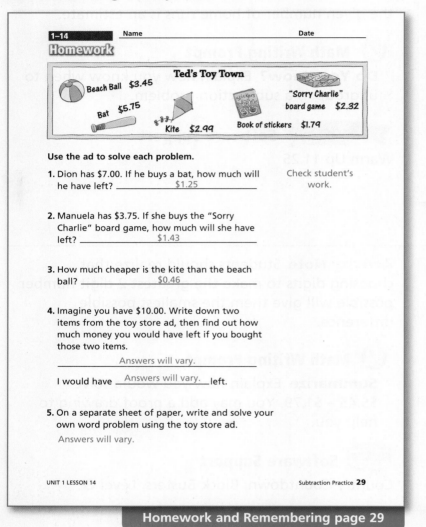

Goal: Additional Practice

The Homework page gives students practice adding and subtracting money amounts.

Goal: Spiral Review

This Remembering page would be appropriate anytime after today's lesson.

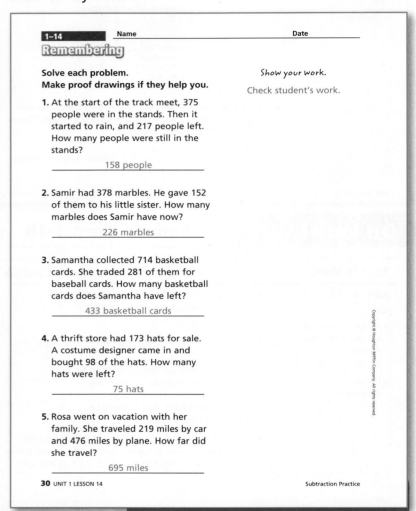

Home and School Activity

 Sports Connection

Baseball Ticket Prices Display the price list shown at the right. Explain that it shows the ticket prices for baseball games at Wrigley Field in Chicago in 1952. Discuss the difference between those prices and what tickets would cost today. In a recent year, tickets for a regular Chicago Cubs game at Wrigley Field cost between $14 and $40.

Have students use the price list to create and solve several addition and subtraction problems based on the price list.

Ticket Prices at Wrigley Field in 1952	
Adults	
Box Seats	$2.50
Grandstand	$1.25
Bleachers	$0.60
Children under 14	
Box Seats	$1.85
Grandstand	$0.60
Bleachers	$0.60

120 UNIT 1 LESSON 14

UNIT 1

LESSON

15

Addition and Subtraction Practice

REAL WORLD Problem Solving

Lesson Objective

● Practice and discuss addition and subtraction methods.

Vocabulary

total   partner
Math Mountain

The Day at a Glance

Today's Goals	Materials
1 **Teaching the Lesson** **A1:** Create and solve addition and subtraction word problems. **A2:** Use ads to practice addition and subtraction of money amounts. **2** **Going Further** ► Math connection: Choose a Computation Method. ► Differentiated Instruction **3** **Homework and Spiral Review**	**Lesson Activities** Homework and Remembering pp. 31–32 Toy store ads from lesson 14 Play money Quick Quiz 3 (Assessment Guide) **Going Further** Student Activity Book pp. 39–40 or Student Hardcover Book pp. 39–40 and Activity Workbook pp. 13–14 (includes Game Rules) Activity Cards 1-15 Calculator Index cards Paper bags MathBoard materials Game Cards (TRB M25) Math Journals

123 Use Math Talk today!

Keeping Skills Sharp

Quick Practice ⏱ 5 MINUTES	Daily Routines
Goal: Subtract hundreds. **Materials:** Demonstration Secret Code Cards (TRB M3–M18) **Subtract Hundreds** Have a **Student Leader** select the 1,000 and 500 cards and assemble them to show a 4-digit number. Then, have the leader choose a hundred card and display it on the right.	**Homework Review** Ask a student volunteer to share a word problem written for problem 5. Invite several students to solve it at the board, while the others work at their seats. **Place Value** Write the least number and the greatest number possible using the digits 6, 1, 4, and 8. Use each digit only once within a number. Least number: 1,468; Greatest number: 8,641

1000	500		900
1	**5 0 0**		**9 0 0**

Have another **Student Leader** say, "Subtract." The class says the equation aloud. The leader selects a student to illustrate the Make a Thousand strategy. Repeat, subtracting different hundreds from combinations between 1,100 and 1,900.

Teaching the Lesson

Create and Solve Problems

 25 MINUTES

Goal: Create and solve addition and subtraction word problems.

✔ **NCTM Standards:**
Number and Operations
Problem Solving
Communication

The Learning Classroom

Math Talk When students discuss how they can solve an addition problem or a subtraction problem without doing any calculations, encourage them to use the words *partner* and *total* in their explanations. For example:

► The total is 900. When I subtract the partner 672, I get the other partner, 228.

► I start with the partner 717. When I add the other partner, 655, I get the total, 1,372.

 Class Management

Students will continue to solve problems using multi-digit addition and subtraction for the next two units. Give the unit test to see where your students are and what you might need to address in the next two units, but move on to Unit 2. Less-advanced students will begin to pull their place value and multi-digit concepts together over the next two units so that they are accurate and fluent. Be sure to discuss the top-from-bottom error if any students are making it, and be sure that those students are making the magnifying glass to inhibit that error in subtraction.

► **Use Math Mountains to Relate Addition and Subtraction** WHOLE CLASS

Write the numbers 672 and 228 on the board. Ask students to think of an addition word problem that has these numbers.

123 **Math Talk** Choose a volunteer to share his or her word problem. Have students solve the problem, using the **Solve and Discuss** structure. Make a Math Mountain for the problem on the board, eliciting the partners and total from students. Then, have a volunteer write an addition and subtraction equation from the Math Mountain.

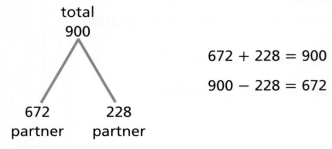

Ask students to think of a subtraction word problem that can be written based on this Math Mountain. Choose a volunteer to share his or her word problem. Then have a student explain how you can find the answer without doing any calculations.

Next, write the numbers 1,372 and 717 on the board. Ask if anyone can think of a subtraction word problem that has these numbers. Choose a volunteer to share his or her problem. Have students solve the problem, using the **Solve and Discuss** structure. Make a Math Mountain for the problem on the board, eliciting the partners and total from students. Then have a volunteer write a subtraction and addition equation from the Math Mountain.

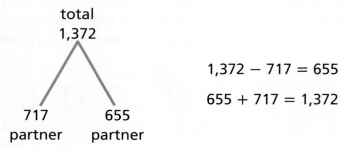

Ask students to think of an addition word problem that can be written based on this Math Mountain. Choose a volunteer to share his or her problem. Then have a student explain how you can find the answer without doing any calculations.

Repeat this process for two more pairs of numbers.

Use Ads to Practice Addition and Subtraction

▶ Add and Subtract Money Amounts PAIRS

Ask **Student Pairs** to take out the toy store ads they made in Lesson 14. Have each pair trade ads with another pair.

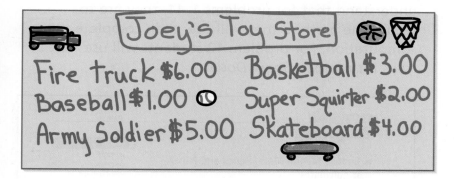

Explain that, as before, students have a different amount to spend each day at the toy store. Write the following amounts on the board.

Monday	$10.00
Tuesday	$15.25
Wednesday	$16.00
Thursday	$18.50
Friday	$20.00

Explain that, just as they did in the previous lesson, **Student Pairs** should choose at least two items they want to buy each day. They should add the prices for the items and figure out if they can afford another item or two. If so, they should add the item(s) to the list of items that they already chose. When the list is complete, they should calculate the total cost and the amount of money they would have left after paying for all of the items.

As students work, walk around the room and provide help if needed.

30 MINUTES

Goal: Use ads to practice addition and subtraction of money amounts.

Materials: Toy store ads from Lesson 14

✔ **NCTM Standards:**
Number and Operations
Problem Solving

English Language Learners

Model a simple math mountain to help students identify the total and partners. Then, write
36 + ____ = 100

• **Beginning** Say: **100 is the ____. total 36 is a ____. partner We need to find the other partner.** Ask: **Do we add or subtract?** subtract

• **Intermediate** Ask: **What is missing?** 1 partner **How do we find the other partner?** 100 − 36

• **Advanced** Ask: **How can we find the missing partner?**

Ongoing Assessment

Ask students to explain how addition and subtraction are related.

Quick Quiz

See Assessment Guide for Unit 1 Quick Quiz 3.

Going Further

Math Connection: Choose a Computation Method

Goal: Choose a computation method to add or subtract.

Materials: Student Activity Book or Hardcover Book pp. 39–40 and Activity Workbook p. 13, calculators (1 per group of three students), index cards (6 per group), paper bags (1 per group)

✓ **NCTM Standards:**
Number and Operations
Problem Solving

▶ Add or Subtract Larger Numbers

WHOLE CLASS

Write the following exercises on the board.

```
  11 15 12 11
  516,219
+ 314,845
  11   1
  831,064
```

```
  11 15 12 11
  2 ₆ 5 ₂ 1 14
  326,324
 −  77,456
  248,868
```

Math Talk Using the **Solve and Discuss** structure, have students solve the examples. Make sure volunteers explain the computation place-by-place, noting and recording all grouping and ungrouping.

Ask students if they had a choice of using a calculator or pencil and paper to add or subtract these exercises, which they would use. Sample response: A calculator. Why? It's faster.

Compare Computation Methods Discuss the uses of the three computation methods (mental math, pencil and paper, and calculator) by asking students the following questions.

● When would you use mental math to find the answer to an exercise? Give an example. Sample response: When you add two numbers that are easy to add such as 150 + 20.

● Would you use pencil and paper or a calculator to find the answer to 428,965 − 325,941? Why? Sample response: A calculator because the numbers are large.

● When would you use pencil and paper instead of a calculator to find the answer? Give an example. Sample response: When the numbers are in the tens, hundreds, or thousands such as 267 + 986.

▶ Choose Mental Math, Pencil and Paper, or Calculator INDIVIDUALS

Direct students' attention to Student Book page 39. Read aloud the directions. Make sure students understand that for problems 1–11, they are to record the method they will use, then complete the computation. For problem 12 students will use the rules for *Method Show Down*.

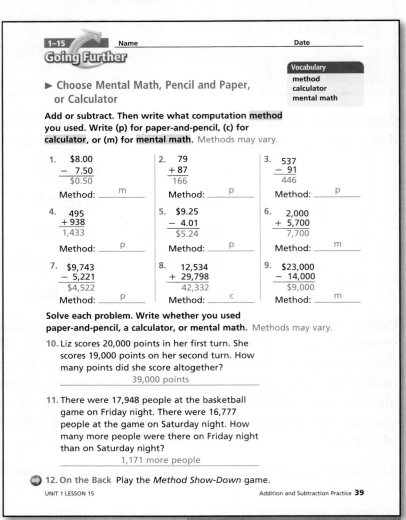

Student Activity Book page 39

Teaching Note

Math Connection This activity is designed to make the connection between the size of the numbers and the most efficient computation method to use.

Intervention   Activity Card 1-15

Help Yourself!   Activity Card 1-15 ●

Work: In pairs

Use:
- MathBoard materials

1. Write a four-digit number on your MathBoard.

2. Find the sum of the number that you wrote and the number that your partner wrote.

$$\begin{array}{r} 4{,}632 \\ +3{,}421 \\ \hline 8{,}053 \end{array}$$

3. If your sum does not match your partner's sum, work together to find the error.

4. Next, subtract the smaller of the two numbers that you and your partner wrote from the sum. Compare results. If they do not match, work together to find the error.

$$\begin{array}{r} ^{7\ 10} \\ 8{,}0\cancel{5}3 \\ -3{,}421 \\ \hline 4{,}632 \end{array}$$

Unit 1, Lesson 15   Copyright © Houghton Mifflin Company

Activity Note To reinforce understanding, point out the relationship between addition and subtraction as shown in each pair of exercises.

 Math Writing Prompt

You Decide Write an addition word problem for this equation: $315 + 277 = 592$.

 **Software Support**

Warm Up 11.26

On Level   Activity Card 1-15

Pass the Arithmetic   Activity Card 1-15 ▲

Work: In small groups

Use:
- Index cards
- Paper bag

1. Each student writes a 5-digit addition or subtraction exercise on a card and places the card in the bag. Work as a group to find each difference.

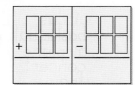

2. Each student picks a card from the bag and adds or subtracts the digits in the ones place.

3. Then each student passes the card to the student on the right to add or subtract the digits in the tens place.

4. Continue passing the cards until each sum or difference is complete. Pass the cards once more to check the results.

Unit 1, Lesson 15   Copyright © Houghton Mifflin Company

Activity Note To facilitate this exercise, students should work from right to left for both addition and subtraction.

 Math Writing Prompt

Real Life Experience Think of a time outside of school when you or someone you were with needed to add or subtract. Describe the situation.

 Software Support

Numberopolis: Carnival Stories, Level R

Challenge   Activity Card 1-15

Use Only Once!   Activity Card 1-15 ■

Work: In pairs

Use:
- TRB M25 (Game Cards)

1. Use 6 game cards to make addition and subtraction exercises as shown below. Use each number card only once in each exercise.

[grid diagram with + and − exercises]

2. What is the least sum you can make? $135 + 204 = 339$

3. What is the greatest sum you can make?
$875 + 964 = 1{,}839$

4. What is the least difference you can make?
$601 - 598 = 3$

5. What is the greatest difference you can make?
$987 - 102 = 885$

Unit 1, Lesson 15   Copyright © Houghton Mifflin Company

Activity Note Students can use the Guess and Check strategy and number sense to answer each question. Students should compare their results to see if they have found the greatest and least sum or difference.

 Math Writing Prompt

Find the Rule What is the next number in the pattern? 25, 51, 77, 93, ____. Give the rule.

 DESTINATION Math· **Software Support**

Course II: Module 2: Unit 1: Estimating and Finding Differences within 1,000

③ Homework and Spiral Review

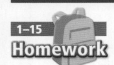

Homework 1–15   **Goal:** Additional Practice

This Homework page provides practice in addition and subtraction.

1–15 Homework   Name _____   Date _____

Solve.

1. Write and solve an addition word problem that has the numbers 268 and 487.

   _____ Answers will vary. _____

   _____

   _____

2. Write and solve a subtraction word problem that has the numbers 194 and 526.

   _____ Answers will vary. _____

   _____

   _____

3. The yearbook staff took a total of 1,005 photographs. They used 487 of the photographs in the yearbook. How many of the photographs were not used?

   _____ 518 photographs _____

4. Mr. Pinsky has to read a 362-page book for his book club. He read the first 129 pages last week. This week he has read 153 pages. How many pages does he have left to read?

   _____ 80 pages _____

5. Josh had $9.00 in his pocket when he left the house this morning. He spent $1.75 on bus fare and $3.48 on lunch. How much does he have left?

   _____ $3.77 _____

UNIT 1 LESSON 15   Addition and Subtraction Practice **31**

Homework and Remembering page 31

Remembering 1–15   **Goal:** Spiral Review

This Remembering page would be appropriate anytime after today's lesson.

1–15 Remembering   Name _____   Date _____

Solve.   *Show your work.*

1. Aimee's dog weighs 58 pounds and her cat weighs 13 pounds. How much do her dog and cat weigh together?

   _____ 71 pounds _____

2. Write a subtraction word problem related to the addition problem in Problem 1. Then solve the problem you wrote without doing any calculations.

   Answers will vary. Problems should involve a

   total of 71 and the partners 58 and 13.

Subtract. Check your answers by adding.

3. $1{,}163 - 793 = \underline{370}$ 4. $1{,}937 - 88 = \underline{1{,}849}$ 5. $627 - 329 = \underline{298}$
   $793 + 370 = 1{,}163$ $88 + 1{,}849 = 1{,}937$ $329 + 298 = 627$

Use mental math to find the answer.

6. $9 + 6 + 1 = \underline{16}$ 7. $5 + 7 + 2 = \underline{14}$ 8. $8 + 6 + 2 = \underline{16}$

9. $40 + 20 + 30 = \underline{90}$ 10. $60 + 60 + 60 = \underline{180}$ 11. $70 + 40 + 20 = \underline{130}$

12. $170 - 80 = \underline{90}$ 13. $140 - 50 = \underline{90}$ 14. $150 - 70 = \underline{80}$

32 UNIT 1 LESSON 15   Addition and Subtraction Practice

Homework and Remembering page 32

Home and School Activity

Social Studies Connection

Where Can You Find 100? Have students list places and situations where they might see more than 100 people at a time. Have students write a short paragraph that describes one of these places or situations. Then ask students to write and solve an addition or subtraction word problem using the paragraph they wrote.

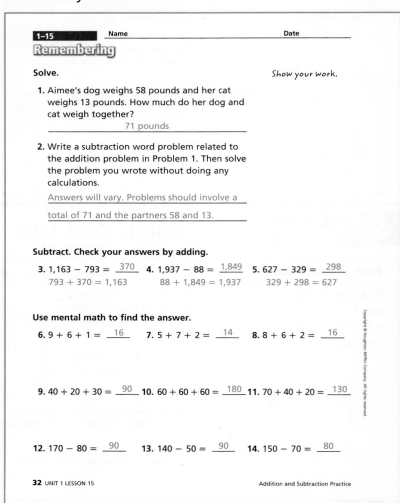

Places with More than 100 People

circus
basketball game
airplane
concert
train

UNIT 1

LESSON

16

Use Mathematical Processes

REAL WORLD Problem Solving

Lesson Objectives

- Apply mathematical concepts and skills in meaningful contexts.
- Reinforce the NCTM process skills embedded in this unit with a variety of problem-solving situations.

The Day at a Glance

Today's Goals	Materials
1 Teaching the Lesson **A1: Art Connections** Solve 2-digit and 3-digit word problems that require addition or subtraction with no regrouping; write word problems; act out and use models to solve addition and subtraction problems. **A2: Problem Solving** List the different outcomes for one round of a game; tell how many different outcomes there are in one round of a game: record the results of a game in a table. **A3: Reasoning and Proof** Use reasoning to solve a problem. **A4: Representation** Use drawings to show two numbers. **A5: Communication** Tell how you solved a problem with multiple solutions.	**Lesson Activities** Student Activity Book or Student Hardcover Book pp. 41–42 Homework and Remembering pp. 33–34 Spinner (TRB M131) Scissors Base ten blocks Paper clips Pencil *Hannah's Collections* by Marther Jocelyn, New York: Dutton Children's Books, 2000 **Going Further** Activity Cards 1-16 MathBoard materials Number Cubes Math Journals
2 Going Further ▶ Differentiated Instruction	
3 Homework and Spiral Review	

Use Math Talk today!

Keeping Skills Sharp

Quick Practice / Daily Routines	
If you wish to include Quick Practice or a Daily Routine, choose content based on the needs of your class.	**Class Management** Select activities from this lesson that support important goals and objectives, or that help students prepare for state or district tests.

Teaching the Lesson

Math and Literature

 30 MINUTES

Goals: Solve 2-digit and 3-digit word problems that require addition or subtraction with no regrouping; write word problems; act out and use models to solve addition and subtraction problems.

Materials: Student Activity Book or Hardcover Book p. 42, TRB M131 (Spinner), scissors, paper clips, pencils, base ten blocks, Math Boards, *Hannah's Collections* by Marther Jocelyn, New York: Dutton Children's Books, 2000.

✓ **NCTM Standards:**
Problem Solving   Communication
Connections   Representation

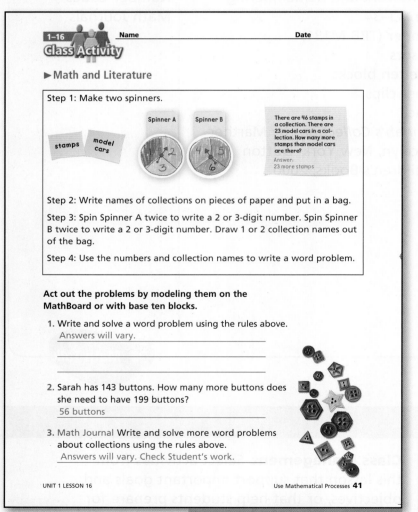

Student Activity Book page 41

▶ Name Types of Collections

Task 1 Get ready to do the activity.

Have students make two spinners using M131. Spinner A has the numbers 1, 2, and 3 on it. Spinner B has the numbers 4, 5, and 6 on it.

Tell students that they are going to be writing and solving problems about collections. Have them write names of collections they would like to have on pieces of paper and put them in a bag.

Read *Hannah's Collections* to the students.

▶ Do you collect anything? What kind of collections would you like to have? Allow students to share. Write the names of collections on the board.

▶ Act Out Problems Involving Collections

Task 2 Write and solve word problems about collections.

You might want to do exercise 1 as a class so that students understand how to get the numbers and collection names and use those to write a word problem. Then use the MathBoard or base ten blocks to model the problem and solve it.

Show the page in *Hannah's Collections* where it says that Hannah has 153 buttons. Have students use their MathBoard or Base Ten Blocks to solve the problem in exercise 2.

In exercise 3, make sure they use Spinner A to get one number and Spinner B to get the other number so that the addition or subtraction they use to solve the problem will not require regrouping.

You may want to have students work in **Student Pairs** to solve each other's problems.

Teaching Note

Creating Collections Have the class collect something simple and small such as bottle caps. Bottle caps can be put in bags of 10 to make them easier to count. 10 bags of 10 can be put in a bigger bag. When enough are collected, students can use these to act out and model problems.

Rock, Paper, Scissors

 30 MINUTES

Goals: List the different outcomes for one round of a game; tell how many different outcomes there are in one round of a game; record the results of a game in a table

Materials: Student Activity Book or Hardcover Book p. 42

 NCTM Standards:

Problem Solving   Communication
Representation   Reasoning and Proof

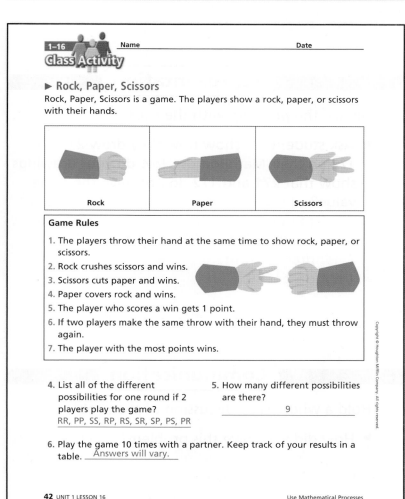

Name _____   Date _____

1-16
Class Activity

▶ **Rock, Paper, Scissors**
Rock, Paper, Scissors is a game. The players show a rock, paper, or scissors with their hands.

Rock	Paper	Scissors

Game Rules

1. The players throw their hand at the same time to show rock, paper, or scissors.
2. Rock crushes scissors and wins.
3. Scissors cuts paper and wins.
4. Paper covers rock and wins.
5. The player who scores a win gets 1 point.
6. If two players make the same throw with their hand, they must throw again.
7. The player with the most points wins.

4. List all of the different possibilities for one round if 2 players play the game?
RR, PP, SS, RP, RS, SR, SP, PS, PR

5. How many different possibilities are there?
9

6. Play the game 10 times with a partner. Keep track of your results in a table. _Answers will vary._

42 UNIT 1 LESSON 16   Use Mathematical Processes

Student Activity Book page 42

▶ **List Possible Outcomes in the Game**

Task 1 Introduce the game Rock, Paper, Scissors to the students.

▶ Have you ever played the game Rock, Paper, Scissors? Allow students to share their experiences.

▶ What are the rules of the game? Have students look at the game rules on their Student Book page 42. Have them demonstrate each of the throws. Play a couple of sample rounds with 2 volunteers for the whole class to see.

Tell students that they are going to figure out how many different possibilities there are for one round of the game with two players. Make sure they understand that Paper Rock and Rock Paper are two different possibilities since a different person gets Rock and a different person gets Paper in each of the possibilities. Then tell them they will play the game with a partner and record their results in a table. **Math Talk** 123

▶ **Discussing the Game Results**

Task 2 Discuss the tables that students made to record the results of the game they played.

▶ Have students show the tables they made. How did you show the throw for each player for the round? Answers will vary.

▶ How did you show who won the round in your table? Answers will vary.

English Language Learners

Draw pictures or show examples of different things people collect.

• **Beginning** Say: **There is a collection of 24 stamps and a collection of 43 coins.** Write the numbers. Say: **Let's write a subtraction problem.** Write: **How many more coins are there than stamps?** Say: **This means subtract 43 – 24.**

• **Intermediate and Advanced** Ask: **Does anyone collect stamps/coins/stickers? How many do you have?** Use two students' collections to write an example word problem.

Activity 3

Reasoning and Proof

A Pocketful of Change

 10 MINUTES

Goal: Use reasoning to solve a problem.

 NCTM Standards:
Problem Solving   Communication
Connections   Reasoning and Proof

Dan has 5 pennies, 5 nickels, and 5 dimes in his pocket. Suppose he takes 2 coins out of his pocket. What are the different amounts of money he could take out? Describe how you found all the possibilities. 2¢, 6¢, 10¢, 11¢, 15¢, 20¢; Sample: I organized my work to make sure I listed all of the ways. There are 6 ways.

Hold a whole-class discussion of the problem.

▶ **How can you organize your work so you make sure you find all the possibilities?** sample: One way is to list all the possibilities with at least 1 penny (pp, pn, pd), then list all the possibilities that haven't been listed yet with 1 nickel (nn, nd), and finally list all the possibilities with 1 dime that haven't been listed yet (dd).

▶ **How do you know that your answer is correct?** sample: If I've done a good job of organizing my work, I'll know that I've covered all the possibilities.

Activity 4

Representation

Same Digits, Different Value

 10 MINUTES

Goal: Use drawings to show two numbers.

 NCTM Standards:
Problem Solving   Representation
Communication

Use your MathBoard. Draw pictures to show that 271 and 172 do not have the same value. Check student's work.

Discuss the problem with the class.

▶ Ask students to show how they drew 271 and 172 on their MathBoards. **How do your drawings show that 271 and 172 do not have the same value?** Allow students to show their picture of the two numbers. In the discussion bring out differences such as: The drawing for 271 has 2 hundreds and the drawing for 172 only has 1 hundred.

Activity 5

Communication

Toys for Tim

 10 MINUTES

Goal: Tell how you solved a problem with multiple solutions.

 NCTM Standards:
Problem Solving   Reasoning and Proof
Connections

Tim has $1 to spend on toys. The toys he wants cost 15¢, 20¢, 65¢, 81¢. Which can he buy and spend $1 or less? How did you solve this problem? The ones that cost 15¢, 20¢, and 65¢; 65¢ and 15¢; 65¢ and 20¢; 81¢ and 15¢. Answers will vary.

Hold a whole-class discussion of the problem.

▶ **How did you solve this problem?** Have different students explain how they solved the problem. Many students will use trial and error. Other students will use estimation to help them figure out what amounts will total $1 or less.

② Going Further

Differentiated Instruction

Intervention — Activity Card 1-16

Roll Three Digits — Activity Card 1-16 ●

Work: In pairs

Use:
- Number cubes
- MathBoard materials

1. Roll three number cubes.

2. Find as many ways as you can to write a number on your MathBoard with the numbers on the cubes as digits. Make a place value drawing of each number.

236
326

Unit 1, Lesson 16   Copyright © Houghton Mifflin Company

Activity Note The activity is a chance for students to practice the problem solving process skill of representation and apply what they learned about place value in this unit.

✐ **Math Writing Prompt**

Drawing a Picture Choose one number you made with your number cubes. Tell how you drew a picture of it on your MathBoard.

Soar to Success Math ★ Software Support

Warm Up 66.2

On Level — Activity Card 1-16

Make a 3-Digit Number — Activity Card 1-16 ▲

Work: In pairs

Use:
- Number cubes
- MathBoard materials

1. Roll three number cubes until you get 3 different numbers.

2. Find as many ways as you can to make a number on your MathBoard using all of the numbers on the cubes as digits.

246 426 624
264 462 642

3. How many ways are there? 6

4. Repeat the activity with 3 other different numbers.

5. **Analyze** Make a generalization about how many different ways there are to make a 3-digit number using 3 different digits. There are 6 ways to make a 3-digit number using 3 different digits.

Unit 1, Lesson 16   Copyright © Houghton Mifflin Company

Activity Note The activity is a chance for students to practice the problem solving process skills of representation and reasoning. They also have an opportunity to apply what they learned about place value in this unit.

✐ **Math Writing Prompt**

How Many Ways? Choose one of your sets of 3 numbers. Tell how you are sure you found all the ways to use the three numbers to make as many 3-digit numbers as you can.

MegaMath Grades K-6 Software Support

Numberopolis: Cross Town Number Line V

Challenge — Activity Card 1-16

Make a Generalization — Activity Card 1-16 ■

Work: In pairs

Use:
- Number cubes
- MathBoard materials

1. Roll three number cubes.

2. Find as many ways as you can to make a number on your MathBoard using all of the numbers on the cubes as digits.

246 426 624
264 462 642

3. Continue the activity and keep a record of each round.

4. **Analyze** Make a generalization about how many different ways there are to make a 3-digit number using 3 different digits. There are 6 ways to make a 3-digit number using 3 different digits.

5. **Analyze** Make a generalization about how many different ways there are to make a 3-digit number if 2 of the digits are the same. There are 3 ways.

Unit 1, Lesson 16   Copyright © Houghton Mifflin Company

Activity Note The activity is a chance for students to practice the problem solving process skills of representation and reasoning. They apply what they learned about place value in this unit.

✐ **Math Writing Prompt**

Tell How You Made a Generalization Choose one of the generalizations you made. Tell how you made it.

✺ **DESTINATION Math® Software Support**

Course II: Module 1: Unit 1: Comparing and Ordering

Use Mathematical Processes   **131**

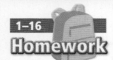

③ Homework and Spiral Review

Homework Goal: Additional Practice

✓ Include student's completed Homework page as part of their portfolios.

Remembering Goal: Spiral Review

This Remembering page would be appropriate anytime after today's lesson.

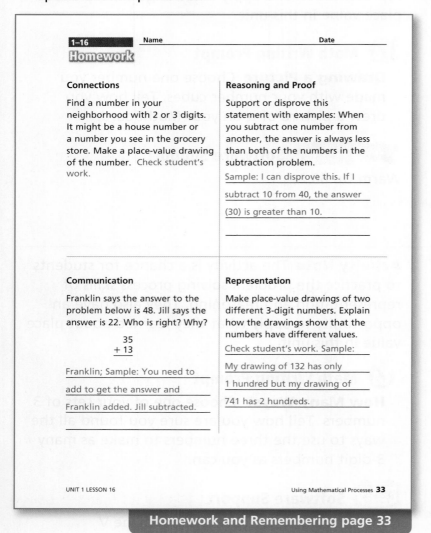

1–16 Homework Name _____ Date _____

Connections

Find a number in your neighborhood with 2 or 3 digits. It might be a house number or a number you see in the grocery store. Make a place-value drawing of the number. Check student's work.

Reasoning and Proof

Support or disprove this statement with examples: When you subtract one number from another, the answer is always less than both of the numbers in the subtraction problem.

Sample: I can disprove this. If I subtract 10 from 40, the answer (30) is greater than 10.

Communication

Franklin says the answer to the problem below is 48. Jill says the answer is 22. Who is right? Why?

```
  35
+ 13
```

Franklin; Sample: You need to add to get the answer and Franklin added. Jill subtracted.

Representation

Make place-value drawings of two different 3-digit numbers. Explain how the drawings show that the numbers have different values.

Check student's work. Sample: My drawing of 132 has only 1 hundred but my drawing of 741 has 2 hundreds.

UNIT 1 LESSON 16   Using Mathematical Processes **33**

Homework and Remembering page 33

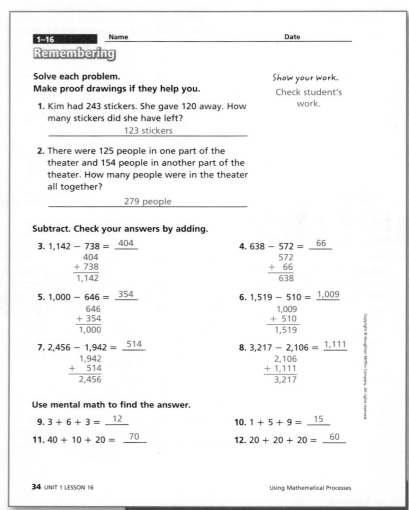

1–16 Remembering Name _____ Date _____

Solve each problem.
Make proof drawings if they help you.

Show your work. Check student's work.

1. Kim had 243 stickers. She gave 120 away. How many stickers did she have left?
   123 stickers

2. There were 125 people in one part of the theater and 154 people in another part of the theater. How many people were in the theater all together?
   279 people

Subtract. Check your answers by adding.

3. $1{,}142 - 738 = \underline{404}$
```
  404
+ 738
1,142
```

4. $638 - 572 = \underline{66}$
```
  572
+  66
  638
```

5. $1{,}000 - 646 = \underline{354}$
```
  646
+ 354
1,000
```

6. $1{,}519 - 510 = \underline{1{,}009}$
```
1,009
+ 510
1,519
```

7. $2{,}456 - 1{,}942 = \underline{514}$
```
1,942
+  514
2,456
```

8. $3{,}217 - 2{,}106 = \underline{1{,}111}$
```
2,106
+ 1,111
3,217
```

Use mental math to find the answer.

9. $3 + 6 + 3 = \underline{12}$

10. $1 + 5 + 9 = \underline{15}$

11. $40 + 10 + 20 = \underline{70}$

12. $20 + 20 + 20 = \underline{60}$

34 UNIT 1 LESSON 16   Using Mathematical Processes

Homework and Remembering page 34

Home or School Activity

 Real-World Connection

Take a Survey Have students think of a question that can be answered with yes or no that they would like to ask their family or friends. Have them ask people the question and record the results. Have them show their results in a table or bar graph.

Do You Like Peas?

Yes or No	Number of People
Yes	////
No	//

Unit Review and Test

Lesson Objective

● **Assess student progress on unit objectives.**

The Day at a Glance

Today's Goals	Materials
1 Assessing the Unit ▶ Assess student progress on unit objectives. ▶ Use activities from unit lessons to reteach content. **2 Extending the Assessment** ▶ Use remediation for common errors. There is no homework assignment on a test day.	Unit 1 Test, Student Activity Book pages 43–44 Unit 1 Test, Form A or B, Assessment Guide (optional) Unit 1 Performance Assessment, Assessment Guide (optional)

Keeping Skills Sharp

Quick Practice 5 MINUTES	
Goal: Review any skills you choose to meet the needs of your class. If you are doing a unit review day, use any of the Quick Practice activities that provide support for your class. If this is a test day, omit Quick Practice.	**Review and Test Day** You may want to choose a quiet game or other activity (reading a book or working on homework for another subject) for students who finish early.

Assessing the Unit

Assess Unit Objectives

45 MINUTES (more if schedule permits)

Goal: Assess student progress on unit objectives.

Materials: Student Activity Book or Hardcover Book pp. 43–44, Assessment Guide Unit 1 Test Form A or B (optional), Assessment Guide Unit 1 Performance Assessment (optional)

▶ Review and Assessment

If your students are ready for assessment on the unit objectives, you may use either the test on the Student Activity Book pages or one of the forms of the Unit 1 Test in the Assessment Guide to assess student progress.

If you feel that students need some review first, you may use the test on the Student Activity Book pages as a review of unit content, and then use one of the forms of the Unit 1 Test in the Assessment Guide to assess student progress.

To assign a numerical score for all of these test forms, use 5 points for each question.

You may also choose to use the Unit 1 Performance Assessment. Scoring for that assessment can be found in its rubric in the Assessment Guide.

▶ Reteaching Resources

The chart at the right lists the test items, the unit objectives they cover, and the lesson activities in which the objective is covered in this unit. You may revisit these activities with students who do not show mastery of the objectives.

Unit Test

Name _____   Date _____

Make a place value drawing for each number.

1. 57

2. 392

Unscramble the place values and write the number.

3. 9 ones + 6 hundreds + 4 tens   649

4. 5 hundreds + 2 ones + 3 tens   532

5. 5 ones + 7 hundreds + 1 thousand + 6 tens   1,765

6. 8 tens + 4 ones + 0 hundreds + 1 thousand   1,084

Write the number for the words.

7. eight hundred seventy-two   872

8. five hundred four   504

9. one thousand fifty   1,050

Add or subtract.

10. 435 + 283 = ___718___   11. 962 − 87 = ___875___

UNIT 1   Test **43**

Student Activity Book page 43

Unit Test Items	Unit Objectives Tested	Activities to Use for Reteaching
1–9, 20	**1.1** Read, write, identify, and represent the place value of whole numbers.	Lesson 1, Activity 2 Lesson 3, Activity 2 Lesson 4, Activity 1
10–14	**1.2** Add and subtract whole numbers.	Lesson 5, Activity 2 Lesson 6, Activity 2 Lesson 8, Activity 3 Lesson 10, Activity 1 Lesson 11, Activity 2 Lesson 12, Activities 1 and 2

Student Activity Book page 44

Unit Test 1

Name _____ Date _____

Add or subtract.

12. 972
    + 129
    ——
    1,101

13. 617
    − 549
    ——
    68

14. 800
    − 684
    ——
    116

15. $3.29
    + 5.98
    ——
    $9.27

16. $5.31
    − 0.32
    ——
    $4.99

17. $10.00
    − 7.54
    ——
    $2.46

18. Gordon baked 346 blueberry muffins and 287 bran muffins. How many muffins did he bake in all?
    633 muffins

19. Write a subtraction word problem related to the addition word problem in problem 18. Then find the answer without doing any calculations.
    Possible answer: Gordon baked 633 muffins. He baked 346 blueberry muffins and the rest were bran muffins. How many were bran muffins? (287 bran muffins)

*20. **Extended Response** Veronica has 423 baseball cards. She put them in piles of 10 cards each.

How many piles of 10 cards did she make? 42 piles

How many extra cards did she have? 3 cards

Explain your reasoning. Possible answer: Four hundreds is the same as 40 tens; 40 tens plus 2 tens makes 42 tens. There are 3 ones in 423, so there are 3 cards left over.

*Item 20 also assesses the Process Skills of Connections, Communication and Reasoning and Proof.

44 UNIT 1   Test

Unit Test Items	Unit Objectives Tested	Activities to Use for Reteaching
15–17	**1.3** Add and subtract money amounts.	Lesson 7, Activity 2
18–19	**1.4** Write a related subtraction word problem for an addition problem and vice versa.	Lesson 13, Activity 1

▶ Assessment Resources

Free Response Tests
Unit 1 Test, Student Book pages 43–44
Unit 1 Test, Form A, Assessment Guide

Extended Response Item
The last item in the Student Activity Book test and in the Form A test will require an extended response as an answer.

Multiple Choice Test
Unit 1 Test, Form B, Assessment Guide

Performance Assessment
Unit 1 Performance Assessment, Assessment Guide
Unit 1 Performance Assessment Rubric, Assessment Guide

▶ Portfolio Assessment

Teacher-selected Items for Student Portfolios:

- Homework, Lessons 3, 4, 10, 11, 13, and 16
- Class Activity work, Lessons 6, 7, 14, and 16

Student-selected Items for Student Portfolios:

- Favorite Home or School Activity
- Best Writing Prompt

② Extending the Assessment

Unit Objective 1.1

Read, write, identify, and represent the place value of whole numbers.

Common Error: Omits Zeros

Given the word form of a number, students may sometimes omit one or more zeros when writing the standard form of the number.

Remediation Use Secret Code Cards to make numbers including numbers with zeros.

Unit Objective 1.2

Add and subtract whole numbers.

Common Error: Incorrect Alignment

When writing an addition or subtraction exercise vertically, some students may not align the places correctly; for example:

$$\begin{array}{r} 267 \\ + \ 32 \\ \hline \end{array} \quad \text{instead of} \quad \begin{array}{r} 267 \\ + \ \ 32 \\ \hline \end{array}$$

Remediation Have students complete their computations in a place value chart or on grid paper.

Common Error: Does Not Group or Ungroup Correctly

Some students make errors when forming new groups in addition or ungrouping in subtraction.

Remediation Distribute base ten blocks and ask students to act out the grouping or ungrouping in each place. Assign a helping partner to help with the student's chosen method. Use proof drawings (Step-by-Step) with the numerical method.

Unit Objective 1.3

Add and subtract money amounts.

Common Error: Difficulty Grouping or Ungrouping

Some students make grouping or ungrouping errors when adding or subtracting money amounts.

Remediation Remind students that even though they are adding and subtracting money amounts, the computations are completed in the same way as whole number computations. For some students, computations with money may be simpler if the numbers are aligned vertically by place value and the decimal point is written in the answer before the answer is found.

Common Error: Does Not Align Decimals

Students may add or subtract money amounts incorrectly because they have misaligned decimal points and place values.

Remediation Have students align the decimals and digits using a place value chart or grid paper.

Common Error: Does Not Record the Decimal Point in the Answer

Students may neglect to write the decimal point when adding money amounts.

Remediation Encourage students to write the decimal point first, before completing the computation.

Unit Objective 1.4

Write a related subtraction word problem for an addition problem and vice versa.

Common Error: Difficulty Deciding Whether to Add or to Subtract

Students may have difficulty determining if a word problem involves addition or subtraction.

Remediation Have students use blocks to act out a problem. As they take various actions, work with them to make the connection to addition or to subtraction by asking questions such as,

- Are you putting groups together? Putting groups together means you are adding.
- Are you separating a group into parts? Separating groups means you are subtracting.
- Are you taking some away? Taking away means you are subtracting.
- Are you comparing numbers? Comparing means you are subtracting.

Common Error: Cannot Explain Why an Operation was Chosen

Students may have difficulty explaining why a word problem involves addition or subtraction.

Remediation Have students make up addition and subtraction problems. Reinforce the language of operations by posing questions similar to the questions above. Have students make lists of words that mean to add or to subtract.

Lines, Line Segments, and Quadrilaterals

UNIT 2 BUILDS UPON the conceptual understanding of linear measurement and the properties of quadrilaterals students developed in previous grade levels. In this unit, students name, sort, and classify quadrilaterals and describe them using geometric terms. Students are expected to apply their understanding of attributes of quadrilaterals to find perimeters of squares and rectangles without measuring all four sides.

Skills Trace

Grade 2	Grade 3	Grade 4
• Measure and draw line segments.	• Measure and draw line segments.	• Draw, name, and identify lines, line segments, and rays.
• Find the perimeter of triangles, squares, and rectangles.	• Find the perimeter of triangles, parallelograms, squares, and rectangles.	• Find the perimeter and area of regular and complex figures.
• Define *parallelogram*, *rectangle*, and *square*.	• Define *parallelogram*, *rectangle*, *square*, and *rhombus*.	• Define *parallelogram*, *rectangle*, *square*, *rhombus*, and *trapezoid*.
• Sort and classify quadrilaterals.	• Sort and classify quadrilaterals.	• Sort and classify quadrilaterals.

Unit 2 Contents

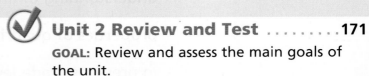

Unit 2 Assessment

✔ Unit Objectives Tested	Unit Test Items	Lessons
2.1 Measure and draw line segments to the nearest centimeter and find the perimeter of geometric figures.	1, 2	1
2.2 Identify lines and line segments.	3, 4, 9, 10	2
2.3 Identify and classify quadrilaterals.	5–8	3, 5

Assessment and Review Resources

Formal Assessment

Student Activity Book
- Unit Review and Test (pp. 65–66)

Assessment Guide
- Quick Quiz (p. A13)
- Test A–Open Response (pp. A14–A15)
- Test B–Multiple Choice (pp. A16–A17)
- Performance Assessment (pp. A18–A20)

Test Generator CD-ROM
- Open Response Test
- Multiple Choice Test
- Test Bank Items

Informal Assessment

Teacher Edition
- Ongoing Assessment (in every lesson)
- Math Talk (in every lesson)
- Portfolio Suggestions (p. 173)

(123) Math Talk
- ▸ Math Talk in Action (p. 168)
- ▸ Student Pairs (p. 154)
- ▸ In Activities (pp. 142, 146, 154, 162, 166)

Review Opportunities

Homework and Remembering
- Review of recently taught topics
- Spiral Review

Teacher Edition
- Unit Review and Test (pp. 171–174)

Test Generator CD-ROM
- Custom Review Sheets

Planning Unit 2

Lesson/NCTM Standards	Resources	Materials for Lesson Activities	Materials for Other Activities
2-1 **Measure Line Segments and Perimeters of Figures** NCTM Focal Points: 5.2, 5.3, 5.4 NCTM Standards: 3, 4	TE pp. 137–144 SAB pp. 45–50 H&R pp. 35–36 AC 2-1 MCC 5	✓ Centimeter rulers Scissors Blank transparency (Optional) Transparent ruler (Optional) Overhead projector (Optional) Overhead transparency of Student Activity Book page 45–46 (Optional)	✓ Centimeter rulers ✓ MathBoard materials ✓ Pattern blocks Math Journals
2-2 **Parallel and Perpendicular Lines and Line Segments** NCTM Focal Points: 3.1, 3.2 NCTM Standards: 3, 4, 10	TE pp. 145–150 SAB pp. 51–54 H&R pp. 37–38 AC 2-2 MCC 6	✓ Centimeter rulers	Geoboards and rubber bands Centimeter Dot Paper (TRB M28) ✓ Pattern blocks Venn Diagram (TRB M29) ✓ MathBoard materials Math Journals
2-3 **Parallelograms, Rectangles, Squares, and Rhombuses** NCTM Focal Points: 3.1, 3.2, 3.3, 3.4, 5.2, 5.3, 5.4 NCTM Standards: 3, 4	TE pp. 151–158 SAB pp. 55–60 H&R pp. 39–40 AC 2-3	✓ Centimeter rulers Tangrams (TRB M30) *Grandfather Tang's Story,* by Ann Tompert	Tangrams (TRB M30) Math Journals

Resources/Materials Key: TE: Teacher Edition   SAB: Student Activity Book   H&R: Homework and Remembering
AC: Activity Cards   MCC: Math Center Challenge   AG: Assessment Guide   ✓: Grade 3 kits   TRB: Teacher's Resource Book

NCTM Standards and Expectations Key: **1.** Number and Operations   **2.** Algebra   **3.** Geometry
4. Measurement   **5.** Data Analysis and Probability   **6.** Problem Solving   **7.** Reasoning and Proof
8. Communication   **9.** Connections   **10.** Representation

Lesson/NCTM Standards	Resources	Materials for Lesson Activities	Materials for Going Further
2-4 **Draw Parallelograms and Rectangles** NCTM Focal Points: 3.1, 3.2, 3.3, 5.2, 5.3, 5.4 NCTM Standards: 3, 4, 10	TE pp. 159–164 SAB pp. 61–62 H&R pp. 41–42 AC 2-4 MCC 7	✓ Rulers Centimeter Grid Paper (TRB 31)	✓ Pattern blocks Rulers Scissors Rectangular sheets of paper Math Journals
2-5 **Classify Quadrilaterals** NCTM Focal Points: 3.1, 3.2, 5.2 NCTM Standard: 3	TE pp. 165–170 SAB pp. 63–64 H&R pp. 43–44 AC 2-5 MCC 8 AG Quick Quiz	✓ Centimeter rulers Quadrilaterals (TRB M32) Scissors Venn Diagram (TRB M29) Sheet protector Dry erase markers ✓ MathBoard materials Geoboards and rubber bands *Squares and Cubes,* by Sally Morgan	Straws or pencils Quadrilaterals (TRB M32) Scissors Math Journals
Unit Review and Test	TE pp. 171–174 SAB pp. 65–66 AG Unit 2 Tests		

Hardcover Student Book

- Together, the Hardcover Student Book and its companion Activity Workbook contain all of the pages in the consumable Student Activity Book.

Manipulatives and Materials

- Essential materials for teaching *Math Expressions* are available in the Grade 3 kits. These materials are indicated by a ✓ in these lists. At the front of this Teacher Edition is more information about kit contents, alternatives for the materials, and use of the materials.

Independent Learning Activities

Ready-Made Math Challenge Centers

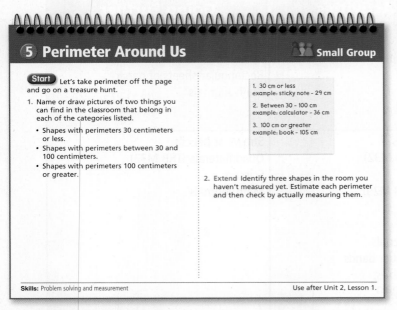

⑤ Perimeter Around Us　　　　Small Group

Start Let's take perimeter off the page and go on a treasure hunt.

1. Name or draw pictures of two things you can find in the classroom that belong in each of the categories listed.
   - Shapes with perimeters 30 centimeters or less.
   - Shapes with perimeters between 30 and 100 centimeters.
   - Shapes with perimeters 100 centimeters or greater.

1. 30 cm or less
   example: sticky note – 29 cm

2. Between 30 – 100 cm
   example: calculator – 36 cm

3. 100 cm or greater
   example: book – 105 cm

2. **Extend** Identify three shapes in the room you haven't measured yet. Estimate each perimeter and then check by actually measuring them.

Skills: Problem solving and measurement　　Use after Unit 2, Lesson 1.

Grouping Small Group

Materials Centimeter rulers, measuring tapes (optional)

Objective Students use estimation and measuring to find real-world objects with specific perimeters.

Connections Measurement and Real World

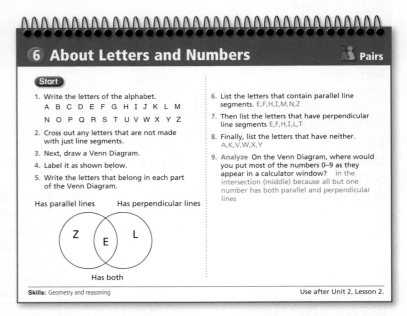

⑥ About Letters and Numbers　　　　Pairs

Start

1. Write the letters of the alphabet.
   A B C D E F G H I J K L M
   N O P Q R S T U V W X Y Z

2. Cross out any letters that are not made with just line segments.

3. Next, draw a Venn Diagram.

4. Label it as shown below.

5. Write the letters that belong in each part of the Venn Diagram.

6. List the letters that contain parallel line segments. E,F,H,I,M,N,Z

7. Then list the letters that have perpendicular line segments E,F,H,I,L,T

8. Finally, list the letters that have neither. A,K,V,W,X,Y

9. **Analyze** On the Venn Diagram, where would you put most of the numbers 0–9 as they appear in a calculator window? in the intersection (middle) because all but one number has both parallel and perpendicular lines

Has parallel lines　　Has perpendicular lines

Z　　E　　L

Has both

Skills: Geometry and reasoning　　Use after Unit 2, Lesson 2.

Grouping Pairs

Materials Calculator

Objective Students identify letters and numbers with parallel and perpendicular line segments.

Connections Geometry and Real World

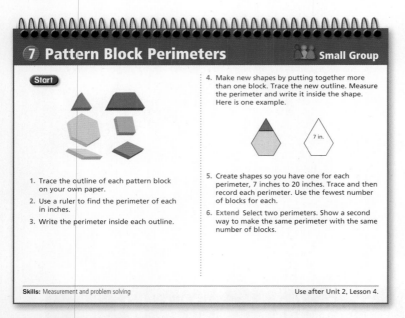

⑦ Pattern Block Perimeters　　　　Small Group

Start

1. Trace the outline of each pattern block on your own paper.

2. Use a ruler to find the perimeter of each in inches.

3. Write the perimeter inside each outline.

4. Make new shapes by putting together more than one block. Trace the new outline. Measure the perimeter and write it inside the shape. Here is one example.

7 in.

5. Create shapes so you have one for each perimeter, 7 inches to 20 inches. Trace and then record each perimeter. Use the fewest number of blocks for each.

6. **Extend** Select two perimeters. Show a second way to make the same perimeter with the same number of blocks.

Skills: Measurement and problem solving　　Use after Unit 2, Lesson 4.

Grouping Small Group

Materials Pattern blocks or Pattern Blocks (TRB M27)

Objective Students use pattern blocks to extend their thinking about perimeter.

Connections Geometry and Reasoning

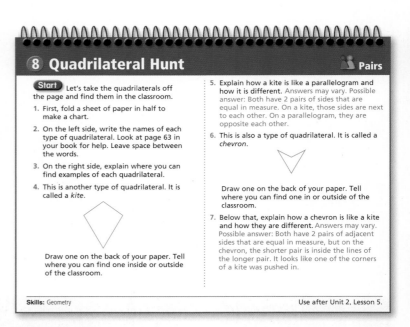

⑧ Quadrilateral Hunt　　　　Pairs

Start Let's take the quadrilaterals off the page and find them in the classroom.

1. First, fold a sheet of paper in half to make a chart.

2. On the left side, write the names of each type of quadrilateral. Look at page 63 in your book for help. Leave space between the words.

3. On the right side, explain where you can find examples of each quadrilateral.

4. This is another type of quadrilateral. It is called a *kite*.

Draw one on the back of your paper. Tell where you can find one inside or outside of the classroom.

5. Explain how a kite is like a parallelogram and how it is different. Answers may vary. Possible answer: Both have 2 pairs of sides that are equal in measure. On a kite, those sides are next to each other. On a parallelogram, they are opposite each other.

6. This is also a type of quadrilateral. It is called a *chevron*.

Draw one on the back of your paper. Tell where you can find one in or outside of the classroom.

7. Below that, explain how a chevron is like a kite and how they are different. Answers may vary. Possible answer: Both have 2 pairs of adjacent sides that are equal in measure, but on the chevron, the shorter pair is inside the lines of the longer pair. It looks like one of the corners of a kite was pushed in.

Skills: Geometry　　Use after Unit 2, Lesson 5.

Grouping Pairs

Materials None

Objective Students expand their understanding of quadrilaterals and find real world examples.

Connections Geometry and Reasoning

Ready-Made Math Resources

Technology — Tutorials, Practice, and Intervention

Use online, individualized intervention and support to bring students to proficiency.

Help students practice skills and apply concepts through exciting math adventures.

Extend and enrich students' understanding of skills and concepts through engaging, interactive lessons and activities.

Visit **Education Place®**
www.eduplace.com

Visit **www.eduplace.com/mx2t/** and find family, teacher, and student materials, activities, games, and more.

Literature Links

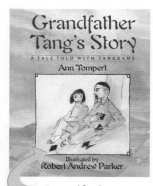

Grandfather Tang's Story: A Tale Told with Tangrams

Grandfather Tang's Story: A Tale Told with Tangrams

This loving story by Ann Tompert, which Grandfather tells to his granddaughter using the traditional seven tangram shapes placed into picture formations, reminds the reader what it means to be a true friend.

Unit 2 Teaching Resources

Differentiated Instruction

Individualizing Instruction

Activities	Level	Frequency
Activities	• Intervention • On Level • Challenge	All 3 in every lesson
	Level	Frequency
Math Writing Prompts	• Intervention • On Level • Challenge	All 3 in every lesson
Math Center Challenges	For advanced students	
	4 in every unit	

Reaching All Learners

English Learners	Lessons	Pages
English Learners	1, 2, 3, 4, 5	137, 145, 151, 159, 165
Extra Help	Lessons	Pages
	1, 4	140, 161
Alternate Approach	Lessons	Pages
	3, 5	154, 156, 168

Strategies for English Language Learners

Present this problem to all students. Offer the different levels of support to meet the students' levels of language proficiency.

Objective Identify and describe two-dimensional shapes.

Problem Show sets of rectangles, circles, squares, and triangles. Say: **These are *figures*.** Name each figure then mix them. Hold up each figure. Help students name and describe it.

Newcomer

- Say: **This is a *rectangle*. This is an *angle*. This is a *side*.** Have children repeat.
- Ask: **How many *angles* does a rectangle have?** 4 Continue with other figures.

Beginning

- Ask: **What *figure* is this?** square Say: **A *square* has 4 equal *sides* and 4 equal *angles*.**
- Say: **Find the figures that have 3 angles.** Ask: **What are these figures?** triangles Continue with other figures.

Intermediate

- Have students mix and sort the shapes. Guide them to describe the shapes using cloze sentences. For example: **A rectangle has __ angles and __ sides.**

Advanced

- Write questions on the board: *How many sides are there? How many angles are there? What figure is it?* Have students take turns asking and answering.

Connections

 Sport Connection
Lesson 2, page 150

 Literature Connection
Lesson 3, page 158

 Art Connection
Lesson 4, page 164

 Social Studies Connection
Lesson 5, page 170

Math Background

Putting Research into Practice for Unit 2

From Current Research: Properties of Quadrilaterals

Learning mathematics involves accumulating ideas and building successively deeper and more refined understanding. A school mathematics curriculum should provide a road map that helps teachers guide students to increasing levels of sophistication and depths of knowledge. Such guidance requires a well-articulated curriculum so that teachers at each level understand the mathematics that has been studied by students at the previous level and what is to be the focus at successive level.

For example:

K–2 Students typically explore similarities and differences among two-dimensional shapes.

3–5 Students can identify characteristics of various quadrilaterals.

6–8 Students may examine and make generalizations about properties of particular quadrilaterals.

9–12 Students may develop logical arguments to justify conjectures about particular polygons.

As they reach higher levels, student should engage more deeply with mathematical ideas and their understanding and ability to use the knowledge is expected to grow.

National Council of Teachers of Mathematics. *Principles and Standards for School Mathematics.* Reston: NCTM, 2000. p. 15

The Use of Tools

The study of geometry in grades 3-5 requires thinking and doing. As students sort, build, draw, model, trace, measure, and construct, their capacity to visualize geometric relationships will develop. At the same time they are learning to reason and to make, test, and justify conjectures about these relationships. This exploration requires access to a variety of tools, such as *graph paper, rulers, pattern blocks, geoboards, and geometric solids*, and is greatly enhanced by electronic tools that support exploration, such as dynamic geometry software.

National Council of Teachers of Mathematics. *Principles and Standards for School Mathematics.* Reston: NCTM, 2000. p. 165

Other Useful References: Measurement, 2-D Shapes, Perimeter

Batista, Michael. T. "Learning Geometry in a Dynamic Computer Environment." *Teaching children Mathematics.* 8.6 (Feb. 2002): p. 333

National Council of Teachers of Mathematics. *Principles and Standards for School Mathematics* (Number and Operations Standard for Grades 3–5). Reston: NCTM, 2000. pp. 97, 103–105.

Getting Ready to Teach Unit 2

In this unit, students build on their understanding of linear measurement and properties of quadrilaterals. Students are expected to use geometric terms when describing quadrilaterals and apply their understanding of attributes to find perimeter.

Concept Building Activities

Linear Measurement
Lesson 1

In this unit, students are provided with an opportunity to further develop then skills in linear measurement. Using centimeter rulers, students will draw and measure line segments with specified lengths. In the previous grade, linear measurement involved counting the number of times a standard unit was needed to match a given length. This idea is further developed with students drawing a collection of line segments from 1 cm to 6 cm marked in 1-cm lengths and then comparing the line segments to a ruler to reinforce.

Attributes of Quadrilaterals
Lessons 2, 3, 4, and 5

In previous grades, students investigated the properties of rectangles, squares, and parallelograms, with students primarily using their own vocabulary to describe the properties of these quadrilaterals. In Lessons 2 and 3, the rhombus is added to the list of quadrilaterals and students see, hear, and use specialized vocabulary like parallel, perpendicular, opposite, and adjacent in their descriptions of quadrilaterals.

To help clarify the relationships between the different quadrilaterals, students draw, name, and sort quadrilaterals according to attributes. This will increase their knowledge about how geometric shapes are related to one another and will provide support for their geometric arguments about the properties of these shapes.

Perimeter
Lessons 1, 3, and 4

Students will calculate the perimeter of quadrilaterals and triangles using informal methods. In the previous grades, class discussion identified that only one side measure is needed to find the perimeter of a square. In this unit, students identify that opposite sides of a rectangle are equal, and students are expected to apply this knowledge to find the perimeter of a rectangle with only two side measures. Calculating perimeter of squares and rectangles with the least number of side measures is a goal for formula development in subsequent years.

In Lesson 4, students will draw rectangles for given perimeters and begin to look at the relationships between dimension and perimeter of rectangles.

Problem Solving

In *Math Expressions,* a research-based, algebraic problem-solving approach that focuses on problem types is used: understand the situation, represent the situation with a math drawing or an equation, solve the problem, and see that the answer makes sense. In this unit, problems involving addition and substraction are reviewed on Remembering pages 36, 38, 40, and 42.

Use Mathematical Processes
Lessons 3, 4, and 5

The mathematical process skills of problem solving, reasoning and proof, communication, connections, and representation are pervasive in this program and underlie all the students' mathematical work. In this unit the skills of Representation and Reasoning and Proof are emphasized as students draw figures from descriptions, describe characteristics and parts of figures, and classify figures.

Measure Line Segments and Perimeters of Figures

Vocabulary

centimeter
line segment
horizontal
vertical
perimeter
triangle
quadrilateral

Lesson Objectives

- Measure lengths to the nearest centimeter.
- Draw line segments of given lengths.
- Find perimeters of triangles and quadrilaterals.

The Day at a Glance

Today's Goals	Materials
1 Teaching the Lesson **A1:** Measure and draw line segments of given lengths. **A2:** Find the perimeters of triangles and quadrilaterals. **2 Going Further** ▶ Differentiated Instruction **3 Homework and Spiral Review**	**Lesson Activities** Student Activity Book pp. 45–50 or Student Hardcover Book pp. 45–50 and Activity Workbook pp. 15–18 (include Family Letter) ✓ Homework and Remembering pp. 35–36 ✓ Centimeter rulers or Centimeter Rulers (TRB M26) ✓ Scissors Blank transparency (optional) Transparent ruler (optional) Overhead projector (optional) Overhead transparency of Student Book pages 45–46 (optional) **Going Further** Student Activity Book p. 46 Activity Cards 2-1 Centimeter rulers Pattern blocks or Pattern Blocks (TRB M27) MathBoard materials Math Journals

123 Use **Math Talk** today!

Keeping Skills Sharp

Daily Routines	English Language Learners
Homework Review Ask students if they had difficulties with any part of their homework. Plan to set aside some time to work with students needing extra help. **Elapsed Time** Susan started painting a picture at 10:00 A.M. She finished at 1:30 P.M. For how long did Susan paint? 3 hours 30 minutes	Guide students to measure objects in centimeters. Model how to measure a classroom object and describe the length. • **Beginning** Display a ruler. Show students where a centimeter begins and ends. Say: **This is one centimeter.** Have them repeat. Have students gesture to show you different lengths. Ask: **About how long is 5 centimeters?** • **Intermediate** Have students work in pairs. Help them to measure different objects and say the length in centimeters. • **Advanced** Show students a book. Ask: **Is the length closer to 5 centimeters or 10 centimeters?** Have them check their estimate.

① Teaching the Lesson

Draw and Measure Line Segments

 20 MINUTES

Goal: Measure and draw line segments of given lengths.

Materials: Centimeter rulers (2 per student) or Centimeter Rulers (TRB M26) printed on card stock, scissors (1 pair per student), blank transparency, transparent ruler, and overhead projector (optional), overhead transparency of Student Book pp. 45–46 (optional)

 NCTM Standard:
Measurement

▶ Measuring with a Ruler WHOLE CLASS

Distribute rulers to each student. If you do not have centimeter rulers, use TRB M26 and give students 2 horizontal and 2 vertical rulers. Students can keep 2 rulers in school and take 2 rulers home. Emphasize that they should find a safe place to keep their rulers at home, as they will need them throughout the year.

● For what do we use rulers for? to draw straight lines; to measure things

Tell students that these rulers are used to measure lengths in centimeters. Explain that the distance between any two numbered marks is 1 cm.

 Class Management

If you have access to the *Math Expressions* Materials Kit, the Centimeter Rulers are included, so you will not have to prepare these materials.

On a blank transparency or the board, draw 1-cm, 2-cm, 3-cm, 4-cm, 5-cm, and 6-cm horizontal lengths directly beneath one another. At the end of each line segment, write its length. Have students do the same on a sheet of paper at their desks.

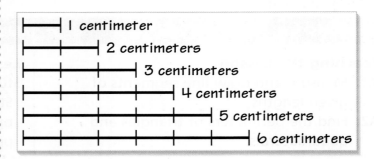

Ask students to imagine what it would look like if they could draw these line segments right on top of one another (they would create a ruler). Emphasize that each number on the ruler refers to the number of 1-cm lengths from the left edge of the ruler to that point.

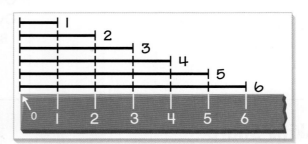

Teaching Note

Language and Vocabulary When you discuss the exercises in this section, use the term *line segment* rather than *line*. Students will learn the difference between a line and a line segment in Lesson 2.

► Measure Line Segments [WHOLE CLASS]

Display a transparency of Student Book page 45. Invite a volunteer to demonstrate how to find the length of the line segment in exercise 1 while other students follow on their pages. Emphasize that the 0-cm mark on the ruler should be lined up with one end of the line segment. The other end of the line segment will be at the 10-cm mark, so the line segment is about 10 cm long.

Not to scale

Have students look at the line segment in exercise 2.

● How is this line segment different from the one in exercise 1? *It goes up and down; the first one went side to side.*

Review the terms *horizontal* (a line segment that goes straight "across," like the line segment in exercise 1) and *vertical* (a line segment that goes straight "up and down," like the one in exercise 2).

Have a volunteer demonstrate how to measure the line segment in exercise 2. Remind students to line up the 0-cm mark on the ruler with one end of the line segment.

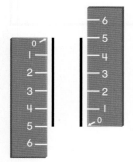

Not to scale

Have the student volunteer report the length. *5 cm*

Repeat for exercise 3.

Invite another volunteer to measure the line segment in exercise 4 for the class, while other students

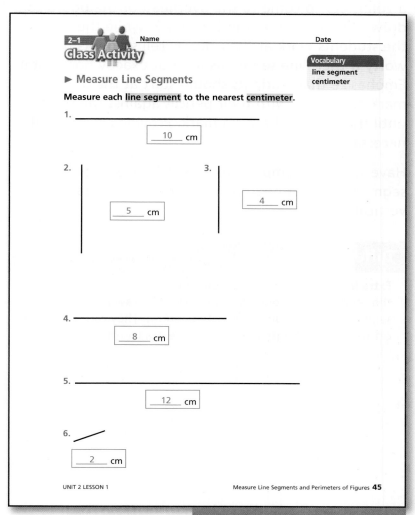

Student Activity Book page 45

measure on their page. Point out that the right end of the line segment falls between the 8-cm mark and the 9-cm mark on the ruler.

● The directions say to measure to the nearest centimeter. What do you think this means? *Find the centimeter measurement the length is closest to.*

● Is the right end of the line segment closer to the 8-cm mark or the 9-cm mark? *the 8-cm mark*

● So, what is the length of the line segment to the nearest centimeter? *8 cm*

Have students complete page 45, and discuss their answers. Have students, who experience difficulty, check their answers with a **Helping Partner**.

Activity continued ▶

① Activity 1 (continued)

▶ Draw Line Segments of Given Lengths [INDIVIDUALS]

Have students look at Student Book page 46. Invite a volunteer to come to the overhead or the board to draw the line segment in exercise 7, while the rest of the students work at their desks. Tell students not to worry if their line segments are not exactly horizontal. Emphasize that students should start at the 0-cm mark and draw, with their pencils against the ruler, until they get to the 7-cm mark. Provide assistance if necessary.

Have students complete exercises 8–11. Students' line segments do not need to be exactly horizontal or vertical.

Differentiated Instruction

Extra Help If students have trouble drawing and measuring at the same time, suggest that they start by drawing a line segment longer than the specified length. They can then mark off the correct length and erase the extra length.

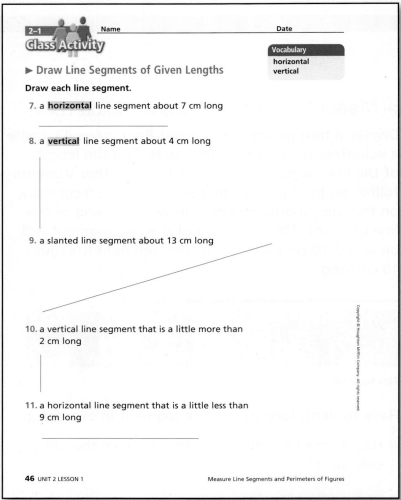

 Ongoing Assessment

Have **Students Pairs** measure and record the lengths of common small objects in the classroom, such as pencils, books, and erasers. If two students get different measurements, ask them to measure again and explain why their measurements were different.

Activity 2

Find Perimeters

 25 MINUTES

Goal: Find the perimeters of triangles and quadrilaterals.

Materials: Student Activity Book or Hardcover Book pp. 47–48 and Activity Workbook pp. 15–18, centimeter rulers (1 per student)

✔ **NCTM Standards:**
Measurement
Geometry

▶ Measure the Perimeter of a Triangle

WHOLE CLASS

Ask for ideas Ask a volunteer to explain what the perimeter of a figure is. Make sure students understand that the perimeter is the distance around a figure. Refer students to Student Book page 47 and have them focus on the triangle in exercise 12.

● This figure is a triangle. What is a triangle? a figure with three sides

● How many line segments will you have to measure to find the perimeter of a triangle? 3

● How can you find the perimeter of this triangle? Find the length of each side and then add the three lengths.

Give students a few minutes to find the perimeter. Suggest that they label each side with its length so they can keep track of their measurements. Invite a student to the board to explain how he or she found the perimeter.

Have students find the perimeter of the other triangles on the page and encourage them to discuss the results.

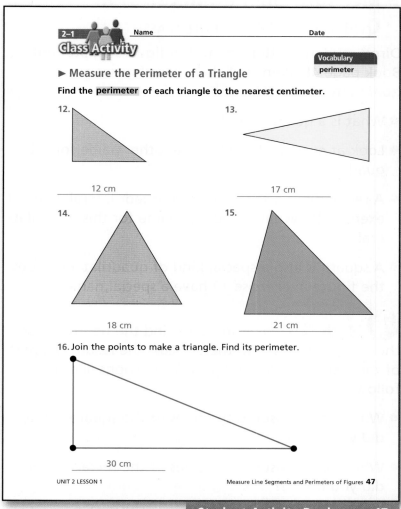

Student Activity Book page 47

Language and Vocabulary

Perimeter—"rim" of the shape—compare to rim of glass as being distance around the opening.

Activity continued ▶

① Activity 2 (continued)

► Measure the Perimeter of a Quadrilateral WHOLE CLASS

Direct students' attention to the figures on Student Book page 48. Point out that these figures are quadrilaterals.

● What is a quadrilateral? a figure with 4 sides

● Look at exercise 17. What is another name for this quadrilateral? a rectangle

● A rectangle is a special kind of quadrilateral. Look at exercise 18. What is another name for this quadrilateral? a square

● A square is also a special kind of quadrilateral. Does the figure in exercise 19 have a special name? no

123 Math Talk Have students find the perimeter of the quadrilaterals, and then discuss the results. As part of the discussion, you might ask questions like the following:

● When you measured the sides of the square, what did you notice? All the sides are the same length.

● When you measured the sides of the rectangle, what did you notice? The opposite sides are the same length.

Have students complete exercise 21.

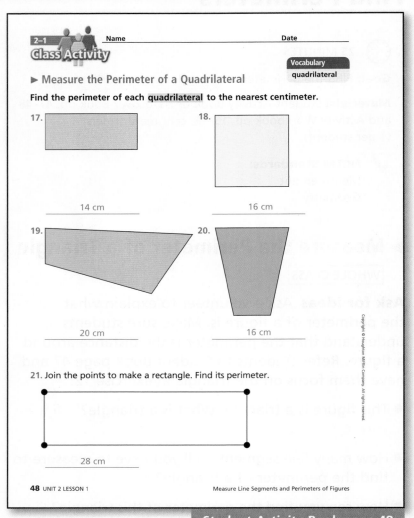

2-1
Class Activity

Name _____ Date _____

Vocabulary
quadrilateral

► Measure the Perimeter of a Quadrilateral

Find the perimeter of each **quadrilateral** to the nearest centimeter.

17.   14 cm

18.   16 cm

19.   20 cm

20.   16 cm

21. Join the points to make a rectangle. Find its perimeter.

28 cm

48 UNIT 2 LESSON 1   Measure Line Segments and Perimeters of Figures

Student Activity Book page 48

The Learning Classroom

Building Concepts Students will look more closely at squares and rectangles in Lesson 3. In that lesson, students learn the important attributes of parallelograms, rectangles, and squares, and explore the relationships among these figures.

② Going Further

Differentiated Instruction

Intervention   Activity Card 2-1

Draw New Line Segments   Activity Card 2-1 ●

Work: On your own

Use:
- Student Activity Book or Hardcover Book page 46
- Centimeter ruler or TRB M26
- MathBoard materials

1. Complete page 46 of the Student Book.

2. On your MathBoard, draw a new line segment in a different position for each exercise you completed.

3. Look at the example below. It shows the line segment in exercise 7 in a different position.

4. Measure to be sure that each line segment you draw on the MathBoard is the same length as the one you drew for Student Book page 46.

Unit 2, Lesson 1   Copyright © Houghton Mifflin Company

Activity Note Be sure that students align the 0 mark on their rulers with the end of each line segment.

 Math Writing Prompt

Define Perimeter How can the word *rim* inside the word *perimeter* help you to remember what perimeter means?

Soar to Success Math ★ **Software Support**

Warm Up 38.11

On Level   Activity Card 2-1

Estimate Perimeter   Activity Card 2-1 ▲

Work: In pairs

Use:
- 2 centimeter rulers
- TRB M27 (Pattern Blocks) or pattern blocks

1. Look at each pattern block in your set.

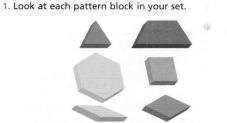

2. **Work Together** Estimate to answer each question:
- Which block has the greatest perimeter?
- Which block has the least perimeter?

3. Measure each perimeter to check your estimates.

Unit 2, Lesson 1   Copyright © Houghton Mifflin Company

Activity Note Students may estimate by using visual comparisons or by counting how many times a small object fits around the perimeter of each block.

 Math Writing Prompt

Explain Your Thinking How can you use a single piece of string to measure the perimeter of a figure?

MEGA MATH Grades K-6 **Software Support**

Shapes Ahoy: Ship Shapes, Level W

Challenge   Activity Card 2-1

Draw a Triangle   Activity Card 2-1 ■

Work: In pairs

Use:
- 2 centimeter rulers
- MathBoard materials

1. **Work Together** Draw at least four triangles. Make one side of each triangle 7 cm long. Make another side of each triangle 9 cm long. Use a centimeter ruler to measure and draw each side.

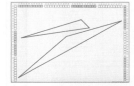

2. Answer the following questions for each triangle you drew.
- How long is the third side to the nearest centimeter?
- What is the perimeter of the triangle?

Unit 2, Lesson 1   Copyright © Houghton Mifflin Company

Activity Note To extend the activity, suggest that students compare the length of the third side with the sum of the other two sides. Ask students what they observe.

 Math Writing Prompt

Investigate Math Try to draw a triangle with sides that are 5 cm, 5 cm, and 15 cm long. Describe what happens.

✳ DESTINATION Math· **Software Support**

Course II: Module 3: Unit 1: Area

③ Homework and Spiral Review

2-1 Homework — Goal: Additional Practice

On this Homework page, students find the perimeters of triangles and quadrilaterals.

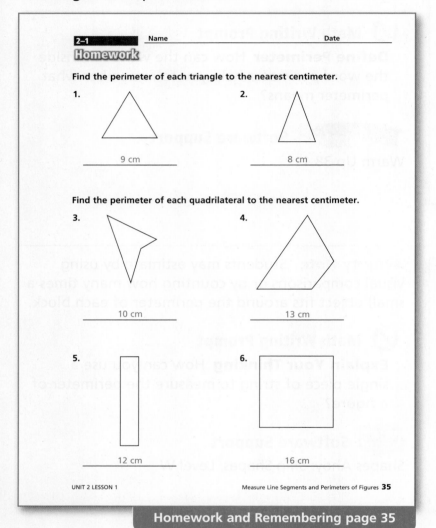

2-1 Remembering — Goal: Spiral Review

This Remembering activity is appropriate anytime after today's lesson.

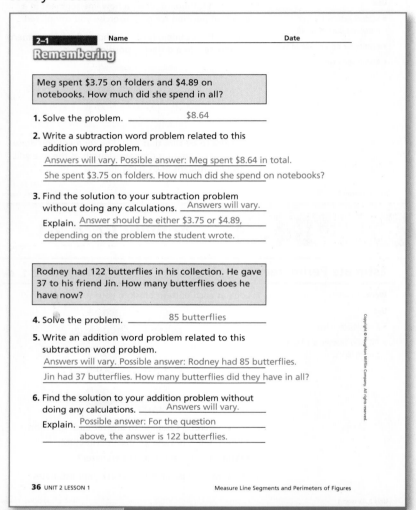

Home and School Connection

Family Letter Have students take home the Family Letter on Student Activity Book page 49 or Activity Book page 17. A Spanish translation of this letter is on the following page. This letter explains how the concept of quadrilaterals is developed in *Math Expressions.* It gives parents and guardians a better understanding of the learning that goes on in math class and creates a bridge between school and home.

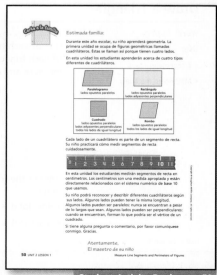

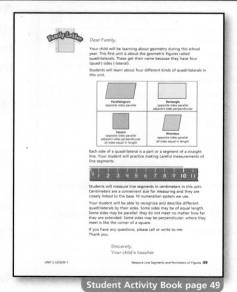
Student Activity Book page 49

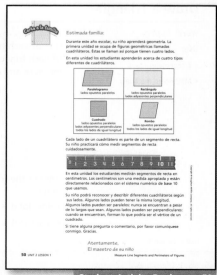
Student Activity Book page 50

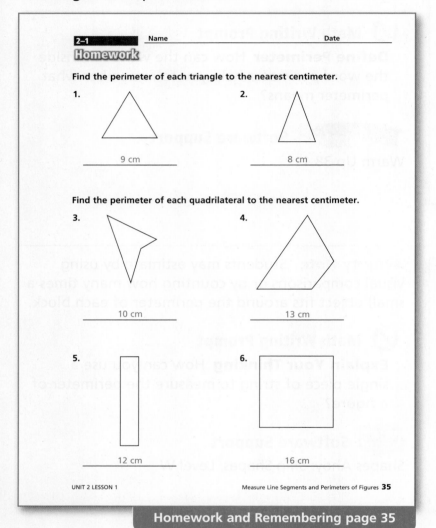
Homework and Remembering page 35

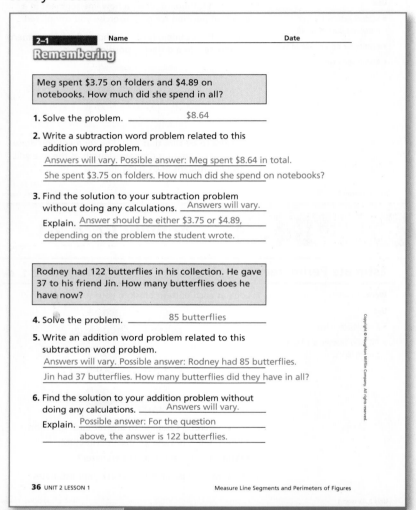
Homework and Remembering page 36

Parallel and Perpendicular Lines and Line Segments

Lesson Objectives

● Identify and find examples to illustrate the terms *line*, *line segment*, *parallel*, and *perpendicular*.

● Identify opposite and adjacent sides of quadrilaterals.

The Day at a Glance

Today's Goals	Materials
1 Teaching the Lesson **A1:** Demonstrate understanding of the meanings of *line*, *line segment*, *parallel*, and *perpendicular* and find examples of each. **A2:** Identify opposite and adjacent sides of quadrilaterals. **A3:** Identify types of lines and line segments. **2 Going Further** ▸ Differentiated Instruction **3 Homework and Spiral Review**	**Lesson Activities** ✓ Student Activity Book pp. 51–54 or Student Hardcover Book pp. 51–54 ✓ Homework and Remembering pp. 37–38 Centimeter rulers **Going Further** Activity Cards 2-2 Geoboards and rubber bands Centimeter Dot Paper (TRB M28) Pattern blocks or Pattern Blocks (TRB M27) Venn Diagram (TRB M29) MathBoard materials Math Journals

123 Use Math Talk today!

Keeping Skills Sharp

Daily Routines	English Language Learners
Homework Review To find if an error is conceptual or procedural, have students explain how they found the answers. **Place Value** Find the number that is 100 less than 1,406. 1,306	Make sure students can identify a line segment and a line. Draw an example of each on the board. ● **Beginning** Ask: **Are these the same?** no Point to each one. Say: **This is a line segment. It ends here and here. These are the endpoints. This is a line.** Ask: **Does it have endpoints?** no ● **Intermediate** Ask: **Which one is a line segment? A line segment has two ____.** endpoints Point to the line. Say: **A line does not have ____.** endpoints ● **Advanced** Encourage students to use short sentences to compare the two drawings.

Teaching the Lesson

Learn about Parallel Lines and Perpendicular Lines

 30 MINUTES

Goal: Demonstrate understanding of the meanings of *line, line segment, parallel,* and *perpendicular* and find examples of each.

Materials: Student Activity Book or Hardcover Book pp. 51–52

 NCTM Standards:
Geometry
Representation

▶ **Define Lines and Line Segments**
WHOLE CLASS

Have students look at the examples of lines on Student Book page 51.

Math Talk Discuss the following key ideas:

● Lines go on forever in both directions.

● When we draw a line, we put arrows on the ends to show the line continues on and on.

Next, have students look at the line segments. Discuss the key ideas about line segments:

● A line segment is part of a line.

● A line segment has two ends, which are called endpoints.

Remind students that they measured line segments in the previous lesson.

Continue the discussion with exercise 1.

Draw examples like those below.

Explain that even though the line on the left looks shorter, it is not shorter. All lines go on forever. Tell students that when they look at a drawing of a line, they need to use their imagination to picture the line extending forever in both directions.

Have students look around the room for examples of lines and line segments. Have students share what they found with the class.

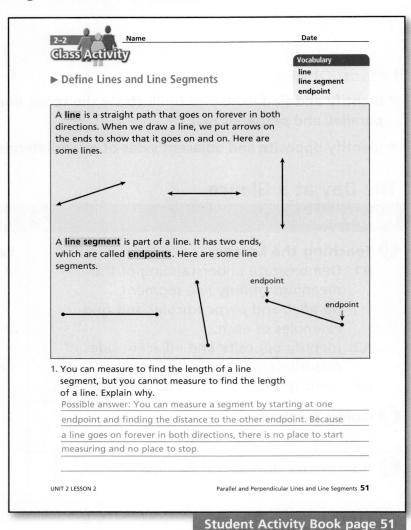

Student Activity Book page 51

Teaching Note

Language and Vocabulary Remind students that many words have more than one meaning. For example, a *line* besides being a straight path that goes on forever may also refer to a fishing line, a clothes line, a line of poetry, a railroad line, line of work, and boundary line.

▶ Define Parallel Lines WHOLE CLASS

Direct students' attention to Student Book page 52. Ask them to examine the parallel lines and the lines that are not parallel. Then ask:

● What do you think it means for two lines to be parallel?

Give students a few minutes to respond in writing, then invite two or three students to share their ideas. Answers will vary, but should include at least these two possibilities:

● Two lines are parallel if they are everywhere the same distance apart.

● Two lines are parallel if they never cross each other.

Note that the drawings of the first two pairs of lines that are not parallel do not cross each other, but because the lines go on forever, they will eventually cross. Students can extend the lines in each pair to check.

Ask students to look at the parallel line segments. Explain that line segments are parallel if the lines they are part of are parallel.

● What examples of parallel line segments do you see in the classroom? Possible answers: opposite sides of the board, lines on notebook paper, opposite sides of a window or door

▶ Define Perpendicular Lines WHOLE CLASS

Ask students to look at the perpendicular and non-perpendicular lines on Student Book page 52. Then ask:

● What do you think it means for two lines to be perpendicular?

Give students a few minutes to respond in writing. Then invite two or three students to share their ideas.

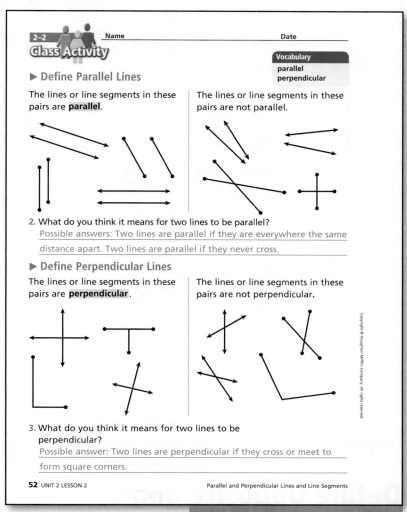

Student Activity Book page 52

Possible answer: Perpendicular lines cross each other to form square corners (some students may use the term *right angles*).

Have students look at the perpendicular line segments. Explain that line segments are perpendicular if they meet to form square corners.

● What examples of perpendicular line segments do you see in the classroom? Possible answers: the edges that form a corner of a desk, door, window, or the cover of a book

✔ Ongoing Assessment

Ask students to think of examples of parallel lines and perpendicular lines in their home or neighborhood or school.

❶ Teaching the Lesson (continued)

Activity 2

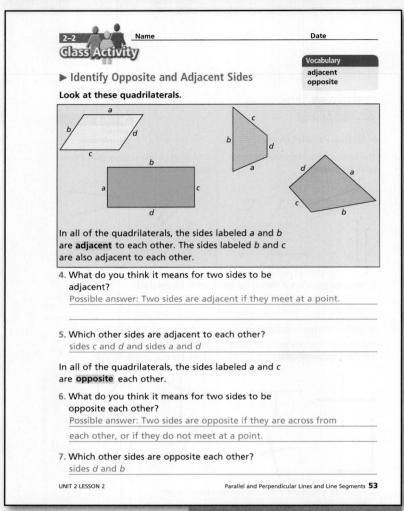

Define Opposite and Adjacent Sides

⏱ **15 MINUTES**

Goal: Identify opposite and adjacent sides of quadrilaterals.

Materials: Student Activity Book or Hardcover Book p. 53

✔ **NCTM Standard:**
Geometry

▶ Identify Opposite and Adjacent Sides

WHOLE CLASS

Have students identify the opposite sides and adjacent sides in each figure and describe opposite sides and adjacent sides in their own words. Then have them complete the page.

148 UNIT 2 LESSON 2

Activity 3

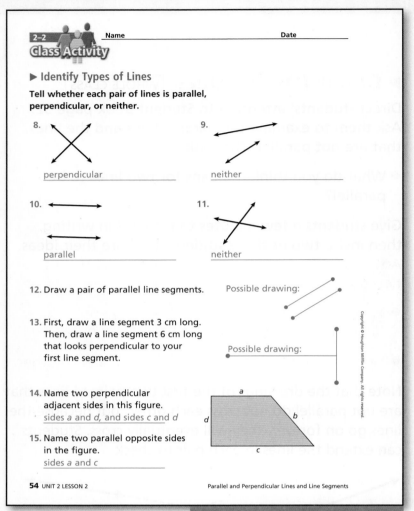

Practice with New Ideas

⏱ **15 MINUTES**

Goal: Identify types of lines and line segments.

Materials: Student Activity Book or Hardcover Book p. 54, centimeter rulers (1 per student)

✔ **NCTM Standards:**
Geometry
Measurement

▶ Identify Types of Lines   INDIVIDUALS

Ask for ideas Elicit from students how to check if two lines are parallel, perpendicular, or neither. Then have them complete the exercises.

②Going Further

Differentiated Instruction

● Intervention   Activity Card 2-2

Make a Quadrangle 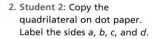   Activity Card 2-2 ●

Work: In pairs

Use:
- Geoboard and rubber bands
- TRB M28 (Centimeter Dot Paper)

Decide:
Who will be Student 1 and who will be Student 2 for the first round.

1. **Student 1:** Make a quadrilateral on the geoboard.

2. **Student 2:** Copy the quadrilateral on dot paper. Label the sides *a*, *b*, *c*, and *d*.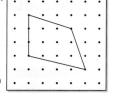

3. Which sides are parallel? Which sides are perpendicular?

4. If no sides are parallel or perpendicular, work together to change your figure to include such sides.

5. Change roles and repeat the activity.

Unit 2, Lesson 2   Copyright © Houghton Mifflin Company

Activity Note To reinforce understanding, first ask students to define *quadrilateral, parallel line segments*, and *perpendicular line segments*.

 Math Writing Prompt

Check Your Answer Explain how you can use lined paper or grid paper to check whether two lines are parallel or perpendicular.

 **Software Support**

Warm Up 35.27

▲ On Level   Activity Card 2-2

Sort Pattern Blocks   Activity Card 2-2 ▲

Work: In pairs

Use:
- Pattern blocks or TRB M27 (Pattern Blocks)
- TRB M29 (Venn Diagram)

1. Use a Venn diagram to sort pattern blocks.

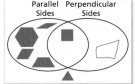

2. Which blocks have parallel sides?

3. Which blocks have perpendicular sides?

4. Which blocks do not belong inside the Venn diagram?

5. Draw a new quadrilateral to go in the empty part of the Venn diagram.

Unit 2, Lesson 2   Copyright © Houghton Mifflin Company

Activity Note To reinforce understanding, have students identify the parallel and perpendicular sides in each shape on their diagram.

 Math Writing Prompt

Use Reasoning Why are opposite sides of a quadrilateral not perpendicular? Why are adjacent sides not parallel?

 Software Support

Shapes Ahoy: Sea Cave Sorting, Level K

■ Challenge   Activity Card 2-2

Investigate Math   Activity Card 2-2 ■

Work: On your own

Use:
- MathBoard materials

1. Explore parallel and perpendicular line segments.

2. Use your MathBoard to draw a vertical line segment.

3. Draw a second line segment perpendicular to the first.

4. Can you draw a third line segment that is also perpendicular to the first but that is *not* parallel to the second line segment?

5. True or false? Any two line segments that are perpendicular to a given line segment will always be parallel to one another. True

Unit 2, Lesson 2   Copyright © Houghton Mifflin Company

Activity Note Extend the activity by having students draw two parallel line segments and then explore whether it is possible to draw a line that intersects both but is perpendicular to only one.

 Math Writing Prompt

Draw a Picture Draw a quadrilateral with no parallel sides and no perpendicular sides. How can you show that the opposite sides are not parallel?

 DESTINATION Math· **Software Support**

Course II: Module 3: Unit 1: Area

3 Homework and Spiral Review

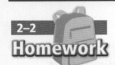

2–2
Homework   Goal: Additional Practice

On this Homework page, students can apply their understanding of the following terms: *adjacent, opposite, parallel,* and *perpendicular*.

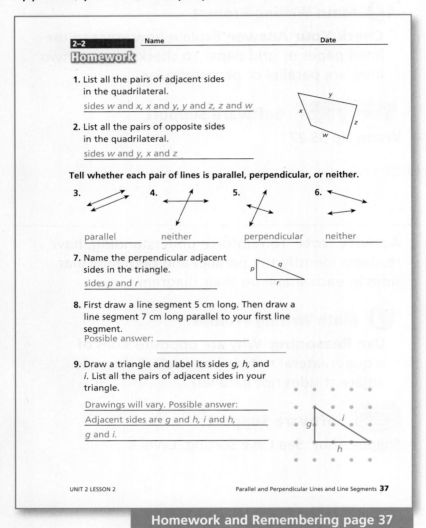

2–2
Remembering   Goal: Spiral Review.

This Remembering activity is appropriate anytime after today's lesson.

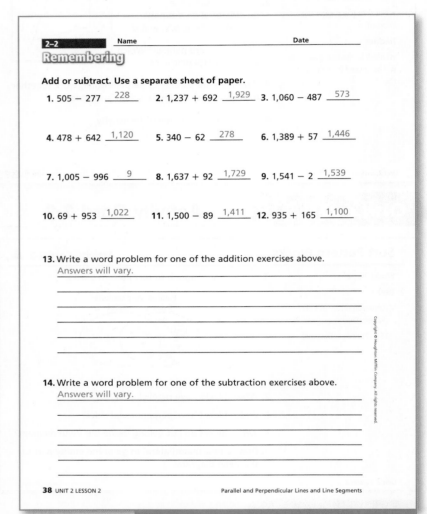

Homework and Remembering page 37

Homework and Remembering page 38

Home or School Activity

 Sports Connection

Lines Around You Have students list examples of parallel and perpendicular lines you might find in a gym or a playing field.

Possible answers: bars on the climber in a playground, uprights and crossbars on a football or soccer field, lines on the gym floor, strings on a racket

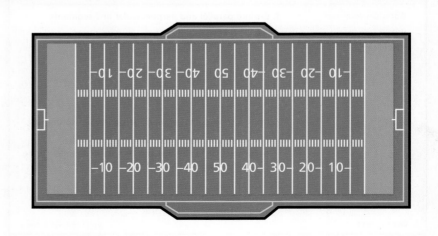

MINI UNIT 2
LESSON 3

Parallelograms, Rectangles, Squares, and Rhombuses

Lesson Objectives

● Develop definitions for *parallelogram, rectangle, square,* and *rhombus.*

● Explore the relationships among parallelograms, rectangles, squares, and rhombuses.

● Find the perimeters of rectangles and squares without measuring all four sides.

Vocabulary

parallelogram
rectangle
square
rhombus
parallel
adjacent
perpendicular

The Day at a Glance

Today's Goals	Materials
1 **Teaching the Lesson** **A1:** Define *parallelogram* and observe, by measuring, that opposite sides of a parallelogram are the same length. **A2:** Define *rectangles, squares,* and *rhombuses* and explain the relationships among them. **A3:** Find perimeters of rectangles and squares by measuring as few sides as possible. **A4:** Identify all names for given quadrilaterals. **2** **Going Further** ▶ Math Connection: Visualize Figures with Tangrams ▶ Differentiated Instruction **3** **Homework and Spiral Review**	**Lesson Activities** Student Activity Book pp. 55–58 or Student Hardcover Book pp. 55–58 Homework and Remembering pp. 39–40 Centimeter rulers Tangrams *Grandfather Tang's Story,* by Ann Tompert (Bantam Doubleday Dell Books for Young Readers, 1997) **Going Further** Student Activity Book pp. 58A–60 or Student Hardcover Book pp. 59–60 and Activity Workbook pp. 19 –21 (includes Cut Outs) Activity Cards 2-3 Tangrams or Tangrams (TRB M30) Math Journals

Use **Math Talk** today!

Keeping Skills Sharp

Daily Routines	English Language Learners
Homework Review Have students discuss any errors made on the homework. Encourage students to help each other resolve these errors. **Create a Pattern** Have students use a triangle, circle, and square to create a repeating pattern. Discuss the patterns students created as a class.	Measure the sides of a book in centimeters and find the perimeter on the board. Review the terms *long* and *length.* ● **Beginning** Measure two sides of the book. Have students measure the other two sides. Model how to describe the length. Have students repeat. ● **Intermediate** Ask: How many centimeters long is each side? What is the length? What is the perimeter? ● **Advanced** Have students measure a book and use *long* and *length* to describe the sides. Then, guide them to describe how to find the *perimeter* using sentence starters such as: **First** ____. **Next** ____. **Last we add** ____.

Parallelograms, Rectangles, Squares, and Rhombuses **151**

① Teaching the Lesson

Define and Measure Parallelograms

 15 MINUTES

Goal: Define *parallelogram* and observe, by measuring, that opposite sides of a parallelogram are the same length.

Materials: Student Activity Book or Hardcover Book p. 55, centimeter rulers (1 per student)

 NCTM Standards:
Geometry
Measurement

▶ Define a Parallelogram WHOLE CLASS

Refer students to the first two rows of figures on Student Book page 55. Ask them to look at the examples of parallelograms and the figures that are not parallelograms.

Ask for Ideas Ask students what they think a parallelogram is. If necessary, suggest that they think about the word *parallel*. (You might write the word *parallelogram* on the board and underline "parallel.") Help students refine and clarify their answers. For example:

• If a student says that a parallelogram is a quadrilateral with parallel sides, point out that figure G is a quadrilateral with parallel sides, but it is not a parallelogram.

• If a student says that a parallelogram is a figure with two pairs of parallel sides, point out that figure J has two pairs of parallel sides, but it is not a parallelogram.

Work as a class to complete the definition: A parallelogram is a quadrilateral in which both pairs of opposite sides are parallel. Record the definition on the board or on a sheet of chart paper and leave it posted for the remainder of the lesson.

Teaching Note

Language and Vocabulary Some students may suggest the following definition: A parallelogram is a quadrilateral in which both pairs of opposite sides are the same length. This definition is also correct. If it is mentioned, record it as well. If not, you do not need to bring it up. This point will be made later.

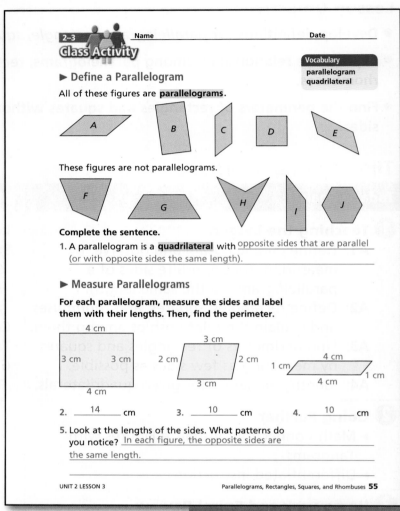

Student Activity Book page 55

▶ Measure Parallelograms INDIVIDUALS

Read aloud the directions in the Measure Parallelograms section and make sure everyone knows what to do. Give students a few minutes to complete exercises 2–5 as you circulate and provide assistance. Then, discuss the answers. Students should notice that in all the parallelograms the opposite sides are the same length.

Rectangles, Squares, and Rhombuses

 15 MINUTES

Goal: Define *rectangles, squares,* and *rhombuses* and explain the relationships among them.

Materials: Student Activity Book or Hardcover Book p. 56

 NCTM Standard:
Geometry

▶ Define a Rectangle | WHOLE CLASS |

Have students look at the rectangles, and read and discuss Adel's statement. If necessary, refer them to the posted definition of *parallelogram.*

● Is Adel right? Are rectangles parallelograms? yes

● How do you know? They are quadrilaterals and both pairs of opposite sides are parallel.

● Adel said that rectangles are special parallelograms. What makes them special?

Allow several students to share their answers and encourage them to use any new words. Work as a class to write at least one of the following definitions:

● A rectangle is a parallelogram with four square corners.

● A rectangle is a parallelogram in which adjacent sides are perpendicular.

Record the definition(s) on the board or chart paper.

▶ Explore Squares and Rhombuses

| WHOLE CLASS |

Refer students to the squares and read aloud Takeshi's statement.

● Is Takeshi right? Are squares rectangles? yes

● How do you know? They are parallelograms and they have four square corners.

● What makes squares special rectangles? All the sides are the same length.

Work as a class to complete the definitions of a square and a rhombus. A square is a rectangle in which all four

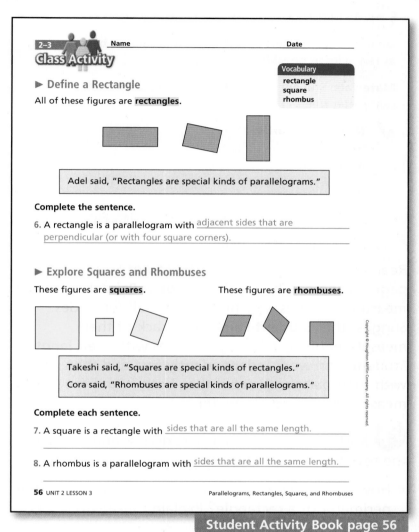

Student Activity Book page 56

sides are the same length. A rhombus is a parallelogram in which all four sides are the same length. Record the definitions under the previous one(s).

▶ Explore Trapezoids (Optional)

| WHOLE CLASS |

Draw three different trapezoids on the board.

● These quadrilaterals are called trapezoids. What do you notice about them? Each has one pair of parallel sides.

Ask students to complete this sentence.

● A trapezoid is a quadrilateral _____ with just one pair of parallel sides.

Teaching the Lesson (continued)

Activity 3

Perimeters of Rectangles and Squares

 15 MINUTES

Goal: Find perimeters of rectangles and squares by measuring as few sides as possible.

Materials: Student Activity Book or Hardcover Book p. 57, centimeter rulers (1 per student)

✓ **NCTM Standards:**
Geometry
Measurement

▶ Find the Perimeters of Rectangles and Squares PAIRS

Read aloud the directions at the top of Student Book page 57 and emphasize that **Student Pairs** should only measure the sides they need to, not all four sides. Suggest that **Student Pairs** keep track of their measurements by labeling the sides with their lengths. Students can work independently first and then check with their partner to see if they both found the same measurements and perimeter.

 Math Talk Then, as a class discuss and summarize the results.

- How many sides do you have to measure to find the perimeter of a rectangle? Explain. 2; The opposite sides are the same length, so you just have to measure the two adjacent sides, and you know the length of the other sides.

- How many sides do you have to measure to find the perimeter of a square? Explain. 1; All the sides are the same length, so if you know the length of one side, you know the length of all four.

Have each student write an answer to exercise 13 and then ask volunteers to share their answers with the class.

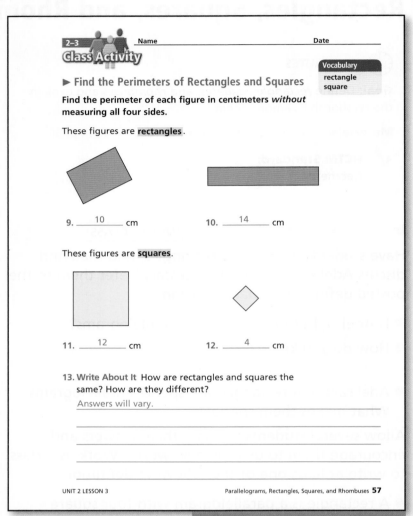

Student Activity Book page 57

✋ Alternate Approach

Act It Out Vocabulary words such as *adjacent* and *perpendicular* may be hard for students to understand. If students can't visualize paper and pencil drawings, have **Small Groups** create human rectangles and squares. When students create these figures, they will clearly see how the opposite or parallel sides are different from the adjacent, perpendicular sides.

Activity 4

Name Quadrilaterals

 15 MINUTES

Goal: Identify all the names for given quadrilaterals.

Materials: Student Activity Book or Hardcover Book p. 58

✔ **NCTM Standard:**
Geometry

▶ Describe Quadrilaterals | WHOLE CLASS |

Refer students to Student Book 58. Discuss the different names a quadrilateral can have. You may have to ask specific questions to get students to realize that there are other possible names for quadrilaterals. For example:

● Are there words in the box that describe the figure in exercise 14? What about the word *quadrilateral*? Can someone remind us what a quadrilateral is? a figure with four sides

● Does this figure have four sides? yes

● So, is it a quadrilateral? yes

● Is this figure a parallelogram? yes

● How do you know? Both pairs of opposite sides are parallel.

● Is this shape a square? no

● Why not? because not all of the sides are the same length

● So, this figure is a quadrilateral, a parallelogram, and a rectangle, but not a square.

Have students complete the page and discuss their answers.

Teaching Note

Watch For! Students may have difficulty understanding the inclusive nature of some of these figures. A square is a kind of rectangle, which is a kind of parallelogram, which is a kind of quadrilateral. This should become clearer as students continue to explore these quadrilaterals in the next geometry unit. To help students understand inclusive relationships, you might mention some examples that are more familiar to them. For example, a beagle is a kind of dog, which is a kind of animal. Point out that we would not say, "This can't be a dog because it is a beagle" or "This can't be an animal because it is a dog." Relate this to the idea that we would not say, "This can't be a parallelogram because it is a rectangle."

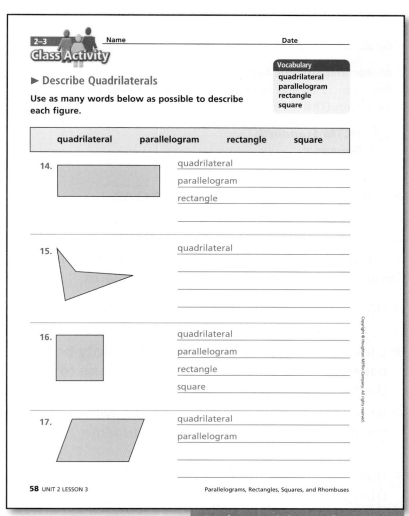

Student Activity Book page 58

Ongoing Assessment

Draw any quadrilateral on the board. Then, have students classify the quadrilateral by writing its name on their MathBoards. Have students hold their MathBoards up so the class can see the different names for one quadrilateral.

Parallelograms, Rectangles, Squares, and Rhombuses **155**

② Going Further

Math Connection: Visualize Figures with Tangrams

Goal: Compose and decompose figures

Materials: Student Activity Book pp. 58A–60 or Hardcover Book pp. 59-60 and Activity Workbook p. 19-21, tangrams or Tangrams (TRB M30)

✓ **NCTM Standard:**
Geometry

▶ Tangram Figures WHOLE CLASS

Have students cut out the tangram pieces on Student Activity Book page 58A or Activity Workbook p. 19. Then use these critical thinking questions to help familiarize students with the tangram pieces.

● How can two tangram pieces become one figure? line up 2 sides to make 1 figure

● Look at the cat pattern on Student Activity Book page 59. What tangram pieces can you use to make the tail? the parallelogram or the 2 small triangles

● What different figures can you make with the two small triangles? a square, a larger triangle, and a parallelogram

● How many small triangles can fit inside the largest triangle? 4

● Two small triangles fit into the square and the medium size triangle. Does that mean that the square fits into the medium size triangle? No; the square has 4 sides and the triangle only has 3 sides.

● Which combination of figures can you use to make the largest triangle? 1 medium size triangle and 2 small triangles; a square and 2 small triangles; a parallelogram and 2 small triangles

Explain that tangram puzzles came from ancient China. Have students try to make the cat puzzle shown on Student Book page 59 using the tangram pieces they cut out from Student Activity Book page 58A or Activity Workbook page 19. If time permits, have students try to create the other tangram patterns on the page and complete the On the Back activity.

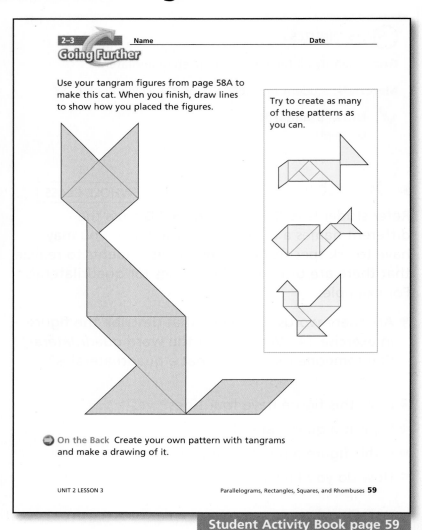

2–3 Going Further Name _____ Date _____

Use your tangram figures from page 58A to make this cat. When you finish, draw lines to show how you placed the figures.

Try to create as many of these patterns as you can.

◗ On the Back Create your own pattern with tangrams and make a drawing of it.

UNIT 2 LESSON 3   Parallelograms, Rectangles, Squares, and Rhombuses **59**

Student Activity Book page 59

✋ Alternate Approach

Tangrams Students can also use foam or plastic tangrams if available. Such materials will be of a precise size and will help students create patterns more accurately.

Teaching Note

Math Connection This activity is designed to make the visual connection between the whole figure and the smaller figures that compose it. Students will use what they know about the shapes of smaller figures to compose and decompose larger figures.

Differentiated Instruction

Just Two Triangles

Activity Card 2-3 ●

Work: On your own

Use:
- TRB M30 or Student Activity Book page 58A (tangrams)

1. Use the two small triangle tangrams to create each figure listed below.

a square

a parallelogram

a larger triangle

- a square
- a parallelogram
- a larger triangle

2. **Analyze** How did you decide how to place the triangles to make a square?
A square has two pairs of perpendicular sides that are equal in length, so the two congruent triangles with perpendicular sides make a square.

Unit 2, Lesson 3   Copyright © Houghton Mifflin Company

Activity Note Focusing on the properties of each shape will help students create each figure.

✎ Math Writing Prompt

Explain Your Answer Isaac wants to find the perimeter of a square. He measures each side with his ruler and adds the measurements together. Explain to Isaac another way to calculate the perimeter.

Soar to Success Math ★ **Software Support**

Warm Up 35.17

Two or More Pieces

Activity Card 2-3 ▲

Work: On your own

Use:
- TRB M30 or Student Activity Book page 58A (tangrams)
- Math Journal

a square   a rectangle

a parallelogram

a triangle twice as big as the medium size triangle

Designs may vary.

1. Use at least two of the tangram pieces to create each figure below. Record how you placed the pieces in your Math Journal.

- a square
- a rectangle that is not a square
- a parallelogram that is not a rectangle
- a triangle twice as big as the medium size triangle

2. **Analyze** What is the least number of tangrams you can use to make a parallelogram that is not a square? 2

Unit 2, Lesson 3   Copyright © Houghton Mifflin Company

Activity Note Students should share their designs with their classmates.

✎ Math Writing Prompt

Explain Your Thinking Takeshi said that squares are special rectangles. Do you think he is correct? Explain your thinking.

MEGA MATH Grades K-6 **Software Support**

Shapes Ahoy: Ship Shapes, Level K

All Seven Pieces

Activity Card 2-3 ■

Work: In pairs

Use:
- TRB M30 or Student Activity Book page 58A (tangrams)

1. Look at the diagram. It shows how to use all seven tangram pieces to make a rectangle.

a rectangle

2. Form the arrangement above with your tangrams.

3. Now change the arrangement of the seven tangrams to make a parallelogram that is *not* a rectangle.

a parallelogram

a square

4. How can you use all seven tangrams to make a square?

Unit 2, Lesson 3   Copyright © Houghton Mifflin Company

Activity Note Repositioning tangrams to make a parallelogram from a rectangle previews the derivation of the area formula for a parallelogram.

✎ Math Writing Prompt

Make a Drawing Cora said that rhombuses are special kinds of parallelograms. Do you think she is correct? Include a drawing in your answer.

✖ DESTINATION Math· **Software Support**

Course II: Module 3: Unit 1: Area

Parallelograms, Rectangles, Squares, and Rhombuses   **157**

③ Homework and Spiral Review

Homework **Goal:** Additional Practice

✓ Include students' completed Homework page as part of their portfolios.

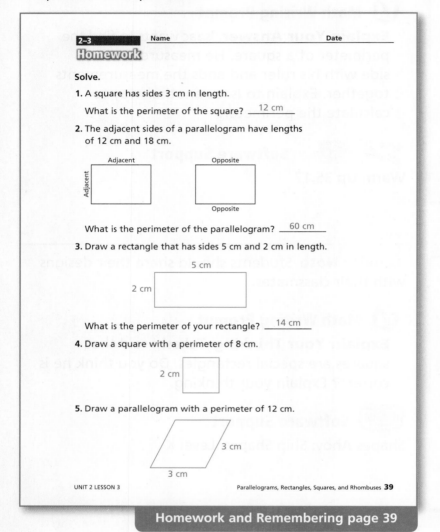

2-3 Homework Name _____ Date _____

Solve.

1. A square has sides 3 cm in length.
What is the perimeter of the square? __12 cm__

2. The adjacent sides of a parallelogram have lengths of 12 cm and 18 cm.

Adjacent / Opposite

What is the perimeter of the parallelogram? __60 cm__

3. Draw a rectangle that has sides 5 cm and 2 cm in length.

5 cm
2 cm

What is the perimeter of your rectangle? __14 cm__

4. Draw a square with a perimeter of 8 cm.

2 cm

5. Draw a parallelogram with a perimeter of 12 cm.

3 cm
3 cm

UNIT 2 LESSON 3   Parallelograms, Rectangles, Squares, and Rhombuses **39**

Homework and Remembering page 39

Remembering **Goal:** Spiral Review

This Remembering activity is appropriate anytime after today's lesson.

2-3 Remembering Name _____ Date _____

Read each sentence and write whether it is true or false.

1. All squares are rectangles. __true__

2. All parallelograms are squares. __false__

3. All quadrilaterals are parallelograms. __false__

4. The opposite sides of a square are always parallel. __true__

5. If you know the lengths of two opposite sides of a parallelogram, you can find its perimeter. __false__

Use the word problem below to complete exercises 6–8.

> Ms. Molina has 148 paperback books and 82 hardcover books. How many books does she have in all?

6. Solve the problem. __230 books__

7. Write a subtraction word problem related to this addition word problem.

Possible answer: Ms. Molina has 230 books. 148 of her books are paperback books. How many of her books are hardcover books?

8. Find the answer to your subtraction problem without doing any calculations.

Answers will vary: For the question above the answer is 82 hardcover books.

40 UNIT 2 LESSON 3   Parallelograms, Rectangles, Squares, and Rhombuses

Homework and Remembering page 40

Home or School Activity

 Literature Connection

Grandfather Tang's Story Have students read Ann Tompert's book, *Grandfather Tang's Story* (Bantam Doubleday Dell Books for Young Readers, 1997). As they read along, have them create the animals in the story with tangrams. As an extension, have students create their own animal pattern out of tangrams and write and illustrate an animal story. If students would like to color their own tangram pattern, they can use TRB M30.

Draw Parallelograms and Rectangles

Lesson Objectives

- Draw parallelograms and rectangles.

- Observe the relationship between the dimensions of a rectangle and its perimeter.

The Day at a Glance

Today's Goals	Materials
1 **Teaching the Lesson** **A1:** Review the attributes of and draw parallelograms. **A2:** Review the attributes of rectangles and draw all possible rectangles with a given perimeter and sides with whole-number lengths. **2** **Going Further** ▶ Differentiated Instruction **3** **Homework and Spiral Review**	**For Lesson Activities** Student Activity Book pp. 61–62 or Student Hardcover Book pp. 61–62 and Activity Workbook pp. 22–23 (includes grids) Homework and Remembering pp. 41–42 Rulers Centimeter-Grid Paper (TRB M31) **Going Further** Activity Cards 2-4 Pattern Blocks (TRB M27) Scissors Rulers Rectangular sheets of paper Math Journals

123 Use **Math Talk** today!

Keeping Skills Sharp

Daily Routines	English Language Learners
Homework Review Ask students if they had difficulties with any part of their homework. Plan to set aside some time to work with students needing extra help. **Elapsed Time** Fred started the drive to his Aunt's house at 11:30 A.M. He arrived at her house at 3:00 P.M. How long was Fred's drive? 3 hours 30 minutes	Review the terms *adjacent, equal, perpendicular* and *parallel*. Write them on the board. Draw a rectangle and a rhombus on the board. Mark the sides A – H. • **Beginning** Point to the rectangle. Say: **Side A is opposite side C.** Have students repeat. Continue with the other terms. • **Intermediate** Ask: **What is opposite side A? What side is adjacent? Which shape has 4 equal sides?** rhombus **2 pairs of parallel sides?** both **4 perpendicular sides?** rectangle • **Advanced** Have students work in pairs and use the terms to describe the shapes.

Teaching the Lesson

Draw Parallelograms

 25 MINUTES

Goal: Review the attributes of and draw parallelograms.

Materials: Student Activity Book or Hardcover Book p. 61 and Activity Workbook p. 22, rulers (one per student)

✔ **NCTM Standards:**
Geometry
Representation

▶ Explore Parallelograms [INDIVIDUALS]

Review what students learned about parallel line segments. Then, have students look at Student Book page 61.

● Look at the parallelogram on the page. Which sides are opposite sides? sides *a* and *c; b* and *d*

● What can you say about the opposite sides of a parallelogram? The opposite sides are parallel.

● What can you say about the length of the opposite sides of a parallelogram? The opposite sides are the same length.

● If you wanted to find the perimeter of this parallelogram, would you have to measure all four sides? no

● Why not? If you know the length of one side, you automatically know the length of the opposite side.

● Which sides would you have to measure? any two adjacent sides: *a* and *b; b* and *c; c* and *d; d* and *a*

Have students complete exercise 1.

Ask students to draw parallelograms of different sizes, shapes, and orientations on the grid provided. Students can use the lines on the grid to draw one pair of parallel sides and draw the other sides by "eyeballing."

Examples of possible drawings are in the following column.

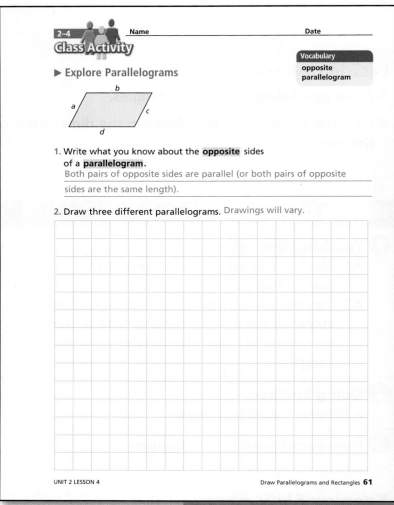

Student Activity Book page 61

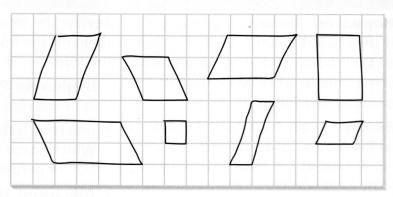

Ask volunteers to share some of the parallelograms they drew. Ask about special parallelograms.

● Did anybody draw a rectangle? Did anybody draw a square? How do you know that a rectangle and a square are parallelograms? In both figures, both pairs of opposite sides are parallel.

Draw Rectangles

 35 MINUTES

Goal: Review the attributes of rectangles and draw all possible rectangles with a given perimeter and sides with whole-number lengths.

Materials: Student Activity Book or Hardcover Book p. 62 and Activity Workbook p. 23, rulers (1 per small group), Centimeter Grid Paper (TRB M31)

 NCTM Standards:
Geometry
Measurement

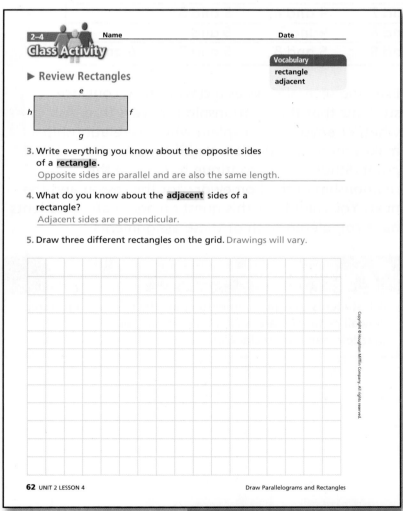

▶ Review Rectangles SMALL GROUPS

Review rectangles by discussing the rectangle on Student Book page 62.

● Rectangles are special kinds of parallelograms. What makes them special? They have four square corners.

● What do you know about the lengths of the sides of a rectangle? The opposite sides are the same length.

● If you wanted to find the perimeter of the rectangle on Student Book page 62, which sides would you have to measure? any two adjacent sides

You might mention that some people refer to the two adjacent sides of a rectangle as the length and the width. These measurements are called the *dimensions* of the rectangle. Have **Small Groups** complete exercises 3–5.

Rectangles with Specific Side Lengths Divide the class into groups of two or three. Assign one of the perimeters below to each group.

10 cm	12 cm
14 cm	16 cm
18 cm	20 cm
22 cm	24 cm

Have each **Small Group** draw, on TRB M31, all the possible rectangles with the given perimeter (and sides with whole-number lengths). Ask students to label the lengths of a pair of adjacent sides for each rectangle. Suggest that **Small Groups** figure out the lengths and widths of all the possible rectangles before they begin drawing.

Differentiated Instruction

Extra Help You may want to have your struggling students work together. Assign the smaller perimeters, which have fewer possible rectangles, to these students. Assist these groups as they draw their rectangles.

Activity continued ▶

① Teaching the Lesson (continued)

On the board, make a chart with a row for each perimeter. Select a spokesperson for each group to come to the board and list the lengths of two adjacent sides for each rectangle the group drew. Students can list just the numbers. They don't need to write "centimeters."

Teaching Note

Watch For! Students may write each pair of dimensions twice. For example, they may write both 3 and 5, and 5 and 3. You can either allow them to do this or point out that these rectangles are really the same; one is simply a rotated copy of the other.

Perimeter (centimeters)	Possible Lengths of Sides (centimeters)				
10	1 and 4	2 and 3			
12	1 and 5	2 and 4	3 and 3		
14	1 and 6	2 and 5	3 and 4		
16	1 and 7	2 and 6	3 and 5	4 and 4	
18	1 and 8	2 and 7	3 and 6	4 and 5	
20	1 and 9	2 and 8	3 and 7	4 and 6	5 and 5
22	1 and 10	2 and 9	3 and 8	4 and 7	5 and 6
24	1 and 11	2 and 10	3 and 9	5 and 8	5 and 7	6 and 6

 Math Talk After all groups have recorded their work, ask students to look closely at the chart and discuss the following questions.

● Which rectangles are also squares? 3 and 3; 4 and 4; 5 and 5; 6 and 6

● How do you know that a square is also a rectangle? Its opposite sides are the same length.

Then, ask students if they see any patterns in the chart. If no one mentions the fact that the total for each pair of lengths is half the perimeter, ask specific questions:

● Look at the row for a rectangle with a perimeter of 16 cm. If you add each pair of lengths of sides, what do you get? 8 cm

● How does this compare to the perimeter? It is half the perimeter.

Challenge students to find similar patterns in other rows of the chart.

Examine several rows as a class to help convince students that this relationship is always true. Ask whether anyone can explain why this relationship makes sense, but don't worry if no one can at this point. Students will continue to explore this relationship in the homework for this lesson and the next. You might ask this question again after students have completed both of these assignments.

✓ **Ongoing Assessment**

Ask students to explain, in writing and by drawing a picture, why all rectangles are also parallelograms, but not all parallelograms are rectangles.

② Going Further

Differentiated Instruction

Geometric Designs

Activity Card 2-4 ●

Work: In pairs

Use:
- Parallelograms and squares from TRB M27 (Pattern Blocks) or from a set of pattern blocks

Decide:

Who will be Student 1 and who will be Student 2 for the first round.

1. **Student 1:** Use your pattern blocks to copy the design below.

2. **Student 2:** How would you describe the design? Use the names of the figures in the design to describe it to your partner.

3. Change roles to create and describe a new design.

Unit 2, Lesson 4   Copyright © Houghton Mifflin Company

Activity Note Point out how the two-dimensional design creates the illusion of a three-dimensional space by the use of shading and shapes. The artist M.C. Escher used these techniques in his work.

 Math Writing Prompt

Organize Data What do you know about the sides and corners of rectangles, squares, and parallelograms? Use a chart to organize your thinking.

 **Software Support**

Warm Up 35.15

Make Parallelograms

Activity Card 2-4 ▲

Work: On your own

Use:
- Scissors
- Ruler
- Rectangular sheets of paper

1. Use a ruler to draw a slanted line segment across a rectangular sheet of paper, as shown below.

2. Cut along the line to make two pieces.

3. Now rearrange the two pieces to make a parallelogram that is *not* a rectangle.

4. **Analyze** How is the parallelogram different from the rectangle? How is it the same? The parallelogram does not have sides that are perpendicular. Both figures are quadrilaterals with opposite sides that are parallel. Both figures have the same area.

Unit 2, Lesson 4   Copyright © Houghton Mifflin Company

Activity Note Students must arrange the pieces so that the two equal sides coincide to create a quadrilateral with two pairs of parallel sides.

 Math Writing Prompt

Explain Your Thinking Draw a quadrilateral that is not a parallelogram. Explain how you can prove that it is not a parallelogram.

 Software Support

Shapes Ahoy: Ship Shapes, Level I

Investigate Math

Activity Card 2-4 ■

Work: On your own

Use:
- 10 squares from a set of pattern blocks or from TRB M27 (Pattern Blocks)

1. Take one square pattern block to begin a design.

2. Add three more blocks to make a larger square.

3. How many *more* blocks do you need to make the next size larger square? 5

4. Now how many *more* blocks do you need to make the next size larger square? 7

5. How would you describe the pattern of blocks that you see? The number of blocks that are added each time increases by 2.

Unit 2, Lesson 4   Copyright © Houghton Mifflin Company

Activity Note Point out that the pattern they create is the sequence of odd numbers: 1, 3, 5, 7,...

 Math Writing Prompt

Investigate Possibilities How many different rectangles can you make with twelve 1-cm squares? Explain your answer.

 DESTINATION Math· **Software Support**

Course II: Module 3: Unit 1: Area

Draw Parallelograms and Rectangles   **163**

③ Homework and Spiral Review

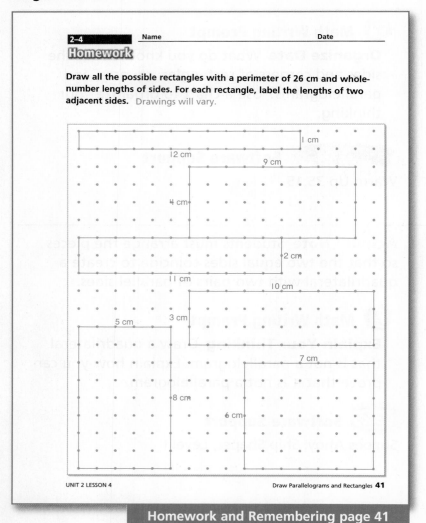

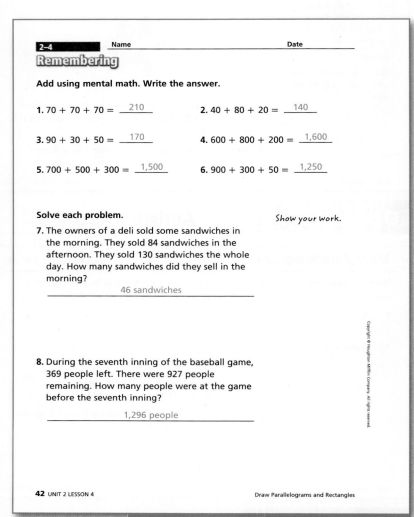

2–4
Homework **Goal:** Additional Practice

For homework, students draw all possible rectangles that have a given perimeter and whole-number lengths of sides.

2–4
Remembering **Goal:** Spiral Review

This Remembering activity is appropriate anytime after today's lesson.

2–4 Name ____ Date ____
Homework

Draw all the possible rectangles with a perimeter of 26 cm and whole-number lengths of sides. For each rectangle, label the lengths of two adjacent sides. Drawings will vary.

I cm
12 cm
9 cm
4 cm
2 cm
11 cm
10 cm
5 cm 3 cm
7 cm
8 cm
6 cm

UNIT 2 LESSON 4   Draw Parallelograms and Rectangles **41**

Homework and Remembering page 41

2–4 Name ____ Date ____
Remembering

Add using mental math. Write the answer.

1. 70 + 70 + 70 = ___210___   2. 40 + 80 + 20 = ___140___

3. 90 + 30 + 50 = ___170___   4. 600 + 800 + 200 = ___1,600___

5. 700 + 500 + 300 = ___1,500___   6. 900 + 300 + 50 = ___1,250___

Solve each problem.   *Show your work.*

7. The owners of a deli sold some sandwiches in the morning. They sold 84 sandwiches in the afternoon. They sold 130 sandwiches the whole day. How many sandwiches did they sell in the morning?

_____46 sandwiches_____

8. During the seventh inning of the baseball game, 369 people left. There were 927 people remaining. How many people were at the game before the seventh inning?

_____1,296 people_____

42 UNIT 2 LESSON 4   Draw Parallelograms and Rectangles

Homework and Remembering page 42

Home or School Activity

🎨 **Art Connection**

Picture Frames Pose this problem to students:
A picture measures 8 inches by 10 inches.

The wooden frame around the picture is one inch wide.

What is the shortest total length of wood you will need to make the frame?

10 + 10 + 12 + 12 = 44 inches

Classify Quadrilaterals

Vocabulary

quadrilateral
parallelogram
rhombus
rectangle
square

Lesson Objectives

● Review the features of quadrilaterals, parallelograms, rectangles, and squares.

● Describe the relationships among various types of quadrilaterals.

The Day at a Glance

Today's Goals	Materials	
1 **Teaching the Lesson** **A1:** Classify quadrilaterals and review the key attributes of quadrilaterals, parallelograms, rectangles, and squares. **A2:** Draw quadrilaterals that match given descriptions. **2** **Going Further** ► Differentiated Instruction **3** **Homework and Spiral Review**	**Lesson Activities** Student Activity Book pp. 63–64 or Student Hardcover Book pp. 63–64 and Activity Workbook p. 24 (includes chart) Homework and Remembering pp. 43–44 Quick Quiz (Assessment Guide) Centimeter rulers Quadrilaterals (TRB M32) Venn Diagram (TRB M29) Sheet protectors, Dry-erase markers MathBoard materials Geoboards, Rubber bands, Scissors *Squares and Cubes,* by Sally Morgan (Thomson Learning, 1994)	**Going Further** Activity Cards 2-5 Straws or pencils Quadrilaterals (TRB M32) Scissors Math Journals 123 *Use* **Math Talk** *today!*

Keeping Skills Sharp

Daily Routines	English Language Learners
Strategy Problem Pat wants to make rectangular cards with a perimeter of 12 inches. How many different cards can Pat make that have a different length and width? 2 cards Make drawings of each card and label the length and width. 5 in. 1 in. 4 in. 2 in.	Draw quadrilaterals on the board to review. Point and say: **This is a square. It has four equal sides.** Ask: **Does it have parallel sides?** yes Continue with other quadrilaterals. • **Beginning** Point to the parallelogram. Ask: **Is this a square corner?** no **Are these sides parallel?** yes **Is this a parallelogram?** yes **Is this a rectangle?** no • **Intermediate** Point to a figure that is not a square, and ask: **Is this a square?** no **Why not?** • **Advanced** Have students describe the corners and sides of a figure then compare two or more figures. Ask: **How are they similar? Different?**

Teaching the Lesson

Activity 1

Different Types of Quadrilaterals

 40 MINUTES

Goal: Classify quadrilaterals and review the key attributes of quadrilaterals, parallelograms, rectangles, and squares.

Materials: Student Activity Book or Hardcover Book pp. 63–64 and Activity Workbook p. 24, centimeter rulers (1 per student), Quadrilaterals (TRB M32), scissors (1 pair per student), Venn Diagram (TRB M29), sheet protector, dry erase markers

✔ **NCTM Standard:**
Geometry

▶ Describe Quadrilaterals [WHOLE CLASS]

Math Talk Read aloud the directions on Student Book page 63 and make sure students know what to do. Have them work independently to complete the page. Review the results, asking students to provide explanations for their answers. For example, for exercise 1:

● Is it a quadrilateral? yes

● How do you know? It has four sides.

● Is it a parallelogram? yes

● How do you know? Both pairs of opposite sides are parallel.

● Is it a rhombus? yes

● How do you know? All sides are the same length.

● Is it a rectangle? no

● How do you know? It doesn't have four square corners.

● How do you know it isn't a square? It's not a rectangle, so it can't be a square.

Have students look at all of their answers and ask whether they see any patterns. Students may notice that the word *quadrilateral* is marked for all the figures. They might also notice that when a name is marked, every name above it is also marked, with the exception of number 4.

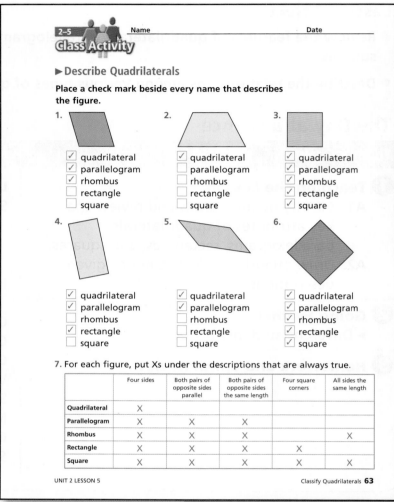

Student Activity Book page 63

Continue eliciting information from students until they have completed the chart together. Ask students what they notice about the completed chart. Make sure they see that each category of figures has all the features of the category above plus some other feature(s). For example, rectangles have all the features of quadrilaterals plus two pairs of parallel opposite sides, two pairs of opposite sides of the same length, and four square corners.

To summarize, have students find objects in the classroom and share how the characteristics of the shapes of the objects match those given in the chart.

Work as a class and use the information on the chart to complete statements 8–12 on Student Book page 64.

2-5

Class Activity

Name _____ Date _____

Use the finished chart on page 63 to complete each statement.

8. Parallelograms have all the features of quadrilaterals *plus*
   opposite sides are parallel and the same length.

9. Rectangles have all the features of parallelograms *plus*
   all four corners are square.

10. Squares have all the features of quadrilaterals *plus*
    both pairs of opposite sides are parallel and the same length;
    there are four square corners; all sides are the same length.

11. Squares have all the features of parallelograms *plus*
    all four corners are square and all sides are the same length.

12. Squares have all the features of rectangles *plus*
    all sides are the same length.

▶ **Draw Quadrilaterals if Possible**

Draw each figure if you can. If it is impossible, explain why.

13. Draw a quadrilateral that is *not* a parallelogram.
    Answers will vary.   Possible answer:

14. Draw a square that is *not* a rectangle.
    Not possible to draw; all squares are rectangles.

15. Draw a parallelogram that is *not* a rectangle.
    Answers will vary.   Possible answer:

16. Draw a rectangle that is *not* a square.
    Answers will vary.   Possible answer:

17. Draw a rhombus that is *not* a parallelogram.
    Not possible to draw; all rhombuses are parallelograms.

64 UNIT 2 LESSON 5   Classify Quadrilaterals

Student Activity Book page 64

- How can you sort the quadrilaterals using the lengths of their sides? equal lengths and different lengths

- How else can you sort the quadrilaterals using descriptions of their sides? parallel sides, perpendicular sides

Give each pair of students a copy of TRB M29, a sheet protector, and dry-erase markers. Students should slip their Venn diagram in the sheet protector and write labels for their Venn diagram on it. Then, they should sort the six quadrilaterals on the Venn diagram. Challenge students to find two rules that will put figures inside all three parts of the circles. Suggest that students can also sort quadrilaterals by name; for example, those that are parallelograms.

Some possible sorting rules are:

- parallelograms/all sides of equal length

- at least one pair of parallel sides/exactly two sides of equal length

- at least one pair of perpendicular sides/at least one pair of sides of equal length

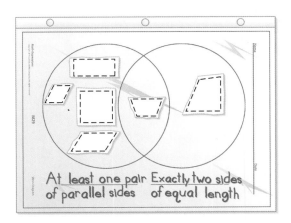

▶ **Classify Quadrilaterals** WHOLE CLASS

Give each pair a copy of TRB M32. The first quadrilateral has two perpendicular adjacent sides of the same length. If you haven't taught trapezoids, they may not know the name of the sixth quadrilateral, but they can still use it for sorting. It is an isosceles trapezoid. Make sure students notice that it has two sides of equal length and one pair of parallel sides.

Have students cut out the six quadrilaterals from TRB M32.

Ask students to note the sides of the quadrilaterals and mark sides of equal length, opposite parallel sides, and adjacent perpendicular sides.

Classify Quadrilaterals   **167**

Teaching the Lesson (continued)

Activity 2

Draw Quadrilaterals

 20 MINUTES

Goal: Draw quadrilaterals that match given descriptions.

Materials: Student Activity Book or Hardcover Book p. 64, centimeter rulers (1 per student), MathBoard materials, geoboards and rubber bands

✓ **NCTM Standard:**
Geometry

▶ Draw Quadrilaterals If Possible

WHOLE CLASS

Re-direct students' attention to Student Book page 64 and read aloud the direction for exercises 13–17. Have students complete these exercises using the **Solve and Discuss** structure. If necessary, students can refer to the chart you completed on the board.

Make sure presenters explain the reasoning they used to draw the figure or to decide that drawing it is impossible. For a sample of classroom dialogue, see **Math Talk in Action** in next column.

 Math Talk in Action

Can you draw the figure in exercise 13?

Aretha: Yes. A parallelogram is a quadrilateral where both pairs of opposite sides are parallel. You can draw a quadrilateral that isn't a parallelogram by drawing a quadrilateral with opposite sides that are not parallel.

What about the figure in exercise 14?

Jeffrey: A square is a rectangle with four square corners, so it is impossible to draw a square that is not a rectangle.

Can you draw the figure in exercise 15?

Diego: Yes. A rectangle is a parallelogram with four square corners. You can draw a parallelogram that isn't a rectangle by drawing a parallelogram that does not have four square corners.

Is the figure in exercise 16 possible?

Alison: Yes. A square is a rectangle with all sides the same length. You can draw a rectangle that is not a square if you draw a rectangle that does not have four sides of the same length.

What about the last figure?

Hoy: It's impossible. The table we completed shows that a rhombus is a parallelogram with some other features. You can't draw a rhombus that is not a parallelogram.

 Alternate Approach

Geoboards Have students use rubber bands to make quadrilaterals on geoboards.

 Ongoing Assessment

Ask students to draw a quadrilateral that is not a parallelogram and then to explain why the quadrilateral cannot be a square or a rectangle.

 Quick Quiz

See Assessment Guide for Unit 2 Quick Quiz.

② Going Further

Differentiated Instruction

Intervention   Activity Card 2-5

Make a Quadrilateral   Activity Card 2-5 ●

Work: In pairs

Use:
- 2 short straws of equal length

- 2 long straws of equal length

1. **Work Together** Use four straws. Try to make and name as many quadrilaterals as you can. Begin with the list below.
   - Quadrilateral
   - Rectangle
   - Parallelogram
   - Square
   - Rhombus

2. **Analyze** Is it possible to make all the figures in the list? If not, explain why not. It is not possible to make the square or the rhombus because you need 4 equal lengths to make both figures.

Unit 2, Lesson 5   Copyright © Houghton Mifflin Company

Activity Note Have students describe the properties of each shape that they make to justify its name.

 Math Writing Prompt

Draw a Picture Draw a parallelogram that is not a rectangle. Explain why it is not a rectangle.

 **Software Support**

Warm Up 35.22

On Level   Activity Card 2-5

Fold Figures   Activity Card 2-5 ▲

Work: In pairs

Use:
- TRB M32 (Quadrilaterals)
- 2 pairs of scissors

1. **Work Together** Find shapes that can be folded into two shapes that are congruent.

2. Cut out each of the following shapes:
   - A square
   - A rhombus that is not a square
   - A rectangle that is not a square
   - A parallelogram that is not a rectangle or rhombus

3. Try to fold each shape in half so that each shape exactly covers the other half.

4. Is there a shape that cannot be folded into two equal shapes? If yes, name the shape. Parallelogram that is not a rectangle or rhombus

Unit 2, Lesson 5   Copyright © Houghton Mifflin Company

Activity Note This activity explores properties of quadrilaterals related to symmetry and congruence.

 Math Writing Prompt

You Decide Write as many true sentences as possible. Copy the sentence and replace the blanks with the words *quadrilateral, parallelogram, rhombus, square,* or *rectangle*.

A_____ is a special kind of _____.

 Software Support

Shapes Ahoy: Ship Shapes, Level L

Challenge   Activity Card 2-5

Investigate Math   Activity Card 2-5 ■

Work: In pairs

1. **Work Together** Explore quadrilaterals.

2. If two sides of a quadrilateral are parallel, what can you say about the lines drawn to extend those sides? They never meet.

3. Look at the figure below. Is it possible to extend the sides of a quadrilateral to show perpendicular lines? Copy the figure and use it to explain your answer.

Unit 2, Lesson 5   Copyright © Houghton Mifflin Company

Activity Note Ask students to define *parallel* and *perpendicular* before they begin the activity.

 Math Writing Prompt

Explain Your Thinking Draw a trapezoid (a quadrilateral with two sides parallel and two sides not parallel). In a trapezoid, can two sides of the same length be parallel? Explain how a trapezoid can have three sides of the same length.

 DESTINATION Math® **Software Support**

Course II: Module 3: Unit 1: Area

③ Homework and Spiral Review

Homework **Goal:** Additional Practice

✓ Include students' completed Homework page as part of their portfolios.

Remembering **Goal:** Spiral Review

This Remembering activity is appropriate anytime after today's lesson.

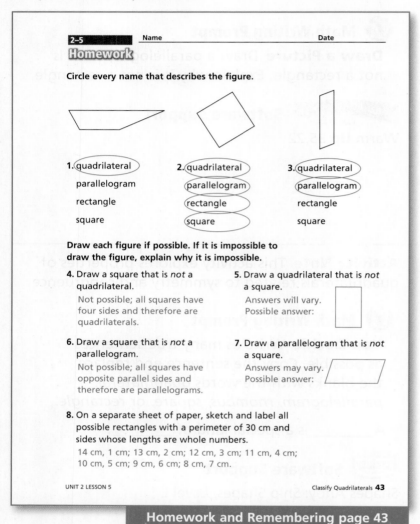

2-5	Name	Date

Homework

Circle every name that describes the figure.

1. (quadrilateral)
   parallelogram
   rectangle
   square

2. quadrilateral
   (parallelogram)
   (rectangle)
   (square)

3. (quadrilateral)
   (parallelogram)
   rectangle
   square

Draw each figure if possible. If it is impossible to draw the figure, explain why it is impossible.

4. Draw a square that is *not* a quadrilateral.
   Not possible; all squares have four sides and therefore are quadrilaterals.

5. Draw a quadrilateral that is *not* a square.
   Answers will vary.
   Possible answer:

6. Draw a square that is *not* a parallelogram.
   Not possible; all squares have opposite parallel sides and therefore are parallelograms.

7. Draw a parallelogram that is *not* a square.
   Answers may vary.
   Possible answer:

8. On a separate sheet of paper, sketch and label all possible rectangles with a perimeter of 30 cm and sides whose lengths are whole numbers.
   14 cm, 1 cm; 13 cm, 2 cm; 12 cm, 3 cm; 11 cm, 4 cm; 10 cm, 5 cm; 9 cm, 6 cm; 8 cm, 7 cm.

UNIT 2 LESSON 5 — Classify Quadrilaterals **43**

Homework and Remembering page 43

2-5	Name	Date

Remembering

Add or subtract.

1.	682 + 245 927	2.	$6.94 + 1.29 $8.23	3.	600 − 187 413
4.	877 − 491 386	5.	2,784 + 3,725 6,509	6.	4,562 − 784 3,778

Solve each problem.   *Show your work.*

7. Waleed barbecued some turkey burgers. He had 16 buns. He put a burger on each bun and had 5 buns left over. How many burgers did he cook?
   ___11 burgers___

8. The drama club sold too many tickets to the play. 782 people bought tickets. 37 people had to stand because there were not enough seats. How many seats are in the auditorium?
   ___745 seats___

9. Sara had $5.00 to buy lunch. She spent $3.49. How much does she have left?
   ___$1.51___

44 UNIT 2 LESSON 5 — Classify Quadrilaterals

Homework and Remembering page 44

Home or School Activity

Social Studies Connection

Quadrilaterals in Architecture Have students look for and list examples of quadrilaterals in buildings. They can look first in books like Sally Morgan's *Squares and Cubes* (Thomson Learning, 1994) and then in their community.

> Quadrilaterals in my Neighborhood
>
> The windows at the community center are squares.
>
> The bricks on my house are rectangles.
>
> The border on the carpet at the library has a pattern made of parallelograms.

Unit Review and Test

Lesson Objective

● **Assess student progress on unit objectives.**

The Day at a Glance

Today's Goals	Materials
1 **Assessing the Unit** ▶ Assess student progress on unit objectives. ▶ Use activities from unit lessons to reteach content. **2** **Extending the Assessment** ▶ Use remediation for common errors. There is no homework assignment on a test day.	Unit 2 Test, Student Activity Book pp. 65–66 or Hardcover Book pp. 65–66 and Activity Workbook pp. 25–26 Unit 2 Test, Form A or B, Assessment Guide (optional) Unit 2 Performance Assessment, Assessment Guide (optional)

Keeping Skills Sharp

Daily Routines 5 MINUTES	
If you are doing a unit review day, go over the homework. If this is a test day, omit the homework review.	**Review and Test Day** You may want to choose a quiet game or other activity (reading a book or working on homework for another subject) for students who finish early.

Assessing the Unit

Assess Unit Objectives

⏱ **45 MINUTES** (more if schedule permits)

Goal: Assess student progress on unit objectives.

Materials: Student Activity Book pp. 65–66 or Hardcover Book pp. 65–66 and Activity Workbook pp. 25–26; Assessment Guide (optional)

▶ Review and Assessment

If your students are ready for assessment on the unit objectives, you may use either the test on the Student Activity Book pages or one of the forms of the Unit 2 Test in the Assessment Guide to assess student progress.

If you feel that students need some review first, you may use the test on the Student Activity Book pages as a review of unit content, and then use one of the forms of the Unit 2 Test in the Assessment Guide to assess student progress.

To assign a numerical score for all of these test forms, use 10 points for each question.

You may also choose to use the Unit 2 Performance Assessment. Scoring for that assessment can be found in its rubric in the Assessment Guide.

▶ Reteaching Resources

The chart lists the test items, the unit objectives they cover, and the lesson activities in which the objective is covered in this unit. You may revisit these activities with students who do not show mastery of the objectives.

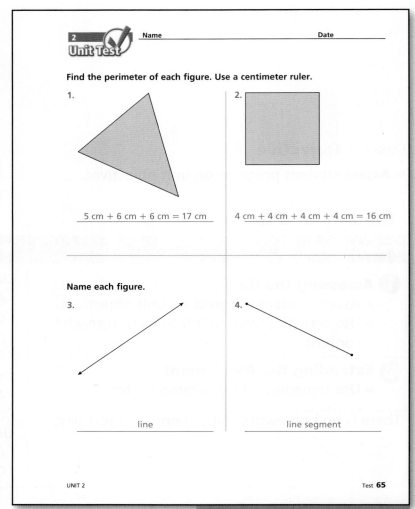

Student Activity Book page 65

Unit Test Items	Unit Objectives Tested	Activities to Use for Reteaching
1, 2	**2.1** Measure and draw line segments to the nearest centimeter and find the perimeter of geometric figures.	Lesson 1, Activities 1 and 2
3, 4, 9, 10	**2.2** Identify lines and line segments.	Lesson 2, Activity 1
5–8	**2.3** Identify and classify quadrilaterals.	Lesson 3, Activity 4 Lesson 5, Activity 1

Student Activity Book page 66

2 Unit Test ✓

Name _____ Date _____

Put a check mark beside every name that describes the figure.

5.

- ☑ quadrilateral
- ☐ not a quadrilateral
- ☑ rectangle
- ☑ square

6.

- ☑ quadrilateral
- ☐ not a quadrilateral
- ☑ rectangle
- ☐ square

7.

- ☑ quadrilateral
- ☐ not a quadrilateral
- ☐ rectangle
- ☐ square

8.

- ☐ quadrilateral
- ☑ not a quadrilateral
- ☐ rectangle
- ☐ square

9. Draw two perpendicular line segments on the dot array.

Sample drawing shown.

10. **Extended Response** Explain what it means for two line segments to be parallel. Draw an example.

Answers may vary. Sample response: Line segments that are parallel
never meet, even if they are extended as lines forever in either
direction.   Example: _____

▶ Assessment Resources

Free Response Tests
Unit 2 Test, Student Book pages 65–66
Unit 2 Test, Form A, Assessment Guide

Extended Response Item
The last item in the Student Activity Book test and in the Form A test will require an extended response as an answer.

Multiple Choice Test
Unit 2 Test, Form B, Assessment Guide

Performance Assessment
Unit 2 Performance Assessment, Assessment Guide
Unit 2 Performance Assessment Rubric, Assessment Guide

▶ Portfolio Assessment

Teacher-selected Items for Student Portfolios:

- Homework, Lessons 3, 5
- Class Activity work, Lessons 2, 4

Student-selected Items for Student Portfolios

- Favorite Home or School Activity
- Best Writing Prompt

② Extending the Assessment

Unit Objective 2.1
Measure and draw line segments to the nearest centimeter and find the perimeter of geometric figures.

Common Error: Uses a Ruler Incorrectly

Students may not line up 0 on the ruler with the endpoint of a line to be measured.

Remediation The exact location of 0 may vary from one ruler to another. Make sure students know where the 0 indicator of their ruler is. If necessary, have them write a 0 on the ruler itself.

Common Error: Doesn't Use All Measurements

In finding perimeter, students may fail to use the lengths of all sides of a polygon.

Remediation Remind students that the number of addends used to find the perimeter must equal the number of sides of the polygon. Suggest that it may help to count the sides and the addends as a check that all sides have been included.

Unit Objective 2.2
Identify lines and line segments.

Common Error: Confuses Lines and Line Segments

Students may say line segments are lines, especially if the endpoints are not specifically marked.

Remediation Explain to students that lines are of infinite (or endless) length. You can't draw a whole line, so you represent a line on paper by putting an arrowhead at each end of a line segment. The arrowheads show that the line continues without end in each direction. Also point out that line segments have endpoints and have length (the distance between the endpoints). Endpoints do not have to be marked, but they are sometimes shown as points at each end or tick marks at each end.

Line segment *AB*

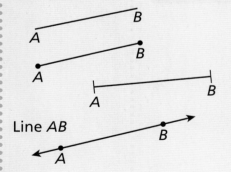

Line *AB*

Unit Objective 2.3
Identify and classify quadrilaterals.

Common Error: Doesn't Identify Irregular 4-Sided Figures as Quadrilaterals

Students usually recognize 4-sided figures such as squares, rectangles (that are not squares), parallelograms, trapezoids, and rhombuses. These routine figures may lead them to believe that irregular 4-sided figures are not quadrilaterals.

Remediation Remind students that "quad" means "four" and that any closed 4-sided figure is a quadrilateral.

Common Error: Doesn't Differentiate Types of Figures

Students may not classify a square or a rectangle as a parallelogram, or classify a square as a rhombus.

Remediation Make side-by-side lists comparing the properties of the different figures, including the kinds of line segments used to make each figure. Remind them that all the basic properties of parallelograms are shared by squares and rectangles, and that the properties of rhombuses are shared by squares.

Addition and Subtraction Word Problems

THE GOAL FOR UNIT 3 is for students to develop effective strategies to solve many types of addition and subtraction word problems involving both single and multi-digit numbers. Students will solve addition and subtraction word problems that involve a total and two partners. One of these three numbers will be unknown. The lessons present a number of math tools that are useful for organizing information in word problems to find the solution.

Skills Trace

Grade 2	Grade 3	Grade 4
• Explore the relationship between addition and subtraction.	• Review the relationship between addition and subtraction.	• Review the relationship between addition and subtraction.
• Represent and solve multi-digit two-step word problems with unknown starts and partners.	• Represent and solve multi-digit, multi-step word problems with unknown starts and partners.	• Represent, solve and write multi-digit, multi-step change and collection word problems.
• Interpret and solve multi-digit comparison word problems.	• Interpret and solve multi-digit comparison word problems.	• Interpret, solve, and write multi-digit comparison word problems.

Unit 3   Contents

Unit 3   Assessment

✓ Unit Objectives Tested	Unit Test Items	Lessons
3.1 Solve a variety of word problems involving addition and subtraction.	1–6	1–4, 6–8
3.2 Express relationships as equations and inequalities; Write equations and use comparison bars to represent and solve word problems.	7–10	1–6

Assessment and Review Resources

Formal Assessment

Student Activity Book
- Unit Review and Test (pp. 95–96)

Assessment Guide
- Quick Quizzes (pp. A21, A22)
- Test A–Open Response (pp. A23–A24)
- Test B–Multiple Choice (pp. A25–A26)
- Performance Assessment (pp. A27–A29)

Test Generator CD-ROM
- Open Response Test
- Multiple Choice Test
- Test Bank Items

Informal Assessment

Teacher Edition
- Ongoing Assessment (in every lesson)
- Math Talk (in every lesson)
- Portfolio Suggestions (p. 249)

123 **Math Talk**
- ▸ Math Talk in Action (pp. 188, 225)
- ▸ Solve and Discuss (pp. 177, 178–179, 179, 181, 182–183, 184, 189, 200–201, 202–204, 216, 217, 218, 219, 220, 224, 226, 227, 228, 229, 234, 242, 243)
- ▸ Student Pairs (pp. 205, 230, 238)
  Helping Partners (p. 228)
- ▸ Small Groups (pp. 210, 211)
- ▸ In Activities (pp. 177, 196, 211, 242, 243)

Review Opportunities

Homework and Remembering
- Review of recently taught topics
- Spiral Review

Teacher Edition
- Unit Review and Test (pp. 247–250)

Test Generator CD-ROM
- Custom Review Sheets

Lesson NCTM Focal Points NCTM Standards	Resources	Materials for Lesson Activities	Materials for Going Further
3-1 **Addition and Subtraction Situations** NCTM Standards: 1, 2, 8	TE pp. 175–186 SAB pp. 67–72 H&R pp. 45–46 AC 3-1 MCC 9	✓ MathBoard Materials Chart paper	✓ Number cubes ✓ MathBoard materials Math Journals
3-2 **Word Problems with Unknown Partners** NCTM Standards: 1, 2, 6, 8	TE pp. 187–192 SAB pp. 73–74 H&R pp. 47–48 AC 3-2	✓ MathBoard materials Chart from Lesson 1 Chart paper *A Bundle of Beasts* by Mark Steele	Chart paper Equation Challenge (TRB M33) ✓ Number cubes Markers Math Journals
3-3 **Word Problems with Unknown Starts** NCTM Standards: 1, 2, 6, 8	TE pp. 193–198 SAB pp. 75–76 H&R pp. 47, 49–50 AC 3-3 MCC 10	✓ MathBoard materials	✓ MathBoard materials Index cards Math Journals
3-4 **Comparison Problems** NCTM Standards: 1, 6, 8	TE pp. 199–208 SAB pp. 77–78 H&R pp. 51–52 AC 3-4	✓ MathBoard materials	✓ Number cubes Spinner B (TRB M35) Paper clips Hundred Chart (TRB M34) ✓ Two-color counters Game Cards (TRB M25) Math Journals
3-5 **Comparison Problems with Misleading Language** NCTM Standards: 1, 6, 8	TE pp. 209–214 SAB pp. 79–80 H&R pp. 53–54 AC 3-5 MCC 11 AG Quick Quiz 1	✓ MathBoard materials	✓ Two-color counters Game cards (TRB 25) Math Journals
3-6 **Multi-Digit Unknown Partner and Unknown Partner Start Problems** NCTM Focal Point: 7.5 NCTM Standards: 1, 2, 6, 10	TE pp. 215–222 SAB pp. 81–84 H&R pp. 55–56 AC 3-6	✓ MathBoard materials	✓ MathBoard materials Calculators Math Journals

Resources/Materials Key: TE: Teacher Edition   SAB: Student Activity Book   H&R: Homework and Remembering
AC: Activity Cards   MCC: Math Center Challenge   AG: Assessment Guide   ✓: Grade 3 kits   TRB: Teacher's Resource Book

NCTM Standards and Expectations Key: **1.** Number and Operations **2.** Algebra **3.** Geometry
4. Measurement **5.** Data Analysis and Probability **6.** Problem Solving **7.** Reasoning and Proof
8. Communication **9.** Connections **10.** Representation

Lesson NCTM Focal Points NCTM Standards	Resources	Materials for Lesson Activities	Materials for Going Further
3-7 **Multi-Digit Comparison Problems** NCTM Focal Point: 7.5 NCTM Standards: 1, 2, 6, 10	TE pp. 223–232 SAB pp. 85–88 H&R pp. 57–58 AC 3-7	✓ MathBoard materials	✓ Number cubes Two-color counters Cross Number Puzzle (TRB M37) Calculators Math Journals
3-8 **Mixed Multi-Digit Word Problems** NCTM Focal Point: 7.5 NCTM Standards: 1, 6, 7, 10	TE pp. 233–240 SAB pp. 89–92 H&R pp. 59–60 MCC 12 ✓ AC 3-8 AG Quick Quiz 2	✓ MathBoard materials	✓ MathBoard materials Math Journals
3-9 **Use Mathematical Processes** NCTM Standards: 6, 7, 8, 9, 10	TE pp. 241–246 SAB pp. 93–94 H&R pp. 61–62 AC 3-9	Stopwatch or watch Ruler Calculators	✓ MathBoard materials Number cubes Math Journals
1Unit Review and Test	TE pp. 247–250 SAB pp. 95–96 AG Unit 3 Tests		

Hardcover Student Book

- Together, the Hardcover Student Book and its companion Activity Workbook contain all of the pages in the consumable Student Activity Book.

Manipulatives and Materials

- Essential materials for teaching *Math Expressions* are available in the Grade 3 kits. These materials are indicated by a ✓ in these lists. At the front of this Teacher Edition is more information about kit contents, alternatives for the materials, and use of the materials.

Independent Learning Activities

Ready-Made Math Challenge Centers

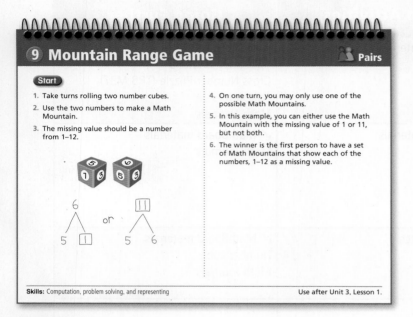

9 Mountain Range Game — Pairs

Start

1. Take turns rolling two number cubes.
2. Use the two numbers to make a Math Mountain.
3. The missing value should be a number from 1–12.
4. On one turn, you may only use one of the possible Math Mountains.
5. In this example, you can either use the Math Mountain with the missing value of 1 or 11, but not both.
6. The winner is the first person to have a set of Math Mountains that show each of the numbers, 1–12 as a missing value.

Skills: Computation, problem solving, and representing

Use after Unit 3, Lesson 1.

Grouping Pairs

Materials 2 number cubes

Objective Students create and solve open equations from numbers rolled on number cubes.

Connections Computation and Representation

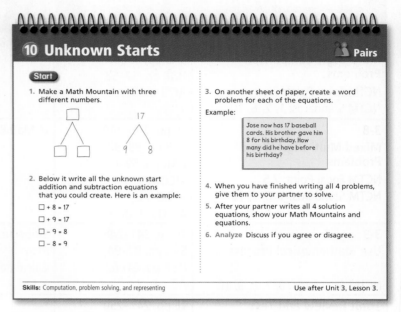

10 Unknown Starts — Pairs

Start

1. Make a Math Mountain with three different numbers.
2. Below it write all the unknown start addition and subtraction equations that you could create. Here is an example:

   $\square + 8 = 17$
   $\square + 9 = 17$
   $\square - 9 = 8$
   $\square - 8 = 9$

3. On another sheet of paper, create a word problem for each of the equations.

   Example:

   > Jose now has 17 baseball cards. His brother gave him 8 for his birthday. How many did he have before his birthday?

4. When you have finished writing all 4 problems, give them to your partner to solve.
5. After your partner writes all 4 solution equations, show your Math Mountains and equations.
6. Analyze Discuss if you agree or disagree.

Skills: Computation, problem solving, and representing

Use after Unit 3, Lesson 3.

Grouping Pairs

Materials None

Objective Students create and solve open equations and word problems from a Math Mountain.

Connections Computation and Reasoning

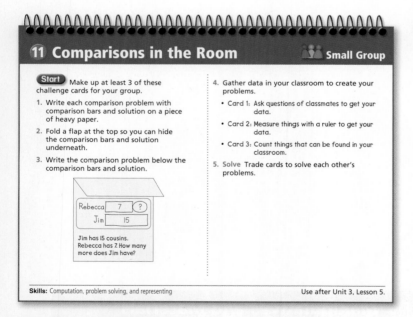

11 Comparisons in the Room — Small Group

Start Make up at least 3 of these challenge cards for your group.

1. Write each comparison problem with comparison bars and solution on a piece of heavy paper.
2. Fold a flap at the top so you can hide the comparison bars and solution underneath.
3. Write the comparison problem below the comparison bars and solution.

   Rebecca 7 ?
   Jim 15

   Jim has 15 cousins. Rebecca has 7. How many more does Jim have?

4. Gather data in your classroom to create your problems.
   • Card 1: Ask questions of classmates to get your data.
   • Card 2: Measure things with a ruler to get your data.
   • Card 3: Count things that can be found in your classroom.
5. Solve Trade cards to solve each other's problems.

Skills: Computation, problem solving, and representing

Use after Unit 3, Lesson 5.

Grouping Small Group

Materials Heavy paper, ruler

Objective Students collect data and use it to create comparison problems and bars.

Connections Computation and Problem Solving

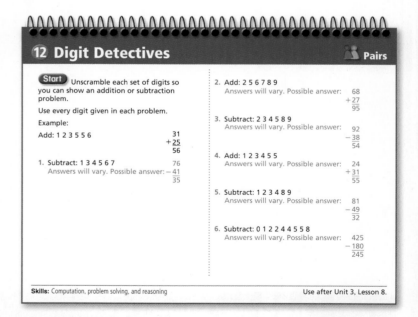

12 Digit Detectives — Pairs

Start Unscramble each set of digits so you can show an addition or subtraction problem.
Use every digit given in each problem.

Example:

Add: 1 2 3 5 5 6
$$\begin{array}{r} 31 \\ +25 \\ \hline 56 \end{array}$$

1. Subtract: 1 3 4 5 6 7
   Answers will vary. Possible answer:
   $$\begin{array}{r} 76 \\ -41 \\ \hline 35 \end{array}$$

2. Add: 2 5 6 7 8 9
   Answers will vary. Possible answer:
   $$\begin{array}{r} 68 \\ +27 \\ \hline 95 \end{array}$$

3. Subtract: 2 3 4 5 8 9
   Answers will vary. Possible answer:
   $$\begin{array}{r} 92 \\ -38 \\ \hline 54 \end{array}$$

4. Add: 1 2 3 4 5 5
   Answers will vary. Possible answer:
   $$\begin{array}{r} 24 \\ +31 \\ \hline 55 \end{array}$$

5. Subtract: 1 2 3 4 8 9
   Answers will vary. Possible answer:
   $$\begin{array}{r} 81 \\ -49 \\ \hline 32 \end{array}$$

6. Subtract: 0 1 2 2 4 4 5 5 8
   Answers will vary. Possible answer:
   $$\begin{array}{r} 425 \\ -180 \\ \hline 245 \end{array}$$

Skills: Computation, problem solving, and reasoning

Use after Unit 3, Lesson 8.

Grouping Pairs

Materials None

Objective Students use reasoning to create addition and subtraction problems from given digits.

Connections Computation and Reasoning

Ready-Made Math Resources

Technology — Tutorial, Practice, and Intervention

Use online, individualized intervention and support to bring students to proficiency.

Help students practice skills and apply concepts through exciting math adventures.

Extend and enrich students' understanding of skills and concepts through engaging, interactive lessons and activities.

Visit **Education Place®**
www.eduplace.com

Visit www.eduplace.com/mx2t/ and find family, teacher, and student materials, activities, games, and more.

Literature Links

One Less Fish

One Less Fish
Prepare to explore the deep blue sea where fish will dazzle your eyes as they swim across the pages of this unique book by Kim Michelle Toft and Allen Sheather. Illustrations will inspire children to think up addition and subtraction word problems, which could then be written and illustrated using bold colors.

Literature Connection
A Bundle of Beasts, by Mark Steele and Patricia Hooper, illustrated by Mark Steele (Houghton Mifflin, 1987)

Unit 3   Teaching Resources

Differentiated Instruction

Individualizing Instruction

Activities	Level	Frequency
	• Intervention • On Level • Challenge	All 3 in every lesson
Math Writing Prompts	Level	Frequency
	• Intervention • On Level • Challenge	All 3 in every lesson
Math Center Challenges	For advanced students	
	4 in every unit	

Reaching All Learners

English Language Learners	Lessons	Pages
	1, 2, 3, 4, 5, 6, 7, 8, 9	178, 190, 196, 201, 211, 218, 227, 235, 243
Extra Help	Lessons	Pages
	1, 2, 3, 4, 5, 7	183, 189, 194, 201, 206, 211, 226, 229, 230
Special Needs	Lesson	Page
	6	220
Alternate Approach	Lesson	Pages
	1	180, 183

Strategies for English Language Learners

Present this problem to all students. Offer the different levels of support to meet students' levels of language proficiency.

Objective Introduce solving word problems with unknowns.

Problem Write a word problem on the board. *Peter has 5 cookies. Before lunch he had 12. How many cookies did Peter eat?* Model the equation $5 + \square = 12$.

Newcomer

• Say: **5 is the start addend. The total is 12. We don't know the other addend.**

• **The box is the *unknown* addend.**

Beginning

• Say: **Now Peter has ___.** 5 cookies **The start addend is 5. We don't know how many cookies Peter ate. It is *unknown*.**

• Say: **Before lunch Peter had ___.** 12 cookies **The total is ___.** 12

Intermediate

• Ask: **What do we know?** Peter has 5 cookies now. He had 12 before lunch. **What don't we know?** How many cookies Peter ate

• Say: **We put together 5 and the *unknown* number to get 12.**

Advanced

• Help students identify the known addend and total. Ask: **Do we know the second addend?** no Say: **It is *unknown*.**

• Ask: **Do we add or subtract the unknown to find the total?** add

Connections

 Literature Connection
Lesson 2, page 192

 Sports Connection
Lesson 3, page 198

 Science Connections
Lesson 4, page 208
Lesson 7, page 232

 Real-World Connection
Lesson 5, page 214

 Language Arts Connection
Lesson 6, page 222

 Art Connection
Lesson 8, page 240

 Social Studies Connection
Lesson 9, page 246

Math Background

Putting Research into Practice for Unit 3

From our Curriculum Research Project: The Meaning and Structure of Word Problems

Word problems form an essential part of the *Math Expressions* curriculum. They reinforce one of the program's main goals: the integration of student's real-world experiences with math concepts. In this unit, students are encouraged to analyze the meaning and structure of different types of addition and subtraction word problems. When analyzing word problems, students are encouraged to look for patterns in the structure of the problems in order to find solution methods.

Research has found that students approach word problems in different ways, and they use various strategies to solve word problems. Some students will use tools such as Math Mountains, equations, and Comparison bars, while others invent methods to solve the word problem.

Because students may use various methods to solve word problems, it is important to use the **Solve and Discuss** structure to have students explain their strategies and solution methods. If students have difficulty explaining their work or are prone to error, others can model other accessible methods for students to use

—Karen Fuson, Author
  Math Expressions

From Current Research: Different Types of Word Problems

Four basic classes of addition and subtraction problems can be identified: problems involving (a) joining, (b) separating, (c) part-part-whole relations, and (d) comparison relations. Problems within a class involve the same type of action or relation, but within each class several distinct types of problems can be identified depending on which quantity is the unknown.

. . . Children's proficiency [in solving problems] gradually develops in two significant directions. One is from having a different solution method for each type of problem to developing a single general method that can be used for classes of problems with a similar mathematical structure. Another direction is toward more efficient calculation procedures. . . . For word problems, these procedures are essentially abstractions of direct modeling that continue to reflect the actions and relations in the problems.

National Research Council. "Developing Proficiency with Whole Numbers." *Adding It Up: Helping Children Learn Mathematics.* Washington, D.C.: National Academy Press, 2001. pp. 184, 186.

Other Useful References: Addition and Subtraction Word Problems

Carpenter, Thomas P., Fennema, E., Franke, M.L., Empson, S.B., & Levi, L.W. *Children's Mathematics: Cognitively Guided Instruction.* Portsmouth, NH: Heinemann, 1999.

Carpenter, Thomas P. "Learning to add and subtract: An exercise in problem solving." *Teaching and learning mathematical problem solving: Multiple research perspectives,* E.A. Silver (Ed.). Hillsdale, NJ: Erlbaum, 1985. pp. 17–40.

Getting Ready to Teach Unit 3

In this unit, students are encouraged to analyze the meaning and structure to addition and subtraction word problems. As they integrate real-world experiences with problem solving, they will develop effective strategies to solve different types of word problems.

Representing Word Problems

Writing Equations
Lessons 1, 2, 3, 6, and 8

One way students represent a word problem in this unit is with a situation equation.

A *situation equation* shows the action or the relationships in a problem.

Then, they may rewrite the situation equation as a solution equation.

A *solution equation* shows the operation that is performed to solve the problem.

When the numbers in a problem are small, students may be able to find the answer from a situation equation without having to write and solve a solution equation. When the numbers are greater (such as the multi-digit numbers in later units) or the situation is more complex, many students will find it helpful to use both equations.

Unknown Partner Problems
Lessons 2, 3, 6, and 8

In "unknown partner" problems, one of the partners is not given—it is unknown. Unknown partners can involve collection situations or change situations, collection situations involve putting together or taking apart in action or conceptually. *Change plus and change minus* problems provide a quantity which is modified by a change—something is added or subtracted—which results in a new quantity.

Put Together
Lessons 1, 2, 3, 6, and 8

Stacy invited 9 girls and some boys to her party. 16 children were invited in all. How many boys were invited?

total
16
/\
9 $\boxed{7}$
girls boys

$9 + \boxed{7} = 16$
girls boys total

Unknown Start Problems
Lessons 3, 6, and 8

In "unknown start" problems, the starting number is the unknown number.

Change Plus
Lessons 1, 2, 3, 6, and 8

Greta's chicken laid some eggs. Then the chicken laid 7 more. Now Greta has 13 eggs. How many eggs did the chicken lay at the start?

total
13
/\
$\boxed{6}$ 7
start more

situation equation:

$\boxed{6} + 7 = 13$
start more now

solution equations:

$7 + \boxed{6} = 13$
$13 - 7 = \boxed{6}$

Patterns in Unknown Partner Problems
Lessons 2, 3, 6, and 8

As students explore the different problem structure described above, they begin to see the following general patterns: If the total is unknown, it can be found by adding the partners. If one of the partners is unknown, it can be found by subtracting the known partner from the total, or adding on from the partner to the total.

As you teach this unit, emphasize understanding of these terms:

Comparison Bars

Math Mountain

situation equation

solution equation

See Glossary on pp. T1–T17.

Take Apart
Lessons 1, 2, 3, 6, and 8

There were 15 people at the park. 7 were playing soccer. The others were playing softball. How many people were playing softball?

total

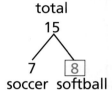

$$15 - 7 = \boxed{8}$$
total   soccer   softball

Change Minus
Lessons 1, 2, 3, 6, and 8

Patricia was carrying some books. Her friend took 3 of them. Patricia has 8 books left. How many books was she carrying at first?

start

situation equation:

$$\boxed{11} - 3 = 8$$
start   friend   now

solution equation:

$$8 + 3 = \boxed{11}$$

Using Math Tools to Represent Word Problems

Student should be encouraged to use a variety of solution strategies for the word problems in this unit. However, the lessons do present math tools that are useful for organizing the information in the problems and finding the solution. These tools become especially important when the focus shifts later in this unit, from word problems with single-digit numbers to those with multi-digit numbers.

Math Tool: Math Mountains
Lessons 1, 2, 3, 6, and 8

Students use Math Mountains to show a total and two partners. The total is written at the top of the mountain, and the partners are written at the bottom. Students can imagine that the total splits into two parts that roll down opposite sides of the mountain. Eight equations can be written for a given Math Mountain.

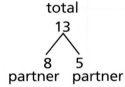

$$13 = 8 + 5 \qquad 8 + 5 = 13$$
$$13 = 5 + 8 \qquad 5 + 8 = 13$$
$$8 = 13 - 5 \qquad 13 - 5 = 8$$
$$5 = 13 - 8 \qquad 13 - 8 = 5$$

Math Tools: Comparison Bars
Lessons 4, 5, 7 and 8

Comparison problems involve one quantity that is more than or less than another quantity. The unknown in a comparison problem may be the smaller quantity, the larger quantity, or the difference between quantities. Making Comparison Bars can help students organize the information in the problem and figure out how to find the unknown.

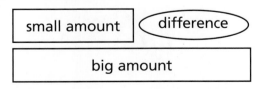

To solve a particular comparison problem, students must ask themselves: *Who has more* (or *fewer*)? and *How many more* (or *fewer*)? They can use this information to label a set of Comparison bars. For example, consider the problem:

Louis ate 14 crackers.

Walt ate 5 fewer crackers than Louis.

How many crackers did Walt eat?

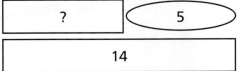

Problem Solving

In *Math Expressions* a research-based, algebraic problem-solving approach that focuses on problem types is used: understand the situation, represent the situation with a math drawing or an equation, solve the problem, and see that the answer makes sense. Lessons that concentrate on developing and applying process skills can be found in every other unit. In this unit students work with problem types and how to solve them.

Use Mathematical Processes
Lesson 9

The NTCM process skills of problem solving, reasoning and proof, communication, connections, and representation are interwoven through all lessons throughout the year. The last lesson of this unit allows students to extend their use of mathematical processes to other situations.

NCTM Process Skill	Activity and Goal
Representation	2: Draw a timeline. 3: Draw examples to support or disprove a problem. 4: Draw a picture to represent a problem.
Communication	2: Share timelines. 3: Express mathematical ideas using correct language. 5: Discuss which solution is correct.
Connections	1: Math and Social Studies: Number Sense and Measurement
Reasoning and Proof	3: Support or disprove statements by using examples. 4: Use a pictorial image to support or disprove a problem. 5: Prove why an answer is correct.
Problem Solving	1: Solve a problem involving measurement. 2: Solve a problem involving a timeline. 3: Solve a problem involving geometry. 4: Draw a picture to solve a problem.

UNIT 3
LESSON
1

Addition and Subtraction Situations

REAL WORLD Problem Solving

Lesson Objectives

● Represent and solve a variety of word problems.

● Review the relationship between addition and subtraction.

Vocabulary

unknown partner	addend
equation	change plus
total	change minus
sum	put together
partner	take apart
equality	expression
inequality	

The Day at a Glance

Today's Goals	Materials	

1 Teaching the Lesson
A1: Discuss Math Mountains.
A2: Review word problems.
A3: Explore equality and inequality.
A4: Explore math language for addition and subtraction equations.
 	
2 Going Further
▶ Differentiated Instruction
 	
3 Homework and Spiral Review
	For Lesson Activities
	Student Activity Book pp. 67–72 or
	  Student Hardcover Book pp. 67–72
	  and Activity Workbook pp. 27–28
	  (includes Family Letter)
	Homework and Remembering
	  pp. 45–46
	MathBoard materials
	Chart paper
		Going Further
		Activity Cards 3-1
		MathBoard materials
		Number cubes
		Math Journals

123 *Use* **Math Talk** *today!*

Keeping Skills Sharp

Quick Practice 🕐 5 MINUTES	Daily Routines
Goal: Find the unknown partner. **Unknown Partner Addition** Write these equations on the board: $9 + \square = 15$ $90 + \square = 150$ $900 + \square = 1,500$ $9 + \square = 17$ $90 + \square = 170$ $900 + \square = 1,700$ Have the **Student Leader** tell the class which equation to complete. Remind the leader to read the box within each equation as "what number." Then, have one student explain the Make a Ten, Make a Hundred, or Make a Thousand strategies. *Leader:* (first equation) Nine plus what number equals 15? *Class:* 9 plus 6 equals 15. *Student:* 9 plus 1 is 10 plus 5 more is 15.	**Function Machine** A function machine subtracts 5 from each input. What is the output when the input is 8? 12? 20? 115? 3; 7; 15; 110

Teaching the Lesson

Discuss Math Mountains

 10 MINUTES

Goal: Discuss Math Mountains.

Materials: Student Activity Book or Hardcover Book p. 67, MathBoard materials

 NCTM Standards:
Number and Operations
Algebra
Communication

Class Management

Math Mountains Students who used *Math Expressions* in a previous grade will be very familiar with Math Mountains. If most of your students understand Math Mountains, you can move through this activity quickly. If they are unfamiliar with them, you may need to spend more than one day on this lesson. Math Mountains are important for solving more complex types of word problems.

The Learning Classroom

Building Concepts To foster algebraic understanding, we associate eight equations, rather than four, with a Math Mountain. It is important for students to see equations with only one number on the left (for example, $11 = 7 + 4$ and $4 = 11 - 7$) as early as possible. In *Math Expressions*, students are introduced to equations such as $5 = 2 + 3$ beginning in kindergarten.

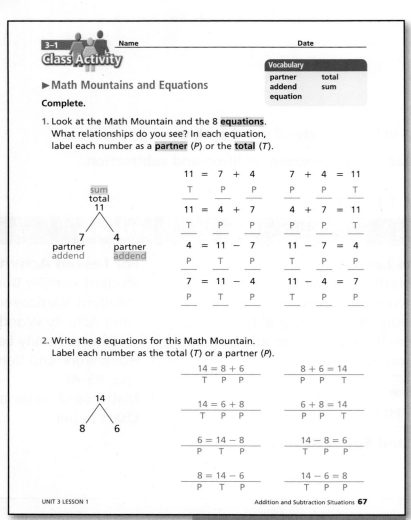

Student Activity Book page 67

▶ Math Mountains and Equations [WHOLE CLASS]

Have students look at the Math Mountain in exercise 1 on Student Book page 67. Explain that a Math Mountain shows the relationship between a total (sum) and its two partners (addends)—that is, the two partners or addends when added equal the total or sum. Eight equations are associated with every Math Mountain.

Discuss the vocabulary associated with Math Mountains.

- **What does the word *partner* or *addend* mean?** one of two numbers that add to make a total

- **How do the two smaller numbers in the Math Mountain work as partners?** They add to make a total.

- **What does *sum* mean?** the result of adding

Discuss the formal math words *addend* and *sum,* relating them to the words *partner* and *total.* Explain that partner and total are used to make the relationships easier to remember.

Ask students how the equations in exercise 1 are related to the Math Mountain and how they are related to one another. Have students label the total and partners in each equation, using the labels *T* and *P.* Then ask students what patterns they notice when they look at where the totals and partners are in the equations.

Have students look at the Math Mountain in exercise 2. Using the **Solve and Discuss** structure, ask them to generate the eight equations associated with it. Tell them to label the partners and total in each equation.

If students need more practice, create additional Math Mountains and have students write the corresponding equations.

123 **Math Talk** Ask questions to check students' understanding of Math Mountains and the corresponding equations:

- **How many numbers does a Math Mountain always have?** 3 numbers

- **Where do we find the total in a Math Mountain?** at the top

- **Where do we find the two partners?** at the bottom

- **Where do we find the total and partners in an addition equation?** The total is on one side of the equals sign, and the two partners are on the other side.

- **Where do we find the total and partners in a subtraction equation?** The total and one partner are on one side, with the total given first, and the other partner is on the other side.

Teaching Note

Language and Vocabulary If your students feel comfortable using the math terms *addend* and *sum,* use those terms instead of *partner* and *total.*

Teaching Note

Math Background When two numbers in a Math Mountain are known, students can find the third number. If the two partners are known, students can add to find the total. If the total and one partner are known, they can subtract or count on to find the *unknown partner.* For example:

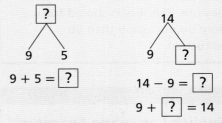

When solving the word problems in Lessons 1–5 of this unit, students will focus on identifying the partners and the total and on using the relationship among these three quantities to find the *unknown number.* In Lessons 6–8, students extend this type of thinking to multi-digit word problems.

Teaching the Lesson (continued)

Activity 2

Introduction to Word Problems

 30 MINUTES

Goal: Review word problems.

Materials: Student Activity Book or Hardcover Book pp. 68–69, MathBoard materials

 NCTM Standards:
Number and Operations
Algebra
Problem Solving
Communication

Class Management

Observing Students Most of the problem types introduced today will be familiar to your students. These activities will give you a chance to observe how your students approach word problems and the strategies they use. This lesson should focus more on discussion than on instruction.

English Language Learners

Review *total, sum, addend,* and *partner.* Write $4 + 8 = 12$ on the board. Say: **Let's draw a Math Mountain.**

- **Beginning** Ask: **Is 12 an** *addend*? no **Is 12 the** *total*? yes Write *sum* above *total.* **Are these the same?** yes **Are 4 and 8** *addends*? yes **Are they** *partners*? yes
- **Intermediate** Ask: **What is the total?** 12 **What is another word for** *total*? sum **What are the addends?** 4 and 8 **What is another word for addend?** partner
- **Advanced** Have students describe the Math Mountain using *addend, partner, total* and *sum.*

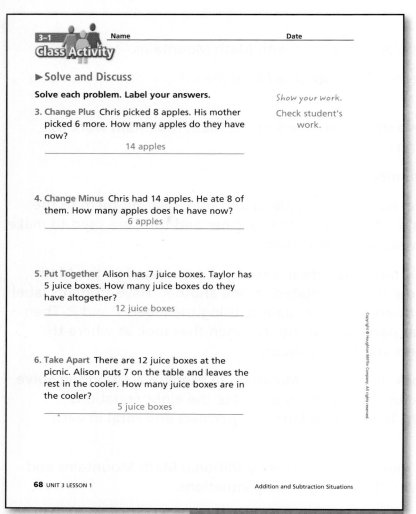

3–1
Class Activity
Name _____ Date _____

▶ **Solve and Discuss**

Solve each problem. Label your answers.

3. **Change Plus** Chris picked 8 apples. His mother picked 6 more. How many apples do they have now?

   ____14 apples____

4. **Change Minus** Chris had 14 apples. He ate 8 of them. How many apples does he have now?

   ____6 apples____

5. **Put Together** Alison has 7 juice boxes. Taylor has 5 juice boxes. How many juice boxes do they have altogether?

   ____12 juice boxes____

6. **Take Apart** There are 12 juice boxes at the picnic. Alison puts 7 on the table and leaves the rest in the cooler. How many juice boxes are in the cooler?

   ____5 juice boxes____

Show your work.

Check student's work.

68 UNIT 3 LESSON 1   Addition and Subtraction Situations

Student Activity Book page 68

▶ **Solve and Discuss** WHOLE CLASS   Math Talk

Read problem 3 on Student Book page 68. Using **Solve and Discuss,** have students solve the problem by making simple drawings on their MathBoards. Although students may not need to make drawings to solve this problem, the drawings can help explain their thinking to their classmates. See sample drawings on the next page.

Here are some drawings students might make.

Math Mountain	Count All
now ↑ T 14 ╱╲ 8　　6 P　　P Chris　Mom	14 now [ooooooo]　[oooooo] Chris　　　　Mom
Equation	**Count On**
8 + 6 = 14 P　P　　T	8 had　[oooooo]　14 　　count on　now 　　6 more

Repeat this process for problem 4.

Here are some drawings students might make.

Math Mountain	Count On to Student
T Chris 14 ╱╲ 8　6 Ate　Now	14 − 8 = ? 8 + ? = 14 8　oooooo 8 + 6 = 14 14 − 8 = 6
Equation	**Use a Drawing**
14 − 8 = 6 T　　P　　P	⊗⊗⊗⊗⊗⊗⊗⊗oooooo 14 − 8 = 6

Next, direct students' attention to the labels for problems 3 and 4. Ask students why they think these problems are labeled *Change Plus* and *Change Minus*. A group of things changes over time because something is either added (*Change Plus*) or taken away (*Change Minus*).

Repeat **Solve and Discuss** for problems 5 and 6. Point out to the class the various solution methods students use (making drawings, writing equations, and so on). Discuss the different ways students labeled their work. Ask students why these problems are labeled *put together* and *take apart*. Two groups of things are put together or a total is taken apart to form two groups.

Activity continued ▶

The Learning Classroom

Building Concepts When solving word problems, it is important that students label their drawings and equations so that they can follow their own thinking and so that others can understand their work. In Change Plus and Change Minus problems, they may want to write action words such as *first, then,* and *now* to help represent the problem situation.

Teaching Note

Watch For! When some students subtract, they start with the total and try to count backward to find the difference. This method is awkward and prone to error. Once students see that subtraction involves finding an unknown partner, they can find the unknown partner by counting on from the known partner to the total. Counting on for subtraction should be encouraged because it is much easier and it makes the connection between subtraction and addition clearer. (The last activity in Unit 1 Lesson 3 reviews subtracting by counting on.)

Alternate Approach

Connecting Cubes In this lesson and in the lessons that follow, students could represent equations with connecting cubes or counters.

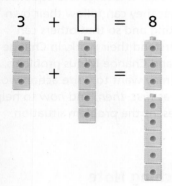

$$3 + \square = 8$$

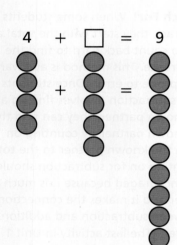

$$4 + \square = 9$$

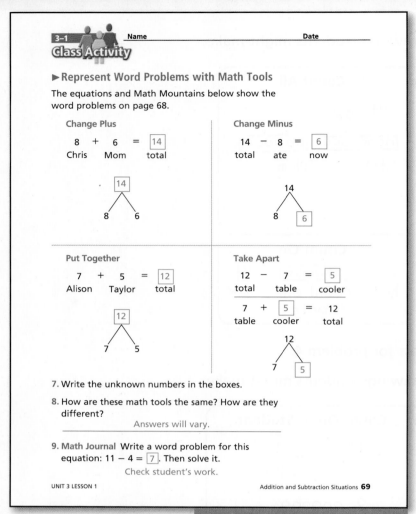

Student Activity Book page 69

▶ Represent Word Problems with Math Tools

WHOLE CLASS

Direct students' attention to the equations and Math Mountains on the top of Student Book page 69. Have students relate these math tools to problems 3–6 on Student Book page 68. Compare the patterns students see in the Math Mountains and the problems. Discuss how they are alike and how they are different.

Be sure students understand that they are finding the unknown partner when they subtract. Have them look at the math tools for a Take Apart problem. Discuss the fact that it is possible to think about this as either an addition or a subtraction problem. Students should understand these points.

● Take Apart as Subtraction: There are a total of 12 juice boxes, and we need to figure out how many are left after we *take away*, or *subtract*, 7.

● Take Apart as Addition: There are 7 juice boxes on the table, and we need to figure out how many boxes we need to *add* to get the total of 12.

Have students complete the page to reinforce the relationships between addition and subtraction problems and between Math Mountains and equations.

▶ Discuss Related Addition and Subtraction Problems WHOLE CLASS Math Talk

Have students look back at problems 3 and 4 on Student Book page 68. Ask them how these problems are related. Discuss that in problem 3 we start with 8 and add 6 to get a total of 14. In problem 4 we start with a total of 14 and take away 8, leaving 6. These problems undo each other.

Next, ask students how the Math Mountains for problems 3 and 4 shown under Change Plus and Change Minus on Student Book page 69 are related. They should notice that in the Math Mountain for problem 3, the total is unknown. In problem 4, a partner is unknown. However, with the unknown numbers filled in, the Math Mountains are the same.

Finally, ask how the equations for problems 3 and 4 shown under Change Plus and Change Minus on Student Book page 69 are related. Discuss the fact that addition and subtraction equations undo each other. In the addition equation, we add two partners to get a total. In the subtraction equation, we start with the total and take away one of the partners to get the other partner. Point out that now that the unknown numbers in the equations are filled in, the partners and totals in the equations are identical.

Have students look back at problems 5 and 6 on Student Activity page 68. Discuss how the problems undo each other.

● In problem 5, we start with 7 and add 5 to get a total of 12. In problem 6, we start with a total of 12 and take away 7, leaving 5.

Ask how the Math Mountains shown under Put Together and Take Apart on Student Activity page 69 are related.

● In the Math Mountain for problem 5, the total is unknown. In the Math Mountain for problem 6, a partner is unknown.

● With the numbers filled in, the Math Mountains are the same.

Ask how the equations for problems 5 and 6 undo each other.

● In the addition equation, we add two partners to get a total.

● In the subtraction equation, we start with a total and take away one of the partners.

① Teaching the Lesson (continued)

Understanding Equality

 20 MINUTES

Goal: Use = and ≠ to make true number sentences.

Materials: Student Activity Book or Hardcover Book p. 70

 NCTM Standards:
Numbers and Operations
Algebra

 Class Management

You can use these exercises as an opportunity for students to practice going to the board quickly and quietly. Emphasize how important it is to save time by doing this quickly and that if students learn to do so, more students can have turns to go to the board.

3–1 Class Activity

Name _____ Date _____

Vocabulary
expression
equation

▶ **Discuss the = and ≠ Signs**

An **expression** is a combination of numbers, variables, and/or operation signs. Expressions do not have an equal sign.

An **equation** is made up of two equal quantities or expressions. An equal sign (=) is used to show that the two sides are equal.

$8 = 5 + 3$ $4 + 2 = 6$ $7 = 7$ $3 + 2 = 2 + 3$ $6 - 2 = 1 + 1 + 2$

The "is not equal to" sign (≠) shows that two quantities are not equal.

$7 \neq 5 + 3$ $4 + 2 \neq 8$ $7 \neq 6$ $6 - 2 \neq 2 + 3$ $5 + 2 \neq 1 + 1 + 3$

10. Use the = sign to write four equations. Vary how many numbers you have on each side.
Equations will vary. _____
_____
_____

11. Use the ≠ sign to write four "is not equal to" statements. Vary how many numbers you have on each side.
Statements will vary. _____
_____
_____

Numbers will vary for inequalities. Descriptions of correct numbers are given.

Write a number to make the number sentence true.

12. $16 = \boxed{7} + 9$ 13. $3 + \boxed{} \neq 12$ 14. $7 + 2 = 2 + \boxed{7}$
Any number except 9.

15. $15 - \boxed{8} = 7$ 16. $\boxed{} \neq 14 - 7$ 17. $6 - 2 \neq 1 + 1 + \boxed{}$
Any number except 7.   Any number except 2.

Write = or ≠ to make a true number sentence.

18. $8 + 2 + 4 \overset{=}{} 9 + 5$ 19. $8 \overset{\neq}{} 6 - 2$ 20. $7 \overset{=}{} 4 + 3$

70 UNIT 3 LESSON 1   Addition and Subtraction Situations

Student Activity Book page 70

▶ Discuss the = and ≠ Signs [WHOLE CLASS] Math Talk

Ask for Ideas Elicit from students what they know about equations.

● What sign does an equation always have? an equals sign

● What does the equal sign show? Possible response: That both sides are equal.

● Are there only numbers in an equation? Explain. No, an equation can have a box for an unknown number

Point out that an equation can have one or more numbers on each side of the equal sign. Write the following on the board as an example.

$$9 - 2 = 1 + 3 + 3$$

$$7 = 7$$

Have students look at the definitions and examples using the "equals" sign and the "is not equal to" sign on Student Activity Book page 70.

Point out and discuss the examples with the "answer" on the left ($8 = 5 + 3$, $7 \neq 5 + 3$. This equation form may be new to some students. It is important for algebraic understanding.

Use **Solve and Discuss** for exercises 10–20. Have some volunteers do exercise 10 at the board while others complete it at their seats. As a class, quickly examine the equations the students wrote at the board. Have students at their seats ask any questions they have of the students at the board. Then ask all students who did not write at least one equation with only one number on the left side to write such an equation.

Send different students to the board and repeat for exercise 11 using the "is not equal to" sign.

Write the following on the board:

$$4 + \square = 11 \qquad 4 + \square \neq 11$$

● What number will make the number sentence on the left true? 7

● What number will make the number sentence on the right true? Any number except 7

Have volunteers give examples of numbers that would make the sentence true and add that number to 4 to prove that it does not equal 11. Then have students complete exercises 12–17. Discuss the results as a class.

Send different students to the board for exercises 18–20 using $=$ or $\neq$. Have volunteers at the board do the additions or subtractions to prove their answers are correct.

Differentiated Instruction

Extra Help Have students make cards showing the $=$ sign and $\neq$ sign. Have students form groups and hold up the appropriate sign. If the groups are of two students each, for example, students should hold up the card with the $=$ sign and say "The groups are equal."

✋ Alternate Approach

Balance Scale Students can use a balance scale and centimeter cubes to model the equations and inequalities.

$$7 \neq 5 + 3$$

Explore Math Language

 10 MINUTES

Goal: Explore math language for addition and subtraction equations.

Materials: Student Activity Book or Hardcover Book p. 68, chart paper

 NCTM Standards:
Number and Operations
Problem Solving
Communication

 Ongoing Assessment

Present the following problem, question, and instructions to the students.

Russ had 12 grapes. He ate 4 of them. How many grapes does he have now?

▶ Is the problem a change plus or a change minus problem?

Then have students:

▶ draw a Math Mountain for the problem,

▶ write an equation for the problem, and

▶ give the solution

 Class Management

Looking Ahead This chart will be used over the next few days, so leave it posted and add new ideas as they emerge.

▶ **Discuss Math Language** WHOLE CLASS   Math Talk

Divide a sheet of chart paper into four sections labeled *Change Plus, Change Minus, Put Together,* and *Take Apart.*

Have students look again at problem 3 on Student Book page 68. Ask students to restate the question in different ways. Possible questions students might generate are:

● What is the total number of apples that they have?

● How many apples do they have altogether?

● How many apples do they have in all?

● How many apples do they have now?

Create a chart like the one below on chart paper. Then fill in the chart with new ways to ask a *change plus* question that were suggested by students. Repeat this process for the other three types of problems. This chart shows some common math questions for each problem type:

Change Plus	Change Minus
What is the total number?	How many are left?
How many altogether?	How many now?
How many in all?	How many remain?
How many now?	How many are still there?
Put Together	**Take Apart**
How many altogether?	How many remain?
How many in all?	How many are left?
How many total?	How many are (the other kind)?

Be sure that **English learners** participate in this important language exercise.

② Going Further

● Intervention   Activity Card 3-I

Roll a Math Mountain   Activity Card 3-1 ●

Work: In pairs

Use:
- 2 number cubes, labeled 0–5 and 1–6
- MathBoard materials

Decide:

Who will be Student 1 and who will be Student 2 for the first round.

1. **Student 1:** Roll both number cubes. Use the numbers to make a Math Mountain as shown. Use the numbers again to write an addition equation on the MathBoard.

2. **Student 2:** Write a related subtraction equation on the MathBoard under the addition equation.

3. **Analyze** In the example above, what other subtraction equation could you write? $9 - 4 = 5$

4. Change roles and repeat the activity three more times.

Unit 3, Lesson 1   Copyright © Houghton Mifflin Company

Activity Note For most pairs of numbers, there are two possible addition equations and two possible subtraction equations.

✎ Math Writing Prompt

Explain How You Know Explain how you can find a missing number in a Math Mountain.

Soar to Success Math ★ Software Support

Warm Up 10.10

▲ On Level   Activity Card 3-I

Math Mountain Equations   Activity Card 3-1 ▲

Work: In pairs

Use:
- 4 number cubes, 2 labeled 1–6 and 2 labeled 4–9
- MathBoard materials

1. **On Your Own** Roll two number cubes. Use the numbers to write as many addition and subtraction equations on your MathBoard as you can. Each equation should have one missing number, as shown in the example.

$2 + 7 = \boxed{9}$ $7 + 2 = \boxed{9}$
$9 - 2 = \boxed{7}$ $\boxed{9} - 7 = 2$

2. Exchange MathBoards with your partner and solve the equations. Then repeat the activity.

3. **Analyze** Is it always possible to write 4 addition and subtraction equations? Explain. No, if the two numbers are the same, you can only write one addition and one subtraction equation.

Unit 3, Lesson 1   Copyright © Houghton Mifflin Company

Activity Note Students can check their work by looking at each equation to be sure that the same two or three numbers are used.

✎ Math Writing Prompt

Compare and Contrast How are a Change Plus problem and a Change Minus problem different? How are they alike?

MegaMath Grades K–6 Software Support

Numberopolis: Carnival Stories, Level H

■ Challenge   Activity Card 3-I

Math Mountain Puzzles   Activity Card 3-1 ■

Work: In pairs

Use:
- 2 number cubes, labeled 1–6 and 4–9
- MathBoard materials

1. **On Your Own** Copy the three blank Math Mountains shown on your MathBoard.

2. Play a game with your partner. Roll both number cubes. Both players use both numbers. The sum or difference of the numbers can be used to fill one blank space on the MathBoard. Or both numbers can be used separately in two blank spaces. If you cannot use both numbers, skip your turn.

3. The first player to fill nine blank spaces wins.

Unit 3, Lesson 1   Copyright © Houghton Mifflin Company

Activity Note Students should not reveal how they will use the two numbers after each roll. After the game ends, the winner's partner checks for errors.

✎ Math Writing Prompt

Explain Your Thinking Joni said, "I can either add or subtract to solve a Take Apart problem." Write an explanation of what Joni means.

✖ DESTINATION Math® Software Support

Course II: Module 2: Unit 1: Sums Less than 100

Addition and Subtraction Situations   **185**

③ Homework and Spiral Review

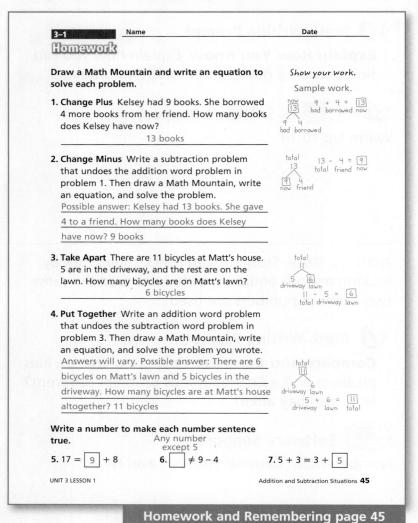

3-1 Homework · Goal: Additional Practice

This Homework page gives students additional practice in solving problems and relating addition and subtraction.

3-1 Homework — Name / Date

Draw a Math Mountain and write an equation to solve each problem.

Show your work.
Sample work.

1. Change Plus Kelsey had 9 books. She borrowed 4 more books from her friend. How many books does Kelsey have now?
13 books

2. Change Minus Write a subtraction problem that undoes the addition word problem in problem 1. Then draw a Math Mountain, write an equation, and solve the problem.
Possible answer: Kelsey had 13 books. She gave 4 to a friend. How many books does Kelsey have now? 9 books

3. Take Apart There are 11 bicycles at Matt's house. 5 are in the driveway, and the rest are on the lawn. How many bicycles are on Matt's lawn?
6 bicycles

4. Put Together Write an addition word problem that undoes the subtraction word problem in problem 3. Then draw a Math Mountain, write an equation, and solve the problem you wrote.
Answers will vary. Possible answer: There are 6 bicycles on Matt's lawn and 5 bicycles in the driveway. How many bicycles are at Matt's house altogether? 11 bicycles

Write a number to make each number sentence true.

Any number except 5

5. $17 = \boxed{9} + 8$

6. $\boxed{} \neq 9 - 4$

7. $5 + 3 = 3 + \boxed{5}$

UNIT 3 LESSON 1 — Addition and Subtraction Situations **45**

Homework and Remembering page 45

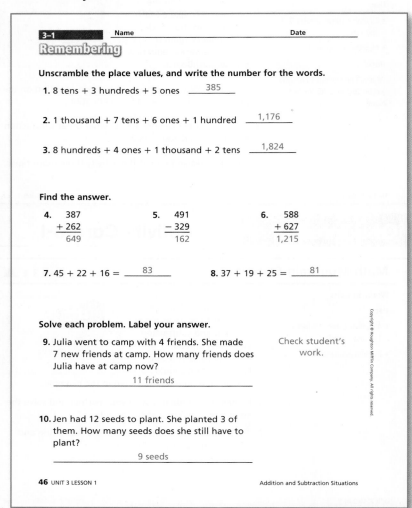

3-1 Remembering · Goal: Spiral Review

This Remembering page would be appropriate anytime after today's lesson.

3-1 Remembering — Name / Date

Unscramble the place values, and write the number for the words.

1. 8 tens + 3 hundreds + 5 ones ____385____

2. 1 thousand + 7 tens + 6 ones + 1 hundred ____1,176____

3. 8 hundreds + 4 ones + 1 thousand + 2 tens ____1,824____

Find the answer.

4.	387	5.	491	6.	588
	+ 262		− 329		+ 627
	649		162		1,215

7. $45 + 22 + 16 = $ ____83____   **8.** $37 + 19 + 25 = $ ____81____

Solve each problem. Label your answer.

9. Julia went to camp with 4 friends. She made 7 new friends at camp. How many friends does Julia have at camp now?
11 friends
Check student's work.

10. Jen had 12 seeds to plant. She planted 3 of them. How many seeds does she still have to plant?
9 seeds

46 UNIT 3 LESSON 1 — Addition and Subtraction Situations

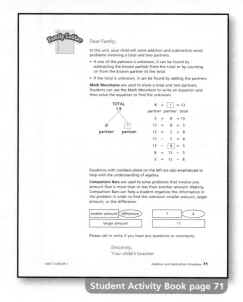

Homework and Remembering page 46

Home and School Connection

Family Letter Have students take home the Family Letter on Student Activity Book page 71 or Activity Workbook page 27. This letter explains how the concept of solving addition and subtraction word problems is developed in *Math Expressions*. It gives parents and guardians a better understanding of the learning that goes on in math class and creates a bridge between school and home. A Spanish translation of this letter is on the following page.

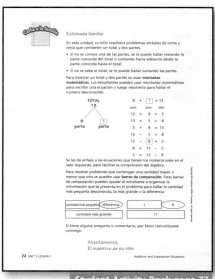

Student Activity Book page 71

Student Activity Book page 72

186 UNIT 3 LESSON 1

Word Problems with Unknown Partners

REAL WORLD Problem Solving

Lesson Objectives

- Represent and solve a variety of word problems.
- Review the relationship between addition and subtraction.

Vocabulary

put together   change plus
take apart   change minus

The Day at a Glance

Today's Goals	Materials
① Teaching the Lesson **A1:** Review the relationship between addition and subtraction. **A2:** Solve word problems with unknown partners. **② Going Further** ▶ Differentiated Instruction **③ Homework and Spiral Review**	**Lesson Activities** Student Activity Book pp. 73–74 or Student Hardcover Book pp. 73–74 Homework and Remembering pp. 47–48 MathBoard materials Chart from Lesson 1 Chart paper A *Bundle of Beasts,* by Mark Steele and Patricia Hooper (Houghton Mifflin, 1987) **Going Further** Activity Cards 3-2 Chart paper Equation Challenge (TRB M33) Number cubes Markers Math Journals 123 *Use* **Math Talk** *today!*

Keeping Skills Sharp

Quick Practice 5 MINUTES	Daily Routines
Goal: Find the unknown partner in addition equations. **Unknown Partner Addition** Write these equations on the board. $9 + \square = 13$ $90 + \square = 130$ $900 + \square = 1{,}300$ $9 + \square = 16$ $90 + \square = 160$ $900 + \square = 1{,}600$ A **Student Leader** directs the class to complete the equations and to explain the Make a Ten, Make a Hundred, or Make a Thousand strategies. (See Unit 3 Lesson 1.)	**Homework Review** Have **Student Pairs** share word problems and solve. **Place Value** Have students write the number for two thousand eight hundred forty and find the number that is 100 more. 2,840; 2,940

Teaching the Lesson

Review Addition and Subtraction Relationships

15 MINUTES

Goal: Review the relationship between addition and subtraction.

Materials: Homework page 45, MathBoard materials, chart from Lesson 1

✓ **NCTM Standards:**
Number and Operations
Problem Solving
Communication

 Math Talk in Action

Write 5 + 7 on the board.

What is the sum?

Clarisse: The sum is 12.

How can you use subtraction to undo the addition?

Gregory: Subtract 7 from 12

Evita: You can also subtract 5 from 12.

Now write 11 − 8 on the board.

What is the difference?

Yuri: 3

How can you use addition to undo the subtraction?

Berta: You can add 3 + 8 or you can add 8 + 3.

► Review How Addition and Subtraction Undo Each Other WHOLE CLASS

Review problems 1–4 from Lesson 1 Homework page 45. Have two or three students present their answers for problems 1 and 2. They should share the Math Mountain and equation for problem 1, the word problem written for problem 2, and the equation and Math Mountain for problem 2.

Here are possible examples of students' answers.

Problem 1: Kelsey had 9 books. She borrowed 4 more books from her friend. How many books does Kelsey have now?

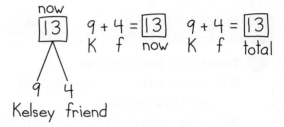

Possible problem for problem 2: Kelsey had 13 books. She gave 4 of the books to a friend. How many books does Kelsey have now?

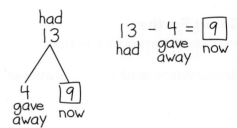

Discuss whether the problem written for problem 2 actually undoes problem 1. Compare the equations and Math Mountains for the two problems. Then repeat the process for problems 3 and 4.

Next, review problem 5. Have students share their new ways of asking the questions. Add any new questions or terms students suggest to the chart your class started in Lesson 1.

Lead students to describe and summarize the relationship between addition and subtraction. See **Math Talk in Action** in side column for a sample of classroom discussion.

Introduce Word Problems with Unknown Partners

 3-2
Class Activity

Name _____ Date _____

▶ **Solve Unknown Partner Word Problems**

Draw a Math Mountain and write and label an equation to solve each problem.

Show your work.
Check student's work.

1. **Put Together: Unknown Partner** Stacy invited 9 girls and some boys to her party. 16 children were invited in all. How many boys were invited?

   _____ 7 boys _____

2. **Take Apart: Unknown Partner** There were 15 people at the park. 7 were playing soccer. The others were playing softball. How many people were playing softball?

   _____ 8 people _____

3. **Change Plus: Unknown Partner** Jan planted 8 tulips last week. Today she planted some lilies. Now she has 17 flowers. How many lilies did she plant?

   _____ 9 lilies _____

4. **Change Minus: Unknown Partner** Tim had 14 tennis balls. Then his brother borrowed some. Now Tim has 6 tennis balls. How many did his brother borrow?

   _____ 8 tennis balls _____

UNIT 3 LESSON 2   Word Problems with Unknown Partners **73**

Student Activity Book page 73

▶ **Solve Unknown Partner Word Problems** | WHOLE CLASS |

Using the **Solve and Discuss** structure, have students solve problem 1 on Student Book page 73. Some students will think of this as an addition, while others will think of it as a subtraction.

$$9 \;+\; \square \;=\; 16 \qquad or \qquad 16 \;-\; 9 \;=\; \square$$

girls   boys   children   children   girls   boys

Ask students why we might call problem 1 an *unknown partner problem.* We don't know one of the partners. It is unknown.

Use **Solve and Discuss** for problems 2–4. Students usually write addition equations for change plus situations (for example, $8 + \square = 17$ for problem 3) and subtraction equations for change minus situations (for example, $14 - \square = 6$ for problem 4). Some students may make math drawings. Leave the equations and Math Mountains on the board.

Activity continued ▶

 40 MINUTES

Goal: Solve word problems with unknown partners.

Materials: Student Activity Book or Hardcover Book pp. 73–74, MathBoard materials, chart paper

✓ **NCTM Standards:**
Number and Operations
Algebra
Problem Solving
Communication

Differentiated Instruction

Extra Help The level of difficulty your students experience with word problems with unknown partners will depend on their familiarity with *Math Expressions,* their reading ability, their English proficiency, and their understanding of addition and subtraction. Help your students, particularly **English Learners,** focus on understanding the situations in the word problems. The math may be easy, but the situations and language may be unfamiliar. Retelling, acting out, or drawing problem situations might be helpful.

 Ongoing Assessment

Circulate around the room as students complete the Math Mountains and equations. Be sure they match the situations described in the word problems. Determine whether student errors stem from misinterpretation of a situation or from incorrect computation.

① Teaching the Lesson (continued)

Teaching Note

Language and Vocabulary Students who are not fluent in English may need extra help with word problems that involve subcategories. Most students will know that *girls* and *boys* belong in the category of *children,* but in other cases the relationship may not be as clear. For example, problem 3 on Student Book page 73 deals with types of flowers, and problem 4 on the Homework page 43 involves types of books. You may want to have the class brainstorm categories that include various subcategories. Make a list of students' ideas on a sheet of chart paper. For example, vehicles include cars, trucks, buses, and boats. Other familiar categories are sports, animals, and food. You can leave the list posted and add to it as you work through the unit.

English Language Learners

Make sure students understand *unknown, put together,* and, *take apart.* Write $5 + \boxed{} = 11$ on the board. Say: **This is an addition equation.** Ask: **Do we *put together* or *take apart*?** put together

- **Beginning** Ask: **Do we know the sum?** yes **Do we know both addends?** no Say: **We know one addend is ___.** 5 **The other addend is *unknown*.**
- **Intermediate** Say: **We *put together* the ___.** partners Ask: **Do we know both partners?** no Say: **One partner is ___.** unknown
- **Advanced** Ask: **What do we *put together*?** the partners **What information is missing?** a partner/an addend Say: **What do we call missing information in an equation?** the unknown

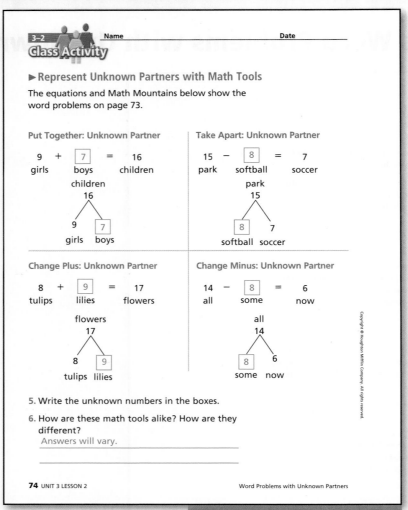

Student Activity Book page 74

▶ Represent Unknown Partners with Math Tools

WHOLE CLASS

Direct students attention to the equations and Math Mountains shown on Student Book page 74, which correspond to problems 1–4. Discuss the relationships students see between these math tools and problems 1–4. Some relationships they might mention are that the Put Together and Change Plus problems both have addition equations and the Take Apart and Change Minus problems both have subtraction equations.

Have students discuss any differences between the Math Mountains and equations they wrote on the board and those on page 74. For example, the order of the partners in the Math Mountains may be different.

If a Math Mountain or equation on the page is not on the board, have a student explain how it models the problem situation. Ask students how they would solve some of the equations.

Have students complete the page to reinforce the relationships between addition and subtraction and between Math Mountains and equations.

② Going Further

Differentiated Instruction

Intervention — Activity Card 3-2

Picture It — Activity Card 3-2 ●

Work: In pairs

Use:
- Chart paper
- Math Journals

1. Copy each problem below into your Math Journal. Then work with your partner to solve them.

> Liz just mailed some party invitations. She'll mail the other 9 after she gets more stamps. She will send 17 invitations in all. How many did Liz already mail?
>
> Liz got a bag of balloons. 7 of them are round. The other 5 are long. How many balloons are in the bag?

2. Design a cartoon, diagram, or other type of drawing to show the main idea of each problem.

3. Make a Math Mountain with labels to show what each box represents. Then write an equation and find the missing number to solve each problem.

Unit 3, Lesson 2   Copyright © Houghton Mifflin Company

Activity Note The unknown start number can be either a total or a partner in the Math Mountain.

 Math Writing Prompt

Explain Your Thinking Identify the partners and the total in this equation: $12 = 5 + 7$. Explain how you know which numbers are the partners and which is the total.

 **Software Support**

Warm Up 10.08

On Level — Activity Card 3-2

Find the Errors — Activity Card 3-2 ▲

Work: On your own

Use:
- Math Journal

1. Each equation below has an error in it. The error can be a wrong number or a wrong symbol.
   - $16 = 8 - 8$
   - $7 - 9 = 16$ $7 \ominus 9 = 16$; $7 + 9 = 16$
   - $14 = 7 + 6$ $14 = 7 + \textcircled{6}$; $14 = 7 + 7$
   - $15 + 7 = 8$ $15 \textcircled{+} 7 = 8$; $15 - 7 = 8$
   - $3 = 10 - 13$ $3 = \textcircled{10} - \textcircled{13}$; $3 = 13 - 10$

2. Copy each equation into your Math Journal. Circle the number or symbol that you need to change to make the equation true.

   $16 = 8 \ominus 8$

3. Then write a true equation.

   $16 = 8 + 8$

Unit 3, Lesson 2   Copyright © Houghton Mifflin Company

Activity Note Be sure that students understand that they can only make one change for each equation.

 Math Writing Prompt

Check for Errors Sonia wrote $15 - 8 = 6$. Explain how you can check if she is correct.

 Software Support

Numberopolis: Carnival Stories, Level O

Challenge — Activity Card 3-2

Equation Challenge — Activity Card 3-2 ■

Work: In pairs

Use:
- TRB M33 (Equation Challenge)
- 2 number cubes labeled 1–6 and 4–9
- 2 different color markers

Decide:
Who will be Student 1 for the first round.

1. Student 1: Roll both number cubes. Use one or both numbers to fill in missing partners or totals, or to begin a new equation on the grid.

2. If you cannot use at least one number, you lose your turn.

3. Continue taking turns until time runs out. The player who has filled in more squares wins.

Unit 3, Lesson 2   Copyright © Houghton Mifflin Company

Activity Note If students complete the grid before time runs out, the game ends. The student with the greater number of squares filled in wins.

 Math Writing Prompt

Relate Use a subtraction equation to solve $22 = \square + 10$. Explain your thinking.

 Software Support

Course II: Module 2: Unit 1: Differences within 100

Word Problems with Unknown Partners   **191**

③ Homework and Spiral Review

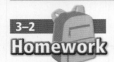

Homework **Goal:** Additional Practice

✓ Include students' completed Homework page as part of their portfolios.

3-2   Name _____ Date _____

Homework

Solve each problem. Label your answers.

Show your work.

Check student's work.

1. Asha made 15 sandwiches. Six were cheese, and the rest were peanut butter. How many peanut butter sandwiches did Asha make?

9 peanut butter sandwiches

2. Farha has 13 CDs. She gave some of them to her sister. Now Farha has 5 CDs. How many did she give to her sister?

8 CDs

3. Joseph did 7 push-ups yesterday. Today he did some more. In all, he has done 14 push-ups. How many did he do today?

7 pushups

4. Devon read 8 chapter books and some picture books. Altogether he read 12 books. How many of them were picture books?

4 picture books

5. Brent has 14 models. 9 are airplane models and the rest are car models. How many are car models?

5 car models

6. Create and Solve Write and solve a word problem in which you must find an unknown partner.

Answers will vary.

UNIT 3 LESSON 2   Word Problems with Unknown Partners **47**

Homework and Remembering page 47

Remembering **Goal:** Spiral Review

This Remembering page would be appropriate anytime after today's lesson.

3-2   Name _____ Date _____

Remembering

Use a ruler to make each drawing.

1. Draw a horizontal line segment about 6 centimeters long.

_____

2. Draw a vertical line segment a little more than 2 centimeters long.

3. Draw two perpendicular lines.

Add or subtract.

4. 926 + 158 = _1,084_   **5.** 803 − 388 = _415_   **6.** 687 − 79 = _608_

Solve each problem. Label your answer.

Show your work.

7. Yolanda had $11. Then she spent some money on a magazine. She has $8 left. How much did she spend on the magazine?

_$3_

8. David is making a comic book. Last week, he finished the first 7 pages. This week, he finished some more pages. He has finished 12 pages in all. How many pages did he draw this week?

5 pages

48 UNIT 3 LESSON 2   Word Problems with Unknown Partners

Homework and Remembering page 48

Home or School Activity

Literature Connection

A Bundle of Beasts In the collection of poems titled A *Bundle of Beasts,* Mark Steele and Patricia Hooper use unusual collective nouns to describe groups of animals. For example, Hooper describes "a *skein* of wildfowl," "a *cast* of hawks," and "an *army* of frogs." Use these poems and group words to initiate a discussion of more common group words for animals, such as *a pride* of lions, *a school* of fish, or a *flock* of geese. Then have students write an unknown partner problem in which they use group words for animals.

Word Problems with Unknown Starts

REAL WORLD
Problem Solving

Lesson Objectives

- Represent and solve word problems with unknown starts.
- Convert situation equations to solution equations.

Vocabulary

unknown start
situation equation
solution equation

The Day at a Glance

Today's Goals	Materials

1 Teaching the Lesson
A1: Review word problems with unknown partners.
A2: Solve and discuss unknown start problems.
 	
2 Going Further
▶ Differentiated Instruction
 	
3 Homework and Spiral Review
	Lesson Activities
	Student Activity Book pp. 75–76 or
	  Student Hardcover Book pp. 75–76
	Homework p. 47
	Homework and Remembering
	  pp. 49–50
	MathBoard materials
	Index cards
		Going Further
		Homework p. 49
		Activity Cards 3-3
		MathBoard materials
		Index cards
		Math Journals

123 *Use* **Math Talk** *today!*

Keeping Skills Sharp

Quick Practice ⏱ 5 MINUTES	Daily Routines
Goal: Find the unknown partner. **Unknown Partner Addition** Write these equations on the board: $8 + \square = 12$ $80 + \square = 120$ $800 + \square = 1{,}200$ $8 + \square = 15$ $80 + \square = 150$ $800 + \square = 1{,}500$ The **Student Leader** directs the class to complete the equations and to explain the Make a Ten, Make a Hundred, or Make a Thousand strategies. (See Unit 3 Lesson 1.)	**Homework Review** Send students to the board to show and explain their solutions. Encourage the rest of the class to ask clarifying questions and make comments. **Skip Count** Have students skip count by 25s from 500 to 975.

① Teaching the Lesson

Activity 1

Review Word Problems with Unknown Partners

 15 MINUTES

Goal: Review word problems with unknown partners.

Materials: Homework p. 47

 NCTM Standards:
Number and Operations
Algebra
Problem Solving
Communication

Differentiated Instruction

Extra Help Students having difficulty generating word problems may choose to draw or diagram their problems first and then work with a partner to find the best words to communicate the problems and their solution strategies.

Teaching Note

Watch For! When discussing students' word problems, watch for students who write word problems in which the answer is the total rather than a partner. Remind students that in a unknown partner problem, the answer is one of the partners.

▶ **Review How to Represent Problems with Unknown Partners** WHOLE CLASS

Review the first section of the Homework page 47, from Lesson 2. Briefly discuss the solutions for problems 1–4 and the ways students represented the problems. Discuss how the various equations and other representations of each problem are related to the same Math Mountain.

Here are the Math Mountains and some possible equations students may present:

Problem 1:
Asha made 15 sandwiches. Six were cheese and the rest were peanut butter. How many peanut butter sandwiches did Asha make?

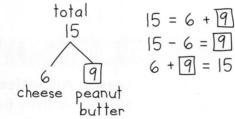 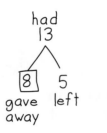

Problem 2:
Farha has 13 CDs. She gave some of them to her sister. Now Farha has 5 CDs. How many did she give to her sister?

Problem 3:
Joseph did 7 push-ups yesterday. Today he did some more. In all, he has done 14 push-ups. How many did he do today?

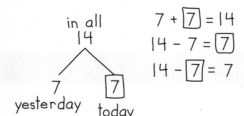 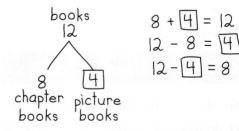

Problem 4:
Devon read 8 chapter books and some picture books. Altogether he read 12 books. How many of them were picture books?

Invite some students to share the word problems they wrote at the bottom of the page. Talk about whether the word problems they wrote are really problems with unknown partners. Make a Math Mountain and write an equation for each problem.

Unknown Starts in Addition and Subtraction

3-3
Class Activity

Name _____   Date _____

▶Solve Unknown Start Problems

Solve each problem. Label your answers.

Show your work.
Check student's work.

1. **Change Plus: Unknown Start** Greta puts some beads on a string. Then she puts on 7 more beads. Now there are 13 beads on the string. How many beads did she put on the string to start?

_____6 beads_____

2. **Change Minus: Unknown Start** Greta puts some beads on a string. Seven of the beads fell off the string. Six beads are still on the string. How many beads were there at first?

_____13 beads_____

3. **Change Plus: Unknown Start** Patrick was carrying some books. His teacher asked him to carry 3 more books. Now he has 11 books. How many books did he start with?

_____8 books_____

4. **Change Minus: Unknown Start** Patricia was carrying some books. Her friend took 3 of them. Patricia has 8 books left. How many books was she carrying at first?

_____11 books_____

UNIT 3 LESSON 3   Word Problems with Unknown Starts **75**

Student Activity Book page 75

---

 40 MINUTES

Goal: Solve unknown start problems.

Materials: Student Activity Book or Hardcover Book p. 75–76, MathBoard materials

 NCTM Standards:
Number and Operations
Algebra
Problem Solving
Communication

Teaching Note

Math Background A Change Plus or Change Minus problem in which the starting number is the unknown number is called an *unknown start problem.* A *situation equation* for an unknown start problem is an equation based directly on the word problem. It shows the unknown number first. Students often find it difficult to solve such equations because it is not obvious how to count on to find the answer. However, a situation equation can be rewritten as a *solution equation* that is easier to solve. For example, students can rewrite the situation equation $\square + 6 = 10$ as $6 + \square = 10$ by switching the partners, or students can use the fact that addition and subtraction undo each other to rewrite $\square + 6 = 10$ as $10 - 6 = \square$.

Do not expect all students to master unknown start problems in this lesson. They will get practice with these types of problems throughout the year.

▶ Solve Unknown Start Problems   WHOLE CLASS

Have the class look at problem 1. Why is the problem called an unknown start problem? The number of beads Greta started with is the unknown number.

Have students solve the problem. Point out different solution methods as students present their work on the board. Here are some possibilities:

● **Switch the Partner:** Students can solve the situation equation $\square + 7 = 13$ by switching the partners to make the solution equation $7 + \square = 13$. This can be solved by counting on or by making a ten.

● **Math Mountain:** Students can draw a Math Mountain to help them see that they need to find the unknown partner.

Activity continued ▶

① Teaching the Lesson (continued)

English Language Learners

Review *situation equation* and *solution equation*. Read problem 1 in the Class Activity. Say: **This says Greta puts on 7 *more* beads. Now there are 13.** Ask: **Do we add or subtract?** add

- **Beginning** Ask: **Is the start addend known?** no Write ☐ + 7 = 13. Say: **The word problem tells us this information. This is the *situation equation*.**

- **Intermediate** Ask: **What is unknown?** the start addend Write the equation. Say: **The word problem gives us this information. This is the *situation equation*.**

- **Advanced** Have students write the equation. Ask: **Is this a *situation equation* or a *solution equation*?**

Ongoing Assessment

Write the following problem on the board:

Ned had some stickers. Susan gave Ned 5 more stickers. Now Ned has 11 stickers.

▶ What situation equation could you use to represent the problem?

▶ What solution equation could you use to solve the problem?

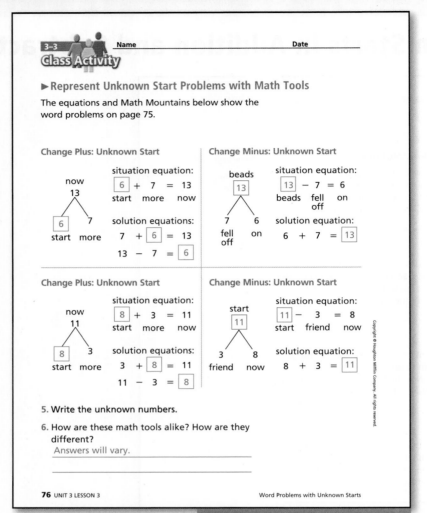

Student Activity Book page 76

▶ Represent Unknown Start Problems with Math Tools [WHOLE CLASS]

Have students look at the equations and Math Mountains shown on Student Book page 76, which correspond to the word problems on Student Book page 75.

Math Talk Discuss the relationships between each situation equation and the solution equation(s). Ask why the solution equations might be easier to solve.

Discuss the fact that the Math Mountains show that there are only two kinds of problems to solve: unknown total (for which you must add the partners) and unknown partner (for which you need to subtract, count on, or make a ten). Discuss any differences in the Math Mountains and equations on this page and those students wrote on the board.

If most students understand unknown start problems, ask them to write their own. Solve their problems as a class, or have students exchange problems with a partner and solve their partner's problems.

②Going Further

Differentiated Instruction

Intervention   Activity Card 3-3

Equation Practice   Activity Card 3-3 ●

Work: In pairs

Use:
• Homework page 49
• MathBoard materials

Decide:
Who will read aloud the first problem.

1. Read aloud Problem 1 on Homework page 49.
2. **On Your Own** Draw a Math Mountain for the problem on your MathBoard. Use words from the problem as labels.
3. Next, write a situation equation with labels.
4. Then write a solution equation and solve.
5. Check your work by exchanging with your partner.
6. Continue with the remaining problems on the page. Take turns reading each problem.

Unit 3, Lesson 3   Copyright © Houghton Mifflin Company

Activity Note Remind students that addition undoes subtraction. A solution can be checked by substituting into the situation equation.

 Math Writing Prompt

Summarize How is an unknown start problem different from an unknown partner problem? Explain.

 **Software Support**

Warm Up 10.08

On Level   Activity Card 3-3

Make Up Unknown Starts   Activity Card 3-3 ▲

Work: In pairs

Use:
• 6 index cards

1. **On Your Own** Write a different equation on three index cards, as described below. A sample for each card is shown at the right.
   • An unknown start equation that uses the number 17
   • A change minus equation with an unknown start and all even numbers
   • A change plus equation in which the unknown start is an odd number

   □ – 23 = 17

   □ – 2 = 6

   □ + 9 = 16

2. Exchange cards with your partner and solve.
3. Exchange cards again to check your results.

Unit 3, Lesson 3   Copyright © Houghton Mifflin Company

Activity Note As students work on the third equation, they will discover that if only one partner is odd, the total is odd. If both are odd, the total is even.

 Math Writing Prompt

Compare and Contrast Explain how you can use a situation equation and a solution equation to solve unknown start problems.

 Software Support

Numberopolis: Carnival Stories, Level O

Challenge   Activity Card 3-3

Make Up Unknown Starts   Activity Card 3-3 ■

Work: On your own

Use:
• Index cards

1. All three clues below describe an unknown start equation.
   • One partner is greater than 6.
   • The second partner is a doubles number.
   • The total is an odd number.
2. **Analyze** How can you be sure that the total is an odd number if one partner is even? The other partner must be odd.
3. Does the equation below fit all three clues? Yes

   ③ + 10 = 13

4. Write at least two other equations that fit all three clues.

Unit 3, Lesson 3   Copyright © Houghton Mifflin Company

Activity Note If time allows, have students write clues to an unknown start equation and exchange with a partner to solve.

 Math Writing Prompt

Multiple Answers Neeraj says, "There are only two kinds of problems. Some have an unknown total. Others have an unknown partner." Do you agree or disagree with Neeraj? Explain.

DESTINATION Math® **Software Support**

Course II: Module 2: Unit 1: Differences within 100

③ Homework and Spiral Review

3–3
Homework Goal: Additional Practice

This Homework page gives students additional practice in solving problems using methods of their choice.

3–3
Remembering Goal: Spiral Review

This Remembering page would be appropriate anytime after today's lesson.

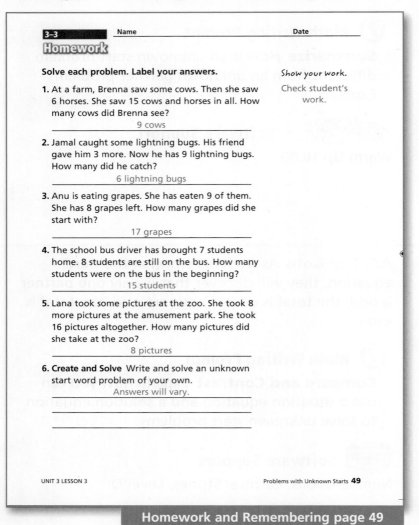

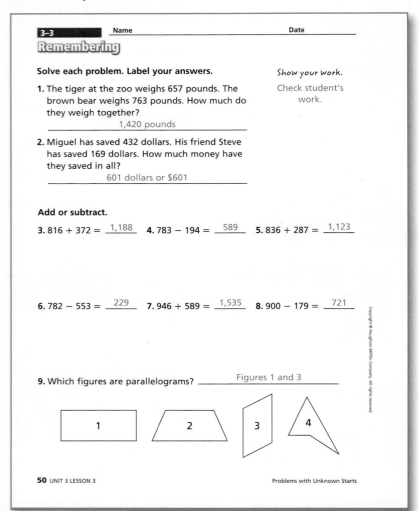

Homework and Remembering page 49

Homework and Remembering page 50

Home or School Activity

 Sports Connection

Sports Problems Have students think about how numbers are used in their favorite sport. For example, in baseball:

- There are 3 outs in an inning.
- There are usually 9 innings in a game.
- Numbers are used to tell how many runs are scored.

Then have students write an unknown start problem about their favorite sport.

> Ryan had some hits in the first game of the doubleheader. He had 4 hits in the second game of the doubleheader. Ryan had 6 hits in the two games. How many hits did Ryan have in the first game?

Comparison Problems

Lesson Objectives

- Interpret and use comparison language such as the words *more* and *fewer* to solve word problems.
- Represent and solve comparison word problems.

Vocabulary

situation equation
difference
solution equation
comparison problem
comparison bars

The Day at a Glance

Today's Goals	Materials	

① Teaching the Lesson
 A1: Represent and solve comparison problems with unknown differences
 A2: Represent and solve comparison problems with unknown larger or smaller amounts.
 A3: Use comparison bars to represent unknown larger or smaller amounts.
 	
 ② Going Further
 ▶ Differentiated Instruction
 	
 ③ Homework and Spiral Review
	Lesson Activities
	 Student Activity Book pp. 77–78 or
	   Student Hardcover Book pp. 77–78
	 Homework and Remembering
	   pp. 51–52
	 MathBoard materials
		Going Further
		 Activity Cards 3-4
		 Number cubes
		 Hundred Chart
		  (TRB M34)
		 Spinner B (TRB M35)
		 Paper clips
		 Two-color counters
		 Game Cards
		  (TRB M25)
		 Math Journals

123 *Use* **Math Talk** *today!*

Keeping Skills Sharp

Quick Practice ⏱ 5 MINUTES	**Daily Routines**
Goal: Find the unknown partner. **Unknown Partner Addition** Write these equations on the board: $7 + \square = 13$ $70 + \square = 130$ $700 + \square = 1{,}300$ $7 + \square = 11$ $70 + \square = 110$ $700 + \square = 1{,}100$ The **Student Leader** directs the class to complete the equations and to explain the Make a Ten, Make a Hundred, or Make a Thousand strategies. (See Unit 3 Lesson 1.)	**Homework Review** Let students work together to check their homework. Pair less able students with more able students. **Calendar** How many days are in 4 weeks? in 6 weeks? 28 days; 42 days

Teaching the Lesson

Introduction to Comparison Problems

 20 MINUTES

Goal: Represent and solve comparison problems with unknown differences.

Materials: Student Activity Book or Hardcover Book p. 77, MathBoard materials

✓ **NCTM Standards:**
Number and Operations
Problem Solving
Communication

Teaching Note

Language and Vocabulary Focus instruction on helping students understand the language in comparison word problems. Comparison problems involve one quantity that is more or less than another quantity. The comparing statement or question has two key pieces of information: *Who has more?* and *How many more?* Asking themselves these two key questions will help students understand the situation. Most students need to show the quantities with a drawing in order to decide whether to add or subtract to solve the problem.

Another needed skill is being able to reverse the comparison statement, which may lead students to an easier solution method. With most comparison problems, the comparison can be stated in two ways:

► How many more does B have than A?

► How many fewer does A have than B?

Comparison bars such as the ones introduced on Student Activity Book page 81 can help students see and solve such problems.

3–4
Class Activity

Name _____   Date _____

►**Discuss Comparison Problems**

Solve each problem. Label your answers.

> David has 5 marbles. Ana has 8 marbles.

1. How many more marbles does Ana have than David? __3 marbles__

2. How many fewer marbles does David have than Ana? __3 marbles__

Here are two ways to represent the comparison situation.

Comparison Drawing

David ○○○○○
Ana ○○○○○○○○

Comparison Bars

David | 5 | ? |
Ana | 8 |

> Claire has 8 marbles. Sasha has 15 marbles.

Show your work.

3. How many more marbles does Sasha have than Claire? __7 marbles__

4. How many fewer marbles does Claire have than Sasha? __7 marbles__

> Rocky has 7 fishing lures. Megan has 12 fishing lures.

5. How many fewer fishing lures does Rocky have than Megan? __5 fishing lures__

UNIT 3 LESSON 4   Comparison Problems **77**

Student Activity Book page 77

► Discuss Comparison Problems [WHOLE CLASS]

Math Talk Read aloud the situation on Student Book page 77, and have students answer questions 1 and 2 using the **Solve and Discuss** structure.

Have students look at the matching drawing and comparison bars for questions 1 and 2 on Student Book page 77.

● How does each drawing show who has more marbles and who has fewer? In the matching drawing, the person with the longer row of circles has more, and the person with the shorter row has fewer. In the comparison bars, the person with the longer bar has more, and the person with the shorter bar has fewer. Both drawings show that Ana has more.

- The amount more or fewer one person has than the other is called the *difference*. How does each drawing show the difference? In the first drawing, the difference is the number of circles in Ana's row that do not have matches in David's row. In the second drawing, the oval shows the difference.

Point out that the difference is the number of marbles David would need to get to have the same number as Ana.

Discuss how the drawings compare to drawings students may have made when they solved the problem.

Have students read problems 3 and 4.

- Which type of drawing is easier to make for this situation? Why? Possible answer: Comparison bars are easier because you don't have to draw each marble.

Using **Solve and Discuss,** have students solve problems 3 and 4. Encourage them to make comparison bars, but allow them to use any method they understand and can explain.

Following are some methods that students might use to solve problems 3 and 4. If none of the presenters draws comparison bars, draw them as a class.

- Students might think, "How many more would Claire need to have 15 like Sasha?" and write $8 + \Box = 15$.

- Students might think, "How many would Sasha have to give away to have as many as Claire?" and write $15 - \Box = 8$.

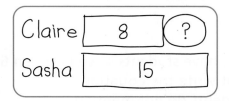

- Students might make comparison bars and write either $8 + \Box = 15$ or $15 - \Box = 8$.

Using **Solve and Discuss,** have students solve problem 5. Then ask students to restate the question in problem 5 using the word *more* instead of *fewer.* How many more fishing lures does Megan have than Rocky?

Activity 2

Comparison Problems with an Unknown Amount

 15 MINUTES

Goal: Represent and solve comparison problems with unknown larger or smaller amounts.

Materials: Student Activity Book or Hardcover Book p. 78

 NCTM Standards:
Number and Operations
Problem Solving
Communication

Teaching Note

What to Expect from Students
Problems in which unknown amounts must be found may be tricky for some students. Now students will be finding *amounts* instead of *differences.* Students will still need to determine who has more and who has fewer as they did with the comparison problems in Activity 1. This knowledge will help them decide what numbers must be added or subtracted.

| 3-4 | Name | Date |

Class Activity

▶ Find an Unknown Larger or Smaller Amount

Solve each problem. Label your answers.

Show your work.

Check student's work.

6. **Unknown Larger Amount** Maribel has 8 stickers. Arnon has 3 more stickers than Maribel. How many stickers does Arnon have?
   _____11 stickers_____

7. **Unknown Smaller Amount** Arnon has 11 stickers. Maribel has 3 fewer stickers than Arnon. How many stickers does Maribel have?
   _____8 stickers_____

8. **Unknown Larger Amount** Ivan has 9 goldfish. Milo has 5 more goldfish than Ivan. How many goldfish does Milo have?
   _____14 goldfish_____

9. **Unknown Smaller Amount** Milo has 14 goldfish. Ivan has 5 fewer goldfish than Milo. How many goldfish does Ivan have?
   _____9 goldfish_____

78 UNIT 3 LESSON 4   Comparison Problems

Student Activity Book page 78

▶ Find an Unknown Larger or Smaller Amount

WHOLE CLASS

123 Math Talk Using **Solve and Discuss,** have students solve problem 6 on Student Book page 78. Students might write the equation $8 + 3 = \square$ or use comparison bars. If students do not mention comparison bars, work as a class to draw them. Start with the basic comparison bar structure, which is shown below.

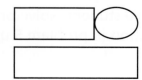

Tell students they can start with this arrangement and then fill in the details.

Elicit the information needed to label the bars.

● Which part of the problem tells us who has more or fewer? Arnon has 3 more stickers than Maribel.

● Who has more? Arnon

● Which bar should I write "Arnon" next to? the longer bar Why? Arnon has more stickers than Maribel.

Write *Arnon* next to the longer bar and *Maribel* next to the shorter bar.

● How many more does Arnon have? 3 more stickers

● Where can we write the "3" to show this difference? in the oval

● What other information does the problem tell us? Maribel has 8 stickers.

● How do we show this in our drawing? Write "8" in Maribel's bar.

● What do we need to find? how many stickers Arnon has

Explain that you can write a question mark in Arnon's bar to show that this is the number that needs to be found.

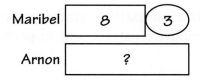

● How do we find out how many stickers Arnon has? We can add 8 and 3.

● How many stickers does Arnon have? 11 stickers

Leave the comparison bars for problem 6 on the board.

Next, use **Solve and Discuss** for problem 7. Encourage students to make comparison bars.

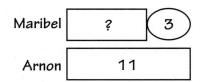

Activity continued ▶

The Learning Classroom

Building Concepts Some students may prefer to draw comparison bars like this:

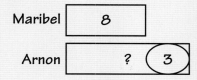

Teaching Note

Language and Vocabulary In English, we say that one person has *less* than the other for a continuous quantity like water. But if we are talking about a discrete, countable quantity, we say *fewer* (for example, "less juice" but "fewer cookies"). We also say *less* for numbers (for example, "5 is less than 7").

Try to use these terms correctly. However, do not tell students they are incorrect for using *less* instead of *fewer*. The distinction is often difficult even for adults. Students will begin to understand the distinction better as they hear the words used correctly.

Teaching the Lesson (continued)

Ask students to compare problems 6 and 7 and the comparison bars for the two problems.

● **How are the situations in the two problems the same? How are they different?** The situations and the amounts are the same, but the unknown number is different. In problem 6, the larger amount (how many Arnon has) is unknown. In problem 7, the smaller amount (how many Maribel has) is unknown.

● **Are the comparison statements in the two problems the same or different?** They are different. Problem 6 says, "Arnon has 3 more stickers than Maribel." Problem 7 says, "Maribel has 3 fewer stickers than Arnon." These two statements give us the same information but in different ways.

● **How are the comparison bars the same and different?** They look the same, but the question mark is in a different place. For problem 6, it is in Arnon's bar. For problem 7, it is in Maribel's bar.

Ask students to restate the comparison statement in problem 6 using the word *fewer,* and the comparison statement in problem 7 using the word *more.*

Using **Solve and Discuss,** have students solve problems 8 and 9. Have students compare the situations and comparison bars for these problems as they did for problems 6 and 7.

Practice with Comparison Bars

▶ Use Comparison Bars to Represent an Unknown Amount PAIRS

Draw the diagram on the board, and ask **Student Pairs** to draw it on their MathBoard.

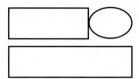

Ask students to listen as you read this comparison statement:

● George has 5 more stamps than Lillian.

Have **Student Pairs** ask themselves, *Who has more (or fewer)?* and *How many more or fewer does that person have?* Students should use the answers to these questions to label the bars with the names and to write the difference in the oval. (If you prefer, have **Student Pairs** label the bars using just the first letter of each name.) Tell them not to worry about the numbers for the larger and smaller amounts right now.

Have **Student Pairs** hold up their MathBoard when they are done so you can check their work.

Now have **Student Pairs** erase the labels from their comparison bars. Read the statement below, and have them label the bars to represent it. Check their work as before.

● Michael has 6 fewer pencils than Lucia.

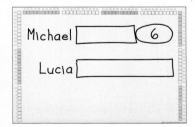

 15 MINUTES

Goal: Use comparison bars to represent unknown larger or smaller amounts.

Materials: MathBoard materials

 NCTM Standards:
Number and Operations
Problem Solving
Communication

Activity continued ▶

Differentiated Instruction

Extra Help Use questioning to help students make the link between the terms *more* and *fewer* and the lengths of the comparison bars. For example:

▶ Which shows more items, the long bar or the short bar?

▶ Which shows fewer items, the long bar or the short bar?

▶ If George has more stamps than Lillian, should his bar be longer or shorter than Lillian's bar?

Repeat this process for the statements below.

● Grace has 4 more comic books than Myles.

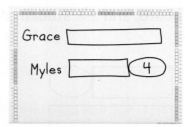

● Kim has 3 fewer grapes than Ramish.

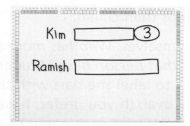

Have **Student Pairs** make up and represent additional statements if they need more practice. Now draw the comparison bars below on the board.

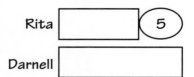

Ask **Student Pairs** to give two comparison statements that match the drawing, one using the word *more* and one using the word *fewer.* Here is one possible answer:

● Darnell has 5 more baseball cards than Rita.

● Rita has 5 fewer baseball cards than Darnell.

Replace the names and the difference, and have students make up comparison statements for the new drawing. Do this several more times.

②Going Further

Intervention   Activity Card 3-4

More or Fewer   Activity Card 3-4 ●

Work: On your own

Use:
- 2 number cubes labeled 0–5 and 4–9
- TRB M35 (Spinner B)
- Paper clips
- TRB M34 (hundred chart)
- 30 counters

1. Roll both number cubes and spin the spinner. Use the cubes to make a 2-digit number.

2. Use a counter to cover a number on the hundreds chart that is *more than* or *fewer than* the 2-digit number, according to the spinner.

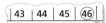

3. Continue rolling the number cubes and spinning the spinner until all the counters are on the chart.

4. **Analyze** How many counters cover numbers that are more than 50? Fewer than 50?

Unit 3, Lesson 4   Copyright © Houghton Mifflin Company

Activity Note Extend this activity by asking students to count the number of counters on numbers that are more than or fewer than 20, 30, and so on.

✎ Math Writing Prompt

Make a Plan Explain how to draw comparison bars for this equation: $8 + 5 = 13$.

Soar to Success Math ★ Software Support

Warm Up 7.17

On Level   Activity Card 3-4

Start with Bars   Activity Card 3-4 ▲

Work: On your own

Use:
- TRB M25 (Game Cards)
- MathBoard materials

1. Shuffle the game cards. Choose 2 without looking.

2. On your MathBoard, make a comparison drawing for the numbers.

3. Now draw comparison bars for the two numbers.

4. Write an equation to compare the two numbers.

5. Repeat the activity three more times.

Unit 3, Lesson 4   Copyright © Houghton Mifflin Company

Activity Note Remind students that the comparison bars do not need to be particular lengths, as long as the greater number has the longer bar.

✎ Math Writing Prompt

Compare and Contrast Explain how comparison drawings and comparison bars are alike and how they are different. Which do you prefer and why?

MegaMath Grades K-6 Software Support

Country Countdown: Harrison's Comparisons, Level I

Challenge   Activity Card 3-4

Create Comparison Problems   Activity Card 3-4 ■

Work: In small groups

Use:
- Math Journals

1. Look at the comparison bars and equation below.

 $57 - 26 = 31$

2. **Predict** Suppose you add the same amount to the number on each comparison bar. What will happen to the difference 31? Try it and see. It stays the same.

3. Choose two new number pairs and draw sets of comparison bars for them in your Journal. Then write an equation for each pair you choose. Test your prediction on these numbers. What do you observe? Students should discover that the difference remains the same when they add the same amount to the numbers on each bar.

Unit 3, Lesson 4   Copyright © Houghton Mifflin Company

Activity Note Students can also try adding numbers other than 3 to the numbers on the comparison bars and then test what happens to the difference.

✎ Math Writing Prompt

Explain Your Thinking Would you solve a comparison problem with an unknown difference the same way you solve a comparison problem with an unknown larger or smaller amount? Explain your thinking.

✦ DESTINATION Math® Software Support

Course II: Module 2: Unit 1: Differences within 100

③ Homework and Spiral Review

Homework **Goal:** Additional Practice

✓ Include students' completed Homework page as part of their portfolios.

Remembering **Goal:** Spiral Review

This Remembering page would be appropriate anytime after today's lesson.

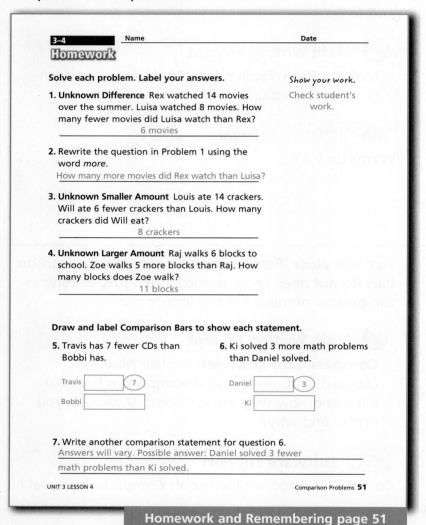

Homework

Name _____ Date _____

Solve each problem. Label your answers.

1. **Unknown Difference** Rex watched 14 movies over the summer. Luisa watched 8 movies. How many fewer movies did Luisa watch than Rex?
   6 movies

2. Rewrite the question in Problem 1 using the word *more*.
   How many more movies did Rex watch than Luisa?

3. **Unknown Smaller Amount** Louis ate 14 crackers. Will ate 6 fewer crackers than Louis. How many crackers did Will eat?
   8 crackers

4. **Unknown Larger Amount** Raj walks 6 blocks to school. Zoe walks 5 more blocks than Raj. How many blocks does Zoe walk?
   11 blocks

Show your work.
Check student's work.

Draw and label Comparison Bars to show each statement.

5. Travis has 7 fewer CDs than Bobbi has.

Travis [7   ]
Bobbi [   ]

6. Ki solved 3 more math problems than Daniel solved.

Daniel [3   ]
Ki [   ]

7. Write another comparison statement for question 6.
   Answers will vary. Possible answer: Daniel solved 3 fewer math problems than Ki solved.

UNIT 3 LESSON 4 — Comparison Problems **51**

Homework and Remembering page 51

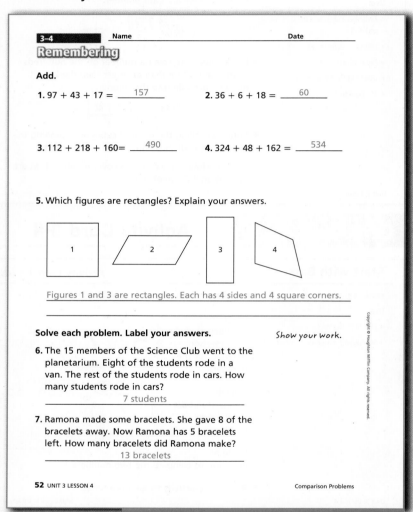

Remembering

Name _____ Date _____

Add.

1. 97 + 43 + 17 = ___157___
2. 36 + 6 + 18 = ___60___
3. 112 + 218 + 160 = ___490___
4. 324 + 48 + 162 = ___534___

5. Which figures are rectangles? Explain your answers.

| 1 | 2 | 3 | 4 |

Figures 1 and 3 are rectangles. Each has 4 sides and 4 square corners.

Solve each problem. Label your answers.

6. The 15 members of the Science Club went to the planetarium. Eight of the students rode in a van. The rest of the students rode in cars. How many students rode in cars?
   7 students

7. Ramona made some bracelets. She gave 8 of the bracelets away. Now Ramona has 5 bracelets left. How many bracelets did Ramona make?
   13 bracelets

Show your work.

52 UNIT 3 LESSON 4 — Comparison Problems

Homework and Remembering page 52

Home or School Activity

Science Connection

Many Moons Provide students with the table shown at the right. Ask students to create comparison problems based on the data in the table. Have students solve each other's problems.

Planet	Moons
Mercury	0
Venus	0
Earth	1
Mars	2
Jupiter	28
Saturn	30
Uranus	21
Neptune	8
Pluto	1

Comparison Problems with Misleading Language

REAL WORLD Problem Solving

Lesson Objectives

- Interpret and apply comparison language.
- Represent and solve comparison word problems with misleading language.

Vocabulary

unknown partner problem	comparison problem
make a ten	comparison bars
make a hundred	unknown amount
make a thousand	

The Day at a Glance

Today's Goals	Materials
1 **Teaching the Lesson** **A1:** Represent and solve comparison problems that have misleading language. **A2:** Solve comparison problems that do not include the words *more* or *fewer*. **2** **Going Further** ▶ Differentiated Instruction **3** **Homework and Spiral Review**	**Lesson Activities** Student Activity Book pp. 79–80 or Student Hardcover Book pp. 79–80 Homework and Remembering pp. 53–54 MathBoard materials Quick Quiz 1 (Assessment Guide) **Going Further** Activity Cards 3-5 Two-color counters Homework p. 53 Game Cards (TRB M25) Math Journals

Use Math Talk today!

Keeping Skills Sharp

Quick Practice ⏱ 5 MINUTES	Daily Routines
Goal: Find the unknown partner. **Unknown Partner Addition** Write these equations on the board: $6 + \square = 11$ $60 + \square = 110$ $600 + \square = 1{,}100$ $6 + \square = 14$ $60 + \square = 140$ $600 + \square = 1{,}400$ The **Student Leader** directs the class to complete the equations and to explain the Make a Ten, Make a Hundred, or Make a Thousand strategies. (See Unit 3 Lesson 1.)	**Homework Review** Have students discuss any errors made on the homework. Encourage students to help each other resolve these errors. **Create a Pattern** Have students choose a number between 15 and 25. Then, have students write a shrinking pattern that starts with this number listing the rule they used.

Teaching the Lesson

Activity 1

Solve Problems with Misleading Language

 30 MINUTES

Goal: Represent and solve comparison problems that have misleading language.

Materials: Student Activity Book or Hardcover Book p. 79, MathBoard materials

✓ **NCTM Standards:**
Number and Operations
Problem Solving
Communication

Teaching Note

Language and Vocabulary
Sometimes comparison problems are stated in a way that is misleading for students. For example, when students read the problem below, they may see the word *fewer* and assume they should subtract 5 from 8.

> Lyle has 8 pencils. Lyle has 5 fewer pencils than Jess. How many pencils does Jess have?

When students are faced with such a problem, they can do one of the following:

▶ Use the problem as it is stated to determine who has more (or fewer) and how many more (or fewer) that person has. Use this information to label comparison bars, and use the bars to decide whether to add or subtract to find the answer.

▶ Find the comparison statement in the problem and state it in terms of the other person in the problem. For example, restating *Lyle has 5 fewer pencils than Jess* as *Jess has 5 more pencils than Lyle* makes it clear that you should start with Lyle's 8 pencils and add 5 to find the number Jess has.

Make sure both methods are mentioned during this activity.

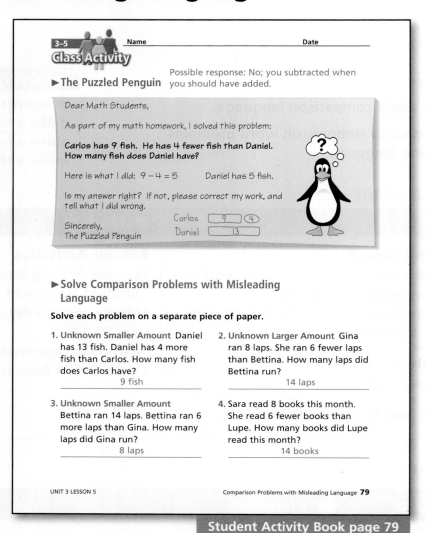

Student Activity Book page 79

▶ The Puzzled Penguin [SMALL GROUPS]

Have **Small Groups** read the problem the Puzzled Penguin solved and discuss the steps the Puzzled Penguin took to solve the problem. After a few minutes, discuss their conclusions.

● Did the Puzzled Penguin do something wrong? yes

● What did he do wrong? He subtracted when he should have added.

● Why do you think he did this? He probably saw the word *fewer* and thought that meant he should subtract.

123 Math Talk Have the **Small Groups** reread the letter and draw comparison bars on their MathBoard to help them solve the problem. After a few minutes, discuss their work.

- Which statement is the comparison statement? He [Carlos] has 4 fewer fish than Daniel.

- Who has fewer fish? Carlos

- Which bar should we label "Carlos"? the shorter one

- How many fewer fish does he have? 4 fewer fish

- Where do we put the number 4? in the oval

- Who has more fish? Daniel

- Where do we put Daniel's name? next to the longer bar

- What else does this problem tell us? that Carlos has 9 fish

- Where do we put the number 9? in the bar for Carlos

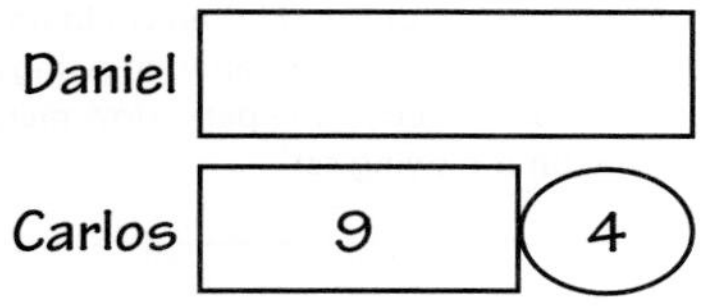

Daniel [ ]

Carlos [9] (4)

Have **Small Groups** look at their comparison bars and tell how they found the missing number.

- How did you find out how many fish Daniel has? by adding 9 and 4

Have **Small Groups** look back at the original problem.

- How could we restate the comparison statement "He had 4 fewer fish than Daniel" using the word more? Daniel has 4 more fish than Carlos.

- Does saying the statement this way make the problem easier to solve? Why? Answers will vary. Possible response: Yes; it makes it clear that we start with Carlos' 9 fish and add 4 more fish.

▶ Solve Comparison Problems SMALL GROUPS

Have **Small Groups** solve problems 1–3. Then discuss the relationship between The Puzzled Penguin problem and problem 1, and between problems 2 and 3. In each pair of problems, the situation is the same but the unknown numbers are different. In one problem, you have to find the larger amount. In the other problem, you have to find the smaller amount.

Have **Small Groups** solve problem 4 and discuss how the comparison statement can be restated using the word *more.*

Teaching the Lesson (continued)

Activity 2

Other Comparison Language

20 MINUTES

Goal: Solve comparison problems that do not include the words *more* or *fewer*.

Materials: Student Activity Book or Hardcover Book p. 80, MathBoard materials

 NCTM Standards:
Number and Operations
Problem Solving
Communication

 Ongoing Assessment

Write this problem on the board:

Diego went on 12 rides at the fair. Janie went on 5 fewer rides. How many rides did Janie go on?

Ask students to:

▶ solve the problem

▶ rewrite the problem using *more* instead of *fewer*.

 Quick Quiz

See Assessment Guide for Unit 3 Quick Quiz 1.

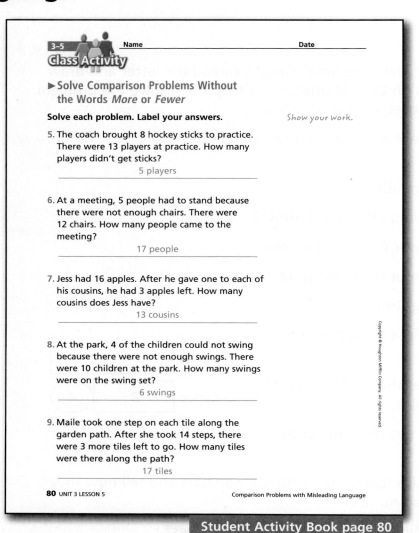

Student Activity Book page 80

▶ Solve Comparison Problems Without the Words *More or Fewer* [WHOLE CLASS]

Discuss problems 5–9 and explain that sometimes comparison problems do not use the words *more* or *fewer*. Students can solve these problems by carefully thinking about which is more and which is fewer. For example, in problem 5, there are fewer hockey sticks than players.

players [13]

hockey sticks [8] (5)

For some students, the comparison may be easier to see with a comparison drawing.

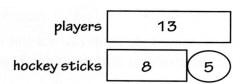

212 UNIT 3 LESSON 5

②Going Further

Intervention — Activity Card 3-5

Another Way — Activity Card 3-5 ●

Work: In pairs

Use:
- 20 two-color counters
- Homework page 53
- Math Journals

1. Using two-color counters can help you solve Problem 1 on Homework page 53. Look at the comparison drawing showing the counters.

> Lucia drew 13 pictures. Lucia drew 6 more pictures than Chelsea. How many pictures did Chelsea draw?

> Lucia ●●●●●●● ●●●●●●
> Chelsea ○○○○○○○
> Chelsea has 7 pictures.

Why are Lucia's counters shown in two groups?
The second group shows how many more counters Lucia has than Chelsea.

2. **Work Together** Use counters to model the remaining problems on page 53. Check each step as you work.

Unit 3, Lesson 5   Copyright © Houghton Mifflin Company

Activity Note Students need to identify which bar represents the category with more items. Then they can decide what number each bar should show.

 Math Writing Prompt

Explain Your Thinking How can you use counters to solve comparison problems? Use an example to explain your thinking.

 **Software Support**

Warm Up 7.17

On Level — Activity Card 3-5

More or Fewer Fishing — Activity Card 3-5 ▲

Work: In pairs

Use:
- 2 copies of TRB M25 (Game Cards)

1. Shuffle the 20 game cards and put them facedown in a pile. Each player takes 5 cards without looking.

2. Take turns collecting matching cards from your partner by asking *more/fewer* questions.

Anya: Do you have a card that's 1 fewer than 5?

Bryce: Yes, I have a 4.

Anya's cards   Bryce's cards

3. When a match is made, put both cards in your pile and ask another question. If a match is not made, pick up another card to end your turn.

4. The greater number of matches wins the game.

Unit 3, Lesson 5   Copyright © Houghton Mifflin Company

Activity Note Students should be careful to ask a question that identifies a number between 0 and 9.

 Math Writing Prompt

Make a Drawing Jeff has 15 pencils. He has 5 fewer than Jan. Draw comparison bars to show the relationship. Explain how you decided which person had the larger amount.

Software Support

Country Countdown: Harrison's Comparisons, Level D

Challenge — Activity Card 3-5

Fill in the Blanks — Activity Card 3-5 ■

Work: On Your Own

Use:
- Math Journals

1. Copy the statements below into your Math Journal. Choose a number to fill in the blank.

Jack has __?__ more books than Judy. They have a total of 12 books.

2. Draw comparison bars to represent the situation. The example below uses the number 6.

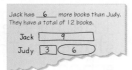

> Jack has __6__ more books than Judy.
> They have a total of 12 books.
> Jack [9]
> Judy [3](6)

3. Repeat the activity with as many different numbers as possible. There are 7 possible combinations: 0, 12; 1, 11; 2, 10; 3, 9; 4, 8; 5, 7; 6, 6

Unit 3, Lesson 5   Copyright © Houghton Mifflin Company

Activity Note The number of possible combinations in the comparison bars depends on the total.

 Math Writing Prompt

Choose a Strategy May has 15 pens. She has 4 more than Kim and 4 fewer than Lynn. Explain what strategy you would use to find how many pencils Kim and Lynn have.

DESTINATION Math· **Software Support**

Course II: Module 1: Unit 1: Comparing and Ordering

Comparison Problems with Misleading Language   **213**

③ Homework and Spiral Review

3–5
Homework **Goal:** Additional Practice

This Homework page provides additional practice in solving comparison problems.

3–5
Remembering **Goal:** Spiral Review

This Remembering page would be appropriate anytime after today's lesson.

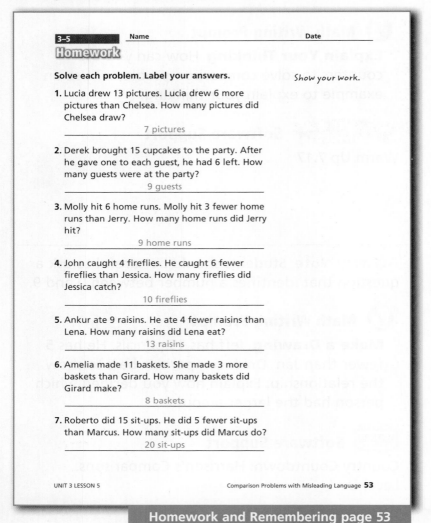

3–5
Homework

Name _____ Date _____

Solve each problem. Label your answers.

Show your work.

1. Lucia drew 13 pictures. Lucia drew 6 more pictures than Chelsea. How many pictures did Chelsea draw?

   7 pictures

2. Derek brought 15 cupcakes to the party. After he gave one to each guest, he had 6 left. How many guests were at the party?

   9 guests

3. Molly hit 6 home runs. Molly hit 3 fewer home runs than Jerry. How many home runs did Jerry hit?

   9 home runs

4. John caught 4 fireflies. He caught 6 fewer fireflies than Jessica. How many fireflies did Jessica catch?

   10 fireflies

5. Ankur ate 9 raisins. He ate 4 fewer raisins than Lena. How many raisins did Lena eat?

   13 raisins

6. Amelia made 11 baskets. She made 3 more baskets than Girard. How many baskets did Girard make?

   8 baskets

7. Roberto did 15 sit-ups. He did 5 fewer sit-ups than Marcus. How many sit-ups did Marcus do?

   20 sit-ups

UNIT 3 LESSON 5   Comparison Problems with Misleading Language **53**

Homework and Remembering page 53

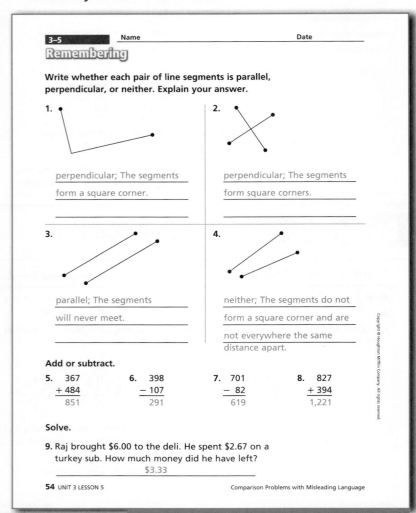

3–5
Remembering

Name _____ Date _____

Write whether each pair of line segments is parallel, perpendicular, or neither. Explain your answer.

1.

perpendicular; The segments form a square corner. _____

2.

perpendicular; The segments form square corners. _____

3.

parallel; The segments will never meet. _____

4.

neither; The segments do not form a square corner and are not everywhere the same distance apart.

Add or subtract.

5. 367	6. 398	7. 701	8. 827
+ 484	− 107	− 82	+ 394
851	291	619	1,221

Solve.

9. Raj brought $6.00 to the deli. He spent $2.67 on a turkey sub. How much money did he have left?

   $3.33

54 UNIT 3 LESSON 5   Comparison Problems with Misleading Language

Homework and Remembering page 54

Home or School Activity

 Real-World Connection

Local Comparisons Have students write pairs of comparison statements in which they compare things in their town or neighborhood. In each pair of statements, students use two different ways to make the same comparison. For example:

● There are more apartment buildings than houses.

● There are fewer houses than apartment buildings.

● The school is farther than the library.

● The library is closer than the school.

> The high school has more students than the middle school.
>
> The middle school has fewer students than the high school.

Multi-Digit Unknown Partner and Unknown Start Problems

Lesson Objectives

● **Represent and solve multi-digit word problems with unknown partners and express relationships as equations and inequalities.**

● **Represent and solve multi-digit word problems with unknown starts.**

Vocabulary

situation equation
solution equation
inequality

The Day at a Glance

Today's Goals	Materials	

① Teaching the Lesson
A1: Represent and solve multi-digit word problems with unknown partners.
A2: Represent and solve multi-digit word problems with unknown starts.
A3: Represent and solve multi-digit unknown partners and unknown start problems.
A4: Express relationships as equations and inequalities.
 	
② Going Further
▶ Differentiated Instruction
 	
③ Homework and Spiral Review
	Lesson Activities
	Student Activity Book pp. 81–84 or
	  Student Hardcover Book pp. 81–84
	Homework and Remembering
	  pp. 55–56
	MathBoard materials
		Going Further
		Activity Cards 3-6
		MathBoard materials
		Calculators
		Math Journals

123 *Use* **Math Talk** *today!*

Keeping Skills Sharp

Quick Practice　🕐 5 MINUTES	Daily Routines
Goal: Find the unknown partner in subtraction equations. **Unknown Partner Subtraction** Write these equations on the board. $14 - \square = 9$　$140 - \square = 90$　$1{,}400 - \square = 900$ $17 - \square = 9$　$170 - \square = 90$　$1{,}700 - \square = 900$ The **Student Leader** tells the class which equation to complete. Then one student explains the Make a Ten, Make a Hundred, or Make a Thousand strategies. *Leader:* (first equation) Fourteen minus what number equals 9? *Class:* 14 minus 5 equals 9. *Student:* 9 plus 1 is 10 plus 4 more is 14. I added 5 in all, so $14 - 9 = 5$.	**Homework Review** If students give incorrect answers, have them explain how they found the answers. This can help you determine whether the error is conceptual or procedural. **Skip Count** Have students skip count backward by 10s from 250.

Teaching the Lesson

Multi-Digit Problems with Unknown Partners

 15 MINUTES

Goal: Represent and solve multi-digit word problems with unknown partners.

Materials: Student Activity Book or Hardcover Book p. 81, MathBoard materials

✔ **NCTM Standards:**
Number and Operations
Problem Solving
Representation

Teaching Note

Language and Vocabulary Make sure students understand the meaning of the words in word problems. In this lesson, check that students understand the meanings of the following words in the context of problems 1-12: collection, pin ball, scored, sheets (of paper), polished, checked out, and section.

Possible Strategies

Add on Numerically

$783 + \boxed{} = 912$ 783   +   7 is 790
   P   P   T   +   10 is 800
                               + 112 is 912
                                    129

Use a Math Mountain to Subtract.

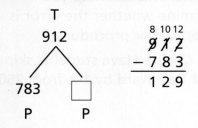

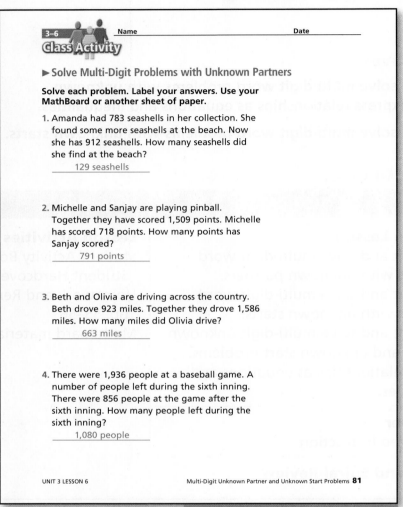

Student Activity Book page 81

▶ Solve Multi-Digit Problems with Unknown Partners   WHOLE CLASS

Using the **Solve and Discuss** structure, have students solve problems 2–4 on Student Book page 81. Emphasize that they should identify the partners and the total, and label them in their equations and drawings. Make sure a variety of methods are presented. Some possible strategies are presented below and in the side column.

Add on with a Drawing

$783 + \boxed{} = 912$
  P   P   T

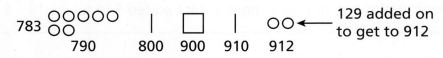

Other Comparison Language

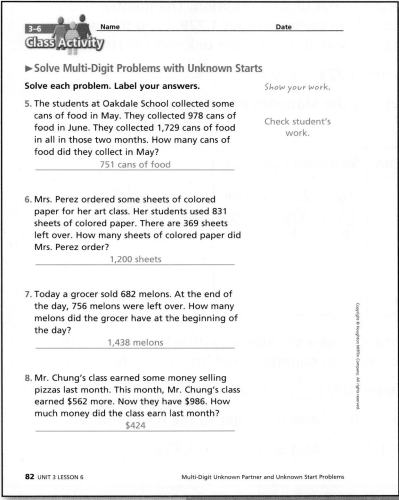

3-6
Class Activity

Name _____ Date _____

▶ Solve Multi-Digit Problems with Unknown Starts

Solve each problem. Label your answers.

Show your work.

5. The students at Oakdale School collected some cans of food in May. They collected 978 cans of food in June. They collected 1,729 cans of food in all in those two months. How many cans of food did they collect in May?

Check student's work.

_____751 cans of food_____

6. Mrs. Perez ordered some sheets of colored paper for her art class. Her students used 831 sheets of colored paper. There are 369 sheets left over. How many sheets of colored paper did Mrs. Perez order?

_____1,200 sheets_____

7. Today a grocer sold 682 melons. At the end of the day, 756 melons were left over. How many melons did the grocer have at the beginning of the day?

_____1,438 melons_____

8. Mr. Chung's class earned some money selling pizzas last month. This month, Mr. Chung's class earned $562 more. Now they have $986. How much money did the class earn last month?

_____$424_____

82 UNIT 3 LESSON 6   Multi-Digit Unknown Partner and Unknown Start Problems

Student Activity Book page 82

▶ Solve Multi-Digit Problems with Unknown Starts INDIVIDUALS

Using the **Solve and Discuss** structure, have students solve problem 5 on Student Book page 82. If students struggle, suggest they use Math Tools like they used in Lesson 3. The Math Mountain and situation equation for problem 5 are shown below.

Math Mountain

two months
T
1,729

□   978
P   P

May   June

Situation Equation

May   June   both
□ + 978 = 1,729
P   P   T

Goal: Represent and solve multi-digit word problems with unknown starts.

Materials: Student Activity Book or Hardcover Book p. 82, MathBoard materials

 NCTM Standards:
Number and Operations
Problem Solving
Representation

Teaching Note

What to Expect from Students
When students solve multi-digit word problems, encourage them to identify and label the partners and the total. When both partners are known, students can add the partners to find the solution. However, when the total and one partner are known, they can either subtract the partner from the total or add on from the partner to make the total. Some students have a strong preference for adding on rather than subtracting. This method is perfectly acceptable and should not be discouraged. Students may add on numerically or by using drawings.

❶ Teaching the Lesson (continued)

The following are some other possible solution strategies for problem 5.

- **Reversing the Situation:** Write a solution equation by thinking about the operation that undoes addition. The number 978 is *added* to the unknown partner to get 1,729. So, if 978 is *taken away* from 1,729, the result will be the unknown partner.

  Solution equation: $1{,}729 - 978 = \square$

- **Math Mountain:** Use the Math Mountain to write and solve a subtraction.

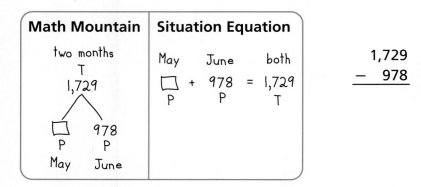

- **Switch the Partner:** Write a solution equation by switching the partners in the situation equation. Add on to find the solution.

  Solution equation: $978 + \square = 1{,}729$

  978 + 22   is 1,000   Add on to get to the next hundred.

  + 729   is 1,729   Add on to get to 1,729.

  751

Have students use **Solve and Discuss** to solve problem 6 on Student Book page 82. The Math Mountain, situation equation, and solution equation for problem 6 are shown below.

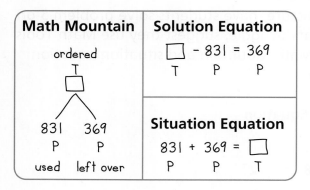

Using **Solve and Discuss,** have students solve problems 7 and 8 on Student Book page 82.

Activity 3

Mixed Problems

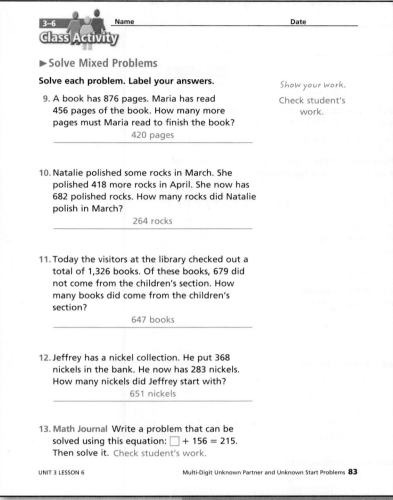

3–6
Class Activity

Name _____   Date _____

▶ Solve Mixed Problems

Solve each problem. Label your answers.

Show your work.
Check student's work.

9. A book has 876 pages. Maria has read 456 pages of the book. How many more pages must Maria read to finish the book?
   _____ 420 pages _____

10. Natalie polished some rocks in March. She polished 418 more rocks in April. She now has 682 polished rocks. How many rocks did Natalie polish in March?
    _____ 264 rocks _____

11. Today the visitors at the library checked out a total of 1,326 books. Of these books, 679 did not come from the children's section. How many books did come from the children's section?
    _____ 647 books _____

12. Jeffrey has a nickel collection. He put 368 nickels in the bank. He now has 283 nickels. How many nickels did Jeffrey start with?
    _____ 651 nickels _____

13. **Math Journal** Write a problem that can be solved using this equation: ☐ + 156 = 215. Then solve it. Check student's work.

UNIT 3 LESSON 6   Multi-Digit Unknown Partner and Unknown Start Problems **83**

Student Activity Book page 83

▶ Solve Mixed Problems [WHOLE CLASS]

Using the **Solve and Discuss** structure, have students solve problems 9–12 on Student Book page 83. The problems are not labeled by type, so students must think carefully about the situation before deciding how to solve the problem. Remind them to label the total and partners. Talk about the Math Mountains and equations students write.

Math Journal If time allows, have students share the problems they created in exercise 13. Have students who used different solution methods present and explain their work.

 20 MINUTES

Goal: Represent and solve multi-digit unknown partner and unknown start word problems.

Materials: Student Activity Book or Hardcover Book p. 83, MathBoard materials

 NCTM Standards:
Number and Operations
Problem Solving
Representation

 Ongoing Assessment

As students solve problem 12, ask questions such as:

▶ How do you know whether 386 is a partner or the total? What about 283?

▶ How did you decide whether to add or subtract the numbers?

Multi-Digit Unknown Partner and Unknown Start Problems   **219**

Teaching The Lesson

Express Relationships as Equations and Inequalities

 20 MINUTES

Goal: Compare numbers and expressions using > and <.

Materials: Student Activity Book or Hardcover Book p. 84

✓ **NCTM Standards:**
Numbers and Operations
Algebra

 Class Management

As you walk around the room to observe how students are completing the exercises, ask any student who has made a mistake to read the statement they have made aloud. This will enable you to identify students who are confusing the inequality symbols. You can remind them that each symbol points to the smaller number.

Students will have an opportunity to compare larger numbers and expressions in Unit 5 and fractions in Unit 11.

Differentiated Instruction

Special Needs If some students consistently confuse the "is greater than sign" and the "is less than sign", allow them to write a capital G or L in the circles on the student page.

3–6 Name _____ Date _____

Class Activity

Vocabulary
inequality

▶ Discuss Equations and Inequalities

An equation shows that two quantities or expressions are equal.
An equal sign (=) is used to show that the two sides are equal.

$8 = 5 + 3$ $4 + 2 = 6$ $7 = 7$ $3 + 2 = 2 + 3$ $6 - 2 = 1 + 1 + 2$

An **inequality** shows that two quantities or expressions are not equal. The signs less than (<), greater than (>), and not equal ($\neq$) show that the two sides are not equal.

$7 < 5 + 3$ $9 + 2 > 8$ $7 \neq 6$ $6 - 2 < 2 + 3$ $5 + 2 > 1 + 1 + 3$

1. Use the > sign to write four inequalities. Vary how many numbers you have on each side.
   Inequalities will vary. _____

2. Use the < sign to write four inequalities. Vary how many numbers you have on each side.
   Inequalities will vary. _____

Write a number to make the inequality true. Numbers will vary. Descriptions of correct numbers are given.

3. $16 > \boxed{} + 9$ 4. $3 + \boxed{} > 12$ 5. $7 + 2 > 2 + \boxed{}$
Any number less than 7. Any number greater than 9. Any number less than 7.

6. $18 - \boxed{} > 9$ 7. $\boxed{} < 15 - 7$ 8. $5 - 2 < 1 + 1 + \boxed{}$
Any number less than 9. Any number less than 8. Any number greater than 1.

Write >, <, or = to make a true number sentence.
9. $5 + 2 + 4 \leq 9 + 5$ 10. $9 \geq 8 - 2$ 11. $12 = 7 + 5$

84 UNIT 3 LESSON 6   Multi-Digit Unknown Partner and Unknown Start Problems

Student Activity Book page 84

▶ Discuss Equations and Inequalities

WHOLE CLASS   **Math Talk**

Explain to the class that >, < and $\neq$ are all symbols of inequality.

Write $5 \neq 8$ on the board. Then ask the students for a more specific statement. $5 < 8$

Have students read the top of Student page 84 to review equations and introduce inequalities. Write all the examples of inequalities on the board and ask the students why each is true.

Use **Solve and Discuss** for exercises 1–11. Have some volunteers do exercises 1 and 2 at the board while others complete them at their seats. Discuss the results as a class.

Send some other students to the board for exercises 3–11. Have volunteers at the board do the additions or subtractions to prove their answers are correct.

② Going Further

Intervention — Activity Card 3-6

Solve a Simpler Problem — Activity Card 3-6 ●

Work: In small groups

Use:
• Math Journals
• MathBoard materials

1. Sometimes solving a simpler problem can help you decide what operation to use to solve an equation. Study the example at the right.

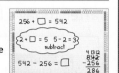

2. Copy each equation below into your Math Journal.
   • $1,278 - \square = 872$ 406
   • $\square + 922 = 1,599$ 677
   • $\square - 489 = 261$ 750

3. Write an equation with smaller numbers to help your decide what operation you need to solve each equation. Then use that operation to solve the original equation with the larger numbers.

Unit 3, Lesson 6   Copyright © Houghton Mifflin Company

Activity Note After writing a simpler equation, students should decide which operation using the two known numbers will give the unknown number.

✏ Math Writing Prompt

Simpler Problem How could you use smaller numbers to help you decide how to solve $524 - \square = 312$?

Soar to Success Math ★ Software Support

Warm Up 59.02

On Level — Activity Card 3-6

Dial a Number — Activity Card 3-6 ▲

Work: In pairs

Use:
• Math Journals
• Calculator

1. **On Your Own** Use the telephone key pad below to make as many words as you can with three or more letters. Record each word that you make and the number it represents.

THE = 843   JAR = 527

2. Use pairs of words that you make to write equations with words and numbers. Exchange equations with your partner and use a calculator to check your work.

THE = 843   JAR = 527

THE + JAR = 1,370

Unit 3, Lesson 6   Copyright © Houghton Mifflin Company

Activity Note Students should exchange only the equations with their partners, not the equivalent values for each word they use in the equations.

✏ Math Writing Prompt

Compare and Contrast In what way is solving a multi-digit problem just like solving a problem with 1-digit numbers? In what ways is it different? Explain your thinking.

HARCOURT MEGA MATH Grades K-6 Software Support

Country Countdown: Harrison's Comparisons, Level J

Challenge — Activity Card 3-6

Break the Code — Activity Card 3-6 ■

Work: In pairs

Use:
• Math Journals

1. **On Your Own** Use the telephone key pad below to make as many words as you can with two or more letters. Record each word you make and the number it represents.

NOW + HI = $\square$

$228 + \square$ = DOG

$\square + \bigcirc$ = LOW

2. Write three equations with unknown numbers. Use the words that you made and numbers with two or more digits, as shown above. Be sure that the last equation has two different unknown numbers.

3. Exchange with your partner to find the unknown numbers in each equation.

Unit 3, Lesson 6   Copyright © Houghton Mifflin Company

Activity Note Students can write addition or subtraction equations. The equation with two unknown numbers can be solved by using the value of one unknown that was found in the first equation.

✏ Math Writing Prompt

Real-World Application Describe a real-life situation where you might need to solve a math problem involving 3-digit numbers.

✖ DESTINATION Math® Software Support

Course II: Module 2: Unit 1: Estimating and Finding Sums less than 1,000

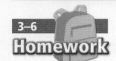 **3** # Homework and Spiral Review

---

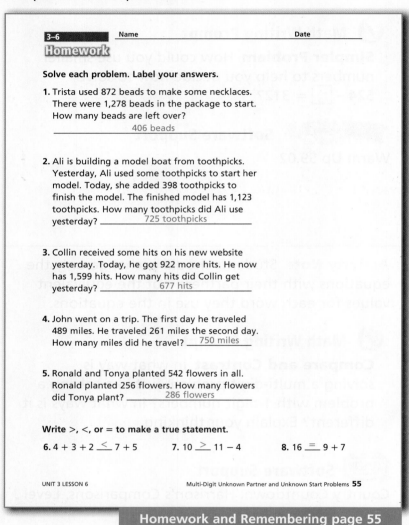

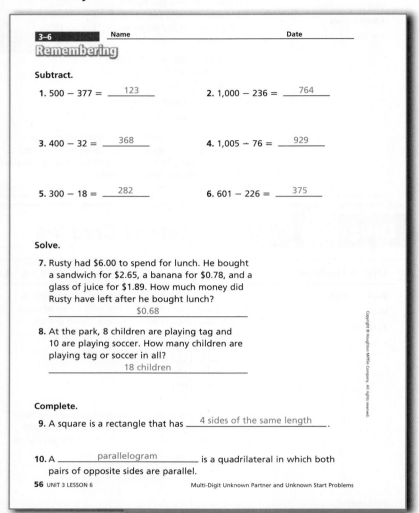

Homework and Remembering page 55

Homework and Remembering page 56

Home or School Activity

 Language Arts Connection

Tall Tales Explain to students that a *tall tale* is a story in which exaggerations are used. Remind students of tall tales they may know, such as the stories of Paul Bunyan, Johnny Appleseed, and Pecos Bill.

Have students write tall tales in which they are the main characters. The tall tales should involve large numbers. Students should give a title to the tall tale and draw a picture that illustrates the situation described in the story. Then they should write and solve an unknown partner or an unknown start problem that is based on their tall tale.

Multi-Digit Comparison Problems

REAL WORLD **Problem Solving**

Lesson Objectives

● Represent and solve multi-digit comparison problems.

● Represent and solve multi-digit comparison problems with misleading language.

Vocabulary
comparison problem
comparison bars

The Day at a Glance

Today's Goals	Materials
1 Teaching the Lesson **A1:** Solve multi-digit comparison word problems using different strategies. **A2:** Represent and solve multi-digit comparison problems with misleading language. **2 Going Further** ▶ Problem Solving Strategy: Use Logical Reasoning ▶ Math Connection: Choose a Number Sentence ▶ Differentiated Instruction **3 Homework and Spiral Review**	**Lesson Activities** Student Activity Book pp. 85–88 or Student Hardcover Book pp. 85–88 Homework and Remembering pp. 57–58 MathBoard materials **Going Further** Student Activity Book pp. 87–88 or Student Hardcover Book pp. 87–88 Activity Cards 3-7 MathBoard materials Two-color counters Calculators (optional) Cross-Number Puzzle (TRB M37) Math Journals

123 *Use* **Math Talk** *today!*

Keeping Skills Sharp

Quick Practice 🕐 5 MINUTES	Daily Routines
Goal: Find the unknown partner. **Unknown Partner Subtraction** Write these equations on the board. $15 - \square = 8$ $150 - \square = 80$ $1{,}500 - \square = 800$ $12 - \square = 8$ $120 - \square = 80$ $1{,}200 - \square = 800$ The **Student Leader** directs the class to complete the equations and to explain the Make a Ten, Make a Hundred, or Make a Thousand strategies. (See Unit 3 Lesson 6.)	**Homework Review** Find students who had difficulty with one specific problem. Work with these students as a group. Strategy Problem A small drink is 72¢, a medium drink is 77¢, and a large drink is 82¢. If the pattern continues, how much is an extra large drink likely to cost? Explain. 87¢; I wrote out the numbers to find the pattern, which is add 5¢. Extra large is after large, so I add 5¢ to 82¢ and get 87¢.

Teaching the Lesson

Multi-Digit Comparison Problems

 20 MINUTES

Goal: Solve multi-digit comparison problems using different strategies.

Materials: Student Activity Book or Hardcover Book p. 85, MathBoard materials

✔ **NCTM Standards:**
Number and Operations
Problem Solving
Representation

The Learning Classroom

Helping Community Students at the board may get stuck at some point. They usually welcome help from another student at that point. Allowing other students to help instead of you will help them to assume responsibility for one another's learning. Ask who they would like to come up to help them. You can move on to another explainer while they redo their work. Of course, sometimes it is fine just to go ahead and have the whole class help the student with you leading with questions.

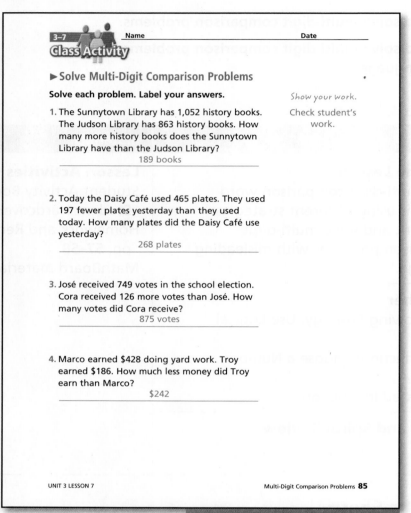

Student Activity Book page 85

▶ Solve Multi-Digit Comparison Problems

WHOLE CLASS

Using the **Solve and Discuss** structure, have students solve problem 1 on Student Book page 85. Select students who used different strategies to present their solutions.

A variety of strategies are presented on the following page.

Comparison Bars

Judson | 863 | ?

Sunnytown | 1,052

Numerical Methods

1,052
− 863

863 + 7 is 870
+ 30 is 900
+152 is 1,052
189

Equation

863 + ☐ = 1,052

Place Value Drawings

863 ooooo ||| ☐ ||||| oo ←189 added
oo   on to get
870 900 1,000 1,050 1,052   1,052

Using **Solve and Discuss,** have students solve problem 2 on Student Activity Book page 89. Select students who used different strategies to present their solutions. Here are the comparison bars for problem 2.

yesterday | ? | (197)

today | 465

Students may also write and solve one of the following equations to solve the problem.

☐ + 197 = 465   197 + ☐ = 465   465 − 197 = ☐

For a sample of classroom dialogue, see **Math Talk in Action** in the side column.

 Math Talk in Action

Jonah: The problem says that the Daisy Café used 465 plates today and yesterday they used 197 fewer plates than they did today.

Carrie: We have to find out how many plates were used yesterday. I think we have to add 465 + 197.

Alexa: No we don't, the word *fewer* means *less than*. They used fewer plates yesterday than they did today. That means they used more plates today.

Carrie: I still don't understand.

Jonah: When we draw the comparison bars, we fill in the bars for the larger amount, 465 and the difference, 197. We can subtract 465 − 197 to find out the smaller amount. That stands for how many plates they used yesterday.

Alexa: 465 − 197 = 268. They used 268 plates yesterday.

Carrie: And that's fewer than they used today. Now I understand!

❶ Teaching the Lesson (continued)

Differentiated Instruction

Extra Help If you think students need practice restating *more* comparisons using *fewer,* and *fewer* comparisons using *more,* go through problems 1–4 on Student Activity Book page 89, asking students to restate each comparison.

Using **Solve and Discuss,** have students solve problem 3 on Student Activity Book page 89. Select students who used different strategies to present their solution. Some possible strategies are shown below.

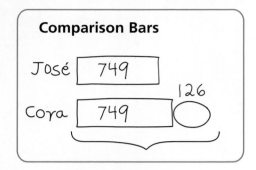

Comparison Bars

José 749
Cora 749 126

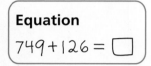

Equation

$749 + 126 = \square$

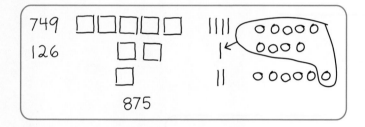

749
126

875

Using **Solve and Discuss,** have students solve Problem 4. Again select students who used different strategies to present their solution. The comparison bars are shown below.

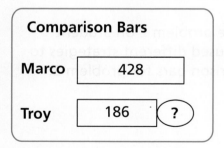

Comparison Bars

Marco 428

Troy 186 ?

Activity 2

Multi-Digit Comparison Problems with Misleading Language

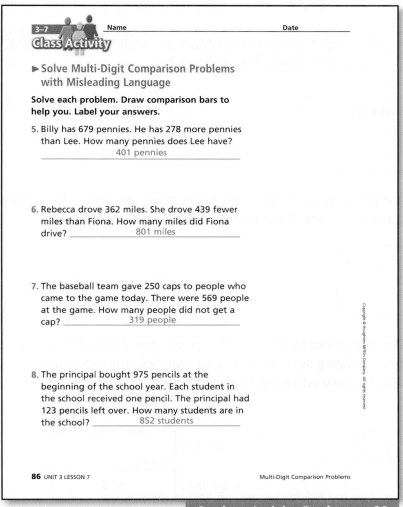

3–7

Class Activity

Name _____ Date _____

▶ Solve Multi-Digit Comparison Problems
with Misleading Language

Solve each problem. Draw comparison bars to
help you. Label your answers.

5. Billy has 679 pennies. He has 278 more pennies
than Lee. How many pennies does Lee have?
_____ 401 pennies

6. Rebecca drove 362 miles. She drove 439 fewer
miles than Fiona. How many miles did Fiona
drive? _____ 801 miles

7. The baseball team gave 250 caps to people who
came to the game today. There were 569 people
at the game. How many people did not get a
cap? _____ 319 people

8. The principal bought 975 pencils at the
beginning of the school year. Each student in
the school received one pencil. The principal had
123 pencils left over. How many students are in
the school? _____ 852 students

Copyright © Houghton Mifflin Company. All rights reserved.

86 UNIT 3 LESSON 7 — Multi-Digit Comparison Problems

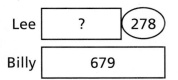
Student Activity Book page 86

 20 MINUTES

Goal: Represent and solve multi-digit
comparison problems with misleading
language.

Materials: Student Activity Book or
Hardcover Book p. 86, MathBoard
materials

 NCTM Standards:
Number and Operations
Problem Solving
Representation

Teaching Note

Critical Thinking Encourage
students to review their answers to
make sure that the answer makes
sense and is reasonable.

English Language Learners

Help students understand *mislead*.
Write *lead* on the board. Have 3
students stand behind you in a line.
Say: **I'm going to *lead* you to the
door. Follow me.** Walk the wrong
way.

• **Beginning** Ask: **Are we walking
to the door?** no Say: **I'm *misleading*
you. We're going the wrong way.**
• **Intermediate** Ask: **Are we going
the right way?** no Say: **I'm
misleading you.** Write *mislead*.
Say: **Sometimes the words *fewer*
and *more* are *misleading* in word
problems.**
• **Advanced** Ask: **Am I leading you
the right way?** no Say: **I was
misleading you.** Ask: **What
comparison words sometimes
mislead you to the wrong
answer?** fewer, more

▶ Solve Multi-Digit Comparison Problems with Misleading Language WHOLE CLASS

Using the **Solve and Discuss** structure, have students solve problem 5 on
Student Book page 86. Here are the comparison bars for problem 5.

Lee | ? | (278)
Billy | 679

Multi-Digit Comparison Problems **227**

Discuss the common error many people make when solving this type of problem.

- The Puzzled Penguin might solve this problem by adding 679 and 278. Why do you think he might make this mistake? He sees the word *more* and thinks he should add.

- How can you avoid this error? Answers will vary. Possible answers: Think carefully about who has more and who has fewer, and draw comparison bars, or say the comparison the other way to see if it makes the problem clearer.

Have students solve problem 6 on Student Book page 86, using the **Solve and Discuss** structure. Here are the comparison bars for problem 6.

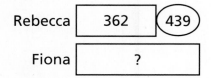

Rebecca | 362 | (439)
Fiona | ?

Using **Solve and Discuss,** have students solve problems 7 and 8 on Student Book page 86. Make sure a variety of solution methods are presented, including the use of comparison bars, which are shown below.

caps | 250 | (?)
people | 569

pencils | ? | (123)
students | 975

Have students who experience difficulty check their comparison bars and answers with a **Helping Partner**.

If time allows, have students brainstorm and write more comparison problems.

Going Further

Problem Solving Strategy: Logical Reasoning

Goal: Use logical reasoning to solve problems.

Materials: Student Activity Book or Hardcover Book p. 87, MathBoard materials

✓ **NCTM Standards:**
Number and Operations
Problem Solving

Teaching Note

Math Background The problem-solving strategy, *Use Logical Reasoning,* can be applied to many different types of situations. On this page, students organize the facts given and use logical reasoning to find unknown facts to solve the problem.

▶ Use Logical Reasoning to Solve Problems | WHOLE CLASS |

Have students read problem 1 on Student Book page 87. Lead students through the logical reasoning process by asking the following questions.

● You know the exact amount that one person spent. Who is it? Darnell How much did he spend? $11

● Whose amount is compared to Darnell's? Mark's What is the comparison? Mark spent $3 less than Darnell. How much did Mark spend? $8

● Whose amount is compared to Marks? Rita's What is the comparison? Rita spent $7 more than Mark. What amount did Rita spend? $15

Have a student read aloud problem 2. Help students start to solve the problem by asking:

● You know one person's house number. Who is it? Lily What is it? 251

Give students a few minutes to finish. Then ask a volunteer to present their method of solving.

Using the **Solve and Discuss** structure, have students solve problems 3–5 on Student Book page 87. As time allows, have students share their strategies for the Math Journal problem.

Student Activity Book page 87

Differentiated Instruction

Extra Help Some students may find it helpful to write each sentence of a problem on a separate strip of paper. Then they can identify a logical order for the given information by rearranging the strips of paper.

> Darnell, Rita and Mark each bought a CD.
>
> Darnell spent $11.
>
> Mark spent $3 less than Darnell.
>
> Rita spent $7 more than Mark.
>
> How much did Rita spend?

Math Connection: Choose a Number Sentence

🕐 **20 MINUTES**

Goal: Match word problems and equations.

Materials: Student Activity Book or Hardcover Book p. 88

✓ **NCTM Standards:**
Numbers and Operations
Algebra

▶ Choose the Equation PAIRS

Have **Student Pairs** complete Student Book page 88.
Then discuss the answers as a class.

● Why can you eliminate $17 - \square = 9$ as the equation
for Problem 1? Possible response: The problem says
Trinh had nine pennies and found some more not
that he had 17 pennies and lost some.

● Why can you eliminate $6 - 13 = \square$ as the equation
that represents Problem 2? Possible response: 13 is
the total students at the park not the number you
need to subtract.

● How do you know that $\square + 8 = 14$ represents
problem 9? Possible response: The first sentence of
the problem has "some" shells and the second sentence shows she found 8 more for a total of
14 shells.

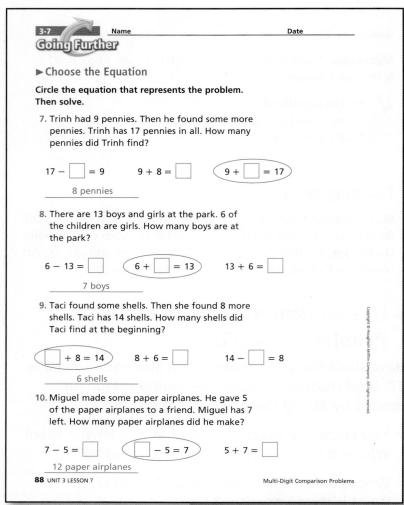

Student Activity Book page 88

Teaching Note

Math Connection This activity is designed to emphasize the
connection between the situation in a word problem and an
equation. Students will use what they know about writing an
equation to represent a problem to choosing the equation that
represents the problem. This activity requires students to use
the process of elimination.

Differentiated Instruction

Extra Help For students that have difficulty choosing the
correct equation, have them work with a **Helping Partner**
and use counters for the numbers and an index card for the
unknown number. As one student reads a part of the problem
the other represents that part with counters or the index card.
Then have them record the steps with the counters and index
card to write an equation.

Differentiated Instruction

Intervention Activity Card 3-7

Multi-Digit Comparisons
Activity Card 3-7 ●

Work: On your own

Use:
- Two number cubes, labeled 0–5 and 4–9
- Math Journal
- Calculator

1. Roll the two number cubes and make two 2-digit numbers with the digits you rolled.

2. Complete the statements below with the two numbers you made.

45   54

- Margot drove _?_ miles today.
- Sean drove _?_ miles today.

3. Find the difference between the numbers. Then use the difference to write two comparison statements, one using the word *fewer* and the other using the word *more*.

4. Use your calculator to check your statements.

5. Repeat the activity two more times.

Unit 3, Lesson 7
Copyright © Houghton Mifflin Company

Activity Note The greater number shows who drove more miles. The lesser number shows who drove fewer miles. The difference tells how many more or how many fewer miles.

✎ Math Writing Prompt

Understand the Problem What questions can you ask yourself after you read a comparison problem to help you label the comparison bars?

Soar to Success Math Software Support

Warm Up 7.17

On Level Activity Card 3-7

Cross-Number Puzzle
Activity Card 3-7 ▲

Work: On your own

Use:
- TRB M37 (Cross-Number Puzzle)
- Calculator

1. Find the missing numbers for each equation clue to complete the puzzle.

2. Use a calculator to check your work.

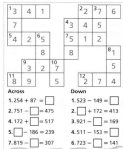

Across
1. $254 + 87 = \square$
2. $751 - \square = 475$
4. $172 + \square = 517$
5. $\square - 186 = 239$
7. $819 - \square = 307$

Down
1. $523 - 149 = \square$
2. $\square + 172 = 413$
3. $921 - \square = 169$
4. $511 - 153 = \square$
6. $723 - \square = 141$

Unit 3, Lesson 7
Copyright © Houghton Mifflin Company

Activity Note To find a missing partner, students need to remember that addition undoes subtraction and subtraction undoes addition.

✎ Math Writing Prompt

Say It Another Way Don has 5 more books than Sarah. What is another way to write this comparison? Which one is clearer? Explain.

MegaMath Grades K-6 Software Support

Numberopolis: Carnival Stories, Level R

Challenge Activity Card 3-7

Pattern Search Rule
Activity Card 3-7 ■

Work: In small groups

Use:
- Math Journals

1. Copy the patterns below into your Math Journal.

1. 123, 345, 567, ____
2. 115, 350, 585, ____
3. 152, 251, 323, ____, 701, 800

1. 789; each 3-digit number is in consecutive order
2. **Work Together** Find the missing number that fits each pattern and write the rule. There may be more than one correct number that fits a pattern.
2. 820; add 235
3. Now make three new patterns with missing numbers. Exchange with another group to find each missing number and write each rule.
3. Possible answer: 440; each of the three digits adds up to 8

Unit 3, Lesson 7
Copyright © Houghton Mifflin Company

Activity Note Encourage students to create patterns with at least four numbers, using addition or subtraction to reinforce the lesson concepts.

✎ Math Writing Prompt

Explain Your Thinking Is the word *more* a clue word to add? Explain.

DESTINATION Math Software Support

Course II: Module 1: Unit 1: Comparing and Ordering

Multi-Digit Comparison Problems **231**

③ Homework and Spiral Review

Homework **Goal:** Additional Practice

The Homework page provides additional practice in solving comparison problems using any method.

Remembering **Goal:** Spiral Review

This Remembering page would be appropriate anytime after today's lesson.

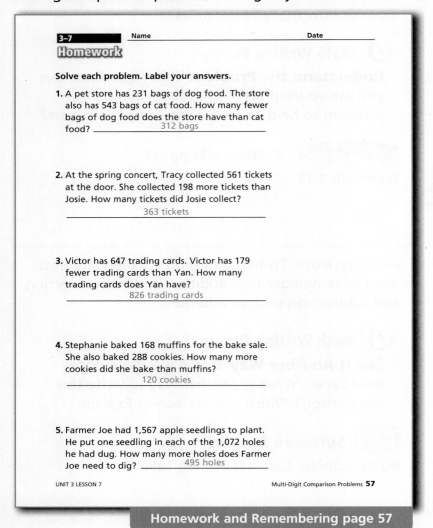

3-7 Name _____ Date _____
Homework

Solve each problem. Label your answers.

1. A pet store has 231 bags of dog food. The store also has 543 bags of cat food. How many fewer bags of dog food does the store have than cat food? _____ 312 bags

2. At the spring concert, Tracy collected 561 tickets at the door. She collected 198 more tickets than Josie. How many tickets did Josie collect?
_____ 363 tickets

3. Victor has 647 trading cards. Victor has 179 fewer trading cards than Yan. How many trading cards does Yan have?
_____ 826 trading cards

4. Stephanie baked 168 muffins for the bake sale. She also baked 288 cookies. How many more cookies did she bake than muffins?
_____ 120 cookies

5. Farmer Joe had 1,567 apple seedlings to plant. He put one seedling in each of the 1,072 holes he had dug. How many more holes does Farmer Joe need to dig? _____ 495 holes

UNIT 3 LESSON 7   Multi-Digit Comparison Problems **57**

Homework and Remembering page 57

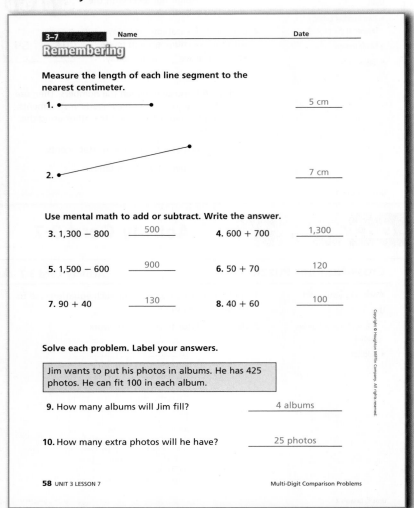

3-7 Name _____ Date _____
Remembering

Measure the length of each line segment to the nearest centimeter.

1. ●——————● _____ 5 cm

2. ●—————————● _____ 7 cm

Use mental math to add or subtract. Write the answer.

3. 1,300 − 800 _____ 500 _____   4. 600 + 700 _____ 1,300 _____

5. 1,500 − 600 _____ 900 _____   6. 50 + 70 _____ 120 _____

7. 90 + 40 _____ 130 _____   8. 40 + 60 _____ 100 _____

Solve each problem. Label your answers.

Jim wants to put his photos in albums. He has 425 photos. He can fit 100 in each album.

9. How many albums will Jim fill? _____ 4 albums

10. How many extra photos will he have? _____ 25 photos

58 UNIT 3 LESSON 7   Multi-Digit Comparison Problems

Homework and Remembering page 58

Home or School Activity

Science Connection

Compare Pulse Rates Explain to students that the number of times the heart beats per minute is called the *pulse rate.* Show students how to take their pulses by pressing two fingers to the side of the neck and counting the number of beats. Then have students do the following:

● Take their resting pulse rate for 1 minute and record the number.

● Run in place for 1 minute and record the number.

● Find the difference between the two pulse rates.

UNIT 3

LESSON 8

Mixed Multi-Digit Word Problems

REAL WORLD Problem Solving

Lesson Objective

- Represent and solve a variety of multi-digit word problems.

The Day at a Glance

Today's Goals	Materials

1 Teaching the Lesson
Represent and solve multi-digit word problems of various types.
 	
2 Going Further
▶ Math Connection: Missing Digits
▶ Differentiated Instruction
 	
3 Homework and Spiral Review
	Lesson Activities
	Student Activity Book pp. 89–90
	  Student Hardcover Book
	  pp. 89–90
	Homework and Remembering
	  pp. 59–60
	MathBoard materials
	Quick Quiz 2 (Assessment Guide) **Going Further**
	Student Activity
	  Book pp. 91–92 or
	  Student Hardcover
	  Book pp. 91–92 and
	  Activity Workbook
	  p. 29 (includes boxes
	  for writing missing
	  digits)
	Activity Cards 3-8
	MathBoard materials
	Math Journals

123 Use Math Talk today!

Keeping Skills Sharp

Quick Practice ⏱ 5 MINUTES	Daily Routines
Goal: Find the unknown partner. **Unknown Partner Subtraction** Write these equations on the board. $11 - \square = 7$ $110 - \square = 70$ $1{,}100 - \square = 700$ $15 - \square = 7$ $150 - \square = 70$ $1{,}500 - \square = 700$ The **Student Leader** directs the class to complete the equations and to explain the Make a Ten, Make a Hundred, or Make a Thousand strategies. (See Unit 3 Lesson 6.)	**Homework Review** Ask students to place their homework at the corner of their desks. As you circulate during Quick Practice, check that students completed the assignment, and see whether any problem caused difficulty for many students. **Coins and Bills** Asa has 3 dollars, 2 quarters, and 2 dimes. How much money does she have? She spends $2.50. How much money does she have left? $3.70; $1.20

Mixed Multi-Digit Word Problems   **233**

① Teaching the Lesson

Activity 1

Mixed Multi-Digit Word Problems

 45 MINUTES

Goal: Represent and solve multi-digit word problems of various types.

Materials: Student Activity Book or Hardcover Book pp. 89–90, MathBoard materials

✔ **NCTM Standards:**
Number and Operations
Problem Solving
Representation

Math Mountain	Situation Equation
T 347 ⟋⟍ 219 ☐ P P	219 + ☐ = 347 P P T

Add on with a Drawing

219 o ☐ ‖ 00000 ←128 added
               00   on to get
220 320 340 347 347

Add on Numerically

219 + 1 is 220
    +100 is 320
    + 20 is 340
    + 7 is 347
      128

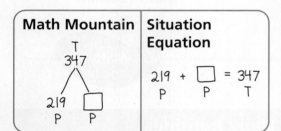

Student Activity Book page 89

▶ Solve Mixed Multi-Digit Word Problems   WHOLE CLASS

123 **Math Talk** Have students use **Solve and Discuss** to solve problems 1–8 on Student Book pages 89–90. For each problem, select two or three students who used different strategies to present their solutions. The following examples are some of the ways students might solve each problem.

Problem 1 is a Change Plus unknown partner problem. Other students may rewrite the equation as 347 − 219 = ☐ and solve it by subtracting. Others may solve 219 + ☐ = 347 by adding on. See the left side column for sample student work.

Problem 2 is a Change Plus unknown start problem. Students might write the situation equation ☐ + 239 = 427 and change it to the solution equation 427 − 239 = ☐.

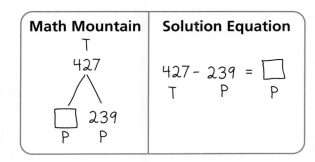

| Math Mountain | Solution Equation |

Problem 3 is a comparison problem with an unknown difference. Students might draw comparison bars and then write and solve the equation 261 − 122 = ☐ or 122 + ☐ = 261.

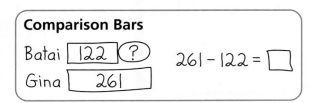

Comparison Bars

Problem 4 is a comparison problem with an unknown smaller amount. Students might draw comparison bars and then write and solve the equation 449 − 110 = ☐.

Comparison Bars

Mitch [?](110)   449 − 110 = ☐
Greta (449)

Students might also write the addition equation ☐ + 110 = 449, rewrite it as 110 + ☐ = 449, and solve by adding on.

Activity continued ▶

English Language Learners

Review vocabulary for the word problems. Write *bottle cap, stamp, phone-a-thon,* and *fence* on the board. Say: **In a *phone-a-thon* people make phone calls and ask for money.** Show pictures of the objects.

- **Beginning** Say: This is a *bottle cap*. It goes on a ___. bottle This is a *stamp*. This is an envelope. We put the *stamp* on the ___. envelope We *stamp* the envelope.
- **Intermediate** Ask: Which of these do people collect? bottle cap, stamp What goes around a house? fence
- **Advanced** Have students identify the objects and say what they are for. Ask: What is a short way to say *make a phone call*? call

3-8
Class Activity

Name _____ Date _____

Solve each problem. Label your answers.

Show your work.

Check student's work.

5. The Grove Street bus carried 798 passengers today. The Elm Street bus carried 298 more passengers today than the Grove Street bus. How many passengers did the Elm Street bus carry today?

_____ 1,096 passengers _____

6. Park City Cycle has 876 bicycles in stock. This is 134 more bicycles than Bentley's Bike Shop has in stock. How many bicycles does Bentley's Bike Shop have in stock?

_____ 742 bicycles _____

7. At Sunflower Bakery's grand opening, the first 250 customers received a free bagel. There were 682 customers at the grand opening. How many customers did not get a free bagel?

_____ 432 customers _____

8. There were some chairs set up for a concert. Then Shantel set up 256 more chairs. Now 610 chairs are set up. How many chairs were set up to start with?

_____ 354 chairs _____

90 UNIT 3 LESSON 8

Mixed Multi-Digit Word Problems

Student Activity Book page 90

Problem 5 is a comparison problem with an unknown larger amount. Students might write the equation $798 + 298 = \square$ or draw comparison bars and then add.

Comparison Bars

Grove Street | 798 | 298 |

Elm Street | ? |

$798 + 298 = \square$

Problem 6 is a comparison problem with misleading language and an unknown smaller amount. Students might draw comparison bars and then write and solve the subtraction equation 876 − 134 = ☐ or the addition equation 134 + ☐ = 876.

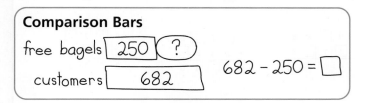

Comparison Bars

Bentley's Bike Shop [?] (134)   876 − 134 = ☐

Park City Cycle [876]

Problem 7 is an unknown difference comparison problem that does not use the word *more* or *fewer*. Students might draw comparison bars and then write and solve 250 + ☐ = 682 or 682 − 250 = ☐.

Comparison Bars

free bagels [250] (?)   682 − 250 = ☐

customers [682]

Problem 8 is a Change Plus unknown start problem. Students might use a Math Mountain to write the subtraction equation 610 − 256 = ☐.
Or they might write a situation equation, reverse the partners to get 256 + ☐ = 610, and solve by counting on.

Math Mountain	Solution Equation
T 610 /\\ ☐ 256 P P	610 − 256 = ☐

If time allows, have groups of students write the following:

● a word problem with an unknown start

● a comparison problem with an unknown difference

● a comparison problem with an unknown amount

Have groups exchange problems, solve, and present their solutions.

Class Management

Looking Ahead Even if your students have not mastered solving multi-digit word problems, move on to Unit 4. Addition and subtraction word problems appear throughout the Remembering section in Unit 4.

Quick Quiz

See Assessment Guide for Unit 3 Quick Quiz 2.

Ongoing Assessment

As students solve and discuss problems 5 through 8, ask students to explain how they decide what kind of problem each one is.

Math Connection: Missing Digits

Goal: Use logical reasoning to identify missing digits in multi-digit additions and subtractions.

Materials: Student Activity Book or Hardcover Book pp. 91–92 and Activity Workbook pp. 29–30

✔ **NCTM Standards:**
Number and Operations
Problem Solving
Reasoning and Proof

▶ Find the Missing Digits PAIRS

Have students look at exercise 1 on Student Book page 91. Ask students to describe what they see. Possible answer: It's an addition exercise. You know the sum. You don't know some of the digits of the numbers that you are adding.

● Now look at the ones places of the numbers. How many ones must be in the second number? 7 How do you know? There are 6 ones in the sum. The only way to get 6 ones in the sum is to add 7 to 9, because 9 plus 7 equals 16. Write 7 in the ones place of the first number.

● Now look at the tens places of the numbers. How many tens must be in the first number? 3 How do you know? There are 12 tens in the sum. There is 1 ten from adding 7 plus 9, and there are 8 tens in the second number. That's 9 tens. So you need 3 more tens to get 12 tens. Write 3 in the tens place of the first number.

● What is the completed addition? 39 plus 87 equals 126.

Using a similar set of questions, lead the class through the solution of exercise 2. Begin by pointing out that this exercise is different because it involves a subtraction.

Have **Student Pairs** solve exercises 3–12.

On the Back If time permits, each student should write an original missing digit addition exercise and subtraction exercise. **Student Pairs** should then work individually to solve each other's exercises.

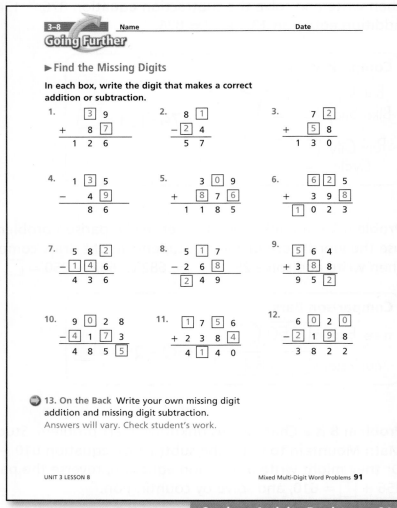

Student Activity Book page 91

Teaching Note

Math Connection This activity is designed to emphasize the connection between the operations of addition and subtraction and the sum or difference. Students use what they know about adding, subtracting, ungrouping, and regrouping to find unknown digits.

Differentiated Instruction

Intervention   Activity Card 3-8

Double-Digit Code Breaker   Activity Card 3-8 ⬤

Work: In small groups

Use:
• MathBoard materials
• Math Journals

1. Study the addition pattern below. Each of the three letters stands for a different digit.

$$\begin{array}{r} A\,A \\ +\,B\,B \\ \hline C\,C \end{array}$$

2. What can you tell about the three numbers in the pattern? Each number has two digits that are the same.

3. **Work Together** Find as many numbers as possible that fit the addition pattern. One example is shown below.

Unit 3, Lesson 8   Copyright © Houghton Mifflin Company

Activity Note Students may recognize from the pattern that the numbers they choose should not involve any regrouping.

 Math Writing Prompt

Create Your Own Write a comparison problem using multi-digit numbers. Explain how to solve your problem.

 **Software Support**

Warm Up 10.09

On Level   Activity Card 3-8

Triple-Digit Code Breaker   Activity Card 3-8 ▲

Work: In small groups

Use:
• MathBoard materials
• Math Journals

1. Study the addition pattern below. Each of the three letters stands for a different digit.

$$\begin{array}{r} A\,A\,A \\ +\,B\,B\,B \\ \hline C\,C\,C \end{array}$$

2. What can you tell about the three numbers in the pattern? Possible answer: Each number has three repeating digits.

3. **Work Together** Find as many numbers as possible that fit the addition pattern. One example is shown below.

Unit 3, Lesson 8   Copyright © Houghton Mifflin Company

Activity Note Students should use an organized list to identify all the possible sets of numbers that make a 3-digit total without regrouping.

 Math Writing Prompt

Justify When you add two 3-digit numbers, will the total always be a 3-digit number? Explain.

 Software Support

Numberopolis: Cross Town Number Line, Level V

Challenge   Activity Card 3-8

Palindrome Total   Activity Card 3-8 ■

Work: In small groups

Use:
• MathBoard materials
• Math Journals

1. Study the addition pattern below. Each of the four letters stands for a different digit.

$$\begin{array}{r} A\,A\,A \\ +\,B\,B\,B \\ \hline D\,C\,C\,D \end{array}$$

2. What can you tell about the three numbers in the pattern? Each number has repeating digits.

3. **Work Together** Find as many numbers as possible that fit the addition pattern. One example is shown below.

Unit 3, Lesson 8   Copyright © Houghton Mifflin Company

Activity Note The sum is a palindrome. A palindrome is a number that reads the same from left to right as from right to left.

 Math Writing Prompt

Predict Do you think 152 − 137 and 155 − 140 have the same difference? Explain your thinking.

 Software Support

Course II: Module 2: Unit 1: Estimating and Finding Sums less than 1,000

Mixed Multi-Digit Word Problems   **239**

 # ③ Homework and Spiral Review

3–8 Homework

Goal: Additional Practice

✓ Include students' completed Homework page as part of their portfolios.

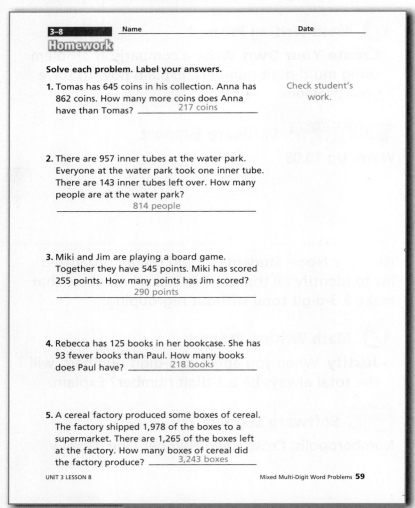

3-8 Homework   Name _____ Date _____

Solve each problem. Label your answers.

Check student's work.

1. Tomas has 645 coins in his collection. Anna has 862 coins. How many more coins does Anna have than Tomas? ___217 coins___

2. There are 957 inner tubes at the water park. Everyone at the water park took one inner tube. There are 143 inner tubes left over. How many people are at the water park? ___814 people___

3. Miki and Jim are playing a board game. Together they have 545 points. Miki has scored 255 points. How many points has Jim scored? ___290 points___

4. Rebecca has 125 books in her bookcase. She has 93 fewer books than Paul. How many books does Paul have? ___218 books___

5. A cereal factory produced some boxes of cereal. The factory shipped 1,978 of the boxes to a supermarket. There are 1,265 of the boxes left at the factory. How many boxes of cereal did the factory produce? ___3,243 boxes___

UNIT 3 LESSON 8   Mixed Multi-Digit Word Problems **59**

Homework and Remembering page 59

3–8 Remembering

Goal: Spiral Review

This Remembering page would be appropriate anytime after today's lesson.

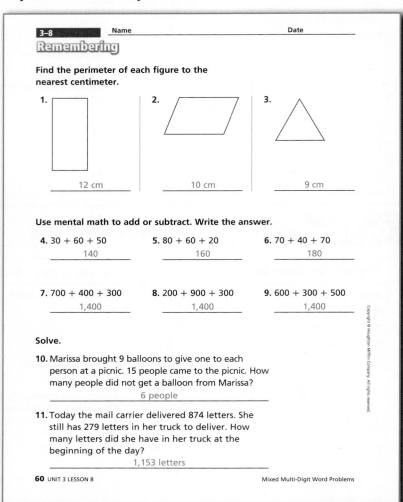

3-8 Remembering   Name _____ Date _____

Find the perimeter of each figure to the nearest centimeter.

1.   12 cm

2.   10 cm

3.   9 cm

Use mental math to add or subtract. Write the answer.

4. 30 + 60 + 50   140
5. 80 + 60 + 20   160
6. 70 + 40 + 70   180

7. 700 + 400 + 300   1,400
8. 200 + 900 + 300   1,400
9. 600 + 300 + 500   1,400

Solve.

10. Marissa brought 9 balloons to give one to each person at a picnic. 15 people came to the picnic. How many people did not get a balloon from Marissa? ___6 people___

11. Today the mail carrier delivered 874 letters. She still has 279 letters in her truck to deliver. How many letters did she have in her truck at the beginning of the day? ___1,153 letters___

60 UNIT 3 LESSON 8   Mixed Multi-Digit Word Problems

Homework and Remembering page 60

Home or School Activity

 ### Arts Connection

Create an Advertisement Have students create an advertisement for a store that is having a sale on items that cost more than $100. Explain that for each item, the advertisement should show the regular price and the sale price. Have students include at least three items in the ad. When students are finished, have them calculate the difference between the regular price and the sale price for each item.

CAL'S WAREHOUSE STUPENDOUS STOREWIDE SALE

22-inch Flat TV
Regular Price: $1,850
Cal's Stupendous Sale Price: $999

Megaram 66 Laptop
Regular Price: $1,248
Cal's Stupendous Sale Price: $677

Port-a-Tune Player
Regular Price: $219
Cal's Stupendous Sale Price: $144

240 UNIT 3 LESSON 8

Use Mathematical Processes

Lesson Objectives

● Apply mathematical concepts and skills in meaningful conexts.

● Reinforce the NCTM process skills embedded in this unit, and in previous units, with a variety of problems-solving situations.

The Day at a Glance

Today's Goals	Materials	
1 Teaching the Lesson **A1: Social Studies Connection** Find the difference between two measurements; Estimate the amount of time something will take. **A2: Problem Solving** Use a timeline to find when an event starts, how long the event will last, and to put events in order mark a time on a timeline Create a timeline. **A3: Reasoning and Proof** Use reasoning to support or disprove a statement. **A4: Representation** Use a drawing to show a problem. **A5: Communication** Tell why one solution to a problem is correct and another solution is incorrect.	**Lesson Activities** Student Activity Book pp. 93–94 or Student Hardcover Book pp. 93–94 Homework and Remembering pp. 61–62 Calculator Stopwatch or Watch Ruler	**Going Further** Activity Cards 3-9 Number Cubes MathBoard materials Math Journals
2 Going Further ▶ Differentiated Instruction		
3 Homework and Spiral Review		123 Use Math Talk today!

Keeping Skills Sharp

Quick Practice/Daily Routines	
If you wish to include Quick Practice or a Daily Routine, choose content based on the needs of your class.	**Class Management** Select activities from this lesson that support important goals and abjectives, or that help students prepare for state or district tests.

Teaching the Lesson

Math and Social Studies

 30 MINUTES

Goal: Find the difference between two measurements; estimate the amount of time something will take.

Materials: Student Activity Book or Hardcover Book p. 93, calculators, stopwatch or watch, foot ruler

✓ **NCTM Standards:**
Problem Solving
Connections
Communication

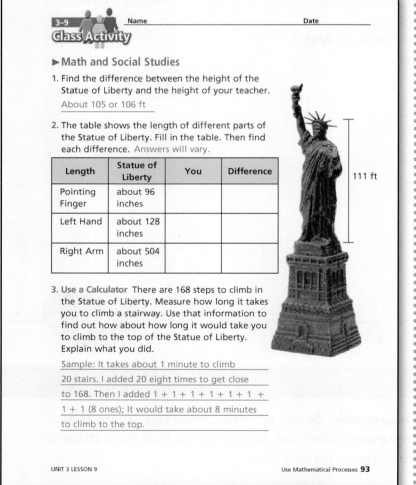

Student Activity Book page 93

Math Talk

▶ Discuss the Statue of Liberty

Task 1 Begin work on the problem with whole class discussion.

● Has anyone ever been to the Statue of Liberty or seen pictures of it? Allow students to share their experiences.

● Have students look at the picture on the Student Book page during the discussion.

● Do you think I am taller or shorter than the Statue of Liberty? Why? Allow students to give their ideas.

● I have a ruler here. How could we use this to find out how tall I am? Allow students to share their ideas. One way is to place a mark on the chalkboard that is level with the top of your head. The class counts how many ruler lengths it takes to get to the top of the mark. Alternatively, you can tell the class your height to the nearest foot.

▶ Size Comparisons to the Statue of Liberty

Task 2 Tell students that they are going to find the difference between the teacher's height and the height of the Statue of Liberty. They are also going to find the difference between some measurements on the Statue of Liberty and some measurements they will make on themselves. This will help them get an idea of how big the Statue of Liberty really is.

If your classroom has 8 foot ceilings, point out to students, that the statue's finger is as long as the distance from the floor to the ceiling.

▶ Find How Long to Climb to the Top

Task 3 Exercise 4 is a good problem to do as a class. Let students offer suggestions about how to solve the problem. Allow students to use a calculator.

Teaching Note

A Statue Where You Live Find a statue of a person where you live. Help the students figure out about how long the pointing finger, hand, and arm are. Have them find the difference in the measurements between the statue where you live and the Statue of Liberty.

A Day at the Amusement Park

 20 MINUTES

Goal: Use a timeline to find when an event starts, how long the event will last, and to put events in order; mark a time on a timeline; create a timeline.

Materials: Student Activity Book or Hardcover Book p. 94

 NCTM Standards:
Problem Solving
Connections
Communication
Representation

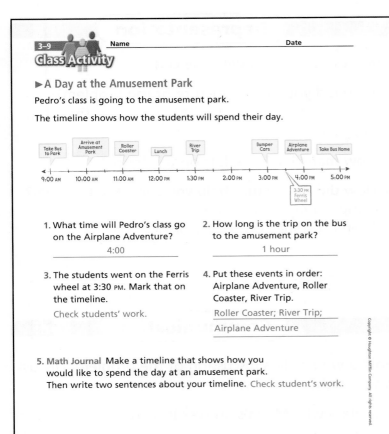

3-9
Class Activity

Name _____ Date _____

▶ **A Day at the Amusement Park**

Pedro's class is going to the amusement park.

The timeline shows how the students will spend their day.

1. What time will Pedro's class go on the Airplane Adventure?
   _____4:00_____

2. How long is the trip on the bus to the amusement park?
   _____1 hour_____

3. The students went on the Ferris wheel at 3:30 PM. Mark that on the timeline.
   Check students' work.

4. Put these events in order: Airplane Adventure, Roller Coaster, River Trip.
   Roller Coaster; River Trip;
   Airplane Adventure

5. Math Journal Make a timeline that shows how you would like to spend the day at an amusement park. Then write two sentences about your timeline. Check student's work.

94 UNIT 3 LESSON 9   Use Mathematical Processes

Student Activity Book page 94

▶ **Discuss Amusement Parks and Timelines**   Math Talk

Task 1 Begin with whole class discussion.

● Have you ever been to an amusement park? What are your favorite rides? Allow students to share their experiences.

● What is a timeline and how is it used? Have students look at the timeline on the SAB page. Bring out in the discussion that a timeline shows the order of events and what time each event occurs. Timelines are used to easily show this information to people.

Explain that Pedro's class is going to an amusement park and the timeline shows their schedule. Tell students that they are going to answer questions about the timeline. Have students complete problems 1–4 and discuss the answers as a class.

▶ **Create Your Own Timeline**

Task 2 Explain that students are going to create a timeline that shows how they would like to spend the day at an amusement park. When students have completed exercise 5, have students share their timelines.

● What can you say about your timeline? Have students show their timelines and share what they wrote about them.

English Language Learners

Show pictures to review *amusement park* and *rides*. Draw the timeline from the SAB without the times. Say: **This is a timeline.** It tells us the order of activities.

● **Beginning** Ask: **Do they take the bus or arrive at the park first?** take the bus Write the times. Ask: **What time is lunch?** noon

● **Intermediate** Ask: **What ride is first?** rollercoaster Write the times. Ask: **What time will they arrive?** 9A.M. **Leave?** 5P.M.

● **Advanced** Have students describe the order of events. Write the times. Ask: **What time is lunch?** noon **The River Trip?** 1:30P.M. Ask: **Is lunch 1 hour or $1\frac{1}{2}$ hours?** $1\frac{1}{2}$

Activity 3

Dividing Rectangles

 10 MINUTES

Goal: Use reasoning to support or disprove a statement.

 NCTM Standards:
Problem Solving   Reasoning and Proof
Communication   Representation

Support or disprove with examples: All rectangles can be divided into two triangles.

Hold a whole-class discussion of the statement.

● Do you think all rectangles can be divided into two triangles? Yes.

● Can you support this with examples? Allow students to show their examples.

● Can anyone find a rectangle that cannot be divided into two triangles? No; If anyone thinks they have a rectangle that cannot be divided into two triangles, ask a volunteer to show a way.

Activity 4

Fly Away

 10 MINUTES

Goal: Use a drawing to show a problem.

 NCTM Standards:
Problem Solving   Connections   Communication
Reasoning and Proof   Representation

Draw a picture to show this problem:
There are 15 birds on a fence. 8 birds fly away. How many birds are left? Check students' art.

Discuss the problem with the class.

● How did you draw a picture of the problem? Allow students to show their picture of the problem.

● How many birds are left on the fence? 7

● How did the picture help you solve the problem? Sample: I drew birds to count on from 8 to 15. Then I counted the birds I drew.

Activity 5

How Many Apples?

 10 MINUTES

Goal: Tell why one solution to a problem is correct and another solution is incorrect.

 NCTM Standards:
Problem Solving   Communication   Connections

Mio bought 2 green apples and 6 red apples. How many apples did she buy altogether?

Jason says Mio bought 4 apples in all. Maria says Mio bought 8 apples in all. Who is right? Maria

Hold a whole-class discussion of the problem. Discuss who is right and why.

● Explain why Maria's answer is correct. You need to add 2 and 6, and $2 + 6 = 8$, Maria's answer is correct.

● What did Jason do wrong? Jason subtracted 2 from 6.

● Why do you think Jason decided to subtract? Answers will vary.

Intervention   Activity Card 3-9

An Animal Story   Activity Card 3-9 ●

Work: In pairs

Use:
• Number cubes

Decide:
Who will be Student 1 and who will be Student 2 for the first round.

1. **Student 1:** Choose an animal. Roll a number cube. Draw a picture of that many animals.

2. Roll the number cube again. Show that many animals coming into the group or leaving the group in your picture.

3. **Student 2:** Write an addition or subtraction story for the picture your partner drew.

There were 8 ducks in the pond. 3 ducks flew away.

Unit 3, Lesson 9   Copyright © Houghton Mifflin Company

Activity Note Students should tell an addition story for things coming into a group. They should tell a subtraction story for things leaving a group.

✎ **Math Writing Prompt**

Add or Subtract Bala drew a picture of 5 ducks in a pond and 3 ducks leaving the pond. What addition or subtraction sentence would you write for that situation? Why?

Soar to Success Math ★ **Software Support**

Warm Up 10.04

On Level   Activity Card 3-9

Tell a Story   Activity Card 3-9 ▲

Work: On your own

Use:
• Number cubes

1. Roll two number cubes.

2. Use the numbers to write an addition or subtraction story.

3. Write a number sentence for your story.

Andy has 7 toys. He gave Imala 2 toys. How many toys does Andy have left?

$7 - 2 = 5$

4. Does your number sentence show subtraction or addition? Explain why you used that operation.

5. Repeat the activity.

Unit 3, Lesson 9   Copyright © Houghton Mifflin Company

Activity Note When students roll the number cubes, they have their choice of telling an addition or a subtraction story.

✎ **Math Writing Prompt**

Same Numbers, Different Story Choose one of your stories. Write another story with the same numbers but with the opposite operation.

MEGA MATH Grades K-6 **Software Support**

Numberopolis: Carnival Stories, Level I

Challenge   Activity Card 3-9

Roll a Cube, Write a Number Sentence   Activity Card 3-9 ■

Work: In pairs

Use:
• Number cube
• MathBoard materials

Decide:
Who will be Student 1 and who will be Student 2 for the first round.

1. **Student 1:** Roll a number cube. Write an addition or subtraction number sentence that has your number for the answer.

$15 - 8 = 7$
$19 - 12 = 7$

2. **Student 2:** Write another number sentence for your partner's number.

3. **Work Together** Think of story problems for your number sentences.

4. Take turns being Student 1 and Student 2.

Unit 3, Lesson 9   Copyright © Houghton Mifflin Company

Activity Note For any number the students roll, they can write an addition sentence or a subtraction sentence.

✎ **Math Writing Prompt**

Write a Story Write a story for one of the number sentences that you wrote.

✳ **DESTINATION** Math **Software Support**

Course II: Module 2: Unit 1: Differences within 100

③ Homework and Spiral Review

✓ Include student's completed Homework page as part of their portfolios.

3-9
Remembering **Goal:** Spiral Review

This Remembering page would be appropriate anytime after today's lesson.

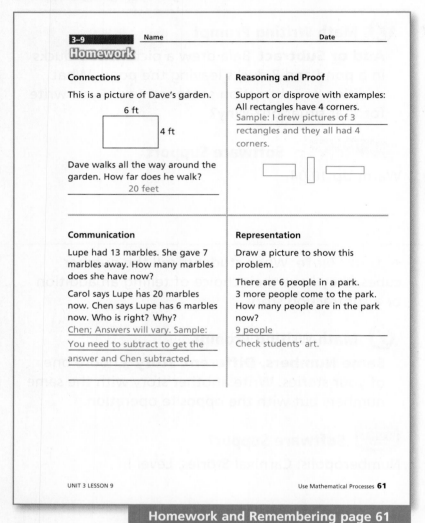

3-9 Name _____ Date _____
Homework

Connections

This is a picture of Dave's garden.

6 ft

4 ft

Dave walks all the way around the garden. How far does he walk?
_____20 feet_____

Communication

Lupe had 13 marbles. She gave 7 marbles away. How many marbles does she have now?

Carol says Lupe has 20 marbles now. Chen says Lupe has 6 marbles now. Who is right? Why?
Chen; Answers will vary. Sample:
You need to subtract to get the
answer and Chen subtracted.

Reasoning and Proof

Support or disprove with examples: All rectangles have 4 corners.
Sample: I drew pictures of 3
rectangles and they all had 4
corners.

Representation

Draw a picture to show this problem.

There are 6 people in a park. 3 more people come to the park. How many people are in the park now?
9 people
Check students' art.

UNIT 3 LESSON 9   Use Mathematical Processes **61**

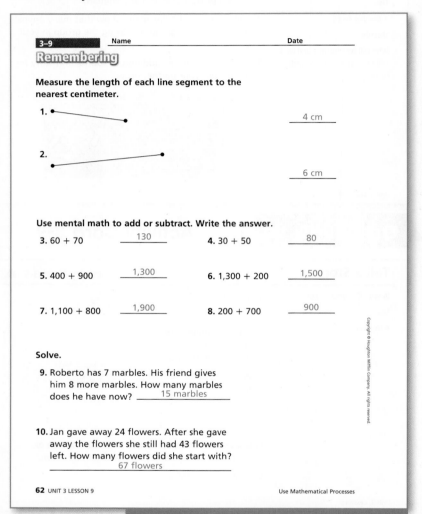

3-9 Name _____ Date _____
Remembering

Measure the length of each line segment to the nearest centimeter.

1. ●————————●   _____4 cm_____

2. ●————————●   _____6 cm_____

Use mental math to add or subtract. Write the answer.

3. 60 + 70   _____130_____   4. 30 + 50   _____80_____

5. 400 + 900   _____1,300_____   6. 1,300 + 200 _____1,500_____

7. 1,100 + 800 _____1,900_____   8. 200 + 700   _____900_____

Solve.

9. Roberto has 7 marbles. His friend gives him 8 more marbles. How many marbles does he have now? _____15 marbles_____

10. Jan gave away 24 flowers. After she gave away the flowers she still had 43 flowers left. How many flowers did she start with?
_____67 flowers_____

62 UNIT 3 LESSON 9   Use Mathematical Processes

Home or School Activity

 Social Studies Connection

Create a Flag Have students look at pictures of flags from different countries on the Internet or in books. Have them talk about the geometric shapes they see in the flags. Have them create their own flag with geometric shapes in the design. Have them talk about the geometric shapes they used in the design.

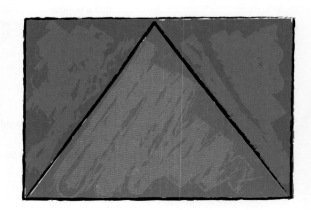

Unit Review and Test

Lesson Objectives

● **Assess student progress on unit objectives.**

The Day at a Glance

Today's Goals	Materials
1 **Teaching the Lesson** ► Assess student progress on unit objectives. ► Use activities from unit lessons to reteach content.	Unit 3 Test, Student Activity Book or Hardcover Book pp. 95–96 Unit 3 Test, Form A or B, Assessment Guide (optional)
2 **Extending the Assessment** ► Use remediation for common errors.	Unit 3 Performance Assessment, Assessment Guide (optional)
There is no homework assignment on a test day.	

Keeping Skills Sharp

Quick Practice 🕐 5 MINUTES	
Goal: Review any skills you choose to meet the needs of your class. If you are doing a unit review day, use any of the Quick Practice activities that provide support for your class. If this is a test day, omit Quick Practice.	**Review and Test Day** You may want to choose a quiet game or other activity (reading a book or working on homework for another subject) for students who finish early.

Assess Unit Objectives

🕐 **45 MINUTES** (more if schedule permits)

Goal: Assess student progress on unit objectives

Materials: Student Activity Book or Hardcover Book pp. 95–96; Assessment Guide Unit 3 Test Form A or B (optional), Unit 3 Performance Assessment (optional)

▶ Review and Assessment

If your students are ready for assessment on the unit objectives, you may use either the test on the Student Activity Book pages or one of the forms of the Unit 3 Test in the Assessment Guide to assess student progress.

If you feel that students need some review first, you may use the test on the Student Book pages as a review of unit content, and then use one of the forms of the Unit 3 Test in the Assessment Guide to assess student progress.

To assign a numerical score for all of these test forms, use 10 points for each question.

You may also choose to use the Unit 3 Performance Assessment. Scoring for that assessment can be found in its rubric in the Assessment Guide.

▶ Reteaching Resources

The chart at the right lists the test items, the unit objectives they cover, and the lesson activities in which the objective is covered in this unit. You may revisit these activities with students who do not show mastery of the objectives.

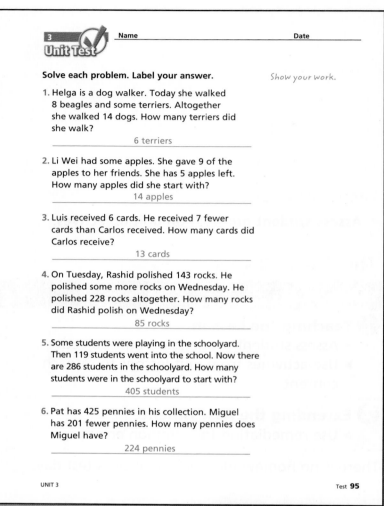

Student Activity Book page 95

Unit Test Items	Unit Objectives Tested	Activities to Use for Reteaching
1–6	**3.1** Solve a variety of word problems involving addition and subtraction.	Lesson 1, Activities 2, 4 Lesson 2, Activity 2 Lesson 3, Activity 2 Lesson 4, Activity 2 Lesson 6, Activity 1 Lesson 7, Activity 1 Lesson 8, Activity 1
7–10	**3.2** Express relationships as equations and inequalities; Write equations and use comparison bars to represent and solve word problems.	Lesson 1, Activity 3 Lesson 2, Activity 2 Lesson 3, Activity 2 Lesson 4, Activity 2 Lesson 5, Activity 1 Lesson 6, Activity 4

Student Activity Book page 96

3 Unit Test

Name _____ Date _____

7. Write a number to make the number sentence true.

a. $10 = \boxed{7} + 3$ b. $8 - \boxed{} \neq 3$
Any number except 5.

c. $5 + \boxed{6} = 11$ d. $15 > \boxed{} + 8$
Any number less than 7.

e. $9 - 2 < \boxed{} + 5$ Any number greater than 2.

Numbers will vary for inequalities. Descriptions of correct numbers are given.

Show your work.

Write an equation and then solve each problem. Label your answer.

8. On Monday and Tuesday, Franco spent 5 hours doing homework altogether. He did homework for 2 hours on Tuesday. How many hours did Franco spend doing homework on Monday?
$5 - 2 = \boxed{}$ or $2 + \boxed{} = 5$; 3 hours

9. Tony had some baseball cards. Jeremy gave him 8 more. Then he had 19 baseball cards. How many did he have to start?
$\boxed{} + 8 = 19$ or $19 - 8 = \boxed{}$; 11 baseball cards

*10. **Extended Response** Elsa read 13 books this month. She read 6 fewer books than Cliff read. Draw Comparison Bars to represent the problem.

Cliff | ? books
Elsa | 13 books | (6 books)

How many books did Cliff read? __19 books__

Explain how you know who read more books, Elsa or Cliff.
Possible answer: Cliff read more books because the problem says Elsa read 6 fewer books than Cliff.

*Item 10 also assesses the Process Skills of Representation, Communication, and Reasoning and Proof.

96 UNIT 3   Test

► Assessment Resources

Free Response Tests
Unit 3 Test, Student Book pages 95–96
Unit 3 Test, Form A, Assessment Guide

Extended Response Item
The last item in the Student Book test and in the Form A test will require an extended response as an answer.

Multiple Choice Test
Unit 3 Test, Form B, Assessment Guide

Performance Assessment
Unit 3 Performance Assessment, Assessment Guide
Unit 3 Performance Assessment Rubric, Assessment Guide

► Portfolio Assessment

Teacher-selected Items for Student Portfolios:

- Homework, Lessons 2, 4, 6, 8, and 9
- Class Activity work, Lessons 5, 7, and 9

Student-selected Items for Student Portfolios:

- Favorite Home or School Activity
- Best Writing Prompt

② Extending the Assessment

Unit Objective 3.1

Solve a variety of word problems involving addition and subtraction.

Common Error: Unable to Identify the Relevant Information

Students may have difficulty identifying what they need to find.

Remediation Have students circle the information provided and label it (for example, total, partner, larger amount, smaller amount).

Common Error: Cannot Explain Why an Operation Was Chosen

Students may have difficulty explaining why a word problem involves addition or subtraction

Remediation Have students make up addition and subtraction problems. Ask them to explain how they know the problem is about addition or subtraction. Reinforce the language of operations by posing questions such as "Are you putting groups together?" or "Are you taking groups apart?".

Common Error: Makes Incorrect Computations

Sometimes students have difficulty solving word problems because they do not know basic additions and subtractions.

Remediation Have students make Math Mountain cards of the basic additions and subtractions they don't know. Or, students can practice with flash cards.

Common Error: Doesn't Know How to Begin When Problems Have Larger Numbers

When problems involve larger numbers, student may have difficulty deciding how to begin.

Remediation Have students rewrite the problem using smaller numbers. Then have students draw a diagram using the smaller numbers (Comparison Bars or a Math Mountain) to help organize the information in the problem. When they've organized the information, have them replace the smaller numbers with the original numbers.

Common Error: Has Difficulty Deciding Whether to Add or to Subtract

Students may have difficulty determining if a word problem involves addition or subtraction.

Remediation Have students use blocks to act out a problem. As they take various actions, help students make connections to addition or subtraction by asking questions such as,

- Are you putting groups together? (add)
- Are you separating a group into parts? (subtract)
- Are you taking some away? (subtract)
- Are you comparing numbers? (subtract)

Have students make lists of words that mean to add or to subtract.

Unit Objective 3.2

Express relationships as equations and inequalities; Write equations and use comparison bars to represent and solve word problems.

Common Error: Draws Comparison Bars Incorrectly

Students may draw and label the Comparison Bars incorrectly.

Remediation Point out to students that the smaller amount and the difference are connected. Have students write "larger", "smaller", and "difference" inside the correct part of the Comparison Bar diagram and have them use this as a reference as they work through problems.

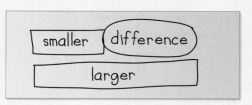

Common Error: Writes an Incorrect Equation

When translating a word problem into a math sentence, students may write the wrong equation.

Remediation Have students work in pairs to solve problems. Partners should read aloud the problems and then work together to identify the unknowns and write the equations. They can draw a picture or model the problems with base-ten blocks to help organize the information and write the equations.

Figures, Angles, and Triangles

UNIT 4 REVIEWS classifying quadrilaterals and identifying parallel sides and perpendicular sides in figures. Lines of symmetry and congruent figures are introduced. Students decompose and compose figures and classify triangles according to lengths of sides and measures of angles. Students estimate the measures of angles using benchmark angles, discover that the sum of the angles in a triangle is 180°, and find the measure of a third angle in a triangle given the measure of two other angles.

Skills Trace

Grade 2	Grade 3	Grade 4
• Explore and create symmetrical shapes. • Compare and sort shapes that are congruent or similar. • Practice with quadrilaterals. • Compose and decompose quadrilaterals.	• Identify figures that are congruent and draw lines of symmetry. • Label figures with letters. • Review quadrilaterals and introduce other polygons, including pentagons, hexagons, and octagons. • Compose and decompose triangles and quadrilaterals. • Classify triangles by the lengths of sides and explore the measures of their angles.	• Identify figures that are congruent and draw lines of symmetry. • Label figures with letters. • Review quadrilaterals and introduce other polygons, including trapezoids. • Compose and decompose triangles and quadrilaterals to find the area of parallelograms. • Classify triangles by the lengths of sides and the measures of their angles.

Unit 4   Contents

Unit 4 Assessment

✔ Unit Objectives Tested	Unit Test Items	Lessons
4.1 Identify figures that are congruent and draw lines of symmetry on figures.	1, 2	1
4.2 Label figures with letters and compose and decompose polygons.	3, 10	2, 3
4.3 Identify polygons; Classify triangles by length of sides or measure of angles.	4–9	3

Assessment and Review Resources

Formal Assessment

Student Activity Book
- Unit Review and Test (pp.119–120)

Assessment Guide
- Quick Quiz (p. A30)
- Test A–Open Response (pp. A31–A32)
- Test B–Multiple Choice (pp. A33–A34)
- Performance Assessment (pp. A35–A37)

Test Generator CD-ROM
- Open Response Test
- Multiple Choice Test
- Test Bank Items

Informal Assessment

Teacher Edition
- Ongoing Assessment (in every lesson)
- Math Talk (in every lesson)
- Portfolio Suggestions (p. 289)

123 **Math Talk**
- ▸ Math Talk in Action (pp. 252, 264, 284)
- ▸ Solve and Discuss (p. 257)
- ▸ Student Pairs (pp. 271, 275, 283, 284)
     Helping Partners (p. 282)
- ▸ Small Groups (p. 274)
- ▸ In Activities (pp. 254, 269)

Review Opportunities

Homework and Remembering
- Review of recently taught topics
- Spiral Review

Teacher Edition
- Unit Review and Test (pp. 287–290)

Test Generator CD-ROM
- Custom Review Sheets

Planning Unit 4

Lesson NCTM Focal Points NCTM Standards	Resources	Materials for Lesson Activities	Materials for Going Further
4-1 Symmetry and Congruence NCTM Focal Points: 3.1, 3.2, 3.4, 3.6 NCTM Standards: 3, 4, 7, 9	TE pp. 251–260 SAB pp. 97–98; 98A–98B; 99–104 H&R pp. 63–64 AC 4-1 MCC 13	Transparency of Student Activity Book page 98 (optional) Overhead projector (optional) Scissors ✓ Rulers Plastic mirrors Envelopes Tracing or unlined paper	Tangrams (TRB 30) Math Journals
4-2 **Label Figures and Draw Diagonals** NCTM Focal Point: 3.6 NCTM Standards: 3, 4, 7, 10	TE pp. 261–266 SAB pp. 105–108 H&R pp. 65–66 AC 4-2 MCC 14	✓ Rulers Scissors Tracing paper (optional)	Quadrilateral Cutouts B, C, G, and I from Student Activity Book page 98 Scissors ✓ Rulers Math Journals
4-3 **Angles and Triangles** NCTM Focal Points: 3.1, 3.2, 3.4, 5.2 NCTM Standards: 3, 7, 9	TE pp. 267–278 SAB pp. 109–114; 112A–112B; 114A–114B H&R pp. 67–68 AC 4-3 MCC 15	Straws Colored, flexible rods (i.e. chenille sticks) ✓ Centimeter rulers Chart paper (optional) Scissors ✓ MathBoard materials	Colored, flexible rods (i.e. chenille sticks) Index cards ✓ MathBoard materials Math Journals

Resources/Materials Key: TE: Teacher Edition SAB: Student Activity Book H&R: Homework and Remembering
AC: Activity Cards MCC: Math Center Challenge AG: Assessment Guide ✓: Grade 3 kits TRB: Teacher's Resource Book

NCTM Standards and Expectations Key: **1.** Number and Operations   **2.** Algebra   **3.** Geometry
4. Measurement   **5.** Data Analysis and Probability   **6.** Problem Solving   **7.** Reasoning and Proof
8. Communication   **9.** Connections   **10.** Representation

Lesson NCTM Focal Points NCTM Standards	Resources	Materials for Lesson Activities	Materials for Going Further
4-4 **Angle Measures** NCTM Focal Point: 5.2 NCTM Standards: 3, 4, 7, 8, 9	TE pp. 279– 286 SAB pp. 115–118 H&R pp. 69–70 AC 4-4 AG Quick Quiz MCC 16	Straws ✓ Centimeter rulers Scissors	Measure by Filling Angles (TRB M38) Scissors ✓ MathBoard materials Math Journals
✓ Unit Review and Test	TE pp. 287–290 SAB pp. 119–120 AG Unit 4 Tests		

Hardcover Student Book

- Together, the Hardcover Student Book and its companion Activity Workbook contain all of the pages in the consumable Student Activity Book.

Manipulatives and Materials

- Essential materials for teaching *Math Expressions* are available in the Grade 3 kits. These materials are indicated by a ✓ in these lists. At the front of this Teacher Edition is more information about kit contents, alternatives for the materials, and use of the materials.

Independent Learning Activities

Ready-Made Math Challenge Centers

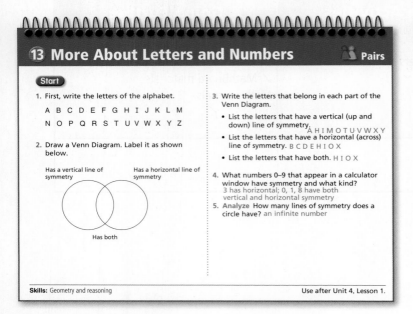

Grouping Pairs

Materials Calculator, Venn Diagram (TRB M29)

Objective Students sort letters and numbers by type of symmetry.

Connections Geometry and Reasoning

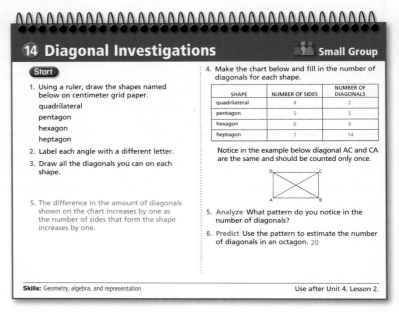

Grouping Small Group

Materials Centimeter Dot Paper (TRB M28), ruler

Objective Students investigate the pattern in the number of diagonals in polygons.

Connections Geometry and Algebra

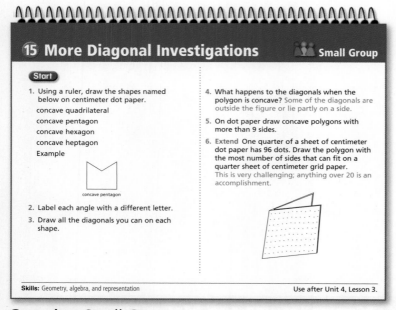

Grouping Small Group

Materials Ruler, Centimeter Grid Paper (TRB M28)

Objective Students investigate concave polygons and their properties.

Connections Geometry and Representation

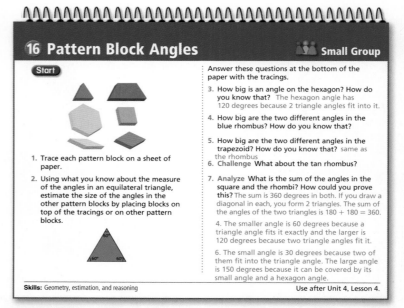

Grouping Small Group

Materials Pattern blocks

Objective Students estimate the angle measures of pattern blocks.

Connections Geometry and Estimation

Ready-Made Math Resources

Technology — Tutorial, Practice, and Intervention

Use online, individualized intervention and support to bring students to proficiency.

Help students practice skills and apply concepts through exciting math adventures.

Extend and enrich students' understanding of skills and concepts through engaging, interactive lessons and activities.

Visit **Education Place**
www.eduplace.com

Visit **www.eduplace.com/mx2t/** and find family, teacher, and student materials, activities, games, and more.

Literature Links

Sam Johnson and the Blue Ribbon Quilt

Sam Johnson and the Blue Ribbon Quilt

Quilts are a marvelous way for children to see symmetrical patterns put to use in real life. In this story by Lisa Campbell Ernst students will find out how collaboration between two quilting clubs ends up winning a quilting contest. As a follow up students could create their own symmetrical quilt squares using cut paper.

Differentiated Instruction

Individualizing Instruction

	Level	Frequency
Activities	• Intervention • On Level • Challenge	All 3 in every lesson
	Level	Frequency
Math Writing Prompts	• Intervention • On Level • Challenge	All 3 in every lesson
Math Center Challenges	For advanced students	
	4 in every unit	

Reaching All Learners

English Language Learners	Lessons	Pages
	1, 2, 3, 4	251, 261, 267, 279
Extra Help	Lessons	Pages
	1, 4	256, 282
Alternate Approach	Lesson	Page
	1	253

Strategies for English Language Learners

Present this problem to all students. Offer the different levels of support to meet students' levels of language proficiency.

Objective Review quadrilaterals and put them into categories based on their properties.

Problem Have students work in groups. Make cut outs of different quadrilaterals. Give each group a set and a sheet of poster paper with empty boxes matching the categories on the Geometry Poster.

Newcomer

• Hold up each figure and describe it. Have children repeat. Invite each group to find the figure and put it in the correct category.

Beginning

• Hold up a square. Ask: **How many sides are there?** 4 **Are the sides equal?** yes **Are opposite sides parallel?** yes **Is this a square?** yes

• Show students where to put the figures on their poster. Continue with other figures.

Intermediate

• Guide students to categorize the figures. First, *Parallelograms/ Not Parallelograms*, then *Rectangles/Not Rectangles*, and finally *Squares/Not Squares*.

• Use sentence frames to review the properties. For example, say: **Parallelogram means both pairs of opposite sides are ___.** parallel

Advanced

• Have students describe the properties of each category then invite them to work in groups to sort the quadrilaterals.

Connections

Science Connection
Lesson 2, page 266

Social Studies Connections
Lesson 3, page 278
Lesson 4, page 286

Math Background

Putting Research into Practice for Unit 4

From Current Research: Mathematical Arguments

In grades 3–5, teachers should emphasize the development of mathematical arguments. As students' ideas about figures evolve, they should formulate conjectures about geometric properties and relationships. Using drawings, concrete materials, and geometry software to develop and test their ideas, they can articulate clear mathematical arguments about why geometric relationships are true. For example: "You can't possibly make a triangle with two right angles because if you start with one side of the triangle across the bottom, the other two sides go straight up. They're parallel, so they can't possibly ever meet, so you can't get it to be a triangle."

National Council of Teachers of Mathematics. *Principles and Standards for School Mathematics.* Reston: NCTM, 2000. p. 165.

Estimating Angles

Students in grades 3–5 should measure the attributes of a variety of physical objects and extend their work to measuring more complex attributes, including area, volume, and angle. They will learn that length measurements in particular contexts are given specific names, such as *perimeter, width, height, circumference,* and *distance.* They can begin to establish some benchmarks by which to estimate or judge the size of objects. For example, they learn that a "square corner" is called a *right angle* and establish this as a benchmark for estimating the size of other angles.

National Council of Teachers of Mathematics. *Principles and Standards for School Mathematics.* Reston: NCTM, 2000. p. 171.

Mathematical Vocabulary

When discussing figures, students in grades 3–5 should be expanding their mathematical vocabulary by hearing terms used repeatedly in context. As they describe shapes, they should hear, understand, and use mathematical terms such as *parallel, perpendicular, face, edge, vertex, angle, trapezoid, prism,* and so forth, to communicate geometric ideas with greater precision. For example, as students develop a more sophisticated understanding of how geometric shapes can be the same or different, the everyday meaning of *same* is no longer sufficient, and they begin to need words such as *congruent* and *similar* to explain their thinking.

National Council of Teachers of Mathematics. *Principles and Standards for School Mathematics.* Reston: NCTM, 2000. p. 166.

Other Useful References: Classifying Quadrilaterals, Classifying Triangles

National Council of Teachers of Mathematics. *Developing Mathematical Reasoning in Grades K–12 (1999 Yearbook).* Ed. Lee V. Stiff. Reston: NCTM, 1999.

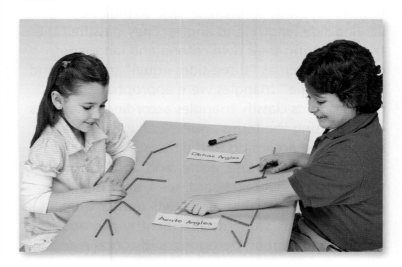

Getting Ready to Teach Unit 4

In this unit, students explore symmetry and congruence and build upon classifying and identifying polygons by their attributes. They also explore the measures of angles and discover that the sum of the measures of the angles of a triangle is 180°.

Geometry Concepts
Symmetry and Congruence
Lesson 1

In Unit 4, students are introduced to lines of symmetry. They will see that a line of symmetry divides a figure in half so that if you fold the figure along the line, the two halves will match exactly. Each half of the figure formed by a line of symmetry is described as a congruent half. Students will also discover that a figure can be divided into congruent halves by lines other than lines of symmetry. For example, in a rectangle, a diagonal is not a line of symmetry, but it does divide the rectangle into two congruent halves. The introduction to congruent halves extends to having students identify congruent figures.

Classifying Polygons
Lesson 3

In grade 2, students drew unique triangles by varying side lengths and angles. They classified these triangles using their own criteria and language: categories such as "three-sides-equal" triangles and "no-big-angle" triangles were appropriate. In this unit, students classify triangles according to lengths of sides using the terms *equilateral, isosceles, and scalene*, and according to the measure of angles using the terms *obtuse, acute*, and *right*. Although these terms should be heard, seen, and used, it is not expected that all students will master them at this grade level. Students also identify pentagons, hexagons, octagons, decagons, and concave and convex figures.

Composing and Decomposing
Lessons 2 and 3

Polygons In this unit, students continue to investigate the relationship between different polygons and triangles by dividing quadrilaterals with diagonals and composing polygons with triangles. Through these investigations, students build their ideas about properties of figures and how they are related, laying the conceptual foundation for development of area formulas of complex figures in subsequent years.

Estimating Measures of Angles
Lesson 4

In grade 2, students experimented with making big angles and small angles and drawing triangles starting with different sizes of angles. In this unit, students use benchmark angles like 90° and 180° to estimate the measures of angles. These skills in estimating angles will provide students with the foundation to use protractors successfully in subsequent years. As with all measurement, estimating is an integral part of the process.

Sum of Measures of Angles in a Triangle
Lesson 4

In this unit, students physically rearrange the angles of a triangle to form a straight angle and discover that the sum of the measures of the angles in a triangle is 180°. They then apply this property of triangles to find the measure of a missing angle in a triangle.

Problem Solving

In *Math Expressions* a research-based, algebraic problem-solving approach that focuses on problem types is used: understand the situation, represent the situation with a math drawing or an equation, solve the problem, and see that the answer makes sense. In this unit problems involving addition, subtraction, and geometry are reviewed on Remembering pages 64, 68, and 70.

MINI UNIT 4

LESSON

1

Symmetry and Congruence

Lesson Objectives

- Draw lines of symmetry.

- Identify congruent halves of figures and congruent figures.

Vocabulary

parallel
perpendicular
line of symmetry
symmetric figure
congruent

The Day at a Glance

Today's Goals	Materials
1 Teaching the Lesson **A1:** Review types of quadrilaterals and the concepts of parallel and perpendicular. **A2:** Draw the lines of symmetry in figures. **A3:** Identify congruent halves of figures and congruent figures. **2 Going Further** ▶ Math Connection: Apply Properties of Congruence and Symmetry ▶ Differentiated Instruction **3 Homework and Spiral Review**	**Lesson Activities** Student Activity Book pp. 97–100, 103–104 or Student Hardcover Book pp. 97–100, 103–104 and Activity Workbook pp. 31–34, 37–38 (includes special formats, cut outs, and Family Letter) Homework and Remembering pp. 63–64 Transparency of Student Activity Book p. 98 (optional) Overhead projector (optional) Scissors, Rulers, Envelopes Plastic mirrors Tracing paper or unlined paper	**Going Further** Student Activity Book pp. 101–102 or Hardcover Book pp. 101–102 and Activity Workbook p. 35 (includes Dot Grid to Complete Figure) Activity Cards 4-1 Tangrams or Tangrams (TRB M30) Math Journals *(123)* **Use Math Talk today!**

Keeping Skills Sharp

Daily Routines	English Language Learners
Reasoning Three people ran in the last race. Jo finished the race after Paul. Paul finished the race before Hanh. Hanh finished the race before Jo. Who finished the race first? Who finished the race last? Paul; Jo	Write *line of symmetry* and *congruent* on the board. Draw the shapes below. Give students cut outs of each. Have them fold along the lines. • **Beginning** Say: **Let's fold the square. Do the parts match?** yes **This is a *line of symmetry*. Now let's fold the rectangle. Do the parts match?** no **This is not a *line of symmetry*.** • **Intermediate** Say: **Fold the rectangle and the square along the lines.** Ask: **Which shape has parts that match?** square Say: **This is a *line of symmetry*.** Have students cut the shapes along the lines and match up the halves. Ask: **Are the parts of each shape equal?** yes Say: **They are *congruent*.** • **Advanced** Ask: **Which shape can you fold in half?** square Say: **This is a *line of symmetry*.** Say: ***Congruent* means the parts are equal.** Have students use the square to show the equal parts.

Teaching the Lesson

Review Geometry Concepts

 15 MINUTES

Goal: Review types of quadrilaterals and the concepts of parallel and perpendicular.

Materials: Student Activity Book or Hardcover Book p. 97 and Activity Workbook p. 31

✔ **NCTM Standards:**
Geometry
Connections

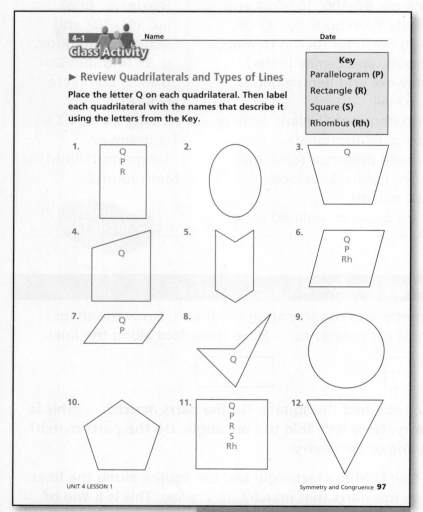

4–1
Class Activity
Name _____ Date _____

▶ Review Quadrilaterals and Types of Lines

Place the letter Q on each quadrilateral. Then label each quadrilateral with the names that describe it using the letters from the Key.

Key
Parallelogram (P)
Rectangle (R)
Square (S)
Rhombus (Rh)

1. Q P R
2.
3. Q
4. Q
5.
6. Q P Rh
7. Q P
8. Q
9.
10.
11. Q P R S Rh
12.

UNIT 4 LESSON 1   Symmetry and Congruence **97**

Student Activity Book page 97

▶ **Review Quadrilaterals and Types of Lines** WHOLE CLASS

Have students complete Student Book page 97. When they are finished, discuss the answers.

Ask for a volunteer to define parallel lines and parallel line segments. Parallel lines are everywhere the same distance apart. They go on forever and never meet. Parallel line segments are parts of parallel lines.

● Which figures on page 97 have parallel sides?
figures 1, 3, 4, 5, 6, 7, and 11

Ask for a volunteer to define perpendicular lines and perpendicular line segments. Perpendicular lines meet at right angles. Perpendicular line segments are parts of perpendicular lines.

● Which figures on page 97 have perpendicular sides?
figures 1, 4, and 11

Some students may also note that in certain figures two line segments may be perpendicular if one side is extended to meet another side.

● Which figures have both parallel sides and perpendicular sides? figures 1, 4, and 11

 Math Talk in Action

How can you remember what *parallel* means?

Juan: The double *l* in the word parallel looks like a pair of parallel lines.

Tina: The word also sounds a bit like "a pair of Ls."

How can you check if two line segments are perpendicular?

Tina: You can put a piece of paper with a square corner along the edge to check. This figure is not perpendicular because the line segments do not meet at a right angle.

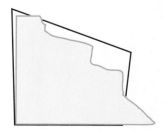

Explore Symmetry

 25 MINUTES

Goal: Draw the lines of symmetry in figures.

Materials: Student Activity Book pp. 98–98B or Hardcover Book p. 98 and Activity Workbook pp. 32–34, transparency of Student Book p. 98 and overhead projector (optional), scissors, rulers (1 per student), plastic mirrors, envelopes (one per student)

 NCTM Standards:
Measurement
Geometry
Reasoning and Proof

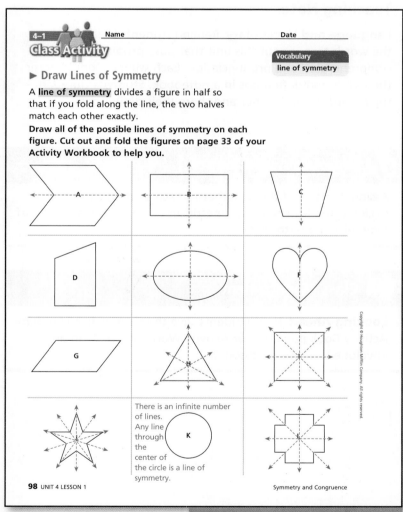

Student Activity Book page 98

▶ **Draw Lines of Symmetry** WHOLE CLASS

On the board or on an overhead transparency of Student Book page 98, draw the line of symmetry for figure A.

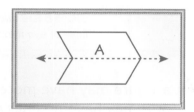

Point out that this line divides figure A into two pieces.

● **How do these two pieces compare?** They are the same size and shape.

● **What will happen if I cut out figure A and fold it along the line?** The two halves will match.

Explain to students that the line you drew is called a line of symmetry. A line of symmetry divides a figure in half so that if you fold the figure along the line, the two halves will match exactly. Point out that a line of symmetry is sometimes called a mirror line because the half on one side of the line looks like the reflection of the other half in a mirror. We say a figure has symmetry if it can be folded along a line so that the two halves match exactly.

✋ **Alternate Approach**

Plastic Mirrors To verify a line of symmetry, students can place a transparent mirror alongside it. If one half of the figure appears to fall directly on top of the other half, the mirror is on a line of symmetry.

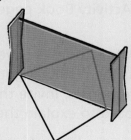

Activity continued ▶

❶ Teaching the Lesson (continued)

Use the overhead transparency of Student Activity Book page 98 or draw an enlarged version of figure B on the board and invite a volunteer to draw a line of symmetry in the figure.

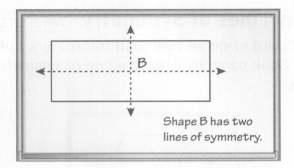

Shape B has two lines of symmetry.

Tell students that a figure may have more than one line of symmetry, or it may have no lines of symmetry. Ask another volunteer to draw a different line of symmetry on figure B.

Some students may suggest a diagonal as a possible line of symmetry for figure B.

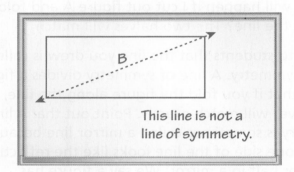

This line is not a line of symmetry.

Demonstrate that this line is not a line of symmetry by cutting out a copy of figure B and folding it along the diagonal. Explain that when two halves do not match when folded, the line is not a line of symmetry.

Have students cut out the copies of the figures on page 98A or Activity Workbook p. 33 so they can fold to test their lines of symmetry. Then have students complete Student Activity Book page 98.

⑫³ Math Talk After students have completed the exercise, discuss the results together. If students disagree on their responses, invite them to the overhead or the board to explain their thinking.

● Which figures have no lines of symmetry?
figures D and G

● Which figures have only one line of symmetry?
figures A, C, F

254 UNIT 4 LESSON 1

● Which figures have exactly two lines of symmetry?
figures B, E

● Which figures have three or more lines of symmetry? figures H, I, J, K, L

● Which figure has the most lines of symmetry?
figure K

● How many lines of symmetry does it have?
an infinite number

● Which figures are not symmetric? How do you know? figures D and G; there are no lines of symmetry.

● How many lines of symmetry does a figure need to be symmetric? at least 1 line of symmetry

Teaching Note

Language and Vocabulary Remind students to identify the words throughout this unit that pose problems in comprehension and pronunciation. Each student should enter the words and definitions in a notebook. Students can read their words to each other and share their definitions.

✓ Ongoing Assessment

Assign 2 letters of the alphabet to each student. Ask them to decide if the letters are symmetric and if so, how many lines of symmetry the letter has.

📁 Class Management

Looking Ahead Have students save the cutouts from Student Activity Book page 98A or Activity Workbook p. 33 in an envelope to reuse in Lesson 2.

Congruent Parts and Figures

 20 MINUTES

Goal: Identify congruent halves of figures and congruent figures.

Materials: Student Activity Book or Hardcover Book pp. 98, 99–100 and Activity Workbook p. 32, rulers (1 per student), tracing paper or unlined paper

 NCTM Standards:
Measurement
Geometry
Reasoning and Proof

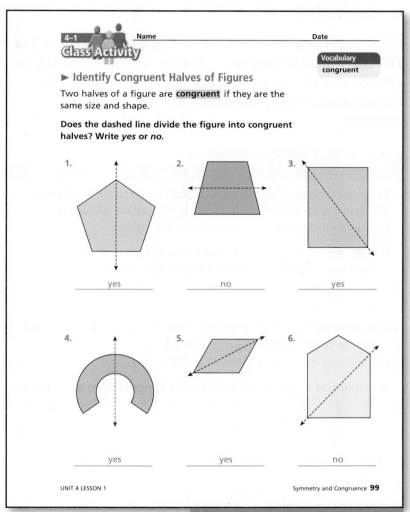

Student Activity Book page 99

▶ Identify Congruent Halves of Figures

WHOLE CLASS

Have students look back at the line of symmetry drawn for figure A on Student Book page 98 or Activity Workbook p. 32. Point out that the two halves are exactly the same size and shape. Explain that when two halves are the same size and the same shape we say they are *congruent.* A line of symmetry divides a figure into congruent halves.

Point out that a line does not have to be a line of symmetry to divide a figure into congruent halves. You can show this by drawing a large rectangle on the board and marking one of the diagonals. Show students that although the line is not a line of symmetry, the two halves are congruent. If necessary, demonstrate by cutting out a copy of the figure, cutting it in half along a diagonal, and matching up the halves so they fit exactly on top of one another.

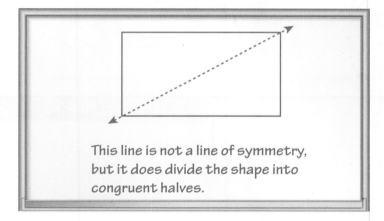

This line is not a line of symmetry, but it does divide the shape into congruent halves.

Direct student's attention to Student Book page 99 and have students complete exercises 1–6 as a class.

Activity continued ▶

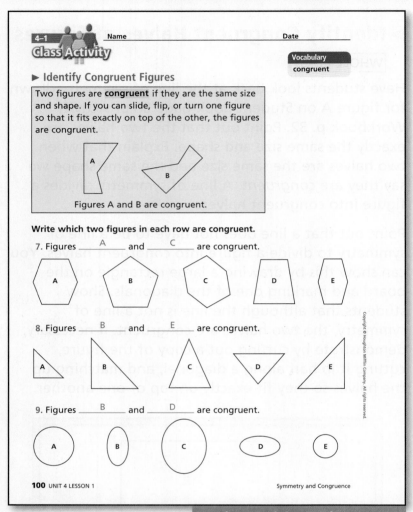

Student Activity Book page 100

▶ Identify Congruent Figures

WHOLE CLASS

Explain that we can also speak of two figures as being congruent. Two figures are congruent if they are the same size and shape. Emphasize that the figures do not have to be positioned in the exact same way. If you can slide, flip, or turn one figure to fit exactly on top of another, the two figures are congruent. Refer students to Student Book page 104 and have them look at congruent figures A and B. Tell students that they can check whether the figures are congruent by tracing one of them and then fitting the tracing exactly over the other.

Give students a few minutes to complete exercises 7–9. Tell them that if they are not sure whether two figures are congruent, they can trace one and try to fit the tracing exactly over the other. Discuss the results together.

Differentiated Instruction

Extra Help Have students look at Student Activity Book page 100 and ask questions to help students quickly eliminate figures that cannot be congruent to the others.

▶ Without tracing, how do you know that figures B and D in exercise 7 aren't congruent to any other figure? Figure B has five sides and figure D has four sides. All of the other figures have six sides.

▶ In exercise 8, how do you know that figures A, B, and E will not be congruent to figures C or D? Figures A, B, and E have right angles; figures C and D don't.

▶ In exercise 9, why can't figure A be congruent to any others? The only one that is the same shape is figure E and it's much smaller than figure A.

② Going Further

Math Connection: Apply Properties of Congruence and Symmetry

Goal: Apply properties of congruence and symmetry to solve problems.

Materials: Student Activity Book or Hardcover Book p. 101 and Activity Workbook p. 35

✓ **NCTM Standards:**
Geometry
Problem Solving
Connections
Representation

4-1
Going Further

Name _____ Date _____

▶ Use Congruence and Symmetry

Solve.

1. The triangles at the right are congruent. Find the missing measure.

   _____4 inches_____

2. Complete the figure so it has the line of symmetry shown.

3. All parts of the two dog houses are congruent. How tall is Fido's dog house?

   _____3 feet_____

4. The lines of symmetry shown in the figure at the right divide the figure into congruent triangles. The base (short side) of one triangle measures 10 inches. What is the perimeter of the figure?

   _____80 inches_____

5. The rectangular field at the right has the lines of symmetry shown. How many feet of fencing are needed?

   _____160 feet_____

6. **Math Journal** Draw a design that has at least one line of symmetry and that uses at least two congruent figures. Check Students' drawings.

UNIT 4 LESSON 1   Symmetry and Congruence **101**

Student Activity Book page 101

Teaching Note

Math Connection Students use what they know about congruence and symmetry to solve problems.

▶ Use Congruence and Symmetry

WHOLE CLASS

Ask for Ideas Elicit from students what they know about congruence and symmetry.

● How can you tell if two figures are congruent? They are the same size and shape and you can put one on top of the other to match exactly.

● What do you know about the parts of figures that are congruent? All the corresponding sides and angles are congruent.

● If a figure has a line of symmetry, what do you know about the figures formed by the line of symmetry? The figures are congruent

● What is the perimeter of a figure? The distance around the figure.

● How can you find the perimeter of a figure? Possible answer: Add the lengths of all the sides.

Using the **Solve and Discuss** structure, have students solve problem 1 on Student Book page 101.

● How do you know the missing measure is 4 inches? Possible answer: If you flip the triangle with the measures over onto the other triangle the 4 inch side fits over the side with the missing measure.

Have students complete Problem 2. Have students share their drawings.

Use **Solve and Discuss** for Problems 3–5. Have volunteers explain how they found the answers.

Give students some time to create the design described in Problem 6. Have students share their designs and point out the congruent figures and lines of symmetry.

Activity continued ▶

Going Further (Continued)

Extension: Similar Figures

Goal: Identify figures that have the same shape but are not necessarily the same size.

Materials: Student Activity Book or Hardcover Book p. 102, tangrams or tangrams (TRB M30)

✓ **NCTM Standard:**
Geometry

▶ Identify Similar Figures WHOLE CLASS

Draw two squares of different sizes on the board.

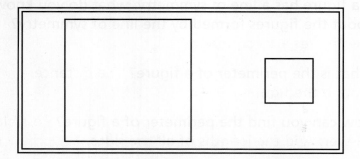

● Do these two quadrilaterals have the same shape? yes

● Are they the same size? no

Explain that we describe figures that have the same shape as similar. The shapes may be the same size but they don't have to be.

Refer students to Students Book page 102 and have them look at the first example.

● Why are these two figures similar? They have the same shape.

Point out that similar figures can also be congruent figures. Reinforce that figures do not have to be different sizes in order to be similar.

Have students look at the second example.

● Why are these two figures similar? They have the same shape

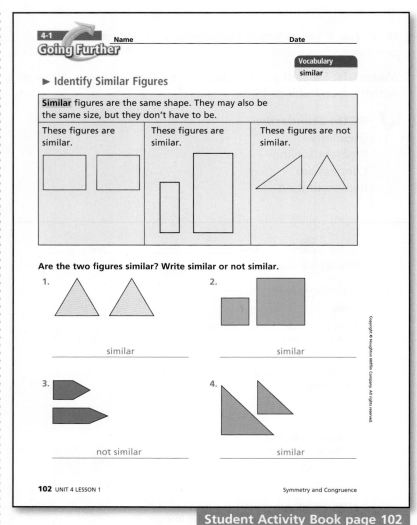

Student Activity Book page 102

Have students look at the third example.

● Why aren't these two figures similar? They are different shapes.

Ask students to complete exercises 1-4 individually. When they are finished, discuss their answers as a class.

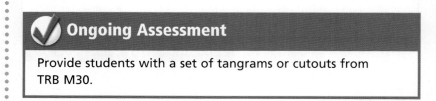

Ongoing Assessment

Provide students with a set of tangrams or cutouts from TRB M30.

② Going Further

Intervention · Activity Card 4-1

Identify Congruent Figures · Activity Card 4-1 ●

Work: On your own

Use:
- Tangrams or TRB M30 (tangrams)

1. What does it mean to say that two shapes are congruent? Copy and complete the sentence below.

   Two shapes are congruent if they are the same _?_ and _?_. size and shape

2. Look at all the tangram shapes that you have. Match the shapes that are congruent.

3. **Analyze** How can you test whether two shapes are congruent? By placing shapes on top of each other to see if they match exactly.
4. How many congruent pairs did you find? 2, the smallest triangles and the largest triangles

Unit 4, Lesson 1   Copyright © Houghton Mifflin Company

Activity Note Point out that the large and small triangles are not congruent to each other because they are the same shape, but not the same size.

 Math Writing Prompt

Explain Your Thinking Lian has two figures but she is not sure that they are congruent. Explain how she can test whether they are congruent.

 **Software Support**

Warm Up 37.05

On Level · Activity Card 4-1

Make Congruent Figures · Activity Card 4-1 ▲

Work: On your own

Use:
- Tangrams or TRB M30 (tangrams)

1. Join together pairs of tangrams. Try to make a shape that is congruent to another tangram.

2. Begin with the square.

   Think What two shapes can be joined together to match the square exactly? the two smallest triangles

3. Now use the same two shapes to form another tangram shape.

4. **Analyze** How many congruent shapes have you found or made in this activity? Three: 2 small triangles; 2 squares; 2 parallelograms

Unit 4, Lesson 1   Copyright © Houghton Mifflin Company

Activity Note Be sure that students check for congruence by stacking the shapes to show that the size and shape are identical.

 Math Writing Prompt

You Decide Benito claims that all triangles are congruent. Do you agree or disagree? Explain your answer.

 Software Support

Shapes Ahoy: Ship Shapes, Level L

Challenge · Activity Card 4-1

Build Two Congruent Figures · Activity Card 4-1 ■

Work: On your own

Use:
- Tangrams or TRB M30 (tangrams)

1. Join the two largest tangram triangles to make another triangle.

2. Now use all the remaining tangram shapes to create a congruent triangle.

3. **Analyze** Which three tangram shapes can you use to make a triangle congruent to *one* of the two large triangles that you joined above? The two smallest triangles and the square or the two smallest triangles and the parallelogram.

Unit 4, Lesson 1   Copyright © Houghton Mifflin Company

Activity Note To answer the analyze question, students should focus on how to make half of the arrangement that they made with the five shapes.

 Math Writing Prompt

Draw a Diagram Draw two congruent figures. Explain why they are congruent.

 DESTINATION Math· **Software Support**

Course II: Module 3: Unit 1: Area

3 Homework and Spiral Review

Homework Goal: Additional Practice

✓ On this Homework page, students draw lines of symmetry and identify congruent pairs of figures.

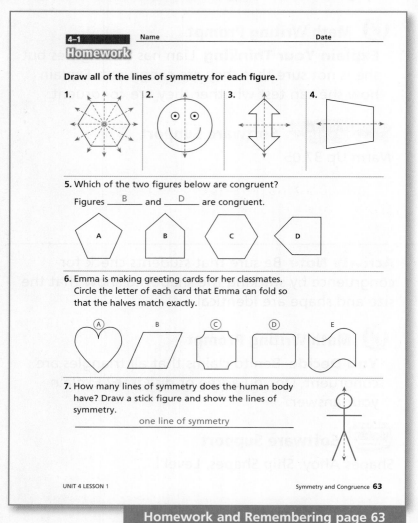

Remembering Goal: Spiral Review

This Remembering page is appropriate anytime after today's lesson.

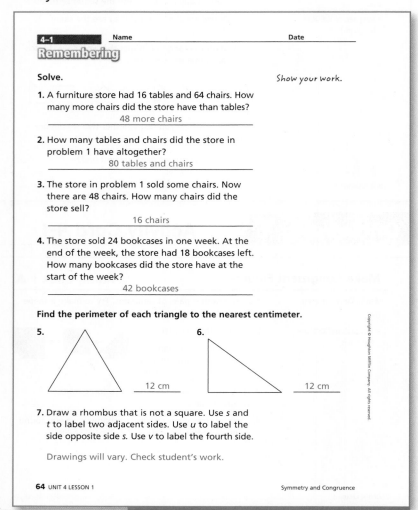

Home and School Connection

Family Letter Have students take home the Family Letter on Student Book page 103 or Activity Workbook p. 37. This letter explains how the concepts of symmetry and congruence are developed in *Math Expressions*. It gives parents and guardians a better understanding of the learning that goes on in math class and creates a bridge between school and home. A Spanish translation of this letter is on the following page.

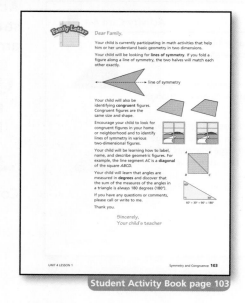

Student Activity Book page 103

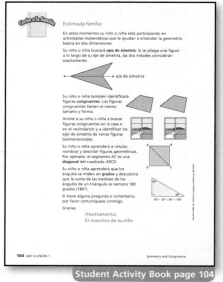

Student Activity Book page 104

Label Figures and Draw Diagonals

Lesson Objectives

- Label and name figures using letters.
- Understand the relationship between the diagonals of quadrilaterals and the triangles they form.

Vocabulary
diagonal
right angle
right triangle
vertex
vertices

The Day at a Glance

Today's Goals	Materials
1 **Teaching the Lesson** **A1:** Label vertices and name figures using letters. **A2:** Draw diagonals in quadrilaterals to form triangles. **2** **Going Further** ▶ Differentiated Instruction **3** **Homework and Spiral Review**	**Lesson Activities** Student Activity Book pp. 105–108 or Student Hardcover Book pp. 105–108 and Activity Workbook pp. 39–40 (includes Figures and Drawing Diagonals) Homework and Remembering pp. 65–66 Rulers Scissors Tracing paper (optional) **Going Further** Activity Cards 4-2 Quadrilateral Cutouts from Student Activity Book p. 98 Rulers Math Journals

123 Use Math Talk today!

Keeping Skills Sharp

Daily Routines	English Language Learners
Homework Review Have students discuss the errors from their homework. Encourage students to help each other understand how to correct the errors. **Elapsed Time** Field hockey practice started at 10:30 A.M. and ended at 1:00 P.M. How long was field hockey practice? 2 hours 30 minutes	Write *vertex* on the board. Draw the shape below. Point to a vertex. Say: **This is a *vertex*.** Count the vertices. Say: **1 vertex, 2 vertices, 3 vertices, 4 vertices.** Have students repeat. ● **Beginning:** Say: **Let's name this shape.** Label the vertices A, B, C, D. Say: **This is shape *ABCD*.** Write the name on the board. ● **Intermediate:** Say: **A *vertex* is where two sides or edges meet.** Draw a circle. Ask: **Does a circle have *vertices*?** no Point to the quadrilateral. Say: **We *label* the *vertices* to name shapes.** Label the vertices A, B, C, D. Say: **This is shape *ABCD*.** ● **Advanced:** Have students name other shapes with vertices. Draw the shapes on the board. Point to the original shape. Say: **We *label* the vertices to name shapes.** Label the vertices A, B, C, D. Say: **This is shape *ABCD*.**

Teaching the Lesson

Label Figures

 15 MINUTES

Goal: Label vertices and name figures using letters.

Materials: Student Activity Book or Hardcover Book p. 105, rulers (1 per student)

✔ **NCTM Standards:**
Geometry
Representation

▶ Label Corners with Letters [WHOLE CLASS]

Draw a quadrilateral on the board.

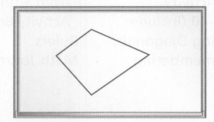

Explain that it is sometimes helpful to give a figure a name with letters. To name this figure with letters, first label its corners with capital letters. Label the vertices *W, X, Y,* and *Z.*

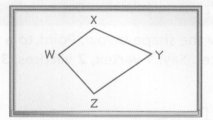

Explain that to name a figure with letters you start at any corner and list the letters in order as you go around the figure clockwise or counterclockwise.

Point out that one name for the figure on the board is *WXYZ.* Point to each vertex as you say its name, and then write *WXYZ* on the board next to the figure.

● What are some other names for this figure? *XYZW, XWZY, YZWX, YXWZ, ZWXY, ZYXW, WZYX*

● Can you name the figure *WYXZ?* no

● Why not? Those letters are not in order around the figure.

Have students complete Student Book page 105. When they are finished, discuss their answers.

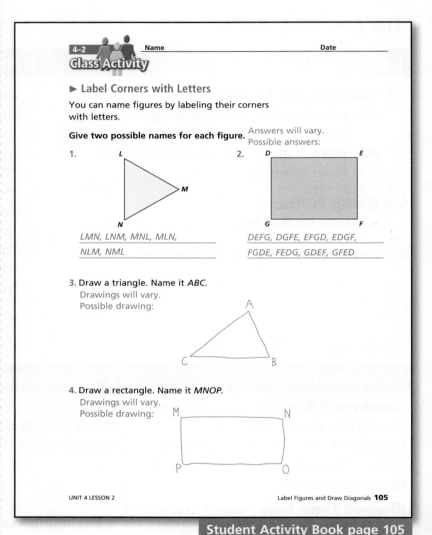

Student Activity Book page 105

 Ongoing Assessment

Ask students to draw a triangle and a rectangle and to label them with letters. Have students provide two possible names for each figure using their letter labels.

Draw Diagonals

 45 MINUTES

Goal: Draw diagonals in quadrilaterals to form triangles.

Materials: Student Activity Book or Hardcover Book pp. 106–108 and Activity Workbook pp. 39–40, rulers (1 per student), scissors (1 pair per student), tracing paper (optional)

 NCTM Standards:
Measurement
Geometry
Reasoning and Proof

▶ Diagonals WHOLE CLASS

Draw quadrilateral *STUV* on the board.

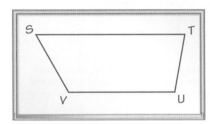

Explain to students that they can name a line segment using the letter labels at each endpoint in either order. Point to side *ST*.

● Give two names for this side. *ST* and *TS*

● Name all the other sides in two ways. *TU* or *UT*, *UV* or *VU*, and *VS* or *SV*

Draw a diagonal from *V* to *T*.

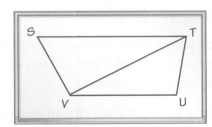

Tell students that a line segment that connects two corners of a quadrilateral and is not a side of the quadrilateral is called a diagonal.

● What is the name of this diagonal? *TV* or *VT*

● How do you know? Its endpoints are *T* and *V*.

Add a second diagonal *SU* to the quadrilateral on the board.

● What is the name of this diagonal? *SU* or *US*

Have students complete exercises 5–14 on Student Book pages 106–107. Some students may want to use tracing paper to trace the triangles formed so that they can check if the triangles are congruent. They can also trace, cut out, and fold the quadrilaterals to check for symmetry.

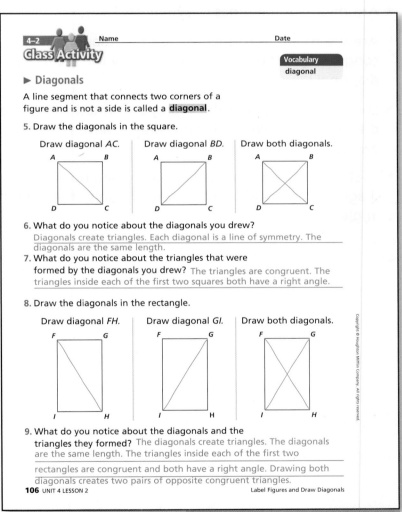

Student Activity Book page 106

Activity continued ▶

Label Figures and Draw Diagonals   **263**

① Teaching the Lesson (continued)

For each exercise, invite students to share their observations. Encourage them to use the geometry words they learned earlier. You may need to review the meanings of such terms as *congruent, line of symmetry,* and *right angle.*

Here are some questions you might ask for each exercise:

● Are the two diagonals the same length?

● Are the two triangles formed by each diagonal congruent?

● When you drew both diagonals, were any pairs of triangles congruent?

● Are the diagonals lines of symmetry?

● Are the triangles formed by the first diagonal congruent to the triangles formed by the second diagonal?

● Look at the angles in the triangles formed when one diagonal is drawn. Do both triangles have right angles?

● Look at the four triangles formed when both diagonals are drawn. Do all four triangles have right angles?

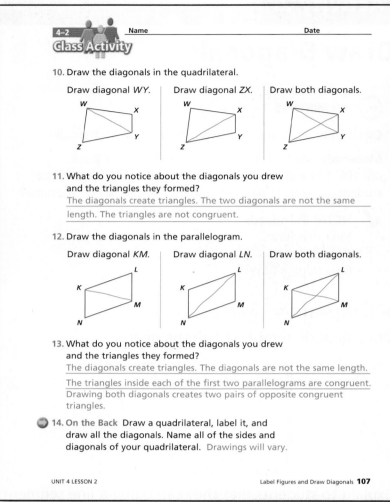

Student Activity Book page 107

 Math Talk in Action

When is a diagonal of a quadrilateral a line of symmetry?

Elia: A diagonal is a line of symmetry when the two triangles it makes are congruent.

Sophie: I'm not sure that is enough. The triangles might be congruent and still not match each other when you fold over the diagonal.

Huy: Yeah. I only think the square matches when you fold along the diagonal.

Why don't you think the other quadrilaterals match when they fold onto themselves?

Huy: The opposite corners aren't in the same place along the diagonal. They have to be opposite each other, exactly halfway along the diagonal for the two triangles to match.

② Going Further

Differentiated Instruction

Intervention Activity Card 4-2

Diagonal Halves Activity Card 4-2 ●

Work: On your own

Use:
• Quadrilateral Cutouts B, C, G, and I from Student Activity Book, page 98
• scissors

1. Cut out the four quadrilaterals shown below from Unit 4, Lesson 1, in your Student Book.

2. Draw a diagonal on each quadrilateral. Cut along each diagonal to make two triangles.

3. **Think** Are the two triangles from each quadrilateral congruent? Slide, flip, and turn each triangle to help you answer the question.

4. Which quadrilaterals can be divided into two congruent triangles? How do you know? rectangle, parallelogram, square; the two triangles match exactly.

Unit 4, Lesson 2   Copyright © Houghton Mifflin Company

Activity Note Remind students that diagonals divide a figure into smaller shapes by connecting opposite corners, not opposite sides.

✎ **Math Writing Prompt**

Explain Your Thinking Luk Sun has drawn a diagonal line in a parallelogram, but he is unsure whether the diagonal is a line of symmetry. Explain what he can do to test whether the diagonal is a line of symmetry.

Soar to Success Math ★ **Software Support**

Warm Up 37.15

On Level Activity Card 4-2

Diagonal Clues Activity Card 4-2 ▲

Work: In pairs

Use:
• 2 inch rulers

1. **On Your Own** Make a secret drawing that shows a quadrilateral and one or two diagonals.

2. On a separate piece of paper, write clues about the diagonals and the shapes that they form. Give no other information about your quadrilateral.

> The diagonals are equal in length and all four triangles they form are congruent. What is the figure?

3. Exchange clues with your partner and try to guess the name of the figure. Draw the figure. Then exchange drawings with your partner.

4. **Analyze** Did more than one figure match the clues? Why or why not?

Unit 4, Lesson 2   Copyright © Houghton Mifflin Company

Activity Note One or more figures may match a single clue. For example, a square and a rectangle, have two equal diagonals. Encourage students to write more than one clue.

✎ **Math Writing Prompt**

Draw a Picture Use a picture to help explain why a triangle does not have any diagonals.

MegaMath Grades K-6 **Software Support**

Shapes Ahoy: Ship Shapes, Level L

Challenge Activity Card 4-2

Compare Diagonals Activity Card 4-2 ■

Work: In small groups

1. **Work Together** Copy and complete the chart below. Write *yes* or *no* in each row under the headings *Square* and *Rectangle*.

Property of diagonals	Square	Rectangle
diagonals are lines of symmetry	yes	no
diagonals are equal in length	yes	yes
one diagonal forms congruent triangles	yes	yes

2. **Think** What other properties can you include in the chart? Possible answer: Two diagonals form four congruent triangles for a square, but not for a rectangle.

Unit 4, Lesson 2   Copyright © Houghton Mifflin Company

Activity Note Suggest that students draw examples of both a square and a rectangle to justify the entries in their chart.

✎ **Math Writing Prompt**

Make a Comparison How are the diagonals of squares and rectangles similar? How are they different?

✸ **DESTINATION** Math® **Software Support**

Course II: Module 3: Unit 1: Area

Label Figures and Draw Diagonals **265**

③ Homework and Spiral Review

4-2 Homework Goal: Additional Practice

On this Homework page, students name figures using letters and draw diagonals on quadrilaterals to form triangles.

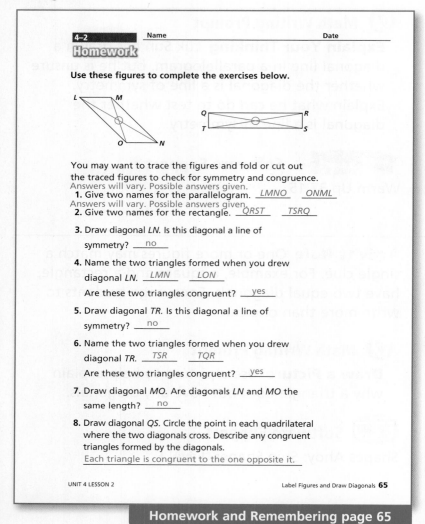

4-2 Homework

Name _____   Date _____

Use these figures to complete the exercises below.

You may want to trace the figures and fold or cut out the traced figures to check for symmetry and congruence.
Answers will vary. Possible answers given.
1. Give two names for the parallelogram. __LMNO__ __ONML__
Answers will vary. Possible answers given.
2. Give two names for the rectangle. __QRST__ __TSRQ__

3. Draw diagonal *LN*. Is this diagonal a line of symmetry? __no__

4. Name the two triangles formed when you drew diagonal *LN*. __LMN__ __LON__
Are these two triangles congruent? __yes__

5. Draw diagonal *TR*. Is this diagonal a line of symmetry? __no__

6. Name the two triangles formed when you drew diagonal *TR*. __TSR__ __TQR__
Are these two triangles congruent? __yes__

7. Draw diagonal *MO*. Are diagonals *LN* and *MO* the same length? __no__

8. Draw diagonal *QS*. Circle the point in each quadrilateral where the two diagonals cross. Describe any congruent triangles formed by the diagonals.
__Each triangle is congruent to the one opposite it.__

UNIT 4 LESSON 2   Label Figures and Draw Diagonals **65**

Homework and Remembering page 65

4-2 Remembering Goal: Spiral Review

This Remembering page is appropriate anytime after today's lesson.

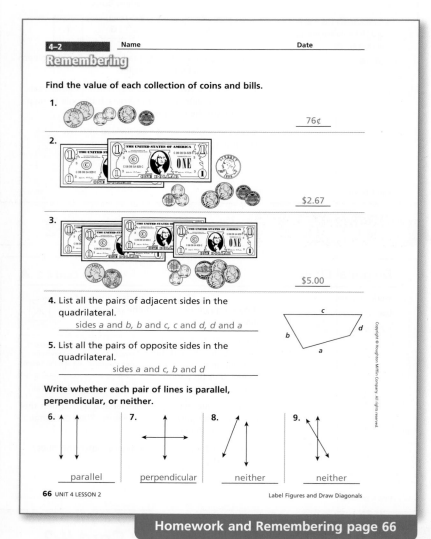

4-2 Remembering

Name _____   Date _____

Find the value of each collection of coins and bills.

1. __76¢__

2. __$2.67__

3. __$5.00__

4. List all the pairs of adjacent sides in the quadrilateral.
__sides *a* and *b*, *b* and *c*, *c* and *d*, *d* and *a*__

5. List all the pairs of opposite sides in the quadrilateral.
__sides *a* and *c*, *b* and *d*__

Write whether each pair of lines is parallel, perpendicular, or neither.

6. __parallel__   7. __perpendicular__   8. __neither__   9. __neither__

66 UNIT 4 LESSON 2   Label Figures and Draw Diagonals

Home or School Activity

🔬 Science Connection

Find the Center of Gravity An object's center of gravity is its balance point.

Invite students to draw quadrilaterals on card stock and to cut out the figures. Next, ask them to draw the two diagonals in all of their figures. Challenge students to try to balance each figure on the eraser end of a pencil at the point where the two diagonals intersect.

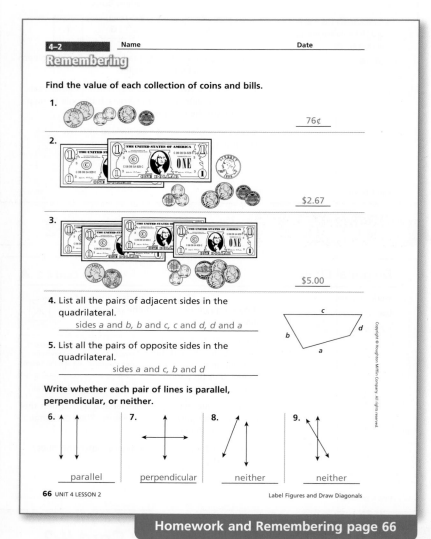

Homework and Remembering page 66

Angles and Triangles

MINI UNIT 4
LESSON 3

Lesson Objectives

- Understand what an angle is and name angles by size.
- Describe and name polygons.
- Understand the relationship between quadrilaterals and triangles.

Vocabulary

angle	right triangle	equilateral triangle
right angle	acute triangle	isosceles triangle
acute angle	obtuse triangle	scalene triangle
obtuse angle	octagon	pentagon
hexagon	polygon	

The Day at a Glance

Today's Goals	Materials	
① Teaching the Lesson **A1:** Compare and name angles. **A2:** Classify triangles by lengths of sides and sizes of angles. **A3:** Build quadrilaterals from two congruent triangles. **A4:** Build a pentagon, hexagon and an octagon from triangles. **② Going Further** ▶ Differentiated Instruction **③ Homework and Spiral Review**	**Lesson Activities** Student Activity Book pp. 109–114B or Student Hardcover Book pp. 109–114 and Activity Workbook pp. 41–44 (includes Cut Outs) Homework and Remembering pp. 67–68 MathBoard materials Straws Colored flexible rods, such as chenille sticks Centimeter rulers Scissors, Chart paper (optional)	**Going Further** Activity Cards 4-3 Colored flexible rods, such as chenille sticks Index cards MathBoard materials Math Journals

123 Use Math Talk today!

Keeping Skills Sharp

Daily Routines	English Language Learners
Homework Review If students give incorrect answers, have them explain how they found the answers. This can help you determine whether the error is conceptual or procedural. **Skip Count** Have students skip count by 50s beginning at 600 and ending at 1,000.	Draw a right triangle. Point to the angles. Say: **These are *angles*.** Point to the right angle. Say: **This triangle has a *right angle*. It is a *right triangle*.** Describe an acute and an obtuse triangle. ● **Beginning** Model an acute triangle with your fingers. Say: **This is an *acute triangle*. The angles are smaller than a *right angle*.** Model an obtuse triangle. Say: **This triangle has one angle that is bigger than a *right angle*. This is an *obtuse angle*.** ● **Intermediate** Say: **Make a triangle with 3 angles smaller than a right angle. That is an *acute angle*. Make a triangle with 1 angle bigger than a right angle. That is an *obtuse angle*.** ● **Advanced** Model the triangles. Ask students if each angle is bigger or smaller than a right angle.

Teaching the Lesson

Introduce Angles

 20 MINUTES

Goal: Compare and name angles.

Materials: Student Activity Book or Hardcover Book p. 109, straws (4 per student), colored flexible rods, such as pipe cleaners or chenille sticks (2 per student)

✓ **NCTM Standards:**
Geometry
Reasoning and Proof

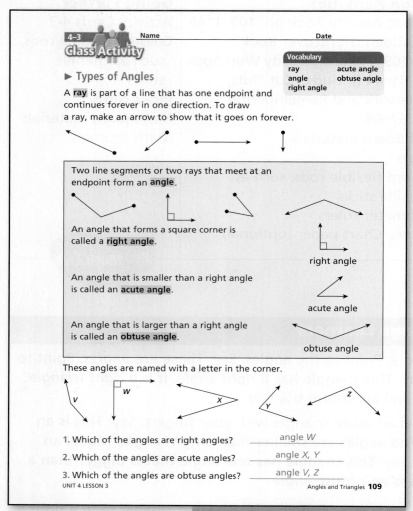

Student Activity Book page 109

Teaching Note

Language and Vocabulary Students should not be expected to master all of the new vocabulary in this lesson. Students will revisit these terms in Remembering problems and in future grades.

▶ Types of Angles WHOLE CLASS

Discuss the meanings of the geometry terms introduced on Student Book page 109.

Explain to students that the size of an angle is the amount of rotation, or turn, from one side to the other. Connect two straws with a pipe cleaner or chenille stick. Leave one straw fixed and rotate the other straw to form angles of different sizes. Tell students that rotating the straw more creates larger angles. Show students pairs of angles and ask them which is larger.

Demonstrate how to make an angle smaller by rotating one straw closer to the other. Next, demonstrate how to make an angle larger by rotating one straw away from the other straw.

Then distribute materials to students and invite them to create a right angle using two of their straws.

Ask students to use their remaining two straws to make an angle smaller than a right angle, or an acute angle.

Have students make an angle larger than a right angle, or an obtuse angle.

Then ask students to complete exercises 1–3 on Student Book page 109.

Classify Triangles

 30 MINUTES

Goal: Classify triangles by lengths of sides and sizes of angles.

Materials: Student Activity Book or Hardcover Book pp. 110–112, centimeter rulers (1 per student), chart paper (optional)

 NCTM Standards:
Geometry
Reasoning and Proof
Connections

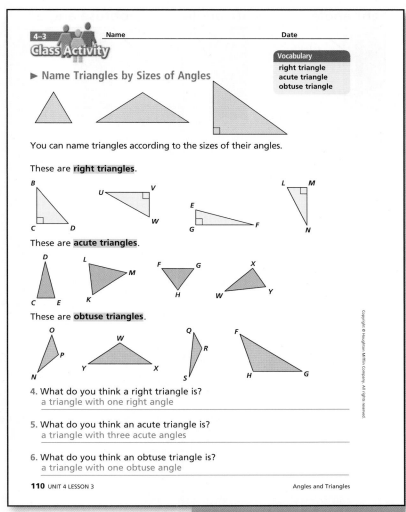

Student Activity Book page 110

► Name Triangles by Sizes of Angles

WHOLE CLASS

(123) **Math Talk** Have students look at the three triangles at the top of Student Book page 110. Talk about the similarities and differences among the three triangles.

● How many angles does each of the triangles have? three

● Do you see a right angle in any of the triangles? yes

● In which triangle? the third triangle

● Do you see an obtuse angle in any of the triangles? yes

● In which triangle? the middle triangle

● What kind of an angle is each angle in the first triangle? acute

Write *obtuse, acute,* and *right* on the board.

Explain that we use these words to name triangles according to the sizes of their angles. Tell students that they will now try to determine which word goes with each of the three triangles.

Turn students' attention to the examples of each type of triangle. Encourage them to think about what is the same about each group of triangles in order to help figure out which word can be used to describe each type of triangle. Students can work in pairs to classify the angles in each triangle and complete exercises 4–6.

As a class, come up with definitions of *right triangle, acute triangle,* and *obtuse triangle* and write them on the board or chart paper.

Here are some possible definitions:

right triangle: a triangle with one right angle

acute triangle: a triangle with three angles, each smaller than right angles

obtuse triangle: a triangle with one angle larger than a right angle

Activity continued ▶

Teaching the Lesson (continued)

Have students look at the three triangles at the top of the Student Book page 110 once again. Ask these questions to help students label each triangle according to the sizes of its angles.

- Check the angles in the first triangle. What kind of triangle is it? *acute*

- Check the angles in the second triangle. What kind of triangle is it? *obtuse*

- Check the angles in the third triangle. What kind of triangle is it? *right*

Draw Triangles with Different Angles

Encourage students to explore the characteristics of triangles. Have them try to draw a variety of triangles, both possible and impossible, such as triangles with the following characteristics:

- two acute angles
- two right angles
- two obtuse angles

Talk about why some of these "triangles" cannot exist. For example, two right angles would prevent two of the sides from joining.

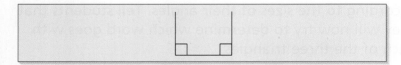

Invite students to share any interesting observations they made while drawing. For example, they might mention that if a triangle has one obtuse angle, the other two angles must be acute.

Teaching Note

Language and Vocabulary *Acute* is derived from Latin and means "sharp." An acute blade, for example, has a very sharp point. *Obtuse* is derived from Latin and means "blunt" or "dull." *Equilateral* is also derived from Latin and means "equal sides." *Scalene* is derived from Greek and means "uneven" or "odd." *Isosceles,* too, is derived from Greek and means "equal leg."

Differentiated Instruction

Extra Help Some students may benefit from using the square corner of a ruler as a tool to help identify the types of angles in a triangle. Demonstrate how to align one side of an angle with the end of a ruler and how to evaluate the position of the angle's other side.

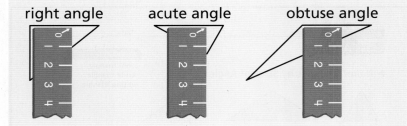

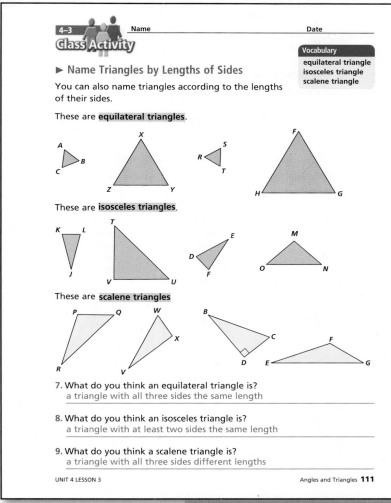

The activity book page shown contains:

4–3
Class Activity

Name _____ Date _____

Vocabulary
equilateral triangle
isosceles triangle
scalene triangle

▶ Name Triangles by Lengths of Sides

You can also name triangles according to the lengths of their sides.

These are **equilateral triangles**.

These are **isosceles triangles**.

These are **scalene triangles**

7. What do you think an equilateral triangle is?
   a triangle with all three sides the same length

8. What do you think an isosceles triangle is?
   a triangle with at least two sides the same length

9. What do you think a scalene triangle is?
   a triangle with all three sides different lengths

UNIT 4 LESSON 3   Angles and Triangles **111**

▶ Name Triangles by Lengths of Sides

PAIRS

Direct students' attention once again to the three triangles at the top of Student Book page 110. This time, have them focus on the side lengths of each triangle. Talk about the similarities and differences among the triangles.

● What do you notice about the lengths of sides of the first triangle? All sides are the same length.

● What about the second triangle? Two sides are the same length and one is of a different length.

● What about the third triangle? All of the sides are different lengths.

Write these words on the board and read them aloud.

scalene   isosceles   equilateral

Explain that we use these words to name triangles based on the length of their sides.

Have **Student Pairs** look at the examples of each type of triangle on Student Book page 111. Encourage them to think about what is the same about each group of triangles in order to help them figure out the meanings of the words on the board. Have **Student Pairs** measure the lengths of the sides of each triangle and complete exercises 7–9.

Together, come up with definitions of *equilateral triangle, isosceles triangle,* and *scalene triangle* and record them on the board or chart paper. Here are some possible definitions:

equilateral triangle: a triangle with all sides the same length

isosceles triangle: a triangle with at least two sides the same length

scalene triangle: a triangle with no sides the same length

Point out that an equilateral triangle can also be classified as isosceles because it has at least two sides the same length.

Teaching Note

Math Background Be aware that definitions may vary slightly among resources. For example, there are two possible definitions of an isosceles triangle:

1. a triangle with at least two sides the same length

2. a triangle with exactly two sides the same length

According to the second definition, an equilateral triangle is not isosceles. *Math Expressions* uses the first definition.

Activity continued ▶

① Teaching the Lesson (continued)

Have students look at the three triangles at the top of the previous page once again. Ask these questions to help students label each triangle according to the lengths of its sides:

● Measure the sides of the first triangle. What kind of triangle is it? equilateral

● How can you name the triangle in two ways? acute, equilateral

● Measure the sides of the second triangle. What kind of triangle is it? isosceles

● How can you name the triangle in two ways? obtuse, isosceles

● Measure the sides of the third triangle. What kind of triangle is it? scalene

● How can you name the triangle in two ways? right, scalene

Challenge students to try to draw these triangles and explain why they cannot exist.

● an equilateral right triangle

● an equilateral obtuse triangle

Encourage students to share their observations. For example, they might mention that all of the angles in an equilateral triangle are acute, so an equilateral triangle cannot be an obtuse or right triangle.

▶ Name Triangles by Sizes of Angles and Lengths of Sides INDIVIDUALS

Have students turn their attention to exercise 10 on Student Book page 112. Explain that the symbol in the corner of the triangle shows that the angle is a right angle.

● If a triangle has a right angle, what kind of triangle is it? It is a right triangle.

Ask students to measure the lengths of the sides of the triangle in exercise 10.

● How many sides are the same length? 2 sides

● If a triangle has two sides the same length, what kind of triangle is it? It is an isosceles triangle.

Ask students to complete exercises 10–15 independently.

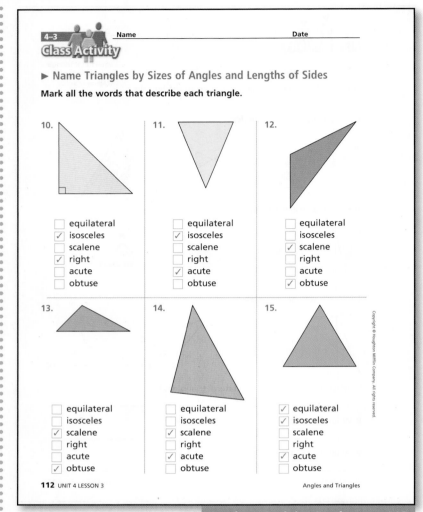

Student Activity Book page 112

After discussing the answers as a class, have students find objects around the room that have the shape of a triangle. Then have students measure the length of each line segment and name the triangle using the lengths of the sides.

Allow students to share their findings. Be sure students use the terms point and line segments in their descriptions and tell how they know the name of the triangle is correct.

Ongoing Assessment

Ask students to draw the following triangles to show their understanding of different types of triangles.

▶ Draw an equilateral triangle.

▶ Draw an obtuse isosceles triangle.

▶ Draw a right scalene triangle.

Activity 3

Build Quadrilaterals from Triangles

 10 MINUTES

Goal: Build quadrilaterals from two congruent triangles.

Materials: Student Activity Book pages 112A–112B or Activity Workbook pp. 41–42, scissors (1 pair per student), centimeter rulers (1 per student)

✔ **NCTM Standards:**
Geometry
Reasoning and Proof
Connections

▶ Build Quadrilaterals from Triangles

INDIVIDUALS

Have students cut out the two obtuse triangles from Student Activity Book page 112A or Activity Workbook page 41.

Borrow a pair of triangles from a student and demonstrate how to make a quadrilateral by matching up two of the sides of equal length.

● There are many ways to form a quadrilateral from these two triangles. Experiment to find as many different ways as you can. Trace each quadrilateral you make.

After a few minutes, invite volunteers to share some of the quadrilaterals they created. There are six possible figures in all.

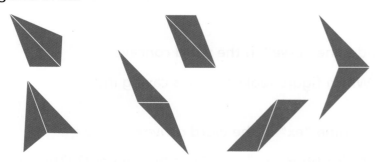

● What do you call the line segment where the two triangles are joined? a diagonal

Ask students to repeat the activity using the acute triangles. Here are three possible quadrilaterals:

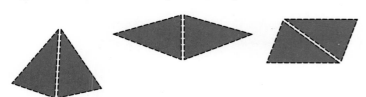

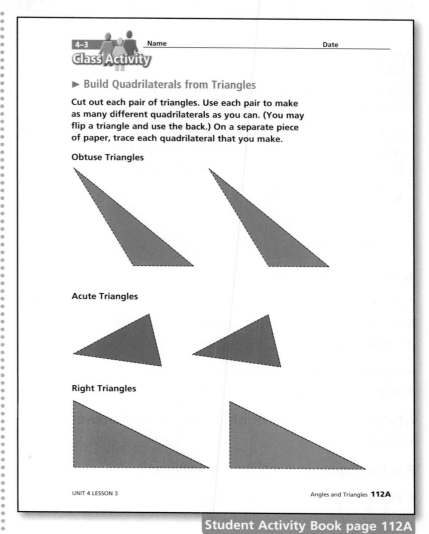

Student Activity Book page 112A

Finally, have students repeat the activity with the right triangles. Here are four possible quadrilaterals:

Challenge students to draw and cut out two congruent triangles, that can be used to build a square.

Then draw a parallelogram and cut it into a rectangle and two right triangles:

Angles and Triangles **273**

Activity 4

Build Polygons from Triangles

 30 MINUTES

Goal: Identify the attributes of polygons; name polygons; compose and decompose polygons

Materials: Student Activity Book or Hardcover Book pp. 113–114, Student Activity Book pp. 114A–114B or Activity Workbook pp. 43–44, TRB M161, MathBoard Materials

 NCTM Standards:
Geometry
Reasoning and Proof
Connections

▶ Polygons SMALL GROUPS

Tell students that the prefix poly- means "many" and the suffix –gon refers to angles. A polygon has "many angles."

Have **Small Groups** complete exercises 1–8 and be ready to explain their answers.

When students have finished, discuss the answers as a class.

- Is the figure in exercise 1 a polygon? yes

- How do you know? It has straight line segments for sides. They are all connected so it is closed and the sides don't cross over each other.

- Is the figure in Exercise 2 a polygon? No; the line segments cross each other.

- Which figure is not made up of line segments? The figure in exercise 5

- Which figures are not closed? The figures in exercises 7 and 8

Discuss the meaning of concave and convex. Draw an example of each on the board.

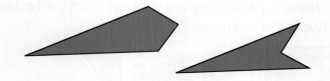

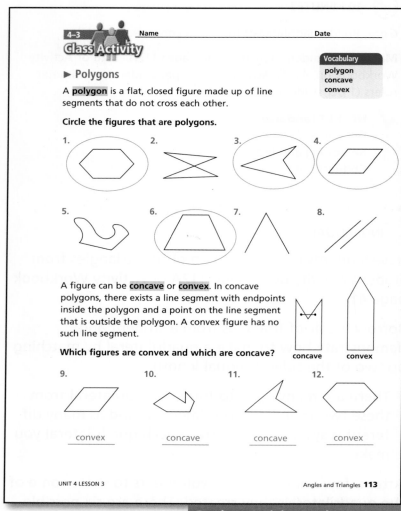

Student Activity Book page 113

Underline "cave" in the word *concave.*

- Which figure looks as if it is caving in? The second one.

Underline "ex" in the word *convex.*

- Which figure looks as if it is bulging out? (Think of *exit*) the first one

- Which figures in exercises 9–12 look like they are caving in? Exercises 10 and 11.

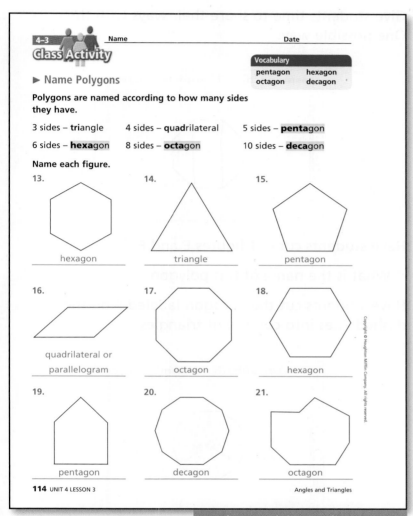

Student Activity Book page 114

The content of Student Activity Book page 114:

► Name Polygons

Vocabulary
pentagon	hexagon
octagon	decagon

Polygons are named according to how many sides they have.

3 sides – triangle 4 sides – quadrilateral 5 sides – **penta**gon
6 sides – **hexa**gon 8 sides – **octa**gon 10 sides – **deca**gon

Name each figure.

13. hexagon

14. triangle

15. pentagon

16. quadrilateral or parallelogram

17. octagon

18. hexagon

19. pentagon

20. decagon

21. octagon

114 UNIT 4 LESSON 3   Angles and Triangles

Copyright © Houghton Mifflin Company. All rights reserved.

► Name Polygons PAIRS

Write these prefixes on the board in random order:
tri- deca-, octa-, quadri-, hexa- penta-

Invite students to discuss what number might match each prefix.

Tell students that all sides are congruent and all angles are congruent in a regular polygon.

● Which polygons on Student Book page 114 are regular? figures in exercises 13, 14, 15, 17, 18, and 20

● Which figure is concave? The figure in exercise 21.

Have **Student Pairs** complete exercises 13–21.

► Build Polygons from Triangles

INDIVIDUALS

Have students cut out all the triangles labeled A on Student Activity Book page 114A or Activity Workbook page 43 and put them together to form a regular polygon on a MathBoard. Have students trace and name the figure.

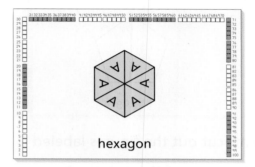

hexagon

Then have students remove the triangles from the MathBoard and draw lines to show how they could compose or make this figure using other figures.

Some possible ways are shown below:

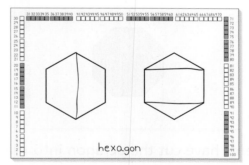

hexagon

Next have students cut out the triangles labeled B and put them together to make a regular polygon on a MathBoard. Have students trace and name the figure.

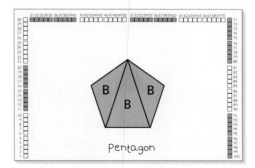

Pentagon

Activity continued ▶

Then have students remove the triangles from the MathBoard and draw lines to show how they could decompose this figure into other figures.

One possible way is shown below.

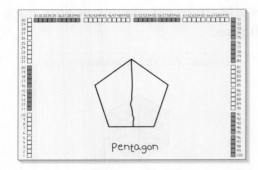

Have students cut out the figures labeled C and D.

● **What is the name of the polygon?** octagon

Have students cut the octagon labeled C on the dashed lines into eight congruent triangles.

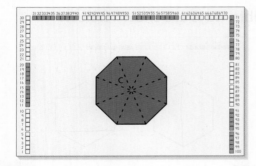

After students have cut the octagon into triangles, ask students to cut one of the triangles into 2 triangles.

● **What type of triangles were formed?** right triangles

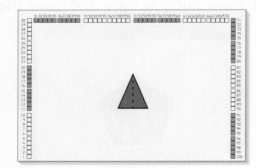

Next ask students to cut the octagon labeled D into other polygons and record how they did it on the MathBoard.

Give students time to share their ways with the class. One possible way:

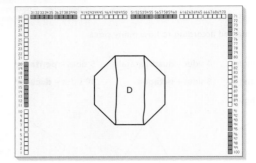

Have students cut out figures E and F.

● **What is the name of this polygon?** decagon

Have students cut the decagon labeled E on the dashed lines into congruent triangles

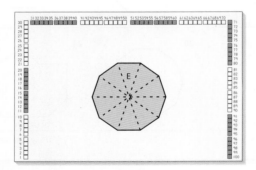

Next ask students to cut the decagon labeled F into other polygons and record how they did it on the MathBoard. Give students time to share their ways with the class.

One possible way:

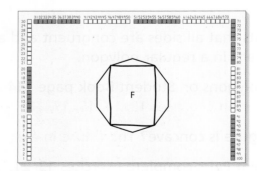

Finally have students use any of their cut out triangles to form concave or convex figures and share their figures with the class.

② Going Further

Differentiated Instruction

Intervention — Activity Card 4-3

Colored Side Lengths
Activity Card 4-3 ●

Work: On your own

Use:

Blue, red, and yellow pipe cleaners or chenille sticks to make rods

- Cut the blue ones into 10-cm rods.
- Cut the red ones into 8-cm rods.
- Cut the yellow ones into 6-cm rods.

1. Use 3 rods to make an equilateral triangle. **Think** How many sides are equal in an equilateral triangle? How many different colors do you need?

2. Use three rods to make an isosceles triangle. **Think** How many sides are equal in an isosceles triangle? 2
How many different colors do you need? 2

3. Use three rods to make a scalene triangle. **Think** How many sides are equal in a scalene triangle? 0
How many different colors do you need? 3

Unit 4, Lesson 3   Copyright © Houghton Mifflin Company

Activity Note Equilateral triangles have all sides equal. Isosceles triangles have at least two equal sides. Only one scalene triangle is possible, using three different color rods.

 Math Writing Prompt

Create Your Own Method Adra wants to check whether or not an angle is a right angle. Suggest a method that she can use.

 **Software Support**

Warm Up 35.26

On Level — Activity Card 4-3

Match Names and Triangles
Activity Card 4-3 ▲

Work: In small groups

Use:

- Index cards

1. Make a set of 14 cards as shown on the right.

2. Turn all the name cards face down in one pile. Turn all the picture cards face down in a second pile.

3. Each player turns over one card from each pile making a match if possible.

4. Continue until all the cards are matched. Keep score by giving one point for each correct match. The person with the higher score wins.

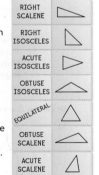

RIGHT SCALENE

RIGHT ISOSCELES

ACUTE ISOSCELES

OBTUSE ISOSCELES

EQUILATERAL

OBTUSE SCALENE

ACUTE SCALENE

Unit 4, Lesson 3   Copyright © Houghton Mifflin Company

Activity Note A right triangle must have exactly one right angle. An obtuse triangle must have exactly one obtuse angle. But an acute triangle must have three acute angles.

 Math Writing Prompt

Draw a Picture Can a triangle have two right angles? Include a drawing with your explanation.

 Software Support

Shapes Ahoy: Ship Shapes, Level H

Challenge — Activity Card 4-3

Angles of Equal Measure
Activity Card 4-3 ■

Work: In small groups

Use:

- MathBoard materials

1. Draw an equilateral triangle. Trace one angle and place it over the other angles to compare.

2. Draw an isosceles triangle. Trace and compare all angles.

3. Draw a scalene triangle. Trace and compare angles.

4. Copy and complete the following.
   - An equilateral triangle has _?_ equal angles. 3
   - An isosceles triangle has _?_ equal angles. 2
   - A scalene triangle has _?_ equal angles. 0

5. **Analyze** What do you notice about your results?
An equilateral triangle has three angles of equal measure. An isosceles triangle has two angles of equal measure. All three angles in a scalene triangle have different measures.

Unit 4, Lesson 3   Copyright © Houghton Mifflin Company

Activity Note For the Analyze question, students may notice that the number of equal sides in a triangle is the same as the number of equal angles.

 Math Writing Prompt

Explain Your Thinking Explain why you cannot draw an obtuse equilateral triangle.

 DESTINATION Math **Software Support**

Course II: Module 3: Unit 1: Area

Angles and Triangles   **277**

③ Homework and Spiral Review

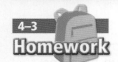

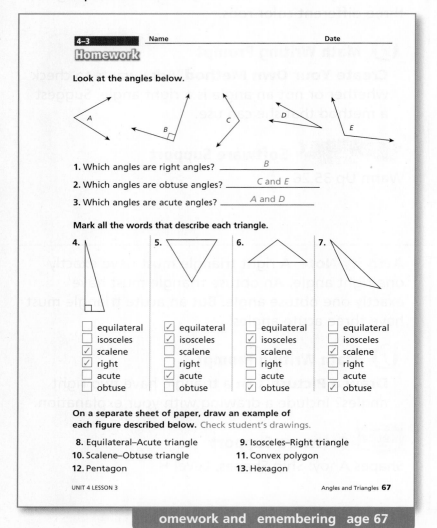

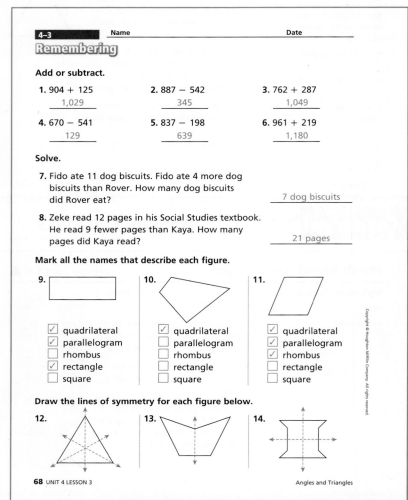

Homework **Goal:** Additional Practice

✓ Include students' work for page 67 as part of their portfolios.

Remembering **Goal:** Spiral Review

This Remembering page is appropriate anytime after today's lesson.

Home or School Activity

🌎 Social Studies Connection

Roof Angles The sides of a peaked roof meet to form an angle. In places where there is frequent snow and rain, roof sides typically meet to form acute angles. A steeper roof allows rain and snow to run off easily. In more arid parts of the world, roof slope is less critical, so roof sides can form obtuse angles.

Invite students to explore their neighborhoods and to sketch the angles formed by different roofs.

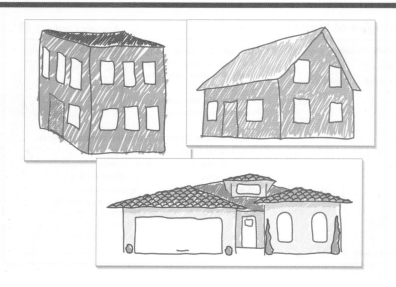

MINI UNIT 4
LESSON 4

Angle Measures

Lesson Objectives

- Estimate angle measures by comparing them to angles with known measures.

- Discover that the sum of the measures of the angles in any triangle is 180 degrees.

- Given the measures of two angles in a triangle, find the measure of the third angle.

Vocabulary

degree
straight angle
ray

The Day at a Glance

Today's Goals	Materials	

1 Teaching the Lesson
A1: Learn about degrees as units of measure and estimate angle measures.
A2: Discover that the sum of the measures of the angles in any triangle is 180 degrees.
A3: Calculate the measure of the third angle, given the measure of the other two angles in a triangle.
 	
2 Going Further
▶ Differentiated Instruction
 	
3 Homework and Spiral Review
	Lesson Activities
	Student Activity Book pp. 115–118
	  Student Hardcover Book
	  pp. 115–118
	Homework and Remembering
	  pp. 69–70
	Straws
	Centimeter rulers
	Scissors
	Quick Quiz (See Assessment Guide)
		Going Further
		Activity Cards 4-4
		Measure by Filling
		  Angles (TRB M38)
		Scissors
		MathBoard materials
		Math Journals

Use **Math Talk** *today!* 123

Keeping Skills Sharp

Daily Routines	English Language Learners
Homework Review Set aside some time to work with students who had difficulty with their homework. **Logic Problems** Use *all*, *some*, or *no* to complete each sentence. 1. If all isosceles triangles have at least two equal sides, then ___ equilateral triangles are isosceles triangles. all 2. If all parallelograms are quadrilaterals, then ___ quadrilaterals are parallelograms. some	Write *degree* and *straight angle*. Turn in place. Ask: **What did I do?** turned around Turn half way. Ask: **Did I turn completely around?** no Say: **I turned half way. We measure turns in** *degrees.* **A complete turn is a circle. It is 360°. Half a turn is 180°.** • **Beginning** Make a right angle with your arms. Ask: **Is this a right angle?** yes Say: **A right angle is a turn in a circle. It is 90°.** Have students repeat. • **Intermediate** Make a right angle with your arms. Ask: **What angle is this?** right angle Say: **A right angle is 90°.** Make a straight angle. Say: **This is half a turn. It is ___.** 180° **180° is a** *straight angle.* • **Advanced** Guide students to make right and straight angles with their arms and describe them. Draw a circle on the board and label rays at 90° and 180°. Ask: **How many degrees is a right angle?** 90° **How many degrees is a** *straight angle?* 180°

Angle Measures **279**

Teaching the Lesson

Estimate Angle Measures

 20 MINUTES

Goal: Learn about degrees as units of measure and estimate angle measures.

Materials: Student Activity Book or Hardcover Book pp. 115–116, straws

✔ **NCTM Standards:**
Geometry
Measurement
Connections

▶ Introduce Degrees   WHOLE CLASS

Invite students to suggest different units of measure and to explain their use. Answers will vary. Possible answers: Centimeters and inches measure length. Pounds measure weight.

Draw several different angles on the board. Remind students that the size of an angle is the amount of rotation, or turn, from one side to the other side.

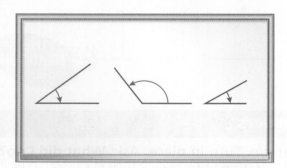

Explain to students that the size of an angle is measured in units called degrees.

Refer students to Student Book page 115. Ask them to examine the 1-degree angle. Point out that 1 degree is a very small rotation.

Refer students to the 5-degree angle and explain that an angle's measure is the total number of 1-degree angles that fit inside it. Then introduce the symbol (°) for degrees.

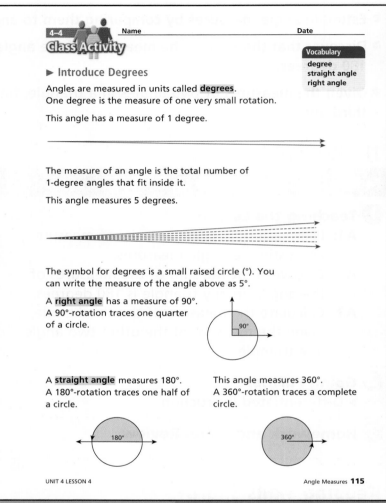

Student Activity Book page 115

Hold up two straws and show students how to rotate one straw to trace a complete circle.

Demonstrate a 90° rotation using the two straws.

● What kind of angle is this? a right angle

Explain to students that the measure of a right angle is 90° and point out that a 90° rotation is one quarter of a circle.

Next, rotate the straw to show a 180° angle and tell students that this angle is twice the size of a 90° angle.

● If this angle is twice the size of a 90° angle, what is its measure? 180°

Emphasize for students that a 180° rotation traces a half-circle. Explain that a 180° angle is called a *straight angle*; it looks like a straight line because the rays that form the sides of the angle point in opposite directions.

Rotate the straw to show a complete circle and indicate that this angle is twice the size of a 180° angle.

● If this angle is twice the size of a 180° angle, what is its measure? 360°

Tell students that a 360° rotation traces a complete circle. Explain that a 360° angle looks like a single ray because the two rays that form the sides of the angle align and point in the same direction.

▶ Angle Measures WHOLE CLASS

Draw an angle that is approximately 80° on the board and include a dashed line at 90° for reference.

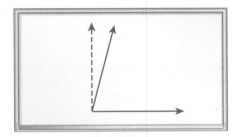

● Is the measure of this angle greater than or less than 90°? It is less than 90°.

Point out that the measure of this angle is slightly less than 90°, so you can estimate that its measure is approximately 80°.

Together, complete exercise 1 on Student Activity Book page 116. Draw a 45° angle on the board and show a dashed line at 90°.

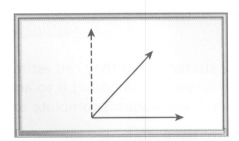

● How many angles like this one will fit inside a 90° angle? two angles

● What number, if you double it, is equal to 90? 45

Tell students that the measure of this angle is approximately 45°.

Activity continued ▶

1 Teaching the Lesson (continued)

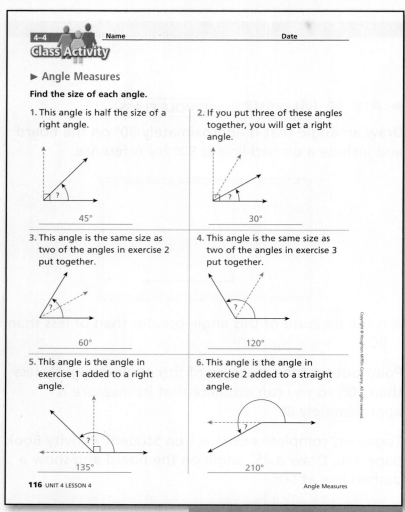

4-4

Class Activity

Name _____ Date _____

▶ Angle Measures

Find the size of each angle.

1. This angle is half the size of a right angle.

45°

2. If you put three of these angles together, you will get a right angle.

30°

3. This angle is the same size as two of the angles in exercise 2 put together.

60°

4. This angle is the same size as two of the angles in exercise 3 put together.

120°

5. This angle is the angle in exercise 1 added to a right angle.

135°

6. This angle is the angle in exercise 2 added to a straight angle.

210°

116 UNIT 4 LESSON 4

Angle Measures

Student Activity Book page 116

Emphasize for students that they can estimate the measure of an angle by comparing it to angles with given measures. Have students complete exercises 2–6.

You may wish to have students experiencing difficulty work with a **Helping Partner**.

Differentiated Instruction

Extra Help Some students will benefit from using their arms to form 90°, 180°, and 360° angles. In pairs, students can take turns making and identifying these angles. When students are comfortable with these benchmark angles, encourage them to experiment with making other angles and estimating their measures.

✓ Ongoing Assessment

Ask students about angles made by the hands of a clock.

▶ What is the measure of the angle formed on a clock when the minute hand points to 12 and the hour hand points to 6?

▶ What is the measure of the angle formed on a clock when the minute hand points to 12 and the hour hand points to 3?

Find the Sum of the Measures of the Angles of a Triangle

 20 MINUTES

Goal: Discover that the sum of the measures of the angles in any triangle is 180 degrees.

Materials: Student Activity Book or Hardcover Book p. 117, centimeter rulers (1 per student), scissors (1 pair per student)

 NCTM Standards:
Geometry
Measurement
Connections

▶ Join Angles of a Triangle PAIRS

Have **Student Pairs** follow the directions on Student Book page 117 to draw a triangle, cut it out, tear off the corners, and rearrange the corners to form a straight angle (180°).

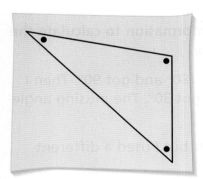

Have **Student Pairs** complete exercises 7–10. Circulate while students are working and help those who are having difficulty.

When students are finished, discuss their answers. Ask students to name the types of triangles they drew. right triangle, isosceles triangle, acute triangle, obtuse triangle, scalene triangle, equilateral triangle

● Did everyone make straight angles when they rearranged the angles of their triangles? yes

Summarize by pointing out that the sum of the measures of the three angles in any triangle is 180°.

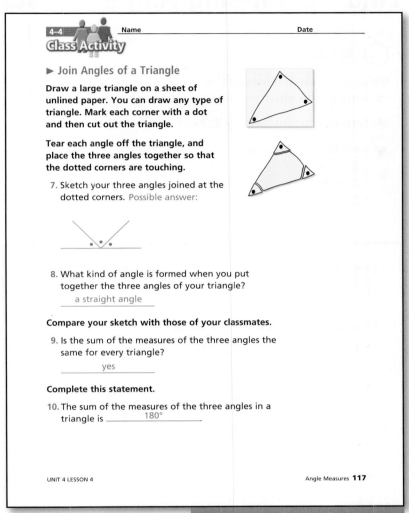

Student Activity Book page 117

Teaching the Lesson (continued)

Activity 3

Find the Missing Angle Measure in a Triangle

 20 MINUTES

Goal: Calculate the measure of the third angle, given the measure of the other two angles in a triangle.

Materials: Student Activity Book or Hardcover Book p. 118

✔ **NCTM Standards:**
Geometry
Connections
Communication

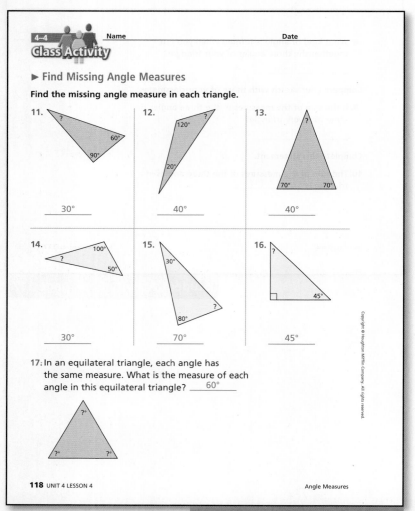

Student Activity Book page 118

Teaching Note

Watch For! You may need to remind some students that the square in the angle in exercise 16 shows that it is a right angle. Ask them to tell you the measure of a right angle. 90°

▶ **Find Missing Angle Measures** [PAIRS]

Have **Student Pairs** find the missing angle measure in exercise 11 on Student Book page 118.

When they are finished, discuss their methods of solving as a class.

Ask **Student Pairs** to complete exercises 12–17. When they are finished, invite volunteers to record their answers on the board.

 Math Talk in Action

What information do we know that can help us calculate the measure of the missing angle measure?

Aida: We know that the sum of the measures of angles in a triangle is 180°.

Explain how you used this information to calculate the measure of the missing angle.

Enrico: I subtracted 90° from 180° and got 90°. Then I subtracted 60° from 90° and got 30°. The missing angle has a measure of 30°.

Seema: I got the same answer but I used a different method.

Enrico: What did you do?

Seema: I added 90° and 60° and got 150°. Then I subtracted 150° from 180° and got 30°.

Both methods are correct. Adding two numbers together before subtracting them from another number is the same as subtracting the two numbers one at a time.

 Quick Quiz

See Assessment Guide for Unit 4
Quick Quiz

Intervention — Activity Card 4-4

Fill-in Angles
Activity Card 4-4

Work: In pairs

Use:
- TRB M38 (Measure by Filling Angles)
- 2 scissors

1. **Work Together** Find the measure of each angle on TRB M38.
2. Cut out the 10° angle. Then place it inside the angle you want to measure, aligned with one of the rays.
3. Trace the 10° angle in position. Then rotate it to align with the tracing and trace it again.
4. Continue moving and tracing the 10° angle until you have filled the entire angle that you are measuring.
5. How many tracings did you make inside the angle? Add 10° that number of times to find the measure of the angle. 8; 80°

Unit 4, Lesson 4   Copyright © Houghton Mifflin Company

Activity Note Students can count by 10s to find the total measure of each angle after they have completed their tracings.

Math Writing Prompt

Draw a Picture If Philip draws an angle that is a straight line, what is the measure of this angle? Include a drawing with your answer.

 **Software Support**

Warm Up 35.23

On Level — Activity Card 4-4

Rays and Angles
Activity Card 4-4 ▲

Work: On your own

Use:
- MathBoard materials

1. Draw angles on your MathBoard. Use them to test the statements below about rays and angles.
2. True or false? The measure of an angle changes when one ray is rotated. true
3. True or false? The measure of an angle does not change when the length of its rays changes. true
4. **Analyze** Think about how you measure an angle. How does that help explain your answers to the questions above? An angle is measured by the size of its opening, not the length of its rays.

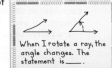
When I rotate a ray, the angle changes. The statement is ____.

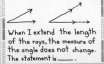
When I extend the length of the rays, the measure of the angle does not change. The statement is ____.

Unit 4, Lesson 4   Copyright © Houghton Mifflin Company

Activity Note To reinforce the underlying concept, suggest that students rotate the ray until the angle becomes a right angle. Then ask students if extending the rays can create a 90° angle.

Math Writing Prompt

Explain Your Thinking Jocelyn draws a right triangle with one angle measuring 30°. What are the measures of the other two angles? Explain your thinking.

 Software Support

Shapes Ahoy: Ship Shapes, Level H

Challenge — Activity Card 4-4

Classroom Angles
Activity Card 4-4 ■

Work: In pairs

1. Work with a partner. Locate as many angles as you can in your classroom.
2. Use what you know about angles. Estimate the measure of each angle you find. Record the angles you see and your estimates.
3. **Remember** A straight angle measures 180°. A right angle measures 90°.
4. **Analyze** How can you use the common angle measures above to help you estimate? Using benchmark angles helps you make angle estimates.

The corner of my desk is a 90° angle.

The W on the wall has 45° angles in it.

Two tiles on the floor meet to form a 180° angle.

The collar of Han's shirt looks like an 80° angle.

Unit 4, Lesson 4   Copyright © Houghton Mifflin Company

Activity Note Be sure that students recognize the importance of using benchmark angles such as 45°, 90°, and 180° when making angle estimates.

Math Writing Prompt

Compare and Contrast How is the process of measuring an angle like measuring a line segment? How is it different?

 DESTINATION Math **Software Support**

Course II: Module 3: Unit 1: Area

③ Homework and Spiral Review

Homework **Goal:** Additional Practice

On this Homework page, students measure angles based on given information.

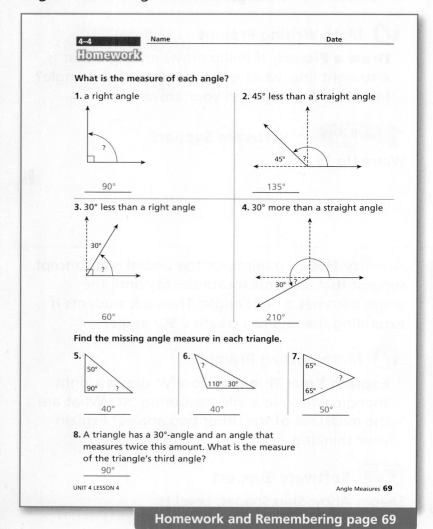

Remembering **Goal:** Spiral Review

This Remembering page is appropriate anytime after today's lesson.

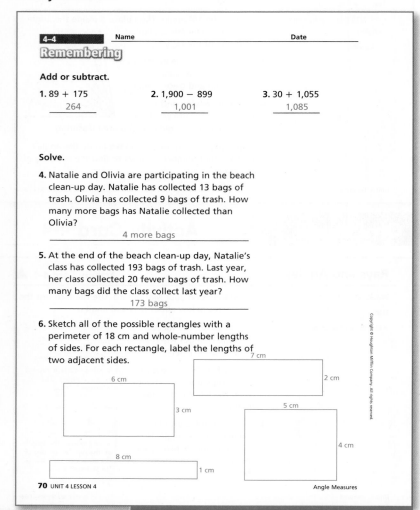

Home or School Activity

 Social Studies Connection

Communication with Symbols Before telecommunications, people sent messages moving wooden arms mounted at the tops of towers. They put the arms at different angles to represent letters.

Challenge students to create their own signaling system by holding their arms at different angles. Ask them to draw diagrams for their system and to test it with a classmate.

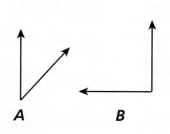

A   *B*

Unit Review and Test

Lesson Objectives

● **Assess student progress on unit objectives.**

The Day at a Glance

Today's Goals	Materials
1 Assessing the Unit ▶ Assess student progress on unit objectives. ▶ Use activities from unit lessons to reteach content. **2 Extending the Assessment** ▶ Use remediation for common errors. There is no homework assignment on a test day.	Unit 4 Test, Student Activity Book pp. 119–120 or Hardcover Book pp.119–120 and Activity Workbook pp. 45–46 Unit 4 Test, Form A or B, Assessment Guide (optional) Unit 4 Performance Assessment, Assessment Guide (optional)

Keeping Skills Sharp

Daily Routines 🕐 5 MINUTES	
If you are doing a unit review day, go over the homework. If this is a test day, omit the homework review.	**Review and Test Day** You may want to choose a quiet game or other activity (reading a book or working on homework for another subject) for students who finish early.

Assessing the Unit

Assess Unit Objectives

45 MINUTES (more if schedule permits)

Goal: Assess student progress on unit objectives.

Materials: Student Activity Book pp.119–120 or Hardcover Book pp. 119–120 and Activity Workbook pp. 45–46; Assessment Guide (optional)

▶ Review and Assessment

If your students are ready for assessment on the unit objectives, you may use either the test on the Student Book pages or one of the forms of the Unit 4 Test in the Assessment Guide to assess student progress.

If you feel that students need some review first, you may use the test on the Student Book pages as a review of unit content, and then use one of the forms of the Unit 4 Test in the Assessment Guide to assess student progress.

To assign a numerical score for all of these test forms, use 10 points for each question.

You may also choose to use the Unit 4 Performance Assessment. Scoring for that assessment can be found in its rubric in the Assessment Guide.

▶ Reteaching Resources

The chart lists the test items, the unit objectives they cover, and the lesson activities in which the objective is covered in this unit. You may revisit these activities with students who do not show mastery of the objectives.

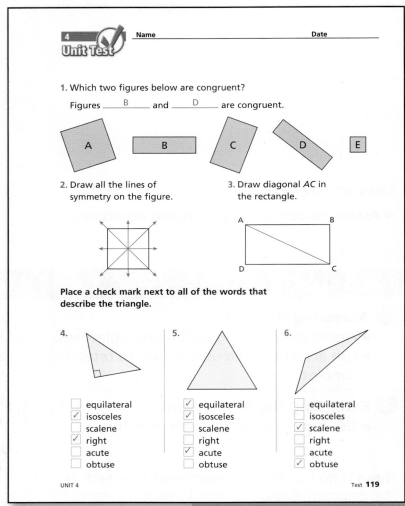

Student Activity Book page 119

Unit Test Items	Unit Objectives Tested	Activities to Use for Reteaching
1, 2	**4.1** Identify figures that are congruent and draw lines of symmetry on figures.	Lesson 1, Activities 2 and 3
3, 10	**4.2** Label figures with letters and compose and decompose polygons.	Lesson 2, Activities 2 and 3 Lesson 3, Activity 3 Lesson 3, Activity 4

Student Activity Book page 120

Unit Test Items	Unit Objectives Tested	Activities to Use for Reteaching
4–9	**4.3** Identify polygons; Classify triangles by length of sides or measure of angles.	Lesson 3, Activity 2 Lesson 3, Activity 4

▶ Assessment Resources

Free Response Tests
Unit 4 Test, Student Book pages 119–120
Unit 4 Test, Form A, Assessment Guide

Extended Response Item
The last item in the Student Book test and in the Form A test will require an extended response as an answer.

Multiple Choice Test
Unit 4 Test, Form B, Assessment Guide

Performance Assessment
Unit 4 Performance Assessment, Assessment Guide
Unit 4 Performance Assessment Rubric, Assessment Guide

▶ Portfolio Assessment

Teacher-selected Items for Student Portfolios:

- Homework, Lesson 3
- Class Activity work, Lessons 1, 4

Student-selected Items for Student Portfolios:

- Favorite Home or School Activity
- Best Writing Prompt

② Extending the Assessment

Unit Objective 4.1

Identify figures that are congruent and draw lines of symmetry on figures.

Common Error: Draws Lines of Symmetry Incorrectly

When drawing lines of symmetry on figures, students may include lines that are not lines of symmetry.

Remediation Have students fold a paper circle or square in half four different ways to demonstrate that lines of symmetry divide a figure into two congruent halves.

Common Error: Identifies Too Few Lines of Symmetry

When drawing lines of symmetry on figures, students may identify some, but not all, of the lines of symmetry. For example, they may recognize the vertical and horizontal lines of symmetry of a square but not the lines of symmetry along the diagonals.

Remediation To help students identify all the lines of symmetry of a figure, encourage them to fold the figure in different ways to try to find lines of symmetry.

Unit Objective 4.2

Label figures with letters and compose and decompose quadrilaterals.

Common Error: Doesn't Identify All of the Quadrilaterals that Can be Composed

When students are asked to compose quadrilaterals from two congruent triangles, they may not identify all possible quadrilaterals.

Remediation Have students compose quadrilaterals from two congruent scalene triangles. They begin by drawing matching color line segments along each congruent side. In each triangle, they might color the longest side red, the next shorter side blue, and the shortest side green. They then make quadrilaterals by joining corresponding sides of the triangles—green to green, red to red, and blue to blue.

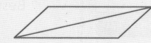

Common Error: Doesn't Recognize Congruent Quadrilaterals

When students are asked to compose quadrilaterals from two congruent triangles, they may not recognize that some of the quadrilaterals they create are congruent.

Remediation Have students compose quadrilaterals from two isosceles triangles. Have them sketch the quadrilaterals, cut them out, and place them on top of each other in different positions to check which ones are congruent.

Unit Objective 4.3

Identify polygons; Classify triangles by length of sides or measure of angles.

Common Error: Identifies Angles Incorrectly

When trying to name triangles by angles, students may incorrectly identify an angle as having a measure equal to, greater than, or less than a right angle.

Remediation Have students use an index card to help decide if an angle has a measure equal to, greater than, or less than a right angle.

Explain that any square corner is a right angle. So the square corner of an index card or piece of paper is a right angle. Demonstrate how students can align the corner of the card or paper to the given angle. The angle will be greater than, less than, or congruent to the angle of the card or paper.

Common Error: Doesn't Distinguish Between Equilateral and Isosceles Triangles

Some students may have difficulty distinguishing between isosceles and equilateral triangles.

Remediation Draw an equilateral and isosceles triangle on the board. Invite students to use a meter stick or yardstick and colored chalk to highlight the sides of equal length in the triangles.

Unit 5 Overview

Use Addition and Subtraction

UNIT 5 PROVIDES EXPERIENCE with various representations and contexts for addition and subtraction, while continuing to develop and practice computation methods that are meaningful and easily used by students. Students apply their knowledge of place value to compare, order, and round numbers, and use rounding to estimate sums and differences. Students extend money skills to make change. More complex word problems are also introduced.

Skills Trace

Grade 2	Grade 3	Grade 4
• Compare, order, and round whole numbers (through the hundreds) to the nearest ten.	• Compare, order, and round whole numbers (through the thousands) to the nearest ten and hundred.	• Compare, order, and round whole numbers and decimals.
• Estimate quantities and sums and differences (through the hundreds).	• Estimate quantities and sums and differences (through the thousands).	• Estimate quantities and sums and differences (including decimal numbers).
• Find the value, represent money amounts, and count change for ten dollars or less.	• Find the value, represent money amounts, and count change for ten dollars or less.	• Analyze, complete, and graph functions.
• Make picture graphs, pictographs, bar graphs, and circle graphs.	• Represent, organize, and analyze data in pictographs, bar graphs, frequency tables, and line plots. (*line graphs, see Extension Lesson 12*)	• Make pictographs, bar graphs, line graphs, and circle graphs.
• Solve word problems with two steps (up to three-digit numbers).	• Solve multi-digit, multi-step problems and problems that have extra, hidden, and insufficient information.	• Solve multi-digit, multi-step word problems.

Unit 5 Contents

Unit 5   Assessment

✓ Unit Objectives Tested	Unit Test Items	Lessons
5.1 Compare, order, and round whole numbers and estimate sums and differences.	1–5, 15	1–3
5.2 Find the value of and represent money amounts with coins and bills, count change, compare, round, and estimate with money.	6, 7, 17–20	4–7
5.3 Interpret data in a table, graph or line plot, make graphs, and complete tables.	8–12	8–10, 16
5.4 Solve word problems with two steps, multi-steps, extra or hidden information, and identify problems with not enough information.	13, 14, 16	11–14

Assessment and Review Resources

Formal Assessment	Informal Assessment	Review Opportunities

Formal Assessment

Student Activity Book
- Unit Review and Test (pp. 177–180)

Assessment Guide
- Quick Quizzes (pp. A38, A39, A40, A41, A42)
- Test A-Open Response (pp. A43–A46)
- Test B-Multiple Choice (pp. A47–A50)
- Performance Assessment (pp. A51–A53)

Test Generator CD-ROM
- Open Response Test
- Multiple Choice Test
- Test Bank Items

Informal Assessment

Teacher Edition
- Ongoing Assessment (in every lesson)
- Quick Practice (in every lesson)
- Portfolio Suggestions (p. 431)

123 Math Talk
  - ▸ Math Talk in Action (pp. 293, 296, 324, 348, 377, 386, 394, 395, 402, 411)
  - ▸ Solve and Discuss (pp. 302, 312, 320, 324, 331, 338, 340, 355, 370, 379, 384, 392)
  - ▸ Student Pairs (pp. 303, 312, 326, 350, 402, 406)
  - ▸ Small Groups (pp. 395, 396, 405, 419) Helping Partners (pp. 332, 348, 378, 404)
  - ▸ In Activities (pp. 292, 325, 330, 344, 365, 371, 394, 419, 420)
  - ▸ Scenarios (pp. 326, 332)

Review Opportunities

Homework and Remembering
- Review of recently taught topics
- Spiral Review

Teacher Edition
- Unit Review and Test (pp. 429–432)

Test Generator CD-ROM
- Custom Review Sheets

Planning Unit 5

Lesson NCTM Focal Points NCTM Standards	Resources	Materials for Lesson Activities	Materials for Going Further
5-1 **Round to the Nearest Hundred** NCTM Focal Points: 7.1, 7.4 NCTM Standards: 1, 7	TE pp. 291–298 SAB pp. 121–124 H&R pp. 71–72 AC 5-1	✓ MathBoard Materials ✓ Demonstration Secret Code Cards	MathBoard materials Calculators Math Journals
5-2 **Round to the Nearest Ten** NCTM Focal Points: 7.1, 7.4 NCTM Standards: 1, 4, 5, 6, 7	TE pp. 299–306 SAB pp. 125–128 H&R pp. 73–74 AC 5-2	Clear jars, Beans ✓ MathBoard materials ✓ Demonstration Secret Code Cards ✓ Secret Code Cards "Geometry Park" CD	✓ Secret Code Cards ✓ MathBoard materials Index cards Calculators Math Journals
5-3 **Compare Whole Numbers** NCTM Focal Point: 7.1 NCTM Standards: 1, 8	TE pp. 307–314 SAB pp. 129–130 H&R pp. 75–76 AG Quick Quiz 1 AC 5-3 MCC 17	✓ MathBoard materials ✓ Base ten blocks *The Greatest Gymnast of All*, by Stuart J. Murphy	✓ Secret Code Cards ✓ MathBoard materials ✓ Number cubes Math Journals
5-4 **Money Values** NCTM Standards: 1, 6, 7, 8, 9, 10	TE pp. 315–322 SAB pp. 131–134 H&R pp. 77–78 AC 5-4	✓ Play money Snack bags or envelopes Overhead money (optional) Overhead projector (optional)	✓ Play money ✓ Number cubes Math Journals
5-5 **Represent Money Amounts in Different Ways** NCTM Standards: 1, 6, 8, 9	TE pp. 323–328 SAB pp. 135–136 H&R pp. 79–80 AC 5-5	✓ MathBoard materials ✓ Play money Coin Strips (TRB M41) Price tags	✓ MathBoard materials ✓ Number cubes ✓ Play money Index cards Math Journals
5-6 **Make Change** NCTM Standards: 1, 6, 8, 9	TE pp. 329–334 SAB pp. 137–138 H&R pp. 81–82 AC 5-6 MCC 18	✓ Play money Overhead projector and overhead coins (optional) *Ox-Cart Man*, by Donald Hall	✓ Play money ✓ MathBoard materials Store flyers Math Journals
5-7 **Round Money Amounts** NCTM Focal Points: 7.3, 7.4 NCTM Standards: 1, 6, 10	TE pp. 335–342 SAB pp. 139–142 H&R pp. 83–84 AC 5-7 AG Quick Quiz 2	✓ MathBoard materials	✓ MathBoard materials Index cards Math Journals
5-8 **Ask Addition and Subtraction Questions from Tables** NCTM Focal Point: 7.5 NCTM Standards: 1, 2, 5, 8	TE pp. 343–352 SAB pp. 143–146 H&R pp. 85–86 AC 5-8	Transparency of Student Activity Book page 143 (optional) Overhead projector (optional) Sticky notes	Math Journals

Resources/Materials Key: TE: Teacher Edition   SAB: Student Activity Book   H&R: Homework and Remembering
AC: Activity Cards   MCC: Math Center Challenge   AG: Assessment Guide   ✓: Grade 3 kits   TRB: Teacher's Resource Book

Lesson NCTM Focal Points NCTM Standards	Resources	Materials for Lesson Activities	Materials for Going Further
5-9 **Complete Tables** NCTM Focal Points: 6.1, 7.5 NCTM Standards: 1, 5, 6, 8	TE pp. 353– 362 SAB pp. 147–150 H&R pp. 87–88 AC 5-9	Crayons or pencils	Inch Grid Paper (TRB M42) Math Journals
5-10 **More Practice with Tables** NCTM Focal Points: 6.1, 7.5 NCTM Standards: 1, 2, 5, 6, 7, 8, 9, 10	TE pp. 363–368 SAB pp. 151–152 H&R pp. 89–90 AC 5-10 AG Quick Quiz 3 MCC 19	✓ Play money Calculators (optional)	Blocks (red and blue) Paper bags ✓ MathBoard materials ✓ Two-color counters Math Journals
5-11 **Word Problems with Extra or Hidden Information** NCTM Standards: 1, 6, 8, 10	TE pp. 369–374 SAB pp. 153–154 H&R pp. 91–92 AC 5-11	Highlighters	Math Journals
5-12 **Word Problems with Not Enough Information** NCTM Standards: 1, 6, 8, 9	TE pp. 375–382 SAB pp. 155–158 H&R pp. 93–94 AC 5-12	None	✓ MathBoard materials Homework p. 93 Math Journals
5-13 **Solve Two-Step Word Problems** NCTM Standards: 1, 6, 7	TE pp. 383–390 SAB pp. 159–160 H&R pp. 95–96 AC 5-13	None	Highlighters (different colors) Homework p. 95 Index Cards Sentence strips Math Journals
5-14 **Solve Multi-Step Word Problems** NCTM Standards: 1, 6, 7, 8, 9, 10	TE pp. 391–398 SAB pp. 161–164 H&R pp. 97–98 AC 5-14 AG Quick Quiz 4	*Math Mysteries*, by Jack Silbert (optional)	✓ MathBoard materials Sentence strips Math Journals
5-15 **Read and Create Pictographs and Bar Graphs** NCTM Focal Point: 6.2 NCTM Standards: 1, 2, 5, 6, 8, 10	TE pp. 399–408 SAB pp. 165–168 H&R pp. 99–100 AC 5-15 MCC 20	Ruler Connecting cubes Yardsticks Index cards Overhead projector (optional) Transparency of Student Activity Book pp. 166, 167 (optional) Class list	✓ Connecting cubes Markers 10 × 10 Grid (TRB M43) Math Journals

Hardcover Student Book

- Together, the Hardcover Student Book and its companion Activity Workbook contain all of the pages in the consumable Student Activity Book.

Manipulatives and Materials

- Essential materials for teaching *Math Expressions* are available in the Grade 3 kits. These materials are indicated by a ✓ in these lists. At the front of this Teacher Edition is more information about kit contents, alternatives for the materials, and use of the materials.

Lesson NCTM Focal Points NCTM Standards	Resources	Materials for Lesson Activities	Materials for Going Further
5-16 **Read and Create Bar Graphs with Multi-Digit Numbers** NCTM Focal Point: 6.2 NCTM Standards: 1, 2, 5, 8, 10	TE pp. 409–416 SAB pp. 169–172 H&R pp. 101–102 AC 5-16	Index cards 10 × 10 Grid (TRB M43)	Data Tables (TRB M44) Centimeter Grid Paper (TRB M31) Crayons Math Journals
5-17 **Represent and Organize Data** NCTM Focal Points: 6.1, 6.2, 6.3, 6.4 NCTM Standards: 1, 2, 5, 10	TE pp. 417– 422 SAB pp. 173–174 H&R pp. 103–104 AC 5-17 AG Quick Quiz 5	None	✓ MathBoard materials Spinner E (TRB M132) ✓ Connecting cubes ✓ Number cubes Paper bag Blank paper Calendar Math Journals
5-18 **Use Mathematical Processes** NCTM Focal Points: 3.6, 6.1, 6.2, 7.4 NCTM Standards: 6, 7, 8, 9, 10	TE pp. 423–428 SAB pp. 175–176 H&R pp. 105–106 AC 5-18	Tape Measuring tapes Grid paper Calculators	Straws Scissors Math Journals
✓ **Unit Review and Test**	TE pp. 429–432 SAB pp. 177–180 AG Unit 5 Tests		

Resources/Materials Key: TE: Teacher Edition   SAB: Student Activity Book   H&R: Homework and Remembering
AC: Activity Cards   MCC: Math Center Challenge   AG: Assessment Guide   ✓: Grade 3 kits   TRB: Teacher's Resource Book

Hardcover Student Book

- Together, the Hardcover Student Book and its companion Activity Workbook contain all of the pages in the consumable Student Activity Book.

Manipulatives and Materials

- Essential materials for teaching *Math Expressions* are available in the Grade 3 kits. These materials are indicated by a ✓ in these lists. At the front of this Teacher Edition is more information about kit contents, alternatives for the materials, and use of the materials.

Unit 5   Teaching Resources

Differentiated Instruction

Individualizing Instruction

Activities	Level	Frequency
	• Intervention • On Level • Challenge	All 3 in every lesson

Math Writing Prompts	Level	Frequency
	• Intervention • On Level • Challenge	All 3 in every lesson

Math Center Challenges	For advanced students
	4 in every unit

Reaching All Learners

English Language Learners	Lessons	Pages
	1, 2, 3, 4, 5, 6, 7, 8, 9, 10, 11, 12, 13, 14, 15, 16, 17, 18	293, 303, 310, 316, 330, 335, 336, 345, 354, 365, 370, 377, 385, 392, 402, 410, 418, 424

Extra Help	Lessons	Pages
	2, 3, 5, 6, 7, 8, 9, 12, 15, 16	301, 308, 324, 325, 331, 337, 345, 347, 348, 354, 376, 402, 411, 413

Alternate Approach	Lessons	Pages
	1, 3, 6, 10, 11, 14, 15	294, 309, 331, 366, 371, 396, 404

Advanced Learners	Lessons	Pages
	5, 10	326, 365

Strategies for English Language Learners

Present this problem to all students. Offer the different levels of support to meet students' levels of language proficiency.

Objective Familiarize students with estimating.

Problem Make 3 stacks of blocks in front of the classroom: 1 with as many blocks as students in the class, 1 with double the amount, 1 stack with half the amount.

Newcomer

- Ask: **How many students are in the class?** Say: **I want to give each student a block.**

- Point to the stacks. Say: **This one is *too* big. This one is *too* small. I *think* this one is right.**

Beginning

- Say: **I want to give every student 1 block. I do not want to count the blocks. We *estimate*.**

- **Do I use the small stack, the middle stack, or the big stack?** middle

Intermediate

- Say: **I want to give every student 1 block.** Ask: **Which stack do you *think* has 1 block for every student?** middle one Say: **Yes. That is an *estimate*.**

Advanced

- Have students estimate which stack has enough to give everyone 1 block. Ask volunteers to describe how they decided.

Connections

 Social Studies Connections
Lesson 4, page 322
Lesson 5, page 328
Lesson 6, page 334
Lesson 13, page 390

 Real-World Connections
Lesson 7, page 342
Lesson 16, page 416

 Language Arts Connections
Lesson 8, page 352
Lesson 11, page 374
Lesson 14, page 398
Lesson 18, page 428

 Math-to-Math Connection
Lesson 12, page 382

 Technology Connection
Lesson 9, page 362

 Music Connection
Lesson 2, page 306

 Science Connections
Lesson 10, page 368
Lesson 15, page 408

 Literature Connection
Lesson 3, page 314

 Physical Education Connection
Lesson 17, page 422

 Real-World Connection
Lesson 18, page 428

Independent Learning Activities

Ready-Made Math Challenge Centers

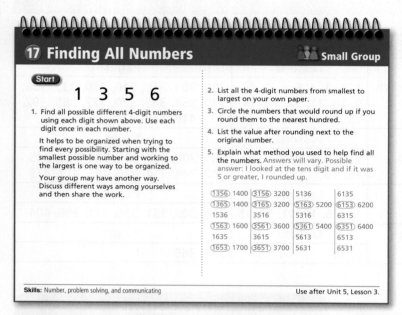

17 Finding All Numbers Small Group

Start

1 3 5 6

1. Find all possible different 4-digit numbers using each digit shown above. Use each digit once in each number.

   It helps to be organized when trying to find every possibility. Starting with the smallest possible number and working to the largest is one way to be organized.

   Your group may have another way. Discuss different ways among yourselves and then share the work.

2. List all the 4-digit numbers from smallest to largest on your own paper.

3. Circle the numbers that would round up if you round them to the nearest hundred.

4. List the value after rounding next to the original number.

5. Explain what method you used to help find all the numbers. Answers will vary. Possible answer: I looked at the tens digit and if it was 5 or greater, I rounded up.

(1356) 1400	(3156) 3200	5136	6135
(1365) 1400	(3165) 3200	(5163) 5200	(6153) 6200
1536	3516	5316	6315
(1563) 1600	(3561) 3600	(5361) 5400	(6351) 6400
1635	3615	5613	6513
(1653) 1700	(3651) 3700	5631	6531

Skills: Number, problem solving, and communicating   Use after Unit 5, Lesson 3.

Grouping Small Group

Materials None

Objective Students find 4-digit numbers, given four digits, and round some to the next hundred.

Connections Number and Problem Solving

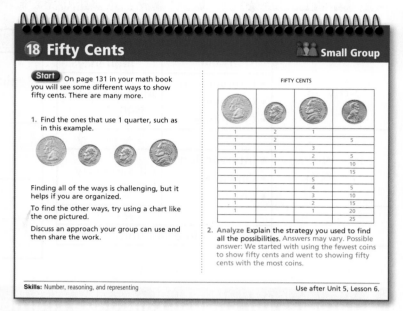

18 Fifty Cents Small Group

Start On page 131 in your math book you will see some different ways to show fifty cents. There are many more.

1. Find the ones that use 1 quarter, such as in this example.

Finding all of the ways is challenging, but it helps if you are organized.

To find the other ways, try using a chart like the one pictured.

Discuss an approach your group can use and then share the work.

FIFTY CENTS

1	2	1	
1	2		5
1		3	
1	1		5
1	1	1	10
1	1		15
1		5	
1		4	5
1		3	10
1		2	15
1		1	20
			25

2. **Analyze** Explain the strategy you used to find all the possibilities. Answers may vary. Possible answer: We started with using the fewest coins to show fifty cents and went to showing fifty cents with the most coins.

Skills: Number, reasoning, and representing   Use after Unit 5, Lesson 6.

Grouping Small Group

Materials Coins (optional), calculator (optional)

Objective Students chart the different ways to represent fifty cents with coins.

Connections Number and Reasoning

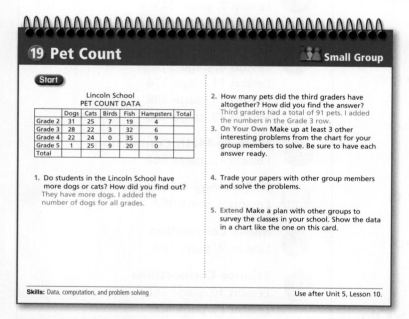

19 Pet Count Small Group

Start

Lincoln School PET COUNT DATA

	Dogs	Cats	Birds	Fish	Hampsters	Total
Grade 2	31	25	7	19	4	
Grade 3	28	22	3	32	6	
Grade 4	22	24	0	35	9	
Grade 5	1	25	9	20	0	
Total						

1. Do students in the Lincoln School have more dogs or cats? How did you find out? They have more dogs. I added the number of dogs for all grades.

2. How many pets did the third graders have altogether? How did you find the answer? Third graders had a total of 91 pets. I added the numbers in the Grade 3 row.

3. On Your Own Make up at least 3 other interesting problems from the chart for your group members to solve. Be sure to have each answer ready.

4. Trade your papers with other group members and solve the problems.

5. Extend Make a plan with other groups to survey the classes in your school. Show the data in a chart like the one on this card.

Skills: Data, computation, and problem solving   Use after Unit 5, Lesson 10.

Grouping Small Group

Materials Calculator

Objective Students analyze data in a table and create word problems.

Connections Data and Computation

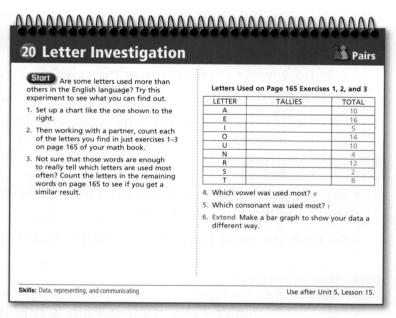

20 Letter Investigation Pairs

Start Are some letters used more than others in the English language? Try this experiment to see what you can find out.

1. Set up a chart like the one shown to the right.

2. Then working with a partner, count each of the letters you find in just exercises 1–3 on page 165 of your math book.

3. Not sure that those words are enough to really tell which letters are used most often? Count the letters in the remaining words on page 165 to see if you get a similar result.

Letters Used on Page 165 Exercises 1, 2, and 3

LETTER	TALLIES	TOTAL
A		10
E		16
I		5
O		14
U		10
N		4
R		12
S		2
T		8

4. Which vowel was used most? e

5. Which consonant was used most? r

6. Extend Make a bar graph to show your data a different way.

Skills: Data, representing, and communicating   Use after Unit 5, Lesson 15.

Grouping Pairs

Materials Ruler, math book

Objective Students count and record the letters most often used on a math book page.

Connections Data and Communication

Ready-Made Math Resources

Technology — Tutorial, Practice, and Intervention

Use online, individualized intervention and support to bring students to proficiency.

Help students practice skills and apply concepts through exciting math adventures.

Extend and enrich students' understanding of skills and concepts through engaging, interactive lessons and activities.

Visit **Education Place**®
www.eduplace.com

Visit **www.eduplace.com/mx2t/** and find family, teacher, and student materials, activities, games, and more.

Literature Links

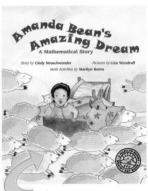

Amanda Bean's
Amazing Dream:
A Mathematical
Story

Amanda Bean's Amazing Dream: A Mathematical Story

This book by Cindy Newschwander introduces adding like sets of objects. Secondly, it presents sets of objects to be counted in rows and columns, as rectangular arrays.

Literature Connection

The Greatest Gymnast of All, by Stuart J. Murphy, illustrated by Cynthia Jabar (Harper Trophy, 1998)

Math Background

Putting Research into Practice for Unit 5

From Current Research: Statistics and Learning to Use Data

Processes like organizing data and conventions like labeling and scaling are crucial to data representation and are strongly connected to the concepts and processes of measurement. Given the difficulties students experience, instruction might need to differentiate these processes and conventions more sharply. Fundamental concepts...such as the conventions of scaling in graphs...need more careful attention in initial instruction.

National Research Council. "Developing Proficiency with Whole Numbers." *Adding It Up: Helping Students Learn Mathematics.* Washington, D.C.: National Academy Press, 2001. pp. 288–294

Estimation

[Computation estimation] requires recognizing that the appropriateness of an estimate is related to the problem and its context . . . Estimating the results of a computation is a complex activity that should integrate all strands of mathematical proficiency.

Its potential benefit is lost, however, if it is treated as a separate skill and taught as a set of isolated rules and techniques. Its benefit is realized when students are allowed to draw on other strands to find ways to simplify calculations and compensate for that simplification. For example, the representation students make of the mathematical situation enables them to make simple, appropriate estimates . . . [E]stimation is a good indicator of students' productive disposition—in this case, their propensity to make sense of mathematical situations so that they understand that estimates are not wild guesses but informed, approximate solutions.

National Research Council. "Developing Proficiency with Whole Numbers."

Adding It Up: Helping Children Learn Mathematics. Washington, D.C.: National Academy Press, 2001. p. 216

Other Useful References: Addition, Subtraction, and Estimating

Rubenstein, R.N. Computational estimation and related mathematical skills. *Journal for Research in Mathematics Education, 16,* 1985. pp. 106–119.

Sowder, J.T., & Wheeler, M.M. The development of concepts and procedures used in computational estimation. *Journal for Research in Mathematics Education, 20,* 1989. pp. 130–146.

Getting Ready to Teach Unit 5

In this unit students round numbers to estimate sums and differences. They organize and analyze data in tables and graphs and solve complex word problems.

Use Rounding to Estimate Sums and Differences

Round to the Nearest Hundred
Lesson 1

3̲64   **Underline the place to which you are rounding.**

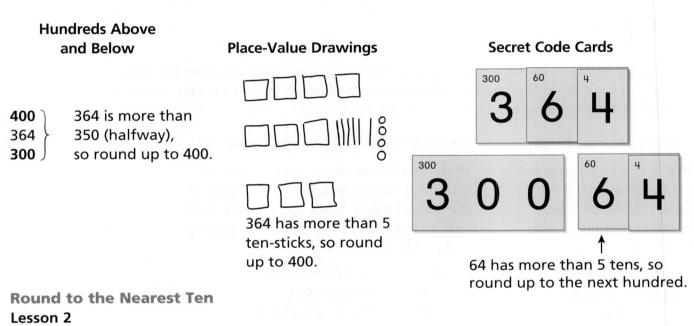

Hundreds Above and Below

400 ⎫
364 ⎬   364 is more than
300 ⎭   350 (halfway),
        so round up to 400.

Place-Value Drawings

364 has more than 5 ten-sticks, so round up to 400.

Secret Code Cards

| 300 | 60 | 4 |
| 3 | 6 | 4 |

| 300 | 60 | 4 |
| 3 0 0 | 6 4 |

64 has more than 5 tens, so round up to the next hundred.

Round to the Nearest Ten
Lesson 2

36̲4   **Underline the place to which you are rounding.**

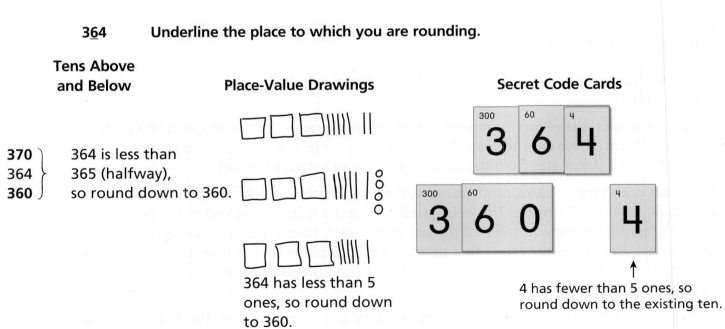

Tens Above and Below

370 ⎫
364 ⎬   364 is less than
360 ⎭   365 (halfway),
        so round down to 360.

Place-Value Drawings

364 has less than 5 ones, so round down to 360.

Secret Code Cards

| 300 | 60 | 4 |
| 3 | 6 | 4 |

| 300 | 60 | 4 |
| 3 6 0 | 4 |

4 has fewer than 5 ones, so round down to the existing ten.

Estimating Sums and Differences
Lessons 1 and 2

For rounding to estimate sums or differences, students round each number to the nearest ten or nearest hundred, and then add or subtract.

There are 48 children on one bus and 33 on another bus. About how many children are there altogether?

48 rounds to 50
33 rounds to 30.

Add 50 and 30 to get an estimate of 80.

Rounding Money Amounts
Lesson 7

Students round money amounts to the nearest dime or nearest dollar, using the rules for rounding. If the amount is equal to or more than half of the next whole dime (or dollar) amount, round up. If it is less than half of the next whole dime (or dollar) amount, round down.

Round $3.62 to the Nearest Dime

Underline the place to which you are rounding. Find the digit to the right of the dimes place. Since 2¢ is less than half of a dime, round down to the lesser dime: $3.60.

$3.70 ⎫
$3.62 ⎬ $3.62 is less than $3.65 (halfway), so round down to $3.60.
$3.60 ⎭

Round $3.62 to the Nearest Dollar

Underline the place to which you are rounding. Find the digits to the right of the dollars place. Since 62¢ is more than half of a dollar, round up to the greater dollar: $4.00.

$4.00 ⎫
$3.62 ⎬ $3.62 is more than $3.50 (halfway), so round up to $4.00.
$3.00 ⎭

Organizing and Analyzing Data

Data in Tables, Pictographs, Bar Graphs, and Line Plots
Lessons 15, 16, and 17

A major focus of this unit is learning to understand tables, pictographs, bar graphs, and line plots. As students interact with these data formats, they continually write and solve problem situations and pose questions for their classmates from the data they can read in these formats.

Working with bar graph scales builds on students' earlier work with understanding the scale in rulers and how it is built from small lengths. This helps students see the lengths involved in bar graphs, and the bars in bar graphs help students think of the bar graph scale, rulers, and number lines as a length model (for example, the 6 does not mean that point, it means 6 of the length units used in the scale). Work with both horizontal and vertical bar graph scales helps to prepare students for work with such scales on coordinate grids in Unit 14.

Working with tables helps students learn to look across rows and down columns. This helps to prepare them for the array and area situations they will encounter in Unit 7 in multiplication and division situations. Students will continue to interact with tables in Units 7 and 9 where they will use the multiplication table and solve small scrambled mini-multiplication tables called Missing Number Puzzles. Students return to a focused use of tables in Unit 13, where tables summarize measurement information.

Problem Solving

In *Math Expressions* a research-based, algebraic problem-solving approach that focuses on problem types is used: understand the situation, represent the situation with a math drawing or an equation, solve the problem, and see that the answer makes sense.

This systematic and research-based focus on word problems has changed the word problem solving modes of many students. They no longer just look at the numbers and do something with them (for example, add or subtract all numbers they see); they think about the situation, try to understand it, and make a drawing if it will help.

Complex Word Problems
Lessons 11, 12, 13, 14, and 17

In this unit using real-world situations, students will solve problems with extra information, determining which of the given information is required for the solution and which information can be ignored. They will solve word problems with implied (hidden) information. Students are presented with problems that cannot be solved because they do not include all the necessary information. Students will need to recognize that this type of problem is unsolvable and tell what additional information is needed. Students also encounter problems that require two or more steps to solve.

Use Mathematical Processes
Lesson 18

The NCTM process skills of problem solving, reasoning and proof, communication, connections, and representation are interwoven through all lessons throughout the year. The last lesson of this unit allows students to extend their use of mathematical processes to other situations.

NCTM Process Skill	Activity and Goal
Representation	2: Record data in a table and on a bar graph. 4: Draw different ways to show an amount of money.
Communication	1: Discuss data in a table and how to solve a problem. 1, 2 : Share reasoning. 2: Discuss the shape of data and the mode. 5: Discuss which estimate is best.
Connections	1: Math and Science: Number Sense and Measurement
Reasoning and Proof	1, 2: Make predictions using data. 3: Use reasoning to decide if figures are symmetrical and support conclusions with examples.
Problem Solving	1: Solve a problem involving length. 2: Solve problems using collected data. 4: Solve a problem with multiple solution. 5: Solve a problem involving estimates.

Round to the Nearest Hundred

REAL WORLD Problem Solving

Lesson Objectives

- Round numbers to the nearest hundred.
- Round to estimate sums and differences and check calculations.

Vocabulary

estimate
round

The Day at a Glance

Today's Goals	Materials	
1 **Teaching the Lesson** **A1:** Round numbers to the nearest hundred. **A2:** Estimate sums and differences and estimate to decide if answers are reasonable. **2** **Going Further** ▶ Differentiated Instruction **3** **Homework and Spiral Review**	**Lesson Activities** Student Activity Book pp. 121–124 or Student Hardcover Book pp. 121–124 and Activity Workbook pp. 47–48 (includes Family Letter) Homework and Remembering pp. 71–72 MathBoard materials Demonstration Secret Code Cards	**Going Further** Activity Cards 5-1 MathBoard Materials Calculators Math Journals

123 *Use* **Math Talk** *today!*

Keeping Skills Sharp

Quick Practice ⏱ 5 MINUTES

Goal: Count by tens and hundreds.

Tens and Hundreds Count Have a **Student Leader** write a number on the board, point to it, say the number aloud, instruct the class whether to add or subtract 10 or 100, and give the class a signal. The class responds by counting in unison and continues the pattern until the leader instructs them to stop. [5]

Leader: (Writes 800 on the board and points to it.) 800. Subtract 100. Begin.

Class: 700, 600, 500, 400, 300

Leader: Stop.

Daily Routines

Reasoning A palindrome is a number that is the same whether read from left to right or from right to left, such as 121. Use the digits 5 and 6 to make all possible three-digit palindromes. Digits can be repeated within a number. Explain how you found your answer. 666, 656, 555, 565; I put the same digit in the front and back. Then, changed the digit in the middle.

Teaching the Lesson

Round Up or Down

 30 MINUTES

Goal: Round numbers to the nearest hundred.

Materials: MathBoard materials, Demonstration Secret Code Cards (TRB M3–M18), Student Activity Book or Hardcover Book p. 121

✔ **NCTM Standard:**
Number and Operations

The Learning Classroom

Building Concepts Point out that estimation is a useful skill in the real world when you don't have pencil and paper or a calculator to use. Estimation is also useful when you use a calculator. If you should press a wrong key or forget to press a key, a quick estimate will tell you that the answer on the calculator is not correct.

Possible strategies students may use to estimate 494 + 128 + 368:

▶ Round to the hundreds place and add: 500 + 100 + 400 = 1,000.

▶ Round the numbers to other numbers that are easy to add. For example, 500 + 125 + 375 = 1,000.

▶ Leave the first digit of each number and change the rest of the digits to 0, and add: 400 + 100 + 300 = 800. (This method is sometimes called *front-end estimation*.)

▶ Round to the tens place and add: 490 + 130 + 370 = 990.

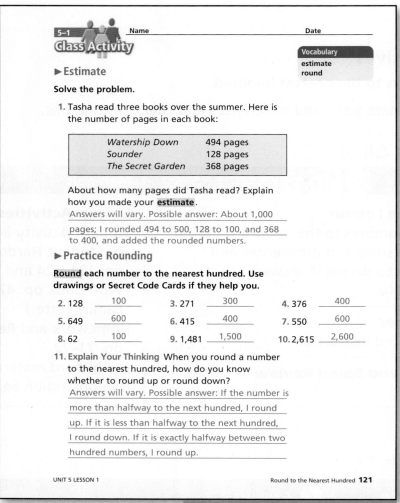

Student Activity Book page 121

▶ Estimate $\boxed{\text{WHOLE CLASS}}$

Math Talk Ask students to share what they know about estimation. Mention these ideas if they do not bring them up.

● An estimate tells *about* how many or *about* how much.

● Estimation is used when an exact number or measurement is not needed, or when there is not an exact number.

Then ask students to describe real-life situations in which someone might make an estimate. Offer some suggestions: shoppers in grocery stores, someone planning a party, or a person going to a movie. Read aloud problem 1 and have students make their estimates. Ask a few students to share their strategies for estimating the answer. Some possible strategies students might suggest are shown in the column to the left.

Round Using Place-Value Drawings Discuss rounding numbers in real-world situations and in mathematics.

- Many of you made your estimates by rounding the number to another number that was easier to add. Every day, you can use many strategies for rounding numbers. For example, if you want to be sure you have enough money to pay for items at a store, you might round all the prices up and then add them. In math, there are rules that tell you when to round up and when to round down. In this lesson, we'll look at the rules for rounding to the hundreds place.

Write 368 on the left side of the board, leaving enough room above and below the number. Ask students to do the same on their MathBoards.

- We are going to round 368 to the hundreds place. What digit is in the hundreds place? 3 Let's underline the 3 so we remember the place we are rounding to.

- We want to round to the nearest hundred. First, let's find the two hundred numbers that 368 is between. Which hundred number is right below 368? 300 Which hundred number is right above 368? 400

Write 300 below 368 and 400 above it, having students do the same. Then ask students to make place-value drawings for the three numbers. Choose one student to draw them on the board.

- Which hundred number is nearest to 368? 400 How can you tell from your drawings? There are more than five ten-sticks.

Have students explain why 400 is the nearest hundred. For a sample of classroom dialogue, see **Math Talk in Action** in the side column.

Have students draw an arrow from 368 to 400 to show that we round up.

 **Math Talk in Action**

Why do you think 400 is the nearest hundred to 368?

Gwen: 368 is about 370. That's closer to 400 than 300.

Did anyone use a different strategy?

Saeed: I did. Halfway between 300 and 400 is 350, so 368 is more than halfway between 300 and 400.

Did anyone use the place-value drawings to help them?

Peter: I did. 300 has 3 hundred-boxes and 400 has 4 hundred-boxes. The number halfway would have 3 hundred-boxes and 5 ten-sticks. 368 has more than 5 ten-sticks, so it must be closer to 400 than 300.

English Language Learners

Write 132 + 189. Say: **When we estimate we *round* the numbers then add.** Use the drawing below.

- **Beginning** Say: We push the ball to 132. It falls on 100. Continue with 189.
- **Intermediate** Say: First, *round* 132. We push the ball to the ___. left It falls on ___. 100 Continue with 189. Have students add the two numbers. Say: **300 is not exact. It is an *estimate*.**
- **Advanced** Have students describe how to roll the ball to round, then add. Ask: **Is 300 exact or an *estimate*?** estimate

Activity continued ▶

Alternate Approach

Use a Number Line Students can draw a number line marked by hundreds from 0 to 900 with tick marks for 50s. When they place the number to be rounded on the number line they can see which hundred it is closer to and round to that hundred.

The Learning Classroom

Building Concepts You may want to extend the activity by asking students to give examples of numbers that round to 400 (350–399; 401–449). This allows students to explore that some numbers round up to 400 and others round down 400.

Round Using Secret Code Cards Demonstrate another way to round with Demonstration Secret Code Cards. Erase the place-value drawings and the arrow, and ask students which Secret Code Cards are needed to build 368. Have a volunteer build the number.

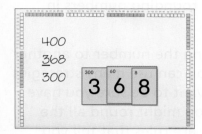

Tell students that to figure out how to round to the hundreds place, they should "open up" the Secret Code Cards, separating 3 hundreds from the rest of the number.

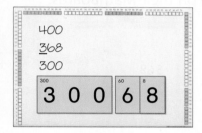

Explain that to determine whether to round up or down, they should look at the 68.

● Does 68 have more than 5 tens or fewer than 5 tens? more than 5 tens

● So, the 68 is closer to 100 than to 0 and is rounded up to the next hundred. *Draw an arrow from 368 to 400.*

Now discuss rounding down.

● When rounding 368 to the nearest hundred, it is rounded *up* to 400. Can anyone think of a number that would be rounded *down* to 300? Possible answer: 349

Erase 368 and replace it with the number suggested. Choose a volunteer to use place-value drawings to explain why we round down. Have a second volunteer explain the rounding, using the Demonstration Secret Code Cards.

Next, erase everything except 300 and 400. Draw a line across the board between the two numbers. Ask students to suggest several numbers that would round up to 400, and write those numbers above the line. Then ask for numbers that would round down to 300, and write them below the line. See sample in the left side column.

► Practice Rounding [INDIVIDUALS]

Have students look back at the Practice Rounding section on Student Book page 121 and make sure each student knows what to do. Give students a few minutes to round the numbers to the nearest hundred in exercises 2–10.

Make sure to discuss exercises 9–10 which show 4-digit numbers. Remind students to underline the number in the hundreds place to help them remember which place to round to. The hundreds above and below 1,481 are 1,400 and 1,500. When using Secret Code Cards, students separate 81 from 1,400 and determine whether 81 has more or fewer than 5 tens. If students need additional practice rounding to the nearest hundred, give them more 4-digit numbers to round.

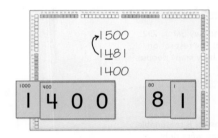

Rounding Rules Write 450 on the board, and ask how students would round it to the nearest hundred. Some may already know the rounding rule. Explain that because 450 is exactly halfway between 400 and 500, it is impossible to figure out how to round it. For this reason, people have agreed to round up whenever a number is exactly halfway between 2 hundred numbers. So we round 450 up to 500.

Problem 11 on Student Book page 121 asks students to explain the rule for rounding to the nearest hundred. Ask for suggestions. Ask a volunteer to explain the rule. The class should listen to the explanations and ask questions to help the presenter clarify their thinking. Here is one way to state the rule:

● If the number is more than halfway to the next hundred, round up.

● If the number is less than halfway to the next hundred, round down.

● If the number is exactly halfway between two hundreds, round up.

Ongoing Assessment

To check that students understand the concept of rounding to the nearest hundred, ask questions such as:

► What is 54 rounded to the nearest hundred? 100 What about 32? 0

► What is 983 rounded to the nearest hundred? 1,000 What about 1,012? 1,000

► What is 750 rounded to the nearest hundred? 800

Teaching the Lesson (continued)

Activity 2

Estimate Sums and Differences

 25 MINUTES

Goal: Estimate sums and differences and estimate to decide if answers are reasonable.

Materials: MathBoard materials, Demonstration Secret Code Cards (TRB M3–M18), Student Activity Book or Hardcover Book p. 122

✔ **NCTM Standards:**
Number and Operations
Reasoning and Proof

 Math Talk in Action

Do you think the answer for exercise 18 is reasonable?

Trevor: I think the answer is reasonable.

Can you explain why?

Trevor: First, I rounded 1,041 to 1,000 and 395 to 400. Next, I subtracted the two rounded numbers and got 600. 600 is pretty close to 646, so it's reasonable.

Did anyone find another answer?

Madeleine: I did. I don't think it's a reasonable answer because you have to add, not subtract. When you add the two rounded numbers, you get 1,400, which is not close to 646. So the answer of 646 is not reasonable.

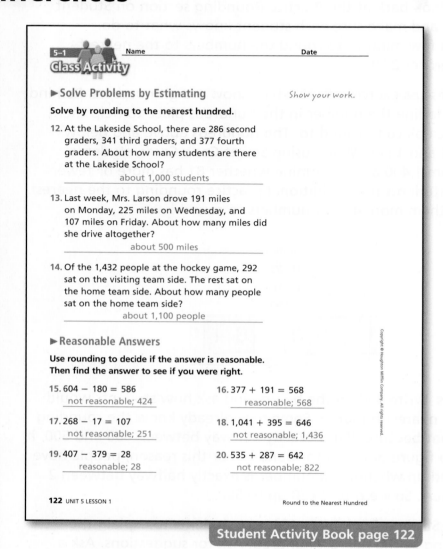

Student Activity Book page 122

▶ Solve Problems by Estimating [WHOLE CLASS]

Explain that one way to estimate a sum or difference is to round each number and then add or subtract. Have a volunteer read aloud problem 12. Point out that the word *about* indicates that the problem is asking for an estimate, not an exact answer. Give students a minute to estimate, and then discuss the answer with the class. Have students complete problems 13 and 14 on their own.

▶ Reasonable Answers [INDIVIDUALS]

Read aloud the directions for exercises 15–20. Explain that rounding and then adding or subtracting is a good way to check if your answer is reasonable. Have a volunteer show how to do exercise 15. Have students complete the rest of the exercises independently, and discuss the answers as a class. For a sample of classroom dialogue, see **Math Talk in Action** in the side column.

②Going Further

Intervention — Activity Card 5-1

Round Using Drawings
Activity Card 5-1

Work: In pairs

Use:
• MathBoard materials

Decide:
Who will be Student 1 and who will be Student 2 for the first round.

1. Student 1: Write a 3-digit number.

2. Student 2: Make a place-value drawing for the number that your partner wrote. Then write 2 hundred numbers, one greater and one less than the 3-digit number.

200
171
100
171 rounds up to 200

3. Student 1: Use your partner's work to help you round the 3-digit number to the nearest hundred.

4. Change roles and repeat the activity.

Unit 5, Lesson 1   Copyright © Houghton Mifflin Company

Activity Note Suggest that students look at the number of tens in the place value drawing. If there are 5 or more, round up. Otherwise, round down.

✎ Math Writing Prompt

Explain the Steps Describe how you would round 274 to the nearest hundred.

 **Software Support**

Warm Up 15.16

On Level — Activity Card 5-1

Estimate and Check
Activity Card 5-1 ▲

Work: In pairs

Use:
• MathBoard materials
• Calculator

Decide:
Who will be Student 1 and who will be Student 2 for the first round.

1. Student 1: Write a 3-digit addition exercise.

2. Student 2: Use rounding to estimate the sum.

568 → 600
+345 → +300
           900

3. Use a calculator to find the actual sum.

4. Analyze Is the estimate close to the actual answer? Can you think of a situation in which such an estimate would be useful?

5. Switch roles and repeat the activity, using a subtraction exercise.

Unit 5, Lesson 1   Copyright © Houghton Mifflin Company

Activity Note Remind students to use the digit in the tens place to help them decide whether to round up or to round down.

✎ Math Writing Prompt

Real-World Application Describe a situation when you or someone you know used estimation to solve a problem.

 Software Support

Numberopolis: Cross Town Number Line, Level U

Challenge — Activity Card 5-1

Find Other Strategies
Activity Card 5-1 ■

Work: In pairs

Use:
• MathBoard materials
• Calculator

1. Rounding to the nearest hundred is one way to estimate sums. Work together to find different strategies to estimate sums.

900
105 + 875
about 100
900 + 100 = 1,000

400
352 + 148
Add just hundreds

219 → 220
+178 → +180
           400
Round to the nearest ten and add

347 → 350
+706 → +700
          1,050
Change to numbers that are easy to add

2. Think Could you round to a different place value? Could you use numbers that are easier to add? Could you just add one place value?

3. Estimate each sum below. Share your strategies with your classmates. Answers may vary. Possible estimates are given.

105 + 875   352 + 148   219 + 178
About 1,000   About 500   About 400
215 + 759   347 + 706   1,255 + 2,812
About 1,000   About 1,050   About 4,000

Unit 5, Lesson 1   Copyright © Houghton Mifflin Company

Activity Note Encourage students to discuss which strategy is likely to give the closest estimate and which is easiest to use.

✎ Math Writing Prompt

Explain Your Thinking The Mississippi River is about 2,340 miles long. The Nile River is about 4,160 miles long. Is the difference more or less than 2,000 miles? Explain.

✖ DESTINATION Math **Software Support**

Course II: Module 2: Unit 1: Estimating and Finding Sums less than 1,000

③ Homework and Spiral Review

5-1 Homework   **Goal:** Additional Practice

✓ This Homework page provides practice in rounding numbers to the nearest hundred.

5-1 Remembering   **Goal:** Spiral Review

This Remembering page would be appropriate anytime after today's lesson.

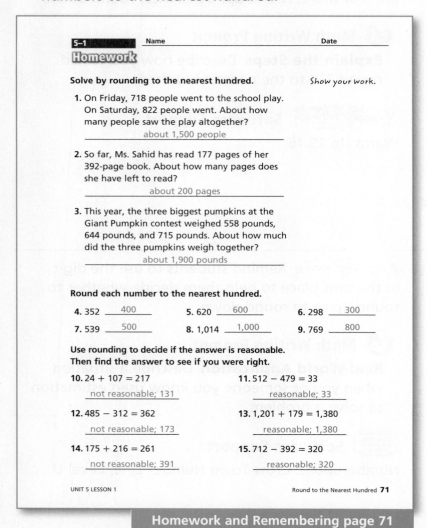

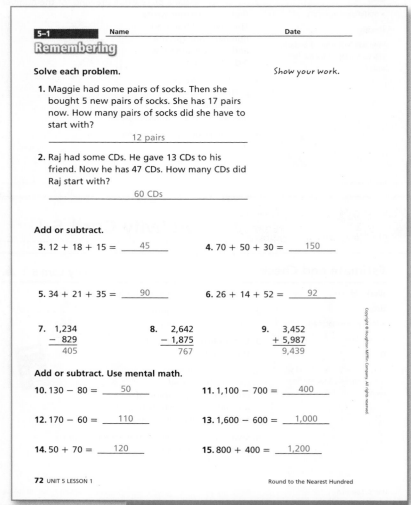

Home and School Connection

Family Letter Have children take home the Family Letter on Student Activity Book page 123 or Activity Book p. 47. This letter explains how the concepts of rounding, ordering, estimating, interpreting data, and solving a variety of words problems are developed in *Math Expressions*. It gives parents and guardians a better understanding of the learning that goes on in math class and creates a bridge between school and home. A Spanish translation of this letter is on the following page.

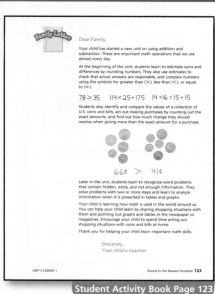

Student Activity Book Page 123

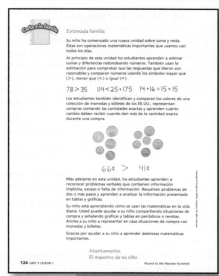

Student Activity Book Page 124

298 UNIT 5 LESSON 1

UNIT 5
LESSON 2

Round to the Nearest Ten

REAL WORLD Problem Solving

Lesson Objectives

- Round numbers to the nearest ten.
- Use rounding to estimate sums and differences.
- Estimate quantities.

Vocabulary
round

The Day at a Glance

Today's Goals	Materials

1 **Teaching the Lesson**
A1: Round numbers to the nearest ten.
A2: Round to estimate sums and differences, and estimate to decide if answers are reasonable.
A3: Estimate Quantities
 	
2 **Going Further**
▶ Extension: Estimation Strategies
▶ Differentiated Instruction
 	
3 **Homework and Spiral Review**
	Lesson Activities
	Student Activity Book pp. 125–128
	  or Student Hardcover Book
	  pp. 125–128
	Homework and Remembering
	  pp. 73–74
	MathBoard materials
	Demonstration Secret Code Cards
	Secret Code Cards
	2 clear jars, beans (at least 250)
	"Geometry Park" CD (Illumisware, 2002)
		Going Further
		Activity Cards 5-2
		Secret Code cards
		MathBoard materials
		  or Number Path
		  (TRB M39)
		Index cards
		Calculators
		Math Journals

123 **Use Math Talk today!**

Keeping Skills Sharp

Quick Practice 🕐 5 MINUTES	Daily Routines
Goal: Round whole numbers to the nearest hundred. **Rounding Practice** Have a **Student Leader** write these six numbers on the board. **241 870 350 562 109 1,722** The **Student Leader** points to each number and says, "Round to the nearest hundred." When the leader gives a signal, students respond in unison with the rounded number. *Leader (pointing to 241):* Round to the nearest hundred. *Class:* 200	**Homework Review** Let students check their work in pairs. Remind students to use what they know about helping others. **Create a Pattern** Ask students for the digit that comes next in this repeating pattern: 4 7 7 4 7 7 4 7 7. 4 Then have students create a repeating pattern using any digit 0 through 9.

Teaching the Lesson

Round Up or Down

 20 MINUTES

Goal: Round numbers to the nearest ten.

Materials: MathBoard materials, Demonstration Secret Code Cards (TRB M3–M18), Secret Code Cards (TRB M19–M22), Student Activity Book or Hardcover Book p. 125-126

✔ **NCTM Standard:**
Number and Operations

Teaching Note

Math Background Remind students that rounding is only one way to estimate. Have students discuss why estimates are useful. They can also generate a list of situations in which estimation is used.

▶ **Round to the Nearest Ten** WHOLE CLASS

Tell students that today they will focus on rounding numbers to the nearest ten.

Round with Place-Value Drawings Write 43 on the board, leaving room above and below the number.

● Which digit is in the tens place? 4 *Underline the 4.*

Ask a volunteer to come to the board and demonstrate how to use a place-value drawing to round 43 to the nearest ten. Provide help as needed. Encourage other students to ask questions if they don't understand. Here are the steps that should be demonstrated.

● Find the tens numbers just below and just above 43. Then make place-value drawings for all three numbers. Since 40 has 4 ten-sticks, and 50 has 5 ten-sticks, the number halfway between 40 and 50 would have 4 ten-sticks and 5 circles. 43 has 4 ten-sticks and 3 circles so it is less than halfway to 50. So 43 rounds down to 40. Draw an arrow from 43 to 40 to indicate that we round down.

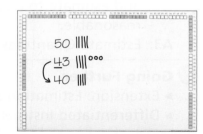

Round with Secret Code Cards Erase the place-value drawings and the arrow on the board, and have a volunteer show how to round the number 43 using the Demonstration Secret Code Cards. Encourage other students to ask questions if they don't understand and offer help as needed. Following are the steps the student should follow.

● Build 43 with Secret Code Cards. Open up the cards, separating the 4 tens from the rest of the number (the 3 ones). The ones card has fewer than 5 ones, so we round down to 40. Draw an arrow from 43 to 40 to show that we round down.

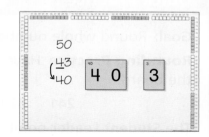

Erase the board and write 276 on the left side, asking students to do the same on their MathBoards. Have them round the number to the nearest ten. Make sure students underline the digit in the tens place. Emphasize that they only look at the digits to the right of the place they are rounding to. In this case, look at the ones. Because there are more than 5 ones, round up.

5-2

Class Activity

Name _____ Date _____

▶ Round 2-Digit Numbers to the Nearest Ten

Round each number to the nearest ten.

1. 63 ___60___

2. 34 ___30___

3. 78 ___80___

4. 25 ___30___

5. 57 ___60___

6. 89 ___90___

7. 42 ___40___

8. 92 ___90___

▶ Round 3-Digit Numbers to the Nearest Ten

Round each number to the nearest ten.

9. 162 ___160___

10. 741 ___740___

11. 309 ___310___

12. 255 ___260___

13. 118 ___120___

14. 197 ___200___

15. 503 ___500___

16. 246 ___250___

17. **Explain Your Thinking** When you round a number to the nearest ten, how do you know whether to round up or round down?

Answers will vary. Possible answer: If the number is less than halfway to the next ten, round down. If the number is exactly halfway between or more than halfway to next ten, round up.

UNIT 5 LESSON 2   Round to the Nearest Ten **125**

▶ Round 2-Digit Numbers to the Nearest Ten

INDIVIDUALS

Have students complete exercises 1–8. Have students discuss how they rounded in exercise 4. Point out that 25 is halfway between 20 and 30. When a number is exactly halfway between two tens, we round up to the next ten.

▶ Round 3-Digit Numbers to the Nearest Ten

INDIVIDUALS

Have students complete exercises 9–16 independently. They can use drawings or cards as needed. Then discuss exercise 17, which asks students to explain the rule for rounding to the nearest ten.

Activity continued ▶

Differentiated Instruction

Extra Help Some students may not see that when rounding to the tens place, the digit in the ones place determines the direction of rounding. It is important that students look at the digit to the right of the place to which they are rounding to determine whether to round a number up or down. Remind students that this is also true when rounding to the nearest hundred. The digit in the tens place tells which direction to round. It is helpful to underline the place to which you are rounding and then look to the next smaller place to decide whether to go up or stay with that number. If students are ready, you may want to demonstrate that when rounding to the nearest thousand, the digit in the hundreds place tells the direction in which any 4-digit number is rounded.

Students who are still struggling should use place-value drawings and Secret Code Cards.

The Learning Classroom

Building Concepts As students discuss the rule for rounding in exercise 17 on Student Book page 125, have them think of a number of different examples before writing their explanation.

Make sure that students understand that most of the time when you round a number to the nearest ten, the number will end in 0. For example, 527 rounds to 530 when you round it to the nearest ten. However, numbers such as 203 and 399 rounded to the nearest ten are 200 and 400, which have two zeros.

Teaching Note

Watch For! Students may round 3-digit numbers to the nearest hundred instead of to the nearest ten. Remind them to underline the digit in the place they are rounding to avoid rounding to the wrong place.

 Ongoing Assessment

To check that students understand the concept of rounding to the nearest ten, ask questions such as:

► What is 37 rounded to the nearest ten? What is 4 rounded to the nearest ten?

► What is 346 rounded to the nearest ten? What is 1,438 rounded to the nearest ten?

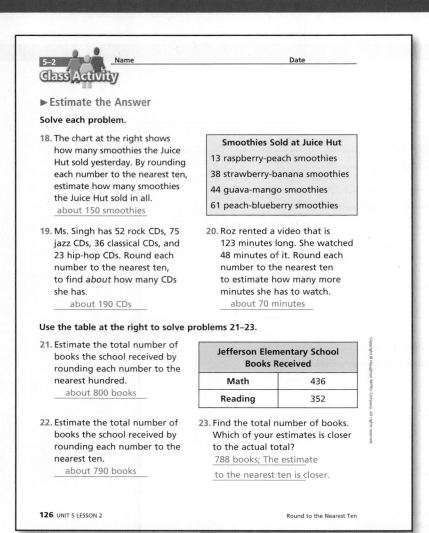

5–2
Class Activity

Name _____ Date _____

► **Estimate the Answer**

Solve each problem.

18. The chart at the right shows how many smoothies the Juice Hut sold yesterday. By rounding each number to the nearest ten, estimate how many smoothies the Juice Hut sold in all.
about 150 smoothies

Smoothies Sold at Juice Hut
13 raspberry-peach smoothies
38 strawberry-banana smoothies
44 guava-mango smoothies
61 peach-blueberry smoothies

19. Ms. Singh has 52 rock CDs, 75 jazz CDs, 36 classical CDs, and 23 hip-hop CDs. Round each number to the nearest ten, to find *about* how many CDs she has.
about 190 CDs

20. Roz rented a video that is 123 minutes long. She watched 48 minutes of it. Round each number to the nearest ten to estimate how many more minutes she has to watch.
about 70 minutes

Use the table at the right to solve problems 21–23.

21. Estimate the total number of books the school received by rounding each number to the nearest hundred.
about 800 books

Jefferson Elementary School Books Received	
Math	436
Reading	352

22. Estimate the total number of books the school received by rounding each number to the nearest ten.
about 790 books

23. Find the total number of books. Which of your estimates is closer to the actual total?
788 books; The estimate to the nearest ten is closer.

126 UNIT 5 LESSON 2   Round to the Nearest Ten

Student Activity Book page 126

► **Estimate the Answer** [INDIVIDUALS]

(123) **Math Talk** Have students independently work on problems 18–23 and then use the **Solve and Discuss** structure to have volunteers share their solutions.

Activity 2

Estimate Sums and Differences

 15 MINUTES

Goal: Estimate to decide if answers are reasonable.

Materials: Student Book p. 127

 NCTM Standards:
Number and Operations
Reasoning and Proof

► **Reasonable Answers** [INDIVIDUALS]

Have a volunteer show how to do exercise 24 on Student Book page 127. The student should round 58 to 60 and 37 to 40 and then add to get an estimate of 100. The answer given, 131, is too big. Have students complete exercises 25–30 independently, and discuss the answers as a class.

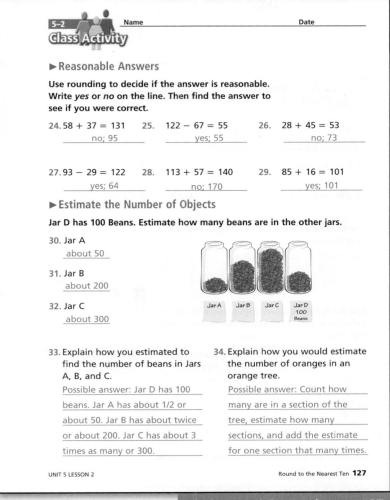

5-2
Class Activity

Name _____ Date _____

▶Reasonable Answers

Use rounding to decide if the answer is reasonable. Write *yes* or *no* on the line. Then find the answer to see if you were correct.

24. 58 + 37 = 131   25. 122 − 67 = 55   26. 28 + 45 = 53
    ___no; 95___   ___yes; 55___   ___no; 73___

27. 93 − 29 = 122   28. 113 + 57 = 140   29. 85 + 16 = 101
    ___yes; 64___   ___no; 170___   ___yes; 101___

▶Estimate the Number of Objects

Jar D has 100 Beans. Estimate how many beans are in the other jars.

30. Jar A
    __about 50__

31. Jar B
    __about 200__

32. Jar C
    __about 300__

Jar A   Jar B   Jar C   Jar D
                        100
                        Beans

33. Explain how you estimated to find the number of beans in Jars A, B, and C.
    Possible answer: Jar D has 100 beans. Jar A has about 1/2 or about 50. Jar B has about twice or about 200. Jar C has about 3 times as many or 300.

34. Explain how you would estimate the number of oranges in an orange tree.
    Possible answer: Count how many are in a section of the tree, estimate how many sections, and add the estimate for one section that many times.

UNIT 5 LESSON 2   Round to the Nearest Ten **127**

Student Activity Book page 127

The Learning Classroom

Helping Community You may want to have students work in **Student Pairs** to complete problems 25–30 on Student Book page 127. Students can work together to round sets of numbers and then add and subtract independently. Have them compare their estimates to check that they added or subtracted the rounded numbers correctly before comparing the estimate with the actual answer.

English Language Learners

Review *reasonable answer*. Write 62 + 87 = 130. Say: **A** *reasonable* **answer is close to the estimate.**

• **Beginning** Say: We round the addends. **60 + 90 = 150.** Ask: **Is 130 close to 150?** no Say: **130 is not** *reasonable*.

• **Intermediate** Have students round 62 and 87. Say: **What is 60 + 90?** 150 Ask: **Is 130 reasonable?** no

• **Advanced** Help students describe the steps to check if 130 is *reasonable*.

Activity 3

Estimate Quantities

▶ Estimate the Number of Objects WHOLE CLASS

Put 50 beans in one jar and at least 200 beans in the other.

Have students use the 50-bean jar to help them estimate about how many beans are in the second jar. Have them explain their estimates and then count the beans. Have students complete exercises 30–34 on Student Book page 127.

 20 MINUTES

Goal: Estimate Quantities

Materials: 2 clear jars, beans (At least 250), Student Activity Book or Hardcover Book p. 127.

 NCTM Standards:
Measurement
Problem Solving

② Going Further

Extension: Estimation Methods

Goal: Use other strategies to estimate.

Materials: Student Activity Book or Hardcover Book p. 128

✔ **NCTM Standards:**
Number and Operations
Problem Solving

▶ Different Ways to Estimate

WHOLE CLASS

Explain that there are a number of other ways to estimate besides rounding the numbers to the nearest ten or hundred and finding the sum or difference as we did in this lesson.

Clustering Point out that when numbers cluster around the same ten or hundred you can use clustering to estimate the sum. Direct students' attention to exercise 1.

● What ten do these numbers cluster around? 60

So we can add 60 three times to get an estimate of 180. Have students complete exercises 1–4.

Front-End Estimation Explain that front-end estimation is another strategy that can be used when you need a quick estimate. In this method, add just the digits farthest to the left. For example, in order to make an estimate of the total weight of 675, 430, 43, and 110 pounds, add 600, 400, and 100 for an estimate of 1,100 pounds.

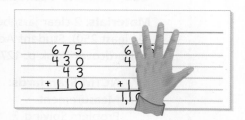

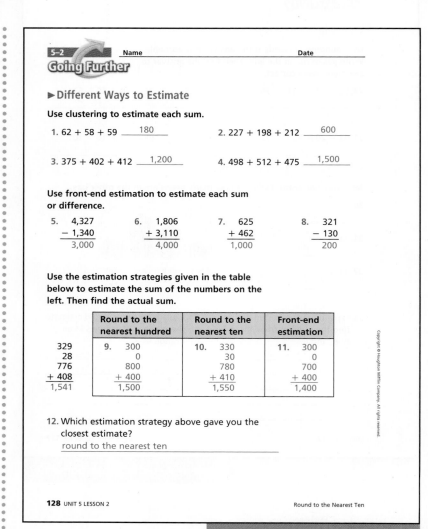

Student Activity Book page 128

Point out to students that you do not add 43 when estimating in this example. In this case, 43 does not have a number in the hundreds place like the other three numbers.

Have students complete exercises 5–12 independently and discuss their answers.

Differentiated Instruction

Intervention — Activity Card 5-2

Around the Path
Activity Card 5-2

Work: On your own

Use:
- Secret Code Cards
- MathBoard materials or TRB M39 (Number Path)

1. Separate the Secret Code cards into two piles of tens and ones. Shuffle each pile and place them face down.

2. Using the top card from each pile, make a 2-digit number and write it on your MathBoard.

3. Shade your 2-digit number on the Number Path. Then circle the tens that come before and after.

4. **Think** Which ten is closer? Round your number to the closer ten and then repeat the activity again.

Unit 5, Lesson 2
Copyright © Houghton Mifflin Company

Activity Note This activity will help students see that the ones digit will tell them how to round to the nearest ten. Point out that if the ones digit is 5 or more, they should round up. Otherwise, round down.

Math Writing Prompt

Explain Your Thinking Describe how you would round the number 867 to the nearest ten.

Soar to Success Math Software Support
Warm Up 15.14

On Level — Activity Card 5-2

Round and Round
Activity Card 5-2

Work: In pairs

Use:
- 20 index cards

1. On your own, write 2- or 3-digit numbers on five index cards. Then make five matching cards for those numbers rounded to the nearest ten.

34	30
88	67
70	245
20	90
250	15

2. Shuffle all 20 cards that you and your partner have made. Give five cards to each player. Place the remaining cards face down in a pile.

3. Take turns. Ask your partner for a card that matches one of your own. If you get a match, ask for another one. If not, take a card from the pile and let your partner take a turn.

4. The player with more matches wins.

Unit 5, Lesson 2
Copyright © Houghton Mifflin Company

Activity Note Students will be asking for the rounded numbers to match numbers that they hold in their hand. They may also use what they know about rounding to ask for the number that was rounded to the ten number they are holding.

Math Writing Prompt

Are They the Same? Round 145 and 153 to the nearest ten. Are the rounded numbers the same? Explain why or why not.

MegaMath Software Support
Numberopolis: Cross Town Number Line, Level U

Challenge — Activity Card 5-2

Select a Strategy
Activity Card 5-2

Work: In pairs

Use:
- Calculator

Decide:
Who will be Student 1 and who will be Student 2 for the first round of the game.

1. **Student 1:** Write an addition expression with three 3-digit numbers.

2. **Student 2:** Estimate the sum. Record your estimate.

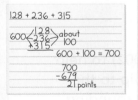

3. **Student 1:** Use a calculator to find the actual sum.

4. **Student 2:** Calculate the difference between the actual sum and your estimate. The difference is the number of points you get for this round.

5. Take turns until each player makes 3 estimates.

6. Whoever has the lower number of points wins.

Unit 5, Lesson 2
Copyright © Houghton Mifflin Company

Activity Note The winner will be the student who makes the closer estimates. Choosing strategies for estimation will make a difference in the game's outcome.

Math Writing Prompt

Greater Than or Less Than? When you round both numbers up to estimate a sum, will your estimate always be greater than or less than the actual sum? Explain your thinking.

DESTINATION Math Software Support
Course II: Module 2: Unit 1: Estimating and Finding Sums less than 1,000

③ Homework and Spiral Review

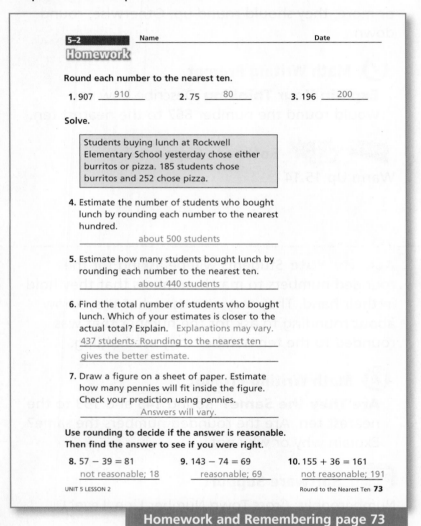

5-2 Homework Goal: Additional Practice

✔ Include children's completed Homework page as part of their portfolios.

5-2 Homework Name _____ Date _____

Round each number to the nearest ten.

1. 907 ___910___   2. 75 ___80___   3. 196 ___200___

Solve.

> Students buying lunch at Rockwell Elementary School yesterday chose either burritos or pizza. 185 students chose burritos and 252 chose pizza.

4. Estimate the number of students who bought lunch by rounding each number to the nearest hundred.
   _____ about 500 students _____

5. Estimate how many students bought lunch by rounding each number to the nearest ten.
   _____ about 440 students _____

6. Find the total number of students who bought lunch. Which of your estimates is closer to the actual total? Explain. Explanations may vary.
   437 students. Rounding to the nearest ten
   gives the better estimate.

7. Draw a figure on a sheet of paper. Estimate how many pennies will fit inside the figure. Check your prediction using pennies.
   _____ Answers will vary. _____

Use rounding to decide if the answer is reasonable. Then find the answer to see if you were right.

8. 57 − 39 = 81   9. 143 − 74 = 69   10. 155 + 36 = 161
   not reasonable; 18   reasonable; 69   not reasonable; 191

UNIT 5 LESSON 2   Round to the Nearest Ten **73**

Homework and Remembering page 73

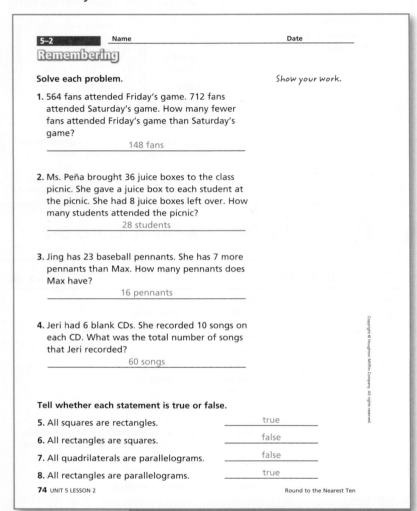

5-2 Remembering Goal: Spiral Review

This Remembering page would be appropriate anytime after today's lesson.

5-2 Remembering Name _____ Date _____

Solve each problem.   *Show your work.*

1. 564 fans attended Friday's game. 712 fans attended Saturday's game. How many fewer fans attended Friday's game than Saturday's game?
   _____ 148 fans _____

2. Ms. Peña brought 36 juice boxes to the class picnic. She gave a juice box to each student at the picnic. She had 8 juice boxes left over. How many students attended the picnic?
   _____ 28 students _____

3. Jing has 23 baseball pennants. She has 7 more pennants than Max. How many pennants does Max have?
   _____ 16 pennants _____

4. Jeri had 6 blank CDs. She recorded 10 songs on each CD. What was the total number of songs that Jeri recorded?
   _____ 60 songs _____

Tell whether each statement is true or false.

5. All squares are rectangles. _____ true
6. All rectangles are squares. _____ false
7. All quadrilaterals are parallelograms. _____ false
8. All rectangles are parallelograms. _____ true

74 UNIT 5 LESSON 2   Round to the Nearest Ten

Homework and Remembering page 74

Home or School Activity

Music Connection

Rap a Round Use the "Geometry Park" CD (Illumisware 2002) to help students with their rounding skills. Students can rap to "Slip to the Side" which reinforces the importance of the number 5 in rounding. After students have learned the lyrics to this, challenge them to make up their own songs, raps, or rhymes. They can share these with classmates to help others with the rules of rounding.

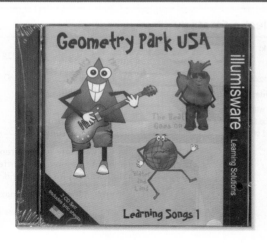

Compare Whole Numbers

REAL WORLD Problem Solving

Lesson Objectives

- Compare and order whole numbers.
- Compare the values of expressions.

The Day at a Glance

Today's Goals	Materials	

1 Teaching the Lesson
A1: Compare and order whole numbers.
A2: Compare values of expressions by calculating and by estimating or by using number sense.
	Lesson Activities
	Student Activity Book pp. 129–130
	  or Student Hardcover Book
	  pp. 129–130
	Homework and Remembering
	  pp. 75–76
	MathBoard materials
	Base ten blocks
	Quick Quiz 1 (Assessment Guide)
	The Greatest Gymnast of All by
	  Stuart J. Murphy (Harper Trophy,
	  1998)
		Going Further
		Activity Cards 5-3
		Secret Code Cards
		  (2 sets)
		MathBoard Materials
		  or Number Path
		  (TRB M39)
		Number cubes
		Math Journals

2 Going Further ▶ Differentiated Instruction		
3 Homework and Spiral Review		

123 Use Math Talk today!

Keeping Skills Sharp

Quick Practice ⏱ 5 MINUTES	**Daily Routines**
Goal: Round whole numbers to the nearest ten or hundred. **Rounding Practice** Have the **Student Leader** write 271, 983, 349, 628, 115, and 1,257 on the board. The leader points to a number and says either, "Round to the nearest hundred," or, "Round to the nearest ten." When the leader gives a signal, students respond in unison with the rounded number. *Leader (pointing to 349):* Round to the nearest ten. *Class:* 350	**Homework Review** Ask students if they had difficulty with any part of the homework. Plan to set aside some to work with students needing extra help. **Skip Count** Have students skip count by 50s beginning at 250 and ending at 1,000.

① Teaching the Lesson

Compare and Order Whole Numbers

 25 MINUTES

Goal: Compare and order whole numbers.

Materials: MathBoard materials, base ten blocks, Student Activity Book or Hardcover Book p. 129

 NCTM Standards:
Number and Operations
Communication

Differentiated Instruction

Extra Help If students have a hard time remembering which way the greater than, less than symbol should point, use the simple drawings below to help them.

First, draw the greater than symbol.

Then, turn the symbol into a fish's mouth.

Explain that the fish's open mouth always faces the larger number.

Show students that the fish's open mouth can go in either direction as long as it still opens to the larger number.

▶ **Compare Numbers** | WHOLE CLASS |

Explain to the class that they will be comparing numbers to decide if one number is greater than or less than another or if the numbers are equal. Point out that we use the symbols for greater than, less than, and equal to show the comparison. Write and label the symbols on the MathBoard and write the two numbers to be compared as shown below.

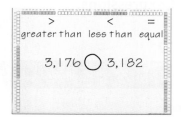

Ask for Ideas Elicit from students different methods to compare numbers. One method is shown below.

Use place-value drawings.

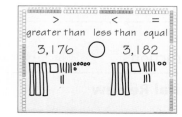

● Do the numbers have the same number of thousands? yes

● Do the numbers have the same number of hundreds? yes

● Do the numbers have the same number of tens? no Which number has the greater number of tens? 3,182

● Which is the greater number? 3,182

● Which symbol should be placed in the circle? <

Point out that the point of the symbol always points to the smaller number and the wide, open part always points to the larger number.

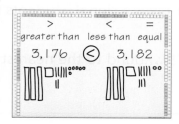

Ask a volunteer to read the comparison statement. Three thousand, one hundred seventy-six is less than three thousand, one hundred eighty-two.

Another way to compare numbers is to line up the numbers as if you were going to add them. Then begin comparing from left to right until the digits are not the same.

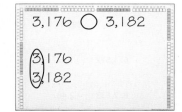

Use place value.

Draw a loop around the digits in the thousands place of both numbers.

● Do the numbers have the same number of thousands? yes

Draw a loop around the digits in the hundreds place of both numbers.

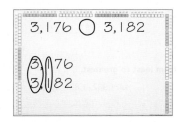

● Do the numbers have the same number of hundreds? yes

Draw a loop around the digits in the tens place of both numbers.

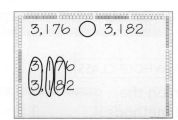

● Do the numbers have the same number of tens? no
● Which number has the greater number of tens? 3,182
● Which symbol should we put in the circle? less than

Have a volunteer write the greater than symbol in the circle.

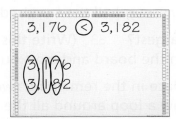

Have students work independently to complete exercises 1–10 on Student Book page 129. Discuss any difficulties student may have had.

Activity continued ▶

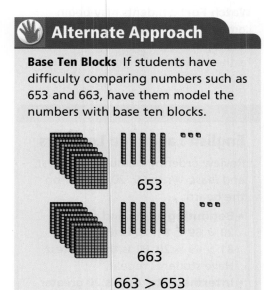

Alternate Approach

Base Ten Blocks If students have difficulty comparing numbers such as 653 and 663, have them model the numbers with base ten blocks.

653

663

663 > 653

Teaching the Lesson (continued)

Teaching Note

Watch For! Students may begin comparing numbers from the right, missing the fact that the place farthest left has the greatest value.

English Language Learners

Review ordering numbers, *greatest*, and *least*. Write 69, 20, and 81 on the board.

- **Beginning** Write and say: 20 < 69 < 81. 20 is the *least*. 81 > 69 > 20. 81 is the *greatest*. Have students repeat.
- **Intermediate** Ask: **Is 20 greater or less than 69?** less **Than 81?** less Say: **20 is the least.** Continue with 81 and *greatest*.
- **Advanced** Have students work in pairs to order the numbers. Ask: **Which number is the least?** 20 Continue with *greatest*.

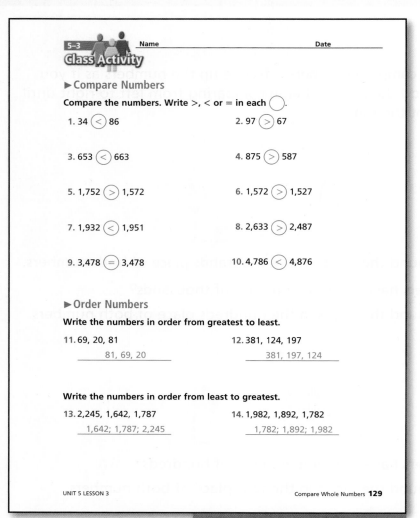

Student Activity Book page 129

► Order Numbers [WHOLE CLASS]

Write the example shown on the right, on the board. Elicit methods from the students on ordering these numbers from least to greatest. One method is shown.

> 1,580
> 1,547
> 1,637
> ___ ___ ___

- What is the greatest place in the numbers in which the digits differ? hundreds (Draw a loop around all the hundreds digits.)

- Which number is the largest? 1,637 (Write this number on the blank farthest to the right on the board and cross out 1,637 above.)

- What is the greatest place in the remaining two numbers in which the digits differ? tens (Draw a loop around all the tens digits.)

- Which number is smaller? 1,547 (Write 1,547 in the first blank and 1,580 in the middle blank.)

Have students complete exercises 11–14 independently.

Compare Values of Expressions

▶ Multi-Step Comparisons | WHOLE CLASS |

Explain to the class that sometimes numbers have to be added or subtracted before they are compared.

Write this problem on the board and read it aloud to students.

Tim has 36 baseball cards and 29 football cards. Pilar has 24 baseball cards and 38 football cards. Who has more cards?

Write this comparison statement on the board. Explain that we can write this open comparison statement to start to solve the problem.

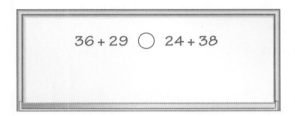

- How much is 36 + 29? 65
- How much is 24 + 38? 62

Write these numbers under the expressions on the board.

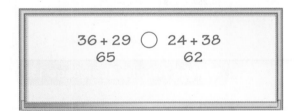

- Which is greater, 65 or 62? 65
- What symbol belongs in the circle? greater than

Have a volunteer write the correct symbol in the circle and read the comparison sentence 36 plus 29 is greater than 24 plus 38.

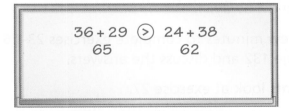

- Who has more cards? Tim

Have students complete exercises 15–22 on Student Book page 130 independently. Have students record the value for each expression under the expression so they can compare the values easily, and write the symbol.

Activity continued ▶

---

 20 MINUTES

Goal: Compare values of expressions by calculating and by estimating or using number sense.

Materials: Student Activity Book or Hardcover Book p. 130

 NCTM Standards:
Number and Operations
Communication

✓ Ongoing Assessment

To check that students understand the concept of comparing and ordering whole numbers, ask questions such as:

▶ In Chicago, Illinois, the three tallest buildings are the Aon Center, which is 1,136 ft tall, the John Hancock Center, which is 1,127 ft tall, and the Sears Tower, which is 1,450 ft tall. Write the heights of these three buildings in order from shortest to tallest.

① Teaching the Lesson (continued)

The Learning Classroom

Helping Community You may want to have students work in **Student Pairs** to complete exercises 15–22 on Student Activity page 132. Students can work independently to find the sums or differences. Then have them compare their sums or differences to be sure they are correct before they write the symbol in the circle.

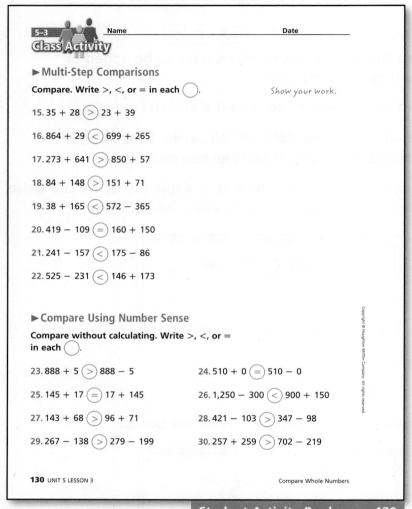

5–3
Class Activity

Name _____ Date _____

► **Multi-Step Comparisons**

Compare. Write >, <, or = in each ◯.   *Show your work.*

15. 35 + 28 (>) 23 + 39

16. 864 + 29 (<) 699 + 265

17. 273 + 641 (>) 850 + 57

18. 84 + 148 (>) 151 + 71

19. 38 + 165 (<) 572 − 365

20. 419 − 109 (=) 160 + 150

21. 241 − 157 (<) 175 − 86

22. 525 − 231 (<) 146 + 173

► **Compare Using Number Sense**

Compare without calculating. Write >, <, or = in each ◯.

23. 888 + 5 (>) 888 − 5   24. 510 + 0 (=) 510 − 0

25. 145 + 17 (=) 17 + 145   26. 1,250 − 300 (<) 900 + 150

27. 143 + 68 (>) 96 + 71   28. 421 − 103 (>) 347 − 98

29. 267 − 138 (>) 279 − 199   30. 257 + 259 (>) 702 − 219

130 UNIT 5 LESSON 3   Compare Whole Numbers

Student Activity Book page 130

► Compare Using Number Sense [WHOLE CLASS]

Read students this problem: Tim and Gail each have 10 apples. Tim gives 4 apples away. Gail picks 4 more apples. Who has more apples? Gail

● Ask students to explain why you do not need to add or subtract to answer the question. Since they both started with 10 apples, the person who got 4 more apples would have more apples than the person who gave 4 away.

Give students a few minutes to complete exercises 23–26 on Student Activity Book page 132 and discuss the answers.

Then have students look at exercise 27.

● Is 143 + 68 more or less than 200? more than 200

● Is 96 + 71 more or less than 200? less than 200

Math Talk Using **Solve and Discuss**, complete exercises 28–30. Then have students discuss how they used number sense to know the comparison are reasonable. Allow students with different strategies to share with the class.

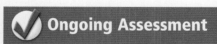

Ongoing Assessment

See Assessment Guide for Unit 5 Quick Quiz 1.

② Going Further

Intervention   Activity Card 5-3

Number Path Comparisons   Activity Card 5-3 ●

Work: In pairs

Use:
• 2 sets of Secret Code Cards
• MathBoard materials or TRB M39 (Number Path)

1. **On Your Own** Divide your set of Secret Code Cards into two separate piles of tens and ones. Shuffle each pile and place it face down. Then use the two top cards to make a 2-digit number. Circle it on the Number Path as shown below.

2. Together with your partner, write two comparisons using the two numbers marked on the Number Path.

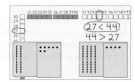

3. Repeat the activity three more times.

Unit 5, Lesson 3   Copyright © Houghton Mifflin Company

Activity Note If students have difficulty choosing the correct comparison symbol, tell them that the symbol always points to the lesser number.

✎ Math Writing Prompt

Connected Math How do you think a Number Path can help you compare numbers? Explain.

Soar to Success Math ✦ **Software Support**

Warm Up 7.17

On Level   Activity Card 5-3

Comparison Toss   Activity Card 5-3 ▲

Work: In pairs

Use:
• Number cube labeled 1–6

Decide:
Who will be Student 1 and who will be Student 2 for the first round.

1. **Student 1:** Write any 2-digit number on a piece of paper and then roll the number cube.

   `53`

2. **Student 2:** If the number on the number cube is a 1, 2, or 3, write a 2-digit number that is less than the number on the MathBoard. Otherwise, write a number that is greater.

    The 2 on the cube means I need a number that is less than 53, so I'll choose 50.

3. Together, write a comparison sentence using the symbol < or >.

4. Switch roles and repeat the activity twice more.

Unit 5, Lesson 3   Copyright © Houghton Mifflin Company

Activity Note Students can check their work by looking at the symbol and making sure that it points to the lesser number.

✎ Math Writing Prompt

Write Your Own Real-World Application A museum has 2,016 gems and 2,061 minerals on display. Does the museum have more gems or more minerals on display? Explain how you decided.

MEGAMATH Grades K-6 **Software Support**

Numberopolis: Carnival Stories, Level R

Challenge   Activity Card 5-3

Ordered Populations   Activity Card 5-3 ■

Work: On your own

1. The populations of the six largest cities and towns in New Mexico are shown alphabetically in the table below.

City	Population
6 Albuquerque	463,874
1 Farmington	40,563
5 Las Cruces	75,015
3 Rio Rancho	56,614
2 Roswell	44,058
4 Santa Fe	65,127

2. Reorder the cities and their populations from least populated to most populated.

Unit 5, Lesson 3   Copyright © Houghton Mifflin Company

Activity Note Students will easily choose the most populated city. Ordering the remaining cities can be done by ordering the numbers 40, 75, 56, 44, and 65.

✎ Math Writing Prompt

Is Ten Dollars Enough? You want to buy three model trucks that cost $2.99 each plus glue. The glue costs $1.25. Is $10 enough? Decide without calculating. Explain your thinking.

✸ DESTINATION Math® Software Support

Course II: Module 1: Unit 2: Comparing and Ordering

5–3
Homework **Goal:** Additional Practice

Use this Homework page to provide students with more practice comparing and ordering numbers.

5–3
Remembering **Goal:** Spiral Review

This Remembering page would be appropriate anytime after today's lesson.

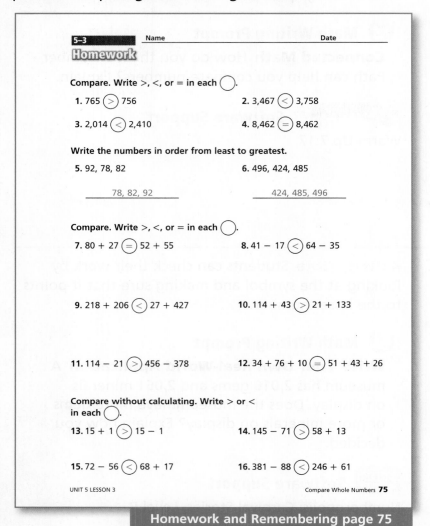

5–3   Name _____   Date _____
Homework

Compare. Write >, <, or = in each ◯.

1. 765 (>) 756

2. 3,467 (<) 3,758

3. 2,014 (<) 2,410

4. 8,462 (=) 8,462

Write the numbers in order from least to greatest.

5. 92, 78, 82

   78, 82, 92

6. 496, 424, 485

   424, 485, 496

Compare. Write >, <, or = in each ◯.

7. 80 + 27 (=) 52 + 55

8. 41 − 17 (<) 64 − 35

9. 218 + 206 (<) 27 + 427

10. 114 + 43 (>) 21 + 133

11. 114 − 21 (>) 456 − 378

12. 34 + 76 + 10 (=) 51 + 43 + 26

Compare without calculating. Write > or < in each ◯.

13. 15 + 1 (>) 15 − 1

14. 145 − 71 (>) 58 + 13

15. 72 − 56 (<) 68 + 17

16. 381 − 88 (<) 246 + 61

UNIT 5 LESSON 3   Compare Whole Numbers **75**

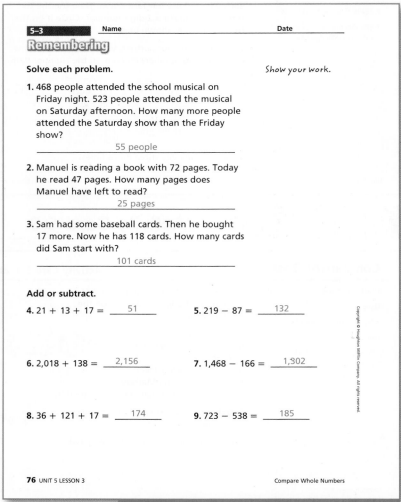

5–3   Name _____   Date _____
Remembering

Solve each problem.   *Show your work.*

1. 468 people attended the school musical on Friday night. 523 people attended the musical on Saturday afternoon. How many more people attended the Saturday show than the Friday show?

   55 people

2. Manuel is reading a book with 72 pages. Today he read 47 pages. How many pages does Manuel have left to read?

   25 pages

3. Sam had some baseball cards. Then he bought 17 more. Now he has 118 cards. How many cards did Sam start with?

   101 cards

Add or subtract.

4. 21 + 13 + 17 = ___51___

5. 219 − 87 = ___132___

6. 2,018 + 138 = ___2,156___

7. 1,468 − 166 = ___1,302___

8. 36 + 121 + 17 = ___174___

9. 723 − 538 = ___185___

76 UNIT 5 LESSON 3   Compare Whole Numbers

Homework and Remembering page 75

Homework and Remembering page 76

Home or School Activity

 Literature Connection

The Greatest Gymnast of All When students are using comparison language in math, such as *greater, less, more,* and *fewer,* it's the perfect time to introduce antonyms. To emphasize the similarity between math and language comparisons, have students read *The Greatest Gymnast of All* by Stuart J. Murphy. After students have read the story, have them write pairs of antonyms and put them in comparison sentences. For example, Joey is *taller* than Ann. Ann is *shorter* than Joey.

Money Values

Vocabulary

penny
nickel
dime
quarter
coin equivalents

Lesson Objectives

- Review the values of a penny, nickel, dime, and quarter.
- Determine and compare the values of collections of coins and bills.

The Day at a Glance

Today's Goals	Materials	
1 **Teaching the Lesson** **A1:** Review the names and values of U.S. coins. **A2:** Use various strategies to find the values of collections of coins and bills. **A3:** Compare the values of collections of coins and bills.	**Lesson Activities** Student Activity Book pp. 131–134 or Student Hardcover Book pp. 131–134 Homework and Remembering pp. 77–78 Play money or Play Money (TRB M40) Snack bags or envelopes Overhead projector and Overhead money (optional)	**Going Further** Activity Cards 5-4 Play money or Play Money (TRB M40) Number cubes Math Journals
2 **Going Further** ▶ Differentiated Instruction		
3 **Homework and Spiral Review**		

Use
Math Talk today!

Keeping Skills Sharp

Quick Practice ⏱ 5 MINUTES	Daily Routines
Goal: Round to the nearest ten or hundred. **Rounding Practice** Have a **Student Leader** write the following six numbers on the board. **168 129 172 354 1,409 240** The **Student Leader** points to each number and says "Round to the nearest ten," or "Round to the nearest hundred." When the leader gives a signal, students respond in unison with the rounded number. *Leader (pointing to 168):* Round to the nearest ten. *Class:* 170	**Homework Review** Ask students to place their homework at the corner of their desks. Check that students completed the assignment and check to see if any one problem caused difficulty. **Calendar** Today is Wednesday, July 13. Tamara has a dance recital on Thursday, July 28. How many days until the dance recital? 15 days

Teaching the Lesson

Reviewing Quarters, Dimes, Nickels, and Pennies

 5 MINUTES

Goal: Review the names and values of U.S. coins.

Materials: sets of play money (1 quarter, 1 dime, 1 nickel, and 1 penny per student) or Play Money (TRB M40); Student Activity Book page or Hardcover Book p. 131, snack bags or envelopes

 NCTM Standards:
Number and Operations
Communication
Representation

Class Management

Looking Ahead Have students keep their money cut-outs in a snack bag or envelope for future use.

English Language Learners

Review coins and their values. Give students play money. Have them hold up a penny. Draw the coins on the board. Write the values.

- **Beginning** Say: **This is a** *penny.* **It is 1¢.** Have students repeat. Continue with *nickel, dime,* and *quarter.*
- **Intermediate** Ask: **Is this a** *nickel* **or a** *penny?* penny **How many cents is a penny?** 1 Continue with other coins.
- **Advanced** Have students hold up each coin, name it, and tell its worth.

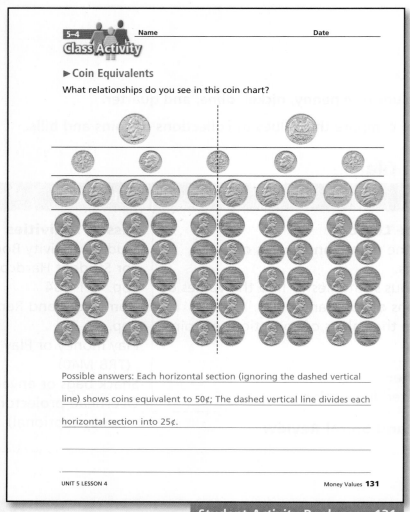

Student Activity Book page 131

▶ Coin Equivalents WHOLE CLASS

Distribute a set of play money to each student or have students cut out the coins on Play Money (TRB M40). Discuss the similarities and differences.

Have students look at the chart on Student Book page 131. Ask them about the relationships they see in the coin chart. They should mention the following points:

- Each horizontal section (ignoring the dashed line) shows coins equivalent to 50¢.

- The dashed vertical line divides each horizontal section in half. The coins in each half are equivalent to 25¢.

Ask a few simple questions about coin equivalents that can be answered using the chart on Student Book page 131.

- What are some combinations of coins that are equivalent to a dime? 2 nickels, 10 pennies, 1 nickel and 5 pennies

- What are some combinations of coins that are equivalent to a quarter? 5 nickels; 25 pennies; 2 dimes and 1 nickel; 4 nickels and 5 pennies, and so on

▶ Coin Values WHOLE CLASS

Hold up each coin, and say its value aloud. Have students respond with the name of the coin.

- A 25¢ coin is a … quarter! A 10¢ coin is a … dime! A 5¢ coin is a … nickel! A 1¢ coin is a … penny!

Repeat this activity. Scramble the order of the coins.

Now hold up the coins one at a time, and have students name each coin.

 Dime!    Quarter!

Finally, hold up the coins one at a time, and have students show fingers to indicate the value. (They can flash 2 tens and a 5 to show a quarter's value.)

 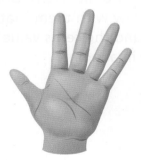

If you think students could benefit from additional practice with naming coins and their values, you might use the above activities as Quick Practice activities at the beginning of the next several lessons.

Teaching Note

Language and Vocabulary The activity will be especially powerful for Spanish and other nonnative English speakers. In Spanish, a quarter is often referred to as a "25¢ coin." The other U.S. coins are referred to in a similar way. The activity will also be helpful for native English speakers who need more practice associating each coin with its name and value.

Activity 2

Find the Value of Collections of Coins

 20 MINUTES

Goal: Use various strategies to find the values of collections of coins and bills.

Materials: sets of money (two $1 bills, 8 quarters, 10 dimes, 10 nickels, and 10 pennies per student), set of overhead money (optional), overhead projector (optional), Student Activity Book or Hardcover Book p. 132

✓ **NCTM Standards:**
Number and Operations
Reasoning and Proof
Communication

Teaching Note

Watch For! Some students might have difficulty counting on. Review how to skip count by 2s, 5s, 10s and 25s. Then as the class is counting on using the coins, ask the students what kind of coin they are counting and what type of skip counting is necessary.

▶ **Ways to Count the Value of Coins** WHOLE CLASS

Ask students to take 1 quarter, 1 dime, and 3 nickels from their sets of coins. Give them a few minutes to find the total value of the coins. Then choose a student to explain the counting method he or she used, using overhead coins to demonstrate if necessary. Ask anyone who used a different counting method to present it. Here are some ways students might count:

● Arrange the coins into groups whose values are easy to add.

● Count up, starting with the coin with the largest value.

Next, have students select one $1 bill, 3 quarters, 4 dimes, and 3 pennies and find the value of this collection. Select students who used different counting strategies to explain them.

Be sure that students understand what the cent sign, dollar sign, and the decimal point stand for. Remind them that cent signs are never shown with decimal points or dollar signs. Dollar signs can be shown with decimal points. Review with them that the dollar value is to the left of the decimal point, and the cents value (the amount under a dollar) is to the right of the decimal point.

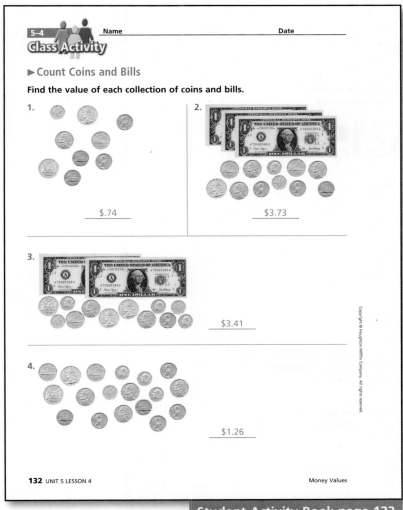

Student Activity Book page 132

Contents of Student Activity Book page 132:

5-4
Class Activity

Name _____ Date _____

▶ Count Coins and Bills

Find the value of each collection of coins and bills.

1. _____ $.74

2. _____ $3.73

3. _____ $3.41

4. _____ $1.26

132 UNIT 5 LESSON 4   Money Values

▶ Count Coins and Bills WHOLE CLASS

Introduce (or review) the idea of counting up from the coin with the greatest value to the coin with the least value. Have students select 1 quarter, 5 dimes, 3 nickels, and 2 pennies and arrange the coins in order of value on their desks. Arrange the corresponding overhead coins on the projector. Have students count up with you to find the value, pointing to each coin as they count it.

25¢ 35¢ 45¢ 55¢ 65¢ 75¢ 80¢ 85¢ 90¢ 91¢ 92¢

Repeat this for two $1 bills, 3 quarters, 2 dimes, 5 nickels, and 1 penny.

Have students complete exercises 1–4 on Student Book page 132. Discuss their results and counting strategies. Some may group coins by circling them. Others may count up, writing the cumulative totals as they count.

Teaching the Lesson (continued)

Activity 3

Compare Money Amounts

 15 MINUTES

Goal: Compare the values of collections of coins and bills.

Materials: Student Activity Book or Hardcover Book p. 133

 NCTM Standards:
Number and Operations
Problem Solving
Reasoning and Proof
Communication
Connections
Representation

✔ Ongoing Assessment

To be sure that students understand how to determine the value of a set of coins and bills, ask questions such as:

► If you had a pocketful of coins, how would you find the total value of the coins?

► Leo has 1 quarter, 2 nickels and 3 dimes. He said he has 65¢. How do you know he is correct?

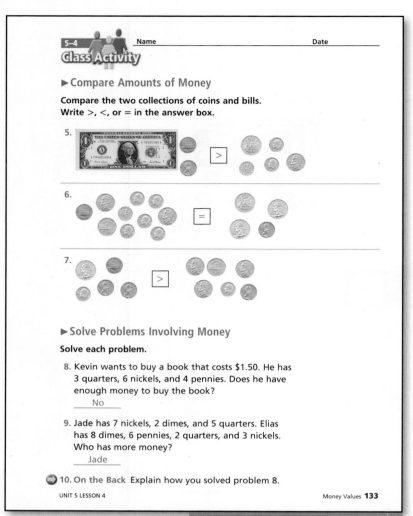

Student Activity Book page 133

► Compare Amounts of Money [WHOLE CLASS]

Read aloud the directions to exercises 5–7 on Student Activity Book page 135. Make sure everyone knows what to do. You may need to review the meaning of the symbols >, < and =. (You might remind students that the bigger part of the < or > symbol opens to the greater amount.)

Give students a few minutes to complete exercises 5–7. Then review the answers.

► Solve Problems Involving Money [WHOLE CLASS]

Math Talk Using **Solve and Discuss,** have students solve problems 8–9. Allow them to use money or to draw coins if they need to. As a class, discuss how students found the total amount of each set of given coins. Students may mention counting the coins with the greatest value first.

On the Back Have students explain how they solved question 8 if there is time.

② Going Further

Differentiated Instruction

Intervention   Activity Card 5-4

Counting Patterns
Activity Card 5-4 ●

Work: In pairs

Use:
• Play Money (10 quarters, 10 dimes, 10 nickels, 10 pennies)

Decide:
Who will be Student 1 and who will be Student 2 for the first round.

1. **Student 1:** Count the pennies by 2s, sliding the coins to your partner.
2. **Student 2:** How much money in pennies do you have? 10¢
3. **Student 1:** Now count the nickels by 5s, sliding the coins to your partner.
4. **Student 2:** What is the total amount in nickels? 50¢
5. **Student 1:** Then count dimes by 10s and quarters by 25s, sliding the coins to your partner.
6. **Student 2:** What is the total for dimes? For quarters? $1; $2.50
7. **Student 2:** Follow the same procedure as your partner for each group of coins. Did you count the same total for each group?

Unit 5, Lesson 4   Copyright © Houghton Mifflin Company

Activity Note After completing the first round of counting, have students repeat the exercise, beginning with the total and counting backward. If times allows, have students create collections of coins for each other to count and find the value.

✏️ Math Writing Prompt

Money Patterns What skip counting patterns do you use when counting quarters, nickels, and dimes? Use drawings to explain the patterns.

Soar to Success Math ★ Software Support
Warm Up 3.08

On Level   Activity Card 5-4

The Banking Game
Activity Card 5-4 ▲

Work: In small groups

Use:
• Several sets of coins

Decide:
Who will be the Banker.

1. Begin by giving all the money to the Banker.
2. The Banker gives a small handful of coins to each player. Each player counts the coins.
3. The player with the most money keeps it. Other players return their coins to the Banker.

> I have $1.22, but I have to give it back to the banker because Hannah has $2.24.

4. The game continues until the Banker has no coins left. The player with the most money wins.

Unit 5, Lesson 4   Copyright © Houghton Mifflin Company

Activity Note The Banker should distribute coins at random, in small handfuls, to each player. Students should verify each others coin counts.

✏️ Math Writing Prompt

Counting Strategy What strategy do you use when you need to find the value of a number of coins and bills? Explain your thinking.

MEGA MATH Grades K-6 Software Support
Numberopolis: Lulu's Lunch Counter, Level N

Challenge   Activity Card 5-4

Coin Combinations...
Activity Card 5-4 ■

Work: In pairs

Use:
• 2 number cubes labeled 1–6

Decide:
Who will be Student 1 and who will be Student 2 for the first round.

1. **Student 1:** Toss both number cubes and use the digits to name an amount of money. If both digits are the same, toss again until the digits are different.
2. Write the fewest coins possible for that amount of money.
3. **Student 2:** Use the same digits to name a different amount of money. Use the fewest coins needed to show that amount.
4. Whoever used fewer coins adds that amount of money to their score and tosses the cubes again.
5. Repeat until one player gets a score greater than $2.00 to win the game.

> 35¢
> That's 1 quarter plus 1 dime, or 2 coins. I can add 35¢ to my score.

> 53¢
> That's 2 quarters plus 3 pennies, or 5 coins.

Unit 5, Lesson 4   Copyright © Houghton Mifflin Company

Activity Note Students should think about which arrangement of digits will take the fewest coins to represent. For example, 35¢ takes a quarter and a dime. 53¢ takes 2 quarters and 3 pennies.

✏️ Math Writing Prompt

Other Ways Danny has 51¢ in his pocket. If he has 5 coins in his pocket, what are the coins? Explain.

✦ DESTINATION Math® Software Support
Course II: Module 3: Unit 2: Money

Money Values   **321**

③ Homework and Spiral Review

Homework **Goal:** Additional Practice

Use this Homework page to provide students with more practice comparing money amounts.

Remembering **Goal:** Spiral Review

This Remembering page would be appropriate anytime after today's lesson.

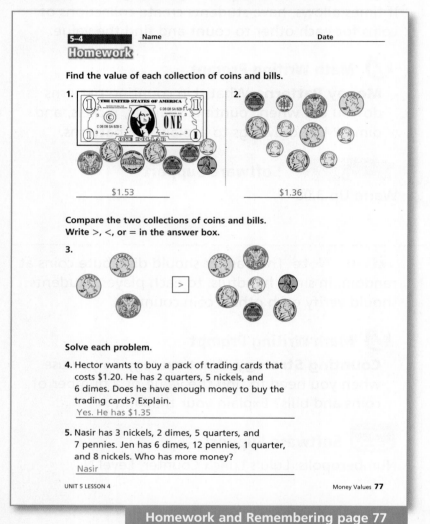

5-4   Name _____ Date _____
Homework

Find the value of each collection of coins and bills.

1. $1.53

2. $1.36

Compare the two collections of coins and bills. Write >, <, or = in the answer box.

3.   >

Solve each problem.

4. Hector wants to buy a pack of trading cards that costs $1.20. He has 2 quarters, 5 nickels, and 6 dimes. Does he have enough money to buy the trading cards? Explain.
Yes. He has $1.35

5. Nasir has 3 nickels, 2 dimes, 5 quarters, and 7 pennies. Jen has 6 dimes, 12 pennies, 1 quarter, and 8 nickels. Who has more money?
Nasir

UNIT 5 LESSON 4   Money Values **77**

Homework and Remembering page 77

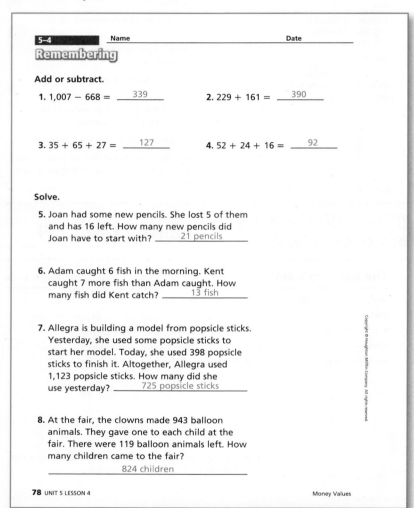

5-4   Name _____ Date _____
Remembering

Add or subtract.

1. 1,007 − 668 = ___339___

2. 229 + 161 = ___390___

3. 35 + 65 + 27 = ___127___

4. 52 + 24 + 16 = ___92___

Solve.

5. Joan had some new pencils. She lost 5 of them and has 16 left. How many new pencils did Joan have to start with? ___21 pencils___

6. Adam caught 6 fish in the morning. Kent caught 7 more fish than Adam caught. How many fish did Kent catch? ___13 fish___

7. Allegra is building a model from popsicle sticks. Yesterday, she used some popsicle sticks to start her model. Today, she used 398 popsicle sticks to finish it. Altogether, Allegra used 1,123 popsicle sticks. How many did she use yesterday? ___725 popsicle sticks___

8. At the fair, the clowns made 943 balloon animals. They gave one to each child at the fair. There were 119 balloon animals left. How many children came to the fair?
___824 children___

78 UNIT 5 LESSON 4   Money Values

Homework and Remembering page 78

Home or School Activity

 Social Studies Connection

Coin Design Have students look at the designs on a penny, a nickel, a dime, a quarter, a half dollar, a Susan B. Anthony dollar, and a Golden dollar. Have students make a poster showing who is on the front and what is on the back of each coin.

Coin	Who's on Front?	What's on Back?
Penny	Abraham Lincoln	The Lincoln Memorial
Nickel	Thomas Jefferson	Jefferson's Home, Monticello
Dime	Franklin Delano Roosevelt	A torch, an oak branch, and an olive branch

Represent Money Amounts in Different Ways

Lesson Objectives

- Represent amounts of money in various ways.
- Practice counting out the exact amount of money to make a purchase.

Vocabulary

dollar
exact

The Day at a Glance

Today's Goals	Materials	
1 Teaching the Lesson **A1:** Determine different coin combinations for given amounts. **A2:** Identify how to pay for items with exact change. **2 Going Further** ▶ Differentiated Instruction **3 Homework and Spiral Review**	**Lesson Activities** Student Activity Book pp. 135–136 or Student Hardcover Book pp. 135–136 Homework and Remembering pp. 79–80 Activity Cards 5-5 MathBoard materials Real or play money or Play Money (TRB M40) Coin Strips (TRB M41) Price tags	**Going Further** MathBoard Materials Number cubes Play Money Index cards Math Journals

123 Use Math Talk today!

Keeping Skills Sharp

Quick Practice ⏱ 5 MINUTES	Daily Routines	
Goal: Round numbers to the nearest ten and hundred. **Rounding Practice** Have the **Student Leader** make two teams and write 238, 721, 364, 1,298, 1,550, and 981 on the board. The leader points to a number and says, "Round to the nearest hundred," or, "Round to the nearest ten." The first team to give the correct rounded number wins a point and the most points wins.	**Homework Review** Send students to the board to show their work for problems 4 and 5. Have each student at the board explain his/her work. Encourage the rest of the class to ask clarifying questions and make comments.	**Strategy Problem** Ty used half of his savings to buy a DVD. The DVD cost $25. Then, he spent $5 on a comic book. How much money does he have left? Explain your answer. $20; Possible explanation: If the DVD cost $25, and that was half of his savings, then Ty had $50 in his savings. Ty then bought a comic for $5, for a total spent of $30. To find out how much money he has left, I subtracted $30 from $50 to get $20.

① Teaching the Lesson

Finding Equivalent Coin Combinations

 15 MINUTES

Goal: Determine different coin combinations for given amounts.

Materials: MathBoard materials, real or play money (8 quarters, 10 dimes, 10 nickels, 10 pennies per student) or Play Money (TRB M40), Coin Strips (TRB M41), Student Activity Book or Hardcover Book p. 135

 NCTM Standards:
Number and Operations
Problem Solving
Communication
Connections

Differentiated Instruction

Extra Help Have students who struggled with the coin activities in Lesson 4 use Coin Strips (TRB M41) that show the coin values by size. Since the pennies are small, students may find it easier to fold a strip of pennies or tear off groups of them than to cut out individual pennies.

 Math Talk in Action

Why do you think it's important to know how to make a certain amount of money in different ways?

Latasha: It's important because you might want to buy something and you need to know that there is more than just one way to get to that amount.

Can you give me an example?

Latasha: If a soda costs 75¢, you might not have 3 quarters, but you might have 1 quarter and 5 dimes. You can still buy the soda because you have the 75¢.

Very good.

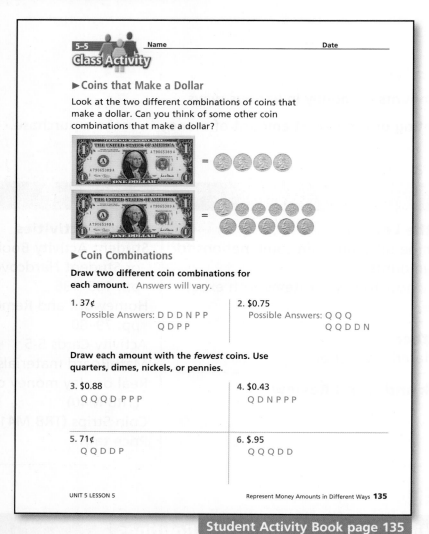

Student Activity Book page 135

► Coins that Make a Dollar [WHOLE CLASS]

Have students look at Student Book page 135 and discuss the different ways to make a dollar. For each set of coins, have the class count the coins (from greatest to least value) in unison to check that the total is a dollar.

Have students suggest other ways to make a dollar while the rest of the class works on their MathBoards. Allow students to use real or play sets of money if they need to, or just represent the coins with circles labeled with letters or their values, or just write letters.

  D

► Coin Combinations [INDIVIDUALS]

Have students complete exercises 1–6 and then use **Solve and Discuss** to have students compare their answers and strategies.

Shopping with Exact Change

▶ Model Making a Purchase [WHOLE CLASS]

Math Talk Have students share what they know about buying things with money.

● the cashier determines the total cost of the items

● the customer pays for the items

● the cashier gives the customer change back if there is any

Put the 37¢ price tag on a pencil and the 56¢ price tag on a ruler. Choose two volunteers to act out purchasing the pencil and the ruler. Have the customer get some play money. Explain that the shopkeeper does not have a cash register or any coins, so the customer will have to pay with the exact amount.

Customer: (Brings pencil and ruler to cashier) I would like to buy these two items.

Shopkeeper: I'll make out a sales slip and find your total cost.

pencil $0.37
ruler $0.56
      ─────
       $0.93

Shopkeeper: Your total cost is 93¢. I do not have any coins, so you will need to give me the exact change.

Customer: Twenty-five, fifty, seventy-five, eighty-five, ninety, ninety-one, ninety-two, ninety-three.

Shopkeeper: I'll draw 3 quarters, 1 dime, 1 nickel, and 3 pennies to record the sale.

pencil $0.37
ruler $0.56
      ─────
       $0.93
    QQQDNPPP

Ask the class to give other coin combinations the customer could have used to make the purchase with the exact amount.

Activity continued ▶

---

 30 MINUTES

Goal: Identify how to pay for items with exact change.

Materials: Price tags: (37¢ and 56¢), play money, Student Activity Book or Hardcover Book p. 136

✓ **NCTM Standards:**
Number and Operations
Problem Solving
Communication
Connections

Differentiated Instruction

Extra Help Some students may not follow the procedures for purchasing items when the steps are presented. Tell these students that in this first activity students will set up a scenario with props to model the activity they will do on the Student Book page.

English Language Learners

Draw a picture of someone buying a 75¢ ruler with $1. Label the *customer* and *cashier*. Write $1 = 100¢.

● **Beginning** Say: A ruler costs __. 75¢. The *customer* gives $1. $1 − 75¢ = 25¢. The *cashier* gives 25¢ *change.*

● **Intermediate** Ask: Does the *customer* buy or sell the ruler? buys the ruler Say. **He gives the cashier $1. What is $1 − 75¢?** 25¢ **25¢ is the *change.***

● **Advanced** Say: The *customer* gives $1 to the ___. cashier Ask: **What is $1 − 75¢?** 25¢ **How much *change* does the customer get?** 25¢

① Teaching the Lesson (continued)

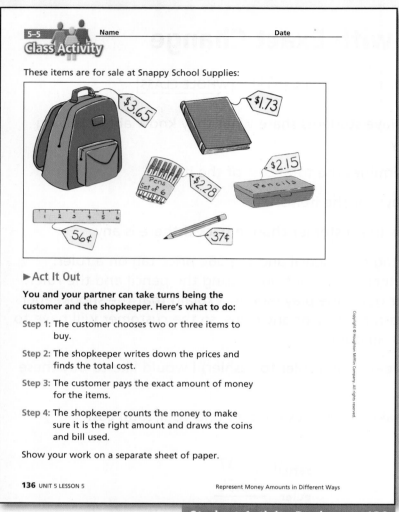

Student Activity Book page 136

▶ Act It Out PAIRS

Divide the class into **Student Pairs** and explain that they are going to act out a sales purchase like the two volunteers just did. Remind them that the shopkeeper will not have any coins or a cash register so the shopkeeper will have to make out a sales slip and the customer will have to pay with the exact amount.

Read aloud the steps on Student Book page 136. Then, have a student give out play money to each **Student Pair**. Allow students to shop for 20 minutes and then choose a few pairs to describe the items the customer bought, how the shopkeeper found the total, and which coins and bills the customer used.

Make sure **Student Pairs** understand that a customer does not always have to pay with an exact amount of money. Sometimes they may not have an exact amount and pay too much. In that case, they need to get change back.

② Going Further

Intervention — Activity Card 5-5

How Many Ways?

Activity Card 5-5 ●

Work: In pairs

Use:
- MathBoard materials

Decide:
Who will be Student 1 and who will be Student 2 for the first round.

1. **Student 1:** Write $0.75 on your MathBoard.
2. **Student 2:** Make a coin drawing to show $0.75 in as many ways as possible. Look at the drawing. What other coin combinations can you make? Possible answers: 15 nickels; 3 quarters; 1 quarter, 5 dimes
3. Change roles and repeat the activity twice for amounts between $0.50 and $1.00.

Unit 5, Lesson 5 — Copyright © Houghton Mifflin Company

Activity Note Students should share their results with other groups. Including pennies will create many different ways to represent each amount.

 **Math Writing Prompt**

Represent Coins Edith counted her coins like this: "10 cents, 15 cents, 20 cents, 21 cents, 22 cents." What coins does Edith have? Use a picture to help you explain your answer.

Soar to Success Math ★ Software Support
Warm Up 3.14

On Level — Activity Card 5-5

Count It Up!

Activity Card 5-5 ▲

Work: In pairs

Use:
- Number cube labeled 1–6
- Play money (16 quarters, 20 dimes, 20 nickels, 20 pennies)

Decide:
Who will roll the number cube first in the first round.

1. Each player takes 8 quarters, 10 dimes, 10 nickels, and 10 pennies. Together, choose a target amount between $3.00 and $5.00. Record the choice. Then take turns repeating the activity below to reach the target amount.
2. Roll the number cube, and take that number of coins or fewer from the pile of money. Write the value of the coins.
3. After the first round, each player adds the value of the coins to the total from the last turn. The first player to reach the target *exactly* wins.

TARGET $4.00
3 quarters is 75¢
5 quarters is $1.25
My total so far is $2.00

Unit 5, Lesson 5 — Copyright © Houghton Mifflin Company

Activity Note Students may choose to take fewer coins on a single turn than the number shown on the number cube to avoid exceeding the target number.

Math Writing Prompt

Make a Drawing Draw three ways a customer can *exactly* pay for something that costs $2.35. Explain how you know you have the correct amount.

MegaMath Grades K–6 Software Support
Numberopolis: Lulu's Lunch Counter, Level V

Challenge — Activity Card 5-5

Drawing for Dollars

Activity Card 5-5 ■

Work: In pairs

Use:
20 index cards cut in half and labeled as follows:
- Ten 1¢ cards
- Ten 5¢ cards
- Eight 10¢ cards
- Eight 25¢ cards
- Four 50¢ cards

Decide:
Who will be Student 1 and who will be Student 2 for the first round.

1. Shuffle the cards and place them face down in a pile. Each player draws five cards from the pile.
2. Take turns asking one another for one card at a time to make a total of $1.00. If your partner does not have the card, draw a card from the pile.
3. Set aside each group of cards equal to $1.00 that you collect.
4. Continue until the pile is gone. Then add the dollar amounts that were made. The player with the most money wins.

Unit 5, Lesson 5 — Copyright © Houghton Mifflin Company

Activity Note By asking for the cards with the greatest values first, students increase their chances of getting $1.00 combinations more quickly.

Math Writing Prompt

Make a List Draw all six ways that you can make $1.50 using dimes, quarters, and dollar bills. Explain how you organized your list so that you didn't miss any ways.

✖ DESTINATION Math· Software Support
Course II: Module 3: Unit 2: Money

③ Homework and Spiral Review

This Homework page gives students practice adding money and counting out exact change.

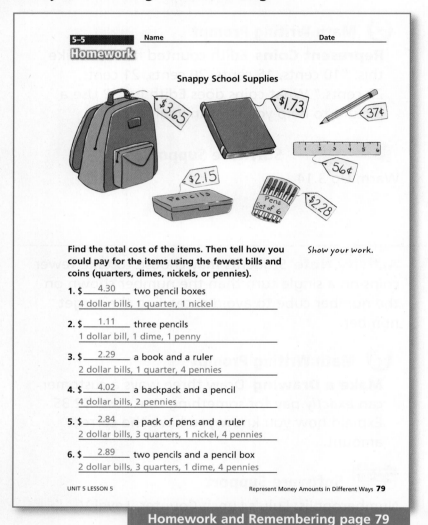

This Remembering page would be appropriate anytime after today's lesson.

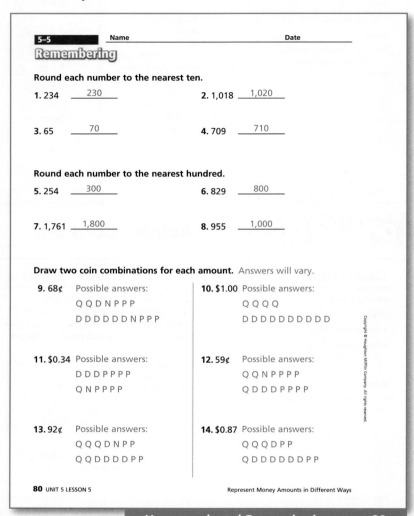

Home or School Activity

 Social Studies Connection

Name That Face Have students find out whose face appears on $1, $5, $10, and $20 bills. Challenge them to also find any other historical information on money.

Make Change

REAL WORLD Problem Solving

Lesson Objective

● **Use the Counting On strategy to make change from purchases.**

Vocabulary

change

The Day at a Glance

Today's Goals	Materials	

1 Teaching the Lesson
A1: Count on to make change.
A2: Act out real-life shopping situations.
 	
2 Going Further
▶ Differentiated Instruction
 	
3 Homework and Spiral Review
	Lesson Activities
	Student Activity Book pp. 137–138
	  or Student Hardcover Book
	  pp. 137–138
	Homework and Remembering
	  pp. 81–82
	Overhead projector and coins
	  (optional)
	Play money or Play Money
	  (TRB M40)
	Ox-Cart Man by Donald Hall
	  (Puffin Books, 1983)
		Going Further
		Activity Cards 5-6
		MathBoard Materials
		Store flyers
		Play money or Play
		  Money (TRB M40)
		Math Journals

123 Use Math Talk today!

Keeping Skills Sharp

Quick Practice ⏱ 5 MINUTES	Daily Routines
Goal: Count coin values. **Counting Coins** Write a sequence of quarters (Qs), dimes (Ds), nickels (Ns), and pennies (Ps) on the board, in that order. Point to the coins in order as the class counts on to find the total. **Q Q Q Q Q D D N N N P** *Teacher:* Count on to find the total amount. *Class:* 25¢, 50¢, 75¢, \$1.00, \$1.25, \$1.35, \$1.45, \$1.50, \$1.55, \$1.60, \$1.65, \$1.66 Then, add coins to or erase coins from the sequence, and the class counts again. Repeat. Have a **Student Leader** lead this activity tomorrow after students learn how it works today.	**Homework Review** Have students discuss the errors from their homework. Encourage students to help each other understand how to correct these errors. **Place Value** Have students find the number that is 100 less than 1,512 and 1,604. 1,412; 1,504

Teaching the Lesson

Use the Counting On Strategy

 15 MINUTES

Goal: Count on to make change.

Materials: Student Activity Book page 137, play money (two $5 bills, five $1 bills, 8 quarters, 10 dimes, 10 nickels, and 10 pennies per student) or, overhead projector and coins, Play Money (TRB M40)

✔ **NCTM Standards:**
Number and Operations
Problem Solving
Communication
Connections

Teaching Note

Language and Vocabulary The word *purchase* is used frequently in this lesson. Some students, especially English learners, might not understand its meaning as both a verb and a noun. Tell students that this word means *to buy* as well as *the item or items bought.*

English Language Learners

Draw different coins on the board. Have students identify them.

- **Beginning** Say: **We also call coins** *change.* Jingle some coins in your pocket. Ask: **Do I have** *change* **in my pocket?** yes
- **Intermediate** Say: *Change* **also means a group of coins.** Jingle some coins in your pocket. Ask: **What is in my pocket?** change/ coins
- **Advanced** Have students tell the definition of change they know. Circle the coins on the board. Say: *Change* **is also a group of coins.**

▶ Share Shopping Experiences [WHOLE CLASS]

 Math Talk Have students talk about getting change back.

- When does someone get money back from a cashier? When they have paid more money than the items cost.

- What word do we use for the money we get back when we buy something? change

Discuss the two ways people use the word *change* when talking about money.

- People sometimes think of *change* as small amounts of money. For example, a person might say that a few coins are "loose change."

- The money a person gets back when they pay more than the total cost is also called *change.*

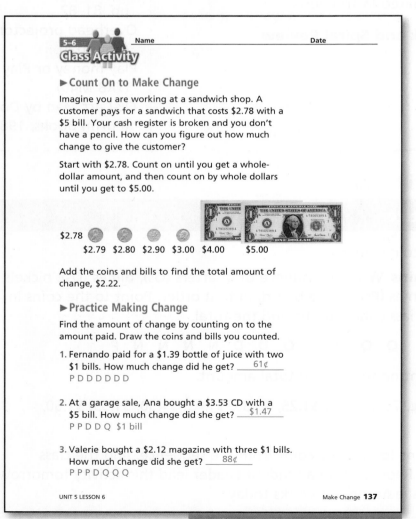

Student Activity Book page 137

▶ Count On to Make Change WHOLE CLASS

Have a student volunteer read aloud the shopping situation on Student Book page 137. Allow several students to share their ideas on how to figure out how much change the customer should get back.

Have students pass out sets of play money or TRB M40 to the class and then read through the Counting On strategy with students. As you read aloud the steps for counting on, students should count on with their money.

● Many cashiers make change by counting on from the total amount the customer pays. Let's try this strategy for this example. Use your coins to count out the change with me.

● What was the total cost for the sandwich? $2.78 How did the customer pay? with a $5.00 bill

● First, let's start by counting on 2 pennies to get to a nice even amount with no extra cents. $2.79, $2.80

● Now we want to count on to get to the next whole dollar. We can add 2 dimes. $2.90, $3.00

● Finally, we'll add on whole dollars until we reach $5.00. $4.00, $5.00

● Now, look at the money we counted. What is the total amount of change we gave back to the customer? 2 dollars and 22 cents. That's $2.22

Explain to students they don't have to use exactly this order. For example, they could have counted on 2 dimes, then 2 pennies, and then 2 dollars. The important thing is to start with the purchase price and count on to the total amount the customer paid.

▶ Practice Making Change INDIVIDUALS

You may want to solve the first word problem as a class, and then use the **Solve and Discuss** structure for problems 2 and 3.

 Alternate Approach

Visual Learners While you demonstrate the Counting On strategy for making change, you may wish to use a transparent set of money on the overhead projector so students can check that they are counting on correctly. If you have large coins, you could also have student volunteers count on to find the change.

Differentiated Instruction

Extra Help Making change can be a tough skill for many students. You might want to begin by having students make change by counting on to $1.00. Give students several examples until you feel they are ready to make change for greater amounts.

 Ongoing Assessment

Observe students as they complete Student Activity Book page 138. Check to make sure students are adding their items correctly. Be sure students are starting from the total amount of their purchases and counting on to the amount paid. Check to see if they are beginning by adding pennies to get to the 5¢ mark, then adding nickels if necessary, then dimes, and so on. Remind student customers that they should always count their change to be sure it is correct.

Teaching the Lesson (continued)

Activity 2

Run a Shop

 30 MINUTES

Goal: Act out real-life shopping situations.

Materials: Student Activity Book or Hardcover Book p. 138

 NCTM Standards:
Number and Operations
Problem Solving
Connections
Communication

The Learning Classroom

Building Concepts When students practice math concepts in real-life situations, they will conceptualize and take ownership of their learning. To create this environment, have students make and use their own lists of items and prices. The price of each item should be less than $3.00. Students can also set up shopping learning centers. They can put price tags on small items they find around the classroom and practice buying items and making change with other classmates.

The Learning Classroom

Scenarios In this Act-It-Out scenario, students role-play being a customer and shopkeeper to find the total cost of two items and make change. This role playing in a real-life situation can foster a sense of involvement and create a meaningful context for adding money amounts and making change.

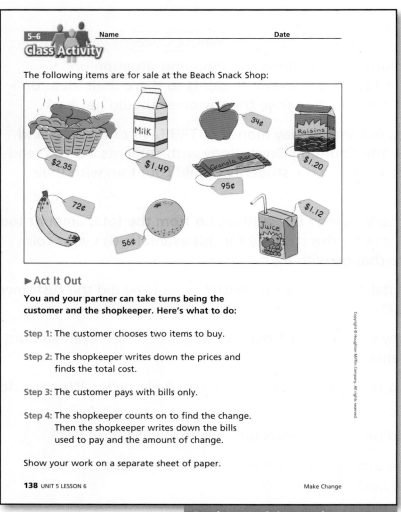

Student Activity Book page 138

► Act It Out PAIRS

Divide the class into pairs. You may wish to pair a student who is skilled at working with coins, a **Helping Partner,** with one who isn't.

Read aloud the instructions for Student Book page 138 and make sure students know what to do. You may want to demonstrate a sales purchase, with a student playing the roles of the shopkeeper and customer. Allow students 25 minutes or so to shop, and then choose a few pairs to demonstrate one of their purchases. They should tell what items were purchased, how they found the total, and how they determined how much change to give.

②Going Further

Differentiated Instruction

Intervention — Activity Card 5-6

The Yard Sale   Activity Card 5-6 ●

Work: In pairs

Use:
- Play Money (8 quarters, 10 dimes, 10 nickels, 8 pennies)
- MathBoard materials

Decide:
Who will be the customer and who will be the shopkeeper for the first round.

1. Work together to list 5 items that might be for sale at a yard or garage sale for 50¢ or less. Draw each item on your MathBoard with its price tag. Then take turns buying and selling each item.

2. **Customer:** Choose an item and give the shopkeeper 50¢ to pay for it.

3. **Shopkeeper:** Use the counting on strategy to give the customer the correct change.

4. Switch roles and repeat the activity until all the items have been sold.

Unit 5, Lesson 6   Copyright © Houghton Mifflin Company

Activity Note After students have mastered the activity as written, change the activity so that the customer pays with one-dollar bills.

✐ Math Writing Prompt

Why Change? As a customer, why is it important to know how to make change?

 **Software Support**

Warm Up 3.17

On Level — Activity Card 5-6

Shopping   Activity Card 5-6 ▲

Work: In small groups

Use:
- Store flyers
- Play Money (two $5 bills, five $1 bills, 8 quarters, 10 dimes, 10 nickels, 10 pennies for each student)

Decide:
Who will be the cashier for the first round.

1. Choose a store flyer for a shopping activity. One student is the cashier and the other students are the customers for each round.

2. One customer chooses three items from the store flyer that will total less than $10. Then the cashier finds the total price.

3. The customer gives the cashier a whole-dollar amount. Then the cashier gives the correct change. The customer checks that the correct amount of change was given.

4. Continue the activity until each customer has bought three items. Then switch roles and start the shopping again.

Unit 5, Lesson 6   Copyright © Houghton Mifflin Company

Activity Note Customers can use estimation to choose the items and check that the amount charged and the change they receive are reasonable amounts.

✐ Math Writing Prompt

From Least to Greatest When people count on to give change, they often start with the coin of least value. Why is this so?

MEGA MATH Grades K-6 **Software Support**

Numberopolis: Lulu's Lunch Counter, Level Q

Challenge — Activity Card 5-6

Larger Purchases   Activity Card 5-6 ■

Work: In pairs

Use:
- Store flyers
- Play Money (two $20 bills, two $10 bills, five $1 bills, 8 quarters, 8 dimes, 10 nickels, 10 pennies)

Decide:
Who will be the cashier for the first round.

1. Choose a store flyer for a shopping activity. One student is the cashier and the other student is the customer for each round.

2. The customer chooses three items from the store flyer that will total less than $60. Then the cashier finds the total price.

3. The customer gives the cashier only enough bills to pay the amount. Then the cashier gives the correct change. The customer checks that the correct amount of change was given.

4. Switch roles and start the shopping again.

Unit 5, Lesson 6   Copyright © Houghton Mifflin Company

Activity Note Be sure to provide flyers that have items with prices between $10 and $40 so that students have a chance to use the larger bills.

✐ Math Writing Prompt

Fewest Number of Bills and Coins Jon buys a toy for $3.12. He pays for it with $5. He estimates and says that he should get $2 and some coins back. Is he correct? Explain.

✖ DESTINATION Math **Software Support**

Course II: Module 3: Unit 2: Money

Make Change   **333**

③ Homework and Spiral Review

This Homework page provides more practice with making change.

This Remembering page would be appropriate anytime after today's lesson.

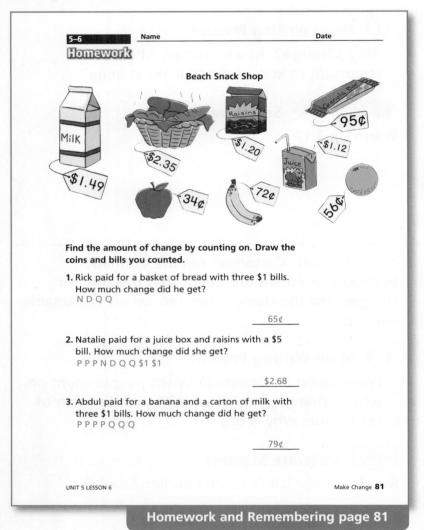

5–6
Homework

Name _____ Date _____

Beach Snack Shop

Milk $1.49
$2.35
34¢
Raisins $1.20
72¢
Juice $1.12
95¢
56¢

Find the amount of change by counting on. Draw the coins and bills you counted.

1. Rick paid for a basket of bread with three $1 bills. How much change did he get?
   N D Q Q
   _____ 65¢

2. Natalie paid for a juice box and raisins with a $5 bill. How much change did she get?
   P P P N D Q Q $1 $1
   _____ $2.68

3. Abdul paid for a banana and a carton of milk with three $1 bills. How much change did he get?
   P P P P Q Q Q
   _____ 79¢

UNIT 5 LESSON 6   Make Change **81**

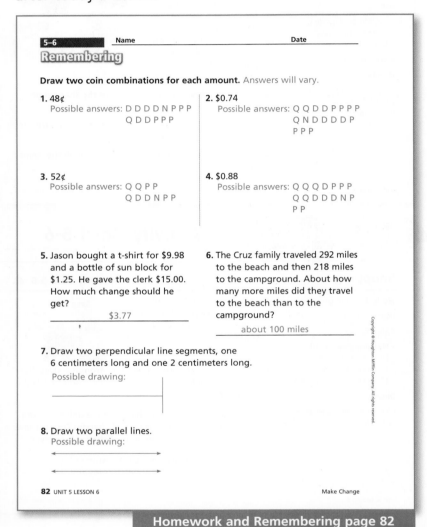

5–6
Remembering

Name _____ Date _____

Draw two coin combinations for each amount. Answers will vary.

1. 48¢
   Possible answers: D D D D N P P P
   Q D D P P P

2. $0.74
   Possible answers: Q Q D D P P P P
   Q N D D D D P
   P P P

3. 52¢
   Possible answers: Q Q P P
   Q D D N P P

4. $0.88
   Possible answers: Q Q Q D P P P
   Q Q D D D N P
   P P

5. Jason bought a t-shirt for $9.98 and a bottle of sun block for $1.25. He gave the clerk $15.00. How much change should he get?
   _____ $3.77

6. The Cruz family traveled 292 miles to the beach and then 218 miles to the campground. About how many more miles did they travel to the beach than to the campground?
   _____ about 100 miles

7. Draw two perpendicular line segments, one 6 centimeters long and one 2 centimeters long.
   Possible drawing:

8. Draw two parallel lines.
   Possible drawing:

82 UNIT 5 LESSON 6   Make Change

Homework and Remembering page 81

Homework and Remembering page 82

Home and School Connection

Social Studies Connection

Bartering Ask students if they have ever bought something without paying money for it. Tell them that before there was money, people traded things instead of buying them. A farmer might trade chickens for fabric to make clothes. This is called *bartering* or *trading*.

Have students read the *Ox Cart Man* by Donald Hall to learn about bartering and shopping practices in earlier times.

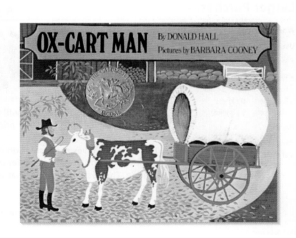

Round Money Amounts

REAL WORLD **Problem Solving**

Lesson Objectives

● **Round money amounts to the nearest dime or dollar.**

● **Make estimates in real-world situations involving money.**

Vocabulary

round
estimate
rounding rules

The Day at a Glance

Today's Goals	Materials	

1 **Teaching the Lesson**
   A1: Round money amounts to the nearest dollar or dime.
   A2: Estimate sums involving money.
 	
 2 **Going Further**
   ▶ Extension: More Estimation Strategies
   ▶ Differentiated Instruction
 	
 3 **Homework and Spiral Review**
	Lesson Activities
	 Student Activity Book pp. 139–141
	   or Student Hardcover Book
	   pp. 139–141
	 Homework and Remembering
	   pp. 83–84
	 MathBoard materials
	 Quick Quiz 2 (Assessment Guide)
		Going Further
		 Student Activity Book
		  p. 142
		 Activity Cards 5-7
		 MathBoard Materials
		 Index cards
		 Math Journals

123 *Use* **Math Talk** *today!*

Keeping Skills Sharp

Quick Practice 🕐 5 MINUTES	**Daily Routines**
Goal: Add the values of different coins to find a total. **Counting Coins** The **Student Leader** writes a sequence of quarters (Qs), dimes (Ds), nickels (Ns), and pennies (Ps) on the board, in that order, such as **Q Q Q Q D D D N N P P P.** $1.43 The leader points to the letters in order as the class counts on to find the total. Have the leader pause after each subtotal to allow time in between for all students to calculate. To do this, the leader may use a signal that tells the class when to answer. Have the leader add or erase coins from the sequence and repeat. (See Unit 5 Lesson 6.)	**Homework Review** If students give incorrect answers, have them explain how they found the answers. This can help you determine whether the error is conceptual or procedural. **Skip Counting** Have students skip count backward by 100s beginning from 850 and stopping with 250.

Teaching the Lesson

Round to the Nearest Dime or Dollar

 20 MINUTES

Goal: Round money amounts to the nearest dollar or dime.

Materials: MathBoard materials, Student Activity Book or Hardcover Book p. 139

✓ **NCTM Standards:**
Number and Operations
Problem Solving
Representation

Teaching Note

Language and Vocabulary
Students may not initially grasp how the *dimes place* and the *tens place* are used interchangeably in this activity. Explain that it is acceptable to use the term *dimes place* when talking about how to round money amounts. If students are confused, reinforce the connection between a dime and ten.

English Language Learners

Write 110¢ on the board. Help students make a place value model with pennies.

• **Beginning** Point to the 10. Say: **This is 1 ten.** Point to a penny ten stick. Say: **10 pennies is 10¢.** Hold up a dime. Write and say: **10¢ = 1 dime = 1 ten.** Have students repeat.

• **Intermediate** Ask: **How many tens are there?** 1 **Does 10¢ = 1 ten?** yes **What coin equals 10¢?** dime **Does 1 dime = 1 ten?** yes

• **Advanced** Have students describe their model and say what coin equals 1 ten. Write $2.30. Ask: **What is the digit in the dimes place?** 3

5–7
Class Activity

Name _____ Date _____

▶ **Round Amounts of Money**

Round each amount first to the nearest dime and then to the nearest dollar.

	Rounded to the nearest dime	Rounded to the nearest dollar
1. $3.62	$3.60	$4.00
2. $5.09	$5.10	$5.00
3. $1.25	$1.30	$1.00
4. $2.99	$3.00	$3.00
5. $7.50	$7.50	$8.00

Solve each problem.   *Show your work.*

6. Carl spent $3.35 on a sandwich and $1.85 on a drink. Estimate the total amount he spent by rounding the prices to the nearest dollar and adding.
   about $5.00

7. Rose spent 85¢ on a pen, 32¢ on an eraser, and 78¢ on a pencil sharpener. Estimate the total amount she spent by rounding the prices to the nearest dime and adding.
   about $2.00

8. Aisha spent $4.12 on a book, $3.65 on a magazine, and $1.75 on a greeting card. Estimate the total amount she spent by rounding the prices to the nearest dollar and adding.
   about $10.00

UNIT 5 LESSON 7   Round Money Amounts **139**

Student Activity Book page 139

▶ Round Amounts of Money [WHOLE CLASS]

Have students look at exercise 1 on Student Book page 139. Ask students how they would round $3.62 to the nearest dime. Possible response: First I looked at the digit to the right of the dimes place. It is a 2, which means 2¢. Since 2¢ is less than half of a dime, we round down to $3.60.

If necessary, write $3.62 on the left side of the board and underline the 6. Ask students what the dime amounts above and below this amount are and write them on the board. $3.60 and $3.70 Have a student create place value drawings for the three numbers and explain how the drawings show that we should round down.

$3.70
$3.62
$3.60

Now ask students how to round $3.62 to the nearest dollar. See the possible explanation below.

● First I looked at the digits to the right of the dollars place. They are 6 and 2, which means 6 dimes and 2 pennies, or 62¢. Since 62¢ is more than half of a dollar, we round up to $4.00.

If necessary, write $3.62 on the board. Then, ask the students what the dollar amounts above and below $3.62 are. $3.00 and $4.00 Write them on the board, above and below the $3.62. Again, have a student create place-value drawings and explain how the drawings show that we should round up to $4.00.

Have students work independently to complete exercises 2–5.

Review Rules of Rounding Remind students of these rules when rounding to the nearest dime:

● If the amount is equal to or more than half of the next ten (or whole dime amount), round up.

● If the amount is less than half of the next ten (or whole dime amount), round down.

Remind students of these rules when rounding to the nearest dollar:

● If the amount is equal to or more than half of the next whole dollar amount, round up.

● If the amount is less than half of the next whole dollar amount, round down.

Have students work independently on problems 6–8, which ask them to estimate sums of money by rounding to the nearest dime or dollar.

Differentiated Instruction

Extra Help Students may need a brief review of the halfway points used when rounding. Explain that when rounding to the nearest ten, if the digit to the right of the tens place is 5 (the halfway point) or higher, you should round up to the next ten. Similarly, when rounding to the nearest dime, if the digit to the right of the dimes place is 5 cents (the halfway point) or higher, you should round up to the next dime. When rounding to the nearest dollar, students should remember that 50 cents is the halfway point.

Ongoing Assessment

Make sure students understand the concept of rounding to the nearest dime or dollar.

▶ What are the dime amounts above and below $4.53?

▶ Which of the two amounts will you round to? Why?

▶ What are the dollar amounts above and below $4.53?

▶ Which of the two amounts will you round to? Why?

Activity 2

Make Estimates Involving Money

 35 MINUTES

Goal: Estimate sums involving money.

Materials: MathBoard materials, Student Activity Book or Hardcover Book p. 140

 NCTM Standards:
Numbers and Operations
Problem Solving

The Learning Classroom

Building Concepts When students solve real-world problems or act out shopping situations, they learn when to round prices up or down. When students make these connections between math and their everyday lives, they see a purpose for their learning.

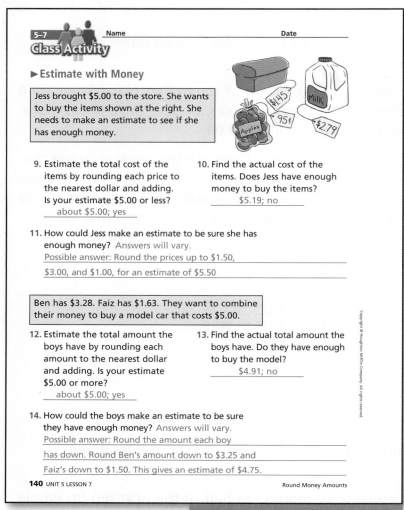

Student Activity Book page 140

► Estimate with Money WHOLE CLASS

Using the **Solve and Discuss** structure, have students solve problems 9–11. Discuss the fact that if Jess estimates by rounding to the nearest dollar, she may think she has enough money, when she actually does not.

Help students see that if Jess rounds all the prices up, she can be sure her estimate is more than the actual total. Students may suggest rounding up to the next dollar or rounding up to other numbers that are easy to add (for example, $1.50 for $1.45).

(123) Math Talk Discuss with the class the benefits of rounding the cost of items up in problems involving money. Students may suggest that:

● overestimating the cost guarantees that you'll know quickly and accurately whether or not you have enough money to make purchases.

● rounding can make it easier to add a series of prices or money amounts.

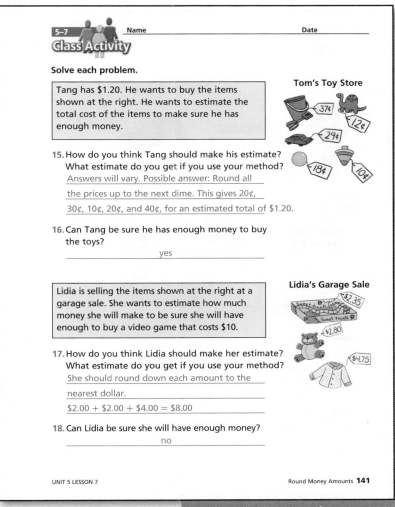

Student Activity Book page 141

Page 141 content:

5-7
Class Activity
Name _____ Date _____

Solve each problem.

> Tang has $1.20. He wants to buy the items shown at the right. He wants to estimate the total cost of the items to make sure he has enough money.

Tom's Toy Store

37¢ 12¢ 29¢ 18¢ 10¢

15. How do you think Tang should make his estimate? What estimate do you get if you use your method?
   Answers will vary. Possible answer: Round all
   the prices up to the next dime. This gives 20¢,
   30¢, 10¢, 20¢, and 40¢, for an estimated total of $1.20.

16. Can Tang be sure he has enough money to buy the toys?
   yes

> Lidia is selling the items shown at the right at a garage sale. She wants to estimate how much money she will make to be sure she will have enough to buy a video game that costs $10.

Lidia's Garage Sale

$2.35 $2.80 $4.75

17. How do you think Lidia should make her estimate? What estimate do you get if you use your method?
   She should round down each amount to the
   nearest dollar.
   $2.00 + $2.00 + $4.00 = $8.00

18. Can Lidia be sure she will have enough money?
   no

UNIT 5 LESSON 7   Round Money Amounts **141**

Teaching Note

Watch For! If students do not fully understand the benefits of estimating by rounding all amounts down or all amounts up, they may simply add the money amounts to find a total, and forgo rounding altogether. Explain that it is best to round prices up when you already know how much money there is to spend (as in problems 11 and 15). On the other hand, it is best to round money amounts down when you don't know if you have enough money (as in problems 14 and 17).

Next have students solve problems 12–14. In this situation, the two boys need to round down to be sure they have enough money. Again, students may suggest rounding down to the next dollar or rounding down to other numbers that are easy to add (for example, $3.25 for $3.28, or $1.50 for $1.63).

Have students solve problems 15–18 on Student Book page 141. In these problems, students will again need to determine when it is beneficial to round up and when it is better to round down.

 Quick Quiz

See Assessment Guide for Unit 3 Quick Quiz 2.

Going Further

Extension: More Estimation Strategies

Goal: Estimate by using compatible numbers and using mental math.

Materials: Student Activity Book or Hardcover Book p. 142

✓ **NCTM Standards:**
Numbers and Operations
Problem Solving

▶ Use Mental Math to Estimate

WHOLE CLASS

Write these money amounts on the board:

$$\$2.89$$
$$\$1.69$$
$$\$4.29$$

Explain that you can use mental math to make a quick estimate by looking for amounts of cents that when added will be close to $1 or for amounts of cents that are close to $1.

● Are there any amounts of cents close to $1? Yes, 89¢

● Are there any amounts of cents that when added are close to $1? Yes, 69¢ and 29¢.

Summarize their thinking by writing this on the board.

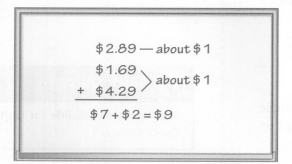

▶ Different Ways to Estimate with Money INDIVIDUALS

Have students look at the items at the top of Student Book page 142. Explain that they will use rounding and mental math to estimate the total cost of the items.

Give students a few minutes to complete the page. Use **Solve and Discuss,** and have students demonstrate how they estimated, checked the reasonableness of an answer, and decided what strategy they would use to be sure they have enough money when shopping.

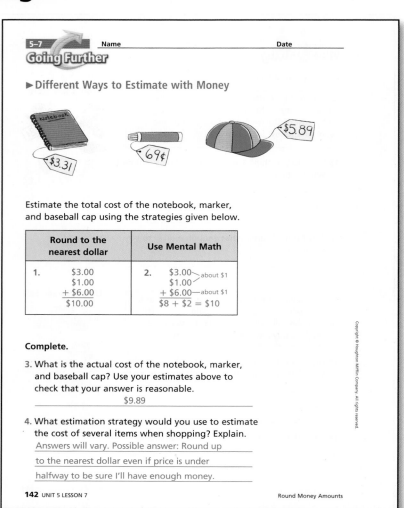

Differentiated Instruction

Money Maker
Activity Card 5-7 ●

Work: On your own

Use:
• MathBoard materials

1. Write the number 345 on your MathBoard. Then write the tens and hundreds numbers that come before and after as shown.

2. **Think** Which digit in the number helps you decide how to round 345 to the nearest ten? to the nearest hundred? 5; 4

3. Circle the numbers that show 345 rounded to the nearest ten and the nearest hundred.

4. Repeat the activity for three more 3-digit numbers. Then place a decimal point and dollar sign in each number to show how to round money amounts.

Unit 5, Lesson 7   Copyright © Houghton Mifflin Company

Activity Note If time permits, extend the activity to have students write money amounts and then round each amount to the nearest dime and nearest dollar.

Math Writing Prompt

Explain Your Thinking Explain how you would round $5.55 to the nearest dollar.

Soar to Success Math ★ **Software Support**

Warm Up 15.16

Money Match Up
Activity Card 5-7 ▲

Work: In pairs

Use:
• 16 index cards

1. Work with your partner. Make 8 pairs of index cards. On the first card, write any money amount less than $4.99 that does not end in a 0.

2. On the second card, write the amount of money rounded to the nearest dime and nearest dollar.

3. Shuffle the cards and place them face down in a 4 × 4 array. Take turns choosing two cards at random and try to make a match.

4. If a match is not made, turn the cards over and let your partner take a turn. When all the cards are matched, the player with the most matches wins.

Unit 5, Lesson 7   Copyright © Houghton Mifflin Company

Activity Note Students should verify each other's matches. To make the game more challenging, restrict the money amounts to less than $1.99

Math Writing Prompt

Explain a Rule Round $1.77 to the nearest dime. Write a rule that could be used to round to the nearest dime.

MEGA MATH Grades K-8 **Software Support**

Numberopolis: Lulu's Lunch Counter, Level O

Round Up or Down?
Activity Card 5-7 ■

Work: In pairs

1. Write a word problem about finding the estimated cost of some items to decide whether you have enough money to buy something.

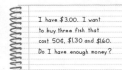

2. Write a second problem about estimating how much money you have to spend after combining your allowance and your savings.

3. **Analyze** In which situation does it make sense to round down? In which situation does it make sense to round up? How do you decide?

Unit 5, Lesson 7   Copyright © Houghton Mifflin Company

Activity Note Estimating the amount needed for a purchase requires rounding up to avoid a shortfall. Estimating the amount accumulated for spending requires estimating down for the same reason.

Math Writing Prompt

Generalize Give an example of when you would round both addends down when estimating a sum of money.

DESTINATION Math **Software Support**

Course II: Module 3: Unit 2: Money

③ Homework and Spiral Review

Homework **Goal:** Additional Practice

This Homework page gives students practice in rounding money amounts.

Remembering **Goal:** Spiral Review

This Remembering page would be appropriate anytime after today's lesson.

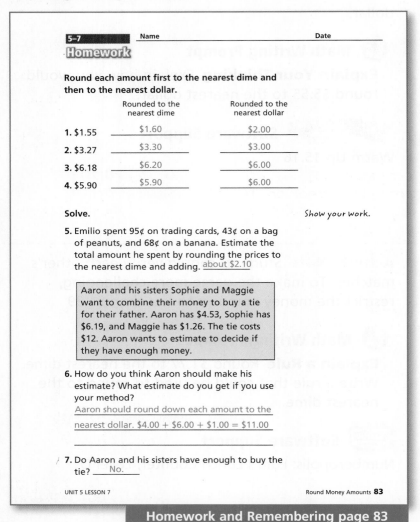

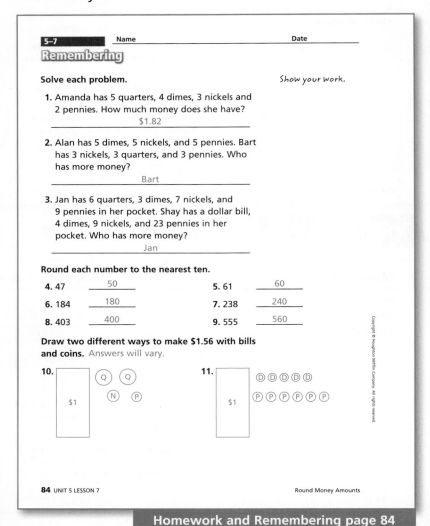

Home or School Activity

 Real-World Connection

Shopping Spree First, have the students decide how much play money under $50 they would like to spend on a shopping spree. Have them record the amount and the prices of several items they would like to buy from a local store flyer. Next, they should estimate the cost of the items to decide if they have enough money. Then they check to see if they are correct by finding the actual cost.

Ask Addition and Subtraction Questions from Tables

Lesson Objectives

● Interpret information in tables.

● Write and solve problems based on tables with data.

Vocabulary

table
row
column
cell
function table

The Day at a Glance

Today's Goals	Materials
1 **Teaching the Lesson** **A1:** Understand how information is organized in a table. **A2:** Use information to ask and answer questions in tables. **2** **Going Further** ► Math Connection: Patterns in Tables ► Differentiated Instruction **3** **Homework and Spiral Review**	**Lesson Activities** Student Activity Book pp. 143–147 or Student Hardcover Book pp. 143–147 and Activity Workbook pp. 49–51 (includes tables) Homework and Remembering pp. 85–86 MathBoard materials Transparency of Student Activity Book page 145 and overhead projector (optional) Sticky notes **Going Further** Student Activity Book pp. 145–146 or Hardcover pp. 145–146 and Activity Workbook pp. 50–51 Activity Cards 5-8 Math Journals

123 *Use* **Math Talk** *today!*

Keeping Skills Sharp

Quick Practice ⏱ 5 MINUTES	Daily Routines
Goal: Count coin values. **Counting Coins** The **Student Leader** writes a sequence of quarters (Qs), dimes (Ds), nickels (Ns), and pennies (Ps) on the board, in that order. The leader points to the coins in order as the class counts on to find the total. The Student Leader should repeat this several times, adding coins to or erasing coins from the sequence. Q Q Q Q Q Q D N N P P *Leader:* (Pointing to the coins) Count on to find the total amount. *Class:* 25¢, 50¢, 75¢, $1.00, $1.25, $1.50, $1.60, $1.65, $1.70, $1.75, $1.76, $1.77	**Homework Review** Let students work together to check their work. Initially, pair less able students with more able students. Remind students to use what they know about helping others. **Mental Math** Use a mental math strategy to add $66 + 25$. Explain how you found your answer. 91; Possible explanation: I added the tens first. $60 + 20$ is 80. Then I added the ones. $6 + 5$ is 11. Then I added $80 + 11$ which is 91.

Teaching the Lesson

Introduce Tables

 15 MINUTES

Goal: Understand how information is organized in a table.

Materials: Student Activity Book or Hardcover Book p. 143, transparency of Student Activity Book or Hardcover Book p. 143 (optional), overhead projector (optional)

✔ **NCTM Standards:**
Number and Operations
Data Analysis and Probability

Teaching Note

Language and Vocabulary
Students often have trouble remembering the distinction between *row* and *column*. To help them remember, gesture from left to right when you talk about rows, and up and down when you talk about columns. To further reinforce that columns are vertical, you may also want to have students connect columns in a table with columns in architecture.

 Class Management

You may want to make a transparency of Student Book page 143 and display it during this discussion.

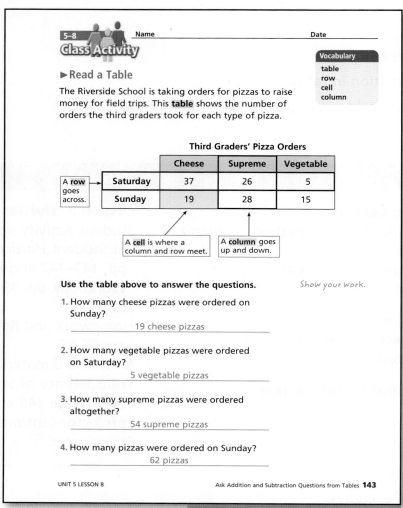

Student Activity Book page 143

▶ Read a Table WHOLE CLASS

Math Talk Ask students where they have seen tables and charts. Possible responses: newspapers, magazines, nutrition labels, textbooks

Turn students' attention to the *Pizza Orders* table on Student Book page 143. Ask students to explain what the table shows.

Explain that tables are arranged in *rows* and *columns,* and ask students to run their fingers across the row for Saturday.

● What do the numbers in the Saturday row tell us? how many of each pizza type was sold on Saturday

Next, have students run their fingers down the column for Supreme pizza.

- What do the numbers in the column labeled *Supreme* tell us? the number of Supreme pizzas sold each day

Explain that the rectangles where a column and row meet are called *cells.*

Have students put one finger on *Sunday* and another on *Cheese.* Ask them to slide their fingers across and down until they meet. If you are using a transparency, demonstrate as students follow along.

- What number is in this cell? 19

- What does this number tell us? The number of cheese pizzas that sold on Sunday.

Have students practice finding particular cells.

- Can someone explain how to find how many Supreme pizzas were sold on Saturday? Move one finger from Supreme and the other from Saturday.

- Find the cell that contains the number 5. What does this number tell us? The number of vegetable pizzas sold on Saturday.

- Can someone explain how to find how many pizzas were sold on Saturday? Add the numbers in the row labeled Saturday.

- Find the cell that contains the number 37. What does this number tell us? The number of cheese pizzas sold on Saturday.

Give students a few minutes to answer questions 1–4, then discuss the answers.

- Suppose someone has an answer of 15 for exercise 2, what did they do wrong? The person went across from Sunday instead of Saturday.

- Suppose someone had an answer of 44 for exercise 3, what did they do wrong? The person didn't carry the ten.

- Suppose someone has an answer of 68 for exercise 4, what did they do wrong? The person added the numbers for Saturday instead of Sunday.

Teaching the Lesson (continued)

Ongoing Assessment

Check to see that students understand how to interpret information in a table. Ask questions such as these:

▶ What does the 5 in the table mean?

▶ How can you find the number of vegetable pizzas sold on Sunday using the table?

▶ Create Your Own WHOLE CLASS

Have a volunteer choose two cells in the table and identify each cell for the class by saying both the day and the pizza type. Ask students to mark the two cells lightly in pencil in their books. Mark the cells on the transparency if you are using one.

Ask if anyone can suggest an addition question based on these two cells. For example, if the student chose the number of cheese pizzas sold on Saturday and the number of cheese pizzas sold on Sunday, the following is a possible question:

● How many cheese pizzas did the third graders sell over the weekend?

Have another volunteer explain how he or she would find the answer to the question. (Do not require the student to actually find the answer.)

Now ask if anyone can think of a subtraction question based on the same two cells. The following is a possible question:

● How many more cheese pizzas did the third graders sell on Saturday than on Sunday?

Again, have a student explain how he or she would find the answer. Repeat this process a few times, with different volunteers choosing the cells and suggesting the questions.

Some possible questions:

● How many pizzas were sold on Sunday?

● How many Vegetable pizzas were sold altogether?

● How many Cheese pizzas were sold altogether?

● How many more Supreme pizzas were sold on Sunday than Saturday?

● How many more Cheese pizzas than Vegetable pizzas were sold on the two days?

Write and Answer Addition and Subtraction Questions

5–8
Class Activity

Name _____ Date _____

▶ **Use a Table**

This table shows the number of animals a veterinarian treated over three months.

Animals Treated

	Dogs	Cats	Birds	Reptiles	All Animals
January	68	118	25	11	222
February	94	106	8	19	227
March	122	77	19	26	244
3-Month Total	284	301	52	56	693

5. Fill in the total for each column and row.

6. Write two addition questions about this table.
   Answers will vary.
   _____
   _____
   _____
   _____

7. Write two subtraction questions about this table.
   Answers will vary.
   _____
   _____
   _____
   _____

Copyright © Houghton Mifflin Company. All rights reserved.

144 UNIT 5 LESSON 8   Ask Addition and Subtraction Questions from Tables

Student Activity Book page 144

35 MINUTES

Goal: Use information to ask and answer questions in tables.

Materials: Student Activity Book or Hardcover Book p. 144 and Activity Workbook p. 49, sticky notes

 NCTM Standards:
Number and Operations
Algebra
Data Analysis and Probability
Communication

Differentiated Instruction

Extra Help When answering addition or subtraction questions some students may have trouble remembering which cell to refer to. To help them remember, have them mark the cells with small sticky notes that remove easily. When they have answered the questions, they can remove the sticky note and use them to mark other cells.

▶ Use a Table WHOLE CLASS

Have students read the table on Student Book page 144 and encourage a volunteer to explain the table. Ask questions like the ones below to make sure students understand how the table is organized.

● How many reptiles did the vet treat in March? 26

● How many cats did the vet treat in February? 106

Point out that the bottom row, *3-Month Total,* and the last column, *All Animals,* are not filled in and prompt students to explain the purpose of the blank cells in the table.

● What information belongs in the bottom row? the total number of each type of animal treated over the 3-month period

● How can you find the number that goes at the bottom of the *Dogs* column? Add 68, 94, and 122

● **What information belongs in the last column?** the total number of animals treated each month

● **How can you find the number that goes at the end of the *January* row?** Add 68, 118, 25, and 11.

Direct students' attention to the blank cell in the lower right corner.

● **What information goes in this cell?** the total number of animals (all types) treated over the 3-month period

Give students a few minutes to complete exercise 5, finding the totals and filling in the blank row and column. Discuss the results with the class and have students explain the two ways to find the overall total.

Have students write addition and subtraction questions about this table in exercises 6 and 7. To demonstrate, ask a volunteer to suggest an addition question, or suggest one yourself. Here is one example:

● **In January, how many dogs and cats did the vet treat altogether?**

Have a student explain how he or she would find the answer.

Have students trade papers to answer each other's questions for exercises 6 and 7. Then have them return the papers and check each other's work using Student Book page 144. For a sample classroom dialogue, see **Math Talk in Action.** If time allows, choose students to share the questions they wrote.

 Math Talk in Action

Amit: How many of the animals treated in February were not dogs?

Rebecca: I know that the vet treated 227 animals in February, and 94 of the animals were dogs. So 227 − 94 is 133. 133 of the animals treated in February were not dogs.

Amit: How did you know that only 94 of the 227 animals treated were dogs?

Rebecca: I looked in the *February* row and the *Dog* column. That cell told me that 94 dogs were treated in February.

② Going Further

Math Connection: Patterns in Tables

Goal: Identify and use patterns in tables.

Materials: Student Activity Book or Hardcover Book p. 145 and Activity Workbook p. 50

✔ **NCTM Standards:**
Number and Operations
Algebra
Data Analysis and Probability

▶ Find a Pattern in a Table WHOLE CLASS

Have students look at the tables on Student Book page 145. Ask the following questions:

● **How are the first two tables different from the last table?** The first two tables have labels for columns, but not for rows.

● **What information does the first table show?** the number of blocks in a tower, starting at Row 1 through Row 7

● **How can you tell how many blocks should be in Row 6 of the block tower?** Subtract 1 block from the number of blocks in Row 5.

● **What pattern do you see in the number of blocks as a row is added to the block tower?** The number of blocks decreases by 1 block.

Have students use the pattern to complete the table and answer question 1. Discuss students' answers as a class.

Have students look at the second table.

● **What information does the second table show?** the amount of money in a savings account

● **How does the amount of money in the savings account change from one week to the next week?** It decreases.

● **What pattern do you see?** The amount of money in the account decreased $15 from Week 1 to Week 2 and Week 4 to Week 5.

Have students complete the second table and answer question 2. Discuss their answers as a class.

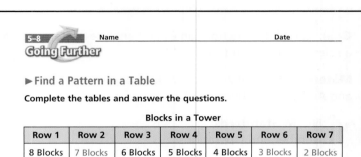

Student Activity Book page 145

Using **Solve and Discuss**, complete the third table and answer question 3.

Math Journal As time allows, have students share their own tables in exercise 4.

The Learning Classroom

Building Concepts Working with tables gives students the opportunity to experience addition and subtraction in an alternate context. Identifying patterns in the tables in this activity gives students practice in identifying and describing quantitative changes involving addition and subtraction.

Ask Addition and Subtraction Questions from Tables **349**

Math Connection: Function Tables

Goal: Complete function tables and analyze patterns to write a rule for a function table.

Materials: Student Activity Book or Hardcover Book p. 146 and Activity Workbook p. 51

✓ **NCTM Standards:**
Number and Operations
Algebra
Representation

Teaching Note

Math Connection This activity is designed to emphasize the connection between finding and using patterns and tables. Students will use what they know about patterns and number relationships to complete and find rules for function tables.

▶ Introduce Function Tables WHOLE CLASS

Tell students that a function table is a table of ordered pairs that follow a rule. The rule tells what to do to the input number to get the output number.

Put the function table on the board and ask students to explain how to complete it using the rule.

Rule: Add 5	
Input	**Output**
5	10
25	30
80	85
95	100

Next put this function table on the board and ask students to find the pattern and give the rule.

Rule: Subtract 8	
Input	**Output**
12	4
28	20
70	62
84	76

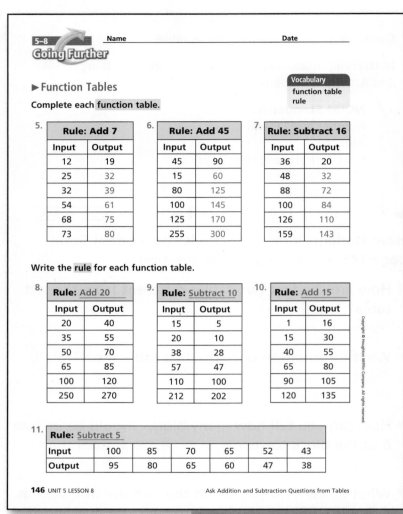

Student Activity Book page 146

▶ Function Tables PAIRS

Have **Student Pairs** work to complete each function table in exercises 5–7 on Student Book page 146. Encourage them to use mental math to complete the tables. Discuss their answers and have them share their solution methods.

Then have **Student Pairs** find the rules for exercises 8–11. Have volunteers explain how they found each rule.

Differentiated Instruction

Topsy-Turvy Tables   Activity Card 5-8

Work: In pairs

1. Copy both tables below. Complete the second table using the information in the first table. Then use both tables to answer the questions below.

Garden Tool Sales			
	Thursday	Friday	Saturday
shovel	13	12	16
rake	15	20	17

Garden Tool Sales		
	shovel	rake
Thursday	13	15
Friday	12	20
Saturday	16	17

2. How many rakes were sold during the three days? 52

3. How many more rakes than shovels were sold? 11

4. **Analyze** How are the tables alike? How are they different? Possible answer: Both tables show the same information even though they look different. The first table has two rows and three columns. The second table has two columns and three rows.

Unit 5, Lesson 8   Copyright © Houghton Mifflin Company

Activity Note Students should recognize that each column of Table 1 has the same information as the corresponding row of Table 2.

✎ Math Writing Prompt

In Your Own Words Explain the difference between rows and columns. Use a drawing to help you explain.

Soar to Success Math ✦ **Software Support**

Warm Up 10.34

What's Missing?   Activity Card 5-8 ▲

Work: In pairs

1. Copy the table below.

Favorite Sports			
	Baseball	Basketball	Soccer
Grade 3			
Grade 4			

2. Use any numbers you choose to complete the table about favorite sports in two classes.

3. Take turns. Ask your partner an addition or subtraction question about the data in the table.

4. Check your partner's answer and then switch roles to ask another question.

Unit 5, Lesson 8   Copyright © Houghton Mifflin Company

Activity Note Encourage students to compare individual numbers as well as total numbers computed from data in the table.

✎ Math Writing Prompt

Critical Thinking Why do you think people use tables to organize data? Explain your thinking.

MegaMath ■ **Software Support**

Country Countdown: White Water Graphing, Level C

This Table Shows ...   Activity Card 5-8 ■

Work: In pairs

1. Three classes sold tickets to a concert on Thursday and Friday. Work together to make up and write sentences telling how many tickets were sold by each class.

On Thursday, Mr. Simon's class sold 54 tickets to the concert, Ms. Tran's class sold 68, and Mrs. Jackson's class sold 57. On Friday, Mr. Simon's class sold 48 tickets, Ms. Tran's class sold 50, and Mrs. Jackson's class sold 62.

2. Make a table to show the data in your sentences.

3. Ask your partner an addition or subtraction question about the data in the table.

4. Check your partner's answer and then switch roles to ask another question.

Unit 5, Lesson 8   Copyright © Houghton Mifflin Company

Activity Note Students should make tables with two rows and three columns, or three rows and two columns.

✎ Math Writing Prompt

Real-World Application Think of a situation when you might use a table to display data. Is a table the best way to organize this information? Explain.

✦ **DESTINATION** Math· **Software Support**

Course II: Module 2: Unit 1: Estimating and Finding Differences within 1,000

Ask Addition and Subtraction Questions from Tables   **351**

③ Homework and Spiral Review

5–8 Homework Goal: Additional Practice

This Homework page helps students use information in tables.

5–8 Homework Name ___ Date ___

This table shows the number of tickets sold for the early and late showings of each movie at the Palace Theater last Saturday.

Saturday Ticket Sales

	Jungle Adventure	Hannah the Hero	Space Race
Early Show	72	109	143
Late Show	126	251	167

1. How many fewer tickets were sold for the early showing of *Jungle Adventure* than for the late showing?
   54 tickets

2. How many more tickets were sold for the late showing of *Hannah the Hero* than for the late showing of *Space Race*?
   84 tickets

This table shows the number of pizza, pasta, and salad orders at Luigi's Pizzeria last Tuesday and Wednesday.

Orders at Luigi's Pizzeria

	Pizza	Pasta	Salads
Tuesday	45	27	18
Wednesday	51	65	29

3. Write one addition question and one subtraction question based on the table above, and then find the answers.
   Answers will vary. Possible questions: How many orders of pasta were taken on Tuesday and Wednesday together?; 92; How many more pizzas were sold on Wednesday than on Tuesday?; 6

UNIT 5 LESSON 8   Ask Addition and Subtraction Questions from Tables **85**

Homework and Remembering page 85

5–8 Remembering Goal: Spiral Review

This Remembering page would be appropriate anytime after today's lesson.

5–8 Remembering Name ___ Date ___

1. Draw a square with a perimeter of 12 centimeters. Label the sides with their lengths.

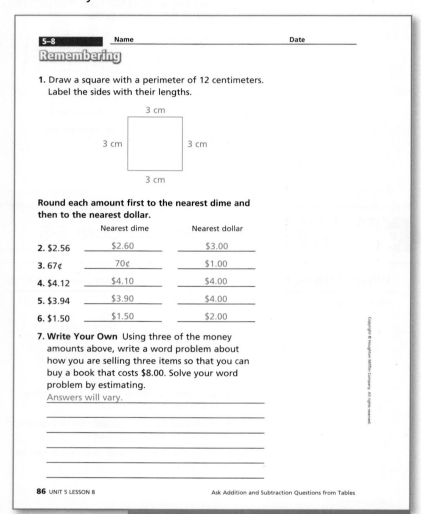

3 cm
3 cm   3 cm
3 cm

Round each amount first to the nearest dime and then to the nearest dollar.

		Nearest dime	Nearest dollar
2.	$2.56	$2.60	$3.00
3.	67¢	70¢	$1.00
4.	$4.12	$4.10	$4.00
5.	$3.94	$3.90	$4.00
6.	$1.50	$1.50	$2.00

7. **Write Your Own** Using three of the money amounts above, write a word problem about how you are selling three items so that you can buy a book that costs $8.00. Solve your word problem by estimating.
   Answers will vary.
   _____
   _____
   _____
   _____
   _____
   _____

86 UNIT 5 LESSON 8   Ask Addition and Subtraction Questions from Tables

Homework and Remembering page 86

Home or School Activity

Language Arts Connection

Homonyms Homonyms are words that are spelled or pronounced the same, but have different meanings. Introduce homonyms to students with the examples *row, table,* and *cell.* Have students think about the meaning of those three words and encourage students to set up a chart to organize their thinking. Students should be thinking of the meaning of the words in mathematics and their meaning outside of math class.

Challenge students to think of other homonyms.

Math	Homonym	Non-math
It goes across in a table.	row	Something you do to move a boat.
Displays data	table	Something you eat on.
A rectangle in a table.	cell	Something in your body.

352 UNIT 5 LESSON 8

Complete Tables

Vocabulary
table
row
column
cell

Lesson Objectives

● Use information in tables to create and solve word problems.

● Complete tables.

The Day at a Glance

Today's Goals	Materials	
1 **Teaching the Lesson** **A1:** Review tables and create word problems based on information in tables. **A2:** Complete tables and ask questions about the data. **2** **Going Further** ▶ Problem Solving Strategy: Logic Problems ▶ Differentiated Instruction **3** **Homework and Spiral Review**	**Lesson Activities** Student Activity Book pp. 148–150 or Student Hardcover Book pp. 148–150 and Activity Workbook pp. 52–54 (includes tables and special format) Homework and Remembering pp. 87–88 Four different colored crayons or pencils	**Going Further** Student Activity Book pp. 149–150 Activity Cards 5-9 Inch Grid Paper (TRB M42) Math Journals

123 Use Math Talk today!

Keeping Skills Sharp

Quick Practice ⏱ 5 MINUTES	Daily Routines
Goal: Round whole numbers to the nearest ten or hundred. **Rounding Practice** The **Student Leader** writes the numbers below on the board, points to each, and says either, "Round to the nearest ten," or, "Round to the nearest hundred." When the leader gives a signal, the class responds with the rounded number. The leader should allow enough time between signals to give all students time to think. Rounding a number in the thousands might require a longer pause. **698 236 459 1,980 2,333 7,777** *Leader (pointing to 698):* Round to the nearest ten. *Class:* 700	**Homework Review** Ask a student volunteer to share the questions he/she wrote for problem 3. Invite a student to answer the questions at the board, while the others work at their seats. **Equations** Write a solution equation for the word problem but do not solve. *In June, To had 5,617 points. By the end of July, she had a total of 8,972 points. How many points did To gain in July?* Possible answer: $8{,}972 - 5{,}617 = \square$

Teaching the Lesson

Review Tables

 20 MINUTES

Goal: Review tables and create word problems based on information in tables.

Materials: Student Activity Book or Hardcover Book p. 147

✔ **NCTM Standards:**
Number and Operations
Data Analysis and Probability
Problem Solving
Communication

Differentiated Instruction

Extra Help Some students may still be struggling to understand what the numbers in a table represent. Have students move one finger from the number to the row and another finger to the column and then tell what the number represents.

English Language Learners

Draw the Class Activity table, a *roller coaster, ferris wheel,* and *bumper car* on the board. Help students make comparisons.

- **Beginning** Say: **383 people rode the roller coaster on Monday.** Ask: **Did *more* people ride it on Tuesday?** yes Ask questions with *fewer.*
- **Intermediate** Ask: **Did *more* people ride the roller coaster or bumper cars on Monday?** roller coaster Continue with *fewer.*
- **Advanced** Have students use *more, fewer,* and *less* to compare the information.

 Name _____ Date _____

▶ **Analyze Tables**

This table shows the number of people who went on different rides at an amusement park.

Number of People Who Went on Rides

	Roller Coaster	Ferris Wheel	Bumper Cars
Monday	383	237	185
Tuesday	459	84	348
Wednesday	106	671	215

Use the table above to answer the questions.

1. What do the numbers in the row for Tuesday stand for?
   The number of people who rode on the Roller Coaster, Ferris Wheel, and Bumper Cars on Tuesday.

2. What do the numbers in the column for bumper cars stand for?
   The number of people who rode on bumper cars on Monday, Tuesday, and Wednesday.

3. Find the cell with 106 in it. What does this number stand for?
   The number of people who rode on the Roller Coaster on Wednesday.

UNIT 5 LESSON 9   Complete Tables **147**

Student Activity Book page 147

▶ **Analyze Tables** WHOLE CLASS

Ask a volunteer to explain what the table shows on Student Book page 147. Review the terms *row, column,* and *cell* with the following questions.

● Run your finger across the row for Wednesday. What do the numbers in this row tell us? the number of people who rode rides on Wednesday

● Run your finger down the column for roller coaster. What do the numbers in this column tell us? the number of people who rode the roller coaster each day

● Find the cell that contains the number 84. What does this number tell us? the number of people who rode the Ferris Wheel on Tuesday

● How many people rode bumper cars on Monday? 185

Math Talk Using **Solve and Discuss,** have students look at and answer questions 1–3 at the bottom of the page. Then discuss the answers as a class.

Comparison Questions Challenge students to think of comparison word problems and questions using data from the table on Student Book page 147. Remind students that comparison questions use the words *more, fewer, less,* and so on. Volunteers should give the complete problem, not just the question. You may need to offer an example.

● On Tuesday, 459 people rode the roller coaster and 106 people rode the roller coaster on Wednesday. How many *more* people rode the roller coaster on Tuesday than on Wednesday?

Choose several students to suggest different word problems. Discuss whether each suggestion is indeed a comparison problem. Then have each student who suggested a word problem discuss how they would solve it. It is not necessary to have students find the solution.

Now ask students to think of some Put Together word problems. Again, allow several students to share their word problems and explain how they would solve them. Here are two examples:

● On Monday, 237 people rode the Ferris Wheel and 185 people rode bumper cars. How many people rode the Ferris Wheel and the bumper cars in all on Monday?

● On Tuesday, 459 people rode the roller coaster and 106 people rode the roller coaster on Wednesday. How many people rode the roller coaster on Tuesday and Wednesday combined?

The Learning Classroom

Building Concepts To refresh students' memory of comparison and Put Together word problems, make two lists of "clue words" on the board, one for each type of word problem. As students volunteer comparison and Put Together problems, add terms they use to these lists, such as *more, in all, fewer,* and *less.* Leave the lists displayed for students to reference throughout the lesson.

① Teaching the Lesson (continued)

Activity 2

Complete Tables

 30 MINUTES

Goal: Complete tables and ask questions about the data.

Materials: Student Activity Book or Hardcover Book p. 148 and Activity Workbook p. 52

 NCTM Standards:
Numbers and Operations
Data Analysis and Probability
Problem Solving
Communication

Teaching Note

Watch For! Since the last column in many tables is a *Total* column, students may begin to automatically add to find values for *every* last column. Remind students to pay close attention to every row and column label. Emphasize that these labels are often hints for how to fill in empty cells. For example, in the first table in Student Book page 148, the word *Left* in the last column's label *Loaves Left* points to the need for subtraction, not addition.

The Learning Classroom

Building Concepts Whole-class practice allows less advanced students to benefit from the knowledge of more advanced students without having to ask for help directly. It also provides the teacher with a quick and easy means of assessing the progress of the class as a whole.

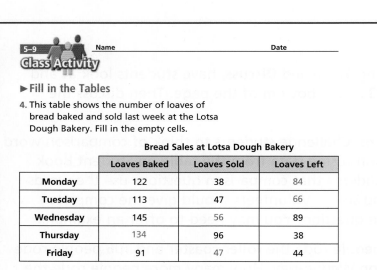

5–9
Class Activity

Name _____ Date _____

▶ **Fill in the Tables**

4. This table shows the number of loaves of bread baked and sold last week at the Lotsa Dough Bakery. Fill in the empty cells.

Bread Sales at Lotsa Dough Bakery

	Loaves Baked	Loaves Sold	Loaves Left
Monday	122	38	84
Tuesday	113	47	66
Wednesday	145	56	89
Thursday	134	96	38
Friday	91	47	44

5. This table shows the number of CDs and videotapes sold at the Sound Out Music Store last week. Fill in the empty cells.

Sound Out Music Sales

	CDs	Videotapes	Total
Monday	62	19	81
Tuesday	73	32	105
Wednesday	88	45	133
Thursday	94	26	120
Friday	155	68	223
Saturday	228	66	294

148 UNIT 5 LESSON 9   Complete Tables

Student Activity Book page 148

▶ Fill in the Tables WHOLE CLASS

Have a student explain what the *Lotsa Dough Bakery* table on Student Book page 148 shows. Make sure students understand how the columns are related: for each day, the number in the first column shows how many loaves were baked, the number in the second column shows how many of those loaves were sold, and the number in the third column shows how many of those loaves were left (that is, how many were *not* sold).

Explain to students that this table has some empty cells. Have students suggest ways to figure out how to fill them in.

● Let's start with the empty cell in the top row. What information should this cell show? the number of loaves left over on Monday

- Can anyone make up a word problem we could use to find the missing number? The bakery made 122 loaves of bread on Monday. They sold 38 of the loaves. How many loaves were left?

Give students time to find the answer, 84, and then have a volunteer show the solution on the board.

Have students work independently to fill in the rest of the table. Students do not need to write the word problems, but they should think carefully about the information they know and the unknown numbers they need to find. After most of the class has finished, choose students to share their answers and explain how they found them. (Students should just describe their solution methods; they do not need to explain every step of their computations.)

Next, have a student explain what the *Sound Out Music Sales* data table shows. Make sure students understand that the Total column shows the total number of CDs and videotapes sold each day. Have students work independently to fill in the empty cells, and then select students to share and explain their answers.

▶ Compare Data INDIVIDUALS

Have students use the completed tables on Student Book page 148 to write two comparison questions using the words *more* or *less*. Here are a few examples of students' questions:

- How many more loaves were baked on Wednesday than on Monday?

- On Tuesday, how many more loaves were baked than were sold?

- How many fewer loaves were left on Thursday than on Friday?

- How many fewer loaves were sold on Tuesday than on Thursday?

- How many more CDs were sold on Saturday than on Monday?

- How many fewer CDs and videotapes were sold on Thursday than on Friday?

- How many fewer videotapes than CDs were sold on Friday?

Select students to read aloud their questions and explain how to find the answers. They do not need to find the solution, unless you feel they need the practice.

 Ongoing Assessment

Check students' understanding of how to locate specific information in tables.

▶ How can you find how much more there is of one thing than another using a table?

▶ How can you find the total of all the items listed in one row?

Problem Solving Strategy: Logic Problems

Goal: Use inductive and deductive reasoning to solve problems.

Materials: Student Activity Book or Hardcover Book pp. 149–150 and Activity Workbook pp. 53–54, four different colored crayons or colored pencils

✓ **NCTM Standards:**
Number and Operations
Data Analysis and Probability
Problem Solving

Teaching Note

Math Background Reasoning by deduction involves rule-based learning, where a rule directs the conclusions. Reasoning by induction, on the other hand, involves recognizing different patterns or parts of rules, and then coming up with a probable rule. Deduction is very important when you have all the rules in hand, but inductive reasoning may be a stronger tool when the rules are incomplete, a completely different approach is desired, or existing information is misleading or contradictory.

▶ Use Deductive Reasoning WHOLE CLASS

Explain that a table can also be used to organize what you know and that you can then use logical reasoning to complete it. Read aloud problem 1 on Student Book page 149. Then draw the table on the board and fill in the table with either *yes* or *no* using the information in the problem.

	Red	Blue	Green	Yellow
Jan	no		no	
Bev	no		no	no
Luis	no			no
Alex	yes	no	no	no

When a *yes* is entered, fill in the rest of that row and the column with *no*. When there is just one empty cell left in a row or a column with all *no*, fill in *yes*.

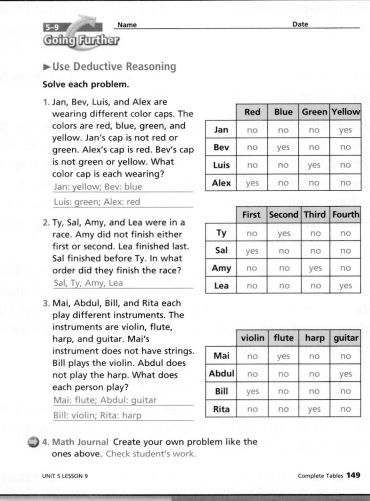

Student Activity Book page 149

Where do you see one empty cell in a row or column? column for green and yellow

Write *yes* in those cells. Then continue in this manner until all cells are filled and the problem is solved.

	Red	Blue	Green	Yellow
Jan	no	no	no	yes
Bev	no	yes	no	no
Luis	no	no	yes	no
Alex	yes	no	no	no

Alex has a red cap, Bev has a blue cap, Luis has a green cap, and Jan has a yellow cap.

Have students complete problems 2–4. Have volunteers demonstrate how they solved the problems and present the ones they wrote in exercise 4.

▶ Use Inductive Reasoning

Explain to students that they will continue to use logical reasoning skills on Student Book page 150, but these types of problems will be different.

In these problems you are not given a pattern, a rule, or generalization. Instead, you will have to look for patterns to make generalizations.

Share this scenario with students for an example of inductive reasoning.

> Sanjay draws connecting cubes out of a bag. Every cube that he draws out of the bag is red. Sanjay then says, "All connecting cubes are red."

● Do you think Sanjay is correct? Possible answer: No, because connecting cubes are *only* red in this situation. There are other colors of connecting cubes that could have been in the bag at another time.

Explain to students that Sanjay observed a pattern and made a generalization from the pattern. Sometimes, however, the conclusion may need further investigation to prove it's always true.

Direct students to Student Book page 150. Use the drawings of the squares to review what a *line of symmetry* is.

● What type of figures do the line segments that are part of the lines of symmetry form? triangles

Extend the line segment in the first square with arrows if needed so students can see the lines of symmetry that the line segments are a part of.

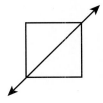

● Look at the first square. How many line segments that are part of a line of symmetry are there? 1

● How many triangles are there? 2

● Look at the second square. How many line segments? 2

● How many triangles? 4

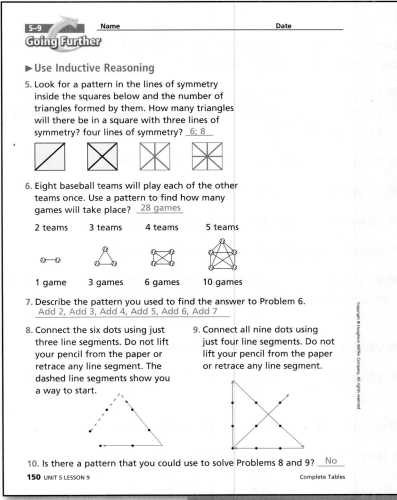

Student Activity Book page 150

Draw a table with this information to help students see the pattern.

Number of Lines of Symmetry	Number of Triangles
1	2
2	4
3	
4	

● The next square will have 3 lines of symmetry. How many triangles do you predict it will have? 6

● What pattern do you see? Possible answer: When a line of symmetry is added the number of triangles doubles from the time before.

Have students check their predictions by drawing the next figures and then have them answer problem 5.

Direct students' attention to Problem 6. Have a volunteer read the problem.

● What do the line segments between the baseballs represent? The number of games that will be played?

● How many games will be played with 2 teams? 1

● How many games will be played with 3 teams? 3

● How many games will be played with 4 teams? 6

● How many games will be played with 5 teams? 10

● What are three strategies you could use to find how many games there would be with 8 teams? Possible answers: Find a pattern or draw a picture.

● Which might be easier? Finding a pattern.

● What pattern do you see? Add 2, then 3, then 4 to the number of games.

Show the pattern on the board or overhead.

1 game   3 games   6 games   10 games

     + 2   + 3   + 4

What will you add to find the number of games for 6 teams? 5

How many games are needed for 6 teams? 15

Have students use the pattern to complete Problems 6 and 7.

Next have students look at problem 8 and have a volunteer read the directions. Explain that they'll need to use reasoning skills in order to solve the problem.

Show them how to use different colors to keep track of the number of edges or line segments they use.

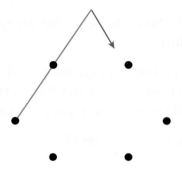

Allow students time to try to draw the three segments on their own. Then use Solve and Discuss to have volunteers share their solution methods.

What do you notice that you have to do to connect the dots using only 3 segments? Move outside the direct routes of the dots.

Do you think you will have to do this in Problem 9? Answers will vary.

Have volunteers share their solution methods and discuss that you can draw a conclusion that you may have to go outside the direct path of the dots to do others of this type, but that there is no rule, pattern, or generalization.

Intervention — Activity Card 5-9

Compare or Put Together
Activity Card 5-9 ●

Work: In pairs

Use:
- TRB M42
  (Inch grid paper)

Decide:
Who will be Student 1 and who will be Student 2 for the first round.

1. Copy the table below on grid paper.

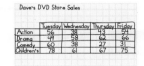

Dave's DVD Store Sales

	Tuesday	Wednesday	Thursday	Friday
Action	56	38	43	54
Drama	49	58	62	66
Comedy	60	38	27	31
Children's	78	61	67	75

2. **Student 1:** Choose two numbers in the table, circle them, and write a word problem about the numbers.

3. **Student 2:** Tell whether the problem that your partner wrote can be solved by comparing the two numbers or putting them together.

4. Switch roles and repeat the activity three more times.

Unit 5, Lesson 9   Copyright © Houghton Mifflin Company

Activity Note Encourage students to write both addition problems and subtraction problems.

 Math Writing Prompt

Clue Words What words are clues that tell you to use addition to solve a word problem using data in a table? What words are clues that tell you to use subtraction?

 **Software Support**

Warm Up 7.15

On Level — Activity Card 5-9

What's Missing?
Activity Card 5-9 ▲

Work: In small groups

Use:
- TRB M42
  (Inch grid paper)

1. Use grid paper to copy the table shown below.

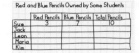

Red and Blue Pencils Owned by Some Students

	Red Pencils	Blue Pencils	Total Pencils
Sue	3	7	10
Jack			
Leon			
Maria			
Kim			

2. Take turns. Write a word problem for each person listed in the table. For example, the word problem for Sue could be the following:
   Sue has 10 pencils. Three of them are red. How many blue pencils does she have?

3. **Think** What data would you put into the first row of the table if you used the problem above? 3, 7, 10

4. Write more word problems to complete the table.

Unit 5, Lesson 9   Copyright © Houghton Mifflin Company

Activity Note Students can use comparisons with data already entered into the table to make their problems more challenging. For example: Jack has 4 more red pencils than Sue and 10 pencils altogether.

 Math Writing Prompt

Justify When would you use exact numbers and when would you use rounded numbers to create a data table? Give an example of each.

 Software Support

<patch 131>

Country Countdown: White Water Graphing, Level C

Challenge — Activity Card 5-9

Take a Survey
Activity Card 5-9 ■

Work: In pairs

Use:
- TRB M42
  (Inch grid paper)

1. Take a survey. Record the hair color of boys and girls in your class. Then use grid paper to draw a table and record the results of your survey as shown below.

Red	Black	Blonde	Brown
boys I	boys III	boys III	boys IIII
girls II	girls IIII	girls IIII	girls III

Hair Color of Students

	Red	Black	Blonde	Brown	Total
Girls	2	5	4	3	14
Boys	1	3	3	4	11
Total	3	8	7	7	25

2. Work together to find the total for each row and each column in your table.

3. Take turns writing one addition word problem and one subtraction word problem, using data in the table. Exchange problems and solve.

Unit 5, Lesson 9   Copyright © Houghton Mifflin Company

Activity Note Have students check their totals by adding both ways and check that the total matches the number of students in their class.

 Math Writing Prompt

Investigate Math Is it easier to create word problems using a list of data or data organized in a table? Explain your reasoning.

 **Software Support**

Course II: Module 2: Unit 1: Sums Less Than 100

③ Homework and Spiral Review

Homework **Goal:** Additional Practice

✔ Include students' completed Homework page as part of their portfolios.

Homework

Name _____ Date _____

1. This table shows how many calendars of each type the third graders ordered from the calendar publisher, the number they sold, and the number they have left. Fill in the empty cells.

Third Grade Calendar Sales

	Number Ordered	Number Sold	Number Left
Playful Puppies	475	387	88
Adorable Kittens	300	123	177
Lovable Lambs	550	471	79

2. Make up a Comparison question about the table that uses the word *more*, and find the answer.
Answers will vary.
_____
_____

3. This table shows the number of students at Lakeside Elementary who participate in various activities. Fill in the empty cells.

Participation in Activities

	Boys	Girls	Total
Band or Chorus	36	43	79
Sports	93	78	171
After-School Clubs	47	39	86

4. Make up a Comparison question about the table that uses the word *fewer*, and write the answer.
Answers will vary.
_____
_____

UNIT 5 LESSON 9   Complete Tables **87**

Homework and Remembering page 87

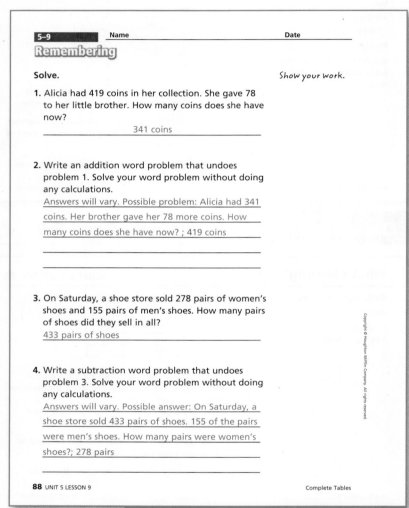

Remembering **Goal:** Spiral Review

This Remembering page would be appropriate anytime after today's lesson.

Remembering

Name _____ Date _____

Solve.   *Show your work.*

1. Alicia had 419 coins in her collection. She gave 78 to her little brother. How many coins does she have now?
_____341 coins_____

2. Write an addition word problem that undoes problem 1. Solve your word problem without doing any calculations.
Answers will vary. Possible problem: Alicia had 341 coins. Her brother gave her 78 more coins. How many coins does she have now? ; 419 coins
_____
_____

3. On Saturday, a shoe store sold 278 pairs of women's shoes and 155 pairs of men's shoes. How many pairs of shoes did they sell in all?
433 pairs of shoes

4. Write a subtraction word problem that undoes problem 3. Solve your word problem without doing any calculations.
Answers will vary. Possible answer: On Saturday, a shoe store sold 433 pairs of shoes. 155 of the pairs were men's shoes. How many pairs were women's shoes?; 278 pairs
_____

88 UNIT 5 LESSON 9   Complete Tables

Homework and Remembering page 88

Home or School Activity

Technology Connection

Computer Art Have students use a computer software program to create tables with graphics. Students can use data from a completed table on a Student Activity Book page or they can create a table with their own data.

	CDs	Videotapes	Total
Monday	62	19	81
Tuesday	73	32	105
Wednesday	88	45	133

More Practice with Tables

REAL WORLD Problem Solving

Lesson Objectives

- Create a simple table.
- Practice completing tables in which there is a mathematical relationship between the columns.

Vocabulary

column	survey
row	tally
cell	data
table	

The Day at a Glance

Today's Goals	Materials	
1 Teaching the Lesson 　**A1:** Gather data and summarize it in a table. 　**A2:** Create word problems based on tables and practice completing tables. **2 Going Further** 　▶ Differentiated Instruction **3 Homework and Spiral Review**	**Lesson Activities** Student Activity Book pp. 151–152 or Student Hardcover Book pp. 151–152 and Activity Workbook pp. 55–56 (includes tables) Homework and Remembering pp. 89–90 Quick Quiz 3 (Assessment Guide) Real or play money Calculators (optional)	**Going Further** Activity Cards 5-10 Blocks (red and blue) Paper bag MathBoard materials Two-color counters Math Journals 123 **Use Math Talk today!**

Keeping Skills Sharp

Quick Practice ⏱ 5 MINUTES	Daily Routines	
Goal: Round whole numbers to the nearest ten or hundred. **Rounding Practice** Have the **Student Leader** write 2,232, 111, 428, 1,220, 278, and 360 on the board and tell the class to round to the nearest ten or hundred. The leader gives a signal and the class says the rounded number. The length of the activity is recorded. Repeat the activity several times to improve the time.	**Homework Review** Ask students to place their homework at the corner of their desks. As you circulate during Quick Practice, check that students completed the assignment, and see whether any problems caused difficulty for many students.	**Nonroutine Problem** Ricardo has 6 coins with a total value of $0.76. What are the six coins that Ricardo has? Explain how you found the answer. 2 quarters, 2 dimes, 1 nickel, and 1 penny; Possible explanation: I kept adding coins to find the group that had 6 coins and a total of $0.76.

Teaching the Lesson

Collect Data and Make a Table

 20 MINUTES

Goal: Gather data and summarize it in a table.

Materials: Real or play money (1 penny), Student Activity Book or Hardcover Book p. 151 and Activity Workbook p. 55

✔ **NCTM Standards:**
Algebra
Data Analysis and Probability
Communication
Connections
Representation

Teaching Note

Language and Vocabulary Use the words *data, survey,* and *tally* in this activity. Explain that one way to collect data, or information, is to take a survey. When you take a survey, you ask people questions and record their answers using tally marks.

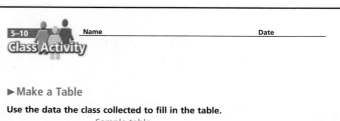

►Make a Table

Use the data the class collected to fill in the table.

Sample table
Sanjay and Gwen's Coin Tosses

	Heads	Tails
Sanjay	9	11
Gwen	12	8

►Use a Table

1. Write a comparison question using data from the table above and the word *more*. Answer your question.

   Possible question: How many more times did Gwen's tosses land on heads than Sanjay's?; 3

2. Write a comparison question using data from the table above and the word *fewer*. Answer your question.

   Possible question: How many fewer times did Gwen's tosses land on tails than Sanjay's?; 3

3. Write a question using data from the table and the word *altogether*. Answer your question.

   Possible question: How many times did Sanjay's and Gwen's tosses land on heads altogether?; 21

UNIT 5 LESSON 10   More Practice With Tables **151**

Student Activity Book page 151

►Coin Toss ⬚WHOLE CLASS⬚

Have a volunteer come to the front of the room and write his or her name on the board. Have the student toss a coin 20 times. Record the result of each toss, H or T, after the student's name. Repeat with another volunteer. Your results should look something like this:

Sanjay: T T H T H T T H H T H H H T H H T
        H T T

Gwen: T H T H H H H T T T H H T T H T H
        H H H

▶ Make a Table   WHOLE CLASS

Now have students look at the blank table on Student Book page 151. Explain that they will fill in the table with the number of heads and tails each student tossed.

Remind students that when they make a table, they should always give it a title. Have students suggest titles for the table. Possible responses: Sanjay and Gwen's Coin Tosses. Have them write the title above the table and label the columns *Heads* and *Tails.*

Have students fill in the table as you provide help to those who need it. Once students are finished with the table, review the results and answer any questions they may have. A sample table is provided.

Sanjay and Gwen's Coin Tosses

	Heads	Tails
Sanjay	9	11
Gwen	12	8

▶ Use a Table   WHOLE CLASS

123 **Math Talk** In order to get students to look closely at their completed tables, ask a few questions such as:

● Who tossed the greatest number of heads? Gwen

● Who tossed the least number of tails? Gwen

Challenge them to suggest addition and subtraction questions based on the table. Have student volunteers share their questions. Some possible questions they might ask are:

● How many fewer times did Sanjay's tosses land on heads than Gwen's tosses? 3

● How many more times did Sanjay's tosses land on tails? 3

● What are the total number of heads tossed by Sanjay and Gwen together? 21

● What are the total number of tails tossed by Sanjay and Gwen? 19

● How do the totals for heads and the total for tails compare? There are more heads than tails.

Then have students complete exercises 1–3.

1 Teaching the Lesson (continued)

Activity 2

More Practice Completing Tables

 25 MINUTES

Goal: Create word problems based on tables and practice completing tables.

Materials: Student Activity Book or Hardcover Book p. 152 and Activity Workbook p. 56, calculators (optional)

✔ **NCTM Standards:**
Number and Operations
Algebra
Data Analysis and Probability
Problem Solving
Reasoning and Proof
Communication
Connections
Representation

 Alternate Approach

Calculators Some students might want to check their answers with a calculator.

 Quick Quiz

See Assessment Guide for Unit 5, Quick Quiz 3.

 Ongoing Assessment

To check that students understand how to use information in tables, ask questions such as:

► How do the column labels help you to fill in missing information in a table?

► If there is an empty cell in a row, how can you find the number that goes there?

5-10 Class Activity

Name _____ Date _____

► Analyze Data

Fill in the missing information in the tables and answer the questions.

This table shows the number of souvenirs the Wildcats baseball team sold last weekend.

Souvenir Sales for Wildcats Baseball Team

	White	Red	Total
Caps	134	77	211
T-shirts	64	109	173
Pennants	59	92	151

4. Which item above had the most total sales? ___caps___

5. Which color T-shirt had the most sales? ___red___

This table shows the number of items the Green Thumb Garden Shop sold at their Spring sale.

Spring Sale at Green Thumb Garden Shop

	Number Before the Sale	Number Sold	Number Left
Spades	232	185	47
Straw Hats	144	68	76
Small Pots	412	342	70
Big Pots	325	227	98

6. Which item had the most sales? ___small pots___

7. Which item has the least number left? ___spades___

152 UNIT 5 LESSON 10   More Practice With Tables

Student Activity Book page 152

► Analyze Data WHOLE CLASS

Have a volunteer explain what the first table on Student Book page 152 shows. Ask what word problem students could solve to find the number that belongs in the empty cell in the first row. Possible response: The team sold 134 white caps and some red caps. They sold 211 caps altogether. How many red caps did they sell?

Give students a minute to solve the problem, and then choose someone to present the solution.

Have students work independently to complete exercises 4–7. Remind them they do not have to write word problems, but they should think carefully about what information they know. Help students who are struggling, or pair struggling students with Helping Partners.

Discuss the results. For each row, have a student state a related word problem and give the answer.

②Going Further

Differentiated Instruction

Intervention — Activity Card 5-10

Picking Blue or Red — Activity Card 5-10 ●

Work: In small groups

Use:
- 2 blue blocks
- 3 red blocks
- paper bag
- MathBoard materials

1. Place the five blocks in the bag.
2. Take turns choosing a block from the bag without looking. Write B for a blue block or R for a red block on the MathBoard beside your name. Then return the block to the bag.
3. Continue taking turns to repeat the activity 20 times.
4. Make a table like the one below with your data.

	Blue	Red

5. **Analyze** Was a red block picked more times than a blue block? Why do you think this happened?

Unit 5, Lesson 10 — Copyright © Houghton Mifflin Company

Activity Note Students should write the name of each person in their group in the leftmost column of the table and use the tally of Bs and Rs for each person's choices to complete the table.

 Math Writing Prompt

Explain Your Thinking Harry tossed a coin fifty times. He made a table to record his results. He wrote 25 under *heads*. What should he write under *tails?* Explain.

 **Software Support**

Warm Up 51.01

On Level — Activity Card 5-10

Cover It! — Activity Card 5-10 ▲

Work: In pairs

Use:
- 2 counters

1. **On Your Own** Make a table showing data that you might have collected in a school survey. Use the example below as a model. Be sure that the last column shows a total for each row.

Favorite Sandwiches of 3rd Graders at Peabody Elementary

	Girls	Boys	Total
Peanut Butter	●	57	65
Ham and Cheese	48	18	●
Tuna	10	3	13

2. Take turns. Cover any two numbers on your table with counters. Then ask your partner to find the missing numbers. Remove the counters to check the answers.

Unit 5, Lesson 10 — Copyright © Houghton Mifflin Company

Activity Note Remind students that when they choose the data for their tables, the totals must be calculated from the other numbers they have chosen.

 Math Writing Prompt

Critical Thinking Sanjay and Gwen each toss a penny 40 times. Then they create a data table showing their results. Is it likely that the same number will appear in every cell? Explain.

 Software Support

Country Countdown: White Water Graphing, Level C

Challenge — Activity Card 5-10

Find the Missing Numbers — Activity Card 5-10 ■

Work: In pairs

1. Make two copies of the table.
2. **Work Together** Find each missing number and record it in the first table. Write the letters A to F in the second table to show the order in which you found the numbers.

Favorite Subjects at Pine Avenue Elementary School

	3rd Graders	4th Graders	Total
Gym	53	44	97
Music	45	39	84
Art	25	44	69
Total Students in Each Grade	123	127	250

3. **Analyze** How did you choose which cell to fill first? Could you have chosen another cell? Is there any cell that you could not have filled first? 4th grade art or music could not have been filled first.

Unit 5, Lesson 10 — Copyright © Houghton Mifflin Company

Activity Note There are several ways to begin calculating the missing numbers. However, the column for 4th Graders cannot be completed until the column for 3rd Graders is complete.

 Math Writing Prompt

Predict If you put 2 red blocks and 1 blue block in a bag, and pick a block without looking 30 times, predict what your data table will look like. Explain.

DESTINATION Math® **Software Support**

Course II: Module 2: Unit 1: Sums Less Than 100

More Practice with Tables **367**

③ Homework and Spiral Review

5–10 Homework **Goal:** Additional Practice

This Homework page provides students with extra practice in completing tables.

5–10 Remembering **Goal:** Spiral Review

This Remembering page would be appropriate anytime after today's lesson.

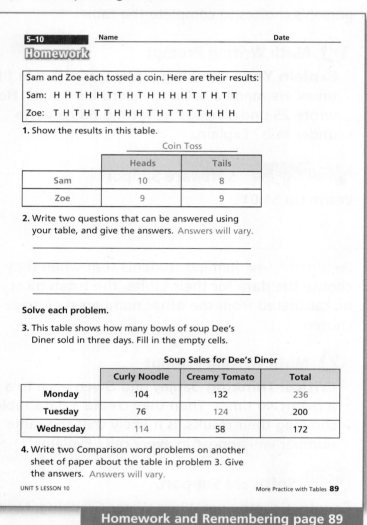

5–10 Homework Name _____ Date _____

Sam and Zoe each tossed a coin. Here are their results:

Sam: H H T H H T T H T H H H H H T T H T T

Zoe: T H T H T T H H H T H T T T T H H H

1. Show the results in this table.

Coin Toss

	Heads	Tails
Sam	10	8
Zoe	9	9

2. Write two questions that can be answered using your table, and give the answers. Answers will vary.

_____

_____

_____

Solve each problem.

3. This table shows how many bowls of soup Dee's Diner sold in three days. Fill in the empty cells.

Soup Sales for Dee's Diner

	Curly Noodle	Creamy Tomato	Total
Monday	104	132	236
Tuesday	76	124	200
Wednesday	114	58	172

4. Write two Comparison word problems on another sheet of paper about the table in problem 3. Give the answers. Answers will vary.

UNIT 5 LESSON 10 • More Practice with Tables **89**

5–10 Remembering Name _____ Date _____

Solve each problem. *Show your work.*

1. Lauren's dog gained 7 pounds since his last visit to the vet. He weighs 54 pounds now. How much did he weigh on his last visit to the vet?
___47 pounds___

2. Carlos's mom measures his height on every birthday. On his seventh birthday, he was 50 inches tall. This is 9 inches taller than he was on his fourth birthday. How tall was Carlos on his fourth birthday?
___41 inches___

3. Toshi lives 229 miles from her grandmother and 405 miles from her cousin Kioko. How much farther does Toshi live from her cousin than from her grandmother?
___176 miles___

Draw each shape if you can. If it is impossible to draw the shape, explain why it is impossible.

4. a quadrilateral that is not a rectangle
___Answers will vary.___

Possible answer for exercise 4.

5. a square that is not a parallelogram
Possible explanation: Impossible because both pairs of opposite sides of a square are parallel, so it must be a parallelogram.

6. a parallelogram that is not a rectangle
___Answers will vary.___

Possible answer for exercise 6.

90 UNIT 5 LESSON 10 • More Practice with Tables

Homework and Remembering page 89

Homework and Remembering page 90

Home or School Activity

Science Connection

Your Town's Weather Remind students that tables provide us with useful information without using a lot of words. Tell students that tables are often used to summarize weather data. Have students use a newspaper or the Internet to find weather data they can display in a table.

Temperatures at Noon

	Reedvale	Jefferson Park
Monday	67°F	68°F
Tuesday	63°F	59°F

Word Problems with Extra or Hidden Information

REAL WORLD **Problem Solving**

Lesson Objective

- Represent and solve word problems with extra or hidden information.

The Day at a Glance

Today's Goals	Materials	

1 Teaching the Lesson
A1: Solve word problems with extra information.
A2: Recognize and solve word problems with hidden information.
	Lesson Activities
	Student Activity Book pp. 153–154
	  or Student Hardcover Book
	  pp. 153–154
	Homework and Remembering
	  pp. 91–92
	Highlighters
		Going Further
		Activity Cards 5-11
		Math Journals

2 Going Further ▶ Differentiated Instruction		
3 Homework and Spiral Review		

123 *Use* **Math Talk** *today!*

Keeping Skills Sharp

Quick Practice   ⏱ 5 MINUTES

Goal: Round whole numbers to the nearest ten or hundred.

Rounding Practice The **Student Leader** writes the six numbers below on the board. The leader points to the numbers one at a time and says either, "Round to the nearest ten," or, "Round to the nearest hundred." When the leader gives a signal, students respond with the rounded number.

$$209 \quad 853 \quad 1,325 \quad 487 \quad 662 \quad 744$$

Leader (pointing to 209): Round to the nearest ten.

Class: 210

Daily Routines

Homework Review Ask students to share the word problems they wrote for homework. Have the class ask clarifying questions about each problem. If necessary, model asking questions.

Mental Math Find each sum using mental math.

1. 5,000 + 3,500 8,500

2. 4,500 + 2,000 6,500

3. 2,200 + 1,500 3,700

Teaching the Lesson

Recognize Extra Information in Word Problems

 25 MINUTES

Goal: Solve word problems with extra information.

Materials: Student Activity Book or Hardcover Book p. 153, highlighters

✔ **NCTM Standards:**
Number and Operations
Problem Solving
Communication
Representation

Teaching Note

What to Expect from Students
Many students will prefer to use the cross-out method when dealing with word problems. Be sure to monitor this closely so that students do not become confused and start crossing out information they need to solve the problem.

English Language Learners

Help children find extra information. Write Class Activity problem 1 on the board. Model how to cross out the extra information.

• **Beginning** Read the question aloud. Circle *math problems*. Point to *7 reading questions*. Say: **This is extra information.**
• **Intermediate** Ask: **Is the question about math problems or reading questions?** math problems
• **Advanced** Ask: **What is the question about?** math problems **What information is extra?** reading problems

---

| 5–11 Class Activity | Name _____ Date _____ |

▶ Solve Problems with Extra Information

Read each problem. Cross out any extra information. Then solve.

1. Emma solved 9 math problems ~~and answered 7 reading questions~~. Her sister solved 8 math problems. How many math problems did they solve in all?

   _____17 math problems_____

2. Mark had 6 shirts ~~and 5 pairs of pants~~. Today his aunt gave him 4 more shirts ~~and another pair of pants~~. How many shirts does he have now?

   _____10 shirts_____

3. A parking lot had 179 cars ~~and 95 trucks~~. Then 85 cars left the lot. How many cars are in the parking lot now?

   _____94 cars_____

4. Laura had some roses in a vase. From her garden, she picked 7 more roses ~~and 6 daisies~~. Now she has 12 roses in all. How many roses did she have at first?

   _____5 roses_____

5. Nikko had 245 pennies ~~and 123 nickels~~. His brother gave him 89 more pennies ~~and 25 more nickels~~. How many pennies does Nikko have now?

   _____334 pennies_____

UNIT 5 LESSON 11   Word Problems with Extra or Hidden Information **153**

Student Activity Book page 153

▶ Solve Problems with Extra Information WHOLE CLASS

Using **Solve and Discuss**, have students solve problem 1 on Student Book page 153. Remember to select students who used different strategies to present their solutions.

● What is difficult about this word problem? Some of the numbers given are not needed to solve the problem.

● How can we figure out which numbers we need and which we don't? Possible response: We can look at what the question is asking and then cross out the information we don't need.

Note Taking If students do not suggest taking notes as a problem-solving strategy, introduce it now. Demonstrate note taking as a quick way to keep track of information in a word problem.

 Math Talk Explain that using abbreviations when taking notes is a way to save time.

● **What information is given first in the problem?** Emma solved 9 math problems. I'll write Emma's name, and then I'll write 9M. I wrote *M* instead of *math problems* to save time.

Emma   9M

● **What information is given next?** She answered 7 reading questions. **What should we add to our notes?** We could add 7R next to Emma's name.

Emma   9M   7R

● **What other information is given?** Her sister solved 8 math problems. **What should we add to our notes now?** We could write down *sister* with 8M next to it.

Emma   9M   7R
Sister   8M

● **What is the question asking us about?** math problems **Do we need the information about reading questions?** no **We can cross that information out.**

Emma   9M   7R̶
Sister   8M

● **What else does the question ask?** How many math problems did they solve in all. **Have a student write the equation on the board.**

$9 + 8 = \boxed{}$

● **What is the total?** 17 math problems

Allow students to share their thoughts on taking notes as a problem-solving strategy. Some may find taking notes helpful; others may not need to take any notes.

Have students solve problems 2–5 independently and then discuss the results in **Student Pairs.**

Alternate Approach

Highlight It Have students read the problem and highlight the information that they need to solve the problem with a highlighter. Then have them read the problem again reading only the highlighted information. Ask them if the problem still makes sense and can be solved without the other information.

 Ongoing Assessment

To be sure that students understand extra information problems, ask questions such as:

► Why is it important to read a word problem carefully?

► How do you decide what information is important?

► How do you know when information is extra?

Teaching the Lesson (continued)

Recognize Hidden Information in Word Problems

25 MINUTES

Goal: Recognize and solve word problems with hidden information.

Materials: Student Activity Book or Hardcover Book p. 154

5–11
Class Activity
Name _____ Date _____

▶ **Solve Problems with Hidden Information**

Read each problem. Circle the hidden information. Then solve.

6. Samuel had 16 horseshoes in the shed yesterday. Today he put a new set of horseshoes on his horse Betsy. How many horseshoes are left in the shed?

   _____12 horseshoes_____

7. Maya is going on a vacation with her family for a week and 3 days. How many days will she be on vacation?

   _____10 days_____

8. Julie bought a dozen eggs at the market. She gave 3 of them to Serge. How many eggs does Julie have left?

   _____9 eggs_____

9. Lisa had 3 quarters and 2 dimes. Then she found 3 nickels and 12 pennies. How many cents does she have now?

   _____122 cents_____

10. Marissa is moving away. She is going to move back in a year and 21 days. How many days will she be gone?

   _____386 days_____

154 UNIT 5 LESSON 11   Word Problems with Extra or Hidden Information

Student Activity Book page 154

Information That Is Hidden in Problems 7–10

Problem 7: There are 7 days in a week.

Problem 8: There are 12 eggs in a dozen.

Problem 9: There are 25 cents in a quarter, 10 cents in a dime, 5 cents in a nickel, and 1 cent in a penny.

Problem 10: A year (usually) has 365 days.

▶ Solve Problems with Hidden Information [WHOLE CLASS]

Have students read problem 6 on Student Book page 154 and ask the following questions.

● **What is different about this word problem?** The problem does not give all the numbers we need in order to solve it.

● **Can we still solve this problem?** Yes. **How do you know?** Even though the number is not given, we still know it.

● **How can we figure out the number that is not given in this problem?** We know that horses have 4 feet.

● **How can we solve this problem?** Subtract the number of feet a horse has (4) from the number of horseshoes Samuel has (16) to get the number of horseshoes left (12).

Have students solve problems 7–10. See the side column for hidden information in problems 7–10.

②Going Further

● Intervention   Activity Card 5-11

What Is Extra?   Activity Card 5-11 ●

Work: In pairs

1. **Think** What information is needed to solve the problem below? What information is extra? 4 packs of gum and 10 packs of gum; 2 bags of candy

> Billy has 4 packs of gum and 2 bags of candy. Jennette has 10 packs of gum. How many packs of gum do they have altogether?

2. **On Your Own** Write a word problem that has extra information.

3. **Exchange** word problems with your partner to solve. Then discuss your answers and strategies.

Unit 5, Lesson 11   Copyright © Houghton Mifflin Company

Activity Note If students have difficulty writing word problems with extra information, tell them to write a problem with the necessary information and then add one piece of extra information.

 Math Writing Prompt

Problem Solving Strategy When you have extra information in a word problem, what is a strategy that you can use to help you solve the problem? Explain your thinking.

 **Software Support**

Warm Up 10.04

▲ On Level   Activity Card 5-11

What Is Extra or Hidden?   Activity Card 5-11 ▲

Work: In small groups

1. **Look** at the problems below. Which one has too much information? Which one has hidden information? Problem 1; Problem 2

>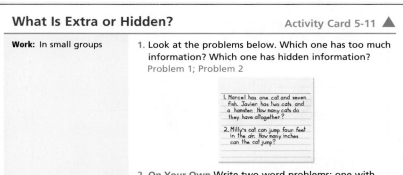
> 1. Marcel has one cat and seven fish. Javier has two cats and a hamster. How many cats do they have altogether?
> 2. Milly's cat can jump four feet in the air. How many inches can the cat jump?

2. **On Your Own** Write two word problems: one with one piece of extra information and the other with one piece of hidden information.

3. **Exchange** problems with the person to your right and solve. Exchange again to check.

Unit 5, Lesson 11   Copyright © Houghton Mifflin Company

Activity Note After students have exchanged and solved their problems, have them discuss any answers that are not correct.

 Math Writing Prompt

You Decide Which kind of word problem is easier for you to solve: one with extra information or one with hidden information? Explain.

 Software Support

Numberopolis: Carnival Stories, Level M

■ Challenge   Activity Card 5-11

Double Hidden and Extra Information   Activity Card 5-11 ■

Work: In small groups

1. **Look** at the problems below. Which one has too much information? Which one has hidden information? Problem 1; Problem 2

> 1. Anita has 3 skirts, 6 pairs of pants, and 5 pairs of shorts. Marina has 4 skirts, 8 pairs of pants, and 2 pairs of shorts. How many skirts do the girls have altogether?
> 2. Arthur has 7 quarters and 2 nickels. How many cents does he have altogether?

2. **On Your Own** Write two word problems: one with two pieces of extra information and the other with two pieces of hidden information.

3. **Exchange** problems with the person to your right and solve. Exchange again to check.

Unit 5, Lesson 11   Copyright © Houghton Mifflin Company

Activity Note Students may need to do more than one conversion if the problem has two pieces of hidden information.

 Math Writing Prompt

Real-World Application Give an example of what you might need to solve a problem with hidden information in real life. How might you find the hidden information?

 **Software Support**

Course II: Module 2: Unit 1: Sums Less Than 100

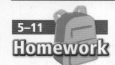

③ Homework and Spiral Review

This Homework page provides students with more practice in solving these types of word problems.

This Remembering page would be appropriate anytime after today's lesson.

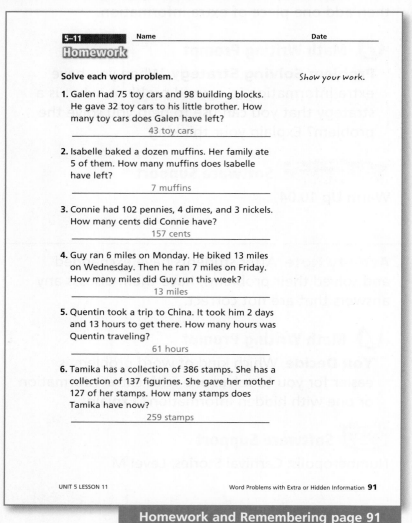

5–11   Name _____ Date _____
Homework

Solve each word problem.   *Show your work.*

1. Galen had 75 toy cars and 98 building blocks. He gave 32 toy cars to his little brother. How many toy cars does Galen have left?
   43 toy cars

2. Isabelle baked a dozen muffins. Her family ate 5 of them. How many muffins does Isabelle have left?
   7 muffins

3. Connie had 102 pennies, 4 dimes, and 3 nickels. How many cents did Connie have?
   157 cents

4. Guy ran 6 miles on Monday. He biked 13 miles on Wednesday. Then he ran 7 miles on Friday. How many miles did Guy run this week?
   13 miles

5. Quentin took a trip to China. It took him 2 days and 13 hours to get there. How many hours was Quentin traveling?
   61 hours

6. Tamika has a collection of 386 stamps. She has a collection of 137 figurines. She gave her mother 127 of her stamps. How many stamps does Tamika have now?
   259 stamps

UNIT 5 LESSON 11   Word Problems with Extra or Hidden Information **91**

Homework and Remembering page 91

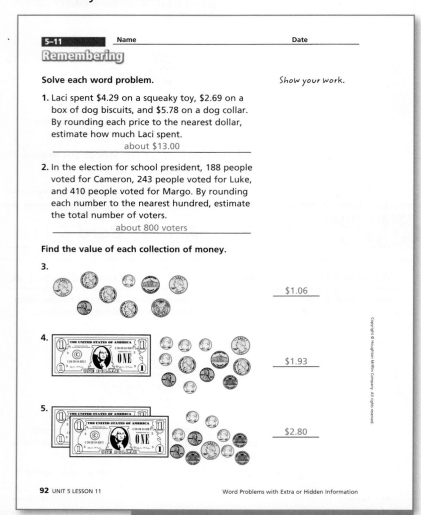

5–11   Name _____ Date _____
Remembering

Solve each word problem.   *Show your work.*

1. Laci spent $4.29 on a squeaky toy, $2.69 on a box of dog biscuits, and $5.78 on a dog collar. By rounding each price to the nearest dollar, estimate how much Laci spent.
   about $13.00

2. In the election for school president, 188 people voted for Cameron, 243 people voted for Luke, and 410 people voted for Margo. By rounding each number to the nearest hundred, estimate the total number of voters.
   about 800 voters

Find the value of each collection of money.

3. $1.06

4. $1.93

5. $2.80

92 UNIT 5 LESSON 11   Word Problems with Extra or Hidden Information

Homework and Remembering page 92

Home or School Activity

 Language Arts Connection

Editing Word Problems Give students a copy of the word problem to the right. It has mistakes in punctuation, capitalization, and spelling. Altogether, there are six errors.

Have students work in pairs to make a list identifying the errors in the word problem. If time allows have students write a problem containing hidden information and a total of six errors in spelling, punctuation, or capitalization.

> Ryan walked 2 blocks; to the library. He borrowed 2 books. Each book weighed 1 Pound. Then he walk 3 blocks two the grocery store. He bought a galon of milk that weighed 3 pounds. Then he walked 5 blocks home? How much weight did he carry from the grocery store to home?

Word Problems with Not Enough Information

Lesson Objectives

● Identify word problems with not enough information to solve and identify the information needed.

● Rewrite word problems with not enough information.

The Day at a Glance

Today's Goals	Materials	

① Teaching the Lesson
A1: Identify information needed to solve word problems.
A2: Rewrite word problems including the needed information.
	Lesson Activities
	Student Activity Book pp. 155–158
	  or Student Hardcover Book
	  pp. 155–158
	Homework and Remembering
	  pp. 93–94
		Going Further
		Activity Cards 5-12
		Homework p. 93
		MathBoard materials
		Math Journals

② Going Further ▶ Differentiated Instruction		
③ Homework and Spiral Review		

123 Use Math Talk today!

Keeping Skills Sharp

Quick Practice 🕐 5 MINUTES

Goal: Count coin values.

Counting Coins The **Student Leader** writes a sequence of quarters (Qs), dimes (Ds), nickels (Ns), and pennies (Ps) on the board, in that order. The leader points to the coins in order as the class counts on to find the total.

Q Q Q D D D D D D N N P

Leader: Count on to find the total amount.

Class: 25¢, 50¢, 75¢, 85¢, 95¢, $1.05, $1.15, $1.25, $1.35, $1.40, $1.45, $1.46

After the first sequence with the class, have the leader assign groups and make one sequence per group. Allow groups to share the total.

Daily Routines

Homework Review If students give incorrect answers, have them explain how they found the answers. This can help you determine whether the error is conceptual or procedural.

Place Value Have students write the number that represents two thousand seven hundred nineteen. Then, have them find the number that is 1,000 more than this number. 2,719; 3,719

Teaching the Lesson

Recognize Word Problems with Not Enough Information

 35 MINUTES

Goal: Identify information needed to solve word problems.

Materials: Student Activity Book or Hardcover Book pp. 155–156

✔ **NCTM Standards:**
Number and Operations
Problem Solving
Communication
Connections

Differentiated Instruction

Extra Help Remind students about note taking from the previous lesson. Have them suggest ways this problem-solving strategy could help them with problems 1, 2, or 3.

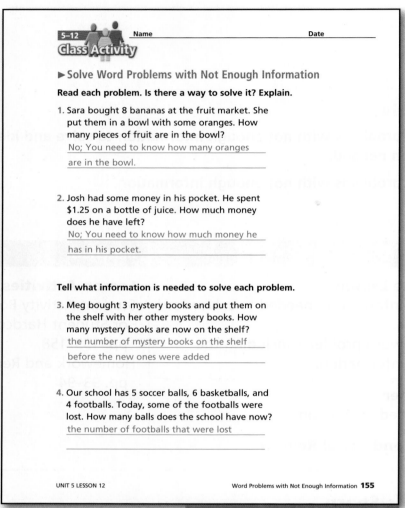

Student Activity Book page 155

▶ Solve Word Problems with Not Enough Information WHOLE CLASS

Allow students a few minutes to try to solve problem 1.

● **What information does this problem give us?** Sara bought 8 bananas and put them in a bowl with oranges.

● **What does the question ask us to find?** the number of pieces of fruit in the bowl

● **What would we need to do to find the answer?** Add the number of bananas and the number of oranges.

● **Do we have enough information to solve the problem?** no **What else do we need to know?** the number of oranges in the bowl

Then have students try to solve problem 2. Discuss the problem together.

- What information does this problem give us? Josh had some money, and he spent $1.25.

- What does the question ask us to find? the amount of money Josh has left

- What would we need to do to find the answer? Subtract the amount he spent from the amount he started with.

- Do we have enough information to solve the problem? no What else do we need to know? the amount Josh started with

Now read problem 3 aloud and have students tell what other information is needed to solve the problem.

 Math Talk in Action

Is there a way to solve problem 3?

Jonelle: I don't think so. I think we need to know how many mystery books Meg had on her shelf to start.

What information could we add to the problem to solve it?

Christopher: We could say that Meg brought 3 mystery books and put them on the shelf with her 11 other mystery books. Then we can find out how many mystery books are on the shelf now.

Very good!

Have students read problem 4 on their own and identify what information is needed to solve it. Then discuss as a class how problem 4 could be rewritten so it can be solved.

Activity continued ▶

Teaching Note

Language and Vocabulary
Problems with not enough information may be particularly difficult for some students because they may think that they have not been able to read well enough to find all of the information. Have these students make up such problems for each other so that they understand that problems can be incomplete. Continue to use your support structures for being sure that students understand the problem before they try to solve it.

English Language Learners
Write Class Activity problem 1 on the board. Read it aloud.

- **Beginning** Circle the question. Say: **We have to add the bananas and oranges.** Ask: **How many bananas are there?** 8 bananas Circle *some oranges*. Say: **We do not know the number of oranges.** Ask: **Can we find the total?** no
- **Intermediate** Ask: **What do we need to add?** bananas and oranges **Do we know how many bananas there are?** yes **Do we know how many oranges?** no **Is there *enough* information?** no
- **Advanced** Say: **We have to find the total ___.** pieces of fruit Ask: **What information do we have?** number of bananas **What is missing?** number of oranges

The Learning Classroom

Helping Community Word problems can present new difficulties for students who are not confident readers. Pair struggling students with **Helping Partners** who are confident readers.

5–12
Class Activity

Name _____ Date _____

Tell what information is needed to solve each problem.

5. A stepladder is 8 feet tall. Two of the steps are broken. How many steps are not broken?

    the total number of steps on the ladder

    _____

6. Rebecca did 112 dives in competition last summer. This summer, she did many more dives in competition. How many competition dives did she do in the two summers?

    the number of competition dives Rebecca

    did this summer

7. Today, Maggie's Café sold more hot chocolate than yesterday. Yesterday, Maggie's Café sold 237 cups of hot chocolate. How many more cups were sold today than yesterday?

    the number of cups sold today

    _____

8. A living room couch is 6 feet long. There are 4 blue pillows and several gray pillows on the couch. How many pillows are on the couch altogether?

    the number of gray pillows on the couch

156 UNIT 5 LESSON 12   Word Problems with Not Enough Information

Student Activity Book page 156

Follow the same procedure for problems 5–8 on Student Book page 156. Ask students if there is enough information to solve each problem. Ask what additional information is needed, and then ask for a way to rewrite the problem so it can be solved. Note that problems 5 and 8 contain extra information: the height of the ladder and the length of the couch are not relevant.

Practice Identifying Problems with Not Enough Information

▶ Practice

Solve each problem if possible. If more information is needed, rewrite the problem to include the necessary information and then solve it.

9. Leah began fishing at 2 o'clock in the afternoon. She stopped at dinnertime. How many hours did Leah fish?
Possible rewrite: Leah began fishing at 2 o'clock in the afternoon. She stopped at 6 o'clock for dinner. How many hours did Leah fish? Answer: 4 hours

10. On Saturday, Maria handed out 646 flyers in the morning and the same number of flyers in the afternoon. How many flyers did Maria hand out on Saturday?
1,292 flyers

11. The Kitchen Store sold 532 pans and 294 pots. Then some pans were returned. How many pans were not returned?
Possible rewrite: The Kitchen Store sold 532 pans and 294 pots. Then 12 pans were returned. How many pans were not returned? Answer: 520 pans

12. There are 3 tables in the room with 4 legs each. One has a broken leg. How many table legs in the room are not broken?
11 legs

UNIT 5 LESSON 12   Word Problems with Not Enough Information **157**

Student Activity Book page 157

 20 MINUTES

Goal: Rewrite word problems including the needed information.

Materials: Student Activity Book or Hardcover Book pp. 157–158

NCTM Standards:
Numbers and Operations
Problem Solving
Communication
Connections

▶ **Practice** [WHOLE CLASS]

Using **Solve and Discuss,** have students solve problems 9–12 if possible. For the problems with not enough information (problems 9 and 11), have students share their rewritten problem and its solution. Possible problems that students may write including the information needed are given below:

Problem 9: Possible rewrite: Leah began fishing at 2 o'clock in the afternoon. She stopped at 6 o'clock for dinner. How many hours did Leah fish? 4 hours

Problem 11: Possible rewrite: The kitchen store sold 532 pans and 294 pots. 12 pans were returned. How many pans were not returned? 520

Activity continued ▶

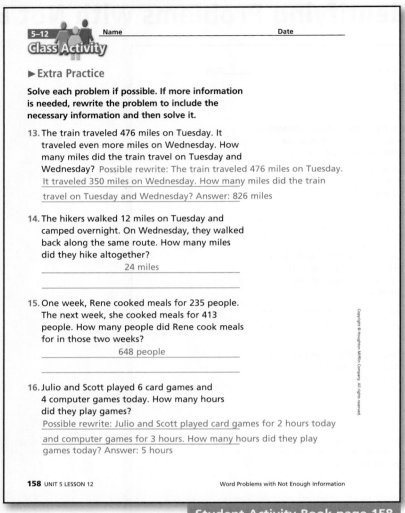

Student Activity Book page 158

The Student Activity Book page 158 shows:

5–12

Class Activity

Name _____ Date _____

▶ **Extra Practice**

Solve each problem if possible. If more information
is needed, rewrite the problem to include the
necessary information and then solve it.

13. The train traveled 476 miles on Tuesday. It
traveled even more miles on Wednesday. How
many miles did the train travel on Tuesday and
Wednesday? Possible rewrite: The train traveled 476 miles on Tuesday.
It traveled 350 miles on Wednesday. How many miles did the train
travel on Tuesday and Wednesday? Answer: 826 miles

14. The hikers walked 12 miles on Tuesday and
camped overnight. On Wednesday, they walked
back along the same route. How many miles
did they hike altogether?
_____ 24 miles _____

15. One week, Rene cooked meals for 235 people.
The next week, she cooked meals for 413
people. How many people did Rene cook meals
for in those two weeks?
_____ 648 people _____

16. Julio and Scott played 6 card games and
4 computer games today. How many hours
did they play games?
Possible rewrite: Julio and Scott played card games for 2 hours today
and computer games for 3 hours. How many hours did they play
games today? Answer: 5 hours

158 UNIT 5 LESSON 12   Word Problems with Not Enough Information

---

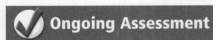

Ongoing Assessment

As students work individually on
Student Book page 158, circulate
around the room and have
students explain the steps they go
through to solve a word problem.
Students should explain the
following:

▶ First, I find out what information
the problem gives me. I can ask
myself, "What do I know?"

▶ Then, I reread the question the
word problem asks. I can say to
myself, "What do I want to
know?"

▶ Finally, I check to be sure if I have
enough information to solve the
problem.

▶ **Extra Practice** [INDIVIDUALS]

Have students independently solve problems 13–16. For the problems
with missing information (problems 13 and 16), students should write
their rewritten problem and its solution. Possible problems that students
may write including the information needed are given below:

Problem 13: Possible rewrite: The train traveled 476 miles on Tuesday. It
traveled 350 miles on Wednesday. How many miles did the train travel
on Tuesday and Wednesday? 826 miles

Problem 16: Possible rewrite: Julio and Scott played card games for
2 hours today and computer games for 3 hours. How many hours did
they play games today? 5 hours

② Going Further

Differentiated Instruction

What's Missing?

Activity Card 5-12 ●

Work: In pairs

Use:
• Homework, page 93
• MathBoard materials

1. **Work Together** Solve each problem on Homework page 93. Follow the steps below.
   • Read the problem aloud.
   • **Think** What do you know? What do you want to know? What strategy will you use?
   • Do you have enough information to solve the problem? If so, solve the problem on your own. Then compare answers with your partner.
   • If you need more information, work together to write the missing information and then solve the problem.

Unit 5, Lesson 12   Copyright © Houghton Mifflin Company

Activity Note Students should use a question format to indicate the missing information. For example, in Problem 2, students could write, "How many ducks flew away?" or "What number of ducks is some?"

🖊 **Math Writing Prompt**

Write About It Explain the steps you use to solve a problem and tell how you know when a problem is missing information.

Soar to Success Math ★ **Software Support**

Warm Up 10.04

Find the Unknown

Activity Card 5-12 ▲

Work: In pairs

Use:
• MathBoard materials

1. **On Your Own** Write a word problem with missing information on your MathBoard. Include an answer that is reasonable.

2. Exchange MathBoards with your partner. Write an equation with an empty box to represent the unknown number.

3. Solve the equation and write what the unknown number represents. Exchange MathBoards with your partner to check your work.

Unit 5, Lesson 12   Copyright © Houghton Mifflin Company

Activity Note Encourage students to use clue words to set up the equation with the appropriate operation. Students should use the opposite operation to check their work.

🖊 **Math Writing Prompt**

Investigate What are two ways you could find the missing number in this equation? $12 - \square = 5$

MEGA MATH Grades K-6 **Software Support**

Numberopolis: Carnival Stories, Level N

Missing Information Detective

Activity Card 5-12 ■

Work: In pairs

Use:
• MathBoard materials

1. Write a word problem with missing information on your MathBoard. Exchange with your partner.

2. Write a reasonable answer for the problem on the MathBoard and exchange problems again. Use the answer to find the missing information.

3. **Analyze** What operation did you use to find the missing information? What operation would you have used to solve the problem?

Unit 5, Lesson 12   Copyright © Houghton Mifflin Company

Activity Note Students should realize that opposite operations are used to find missing information and solve the problem using that information.

🖊 **Math Writing Prompt**

Explain Your Thinking How can you use the note taking strategy to help you solve problems with missing information?

✖ **DESTINATION** Math® **Software Support**

Course II: Module 2: Unit 1: Differences within 100

Word Problems with Not Enough Information   **381**

③ Homework and Spiral Review

Homework **Goal:** Additional Practice

This Homework page gives students practice identifying problems with not enough information.

Remembering **Goal:** Spiral Review

This Remembering page would be appropriate anytime after today's lesson.

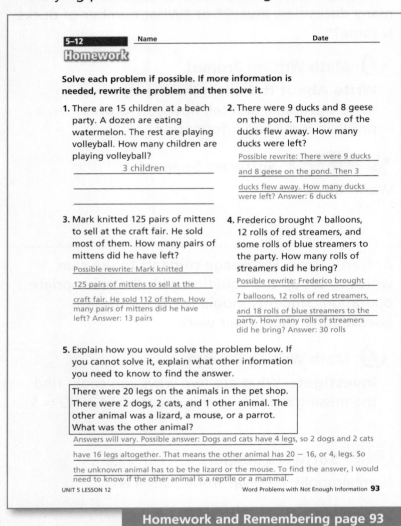

5–12
Homework

Name _____ Date _____

Solve each problem if possible. If more information is needed, rewrite the problem and then solve it.

1. There are 15 children at a beach party. A dozen are eating watermelon. The rest are playing volleyball. How many children are playing volleyball?
   _____ 3 children _____

2. There were 9 ducks and 8 geese on the pond. Then some of the ducks flew away. How many ducks were left?
   Possible rewrite: There were 9 ducks and 8 geese on the pond. Then 3 ducks flew away. How many ducks were left? Answer: 6 ducks

3. Mark knitted 125 pairs of mittens to sell at the craft fair. He sold most of them. How many pairs of mittens did he have left?
   Possible rewrite: Mark knitted 125 pairs of mittens to sell at the craft fair. He sold 112 of them. How many pairs of mittens did he have left? Answer: 13 pairs

4. Frederico brought 7 balloons, 12 rolls of red streamers, and some rolls of blue streamers to the party. How many rolls of streamers did he bring?
   Possible rewrite: Frederico brought 7 balloons, 12 rolls of red streamers, and 18 rolls of blue streamers to the party. How many rolls of streamers did he bring? Answer: 30 rolls

5. Explain how you would solve the problem below. If you cannot solve it, explain what other information you need to know to find the answer.

   > There were 20 legs on the animals in the pet shop. There were 2 dogs, 2 cats, and 1 other animal. The other animal was a lizard, a mouse, or a parrot. What was the other animal?

   Answers will vary. Possible answer: Dogs and cats have 4 legs, so 2 dogs and 2 cats have 16 legs altogether. That means the other animal has 20 − 16, or 4, legs. So the unknown animal has to be the lizard or the mouse. To find the answer, I would need to know if the other animal is a reptile or a mammal.

   UNIT 5 LESSON 12   Word Problems with Not Enough Information **93**

Homework and Remembering page 93

5–12
Remembering

Name _____ Date _____

Solve each problem.   *Show your work.*

1. Matt spent some time practicing the piano. Then he spent 25 minutes practicing the guitar. He spent a total of 60 minutes practicing. How much time did he practice the piano?
   _____ 35 minutes _____

2. A vendor at the park sold 415 bottles of water on Saturday. She sold 137 fewer bottles of water than cups of lemonade. How many cups of lemonade did she sell?
   _____ 552 cups _____

3. The table shows the Bagel Shop's sales last Monday morning. Fill in the empty cells.

Monday Morning Bagel Sales

	Number Made	Number Sold	Number Left
Plain	420	385	35
Cinnamon Raisin	336	208	128
Sesame	288	249	39
Onion	216	127	89

Write two Comparison questions that can be answered by using the table. Give the answers. Answers will vary.

4. _____
   _____

5. _____
   _____

94 UNIT 5 LESSON 12   Word Problems with Not Enough Information

Homework and Remembering page 94

Home or School Activity

 Math-to-Math Connection

Pattern Puzzle Write these pattern puzzles on the board and have students copy them. Then have students try to determine a rule so that each sequence follows a pattern. Once students are done, have them compare their completed patterns, and encourage them to discuss the similarities and differences between each of the solutions. Make sure students see that some of the puzzles do not have enough information, and in these cases, students will find that many solutions may be correct for one pattern puzzle.

2, 4, ___, ___, 10, ___

___, 3, ___, ___, ___, ___

AA, ZZ, ___, YY, CC, ___, DD, WW, ___

Ab, ___, Cd, De, ___, ___

Aa, ___, ___, ___, ___

Solve Two-Step Word Problems

Lesson Objective

● **Solve word problems requiring two steps.**

Vocabulary

net gain

The Day at a Glance

Today's Goals	Materials	
1 **Teaching the Lesson** **A1:** Represent and solve two-step word problems. **2** **Going Further** ▸ Differentiated Instruction **3** **Homework and Spiral Review**	**Lesson Activities** Student Activity Book pp. 159–160 or Student Hardcover Book pp. 159–160 Homework and Remembering pp. 95–96	**Going Further** Activity Cards 5-13 Highlighters (2 different colors) Index cards 4 strips of paper Homework p.95 Math Journals

123 *Use* **Math Talk** *today!*

Keeping Skills Sharp

Quick Practice ⏱ 5 MINUTES	Daily Routines	
Goal: Count coin values. **Counting Coins** The **Student Leader** writes a sequence of quarters (Qs), dimes (Ds), nickels (Ns), and pennies (Ps) on the board, in that order. The leader points to the coins in order as the class counts on to find the total. Have the leader add coins to or erase coins from the sequence and repeat.	**Homework Review** Ask students if they had difficulty with any part of the homework. Plan to set aside some time to work with students needing extra help.	**Strategy Problem** Tyra has 10 fewer stickers than Giselle. Together, they have 50 stickers in all. How many stickers does Giselle have? Explain how you found your answer. 30 stickers; Possible explanation: I looked for two addends with a difference of 10 and a sum of 50. 5 and 15: sum: 25 - too low 10 and 20: sum: 30 - too low 20 and 30: sum: 50 - just right. Giselle has more stickers; 30 > 20.

Teaching the Lesson

Solve Two-Step Word Problems

 55 MINUTES

Goal: Represent and solve two-step word problems.

Materials: Student Activity Book or Hardcover Book pp. 159–160

 NCTM Standards:
Number and Operations
Problem Solving
Reasoning and Proof

Class Management

To keep students interested and to check they understand how to solve problems with two steps, you may want to divide the problems in this activity into two or three sections. Have students solve problem 1 and have the class review it. Proceed in this manner by solving problems 2 and 3 and then work on problems 4–6 and finally problems 7–10.

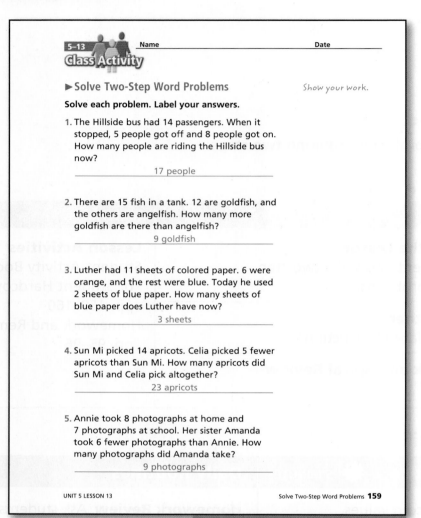

Student Activity Book page 159

▶ Solve Two-Step Word Problems [WHOLE CLASS]

Using **Solve and Discuss**, have students solve problems 1–5 on Student Book page 159. Make sure a variety of methods are presented. There are different ways to approach the problems on the next page. Equations and diagrams are shown in the descriptions, but many students will use representations that differ from those shown, and will be able to do some or all of the steps mentally.

Problem 1: Add and subtract according to how the problem is presented.

$$14 - 5 + 8 = \boxed{17}$$

start got got now
        off   on

Another way to solve the problem is to subtract the number of people who got off from the number who got on, and add the result to the original number of passengers.

$$8 - 5 = 3 \quad \rightarrow \quad 14 + 3 = \boxed{17}$$

got got   start   now
on   off

Problem 2: Find the number of angelfish, and then find the difference between this number and the number of goldfish.

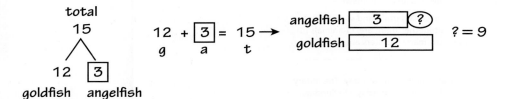

total
15
12   3
goldfish angelfish

$$12 + \boxed{3} = 15 \rightarrow$$
     g   a   t

angelfish $\boxed{3}$ (?)
goldfish   12   ? = 9

Problem 3: Find the number of blue sheets Luther started with, and subtract 2 to find the number he has now.

total
11
6   5
orange blue

$$6 + \boxed{5} = 11 \rightarrow 5 - \boxed{2} = 3$$
  o   b   t   had used now

Another way to figure it out is to subtract the 2 sheets Luther used from the original 11, and then figure out how many of the remaining sheets must be blue if 6 are orange.

$$11 - 2 = \boxed{9} \quad \rightarrow$$
had used now

9
6   3
orange blue

$$6 + \boxed{3} = 9$$
  o   b   t

Activity continued ▶

English Language Learners

Write Class Activity problem 1 on the board. Read it aloud. Say: **This problem has *two steps*.**

- **Beginning** Say: **First there were 14 people.** Circle and say: *5 people got off.* Say and write: **14 − 5.** Circle and say: *8 people got on.* Say and write: **14 − 5 + 8.**
- **Intermediate** Ask: **How many people were on the bus?** 14 people Say: **First, 5 people got off. We subtract ___.** 5 **Then, 8 people got on. We add ___.** 8
- **Advanced** Ask: **What number do we start with?** 14 **What is the first change?** 5 people got off **What is the second change?** 8 people got on

Problem 4: Find the number of apricots Celia picked, and add the result to the 14 Sun Mi picked.

Celia [?] (5)   ? = 9 → 9 + 14 = [23]
Sun Mi [14]   c   s   total

Problem 5: Add 8 and 7 to find the total number of photographs Annie took, and subtract 6 to find the number Amanda took.

8 + 7 = [15] → Amanda [?] (6)   ? = 9
home school total   Annie [15]

▶ **Solve and Discuss** | WHOLE CLASS |

5–13	Name	Date
Class Activity		Show your work.

▶ Solve and Discuss

Solve each problem. Label your answers.

6. There are 5 mice, 3 gerbils, and some hamsters in a cage. Altogether there are 15 animals in the cage. How many hamsters are there?
_____7 hamsters_____

7. A new library opened on Saturday. The library lent out 234 books on Saturday. On Sunday, they lent out 138 books. That day, 78 books were returned. How many books were not returned?
_____294 books_____

8. Katie had 8 dimes and some nickels in her duck bank. She had 4 more nickels than dimes. She took out 5 nickels to buy a newspaper. How many nickels are in her duck bank now?
_____7 nickels_____

9. Tony had 14 colored pencils. 9 of them needed sharpening, and the rest were sharp. Yesterday, his uncle gave him some new colored pencils. Now Tony has 12 sharp colored pencils. How many colored pencils did his uncle give him?
_____7 colored pencils_____

10. José ate 6 strawberries. Then he ate 7 more. Lori ate 9 strawberries. How many fewer strawberries did Lori eat than José?
_____4 strawberries_____

160 UNIT 5 LESSON 13   Solve Two-Step Word Problems

Student Activity Book page 160

123 **Math Talk in Action**

Will someone share how they solved Problem 8?

Carlo: Well, I started by figuring out that eight dimes is the same as 80¢. But that's not what the problem is about.

That's right. What did you do next?

Carlo: I added 4 to 8 to find out how many nickels Katie had. She had 12 nickels.

Good. Then what?

Carlo: I subtracted 5 from 12. Now Katie has 7 nickels.

That's right. One important thing to do every time you solve a word problem is to read it all the way through before you try to solve it. Why do you think that's a good idea?

Lewis: That way you know what the problem is about.

Continue working through problems 6–10 on Student Book page 160 with the class. Possible approaches students may use are described on the next page. For a sample classroom dialogue, see **Math Talk in Action** in the side column.

Problem 6: Add to find the number of mice and gerbils, and subtract the result from 16 or use a Math Mountain to find the number of hamsters.

$$15 \; - \; 8 \; = \boxed{7}$$
$$a \quad\; m+g \quad\; h$$

$$5 \; + \; 3 \; = \boxed{8} \quad \longrightarrow$$
mice gerbils total

animals
15

$$\begin{array}{c} \diagup \diagdown \\ m+g \; 8 \quad \boxed{7} \; \text{hamsters} \end{array}$$

or

$$8 \; + \boxed{7} = \; 15$$
$$m+g \quad h \qquad a$$

You could also start with 15, subtract the number of mice, and then subtract the number of gerbils.

$$15 \quad - \quad 5 \quad - \quad 3 \quad = \quad \boxed{7}$$
animals mice gerbils hamsters

Problem 7: Add 234 and 138 to find the total number of books lent out, and then subtract the 78 books that were returned.

$$234 \quad + \quad 138 \quad = \boxed{372} \; \longrightarrow \quad 372 \quad - \quad 78 \quad = \boxed{294}$$

| Saturday | Sunday | total lent out | lent out | returned | not returned |

Another way is to subtract 78 from 138 to get the "net lent out" for Sunday, and add this to the number lent out on Saturday.

$$138 \quad - \quad 78 \quad = \boxed{60} \; \longrightarrow \quad 234 \quad + \quad 60 \quad = \boxed{294}$$

lent out Sunday   returned Sunday   lent out Saturday   not returned

Activity continued ▶

❶ Teaching the Lesson (continued)

Problem 8: Find the number of nickels Katie had to start with, and then subtract 5 nickels.

Dimes $\boxed{8}$ $\textcircled{4}$? $= 12 \rightarrow$ $12 - 5 = \boxed{7}$
Nickels $\boxed{?}$ had took left
                                                      out

Or you might reason that if Katie started with 4 more nickels than dimes, and then takes out 5 nickels, she will have 1 fewer nickel than dimes, or 7 nickels.

Problem 9: First find the number of sharp colored pencils Tony had to start with, and subtract the result from 12, or use a Math Mountain to figure out how many colored pencils his uncle gave him.

total
14
$9 + \boxed{5} = 14 \rightarrow$ sharp now 12 $5 + \boxed{7} = 12$
    dull sharp total   sharp not sharp
                                  then sharp now
9   5   5   7
dull sharp   sharp not
                               then sharp

You could also add 9 to 12 to find the number of colored pencils Tony has now, and subtract the 14 colored pencils he had to start with.

$9 + 12 = \boxed{21}$ $\rightarrow$ $21 - 14 = \boxed{7}$
dull sharp total   total before now
          now   now   sharp

Problem 10: Find the total number of strawberries José ate, and then find the difference between that total and the 9 strawberries Lori ate.

$6 + 7 = 13 \rightarrow$ Lori $\boxed{9}$ $\textcircled{?}$? $= 4$
start more total   José $\boxed{13}$
          José

✓ Ongoing Assessment

To check that students understand the process of solving two-step word problems, ask them to read one of the problems in this lesson and identify what their first step would be when solving it. Ask if it is possible to solve the problem by using a different first step.

② Going Further

Intervention   Activity Card 5-13

Color the Steps   Activity Card 5-13 ●

Work: In pairs

Use:
- Highlighters (4 different colors)
- Homework, page 95

1. Use different-colored highlighters to help you solve the problems on Homework page 95. Look at the example to the right for solving Problem 1.

> *Show your work.*
> Todd's Dad cut 12 slices of mango. Then Todd's mom cut 6 more slices. How many slices of mango were left?
>
> **Step 1**
> 12 – 4 = 8
> **Step 2**
> 8 + 6 = 14 slices

2. **Analyze** Why is the first step a subtraction? Could you solve the problem with a different first step? Four slices were eaten from the original 12; Add 12 + 6 and then subtract 4.

3. **On Your Own** Repeat the activity for each problem on page 95. Compare your work with your partner's work. Discuss how your solutions are the same and how they are different.

Unit 5, Lesson 13   Copyright © Houghton Mifflin Company

Activity Note Students use the highlighting to group each set of data that will be used in the two-step solution. Depending on the two steps chosen, the data may be grouped in different ways.

 Math Writing Prompt

In Your Own Words How can you check that your answer to a two-step word problem is correct?

 **Software Support**

Warm Up 11.04

On Level   Activity Card 5-13

Match It   Activity Card 5-13 ▲

Work: In pairs

Use:
- 2 index cards
- 2 strips of paper

1. **On Your Own** Write a two-step word problem on an index card. Then write the equation you would use to solve the problem on a strip of paper. Use the problem below as an example.

> Eliza took 13 photos from inside her car and 5 photos from outside her car. If she has a roll of 24 pictures, how many photos can she still take?
>
> 24 – 13 – 5 = 6 photos

2. Exchange problems with your partner to solve, but do not share the equation you wrote.

3. **Analyze** Does your solution use the same equation as the one your partner wrote? Is there more than one way to solve the problem?

Unit 5, Lesson 13   Copyright © Houghton Mifflin Company

Activity Note Be sure that students understand how a single equation represents a solution to a two-step problem when two operations are involved.

 Math Writing Prompt

Write Your Own Brynne wrote this equation to solve a word problem: 8 – 4 + 2 = 6. Write a word problem that Brynne may have solved.

 Software Support

Numberopolis: Carnival Stories, Level L

Challenge   Activity Card 5-13

The Ultimate Word Problem   Activity Card 5-13 ■

Work: In small groups

Use:
- 1 index card for each student

1. **On Your Own** Use an index card to write a two-step word problem that includes extra information and hidden information. A sample problem and solution are shown below.

> Nick has 180 pennies and 12 nickels. His sister has 9 quarters. Nick spent 50¢. How much money does he have left?
>
> $1.80 + $.60 – $.50 = $1.90

2. **Think** Did you include all the information that is necessary to solve the problem? Can you find some information by changing units of measure or money? Did you include extra information?

3. Exchange your problem with the student to your right. Then solve the problem you receive.

Unit 5, Lesson 13   Copyright © Houghton Mifflin Company

Activity Note Have students discuss their solutions and challenge them to find more than one way to solve each problem.

 Math Writing Prompt

Investigate Math Write a two-step word problem and explain how to solve it in two different ways.

 DESTINATION Math **Software Support**

Course II: Module 2: Unit 1: Differences within 100

 **Homework and Spiral Review**

5–13
Homework **Goal:** Additional Practice

This Homework page allows students to practice solving two-step word problems.

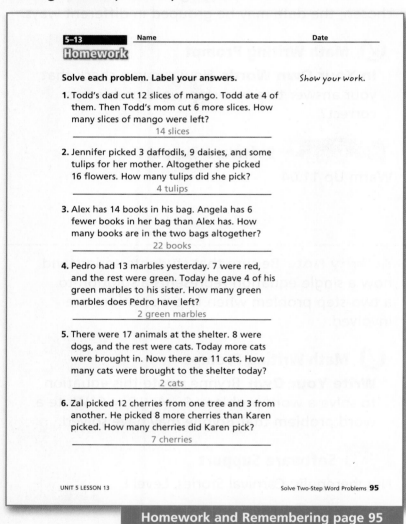

5–13   Name _____ Date _____
Homework

Solve each problem. Label your answers.   *Show your work.*

1. Todd's dad cut 12 slices of mango. Todd ate 4 of them. Then Todd's mom cut 6 more slices. How many slices of mango were left?
   _____ 14 slices _____

2. Jennifer picked 3 daffodils, 9 daisies, and some tulips for her mother. Altogether she picked 16 flowers. How many tulips did she pick?
   _____ 4 tulips _____

3. Alex has 14 books in his bag. Angela has 6 fewer books in her bag than Alex has. How many books are in the two bags altogether?
   _____ 22 books _____

4. Pedro had 13 marbles yesterday. 7 were red, and the rest were green. Today he gave 4 of his green marbles to his sister. How many green marbles does Pedro have left?
   _____ 2 green marbles _____

5. There were 17 animals at the shelter. 8 were dogs, and the rest were cats. Today more cats were brought in. Now there are 11 cats. How many cats were brought to the shelter today?
   _____ 2 cats _____

6. Zal picked 12 cherries from one tree and 3 from another. He picked 8 more cherries than Karen picked. How many cherries did Karen pick?
   _____ 7 cherries _____

UNIT 5 LESSON 13   Solve Two-Step Word Problems **95**

Homework and Remembering page 95

5–13
Remembering **Goal:** Spiral Review

This Remembering page would be appropriate anytime after today's lesson.

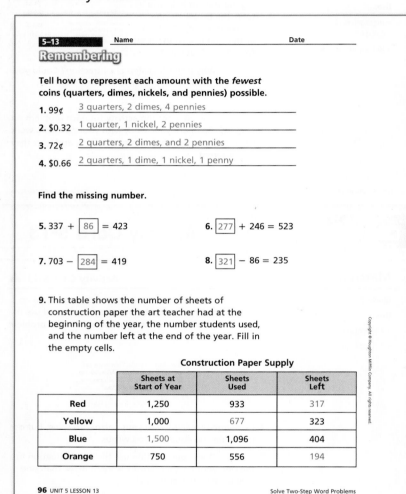

5–13   Name _____ Date _____
Remembering

Tell how to represent each amount with the *fewest* coins (quarters, dimes, nickels, and pennies) possible.

1. 99¢   3 quarters, 2 dimes, 4 pennies
2. $0.32   1 quarter, 1 nickel, 2 pennies
3. 72¢   2 quarters, 2 dimes, and 2 pennies
4. $0.66   2 quarters, 1 dime, 1 nickel, 1 penny

Find the missing number.

5. $337 + \boxed{86} = 423$ 6. $\boxed{277} + 246 = 523$

7. $703 - \boxed{284} = 419$ 8. $\boxed{321} - 86 = 235$

9. This table shows the number of sheets of construction paper the art teacher had at the beginning of the year, the number students used, and the number left at the end of the year. Fill in the empty cells.

Construction Paper Supply

	Sheets at Start of Year	Sheets Used	Sheets Left
Red	1,250	933	317
Yellow	1,000	677	323
Blue	1,500	1,096	404
Orange	750	556	194

96 UNIT 5 LESSON 13   Solve Two-Step Word Problems

Homework and Remembering page 96

Home or School Activity

 Social Studies Connection

Mathematicians in History Throughout history there have been many successful mathematicians whose ideas and discoveries are still used today. For example, Ada Byron Lovelace (1815–1852) used mathematics to help design and explain the Analytical Engine (the first computer). Divide students into small groups and have them research assigned mathematicians. A sample list is provided at the right. Have students determine when and where their mathematician lived, and find one contribution they made to mathematics.

Famous Mathematicians

Ada Byron Lovelace (1815–1852)
Leonardo Fibonacci (1170–1250)
Herman Hollerith (1860–1929)
Evelyn Boyd Granville (1924–)
J. Napier (1550–1617)
Sophie Germain (1776–1831)

Solve Multi-Step Word Problems

REAL WORLD Problem Solving

Vocabulary

Associative Property of Addition
Commulative Property of Addition
Indentity Property of Addition

Lesson Objective

● Solve multi-step word problems requiring two or more steps.

The Day at a Glance

Today's Goals	Materials

❶ Teaching the Lesson
A1: Solve multi-step word problems.
A2: Work in small groups to solve a challenging problem.
 	
❷ Going Further
▶ Problem Solving Strategy: Work Backward
▶ Differentiated Instruction
 	
❸ Homework and Spiral Review
	Lesson Activities
	Student Activity Book pp. 161–164
	  or Student Hardcover Book
	  pp. 161–164
	Homework and Remembering
	  pp. 97–98
	Quick Quiz 4 (Assessment Guide)
	Math Mysteries by Jack Silbert
	(Scholastic, 1995)
		Going Further
		Student Activity Book
		  pp. 163–164
		Activity Cards 5-14
		MathBoard materials
		Sentence strips
		Math Journals
		
		123 Use **Math Talk** today!

Keeping Skills Sharp

Quick Practice 🕐 5 MINUTES	**Daily Routines**
Goal: Count coin values. **Counting Coins** The **Student Leader** writes a sequence of quarters (Qs), dimes (Ds), nickels (Ns), and pennies (Ps) on the board, in that order. The leader points to the coins in order as the class counts on to find the total and times the length of the activity. **Q Q Q Q Q Q D D D N P** *Leader:* Count on to find the total amount. *Class:* 25¢, 50¢, 75¢, $1.00, $1.25, $1.50, $1.60, $1.70, $1.80, $1.85, $1.86 The leader adds coins to or erases coins from the sequence, and the class counts again. With each new sequence, the class should try to improve its time.	**Homework Review** If students have difficulty with word problems, encourage them to write situation equations and then change them to solution equations. **Coins and Bills** Jolon has 6 dollars, 3 quarters, 1 dime, and 1 nickel. He uses this money to buy a pencil for $0.25 and a notebook for $4.75. How much money does he have left? $1.90

Teaching the Lesson

Use Properties to Solve Multi-Step Word Problems

 25 MINUTES

Goal: Solve multi-step word problems.

Materials: Student Activity Book or Hardcover Book p. 161

 NCTM Standards:
Number and Operations
Problem Solving
Reasoning and Proof
Communication

Class Management

Because of the number and complexity of the word problems in this lesson, be sure to allow enough time for this activity. Have students solve problem 1 and then have the class review it. Continue with problems 2–6 and have the class ask questions and review the steps they took to solve the word problems.

English Language Learners

Write Class Activity problem 1 on the board. Say: **This problem has** *more* **than 2 steps.** Circle the first sentence. Use the equations on page 393 to model the steps.

• **Beginning** Say: **First we find how many pears she had.** Model the steps. Say: **Now we find how many pears she bought.**

• **Intermediate** Ask: **Do we know how many pears she started with?** no Model the steps. Say: **Now we find how many pears she ___.** bought

• **Advanced** Have students work in pairs to solve each part of the problem. Have volunteers describe the steps.

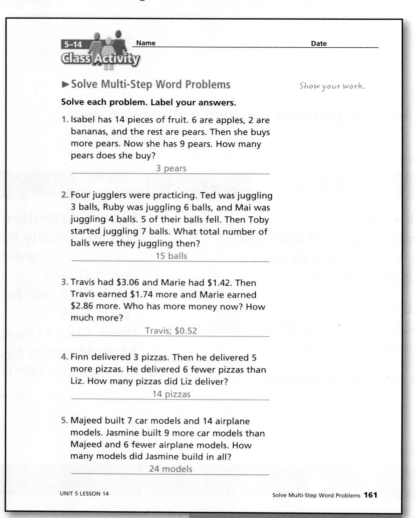

Student Activity Book page 161

▶ Solve Multi-Step Word Problems [WHOLE CLASS]

The multi-step word problems in this lesson are more complex than those in Lesson 13.

Encourage students to organize and keep track of their work by taking notes and labeling their drawings and equations.

Using **Solve and Discuss**, have students solve problems 1–5 on Student Book page 161. There are some ways to approach the problems on the next page. Equations and diagrams are described, but many students will use representations that differ from those shown, and some will be able to do some or all of the steps mentally.

Problem 1: First, find the total number of apples and bananas. Then figure out how many pears Isabel started with. Finally, figure out how many pears she bought.

$$
\begin{array}{ccccc}
6 & + & 2 & = & \boxed{8} \\
\text{apples} & & \text{bananas} & & a+b
\end{array}
\quad \longrightarrow \quad
\begin{array}{c}
\text{total} \\
14 \\
\diagdown \\
8 \quad \boxed{6} \\
a+b \quad \text{pears}
\end{array}
$$

$$
\begin{array}{ccccc}
8 & + & 6 & = & \boxed{14} \\
a+b & & \text{pears} & & \text{total}
\end{array}
\quad \longrightarrow \quad
\begin{array}{c}
\text{total} \\
\text{pears} \\
9 \\
\diagdown \\
6 \quad \boxed{3} \\
\text{pears} \quad \text{pears} \\
\text{at start} \quad \text{bought}
\end{array}
\qquad
\begin{array}{ccccccc}
6 & + & \boxed{3} & = & 9 \\
\text{start} & & \text{bought} & & \text{total}
\end{array}
$$

Problem 2: Add and subtract in the order the information is given.

$$
\begin{array}{ccccccccc}
3 & + & 6 & + & 4 & - & 5 & + & 7 \\
\text{Ted} & & \text{Ruby} & & \text{Mai} & & \text{Fell} & & \text{Toby}
\end{array}
$$

Another way to solve this problem is to first find the total number of balls in the air, and then subtract the number that fell.

$$
\begin{array}{ccccccccc}
3 & + & 6 & + & 4 & + & 7 & - & 5 \\
\text{Ted} & & \text{Ruby} & & \text{Mai} & & \text{Toby} & & \text{Fell}
\end{array}
$$

In either case, the numbers can be grouped to simplify the calculations. Here we group to get two 10s.

$$
\begin{array}{ccccccccccc}
& & & 10 & & & & & & & \\
③ & + & ⑥ & + & ④ & + & ⑦ & - & 5 & = & 10 + 10 - 5 \\
\text{Ted} & & \text{Ruby} & & \text{Mai} & & \text{Toby} & & \text{Fell} & & \\
& & & 10 & & & & & & &
\end{array}
$$

Problem 3: First find the amount each person has.

Travis: $3.06 + $1.74 = $4.80

Marie: $1.42 + $2.86 = $4.28

Travis has more money. Find how much more by subtracting, or by adding on from $4.28 to $4.80.

Activity continued ▶

Teaching Note

Math Background Grouping the numbers as described in this activity involves applying the Commutative and Associative Properties of Addition.

The Commutative Property says that for any real numbers a and b,

$$a + b = b + a$$

This means we can switch the order in which two numbers are added and the sum will remain the same. For example, $3 + 5 = 5 + 3$.

The Associative Property says that for any real numbers a, b, and c,

$$a + (b + c) = (a + b) + c$$

This means we can group the numbers in an addition expression in any way we want and the sum will remain the same. For example, $3 + (5 + 2) = (3 + 5) + 2$.

Students should be aware that not all mathematical operations are commutative. For example, subtraction is not commutative. To stress this point, you might discuss some real-life situations that are not "Commutative" Here are two examples.

▶ Does it make a difference whether you first put on your socks or put on your shoes? Yes, you have to put on your socks first, so these two "operations" are not commutative.

▶ Does it make a difference whether you first put on your left sock or put on your right sock? No, it does not make a difference, so these two "operations" are commutative.

You might want to have a discussion in which students suggest other examples of real-life "operations" that are and are not commutative.

Math Talk in Action

Can you change the order of the steps to figure out problem 4?

Matilda: No.

Why not?

Matilda: Because finding the number of pizzas Liz delivered depends on knowing the number of pizzas Finn delivered.

Problem 5: Find the number of car models and airplane models Jasmine built, and then add the results.

J's cars	7	9		J's planes	?	6
M's cars	?			M's planes	14	
	? = 16				? = 8	

16	+	8	=	24
J's cars		J's planes		total

Ongoing Assessment

To check understanding of solving multi-step word problems, have students solve these problems or others like them.

▶ Jamil had 7 dimes in his pocket. Then he put one dollar's worth of quarters in the same pocket. How many coins does he have now?

▶ Yvette has 17 books. Eight are mysteries and the rest are science fiction books. Then she received 3 more science fiction books. How many science fiction books does she have now?

Problem 4: First, find the total number of pizzas Finn delivered. Then use the fact that Liz delivered 6 more to figure out how many she delivered.

3	+	5	=	8
pizza		more		total Finn

→

Finn	8	6
Liz	?	

? = 14

See **Math Talk in Action** in the side column for problems 4 and 5.

▶ Discuss Properties of Addition | WHOLE CLASS |

 Math Talk Have students look back at problem 1 on Student Book page 161. Remind students that 6 apples and then 2 bananas were added to find a total of 8 pieces of fruit. Write 6 + 2 = 8 on the board.

● Can you switch the order in which you added the apples and bananas? Yes, 2 + 6 = 8 or 6 + 2 = 2 + 6

This is an example of the **Commutative Property of Addition,** which states that addition can be done in any order.

Now have students look back at Problem 2 on Student Book page 161. Remind students that Ted was juggling 3 balls, Ruby was juggling 6 balls, and Mai was juggling 4 balls. Write this equation on the board.

$$3 + 6 + 4 = \boxed{}$$

● How can we group these numbers to make the addition easier? Possible answer: Add 6 + 4 first, then add 3 for a total of 13.

● Show how to group the addends in a different way.

3 + (6 + 4) = 3 + 10 = 13   (3 + 6) + 4 = 9 = 4 = 13

This is an example of the **Associative Property of Addition,** which states that grouping the addends in different ways does not change the sum.

● Do you think these properties work for subtraction, too? Explain. No, because 6 − 2 = 4, but 2 − 6 does not equal 4; 5 − (2 − 1) = 4 but (5 − 2) − 1 = 2.

Write 45 + 0 = 45 and 0 + 8 = 8 on the board, and explain that this is an example of the **Identity Property of Addition,** which states that the sum of 0 and any number is that number.

Write these equations on the board.

3 + 4 = 3 + ☐ 3; Commutative property 2 + (7 + 6) = (2 + 6) + ☐ 6; Associative property 25 + 0 = ☐ 25; Identity property (4 + 7) + ☐ = 4 + (7 + 2) 7; Associative property 2 + ☐ = 7 + 2 2; Commutative property 0 + 50 = ☐ 50; Identity property

Ask volunteers to tell what goes in the box by using the properties of addition. Then ask them to tell what property they used.

Solve Challenging Word Problems

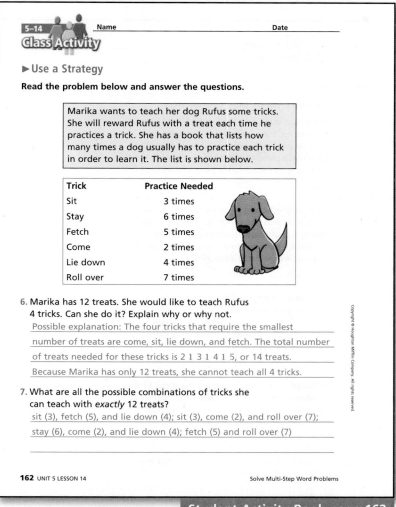

Student Activity Book page 162

⏱ 20 MINUTES

Goal: Work in small groups to solve a challenging problem.

Materials: Student Activity Book or Hardcover Book p. 162

 NCTM Standards:
Number and Operations
Problem Solving
Reasoning and Proof
Connections
Representations

The Learning Classroom

Math Talk Working in small groups of 4 to 6 should be a student-to-student interactive process. Spontaneous helping is encouraged throughout. Students can all solve the problem, and then they all explain their thinking to their small group or, half could explain for each problem. It is important that other students ask questions and help to clarify the explanation. At the end a reporter could report on important issues about the problems or about explaining.

 Quick Quiz

See Assessment Guide for Unit 5, Quick Quiz 4.

► Use a Strategy SMALL GROUPS

Have **Small Groups** work to solve the multi-step word problems on Student Book page 162. Select several groups to share their strategies and solutions.

One strategy for finding all the possible combinations in problem 6 is to start with the first item on the list (sit), which requires 3 treats. Then, figure out how many treats Marika would have left after teaching this trick; in this case, 9. Finally, look for combinations of two tricks (or one additional trick) with this number as the "treat total." Repeat this process for the other items on the list.

Problem Solving Strategy: Work Backward

Goal: Use the Work Backward strategy to solve word problems.

Materials: Student Activity Book or Hardcover Book p. 163, *Math Mysteries* by Jack Silbert

✔ **NCTM Standards:**
Number and Operations
Problem Solving
Reasoning and Proof

▶ Introduce the Work Backward Strategy WHOLE CLASS

Explain to students that the word problems they have solved so far involved following steps in the order they happen to find an answer. In the problems in this activity, an end result is given and they will need to work backward to find what number there was to start with.

Write the following word problem on the board and work though the problem with students.

There were 4 pies left over from a feast. 12 pies were eaten at the feast. Princess May took 2 pies back to her castle before the feast was over. How many pies were at the feast at the beginning?

● How many pies were left over at the feast? 4 pies

● How many pies were eaten or taken by someone? 14: 12 pies were eaten and Princess May took 2.

● How can I find out how many pies there were in the beginning? You can add 4 and 14 which is 18 pies.

▶ Use the Work Backward Strategy

SMALL GROUPS

Have students solve problem 1 on Student Activity Book page 165 in **Small Groups**. Select several groups to share their solutions. Students may use different representations than those shown below, and some will be able to do some or all of the steps mentally.

Problem 1: Start with the final length of fishing line. Work backward by adding 8 then keep working backward by adding the lengths of the 2 pieces of fishing line.

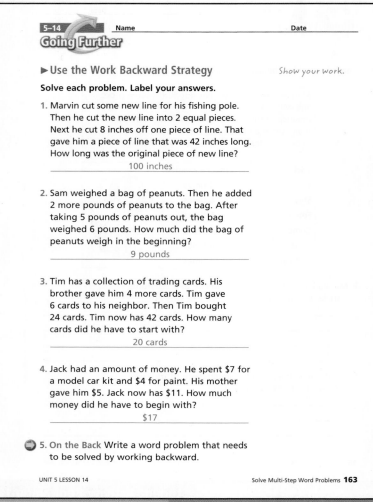

Student Activity Book page 163

Final length	put length back on		1st piece of fishing line		2nd piece of fishing line		original piece of fishing line
42	+	8 = 50	50	+	50	=	100

Have students complete the remaining problems on the page in small groups. Ask students how they can check their answers to word problems by working backward. Possible response: Put the answer back into the original problem and check that it works.

 Alternate Approach

Literature Connection Read aloud or give students a copy of "The Backward Burglar," a short story from Jack Silbert's *Math Mysteries*. Have students work in small groups to solve the problem by using the Work Backward strategy.

Differentiated Instruction

Cut It Out!
Activity Card 5-14

Work: In small groups

Use:
- MathBoard materials
- Strips of paper

1. Write each sentence below on a strip of paper.

   > Ravati put 5 more mysteries on the shelf.
   >
   > There are 18 books on Ravati's book shelf.
   >
   > Eight are novels.
   >
   > Three are science fiction and the rest are mysteries.
   >
   > How many mysteries are on her shelf now?

2. **Work Together** Arrange the strips in a way that helps you organize the information given. Then solve the problem.

3. **Analyze** How did you choose the first step to solve the problem? Could you have chosen a different first step? How many steps in all did you need to solve it?

Unit 5, Lesson 14   Copyright © Houghton Mifflin Company

Activity Note Possible answer: 8N + 3 SF = 11; 18 − 11 = 7 mysteries; 7M + 5M = 12 mysteries

 **Math Writing Prompt**

Explain Your Thinking How can you check your answer to a multi-step word problem?

Soar to Success Math **Software Support**

Warm Up 67.02

Error Detector
Activity Card 5-14 ▲

Work: In pairs

1. Together with your partner, read the problem below. Check the solution to decide if it is reasonable and correct.

   > Salma sold some of her old postcards. Saul bought 12 of the postcards. Then Salma sold postcards to Sam, who bought 9 more than Saul. How many postcards did Salma sell?
   >
   > Solution steps:
   >   1. Start with the 12 postcards Saul bought.
   >   2. Add the 9 postcards Sam bought.
   >   3. That's how many postcards Salma sold.
   >   12 + 9 = 21 ANSWER
   >
   > The answer is not correct. They may have read the problem wrong and did not see that Sam has "9 more than Saul". It should be 12 + 12 + 9 = 33 postcards.

2. If the solution is correct, find another way to solve the problem. If the solution is not correct, tell why and find the correct solution.

Unit 5, Lesson 14   Copyright © Houghton Mifflin Company

Activity Note The answer is not correct. Sam has 9 *more than* Saul. So the solution should be 12 + 12 + 9 = 33 postcards.

 Math Writing Prompt

Reasonable Answers Is there more than one way to solve a multi-step problem? Give an example.

MegaMath Grades K–6 **Software Support**

Numberopolis: Carnival Stories, Level P

Build a Problem
Activity Card 5-14 ■

Work: In small groups

Use:
- MathBoard materials

1. Take turns writing sentences to create multi-step word problems.

2. Have each member of your group write the first sentence of a problem on their MathBoard. Then pass that MathBoard to the next student who writes the next sentence.

   > Alice delivered 8 pizzas. Then she delivered 6 more to another party. Each pizza cost $5. Liz delivered 5 more pizzas than Alice. How much money did Liz make?
   >   8 + 6 = 14 Alice
   >   14 + 5 = 19 Liz   5,5,5,5,5   5,5,5,5
   >   5,5,5,5,5   5,5,5,5
   > $95

3. Continue until every person in your group has written a sentence for each problem and each problem is complete.

4. Return each MathBoard to the student who wrote the first sentence. Each student then solves that problem.

Unit 5, Lesson 14   Copyright © Houghton Mifflin Company

Activity Note This activity works best with four or more students per group.

 Math Writing Prompt

Describe Your Method In a multi-step problem, how do you know when you have found the solution?

DESTINATION Math **Software Support**

Course II: Module 2: Unit 1: Sums Less Than 100

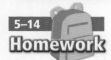

③ Homework and Spiral Review

Homework **Goal:** Additional Practice

✓ Include students' completed Homework page as part of their portfolios.

Remembering **Goal:** Spiral Review

This Remembering page would be appropriate anytime after today's lesson.

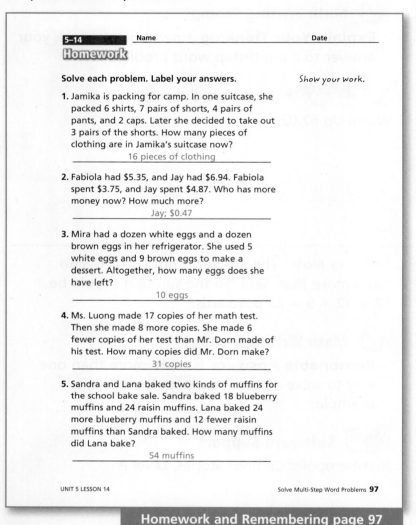

5–14 Homework

Name _____ Date _____

Solve each problem. Label your answers. *Show your work.*

1. Jamika is packing for camp. In one suitcase, she packed 6 shirts, 7 pairs of shorts, 4 pairs of pants, and 2 caps. Later she decided to take out 3 pairs of the shorts. How many pieces of clothing are in Jamika's suitcase now?

   16 pieces of clothing

2. Fabiola had $5.35, and Jay had $6.94. Fabiola spent $3.75, and Jay spent $4.87. Who has more money now? How much more?

   Jay; $0.47

3. Mira had a dozen white eggs and a dozen brown eggs in her refrigerator. She used 5 white eggs and 9 brown eggs to make a dessert. Altogether, how many eggs does she have left?

   10 eggs

4. Ms. Luong made 17 copies of her math test. Then she made 8 more copies. She made 6 fewer copies of her test than Mr. Dorn made of his test. How many copies did Mr. Dorn make?

   31 copies

5. Sandra and Lana baked two kinds of muffins for the school bake sale. Sandra baked 18 blueberry muffins and 24 raisin muffins. Lana baked 24 more blueberry muffins and 12 fewer raisin muffins than Sandra baked. How many muffins did Lana bake?

   54 muffins

UNIT 5 LESSON 14 Solve Multi-Step Word Problems **97**

Homework and Remembering page 97

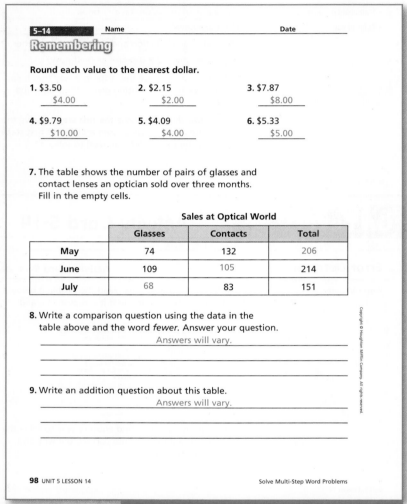

5–14 Remembering

Name _____ Date _____

Round each value to the nearest dollar.

1. $3.50   _$4.00_   2. $2.15   _$2.00_   3. $7.87   _$8.00_

4. $9.79   _$10.00_   5. $4.09   _$4.00_   6. $5.33   _$5.00_

7. The table shows the number of pairs of glasses and contact lenses an optician sold over three months. Fill in the empty cells.

Sales at Optical World

	Glasses	Contacts	Total
May	74	132	206
June	109	105	214
July	68	83	151

8. Write a comparison question using the data in the table above and the word *fewer.* Answer your question.

   Answers will vary.

9. Write an addition question about this table.

   Answers will vary.

98 UNIT 5 LESSON 14 Solve Multi-Step Word Problems

Homework and Remembering page 98

Home or School Activity

Language Arts Connection

Step-by-Step Directions Have students brainstorm a list of activities that need to be done in a special order (brushing their teeth, making a sandwich, and so on). Then have them list as many "time-order" words they can think of that help them explain these activities in sequential order (*first, then, next, finally, lastly,* and so on). Finally, have students write a "How-To" paragraph explaining how to do something in order. Their paragraphs should include a topic sentence, the steps in sequential order, and a closing sentence.

<u>How to Brush Your Teeth</u>

You need to brush your teeth to keep your mouth healthy. First, you open the toothpaste. Then, you squirt the toothpaste on your brush. Next, you move the brush all over your teeth. Finally, you wash your toothbrush off and put it away. Brushing your teeth every day will keep the cavities away.

Read and Create Pictographs and Bar Graphs

REAL WORLD Problem Solving

Lesson Objectives

- Write and answer questions using horizontal and vertical bar graphs.
- Create bar graphs to represent data from tables.
- Find mode and range of data.

Vocabulary	
vertical axis	pictograph
horizontal axis	axes
vertical bar graph	mode
horizontal bar graph	range
maximum value	scale
minimum value	

The Day at a Glance

Today's Goals	Materials
1 **Teaching the Lesson** **A1:** Read, create, and interpret pictographs. **A2:** Read and interpret bar graphs. **A3:** Create bar graphs. **A4:** Find the mode and range of the data. **2** **Going Further** ▶ Extension: Surveys ▶ Differentiated Instruction **3** **Homework and Spiral Review**	**Lesson Activities** Student Activity Book pp. 165–168 or Student Hardcover Book pp. 165–168 and Activity Workbook pp. 57–59 (includes grids for graphs) Homework and Remembering pp. 99–100 Overhead projector and transparency of Student Book pp. 166, 167 (optional) Index cards Rulers, Class list	Connecting cubes Yardsticks **Going Further** Activity Cards 5-15 Connecting Cubes Markers 10 × 10 Grid (TRB M43) Math Journals

123 Use Math Talk today!

Keeping Skills Sharp

Quick Practice ⏱ 5 MINUTES

Goal: Round whole numbers to the nearest ten or hundred.

Rounding Practice The **Student Leader** writes 617, 382, 455, 621, 1,792, and 748 on the board. The leader points to the numbers one at a time and says either, "Round to the nearest ten," or, "Round to the nearest hundred." When the leader gives a signal, students respond in unison with the rounded number.

Leader (pointing to 617): Round to the nearest hundred.

Class: 600

Daily Routines

Homework Review Have students describe strategies they used. Students may solve the problem correctly but use an inefficient strategy.

Estimation Kate drove 215 miles on Monday and 175 miles on Tuesday. About how many miles did Kate drive in all on both days? **Explain.** Possible answer: about 400 miles; Round to the nearest hundred, 200 and 200, and add.

Teaching the Lesson

Pictographs

 10 MINUTES

Goal: Interpret and make pictographs in which symbols represent more than one object.

Materials: Student Activity Book or Hardcover Book p. 165 and Activity Workbook p. 57.

✔ **NCTM Standards:**
Number and Operations
Algebra
Data Analysis and Probability
Representation

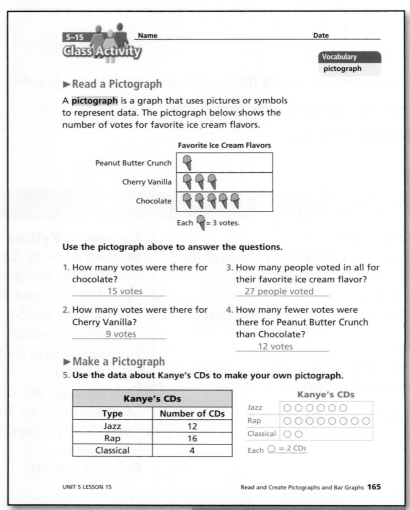

Student Activity Book page 165

▶ Read a Pictograph WHOLE CLASS

Discuss the pictograph on Student Book page 165. Have students name the title, the types of flavors, the symbols, and the key.

● How would the data for Chocolate be displayed if each cone equaled 5 votes? There would only be 3 cones.

Have students complete exercises 1–4 and use Solve and Discuss to check the answers.

▶ Make a Pictograph WHOLE CLASS

Direct students to the data table about Kanye's CDs at the bottom of Student Book page 165. Have students make their own pictographs and have volunteers share them with the class. Make sure to note that students may choose to use 2 or 4 for the key in this pictograph.

1 Teaching the Lesson

Read Bar Graphs

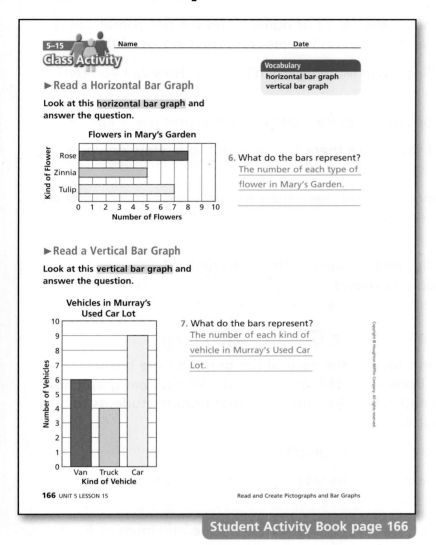

Student Activity Book page 166

The Student Activity Book page shows:

5-15 Class Activity

Name _____ Date _____

Vocabulary
horizontal bar graph
vertical bar graph

▶ **Read a Horizontal Bar Graph**

Look at this **horizontal bar graph** and answer the question.

Flowers in Mary's Garden

Kind of Flower: Rose, Zinnia, Tulip

Number of Flowers: 0 1 2 3 4 5 6 7 8 9 10

6. What do the bars represent?
   The number of each type of flower in Mary's Garden.

▶ **Read a Vertical Bar Graph**

Look at this **vertical bar graph** and answer the question.

Vehicles in Murray's Used Car Lot

Number of Vehicles: 0–10

Kind of Vehicle: Van, Truck, Car

7. What do the bars represent?
   The number of each kind of vehicle in Murray's Used Car Lot.

166 UNIT 5 LESSON 15   Read and Create Pictographs and Bar Graphs

▶ Read a Horizontal Bar Graph WHOLE CLASS

Have students look at the bar graph at the top of Student Book page 166 or display a transparency of this page. Explain to students that *bar graphs* use bars to show information. Explain that a horizontal bar graph has bars that go across. Discuss what the bar graph shows and how to read it.

- What is the title of this graph? *Flowers in Mary's Garden*

- What is the label on the vertical axis? *Kind of Flower*

- What kinds of flowers are there? roses, zinnias, and tulips

- What does each bar represent? a different kind of flower

- What is the label on the horizontal axis? *Number of Flowers*

- What do the numbers along the horizontal axis represent? number of flowers

 15 MINUTES

Goal: Read and interpret bar graphs.

Materials: Student Activity Book or Hardcover Book p. 166, index cards, overhead projector (optional), transparency of Student Activity Book or Hardcover Book p. 166 (optional)

 NCTM Standards:
Number and Operations
Data Analysis and Probability
Problem Solving
Communication

Teaching Note

Language and Vocabulary Review the words *vertical* and *horizontal* with students. Draw the letter T on the chalkboard. Explain that when we say that a line is vertical, it means that the line goes straight up and down.

▶ Which part of the letter **T** is vertical? the bottom part of the T

Explain that when we say that a line is horizontal, it means that the line goes straight across.

▶ Which part of the letter **T** is horizontal? the top part of the T

Explain to students that an *axis* is at the side or bottom of a graph, and that an axis has labels. Have them look at the graph *Flowers in Mary's Garden.*

▶ Find the axis called *Number of Flowers.* Is this the horizontal axis or the vertical axis? horizontal How do you know? It goes straight across.

▶ Find the axis called *Kind of Flower.* Is this the horizontal axis or the vertical axis? vertical How do you know? It goes straight up and down.

(123) Math Talk in Action

Juan: How many more cars than trucks are in Murray's used car lot?

Tina: There are 5 more cars than trucks.

Juan: How did you get 5?

Tina: The bar for car goes up to the line for 9. The bar for truck goes up to the line 4. 9 minus 4 equals 5.

Point out that the arrangement of numbers on the horizontal axis is called the *scale,* and that is used to measure the lengths of the bars.

- How many tulips are in Mary's garden? 7 tulips How can you tell? The bar for Tulip goes to the line for the number 7 on the scale.

Then ask questions that require students to interpret the graph.

- Which type of flower are there the most of? roses How do you know? The bar for Rose is the longest.

- How many more roses are there than zinnias? 3 more roses How do you know? The bar for Rose is 3 units longer than the bar for Zinnia; The graph shows there are 8 roses and 5 zinnias, and $8 - 5 = 3$.

- How many tulips and zinnias are there altogether? 12 tulips and zinnias How do you know? The bar for Tulip shows there are 7 tulips and the bar for Zinnia shows there are 5 zinnias, and $7 + 5 = 12$.

▶ Read a Vertical Bar Graph [WHOLE CLASS]

Now have students look at the vertical bar graph on the bottom of Student Activity Book page 167. Explain that a vertical bar graph has bars that go up and down. Ask questions that require students to interpret the graph.

- What is the title of this bar graph? *Vehicles in Murray's Used Car Lot*

- How many trucks are in the lot? 4 trucks How do you know? The bar for Truck goes up to the line for 4; The bar for Truck is 4 units long.

Explain to students that this is an example of the *minimum* or *least value* on the graph.

- Are there more vans or more cars in the lot? more cars How can you tell? The bar for Car is longer than the bar for Van.

Explain to students that this is an example of the *maximum* or *greatest value* on the graph.

Have students subtract the minimum value from the maximum value ($9 - 4 = 5$). Explain that 5 is the **range** of the data.

- How many vehicles are there in the lot altogether? 19 vehicles How did you know? There are 6 vans, 4 trucks, and 9 cars, and $6 + 4 + 9 = 19$.

Have **Student Pairs** create and answer more questions based on either graph on Student Book page 166. **See Math Talk in Action** in the side column.

① Teaching the Lesson (continued)

Activity 3

Create Bar Graphs

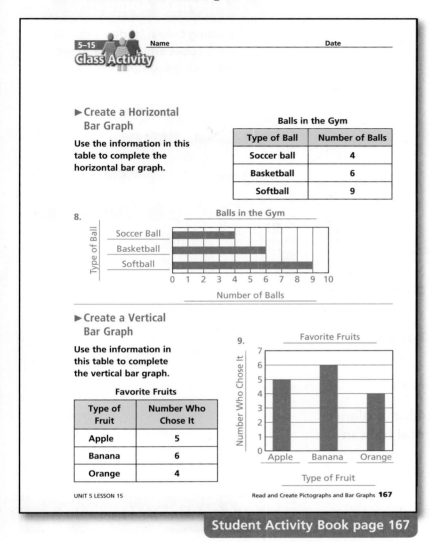

Create a Horizontal Bar Graph

Use the information in this table to complete the horizontal bar graph.

Balls in the Gym

Type of Ball	Number of Balls
Soccer ball	4
Basketball	6
Softball	9

8.

Balls in the Gym

Type of Ball: Soccer Ball, Basketball, Softball
Number of Balls: 0 1 2 3 4 5 6 7 8 9 10

Create a Vertical Bar Graph

Use the information in this table to complete the vertical bar graph.

Favorite Fruits

Type of Fruit	Number Who Chose It
Apple	5
Banana	6
Orange	4

9.

Favorite Fruits

Number Who Chose It: 0 1 2 3 4 5 6 7
Type of Fruit: Apple, Banana, Orange

UNIT 5 LESSON 15   Read and Create Pictographs and Bar Graphs **167**

Student Activity Book page 167

  15 MINUTES

Goal: Create bar graphs.

Materials: Student Activity Book or Hardcover Book p. 167 and Activity Workbook p. 58, overhead projector (optional), transparency of Student Activity Book or Hardcover Book p. 167 (optional), ruler, connecting cubes, index cards

✓ **NCTM Standards:**
Number and Operations
Data Analysis and Probability
Problem Solving
Communication

▶ Create a Horizontal Bar Graph WHOLE CLASS

Have students look at the table at the top of Student Book page 168 or display a transparency of the page. Then ask:

● What does this table show? the number of different kinds of balls in the gym

Tell students that they will make a horizontal bar graph showing the information in the table.

Guide students with their graphs by asking the following questions.

● What should the title of our graph be? Balls in the Gym

● What should the label for the vertical axis be? Type of Ball

● What should we write for the three types of balls? Soccer ball, Basketball, and Softball

Teaching Note

Watch For! Watch for students who begin their graph scales by writing 1 instead of 0 as the first number.

- What should we label the horizontal axis? Number of Balls

- What scale should we use? Start at 0 and go to 10.

The graph should now look like this:

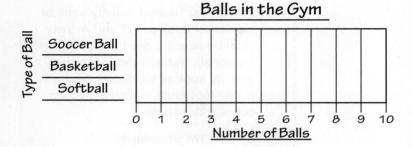

Balls in the Gym

- How do we show 4 soccer balls on our graph? After "Soccer Ball," draw a bar from 0 to the line for 4 and shade it in.
Draw this bar on your graph. Use your ruler to help you draw straight segments.

- What should the bar for "Basketball" look like? It should go from 0 to the line for 6.

- What about the bar for "Softball"? It should go from 0 to 9.

- Which display—the table or the bar graph—is easier to tell at a glance which type of ball there is the most of in the gym? The total balls in the gym? The bar graph; the table

▶ Create a Vertical Bar Graph INDIVIDUALS

Have students look at the table at the bottom of Student Book page 167.

- What does this table show? favorite fruits

Have students work independently to make a vertical bar graph that shows the information in the table. Suggest they look at the vertical bar graph on Student Book page 166 to help them figure out where the labels go.

- When you make a vertical bar graph, should the bars go up and down or across? up and down

- Where will the scale be? on the left axis

- Suppose you surveyed a larger group than shown here. What do you predict would be the favorite fruit? banana

Assist students who are struggling, and allow students to work with a **Helping Partner.**

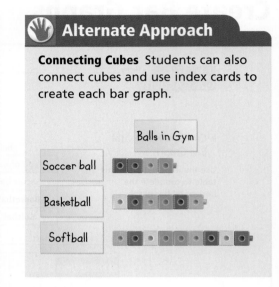

Alternate Approach

Connecting Cubes Students can also connect cubes and use index cards to create each bar graph.

Ongoing Assessment

Observe students as they complete the vertical bar graph on Student Book page 168. Check to see that they label the parts of the graph correctly. Use questioning to assess students understanding.

▶ What does the vertical axis show?

▶ What does the horizontal axis show?

▶ How do you know how long to make the bar for apples?

Teaching the Lesson (continued)

Activity 4

Mode and Range

▶ Record Data in a Tally Chart | SMALL GROUPS |

Have students measure each other's heights (in inches). Once groups have recorded each student's height, work together as a class to make a tally chart and bar graph of all the heights.

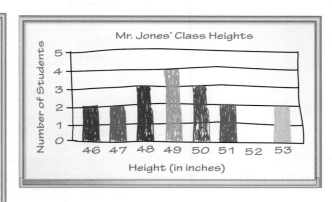

Then have students look at the tally chart and organize the data in a list.
46, 46, 47, 47, 48, 48, 48, 49, 49, 49, 49, 50, 50, 50, 51, 53, 53

▶ Find Range and Mode | WHOLE CLASS |

Write the following definitions on the board and discuss them with students.

Range- The difference between the greatest number or maximum value and the least number or minimum value in a set of data.

Mode- The number that occurs most often in a set of data.

Explain to students that there can be one, more than one, on no mode for a set of data.

Use these questions to help them find the range and mode of the data.

● What is the maximum or greatest value in the set? 53

● What is the minimum or least value in the set? 46

● What is the range of the data? 7

● Look at the set of data. What is the mode? 49

Discuss which display they used to answer each question and why they chose that display.

If time allows, have students work in pairs to find the mode and range of the set of data below about the number of hours that students spent on homework this week: 4, 7, 2, 3, 8, 1, 3, 5, 3, 2, 2, 1, 5, 2 range: 7; mode: 2

 15 MINUTES

Goal: Find the mode and range of a set of data.

Materials: yardsticks

 NCTM Standards:
Number and Operations
Algebra
Data Analysis and Probability
Representation

Going Further

Extension: Surveys

▶ Take a Survey and Record Results

PAIRS

Choose a Topic Have **Students Pairs** work to choose a survey topic and write four answer choices in the tally chart on Student Book page 168.

Predict Ask students to predict which of the choices will be chosen most often and to write their predictions on a separate piece of paper. After students finish collecting the data, they can check their predictions.

Conduct the Survey Pairs can meet with other students to conduct their survey and record the results. Provide students with a class list to help them keep track of the students they have surveyed.

Remind students how to make tally marks. They should group tally marks and represent 5 votes like this: ⊞

Graph the Results Once the surveys are complete, have students graph the data from their tally charts and describe their results. Then have them find the mode and range of the data and explain what the numbers means.

Prediction for a Larger Group If you surveyed a larger group, what do you predict would be the result?
Answers will vary.

 Class Management

Walk around the room and observe as pairs use their tally charts to create their horizontal bar graphs. Watch for students who omit labels or use incorrect labels on their graphs. Ask questions about their favorites or if their predictions were close.

5–15
Going Further

▶ Take a Survey and Record Results

Topics
Sports
Animals
Colors
School Subjects
Snacks

10. Choose a survey topic from the box or make up one of your own. Then take a survey to find the favorite.

Which _____ is your favorite?	
Answer Choice	**Tally**

11. Use the tally chart to complete the horizontal bar graph.

Check students' graphs.

12. Math Journal Write two questions that can be answered using the bar graph. Then answer them.

Student Activity Book page 168

▶ Compare Data in Two Forms

WHOLE CLASS

Have students present their data and discuss the two ways they displayed the data.

● Why might you make a tally chart instead of just writing down each answer to the survey question? It is easier to count tallies than to sort and count answers.

● How does a bar graph make it easy to compare data? You can compare different amounts just by comparing the lengths of the bars.

Differentiated Instruction

Cube Count

Activity Card 5-15 ●

Work: In pairs

Use:

- Red, blue, and green connecting cubes
- Red, blue, and green markers
- TRB M43 (10 × 10 grid)

Decide:

Who will be Student 1 and who will be Student 2 for the first round.

1. **Student 1:** Take a handful of cubes. Connect cubes of the same color into cube trains.

2. **Student 2:** Make a graph on the 10 × 10 grid. Show how many cubes of each color your partner used. Color one square on the grid for each cube.

3. Check your work. How many cubes did your partner use altogether? How many squares did you color on the grid?

4. Change roles and repeat the activity.

Unit 5, Lesson 15   Copyright © Houghton Mifflin Company

Activity Note Suggest that students create horizontal bar graphs. This will reinforce the connection between the cubes and the data that the graph represents.

 Math Writing Prompt

Interpret Data Look at Student Activity Book page 167. Tell two things the graph shows.

Soar to Success Math **Software Support**

Warm Up 50.07

Team Totals

Activity Card 5-15 ▲

Work: In small groups

1. **Work Together** Choose four team sports from this list: tennis, softball, lacrosse, hockey, or soccer.

2. For each sport, find the greatest number of players that a team can have playing at one time.

3. Make a graph that shows your findings.

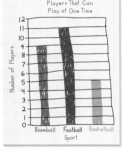

Unit 5, Lesson 15   Copyright © Houghton Mifflin Company

Activity Note Students may create vertical or horizontal graphs. To make it easier to show equal intervals on the numerical axis, be sure that students use ruled paper for their graphs.

 Math Writing Prompt

Explain Your Thinking Think of a few situations in which you might use a bar graph to show data. Explain why a bar graph might be a good way to show the data.

MEGA MATH Grades K-6 **Software Support**

Country Countdown: White Water Graphing, Level F

Explore Scales

Activity Card 5-15 ■

Work: In small groups

1. Look at the bar graph. How many items does each space on the vertical axis represent? 2

2. Use what you know to find the number of bookcases, desks, and chairs shown on the graph. 8; 15; 19

3. **Analyze** Write three questions using the information on the graph and find the answers.

Unit 5, Lesson 15   Copyright © Houghton Mifflin Company

Activity Note Encourage students to create questions that compare the bar lengths either directly or indirectly.

 Math Writing Prompt

Draw a Bar Graph The first bar shows 10 students. The second bar is twice as long as the first bar. The third bar is the same length as the second. How many students does the graph show?

 DESTINATION Math **Software Support**

Course II: Module 3: Unit 1: Area

③ Homework and Spiral Review

Homework **Goal:** Additional Practice

This Homework page provides students with more practice reading and making bar graphs.

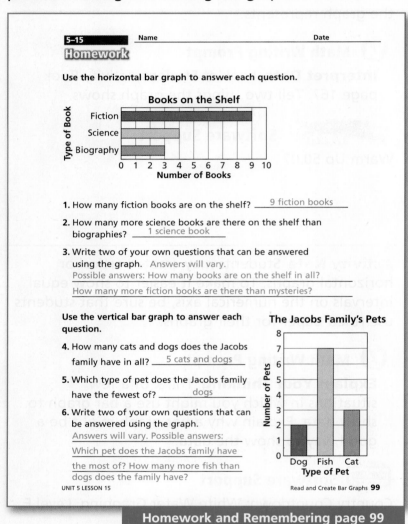

Remembering **Goal:** Spiral Review

This Remembering page would be appropriate anytime after today's lesson.

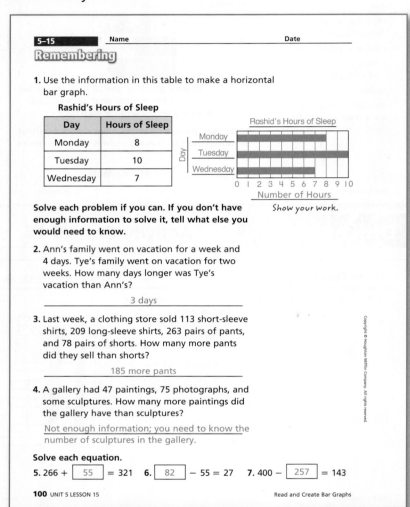

Homework and Remembering page 99

Homework and Remembering page 100

Home or School Activity

Science Connection

How Many Legs? Have students make a bar graph that shows the number of legs on each of the following animals: a chicken, a horse, an ant, and a spider.

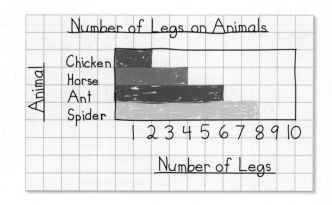

Read and Create Bar Graphs with Multi-Digit Numbers

REAL WORLD Problem Solving

Vocabulary

bar graph
axes
horizontal axis
vertical axis
scale

Lesson Objectives

● Analyze data in horizontal and vertical bar graphs.

● Use information in a table to create horizontal and vertical bar graphs.

The Day at a Glance

Today's Goals	Materials
1 Teaching the Lesson **A1:** Interpret bar graphs with scales that include multi-digit numbers. **A2:** Represent multi-digit data tables with bar graphs. **2 Going Further** ▶ Differentiated Instruction **3 Homework and Spiral Review**	**Lesson Activities** Student Activity Book pp. 169–172 or Student Hardcover Book pp. 169–172 and Activity Workbook p. 60 (includes grids for graphs) Homework and Remembering pp. 101–102 Index cards 10 × 10 Grid (TRB M43)	**Going Further** Student Activity Book p. 171 Activity Cards 5-16 Centimeter Grid Paper (TRB M31) Crayons Data tables (TRB M44) Math Journals

123 Use Math Talk today!

Keeping Skills Sharp

Quick Practice ⏱ 5 MINUTES	**Daily Routines**
Goal: Round whole numbers to the nearest ten or hundred. **Rounding Practice** The **Student Leader** writes 574, 105, 650, 488, 1,642, and 527 on the board, points to the numbers one at a time, and says either, "Round to the nearest ten," or, "Round to the nearest hundred." When the leader gives a signal, students respond in unison with the rounded number. Have the leader repeat the series of numbers so that each number is rounded to both the nearest ten and hundred. Monitor the quickness and volume of responses to identify any problems with rounding.	**Homework Review** If students give incorrect answers, have them explain how they found the answers. This can help you determine if the error is procedural or from reading the graph. **Mental Math** Use mental math to subtract. 1. 84 − 31 53 2. 25 − 16 9

Teaching the Lesson

Read Bar Graphs with Multi-Digit Numbers

 25 MINUTES

Goal: Interpret bar graphs with scales that include multi-digit numbers.

Materials: Student Activity Book or Hardcover Book pp. 169–170, index cards

✔ **NCTM Standards:**
Number and Operations
Algebra
Data Analysis and Probability
Representation

Teaching Note

Language and Vocabulary Review the words *horizontal, vertical,* and *axis.* Ask students to find a horizontal bar and vertical bar graph in this lesson. Also ask students to tell what information is on the horizontal axis and vertical axis of a graph in this lesson.

English Language Learners

Review *horizontal, vertical,* and *axis.* Draw the bar graph from the Class Activity on the board.

• **Beginning** Ask: **Is this a horizontal bar graph** yes Point to each axis. Identify them and have students trace them in the air with a finger.

• **Intermediate** Ask: **Are the drivers on the *vertical* or *horizontal axis*?** vertical **What information is on the *horizontal axis*?** miles

• **Advanced** Have students use short sentences to describe the information on each axis.

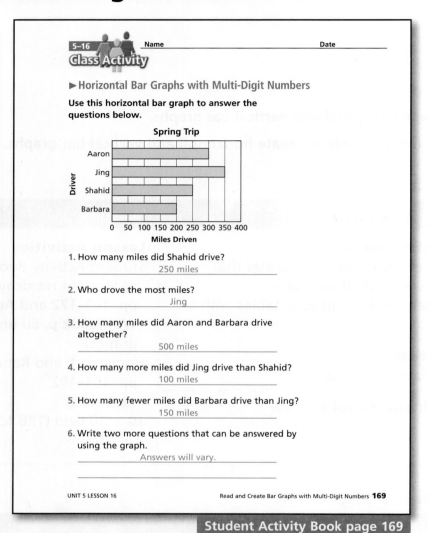

Student Activity Book page 169

► Horizontal Bar Graphs with Multi-Digit Numbers

WHOLE CLASS

Direct students' attention to the horizontal bar graph at the top of Student Book page 169. As a class, examine the graph and its scale.

● **What type of bar graph is this?** horizontal bar graph

● **What does this graph show?** the number of miles different people drove on a trip in the spring

● **How is the scale of this graph different from the scale of other graphs you have worked on? How is it the same?** The scale still starts at 0, but the numbers go much higher than 10.

Check students' understanding of the multi-digit numbers on the scale. Then have students complete p. 169.

Ask these questions to check that students understand how to read the graph:

● How many miles did Aaron drive? 300 How do you know? The bar next to Aaron's name stops at the 300 line on the graph.

● Who drove the least number of miles? Barbara How do you know? She has the shortest bar in the graph

Have students work independently to answer the questions following the graph on Student Book page 169. Discuss the answers as a class. Have a few students share the questions they wrote.

 Math Talk in Action

Who wants to share one of the questions you wrote and then answered for this graph?

Mia: Who drove the second greatest number of miles?

Can we answer this question by reading the graph?

Sam: Yes.

Okay. Who can answer Mia's question?

Tom: After Jing, Aaron drove the most miles. His bar on the graph is the second longest.

Correct! Now who else wants to share a question?

Sudir: How long did it take Barbara to drive 200 miles?

Can we answer this question by reading the graph?

Liz: No.

Liz, why don't you think we can answer Sudir's question using the bar graph?

Liz: There is no information on time, so we don't know how long Barbara was driving.

Liz is correct. We don't know the length of each driver's trip. What information would we need to know in order to answer Sudir's question?

Mia: What if we knew how many miles each person was driving per hour?

Great idea, Mia. That information would definitely help us answer the question.

Activity continued ▶

❶ Teaching the Lesson (continued)

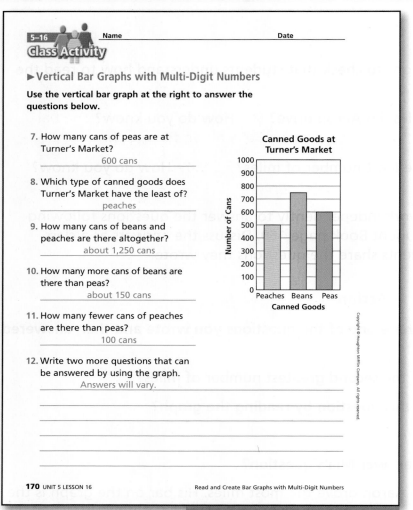

5–16

Class Activity

Name _____ Date _____

▶ **Vertical Bar Graphs with Multi-Digit Numbers**

Use the vertical bar graph at the right to answer the questions below.

7. How many cans of peas are at Turner's Market?
   _____ 600 cans _____

8. Which type of canned goods does Turner's Market have the least of?
   _____ peaches _____

9. How many cans of beans and peaches are there altogether?
   _____ about 1,250 cans _____

10. How many more cans of beans are there than peas?
    _____ about 150 cans _____

11. How many fewer cans of peaches are there than peas?
    _____ 100 cans _____

12. Write two more questions that can be answered by using the graph.
    _____ Answers will vary. _____
    _____
    _____
    _____
    _____
    _____
    _____

Canned Goods at Turner's Market

(Number of Cans vs Canned Goods: Peaches, Beans, Peas)

170 UNIT 5 LESSON 16   Read and Create Bar Graphs with Multi-Digit Numbers

Student Activity Book page 170

▶ Vertical Bar Graphs with Multi-Digit Numbers

WHOLE CLASS

As a class, discuss what the bar graph on Student Book page 170 shows and how to read it. Ask about the title and axis labels. Draw students' attention to the bar labeled *Beans.*

● **How is the bar for the cans of beans different from the other bars?** It ends between two lines. There is not a number on the scale to go with it.

● **Can you still figure out how many cans of beans are at the market?** yes **How?** The top of the bar looks like it is halfway between 700 and 800, so there are about 750 cans of beans.

Have students work independently to complete exercises 7–12. Discuss the answers, and have a few students share the questions they wrote.

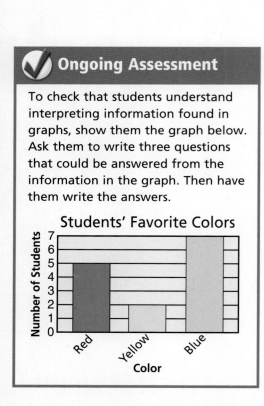
412 UNIT 5 LESSON 16

Create Bar Graphs with Multi-Digit Numbers

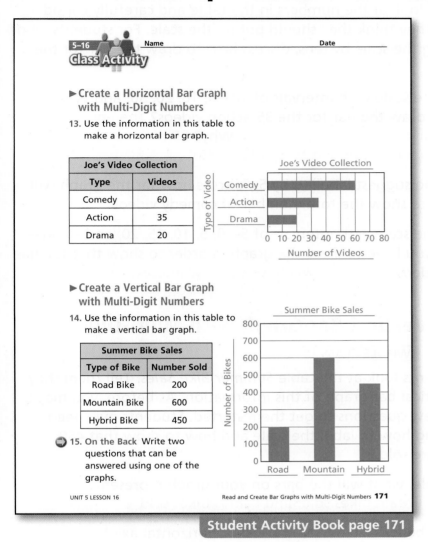

Student Activity Book page 171

Contents of the Student Activity Book page:

5–16 Class Activity

Name _____ Date _____

▶ Create a Horizontal Bar Graph with Multi-Digit Numbers

13. Use the information in this table to make a horizontal bar graph.

Joe's Video Collection	
Type	**Videos**
Comedy	60
Action	35
Drama	20

Joe's Video Collection (bar graph) — Type of Video: Comedy, Action, Drama; Number of Videos: 0 10 20 30 40 50 60 70 80

▶ Create a Vertical Bar Graph with Multi-Digit Numbers

14. Use the information in this table to make a vertical bar graph.

Summer Bike Sales	
Type of Bike	**Number Sold**
Road Bike	200
Mountain Bike	600
Hybrid Bike	450

Summer Bike Sales (bar graph) — Number of Bikes: 0 100 200 300 400 500 600 700 800; Road, Mountain, Hybrid

15. **On the Back** Write two questions that can be answered using one of the graphs.

UNIT 5 LESSON 16   Read and Create Bar Graphs with Multi-Digit Numbers **171**

---

 25 MINUTES

Goal: Represent multi-digit data tables with bar graphs.

Materials: MathBoard materials, Student Activity Book or Hardcover Book p. 171 and Activity Workbook p. 60, 10 × 10 Grid (TRB M43)

 NCTM Standards:
Number and Operations
Algebra
Data Analysis and Probability
Representation
Communication

Differentiated Instruction

Extra Help Have students use 10 × 10 Grid (TRB M43) to plan what the scales for their bar graphs should be. Have students label each block at the bottom row of the grid in intervals of 5, 10, 100, or any number that makes sense for the table. Students may want to test different scales before deciding which one to use. They can draw and erase bars of varied lengths to help them decide which scale works best.

▶ Create a Horizontal Bar Graph with Multi-Digit Numbers WHOLE CLASS

Ask the class to look at the table at the top of Student Book page 171. Tell students that they will make a horizontal bar graph to represent the data in the table. Ask these questions to help students begin their graphs.

● What does the table show? the number of videos of various types in Joe's collection

● Judging from the data in the table, how many bars will your graph have? 3 bars What will the bars represent? comedy, action, and drama

● You will be making a horizontal bar graph. Should the bars go up and down or across? across Where will the scale go? on the horizontal axis

Activity continued ▶

Teaching the Lesson (continued)

Ask students to look at the numbers in the table and carefully consider what numbers they think they should put on the scale. For students who suggest labeling the scale by tens, discuss how to draw the bar for the action videos.

● If you label the scale with intervals of 10—0, 10, 20, 30, and so on—how will you draw the bar for the 35 action videos? The end of the bar will be halfway between 30 and 40. Why? 35 is not a 10, but it is exactly halfway between two tens, 30 and 40.

For students who suggest labeling by 5s, discuss how far the graph will have to extend to show the total number of comedy videos.

● If you label the scale with intervals of 5—0, 5, 10, 15, 20, and so on—how far will you have to draw the graph in order to show that Joe has 60 comedy videos? The scale will have to show intervals of 5 until at least 60.

▶ Create a Vertical Bar Graph with Multi-Digit Numbers [WHOLE CLASS]

Now have students look at the table *Summer Bike Sales.* Tell them they will make a vertical bar graph of this information. As before, you may want to ask a few questions to get them started. Students may need help determining how to label the scale and how to show that 450 hybrid bikes were sold.

● Using this table, what will the bars on your graph represent? road bikes sold, mountain bikes sold, and hybrid bikes sold

● Will the scale be located on the vertical or horizontal axis? vertical axis

● If you label the scale with intervals of 100—0, 100, 200, 300, 400, and so on—how will you draw the bar for 450 hybrid bikes? The end of the bar will be halfway between 400 and 500.

● If you label the scale with intervals of 50—0, 50, 100, 150, 200, and so on—how will you draw the bar for the hybrid bikes? The bar will end at the 450 line on the graph.

Intervention   Activity Card 5-16

Scales for Graphs   Activity Card 5-16 ●

Work: In pairs

Use:
- TRB M44 (Data Tables)
- TRB M31 (Centimeter Grid Paper)

1. **Work Together** Choose a data table from TRB M44 to graph.

2. **On Your Own** Outline the graph and show the scale that you would use to graph the data. The graphs below show two scales for a set of data.

3. **Compare** graphs with your partner to be sure that both scales are reasonable. Then complete your graph. Compare results with your partner.

Unit 5, Lesson 16   Copyright © Houghton Mifflin Company

Activity Note Encourage students to identify the range of the data in the table they have chosen and then choose reasonable intervals that will represent the data clearly within available space.

 Math Writing Prompt

Suggest Ideas List three different things a person could show using a bar graph with multi-digit numbers.

 **Software Support**

Warm Up 50.12

On Level   Activity Card 5-16

Graph Data   Activity Card 5-16 ▲

Work: In pairs

Use:
- TRB M31 (Centimeter Grid Paper)
- Crayons

1. Read the information below.

> In one month, Miranda's Dogwalking Service walks 40 Siberian huskies, 25 German shepherds, and 60 golden retrievers.

2. Work with your partner. Choose two scales that would be reasonable to display the data on a bar graph and decide who will work with each scale.

3. **On Your Own** Make a graph using your scale and the given data. Then compare your graph with your partner's graph.

4. **Analyze** Which scale increases the difference between the lengths of the bars on the graph?

Unit 5, Lesson 16   Copyright © Houghton Mifflin Company

Activity Note A scale of 5 or 10 would be reasonable for the axis showing number of dogs. The scale of 5 will show a greater difference in the length of the bars.

 Math Writing Prompt

Explain Your Reasoning Explain what you need to do to draw a bar to 25 when you are using the scale 0, 10, 20, 30, and so on.

 Software Support

Country Countdown: White Water Graphing, Level F

Challenge   Activity Card 5-16

Double Bar Graphs   Activity Card 5-16 ■

Work: In small groups

Use:
- Student Activity Book or Hardcover Book, p. 171
- Crayons

2. The number of videos Joe will have in 6 months; a second bar for each type of video in a different color.

3. Drama; 115; 140

1. Look at the table about Joe's video collection on Student Activity Book, page 171. Then look at the graph below.

2. What data is included in the graph that is not in the table? How does the graph show this data?

3. **Analyze** Which type of video will increase the least in the next 6 months? How many videos does Joe have now? How many will Joe have in 6 months?

Unit 5, Lesson 16   Copyright © Houghton Mifflin Company

Activity Note Some students may not realize that the red bars showing videos represent the anticipated total after 6 months, not the number added.

 Math Writing Prompt

Difficult Numbers? Think of three numbers that might be difficult to represent accurately on a bar graph with a scale showing intervals of 50. How could you change the scale? Explain.

 DESTINATION
Math® **Software Support**

Course II: Module 3: Unit 1: Area

Read and Create Bar Graphs with Multi-Digit Numbers   **415**

 # Homework and Spiral Review

Homework **Goal:** Additional Practice

✓ Include students' completed Homework page as part of their portfolios.

Remembering **Goal:** Spiral Review

This Remembering page would be appropriate anytime after today's lesson.

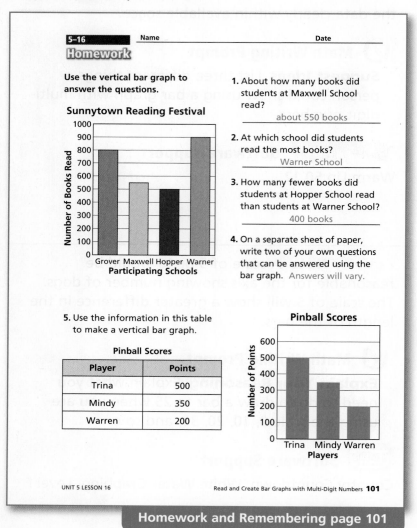

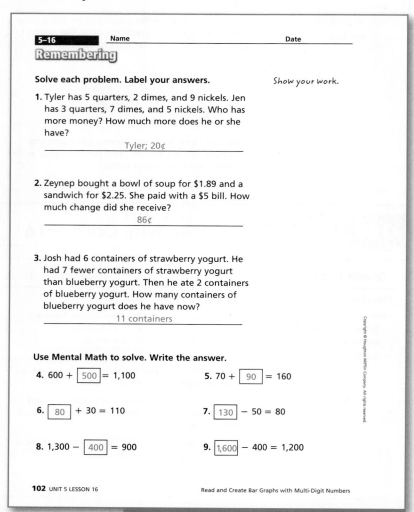

Homework and Remembering page 101

Homework and Remembering page 102

Home or School Activity

 ### Real-World Connection

Surveying and Reporting Have students survey at least 10 classmates, friends, or family members to find out which of three things they like best. For example, the topic of the survey could be favorite sports (soccer, baseball, or basketball) or favorite desserts (cookies, ice cream, or cake). Students should report the results of their survey in a simple table, then use the table to create a bar graph.

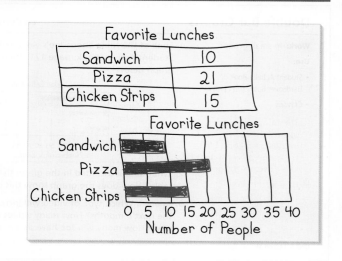

UNIT 5

LESSON 17

Represent and Organize Data

REAL WORLD Problem Solving

Lesson Objectives

- Construct and analyze frequency tables and line plots
- Match a set of data with a graph of the data and describe the important features.

Vocabulary
frequency table
line plot
tally chart
mode
range

The Day at a Glance

Today's Goals	Materials
1 **Teaching the Lesson** **A1:** Make and use frequency tables and line plots to find the mode and range of the data. **A2:** Match conclusions with graphs. **2** **Going Further** ▶ Differentiated Instruction **3** **Homework and Spiral Review**	**Lesson Activities** Student Activity Book pp. 173–174 or Student Hardcover Book pp. 173–174 Homework and Remembering pp. 103–104 Quick Quiz 5 (Assessment Guide) **Going Further** Activity Cards 5-17 MathBoard Materials Spinner E (TRB M132) Connecting cubes Paper bag Number cubes Calendar Math Journals 123 *Use* **Math Talk** *today!*

Keeping Skills Sharp

Quick Practice ⏱ 5 MINUTES	**Daily Routines**
Goal: Round whole numbers to the nearest ten or hundred. **Rounding Practice** The **Student Leader** writes 532, 279, 349, 1,151, 1,837, and 693 on the board. The leader points to the numbers one at a time and says either, "Round to the nearest ten," or, "Round to the nearest hundred." When the leader gives a signal, students respond in unison with the rounded number. *Leader (pointing to 532):* Round to the nearest ten. *Class:* 530	**Homework Review** Have students place their homework at the corner of their desks. Check that students completed the homework and if any problem(s) caused difficulty for many students. **Estimation** Pablo bought 568 cards to sell in his store. His store sold 326 of these cards. About how many cards does his store have left to sell? Explain. Possible answer: about 300 cards; Round to the nearest hundred, 600 and 300, and then subtract.

Teaching the Lesson

Frequency Tables and Line Plots

 30 MINUTES

Goals: Construct and analyze frequency tables and line plots from data. Find mode and range using a line plot.

Materials: Student Activity Book or Hardcover Book p. 173.

✔ **NCTM Standards:**
Number and Operations
Algebra
Data Analysis and Probability
Representation

English Language Learners

Write {2, 3, 3, 4, 4, 4, 7}, *range*, and *mode* on the board. Say: *Range* is the greatest number minus the least number. *Mode* is the number that repeats most.

- **Beginning** Say: What is 7 – 2? 5 **5 is the** *range*. **4 repeats the most. 4 is the** *mode*. **Have students repeat.**
- **Intermediate** Say: The greatest number is __. 7 The least number is __. 2 What is 7 – 2? 5 **5 is the** *range*. Ask: Which number repeats the most? 4 Say: **4 is the** *mode*.
- **Advanced** Have students find the range and mode in different sets of numbers.

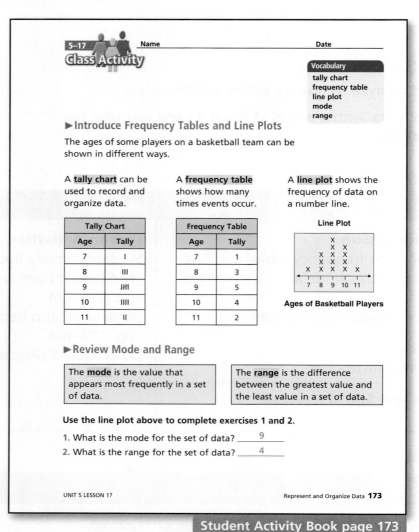

Student Activity Book page 173

▶ Introduce Frequency Tables and Line Plots

WHOLE CLASS

Have students look at the tally chart, frequency table, and line plot on the top of Student Book page 173. Discuss how the same data is shown in three different ways, comparing the benefits of each.

▶ Review Mode and Range WHOLE CLASS

Have students complete exercises 1 and 2. As time allows, have students create their own tally charts, frequency tables, and line plots. You can organize the heights of students in the class collected in Lesson 15, measure the length of each person's foot or forearm length, count the number of letters in each month's name, or conduct an experiment, such as pulling colored cubes or coins out of a bag.

Match Graphs and Data

 25 MINUTES

Goal: Match a set of data with a graphical representation. Match a conclusion to a set of data.

Materials: Student Activity Book or Hardcover Book p. 174

 NCTM Standards:
Number and Operations
Algebra
Data Analysis and Probability
Representation

▶ **Choose an Appropriate Display** [SMALL GROUPS]

Math Talk Write these following types of graphs on the board and discuss with students why they might choose a certain type of graph to display data.

> bar graph
> pictograph
> line plot
> frequency table

● Which graphs can be used to compare data? *bar graphs* and *pictographs.*

● Which graphs are used to show how often things occur? *line plots* and *frequency tables.*

You may also want to review and discuss all the parts of the different types of graphs (i.e. axes, symbols, keys, titles, labels, etc.)

Then have students work in three **Small Groups**, one creating data and a bar graph, another creating data and a pictograph, and another creating data and a frequency table and line plot. Once students have finished their graphs have groups display and explain how they chose their data and created their graphs and tell why they chose the display they did.

Encourage other students and groups to ask questions about each other's graphs. Guide the discussion and make sure to discuss how groups decided on the type of data they wanted to graph, how they wanted to set up the graph, and if there are other ways to display the same data. Then for each graph ask:

● What are some conclusions you can make looking at the graph?

● What predictions can you make by interpreting the graphs?

Then have groups choose a graph that another group created and write two word problems that can be solved using the graph.
Have students share their predictions, problems, and solutions with the class.

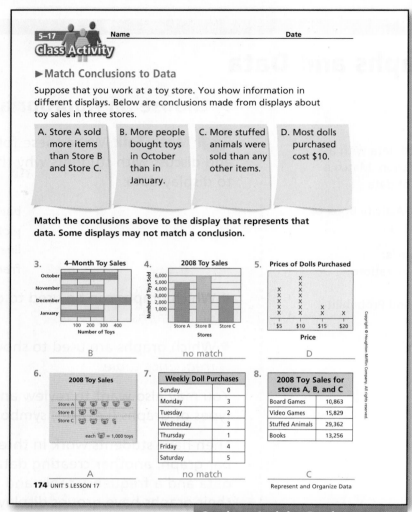

▶ Match Conclusions to Data INDIVIDUALS

 **Math Talk** Have a student volunteer read aloud the scenario described on the top of the Student Book page 174. Then have students read aloud the conclusions and have them decide what type of graph might have been used to display each set of data to get that conclusion. (Possible response: A, B, and C could be shown in a pictograph if the data is not too far spread or very large numbers. A bar graph would also be the good choice for A. B. and C. D could be shown in a line plot.)

Have students complete exercises 3-8 on Student Book page 174 and discuss the results as a class.

Make sure to point out that it is important to look closely at graphs to decide what the graphs show.

 Quick Quiz

See the Assessment Guide for Unit 5, Quick Quiz 5.

Intervention   Activity Card 5-17

Spin a Line Plot   Activity Card 5-17 ●

Work: In pairs

Use:
- MathBoard materials,
- TRB M132 (Spinner E)

1. **Work Together** Set up a line plot on your MathBoard with the numbers 1, 2, 3, and 4 on the horizontal axis. Use the top spinner on TRB M132. Write one of the numbers 1, 2, 3, and 4 in each section.

2. Take turns spinning the spinner 20 times and recording the result on the line plot.

 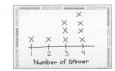

3. **Analyze** Which number did the spinner point to most often? Why do you think this happened? *Possible answer: 4; because it was in the largest section*

Unit 5, Lesson 17   Copyright © Houghton Mifflin Company

Activity Note Students should make sure their line plot is complete. Encourage them to count and add up the number of Xs to make sure that there are a total of 20 Xs.

 Math Writing Prompt

Multi-Step Explain how to find the range for any set of data. Use words like *first*, *next*, *then*, and so on to help explain your thinking

Soar to Success Math ★ **Software Support**

Warm Up 50.07

On Level   Activity Card 5-17

Roll It!   Activity Card 5-17 ▲

Work: In pairs

Use:
- MathBoard materials or blank paper, 4 number cubes (labeled 1-6)

Decide:
Who will be Student 1 and who will be Student 2 for the first round.

1. **Student 1:** Roll both number cubes and add them together to find the sum. Continue this for 10 times and record data in a tally chart. Then organize the data in a frequency table and line plot.

2. **Student 2:** Roll both number cubes and add them together to find the sum. Continue this for 10 times and record the data in a tally chart. Then organize the data in a frequency table and line plot.

3. Compare both line plots and discuss the similarities and differences.

4. **Analyze** What would you predict is the sum that would occur most often? *Answers may vary. The sum of 7 has the greatest probability of occurring ($\frac{6}{36}$).*

Unit 5, Lesson 17   Copyright © Houghton Mifflin Company

Activity Note Students should check their work and make sure they don't have any sums greater than 12. Since the number cube is labeled 1-6, the greatest possible sum is 12.

 Math Writing Prompt

Analyze Do you think it is easier to find the mode when you look at a tally chart, frequency table, or a line plot?

 Software Support

Country Countdown: White Water Graphing, Level D

Challenge   Activity Card 5-17

Alphamode   Activity Card 5-17 ■

Work: On your own

Use:
- MathBoard materials or blank paper, calendar

1. Use a calendar to count the number of letters in each month's name. Record the data in a tally chart.

2. Organize the data in a frequency table and a line plot.

3. Use the line plot to find the mode and range of the set of data.

Unit 5, Lesson 17   Copyright © Houghton Mifflin Company

Activity Note Challenge students to write out and spell each of the months without looking at a calendar. Then have children check their work by looking at a calendar.

 Math Writing Prompt

Reason Sean rolls a number cube (labeled 1-6) and records the data in a line plot. Sean looks at his data and says the range is 6. Is this possible?

 DESTINATION Math· **Software Support**

Course II: Module 3: Unit 1: Area

③ Homework and Spiral Review

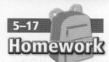
This Homework page provides students with more practice with frequency tables and line plots.

This Remembering page would be appropriate any time after today's lesson.

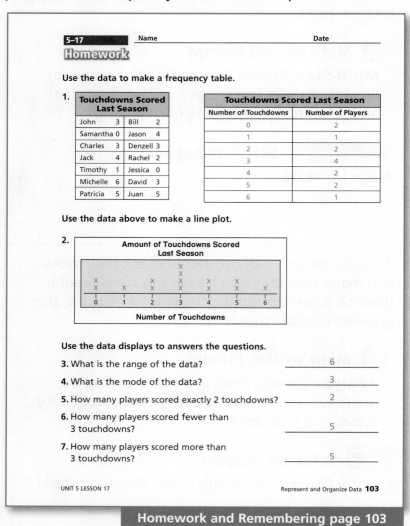

5-17   Name _____   Date _____
Homework

Use the data to make a frequency table.

1.

Touchdowns Scored Last Season			
John	3	Bill	2
Samantha	0	Jason	4
Charles	3	Denzell	3
Jack	4	Rachel	2
Timothy	1	Jessica	0
Michelle	6	David	3
Patricia	5	Juan	5

Touchdowns Scored Last Season	
Number of Touchdowns	Number of Players
0	2
1	1
2	2
3	4
4	2
5	2
6	1

Use the data above to make a line plot.

2.

Amount of Touchdowns Scored Last Season

```
                         X
                         X
X        X       X   X       X
X    X   X   X   X   X   X       X
0    1   2   3   4   5   6
```

Number of Touchdowns

Use the data displays to answers the questions.

3. What is the range of the data? _____ 6

4. What is the mode of the data? _____ 3

5. How many players scored exactly 2 touchdowns? _____ 2

6. How many players scored fewer than 3 touchdowns? _____ 5

7. How many players scored more than 3 touchdowns? _____ 5

UNIT 5 LESSON 17   Represent and Organize Data **103**

Homework and Remembering page 103

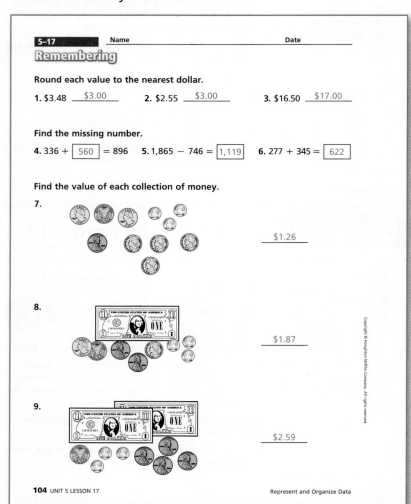

5-17   Name _____   Date _____
Remembering

Round each value to the nearest dollar.

1. $3.48 $3.00   2. $2.55 $3.00   3. $16.50 $17.00

Find the missing number.

4. 336 + 560 = 896   5. 1,865 − 746 = 1,119   6. 277 + 345 = 622

Find the value of each collection of money.

7. $1.26

8. $1.87

9. $2.59

104 UNIT 5 LESSON 17   Represent and Organize Data

Homework and Remembering page 104

Home or School Activity

 Physical Education Connection

Have students stand behind a masking tape line on a gym mat and jump as far as they can two times. Another student measures and records the length of each jump to the nearest foot. Have students create a frequency table and line plot to organize and display the data. Challenge students to find the mode and range of the data using the line plot.

Use Mathematical Processes

Lesson Objectives

● Apply mathematical concepts and skills in meaningful contexts.

● Reinforce the NCTM process skills embedded in this unit, and in previous
units, with a variety of problem-solving situations.

The Day at a Glance

Today's Goals	Materials	

1 Teaching the Lesson
A1: Math Connections Find how many jumps a frog needs to make to go a given distance; find the number of body lengths a frog can jump.
A2: Problem Solving Measure the length of a jump; record data in a table and on a bar graph; describe the shape of the data; find the mode; make a prediction based on data.
A3: Reasoning and Proof Use reasoning to support or disprove a statement.
A4: Representation Use a drawing to show an amount of money in three different ways.
A5: Communication Tell why an estimate is the best of three estimates.
 	
2 Going Further
▶ Differentiated Instruction
 	
3 Homework and Spiral Review
	Lesson Activities
	Student Activity Book pp. 175–176
	  or Student Hardcover Book
	  pp. 175–176
	Homework and Remembering
	  pp. 105–106
	Calculators
	Tap
	Measuring tape
	Grid Paper (TRB M31)
		Going Further
		Activity Cards 5-18
		Straws
		Scissors
		Math Journals
		
		123 Use
		Math Talk
		today!

Keeping Skills Sharp

Quick Practice/Daily Routines	
If you wish to include Quick Practice or a Daily Routine, choose content based on the needs of your class.	**Class Management** Select activities from this lesson that support important goals and objectives, or that help students prepare for state or district tests.

Teaching the Lesson

Math and Science

 45 MINUTES

Goals: Find how many jumps a frog needs to make to go a given distance; find the number of body lengths a frog can jump.

Materials: Student Activity Book or Hardcover Book p. 175, calculators

✓ **NCTM Standards:**
Problem Solving
Connections
Communication
Reasoning and Proof

▶ Who Will Win the Race   Math Talk

Task 1 Begin work on the problem with whole class discussion.

● Look at the table. Which frog do you think will win the race? Answers will vary. Many students will likely think that Flora will win the race since she has the longest jump.

● How could you figure out how many jumps it will take for a frog to cross the finish line? Allow students to share their ideas. One way is to take the length of a frog's jump and see how many times you have to add it to get 1,000 cm or greater.

▶ How Many Of His Body Lengths Can Freddie Jump?

Task 2 Tell students that they are going to find how many body lengths Freddie the Frog can jump.

● How could you figure out how many of his body lengths Freddie the Frog can jump? Allow students to share their ideas. One way is to take the length of Freddie's body (20 cm) and see how many times you have to add it to get 200 cm, the length of his jump.

 5–18 **Class Activity**   Name _____ Date _____

▶ Math and Science

Three frogs are having a Frog Jumping Contest.
The length of the race is 1,000 cm.
The table shows how far each frog goes in 1 jump.

Name of Frog	Length of Jump
Freddie	about 200 cm
Flora	about 315 cm
Frankie	about 144 cm

Use a Calculator.

1. Bena says it will take Flora about 3 jumps to cross the finish line? Is she right?
   No. It will take Flora about 4 jumps.

2. What conclusions can you make about how many jumps it will take the other frogs to cross the finish line?
   Freddie: 5 jumps; Frankie: 7 jumps

3. What conclusion can you make about how many of his body lengths Freddie the Frog can jump?
   Freddie can jump 10 of his body lengths

Freddie's Body Length

← 20 cm →

UNIT 5 LESSON 18   Use Mathematical Processes **175**

Student Activity Book page 175

Teaching Note

More About Frogs Freddie is a Bullfrog, Flora is a South-African Sharp-Nosed Frog, and Frankie is a Leopard Frog. Have students do research on these kinds of frogs and get pictures of what they look like. Flora is about 7 cm long. Have students find out how many body lengths Flora can jump using a calculator. (about 45 body lengths)

English Language Learners

Help students describe the data in the table.

● **Beginning** Ask: **What data is in the rows? In the columns?**
● **Intermediate** Ask: **Does Flora have the longest or shortest jump?** longest **Do you think Flora will win the race?**
● **Advanced** Have students work in pairs to describe the data and make predictions. Have volunteers share their predictions.

Activity 2

Problem Solving

How Far Can You Jump?

 45 MINUTES

Goals: Measure the length of a jump; record data in a table and on a bar graph; describe the shape of the data; find the mode; make a prediction based on data.

Materials: Student Activity Book or Hardcover Book p. 176 and Activity Workbook p. 62, tape, measuring tapes, Grid Paper (TRB M31)

✓ **NCTM Standards:**
Problem Solving
Connections
Communication
Reasoning and Proof
Representation

► How Far Can You Jump?

4. Ask 10 students to jump. Measure the length of each jump. Record the names of the students and the length of the jumps in a table. Data will vary.

5. Make a bar graph on grid paper that shows the length of each jump. Put the data in order from shortest jump to longest jump. Check students' graphs.

6. Look at the graph you made. What is the shape of the data? Answers will vary.

7. What is the mode and range? Answers will vary.

8. What is your prediction for the jump of another student who has not jumped yet? Why do you think that is a good prediction? Answers will vary.

9. What conclusion can you make about how far the 10 students can jump? Possible answer: Most students can jump 3 feet.

176 UNIT 5 LESSON 18

Use Mathematical Processes

Student Activity Book page 176

► The Length of a Jump

Task 1 Begin with whole class discussion.

● How do you think we could measure how far each of you can jump? Allow students to share their ideas. One way is to put a piece of tape on the floor. A student stands at the tape and then jumps as far as they can. Another student measures the length of the jump.

● How far do you think you can jump? Allow students to share their guesses.

Tell students that they will measure how far they can jump and record the length of the jumps of 10 different students in a table and on a bar graph. Help students as needed with measuring the jumps and recording the data. Make sure they put the data in the graph in numerical order so they will be able to discuss the shape of the data.

► Analyze the Data   Math Talk

Task 2 Discuss the data that students have collected.

● What is the shape of the data? Answers will vary. Students may notice places where the data is clustered and places where there are holes.

● What is the mode? Answers will vary. Have students look for the number that showed up most frequently.

► Make a Prediction

Task 3 Discuss how data can be used to make predictions.

● Suppose you asked someone that has not jumped yet to jump. How could you use the data you have collected to make a prediction? Answers will vary. Possible answer. If the person is about the same height as the other jumpers, a good prediction would be a measurement that came up frequently in the data.

● Which display—the table or the bar graph—was easier to use to make your prediction? Possible response: The bar graph was easier to use because the bars show the length at a glance.

Use Mathematical Processes   **425**

Activity 3

Are All Letters Symmetrical?

 10–20 MINUTES

Goal: Use reasoning to support or disprove a statement.

✓ **NCTM Standards:**
Problem Solving   Communication
Connections   Reasoning and Proof

Support or disprove with examples: All letters of the alphabet are symmetrical. Students will not have to go very far in the alphabet to find letters that are not symmetrical. For example, F and G are not symmetrical

Hold a whole-class discussion of the problem.

▶ Do you think all letters of the alphabet are symmetrical? Allow students to give their opinions.

▶ Can anyone give me an example of a letter that is not symmetrical? Record examples on the board.

▶ Should we conclude that all letters are symmetrical or that there are some letters that are not symmetrical? There are some letters that are not symmetrical.

Activity 4

36¢ Three Ways

 10–20 MINUTES

Goal: Use a drawing to show an amount of money in three different ways.

✓ **NCTM Standards:**
Problem Solving   Representation
Connections

Draw 3 ways to show 36¢. Answers will vary. Sample: 1 quarter, 1 dime, 1 penny; 36 pennies; 3 dimes, 1 nickel, 1 penny

Discuss the problem with the class.

▶ How many different ways do you think there are to make 36¢? Allow students to share their guesses.

▶ Let's find out. List all of the ways the students found on the board

▶ Do you think there might be even more ways? See if anyone can find a way that hasn't been listed.

Activity 5

The Best Estimate

 10–20 MINUTES

Goal: Tell why an estimate is the best of three estimates.

✓ **NCTM Standards:**
Problem Solving   Reasoning and Proof
Communication

$39 + 21 + 48 + 33$.

What is the best estimate? 160, 120, or 140. 140 Why? sample: It is the estimate you get when you round each number to the nearest ten.

Hold a whole-class discussion of the problem.

▶ What is the best estimate? 140

▶ Why is 140 the best estimate? You get 140 when you round to the ten that is closest to each number. You get 160 if you round all of the numbers up. You get 120 if you round all of the numbers down. But the best estimate is the estimate you get when you round each number to the nearest ten. If you find the exact answer it is 141. 140 is the estimate that is closest to the exact answer.

② Going Further

Differentiated Instruction

Intervention — Activity Card 5-18

Straw Triangles
Activity Card 5-18 ●

Work: In pairs

Use:
• Straws
• Scissors

1. Cut straws into different lengths.

2. Find straw pieces that you can put together to make triangles.

3. How many different types of triangles can you make? Make a list. Students should be able to make triangles that are right, acute, obtuse, scalene, equilateral, and isosceles.

Unit 5, Lesson 18

Copyright © Houghton Mifflin Company

Activity Note Give students an opportunity to make a poster by taping (or tracing) the different triangles onto poster board and labeling each triangle with its appropriate names.

 Math Writing Prompt

Make an Equilateral Triangle How would you cut the straw pieces if you wanted to make an equilateral triangle?

 **Software Support**

Warm Up 35.07

On Level — Activity Card 5-18

Try to Make a Quadrilateral
Activity Card 5-18 ▲

Work: In pairs

Use:
• Straws
• Scissors

1. Cut straws into different lengths.

2. Find straw pieces that you can put together to make a quadrilateral.

3. How many different types of quadrilaterals can you make? Make a list. Students should be able to make squares, rectangles, trapezoids, rhombuses, parallelograms and irregular quadrilaterals.

Unit 5, Lesson 18

Copyright © Houghton Mifflin Company

Activity Note Give students an opportunity to make a poster by taping (or tracing) the different quadrilaterals onto poster board and labeling each quadrilateral with its appropriate names.

 Math Writing Prompt

Make a Parallelogram How would you use the straws to make a parallelogram that is not a square or a rectangle that is not a square?

 Software Support

Shapes Ahoy: Ship Shapes, Level G

Challenge — Activity Card 5-18

A Generalization About Triangles
Activity Card 5-18 ■

Work: In pairs

Use:
• Straws
• Scissors

Students should generalize that the sum of the lengths of any two sides of a triangle must be greater than the length of the third side; otherwise the ends will not meet to form a triangle.

1. Cut straws into different lengths.

2. Find straw pieces that you can put together to make a triangle. Measure them and record their lengths.

3. Find straw pieces that you cannot put together to make a triangle. Measure them and record their lengths.

4. Generalize When can you make a triangle and when can't you make a triangle?

Unit 5, Lesson 18

Copyright © Houghton Mifflin Company

Activity Note Students may find it helpful to make tables to record the lengths. Each table can be labeled **Can Make a Triangle** or **Cannot Make a Triangle**. This will help them analyze the data.

 Math Writing Prompt

Make Lines How would you use the straws to make parallel and perpendicular lines?

 DESTINATION Math **Software Support**

Course II: Module 3: Unit 1: Area

Use Mathematical Processes   **427**

③ Homework and Spiral Review

Homework　**Goal:** Additional Practice

✓ Include student's completed Homework page as part of their portfolios.

Targeted Practice　**Goal:** Spiral Review

This Remembering page would be appropriate anytime after today's lesson.

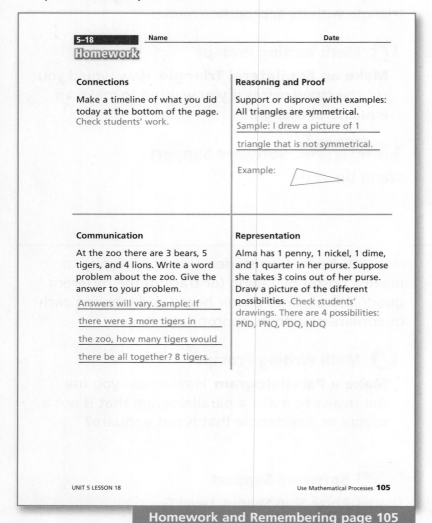

5–18　Name　Date
Homework

Connections

Make a timeline of what you did today at the bottom of the page. Check students' work.

Reasoning and Proof

Support or disprove with examples: All triangles are symmetrical.

Sample: I drew a picture of 1 triangle that is not symmetrical.

Example:

Communication

At the zoo there are 3 bears, 5 tigers, and 4 lions. Write a word problem about the zoo. Give the answer to your problem.

Answers will vary. Sample: If there were 3 more tigers in the zoo, how many tigers would there be all together? 8 tigers.

Representation

Alma has 1 penny, 1 nickel, 1 dime, and 1 quarter in her purse. Suppose she takes 3 coins out of her purse. Draw a picture of the different possibilities. Check students' drawings. There are 4 possibilities: PND, PNQ, PDQ, NDQ

UNIT 5 LESSON 18　Use Mathematical Processes **105**

Homework and Remembering page 105

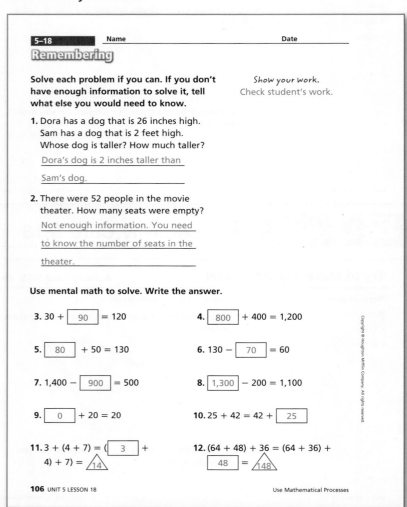

5–18　Name　Date
Remembering

Solve each problem if you can. If you don't have enough information to solve it, tell what else you would need to know.

Show your work.
Check student's work.

1. Dora has a dog that is 26 inches high. Sam has a dog that is 2 feet high. Whose dog is taller? How much taller?

   Dora's dog is 2 inches taller than Sam's dog.

2. There were 52 people in the movie theater. How many seats were empty?

   Not enough information. You need to know the number of seats in the theater.

Use mental math to solve. Write the answer.

3. $30 + \boxed{90} = 120$

4. $\boxed{800} + 400 = 1{,}200$

5. $\boxed{80} + 50 = 130$

6. $130 - \boxed{70} = 60$

7. $1{,}400 - \boxed{900} = 500$

8. $\boxed{1{,}300} - 200 = 1{,}100$

9. $\boxed{0} + 20 = 20$

10. $25 + 42 = 42 + \boxed{25}$

11. $3 + (4 + 7) = (\boxed{3} + 4) + 7) = \triangle{14}$

12. $(64 + 48) + 36 = (64 + 36) + \boxed{48} = \triangle{148}$

106 UNIT 5 LESSON 18　Use Mathematical Processes

Homework and Remembering page 106

Home or School Activity

 Real-Word Connection

Favorite Animal Have students each choose two favorite animals. Have them do some research in books or on the Internet to collect some data on the animals. Have them make a poster that shows what they learned. Ask them to write a word problem about the animals on their poster. Have students solve each other's problems.

Height of Giraffe: 18 feet

Height of Lion: 4 feet

Unit Review and Test

Lesson Objective

● **Assess student progress on unit objectives.**

The Day at a Glance

Today's Goals	Materials
1 **Assessing the Unit** ▶ Assess student progress on unit objectives. ▶ Use activities from unit lessons to reteach content. **2** **Extending the Assessment** ▶ Use remediation for common errors. There is no homework assignment on a test day.	Unit 5 Test, Student Activity Book pp. 177–180 or Hardcover Book pp. 177–180 and Activity Workbook pp. 61–64 Unit 5 Test, Form A or B, Assessment Guide (optional) Unit 5 Performance Assessment, Assessment Guide (optional)

Keeping Skills Sharp

Quick Practice 🕐 5 MINUTES	
Goal: Review any skills you choose to meet the needs of your class. If you are doing a unit review day, use any of the Quick Practice activities that provide support for your class. If this is a test day, omit Quick Practice.	**Review and Test Day** You may want to choose a quiet game or other activity (reading a book or working on homework for another subject) for students who finish early.

1 Assessing the Unit

Assess Unit Objectives

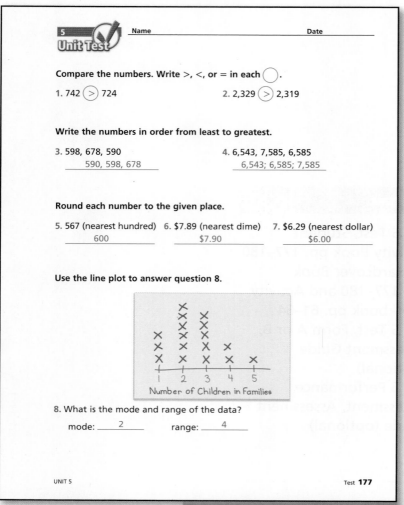

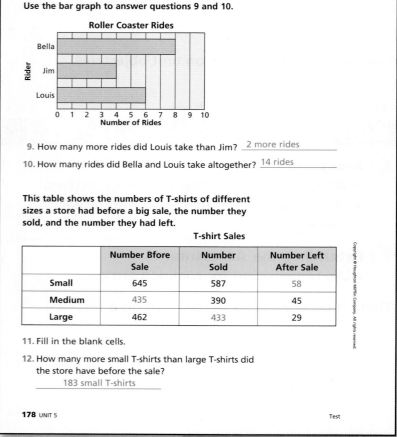

🕐 **45 MINUTES** (more if schedule permits)

Goal: Assess student progress on unit objectives.

Materials: Student Activity Book or Hardcover pp. 177–180 and Activity Workbook pp. 61–64; Assessment Guide (optional)

▶ Review and Assessment

If your students are ready for assessment on the unit objectives, use either the test on the Student Activity Book pages or one of the forms of the Unit 5 Test in the Assessment Guide to assess student progress. To assign a numerical score for all of these test forms, use 5 points for each question.

The chart to the right lists the test items, the unit objectives they cover, and the lesson activities in which the objective is covered in this unit.

Unit Test Items	Unit Objectives Tested	Activities to Use for Reteaching
1–5, 15	5.1 Compare, order, and round whole numbers and estimate sums and differences.	Lesson 1, Activities 1 and 2 Lesson 2, Activity 1 Lesson 3, Activity 1
6, 7, 17–20	5.2 Find the value of and represent money amounts with coins and bills, count change, compare, round, and estimate with money.	Lesson 4, Activity 2 Lesson 5, Activity 1 Lesson 6, Activity 1 Lesson 7, Activities 1 and 2

430 UNIT 5

Name _____ **Date** _____

Solve. Cross out any extra information. Circle any hidden information.

Show your work.

13. Becky has 20 fish ~~and 2 hamsters~~. There are 8 angelfish and the rest of the fish are goldfish. She gets 7 more goldfish. How many goldfish does she have now?

    19 goldfish

14. Raj is going on vacation for (a week) and 5 days. How many days will Raj be gone?

    12 days

Solve. Label your answer.

15. Jason has 485 toy dinosaurs in his collection. He plans to sell 243 toy dinosaurs. Round each number to the nearest ten to estimate how many he will have left.

    250 toy dinosaurs

Solve the problem if possible. If more information is needed, rewrite the problem to include the necessary information and then solve it.

16. Julie and Sam grew tomato plants. Julie's plant grew 16 inches. How much taller did Sam's plant grow?

    Possible answer: Julie and Sam grew tomato
    plants. Julie's plant grew 16 inches. Sam's
    plant grew 20 inches. How much taller did
    Sam's plant grow than Julie's plant?; 4 inches

UNIT 5

Test **179**

Name _____ **Date** _____

Compare the two collections of coins and bills. Write >, <, or = in the ◯.

17.

18. Draw two different coin combinations for 78¢.

    Possible answers: Q Q Q P P P   Q Q D D N P P P

Solve.

19. Uri bought a tube of toothpaste for $2.58. He paid with a $5.00 bill. Find the amount of change by counting on. Draw the coins and bills you counted. How much change did he get?

    Show your work.

    Possible answer: P P N D Q $1 $1: $2.42

*20. **Extended Response** Alexa has $5.00. She wants to order a sandwich for $3.65 and a drink for $1.48. How can she estimate to be sure she has enough money? Alexa should round up each
    amount to the next dollar to see if she has
    enough money. $4.00 + $2.00 = $6.00

    What estimate do you get using your method? Can Alexa be sure she has enough money to buy the sandwich and the drink?
    $6.00; No

    * Item 20 also assesses the Process Skills of Communication, Connections, and Reasoning and Proof.

180 UNIT 5

Test

Unit Test Items	Unit Objectives Tested	Activities to Use for Reteaching
8–12	**5.3** Interpret data in a table, graph, or line plot, make graphs, and complete tables.	Lesson 8, Activity 2 Lesson 9, Activity 2 Lesson 10, Activity 1 Lesson 16, Activity 2
13, 14, 16	**5.4** Solve word problems with two steps, multi-steps, extra or hidden information, and identify problems with not enough information.	Lesson 11, Activities 1 and 2 Lesson 12, Activity 1 Lesson 13, Activity 1 Lesson 14, Activity 1

▶ **Assessment Resources**

Form A, Free Response Test (Assessment Guide)

Form B, Multiple-Choice Test (Assessment Guide)

Performance Assessment (Assessment Guide)

▶ **Portfolio Assessment**

Teacher-selected Items for Student Portfolios:

● Homework, Lessons 2, 9, 14, 16, and 18

● Class Activity work, Lessons 4, 7, 12, and 18

Student-selected Items for Student Portfolios:

● Favorite Home or School Activity

● Best Writing Prompt

Unit Review and Test   **431**

② Extending the Assessment

Unit Objective 5.1

Compare, order, and round whole numbers and estimate sums and differences.

Common Error: Rounds to an Incorrect Place

Students may confuse the place to be rounded with the place that is used to decide how to round the number.

Remediation Remind students to underline the place to which they are rounding and use Secret Code Cards and drawings to help them conclude that they need to look at the next smaller place to decide which way to round.

Common Error: Reverses Inequality Symbols

Students may have difficulty deciding whether the sign is pointing to the smaller or larger number.

Remediation Help students remember the difference between the symbols by pointing out that the symbols are like arrows and the small point of the arrow always points to the smaller number, or that the fish's mouth always faces the larger number.

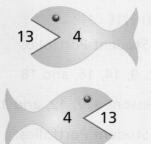

Unit Objective 5.2

Find the value of and represent money amounts with coins and bills, count change, compare, round and estimate with money.

Common Error: Counts Coins Incorrectly

Students must be proficient in skip counting by fives, tens, and twenty-fives to be successful with counting coins.

Remediation Have a group of students take turns saying the next number when counting by fives, tens, or twenty-fives. Then switch counting rules while students are counting. For example, when 4 students have counted by tens, say to the next student, "switch to fives."

Remind students always to count coins starting with the coins that have the greatest value.

Unit Objective 5.3

Interpret data in a table or graph, make bar graphs, and complete tables.

Common Error: Does Not Give Adequate Titles to Tables or Graphs

Students may not be able to use a table or bar graph to solve a problem because the information is not organized clearly.

Remediation Give students practice in saying titles and choosing the labels for the axes in bar graphs by giving various situations.

Unit Objective 5.4

Solve word problems with two steps, multi-steps, and extra or hidden information, and identify problems with not enough information.

Common Error: Has Difficulty with Multi-Step Problems

Students may have difficulty deciding when and how to break a problem into simpler parts.

Remediation Have students act out problems using lists, drawings, manipulatives, or money. This will allow them to see concretely which steps must be performed and how to order the steps.

Common Error: Unable to Identify the Relevant Information

Students may have difficulty identifying if there is too much or too little information in a problem.

Remediation Have students first identify what they need to find. Then have them go back to the beginning of the problem and circle the information they need, and cross out the information they do not need.

Patterns

UNIT 6 CONTINUES TO develop students' algebraic thinking through patterning. The activities in this unit give students the opportunity to identify, extend, and create repeating number patterns, repeating geometric patterns, growing and shrinking number patterns, and growing and shrinking geometric patterns. Students also explore transformations: flips, slides, and turns, and create motion geometry patterns with flips. Students apply their patterning skills to solve problems by using the strategy of solving a simpler related problem.

Skills Trace

Grade 2	Grade 3	Grade 4
• Explore patterns with slides, flips, and turns. • Create and extend repeating and growing patterns. • Identify the rule, and extend number patterns.	• Recognize and describe slides, flips, and turns, and recognize them in geometric patterns. • Identify the rule, and extend number or geometric repeating patterns. • Identify the rule, and extend number or geometric growing and shrinking patterns using addition and subtraction. • Solve real-world problems with patterns.	• Apply geometric transformations in Quadrant 1 of the coordinate plane. • Identify the rule, and extend number or geometric repeating patterns. • Extend number or geometric growing and shrinking patterns using multiplication and division. • Complete function tables, and represent patterns algebraically.

Unit 6   Contents

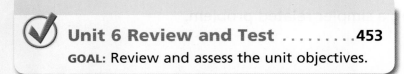

Planning Unit 6

Lesson NCTM Focal Points NCTM Standards	Resources	Materials for Lesson Activities	Materials for Going Further
6-1 **Motion Geometry Patterns** NCTM Focal Point: 3.5 NCTM Standards: 3, 10	TE pp. 433–438 SAB pp. 181–186 H&R pp. 107–108 AC 6-1 MCC 21, 22	✓ Rulers Plastic mirrors (optional) Dot paper (optional)	Pattern Blocks (TRB M27) Pattern Block Grid Paper (TRB M47) Math Journals
6-2 **Repeating Patterns** NCTM Standards: 2, 3, 7	TE pp. 439–444 SAB pp. 187–188 H&R pp. 109–110 AC 6-2 MCC 23	Hundred Grid (TRB M48) Sheet protectors Dry-erase materials ✓ Two-color counter Calculators	Pattern Blocks (TRB M27) Math Journals
6-3 **Growing and Shrinking Patterns** NCTM Standards: 2, 3, 7	TE pp. 445–452 SAB pp. 189–192 H&R pp. 111–112 AC 6-3 MCC 24 AG Quick Quiz	Calculators *One Grain of Rice*, by Demi	Paper squares or square pattern blocks Skip Counting Circle (TRB M49) Math Journals
Unit Review and Test	TE pp. 453–456 SAB pp. 193–194 AG Unit 6 Tests		

Resources/Materials Key: TE: Teacher Edition SAB: Student Activity Book H&R: Homework and Remembering
AC: Activity Cards MCC: Math Center Challenge AG: Assessment Guide ✓: Grade 3 kits TRB: Teacher's Resource Book

NCTM Standards and Expectations Key: 1. Number and Operations 2. Algebra 3. Geometry 4. Measurement
5. Data Analysis and Probability 6. Problem Solving 7. Reasoning and Proof 8. Communication 9. Connections 10. Representation

Hardcover Student Book

- Together, the Hardcover Student Book and its companion Activity Workbook contain all of the pages in the consumable Student Activity Book.

Manipulatives and Materials

- Essential materials for teaching *Math Expressions* are available in the Grade 3 kits. These materials are indicated by a ✓ in these lists. At the front of this Teacher Edition is more information about kit contents, alternatives for the materials, and use of the materials.

Independent Learning Activities

Ready-Made Math Challenge Centers

21 Tiling the Floor — On Your Own

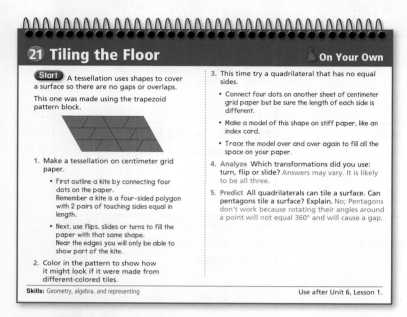

Start A tessellation uses shapes to cover a surface so there are no gaps or overlaps.

This one was made using the trapezoid pattern block.

1. Make a tessellation on centimeter grid paper.
   - First outline a kite by connecting four dots on the paper. Remember a kite is a four-sided polygon with 2 pairs of touching sides equal in length.
   - Next, use flips, slides or turns to fill the paper with that same shape. Near the edges you will only be able to show part of the kite.

2. Color in the pattern to show how it might look if it were made from different-colored tiles.

3. This time try a quadrilateral that has no equal sides.
   - Connect four dots on another sheet of centimeter grid paper but be sure the length of each side is different.
   - Make a model of this shape on stiff paper, like an index card.
   - Trace the model over and over again to fill all the space on your paper.

4. Analyze Which transformations did you use: turn, flip or slide? Answers may vary. It is likely to be all three.

5. Predict All quadrilaterals can tile a surface. Can pentagons tile a surface? Explain. No; Pentagons don't work because rotating their angles around a point will not equal 360° and will cause a gap.

Skills: Geometry, algebra, and representing
Use after Unit 6, Lesson 1.

Grouping Individuals

Materials Ruler, Centimeter Grid Paper (TRB M28), index cards, crayons or markers

Objective Students study patterns when tiling a surface by transforming polygons.

Connections Geometry and Representation

22 Stained Glass Window — On Your Own

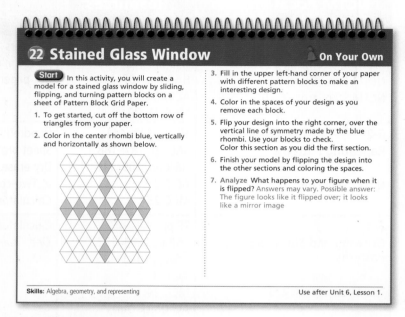

Start In this activity, you will create a model for a stained glass window by sliding, flipping, and turning pattern blocks on a sheet of Pattern Block Grid Paper.

1. To get started, cut off the bottom row of triangles from your paper.

2. Color in the center rhombi blue, vertically and horizontally as shown below.

3. Fill in the upper left-hand corner of your paper with different pattern blocks to make an interesting design.

4. Color in the spaces of your design as you remove each block.

5. Flip your design into the right corner, over the vertical line of symmetry made by the blue rhombi. Use your blocks to check. Color this section as you did the first section.

6. Finish your model by flipping the design into the other sections and coloring the spaces.

7. Analyze What happens to your figure when it is flipped? Answers may vary. Possible answer: The figure looks like it flipped over; it looks like a mirror image

Skills: Algebra, geometry, and representing
Use after Unit 6, Lesson 1.

Grouping Individuals

Materials Pattern blocks, crayons or markers, Pattern Block Grid Paper (TRB M47)

Objective Students study patterns when tiling a surface by transforming polygons.

Connections Geometry and Representation

23 Addition Table Patterns — Pairs

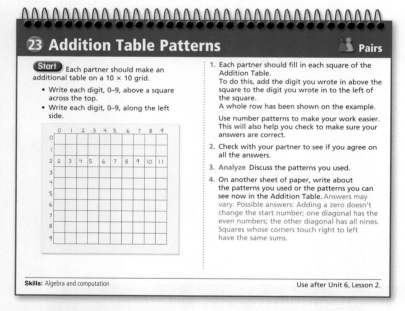

Start Each partner should make an additional table on a 10 × 10 grid.
- Write each digit, 0–9, above a square across the top.
- Write each digit, 0–9, along the left side.

1. Each partner should fill in each square of the Addition Table.
   To do this, add the digit you wrote in above the square to the digit you wrote in to the left of the square.
   A whole row has been shown on the example.
   Use number patterns to make your work easier. This will also help you check to make sure your answers are correct.

2. Check with your partner to see if you agree on all the answers.

3. Analyze Discuss the patterns you used.

4. On another sheet of paper, write about the patterns you used or the patterns you can see now in the Addition Table. Answers may vary. Possible answers: Adding a zero doesn't change the start number; one diagonal has the even numbers; the other diagonal has all nines. Squares whose corners touch right to left have the same sums.

Skills: Algebra and computation
Use after Unit 6, Lesson 2.

Grouping Pairs

Materials 10 × 10 Grid (TRB M43)

Objective Students fill in and study patterns in an Addition Table.

Connections Algebra and Communication

24 Table Seatings — Small Groups

Start Imagine that you plan parties for groups and have tables shaped like triangle pattern blocks. The room where you host the parties is long and narrow so tables must be arranged side by side.

▲	3
◢◣	4
◢◣◢	5
◢◣◢◣	6

1. On another sheet of paper, copy the drawing and the chart that shows the number of chairs that can be used with the number of triangular tables.

Triangle Tables	Chairs
1	3
2	4
3	5
4	6
T	T + 1 Or add one chair for each new table

2. Now work with square tables using the square pattern blocks. Each side fits one chair unless it is next to another side.
   Make a drawing and a chart. Write about the pattern you see in the number of chairs.

3. Do the same for trapezoids tables using the trapezoid pattern blocks.
   Note: the long side of the trapezoid tables can fit two chairs.

4. Do the same for hexagon tables using the hexagon pattern blocks. Each side fits one chair.

Square Tables	Chairs
1	4
2	6
3	8
4	10
T	2T + 2 or add two more chairs for each table

Trapezoid Tables	Chairs
1	5
2	8
3	11
4	14
T	3T + 2 or add three more chairs for each table

Hexagon Tables	Chairs
1	6
2	10
3	14
4	18
T	4T + 2 or add four more chairs for each table

Skills: Algebra and representing
Use after Unit 6, Lesson 3.

Grouping Small Group

Materials Ruler, pattern blocks

Objective Students chart and identify the patterns created by different arrangements of shapes.

Connections Algebra and Representation

Ready-Made Math Resources

Technology — Tutorials, Practice, and Intervention

Use online, individualized intervention and support to bring students to proficiency.

Help students practice skills and apply concepts through exciting math adventures.

Extend and enrich students' understanding of skills and concepts through engaging, interactive lessons and activities.

Visit **Education Place**
www.eduplace.com

Visit **www.eduplace.com/mx2t/** and find family, teacher, and student materials, activities, games, and more.

Literature Links

One Hundred Hungry Ants

One Hundred Hungry Ants

Imagine organizing an army of 100 ants into various marching patterns, so as to reach the destination (the picnic) more quickly! The woodcut illustrations by Bonnie Mackain are incredible, as is the fun of following this ant adventure written by Elinor J. Pinczes.

Literature Connection

One Grain of Rice, by Demi (Scholastic Press, 1997)

Unit 6 Assessment

✓ Unit Objectives Tested	Unit Test Items	Lessons
6.1 Recognize and describe slides, flips, and turns and recognize them in geometric patterns.	1, 2	1, 2
6.2 Identify the rule for number or geometric repeating patterns and continue the patterns.	3, 4, 5	2
6.3 Identify the rule for growing and shrinking number or geometric patterns and continue the patterns.	6, 7, 8, 9	3
6.4 Solve real-world problems with patterns.	10	3

Assessment and Review Resources

Formal Assessment	Informal Assessment	Review Opportunities
Student Activity Book • Unit Review and Test (pp. 193–194) **Assessment Guide** • Quick Quiz (p. A54) • Test A–Open Response (pp. A55–A56) • Test B–Multiple Choice (pp. A57–58) • Performance Assessment (pp. A59–61) **Test Generator CD-ROM** • Open Response Test • Multiple Choice Test • Test Bank Items	**Teacher Edition** • Ongoing Assessment (in every lesson) • Math Talk (in every lesson) • Portfolio Suggestions (p. 455) ⑫③ **Math Talk** ▸ Math Talk in Action (p. 450) ▸ Student Pairs (pp. 435, 447) Helping Partner (p. 440) ▸ In Activities (pp. 436, 442, 446)	**Homework and Remembering** • Review of recently taught topics • Spiral Review **Teacher Edition** • Unit Review and Test (pp. 453–456) **Test Generator CD-ROM** • Custom Review Sheets

Unit 6   Teaching Resources

Differentiated Instruction

Individualizing Instruction

Activities	Level	Frequency
	• Intervention • On Level • Challenge	All 3 in every lesson
Math Writing Prompts	Level	Frequency
	• Intervention • On Level • Challenge	All 3 in every lesson
Math Center Challenges	For advanced students	
	4 in every unit	

Reaching All Learners

English Language Learners	Lessons	Pages
	1, 2, 3	433, 439, 445
Extra Help	Lesson	Page
	2	441
Advanced Learners	Lesson	Page
	2	441

Strategies for English Language Learners

Present this problem to all students. Offer the different levels of support to meet students' levels of language proficiency.

Objective Review triangles, squares, and patterns

Problem Show the following pattern: ▲■▲■▲■▲■.   Have students identify the shapes and read the pattern.

Newcomer

• Point to each shape. Say: **This is a triangle. This is a square.** Have students repeat.

• Point to each shape as you read the pattern. Say: **This is a pattern of triangles and squares.** Have students repeat the pattern.

Beginning

• Point and say: **This is a ___.** triangle, square Have students repeat.

• Point to the pattern. Say: **This is a pattern. What is it a pattern of?** triangles and squares Guide students to read the pattern.

Intermediate

• Ask: **What are the shapes in this pattern?** Invite students to read the pattern and identify what would come next.

Advanced

• Have students describe the pattern.

• Invite them to draw or name another pattern like this, using different shapes.

Connections

Language Arts Connection
Lesson 2, page 444

Literature Connection
Lesson 3, page 452

Math Background

Putting Research into Practice for Unit 6

From Current Research: Transformation

Students in grades 3–5 should consider three important kinds of transformations: reflections, translations, and rotations (flips, slides, and turns). Younger students generally "prove" that two shapes are congruent by physically fitting one on top of the other, but students in grades 3–5 can develop greater precision as they describe the motions needed to show congruence ("turn it 90°" or "flip it vertically, then rotate it 180°"). They should also be able to visualize what will happen when a shape is rotated or reflected and predict the result.

National Council of Teachers of Mathematics. *Principles and Standards for School Mathematics.* Reston: NCTM, 2000. p. 167.

Patterns

Although *algebra* is a word that has not commonly been heard in grades 3–5 classrooms, the mathematical investigations and conversations of students in these grades frequently include elements of algebraic reasoning. These experiences and conversations provide rich contexts for advancing mathematical understanding and are also an important precursor to the more formalized study of algebra in the middle and secondary grades. In grades 3–5, algebraic ideas should emerge and be investigated as students—

- identify or build numerical and geometric patterns;

- describe patterns verbally and represent them with tables or symbols;

- look for and apply relationships between varying quantities to make predictions;

- make and explain generalizations that seem to always work in particular situations;

- use graphs to describe patterns and make predictions;

- explore number properties;

- use invented notation, standard symbols, and variables to express a pattern, generalization, or situation.

National Council of Teachers of Mathematics. *Principles and Standards for School Mathematics.* Reston: NCTM, 2000. p. 159.

Other Useful References: Patterns

Bay-Williams, Jennifer M. "What Is Algebra in Elementary School?" *Teaching Children Mathematics* 8.4 (Dec. 2001): p. 196.

Coburn, Terrence G., et al. *Patterns: Addenda Series, Grades K–6.* Reston: NCTM, 1993. p. 53.

Curcio, Frances R., et al. "Exploring Patterns in Nonroutine Problems." *Mathematics Teaching in the Middle School* 2.4 (Feb. 1997): p. 262.

Ferrini-Mundy, Joan, et al. "Experiences with Patterning." *Teaching Children Mathematics* 3.6 (Feb. 1997): p. 282.

National Council of Teachers of Mathematics. "Creating, Describing, and Analyzing Patterns to Recognize Relationships and Make Predictions: Making Patterns." *Principles and Standards for School Mathematics.* Reston: NCTM, 2000.

National Council of Teachers of Mathematics. *Teaching Children Mathematics* (Focus Issue: Algebraic Thinking) 3.6 (Feb. 1997).

Getting Ready to Teach Unit 6

In this unit, students continue to develop algebraic thinking through patterning. The activities allow students the opportunity to identify, extend, and create patterns, including motion patterns that involve geometric transformations.

Transformations
Lesson 1

In the previous grade, students identified slides, flips, and turns, and created patterns using these transformations. In this unit, students draw flipped images of figures, describe slides, and describe and draw turned figures. When describing a turn, students use the vocabulary *quarter turn* and *half turn* and include an arrow showing the direction of the turn. The terms *clockwise* and *counterclockwise* are reserved for future work with transformations.

Repeating Patterns
Lesson 2

In the previous grade, students extended repeating number and shape patterns. They also had opportunities to create their own repeating patterns. In this unit, students extend repeating patterns, identify patterns on hundred grids, work with open-ended pattern problems, and write rules for patterns. The process of writing a pattern rule, telling how the pattern begins and how it continues, is an important stage in the development of algebraic thinking.

Growing and Shrinking Patterns
Lesson 3

In this unit, students' experiences with growing and shrinking patterns help them to continue making connections between physical representations and verbal descriptions. In the previous grade, students extended growing and shrinking patterns and created their own patterns but they were not required to describe the patterns. In this unit, students identify pattern rules as an integral part of the activities.

Problem Solving
Lesson 3

By developing proficiency in identifying and extending patterns, students acquire the skills and confidence to make sense of the regularities of their worlds. In the final lesson of this unit, students use simpler problems to help solve more complex problems, and solve real-world problems involving patterns. The goal at this grade is to have students recognize patterns, express the patterns they observe, and make predictions based on those patterns. In meeting those objectives, students think mathematically and begin to bridge the gap between arithmetic and algebra.

The process skills of reasoning and proof and communication are exphasized in this unit as students discover, test, and discuss patterns.

Motion Geometry Patterns

Lesson Objectives

- Recognize and describe slides, flips, and turns.
- Recognize slides, flips, and turns in geometric patterns and create patterns.

Vocabulary
flip
slide
turn

The Day at a Glance

Today's Goals	Materials
1 Teaching the Lesson A1: Recognize, describe, and draw flips of geometric figures. A2: Recognize, describe, and draw slides and turns of geometric figures. **2 Going Further** ▶ Differentiated Instruction **3 Homework and Spiral Review**	**Lesson Activities** Student Activity Book pp. 181–186 or Student Hardcover Book pp. 181–186 and Activity Workbook pp. 65–70 (includes Family Letter and special format pages) Homework and Remembering pp. 107–108 Rulers Plastic mirror (optional) Dot paper (optional) **Going Further** Activity Cards 6-1 Pattern blocks or Pattern Blocks (TRB M27) Pattern Block Grid Paper (TRB M47) Math Journals 123 Use Math Talk today!

Keeping Skills Sharp

Daily Routines	English Language Learners
Equations Tenisha had 12 seeds when she started. Now, she has 5 seeds left to plant. How many seeds did Tenisha plant? Write a situation equation for the problem and then solve. 7 seeds; $12 - \square = 5$	Draw a Z on the board next to a line. Say: **This is Z.** Draw a flip of Z. • **Beginning** Point to the flip. Say: **This is Z after a _flip_.** Have students repeat. • **Intermediate** Say: **When you _flip_ a figure, it gets reversed, like a mirror image.** Ask: **Is this a _flip_ of Z?** yes • **Advanced** Have students use short sentences to explain how to flip letter B.

Teaching the Lesson

Learn About Flips

 30 MINUTES

Goal: Recognize, describe, and draw flips of geometric figures.

Materials: Rulers (1 per student), Student Activity Book or Hardcover Book pp. 181–182 and Activity Workbook pp. 65–66, plastic mirrors (optional), dot paper (optional)

✓ **NCTM Standards:**
Geometry
Representation

▶ Describe Flips [WHOLE CLASS]

Have students draw any figure on the bottom half of a sheet of paper. They should draw the figure using dark line segments so that they can see it through the paper to trace.

Ask students to fold the paper in half and trace the figure on the outside of the paper.

Then have them unfold the paper and redraw the tracing on the side of the paper facing them.

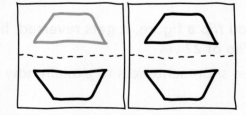

Explain that the new figure is called a flip of the original figure.

● **Why do you think it's called a flip?** The figure looks as if it has flipped over.

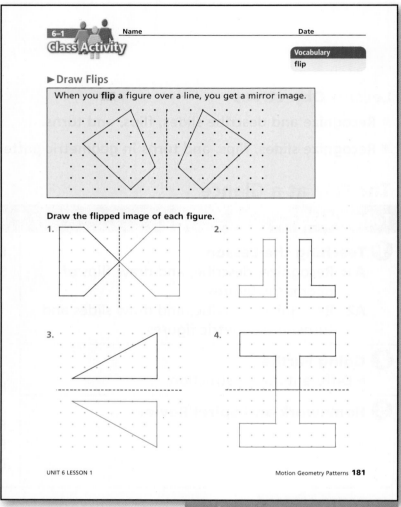

Student Activity Book page 181

● **What happens to a figure when it is flipped?** It gets reversed; it looks like a mirror image.

● **What stays the same?** size and shape

▶ Draw Flips [WHOLE CLASS]

Have students look at the flip of the figure on Student Book page 181.

● **What do you notice about matching corners of the figure and the flipped image?** They are all the same distance from the dashed line.

● **How will this help you to draw flips?** I can measure the distance of each point from the dashed line.

Have the students complete exercises 1–4.

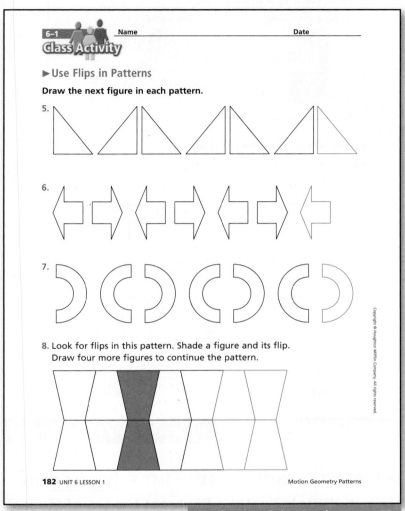

Student Activity Book page 182

► Use Flips in Patterns [PAIRS]

Have students look at the patterns in exercises 5–7 on Student Book page 182 and discuss how the figures were moved to make the patterns. Ask **Student Pairs** to draw the next figure in each pattern and then to complete exercise 8.

Alternate Approach

Use a Plastic Mirror Have the students place the mirror on the dotted line on Student Book page 181. When they look through the mirror, they will see that the image is exactly superimposed on the flipped figure.

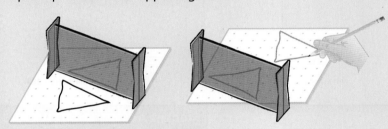

Students can draw a figure, choose a flip line, place the plastic mirror on the line, and trace the image they see when they look through the mirror. Using dot paper will help students to draw accurate images.

Activity 2

Explore Slides and Turns

 30 MINUTES

Goal: Recognize, describe, and draw slides and turns of geometric figures.

Materials: rulers (1 per student), Student Activity Book or Hardcover Book pp. 183–184 and Activity Workbook pp. 67–68

 NCTM Standards:
Geometry
Representation

► Recognize Slides [WHOLE CLASS]

Draw a straight line on the board. Choose any flat object and slide it along the line without turning it.

● What changes when you slide along a straight line? The object moves to another place.

● What doesn't change? The object looks exactly the same after a slide. It's just in a different place.

● What words can you use to describe the new position of an object after a slide? left, right, up, down

Motion Geometry Patterns **435**

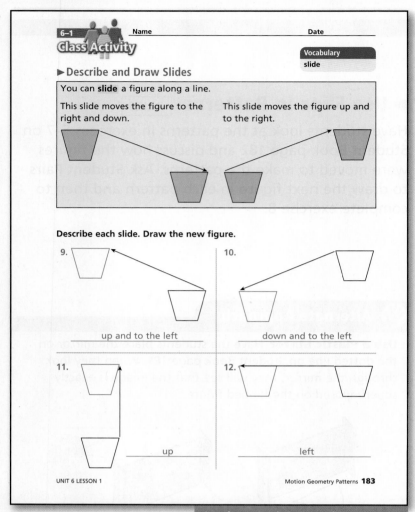

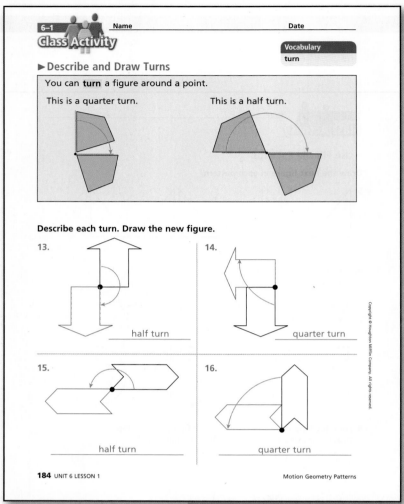

▶ Describe and Draw Slides [INDIVIDUALS]

Have the students complete exercises 9–12. Ask them to describe the new position of each figure.

Teaching Note

Language and Vocabulary The direction of a turn is described as clockwise or counterclockwise. Students need not use these terms, but they need to show the direction of a quarter turn they perform with an arrow.

✓ Ongoing Assessment

After students have completed Student Activity Book pages 181–184, ask them to write a large capital letter F.

▶ Show what the F would look like after a flip about a vertical line.

▶ Show what it would look like after a turn.

▶ Describe and Draw Turns [WHOLE CLASS]

Have students look at the figures at the top of Student Book page 184.

[123] Math Talk Discuss these questions to help students discover and describe the turns.

● Why is the first figure called a quarter turn? It goes a quarter of the way around a circle.

● What is a half turn? a turn that goes halfway around a circle

● Why is showing the direction of a quarter turn important? The figure ends up in a different place if you turn it in the opposite direction.

● Is this true for a half turn? No, the figure ends up in the same place after a half turn in either direction.

Assign exercises 13–16, and have students describe each turn as a half or a quarter turn.

② Going Further

Differentiated Instruction

Intervention — Activity Card 6-1

Model Transformations — Activity Card 6-1 ●

Work: In pairs

Use:
- TRB M27 (Pattern Blocks)
- TRB M47 (Pattern Block Grid Paper)

1. Choose a pattern block and trace it on the grid.

2. Draw a line along one side of the block and slide the block along the line. Trace the block again.

3. Now flip the block over the line and trace it again.

4. Next, choose one corner of the block as a turning point. Turn the block halfway around that corner and then trace the new position.

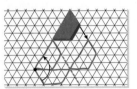

5. Choose another block and repeat the activity.

6. **Analyze** Is there more than one transformation that can move a block from one position to another? Yes

Unit 6, Lesson 1 — Copyright © Houghton Mifflin Company

Activity Note Students should notice that sliding and flipping often result in the same position. For shapes with rotational symmetry, flipping and rotating may also result in the same outcome.

 Math Writing Prompt

Use Reasoning Predict what you will see if you draw a flip about a vertical line of a capital Z. Will it still be a proper Z after this flip? Explain your thinking.

 **Software Support**

Warm Up 37.20

On Level — Activity Card 6-1

Make a Pattern — Activity Card 6-1 ▲

Work: In pairs

Use:
- TRB M27 (Pattern Blocks)
- TRB M47 (Pattern Block Grid Paper)

1. Work together to make a pattern of shapes. Choose a block and trace it on the grid.

2. Use slides, flips, or turns to move the block into new positions. Trace the result of each movement on the grid. Repeat movements to create a pattern.

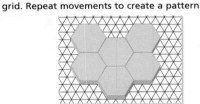

3. **Analyze** In how many ways can you describe a sequence of movements to make the pattern you created?

Unit 6, Lesson 1 — Copyright © Houghton Mifflin Company

Activity Note Patterns may or may not be tessellations, depending on the transformations being used. Some students may enjoy making patterns with more than one shape.

 Math Writing Prompt

Explain Your Thinking How are turns and flips different? How are they the same? Use drawings to explain your thinking.

 Software Support

Shapes Ahoy: Ship Shapes, Level O

Challenge — Activity Card 6-1

Investigate Math — Activity Card 6-1 ■

Work: On your own

Use:
- TRB M27 (Pattern Blocks)

1. Trace a square, a parallelogram, and a rhombus.

2. Turn each shape around its center until it fits onto the tracing again.

3. Describe how far you turned each shape to match the original tracing. Square: quarter turn; rhombus: half turn; parallelogram: half turn

4. **Analyze** How often will each shape match its original position during a complete turn? Square: 4 times; rhombus and parallelogram: twice

Unit 6, Lesson 1 — Copyright © Houghton Mifflin Company

Activity Note Students should describe the turn they use for each shape by writing *quarter turn*, *half turn*, or *full turn*. Demonstrate these terms if necessary before students begin the activity.

 Math Writing Prompt

Investigate Math Explain what happens when you turn a circle around its center.

 DESTINATION Math® **Software Support**

Course II: Module 3: Unit 1: Area

③ Homework and Spiral Review

Homework **Goal:** Additional Practice

For homework, students practice with slides, flips, and turns.

Remembering **Goal:** Spiral Review

This Remembering page is appropriate anytime after today's lesson.

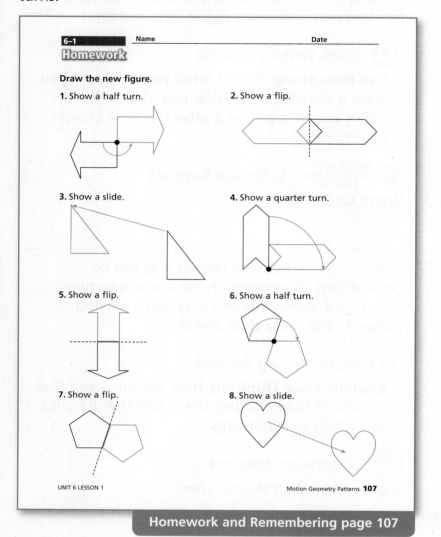

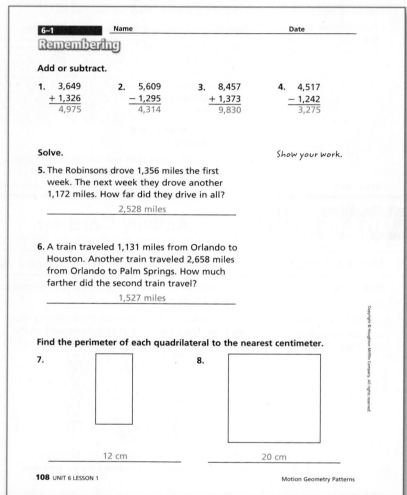

Home and School Connection

Family Letter Have students take home the Family Letter on Student Activity Book page 185 or Activity Workbook page 69. This letter explains how the concept of repeating, growing, and shrinking patterns is developed in *Math Expressions*. It gives parents and guardians a better understanding of the learning that goes on in math class and creates a bridge between school and home. A Spanish translation of this letter is on the following

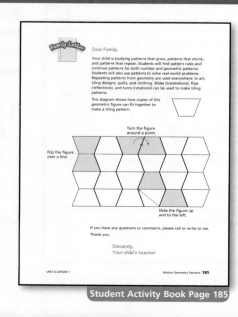

Student Activity Book Page 185

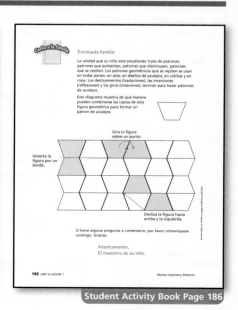

Student Activity Book Page 186

438 UNIT 6 LESSON 1

Repeating Patterns

Lesson Objectives

- Identify and continue a repeating number pattern.

- Identify and continue a repeating geometric pattern.

Vocabulary
repeating pattern

The Day at a Glance

Today's Goals	Materials	

1 Teaching the Lesson
A1: Recognize and describe a repeating number pattern.
A2: Recognize and describe a repeating geometric pattern.
 	
2 Going Further
▶ Differentiated Instruction
 	
3 Homework and Spiral Review
	Lesson Activities
	Student Activity Book pp. 187–188
	  Student Hardcover Book
	  pp. 187–188
	Homework and Remembering
	  pp. 109–110
	Hundred Grid (TRB M48)
	Sheet protectors
	Dry-erase materials
	Two-color counters
	Calculators
		Going Further
		Activity Cards 6-2
		Pattern blocks or
		  Pattern Blocks
		  (TRB M27)
		Math Journals
		
		(123) *Use* **Math Talk** *today!*

Keeping Skills Sharp

Daily Routines	English Language Learners
Homework Review If students give incorrect answers, have them explain how they found the answers. This can help you determine whether the error is conceptual or procedural. **Coins and Bills** Ayita had a $10 bill, three $1 bills, and 3 quarters. She decided to buy a new backpack and spent $12.50. How much money does Ayita have left? $1.25	Write 1, 2, 3, 1, 2, 3, 1, 2, 3 on the board. Guide students to read the pattern. • **Beginning** Say: **This is a *repeating number pattern*. The *numbers* 1, 2, and 3 happen again and again. They *repeat*.** • **Intermediate** Ask: **What is this a pattern of?** numbers **What numbers *repeat*?** 1,2,3 Say: **This is a *repeating number pattern*.** • **Advanced** Have students write their own repeating number pattern and tell it to a partner.

1 **Teaching the Lesson**

Repeating Number Patterns

 30 MINUTES

Goal: Recognize and describe a repeating number pattern.

Materials: Student Activity Book or Hardcover Book p. 187, Hundred Grid (TRB M48), sheet protectors, dry-erase materials, counters, calculators

✓ **NCTM Standards:**
Algebra
Reasoning and Proof

► Explore Repeating Number Patterns

WHOLE CLASS

Write a simple repeating pattern of numbers on the board.

2 4 4 2 4 4 2 4 4 2 4 4 2 4

● **Look at the list of numbers. What pattern do you notice?** Possible responses: It repeats the 3 numbers 2, 4, and 4 (or 2 and 44; or 24 and 4) or the number 244 repeats.

● **What is the next number in the pattern?** 4

● **Why isn't it 2?** because every 2 is followed by two 4s

Explain that you can write a rule to describe any pattern. The rule must say how the pattern starts and how it continues.

● **How does it start?** Possible responses: With the numbers 2, 4, and 4; with 244; with the numbers 2 and 44; with the numbers 24 and 4

● **How does it continue?** It repeats the starting numbers over and over.

Direct students' attention to Student Book page 187 and have students complete exercises 1–4 with a **Helping Partner** if needed.

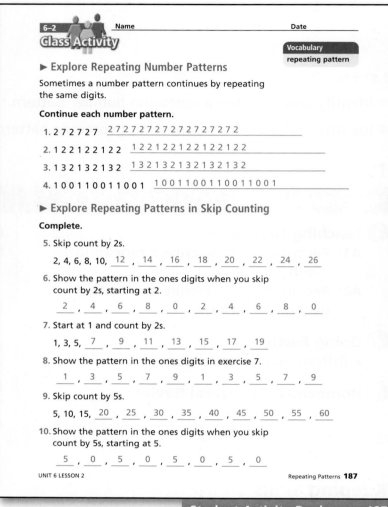

Student Activity Book page 187

► Explore Repeating Patterns in Skip Counting WHOLE CLASS

Distribute a Hundred Grid (TRB M48) and sheet protectors to students and have them explore patterns.

● **What pattern do you see in each column of the grid?** The tens digit repeats except for the last number in each column.

● **What pattern do you see in each row?** The ones digit repeats.

Activity continued ▶

Ask the students to apply this pattern rule: "Start at 3 and count by 3s." Have them mark each number on the grid with a circle.

1	11	㉑	31	41	51	61	71	81	91
2	⑫	22	32	42	52	62	72	82	92
③	13	23	33	43	53	63	73	83	93
4	14	㉔	34	44	54	64	74	84	94
5	⑮	25	35	45	55	65	75	85	95
⑥	16	26	36	46	56	66	76	86	96
7	17	㉗	37	47	57	67	77	87	97
8	⑱	28	38	48	58	68	78	88	98
⑨	19	29	39	49	59	69	79	89	99
10	20	㉚	40	50	60	70	80	90	100

- Describe the pattern of the circles in the grid. The circles go down one square and left one square and line up along diagonals.

Then have students erase their circles and ask them to name other pattern rules and use the rules to mark the hundred grid.

- Choose a starting number from the first column of the grid, and then choose a number to skip count by. Mark the numbers on the chart.

- Describe the pattern your rule makes in the grid.

Explain that whenever you skip count by the same number, the ones digits will eventually make a repeating pattern. Have students complete exercises 5–10 on Student Book page 187.

▶ Calculator Patterns [WHOLE CLASS]

Explain to students that they are going to compare repeating patterns on the calculator with those that they record on the hundred grid. The following example is an example of skip counting by 4.

First, have students follow these steps on the hundred grid:

- Skip count by 4 on the hundred grid.

- Continue circling the numbers in the pattern for the first two columns.

Then, have students follow these steps on the calculator:

- Press the 4, then +4, then =, then continue to press the = key.

- Each time they press the = key, have them compare the calculator results with what is on the hundred grid.

Guide students in a discussion that compares and contrasts finding number patterns on a calculator and a hundred grid. Students should see that it's sometimes quicker to find patterns on the calculator, but on the hundred grid you can see a visual which can help you predict the next number. As time allows, have students work in pairs and practice other skip counting patterns on the calculator.

 Alternate Approach

Counters If sheet protectors are unavailable, have students use counters to record the patterns on the Hundred Grid. This will allow students to reuse their grids.

Differentiated Instruction

Extra Help Explain to students that a *pattern rule* describes how to get the numbers or figures in a pattern. For example, "Start at 3 and count by three" or "triangle, flipped triangle, square, repeat." You can also describe the first pattern as "Each number increases by 3." All three activities on p. 443 are excellent for students to practice describing patterns and reading decoded messages.

✓ Ongoing Assessment

Ask students to make a repeating number pattern. Have them choose a sequence of starting numbers that will repeat, and ask them to write the repeating pattern three times.

Teaching the Lesson (continued)

Repeating Geometric Patterns

 30 MINUTES

Goal: Recognize and describe a repeating geometric pattern.

Materials: Student Activity Book or Hardcover Book p. 188

 NCTM Standard:
Geometry

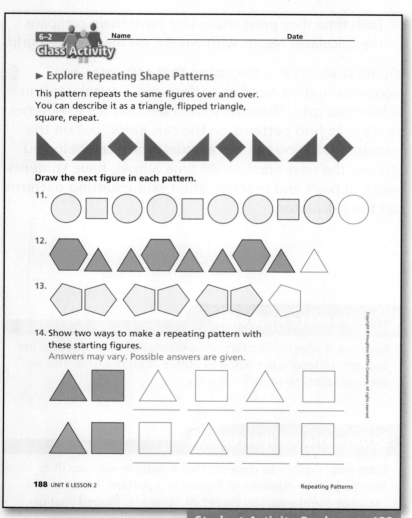

Student Activity Book page 188

▶ **Explore Repeating Shape Patterns**

INDIVIDUALS

Have students look at the pattern of figures at the top of Student Book page 188.

Math Talk To discuss this pattern, use the following questions:

● Look at the figures. What pattern do you notice? Groups of the same 3 figures repeat.

● What is the next figure in the pattern? a triangle that looks exactly like the first triangle

● How are the first and second triangles related? The second triangle is a flip of the first triangle.

● What is the pattern rule? a triangle, a flip of the triangle, and a square; How does it start? with a triangle

● How does the pattern continue? The first 3 figures repeat.

Assign exercises 11–13.

As a class, discuss how the next figure in each pattern was found. Be sure to discuss each pattern, pattern rule, and the relation between any figures in each pattern.

Open-ended Patterns Have students complete exercise 14 and discuss their patterns. Explain that without a given rule, there is no single correct pattern, especially when there are only a few starting numbers or figures. Any pattern that starts with a triangle and a square would be correct.

Teaching Note

Math Background Analyzing mathematical patterns is important to future success in algebra and geometry. A number pattern can usually be modeled as a simple algebraic function. When slides, flips, and turns are done on coordinate grids, the patterns in the coordinates can also be modeled using algebraic functions. Through patterns, these two branches of mathematics become interconnected.

② Going Further

Intervention   Activity Card 6-2

Describe a Pattern   Activity Card 6-2 ●

Work: In pairs

Use:
• TRB M27 (Pattern Blocks)

1. You can describe a repeating block pattern by using figure, color, or transformation. For example, in the first pattern below, the rule could be the following: Draw a vertical line to the right of a red trapezoid and flip it over the line.

2. How would you describe the rule for the second pattern above? Possible answer: Two green triangles in a row, followed by one yellow hexagon

3. Take turns making and describing a repeating pattern, using one or more pattern blocks.

Unit 6, Lesson 2   Copyright © Houghton Mifflin Company

Activity Note The first pattern can also be described as a half turn that moves to the right. The second pattern can also be described as a triangle slid horizontally, followed by a hexagon.

 Math Writing Prompt

Explain Your Thinking What do you need to know to extend a pattern? Give an example.

Soar to Success Math ★ **Software Support**

Warm Up 37.20

On Level   Activity Card 6-2

Make Patterns   Activity Card 6-2 ▲

Work: In pairs

• Look at the number pattern below.

   19, 38, 17, 39, 18, 37, …

• What do you notice about the first digit of each number? It alternates between 1 and 3.

   ⑲, 38, ⑰, 39, ⑱, 37, …

• What do you notice about the second digit of each number? It repeats in the sequence 9, 8, 7.

   19, 38, 17, 39, 18, 37, …

• Make your own number pattern and exchange with your partner to find the next number in the pattern. Be sure to include at least three repetitions of the entire pattern in the sequence of numbers that you give your partner.

Unit 6, Lesson 2   Copyright © Houghton Mifflin Company

Activity Note Students will need to give 6 or more terms in their pattern so that their partner can determine the next term with certainty.

 Math Writing Prompt

Use Reasoning If you know the first three numbers in a number pattern, can you be sure what the next number will be? Give an example.

 Software Support

Numberopolis: Cross Town Number Line, Level R

Challenge   Activity Card 6-2

Make a Secret Code   Activity Card 6-2 ■

Work: In pairs

1. You can use a repeating number pattern to make a coded message like the one below.

> Number pattern: 1, 3, 1, 3, 1, 3, …
> Count on by each number to change each letter of your message.
> If the first letter is Y, Y+1 becomes Z.
> If the second letter is O, O+3 becomes R.
> If the third letter is U, U+1 becomes V.
>
> Message:
>   YOU ARE MY BEST FRIEND
> Coded message:
>   ZRV DSH NB CHTW GUJHOG

2. **Think** How would you code the letter Z as the fourth letter of a message, using the code above? Z + 3, or C.

3. Write a coded message for your partner. Give your partner the coded message and the pattern to decode the message.

Unit 6, Lesson 2   Copyright © Houghton Mifflin Company

Activity Note The example given requires going back to the beginning of the alphabet to code the letters X and Y when they appear as even-numbered letters in a message, and the letter Z in any position.

 Math Writing Prompt

Investigate Math Write a rule for a repeating number pattern and a rule for a repeating shape pattern. Use the rules to make the patterns.

 DESTINATION Math® **Software Support**

Course II: Module 1: Unit 1: Comparing and Ordering

3 Homework and Spiral Review

 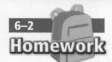

Homework Goal: Additional Practice

✓ Include students' work for page 109 as part of their portfolios.

Remembering Goal: Spiral Review

This Remembering page is appropriate anytime after today's lesson.

6-2	Name		Date	

Homework

Write the next 3 numbers in the pattern.

1. 9 8 7 9 8 7 9 8 7 9 8 7 9 8 ___7___ ___9___ ___8___

2. 1 0 1 1 0 1 1 0 1 1 0 1 1 0 1 ___1___ ___0___ ___1___

3. 6 6 1 1 1 6 6 1 1 1 6 6 1 1 ___1___ ___6___ ___6___

4. 1 2 3 4 3 2 1 2 3 4 3 2 1 2 ___3___ ___4___ ___3___

Draw the next figure in the pattern.

5. ▭ ▭ ▭ ▭ ▭ ▭   ▭

6. △▽ △▽ △▽ △▽   ▽

7. ◹ △ ◯ ◹ △ ◯   ◹

How will you move the last figure to continue the pattern: slide, flip, or turn? Draw the next figure in the pattern.

8. F ꟻ F ꟻ F ꟻ F ꟻ   ꟻ   ___flip___

9. ⚡⚡⚡⚡⚡⚡⚡⚡   ⚡   ___slide___

10. ☺ ☺ ☺ ☺ ☺ ☺   ___turn___

Repeating Patterns **109**

6-2	Name		Date	

Remembering

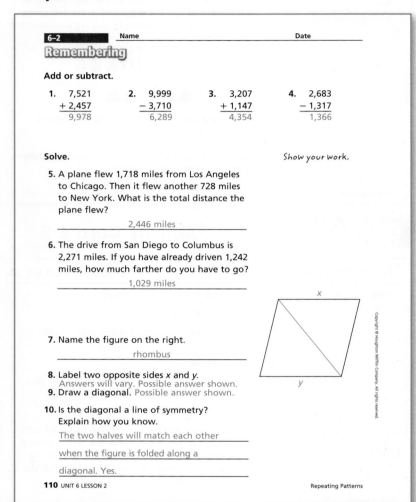

Add or subtract.

1. $7,521$
   $+ 2,457$
   $\overline{9,978}$

2. $9,999$
   $- 3,710$
   $\overline{6,289}$

3. $3,207$
   $+ 1,147$
   $\overline{4,354}$

4. $2,683$
   $- 1,317$
   $\overline{1,366}$

Solve.   *Show your work.*

5. A plane flew 1,718 miles from Los Angeles to Chicago. Then it flew another 728 miles to New York. What is the total distance the plane flew?
   ___2,446 miles___

6. The drive from San Diego to Columbus is 2,271 miles. If you have already driven 1,242 miles, how much farther do you have to go?
   ___1,029 miles___

7. Name the figure on the right.
   ___rhombus___

8. Label two opposite sides *x* and *y*.
   Answers will vary. Possible answer shown.
9. Draw a diagonal. Possible answer shown.

10. Is the diagonal a line of symmetry? Explain how you know.
    The two halves will match each other
    when the figure is folded along a
    diagonal. Yes.

Repeating Patterns

Homework and Remembering page 109   **Homework and Remembering page 110**

Home or School Activity

 Language Arts Connection

Rhyming Patterns Find an example of a rhyming poem. Explain the rhyming pattern. For example, every other line rhymes (ABAB) or every pair of lines rhyme (AABB).

MY SHADOW

Robert Louis Stevenson

I have a little shadow that goes in and out with me, **A**

And what can be the use of him is more than I can see. **A**

He is very, very like me from the heels up to the head; **B**

And I see him jump before me, when I jump into my bed. **B**

Growing and Shrinking Patterns

Lesson Objectives

- Identify and continue a number pattern that grows or shrinks.
- Identify and continue a geometric pattern that grows or shrinks.

Vocabulary

growing pattern
shrinking pattern

The Day at a Glance

Today's Goals	Materials
1 **Teaching the Lesson** **A1:** Continue a number pattern that grows or shrinks. **A2:** Identify and use a table to analyze a growing pattern. **A3:** Solve a problem by solving a simpler problem using tables and patterns. **2** **Going Further** ▶ Differentiated Instruction **3** **Homework and Spiral Review**	**Lesson Activities** Student Activity Book pp. 189–192 or Student Hardcover Book pp. 189–192 and Activity Workbook pp. 71–72 (includes table) Homework and Remembering pp. 111–112 Quick Quiz (Assessment Guide) Calculators *One Grain of Rice,* by Demi (Scholastic Press, 1997)	**Going Further** Activity Cards 6-3 Paper squares or square pattern blocks Skip Counting Circle (TRB M49) Math Journals 123 *Use* **Math Talk** *today!*

Keeping Skills Sharp

Daily Routines	English Language Learners
Homework Review Ask students if they had difficulty with any part of the homework. Plan to set aside some time to work with students needing extra help. **Act it Out** Paul flipped a rectangle along the given line. The rectangle ended horizontally as shown. Show how the rectangle was facing before the flip. Explain how you found your answer. Possible explanation: Fold the paper on the line. Trace the rectangle through the paper. Unfold the paper. The rectangle was horizontal on the right side of the line.	Gradually inflate a balloon. Have students identify whether the balloon is growing or shrinking. Gradually deflate the balloon. • **Beginning** Say: *Growing* means getting larger. *Shrinking* means getting smaller. Have students repeat. • **Intermediate** Ask: **Is the balloon growing or shrinking?** growing Ask: **Is it still** *growing?* no Say: **Now it is** *shrinking.* • **Advanced** Have students use short sentences to tell about growing and shrinking.

Teaching the Lesson

Activity 1

Growing and Shrinking Number Patterns

 15 MINUTES

Goal: Continue a number pattern that grows or shrinks.

Materials: Student Activity Book or Hardcover Book p. 189, calculators

✓ **NCTM Standards:**
Algebra Reasoning and Proof

▶ **Continue a Growing or Shrinking Number Pattern** [INDIVIDUALS]

Remind students that they can write a rule to describe any pattern. The rule must say how the pattern starts and how it continues. Explain that some patterns grow by the same amount each time, while others grow by amounts that change. Write this counting pattern on the board:

$$3, 6, 9, 12, 15, \ldots$$

● What is the rule for this number pattern? It starts at 3 and grows by 3 each time. Write this counting pattern on the board:

$$1, 2, 4, 7, 11, 16, \ldots$$

● What is the rule for this number pattern? It starts at 1 and grows by 1, then by 2, then by 3, then by 4, and so on.

Have students complete exercises 1–6. Remind them some of the patterns grow or shrink by the same amount while others grow or shrink by changing amounts. When they finish, invite volunteers to share their answers with the class.

▶ **Number Patterns on a Calculator**

[WHOLE CLASS]

Complete exercise 7 as a class. Have students look back at exercises 1 and 2 and the pattern rules. For exercise 1, have students push the following keys to see the number pattern:

● Push the 5, then + 3, then =.

As students continue to push the equals key, they will see the same growing pattern appear on the calculator as on their page.

Then have students use their calculators to see the

6-3
Class Activity

Vocabulary
growing pattern
shrinking pattern

▶ Continue a Growing or Shrinking Number Pattern

A number pattern can grow or shrink by the same amount.

Continue the pattern and write the rule.

1. 5, 8, 11, 14, 17, 20 , 23 , 26 , 29 , 32 , 35 , 38
   Add 3 to the previous number to get the next number.

2. 30, 27, 24, 21, 18 , 15 , 12 , 9 , 6 , 3
   Subtract 3 from the previous number to get the next number.

A number pattern can grow or shrink by a changing amount. When this happens, look for a pattern in the changes.

Continue the pattern and write the rule.

3. 6, 7, 9, 12, 16, 21 , 27 , 34 , 42 , 51 , 61 , 72
   Add 1, then add 2, then add 3, then add 4, and so on.

4. 2, 6, 11, 15, 20, 24, 29, 33 , 38 , 42 , 47 , 51 , 56
   Add 4, then add 5, then 4, then 5, and so on.

Make two patterns with these starting numbers.
Write the rule. Answers will vary. Possible answers are given.

5. 2, 4, 6 , 8 , 10   Skip count by 2s.

   2, 4, 7 , 11 , 16   Add 2, then add 3, then add 4, and so on.

6. 50, 45, 40 , 35 , 30   Skip count backward by 5s.

   50, 45, 35 , 20 , 0   Subtract 5, then subtract 10, then subtract 15, and so on.

▶ Number Patterns on a Calculator

7. Use a calculator to check your pattern and rule in exercises 1 and 2.

UNIT 6 LESSON 3   Growing and Shrinking Patterns **189**

Student Activity Book page 189

number pattern in exercise 2. Check that students followed the same steps for continuing the pattern in exercise 1, but used the minus sign key instead of the plus sign.

Math Talk Guide a student discussion that investigates whether a calculator can be used to continue the pattern for exercises 3–4. Students should realize that they can manually enter the pattern on the calculator, but they will not be able to continue hitting the equals key because the pattern rule does not change by the same number.

Growing and Shrinking Geometric Patterns

🕐 **15 MINUTES**

Goal: Identify and use a table to analyze a growing pattern.

Materials: Student Activity Book or Hardcover Book p. 190

✓ **NCTM Standards:**
Geometry
Algebra
Reasoning and Proof

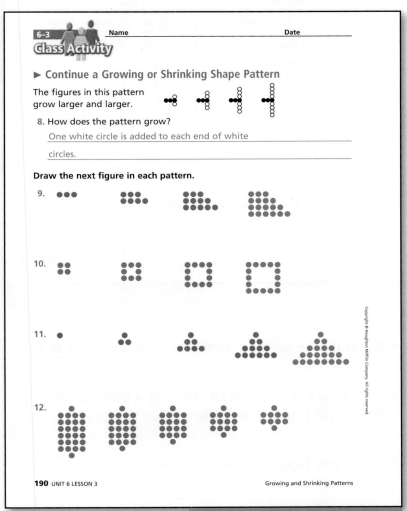

Student Activity Book page 190

► Continue a Growing or Shrinking Shape Pattern WHOLE CLASS

Discuss the pattern of figures at the top of Student Book page 190.

● **How does the growing pattern start?** with a T-shape that has 3 black circles with 1 white circle on each side.

● **How does it continue?** The number of black circles is always the same, but the number of white circles increases by 2 each time.

Have students look at the pattern in exercise 9.

● **What is the rule for the pattern?** It starts with 1 row of 3 dots and adds a new row of dots each time. Each new row has 1 more dot than the row before it.

Ask students to draw the next figure. Ask a volunteer to draw the figure on the board. Then, give students time to complete the patterns in exercises 10 and 11. Ask volunteers to draw the figures on the board.

Next, direct students to the pattern in exercise 12.

● **How is this like the patterns in exercises 8–11?** It's a dot pattern.

● **How is it different?** The dot pictures get smaller instead of bigger.

● **What is the pattern?** Each time the pattern shrinks, 1 row of 4 dots is taken away.

Have students draw the next figure.

● **How many more times can this pattern repeat?** twice

● **What makes a shrinking pattern different from a growing pattern?** A growing pattern gets larger, but a shrinking pattern gets smaller. A growing pattern can continue forever, but a shrinking pattern ends.

If time allows, have students create a growing or shrinking dot pattern of their own and write the rule. You may want students to work in **Student Pairs.**

Activity 3

Patterns in the Real World

 30 MINUTES

Goal: Solve a problem by solving a simpler problem using tables and patterns.

Materials: Student Activity Book or Hardcover Book pp. 191–192 and Activity Workbook p. 71

✔ **NCTM Standards:**
Geometry
Algebra

▶ Solve a Simpler Problem [WHOLE CLASS]

Explain that sometimes we can solve a problem by looking for a pattern in a simpler problem. Then we can use the pattern to solve the original problem. You can often use a table like the one shown on Student Book page 191 to help you see the pattern and extend it to solve the problem. Explain that you could draw the tenth triangle and count the small triangles, but it is easier and quicker to look for a pattern in a smaller number of triangles and extend the pattern.

Draw the table on chart paper or the board, and ask the students to help you complete it.

● **How does the table tell how the pattern starts?** The top row shows that the first figure has 1 triangle.

● **How does it show how the pattern continues?** The right column shows the number of small triangles in each figure: 1, 4, 9, 16.

● **What pattern do you see in the way the number of figures is growing?** Add 3, 5, 7, and so on.

Give students a few minutes to complete exercises 13–16. Then discuss the answers.

● **Write 1 for figure 1. How many triangles do you add to get figure 2?** 3

● **Write 1 + 3. How many triangles do you add to get figure 3?** 5

● **Write 1 + 3 + 5. How many triangles do you add to get figure 4?** 7

● **Write 1 + 3 + 5 + 7. How many triangles do you add to get figure 5?** 9

6–3
Class Activity

Name _____ Date _____

▶ Solve a Simpler Problem

How many small triangles will be in triangle number 10? One way to solve problems like this one is to solve a simpler problem and look for a pattern.

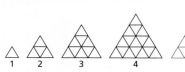
1   2   3   4   5

13. Complete the table to show how the number of small triangles grows.

14. Draw figure 5 in the pattern above. In the table, record the number of triangles it has.

15. Describe how the pattern grows.
The pattern grows by adding 3, 5, 7, 9, … to the previous number. Or, the triangle number multiplied by itself.

Triangle Number	Number of Small Triangles
1	1
2	4
3	9
4	16
5	25

16. Use this pattern to find how many small triangles are in triangle number 10. _____ 100

Solve.

17. If 8 friends all shake hands with each other once, how many handshakes will take place?
28 handshakes

UNIT 6 LESSON 3   Growing and Shrinking Patterns **191**

Student Activity Book page 191

● **What do we call the numbers, 1, 3, 5, 7, and so on?** odd numbers

● **So figure 4 is the sum of the first 4 odd numbers. What will figure 5 be?** the sum of the first 5 odd numbers; 1 + 3 + 5 + 7 + 9

● **What will figure 10 be?** the sum of the first 10 odd numbers

Activity continued ▶

Teaching Note

Math Background The number pattern in the table also represents square numbers. Square numbers will be studied in Unit 9.

● Now solve the problem. Tell students to look for numbers that make a ten to make adding easier.

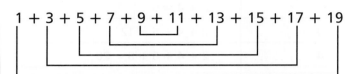

$$20 + 20 + 20 + 20 + 20 = 100$$

Ask these questions to help students solve problem 17. Encourage them to draw diagrams.

● How many handshakes would two friends have? 1

● three friends? 3

● four and five friends? 6; 10

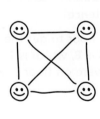 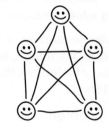

● The pattern is 1, 3, 6, 10, … What is the pattern rule? Add 2, then 3, then 4, and so on.

● Use the pattern rule to solve the problem.

	+2	+3	+4	+5	+6	+7
1	3	6	10	15	21	28

So with 8 friends, there would be 28 handshakes

▶ Make a Number-Chain Pattern
SMALL GROUPS

A "Number Chain" is a series of triangles with numbers inside them and at their corners. Draw this Number Chain on the board.

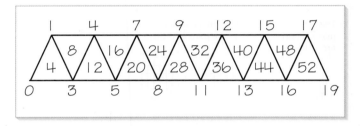

The sum of the numbers on the corners of each triangle is equal to the number inside.

● What pattern do you see inside the triangles? The numbers grow by adding 4 each time.

● What pattern do you see across the top? The numbers grow by adding 3, then 3, then 2, and repeating 3, 3, 2 each time.

● What pattern do you see across the bottom? The numbers grow by adding 3, then 2, then 3, and then repeating 3, 2, 3 each time.

● What zigzag pattern from bottom to top to bottom and so on do you see? The numbers grow by adding 1, then 2, then 1, and then repeating 1, 2, 1 each time.

● What will go inside the next triangle? 56

● What will be at the new corner of the next triangle? 20

Change the numbers in the chain, and ask students to describe the patterns and complete the missing triangles.

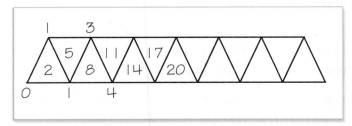

Challenge students to make up their own chains.

Activity continued ▶

① Teaching the Lesson (continued)

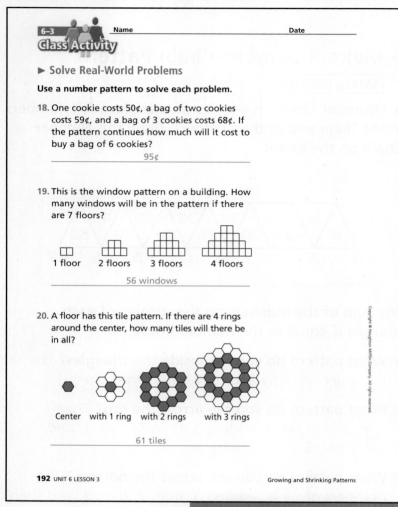

Student Activity Book page 192

▶ Solve Real-World Problems

INDIVIDUALS

Ask students to work independently on problems 18–20. Then discuss and summarize the results.

● **What is the rule for the pattern in problem 18?** Start at 50¢ and add 9¢ for each additional bag of cookies. A bag of 6 cookies would cost 95¢.

● **What pattern do you see in the ones digits when you add 9¢ to each price?** The ones digit decreases by 1.

● **If I started with 63 and added 9, what would the ones digit be in the answer?** 2 **What is 63 + 9?** 72

● **What is the rule for the pattern in problem 19?** Start at 2 and add 4, then 6, then 8, and so on.

To analyze this pattern, make a table like this:

Number of Floors	Number of Windows
1	2
2	2 + 4 = 6
3	2 + 4 + 6 = 12
4	2 + 4 + 6 + 8 = 20
5	2 + 4 + 6 + 8 + 10 = 30
6	2 + 4 + 6 + 8 + 10 + 12 = 42
7	2 + 4 + 6 + 8 + 10 + 12 + 14 = 56

Encourage students to discuss the patterns they see. A sample discussion follows.

Math Talk in Action

What do you notice about the beginning of each addition sentence in column 2?

Melor: It has all the numbers from the row above it.

Samantha: And the last number in each sentence is double the number of the floor. For floor 6, the last number in the addition sentence is 12.

Great. How can you use that information to complete the chart without writing a long addition sentence?

Marshall: Double the number of the floor to get the number of windows to add, so for floor 8, it's 8 + 8, which is 16. Then add 16 to the number of windows that were on floor 7, which was 56. Then 56 + 16 = 72.

Then discuss problem 20.

● **What is the rule for the pattern in problem 19?** Start at 1 and add 6, then 12, then 18, and so on.

● **What do you notice about all the numbers you're adding in this pattern?** They're the "count-by-6" numbers.

● **How did you find the number of tiles needed for four rings?** 1 + 6 + 12 + 18 + 24 = 61

 Quick Quiz

See Assessment Guide for Unit 6 Quick Quiz.

② Going Further

● Intervention   Activity Card 6-3

Continue a Pattern   Activity Card 6-3 ●

Work: In pairs

Use:
• Paper squares or square pattern blocks

1. Make a pattern using squares. Begin with one square for the first figure in the pattern.

2. Add two more squares to make an L shape for the second figure, as shown below.

3. Continue adding two squares to make a larger L shape for each new figure in the pattern.

4. Write a number pattern to match the geometry pattern. 1, 3, 5, 7...

Unit 6, Lesson 3   Copyright © Houghton Mifflin Company

Activity Note The number pattern is the counting pattern of odd numbers. Challenge students to predict the number of squares in the tenth figure. 19

✎ Math Writing Prompt

Explain Your Thinking How do you know if a pattern is growing or shrinking?

Soar to Success Math ★ Software Support

Warm Up 31.08

▲ On Level   Activity Card 6-3

Make a Pattern   Activity Card 6-3 ▲

Work: In pairs

Use:
• Paper squares or square pattern blocks

1. Use squares to make a geometric pattern. Begin with a single square.

2. Add squares to make larger squares for each new figure in the pattern.

3. How many squares did you add for the second shape? How many for the third? 3; 5

4. Write a description of the rule for your pattern, using numbers. Possible answer: Start with 1, Add 3, add 5, add 7, and so on. The pattern is 1, 4, 9, 16,...

Unit 6, Lesson 3   Copyright © Houghton Mifflin Company

Activity Note This geometric pattern illustrates the sequence of perfect squares (1 × 1, 2 × 2, 3 × 3, etc.). Challenge students to predict the number of squares in the tenth figure. 100

✎ Math Writing Prompt

Make a Pattern Make a number pattern that grows or shrinks. Write your pattern rule.

MegaMath Grades K-6 Software Support

Shapes Ahoy: Ship Shapes, Level K

■ Challenge   Activity Card 6-3

Make Patterns   Activity Card 6-3 ■

Work: On your own

Use:
• TRB M49 (Skip Counting Circle)

1. Use the skip-counting circle to draw a pattern. First choose a counting rule for a number pattern. Begin at 0 on the circle, and draw straight lines to each number in pattern that you choose.

2. Look at the circle on the right. It shows the pattern formed when you count by 3s. **Think** How do you show the number after 9? Count three more numbers around the circle to 2.

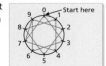

3. How would you describe the geometric figure that represents the number pattern? A star

4. Repeat the activity with another number pattern and describe what you discover.

Unit 6, Lesson 3   Copyright © Houghton Mifflin Company

Activity Note The figure traces over itself when the pattern reaches the number 30. Ask students to notice if and when a figure displays this characteristic.

✎ Math Writing Prompt

Investigate Mathematics Make a number pattern that grows by a different amount each time. What's your pattern rule?

✦ DESTINATION Math® Software Support

Course II: Module 1: Unit 1: Comparing and Ordering

Growing and Shrinking Patterns   **451**

③ Homework and Spiral Review

For homework, students continue practicing number patterns.

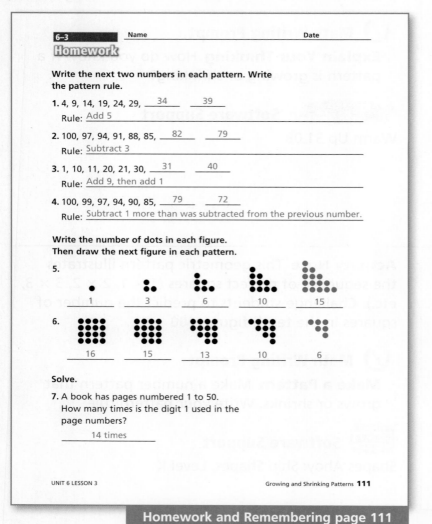

Homework 6–3 Name _____ Date _____

Write the next two numbers in each pattern. Write the pattern rule.

1. 4, 9, 14, 19, 24, 29, __34__ __39__
   Rule: Add 5

2. 100, 97, 94, 91, 88, 85, __82__ __79__
   Rule: Subtract 3

3. 1, 10, 11, 20, 21, 30, __31__ __40__
   Rule: Add 9, then add 1

4. 100, 99, 97, 94, 90, 85, __79__ __72__
   Rule: Subtract 1 more than was subtracted from the previous number.

Write the number of dots in each figure. Then draw the next figure in each pattern.

5.   1   3   6   10   15

6.   16   15   13   10   6

Solve.

7. A book has pages numbered 1 to 50. How many times is the digit 1 used in the page numbers?
   14 times

UNIT 6 LESSON 3   Growing and Shrinking Patterns **111**

Homework and Remembering page 111

This Remembering page is appropriate anytime after today's lesson.

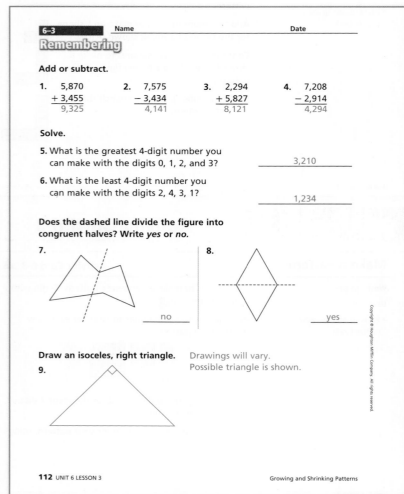

Remembering 6–3 Name _____ Date _____

Add or subtract.

1. 5,870
   + 3,455
   ‾‾‾‾‾‾
   9,325

2. 7,575
   − 3,434
   ‾‾‾‾‾‾
   4,141

3. 2,294
   + 5,827
   ‾‾‾‾‾‾
   8,121

4. 7,208
   − 2,914
   ‾‾‾‾‾‾
   4,294

Solve.

5. What is the greatest 4-digit number you can make with the digits 0, 1, 2, and 3?   3,210

6. What is the least 4-digit number you can make with the digits 2, 4, 3, 1?   1,234

Does the dashed line divide the figure into congruent halves? Write yes or no.

7.   no

8.   yes

Draw an isoceles, right triangle.   Drawings will vary. Possible triangle is shown.

9.

112 UNIT 6 LESSON 3   Growing and Shrinking Patterns

Homework and Remembering page 112

Home or School Activity

 Literature Connection

One Grain of Rice Have students read *One Grain of Rice*, by Demi (Scholastic Press, 1997). When you reach the part of the story where Rani asks for her reward, ask the students if they think her request (1 grain of rice the first day, 2 the second day, 4 the third day, and so on) is a wise one. Have them identify the pattern rule and continue the pattern for seven days to see how the amount of rice is growing. Then read the rest of the story.

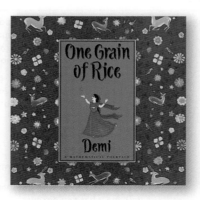

Unit Review and Test

Lesson Objective
● **Assess student progress on unit objectives.**

The Day at a Glance

Today's Goals	Materials
1 Assessing the Unit ▶ Assess student progress on unit objectives. ▶ Use activities from unit lessons to reteach content. **2 Extending the Assessment** ▶ Use remediation for common errors. There is no homework assignment on a test day.	Unit 6 Test, Student Activity Book pp. 193–194 or Student Hardcover Book pp. 193–194 Unit 6 Test, Form A or B, Assessment Guide (optional) Unit 6 Performance Assessment, Assessment Guide (optional)

Keeping Skills Sharp

Daily Routines 🕐 5 MINUTES	
If you are doing a unit review day, go over the homework. If this is a test day, omit the homework review.	**Review and Test Day** You may want to choose a quiet game or other activity (reading a book or working on homework for another subject) for students who finish early.

① Assessing the Unit

Assess Unit Objectives

🕐 **45 MINUTES (more if schedule permits)**

Goal: Assess student progress on unit objectives.

Materials: Student Activity Book or Hardcover Book pp. 193–194; Assessment Guide (optional)

▶ Review and Assessment

If your students are ready for assessment on the unit objectives, you may use either the test on the Student Book pages or one of the forms of the Unit 6 Test in the Assessment Guide to assess student progress.

If you feel that students need some review first, you may use the test on the Student Book pages as a review of unit content, and then use one of the forms of the Unit 6 Test in the Assessment Guide to assess student progress.

To assign a numerical score for all of these test forms, use 10 points for each question.

You may also choose to use the Unit 6 Performance Assessment. Scoring for that assessment can be found in its rubric in the Assessment Guide.

▶ Reteaching Resources

The chart lists the test items, the unit objectives they cover, and the lesson activities in which the objective is covered in this unit. You may revisit these activities with students who do not show mastery of the objectives.

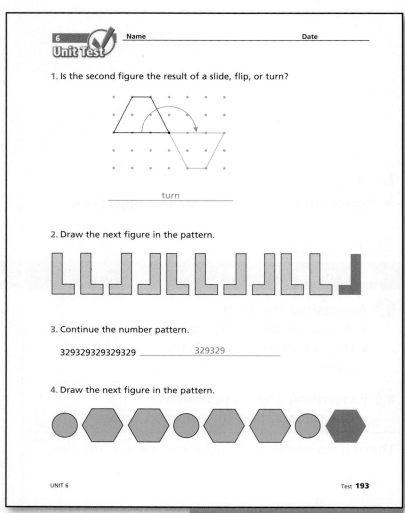

Student Activity Book page 193

Unit Test Items	Unit Objectives Tested	Activities to Use for Reteaching
1, 2	**6.1** Recognize and describe slides, flips, and turns and recognize them in geometric patterns.	Lesson 1, Activities 1 and 2 Lesson 2, Activity 2
3, 4, 5	**6.2** Identify the rule for number or geometric repeating patterns and continue the patterns.	Lesson 2, Activities 1 and 2

6 Unit Test

Name _____ Date _____

5. Write a rule for this pattern.

□ △ △ ○ □ △ △ ○

square, triangle, triangle, circle, repeat

6. Continue this pattern.

65, 62, 59, 56, 53, 50, 47, _44_ , _41_ , _38_ , _35_ , _32_

7. Continue this pattern.

12, 16, 20, 24, 28, 32, 36, _40_ , _44_ , _48_ , _52_ , _56_

8. Continue this pattern.

5, 6, 8, 11, 15, 20, 26, _33_ , _41_ , _50_ , _60_ , _71_

9. Write a rule for this pattern.

69, 64, 59, 54, 49, 44, 39

Start with 69. Then subtract 5.

10. **Extended Response** In September, Elisa walks dogs for $1.25 per walk. In October, she charges $1.50 per walk. In November, she charges $1.75 per walk. If the pattern continues, how much will she charge per walk in December and January? Describe the pattern rule you used to solve the problem.

$2.00, $2.25; The pattern rule is that Elisa raises her price by $0.25 each month. December is the next month after November, so in December she will charge $1.75 + $0.25 = $2.00. January is the next month after December, so in January she will charge $2.00 + $0.25 = $2.25.

194 UNIT 6   Test

Student Activity Book page 194

Unit Test Items	Unit Objectives Tested	Activities to Use for Reteaching
6, 7, 8, 9	**6.3** Identify the rule for growing and shrinking number or geometric patterns and continue the patterns.	Lesson 3, Activities 1 and 2
10	**6.4** Solve real-world problems with patterns.	Lesson 3, Activity 3

▶ Assessment Resources

Free Response Tests
Unit 6 Test, Student Book pages 193–194
Unit 6 Test, Form A, Assessment Guide

Extended Response Item
The last item in the Student Book test and in the Form A test will require an extended response as an answer.

Multiple Choice Test
Unit 6 Test, Form B, Assessment Guide

Performance Assessment
Unit 6 Performance Assessment, Assessment Guide
Unit 6 Performance Assessment Rubric, Assessment Guide

▶ Portfolio Assessment

Teacher-selected Items for Student Portfolios:

- Homework, Lesson 2
- Class Activity work, Lessons 1, 3

Student-selected Items for Student Portfolios:

- Favorite Home or School Activity
- Best Writing Prompt

② Extending the Assessment

Unit Objective 6.1
Recognize and describe slides, flips, and turns and recognize them in geometric patterns.

Common Error: Confuses Slides, Flips, and Turns

Some students may confuse slides, flips, and turns.

Remediation Have students make cutouts of the figures they are working with and mark a dot in one corner of each. Students can then note the position of the dot to help them determine if a transformation is a slide, flip, or turn.

Unit Objective 6.2
Identify the rule for number or geometric repeating patterns and continue the patterns.

Common Error: Does Not Recognize a Visual Pattern

Sometimes students have difficulty identifying patterns that involve figures.

Remediation If students have difficulty recognizing visual patterns, encourage them to use words to describe the patterns. As they repeat the pattern aloud, they may begin to feel the rhythm of the words and more easily recognize the pattern.

For example: triangle, square, triangle, square, triangle, square, triangle, square . . .

- What comes next?

Unit Objective 6.3
Identify the rule for growing and shrinking number or geometric patterns and continue the patterns.

Common Error: Does Not Correctly Identify a Pattern Rule for a Growing or Shrinking Pattern

Students may make errors in extending growing or shrinking patterns because they have not successfully found the pattern rule.

Remediation Encourage those students having difficulty finding pattern rules for growing or shrinking patterns to draw diagrams showing the change between consecutive numbers in the pattern.

Common Error: Does Not Correctly Extend a Growing or Shrinking Pattern

Some students may correctly identify a growing or shrinking pattern rule but then make errors using the pattern rule to extend the pattern.

Remediation For students having difficulty extending number patterns using a pattern rule, suggest that they use an arrow with numbers to help them find the next number in the pattern

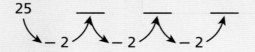

Unit Objective 6.4
Solve real-world problems with patterns.

Common Error: Does Not Recognize the Information Given as a Pattern Rule

Some students may not recognize that a problem provides them with the information to extend a pattern.

Remediation Provide students with opportunities to practice identifying pattern rules in word problems. For example, consider the word problem in the Unit Test: In September, Elisa walks dogs for $1.25 per walk. In October, she charges $1.50 per walk. In November, she charges $1.75 per walk. If the pattern continues, how much does she charge per walk in December and January?

Ask students what the starting cost is per walk, and how much is added each time. Then ask them to determine how far they need to extend the pattern to solve the problem.

Common Error: Records Incorrect Information

Some students may incorrectly record information they are given so they are unable to identify patterns.

Remediation Remind students to check the numbers they write in their tables to be sure they are recording the correct information. Suggest that they have a partner check their data to be sure they entered the correct numbers in their tables before trying to find a pattern.

Multiplication and Division with 0–5, 9, and 10

THIS UNIT USES THREE models to introduce students to multiplication and division: repeated groups, arrays, and area. The lessons emphasize the inverse relationship between multiplication and division—division undoes multiplication and vice versa. Through daily in-class and at-home practice and assessment, students will develop fluency with multiplication and division. This unit covers multiplications and divisions with 1, 2, 3, 4, 5, 9, and 10.

Skills Trace

Grade 2	Grade 3	Grade 4
• Recall basic multiplications and divisions with 2–5. • Explore equal groups and array models. • Write related addition and multiplication equations. • Solve a variety of word problems involving multiplication.	• Recall basic multiplications and divisions with 0–4, 5, 9, and 10. • Write multiplication equations to represent repeated groups, arrays, and area models. • Write related addition and multiplication and multiplication and division equations. • Solve a variety of word problems involving multiplication and division.	• Review basic multiplication and divisions with 0–10 and introduce factors of 11 and 12. • Explore factors, multiples, and prime numbers. • Write situation and solution *equations* for multiplication and division. • Solve a variety of word problems involving multiplication and division, including combination problems.

Unit 7   Contents

Unit 7   Assessment

✓ Unit Objectives Tested	Unit Test Items	Lessons
7.1 Recall basic multiplications and divisions with 0, 1, 2, 3, 4, 5, 9, and 10; use properties and rules.	1–12	1, 4–7, 9, 12, 14
7.2 Write multiplication equations to represent repeated groups, arrays, and area models.	13–15	2, 3, 10
7.3 Write related addition and multiplication equations and related multiplication and division equations.	16–18	1, 4–7, 9, 12
7.4 Solve a variety of word problems involving multiplication and division.	19–20	2–4, 6, 8, 11, 16

Assessment and Review Resources

Formal Assessment

Student Activity Book
- Unit Review and Test (pp. 283–284)

Assessment Guide
- Quick Quizzes (pp. A62, A63, A64)
- Test A–Open Response (pp. A65–A66)
- Test B–Multiple Choice (pp. A67–A69)
- Performance Assessment (pp. A70–A72)

Test Generator CD-ROM
- Open Response Test
- Multiple Choice Test
- Test Bank Items

Informal Assessment

Teacher Edition
- Ongoing Assessment (in every lesson)
- Quick Practice (in every lesson)
- Portfolio Suggestions (p. 607)

📟 **Math Talk**
  ▶ The Learning Classroom (pp. 493, 523, 539, 562)
  ▶ Math Talk in Action (pp. 461, 514, 538, 550, 561, 564, 569)
  ▶ Solve and Discuss (pp. 470, 471, 482, 493, 495, 496, 514, 530, 532, 541, 542, 555, 584, 595)
  ▶ Student Pairs (pp. 476, 490, 500, 510, 518, 528, 532, 536, 546, 554, 555, 560, 568, 576, 584, 588, 590)
      Helping Partners (pp. 472, 494, 531)
  ▶ Small Groups (p. 572)
  ▶ In Activities (pp. 480, 486, 502, 511, 519, 529, 576, 578, 600, 601)

Review Opportunities

Homework and Remembering
- Review of recently taught topics
- Spiral Review

Teacher Edition
- Unit Review and Test (pp. 605–608)

Test Generator CD-ROM
- Custom Review Sheets

Planning Unit 7

Lesson NCTM Focal Points NCTM Standards	Resources	Materials for Lesson Activities	Materials for Going Further
7-1 **Multiply with 5** NCTM Focal Points: 1.1, 1.4, 4.5 NCTM Standards: 1, 10	TE pp. 457–466 SAB pp. 195–200 H&R pp. 113–116 AC 7-1	✓ MathBoard materials Number Path (TRB M39) Centimeter Grid Paper (TRB M31) ✓ Class Multiplication Table Poster ✓ Pointer Class Multiplication Table (TRB M50)	✓ Play money Game Cards (TRB M25) Math Journals
7-2 **Multiplication as Repeated Groups** NCTM Focal Points: 1.1, 4.3, 4.5 NCTM Standards: 1, 2, 6, 10	TE pp. 467–474 SAB pp. 201–204 H&R pp. 117–118 AC 7-2	Chart paper Paper plates ✓ Two-color counters	Index cards Calculator Math Journals
7-3 **Multiplication and Arrays** NCTM Focal Points: 1.1, 1.2, 1.7, 4.1 NCTM Standards: 1, 2, 6, 10	TE pp. 475–488 SAB pp. 205–216 H&R pp. 119–122 AC 7-3	Folders Check up Materials ✓ MathBoard materials ✓ Connecting Cubes	Game Cards ✓ Two–color counters Centimeter-Grid Paper (TRB M31) Math Journals
7-4 **The Meaning of Division** NCTM Focal Points: 1.6, 1.10, 4.2 NCTM Standards: 1, 6, 10	TE pp. 489–498 SAB pp. 217–220 H&R pp. 123–126 AC 7-4	Check up Materials ✓ MathBoard materials ✓ Connecting Cubes Plastic cups ✓ Two-color counters	✓ Play money Inch-Grid Paper (TRB M42) Math Journals
7-5 **Multiply and Divide with 2** NCTM Focal Points: 1.4, 1.9, 1.10, 4.2, 4.3, 4.4 NCTM Standards: 1, 5, 6, 10	TE pp. 499–508 SAB pp. 221–224 H&R pp. 127–132 AC 7-5 AG Quick Quiz 1	✓ Class Multiplication Table Poster ✓ Pointer Check up materials ✓ MathBoard materials Folders Card stock Check sheet 1	Mirrors ✓ Two–color counters Index cards Math Journals
7-6 **Multiply and Divide with 10** NCTM Focal Points: 1.10, 4.2, 4.3, 4.4 NCTM Standards: 1, 6	TE pp. 509–516 SAB pp. 225–228 H&R pp. 133–136 AC 7-6 MCC 25	Blank Sprint Answer Sheet (TRB M57) Check up materials ✓ MathBoard materials 120 Poster (TRB M60) ✓ Base ten blocks Card stock	✓ Play money Math Journals
7-7 **Multiply and Divide with 9** NCTM Focal Points: 1.2, 1.8, 1.10, 4.1, 4.2, 4.3, 4.4 NCTM Standards: 1, 10	TE pp. 517–526 SAB pp. 229–232 H&R pp. 137–142 AC 7-7	Check up materials ✓ MathBoard materials Card stock	Centimeter-Grid Paper (TRB M31) Scissors Index cards Red and blue markers Math Journals
7-8 **Fluency Days for 2s, 5s, 9s, and 10s** NCTM Focal Points: 1.2, 1.9, 4.2, 4.3 NCTM Standards: 1, 6, 8, 10	TE pp. 527–534 SAB pp. 233–236 H&R pp. 143–146, 145 AC 7–8 MCC 26 AG Quick Quiz 2	Blank Sprint Answer Sheet (TRB M57) Check up materials ✓ 120 Poster Red, yellow, blue, and green color tiles *Amanda Bean's Amazing Dream*, by Cindy Neuschwander	Poster paper Crayons Study Sheet A Spinner C (TRB M61) Paper clips Game Cards (TRB M25) Math Journals

Resources/Materials Key: TE: Teacher Edition   SAB: Student Activity Book   H&R: Homework and Remembering   AC: Activity Cards   MCC: Math Center Challenge   AG: Assessment Guide   ✓: Grade 3 kits   TRB: Teacher's Resource Book

NCTM Standards and Expectations Key: **1.** Number and Operations **2.** Algebra **3.** Geometry
4. Measurement **5.** Data Analysis and Probability **6.** Problem Solving **7.** Reasoning and Proof
8. Communication **9.** Connections **10.** Representation

Lesson NCTM Focal Points NCTM Standards	Resources	Materials for Lesson Activities	Materials for Going Further
7-9 **Multiply and Divide with 3** NCTM Focal Points: 1.7, 1.10, 4.1, 4.2, 4.3, 4.4 NCTM Standards: 1, 2	TE pp. 535–544 SAB pp. 237–242 H&R pp. 147–150 AC 7-9	✓ Class Multiplication Table Poster Blank Sprint Answer Sheet (TRB 57) Check Up materials Transparency of Student Activity Book pp. 239–240 (optional) Overhead projector (optional) ✓ Two-color counters	Game Cards (TRB M25) ✓ MathBoard materials Math Journals
7-10 **Multiplication and Area** NCTM Focal Point: 1.3 NCTM Standards: 1, 3, 4, 6	TE pp. 545–552 SAB pp. 243–246; 244A–244Z H&R pp. 151–180 AC 7-10	Blank sprint answer sheet Folders Check Up materials ✓ Strategy Cards Paper clips Plastic bags or envelopes ✓ MathBoard materials Dot Array (TRB 245)	✓ MathBoard materials or Dot Array (TRB M1) ✓ Rulers Square corner Math Journals
7-11 **Solve and Create Word Problems** NCTM Focal Points: 1.9, 4.3 NCTM Standards: 1, 6, 8, 9	TE pp. 553–558 SAB pp. 247–250 H&R pp. 181–182 AC 7-11 MCC 27	Signature Sheet Blank Sprint Answer Sheet (TRB 57) Check up materials Estimating Cards ✓ MathBoard materials	Centimeter-Grid Paper (TRB M31) Math Journals
7-12 **Multiply and Divide with 4** NCTM Focal Points: 1.2, 1.3, 1.7, 1.10, 4.1, 4.2, 4.3, 4.4, 4.5 NCTM Standards: 1, 6, 9	TE pp. 559–566 SAB pp. 251–256 H&R pp. 183–188 AC 7-12	✓ Class Multiplication Table Poster Blank Sprint Answer Sheet (TRB M57) Check Up materials ✓ Strategy Cards ✓ MathBoard materials	Shoe box or paper bag Markers (red and blue) Centimeter-Grid Paper (TRB M31) Crayons Math Journals
7-13 **Use the Strategy Cards** NCTM Focal Points: 1.2, 1.10 NCTM Standards: 1, 8, 9	TE pp. 567–574 SAB pp. 257–260 H&R pp. 189–190 AC 7-13	✓ Class Multiplication Table Poster ✓ Pointer Blank Sprint Answer Sheet (TRB M57) Check Up materials ✓ Strategy Cards Rubber bands Small bags Signature Sheet	Empty egg cartons Art supplies ✓ Number Cubes Hexagon pattern blocks ✓ MathBoard materials Calculator Math Journals
7-14 **Multiply and Divide with 1 and 0** NCTM Focal Points: 1.7, 1.10, 4.1, 4.2, 4.3, 4.4 NCTM Standards: 1, 2	TE pp. 575–586 SAB pp. 261–264 H&R pp. 191–194 AC 7-14 MCC 28	✓ Class Multiplication Table Poster Check Up materials ✓ MathBoard materials	✓ Two-color counters Lined paper ✓ Rulers Math Journals

Hardcover Student Book

- Together, the Hardcover Student Book and its companion Activity Workbook contain all of the pages in the consumable Student Activity Book.

Manipulatives and Materials

- Essential materials for teaching *Math Expressions* are available in the Grade 3 kits. These materials are indicated by a ✓ in these lists. At the front of this Teacher Edition is more information about kit contents, alternatives for the materials, and use of the materials.

Lesson NCTM Focal Points NCTM Standards	Resources	Materials for Lesson Activities	Materials for Going Further
7-15 **Play Multiplication and Division Games** NCTM Focal Point: 1.9 NCTM Standard: 1	TE pp. 587–592 SAB pp. 265–272 H&R pp. 195–198 AC 7-15	✓ Class Multiplication Table Poster ✓ Pointer Blank Sprint Answer Sheet (TRB M57) Check Up materials ✓ Strategy Cards Game pieces (i.e. coins, buttons)	Index cards Math Journals
7-16 **Practice with 0s, 1s, 2s, 3s, 4s, 5s, 9s, and 10s** NCTM Focal Point: 1.9 NCTM Standards: 1, 8, 10	TE pp. 593–598 SAB pp. 273–280 H&R pp. 199–202 AC 7-16 AG Quick Quiz 3	Check Up materials ✓ Strategy Cards Game pieces (i.e. coins, buttons) ✓ MathBoard materials	Game Cards (TRB M25) Index cards ✓ Strategy Cards ✓ Rulers Math Journals
7-17 **Use Mathematical Processes** NCTM Standards:	TE pp. 599–604 SAB pp. 281–282 H&R pp. 203–204 AC 7-17	Grid paper	Square pieces of paper Rectangular pieces of paper Math Journals
Unit Review and Test	TE pp. 605–608 SAB pp. 283–284 AG Unit 7 Tests		

Resources/Materials Key: TE: Teacher Edition   SAB: Student Activity Book   H&R: Homework and Remembering
AC: Activity Cards   MCC: Math Center Challenge   AG: Assessment Guide   ✓: Grade 3 kits   TRB: Teacher's Resource Book

Hardcover Student Book

- Together, the Hardcover Student Book and its companion Activity Workbook contain all of the pages in the consumable Student Activity Book.

Manipulatives and Materials

- Essential materials for teaching *Math Expressions* are available in the Grade 3 kits. These materials are indicated by a ✓ in these lists. At the front of this Teacher Edition is more information about kit contents, alternatives for the materials, and use of the materials.

Unit 7   Teaching Resources

Individualizing Instruction

Activities	Level	Frequency
	• Intervention • On Level • Challenge	All 3 in every lesson

Math Writing Prompts	Level	Frequency
	• Intervention • On Level • Challenge	All 3 in every lesson

Math Center Challenges	For advanced students
	4 in every unit

Reaching All Learners

English Language Learners	Lessons	Pages
	1, 2, 3, 4, 5, 6, 7, 8, 9, 10, 11, 12, 13, 14, 15, 16, 17	449, 468, 485, 492, 505, 512, 524, 529, 537, 549, 555, 561, 570, 581, 589, 601

Extra Help	Lessons	Pages
	1, 2, 4, 6, 7, 11	460, 461, 470, 472, 493, 495, 510, 511, 519, 555

Special Needs	Lesson	Page
	5	504

Alternate Approach	Lessons	Pages
	3, 4, 5, 6, 10, 12, 13	479, 490, 491, 500, 502, 513, 547, 562, 577

Advanced Learners	Lesson	Page
	1	460

Strategies for English Language Learners

Present this problem to all students. Offer the different levels of support to meet student's levels of language proficiency.

Objective Write a multiplication fact given a group of objects.

Problem Draw 3 groups of 5 stars on the board. Ask: **How many groups?** 3 **How many stars in each group?** 5 **How many stars in all?** 15

Newcomer

• Have students count the stars.

• Provide number words as needed.

Beginning

• Point and say: **There are 3 groups. Each group has 5 stars. There are 15 stars in all.** Have students repeat.

• Write $3 \times 5 = 15$ on the board. Say: **3×5 is 15. There are 15 stars.**

Intermediate

• Point and ask: **How many groups?** 3 **How many stars in each group?** 5

• Say: **This is 3×5.** Ask: **How many stars in all?** 15 **What is 3×5?** 15

Advanced

• Have students draw their own groups and write the multiplication fact that represents them.

Connections

Art Connections
Lesson 2, page 474
Lesson 4, page 498
Lesson 11, page 558

Math-to-Math Connection
Lesson 5, page 508

Music Connections
Lesson 7, page 526
Lesson 12, page 566

Social Studies Connection
Lesson 15, page 592

Multi-Cultural Connection
Lesson 14, page 586

Physical Education Connection
Lesson 13, page 574

Language Arts Connection
Lesson 6, page 516

Real-World Connection
Lesson 10, page 552
Lesson 17, page 604

Sports Connection
Lesson 9, page 544

Technology Connection
Lesson 16, page 598

Literature Connection
Lesson 8, page 534

Independent Learning Activities

Ready-Made Math Challenge Centers

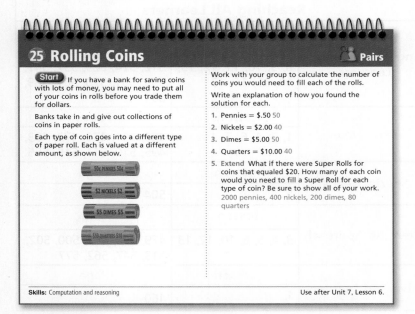

25 Rolling Coins
Pairs

Start If you have a bank for saving coins with lots of money, you may need to put all of your coins in rolls before you trade them for dollars.

Banks take in and give out collections of coins in paper rolls.

Each type of coin goes into a different type of paper roll. Each is valued at a different amount, as shown below.

Work with your group to calculate the number of coins you would need to fill each of the rolls.

Write an explanation of how you found the solution for each.

1. Pennies = $.50 50
2. Nickels = $2.00 40
3. Dimes = $5.00 50
4. Quarters = $10.00 40
5. **Extend** What if there were Super Rolls for coins that equaled $20. How many of each coin would you need to fill a Super Roll for each type of coin? Be sure to show all of your work. 2000 pennies, 400 nickels, 200 dimes, 80 quarters

Skills: Computation and reasoning   Use after Unit 7, Lesson 6.

Grouping Pairs

Materials Calculator (optional)

Objective Students use multiplication or division to determine the amount of coins contained in a roll.

Connections Computation and Reasoning

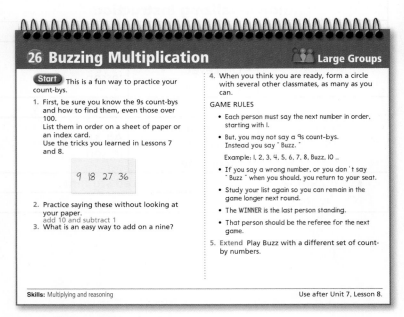

26 Buzzing Multiplication
Large Groups

Start This is a fun way to practice your count-bys.

1. First, be sure you know the 9s count-bys and how to find them, even those over 100.
   List them in order on a sheet of paper or an index card.
   Use the tricks you learned in Lessons 7 and 8.

   9 18 27 36

2. Practice saying these without looking at your paper.
   add 10 and subtract 1
3. What is an easy way to add on a nine?

4. When you think you are ready, form a circle with several other classmates, as many as you can.

GAME RULES
- Each person must say the next number in order, starting with 1.
- But, you may not say a 9s count-bys. Instead you say "Buzz."
  Example: 1, 2, 3, 4, 5, 6, 7, 8, Buzz, 10 …
- If you say a wrong number, or you don't say "Buzz" when you should, you return to your seat.
- Study your list again so you can remain in the game longer next round.
- The WINNER is the last person standing.
- That person should be the referee for the next game.
5. **Extend** Play Buzz with a different set of count-by numbers.

Skills: Multiplying and reasoning   Use after Unit 7, Lesson 8.

Grouping Large Groups

Materials Index cards

Objective Students study and use multiples of nine to play a game.

Connections Computation and Communication

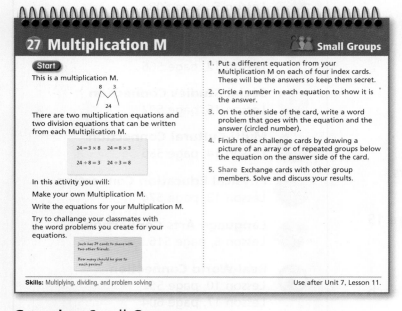

27 Multiplication M
Small Groups

Start
This is a multiplication M.

There are two multiplication equations and two division equations that can be written from each Multiplication M.

$24 = 3 \times 8$ $24 = 8 \times 3$
$24 \div 8 = 3$ $24 \div 3 = 8$

In this activity you will:

Make your own Multiplication M.

Write the equations for your Multiplication M.

Try to challange your classmates with the word problems you create for your equations.

Jack has 24 cards to share with two other friends.
How many should he give to each person?

1. Put a different equation from your Multiplication M on each of four index cards. These will be the answers so keep them secret.
2. Circle a number in each equation to show it is the answer.
3. On the other side of the card, write a word problem that goes with the equation and the answer (circled number).
4. Finish these challenge cards by drawing a picture of an array or of repeated groups below the equation on the answer side of the card.
5. Share Exchange cards with other group members. Solve and discuss your results.

Skills: Multiplying, dividing, and problem solving   Use after Unit 7, Lesson 11.

Grouping Small Groups

Materials Index cards

Objective Students create equations and word problems from a multiplication fact.

Connections Computation and Problem Solving

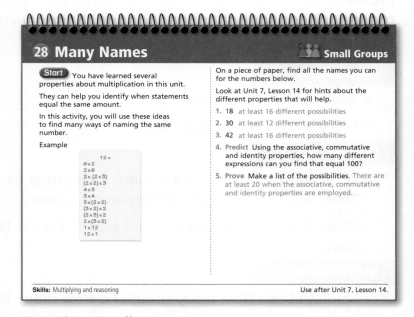

28 Many Names
Small Groups

Start You have learned several properties about multiplication in this unit.

They can help you identify when statements equal the same amount.

In this activity, you will use these ideas to find many ways of naming the same number.

Example

12 =
6 × 2
2 × 6
2 × (2 × 3)
(2 × 2) × 3
4 × 3
3 × 4
3 × (2 × 2)
(3 × 2) × 2
(2 × 2) × 3
2 × (3 × 2)
1 × 12
12 × 1

On a piece of paper, find all the names you can for the numbers below.

Look at Unit 7, Lesson 14 for hints about the different properties that will help.

1. 18 at least 16 different possibilities
2. 30 at least 12 different possibilities
3. 42 at least 16 different possibilities
4. **Predict** Using the associative, commutative and identity properties, how many different expressions can you find that equal 100?
5. **Prove** Make a list of the possibilities. There are at least 20 when the associative, commutative and identity properties are employed.

Skills: Multiplying and reasoning   Use after Unit 7, Lesson 14.

Grouping Small Groups

Materials None

Objective Students use the properties of multiplication to write different names for the same number.

Connections Computation and Reasoning

Ready-Made Math Resources

Technology — Tutorials, Practice, and Intervention

Go Digital

Use online, individualized intervention and support to bring students to proficiency.

HARCOURT
MEGA MATH
Grades K-6

Help students practice skills and apply concepts through exciting math adventures.

DESTINATION Math®

Extend and enrich students' understanding of skills and concepts through engaging, interactive lessons and activities.

Visit **Education Place**®
www.eduplace.com

Visit www.eduplace.com/mx2t/ and find family, teacher, and student materials, activities, games, and more.

Literature Links

A Grain of Rice

A Grain of Rice
Pong Lo, using his knowledge of multiplication, is able to win a bride and a kingdom. Your students will enjoy the wisdom and humor of this tale by Helena Clare Pittman.

Literature Connection
- *Amanda Bean's Amazing Dream,* by Cindy Neuschwander, illustrated by Liza Woodruff, Math Activities by Marilyn Burns (Scholastic Press, 1998)

Math Background

Putting Research into Practice for Unit 7

From our Curriculum Research Project: Multiplication and Division

A core concept that students will learn is that multiplication and division are inverse operations. The students, with the teacher's help, will learn to use and understand the language to describe underlying concepts and situations of multiplication and division including repeated equal groups and arrays.

Students will learn multiplications and divisions for each number by looking for patterns that become the basis for count-bys for that number.

Students will learn how to use products they know to find products they don't know or don't recall. Students study division almost as soon as they learn multiplication. Studying these together makes the process faster because each division is just finding an unknown factor. Through their daily in-class work and goal-setting, students build fluency with multiplication and division.

–Karen Fuson, Author
Math Expressions

From Current Research: Multiplication

[C]hildren learn skip-count lists for different multipliers (e.g., they count 4, 8, 12, 16, 20, … to multiply by four). They then count on and count down these lists using their fingers to keep track of different products. They invent thinking strategies in which they derive related products from products they know.

As with addition and subtraction, children invent many of the procedures they use for multiplication. They find patterns and use skip counting (e.g., multiplying 4 × 3 by counting "3, 6, 9, 12"). Finding and using patterns and other thinking strategies greatly simplifies the task of learning multiplication tables. Moreover, finding and describing patterns are a hallmark of mathematics. Thus, treating multiplication learning as pattern finding both simplifies the task and uses a core mathematical idea.

National Research Council. "Developing Proficiency with Whole Numbers."

Adding It Up: Helping Students Learn Mathematics. Washington, D.C.: National Academy Press, 2001. pages 191–192.

Other Useful References: Multiplication

Lemaire, P., and R.S. Siegler, "Four aspects of strategic change: Contributions to children's learning of multiplication." *Journal of Experimental Psychology: General,* 124, (1995): 83–97.

Mulligan, J., and M. Mitchelmore, "Young children's intuitive models of multiplication and division." *Journal for Research in Mathematics Education,* 28 (1997): 309–330.

Steffe, L. "Children's multiplying schemes." *The Development of Multiplicative Reasoning in the Learning of Mathematics.* Eds. G. Harel and J. Confrey, Albany: State University of New York Press, 1994. 3–39.

Getting Ready to Teach Unit 7

In this unit and unit 9, students will participate in testing and goal directed practice in school and at home. A variety of practice sheets, check sheets and routines will help students learn the basic multiplications and divisions and keep track of their progress. This is also an important opportunity for students to become self-directed and organized.

Math Expressions Vocabulary

As you teach this unit, check understanding of these terms:

- Equal Shares drawing
- count-bys
- Fast-Array drawing
- Repeated Groups drawing

See Glossary on pages T1–T17.

Practice Materials and Routines for Learning the Basic Multiplications and Divisions

Lessons 1, 2, 3, 4, 5, 6, 7, 8, 9, 10, 11, 12, 13, 14, 15, and 16

Study Plans Each day students will fill out a study plan at the top of a homework page, indicating which basic multiplications and divisions he or she will study that evening at home. At first it contains just the count-bys, multiplications, and divisions for the new number introduced. Later it will be the new number and any count-bys, multiplications, or divisions they do not recall when tested by their partner during the Check Up.

4–1	Name	Date
Homework		

Study Plan

5s count bys
5s multiplications

Homework Helper

When a student has finished practicing/studying, the Homework Helper should sign the study plan.

Practice Charts Each time a new number is introduced, a student's homework page will include a practice chart. See Teacher Edition page 464 for an explanation of how to practice the count-bys, multiplications, and divisions by covering the answers with a pencil and sliding it.

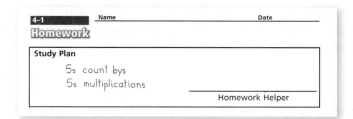

	In Order	Mixed Up
5s	1 × 5 = 5	9 × 5 = 45
	2 × 5 = 10	5 × 5 = 25
	3 × 5 = 15	2 × 5 = 10
	4 × 5 = 20	7 × 5 = 35
	5 × 5 = 25	4 × 5 = 20
	6 × 5 = 30	6 × 5 = 30
	7 × 5 = 35	10 × 5 = 50
	8 × 5 = 40	8 × 5 = 40
	9 × 5 = 45	1 × 5 = 5
	10 × 5 = 50	3 × 5 = 15

Study Sheets Students use both a class and home study sheet, which includes 3 or 4 practice charts on one page. This sheet can be used to practice all the count-bys, multiplications, and divisions or to practice just the ones a student doesn't know.

Home Study Sheet A

Count-bys	Mixed Up ×	Mixed Up ÷	Count-bys	Mixed Up ×	Mixed Up ÷
	5s			**2s**	
1 × 5 = 5	2 × 5 = 10	10 ÷ 5 = 2	1 × 2 = 2	7 × 2 = 14	20 ÷ 2 = 10
2 × 5 = 10	9 × 5 = 45	35 ÷ 5 = 7	2 × 2 = 4	1 × 2 = 2	2 ÷ 2 = 1
3 × 5 = 15	1 × 5 = 5	50 ÷ 5 = 10	3 × 2 = 6	3 × 2 = 6	6 ÷ 2 = 3
4 × 5 = 20	5 × 5 = 25	5 ÷ 5 = 1	4 × 2 = 8	5 × 2 = 10	16 ÷ 2 = 8
5 × 5 = 25	7 × 5 = 35	20 ÷ 5 = 4	5 × 2 = 10	6 × 2 = 12	12 ÷ 2 = 6
6 × 5 = 30	3 × 5 = 15	15 ÷ 5 = 3	6 × 2 = 12	8 × 2 = 16	4 ÷ 2 = 2
7 × 5 = 35	10 × 5 = 50	30 ÷ 5 = 6	7 × 2 = 14	2 × 2 = 4	10 ÷ 2 = 5
8 × 5 = 40	6 × 5 = 30	40 ÷ 5 = 8	8 × 2 = 16	10 × 2 = 20	8 ÷ 2 = 4
9 × 5 = 45	4 × 5 = 20	25 ÷ 5 = 5	9 × 2 = 18	4 × 2 = 8	14 ÷ 2 = 7
10 × 5 = 50	8 × 5 = 40	45 ÷ 5 = 9	10 × 2 = 20	9 × 2 = 18	18 ÷ 2 = 9

7–3	Name	Date
Homework		

Home Signature Sheet

	Count-Bys Homework Helper	Multiplications Homework Helper	Divisions Homework Helper
0			
1			

A routine is built into this program so each day at school and at home student's practice count-bys, multiplications, and divisions and are tested when ready. When a student is ready for a Check Up on a number, a student's partner or Homework Helper tests the student marking any missed exercises lightly with a pencils. If a student gets all the answers in a column correct, the partner or Homework Helper signs the Home Signature Sheet.

Practice Materials and Routines (continued)

Signature Sheet When a student gets all the answers in a column on the Study Sheet correct, the partner or Homework Helper signs the appropriate column on the Signature Sheet. When signatures are in all the columns, the student turns the Signature Sheet into the teacher so there is a record that the multiplications and divisions have been mastered.

Signature Sheet

	Count-Bys Partner	Multiplications Partner	Divisions Partner	Multiplications Sprint	Divisions Sprint
0					
1					
2					
3					
4					

Check Sheets Both the class and home check sheets include columns of 20 multiplications and divisions in mixed order. These sheets can be used as a more challenging alternative to the Study Sheets. They can also be used as reinforcement for students who already have signatures for all the multiplications and divisions on the study sheets.

▶ Check Sheet 1: 5s and 2s

5s Multiplications	5s Divisions	2s Multiplications	2s Divisions
2 × 5 = 10	30 / 5 = 6	4 × 2 = 8	8 / 2 = 4
5 • 6 = 30	5 ÷ 5 = 1	2 • 8 = 16	18 ÷ 2 = 9
5 • 9 = 45	15 / 5 = 3	1 • 2 = 2	2 / 2 = 1
4 × 5 = 20	50 ÷ 5 = 10	6 × 2 = 12	16 ÷ 2 = 8
5 • 7 = 35	20 / 5 = 4	2 • 9 = 18	4 / 2 = 2
10 • 5 = 50	10 ÷ 5 = 2	2 • 2 = 4	20 ÷ 2 = 10
1 × 5 = 5	35 / 5 = 7	3 × 2 = 6	10 / 2 = 5
5 • 3 = 15	40 ÷ 5 = 8	2 • 5 = 10	12 ÷ 2 = 6
8 • 5 = 40	25 / 5 = 5	10 • 2 = 20	6 / 2 = 3
	45 / 5 = 9	2 × 7 = 14	14 / 2 = 7

Sprints A Sprint is the last test that most students take on a number. Those that miss a multiplication or division will need to keep practicing and be re-tested. This test is read orally to the class. Students write only the answer and a partner checks the answers as you read them. If a student gets all answers on a Sprint correct, the partner signs the sheet in the appropriate column.

▶ Sprints for 9s

As your teacher reads each multiplication or division, write your answer in the space provided.

× 9	÷ 9
a. _____	a. _____
b. _____	b. _____
c. _____	c. _____
d. _____	d. _____
e. _____	e. _____
f. _____	f. _____
g. _____	g. _____
h. _____	h. _____
i. _____	i. _____
j. _____	j. _____

Strategies for Multiplying and Dividing

Sequential Groups on a Number Path

Lessons 1, 5, 6, 7, 9, and 12

Students circle sequential groups of a given number (such as 4) on their Number Path and write the sequential totals. The totals show the multiplication products. Students analyze patterns they see in the count-bys for each number.

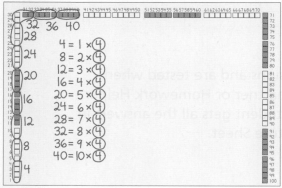

Division on the MathBoard

Lessons 5, 6, 7, 9, and 12

Students use their circled sequential groups on the Number Path, and their knowledge of multiplication, to write the related division equations.

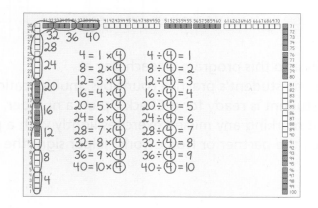

Problem Solving

Representing Word Problems

Lessons 2, 3, and 10

Students using *Math Expressions* are taught a variety of ways to represent word problems. Some are conceptual in nature (making math drawings), while others are symbolic (writing equations). Students move from using math drawings to solving problems symbolically with equations. The following are the math drawings students use to represent multiplication and division word problems in this unit.

Repeated Groups Drawing

bags of lemons

$4 \times 6 = 24$ $24 \div 4 = 6$

Equal Shares Drawing

$4 \times$ 24

6 6 6 6

Array Drawing

$4 \times 6 = 24$ $6 \times 4 = 24$

Area Model

6

4

$4 \times 6 = 24$

Use Mathematical Processes

Lesson 17

The NCTM process skills of problem solving, reasoning and proof, communication, connections, and representation are interwoven through all lessons throughout the year. The last lesson of this unit allows students to extend their use of mathematical processes to other situations.

NCTM Process Skill	Activity and Goal
Representation	1, 2: Display results of a survey in tally charts or bar graphs. 4: Use arrays to represent a problem.
Communication	1: Discuss survey results. 2: Discuss how to conduct a survey. 3, 5: Discuss generalizations about even and odd numbers.
Connections	1: Math and Science: Number Sense and Data
Reasoning and Proof	1, 2: Interpret information in charts and graphs to draw conclusions. 3: Make generalizations and test them.
Problem Solving	1, 2: Solve problems involving information in a tally chart or bar graph. 3, 5: Solve problems involving even and odd numbers. 4: Solve problems involving arrays.

Multiply with 5

Lesson Objectives

- Explore patterns in 5s count-bys and multiplications.
- Learn important multiplication vocabulary.

The Day at a Glance

Today's Goals	Materials
1 **Teaching the Lesson** **A1:** Explore patterns in 5s count-bys and multiplications. **A2:** Use the Class Multiplication Table Poster to practice 5s multiplications and count-bys. **A3:** Use fingers and count-bys to multiply by 5. **A4:** Introduce the home practice routine. **2** **Going Further** ▶ Differentiated Instruction **3** **Homework and Spiral Review**	**Lesson Activities** Student Activity Book pp. 195–200 or Student Hardcover Book pp. 195–200 and Activity Workbook pp. 73–76 (includes Family Letter) Homework and Remembering pp. 113–116 MathBoard materials or Number Path (TRB M39) Centimeter-Grid Paper (TRB M31) Class Multiplication Table Poster Pointer Class Multiplication Table (TRB M50) **Going Further** Activity Cards 7-1 Play money (nickels) Game Cards (TRB M25) Math Journals Use Math Talk today!

Keeping Skills Sharp

Quick Practice 🕐 5 MINUTES	Daily Routines
Quick Practice for this unit will begin in Lesson 2.	**Nonroutine Problem** Traci paid $2 for a book that cost $1.25. What is one combination of coins she got as change? Explain your answer. Possible answer: 3 quarters; $2.00 − $1.25 = $0.75 change; $0.25 + $0.25 + $0.25 = $0.75

① Teaching the Lesson

5s Multiplications

 20 MINUTES

Goal: Explore patterns in 5s count-bys and multiplications.

Materials: MathBoard materials or Number Path (TRB M39), Centimeter-Grid Paper (TRB M31), Student Activity Book or Hardcover Book p. 195

 NCTM Standards:
Number and Operations
Representation

Class Management

Looking Ahead In the next two units, students have many Student Activity Book pages and other materials they need to keep organized. For example, students use Study Sheets, Signature Sheets, and sheet protectors on a daily basis. To help students keep organized, have them store all their materials in a folder.

Teaching Note

Language and Vocabulary The first few lessons of this unit introduce many new vocabulary terms. Students will develop understanding of these terms over the course of the unit. Use the terms frequently, and encourage students to use them when they explain their thinking or ask questions. You may want to post new vocabulary on a sheet of chart paper and keep it posted throughout the unit.

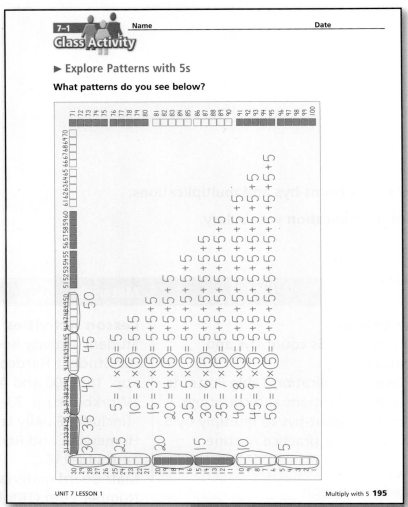

Student Activity Book page 195

▶ Explore Patterns with 5s WHOLE CLASS

Count-bys Model the steps of this activity on the Class MathBoard as students follow along on their MathBoards. Use Number Path (TRB M39) for this activity if MathBoards are not available for students. The completed board is shown alone on Student Book page 195. You can use this page to facilitate a summary discussion of the patterns in 5s multiplications. If a class MathBoard is not available, use a student's MathBoard to model the steps.

First have students circle sequential groups of 5 on the Number Path, up to 50, and write the totals so far next to each group. After they circle the first group, have them say in unison, "1 group of 5 is 5"; after they circle the second group have them say, "2 groups of 5 are 10"; and so on.

After students have circled all ten groups, the board should appear as shown below. Point to each group in order as students say, "1 group of 5 is 5," "2 groups of 5 are 10," "3 groups of 5 are 15," and so on.

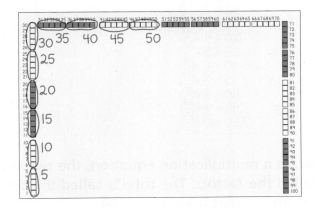

Now point to the totals on the Class MathBoard and have students read them aloud. 5, 10, 15, 20, 25, 30, 35, 40, 45, 50

Tell students we can call these numbers the 5s count-bys. They are the numbers we say when we count by groups of 5.

Multiplication Equations Tell students they can use multiplication to represent the total for repeated groups of 5. Write the following equation on the left side of the Class MathBoard as students write it on their boards.

$$5 = 1 \times \text{⑤}$$

● This equation means "5 is 1 group of 5." It is read as "5 equals 1 times 5." The group size, 5, is circled to help remember which of the numbers being multiplied is the group size and which is the number of groups. In the real world, people do not circle the group size in multiplication equations.

Have students write the next multiplication equation beneath the first.

$$10 = 2 \times \text{⑤}$$

● What does the equation mean? 10 is 2 groups of 5. How do we read it? 10 equals 2 times 5.

Activity Continued ▶

Teaching Note

Math Background In *Math Expressions,* we consider the second factor in a multiplication expression to be the group size. For example, 3 × 5 means "3 groups of 5." We circle the group size in early lessons to make this point clear.

$$3 \times \text{⑤} = 15$$

In many other countries, and in some parts of the United States, people interpret this expression as "a group of 3 taken 5 times." In other words, the first factor is considered to be the group size. (The product is the same either way.) Students may be confused if members of their family use the latter interpretation. You might explain that either way of writing a multiplication expression and either way of interpreting it are correct. However, at least for the first few lessons, encourage students to circle the group size so that everyone understands what their expressions mean.

English Language Learners

Review *count-by* with 5s count-bys. Write 5, 10, 15, 20, 25 on the board.

● **Beginning** Say: These are 5s count-bys. They show counting by 5s. Have students repeat.
● **Intermediate** Ask: What kind of count-bys are these? 5s count-bys
● **Advanced** Have students explain how to tell if a number is a 5s count-by.

Number Line Some students might find it helpful to visualize repeated additions as "jumps" across equal-size intervals on a number line.

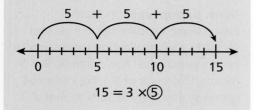

$$15 = 3 \times \textcircled{5}$$

Differentiated Instruction

Extra Help Provide Centimeter-Grid Paper (TRB M31) for writing the multiplications and repeated additions. The rows and columns of the paper might help them align the numbers and symbols more easily.

5 =	1 × 5 = 5	
10 =	2 × 5 = 5 + 5	
15 =	3 × 5 = 5 + 5 + 5	
20 =	4 × 5 = 5 + 5 + 5 + 5	
25 =	5 × 5 = 5 + 5 + 5 + 5 + 5	

As a class, continue to write multiplication equations up to 50 = 10 × 5. Have students, in unison, read each equation after writing it: "15 equals 3 times 5," "20 equals 4 times 5," and so on. After all the equations are written, the board should appear as shown below.

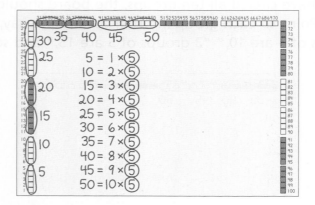

Tell students that, in a multiplication equation, the two numbers being multiplied are called the *factors*. The total is called the *product*. These terms are defined on Student Book page 194.

Repeated Additions Point out that the totals could also be found by adding 5 repeatedly. After each multiplication equation on the MathBoard, write a repeated addition expression. For the first several, ask what you should write.

● For 3 × 5, how many 5s would we add together? 3 So what should I write? 5 + 5 + 5

After all the equations are written, the board should appear as shown below and on Student Book page 193.

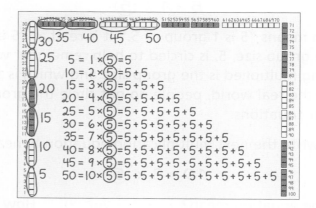

Help students compare multiplication with addition.

● What does the *multiplier,* the number we are multiplying 5 by, tell us? how many 5s we have

Look for Patterns Now ask students to look at *every other* count-by, starting with 10. Have a volunteer read the numbers aloud. 10, 20, 30, 40, 50

- What do you notice about these numbers? They are all tens numbers.
- Can someone explain why every other 5s count-by is a tens number? Because two 5s make 10.

Have students look at the completed MathBoard shown on Student Book page 195 and have them discuss patterns they see. See **Math Talk in Action** for a sample classroom discussion.

 Math Talk in Action

What patterns do you see in the count-bys or products?

Shali: The ones digits of the count-bys alternate between 5 and 0.

Greta: The tens digits of the products follow the pattern 0, 1, 1, 2, 2, 3, 3, 4, 4, 5.

Does anyone see any patterns with the factors?

Shane: I notice that if one factor is an even number, and the other factor is odd, the product is even. For example, 2 × 5 = 10.

Brandi: Yes, and if one factor is odd, and the other factor is odd, the product is odd. For example, 3 × 5 = 15.

What pattern do you see on the Number Path?

Sarah: I also noticed that two 5s (2 × 5 = 10) are half of two 10s (2 × 10 = 20).

Which pattern mentioned earlier from the count-bys can help you decide when 5 is a factor of a number?

Marita: The ones digit of the number is a 5.

Chi: The ones digit of the number is a 0.

What rule can you make?

Camila: If the ones digit of the number is a 5 or 0, then 5 is a factor of that number.

How can you test this rule?

Wapi: Try to divide a number with a ones digit of 0 and another number with a ones digit of 5 by 5. If the answer is a whole number, then the rule works.

Mavis: Divide 40 by 5. The answer is 8. So, any number with a ones digit of 0 such as 10 has a factor of 5.

Liang: Divide 35 by 5. The answer is 7. So, any number with a ones digit of 5 such as 35 has a factor of 5.

Teaching the Lesson (continued)

Activity 2

Introduce the Class Multiplication Table Poster

 15 MINUTES

Goal: Use the Class Multiplication Table Poster to practice 5s multiplications and count-bys.

Materials: Class Multiplication Table Poster, pointer, Class Multiplication Table (TRB M50)

✔ **NCTM Standards:**
Number and Operations
Representation

Teaching Note

Math Symbols In this lesson, students learn three symbols that are commonly used to represent multiplication.

3 × 5
3 * 5
3 • 5

Multiplication exercises should be presented in all three forms so students become comfortable with these symbols.

In later grades students will also learn the use of parentheses to represent multiplication.

3(5)

As they progress in their study of algebra, they will learn that multiplying with variables is often expressed by simply writing the factors in succession. For instance, $a × b$ is usually written as ab, and $3 × n$ is usually written as $3n$.

 Class Management

Distribute Class Multiplication Table (TRB M50) so that students can study their multiplications at home. If you have access to the *Math Expressions* Materials Kit, the Class Multiplication Table Poster is included, so you will not have to prepare these materials.

▶ Introduce the Class Multiplication Table Poster

WHOLE CLASS

Post the Class Multiplication Table Poster where everyone can see it. Explain that each column shows the multiplication equations for a different number. Point out that the group size is not circled but, for now, students should think of the second number in each equation as the group size.

Multiplication Table

X	1	2	3	4	5	6	7	8	9
1	1·1=1	1·2=2	1·3=3	1·4=4	1·5=5	1·6=6	1·7=7	1·8=8	1·9=9
2	2×1=2	2×2=4	2×3=6	2×4=8	2×5=10	2×6=12	2×7=14	2×8=16	2×9=18
3	3·1=3	3·2=6	3·3=9	3·4=12	3·5=15	3·6=18	3·7=21	3·8=24	3·9=27
4	4·1=4	4·2=8	4·3=12	4·4=16	4·5=20	4·6=24	4·7=28	4·8=32	4·9=36
5	5×1=5	5×2=10	5×3=15	5×4=20	5×5=25	5×6=30	5×7=35	5×8=40	5×9=45
6	6·1=6	6·2=12	6·3=18	6·4=24	6·5=30	6·6=36	6·7=42	6·8=48	6·9=54
7	7·1=7	7·2=14	7·3=21	7·4=28	7·5=35	7·6=42	7·7=49	7·8=56	7·9=63
8	8×1=8	8×2=16	8×3=24	8×4=32	8×5=40	8×6=48	8×7=56	8×8=64	8×9=72
9	9·1=9	9·2=18	9·3=27	9·4=36	9·5=45	9·6=54	9·7=63	9·8=72	9·9=81
10	10·1=10	10·2=20	10·3=30	10·4=40	10·5=50	10·6=60	10·7=70	10·8=80	10·9=90

Move the pointer down the 5s column. Tell students that this column shows all the 5s multiplications in order. Point out the various symbols used to represent multiplication. Explain that ×, *, and • all mean the same thing. Also point out that the count-bys, or products, are in bold type.

As you point to the 5s column, have the class read aloud each equation, raising a finger to show each multiplier.

1 times 5 equals 5.   2 times 5 equals 10.   3 times 5 equals 15.

Move down the column again, this time having students say only the count-bys (5, 10, 15, and so on). Have them use their fingers to indicate the multipliers, even though they do not say them. This is an important kinesthetic technique for learning the 5s count-bys.

5   10   15

Activity 3

Use Fingers to Multiply

▶ Multiply 5s Using Fingers WHOLE CLASS

Present 5s multiplication expressions (such as 4 × 5 and 6 × 5), and have students count on with their fingers to find the products. For example, to find 4 × 5, they should count by 5s, raising a finger for each count-by, until four fingers are raised.

10 15 20
5   4 times 5 equals 20.

▶ Practice Multiplications with 5 WHOLE CLASS

Have students look at the top of Student Activity Book page 196. Point out the three important vocabulary words in this lesson: *multiplication, factor,* and *product.* You may want to add these new vocabulary words to your chart paper vocabulary list. The three symbols for multiplication are also shown. Have students work individually to complete exercises 1–12.

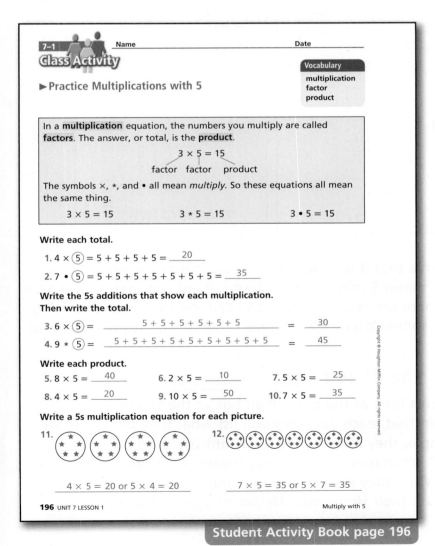

 10 MINUTES

Goal: Use fingers and count-bys to multiply by 5.

Materials: Student Activity Book or Hardcover Book p. 196

 NCTM Standards:
Number and Operations
Representation

The Learning Classroom

Helping Community When students finish their work early, let them help their classmates. Students like to take on this role and enjoy helping each other. Sometimes students who finish early may become bored, and challenging them to explain math content to others may prevent this.

Teaching Note

Language and Vocabulary Students may not be familiar with the various meanings of the words *factor* and *product.* For example, the word *product* may be used in the context of "a product made by a company" vs. the mathematical meaning used in "find the product of 8 and 2". Similarly, the word *factor* may be used as "studying hard is one factor in receiving good grades" vs. the mathematical meaning used in "the number 5 is one factor in the equation 5 × 6 = 30.

Student Activity Book page 196

① Teaching the Lesson (continued)

Activity 4

Introduce the Home Practice Routine

 5 MINUTES

Goal: Introduce the home practice routine.

Materials: Homework and Remembering pages 113–115

 NCTM Standard:
Number and Operations

 Class Management

Practice Materials and Routines See pages I and J of the overview for an explanation of the practice materials and routines used for learning the basic multiplications and divisions.

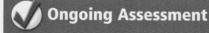 **Ongoing Assessment**

Ask students questions such as the following:

▶ What 5s addition is equal to 7 × 5? How do you know?

▶ What 5s multiplication is equal to 5 + 5 + 5 + 5 + 5 + 5? How do you know?

▶ **Introduce the Practice Chart** WHOLE CLASS

Have students look at the 5s chart on Homework page 113. Explain that each time they learn count-bys for a new number, their first page of homework will include a practice chart like the one below followed by a second page of multiplication and division exercises. Explain that they should think of 5 as the group size, even though it is not circled. Show them how to use the chart to practice their 5s count-bys and multiplications.

● To practice the count-bys, cover the count-bys (the products) in the *In Order* column with a pencil or a strip of heavy paper. Say the count-bys, sliding the pencil or paper down the column to see each count-by.

● To practice the multiplications, cover the products in either the *In Order* or *Mixed Up* column. As you multiply, slide the pencil or strip of paper down to see the answer. Repeat for all the multiplications in the column. You can also start with the last multiplication in a column and slide up.

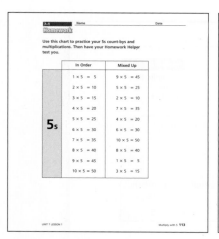 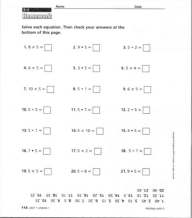

Explain to students that it is important to study count-bys and multiplications at least 5 minutes every night. Point out that on the back of their charts there are multiplication and division exercises which they should do. They should check their answers themselves at the bottom of the page.

▶ **Introduce the Study Plan** WHOLE CLASS

Now have students look at the Study Plan box at the top of Homework page 115. Explain that, each day, they will list what they plan to study. Today, for example, they might write "5s count-bys" and "5s multiplications." Emphasize that studying means practicing a column at least six times. When they are done, they should check the items they completed and ask their Homework Helper to sign on the line.

② Going Further

● Intervention   Activity Card 7-1

Nickel Values   Activity Card 7-1 ●

Work: In pairs

Use:
• Play money (10 nickels)

1. What is the total value of 10 nickels? Work together to count by 5s to find the answer. $0.50

2. Copy the table below. Count by 5s to complete the table.

Number of Nickels	Total Value
3	? $0.15
5	? $0.25
9	? $0.45
8	? $0.40
6	? $0.30

3. **Analyze** Describe at least two ways to find the value of 4 nickels.   Possible answers: Count by 5s to 4 × 5 = 20, or $0.20; Subtract 5 cents from the value of 5 nickels; Add 5 cents to the value of 3 nickels

Unit 7, Lesson 1   Copyright © Houghton Mifflin Company

Activity Note If students have difficulty completing the table as shown, reorder the numbers to show a consecutive counting sequence from 3 to 7 so that students develop a pattern to reinforce understanding.

 Math Writing Prompt

Draw a Picture Draw a picture to show that 6 × 5 = 30. Explain your picture.

Soar to Success Math ★ Software Support

Warm Up 12.12

▲ On Level   Activity Card 7-1

Count-by Cross-out   Activity Card 7-1 ▲

Work: In pairs

Use:
• TRB M25 (Game Cards)

1. Shuffle the Game Cards and place them face down in a stack. On your own, make a score card showing the numbers from 1 to 9 multiplied by 5.

2. Take turns. Draw the top card from the stack. Multiply the number on the card by 5. Then cross out the matching number on your score card. Discard the number card at the end of your turn.

3. When all the number cards have been drawn and discarded, shuffle the cards and continue playing. The first player to cross out all the numbers on the score card wins.

Unit 7, Lesson 1   Copyright © Houghton Mifflin Company

Activity Note Encourage students to say aloud the product they are calculating to reinforce learning and allow partners to check results.

 Math Writing Prompt

Explain Your Thinking Hector has some nickels in his pocket. He has no other coins. Could he have exactly 28¢? Explain.

MEGA MATH Grades K-6 Software Support

Country Countdown, Counting Critters, Level V

■ Challenge   Activity Card 7-1

Roman Numeral Multiplication   Activity Card 7-1 ■

Work: In pairs

1. Look at the Roman numeral chart below.

1	5	10	50	100
I	V	X	L	C

2. Roman numerals can be combined to form new numbers. Use the chart and the examples on the right to help you find the value of other Roman numerals.

    III = 1 + 1 + 1 = 3
    VII = 5 + 1 + 1 = 7
    IV = 5 − 1 = 4
    XC = 100 − 10 = 90

3. Notice that the values are added if the numerals are alike or if the lesser one is on the right. If the numeral of lesser value is on the left, the values are subtracted.

4. Take turns writing and solving Roman numeral multiplication exercises with 5, such as V × III = XV.

Unit 7, Lesson 1   Copyright © Houghton Mifflin Company

Activity Note If students are having difficulty writing other Roman numerals, have them first expand the chart to include the counting numbers from 1 through 12 and multiples of 3 from 15 through 60.

 Math Writing Prompt

Investigate Math Is (4 × 5) + (2 × 5) = 6 × 5? Explain why or why not.

✳ DESTINATION Math· Software Support

Course II: Module 2: Unit 2: Repeated Addition and Arrays

③ Homework and Spiral Review

7–1
Homework **Goal:** Additional Practice

This Homework page provides practice in multiplying by 5.

7–1
Remembering **Goal:** Spiral Review

This Remembering page would be appropriate anytime after today's lesson.

7–1 Name _____ Date _____
Homework

> **Study Plan**
>
> Homework Helper

Write each total.

1. $2 \times \text{\textcircled{5}} = 5 + 5 = $ _____10_____

2. $4 \cdot \text{\textcircled{5}} = 5 + 5 + 5 + 5 = $ _____20_____

3. $6 \cdot \text{\textcircled{5}} = 5 + 5 + 5 + 5 + 5 + 5 = $ _____30_____

Write the 5s additions that show each multiplication. Then write the total.

4. $3 \times \text{\textcircled{5}} = $ _____5 + 5 + 5_____ = _____15_____

5. $5 * \text{\textcircled{5}} = $ _____5 + 5 + 5 + 5 + 5_____ = _____25_____

6. $1 \cdot \text{\textcircled{5}} = $ _____5_____ = _____5_____

7. $8 \cdot \text{\textcircled{5}} = $ _____5 + 5 + 5 + 5 + 5 + 5 + 5 + 5_____ = _____40_____

8. $7 \times \text{\textcircled{5}} = $ _____5 + 5 + 5 + 5 + 5 + 5 + 5_____ = _____35_____

UNIT 7 LESSON 1   Multiply with 5 **115**

Homework and Remembering page 115

7–1 Name _____ Date _____
Remembering

Add or subtract.

1. $836 - 421 = $ _____415_____   2. $378 + 448 + 271 = $ _____1,097_____

Use mental math to add or subtract.

3. $60 + 100 = $ _____160_____ 4. $500 - 80 = $ _____420_____ 5. $600 + 200 = $ _____800_____

Solve each problem.   *Show your work.*

6. Carrie picked 8 carrots from her garden. Then she picked 6 more. How many carrots did Carrie pick in all?
   _____14 carrots_____

7. On Tuesday, the workers at the Tidy Pet Salon groomed 126 dogs. On Wednesday, they groomed 167 dogs. How many fewer dogs did they groom on Tuesday than on Wednesday?
   _____41 fewer dogs_____

8. Darren packed a picnic basket. He packed 5 sandwiches, 8 boxes of juice, 6 bags of pretzels, and 5 apples. Later he took 3 bags of pretzels out of the basket. How many items were in the basket then?
   _____21 items_____

9. Marlena had 379 baseball cards. Then her brother gave her 122 more. How many baseball cards does she have now?
   _____501 baseball cards_____

116 UNIT 7 LESSON 1   Multiply with 5

Homework and Remembering page 116

Home and School Connection

Family Letter Have students take home the Family Letter on Student Activity Book pp. 193–199 or Activity Workbook pp. 73–76. This letter explains how multiplication is developed in *Math Expressions*. A Spanish translation of this letter is on the following pages.

The information in the letter may help family members to talk about math with the children. It gives parents and guardians a better understanding of the learning that goes on in math class and creates a bridge between school and home.

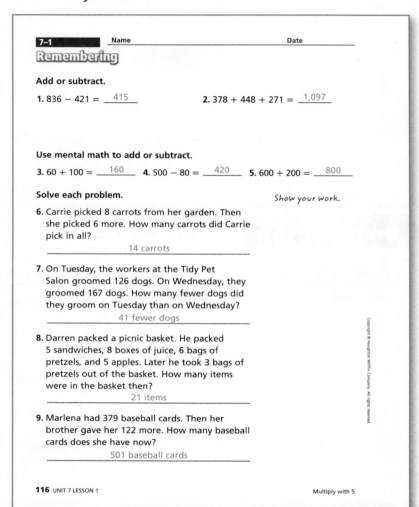
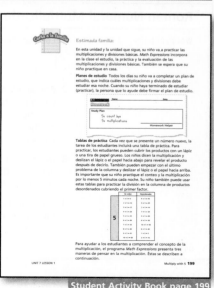

Student Activity Book page 197   Student Activity Book page 199

466 UNIT 7 LESSON 1

Multiplication as Repeated Groups

Vocabulary

repeated groups
in each
in every
per
Equal Shares drawing

Lesson Objectives

● Use multiplication to represent repeated groups situations.

● Use drawings to help solve word problems involving repeated groups.

The Day at a Glance

Today's Goals	Materials
1 **Teaching the Lesson** **A1:** Write multiplication equations for repeated groups pictures. **A2:** Make math drawings to help solve repeated groups word problems. **A3:** Make Equal Shares Drawings to represent repeated groups. **2** **Going Further** ▸ Math Connection: Function Tables ▸ Differentiated Instruction **3** **Homework and Spiral Review**	**Lesson Activities** Student Activity Book pp. 201–204 or Student Hardcover Book pp. 201–204 Homework and Remembering pp. 117–118 Chart paper Paper plates Two-color counters **Going Further** Student Activity Book p. 205 Activity Cards 7-2 Index cards Calculator Math Journals 123 Use Math Talk today!

Keeping Skills Sharp

Quick Practice ⏱ 5 MINUTES

Goal: Multiply with 5s.

Materials: Class Multiplication Table Poster, pointer

Mixed 5s Multiplications Display the Class Multiplication Table Poster. A **Student Leader** has students close their eyes and then points to any equation in the 5s column. The leader reads aloud the multiplication, pauses, and then says, "Answer." Students say the answer in unison and then open their eyes and say the complete equation. Repeat in a mixed order for all equations.

Leader: Close your eyes. 8 times 5 equals? (Pause) Answer.

Class: 40. 8 times 5 equals 40.

Daily Routines

Homework Review Have students explain their incorrect answers.

Logical Reasoning Dulal, Lien, and Kate have either the bird, the cat, or the fish. Dulal does not have the bird. Lien does not have the cat. Kate does not have the fish or the cat. Which pet does each person have? Explain. Dulal: Cat; Lien: Fish; Kate: Bird; Used a table.

	Bird	Cat	Fish
Dulal	no	yes	no
Lien	no	no	yes
Kate	yes	no	no

Teaching the Lesson

Writing Equations for Repeated Groups

 15 MINUTES

Goal: Write multiplication equations for repeated groups pictures.

Materials: Student Activity Book or Hardcover Book p. 201

✓ **NCTM Standards:**
Number and Operations
Algebra
Problem Solving
Representation

English Language Learners

Draw 3 groups of 5 apples on the board. Write *repeated group*.

• **Beginning** Say: **This is a** *repeated group* **of 5.** Have students repeat.
• **Intermediate** Ask: **How many apples are in each** *repeated group?* 5 **How many times does it repeat?** 3
• **Advanced** Have students describe the repeated group. The repeated group shows 5 apples repeated 3 times.

Teaching Note

Math Background In this lesson, a circle around a number indicates that the number represents *a group size*. This distinguishes it from *the number of groups*. Therefore, while it is true that 2 × 5 and 5 × 2 are both equal to 10, the notation 2 × ⑤ represents 2 *groups of* 5 *objects*, whereas 5 × ② represents 5 *groups of* 2 *objects*.

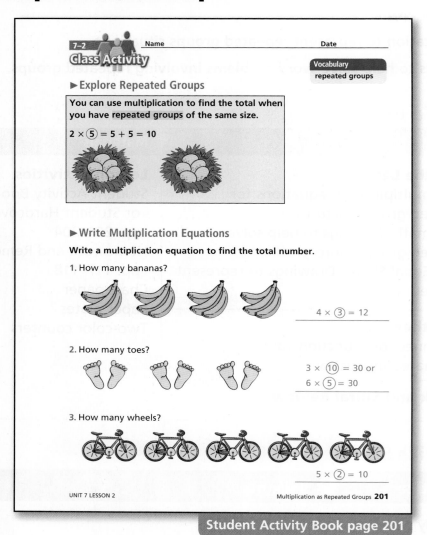

Student Activity Book page 201

► Explore Repeated Groups WHOLE CLASS

Ask for Ideas Briefly review what students learned in Lesson 1. Ask a volunteer to describe how multiplication can be used to show the total of several groups of 5.

Have students look at the information at the top of Student Book page 201.

● **What does the first picture show?** 2 nests with 5 eggs in each nest.

● **What multiplication equation shows the total number of eggs?** 2 × 5 = 10

Write 2 × ⑤ = 10 on the board.

● **What does this equation mean?** 2 groups of 5 are 10.

● **What are the factors in this equation?** 2 and 5

● **What does the 5 tell us?** The group size, or the number of eggs in each nest.

- **What does the 2 tell us?** how many groups, or nests, we have
- **What is the product in this equation?** 10
- **What does the 10 tell us?** the total number of eggs

▶ Write Multiplication Equations WHOLE CLASS

Ask students to answer questions 1–3 by looking at the pictures and writing multiplication equations. For each question, discuss their answers and ask students to circle the number that shows the group size. Explain that toes in problem 2 may be seen as 6 groups of 5 or as 3 groups of 10, depending on whether we think of each group as one foot or as a pair of feet.

Activity 2

Solving Repeated Groups Problems

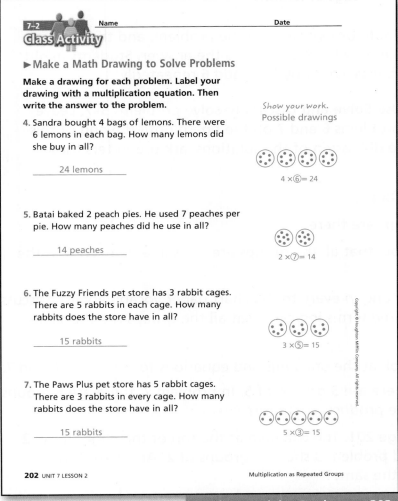

7-2
Class Activity

Name _____ Date _____

▶ Make a Math Drawing to Solve Problems

Make a drawing for each problem. Label your drawing with a multiplication equation. Then write the answer to the problem.

Show your work.
Possible drawings

4. Sandra bought 4 bags of lemons. There were 6 lemons in each bag. How many lemons did she buy in all?

____24 lemons____

$4 \times \text{⑥} = 24$

5. Batai baked 2 peach pies. He used 7 peaches per pie. How many peaches did he use in all?

____14 peaches____

$2 \times \text{⑦} = 14$

6. The Fuzzy Friends pet store has 3 rabbit cages. There are 5 rabbits in each cage. How many rabbits does the store have in all?

____15 rabbits____

$3 \times \text{⑤} = 15$

7. The Paws Plus pet store has 5 rabbit cages. There are 3 rabbits in every cage. How many rabbits does the store have in all?

____15 rabbits____

$5 \times \text{③} = 15$

202 UNIT 7 LESSON 2   Multiplication as Repeated Groups

Student Activity Book page 202

⏱ **20 MINUTES**

Goal: Make math drawings to help solve repeated groups word problems.

Materials: Student Activity Book or Hardcover Book p. 202, chart paper, paper plates, counters

✔ **NCTM Standards:**
Number and Operations
Algebra
Problem Solving
Representation

$$4 \times ⑥ = 24$$

▶ Make a Math Drawing to Solve Problems [WHOLE CLASS]

Read aloud problem 4. Remind students that multiplication can be used to represent repeated groups of the same size.

● Does this problem involve groups? yes What are the groups? the bags of lemons

● How do you know all the groups are the same size? There are 6 lemons in each bag.

On the chart paper vocabulary list, add the term *in each*.

Ask students to make a simple math drawing to represent problem 4. Explain that math drawings don't have to look like real objects; they just need to show the number of groups and the number of items in each group. Select a couple of students to share their drawings. A possible Repeated-Groups drawing is shown below.

$$4 \times ⑥ = 24$$

bags of lemons

Give students a minute or two to solve the problem, and then select a volunteer to explain how he or she found the answer. Students might count individual objects, count by 6, or add 6 repeatedly.

Math Talk Use **Solve and Discuss** to solve problems 5–7. Leave the drawings for problems 6 and 7 on the board until the end of this activity. During the discussion of the solutions, ask presenters these questions:

● What are the groups?

● How many groups are there?

● How do you know that all the groups are the same size? What is the group size?

Add the terms *per* and *in every* to the chart paper vocabulary list. Discuss the fact that all three terms indicate that all the groups are the same size.

Ask students to look at the drawings and equations for problems 6 and 7.

● In problem 6, there are 3 groups of 5. In problem 7, there are 5 groups of 3. How do the products compare? They are the same.

● Look back at page 201. The example at the top of the page shows 2 groups of 5, and problem 3 shows 5 groups of 2. Are the totals in these problems the same? yes, 10

● In these examples, switching the group size and the number of groups did not change the product. Do you think this will always be true? yes

Math Tools: Equal-Shares Drawings

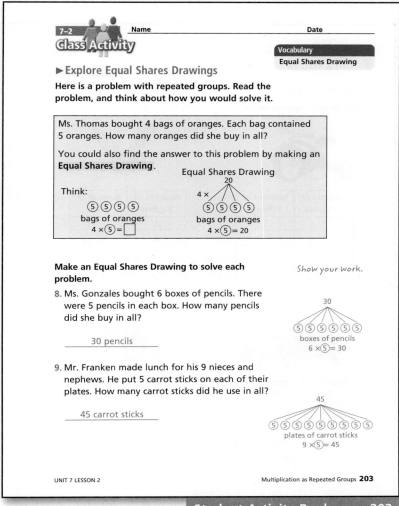

Student Activity Book page 203

The activity book page shows:

7-2
Class Activity

Name _____ Date _____

Vocabulary
Equal Shares Drawing

▶ **Explore Equal Shares Drawings**

Here is a problem with repeated groups. Read the problem, and think about how you would solve it.

Ms. Thomas bought 4 bags of oranges. Each bag contained 5 oranges. How many oranges did she buy in all?

You could also find the answer to this problem by making an **Equal Shares Drawing**.

Think:

Ⓢ Ⓢ Ⓢ Ⓢ
bags of oranges
$4 \times 5 = \square$

Equal Shares Drawing

20
$4 \times$
Ⓢ Ⓢ Ⓢ Ⓢ
bags of oranges
$4 \times 5 = 20$

Make an Equal Shares Drawing to solve each problem.

Show your work.

8. Ms. Gonzales bought 6 boxes of pencils. There were 5 pencils in each box. How many pencils did she buy in all?

____ 30 pencils ____

30
Ⓢ Ⓢ Ⓢ Ⓢ Ⓢ Ⓢ
boxes of pencils
$6 \times 5 = 30$

9. Mr. Franken made lunch for his 9 nieces and nephews. He put 5 carrot sticks on each of their plates. How many carrot sticks did he use in all?

____ 45 carrot sticks ____

45
Ⓢ Ⓢ Ⓢ Ⓢ Ⓢ Ⓢ Ⓢ Ⓢ Ⓢ
plates of carrot sticks
$9 \times 5 = 45$

UNIT 7 LESSON 2   Multiplication as Repeated Groups **203**

▶ Explore Equal Shares Drawings [WHOLE CLASS]

Discuss that even though math drawings are fairly simple, they can take a long time to draw. This is especially true if there are many things in each group. Introduce the idea of using an Equal Shares drawing as a quick way to show a repeated groups situation. Discuss the problem and Equal Shares drawing at the top of page 203.

Have students use **Solve and Discuss** to solve problems 8 and 9, representing the situations with Equal-Shares Drawings.

---

 15 MINUTES

Goal: Make Equal Shares drawings to represent repeated groups.

Materials: Student Activity Book or Hardcover Book p. 203

 NCTM Standards:
Number and Operations
Problem Solving
Representation

The Learning Classroom

Building Concepts You might ask students to compare Equal Shares drawings to the Math Mountains they used for addition and subtraction. One difference is that a Math Mountain always shows two partners, while an Equal-Shares Drawing may show more than two groups.

The most important difference is that the groups in an Equal Shares drawing are always equal. In Math Mountains, the partners can be equal or unequal.

Comparing the two types of drawings should also help students recognize that multiplication can be thought of as repeated addition of the same number.

Going Further

Going Further: Multiplication and Division

Goal: Complete and create function tables using repeated groups.

Materials: Student Activity Book or Hardcover Book p. 204, counters

✔ **NCTM Standards:**
Numbers and Operations
Algebra
Representation

Teaching Note

Math Background A function is a relationship between two sets of numbers in which each number in the first set is paired with exactly one number in the second set. The relationship between the number of equal-size groups and the total number of objects in all the groups is an example of a function. On this page, students see how they can use a function table to pair these numbers in an organized way.

▶ Review Function Tables   WHOLE CLASS

A function table is a table of ordered pairs that follows a rule. The rule tells what to do to the first number to get the second number.

Put the function table at the right on the board and ask students to give the rule.
multiply by 4

Number of Horses	Number of Legs
1	4
2	8
3	12
4	16

▶ Function Tables   INDIVIDUALS

Have students discover the rules and complete each function table in exercises 1–4 on Student Book page 204. Discuss their answers and have them share solution methods. If time permits, suggest that students think of everyday objects that come in equal-size groups, such as pairs of socks or packages of stickers. On a separate sheet of paper, ask students to draw pictures of their objects and then use their pictures to create tables similar to those on Student Book page 204. Have struggling students work with a **Helping Partner.**

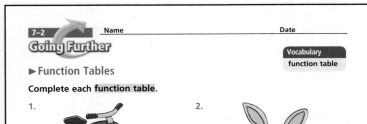

Vocabulary
function table

▶ **Function Tables**

Complete each function table.

1.

Number of Tricycles	Number of Wheels
1	3
2	6
3	9
4	12
5	15

2.

Number of Rabbits	Number of Ears
1	2
2	4
3	6
4	8
5	10

3.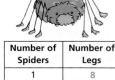

Number of Cars	Number of Wheels
1	4
2	8
3	12
4	16
5	20

4.

Number of Spiders	Number of Legs
1	8
2	16
3	24
4	32
5	40

204 UNIT 7 LESSON 2   Multiplication as Repeated Groups

Student Activity Book page 204

Differentiated Instruction

Extra Help Some students may not see the relationship between the two sets of numbers in the table. Have students use counters to represent each pair of numbers in the function tables.

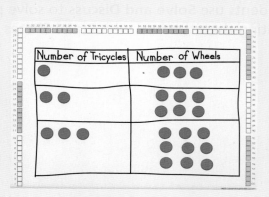

Number of Tricycles	Number of Wheels

Differentiated Instruction

Match Up Activity Card 7-2

Work: In pairs

Use:
- 12 Index cards

1. Write each of the following addition and multiplication expressions on separate index cards:

3 × 5	9 + 9	3 × 3
5 × 2	5 + 5 + 5	5 × 3
2 × 9	9 + 9 + 9 + 9	3 + 3 + 3
4 × 9	2 + 2 + 2 + 2 + 2	3 × 3 × 3 × 3 × 3

2. Shuffle the cards and arrange them in rows face down on the table. Take turns selecting two cards. If the cards match, keep the cards. If they don't match, replace them in their positions face down on the table.

3. When all the cards have been matched, the player with more cards wins.

Unit 7, Lesson 2   Copyright © Houghton Mifflin Company

Activity Note Remind students that the first factor in a multiplication expression tells how many times the second factor is added in the equivalent repeated addition expression.

Math Writing Prompt

Understanding Repeated Groups Explain why you can write 5 + 5 + 5 as a multiplication expression, but you cannot write 5 + 6 + 7 as a multiplication expression.

Soar to Success Math **Software Support**

Warm Up 12.17

Repeated Groups of Tens Activity Card 7-2 ▲

Work: On your own

Use:
- Calculator

1. You can use repeated addition to find products. Look at the example below.

60 + 60 + 60 = 180

2. What addition equation can you use to find the following products?

2 × 40   40 + 40 = 80

4 × 30   30 + 30 + 30 + 30 = 120

5 × 20   20 + 20 + 20 + 20 + 20 = 100

3. Find each product and check your answer with a calculator.

Unit 7, Lesson 2   Copyright © Houghton Mifflin Company

Activity Note As an extension of the activity, have students explain how they can use counting by 6s, 4s, 3s, and 2s to find the equivalent sums.

Math Writing Prompt

Explain Your Thinking You know that 2 × 4 = 8 and that 40 is the same as 4 tens. Explain how you could use this information to find 2 × 40.

MegaMath Grades K-6 **Software Support**

Country Countdown, Counting Critters, Level V

Repeated Groups of Tens and Ones Activity Card 7-2 ■

Work: On your own

Use:
- Calculator

1. You can use repeated addition to find products. Look at the example below.

76 + 76 + 76 = 228

2. What addition equation can you use to find the following products?

2 × 98   98 + 98 = 196

4 × 52   52 + 52 + 52 + 52 = 208

5 × 23   23 + 23 + 23 + 23 + 23 = 115

3. Find each product and check your answer with a calculator.

Unit 7, Lesson 2   Copyright © Houghton Mifflin Company

Activity Note Challenge students to discover ways to find each sum using mental math and groups of tens and ones.

Math Writing Prompt

Investigate Math Suppose you know 8 × 15 = 120. How could you use this information to find the product 7 × 15? Explain your thinking.

DESTINATION Math **Software Support**

Course II: Module 2: Unit 2: Repeated Addition and Arrays

③ Homework and Spiral Review

Left side - Homework 7-2, Goal: Additional Practice

Right side - Remembering 7-2, Goal: Spiral Review

Then Home or School Activity.

7-2

Homework **Goal:** Additional Practice

✓ Include students' completed Homework page as part of their portfolios.

7-2

Remembering **Goal:** Spiral Review

This Remembering page would be appropriate anytime after today's lesson.

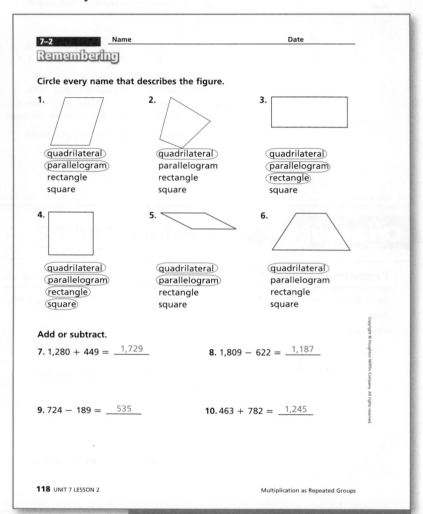

Homework page 117:

7-2 Name _____ Date _____
Homework

Study Plan
_____
Homework Helper

Write a multiplication equation to show how many.

1. How many apples?

$4 \times \boxed{6} = 24$

2. How many lenses?

$7 \times \boxed{2} = 14$

Make a math drawing and label it. Write a multiplication equation that gives the answer.

3. Beth put the dinner rolls she baked in 5 bags, with 6 rolls per bag. How many rolls did Beth bake?
$5 \times \boxed{6} = 30$; 30 rolls

4. Baya arranged her pennies into 7 piles of 5. How many pennies did she have?
$7 \times \boxed{5} = 35$; 35 pennies

UNIT 7 LESSON 2 — Multiplication as Repeated Groups **117**

Remembering page 118:

7-2 Name _____ Date _____
Remembering

Circle every name that describes the figure.

1. quadrilateral / parallelogram / rectangle / square

2. quadrilateral / parallelogram / rectangle / square

3. quadrilateral / parallelogram / rectangle / square

4. quadrilateral / parallelogram / rectangle / square

5. quadrilateral / parallelogram / rectangle / square

6. quadrilateral / parallelogram / rectangle / square

Add or subtract.

7. $1,280 + 449 = \underline{1,729}$

8. $1,809 - 622 = \underline{1,187}$

9. $724 - 189 = \underline{535}$

10. $463 + 782 = \underline{1,245}$

118 UNIT 7 LESSON 2 — Multiplication as Repeated Groups

Homework and Remembering page 117

Homework and Remembering page 118

Home or School Activity

Art Connection

Repeated Groups Drawings Have students make drawings of familiar objects that can show repeated groups. For example, have them draw 3 flowers with 5 petals per flower, and then label the total number of petals. When students' drawings are complete, have them draw and label other elements such as 3 leaves per stem and 2 bees per flower.

15 petals

Multiplication and Arrays

REAL
WORLD
**Problem
Solving**

Lesson Objectives

- **Use multiplication to represent array situations.**
- **Use drawings to help solve word problems involving arrays.**
- **Understand that multiplication is commutative.**

Vocabulary

array
row
column
**Commutative Property
  of Multiplication**

The Day at a Glance

Today's Goals	Materials	

1 **Teaching the Lesson**
   A1: Introduce the Signature and Study Sheets and Check Up procedures.
   A2: Write multiplication equations for arrays.
   A3: Make drawings to help solve word problems involving arrays.
   A4: Recognize that switching the order of the factors in a multiplication equation does not change the product.
 	
 2 **Going Further**
   ▶ Differentiated Instruction
 	
 3 **Homework and Spiral Review**
	Lesson Activities
	 Student Activity Book pp. 205–216 or Student Hardcover Book pp. 205–216 and Activity Workbook pp. 77–82 (includes Signature Sheet, Study Sheet, and Family Letter)
	 Homework and Remembering pp. 119–122
	 Folders
	 Signature Sheet
	 Study Sheet A
	 Dry-erase markers
	 Sheet protectors
	 Connecting cubes
	 MathBoard materials
		Going Further
		 Activity Cards 7-3
		 Game Cards (TRB M25)
		 Counters
		 Centimeter Grid Paper (TRB M31)
		 Math Journals
		
		 123 Use **Math Talk** today!

Keeping Skills Sharp

Quick Practice ⏱ 5 MINUTES	**Daily Routines**
Goal: Practice 5s count-bys and multiplications. **Materials:** Class Multiplication Table Poster, pointer **Mixed 5s Multiplications** Have a **Student Leader** direct the class in practicing their 5s multiplications in a mixed order. (See Unit 7 Lesson 2.)	**Homework Review** Let students work together to check their homework. **Symmetry** Draw a figure that has two lines of symmetry. Possible answer: Rectangle

Teaching the Lesson

Introduce the Signature and Study Sheets

 5 MINUTES

Goal: Introduce the Signature and Study Sheets and Check Up procedures.

Materials: Folders, Check Up materials: Signature Sheet (Student Activity Book pages 205–206 or Activity Workbook p. 77), Study Sheet A (Student Activity Book pages 207–208 or Activity Workbook p. 78), dry-erase markers (1 per student), sheet protectors (1 per student); Homework and Remembering Book pages 119–120

✔ **NCTM Standard:**
Number and Operations

 Class Management

Throughout the unit, students will repeatedly use the Signature Sheet and Study Sheet A. If you need to replace these, use Signature Sheet (TRB M51) and Study Sheet A (TRB M52).

▶ **Introduce the Signature Sheet** PAIRS

Have **Student Pairs** look at the Signature Sheet on Student Book page 205 or Activity Workbook p. 77. Explain that, throughout the unit, they will be using Study Sheets to test each other on count-bys, multiplications, and divisions. If a student gets all the answers on a particular set correct, the partner will sign his or her initials in the appropriate place on the Signature Sheet. Explain that students must get signatures from a partner for each set of count-bys, multiplications, and divisions.

Point out the 2 columns labeled *Sprint.* Explain that Sprints are quick, written tests. Students will take their first Sprint in Lesson 6.

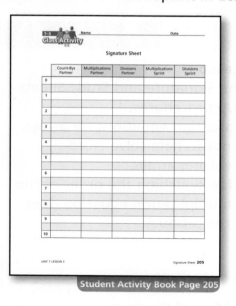

Student Activity Book Page 205

▶ **Introduce the Procedure for Check Ups** PAIRS

Organize students into pairs. Give each student a sheet protector and a dry-erase marker. Have **Student Pairs** write their names on Study Sheet A (Student Activity Book page 207 or Activity Workbook p. 78), and place it into a sheet protector.

Study Sheet A

5s			2s		
Count-bys	Mixed Up ×	Mixed Up ÷	Count-bys	Mixed Up ×	Mixed Up ÷
1 × 5 = 5	2 × 5 = 10	10 ÷ 5 = 2	1 × 2 = 2	7 × 2 = 14	20 ÷ 2 = 10
2 × 5 = 10	9 × 5 = 45	35 ÷ 5 = 7	2 × 2 = 4	1 × 2 = 2	2 ÷ 2 = 1
3 × 5 = 15	1 × 5 = 5	50 ÷ 5 = 10	3 × 2 = 6	3 × 2 = 6	6 ÷ 2 = 3
4 × 5 = 20	5 × 5 = 25	5 ÷ 5 = 1	4 × 2 = 8	5 × 2 = 10	16 ÷ 2 = 8
5 × 5 = 25	7 × 5 = 35	20 ÷ 5 = 4	5 × 2 = 10	6 × 2 = 12	12 ÷ 2 = 6
6 × 5 = 30	3 × 5 = 15	15 ÷ 5 = 3	6 × 2 = 12	8 × 2 = 16	4 ÷ 2 = 2
7 × 5 = 35	10 × 5 = 50	30 ÷ 5 = 6	7 × 2 = 14	2 × 2 = 4	10 ÷ 2 = 5
8 × 5 = 40	6 × 5 = 30	40 ÷ 5 = 8	8 × 2 = 16	10 × 2 = 20	8 ÷ 2 = 4
9 × 5 = 45	4 × 5 = 20	25 ÷ 5 = 5	9 × 2 = 18	4 × 2 = 8	14 ÷ 2 = 7
10 × 5 = 50	8 × 5 = 40	45 ÷ 5 = 9	10 × 2 = 20	9 × 2 = 18	18 ÷ 2 = 9

10s			9s		
Count-bys	Mixed Up ×	Mixed Up ÷	Count-bys	Mixed Up ×	Mixed Up ÷
1 × 10 = 10	1 × 10 = 10	80 ÷ 10 = 8	1 × 9 = 9	2 × 9 = 18	81 ÷ 9 = 9
2 × 10 = 20	5 × 10 = 50	10 ÷ 10 = 1	2 × 9 = 18	4 × 9 = 36	18 ÷ 9 = 2
3 × 10 = 30	2 × 10 = 20	50 ÷ 10 = 5	3 × 9 = 27	7 × 9 = 63	36 ÷ 9 = 4
4 × 10 = 40	8 × 10 = 80	90 ÷ 10 = 9	4 × 9 = 36	8 × 9 = 72	9 ÷ 9 = 1
5 × 10 = 50	7 × 10 = 70	40 ÷ 10 = 4	5 × 9 = 45	3 × 9 = 27	54 ÷ 9 = 6
6 × 10 = 60	3 × 10 = 30	100 ÷ 10 = 10	6 × 9 = 54	10 × 9 = 90	27 ÷ 9 = 3
7 × 10 = 70	4 × 10 = 40	30 ÷ 10 = 3	7 × 9 = 63	1 × 9 = 9	63 ÷ 9 = 7
8 × 10 = 80	6 × 10 = 60	20 ÷ 10 = 2	8 × 9 = 72	6 × 9 = 54	72 ÷ 9 = 8
9 × 10 = 90	10 × 10 = 100	70 ÷ 10 = 7	9 × 9 = 81	5 × 9 = 45	90 ÷ 9 = 10
10 × 10 = 100	9 × 10 = 90	60 ÷ 10 = 6	10 × 9 = 90	9 × 9 = 81	45 ÷ 9 = 5

Discuss the following steps for Check Ups on the count-bys.

● Partner 1 gives his or her Study Sheet (in the sheet protector) to Partner 2.

● Partner 1 says the count-bys from memory as Partner 2 follows along on the Study Sheet.

● Partner 2 puts check marks next to the count-bys that Partner 1 answers incorrectly.

● If Partner 1 answers all the count-bys correctly, Partner 2 signs the appropriate section of Partner 1's Signature Sheet.

● Partner 2 returns the Study Sheet to Partner 1.

● The partners switch roles.

Students can use the marked-up Study Sheet to study from, paying special attention to the count-bys they missed. Demonstrate the procedure by choosing a volunteer to say all the 5s count-bys from memory as you follow along on Study Sheet A. If the student does not make any errors, hold up his or her Signature Sheet and indicate where the partner should sign it. If the student makes a mistake, place a check mark next to that count-by on the Study Sheet.

Give pairs a few minutes to test each other on the 5s count-bys. Tell students they will have only one chance to say the count-bys today. If they make a mistake, they can try again tomorrow. Tell students to write any count-bys they missed in the Study Plan box on Homework page 121.

Have students look at Home Study Sheet A and the Home Signature Sheet on Homework and Remembering pages 119–120. Tell them to take these sheets home, keep them in a safe place, and use them to study.

After students have studied, their Homework Helpers can use Home Study Sheet A to test them. The helper should mark any missed problems lightly with a pencil. If a student gets all the answers on a test correct, the helper should sign his or her initials on the Home Signature Sheet. A student who has collected signatures for the whole sheet should bring in the sheet for you to check.

The Learning Classroom

Helping Community Using a Signature Sheet helps build a supportive classroom in which students help one another learn. Because students get excited about collecting signatures, they are motivated to study at home.

You may want students to work with the same partner for several days or weeks, or you may want to reassign partners frequently. It is important to establish a routine so that Check Ups do not take too long. After testing, students can study individually or with others, preparing for the next day's test.

Class Management

Remind students to keep their Study Sheets, Signature Sheets, sheet protectors, and dry-erase markers in their folders.

Homework and Remembering Book page 120

Activity 2

Explore and Use Arrays

 15 MINUTES

Goal: Write multiplication equations for arrays.

Materials: MathBoard materials, Student Activity Book or Hardcover Book pp. 209–210

✔ **NCTM Standards:**
Number and Operations
Representation

Teaching Note

Math Background The array model for multiplication is important because it has many applications throughout mathematics. For instance, it can be used to demonstrate algebraic properties of operations, as in this lesson where the array model is used to show that multiplication is commutative.

$4 \times 5 = 20$ $5 \times 4 = 20$
$4 \times 5 = 5 \times 4$

Later in this unit students will learn to find the area of a rectangle by viewing its interior as an array of square units.

4-by-5 Array of Square Units

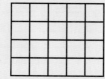

Area = 4×5 square units
Area = 20 square units

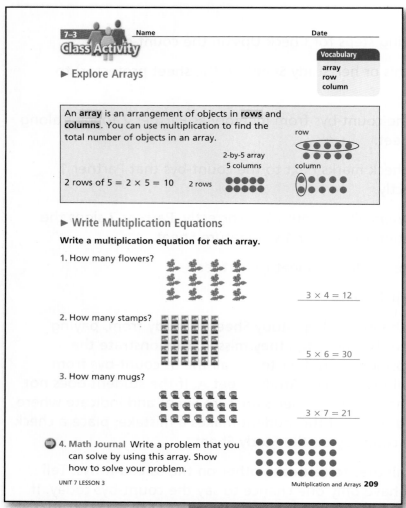

Student Activity Book page 209

► Explore Arrays [WHOLE CLASS]

Refer students to Student Book page 209. Tell them that, in each of the pictures, the arrangement of objects is called an *array*. Ask students to describe the characteristics of an array. Make sure the following points are mentioned.

● An array has *rows* and *columns* of objects.

● Each row has the same number of equally spaced objects.

● Each column has the same number of equally spaced objects.

Review the meanings of row and column by looking at the top of Student Book page 209. Remind students that they learned about rows and columns when they studied tables. As with tables, the rows of an array go across, and the columns go up and down.

Explain that an array with 2 rows and 5 columns is called a 2-by-5 array. Ask students to use the word *by* to describe the arrays shown in exercises 1–3. 4-by-3; 6-by-5; 3-by-7

► Write Multiplication Equations WHOLE CLASS

Have students look at the array of counters at the top of Student Book page 209.

● If the rows of counters are thought of as groups, how many groups are there? 2 groups How many counters are in each group? 5 counters What equation can we write to show the total number of counters? 2 × 5 = 10 Which number should be circled? 5

Write the following equation on the board.

$$2 \times ⑤ = 10$$

● If the columns of counters are groups, how many groups are there? 5 groups How many counters are in each group? 2 counters What equation can be written to show the total number of counters? 5 × 2 = 10 Which number should be circled? 2

Write the following equation on the board.

$$5 \times ② = 10$$

● Because either the rows or the columns can be thought of as the groups, don't circle either factor when writing a multiplication equation for an array.

Tell students we usually write the number of rows first in the equation for an array. Erase the other equations, and write this equation on the board.

$$2 \times 5 = 10$$

Ask students to write multiplication equations for exercises 1–3 on Student Activity Book page 209. Discuss the answers. Then have students complete exercise 4 and present their problems to the class.

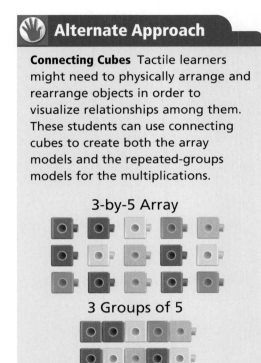

Alternate Approach

Connecting Cubes Tactile learners might need to physically arrange and rearrange objects in order to visualize relationships among them. These students can use connecting cubes to create both the array models and the repeated-groups models for the multiplications.

3-by-5 Array

3 Groups of 5

Activity Continued ▶

▶ **Discuss Comparing Arrays** | WHOLE CLASS | Math Talk 123

Draw the following two arrays on the board.

- Without counting each individual dot, compare the arrays. Do both arrays have the same amount of dots? Or, does one array have more or less than the other? The array on the left has more dots.

- What symbol can we use to show that one array has more dots than the other. We can use a greater than symbol to show that one array has more dots than the other.
  Write in the symbol.

- How could you tell just by looking that the array on the left has more dots? Possible answer: The array on the left has one more row of dots

- What equation can you write for each array to show that the comparison is reasonable and correct? $4 \times 2 = 8$ is greater than $2 \times 3 = 6$.

Now add two dots to the second array in another color and ask these questions.

- Now compare the arrays. Do both arrays have the same amount of dots? Or, does one array have more or less than the other? Both arrays have the same number of dots. Write in the symbol to show this.

- What equation can you write for each array to show that the comparison is reasonable and correct? $4 \times 2 = 8$ is equal to $2 \times 4 = 8$.

Remind students that using multiplication is a quick way to find how many items are in an array without counting all the objects. Draw a circle around the top row and one of the columns to illustrate this.

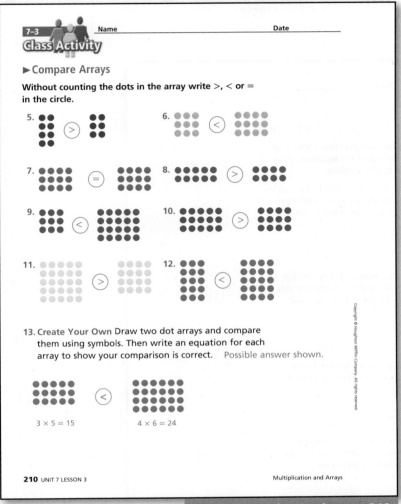

Student Activity Book page 210

▶ Compare Arrays INDIVIDUALS

Have a volunteer read aloud the directions on the top of Student Book page 210 and have students complete exercises 5–12 independently. You may want to encourage students to check their comparisons by writing equations for each array. Then, using the **Solve and Discuss** structure, have students share their arrays, comparisons, and equations for problem 13.

Teaching the Lesson (continued)

Solve Array Problems

 15 MINUTES

Goal: Make drawings to help solve word problems involving arrays.

Materials: MathBoard materials, Student Activity Book or Hardcover Book p. 211

✔ **NCTM Standards:**
Number and Operations
Representation
Problem Solving

Teaching Note

Watch For! Students who draw arrays for problems 5–8 might mix up the number of rows and the number of columns when writing multiplication equations for their arrays. Suggest that they circle each row of an array to show that each row is a group. Remind them that the first number in a multiplication equation represents the number of groups.

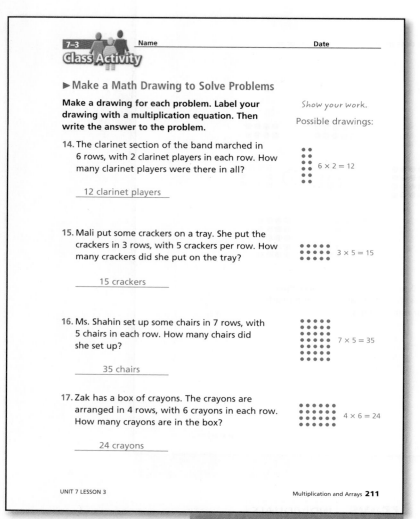

Student Activity Book page 211

▶ Make a Math Drawing to Solve Problems   WHOLE CLASS

Read aloud the directions at the top of Student Activity Book page 211. Using the **Solve and Discuss** structure, have students solve problem 5. Encourage them to make very simple drawings. Make sure various drawings and solution methods are presented. Below are two possible drawings. The second is a form of the Equal-Shares Drawings students made in Lesson 2. If no one makes drawings like these, you may want to suggest them yourself.

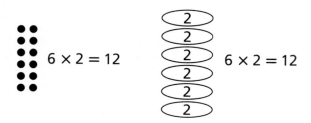

Using **Solve and Discuss,** have students solve problems 14–17.

Activity 4

Commutativity

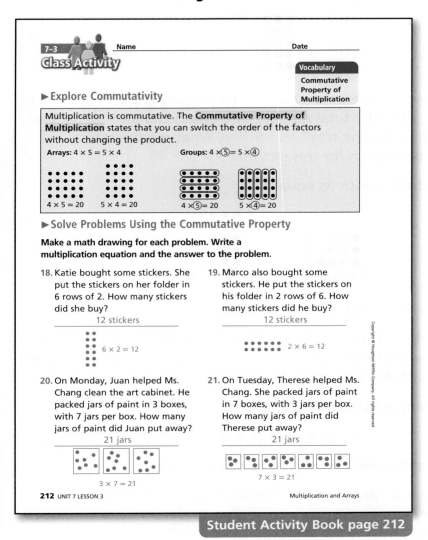

Student Activity Book page 212

▶ Explore Commutativity [WHOLE CLASS]

Revisit problem 6 on Student Book page 211. Draw an array for the problem on the board, and have students do the same on their MathBoards.

● How many rows are in this array? 3 rows How many crackers are in each row? 5 crackers How many crackers are there altogether? 15 crackers What multiplication equation can we write for this array? 3 × 5 = 15

Write the equation beneath the array.

3 × 5 = 15

Activity continued ▶

Goal: Recognize that switching the order of the factors in a multiplication equation does not change the product.

Materials: MathBoard materials, Student Activity Book or Hardcover Book pp. 211–213

 NCTM Standards:
Number and Operations
Representation
Problem Solving
Algebra

Teaching Note

Math Background Students have already learned that addition is commutative. That is, in an addition the order of two addends can be switched without changing the sum. In Activity 4, students use arrays to discover that multiplication has a similar property: The order of two factors can be switched without changing the product.

Students have also already learned that there is an Associative Property of Addition (changing the grouping of addends does not change the sum). For example (3 + 4) + 2 = 3 + (4 + 2) and an Identity Property of Addition (the sum of 0 and any number is that number). For example 0 + 25 is 25 and 156 + 0 is 156. Students should also be aware that multiplication has similar properties. Associative Property of Multiplication: (3 × 4) × 2 = 3 × (4 × 2). Identity Property of Multiplication: *when any number is multiplied by 1, the result is that number.* For example 3 × 1 = 3 and 1 × 5 = 5. Students will be able to practice and explore the Associative, Identity and Zero Properties of Multiplication in Lesson 14 of this unit.

Multiplication and Arrays **483**

① Teaching the Lesson (continued)

Teaching Note

Math Background The activities in this lesson illustrate the flexibility of multiplication models.

▶ In any repeated-groups situation, the groups can be arranged to form the rows or columns of an array. In other words, any repeated-groups situation can be converted to an array situation.

▶ In any array situation, the rows or columns can be thought of as groups. In other words, any array situation can be converted to a repeated-groups situation.

▶ A problem involving *M* rows of *N* can be converted to one involving *N* rows of *M*. The total will be the same.

▶ A problem involving *M* groups of *N* can be converted to one involving *N* groups of *M*. The total will be the same.

Students may use these facts to change a given problem into an equivalent problem that is easier to solve. For example, if a problem requires finding the total of 5 groups of 7, students might think about 7 groups of 5 instead and simply count by 5s to find the answer.

Bring up these ideas as they arise during discussions of word problems. Students will develop flexibility with these models over time.

Now tell students to imagine turning the array so the rows become columns. Ask them to draw the rotated array on their MathBoards as you draw it on the board.

● How many rows are there now? 5 rows How many crackers are in each row? 3 crackers Did the total number of crackers change? no So how many crackers are on the tray? 15 crackers What multiplication equation can be written for this picture? $5 \times 3 = 15$

Label the second array with its equation.

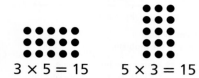

$3 \times 5 = 15$ $5 \times 3 = 15$

Point to the two equations.

● The number of crackers in the two situations is the same. It doesn't matter which way the array is turned. So 3×5 and 5×3 both equal 15. This means that 3×5 equals 5×3.

Write the following equation on the board:

$$3 \times 5 = 5 \times 3$$

Help students generalize this concept to other situations.

● Suppose there is an array with 2 rows and 7 columns. Can it be rotated? yes What equation can be written to show that the number of things in the arrays is the same? $2 \times 7 = 7 \times 2$

Write this equation on the board:

$$2 \times 7 = 7 \times 2$$

● Suppose there is an array with 4 rows and 9 columns. Can it be rotated? yes What equation can be written to show that the number of things in the arrays is the same? $4 \times 9 = 9 \times 4$

Write this equation on the board:

$$4 \times 9 = 9 \times 4$$

● Can any array be rotated, no matter how many rows and columns it has? yes Use the letters *M* and *N* to stand for any two numbers. If an array has *M* rows and *N* columns, how many things does it have altogether? $M \times N$

Write $M \times N$ under 4×9.

• Suppose this array with *M* rows and *N* columns is rotated. How many rows would the new array have? *N* How many columns would it have? *M* So how many things would it have altogether? *N* × *M*

Complete the equation you started above. Leave it on the board until the end of the activity.

$$M \times N = N \times M$$

Remind students that, in the last lesson, they found that 3 groups of 5 have the same total as 5 groups of 3. Tell them that arrays can help them see why this is true. Draw and label a picture of 3 groups of 5.

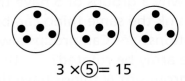

3 ×⑤= 15

• Now, rearrange the groups to form rows. Make the drawing on the right next to the first drawing.

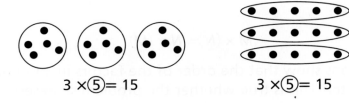

3 ×⑤= 15   3 ×⑤= 15

• Now the drawing looks like an array. Rotate this array. Draw the rotated array next to the first array.

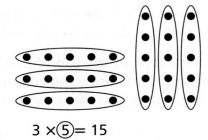

3 ×⑤= 15

• Now the groups of 5 are in columns. We can erase the circles around these groups and think of the rows as the groups instead. Erase the circles around the columns, and circle the rows.

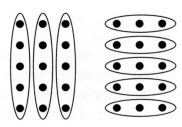

• How many groups are there now? 5 groups And how many things are in each group? 3 things Did the total change? no What is it? 15

Activity continued ▶

Teaching Note

Math Symbols Don't worry if students are confused about the algebraic notation used in the general equations. It is more important that they can describe the concept of commutativity in their own words and apply it in their work.

English Language Learners

Write 2 × 4 = 8 and 4 × 2 = 8. Say: Multiplication is *commutative*. The order of the factors does not matter.

• **Beginning** Say: The order of the factors 2 and 4 does not matter. The factors are *commutative*. Have students repeat.

• **Intermediate** Ask: What are the factors? 2 and 4 Does the order of the factors matter? no The factors are *commutative*.

• **Advanced** Have students give an example of the commutative property.

Label the second array with the related equation.

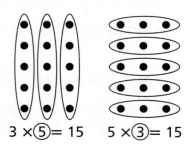

$3 \times \text{⑤} = 15$ $5 \times \text{③} = 15$

● These drawings show why 3 groups of 5 have the same total as 5 groups of 3. Do you think the same thing can be done for other repeated-groups situations? yes Can groups always be arranged into rows and then can the array be rotated? yes Use *M* and *N* to stand for any two numbers. *M* groups of *N* things have the same total as *N* groups of *M* things.

Write the following equation near the equation $M \times N = N \times M$ that you wrote earlier.

$$M \times \text{Ⓝ} = N \times \text{Ⓜ}$$

● These equations show that the order of the factors in a multiplication does not matter. This is true whether the problem represents an array or repeated groups. In math, we say that multiplication is *commutative* or has the *commutative property*. This means that if the order of the factors is switched, the product is the same.

Have students look at the top of Student Book page 212. Tell them that these diagrams summarize the commutative property of multiplication and they can use these diagrams for reference.

▶ Solve Problems Using the Commutative Property
WHOLE CLASS

 Math Talk Problems 18–21 give further examples of the commutative property. Have students solve them, and then discuss the answers. Have students share the drawings and multiplication equations for each problem. As a class, discuss which of these problems are related and how. Be sure the following points are emphasized.

● Problems 18 and 19 are a pair. The array in problem 18 has 6 rows and 2 columns, while the array in problem 19 has 2 rows and 6 columns. In other words, one array is a rotated version of the other. The factors are in a different order, but the product is the same.

● Problems 20 and 21 are a pair. Problem 20 involves 3 groups of 7, while problem 21 involves 7 groups of 3. The factors are in a different order, but the product is the same.

Intervention   Activity Card 7-3

Model Arrays   Activity Card 7-3 ●

Work: In pairs

Use:
- TRB M25 (Game Cards 2 – 7)
- Counters

Decide:
Who will be Student 1 and who will be Student 2 for the first round.

1. Shuffle the Game Cards and place them in a stack. Then draw the top two cards.

2. Student 1: Make an array of counters. Use the first digit as the number of rows and the second digit as the number of columns.

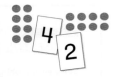

3. Student 2: Make a second array. Use the second digit as the number of rows and the first digit as the number of columns.

$4 \times 2 = 8$ $2 \times 4 = 8$

4. Write a multiplication equation for each array. Then repeat the activity with the remaining cards. What do you notice about each pair of products? They are equal.

Unit 7, Lesson 3   Copyright © Houghton Mifflin Company

Activity Note Transposing rows and columns is easily done by rotating the array of counters 90 degrees. The first factor in the multiplication sentence is always the number of rows in the array.

✐ **Math Writing Prompt**

Draw a Picture Draw a picture to show why $4 \times 7 = 7 \times 4$. Explain your picture.

Soar to Success Math ★ **Software Support**

Warm Up 12.20

On Level   Activity Card 7-3

Multiple Arrays   Activity Card 7-3 ▲

Work: In small groups

1. The drawing below shows two possible ways to arrange 24 counters in an array.

2. Copy the two arrays shown and then add other arrays to show all the possible arrays for 24 counters.

3. Repeat the activity showing all the possible arrays for 30 counters.

Unit 7, Lesson 3   Copyright © Houghton Mifflin Company

Activity Note Have students discuss their strategies for finding all the possible ways to make an array for a given number of objects.

✐ **Math Writing Prompt**

Investigate Math How can you use $7 \times 9 = 63$ to find the missing number in the equation $9 \times \square = 63$?

MEGAMATH Grades K-6 **Software Support**

Country Countdown, Counting Critters, Level V

Challenge   Activity Card 7-3

Array Designs   Activity Card 7-3 ■

Work: On your own

Use:
- TRB M31 (Centimeter Grid Paper)

1. Draw a 10-by-10 square on your grid paper.

2. Make a design by outlining five or more smaller arrays of squares inside the large 10-by-10 square. Be sure that the outlined arrays cover the entire 10-by-10 square. Look at the example below.

3. Label each small array with a multiplication equation.

4. **Analyze** What do you notice about the sum of all the products? They equal 100, which is the product represented by the 10-by-10 array.

Unit 7, Lesson 3   Copyright © Houghton Mifflin Company

Activity Note Encourage students to work from the middle outward or from one side across to the other side to make it easier to include all the squares in the outlined arrays.

✐ **Math Writing Prompt**

Organize Your Thinking Explain how to find all possible arrays for the number 36.

✳ **DESTINATION** Math® **Software Support**

Course II: Module 2: Unit 2: Repeated Addition and Arrays

③ Homework and Spiral Review

This Homework page provides practice in using arrays for multiplication.

This Remembering page would be appropriate anytime after today's lesson.

7-3	Name		Date
Homework			

Study Plan

_____
Homework Helper

Write a multiplication equation for each array.

1. How many muffins?

$3 \times 4 = 12$ muffins

2. How many basketballs?

$5 \times 6 = 30$ basketballs

Make a math drawing for the problem and label it. Write a multiplication equation that gives the answer.

3. Ellie arranged her trophies in 3 rows, with 6 trophies in each row. How many trophies does she have?

18 trophies

Possible drawing:

$3 \times 6 = 18$

4. Maribel planted a garden with 9 tomato plants in each of 2 rows. How many tomato plants did she plant?

18 tomato plants

Possible drawing:

$2 \times 9 = 18$

UNIT 7 LESSON 3 — Multiplication and Arrays **121**

Homework and Remembering page 121

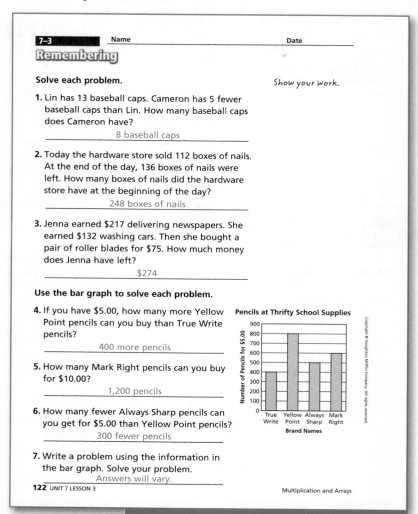

7-3	Name	Date
Remembering		

Solve each problem.   *Show your work.*

1. Lin has 13 baseball caps. Cameron has 5 fewer baseball caps than Lin. How many baseball caps does Cameron have?

8 baseball caps

2. Today the hardware store sold 112 boxes of nails. At the end of the day, 136 boxes of nails were left. How many boxes of nails did the hardware store have at the beginning of the day?

248 boxes of nails

3. Jenna earned $217 delivering newspapers. She earned $132 washing cars. Then she bought a pair of roller blades for $75. How much money does Jenna have left?

$274

Use the bar graph to solve each problem.

4. If you have $5.00, how many more Yellow Point pencils can you buy than True Write pencils?

400 more pencils

5. How many Mark Right pencils can you buy for $10.00?

1,200 pencils

6. How many fewer Always Sharp pencils can you get for $5.00 than Yellow Point pencils?

300 fewer pencils

7. Write a problem using the information in the bar graph. Solve your problem.

Answers will vary.

122 UNIT 7 LESSON 3 — Multiplication and Arrays

Homework and Remembering page 122

Home and School Connection

Family Letter Have students take home the Family Letter on Student Activity Book pages 213–216 or Activity Workbook pages 79–82. This letter explains the home practice expectations in *Math Expressions*. A Spanish translation of this letter is on the following pages.

The information in the letter may help family members to talk about math with the children. It gives parents and guardians a better understanding of the learning that goes on in math class and creates a bridge between school and home.

488 UNIT 7 LESSON 3

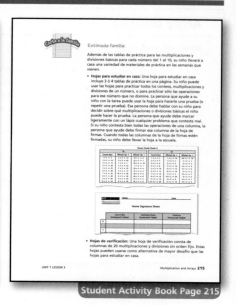

Student Activity Book Page 213

Student Activity Book Page 215

The Meaning of Division

REAL WORLD Problem Solving

Lesson Objectives

- Relate division to multiplication.
- Represent and solve division word problems.

The Day at a Glance

Today's Goals	Materials	

1 Teaching the Lesson
A1: Practice count-bys and multiplications.
A2: Solve division word problems in which the number of groups is unknown.
A3: Solve 5s division and multiplication equations.
A4: Solve division word problems in which the group size is unknown.
	Lesson Activities
	Student Activity Book pp. 217–220
	  or Student Hardcover Book
	  pp. 217–220
	Homework and Remembering
	  pp. 123–126
	Check Up materials
	Signature Sheet
	Study Sheet A
	Study Sheet Answer Strips
	Dry-erase markers
	Sheet protectors
	MathBoard materials
	Connecting cubes
	Plastic cups
		Going Further
		Activity Cards 7-4
		Play money (nickels)
		Inch-Grid Paper
		  (TRB M42)
		Math Journals

2 Going Further ▶ Differentiated Instruction		
3 Homework and Spiral Review		

123 Use Math Talk today!

Keeping Skills Sharp

Quick Practice   ⏱ 5 MINUTES

Goal: Practice 5s count-bys and multiplications.

Materials: Class Multiplication Table Poster, pointer

5s Multiplications in Order The **Student Leader** points to the equations in the 5s column (in order) as students say them in unison, such as "1 times 5 equals 5." Students raise fingers to keep track of the multiplier.

Daily Routines

Strategy Problem Mark cut a ribbon in half. He kept one half and gave $\frac{1}{2}$ of the other half to each of 2 people. Juan got 4 inches. How much ribbon did Mark have to begin with? Explain how you found your answer.

16 inches; I drew a rectangle and filled in what I know.

Whole Ribbon

Mark 8in.	Juan 4in.	? 4in.

8 + 8 = 16 in.

Teaching the Lesson

Check Up and Independent Study

 10 MINUTES

Goal: Practice count-bys and multiplications.

Materials: Check Up materials: Signature Sheet (Student Activity Book pages 205–206 or Activity Workbook p. 77), Study Sheet A (Student Activity Book pages 207–208 or Activity Workbook p. 78), Study Sheet Answer Strips (TRB M54), dry-erase markers (1 per student), sheet protectors (1 per student); Homework and Remembering p. 125

 NCTM Standard:
Number and Operations

✋ Alternate Approach

Study Sheet Answer Strips As one partner reads aloud each multiplication, the other partner writes the equations on the strip.

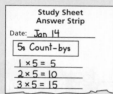

▶ Check Up with 5s PAIRS

Have **Student Pairs** take out their folders with Check Up materials and remind them how to use Study Sheet A to test one another.

- Partner 1 gives his or her Study Sheet (in a sheet protector) to Partner 2.
- Partner 2 reads aloud each multiplication (not the answer) in the *Mixed Up ×* column of the 5s chart, and Partner 1 says the answer.
- Partner 2 puts a check mark next to any multiplications that Partner 1 answers incorrectly.
- If all the answers are correct, Partner 2 signs the appropriate section of Partner 1's Signature Sheet.
- Partners switch roles.

Give **Student Pairs** a few minutes to test each other on 5s multiplications and count-bys. Remind them that today they may try as many *different* 5s tests as they want and have time for, but they can only try any particular test once a day. Some students may have difficulties doing the check ups in this manner. You may wish to use Study Sheet Answer Strips (TRB M54). See side column for instructions.

After partners have tested each other, give students 2 to 3 minutes to independently study their Study Sheets.

Have students complete the Study Plan box on Homework and Remembering page 125, listing any 5s multiplications they missed and 5s divisions. Remind students to put their Check Up materials back in their folders.

Divide to Find the Number of Groups

 15 MINUTES

Goal: Solve division word problems in which the number of groups is unknown.

Materials: MathBoard materials, Student Activity Book or Hardcover Book pp. 217–218

 NCTM Standards:
Number and Operations
Representation
Problem Solving

▶ Explore Division WHOLE CLASS

Have students solve problems 1 and 2 on Student Activity Book page 217. For problem 1, they may make math drawings or variations of the Equal Shares Drawings they learned about in Lesson 3. Alternatively, they may count by 5s until they reach 15 and note that they counted 3 groups of 5.

Tell students you want to write a multiplication equation for problem 1. Write this general equation on the board.

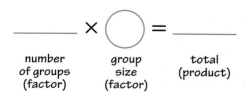

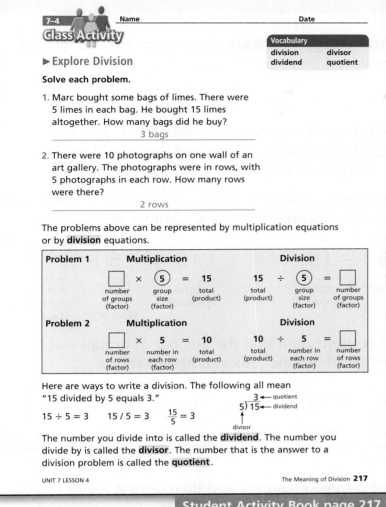

7-4
Class Activity

Name _____ Date _____

▶ **Explore Division**

Solve each problem.

1. Marc bought some bags of limes. There were 5 limes in each bag. He bought 15 limes altogether. How many bags did he buy?

_____3 bags_____

2. There were 10 photographs on one wall of an art gallery. The photographs were in rows, with 5 photographs in each row. How many rows were there?

_____2 rows_____

The problems above can be represented by multiplication equations or by **division** equations.

Problem 1	Multiplication			Division		

□ × ⑤ = 15   15 ÷ ⑤ = □

number of groups (factor) · group size (factor) · total (product)   total (product) · group size (factor) · number of groups (factor)

Problem 2	Multiplication			Division		

□ × 5 = 10   10 ÷ 5 = □

number of rows (factor) · number in each row (factor) · total (product)   total (product) · number in each row (factor) · number of rows (factor)

Here are ways to write a division. The following all mean "15 divided by 5 equals 3."

$15 \div 5 = 3$ $15 / 5 = 3$ $\frac{15}{5} = 3$

3 ← quotient
5)15 ← dividend
↑ divisor

The number you divide into is called the **dividend**. The number you divide by is called the **divisor**. The number that is the answer to a division problem is called the **quotient**.

UNIT 7 LESSON 4   The Meaning of Division **217**

Student Activity Book page 217

Work with students to fill in the information from the problem.

● **What are the groups in this problem?** the bags of limes **Does the problem tell us how many groups, or bags, we have?** no, so we'll make a box for the number of groups.

Replace the answer blank for "number of groups" with a box.

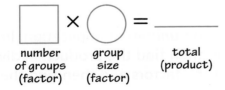

□ × ○ = _____
number of groups (factor) · group size (factor) · total (product)

● **Does the problem tell us the group size?** Yes, there are 5 limes in each bag.

Write 5 in the "group size" circle.

● **Does the problem tell us the total, or product?** Yes, there are 15 limes altogether.

Replace the answer blank for "total" with the number 15.

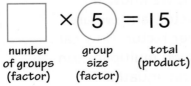

□ × ⑤ = 15
number of groups (factor) · group size (factor) · total (product)

Activity continued ▶

Connecting Cubes Students can use connecting cubes to model divisions.

Total: 15

In Activity 2, tell them the desired group size and have them split the tower apart to find the number of groups.

5 in each group → 3 groups

In Activity 4, tell them the desired number of groups and have them split the tower apart to find the group size.

5 groups → 3 in each group

Ask students how this problem is different from the repeated-groups problems they have solved. In this problem, we need to find the number of groups, which is one of the factors. In the problems so far, we have always found the total, or product.

● When you found the number of groups in problem 1, you were dividing. You were finding how many groups you would get if you *divided* 15 limes into groups of 5.

Next to the multiplication equation, write the related division equation. Point to the ÷ sign, and explain that it is a symbol for division.

$$\boxed{} \times \enclose{circle}{5} = 15 \qquad 15 \div \enclose{circle}{5} = \boxed{}$$

number of groups (factor) · group size (factor) · total (product) · · · total (product) · group size (factor) · number of groups (factor)

Remind students that they found that the number of groups was 3. Write 3 in the "number of groups" box in both equations.

$$\boxed{3} \times \enclose{circle}{5} = 15 \qquad 15 \div \enclose{circle}{5} = \boxed{3}$$

number of groups (factor) · group size (factor) · total (product) · · · total (product) · group size (factor) · number of groups (factor)

Read the completed division equation, and then have students read it with you: "15 divided by 5 equals 3." Introduce the terms *dividend*, *divisor*, and *quotient*.

● The dividend is the number we divide into; it is the product. The divisor is the factor we divide by; in this case, 5. The quotient is the unknown factor; in this case, 3.

Explain that solving a division problem always involves finding an unknown factor.

Emphasize that division *undoes* multiplication. In multiplication, start with the factors and then find the product. In division, start with the product and one of the factors and then find the other factor.

● Problem 2 is also a division problem. You found the number of rows you would have if you *divided* 10 photographs into rows of 5. Can someone help me write an unknown multiplication equation for this problem?

Write the problem on the board and label it.

$$\boxed{} \times \enclose{circle}{5} = 10$$

number of rows (factor) · number in each row (factor) · total (product)

● Just as in problem 1, we know the product and one factor, and we are looking for the other factor. How can I rewrite this unknown multiplication equation as a division equation?

7-4

Name _____ Date _____

Class Activity

▶ Math Tools: Equal Shares Drawings

You can use Equal Shares Drawings to help solve division problems. Here is how you might solve problem 1 on Student Activity Book page 217.

Start with the total, 15.

$15 \div \text{⑤} = \square$

Draw groups of 5, and connect them to the total. Count by 5s as you draw the groups. Stop when you reach 15, the total. Count how many groups you have: 3 groups.

$$\square \times \begin{array}{c} \text{Total:} \\ 15 \end{array}$$
⑤ ⑤ ⑤ $15 \div \text{⑤} = \boxed{3}$
Say: 5 10 15

You can use a similar type of drawing to find the number of rows or columns in an array. Here is how you might solve problem 2.

Start with the total, 10.

$10 \div \text{⑤} = \square$

Draw rows of 5, and connect them to the total. Count by 5s as you draw the rows. Stop when you reach 10, the total. Count how many rows you have: 2 rows.

5 — 5   Total:
10 — 5   10 $10 \div \text{⑤} = \boxed{2}$

Solve each problem.

3. At a bake sale, Luisa bought a lemon square for 35¢. If she paid using only nickels, how many nickels did she spend? _____ 7 nickels

4. Mr. Su bought a sheet of 20 stamps. There were 5 stamps in each row. How many columns of stamps were there? _____ 4 columns

218 UNIT 7 LESSON 4   The Meaning of Division

Write the labeled division equation next to the multiplication equation.

$\boxed{} \times \text{⑤} = 10$

number of rows (factor) | number in each row (factor) | total (product)

$10 \div \text{⑤} = \boxed{}$

total (product) | number in each row (factor) | number of rows (factor)

Ask students what the unknown factor is, and fill in the box in both equations.

▶ Math Tools: Equal Shares Drawings WHOLE CLASS

Discuss the Equal Shares Drawings on Student Book page 218. Compare the process of making drawings for division situations to making them for multiplication situations.

Using **Solve and Discuss,** have students solve problems 3 and 4 on Student Book page 218. Encourage them to make Equal Shares Drawings, but allow them to use any method that makes sense to them.

Differentiated Instruction

Extra Help Discuss the special names given to the factors in a division equation: *divisor* and *quotient*. Talk about the locations of the divisor and the quotient in each example.

To help students become accustomed to the different notations for division, you might use color-coding to highlight the position of the dividend, divisor, and quotient in each form. See definitions on page 452.

dividend divisor quotient
$$15 \div 5 = 3$$

$$15 / 5 = 3$$

$$\frac{15}{5} = 3$$

$$5\overline{)15}^{3}$$

The Learning Classroom

Math Talk You must direct student math talk for it to be productive. Over time as students become more skilled at discussing their thinking and talking directly with each other, you will fade into the background more. But you will always monitor, clarify, extend, and ultimately make the decisions about how to direct the math conversation so that it is productive for your students.

Teaching the Lesson (continued)

Activity 3

Relate Multiplication and Division

 10 MINUTES

Goal: Solve 5s division and multiplication equations.

Materials: MathBoard materials, Student Activity Book or Hardcover Book p. 219

✔ **NCTM Standard:**
Number and Operations

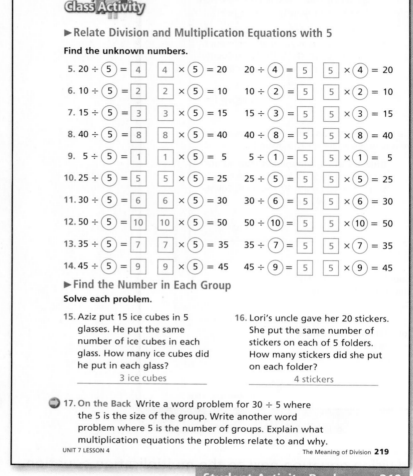

7-4
Class Activity

Name _____ Date _____

▶ Relate Division and Multiplication Equations with 5

Find the unknown numbers.

5. 20 ÷ ⑤ = 4   4 × ⑤ = 20   20 ÷ ④ = 5   5 × ④ = 20
6. 10 ÷ ⑤ = 2   2 × ⑤ = 10   10 ÷ ② = 5   5 × ② = 10
7. 15 ÷ ⑤ = 3   3 × ⑤ = 15   15 ÷ ③ = 5   5 × ③ = 15
8. 40 ÷ ⑤ = 8   8 × ⑤ = 40   40 ÷ ⑧ = 5   5 × ⑧ = 40
9.   5 ÷ ⑤ = 1   1 × ⑤ = 5   5 ÷ ① = 5   5 × ① = 5
10. 25 ÷ ⑤ = 5   5 × ⑤ = 25   25 ÷ ⑤ = 5   5 × ⑤ = 25
11. 30 ÷ ⑤ = 6   6 × ⑤ = 30   30 ÷ ⑥ = 5   5 × ⑥ = 30
12. 50 ÷ ⑤ = 10   10 × ⑤ = 50   50 ÷ ⑩ = 5   5 × ⑩ = 50
13. 35 ÷ ⑤ = 7   7 × ⑤ = 35   35 ÷ ⑦ = 5   5 × ⑦ = 35
14. 45 ÷ ⑤ = 9   9 × ⑤ = 45   45 ÷ ⑨ = 5   5 × ⑨ = 45

▶ Find the Number in Each Group

Solve each problem.

15. Aziz put 15 ice cubes in 5 glasses. He put the same number of ice cubes in each glass. How many ice cubes did he put in each glass?
_____ 3 ice cubes _____

16. Lori's uncle gave her 20 stickers. She put the same number of stickers on each of 5 folders. How many stickers did she put on each folder?
_____ 4 stickers _____

17. **On the Back** Write a word problem for 30 ÷ 5 where the 5 is the size of the group. Write another word problem where 5 is the number of groups. Explain what multiplication equations the problems relate to and why.

UNIT 7 LESSON 4   The Meaning of Division **219**

Student Activity Book page 219

Teaching Note

Watch For! Some students might do the 5s count-bys on their fingers and record the last number they say as the quotient. For instance, after counting 5, 10, 15, 20 for exercise 5, they might write 20 as the quotient. Stress that the quotient is the answer to the question *How many groups of 5?*, which is the number of fingers they raised. Remind them that the multiplication equation to the right of each division equation is a way to check that they have the correct quotient. That is, the quotient must be the unknown number that makes the multiplication equation true.

▶ Relate Division and Multiplication Equations with 5 [WHOLE CLASS]

Direct students to exercises 5–14 on Student Book page 219. Point out that each exercise shows two division equations and the corresponding multiplication equations. In exercise 5, we need to find the number of groups of 5 in 20. Ask if anyone can think of a way to do this using their fingers to count by 5s. If no one can, explain the method yourself: Count by 5s, raising a finger for each count-by until you reach 20. Four raised fingers means there are 4 groups of 5 in 20. In other words, 20 ÷ 5 = 4.

20 divided by 5 equals 4.

Have students complete exercises 5–14 independently, and then check the answers. Have students who experience difficulty discuss their answers with a **Helping Partner**.

494 UNIT 7 LESSON 4

Divide to Find the Group Size

▶ Find the Number in Each Group   WHOLE CLASS

Using **Solve and Discuss,** have students solve problem 15 on Student Book page 219. In this division problem, the group size, rather than the number of groups, is the unknown number. Many students find such division problems difficult because it is not obvious that they can count up or use repeated addition to find the answer.

Some students may make circles to represent the glasses and then pass out the ice cubes, putting one in each glass, then a second in each glass, and so on, until all 15 have been distributed. Others may write an unknown multiplication equation and use their knowledge of 5s multiplication to reason that the unknown factor—in this case, the group size—must be 3.

Work with the class to write an unknown multiplication equation for problem 15.

$$5 \times \bigcirc = 15$$

number   group   total
of groups   size   (product)
(factor)   (factor)

Ask students how this problem is different from problems 1–4. In this problem, the group size is the unknown number. In problems 1–4, the number of groups or rows was the unknown number.

Explain that, like problems 1–4 on Student Book pages 217–218, problem 15 is a division problem— students are finding the number of ice cubes in each glass if the ice cubes are divided equally among the glasses. As in the previous problems, they start with a total and one factor and find the other factor. Add the division equation to the board.

$$5 \times \bigcirc = 15 \qquad 15 \div 5 = \bigcirc$$

number group   total   total   number   group
of groups size (product)   (product) of groups size
(factor) (factor)   (factor) (factor)

Fill in the unknown number—the group size—in each equation. Leave the equations on the board.

$$5 \times \enclose{circle}{3} = 15 \qquad 15 \div 5 = \enclose{circle}{3}$$

number group   total   total   number   group
of groups size (product)   (product) of groups size
(factor) (factor)   (factor) (factor)

- Here is an interesting way to look at this problem. Let's draw tall, thin glasses.

Lightly draw five tall, thin rectangles.

- We'll start by putting one ice cube in each glass. That's one "round" of passing out cubes.

Activity continued ▶

⏱ **15 MINUTES**

Goal: Solve division word problems in which the group size is unknown.

Materials: MathBoard materials, Student Activity Book or Hardcover Book pp. 219–220

✓ **NCTM Standards:**
Number and Operations
Representation
Problem Solving

Differentiated Instruction

Extra Help Tactile learners can act out problem 15 using plastic cups for the glasses and counters for the ice cubes.

Teaching Note

Language and Vocabulary As you discuss problems 15–17 on Student Book page 219, be sure to talk about the language that indicates that the problems involve equal groups. Problem 15 says Aziz put the *same number* of cubes *in each* glass. Problem 16 says Lori put the *same number* of stickers *on each* of the 5 folders. Add these new terms to your chart paper vocabulary list.

📁 Class Management

Looking Ahead Remind students to take home the 5s chart on Homework and Remembering page 123.

✅ Ongoing Assessment

Give students the following equation.

$$40 \div ⑤ = \square$$

Ask questions such as the following:

▶ What does it mean to divide 40 by 5?

▶ Which part of the equation is the dividend? the divisor? the quotient?

▶ How can you use a multiplication equation to find the number that belongs in the box?

Draw an "ice cube" in each "glass." Then circle the row of cubes and label it "1 round."

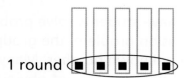

● How many cubes have we passed out so far? 5 We'll keep putting one cube in each glass until we have passed out all 15 ice cubes.

Draw, circle, and label two more rows of cubes. After each row, ask students how many cubes you have drawn so far.

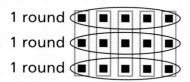

● When we solved this problem before, we looked at the glasses as the groups. This drawing shows that we can instead think of the "rounds" as the groups. To solve the problem, we can answer the question, "How many rounds does it take to pass out all 15 cubes?"

The 5 in the problem is now the group size. This gives the equations:

$$\underset{\substack{\text{number} \\ \text{of groups} \\ \text{(factor)}}}{\boxed{}} \times \underset{\substack{\text{group} \\ \text{size} \\ \text{(factor)}}}{⑤} = \underset{\substack{\text{total} \\ \text{(product)}}}{15} \qquad \underset{\substack{\text{total} \\ \text{(product)}}}{15} \div \underset{\substack{\text{group} \\ \text{size} \\ \text{(factor)}}}{⑤} = \underset{\substack{\text{number} \\ \text{of groups} \\ \text{(factor)}}}{\boxed{}}$$

● Count up to find the number of groups of 5 in 15: 5, 10, 15. (Raise one finger for each number you say.) There are 3 groups of 5 in 15.

Fill in the unknown number in your equations.

$$\underset{\substack{\text{number} \\ \text{of groups} \\ \text{(factor)}}}{\boxed{3}} \times \underset{\substack{\text{group} \\ \text{size} \\ \text{(factor)}}}{⑤} = \underset{\substack{\text{total} \\ \text{(product)}}}{15} \qquad \underset{\substack{\text{total} \\ \text{(product)}}}{15} \div \underset{\substack{\text{group} \\ \text{size} \\ \text{(factor)}}}{⑤} = \underset{\substack{\text{number} \\ \text{of groups} \\ \text{(factor)}}}{\boxed{3}}$$

● Whenever you have a division problem that gives the number of groups, you can think of that number as the group size instead, if that makes solving the problem easier for you. The answer will be the same.

Using **Solve and Discuss,** have students solve problems 16 and 17 on Student Activity Book page 219. For each problem, if possible, choose one presenter who thought of 5 as the group size and one who didn't.

② Going Further

Differentiated Instruction

More About Nickel Money
Activity Card 7-4 ●

Work: In pairs

Use:
• Play Money (10 nickels)

1. Explain how you can use counting by 5s to find the value of any group of nickels. Each nickel is 5 cents, so counting by 5s names the number of cents in each group of nickels starting from 1.

2. Copy the table at right. Use what you know about counting by 5s to find the missing numbers.

Total Value	Number of Nickels
40¢	? 8
25¢	? 5
35¢	? 7
15¢	? 3
30¢	? 6

3. Read the number of nickels that each value in the table represents. Then make a division statement about dividing by 5 that matches each row.

Unit 7, Lesson 4   Copyright © Houghton Mifflin Company

Activity Note If time permits, have students extend the table to include $0.10, $0.20, $0.45, and $0.50.

✏ **Math Writing Prompt**

Draw a Picture Draw a picture to show why 45 ÷ 5 = 9. Explain your picture.

 **Software Support**

Warm Up 13.05

Division Word Problems
Activity Card 7-4 ▲

Work: In pairs

1. Look at the two types of division equations below.

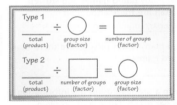

2. On Your Own Write two word problems to show an example of a problem that can be solved using each type of equation.

3. Exchange problems with your partner. Solve the problems and tell which type of equation you used for each one.

Unit 7, Lesson 4   Copyright © Houghton Mifflin Company

Activity Note Be sure that students understand that the Type 1 equation is used when the number of groups is unknown. Type 2 is used when the group size is unknown.

 Math Writing Prompt

Explain Your Thinking Explain how you can use a multiplication equation to find the quotient 40 ÷ 5.

MEGA MATH Grades K-6 **Software Support**

Numberopolis: Carnival Stories, Level T

Search for 5s
Activity Card 7-4 ■

Work: On your own

Use:
• TRB M42 (Inch-Grid Paper)

1. Copy the number grid below on inch-grid paper.

5	2	7	9	8	25
8	4	6	30	5	6
40	15	3	5	40	45
1	4	3	1	25	7
5	2	10	15	5	3
5	6	35	8	5	45

2. Look for groups of three numbers that you can use to make a multiplication or division equation. Check each row, column, and diagonal. Circle each group that you find. The first one is done for you.

Unit 7, Lesson 4   Copyright © Houghton Mifflin Company

Activity Note If time permits, have students make a Search for 5s puzzle for a classmate to do.

 Math Writing Prompt

Investigate Math How can you use 15 ÷ 5 = 3 to find 150 ÷ 5 and 1,500 ÷ 5?

 DESTINATION Math· **Software Support**

Course II: Module 2: Unit 3: Meaning of Divisionπ

③ Homework and Spiral Review

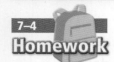

7-4
Homework **Goal:** Additional Practice

This Homework page provides practice in division and multiplication.

Name _____ Date _____

Homework

Study Plan
_____
_____
_____ Homework Helper

Write a multiplication equation and a division equation for each problem. Then solve the problem.

1. Mandy's Diner has a total of 20 chairs. The chairs are divided equally among 5 tables. How many chairs are at each table?

   Show your work.

   $5 \times \square = 20$; $20 \div 5 = \square$; 4 chairs

2. Tarek divided 30 nickels into 5 piles. He put the same number of nickels in each pile. How many nickels were in each pile?

   $5 \times \square = 30$; $30 \div 5 = \square$; 6 nickels

3. A group of singers has 45 members. The singers are arranged in groups of 5 on the stage. How many groups are there?

   $5 \times \square = 45$; $45 \div 5 = \square$; 9 groups

4. Brianna arranged 40 marbles into an array with 5 marbles in each row. How many rows of marbles were in her array?

   $5 \times \square = 40$; $40 \div 5 = \square$; 8 rows

UNIT 7 LESSON 4   The Meaning of Division **125**

Homework and Remembering page 125

7-4
Remembering **Goal:** Spiral Review

This Remembering page would be appropriate anytime after today's lesson.

7-4 Name _____ Date _____

Remembering

Solve each problem. If there is not enough information to solve the problem, tell what else you would need to know.

Show your work.

1. Mona wrote 7 serious poems and some funny poems. She wrote 12 poems in all. How many funny poems did she write?

   5 funny poems

2. Lidia baked 14 cakes. She gave some cakes to her neighbors. How many cakes does Lidia have left?

   Not enough information; need to know how many cakes she gave away.

Use the bar graph to solve each problem.

3. How many more stuffed animals are there than bicycles?

   5 more stuffed animals

4. How many board games and stuffed animals are there altogether?

   15 board games and stuffed animals

5. How many fewer bicycles are there than board games?

   2 fewer bicycles

6. Write a problem using the information in the bar graph. Solve your problem.

   Answers will vary.
   _____
   _____
   _____
   _____

Toys at Mayfield Toy Store

(Bar graph: Types of Toys — Board Games, Stuffed Animals, Bicycles; horizontal axis: Number of Toys, 0 2 4 6 8 10)

126 UNIT 7 LESSON 4   The Meaning of Division

Homework and Remembering page 126

Home and School Activity

 Art Connection

A Show of Hands Have students use finger paints to create a large bulletin board of their hand prints. As students place their hands in different combinations on the bulletin board, they can visualize how to multiply and divide with 5. Have them write a multiplication and division equation below each set of hands.

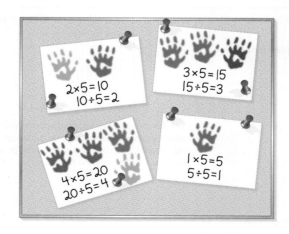

Multiply and Divide with 2

Lesson Objectives

● Explore patterns in 2s count-bys and multiplications.

● Interpret a pictograph.

Vocabulary

count-bys	even number
multiplier	odd number
pictograph	

The Day at a Glance

Today's Goals	Materials
① Teaching the Lesson **A1:** Practice 5s count-bys and multiplications. **A2:** Explore patterns in 2s count-bys and multiplications. **A3:** Solve 2s word problems. **A4:** Practice 5s and 2s multiplications and divisions using a Check Sheet. **② Going Further** ► Differentiated Instruction **③ Homework and Spiral Review**	**Lesson Activities** Student Activity Book pp. 221–224 or Student Hardcover Book pp. 221–224 and Activity Workbook p. 83 (includes Check Sheet) Homework and Remembering pp. 127–132 Check Up materials Signature Sheet, Study Sheet A Study Sheet Answer Strips Dry-erase markers, Sheet protectors MathBoard materials Class Multiplication Table Poster Pointer, Folders Check Sheet 1 Check Sheet Answer Strips Card stock, Quick Quiz 1	**Going Further** Activity Cards 7-5 Mirrors Two-color counters Index cards Math Journals 123 Use Math Talk today!

Keeping Skills Sharp

Quick Practice ⏱ 5 MINUTES	Daily Routines
Goal: Practice 5s count-bys, multiplications, and divisions. **Materials:** Class Multiplication Table Poster, pointer **Mixed 5s Divisions** The **Student Leader** says "Close your eyes," points to an equation in the 5s column, reads aloud the related division problem, pauses, and says "Answer." Students say the answer in unison, open their eyes and say the complete equation. Repeat for all the equations, in a random order. **Repeated Quick Practice** Use this Quick Practice activity from a previous lesson. **Mixed 5s Multiplications** (See Unit 7 Lesson 2.)	**Analyze Data** The class voted for their favorite sport. 5 students voted for football. 7 students voted for soccer. 8 students voted for baseball. Create a tally chart and write a conclusion using the data. Possible answer: Most students liked soccer.

Favorite Sport	
Sport	Number of Votes
Football	ⅢⅢ
Soccer	ⅢⅢ ⅠⅠ
Baseball	ⅢⅢ ⅠⅠⅠ

① Teaching the Lesson

Check Up and Independent Study

 10 MINUTES

Goal: Practice 5s count-bys and multiplications.

Materials: Check Up materials: Signature Sheet (Student Activity Book pp. 205–206 or Activity Workbook p. 77), Study Sheet A (Student Activity Book pp. 207–208 or Activity Workbook p. 78), Study Sheet Answer Strips (TRB M54), dry-erase markers (1 per student), sheet protectors (1 per student); Homework and Remembering page 131

 NCTM Standard:
Number and Operations

 Class Management

Establishing Routines Develop an efficient routine for daily Check Ups and independent study. Students need to take out the materials quickly and get started. You may want to use a timer to keep them on task. Set the timer for two to three minutes, and have one partner test the other. When the time is up, set the timer again and have partners switch roles. Give students another one to two minutes to study independently and then a minute to complete their Study Plan boxes on their Homework page.

 Alternate Approach

Study Sheet Answer Strips As one partner reads aloud each multiplication, the other partner writes their equations on the strip.

> **Study Sheet Answer Strip**
> Date: Jan 14
> 5s Multiplications
> 2 × 5 = 10
> 9 × 5 = 45
> 1 × 5 = 5

▶ **Check Up with 5s** PAIRS

Give **Student Pairs** a few minutes to test each other on 5s count-bys, multiplications, and divisions using Study Sheet A and collect signatures on their Signature Sheets. Remind them that they may try as many different 5s tests as they have time for in one day, but may try each test only once per day. After partners test one another, give them a minute or two to study independently.

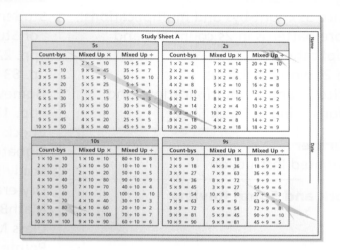

Tell students their homework will include a Practice Chart for 2s. Have students complete the Study Plan box at the top of Homework and Remembering page, indicating any missed multiplications or divisions from the Check Up and what they plan to study that night. (Students should practice 2s count-bys, multiplications, and divisions.) Remind students to put all Check Up materials back in their folders.

Activity 2

Explore 2s Patterns

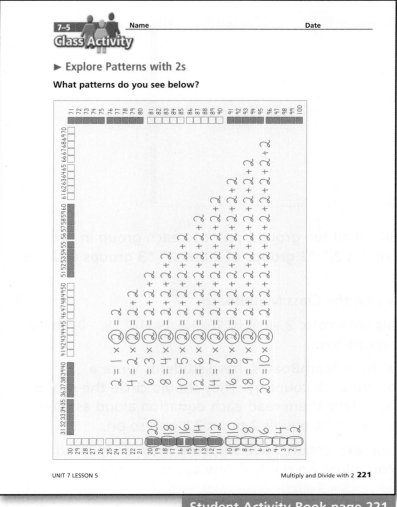

7-5
Class Activity

Name _____ Date _____

▶ Explore Patterns with 2s

What patterns do you see below?

UNIT 7 LESSON 5   Multiply and Divide with 2 **221**

Student Activity Book page 221

▶ Explore Patterns with 2s WHOLE CLASS

Tell students that today they will be thinking about groups of 2. Ask what things in the real world come in groups of 2. eyes, ears, wheels on a bike, shoes, nickels in a dime, and so on

Model the steps of this activity on the Class MathBoard as students follow along on their MathBoards. The completed board is shown above on Student Book page 221. You can use this page to facilitate a summary discussion of the patterns in 2s multiplications.

Activity continued ▶

20 MINUTES

Goal: Explore patterns in 2s count-bys and multiplications.

Materials: MathBoard materials, Class Multiplication Table Poster, pointer, Student Activity Book or Hardcover Book p. 221

✓ **NCTM Standards:**
Number and Operations
Representation

Teaching the Lesson (continued)

Alternate Approach

Number Line Students can picture the 2s count-bys as "jumps" across intervals of 2 on a number line.

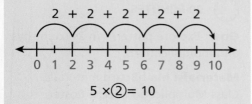

$$5 \times ② = 10$$

Color-coding this number line can help students visualize even and odd numbers in Activity 3. In the picture above, for instance, 0 and the 2s count-bys are colored red, and these are the even numbers. The "in-between" numbers, color-coded blue, are the odd numbers.

Teaching Note

Math Background If your state standards require you to show multiplication as jumps on a number line, this lesson provides an opportunity to use this model. You can draw a number line on the board and demonstrate drawing half-circles to the show jumps. You may wish to connect this model to counting circles on the Number Path. It is important to emphasize that when using the number line, you are counting the lengths from 0, or the small segments, not the numerals.

Have students circle sequential groups of 2, up to 20, on the Number Path and write the totals so far next to each group. After they circle the first group, have them say in unison, "1 group of 2 is 2"; after they circle the second group, have them say, "2 groups of 2 are 4"; and so on.

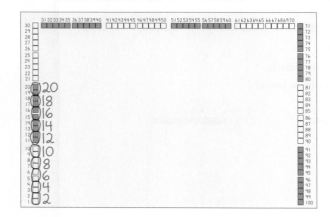

After students have circled all ten groups, point to each group in order as they say, "1 group of 2 is 2," "2 groups of 2 are 4," "3 groups of 2 are 6," and so on.

Now point to the totals on the Class MathBoard.

● Read aloud the totals we wrote: 2, 4, 6, 8, 10, 12, 14, 16, 18, 20. These numbers are the 2s count-bys.

Toward the left side of their MathBoards, have students write a multiplication equation for each count-by. They should circle the group size (2) in each equation. Have them read each equation aloud as they write it: "2 equals 1 times 2," "4 equals 2 times 2," and so on.

After each multiplication expression, have students write a repeated addition expression. You might do the first few as a class, asking what you should write.

● For 3 × 2, how many 2s would we add together? 3 So what should I write? 2 + 2 + 2

Ask students to compare the multiplication expressions to the addition expressions. Then have them summarize what the multiplier, the number we are multiplying 2 by, tells us. It tells how many 2s we have.

(123) **Math Talk** Have students look at their MathBoard or the MathBoard shown on Student Book page 221. Ask them to describe any patterns they see in the count-bys and equations. The following are a few possibilities to discuss as a class.

● All the products are even numbers.

● The pattern of the ones digits of the products is 2, 4, 6, 8, 0, 2, 4, 6, 8, 0.

● The count-bys skip a number between them.

● If you ignore 20, and then start with the outside pair of products, 2 and 18, and move in, the ones digit of each pair of products (2 and 18, 4 and 16, 6 and 14, and 8 and 12) add to 10.

Have students put their MathBoards aside. They should not erase the boards.

► Use the Class Multiplication Table Poster

WHOLE CLASS

Point to the equations in the 2s column of the Class Multiplication Table Poster, in order, as the class reads them aloud, raising a finger for each multiplier.

1 times 2 equals 2.　　2 times 2 equals 4.　　3 times 2 equals 6.

Move down the column again, this time having students say only the count-bys. Again, have them use fingers to indicate the multipliers.

2　　　　　　　　4　　　　　　　　6

► Use Fingers to Multiply WHOLE CLASS

Present 2s multiplications (such as 5 × 2 and 6 × 2), and have students count up on their fingers to find the answers. For example, to find 5 × 2, they should count by 2s, raising a finger for each count-by, until five fingers are raised.

5 times 2 equals 10.

You might show students that for multipliers greater than 5, they can start with all 5 fingers up on one hand to make 10 and count up from there. They will explore this "5s shortcut" in later lessons.

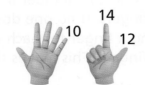

7 times 2 equals 14.

Activity continued ►

Teaching Note

Watch For! Some students may become confused when counting by 2s while counting the number of fingers raised at the same time. You may want to have those students count groups of two connecting cubes instead of using their fingers.

Differentiated Instruction

Special Needs Students with limited dexterity or poor coordination might have difficulty using their fingers to multiply or divide. Provide them with ten pencils or other objects that they can manipulate more easily. Instead of raising a finger for each count-by, have them count aloud as they lay one of the objects on a blank sheet of paper.

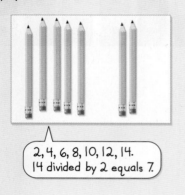

2, 4, 6, 8, 10, 12, 14.
14 divided by 2 equals 7.

▶ Divide with 2s   WHOLE CLASS

Have students erase the repeated addition parts of the equations on their MathBoards. As a class, write the first three division equations ($2 \div 2 = 1$, $4 \div 2 = 2$, $6 \div 2 = 3$) next to the corresponding multiplication equations. Have students provide you with the information needed to write these equations.

Write $6 \div 2 =$ next to $6 = 3 \times ②$ on the class MathBoard.

● How many groups of 2 are in 6? 3

● Point to and count the circled groups on the Number Path until you get to 6. There are 3 groups of 2.

Complete the equation: $6 \div ② = 3$, and have the class read the equation with you. 6 divided by 2 equals 3.

Have students work independently to write the remaining division equations, up to $20 \div ② = 10$.

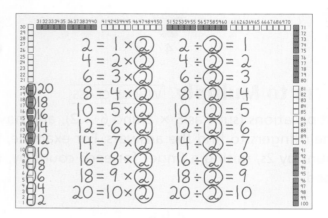

Ask students how the division equations are related to the multiplication equations. Then have them erase their MathBoards and put them aside.

▶ Use Fingers to Divide   WHOLE CLASS

Write this division and related unknown multiplication equation on the board.

$$16 \div 2 = \Box \qquad \Box \times 2 = 16$$

Ask if anyone has a way to find the number in the division equation by counting up on his or her fingers. If no one does, show students this method: Count by 2s, raising a finger for each count-by, until you reach 16. You will have raised 8 fingers. This means there are 8 groups of 2 in 16. That is, $16 \div 2 = 8$.

16 divided by 2 equals 8.

Present several more divisions with a divisor of 2 for students to solve.

Solve 2s Problems

7-5

Class Activity

Name _____ Date _____

Vocabulary
even number
odd number

▶ **Even and Odd Numbers**

The 2s count-bys are called *even numbers* because they are multiples of 2. In an **even number**, the ones digit is 0, 2, 4, 6, or 8. If a number is not a multiple of two, it is called an **odd number**.

Tell whether each number is even or odd.

1. 7   2. 4   3. 20   4. 15
   odd   _even_   _even_   _odd_

▶ **Solve Multiplication and Division Problems with 2s**

Write an equation to represent each situation. Then solve the problem.

5. At the art fair, Tamika sold 9 pairs of earrings. How many individual earrings did she sell?
$9 \times \boxed{2} = \boxed{}$; 18 earrings

6. Rhonda divided 8 crayons equally between her twin brothers. How many crayons did each boy get?
$8 \div \boxed{2} = \boxed{}$ or $\boxed{} \times \boxed{2} = 8$
4 crayons

Use the pictograph to solve each problem.

7. How many Peach-Banana Blast drinks were sold?
15 Peach-Banana Blast drinks

8. In all, how many Strawberry Sensation and Citrus Surprise drinks were sold?
16 drinks

9. How many more Peach-Banana Blast drinks were sold than Mango Madness drinks?
11 more drinks

Drinks Sold at the Smoothie Shop
Strawberry Sensation
Peach-Banana Blast
Mango-Madness
Citrus Surprise

Each stands for 2 drinks.

222 UNIT 7 LESSON 5   Multiply and Divide with 2

Student Activity Book page 222

▶ Even and Odd Numbers WHOLE CLASS

Have a volunteer read aloud the description of even and odd numbers at the top of Student Book page 222. Point out that every whole number is either odd or even. Be sure they understand that, no matter how large the number, it is possible to tell if it is even or odd simply by looking at its ones digit. Then have students complete exercises 1–4.

▶ Solve Multiplication and Division Problems with 2s WHOLE CLASS

Have students solve problems 5–6 on Student Book page 222. These problems have hidden information.

For problems 7–9, make sure students understand that each picture of a drink on the pictograph represents 2 drinks. Ask students to look at the Peach-Banana Blast Smoothie section of the pictograph, and have them discuss what they think the half-picture stands for. 1 smoothie Ask a volunteer to show how to count by 2s to find the number of Strawberry Sensation drinks sold. Then have students complete problems 7–9.

---

 15 MINUTES

Goal: Solve 2s word problems.

Materials: MathBoard materials, Student Activity Book or Hardcover Book p. 222

 NCTM Standards:
Number and Operations
Data Analysis and Probability
Problem Solving

Teaching Note

Watch For! In solving problems about the pictograph, students might simply count the symbols to find the number for each type of drink. Remind them that, on a pictograph, they must always look for the key to understand what each symbol represents. In the pictograph on Student Book page 222, the key is "Each 🥤 stands for 2 drinks."

English Language Learners

Write 1, 3 ,5, 7, 9. Write 0, 2, 4, 6, 8. Write *odd* and *even*.

- **Beginning** Say: Numbers ending in **1, 3, 5, 7,** or **9** are *odd*. **Numbers ending in 0, 2, 4, 6,** or **8** are *even*. Have students repeat.
- **Intermediate** Say: Numbers ending in **1, 3, 5, 7,** or **9** are *odd*. Ask: **Is 21 *odd*?** yes **Is 34 *odd*?** no Say: **Numbers ending in 0, 2, 4, 6, or 8** are *even*.
- **Advanced** Have students say how to tell if numbers are even or odd.

Teaching the Lesson (continued)

Introduce Check Sheets

 5 MINUTES

Goal: Practice 5s and 2s multiplications and divisions using a Check Sheet.

Materials: Folders, Check Sheet 1 (Student Activity Book pp. 223–224 or Activity Workbook p. 83), Check Sheet Answer Strips (TRB M55), cardstock, Homework and Remembering pp. 129–130

✓ **NCTM Standard:**
Number and Operations

 Class Management

Looking Ahead After students have finished practicing, have students place their Check Sheets in their folders with the rest of their Check Up materials. Also, remind students to take home their 2s Charts and Home Check Sheets on Homework and Remembering pp. 127 and 129.

 Ongoing Assessment

Ask questions such as the following:

▶ Name a 2s count-by that is less than 20. What 2s multiplication is related to that number? What 2s division is related to it?

▶ How can you tell if a number is an even number or an odd number?

 Quick Quiz

See Assessment Guide for Unit 4 Quick Quiz 1.

▶ Introduce Check Sheet 1 │ WHOLE CLASS │

Direct students to Check Sheet 1 on Student Activity Book pages 223–224 or Activity Workbook page 83. Point out that it is identical to Home Check Sheet 1 on Homework and Remembering pages 129–130.

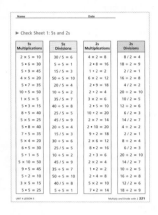

Explain that students can use these sheets to practice their multiplications and divisions. Check Sheets can be used by students individually, with partners, or in groups.

● To practice individually, students cover an answer column with a pencil or a strip of paper and then slide the pencil or paper up or down to reveal the answers as they say them. They can practice finding unknown factors by covering one of the factor columns.

● To practice in pairs, one partner reads the problems aloud and the other says the answers.

● To practice in groups, one group member reads the problems aloud and the other students take turns saying the answers.

Check Sheets can also be used by students who already have signatures for all the multiplications and divisions introduced so far as a more challenging Check Up and for maintenance of recall of these basic multiplications and divisions. To use these sheets as a Check Up, have students use Check Sheet Answer Strips (TRB M55) to record their answers. Have students place a strip of cardstock under their Answer Strip to completely block out the answers.

② Going Further

Intervention — Activity Card 7-5

Mirror Doubles
Activity Card 7-5 ●

Work: In pairs

Use:
- Mirrors
- Counters

1. Multiplying by 2 is like adding doubles. What is the result when you double 6? Think 6 + 6 = 12.

2. Use a mirror to model multiplying 6 by 2. How many counters do you see in all? 12

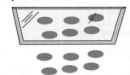

3. Write 10 expressions showing the multiplication of each of the numbers 1 through 10 by 2. Then model each multiplication with the mirror. Write the result to complete each equation.

Unit 7, Lesson 5 — Copyright © Houghton Mifflin Company

Activity Note Students can use Study Sheet A to check their work with the mirror model. Remind students that the commutative property says that the product 6 × 2 is the same as the product 2 × 6.

 Math Writing Prompt

Summarize Explain how to find 5 × 2 = □.

Soar to Success Math  **Software Support**

Warm Up 12.09

On Level — Activity Card 7-5

Create a Pictograph
Activity Card 7-5 ▲

Work: In pairs

1. Study the data shown in the chart below. What does the data show? Number of muffins for each of 4 types that were sold at the bakery

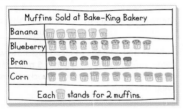

Muffins Sold at Bake-King Bakery

2. Use the data to make a pictograph. Make each symbol on the graph stand for 2 muffins.

3. **Analyze** How many muffins were sold altogether? How many symbols do you have on the graph? 70; 35

Unit 7, Lesson 5 — Copyright © Houghton Mifflin Company

Activity Note The correct number of symbols in the pictograph is as follows: Banana – 6; Blueberry – 10; Bran – 8; Corn – 12.

 Math Writing Prompt

Make a Comparison How is finding the number of earrings in 6 pairs different from finding how many pairs you can make with 6 earrings?

 Software Support

Country Countdown: White Water Graphing, Level D

Challenge — Activity Card 7-5

Divide by 2s or 5s Game
Activity Card 7-5 ■

Work: In pairs

Use:
- 16 Index cards

1. Write the whole numbers from 5 through 20 on the index cards, one number per card. Shuffle the cards and place them in a stack face down.

2. Take turns. Draw a card and decide if the number belongs to the group of count-by-2s, count-by-5s, or both.

3. If the number does not belong to either group, your turn ends. Otherwise, write a correct 2s or 5s division, using the number. Earn 1 point for each division sentence you write.

4. Continue taking turns until all the cards have been used. The player with the higher score wins.

Unit 7, Lesson 5 — Copyright © Houghton Mifflin Company

Activity Note The numbers 10 and 20 each have 2 possible equations. The numbers 5, 6, 8, 12, 14, 15, 16, and 18 each have 1 possible equation. The numbers 7, 9, 11, 13, 17, and 19 have none.

 Math Writing Prompt

Investigate Math How can you tell without multiplying if 5 × 27 = 134 is correct?

 DESTINATION Math **Software Support**

Course II: Module 2: Unit 2: Skip-Counting to Solve Multiplication

Homework and Spiral Review

7-5 Homework — Goal: Additional Practice

This Homework page provides practice in multiplying 2s.

7-5 Remembering — Goal: Spiral Review

This Remembering page would be appropriate anytime after today's lesson.

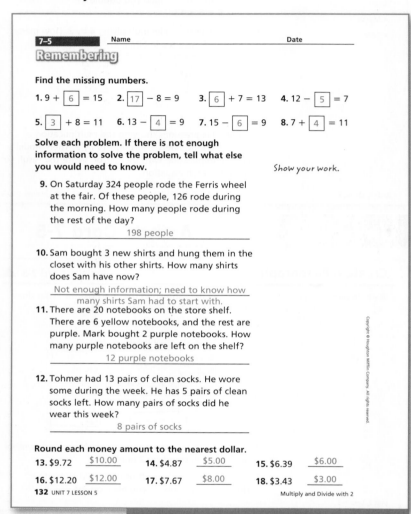

7-5 Homework

Name _____ Date _____

Study Plan

_____

Homework Helper

Solve each problem.

1. Tanya had 14 cups to fill with juice. She put them in 2 equal rows. How many cups were in each row?

   7 cups

2. Rebecca has 3 pairs of running shoes. She bought new shoelaces for each pair. How many shoelaces did she buy?

   6 shoelaces

3. Jason served his family dinner. He put 5 carrots on each of the 4 plates. How many carrots did Jason serve in all?

   20 carrots

4. Olivia filled 8 vases with flowers. She put 5 flowers in each vase. How many flowers did she put in the vases?

   40 flowers

5. Devon has 30 model airplanes. He put the same number on each of the 5 shelves of his bookcase. How many model airplanes did Devon put on each shelf?

   6 model airplanes

6. There are 12 eggs in a carton. They are arranged in 2 rows with the same number of eggs in each row. How many eggs are in each row?

   6 eggs

UNIT 7 LESSON 5 — Multiply and Divide with 2 **131**

Homework and Remembering page 131

7-5 Remembering

Name _____ Date _____

Find the missing numbers.

1. $9 + \boxed{6} = 15$
2. $\boxed{17} - 8 = 9$
3. $\boxed{6} + 7 = 13$
4. $12 - \boxed{5} = 7$
5. $\boxed{3} + 8 = 11$
6. $13 - \boxed{4} = 9$
7. $15 - \boxed{6} = 9$
8. $7 + \boxed{4} = 11$

Solve each problem. If there is not enough information to solve the problem, tell what else you would need to know.

Show your work.

9. On Saturday 324 people rode the Ferris wheel at the fair. Of these people, 126 rode during the morning. How many people rode during the rest of the day?

   198 people

10. Sam bought 3 new shirts and hung them in the closet with his other shirts. How many shirts does Sam have now?

    Not enough information; need to know how many shirts Sam had to start with.

11. There are 20 notebooks on the store shelf. There are 6 yellow notebooks, and the rest are purple. Mark bought 2 purple notebooks. How many purple notebooks are left on the shelf?

    12 purple notebooks

12. Tohmer had 13 pairs of clean socks. He wore some during the week. He has 5 pairs of clean socks left. How many pairs of socks did he wear this week?

    8 pairs of socks

Round each money amount to the nearest dollar.

13. $9.72 $10.00
14. $4.87 $5.00
15. $6.39 $6.00
16. $12.20 $12.00
17. $7.67 $8.00
18. $3.43 $3.00

132 UNIT 7 LESSON 5 — Multiply and Divide with 2

Homework and Remembering page 132

Home or School Activity

Math-to-Math Connection

Doubling Pennies Suppose you have the choice of receiving $1.00 per week allowance or 1 penny on Sunday, 2 pennies on Monday, 4 pennies on Tuesday, and so on until Saturday. Which is more? How much money would you have if you doubled the number of pennies you receive each day for one month (30 days)?

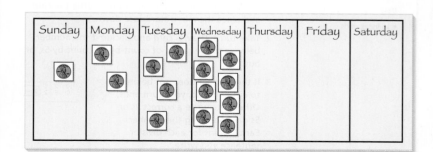

Multiply and Divide with 10

REAL WORLD **Problem Solving**

Lesson Objective

● **Explore patterns in 10s count-bys, multiplications, and divisions.**

The Day at a Glance

Today's Goals	Materials
1 Teaching the Lesson **A1:** Take Sprints for 5s multiplications and divisions. **A2:** Practice count-bys, multiplications, and divisions. **A3:** Explore patterns in 10s count-bys, multiplications, and divisions. **A4:** Practice 10s multiplications and divisions. **A5:** Solve 10s word problems. **2 Going Further** ▶ Differentiated Instruction **3 Homework and Spiral Review**	**Lesson Activities** Student Activity Book pp. 225–228 or Student Hardcover Book pp. 225–228 and Activity Workbook p. 84 (includes Check Sheet) Homework and Remembering pp. 133–136 Blank Sprint Answer Sheet (TRB M57) Check Up materials Signature Sheet Study Sheet A Check Sheet 1 Dry-erase markers	Sheet protectors Study Sheet Answer Strips (TRB M54) Check Sheet Answer Strips (TRB M55) Card stock MathBoard materials 120 Poster (TRB M60) Base ten blocks **Going Further** Activity Cards 7-6 Play money (dimes) Math Journals

123 Use Math Talk today!

Keeping Skills Sharp

Quick Practice ⏱ 5 MINUTES	Daily Routines
Goal: Practice 2s count-bys, multiplications, and divisions. **Materials:** Class Multiplication Table Poster, pointer Display the Class Multiplication Table Poster. Use the number "2" for these activities. **Repeated Quick Practice** Use these Quick Practice activities from previous lessons. **2s Multiplications in Order** (See Unit 7 Lesson 4.) **Mixed 2s Multiplications** (See Unit 7 Lesson 2.) **Mixed 2s Divisions** (See Unit 7 Lesson 5.)	**Homework Review** For word problems, have students write situation equations and then change them to solution equations. **Estimation** In the first game, Gina earned 339 points. In the second game, she earned 178 points. About how many points does Gina earn in all? Explain. Possible answer: about 500 points; Round to the nearest hundred, 300 and 200, and add.

1 Teaching the Lesson

Activity 1

Assess 5s

 10 MINUTES

Goal: Take Sprints for 5s multiplications and divisions.

Materials: Student Activity Book p. 225 or Activity Workbook p. 84, Blank Sprint Answer Sheet (TRB M57)

✔ **NCTM Standard:**
Number and Operations

Differentiated Instruction

Extra Help Adapt Sprints to meet the needs of your students. If your students are struggling with count-bys, you might give a count-by Sprint. Simply have students write the count-bys in order on Blank Sprint Answer Sheet (TRB M57). If most students seem to know the multiplications and divisions, challenge them by giving a Sprint with 10 mixed multiplications and divisions.

▶ Sprints for 5s INDIVIDUALS

Direct students to Student Book page 225 or Activity Workbook p. 84. Explain that they will use the two columns to record their answers for two quick tests, or Sprints, that you will now give.

For the first Sprint, read the × 5 exercises below aloud, pausing a few seconds between exercises to allow students to write the answer. For the second Sprint, read the ÷ 5 exercises aloud.

× 5	÷ 5
a. 6 × 5 30	a. 50 ÷ 5 10
b. 1 × 5 5	b. 15 ÷ 5 3
c. 2 × 5 10	c. 25 ÷ 5 5
d. 9 × 5 45	d. 40 ÷ 5 8
e. 7 × 5 35	e. 30 ÷ 5 6
f. 3 × 5 15	f. 45 ÷ 5 9
g. 8 × 5 40	g. 10 ÷ 5 2
h. 5 × 5 25	h. 35 ÷ 5 7
i. 4 × 5 20	i. 5 ÷ 5 1
j. 10 × 5 50	j. 20 ÷ 5 4

Have **Student Pairs** check one another's work as you read the answers, marking any incorrect answers. If a student gets all the answers on a Sprint correct, have his or her partner initial the Signature Sheet.

Activity 2

Check Up and Independent Study

 5 MINUTES

Goal: Practice count-bys, multiplications, and divisions.

Materials: Check Up materials: Signature Sheet, Study Sheet A, Check Sheet 1, dry-erase markers (1 per student), sheet protectors (1 per student), Study Sheet Answer Strips (TRB M54), Check Sheet Answer Strips (TRB M55), cardstock; Homework and Remembering p. 135

✔ **NCTM Standard:**
Number and Operations

▶ Check Up with 2s and 5s PAIRS

Give students a minute or two to study independently using Check Sheet 1 or Study Sheet A. Remind students to place their Check Sheets or Study Sheets in sheet protectors. Then have **Student Pairs** test one another and collect signatures. You may want to have Study Sheet Answer Strips (TRB M54) or Check Sheet Answer Strips (TRB M55) available to use instead of using sheet protectors.

Have students complete the Study Plan box at the top of Homework and Remembering page 135. They should include 10s practice along with any multiplications or divisions they missed in the Sprint or Check Up.

Explore 10s Patterns

▶ Explore and Discuss Patterns with 10s

WHOLE CLASS   Math Talk

Tell students that today they will be thinking about groups of 10. Ask what things in the real world come in groups of 10. dimes in a dollar, years in a decade, decades in a century, and so on

Model the steps of this activity on the Class MathBoard as students follow along on their MathBoards. The completed board is reproduced on Student Activity Book page 226. You can use it to facilitate a summary discussion of the patterns in 10s multiplications.

Have students draw line segments separating sequential groups of 10, up to 100, on the Number Path and write the totals so far next to each group. As they work, have students say in unison, "1 group of 10 is 10," "2 groups of 10 are 20," and so on.

Have students say the 10s count-bys in unison as you point to them: 10, 20, 30, 40, 50, 60, 70, 80, 90, 100.

Discuss the patterns in the tens words.

● When you said the 10s count-bys, did you notice anything about the words you said? Most end in "ty."

● Let's read them again, this time saying the "ty" part of each word louder: ten, twenTY, thirTY, forTY, fifTY, sixTY, sevenTY, eighTY, nineTY, one hundred.

On the left side of their MathBoards, have students write a multiplication equation for each count-by, reading each aloud as they write it.

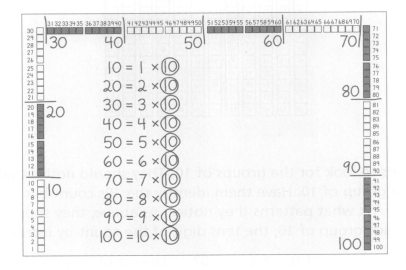

Activity continued ▶

---

 15 MINUTES

Goal: Explore patterns in 10s count-bys, multiplications, and divisions.

Materials: MathBoard materials, 120 Poster (TRB M60), Student Activity Book or Hardcover Book p. 226

 NCTM Standard:
Number and Operations

Teaching Note

Math Background We will continue to circle the group size in these MathBoard activities (though not in the answers), but suggest you let students decide for themselves whether to do so in their own work. Some find that this helps them visualize the situation. As students become more familiar with multiplication and division and learn to think flexibly about the meaning of the operations, they will no longer need to circle the group size.

Differentiated Instruction

Extra Help Help students see that the first part of the word tells us how many tens we have and the second part, "ty," means tens. For example, *sixty* means "six tens." Have students identify the tens words in which the first part is not the same as the number name. We say *twenty*, not *two-ty*; *thirty*, not *three-ty*; and *fifty*, not *five-ty*.

❶ Teaching the Lesson (continued)

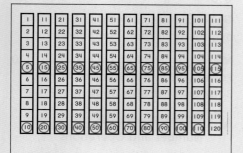
Have students use Student Book page 226 or their MathBoards to describe the patterns they see in the count-bys and equations. The following are a few possibilities.

● All the count-bys end in 0.

● The tens digit of each product is the multiplier, and the ones digit is 0.

● The 10s count-bys are the 1s count-bys (1, 2, 3, 4, . . .) with an added 0.

● Each 10s count-by or product is twice the corresponding 5s count-by or product. For example, 3 × 10 is twice 3 × 5.

Encourage students to try to explain the patterns they see. For example, the tens digit of each product is the multiplier because the multiplier tells the number of tens. The ones digit is 0 because there are only groups of ten with zero ones left over.

Write the first few 10s division equations as a class, and then have students work independently to write the rest. Discuss any patterns they see in the equations.

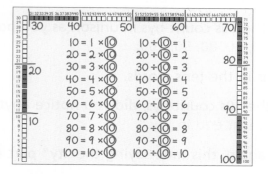

▶ 10s Patterns on the 120 Poster WHOLE CLASS

Display the 120 Poster or distribute TRB M60.

Ask students to look for the groups of 10. They should notice that each column is a group of 10. Have them identify the 10s count-bys as you circle them. Ask what patterns they notice. As above, they should see that with each group of 10, the tens digit of the count-by increases by 1.

● How many groups of ten are in 110? 11 How many groups of 10 are in 120? 12

10s Multiplications and Divisions

▶ Practice WHOLE CLASS

10s Multiplications Present students with several 10s multiplications.

● I'm going to write some multiplications on the board. I'll give you a few seconds to think about each. When I raise my hand, I want you to read the multiplication aloud, all together, and give the answer.

Write a 10s multiplication like the following on the board.

$$3 \times 10$$

Wait a few seconds before raising your hand. Students should say, "3 times 10 equals 30." Give three or four more 10s multiplications, and then have a volunteer summarize the pattern he or she is using to find the answers.

10s Unknown Multiplication Equations Next have students practice solving unknown multiplication equations. Write the following on the board.

$$60 = \boxed{} \times 10$$

On your signal, students should say, "60 equals 6 times 10." Write 6 in the answer box.

● What 10s division equation is related to this multiplication equation? $60 \div 10 = 6$

Give the class three or four more unknown multiplication equations in which the known factor is 10. Again, have a volunteer explain the pattern he or she is using to find the answers.

10s Divisions Finally, have students practice divisions. Write the following on the board.

$$50 \div 10$$

On your signal, students should say, "50 divided by 10 equals 5." Repeat this for several more divisions with divisor 10, and have a volunteer explain the pattern he or she is using to find the answer.

 10 MINUTES

Goal: Practice 10s multiplications and divisions.

Materials: MathBoard materials, base ten blocks

 NCTM Standard:
Number and Operations

 Alternate Approach

Base Ten Blocks Students can use base ten blocks to model the 10s multiplications and divisions in Activity 4.

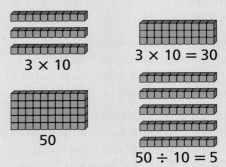

3×10

$3 \times 10 = 30$

50

$50 \div 10 = 5$

 Ongoing Assessment

Write a 10s count-by like 40 on the board. Ask questions such as the following:

▶ Is this a 10s count-by? How do you know?

▶ What 10s multiplication equation can you write for this number?

▶ What 10s division equation can you write for this number?

Teaching the Lesson (continued)

Activity 5

Solve Multiplication and Division Problems with 10s

 10 MINUTES

Goal: Solve 10s word problems.

Materials: MathBoard materials, Student Activity Book or Hardcover Book pp. 227–228

✓ **NCTM Standards:**
Number and Operations
Problem Solving

 Math Talk in Action

Jorge: A dime is 10 cents. I did 10-cent count-bys on my fingers: 10 cents, 20 cents, 30 cents, 40 cents, 50 cents, 60 cents, 70 cents. That's 7 fingers. So Yoko has 7 dimes.

Melissa: I did an unknown multiplication equation, like this: $70 = \boxed{} \times 10$. The missing number is 7. That means 7 dimes.

Danny: I thought of each dime as 10. You want to know how many 10s are in 70. You figure that out by dividing: $70 \div 10 = 7$. I think there are 7 dimes.

 Class Management

Looking Ahead Remind students to take home the 10s chart on Homework and Remembering page 133.

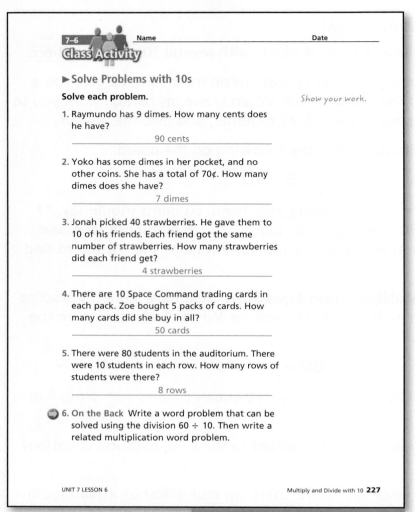

7-6
Class Activity

Name _____ Date _____

▶ Solve Problems with 10s

Solve each problem.   *Show your work.*

1. Raymundo has 9 dimes. How many cents does he have?
   _____ 90 cents _____

2. Yoko has some dimes in her pocket, and no other coins. She has a total of 70¢. How many dimes does she have?
   _____ 7 dimes _____

3. Jonah picked 40 strawberries. He gave them to 10 of his friends. Each friend got the same number of strawberries. How many strawberries did each friend get?
   _____ 4 strawberries _____

4. There are 10 Space Command trading cards in each pack. Zoe bought 5 packs of cards. How many cards did she buy in all?
   _____ 50 cards _____

5. There were 80 students in the auditorium. There were 10 students in each row. How many rows of students were there?
   _____ 8 rows _____

6. **On the Back** Write a word problem that can be solved using the division $60 \div 10$. Then write a related multiplication word problem.

UNIT 7 LESSON 6   Multiply and Divide with 10 **227**

Student Activity Book page 227

▶ Solve Problems with 10s [WHOLE CLASS]

Using **Solve and Discuss,** have students solve problems 1–5 on Student Book page 227. These should go quickly because of the 10s pattern. See **Math Talk in Action** for a sample classroom discussion about problem 2. Encourage students to use patterns rather than make drawings.

Give students an opportunity to share the word problems they wrote for exercise 6.

② Going Further

Differentiated Instruction

Intervention   Activity Card 7-6

Dime Time   Activity Card 7-6 ●

Work: In pairs
Use:
• Play money (10 dimes)

1. What is the total value of 10 dimes? Work together to count by 10s to find the answer. $1.00

2. Copy the table below. Count by 10s to complete the table.

Number of Dimes	Total Value
4	$0.40
? 7	$0.70
6	? $0.60
10	? $1.00
? 9	$0.90

2. **Analyze** Describe at least two ways to find the value of 5 dimes.   Possible answers: Count by 10s to 5 × 10 = 50, or $0.50; Subtract 10 cents from the value of 5 dimes; Add 10 cents to the value of 4 dimes.

Unit 7, Lesson 6   Copyright © Houghton Mifflin Company

Activity Note After students have completed the table, have them say aloud the multiplication and division each row represents. For example: Four dimes equal 40¢. 4 × 10 = 40. 40 ÷ 10 = 4.

✎ Math Writing Prompt

Explain Your Thinking Celia has some dimes in her pocket, and no other coins. She says that she has exactly 85¢. Could this be true? Explain.

 **Software Support**

Warm Up 12.11

On Level   Activity Card 7-6

A 10s Pictograph   Activity Card 7-6 ▲

Work: On your own

1. Study the information in the pictograph.

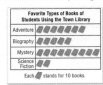

2. Write your answers to the questions below on a separate sheet of paper.
• How many students chose *Biography*? 50
• How many more students chose *Mystery* than *Science Fiction*? 70
• If 60 students chose *Other Fiction*, how many symbols would you use to show that? 6

Unit 7, Lesson 6   Copyright © Houghton Mifflin Company

Activity Note After answering the questions on the activity card, students should make up their own questions and trade with another student to answer each other's questions.

✎ Math Writing Prompt

Summarize Explain how multiplying by 10 is related to multiplying by 2 and multiplying by 5.

MEGAMATH Grades K-6 **Software Support**

Country Countdown: White Water Graphing, Level E

Challenge   Activity Card 7-6

Sticker Sale   Activity Card 7-6 ■

Work: In small groups

1. Suppose that you have exactly $0.50 to spend on these stickers.

2. **Work Together** Make an organized list that shows all the possible combinations of stickers that you can buy. Be sure that you include at least one of each type of sticker in each combination.

3. **Analyze** What strategy did you use to organize your list?

Unit 7, Lesson 6   Copyright © Houghton Mifflin Company

Activity Note If time permits, discuss with students why it is only possible to buy 5, 10, or 15 note stickers with a total of 50¢ to spend.

✎ Math Writing Prompt

Critical Thinking Suppose you know that ♥ × 10 = * × 5. What is the relationship between ♥ and *? Explain your answer.

✦ DESTINATION Math· Software Support

Course II: Module 2: Unit 3: Meaning of Division

Multiply and Divide with 10   **515**

3 Homework and Spiral Review

Homework **Goal:** Additional Practice

This Homework page provides practice with 10s multiplication and division.

7–6 Name _____ Date _____

Homework

Study Plan

Homework Helper

Solve each problem.

1. Wendy has $2.00. She wants to buy some marbles that cost $0.10 each. How many marbles can she buy?

   _____ 20 marbles _____

2. Natalie turned off 2 lights in each of the 6 rooms of her house. How many lights did she turn off?

   _____ 12 lights _____

3. Luis has 18 single socks. How many pairs of socks does he have?

   _____ 9 pairs _____

4. Lana has 9 nickels. She wants to buy an apple that cost $0.40. Does she have enough money?

   _____ yes _____

5. Annabelle had 20 crayons. She gave 5 of them to each of her sisters. How many sisters does Annabelle have?

   _____ 4 sisters _____

6. Harvey wrote letters to 10 of his friends. Each letter was 3 pages long. How many pages did Harvey write?

   _____ 30 pages _____

Complete the table.

7.

Number of Nickels	1	3	5	8	9	10
Total Amount	5¢	15¢	25¢	40¢	45¢	50¢

UNIT 7 LESSON 6 — Multiply and Divide with 10 **135**

Homework and Remembering page 135

Remembering **Goal:** Spiral Review

This Remembering page would be appropriate anytime after today's lesson.

7–6 Name _____ Date _____

Remembering

Vera had 163 marbles. Her older brother gave her his collection of 297 marbles. How many marbles does Vera have now?

1. Solve the problem. _____ 460 marbles _____   *Show your work.*

2. Write a subtraction word problem related to the addition word problem. Possible answer: Vera has 460 marbles. She gave her brother 297 of the marbles. How many marbles does Vera have now?

3. Without doing any calculations, find the solution to the problem you wrote. 163 marbles or 297 marbles, depending on the problem students wrote.

Jose spent $6.87 at the store. He spent $3.96 on markers and the rest on crayons. How much money did he spend on crayons?

4. Solve the problem. _____ $2.91 _____   *Show your work.*

5. Write an addition word problem related to the subtraction word problem. Possible answer: Jose spent $3.96 on markers and $2.91 on crayons. How much money did he spend in all?

6. Without doing any calculations, find the solution to the problem you wrote. $6.87

Use mental math to add or subtract.

7. 800 + 100 = _____ 900 _____

8. 540 − 20 = _____ 520 _____

9. 630 + 300 = _____ 930 _____

10. 300 − 150 = _____ 150 _____

136 UNIT 7 LESSON 6 — Multiply and Divide with 10

Homework and Remembering page 136

Home or School Activity

 Language Arts Connection

Number Prefixes In English, words that begin with "bi" or "duo" mean "two of something". Words that begin with "quint" or "pent" mean "five of something", and words that begin with "deca" mean "ten of something." Have students create a list of "2", "5", and "10" words along with their meanings.

biped	an animal with two legs
duet	a musical composition for two performers
pentagon	a figure with 5 sides
quintuplets	five children born at the same time
decagon	a figure with 10 sides

Multiply and Divide with 9

Lesson Objectives

- Explore patterns in 9s multiplications and divisions.
- Learn a strategy for multiplying and dividing with 9s quickly.

Vocabulary

Quick 9s
multiplier finger

The Day at a Glance

Today's Goals	Materials
1 Teaching the Lesson A1: Practice count-bys, multiplications, and divisions. A2: Explore patterns in 9s count-bys and use them to multiply by 9 on the fingers. A3: Explore patterns in 9s divisions. **2 Going Further** ▶ Differentiated Instruction **3 Homework and Spiral Review**	**Lesson Activities** Student Activity Book pp. 229–232 or Student Hardcover Book pp. 229–232 and Activity Workbook p. 85 (includes Check Sheet) Homework and Remembering pp. 137–142 Check Up materials Signature Sheet Blank Sprint Answer Sheet Study Sheet A, Check Sheet 1 or 2 Dry-erase markers, Sheet protectors Study and Check Sheet Answer Strips	Card stock MathBoard materials or Number Path Multiplication Rap (Rock N' Learn) **Going Further** Activity Cards 7-7 Centimeter-Grid Paper (TRB M31) Scissors, Index cards Red and blue markers Math Journals

123 *Use* **Math Talk** *today!*

Keeping Skills Sharp

Quick Practice ⏱ 5 MINUTES	Daily Routines
Goal: Practice 2s count-bys, multiplications, and divisions. **Materials:** Class Multiplication Table Poster, pointer Use the Multiplication Table and the number "2" for the activities. **Repeated Quick Practice** Use these Quick Practice activities from previous lessons. **2s Multiplications in Order** (See Unit 7 Lesson 4.) **Mixed 2s Multiplications** (See Unit 7 Lesson 2.) **Mixed 2s Divisions** (See Unit 7 Lesson 5.)	**Homework Review** Have students discuss their homework and help each other with any corrections. **Reasoning** Tom finished the race 4 seconds behind Jane. Lou finished 7 seconds ahead of Tom. Write the order in which they finished the race. Explain. Lou, Jane, Tom; I made a drawing using the given data.

① Teaching the Lesson

Check Up and Independent Study

 10 MINUTES

Goal: Practice count-bys, multiplications, and divisions.

Materials: Check Up materials: Signature Sheet (Student Activity Book pp. 205–206 or Activity Workbook p. 77), Blank Sprint Answer Sheet (TRB M57), Study Sheet A (Student Activity Book pages 207–208 or Activity Workbook p. 78), Check Sheet 1 or 2 (Student Activity Book pp. 223–224; 229–230 or Activity Workbook p. 83; 85), dry-erase markers (1 per student), sheet protectors (1 per student), Study Sheet Answer Strips (TRB M54), Check Sheet Answer Strips (TRB M55), cardstock; Homework and Remembering p. 141

✔ **NCTM Standard:**
Number and Operations

▶ Check Up with 2s, 5s, and 10s [PAIRS]

Give **Student Pairs** a few minutes to test each other using Study Sheet A. The student's partner reads the problem from Study Sheet A as the student writes the answers. The partner checks the answers and, if the student makes no errors, initials the appropriate section of the Signature Sheet. For students who have already collected signatures on their Study Sheets, have them study with Check Sheet 1 or Check Sheet 2 on Student Activity book page 229 (10s only) or Activity Workbook page 85.

Students who made mistakes on the 5s Sprints in Lesson 6 (or who were absent) may take repeat or make-up Sprints at this time. Students can record their answers on Blank Sprint Answer Sheet (TRB M57).

Have students complete the Study Plan box on Homework and Remembering page 141. They should include 9s practice along with any multiplications or divisions they missed in the Check Up.

Explore 9s Multiplication Patterns

 20 MINUTES

Goal: Explore patterns in 9s count-bys and use them to multiply by 9 on the fingers.

Materials: MathBoard materials or Number Path (TRB M39), Student Activity Book or Hardcover Book pp. 231–232

✔ **NCTM Standards:**
Number and Operations
Representation

▶ Explore Patterns with 9s [WHOLE CLASS]

Have students think about groups of 9. Ask what things in the real world come in groups of 9. baseball innings

Model this activity on the Class MathBoard as students follow along on their MathBoards.

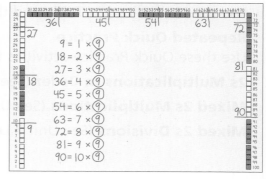

Have students draw line segments separating sequential groups of 9, up to 90, on the Number Path and write the totals so far next to each group. As they work, have them say in unison, "1 group of 9 is 9," "2 groups of 9 are 18," and so on. Then, have students say the 9s count-bys as you point to them: 9, 18, 27, 36, 45, 54, 63, 72, 81, 90. On the left side of their MathBoards, have students write a multiplication equation for each count-by, reading each aloud as they write it.

123 Math Talk Ask students to describe any patterns they see on their MathBoard or on Student Book page 231. The following are a few possibilities. Note that the first pattern given here is perhaps the most important; in a way, it explains all the others. This pattern is explored further in the next part of Activity 2.

- 1 × 9 is 1 less than 1 ten, 2 × 9 is 2 less than 2 tens, 3 × 9 is 3 less than 3 tens, and so on.

- The digits of each count-by have a sum of 9.

- The tens digit of each product is 1 less than the multiplier.

- Moving down the column of products, the tens digit increases by 1, while the ones digit decreases by 1.

- The digits of the larger count-bys are the reverse of the digits of the smaller count-bys. For example, the digits of 81 are the reverse of the digits of 18.

Relate 10s and 9s Remind students that the squares on the Number Path are grouped by tens. As you say the following, point to 10 on the number path and then "slide" back one to 9.

- One group of 9, or 9, is one group of 10 *(point to 10)* minus 1 *(slide back to 9)*.

On the Class MathBoard, after the equation 9 = 1 ×⑨, write = 10 − 1. Point out the relationship between the 9s multiplication and the 10s count-by.

- 1 times 9 equals 10 minus 1.

As you say the following, point to 20 on the number path and then slide back 2 to 18.

- Two groups of 9, or 18, is two groups of 10 *(point to 20)* minus 2 *(slide back to 18)*.

On the Class MathBoard, after the equation 18 = 2 ×⑨, write = 20 − 2. Point out the relationship between the 9s multiplication and the 10s count-by.

- 2 times 9 equals 20 minus 2.

As you say the following, point to 30 on the number path and then slide back 3 to 27.

- Three groups of 9, or 27, is three groups of 10 *(point to 30)* minus 3 *(slide back to 27)*.

After the equation 27 = 3 ×⑨, write = 30 − 3. Point out the relationship between the 9s multiplication and the 10s count-by.

- 3 times 9 equals 30 minus 3.

Activity continued ▶

Differentiated Instruction

Extra Help If students have difficulty seeing the relationship between the 10s count-bys and the 9s multiplications, have them model it by using connecting cubes that have been joined to form ten-towers. The following example shows how to model 2 ×⑨ = [2 × ⑩] − 2 = 20 − 2 = 18.

Have students start with two ten-towers, which represent two groups of 10, or 20.

Tell them to subtract 2 by removing one cube from each tower.

Point out that they are left with two groups of 9, or 18.

So they have demonstrated that two groups of 9, or 18, is two groups of 10 minus 2.

Teaching Note

Language and Vocabulary
Describing patterns in basic multiplications and divisions in their own words and understanding the descriptions by others is critical to understanding what is being addressed in the classroom. Students who are experiencing difficulty expressing themselves can practice describing the patterns aloud to a partner.

Teaching the Lesson (continued)

Teaching Note

Math Background In Activity 2, students discover a relationship between 10s count-bys and 9s multiplications. This relationship can be justified—and generalized—by the following reasoning, which uses some simple algebra and the properties of our number system.

▶ Let the variable n represent the multiplier. Then $n \times 9$ represents the product of n and 9.

▶ Any number or expression may be replaced by a number or expression of equal value. So $n \times 9$ is equal to $n \times (10 - 1)$.

▶ By the Distributive Property, any factor outside a set of parentheses multiplies each term of an addition or subtraction inside the parentheses. Therefore:

$$n \times 9 = n \times (10 - 1) =$$
$$n \times 10 - n \times 1$$

This is the general relationship that students have learned to apply to values of n from 1 through 10:

$1 \times 9 = 1 \times (10 - 1) = 1 \times 10 - 1 \times 1,$
$2 \times 9 = 2 \times (10 - 1) = 2 \times 10 - 2 \times 1,$

and so on.

This pattern can help students with 9s:

$1 \times 9 = 10 - 1 = 9$
$2 \times 9 = 20 - 2 = 18$
$3 \times 9 = 30 - 3 = 27$
$4 \times 9 = 40 - 4 = 36$
$5 \times 9 = 50 - 5 = 45$
$6 \times 9 = 60 - 6 = 54$
$7 \times 9 = 70 - 7 = 63$
$8 \times 9 = 80 - 8 = 72$
$9 \times 9 = 90 - 9 = 81$

Continue up to $90 = 10 \times \textcircled{9}$, encouraging students to say the equations with you once they see the pattern.

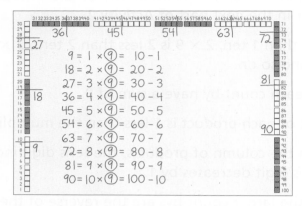

Tell students to turn over their MathBoards as you cover or turn over the Class MathBoard. Write the following multiplication on the board.

$$3 \times 9$$

Have students try to mentally find the product. Suggest they think about the patterns you have just discussed. After a few seconds, ask a volunteer to explain how he or she found the answer. If the student did not find 3 tens minus 3, ask if anyone used this method. Present two or three more 9s multiplications for students to do mentally.

▶ Math Tools: Quick 9s Multiplication WHOLE CLASS

Tell students you will now show them a method called *Quick 9s* that will help them learn and remember their 9s multiplications. Model the process, which is summarized on Student Activity Book page 230, as students follow along. As students work through this process, ask them to relate it to the 9s patterns they found earlier.

Have students hold their hands with their palms facing them and their fingers extended. Note that, for your fingers to be in the correct position, you must stand with your back to the class.

● To find 1×9, bend down your left thumb, which is the first finger as you go from left to right. The fingers to the right of your thumb represent 9 ones. This is the answer: $1 \times 9 = 9$.

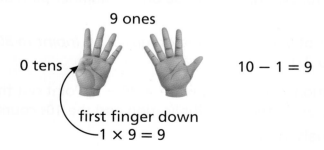

9 ones

0 tens

$10 - 1 = 9$

first finger down
$1 \times 9 = 9$

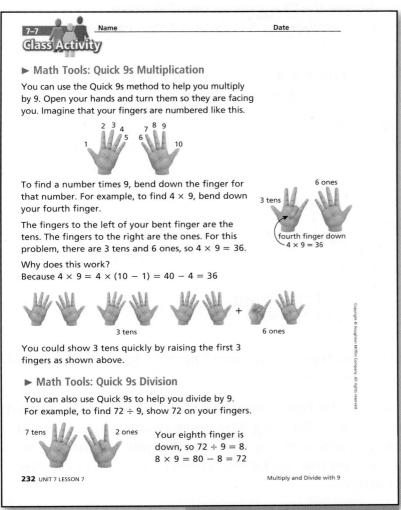

Student Activity Book page 232

On page 232:

7-7
Class Activity

Name _____ Date _____

▶ **Math Tools: Quick 9s Multiplication**

You can use the Quick 9s method to help you multiply by 9. Open your hands and turn them so they are facing you. Imagine that your fingers are numbered like this.

To find a number times 9, bend down the finger for that number. For example, to find 4×9, bend down your fourth finger.

The fingers to the left of your bent finger are the tens. The fingers to the right are the ones. For this problem, there are 3 tens and 6 ones, so $4 \times 9 = 36$.

fourth finger down
$4 \times 9 = 36$

Why does this work?
Because $4 \times 9 = 4 \times (10 - 1) = 40 - 4 = 36$

3 tens + 6 ones

You could show 3 tens quickly by raising the first 3 fingers as shown above.

▶ **Math Tools: Quick 9s Division**

You can also use Quick 9s to help you divide by 9. For example, to find $72 \div 9$, show 72 on your fingers.

7 tens   2 ones   Your eighth finger is down, so $72 \div 9 = 8$.
$8 \times 9 = 80 - 8 = 72$

232 UNIT 7 LESSON 7   Multiply and Divide with 9

- To find 2×9, bend down the second finger. Leave the rest of your fingers up.

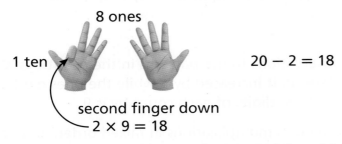

8 ones

1 ten

second finger down
$2 \times 9 = 18$

$20 - 2 = 18$

Walk around the room to make sure students are doing this correctly.

- We know that 2×9 is 18. Can you see how your fingers show 18?

Help students see that the one finger to the left of the bent finger represents 1 ten, and the 8 fingers to the right represent 8 ones.

Activity continued ▶

Teaching Note

Watch For! In previous multiplication lessons, students have used their fingers as a means of keeping track of count-bys. So some students may initially be confused by the different use of the fingers in 9s multiplications. Stress the fact that this method of 9s multiplications and divisions is special because they can actually "read" the product on their hands. That is why this method is given a special name—Quick 9s.

Conversely, when faced with mixed multiplications and divisions, some students may attempt to apply the method to all multiplications and divisions. Ask students to recall the name of the method—Quick 9s—and point out that it applies only to 9s multiplications and divisions.

English Language Learners

Help students describe the 9s multiplications patterns. Write $18 = 2 \times 9 = 20 - 2$ on the board.

- **Beginning** Say: **18 is 2 groups of 9. 18 is 2 less than 20.** Have students repeat.
- **Intermediate** Ask: **18 is how many groups of 9?** 2 groups **18 is 2 less than what number?** 20
- **Advanced** Have students tell why 18 can be represented using 2×9 or $20 - 2$.

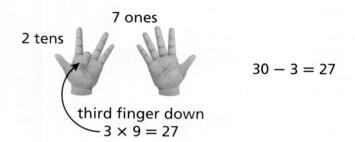

Make sure students also see the "tens minus ones" pattern:
2 × 9 is 2 tens − 2, so the answer has 8 ones and 1 ten less than 2 tens, which is 1 ten.

● **How do you think we find 3 × 9?** Bend down the third finger. Have everyone demonstrate 3 × 9 with their fingers.

● **How do your fingers show the answer?** There are 2 fingers to the left of the bent finger and 7 fingers to the right. This shows 2 tens and 7 ones. So the answer is 27.

● **Can anyone explain the "tens minus ones" pattern for 3 × 9?** 3 × 9 is 3 tens − 3, so the answer has 7 ones and 1 less than 3 tens.

Mention that we can call the bent finger the *multiplier finger* because it shows the number we are multiplying 9 by. Have students use Quick 9s to find the remaining 9s products in order. Provide help to students who need it. Use the pattern on the MathBoard connecting the 9s multiples to the $n × 10 − n$ patterns.

● **As you did each multiplication in order, how did the number of fingers to the left of your bent finger change?** It increased by 1. **How did the number of fingers to the right of your bent finger change?** It decreased by 1.

● **For all the 9s multiplications, how many fingers did you have up?** 9 **Why?** One finger was bent because the number of tens was always 1 less than $n × 10$.

Relate these observations to the patterns in the count-bys. With each count-by, the tens digit increased by 1 while the ones digit decreased by 1, and the sum of the digits of each count-by is 9.

Give students some 9s multiplications in mixed order, and have them find the products by using Quick 9s or the "tens minus ones" pattern they discovered earlier. Have student volunteers demonstrate these multiplications for the class.

For 9 × 6, ask:

● **Which multiplier finger will be down to show 5 tens and 4 ones?** The 6th.

This shows that 54 ÷ 9 = 6. So you can use the multiplier finger that is down for the answer to a 9s division.

Explore 9s Division Patterns

▶ Use Patterns to Find Quotients [WHOLE CLASS]

Erase the subtraction expressions from the Class MathBoard as students do the same on their MathBoards (so all that remains are the 9s multiplication equations).

As a class, write the first two or three division equations next to the corresponding multiplication equations. Have students work independently to write the remaining equations. Walk around the classroom and observe students as they write the remaining equations. Assist students who need help or have them work in Helping Pairs.

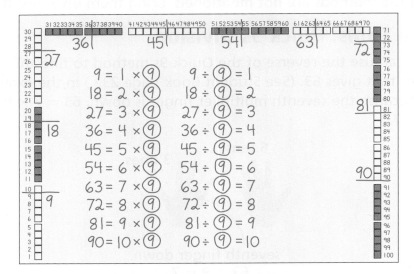

Discuss any patterns students see in the division equations. The following are some possibilities.

● The quotient, or unknown factor, is 1 more than the tens digit of the product. For example, in $27 \div 9 = 3$, 3 is 1 more than the tens digit of 27.

● The unknown factor and the ones digit of the product add to 10. For example, in $72 \div 9 = 8$, 8 and 2 add to 10.

● The unknown factor is the difference between the next ten and the product. For example, consider $54 \div 9 = 6$. The next ten after 54 is 60, and the difference between 54 and 60 is 6.

 20 MINUTES

Goal: Explore patterns in 9s divisions.

Materials: MathBoard materials, Student Activity Book or Hardcover Book p. 232

 NCTM Standards:
Number and Operations
Representation

The Learning Classroom

Math Talk Encourage students to identify and describe the patterns before you do. Allow time for students to make comments or ask questions about each other's patterns before you begin to speak. If you tend to speak first, the students will not take ownership of their role as crucial participants in the discourse; they will look to you instead.

Activity continued ▶

Teaching the Lesson (continued)

 Class Management

Looking Ahead Remind students to take home the 9s chart and Home Check Sheet 2 on Homework and Remembering pages 137–140.

Ongoing Assessment

Ask questions such as the following:

▶ How can you find the product 4 × 9 using a 10s multiplication? using your fingers?

▶ Suppose you know that the product of an unknown factor and 9 is 45. How can you find the mystery factor?

▶ What multiplication equation can you write with the factors 2 and 9? What division equation is related to it?

Have students turn over their MathBoards. Hide the Class MathBoard. Write the following division on the board.

$$63 \div 9$$

Tell students to use the patterns they have found to figure out the answer mentally. Students may identify these strategies:

63 would be 1 more ten 70 − 7, so 7 × 9 = 63

3 ones means it is 7 (70 − 7 = 63)

Open 6 fingers to make 6 tens and bend down the next finger so it is 7.

If any of the methods are not mentioned, bring them up yourself.

▶ Math Tools: Quick 9s Division

Students can use the reverse of the Quick 9s method to find the multiplier that gives 63. (See Student Book page 232.) In the example below, because the seventh multiplier finger is down, 63 = 7 × 9, or 63 ÷ 9 = 7.

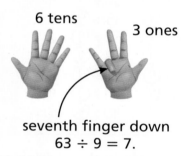

6 tens   3 ones

seventh finger down
63 ÷ 9 = 7.

Have students find the quotients of two or three more 9s divisions by finding the multiplier finger or using the $n \times 10 - n$ pattern.

②Going Further

Differentiated Instruction

Intervention   Activity Card 7-7

Arrays for 10s and 9s Multiplications   Activity Card 7-7 ●

Work: In pairs

Use:
• TRB M31 (Centimeter-Grid Paper)
• Scissors
• Red and blue markers

1. Draw a 4-by-10 rectangle of squares on your grid paper and color it red. Next, draw a 4-by-9 rectangle of squares and color it blue. Write on each rectangle the multiplication it represents.

2. Cut out each rectangle and line up both rectangles along their left edges, with the blue rectangle on top.

3. **Analyze** How many fewer squares are in the blue rectangle? How does that help you to describe the relationship between 4 × 9 and 4 × 10? 4 fewer squares; 4 × 9 is 4 less than 4 × 10.

Unit 7, Lesson 7   Copyright © Houghton Mifflin Company

Activity Note Have students repeat the activity for 7 × 10 and 7 × 9. Discuss why knowing the 10s multiplications makes it easier to find the answer to many 9s multiplication problems.

 Math Writing Prompt

Explain Your Thinking You know that 4 × 9 = 36. Explain how to find 5 × 9 without multiplying.

 **Software Support**

Warm Up 12.20

On Level   Activity Card 7-7

Missing Number Game   Activity Card 7-7 ▲

Work: In pairs

Use:
• 20 index cards

1. Copy the 20 equations below onto index cards.

□×9=9 □×9=54 9÷9=□ 54÷9=□
□×9=18 □×9=63 18÷9=□ 63÷9=□
□×9=27 □×9=72 27÷9=□ 72÷9=□
□×9=36 □×9=81 36÷9=□ 81÷9=□
□×9=45 □×9=90 45÷9=□ 90÷9=□

2. Shuffle the cards and stack them face down. Take turns. Draw the top card from the stack. Read the equation, saying the missing number.

3. If your answer is correct, you get a number of points equal to the missing number. When all the cards are used, the player with the greater number of points wins.

Unit 7, Lesson 7   Copyright © Houghton Mifflin Company

Activity Note For a more challenging game, use a timer to limit the time for each player's turn. Students can use a calculator to help them keep score.

 Math Writing Prompt

Choose a Method What method would you use to find 6 × 10? Explain.

 Software Support

Country Countdown, Counting Critters, Level Z

Challenge   Activity Card 7-7

Choose the Operations   Activity Card 7-7 ■

Work: In pairs

1. Copy the equations below and work together to fill in each circle with one of the following symbols: +, −, ×, or ÷.

```
20 ○ 5 = 5 ○ 5
 9 ○ 4 = 40 ○ 4
16 ○ 2 = 10 ○ 2
90 ○ 9 = 100 ○ 10
45 ○ 5 = 9 ○ 1
```

20 ÷ 5 = 5 × 5
9 × 4 = 40 − 4
16 ÷ 2 = 10 − 2
90 ÷ 9 = 100 ÷ 10
45 ÷ 5 = 9 × 1

2. **On Your Own** Write two new operation exercises like the ones above on a sheet of paper and exchange with your partner to solve.

Unit 7, Lesson 7   Copyright © Houghton Mifflin Company

Activity Note If students have difficulty finding a strategy for this activity, suggest choosing a symbol for the first expression and then trying different symbols for the second expression to find a match.

 Math Writing Prompt

Investigate Math Explain how to use 10s count-bys to find 11 × 9 and 12 × 9.

 DESTINATION Math **Software Support**

Course II: Module 2: Unit 3: Dividing by a 1-digit Number

③ Homework and Spiral Review

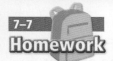

7-7 Homework
Goal: Additional Practice

This Homework page provides practice in 9s multiplications and divisions.

7-7 Name _____ Date _____
Homework

Study Plan
_____
_____
Homework Helper

Write an equation for each situation. Then solve the problem.

Show your work.

1. The pet store has 54 birds. There are 9 birds in each cage. How many cages are there?
$54 \div 9 = \square$ or $\square \times 9 = 54$; 6 cages

2. George told 2 stories each night of the camping trip. The camping trip was 3 nights long. How many stories did George tell?
$3 \times 2 = \square$; 6 stories

3. LaShawna blew up 40 balloons for a party. She made 10 equal bunches of balloons to put on the tables. How many balloons were in each bunch?
$40 \div 10 = \square$ or $10 \times \square = 40$; 4 balloons

4. There are 4 floors in Redville City Hall. Every floor has 9 offices. How many offices are in the building?
$4 \times 9 = \square$; 36 offices

5. Brigitte has 15 CDs. She can put 5 CDs in the CD player at one time. How many times does she have to change the CDs to listen to all of them?
$15 \div 5 = \square$; 3 times

UNIT 7 LESSON 7   Multiply and Divide with 9 **141**

Homework and Remembering page 141

7-7 Remembering
Goal: Spiral Review

This Remembering page would be appropriate anytime after today's lesson.

7-7 Name _____ Date _____
Remembering

Round each number to the nearest hundred.

1. 359	400	2. 642	600	3. 121	100
4. 298	300	5. 971	1,000	6. 750	800

Round each number to the nearest ten.

7. 676	680	8. 94	90	9. 43	40
10. 532	530	11. 67	70	12. 198	200

Draw each figure if you can. If it is not possible, explain why.

13. a quadrilateral that is not a square
Possible answer:

14. a parallelogram that is not a square
Possible answer:

15. a rectangle that is not a parallelogram
Not possible. Every rectangle is a parallelogram.

16. a rectangle that is not a square
Possible answer:

17. a square that is not a rectangle
Not possible. Every square is a rectangle.

18. a square that is not a parallelogram
Not possible. Every square is a parallelogram.

142 UNIT 7 LESSON 7   Multiply and Divide with 9

Homework and Remembering page 142

Home or School Activity

Music Connection

Multiplication Rap Rock N' Learn's *Multiplication Rap* CD can help students master their basic multiplications. Review the nines with students and listen to other multiplication raps as the unit progresses. Challenge students to write their own multiplication raps. You can use this CD in Unit 5 as well.

Fluency Day for 2s, 5s, 9s, and 10s

REAL WORLD Problem Solving

Lesson Objective

● Practice 2s, 5s, 9s, and 10s multiplications and divisions.

Vocabulary

Fast-Array drawing

The Day at a Glance

Today's Goals	Materials	
1 Teaching the Lesson **A1:** Take Sprints for 2s multiplications and divisions. **A2:** Practice count-bys, multiplications, and divisions. **A3:** Discuss 9s patterns on the 120 Poster. **A4:** Solve multiplication and division word problems. **2 Going Further** ▶ Problem Solving Strategy: Organized Lists ▶ Differentiated Instruction **3 Homework and Spiral Review**	**Lesson Activities** Student Activity Book pp. 233–236 or Student Hardcover Book pp. 233–236 and Activity Workbook pp. 86–87 (includes Check Sheet) Homework and Remembering pp. 143–146 Signature Sheet Blank Sprint Answer Sheet Study Sheet A Check Sheets 1, 2 and 3 Study Sheet Answer Strips (TRB M54) Check Answer Strips (TRB M55) Check Up materials Dry-erase markers Sheet protectors 120 Poster	*Amanda Bean's Amazing Dream* by Cindy Neuschwander (Scholastic Press, 1998) Quick Quiz 2 **Going Further** Activity Cards 7-8 Red, yellow, blue, and green color tiles Spinner C (TRB M61) Game Cards (TRB M25) Poster paper Paper clips Crayons or markers Study Sheet A Math Journals

123 **Use Math Talk today!**

Keeping Skills Sharp

Quick Practice ⏱ 5 MINUTES	**Daily Routines**
Goal: Practice 2s count-bys, multiplications, and divisions. **Materials:** Class Multiplication Table Poster, pointer Use the Multiplication Table and the number "2" for the activities. **Repeated Quick Practice** Use these Quick Practice activities from previous lessons. **2s Multiplications in Order** (See Unit 7 Lesson 4.) **Mixed 2s Multiplications** (See Unit 7 Lesson 2.) **Mixed 2s Divisions** (See Unit 7 Lesson 5.)	**Homework Review** Check that students completed the assignment and check to see if any problem(s) caused difficulty. **Function Machine** A function machine multiplies each input by 9. What is the output when the input is 1? 9? 8? 10? 9; 81; 72; 90

Teaching the Lesson

Activity 1

Assess 2s

 10 MINUTES

Goal: Take Sprints for 2s multiplications and divisions.

Materials: Student Activity Book p. 233 or Activity Workbook p. 86, Signature Sheet (Student Activity Book pp. 205–206 or Activity Workbook p. 78), Blank Sprint Answer Sheet (TRB M57)

✔ **NCTM Standard:**
Number and Operations

 Class Management

If students are struggling with count-bys, you might give a count-by Sprint.

▶ Sprints for 2s PAIRS

Direct students to Student Book page 231 or Activity Workbook page 86 and read aloud the two sprints below.

× 2			÷ 2		
a.	4 × 2	8	a.	12 ÷ 2	6
b.	9 × 2	18	b.	8 ÷ 2	4
c.	1 × 2	2	c.	16 ÷ 2	8
d.	5 × 2	10	d.	10 ÷ 2	5
e.	7 × 2	14	e.	4 ÷ 2	2
f.	3 × 2	6	f.	20 ÷ 2	10
g.	6 × 2	12	g.	2 ÷ 2	1
h.	10 × 2	20	h.	6 ÷ 2	3
i.	2 × 2	4	i.	14 ÷ 2	7
j.	8 × 2	16	j.	18 ÷ 2	9

Have **Student Pairs** check one another's work as you read the answers, marking any incorrect answers and getting signatures.

Activity 2

 5 MINUTES

Goal: Practice count-bys, multiplications, and divisions.

Materials: Check Up materials: Signature Sheet (Student Activity Book pages 205–206 or Activity Workbook p. 77), Blank Sprint Answer Sheet (TRB M57), Study Sheet A (Student Activity Book pp. 207–208 Activity Workbook p. 78), Check Sheet 1, 2, or 3 (Student Activity Book pages 223–224; 229–230; 234–235 or Activity Workbook pp. 83; 85; 87), dry-erase markers (1 per student), sheet protectors (1 per student), Study Sheet Answer Strips (TRB M54), Check Sheet Answer Strips (TRB M55), cardstock; Homework and Remembering p. 145

✔ **NCTM Standard:**
Number and Operations

Check Up and Independent Study

▶ Check Up with 2s, 5s, 9s, and 10s PAIRS

Give **Student Pairs** a few minutes to test one another using Study Sheet A and collecting signatures. For students who have already collected signatures on Study Sheet A, have them study with Check Sheets 1, 2, and 3. You may want to provide Study Sheet Answer Strips or Check Sheet Answer Strips for students to record their answers.

Then have students complete their Study Plan boxes including any multiplications and divisions they missed in the Check Up on Homework and Remembering page 139.

Discuss 9s Patterns

▶ Discuss Patterns on the 120 Poster

WHOLE CLASS

Math Talk

Display the 120 Poster. Review 2s, 5s, and 10s patterns on the poster, and then review the 9s patterns that students explored yesterday. Have a volunteer draw line segments separating groups of 9, up to 90, and then draw a square around each 9s count-by.

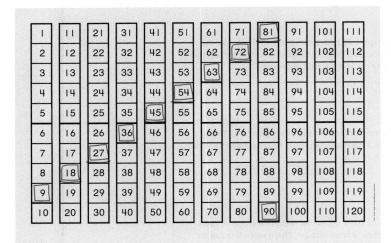

Ask students what patterns they see. The following are some examples.

- The count-bys form a diagonal. When the diagonal reaches the top at 81, it starts again at the bottom at 90.

- Moving up the diagonal, the tens digit increases by 1, while the ones digit decreases by 1.

- The digits of the larger count-bys are the reverse of the digits of the smaller count-bys. For example, the digits of 81 are the reverse of the digits of 18.

- The digits of each count-by have a sum of 9.

- The first count-by is 1 up from the bottom row, the second count-by is 2 up from the bottom row, the third count-by is 3 up from the bottom row, and so on. Because the bottom row is the tens, this shows visually that 9 is 10 − 1, 18 is 20 − 2, 27 is 30 − 3, and so on. You may want to write 10 − 1, 20 − 2, and so on at the bottom of the columns.

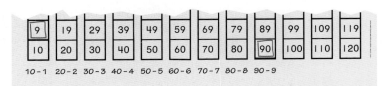

 10 MINUTES

Goal: Discuss 9s patterns on the 120 Poster.

Materials: 120 Poster or 120 Poster (TRB M60)

 NCTM Standard:
Number and Operations

Teaching Note

Math Background As students become more familiar with basic multiplications and divisions, you may want to explore some common divisibility shortcuts. In this lesson, it is noted that the sum of the digits in each 9 count-by is 9. In fact, if the sum of the digits in any number is 9 or a multiple of 9, then the number is divisible by 9.

English Language Learners

Draw a 3 × 4 array. Write the words *row* and *column*.

- **Beginning** Point and say: *Rows go across. There are 3 rows. Columns go down. There are 4 columns.* Have students repeat.
- **Intermediate** Say: *Rows go across.* Ask: **How many** *rows are there*? 3 rows Say: *Columns go down.* Ask: **How many** *columns are there*? 4 columns
- **Advanced** Have students tell the difference between rows and columns.

Teaching the Lesson (continued)

Activity 4

Mixed Word Problems

 15 MINUTES

Goal: Solve multiplication and division word problems.

Materials: Student Activity Book or Hardcover Book pp. 235–236

✔ **NCTM Standards:**
Number and Operations
Representation
Problem Solving

Teaching Note

Making Drawings Drawings are useful for organizing and representing the information in a problem. However, if students always draw and count each individual item, they will not develop an understanding of the meanings of multiplication and division. Equal-Shares drawings and Fast-Array drawings help students understand operations and lead to more efficient computation methods.

As students work on word problems, watch for those who continue to draw individual items, and encourage them to try other types of drawings. When choosing students to present solutions, be sure to select some students who are making quick drawings so the process is modeled for less-advanced students.

7–8
Class Activity

Name _____ Date _____

▶ Solve Word Problems with 2s, 5s, 9s, and 10s

Write an equation to represent each problem. Then solve the problem.

1. Ian planted tulip bulbs in an array with 5 rows and 10 columns. How many bulbs did he plant?
   $5 \times 10 = \square$; 50 bulbs

2. Erin gave 30 basketball cards to her 5 cousins. Each cousin got the same number of cards. How many cards did each cousin get?
   $30 \div 5 = \square$ or $5 \times \square = 30$; 6 cards

3. Martina bought 7 cans of racquetballs. There were 2 balls per can. How many racquetballs did she buy in all?
   $7 \times 2 = \square$; 14 racquetballs

4. The 27 students in the orchestra stood in rows for their school picture. There were 9 students in every row. How many rows of students were there?
   $27 \div 9 = \square$ or $\square \times 9 = 27$; 3 rows

UNIT 7 LESSON 8   Fluency Day for 2s, 5s, 9s, and 10s **235**

Student Activity Book page 235

▶ Solve Word Problems with 2s, 5s, 9s, and 10s

WHOLE CLASS

Using **Solve and Discuss,** have students solve problems 1–4 on Student Activity Book page 235. Circulate as students work and observe the types of drawings they make. Encourage them to make drawings that don't show each individual item, such as Equal-Shares drawings. Make sure a variety of drawings and solution methods are presented.

7–8
Class Activity

Name _____ Date _____

▶ **Math Tools: Fast-Array Drawings**

When you solve a word problem involving an array, you can save time by making a Fast-Array drawing. This type of drawing shows the number of items in each row and column, but does not show every single item.

> **Here is how you might use a Fast-Array drawing for problem 1 on Student Activity Book page 235.**
>
> Show the number of rows and the number of columns. Make a box in the center to show that you don't know the total.
>
> Here are three ways to find the total.
> • Find 5 × 10.
> • Use 10s count-bys to find the total in 5 rows of 10: 10, 20, 30, 40, 50.
> • Use 5s count-bys to find the total in 10 rows of 5: 5, 10, 15, 20, 25, 30, 35, 40, 45, 50.
>
> **Here is how you might use a Fast-Array drawing for problem 4.**
>
> Show the number in each row and the total. Make a box to show that you don't know the number of rows.
>
> Here are two ways to find the number of rows.
> • Find 27 ÷ 9 or solve ☐ × 9 = 27.
> • Count by 9s until you reach 27: 9, 18, 27.

🟡 **Math Journal** **Make a Fast-Array Drawing to solve each problem.**

5. Beth planted tulip bulbs in an array with 9 rows and 6 columns. How many bulbs did she plant?

    54 bulbs

6. The 36 students in the chorus stood in 4 rows for their school picture. How many students were in each row?

    9 students

236 UNIT 7 LESSON 8   Fluency Day for 2s, 5s, 9s, and 10s

Student Activity Book page 236

▶ Math Tools: Fast-Array Drawings WHOLE CLASS

Discuss the Fast-Array drawings shown on Student Book page 236. These are ways to represent an array without drawing each item. Ask students to solve problems 5 and 6 using a Fast-Array drawing, but don't worry if some students have difficulty with this. Some may not be ready for this level of abstraction, and others may have developed their own quick drawing methods. You may wish to have struggling students work with a **Helping Partner**. When students solve array problems in the homework and in upcoming lessons, let them make any type of drawing.

📁 Class Management

Looking Ahead Remind students to take home the Home Check Sheet 3 on Homework and Remembering page 143.

✓ Ongoing Assessment

Write the number 18 on the board. Ask questions such as the following:

▶ How do you know 18 is a 2s count-by? What 2s multiplication can you write for 18? What 2s division is related to that?

▶ How do you know 18 is a 9s count-by? What 9s multiplication can you write for 18? What 9s division is related to that?

▶ How do you know 18 is not a 5s count-by? a 10s count-by?

✓ Quick Quiz

See Assessment Guide for Unit 7 Quick Quiz 2.

② Going Further

Problem Solving Strategy: Organized Lists

▶ Introduce Organized Lists WHOLE CLASS

Discuss with students the meaning of an organized list. Be sure they understand that it is a way to list things in an orderly way to account for all possibilities. Emphasize that an organized list helps us avoid repeating items or forgetting items.

Then write the following problem on the board and work together as a class to solve it.

> Luis has 3 tiles that he wants to put in a row. One tile is red, one is yellow, and one is blue. How many different ways can Luis put the tiles in a row?

● Let's make an organized list to find all the different ways to put the tiles in order. First, let's find all the different ways to arrange the tiles with red being first.

● Who can tell me the ways to list the tiles starting with red? red, yellow, blue; red, blue, yellow

Write the two different ways underneath each other on the board and have a volunteer use the tiles to model the two different ways.

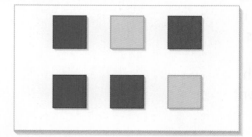

Then repeat this process with yellow first and then blue first. yellow, blue, red; yellow, red, blue; blue, red, yellow; blue, yellow, red

After the organized list is complete, ask how many different ways the tiles can be put in order. 6 different ways

▶ Make Organized Lists INDIVIDUALS

Now present the following problems to students and challenge them to solve them by making organized lists.

> Jo, Marda, and Rob are standing in line to get movie tickets. How many different ways can they be in line? 6 different ways

> Cindy is using the digits 4, 5, and 8 to make as many 3-digit numbers as she can. List all the numbers that Cindy can make. 458, 485, 548, 584, 845, 854

Give the students a few minutes to solve the problems. Then using **Solve and Discuss** have volunteers come to the board and explain how they solved each problem. Encourage the other students to ask questions and make comments.

▶ Make an Organized List with Four Items PAIRS

Have **Student Pairs** solve this variation of the first problem

> Luis has 4 tiles—1 red, 1 yellow, 1 blue, and 1 green. How many different ways can Luis put the tiles in a row if red is always first?

After giving **Student Pairs** some time to solve the problem, have volunteers come to the board and share their organized list with the class.

Students' lists should indicate that there are 6 different ways to arrange the tiles, with red always being first. Then ask students to make an organized list with the other colors being first and find the total number of possible arrangements of the four tiles. A sample student list is shown below.

r, y, b, g	y, r, b, g	b, y, r, g	g, b, r, y
r, y, g, b,	y, r, g, b	b, y, g, r	g, b, y, r
r, b, y, g	y, b, g, r	b, r, g, y	g, r, y, b
r, b g, y	y, b, r, g	b, r, y, g	g, r, b, y
r, g y, b	y, g, b, r	b, g, y, r	g, y, b, r
r, g, b, y	y, g, r, b	b, g, r, y	g, y, r, b

Differentiated Instruction

Write the Story of a Multiplication
Activity Card 7-8

Work: In pairs

Use:
- Poster paper
- Crayons or markers
- Study Sheet A

1. Choose a multiplication from Study Sheet A.

2. Work together to make a poster about your multiplication. The example below shows a poster for the multiplication 4 × 9.

> The Story of 4 × 9   by Chan and Lisa
> Here is a picture   4×9 = 9+9+9+9
> of 4 × 9.   4×9 = 36
>   4 and 9 are factors.
> ○○○○○○○○○   The product is 36.
> ○○○○○○○○○
> ○○○○○○○○○   The division for
>   4 × 9 = 36 is 36 ÷ 9 = 4.

3. Show different ways to represent your multiplication. Be sure to include an array. What addition is related to your multiplication? What division can you show?

Unit 7, Lesson 8   Copyright © Houghton Mifflin Company

Activity Note This activity will help students organize their understanding of multiplication and division. If time permits, have students choose more than one multiplication to illustrate.

Math Writing Prompt

Summarize Complete the following two sentences: One thing I have learned about multiplication is _____. One thing I have learned about division is _____.

Soar to Success Math **Software Support**

Warm Up 12.23

2-5-9-10 Multiplication Spin
Activity Card 7-8 ▲

Work: In pairs

Use:
- TRB M61 (Spinner C)
- Paper clip
- TRB M25 (Game Cards)

1. Make a spinner like the one shown. Shuffle the Game Cards and place them in a stack face down.

2. Take turns. Spin the spinner and draw the top card from the stack. Multiply the two numbers and record the product on a sheet of paper.

2 × 8 = 16

3. Continue taking turns until each player has found four products.

4. Find the total of your products. The player with the greater total wins.

Unit 7, Lesson 8   Copyright © Houghton Mifflin Company

Activity Note Players should verify the products their partners have calculated. Using a timer for each turn and subtracting incorrect answers from the total could make the game more challenging.

Math Writing Prompt

Compare How is multiplication related to addition? How is multiplication related to division? Give examples to explain your answers.

MegaMath Grades K-6 **Software Support**

Country Countdown, Counting Critters, Level Z

Multiplication Riddles
Activity Card 7-8 ■

Work: In pairs

1. **Work Together** Solve each riddle below.

> I am an odd number between 1 and 10.
> I am a factor of 30.
> I am also a factor of 50.
> What number am I? 5

> I am greater than 36 and less than 70.
> One of my factors is 9.
> I am an even number.
> What number am I? 54

2. Now make up your own multiplication riddle and exchange with your partner to solve.

Unit 7, Lesson 8   Copyright © Houghton Mifflin Company

Activity Note Tell students that a good riddle will have only one possible answer. Challenge students to use just enough clues to allow only one possible answer.

Math Writing Prompt

Investigate Math Suppose you cannot remember how to find 7 × 9. Explain two different ways you could use to find the product.

DESTINATION Math **Software Support**

Course II: Module 2: Unit 2: Finding Products less than 100

3 Homework and Spiral Review

Homework **Goal:** Additional Practice

✓ Include students' completed Homework page as part of their portfolios.

7–8	Name _____	Date _____
Homework

Study Plan
_____
_____
                              Homework Helper

Write an equation for each situation. Then solve the problem.

1. Quinn rode his bike 35 miles. He stopped for water every 5 miles. How many times did Quinn stop for water?
$35 \div 5 = \square$ or
$\square \times 5 = 35$; 7 times

2. Roy had 12 bottles of juice. He put them in the refrigerator in 2 rows. How many bottles were in each row?
$12 \div 2 = \square$ or
$2 \times \square = 12$; 6 bottles

3. Melinda has 5 cousins. She called each one on the phone 4 times this month. How many phone calls did she make to her cousins this month?
$5 \times 4 = \square$; 20 phone calls

4. Janelle won 27 tickets at the fair. She traded the tickets for 9 prizes. Each prize was worth the same number of tickets. How many tickets were each prize worth?
$27 \div 9 = \square$ or
$9 \times \square = 27$; 3 tickets

5. Eric had 2 picnic baskets. He put 7 apples in each one. How many apples did he put into the picnic baskets?
$2 \times 7 = \square$ or
$\square \div 2 = 7$; 14 apples

6. Grace has read 2 chapters in each of her 9 books. How many chapters has she read in all?
$2 \times 9 = \square$ or $\square \div 2 = 9$;
18 chapters

UNIT 7 LESSON 8   Fluency Day for 2s, 5s, 9s, and 10s **145**

Homework and Remembering page 145

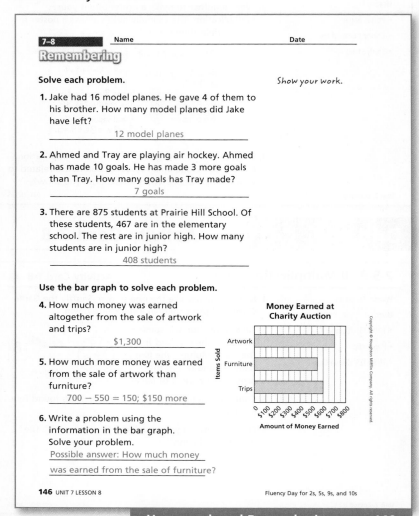

Remembering **Goal:** Spiral Review

This Remembering page would be appropriate anytime after today's lesson.

7–8	Name _____	Date _____
Remembering

Solve each problem.   *Show your work.*

1. Jake had 16 model planes. He gave 4 of them to his brother. How many model planes did Jake have left?
12 model planes

2. Ahmed and Tray are playing air hockey. Ahmed has made 10 goals. He has made 3 more goals than Tray. How many goals has Tray made?
7 goals

3. There are 875 students at Prairie Hill School. Of these students, 467 are in the elementary school. The rest are in junior high. How many students are in junior high?
408 students

Use the bar graph to solve each problem.

4. How much money was earned altogether from the sale of artwork and trips?
$1,300

5. How much more money was earned from the sale of artwork than furniture?
$700 - 550 = 150$; $150 more

6. Write a problem using the information in the bar graph. Solve your problem.
Possible answer: How much money was earned from the sale of furniture?

Money Earned at Charity Auction

(bar graph: Items Sold — Artwork, Furniture, Trips vs. Amount of Money Earned $0–$800)

146 UNIT 7 LESSON 8   Fluency Day for 2s, 5s, 9s, and 10s

Homework and Remembering page 146

Home or School Activity

Literature Connection

Amanda Bean's Amazing Dream Read aloud Cindy Neuschwander's book about moving from counting to multiplying. In this book, Amanda Bean counts everything by ones, twos, fives, and tens until she learns to use multiplication instead of skip counting. Have students discuss how the story shows that multiplication can be used instead of counting.

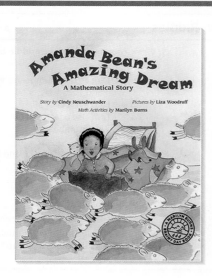

UNIT 7

LESSON

9

Multiply and Divide with 3

REAL WORLD Problem Solving

Lesson Objectives

- Explore patterns in 3s count-bys, multiplications, and divisions.
- Learn a strategy for finding count-bys and products for multipliers greater than 5.

Vocabulary

product
multiplier
commutative
divisor

The Day at a Glance

Today's Goals	Materials
① Teaching the Lesson **A1:** Take Sprints for 10s multiplications and divisions. **A2:** Practice 3s count-bys, multiplications, and divisions. **A3:** Explore patterns in 3s count-bys, multiplications, and divisions. **A4:** Review 5s patterns and count-bys. **② Going Further** ▶ Extension: Represent Numbers Different Ways ▶ Differentiated Instruction **③ Homework and Spiral Review**	**Lesson Activities** Student Activity Book pp. 237–242 or Student Hardcover Book pp. 237–242 and Activity Workbook p. 88 (includes Check Sheet) Homework and Remembering pp. 147–150 Signature Sheet Blank Sprint Answer Sheet Check Up materials Study Sheet A Check Sheet 1, 2, or 3 Dry-erase markers Sheet protectors Study Sheet Answer Strips (TRB M54) Check Sheet Answer Strips (TRB M55)	Card stock Class Multiplication Table Transparency of Student Activity Book pages 239–240 (optional) Overhead projector (optional) **Going Further** Activity Cards 7-9 Game Cards (TRB M25) MathBoard materials Math Journals

123 Use Math Talk today!

Keeping Skills Sharp

Quick Practice ⏱ 5 MINUTES	Daily Routines
Goal: Practice 9s count-bys, multiplications, and divisions. **Materials:** Class Multiplication Table Poster, pointer Use the Multiplication Table and the number "9" for the activities. **Repeated Quick Practice** Use these Quick Practice activities from previous lessons. **9s Multiplications in Order** (See Unit 7 Lesson 4.) **Mixed 9s Multiplications** (See Unit 7 Lesson 2.) **Mixed 9s Divisions** (See Unit 7 Lesson 5.)	**Homework Review** If students give incorrect answers, have them explain how they found the answers. **Write Numbers Different Ways** Write the number 18 on the board. Have students write multiplication expressions that equal this product. Possible answer: 9 × 2

Teaching the Lesson

Activity 1

Assess 10s

 5 MINUTES

Goal: Take Sprints for 10s multiplications and divisions.

Materials: Student Activity Book page 237 or Activity Workbook p. 88, Signature Sheet (Student Activity Book pages 205–206 or Activity Workbook p. 77), Blank Sprint Answer Sheet (TRB M57)

✔ **NCTM Standard:**
Number and Operations

 Class Management

If students are struggling with count-bys, you might give a count-by Sprint.

▶ Sprints for 10s [INDIVIDUALS]

Direct students to Student Book page 237 or Activity Workbook page 88 and read aloud the two Sprints below.

	× 10			÷ 10	
a.	2 × 10	20	a.	50 ÷ 10	5
b.	7 × 10	70	b.	100 ÷ 10	10
c.	4 × 10	40	c.	20 ÷ 10	2
d.	1 × 10	10	d.	10 ÷ 10	1
e.	10 × 10	100	e.	70 ÷ 10	7
f.	8 × 10	80	f.	90 ÷ 10	9
g.	3 × 10	30	g.	30 ÷ 10	3
h.	6 × 10	60	h.	60 ÷ 10	6
i.	9 × 10	90	i.	40 ÷ 10	4
j.	5 × 10	50	j.	80 ÷ 10	8

Have **Student Pairs** check one another's work as you read the answers, marking any incorrect answers and getting signatures.

Activity 2

Check Up and Independent Study

 5 MINUTES

Goal: Practice 3s count-bys, multiplications, and divisions.

Materials: Check Up materials: Signature Sheet, Blank Sprint Answer Sheet (TRB M57), Study Sheet A, Check Sheet 1, 2, or 3, dry-erase markers (1 per student), sheet protectors (1 per student), Study Sheet Answer Strips (TRB M54), Check Sheet Answer Strips (TRB M55), cardstock; Homework and Remembering page 149

✔ **NCTM Standard:**
Number and Operations

▶ Check Up with 2s, 5s, 9s, and 10s [PAIRS]

Give **Student Pairs** a few minutes to test each other using Study Sheet A. The student's partner reads the exercise from the study sheet as the student writes the answers. The partner checks the answers, and initials the appropriate section of the Signature Sheet if the student doesn't make any mistakes. For students who have collected signatures for Study Sheet A, have them study with Check Sheets 1, 2, or 3.

Students who made mistakes on the 2s Sprints in Lesson 8 (or who were absent) may take repeat or make-up Sprints at this time. Students can record their answers on Blank Sprint Answer Sheet (TRB M57).

Have students complete the Study Plan box on the top of Homework and Remembering page 149. They should include 3s practice along with any multiplications or divisions they missed in the Check Up.

Explore 3s Patterns

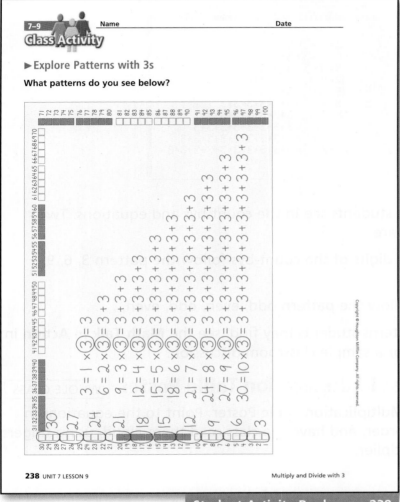

Student Activity Book page 238

 15 MINUTES

Goal: Explore patterns in 3s count-bys, multiplications, and divisions.

Materials: Student Activity Book or Hardcover Book p. 238, Class Multiplication Table Poster

 NCTM Standard:
Number and Operations

English Language Learners

Write 2 × 3 = 6 on the board. Write *product* and *factors*.

- **Beginning** Say: The *factors* are 2 and 3. The *product* is 6. Have students repeat.
- **Intermediate** Ask: What are the *factors*? 2, 3 What is the *product*? 6
- **Advanced** Say: The numbers we multiply are the ___. factors Ask: What do we call the answer? product

---

▶ Explore Patterns with 3s WHOLE CLASS

Tell students that today they will be thinking about groups of 3. Have students brainstorm a list of things in the real world that come in groups of 3. wheels on a tricycle, teaspoons in a tablespoon, leaves on a clover, sides on a triangle, legs on a tripod, and so on

Have students look at Student Book page 238. Model the steps of this activity on the Class MathBoard as students follow along on their MathBoards.

Have students circle sequential groups of 3, up to 30, on the Number Path and write the totals so far next to each group. After they circle the first group, have them say in unison "1 group of 3 is 3"; after they circle the second group, have them say "2 groups of 3 are 6"; and so on. Then point to the totals and have students read them aloud: 3, 6, and so on. Use this to facilitate a discussion of the patterns in 3s multiplications.

Activity continued ▶

❶ Teaching the Lesson (continued)

Teaching Note

Commutativity You may need to remind students that multiplication is commutative. For example, if they know 3 × 2, they also know 2 × 3.

To underscore the fact that 2 × 3 = 3 × 2, write "= 2 + 2 + 2" after "3 + 3" on the Class MathBoard. Similarly, illustrate that 5 × 3 = 3 × 5 and 10 × 3 = 3 × 10.

 Math Talk in Action

Jose: I think I see a pattern in the products. The tens digits are 0, 0, 0, 1, 1, 1, 2, 2, 2 and then a 3. They look like they go in order.

Shayna: I see that too, and I see another pattern. If you add 3 + 27, you get 30. If you add 6 + 24, you also get 30.

Larry: And if you add 9 + 21 or 12 + 18, that's 30 also!

As students follow along, write and read a multiplication equation for each count-by. Then have students write a repeated addition expression for each multiplication equation. For example, for 2 × 3, ask students: How many 3s do we need to add together? 2 So what should I write? 3 + 3

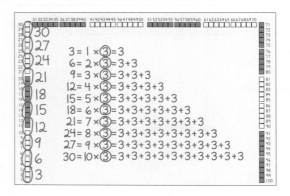

Ask what patterns students see in the count-bys and equations. Two common patterns are:

- The sums of the digits of the count-bys follow the pattern 3, 6, 9, 3, 6, 9, ...

- The products follow the pattern odd, even, odd, even, ...

For additional patterns students may find, see the **Math Talk in Action** in the side column for a sample classroom discussion.

▶ Use the Class Multiplication Table Poster   WHOLE CLASS

Display the Class Multiplication Table Poster. Point to the equations in the 3s column in order, and have the class read them aloud, using fingers to show each multiplier.

1 times 3 equals 3.   2 times 3 equals 6.   3 times 3 equals 9.

Point to each equation in the 3s column again, this time having students say only the count-bys. Again, have them use their fingers to indicate the multipliers.

3   6   9

Present several 3s multiplications (such as 5 × 3 and 7 × 3), and have students count up on their fingers to find the answers. For example, to find 5 × 3, they should count by 3s, raising a finger for each count-by, until five fingers are raised.

5 times 3 equals 15.

▶ Divide with 3s [WHOLE CLASS]

Have students erase the repeated addition parts of the equations on their MathBoards. Write the first two or three division equations as a class, and then have students work independently to write the rest.

$3 = 1 \times 3$	$3 \div 3 = 1$
$6 = 2 \times 3$	$6 \div 3 = 2$
$9 = 3 \times 3$	$9 \div 3 = 3$
$12 = 4 \times 3$	$12 \div 3 = 4$
$15 = 5 \times 3$	$15 \div 3 = 5$
$18 = 6 \times 3$	$18 \div 3 = 6$
$21 = 7 \times 3$	$21 \div 3 = 7$
$24 = 8 \times 3$	$24 \div 3 = 8$
$27 = 9 \times 3$	$27 \div 3 = 9$
$30 = 10 \times 3$	$30 \div 3 = 10$

▶ Use Fingers to Divide [WHOLE CLASS]

Write this division and related multiplication on the board:

$$24 \div 3 = \square$$
$$\square \times 3 = 24$$

Have students find the answer by counting by 3s on their fingers up to 24. Eight fingers will be raised, so there are 8 groups of 3 in 24. So, $24 \div 3 = 8$.

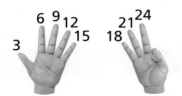

24 divided by 3 equals 8.

Repeat this for several more divisions with a divisor of 3. Have student volunteers demonstrate this in front of the class. After students have modeled divisions with their fingers, encourage the class to say or write the related multiplication.

The Learning Classroom

Math Talk Aspire to make your classroom a place where all students listen to understand one another. Explain to students that this is different from just being quiet when someone else is talking. This involves thinking about what a person is saying so that you could explain it yourself or help them explain it more clearly. Also, they need to listen so that they can ask a question or help the explainer. Explain that listening carefully can help learn a concept better.

Teaching Note

Home Practice Charts For variation and to emphasize the relationship between multiplication and division, have students look at the home practice chart for the 3s on page 147 of the Homework and Remembering book. Students can practice divisions using the middle mixed up multiplication column by covering the left column factors with a pencil or pen (use one that does not roll) and finding the unknown factor. They can practice multiplications using the right mixed up division column by covering the left column products. As they solve each problem, they uncover the answer to check. Have students try both of these practice methods and discuss in general how students are organizing their time at home to do their practice (e.g., quiet place, alone or with their Home Helper or both, every night at a regular time, etc.).

Activity 4

Use Shortcuts

 15 MINUTES

Goal: Review 5s patterns and count-bys.

Materials: Student Activity Book or Hardcover Book pp. 239–240, transparency of Student Book pages 239–240 (optional), overhead projector (optional), counters

 NCTM Standard:
Number and Operations

 Class Management

For this activity, you may want to copy Student Book pages 239–240 onto overhead transparencies and teach this activity using an overhead projector.

The Learning Classroom

Helping Community Students at the board may get stuck at some point. They usually welcome help from another student at that point. Allowing other students to help instead of you will enable them to assume responsibility for each other's learning. Ask who they would like to help them. You can move on to another explainer while they redo their work. Of course, sometimes it is fine just to go ahead and have the whole class help the student with you leading with questions.

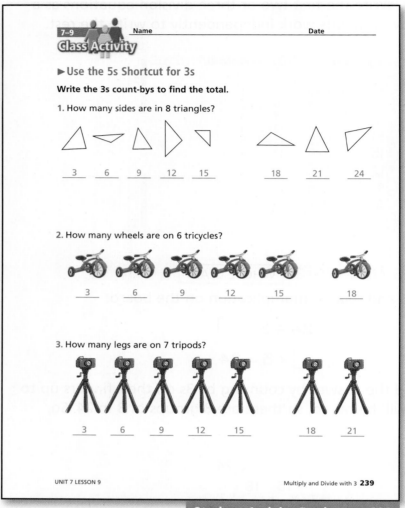

Student Activity Book page 239

▶ Use the 5s Shortcut for 3s [WHOLE CLASS]

Have students complete exercises 1–3 on Student Book page 239. Draw eight triangles on the board as they are grouped on the page.

Have a volunteer come to the board and write in the count-bys. Ask students what they notice about how the triangles are grouped. The first five objects are grouped together.

● In exercise 1, there are 5 triangles plus 3 more triangles. How can we use the fact that five 3s is equal to 15 to count the number of sides in the triangles faster? Write 15 under the fifth triangle, and then count up by three more 3s.

Repeat the same process as above to count the tricycle wheels in exercise 2 and the tripod legs in exercise 3.

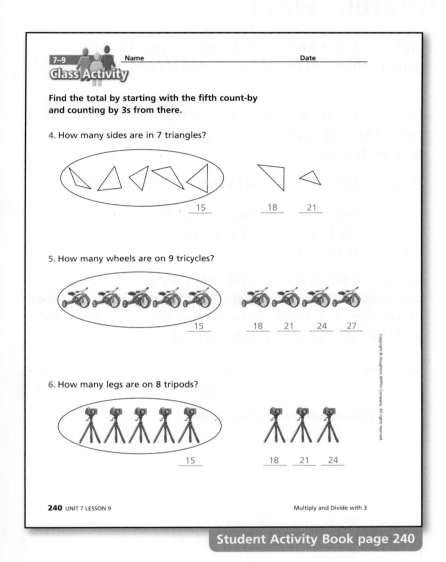

7-9 Name _____ Date _____

Class Activity

Find the total by starting with the fifth count-by and counting by 3s from there.

4. How many sides are in 7 triangles?

15   18   21

5. How many wheels are on 9 tricycles?

15   18   21   24   27

6. How many legs are on 8 tripods?

15   18   21   24

240 UNIT 7 LESSON 9   Multiply and Divide with 3

Student Activity Book page 240

Direct students to Student Book page 240. Using the **Solve and Discuss** structure, have students complete exercises 4–6.

Write 7 × 3 on the board. Ask if anyone can think of a way to use the "5s shortcut" to find the product. Start with all 5 fingers on one hand up to make 15, and then count on two more 3s.

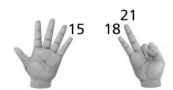

21
15 18

7 times 3 equals 21.

Have students use this shortcut to find 6 × 3 and 9 × 3.

Ongoing Assessment

Ask students the following question.

► How do you use the 5s shortcut to find the product of 9 × 3?

► Draw triangles to explain your answer.

Multiply and Divide with 3   **541**

② Going Further

Extension: Represent Numbers Different Ways

Goals: Represent numbers in different ways; Identify and generate equivalent forms of whole numbers.

Materials: Student Activity Book or Hardcover Book pp. 241–242

✓ **NCTM Standards:**
Number and Operations   Algebra and Functions

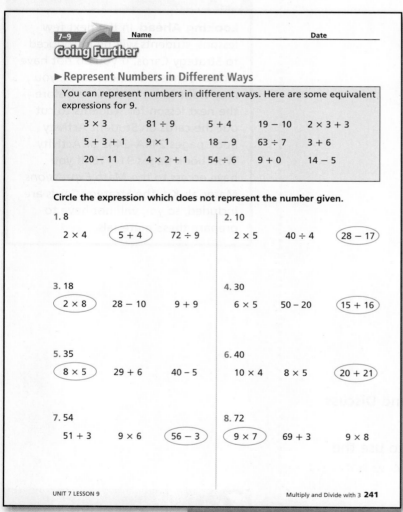

Student Activity Book page 241

▶ **Represent Numbers in Different Ways**

WHOLE CLASS

Ask for Ideas Elicit from students in what different ways they have already represented numbers. (word form, expanded form with numbers (125 = 100 + 20 + 5), and expanded form with place value names

(125 = 12 tens and 7 ones). Explain that in this activity they will represent numbers using different expressions.

Direct students' attention to the top of Student Book page 241 and have a volunteer read aloud the first two sentences.

● What does 3 × 3 equal? What is 81 divided by 9? 9; 9

Give students a few minutes to perform the calculations to check that each expression shown is an equivalent form for 9.

Be sure students understand that they are to find the expression that is not an equivalent form for the number in exercises 1–8. Have students complete exercises 1–16 and then use **Solve and Discuss** to check the answers.

Name _____   Date _____

Write 3 equivalent expressions for each number.
Answers will vary.   Check student's answers.

9. 2
_____

10. 3
_____

11. 5
_____

12. 24
_____

13. 36
_____

14. 50
_____

15. 63
_____

16. 100
_____

242 UNIT 7 LESSON 9   Multiply and Divide with 3

Student Activity Book page 242

Differentiated Instruction

Act It Out!

Activity Card 7-9 ●

Work: In pairs

Decide:

Who will be Student 1 and who will be Student 2 for the first round.

1. Use the price list below for a shopping trip activity.

> 1 lemon – 5¢
> 1 apple – 9¢
> 1 bunch of carrots – 10¢
> 1 banana – 7¢
> 1 orange – 8¢
> 1 tomato – 6¢
> 1 cherry – 3¢

2. Student 1: Choose one or more items to buy, and list the items on a sheet of paper.

3. Student 2: Say aloud the total cost of 3 of each item chosen. Put the cost beside each item on the list.

4. **Work Together** Check the totals. Then switch roles and make another shopping trip.

Unit 7, Lesson 9   Copyright © Houghton Mifflin Company

Activity Note If students have difficulty with this activity, suggest that they count by 3s from 1 through 10 before beginning the activity.

 Math Writing Prompt

Inverse Relationships Write two multiplication equations using the numbers 3, 7, and 21. Then write two related division sentences.

 **Software Support**

Warm Up 12.14

Call It

Activity Card 7-9 ▲

Work: In pairs

Use:

• TRB M25 (Game Cards 1–10)

1. Take turns. Shuffle the cards and put them in a pile face down.

2. Hold up each card, one at a time. Your partner multiplies the number by 3 and calls out the answer.

 9   (9 × 3 = 27)

3. Check each answer and set aside any cards that had wrong answers.

4. Repeat the activity with any cards in the wrong answer pile until all of your partner's answers are correct. Then switch roles and repeat the activity again.

Unit 7, Lesson 9   Copyright © Houghton Mifflin Company

Activity Note Remind students that knowing 10 times a number can help them find the product of that number times 9. For example, 9 × 3 = (10 × 3) − 3, or 30 − 3 = 27.

 Math Writing Prompt

Explain Your Thinking Explain how the 5s shortcut can help when you don't know the answer to a multiplication.

MEGA MATH Grades K-6 **Software Support**

Country Countdown, Counting Critters, Level V

Mayan Multiplication

Activity Card 7-9 ■

Work: In pairs

Use:

• MathBoard materials

1. The Mayans lived in Central America about 3,000 years ago. Their number system included only these three symbols.

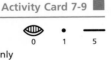
0   1   5

2. Study the examples below. They show how the Mayans combined their three symbols to write other numbers.

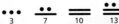
3   7   10   13

3. Take turns writing and solving multiplications with the 3 Mayan symbols. The multiplication 3 × 7 is shown below.

••• × •• = 21

Unit 7, Lesson 9   Copyright © Houghton Mifflin Company

Activity Note Be sure students understand that combining numbers in the Mayan system is done by first adding 5s, if possible, and then 1s.

 Math Writing Prompt

Investigate Math How can you use repeated subtraction to find the answer to 21 ÷ 3?

DESTINATION Math **Software Support**

Course II: Module 2: Unit 2: Repeated Addition and Arrays

③ Homework and Spiral Review

Homework 7-9 **Goal:** Additional Practice

This Homework page provides practice in 3s multiplications and divisions.

Remembering 7-9 **Goal:** Spiral Review

This Remembering page would be appropriate anytime after today's lesson.

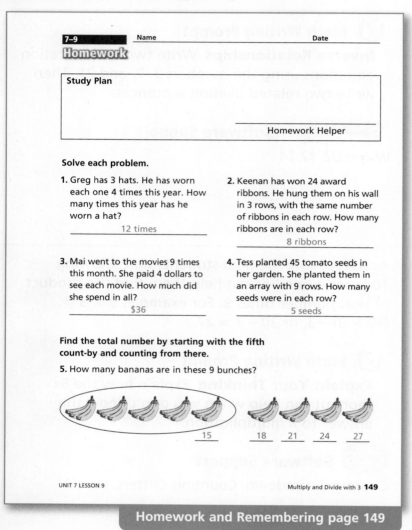

7-9	Name	Date

Homework

Study Plan

_____

Homework Helper

Solve each problem.

1. Greg has 3 hats. He has worn each one 4 times this year. How many times this year has he worn a hat?

   12 times

2. Keenan has won 24 award ribbons. He hung them on his wall in 3 rows, with the same number of ribbons in each row. How many ribbons are in each row?

   8 ribbons

3. Mai went to the movies 9 times this month. She paid 4 dollars to see each movie. How much did she spend in all?

   _$36_

4. Tess planted 45 tomato seeds in her garden. She planted them in an array with 9 rows. How many seeds were in each row?

   5 seeds

Find the total number by starting with the fifth count-by and counting from there.

5. How many bananas are in these 9 bunches?

   15   18   21   24   27

UNIT 7 LESSON 9   Multiply and Divide with 3 **149**

Homework and Remembering page 149

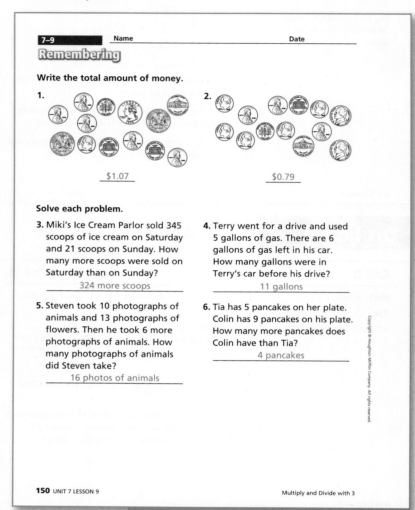

7-9	Name	Date

Remembering

Write the total amount of money.

1. $1.07

2. $0.79

Solve each problem.

3. Miki's Ice Cream Parlor sold 345 scoops of ice cream on Saturday and 21 scoops on Sunday. How many more scoops were sold on Saturday than on Sunday?

   324 more scoops

4. Terry went for a drive and used 5 gallons of gas. There are 6 gallons of gas left in his car. How many gallons were in Terry's car before his drive?

   11 gallons

5. Steven took 10 photographs of animals and 13 photographs of flowers. Then he took 6 more photographs of animals. How many photographs of animals did Steven take?

   16 photos of animals

6. Tia has 5 pancakes on her plate. Colin has 9 pancakes on his plate. How many more pancakes does Colin have than Tia?

   4 pancakes

150 UNIT 7 LESSON 9   Multiply and Divide with 3

Homework and Remembering page 150

Home and School Activity

 Sports Connection

Numbers in Sports Numbers and sports are connected in many ways. There are a certain number of players on a field, teams tally up points to determine the winner, players are identified by a number, and so on. The number 3 is important in baseball, football, and basketball. In baseball, for example, if there are three strikes, the batter is out. Have students find out why 3 is important in these sports. Have students share their answers.

Multiplication and Area

Lesson Objectives

- Understand the area model for multiplications.
- Learn a shortcut for solving multiplication problems.

The Day at a Glance

Today's Goals	Materials
1 Teaching the Lesson **A1:** Practice count-bys, multiplications, and divisions. **A2:** Introduce Strategy Cards. **A3:** Write multiplication equations to represent areas of rectangles and draw rectangles whose areas represent multiplication equations. **A4:** Use the area model to develop a multiplication strategy. **2 Going Further** ► Differentiated Instruction **3 Homework and Spiral Review**	**Lesson Activities** Student Activity Book pp. 243–246 or Student Hardcover Book pp. 243–246 and Activity Workbook pp. 89–116 (includes Check Sheets, Study Sheet, and Strategy Cards) Homework and Remembering pp. 151–180 Check Up materials Folders Signature Sheet Blank Sprint Answer Sheet Study Sheet A or B Check Sheet 1, 2, or 3 Dry-erase markers Sheet protectors Study Sheet Answer Strips Check Sheet Answer Strips Card stock Strategy Cards Paper clips Plastic bags or envelopes MathBoard materials Dot Array (TRB M1) **Going Further** Activity Cards 7-10 MathBoard materials or Dot Grid (TRB M1) Inch Rulers Centimeter Rulers or (TRB M26) Square corner (a piece of paper, index card or envelope) Math Journals 123 *Use* **Math Talk** *today!*

Keeping Skills Sharp

Quick Practice ⏱ 5 MINUTES

Goal: Practice 9s count-bys, multiplications, and divisions.

Materials: Class Multiplication Table Poster, pointer Use the Class Multiplication Table Poster and the number "9" for these activities.

Repeated Quick Practice
Use these Quick Practice activities from previous lessons.

9s Multiplications in Order (See Unit 7 Lesson 4.)

Mixed 9s Multiplications (See Unit 7 Lesson 2.)

Mixed 9s Divisions (See Unit 7 Lesson 5.)

Daily Routines

Strategy Problem At the park, there are birds and dogs. Altogether there are 6 animals and 16 legs. How many birds and dogs are at the park? Show your work. 4 birds, 2 dogs;

	Amount	Legs	Amount	Legs
Birds	3	6	4	8
Dogs	3	12	2	8
Total	6	18>16	6	16

Teaching the Lesson

Check Up and Independent Study

 5 MINUTES

Goal: Practice count-bys, multiplications, and divisions.

Materials: Folders, Check Up materials: Signature Sheet (Student Activity Book pp. 205–206 or Activity Workbook p. 77), Blank Sprint Answer Sheet (TRB M57), Study Sheet A or B (Student Activity Book pages 207–208; 243–244 or Activity Workbook p. 78; 89), Check Sheet 1, 2, or 3 (Student Activity Book pages 223–224; 229–230; 235 or Activity Workbook pp. 83; 85; 87), dry-erase markers (1 per student), sheet protectors (1 per student), Study Sheet Answer Strips (TRB M54), Check Sheet Answer Strips (TRB M55), cardstock; Homework and Remembering Book p. 179

✔ **NCTM Standard:**
Number and Operations

The Learning Classroom

Helping Community When giving students a few minutes to test one another, encourage an environment of communication, collaboration, and patience, rather than one of competition. While some students may understand the answers faster than others, remind students that everyone can learn from each other, and it is important to be patient and helpful.

▶ **Check Up with 2s, 3s, 5s, 9s, and 10s** PAIRS

Have each student write his or her name on Study Sheet B and slide it into a sheet protector. Explain that this sheet includes count-bys, multiplications, and divisions for 3s and for the next few factors students will study. Give **Student Pairs** a few minutes to test each other using Study Sheets A or B and get signatures.

For students who have already collected signatures on Study Sheet A, have students study with Check Sheets 1–3. You may want to have extra Study Sheet and Check Sheet Answer Strips available for students who prefer writing their answers down. Then give students a minute or two to study independently.

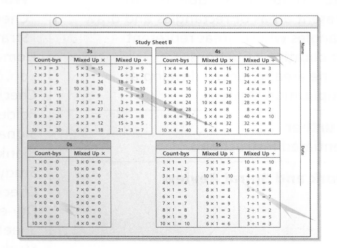

Students who made mistakes on the 10s Sprints from lesson 9 (or who were absent) may take repeat or make-up Sprints at this time. Students can record their answers on Blank Sprint Answer Sheet (Copymaster M57)

Have students complete the Study Plan box on Homework and Remembering page 179. They should include any multiplications or divisions they missed in the check up.

Strategy Cards

▶ Introduce the Strategy Cards WHOLE CLASS

Distribute a set of Strategy Cards for 2s, 5s, and 9s multiplications and divisions to each student. If you have access to the *Math Expressions* materials kits, you will not have to prepare these. If you do not have Strategy Cards, have students cut out the 2s, 5s, and 9s cards on Student Activity Book pages 244A–244Z or Activity Workbook pp. 91–116. Allow students a minute or two to examine the fronts and backs of the cards.

Sample Multiplication Card

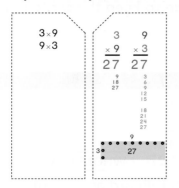

Sample Division Card

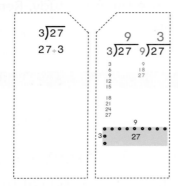

Ask students to describe the features of the cards. Make sure these things are mentioned:

- The front side of each card (the exercises side) has two exercises.
- The two exercises on the multiplication cards have the same two factors, in different orders.
- The two exercises on a multiplication card have the same answer.
- On the division cards, the same exercise is written in two different ways.
- The back side of each card (the equation side) shows the complete equations, including the answers, for both exercises.
- There are count-bys, up to the product, for both factors.
- There is a space between the fifth count-by and the rest of the count-bys.
- There is a Fast-Array drawing that shows the product and the two factors.
- On the division cards, one equation shows a product divided by one number in a factor pair, and the other shows the product divided by the other factor.

Explain to students that the Fast-Array drawing shows the relationships among two factors and their product and are called factor rectangles on the cards. The product is in the center, and the two factors are on the sides.

Activity continued ▶

---

 10 MINUTES

Goal: Introduce Strategy Cards.

Materials: Student Activity Book pages 244A–244Z or Activity Workbook pp. 91–116, paper clips, plastic bags or envelopes

 NCTM Standard: Number and Operations

Teaching Note

What to Expect from Students As students use the Strategy Cards over the next few lessons, some will find ways to use the count-bys and fast-array drawings to help them solve multiplications and divisions. In Lesson 13, students will have the opportunity to share and discuss the strategies they have developed.

Alternate Approach

Students can also use the cards in other ways:

▶ As flashcards: Students can look at the exercise side of the card, say the answer, and turn the card over to check, or the student's partner can hold up a card with the exercise side facing the student. The student says the answer, and the partner says whether the answer is right or wrong.

▶ As a study tool: Students can use the exercise side of the cards to learn and study multiplications and divisions. Students can cut out the home set of Strategy Cards on Homework and Remembering pages 141–166, and use them as part of their homework study routine.

Teaching the Lesson (continued)

📁 **Class Management**

Looking Ahead If you have access to the *Math Expressions* Materials kit, the Strategy Cards are included, so you will not have to prepare these materials. If students need replacement Strategy Cards use TRB M63–M88.

Have students sort their cards into three piles: those with answers they know quickly, those with answers they know slowly, and those with answers they don't know yet. Give them a few minutes to study and practice with the cards in the "know slowly" and "don't know" piles. As they practice, they may be able to move some of the cards into other piles.

Give paper clips to each student to put around the three piles and have them store the piles in plastic bags or envelopes. Tell them they can use the cards to study during the daily class Check Up. They should update their piles as they learn more multiplications and divisions.

There is a home set of Strategy Cards on Homework and Remembering pages 151–176. As part of their homework, students should cut out the cards and use them to study. Remind them to keep the cards in a safe place at home.

Activity 3

Multiplication as Area

 20 MINUTES

Goal: Write multiplication equations to represent areas of rectangles and draw rectangles whose areas represent multiplication equations.

Materials: MathBoard materials, Dot Array (TRB M1), Student Activity Book or Hardcover Book p. 245

✔ **NCTM Standards:**
Number and Operations
Geometry
Measurement

 Teaching Note

Math Background Here multiplication is represented visually using the area of a rectangle. Students will multiply the number of units in a row of a rectangle by the number of rows. Combining areas of adjoining rectangles or breaking one rectangle apart into two rectangles helps form the foundation for discussion of the Distributive property and the development of the skills needed for multi-digit multiplication.

▶ Explore Multiplication as Area WHOLE CLASS

Work on the dot array side of the Class MathBoard as students work on their MathBoards. You can also use the Dot Array (Copymaster M1).

First have students draw a unit square by connecting four dots as shown.

● This small square is called 1 square unit. Use this small square to measure the sizes of other squares and rectangles.

Have students add two more squares to form a rectangle.

● This rectangle contains 3 of our little squares. It has an area of 3 square units. The area of a rectangle, or any shape, is the number of square units that fit inside it.

Have students add a second row of three squares.

● Count the square units in this rectangle. What is the area of this rectangle? 6 square units

● How many rows of square units are in this rectangle? 2 How many square units are in each row? 3

● We can call this a 2-by-3 rectangle, just as we call an array with 2 rows and 3 columns a 2-by-3 array.

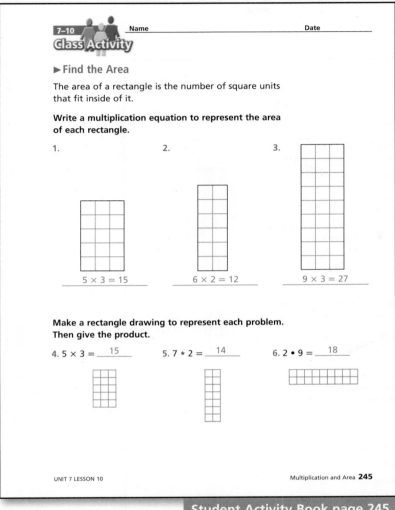

The Student Activity Book page shows:

7-10
Class Activity

Name _____ Date _____

▶ Find the Area

The area of a rectangle is the number of square units that fit inside of it.

Write a multiplication equation to represent the area of each rectangle.

1.

2.

3.

5 × 3 = 15   6 × 2 = 12   9 × 3 = 27

Make a rectangle drawing to represent each problem. Then give the product.

4. 5 × 3 = ___15___   5. 7 * 2 = ___14___   6. 2 • 9 = ___18___

UNIT 7 LESSON 10   Multiplication and Area **245**

▶ Find the Area WHOLE CLASS

Have students add a third row of three squares.

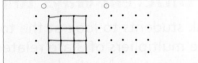

- How many rows of square units are in this rectangle? 3 How many square units are in each row? 3

- If the number of rows of square units in a rectangle is known and the number of square units in each row is known, how can the area be found? Multiply the number of rows by the number of square units in each row. What is the area of this rectangle? 9 square units

Have students add another row of squares to their rectangles and find the area. 12 units Have students continue adding more rows to the square until they have 8 rows of 3 square units.

Have students work independently to complete exercises 1–6 on Student Book page 245. Point out that students now have three ways to think about a multiplication situation: as the total in repeated groups of the same size, as the number of objects in an array, and as the area of a rectangle.

Teaching Note

Watch For! Watch for students who simply count the total number of units to arrive at the area. Encourage them to use multiplication instead. To help them do this, have them shade the top row and left column in order to visualize their multiplication equation.

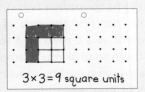

3×3 = 9 square units

Multiplication and Area   **549**

Teaching the Lesson (continued)

Activity 4

Combine Areas

 Math Talk in Action

Ashley: I can't remember what 8 × 3 is.

Sanjay: Do you know the answer to 5 × 3?

Ashley: Sure, it's 15.

Sanjay: What about 3 × 3? Do you know that one?

Ashley: Yes, it's 9.

Sanjay: Well, since 8 = 5 + 3, you can find 8 × 3 by adding 5 × 3 and 3 × 3.

Ashley: So the answer is 15 + 9, which is 24. That's a great strategy!

 Class Management

Looking Ahead Remind students to take home the Home Study Sheet B on Homework and Remembering page 177.

 Ongoing Assessment

Ask students to explain two different ways they can find the area of a rectangle that is 6 rows by 4 columns. Direct them to give you examples by using a drawing and by showing you a multiplication equation.

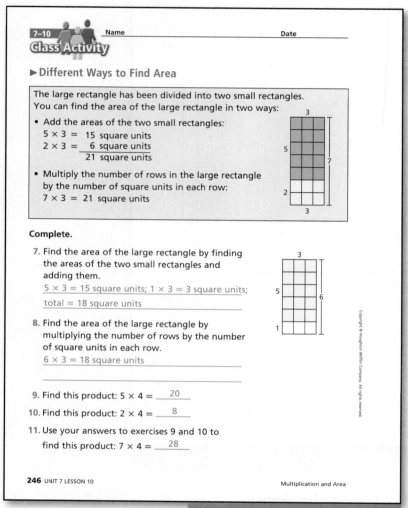

Student Activity Book page 246

▶ Different Ways to Find Area WHOLE CLASS

Ask students to look at the top of Student Book page 246. Discuss how the multipliers of 3 are related. They should see that the multiplier in the equation for the large rectangle is the total of the multipliers in the equations for the small rectangles. Then have students look at exercises 7–8 on Student Book page 246. Discuss the two ways to find the area of the large rectangle.

Give students a few minutes to complete exercises 7–8, and then discuss the answers. For a sample of classroom discussion see the **Math Talk in Action** in the side column. Then have students work on problems 9–11 on Student Book page 246.

②Going Further

Differentiated Instruction

Intervention Activity Card 7-10

Rectangles Everywhere
Activity Card 7-10 ●

Work: In pairs

Use:
• MathBoard materials or TRB M1 (Dot Grid)

Decide:
Who will be Student 1 and who will be Student 2 for the first round.

1. **Student 1:** On your dot grid paper, copy the rectangle shown in the picture.

2. **Student 2:** Write the multiplication for the rectangle. $3 \times 2 = 6$

3. Draw four more rectangles and write the multiplication for each one.
   • 5 units tall and 3 units wide $3 \times 5 = 15$
   • 4 units tall and 9 units wide $9 \times 4 = 36$
   • 7 units tall and 4 units wide $4 \times 7 = 28$
   • 8 units tall and 6 units wide $6 \times 8 = 48$

   Change roles for each new rectangle.

Unit 7, Lesson 10   Copyright © Houghton Mifflin Company

Activity Note To reinforce understanding, tell students to check their work by counting the number of square units in each rectangle.

 Math Writing Prompt

Explain Your Thinking Explain how $3 \times 7 = 21$ can be related to a division situation.

Soar to Success Math **Software Support**

Warm Up 12.23

On Level Activity Card 7-10

Measure and Multiply
Activity Card 7-10 ▲

Work: In pairs

Use:
• Inch rulers

1. Find three small items that are shaped like rectangles. Look for items that measure less than 10 inches on each side.

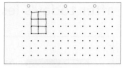

2. Measure the length and the width of each item to the nearest whole inch.

3. Draw a picture of each item and label the length and width, using the measurements you made.

4. Write a multiplication equation to find the area of each rectangle shown on your drawings.

Unit 7, Lesson 10   Copyright © Houghton Mifflin Company

Activity Note Be sure that students multiply only two numbers, the length and the width, to find the area.

 Math Writing Prompt

Investigate Math Explain how to find the length of a fence to enclose a rectangle-shaped swimming pool.

MEGA MATH Grades K-6 **Software Support**

Shapes Ahoy: Ship Shapes, Level X

Challenge Activity Card 7-10

Measure with Multiplications
Activity Card 7-10 ■

Work: In pairs

Use:
• Centimeter rulers or TRB M26 (Centimeter Ruler)
• a square corner (a piece of paper, an index card, or envelope)

Decide:
Who will be Student 1 and who will be Student 2 for the first round.

1. **Student 1:** Use four separate sheets of paper to draw four rectangles. Choose a whole number between 1 and 10 for each length and width.

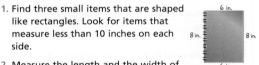

   Use a centimeter ruler to measure and draw each side.

2. **Student 2:** Measure the sides of the rectangles. Label each side in centimeters.

3. Take turns finding the area of each rectangle. Write each area as square centimeters.

   | Area = Length × Width |

4. **Work Together** Check your work.

Unit 7, Lesson 10   Copyright © Houghton Mifflin Company

Activity Note Be sure that students make square corners on each rectangle. This will ensure parallel and congruent sides for measurement purposes.

 Math Writing Prompt

Summarize Explain how you can combine two rectangles with the same width to find the answer to a multiplication that you don't know.

✖ DESTINATION Math· **Software Support**

Course II: Module 3: Unit 1: Area

Multiplication and Area **551**

③ Homework and Spiral Review

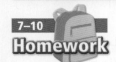
Homework **Goal:** Additional Practice

This Homework page provides practice on multiplication and division and finding area.

Remembering **Goal:** Spiral Review

This Remembering page would be appropriate anytime after today's lesson.

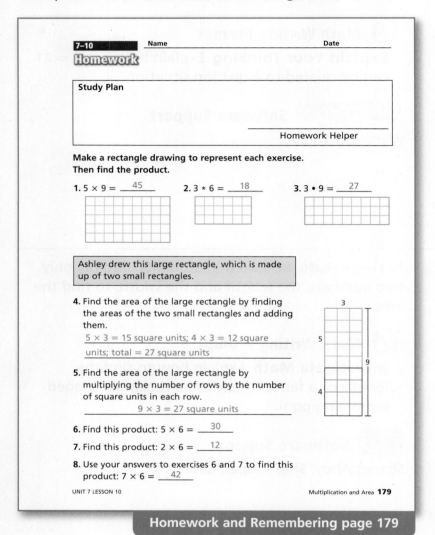

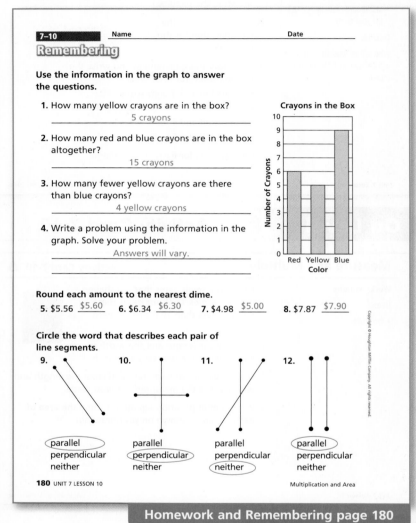

Homework and Remembering page 179

Homework and Remembering page 180

Home and School Activity

 Real-World Connection

Floor Tiles Explain that floors can be covered with squares of tile or carpet. Have students measure the length and width of the classroom or a room at home to the nearest foot. Then ask students to use the measurements to figure out about how many one-foot squares they would need to cover the floor.

Solve and Create Word Problems

Lesson Objectives

- Recognize and identify multiplication and division word problems.
- Write and solve multiplication and division word problems.

> **Vocabulary**
> Repeated-group
> array
> Equal Shares drawing
> Fast-Array drawing

The Day at a Glance

Today's Goals	Materials
1 Teaching the Lesson **A1:** Take Sprints for 9s multiplications and divisions. **A2:** Practice 9s count-bys, multiplications, and divisions. **A3:** Identify word problems by type and then solve them. Create word problems. **2 Going Further** ► Math Connection: Use Mental Math to Solve Related Multiplications ► Differentiated Instruction **3 Homework and Spiral Review**	**Lesson Activities** Student Activity Book pp. 247–250 or Student Hardcover Book pp. 247–250 and Activity Workbook p. 117 (includes Check Sheet) Homework and Remembering pp. 181–182 Signature sheet Blank Sprint Answer Sheet (TRB M57) Check Up materials Study Sheet A or B Check Sheet 1, 2, or 3 Dry-erase markers Study Sheet Answer Strips (TRB M54) Check Sheet Answer Strips (TRB M55) Card stock Estimating cards **Going Further** Activity Cards 7-11 Centimeter-Grid Paper (TRB M31) Homework p. 181 Math Journals

123 *Use Math Talk today!*

Keeping Skills Sharp

Quick Practice ⏱ 5 MINUTES	Daily Routines
Goal: Practice 3s count-bys, multiplications, and divisions. **Materials:** Class Multiplication Table Poster, pointer Use the Multiplication Table and the number "3" for the activities. **Repeated Quick Practice** Use these Quick Practice activities from previous lessons. **3s Multiplications in Order** (See Unit 7 Lesson 4.) **Mixed 3s Multiplications** (See Unit 7 Lesson 2.) **Mixed 3s Divisions** (See Unit 7 Lesson 5.)	**Homework Review** Let students work together and help each other check their answers. **Mental Math** Use a mental math strategy to subtract 74 – 36. Explain how you found your answer. 38; Subtract 4 of the 36 to get 74 to 70; Subtract 2 of the 32 to get 70 to 68; Subtract 3 tens, 30, to get 68 to 38.

Teaching the Lesson

Activity 1

Assess 9s

 5 MINUTES

Goal: Take Sprints for 9s multiplications and divisions.

Materials: Student Activity Book p. 247 or Activity Workbook p. 117, Signature Sheet (Student Activity Book pages 205–206 or Activity Workbook p. 78), Blank Sprint Answer Sheet (TRB M57)

✔ **NCTM Standard:**
Number and Operations

 Class Management

If students are struggling with count-bys, you might give a count-by Sprint.

▶ **Sprints for 9s** INDIVIDUALS

Have students turn to Student Book page 247 or Activity Workbook p. 117 and read aloud the two Sprints below.

× 9	÷ 9
a. 2 × 9 18	a. 81 ÷ 9 9
b. 4 × 9 36	b. 9 ÷ 9 1
c. 7 × 9 63	c. 27 ÷ 9 3
d. 3 × 9 27	d. 90 ÷ 9 10
e. 9 × 9 81	e. 36 ÷ 9 4
f. 5 × 9 45	f. 63 ÷ 9 7
g. 1 × 9 9	g. 72 ÷ 9 8
h. 6 × 9 54	h. 18 ÷ 9 2
i. 10 × 9 90	i. 45 ÷ 9 5
j. 8 × 9 72	j. 54 ÷ 9 6

Have **Student Pairs** check one another's work as you read the answers, marking any incorrect answers, and getting signatures.

Activity 2

Check Up and Independent Study

 5 MINUTES

Goal: Practice 9s count-bys, multiplications, and divisions.

Materials: Check Up materials: Signature Sheet Study Sheet A or B, Check Sheets 1, 2, or 3, dry-erase markers (1 per student), sheet protectors (1 per student), Study Sheet Answer Strips (TRB M54), Check Sheet Answer Strips (TRB M55), cardstock; Estimating Cards, Homework and Remembering page 181

✔ **NCTM Standard:**
Number and Operations

▶ **Check Up with 2s, 3s, 5s, 9s, and 10s** PAIRS

Give **Student Pairs** a few minutes to test one another using Study Sheets A or B and collect signatures. For students who have already collected signatures on Study Sheets A or B, have them use Check Sheets 1–3. You may want to have Study Sheet Answer Strips or Check Sheet Answer Strips (TRB M54–M55) available.

Then give students 2 or 3 minutes to study independently using Study Sheets, Check Sheets, or Strategy Cards. Have them complete the Study Plan box on Homework and Remembering page 181. They should include any multiplication or divisions they missed in the Sprint or Check Up. Remind students to put all their Check Up materials in their folders.

Activity 3

Identify, Solve, and Create Word Problems

7–11 Class Activity   Name ____________ Date ________

► Identify Types of Problems

Read each problem and decide what type of problem it is. Write the letter from the list below. Then write an equation to solve the problem.

a. Array Multiplication
b. Array Division
c. Repeated Groups Multiplication
d. Repeated Groups Division with an Unknown Group Size
e. Repeated Groups Division with an Unknown Multiplier (number of groups)
f. None of the above

1. Mrs. Ostrega has 3 children. She wants to buy 5 juice boxes for each child. How many juice boxes does she need?
   c; 3 × 5 = 15 juice boxes
2. Sophie picked 15 peaches from one tree and 3 peaches from another. How many peaches did she pick in all?
   f; 15 + 3 = 18 peaches
3. Zamir brought 21 treats to the dog park. He divided the treats equally among the 7 dogs that were there. How many treats did each dog get?
   d; 21 ÷ 7 = 3 treats
4. Art said he could make 12 muffins in his muffin pan. The pan has space for 3 muffins in a row. How many rows does the muffin pan have?
   b; 12 ÷ 3 = 4 rows
5. Bia is helping with the lights for the school play. Each box of light bulbs has 6 rows, with 3 bulbs in each row. How many light bulbs are in each box?
   a; 6 × 3 = 18 light bulbs
6. Tryouts were held to find triplets to act in a commercial for Triple-Crunch Peanut Butter. If 24 children tried out for the commercial, how many sets of triplets tried out?
   e; 24 ÷ 3 = 8 sets

248 UNIT 7 LESSON 11   Solve and Create Word Problems

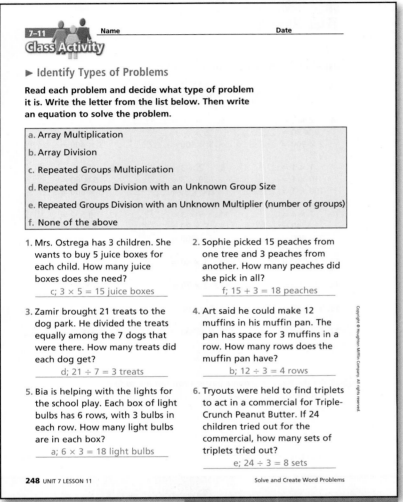

Student Activity Book page 248

► Identify Types of Problems WHOLE CLASS

Math Talk Read aloud the instructions on Student Book page 248. Have students solve problems 1–6 using **Solve and Discuss**. To discuss each problem, ask questions such as:

- How did you decide which type of problem it is?
- Do we know the group size and number of groups?
- Is the unknown number a factor or the product?
- Why is problem 2 an addition problem?

► Create Word Problems PAIRS

Have **Student Pairs** create their own word problems using the list on Student Book page 248. Have **Student Pairs** exchange problems with each other. Have struggling students work with a **Helping Partner**.

25 MINUTES

Goals: Identify word problems by type and then solve them. Create word problems.

Materials: Student Activity Book or Hardcover Book p. 248

NCTM Standards:
Number and Operations
Problem Solving
Communication

Differentiated Instruction

Extra Help If students have trouble identifying the problem type, suggest they first think about whether the problem involves repeated-groups or arrays and whether they need to multiply or divide to find the answer. Have students make a sample drawing for each type of problem listed and label it for reference while completing this page.

Ongoing Assessment

Give students the following problems:

► If I had 5 goldfish and bought 2 plants for each fish, how many plants did I buy?

► I brought a box of crackers. Each box has 2 packages of crackers with 10 crackers in each package. How many crackers are in the box?

Ask students to identify what kind of problem each is and then to write an equation to solve each problem.

English Language Learners

Students may benefit from studying in pairs and practicing the multiplications aloud.

Going Further

Math Connection: Use Mental Math to Solve Related Multiplications

Goal: Use mental math and number patterns to solve related multiplications.

Materials: MathBoard materials, Student Activity Book or Hardcover Book pp. 249–250

✓ **NCTM Standards:**
Number and Operations
Problem Solving
Connections

▶ Introduce Multiplying with Multiples of 10 [WHOLE CLASS]

Ask students the following questions:

- If you have five $1 bills, how much money do you have? $5

- If you have five $10 bills, how much money do you have? $50

- If you have five $100 dollar bills, how much money do you have? $500

- If you have five $1,000 dollar bills, how much money do you have? $5,000

Write the following on the board:

$$5 \times 1 = 5$$
$$5 \times 10 = 50$$
$$5 \times 100 = 500$$
$$5 \times 1,000 = 5,000$$

- What pattern do you see? The answer has the same number of zeros as the number of zeros in the multiple of 10.

Write 8×70 on the board. How can you use the pattern to find 8×70? Write the answer to the basic multiplication 8×7. Then write 1 zero because the multiple of 10 has 1 zero. $8 \times 70 = 560$.

$$8 \times 70 = 560$$

Explain that this pattern works because you can write the multiple of 10 as a number times 10, 100, and so on and use the associative property.

$$8 \times 70 = 8 \times (7 \times 10)$$
$$= (8 \times 7) \times 10$$
$$= 56 \times 10 = 560$$

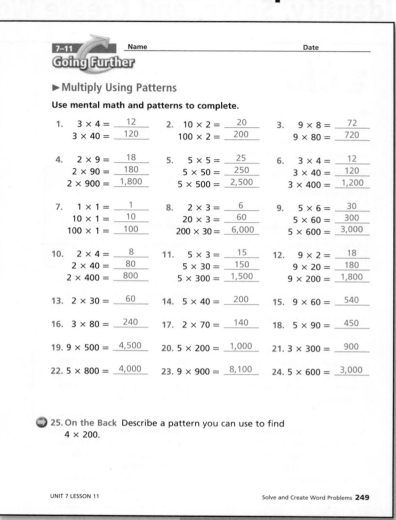

Student Activity Book page 249

▶ Multiply Using Patterns [WHOLE CLASS]

Discuss these 4 *tricky* products for this pattern:
5×2 5×4 5×6 5×8

Ask students to compare these products with other 5s multiplications. They end in 0.

Some students may think it's an exception, but it really is not. These products end in 0 so there is one more 0 than in the pattern, but that 0 is part of the product so it is really not an exception.

Refer students to Student Book page 249.

Have students complete exercises 1–25. Check the answers as a class. Have a volunteer come to the board and describe the pattern they used to find the answer to exercise 25. Encourage the volunteer to circle the 0s in the factor and in the product. For example, they will circle two 0s in 200 and two 0s in 800.

Differentiated Instruction

Write Equations   Activity Card 7-11 ●

Work: In pairs

Use:
• Homework and Remembering; page 181

1. Read Problem 1 on the Homework page together. Then work together to answer the following questions on a separate sheet of paper.
   • How can you decide which type of problem it is?
   • Do you know the group size and number of groups?
   • Is the unknown number a factor or the product?
   • What equation can you write to solve the problem?

2. Now use your answers to help you solve the problem.

3. Answer the questions and write an equation to find the solution for as many of the remaining problems on the page as time allows.

Unit 7, Lesson 11   Copyright © Houghton Mifflin Company

Activity Note Before students begin the activity, be sure they can identify the possible types of problems they are solving. The types are listed at the top of Homework page 181.

 Math Writing Prompt

Language and Vocabulary Make a list of words or phrases that tell you to multiply. Make a list of words or phrases that tell you to divide.

 **Software Support**

Warm Up 12.31

Bagel Count   Activity Card 7-11 ▲

Work: In small groups

Use the pictograph below to answer questions about raisin bagel sales at Murphy's Bakery. Write your answers on a separate sheet of paper.

Raisin Bagels Sold at Murphy's Bakery Last Week	
Monday	◉ ◉ ◉ ◉
Tuesday	◉ ◉ ◉
Wednesday	◉ ◉ ◉ ◉ ◉
Thursday	◉ ◉
Friday	◉ ◉ ◉ ◉

◉ = 3 bagels

• How many bagels were sold on Wednesday? 15
• How many bagels were sold on Tuesday and Thursday altogether? 15
• How many more bagels were sold on Friday than on Thursday? 6
• How many fewer bagels were sold on Monday than on Wednesday? 3

Unit 7, Lesson 11   Copyright © Houghton Mifflin Company

Activity Note Before students begin the activity, ask them to identify the value of the symbol used in the pictograph. Students can use their skills with counting by 3s to help them answer the questions.

 Math Writing Prompt

Summarize Explain how you can tell if a problem can be solved using a multiplication equation or a division equation.

 Software Support

Country Countdown: White Water Graphing, Level E

Math Word Search   Activity Card 7-11 ■

Work: In pairs

Use:
• TRB M31 (Centimeter-Grid Paper)

1. Make a list of at least 8 words that are associated with multiplication and division.

2. Use the words to create a math puzzle like the one shown below.

3. Trade papers with other students to solve the puzzle. Find and circle as many words as you can.

Unit 7, Lesson 11   Copyright © Houghton Mifflin Company

Activity Note Additional words that students might use include *multiplier, division,* and *equation.* Words can appear in any direction on the puzzle, and can also be spelled from right to left or bottom to top.

 Math Writing Prompt

Compare and Contrast How is a repeated-groups multiplication problem like an array multiplication problem? How is it different?

 Software Support

Course II: Module 2: Unit 2: Finding Products less than 100

③ Homework and Spiral Review

7–11
Homework   **Goal:** Additional Practice

This Homework page provides practice in multiplication and division and in identifying types of word problems.

7–11
Remembering   **Goal:** Spiral Review

This Remembering page would be appropriate anytime after today's lesson.

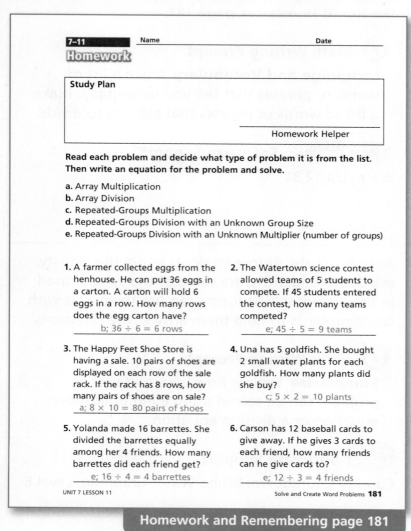

7–11   Name _____ Date _____
Homework

Study Plan
_____
_____
Homework Helper

Read each problem and decide what type of problem it is from the list. Then write an equation for the problem and solve.

a. Array Multiplication
b. Array Division
c. Repeated-Groups Multiplication
d. Repeated-Groups Division with an Unknown Group Size
e. Repeated-Groups Division with an Unknown Multiplier (number of groups)

1. A farmer collected eggs from the henhouse. He can put 36 eggs in a carton. A carton will hold 6 eggs in a row. How many rows does the egg carton have?
   b; 36 ÷ 6 = 6 rows

2. The Watertown science contest allowed teams of 5 students to compete. If 45 students entered the contest, how many teams competed?
   e; 45 ÷ 5 = 9 teams

3. The Happy Feet Shoe Store is having a sale. 10 pairs of shoes are displayed on each row of the sale rack. If the rack has 8 rows, how many pairs of shoes are on sale?
   a; 8 × 10 = 80 pairs of shoes

4. Una has 5 goldfish. She bought 2 small water plants for each goldfish. How many plants did she buy?
   c; 5 × 2 = 10 plants

5. Yolanda made 16 barrettes. She divided the barrettes equally among her 4 friends. How many barrettes did each friend get?
   e; 16 ÷ 4 = 4 barrettes

6. Carson has 12 baseball cards to give away. If he gives 3 cards to each friend, how many friends can he give cards to?
   e; 12 ÷ 3 = 4 friends

UNIT 7 LESSON 11   Solve and Create Word Problems **181**

Homework and Remembering page 181

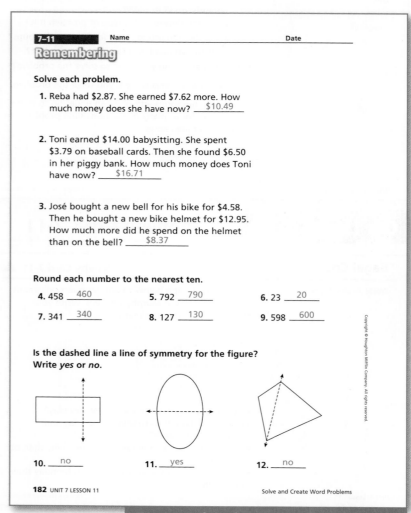

7–11   Name _____ Date _____
Remembering

Solve each problem.

1. Reba had $2.87. She earned $7.62 more. How much money does she have now? $10.49

2. Toni earned $14.00 babysitting. She spent $3.79 on baseball cards. Then she found $6.50 in her piggy bank. How much money does Toni have now? $16.71

3. José bought a new bell for his bike for $4.58. Then he bought a new bike helmet for $12.95. How much more did he spend on the helmet than on the bell? $8.37

Round each number to the nearest ten.

4. 458 __460__   5. 792 __790__   6. 23 __20__

7. 341 __340__   8. 127 __130__   9. 598 __600__

Is the dashed line a line of symmetry for the figure? Write yes or no.

10. __no__   11. __yes__   12. __no__

182 UNIT 7 LESSON 11   Solve and Create Word Problems

Homework and Remembering page 182

Home or School Activity

 Art Connection

Word Problem Drawings Have students choose a type of word problem—an array or repeated-groups—and draw a picture of it. They can choose a word problem from Student Book page 248 or create one of their own. Students should draw pictures instead of using circles as they did in the lesson. When students' drawings are complete, ask volunteers to share their creations with the class. Have other students write new word problems to fit the drawing.

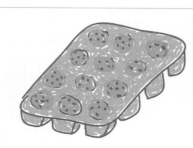

Billy could make 12 muffins in his pan. The pan has room for 4 muffins in each row. How many rows of muffins can he make?

Multiply and Divide with 4

Vocabulary

repeated addition
multiplication
Equal Shares drawing
product
multiplier

Lesson Objectives

● Explore patterns in 4s multiplications and count-bys.

● Learn a strategy for finding 4s count-bys and solving problems involving 4s.

The Day at a Glance

Today's Goals	Materials
1 **Teaching the Lesson** **A1:** Practice count-bys, multiplications, and divisions. **A2:** Explore patterns in 4s count-bys, multiplications, and divisions. **A3:** Use a shortcut for finding 4s count-bys and solving 4s multiplication problems. **2** **Going Further** ▶ Differentiated Instruction **3** **Homework and Spiral Review**	**Lesson Activities** Student Activity Book pp. 251–256 or Student Hardcover Book pp. 251–256 and Activity Workbook p. 118 (includes Check Sheet) Homework and Remembering pp. 183–188 Blank Sprint Answer Sheet (TRB M57) Check Up materials Signature Sheet Check Sheet 1, 2, 3 or 4 Study Sheet A or B Dry-erase markers Sheet protectors Study Sheet Answer Strips Check Sheet Answer Strips Card stock Strategy Cards	MathBoard materials or Number Path (TRB M39) Class Multiplication Table **Going Further** Activity Cards 7-12 Shoebox Red and blue markers Centimeter-Grid Paper (TRB M31) Markers or crayons Math Journals 123 Use Math Talk today!

Keeping Skills Sharp

Quick Practice ⏱ 5 MINUTES	Daily Routines
Goal: Practice 3s count-bys, multiplications, and divisions. Use the Multiplication Table and the number "3" for the activities. **Repeated Quick Practice** Use these Quick Practice activities from previous lessons. **3s Multiplications in Order** (See Unit 7 Lesson 4.) **Mixed 3s Multiplications** (See Unit 7 Lesson 2.) **Mixed 3s Divisions** (See Unit 7 Lesson 5.)	**Homework Review** Have students discuss and correct the errors from their homework. **Place Value** Find the number that is 1,000 more than three thousand five hundred thirty-four. 4,534

1 Teaching the Lesson

Check Up and Independent Study

 5 MINUTES

Goal: Practice count-bys, multiplications, and divisions.

Materials: Check Up materials: Signature Sheet (Student Activity Book pages 205–206 or Activity Workbook p. 77), Blank Sprint Answer Sheet (TRB M57), Study Sheets A or B (Student Activity Book pages 207–208; 243–244 or Activity Workbook pp. 78; 89), Check Sheets 1, 2, 3, or 4 (Student Activity Book pages 223–224; 229–230; 234–235; 251–252 or Activity Workbook pp. 83; 85; 87), dry-erase markers (1 per student), sheet protectors (1 per student), Study Sheet Answer Strips (TRB M54), Check Sheet Answer Strips (TRB M55), cardstock; Strategy Cards, Homework and Remembering page 187.

✔ **NCTM Standard:**
Number and Operations

▶ **Check Up with 2s, 3s, 5s, 9s, and 10s** WHOLE CLASS

Direct students to Check Sheet 4 on Student Activity Book page 251 or Activity Workbook page 118 to use as an alternate Check Up for 3s.

Give **Student Pairs** a few minutes to test one another on Study Sheets A or B and collect signatures. For any students who have already collected signatures on Study Sheets A or B, have them use Check Sheets 1–4. You may want to have Study Sheet and Check Sheet Answer Strips (TRB M54–M55) available. Give them another two or three minutes to study independently using their Check Sheets or Strategy Cards.

Students who made mistakes on Sprints for 9s in lesson 11 (or who were absent) may take repeat or make-up Sprints at this time.

Have students complete their Study Plan box on Homework and Remembering page 187. They should include 4s practice along with any multiplications and divisions they missed in the Check Up. Remind students to place all their Check Up materials in their folders.

Explore 4s Patterns

 20 MINUTES

Goal: Explore patterns in 4s count-bys, multiplications, and divisions.

Materials: MathBoard materials or Number Path (TRB M39), Student Activity Book or Hardcover Book p. 253, Class Multiplication Table Poster

 NCTM Standard:
Number and Operations

▶ **Explore Patterns with 4s** WHOLE CLASS

Tell students that today they will be thinking about groups of 4. Ask what things in the real world come in groups of 4. Possible responses: wheels on a car, sides on a square, leaves on a four-leaf clover, seasons in a year, points on a compass, quarters in a dollar, suits in a deck of cards, and so on

Model the steps of this activity on the Class MathBoard as students follow along on their MathBoards. The completed board is reproduced in Student Activity Book page 253. You can use it to facilitate a discussion of the patterns in 4s multiplications.

Have students circle sequential groups of 4, up to 40, on the Number Path and write the totals so far next to each group. Point to each group as the students circle them, and have students say in unison, "1 group of 4 is 4," "2 groups of 4 are 8," and so on. Then point to the totals as students read them aloud: 4, 8, 12, 16, 20, 24, 28, 32, 36, 40.

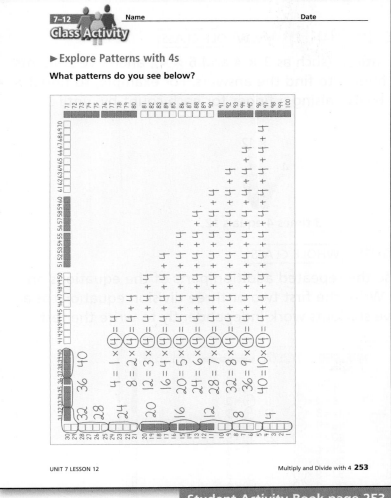

Student Activity Book page 253

Student Activity Book page 253

As students follow along, write and read a multiplication equation for each count-by. Then have students write a repeated addition expression for each multiplication equation.

Have students use Student Book page 253 or their MathBoards to describe any patterns they see in the count-bys and equations. For a sample classroom discussion, see **Math Talk in Action** in the side column.

▶ Use the Class Multiplication Table Poster WHOLE CLASS

Display the Class Multiplication Table Poster. Point to the equations in the 4s column and have the class read them aloud, using fingers to show the multiplier.

1 times 4 equals 4.   2 times 4 equals 8.   3 times 4 equals 12.

Point to each equation in the 4s column again, this time having students say only the count-bys. Again, have them use their fingers to indicate the multipliers.

Activity continued ▶

English Language Learners

Write: *I had 5 dogs. I bought 3 bones for each dog. How many bones did I buy?* Write 3×5 and $5 + 5 + 5$.

- **Beginning** Say: $3 \times 5 = 5 + 5 + 5$. Multiplication is the same as *repeated addition*. Have students repeat.
- **Intermediate** Say: 3×5 is the same as adding 3 groups of ___. 5 Multiplcation is the same as *repeated addition*.
- **Advanced** Have students work in pairs. One writes a multiplication fact. The other tells how to solve it with *repeated addition*.

 Math Talk in Action

What patterns do you see in the 4s count-bys and equations?

Kim: All the products are even numbers and the ones digits follow the pattern 4, 8, 2, 6, 0 and so on.

Jameelah: I think I see another pattern with 4s count-bys. 4s count-bys are also 2s count-bys—the 4s count-bys are every other 2s count-by.

Viktor: I see that too, and I see another pattern. If you ignore 40, and then start with the outside pair of products, 4 and 36, and move in, the ones digit of each pair of products (4 and 36, 8 and 32, 12 and 28, and 16 and 24) add to 10.

Kim: You're right!

Multiply and Divide with 4   **561**

▶ Use Fingers to Multiply WHOLE CLASS

Present 4s multiplications (such as 3×4 and 6×4), and have students count up on their fingers to find the answers. For example, to find 3×4, they should count by 4s, raising a finger for each count-by, until 3 fingers are raised.

3 times 4 equals 12.

▶ Divide with 4s WHOLE CLASS

Have students erase the repeated addition parts of the equations on their MathBoards. Write the first two or three division equations as a class, and then have students work independently to write the rest.

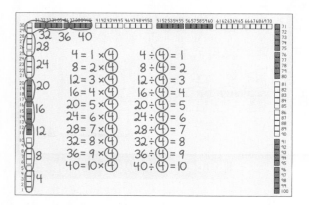

▶ Use Fingers to Divide WHOLE CLASS

Write this division and the related multiplication equation on the board:

$$28 \div 4 = \boxed{} \quad \text{and} \quad \boxed{} \times 4 = 28.$$

Have students count up on their fingers to find the answer. Seven fingers will be raised, indicating that there are 7 groups of 4 in 28. So, $28 \div 4 = 7$.

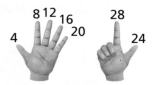

28 divided by 4 equals 7.

Repeat this procedure for several more equations with a divisor of 4.

Use the 5s Shortcut

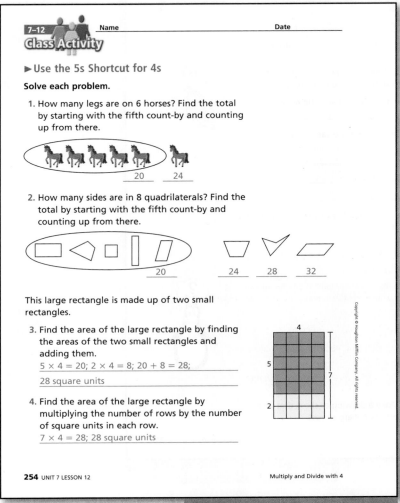

Student Activity Book page 254

▶ Use the 5s Shortcut for 4s INDIVIDUALS

Have students work independently to complete Student Book page 254, and then discuss the answers.

All of these problems illustrate that, if students know $5 \times 4 = 20$, they can count up by 4s or add other 4s multiplications to find count-bys and products for multipliers greater than 5. Be sure to bring this out during the discussion. (Students explored this idea for 3s multiplications in Lesson 9.)

To better illustrate the 5s pattern, you may wish to walk through each problem and identify the group of 5 being called out.

 10 MINUTES

Goal: Use a shortcut for finding 4s count-bys and solving 4s multiplication problems.

Materials: Student Activity Book or Hardcover Book pp. 254–256

 NCTM Standards:
Number and Operations
Problem Solving
Connections

Teaching Note

Start from Other Count-bys There is nothing special about $5 \times 4 = 20$, except that most students find multiplications with factors of 5 easy to learn. Students can start with any 4s count-by they know and count up by 4s to find other 4s count-bys. They can also combine any two 4s multiplications to get another 4s multiplication.

For example, if students know that $3 \times 4 = 12$, they can combine this equation with itself to get $6 \times 4 = 24$ and $9 \times 4 = 36$. They can also count up by 4s to determine that $4 \times 4 = 16$, $5 \times 4 = 20$, and so on.

These ideas will be explored in more depth later, but if you feel your students are ready, you may want to introduce them now.

 Class Management

Looking Ahead Remind students to take home their 4s chart and Home Check Sheet 4 on Homework and Remembering pages 183–186.

Activity continued ▶

❶ Teaching the Lesson (continued)

 Math Talk in Action

The Puzzled Penguin seems to think that combining multiplication equations involves adding *both* factors. Why doesn't this work?

Curt: I think I know... 8 × 4 is 8 groups of 4. This is the same as 5 groups of 4 plus 3 groups of 4 (that is, 5 × 4 plus 3 × 4) *not* 5 groups of 2 plus 3 groups of 2.

Perry: Curt, there's another reason why that doesn't work. 8 × 4 is the area of a rectangle with 8 rows of 4 square units. You can get an 8-by-4 rectangle by putting together a 5-by-4 rectangle and a 3-by-4 rectangle. Combining a 5-by-2 rectangle and a 3-by-2 rectangle gives an 8-by-2 rectangle, which has area 8 × 2.

Tom: I can show you why it doesn't work with a drawing.

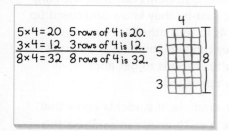

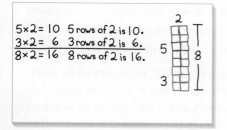

You are all correct!

✔ **Ongoing Assessment**

Ask students to find 2 × 4 and 6 × 4 and then use their answers to find 8 × 4. Ask them to make a drawing to show why the answer is correct.

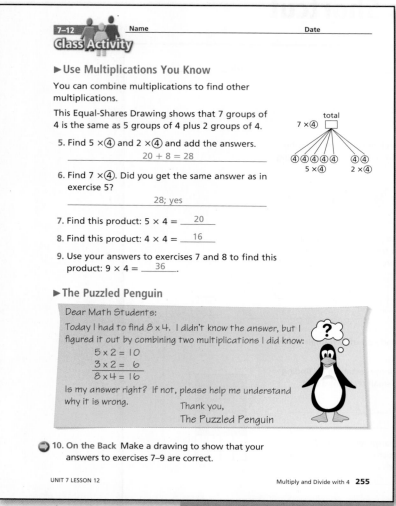

Student Activity Book page 255

▶ Use Multiplications You Know INDIVIDUALS

Have students complete problems 5–9 on Student Book page 255. Students might draw a rectangle, make an Equal-Shares Drawing, or use another method to show their answer is correct.

▶ The Puzzled Penguin INDIVIDUALS

Have students read the letter from the Puzzled Penguin. Allow several students to share their ideas about what the Puzzled Penguin did wrong. Encourage them to make drawings on the board if it helps them explain.

See the **Math Talk in Action** in the side column for a sample classroom dialogue.

② Going Further

Intervention   Activity Card 7-12

Multiply if Red, Divide if Blue   Activity Card 7-12 ●

Work: In pairs

Use:

• Cardboard box

• Red and blue markers, one each

1. Write the numbers 1 through 10 in red on small strips of paper, and fold each paper in half.

2. Write the numbers 4, 8, 12, 16, 20, 24, 28, 32, 36, and 40 in blue on small strips of paper and fold each paper in half. Put the strips of paper in a box. Take turns choosing a number from the box.

3. If the number is red, multiply by 4. If the number is blue, divide by 4. Record your work on a separate sheet of paper. Continue taking turns until the box is empty.

4. **Compare** Which do you find easier to do, multiplying or dividing by 4?

Unit 7, Lesson 12   Copyright © Houghton Mifflin Company

Activity Note Have students check each other's calculations. If students disagree on a product or quotient, have them justify their results by counting by 4s.

 Math Writing Prompt

Real-World Application A bookcase has 4 shelves. Each shelf can hold 9 books. Explain two different ways to find out how many books will fit in the bookcase.

 **Software Support**

Warm Up 13.13

On Level   Activity Card 7-12

Function Tables   Activity Card 7-12 ▲

Work: On your own

1. Copy the function table below onto a separate sheet of paper.

Number of Monkeys	Number of Paws
2	8
3	12
5	20
9	36
10	40

2. What is the relationship between the number of monkeys and the number of paws? Each monkey has 4 paws.

3. Write the missing numbers in the table that you copied. What operation did you use to find each number? Division by 4 for the numbers in column 1; multiplication by 4 for the numbers in column 2.

Unit 7, Lesson 12   Copyright © Houghton Mifflin Company

Activity Note When students have completed the function table, ask them to write the rule that describes the relationship between the values in the table. If time allows have them create another function table using multiplication and division by 4.

 Math Writing Prompt

Write a Rule Create a function table that shows the relationship between a number of squares and the number of sides in the squares. The table should have at least 5 rows. Then write the rule.

 Software Support

Numberopolis: Carnival Stories, Level U

Challenge   Activity Card 7-12

Distribute This   Activity Card 7-12 ■

Work: In small groups

Use:

• TRB M31 (Centimeter-Grid Paper)

• Markers or crayons

1. You can use two or more products to help you find the product 24 × 6.

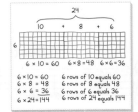

2. **Work Together** Draw as many combinations of arrays as possible to represent 24 × 6.

Unit 7, Lesson 12   Copyright © Houghton Mifflin Company

Activity Note There are many possible combinations of products that equate with 24 × 6. Ask students to explain why using this method of finding an unknown product works.

 Math Writing Prompt

Investigate Math Jerry says that to find 4 × 6, he can find 2 × 3 and then double the answer. Is he correct? Explain.

 DESTINATION Math Software Support

Course II: Module 2: Unit 2: Repeated Addition and Arrays

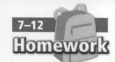

③ Homework and Spiral Review

✓ Include students' completed Homework page as part of their portfolios.

This Remembering page would be appropriate anytime after today's lesson.

7–12	Name	Date

Homework

Study Plan

_____

Homework Helper

Solve each problem.

1. Colin had 16 puzzles. He gave 4 puzzles to each of his nephews. How many nephews does Colin have?

   4 nephews

2. Allegra listed the names of her classmates in 4 columns, with 7 names in each column. How many classmates does Allegra have?

   28 classmates

This large rectangle is made up of two small rectangles.

3. Find the area of the large rectangle by finding the areas of the two small rectangles and adding them.

   $5 \times 4 = 20$; $3 \times 4 = 12$; $20 + 12 = 32$; 32 square units

4. Find the area of the large rectangle by multiplying the number of rows by the number of square units in each row.

   $8 \times 4 = 32$; 32 square units

This Equal-Shares drawing shows that 6 groups of 9 is the same as 5 groups of 9 plus 1 group of 9.

5. Find 5×9 and 1×9, and add the answers.

   $45 + 9 = 54$

6. Find 6×9. Did you get the same answer as in question 5?

   54, yes

UNIT 7 LESSON 12   Multiply and Divide with 4 **187**

Homework and Remembering page 187

7–12	Name	Date

Remembering

Solve each word problem. Label your answer.

Lewis had 542 seashells. His sister gave him her collection of 231 seashells.

1. How many seashells does Lewis have now?

   773 seashells

2. Write a subtraction word problem related to the addition word problem. Possible answer: Lewis had 773 seashells. He gave his sister 231 seashells. How many seashells does he have now?

3. Without doing any calculations, find the solution to the problem you wrote.

   542 or 231, depending on the problem students wrote.

4. Gina read 14 pages of her book on Tuesday and some more pages on Wednesday. She read a total of 26 pages in those two days. How many pages did she read on Wednesday?

   12 pages

5. Troy has 17 goldfish. He has 8 more goldfish than Tomas. How many goldfish does Tomas have?

   9 goldfish

Round each amount to the nearest dollar.

6. $4.56 $5.00
7. $5.67 $6.00
8. $3.21 $3.00
9. $8.34 $8.00
10. $4.17 $4.00
11. $9.85 $10.00

188 UNIT 7 LESSON 12   Multiply and Divide with 4

Homework and Remembering page 188

Home or School Activity

Music Connection

Count the Beats Music is sometimes counted in beats of 4. When writing music in $\frac{4}{4}$ time, musicians write notes and rests that combine to make 4 beats in each measure. This helps musicians keep tempo with each other. Find a song you know with a time signature of $\frac{4}{4}$. Have one person clap a steady beat of four while the other person claps the notes in the time they should be played. Did you end the song at the same time?

4 beats | 4 beats

Use the Strategy Cards

Lesson Objectives

- Understand the relationships in the fast array.
- Develop multiplication and division strategies.

Vocabulary

count-bys
fast array
5s shortcut

The Day at a Glance

Today's Goals	Materials
1 **Teaching the Lesson** **A1:** Take Sprints for 3s multiplications and divisions. **A2:** Review count-bys, multiplications, and divisions. **A3:** Discuss the Strategy Cards. **A4:** Practice with the 3s and 4s Strategy Cards. **A5:** Play *Solve the Stack*. **2** **Going Further** ► Differentiated Instruction **3** **Homework and Spiral Review**	**Lesson Activities** Student Activity Book pp. 257–260 or Student Hardcover Book pp. 257–260 and Activity Workbook pp. 119–120 (includes Check Sheet and Game Rules) Homework and Remembering pp. 189–190 Signature Sheet Blank Sprint Answer Sheet (TRB M57) Check Up materials Study Sheet A or B Check Sheet 1, 2, 3, or 4 Dry-erase markers Sheet protectors Study Sheet Answer Strips Check Sheet Answer Strips Card stock	Strategy Cards Rubber bands Small bags **Going Further** Activity Cards 7-13 Egg carton Construction paper Scissors Red, blue, yellow and green crayons or markers Number cubes Hexagon pattern blocks MathBoard materials Calculator Math Journals

123 Use Math Talk today!

Keeping Skills Sharp

Quick Practice ⏱ 5 MINUTES	Daily Routines
Goal: Practice 4s count-bys, multiplications, and divisions. Use the Multiplication Table and the number "4" for the activities. **Repeated Quick Practice** Use these Quick Practice activities from previous lessons. **4s Multiplications in Order** (See Unit 7 Lesson 4.) **Mixed 4s Multiplications** (See Unit 7 Lesson 2.) **Mixed 4s Divisions** (See Unit 7 Lesson 5.)	**Homework Review** Send students to the board to show their work. **Equations** Carl had 14 points left after he used 12 points to get a game. How many points did Carl have before the game? Write a situation equation and solve. 26 points; □ − 12 = 14

Teaching the Lesson

Assess 3s

 5 MINUTES

Goal: Take Sprints for 3s multiplications and divisions.

Materials: Student Activity Book p. 257 or Activity Workbook p. 119, Signature Sheet (Student Activity Book p. 205–206 or Activity Workbook p. 77), Blank Sprint Answer Sheet (TRB M57)

✔ **NCTM Standard:**
Number and Operations

▶ Sprints for 3s INDIVIDUALS

Direct students to Student Book page 257 or Activity Workbook p. 119. Read aloud the 3s Sprints below, and then have students check one another's work as before.

× 3	÷ 3
a. 6 × 3 = 18	a. 12 ÷ 3 = 4
b. 10 × 3 = 30	b. 18 ÷ 3 = 6
c. 3 × 3 = 9	c. 3 ÷ 3 = 1
d. 7 × 3 = 21	d. 21 ÷ 3 = 7
e. 1 × 3 = 3	e. 6 ÷ 3 = 2
f. 8 × 3 = 24	f. 30 ÷ 3 = 10
g. 2 × 3 = 6	g. 9 ÷ 3 = 3
h. 9 × 3 = 27	h. 24 ÷ 3 = 8
i. 4 × 3 = 12	i. 15 ÷ 3 = 5
j. 5 × 3 = 15	j. 27 ÷ 3 = 9

Have partners check one anothers' work as you read the answers, marking any incorrect answers, and getting signatures.

Check Up and Independent Study

 5 MINUTES

Goal: Review count-bys, multiplications, and divisions

Materials: Check Up materials: Signature Sheet, Study Sheets A or B, Check Sheets 1, 2, 3, or 4, dry-erase markers (1 per student), sheet protectors (1 per student), Study Sheet Answer Strips (TRB M54), Check Sheet Answer Strips (TRB M55), cardstock; Strategy Cards, Homework and Remembering p. 189

✔ **NCTM Standard:**
Number and Operations

▶ Check Up with 2s, 3s, 4s, 5s, 9s, and 10s WHOLE CLASS

Give **Student Pairs** a few minutes to test one another using Study Sheets A or B and collect signatures. For students who have already collected signatures on Study Sheets A or B, have them use Check Sheets 1–4. You may want to have extra Study Sheet and Check Sheet Answer Strips, (TRB M54–M55) available.

Then give them 2 or 3 minutes to study independently using their Study Sheets, Check Sheets, or Strategy Cards. Have them complete the Study Plan box on Homework and Remembering page 189. They should include any multiplications or divisions they missed in the Sprint or the Check Up. Remind students to put all their Check Up materials in their folders.

Strategy Cards and Fast Arrays

▶ Use Strategy Cards WHOLE CLASS

Have students take out their Strategy Cards. Discuss cards with students and ask how they can use count-bys to find products and quotients. See **Math Talk in Action** in the side column for a sample classroom dialogue.

Each multiplication card can be paired with a division card that has the same count-by lists and the same fast array drawing. Here is one such pair:

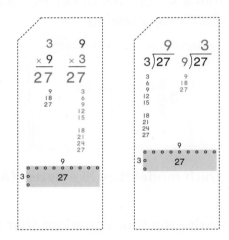

Be sure to mention this last point. Talk about the relationships in a fast array. Make sure students understand that for any factor-factor-product combination, they can write two multiplication equations and two division equations. To emphasize this, draw the array for 3 × 9 on the board.

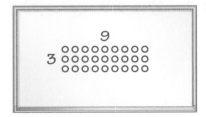

● **How can we use this array to help us multiply 3 × 9?** Possible response: We can count all the circles; We can multiply the number of circles in the far left with the number of circles in the top row.

Encourage students to use the array method rather than counting all the circles.

---

 15 MINUTES

Goal: Discuss the Strategy Cards.

Materials: Strategy Cards (Student Activity Book pp. 244A–244Z or Activity Workbook pp. 91–116)

 NCTM Standards:
Number and Operations
Communication
Connections

 Math Talk in Action

You have been using the Strategy Cards for a few days now. Have any of you noticed anything interesting about them that you would like to share?

Lita: I noticed that the answers to both problems on the multiplication cards are the same.

Pedro: But, on the division cards, the answers are different. The known factor in one problem is the missing quotient in the other.

Lita: I also saw that each count-by list starts with one of the two factors and ends with the product.

Pedro: Did you also notice that the number of count-bys on the list for one factor is equal to the other factor?

Lita: Really?

Pedro: Yes! For example, to find 9 × 3, you can count by 3s until you have said 9 count-bys. The ninth count-by, 27, is the product. To find 27 ÷ 9, you count by 9s until you reach 27.

Lita: Yes, and the number of count-bys you have said, 3, is the quotient!

Activity continued ▶

① Teaching the Lesson (continued)

Activity 3

● From this one fast array, we can write four equations. What are they?

Have a student demonstrate how to put an oval around the far left column of circles and the top row of circles in an array model.

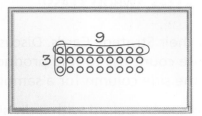

Then have another student volunteer erase all the circles inside the array except for the left column and top row of circles. Have the student write the product inside the fast array drawing.

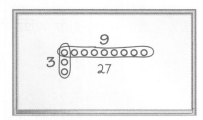

Discuss with students which model they like better (Array model or Fast Array drawings).

Work with students to write the four equations that go along with their Fast Array drawings.

$$3 \times 9 = 27 \qquad 9 \times 3 = 27$$
$$27 \div 9 = 3 \qquad 27 \div 3 = 9$$

(There are actually eight different equations, the four above, plus $27 = 3 \times 9$, $27 = 9 \times 3$, $3 = 27 \div 9$, $9 = 27 \div 3$.)

Next, discuss how students have been using the Strategy Cards to study.

● As you have used the cards, have you discovered any good strategies for finding and learning your multiplications and divisions?

Allow several students to share their ideas. If they do not mention the two points below, bring them up yourself.

● The cards show that you can find a product you don't know by starting at a product you do know and counting up. For example, to find 9 × 3, start at 5 × 3, or 15, and count up by 4 more 3s.

Connect this idea to the 5s shortcut students explored earlier. On the cards, there is a space after the first five count-bys to help facilitate this shortcut. However, students do not have to start at the fifth count-by; they can start at any count-by they know. For example, if they know that 7 × 3 = 21, they can count up by two more 3s to find 9 × 3.

● You can use the relationships in the fast array to find multiplications and divisions you don't know based on those you do. For example, if you know that 3 × 9 = 27, you also know that 27 ÷ 3 = 9, 27 ÷ 9 = 3, and 9 × 3 = 27.

Strategy Cards for 3s and 4s

▶ Practice with 3s and 4s Strategy Cards INDIVIDUALS

Ask students to sort the 3s and 4s Strategy Cards into three piles: those with multiplications and divisions they know quickly, those with multiplications and divisions they know slowly, and those with multiplications and divisions they don't know yet. Give them a few minutes to study and practice with the cards in the "know slowly" and "don't know" piles. Then, have them combine the cards with their other cards (2s, 5s, and 9s) and separate the entire set into "know", "know quickly", and "don't know" piles.

Remind students they have already cut out all the Strategy Cards when they were introduced in Lesson 10. As part of their homework they should add the 3s and 4s cards from the Home Strategy Cards to what they've already been practicing at home. Tell them to keep the rest of the cards in a safe place because they will need them in Unit 9.

 5 MINUTES

Goal: Practice with the 3s and 4s Strategy Cards.

Materials: Strategy Cards for 2s, 3s, 4s, 5s, and 9s (1 set per student), rubber bands, small bags

 NCTM Standard:
Number and Operations

Teaching the Lesson (continued)

Activity 5

Play a Multiplication and Division Game

 10 MINUTES

Goal: Play *Solve the Stack.*

Materials: Student Activity Book or Hardcover Book pages 259–260 and Activity Workbook p. 120, Strategy Cards

 NCTM Standard:
Number and Operations

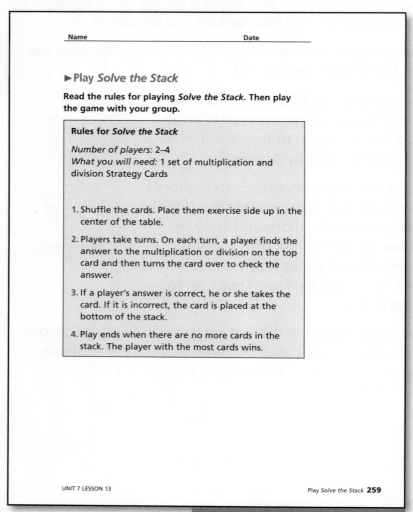

Name _____ Date _____

▶Play *Solve the Stack*

Read the rules for playing *Solve the Stack*. Then play the game with your group.

Rules for *Solve the Stack*

Number of players: 2–4
What you will need: 1 set of multiplication and division Strategy Cards

1. Shuffle the cards. Place them exercise side up in the center of the table.

2. Players take turns. On each turn, a player finds the answer to the multiplication or division on the top card and then turns the card over to check the answer.

3. If a player's answer is correct, he or she takes the card. If it is incorrect, the card is placed at the bottom of the stack.

4. Play ends when there are no more cards in the stack. The player with the most cards wins.

UNIT 7 LESSON 13   Play *Solve the Stack* **259**

Student Activity Book page 259

▶ Play *Solve the Stack* SMALL GROUPS

Give each **Small Group** of students one set of multiplication and division Strategy Cards or have them use the Strategy Cards they cut out in Unit 4 Lesson 10. Students should sort out and not use the 0s, 1s, 6s, 7s, or 8s Cards. Read aloud the rules on Student Book page 259 and make sure students understand the rules for the *Solve the Stack* game. Allow them to play the game for a few minutes.

②Going Further

Intervention | Activity Card 7-13

How Many Eggs?
Activity Card 7-13 ●

Work: In pairs

Use:
- Empty egg carton that holds 12 eggs
- Construction paper
- Scissors
- Red, blue, yellow, and green crayons or markers

1. **Work Together** Cut 12 paper eggs from construction paper. Color groups of 3 eggs in each of the following colors: red, blue, yellow, and green.

2. Group the eggs in the carton by color. Answer the questions below on a separate sheet of paper.

- What is the total number of eggs? 12
- How many color groups are in the carton? 4
- How many eggs are in each group? 3
- Which strategy cards for 3s and 4s are represented by your model?

Unit 7, Lesson 13   Copyright © Houghton Mifflin Company

Activity Note Students should recognize that the number of colors and the number of groups model the factors for the multiplication 3 × 4 and that the total number of eggs is the product 12.

 Math Writing Prompt

Explain How You Know Mrs. Davis uses 3 eggs in every cake she makes. She has 18 eggs. How many cakes can she make? Explain how you found your answer.

 **Software Support**

Warm Up 12.14

On Level | Activity Card 7-13

Go Around in Circles
Activity Card 7-13 ▲

Work: In groups of 5

Decide:
Who will be Student 1 for the first round.

1. Go around a circle to find products and quotients.

2. Student 1 calls out either "3" or "4." Student 2 calls out "times." Student 3 calls out a number greater than 1 but less than 11.

3. Student 4 calls out "equals." Student 5 names the product, and then repeats the product again.

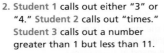

4. Reverse the order now. Student 4 calls out "divide by." Student 3 calls out the same number as before. Student 2 calls out "equals." Student 1 calls out the same number as before.

Unit 7, Lesson 13   Copyright © Houghton Mifflin Company

Activity Note Repeat the activity several times with different students beginning the equations. As students become familiar with the sequence of calls, they will work more quickly around the circle.

 Math Writing Prompt

Investigate Math Les said that anyone who knows 3s multiplications also knows 3s divisions. Do you agree with Les? Explain.

 Software Support

Numberopolis: Carnival Stories, Level S

Challenge | Activity Card 7-13

Hex-a-Product
Activity Card 7-13 ■

Work: In pairs

Use:
- Number cube labeled 2, 3, 4, 5, 9, 10
- Hexagon pattern blocks
- MathBoards
- calculator

1. Each player makes the game board shown below by tracing a hexagon block pattern.

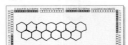

2. Roll the number cube and place the number in any empty hexagon. After all the spaces on your board are filled, find the product of each number pair along all the diagonals. Record each product and find the sum.

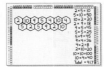

Unit 7, Lesson 13   Copyright © Houghton Mifflin Company

Activity Note Be sure that students see that there are a total of 12 diagonal products represented on the game board. Use the model to illustrate how to identify the products.

 Math Writing Prompt

Mental Math If you know the answer to 3 × 3, do you also know the answer to 30 × 3, 30 × 30, 300 × 300? Explain your thinking.

 DESTINATION Math· **Software Support**

Course II: Module 2: Unit 2: Finding Products less than 100

③ Homework and Spiral Review

7–13
Homework   **Goal:** Additional Practice

This Homework page provides practice with 3s and 4s multiplications and divisions.

7–13	Name	Date
Homework		

Study Plan

_____

_____

                   Homework Helper

Solve.

1. Pablo hung his watercolor paintings in an array with 3 rows and 4 columns. How many paintings did Pablo hang?
   _____ 12 paintings _____

2. A group of 7 friends went on a hiking trip. Each person took 3 granola bars. What total number of granola bars did the friends take?
   _____ 21 granola bars _____

3. Jon had 45 sheets of construction paper. He used 9 sheets to make paper snowflakes. How many sheets does he have now?
   _____ 36 sheets _____

You can combine multiplications you know to find multiplications you don't know.

4. Find this product: $5 \times 8 =$ ___40___

5. Find this product: $1 \times 8 =$ ___8___

6. Use the answers to numbers 4 and 5 to find this product: $6 \times 8 =$ ___48___

UNIT 7 LESSON 13   Use the Strategy Cards **189**

Homework and Remembering page 189

7–13
Remembering   **Goal:** Spiral Review

This Remembering page would be appropriate anytime after today's lesson.

7–13	Name	Date
Remembering		

Use mental math to subtract.

1. $130 - 60 =$ ___70___   2. $1{,}100 - 700 =$ ___400___   3. $150 - 90 =$ ___60___

4. $1{,}600 - 800 =$ ___800___   5. $120 - 80 =$ ___40___   6. $1{,}300 - 400 =$ ___900___

Write a multiplication equation to represent the area of each rectangle.

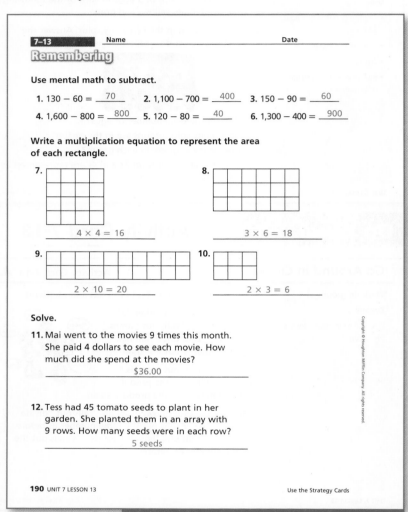

7. $4 \times 4 = 16$

8. $3 \times 6 = 18$

9. $2 \times 10 = 20$

10. $2 \times 3 = 6$

Solve.

11. Mai went to the movies 9 times this month. She paid 4 dollars to see each movie. How much did she spend at the movies?
    _____ $36.00 _____

12. Tess had 45 tomato seeds to plant in her garden. She planted them in an array with 9 rows. How many seeds were in each row?
    _____ 5 seeds _____

190 UNIT 7 LESSON 13   Use the Strategy Cards

Homework and Remembering page 190

Home and School Activity

 Physical Education Connection

3s and 4s Toss Use paper and tape to set up a large target like the one shown at the right. Have students toss a bean bag towards the target and multiply the number they land on with the factor they are practicing (for example 3×2 or 4×2). Have students practice saying the equation out loud and have other students listen to see if they are correct. This game can be modified to practice any basic multiplication.

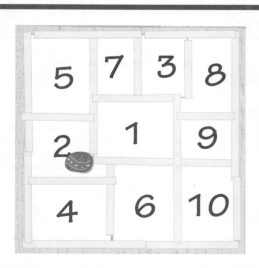

UNIT 7
LESSON 14

Multiply and Divide with 1 and 0

REAL WORLD Problem Solving

Lesson Objectives

- Look for patterns in 1s multiplications, count-bys, and divisions.
- Explore multiplications and divisions with zero and learn that divisions by zero are not possible.
- Investigate the Properties of Addition and Multiplication.

Vocabulary

product	multiplier
factors	quotient
dividend	volume
divisor	

Commutative Property of Multiplication
Associative Property of Multiplication
Identity Property of Multiplication
Zero Property of Multiplication

The Day at a Glance

Today's Goals	Materials

1 Teaching the Lesson
A1: Practice count-bys, multiplications, and divisions.
A2: Explore patterns in 1s count-bys, multiplications, and divisions.
A3: Explore multiplications and divisions with zero and learn that divisions by zero are not possible.
A4: Explore the Properties of Addition, Multiplication, and Division.
 	
2 Going Further
▶ Differentiated Instruction
 	
3 Homework and Spiral Review
	Lesson Activities
	Student Activity Book pp. 261–264
	  or Student Hardcover Book
	  pp. 261–264 and
	Homework and Remembering
	  pp. 191–194
	Check Up materials
	Signature Sheet
	Blank Sprint Answer Sheet (TRB M57)
	Study Sheet A or B
	Check Sheets 1-4
	Dry-erase markers
	Sheet protectors
	Study Sheet Answer Strips
		Check Sheet Answer
		  Strips
		Card stock
		MathBoard materials
		Class Multiplication
		  Tables
		
		Going Further
		Activity Cards 7-14
		Two-color counters
		Lined paper
		Rulers or straight-
		  edges
		Math Journals

Use Math Talk today!

Keeping Skills Sharp

Quick Practice 5 MINUTES	Daily Routines
Goal: Practice 4s count-bys, multiplications, and divisions. Use the Multiplication Table and the number "4" for the activities. **Repeated Quick Practice** Use these Quick Practice activities from previous lessons. **4s Multiplications in Order** (See Unit 7 Lesson 4.) **Mixed 4s Multiplications** (See Unit 7 Lesson 2.) **Mixed 4s Divisions** (See Unit 7 Lesson 5.)	**Homework Review** Have students work together to check their homework. **Coins and Bills** Carlos had two $5 bills, three dimes, and two nickels. He spent $9.65. How much money does Carlos have left? $0.75

① Teaching the Lesson

Activity 1

Check Up and Independent Study

 10 MINUTES

Goal: Practice count-bys, multiplications, and divisions.

Materials: Check Up materials: Signature Sheet, Blank Sprint Answer Sheet (TRB M57), Study Sheet A or B, Check Sheets 1–4, dry-erase markers, sheet protectors, Study Sheet Answer Strips (TRB M54), Check Sheet Answer Strips (TRB M55), cardstock; Homework and Remembering page 193

✔ **NCTM Standard:**
Number and Operations

▶ Check Up with 2s, 3s, 4s, 5s, 9s, and 10s PAIRS

Give **Student Pairs** a few minutes to test each other using Study Sheets A or B and collect signatures. For students who have already collected signatures on Study Sheets A and B, have them use Check Sheets 1, 2, 3, or 4. You may want to have Study Sheet and Check Sheet Answer Strips (TRB M54–M55) available. Students who made mistakes on Sprints for 3s in Lesson 13 (or who were absent) may take repeat or make-up Sprints at this time.

Then have students complete the Study Plan box on Homework and Remembering page 193. They should include 1s and 0s practice, along with any multiplications and divisions they missed in the Check Up.

Activity 2

Patterns in 1s

 15 MINUTES

Goal: Explore patterns in 1s count-bys, multiplications, and divisions.

Materials: MathBoard materials, Class Multiplication Tables, Student Activity Book or Hardcover Book p. 261

✔ **NCTM Standards:**
Number and Operations
Algebra

▶ Explore and Discuss Patterns with 1s

WHOLE CLASS   **Math Talk**

Tell students that today they will be thinking about groups of 1. Ask what things in the real world come in groups of 1. noses, mouths, steering wheels on cars, presidents of countries, and so on.

Have students circle sequential groups of 1, up to 10, on their MathBoards. The completed board is reproduced on Student Activity Book page 287. Then have them follow along as you point to each number from 1 to 10 on the Number Path and write the totals so far next to each group. After they circle each group, have them say in unison "1 group of 1 is 1," "2 groups of 1 are 2," "3 groups of 1 are 3," and so on.

● Let's say the 1s count-bys from 1 to 10. 1, 2, 3, 4, 5, 6, 7, 8, 9, 10

● What do you notice about these count-bys? Possible answer: They are the numbers we say when we count things.

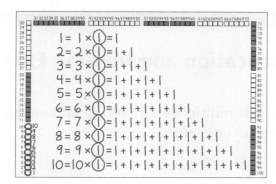

Have students write a multiplication equation for each count-by, reading each equation aloud as they write it. Then, after each multiplication equation, have them write a repeated addition expression.

Ask students to describe patterns they see in the count-bys and equations. Possible responses: The count-bys are just the counting numbers. In each equation, the product is the same as the multiplier. In other words, any number times 1 is that number.

▶ Use the Class Multiplication Table Poster

WHOLE CLASS

As you point to the equations in the 1s column, in order, have the class read them aloud, raising a finger for each new multiplier. As before, have the students use their left hand for these, facing the reader. Raise fingers from the left.

1 times 1 equals 1.   2 times 1 equals 2.   3 times 1 equals 3.

Move down the column again, this time having students say only the count-bys. Again, have them use their fingers to indicate the multipliers.

1   2   3

▶ Divide by Groups of 1   WHOLE CLASS

Have students erase the repeated addition parts of the equations on their MathBoards. Then lead them to write division equations by asking the following questions.

● If you divide 1 thing into groups of 1, how many groups do you get? 1 group (Write 1 ÷ ① = 1 next to 1 = 1 × ①.)1

● If you divide 2 things into groups of 1, how many groups do you get? 2 groups (Write 2 ÷ ① = 2 next to 2 = 2 × ①.)1

Repeat this process for one or two more division equations, and then have the students write the remaining division equations on their own. See side column for the completed MathBoard.

Activity continued ▶

✋ **Alternate Approach**

Use Counters Some children, especially tactile learners, may benefit by modeling the division before writing the equations. Have them use counters to model dividing each number into groups of 1, prior to writing the equations on their MathBoards.

Teaching Note

Math Background When any number is multiplied by 1, the result is that number; therefore, 1 is called the *multiplicative identity*. When any number is added to 0, the result is that number; therefore, 0 is called the *additive identity*.

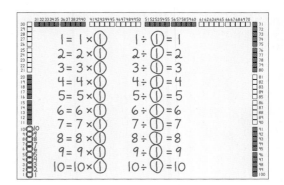

Multiply and Divide with 1 and 0   **577**

1 Teaching the Lesson (continued)

▶ Solve Multiplication and Division Exercises

WHOLE CLASS

Give the class several 1s multiplication and division exercises, and have them say the answer on your signal.

$1 \times 8 = \square$ $9 \times 1 = \square$ $6 \div 1 = \square$ $4 \div 1 = \square$

$1 \div 1 = \square$ $3 \times 1 = \square$ $2 \div 1 = \square$ $10 \times 1 = \square$

Then have a volunteer summarize what students have learned about multiplying and dividing by 1. When you multiply or divide a (nonzero) number by 1, you get that number.

Activity 3

Patterns in 0s

 15 MINUTES

Goal: Explore multiplications and divisions with zero and learn that divisions by zero are not possible.

Materials: MathBoard materials, Student Activity Book or Hardcover Book p. 261

 NCTM Standards:
Number and Operations
Algebra

▶ Explore and Discuss Patterns with 0s

WHOLE CLASS

Math Talk

Tell students that they will now explore groups of 0.

● What is the total in 1 group of 0? 0 What is the total in 2 groups of 0? 0 What about 3 groups of 0? 0 What about 10 groups of 0? 0

● Can we circle groups of 0 on the Number Path? no Why not? A group of 0 is nothing, so there is nothing to circle.

● What if we try to count by 0? What numbers would we say? 0, 0, 0, 0, . . . When we count by 0, we don't get anywhere; we are always stuck at 0!

Write the first few 0s multiplications together as a class. Then have students write the rest independently on their MathBoards. The completed board is reproduced on Student Activity Book page 287. Then, after each multiplication expression, have them write a repeated addition expression.

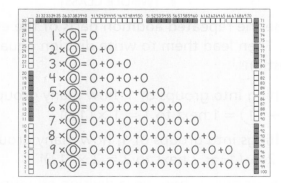

Ask students to describe any patterns they see in the count-bys and equations. Possible responses: The count-bys are always 0. In each equation, the product is always 0. In other words, any number times 0 is 0.

Zero as a Multiplier Write these multiplication expressions on the board:

$$4 \times 0 \qquad 0 \times 4$$

Then ask the following questions to review the Commutative Property.

- We know that 4 groups of 0 is 0, but what about 0 groups of 4? What is the total in 0 groups of 4? 0

- What is the total in 0 groups of 7? 0

- What is the total in 0 groups of 10? 0

- That's right, 0 groups of any number is 0. So it doesn't matter whether 0 is the group size or the multiplier, the total will be 0.

Divide by Zero Tell students that now they will explore dividing by 0. Write the following on the board:

Dividing by 0

$$5 \div 0 = \square$$

Then tell students in order to solve this problem, they need to figure out how many groups of 0 are in 5. Point out that this is a little hard to imagine so it may help to write the division as a multiplication with a missing number. Then write the related multiplication equation on the board.

Dividing by 0

$$5 \div 0 = \square \qquad \square \times 0 = 5$$

- Look at the multiplication equation, $\square \times 0 = 5$. Is there any number we can put in the box to get 5? no How do you know? Any number times 0 is 0 not 5.

Explain that it is impossible to divide 5 by 0 because there is no number we can multiply 0 by to get 5. Write "Impossible" next to the equations.

Dividing by 0

$$5 \div 0 = \square \qquad \square \times 0 = 5 \qquad \text{Impossible}$$

Point out that if we substitute any number (except 0) for 5, we get the same result. For example, finding $9 \div 0$ is impossible because we can't solve $\square \times 0 = 9$. In other words, dividing any number by 0 is impossible.

Activity continued ▶

Teaching Note

What to Expect from Students
Students are often confused by the use of zeros in division. When zero is the dividend, as in $0 \div 5$, the quotient is always zero.

$$0 \div 5 = 0 \text{ because}$$
$$\downarrow \qquad \qquad \downarrow$$
$$0 = 5 \times 0$$

However mathematicians agree that zero as a divisor, such as $5 \div 0$ is impossible.

This is because any solution for the related multiplication gives a false equation. Suppose $5 \div 0 = n$. Then $0 \times n = 5$. But that is not true $0 \times n = 0$.

① Teaching the Lesson (continued)

Teaching Note

Math Background If you feel that your students are ready, you may want to summarize the following points algebraically. Explain that you are using N to represent any number and that $N \neq 0$.

► The product of any number and 0 is 0.

$$N \times 0 = 0$$

► Zero divided by any number is 0.

$$0 \div N = 0$$

► It is impossible to divide any number by 0.

$$N \div 0 \text{ is impossible}$$

Divide Into Zero Leave the "Dividing by 0" equations on the board. To the right of them, write "Dividing into 0" with $0 \div 5 = \square$ beneath it. Ask students to help you write the corresponding mystery multiplication equation, $\square \times 5 = 0$.

Dividing by 0

$$5 \div 0 = \square \qquad \square \times 0 = 5$$

Dividing into 0

$$0 \div 5 = \square \qquad \square \times 5 = 0$$

Ask how this example is different from the example they just looked at. In the previous example, we were dividing 5 by 0. In this example, we are dividing 0 by 5.

Point to $0 \div 5 = \square$ and ask how many groups of 5 are in 0. 0 groups

Then point to the multiplication equation, $\square \times 5 = 0$ and explain that they can also solve the division equation by thinking of this multiplication equation.

● You can think, "What number times 5 equals 0?" What is the answer? 0 That's correct, zero 5s make 0. (Write 0 in both mystery boxes.)

Then ask students if we would get the same answer if we divided 0 by a different number, say 8. They should see that, no matter what nonzero number we divide 0 by, we get 0.

Give the class several 0s multiplications and divisions, both dividing by 0 and dividing into 0.

$$0 \div 8 = \square \qquad 8 \times 0 = \square \qquad 0 \times 3 = \square \qquad 3 \div 0 = \square$$

$$7 \times 0 = \square \qquad 0 \div 4 = \square \qquad 10 \div 0 = \square$$

Tell students to give the answer on your signal. If an exercise is impossible to solve, they should say "Impossible."

Ask students to summarize what they have learned about multiplying and dividing with 0. Make sure these three points are made:

● The product of any number and 0 is 0.

● Zero divided by any (nonzero) number is 0.

● It is impossible to divide a number by 0.

Addition, Multiplication, and Division Properties

▶ Introduce the Associative Property WHOLE CLASS

Draw the following pictures and write the following expressions on the classroom board.

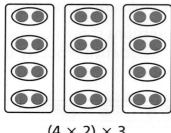

(4 × 2) × 3

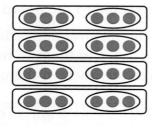

4 × (2 × 3)

Ask the students to discuss how the expressions underneath each picture are the same and how they are different. Both expressions use the same numbers, but the parentheses are in different positions.

Point to the first picture and explain that it shows 3 sets of 4 groups with 2 counters in each group. Tell the students that the parentheses tell us which two factors to multiply first.

- Which two factors should we multiply first? 4 and 2 What is the product of 4 and 2? 8

- Which two numbers should we multiply next? 8 and 3 What is the product of 8 and 3? 24 (Write 8 × 3 = 24 underneath the expression.)

Ask for a volunteer to come to the board and count the counters in the first picture to check that there are 24 counters in the picture.

Then point to the second picture and explain that it shows 4 sets of 2 groups with 3 counters in each group.

- Which two factors should we multiply first? 2 and 3 What is the product of 2 and 3? 6

- Which two numbers should we multiply next? 4 and 6 What is the product of 4 and 6? 24 (Write 4 × 6 = 24 underneath the expression.)

Ask for a volunteer to come to the board and count the counters in the second picture to check that there are 24 counters in the picture.

 20 MINUTES

Goal: Explore the Associative Property of Multiplication.

Materials: Student Activity Book or Hardcover Book p. 262

✔ **NCTM Standards:**
Number and Operations
Algebra

Teaching Note

Math Background Discuss with students that the Associative Property of Addition shows that changing the way addends are grouped does not change the sum.

(4 + 3) + 5 = ☐   4 + (3 + 5) = ☐

7 + 5 = 12   4 + 8 = 12

Then discuss the similarities between the Associative Property of Addition and the Associative Property of Multiplication.

English Language Learners

Write *associative property*, (4 × 2) × 3 = 24, and 4 × (2 × 3) = 24 on the board.

- **Beginning** Say: We can change the way the numbers are grouped. The product is the same. This is the *associative property*. Have students repeat.
- **Intermediate** Ask: Are the numbers grouped the same way? no Does the answer change? no Is this the *associative property*? yes
- **Advanced** Have students write two expressions that show the associative property.

Activity continued ▶

Teaching Note

What to Expect from Students
Some children may be confused by the mathematical names for the multiplication properties and division rules. At this point, it is more important that students know how to use the properties and rules correctly. Continue to use the correct terminology in subsequent lessons and over time students will begin to incorporate the math terms into their own vocabulary.

✔ Ongoing Assessment

Ask students the following questions.

▶ You know that $5 \times 8 = 40$. What is 6×8? 48

▶ What do you get when you multiply any number by 0? 0

▶ What do you get when you multiply or divide any number by 1? You get the number you started with.

▶ Can you find the quotient for $9 \div 0$? No, it is impossible to divide by 0.

▶ # Multiplication Properties and Division Rules WHOLE CLASS

Direct students to Student Book page 262 and have the students discuss the multiplication properties and division rules for 1 and 0. Ask for volunteers to come to the board and draw a picture to show each rule.

Then draw the pictures and write the expressions shown below on the classroom board. Use them to review the Associative Property by asking questions like the ones on the previous page.

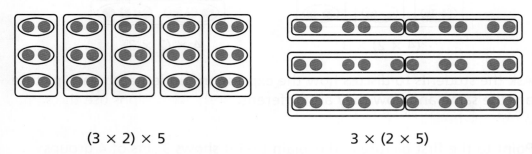

$(3 \times 2) \times 5$ $3 \times (2 \times 5)$

Have the students complete the page independently or in Helping Pairs.

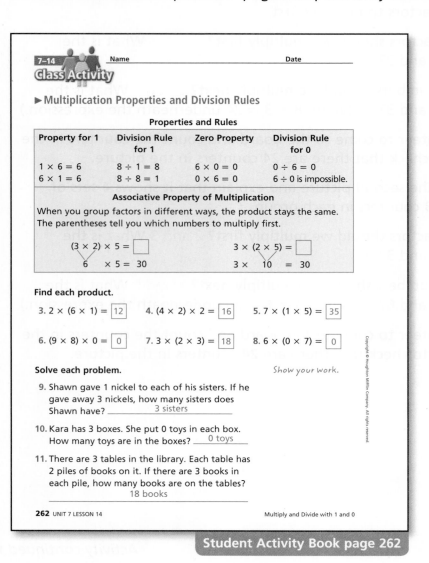

Student Activity Book page 262

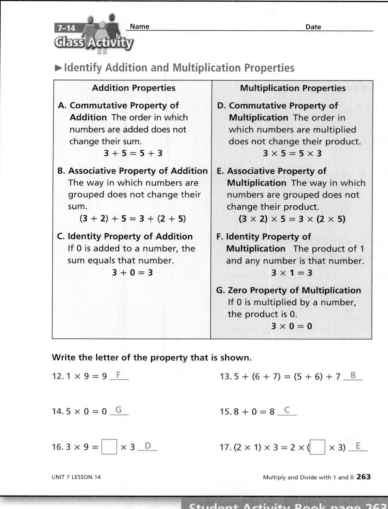

Student Activity Book page 263

▶ Identify Addition and Multiplication Properties

WHOLE CLASS

Have students look at Student Book page 263 and review the addition and multiplication properties that they have already studied and identify the new properties. Point out the similarity and difference between the Identity Properties of Addition and Multiplication: with addition, you are adding zero to get the same number; for multiplication, you are multiplying by one to get the same number.

Discuss if the properties of addition are true for subtraction and if the properties of multiplication are true for division. Have students give examples to support their reasoning. (The identity properties are true for subtraction and division. Division by zero is undefined)

Have students complete exercises 13–17 independently.

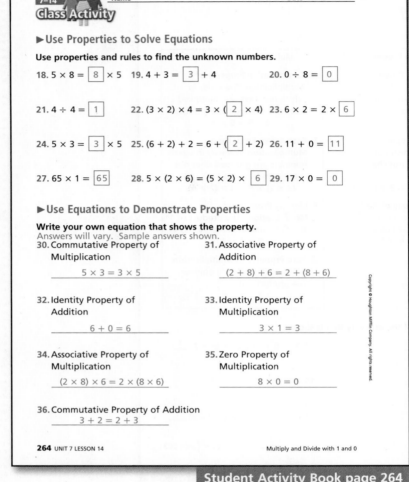

Student Activity Book page 264

The image shows:

7–14
Class Activity
Name _____ Date _____

▶**Use Properties to Solve Equations**

Use properties and rules to find the unknown numbers.

18. 5 × 8 = ⬚8⬚ × 5   19. 4 + 3 = ⬚3⬚ + 4   20. 0 ÷ 8 = ⬚0⬚

21. 4 ÷ 4 = ⬚1⬚   22. (3 × 2) × 4 = 3 × (⬚2⬚ × 4) 23. 6 × 2 = 2 × ⬚6⬚

24. 5 × 3 = ⬚3⬚ × 5   25. (6 + 2) + 2 = 6 + (⬚2⬚ + 2) 26. 11 + 0 = ⬚11⬚

27. 65 × 1 = ⬚65⬚   28. 5 × (2 × 6) = (5 × 2) × ⬚6⬚ 29. 17 × 0 = ⬚0⬚

▶**Use Equations to Demonstrate Properties**

Write your own equation that shows the property.
Answers will vary. Sample answers shown.

30. Commutative Property of Multiplication
    5 × 3 = 3 × 5

31. Associative Property of Addition
    (2 + 8) + 6 = 2 + (8 + 6)

32. Identity Property of Addition
    6 + 0 = 6

33. Identity Property of Multiplication
    3 × 1 = 3

34. Associative Property of Multiplication
    (2 × 8) × 6 = 2 × (8 × 6)

35. Zero Property of Multiplication
    8 × 0 = 0

36. Commutative Property of Addition
    3 + 2 = 2 + 3

264 UNIT 7 LESSON 14   Multiply and Divide with 1 and 0

Class Management

Looking Ahead Remind students to take home their 1s and 0s charts on Homework and Remembering page 191.

▶ **Use Properties to Solve Equations** PAIRS

Have **Students Pairs** solve exercises 18–29. If students need assistance, encourage them to look back at the definitions and examples of each property on Student Book pages 262–263.

Then use **Solve and Discuss** to have students explain what properties they used to solve each equation.

▶ **Use Equations to Demonstrate Properties** PAIRS

Read aloud the directions at the bottom of Student Book page 264. Allow time for **Student Pairs** to complete exercises 30–36 then share their equations with the class.

❷ Going Further

Differentiated Instruction

● Intervention   Activity Card 7-14

Use Counters to Multiply   Activity Card 7-14 ●

Work: In pairs

Use:
• 10 counters

Decide:
Who will be Student 1 and who will be Student 2 for the first round.

1. **Student 1:** Write a multiplication example using the number 0 or 1 as one of the factors.

2. **Student 2:** Use counters to model the example and find the product.

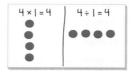

3. Change roles. Write and model a division example using the number 0 or 1. Remember: You cannot divide by 0.

Unit 7, Lesson 14   Copyright © Houghton Mifflin Company

Activity Note Because zero cannot be the divisor in a division equation, the only possible division examples using zero will show zero divided by any other number. The model is simply a blank space.

 Math Writing Prompt

Which Is Easier? Which of these exercises below is easier to solve: 438×1 or 38×2? Explain your thinking.

 **Software Support**

Warm Up 12.24

▲ On Level   Activity Card 7-14

Input/Output Tables   Activity Card 7-14 ▲

Work: In pairs

Use:
• Lined paper
• Ruler or straightedge

1. **On Your Own** Draw an input/output table for multiplying by 1. Use the table below as an example.

Multiply by 1	
Input	Output
4	? 4
36	? 36
279	? 279
7,358	? 7,358

2. Be sure to include a 1-digit, 2-digit, 3-digit, and 4-digit number in your table.

3. Now make an input/output table for dividing by 1.

4. Exchange both tables with your partner and complete each table.

Unit 7, Lesson 14   Copyright © Houghton Mifflin Company

Activity Note Have students discuss why both columns in the table match for both multiplication and division, regardless of the numbers chosen.

 Math Writing Prompt

Draw a Picture Draw pictures or arrays to show why $6 \times 1 = 1 \times 6 = 6$. Use labels to explain your drawing.

 Software Support

Country Countdown, Counting Critters, Level Z

■ Challenge   Activity Card 7-14

Three in a Row   Activity Card 7-14 ■

Work: In pairs

1. **On Your Own** Think of three multiplications that have the same product. Then create a 3-by-3 multiplication grid as shown below.

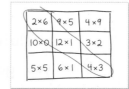

2. Be sure that one row, column, or diagonal of your grid shows the three multiplications with the same product.

3. Exchange puzzles with your partner and circle the three multiplications that are equal.

Unit 7, Lesson 14   Copyright © Houghton Mifflin Company

Activity Note If students have difficulty finding three multiplications with the same product, remind them that the multiplication property of 1 makes it easy to write a multiplication for any product.

 Math Writing Prompt

Write the Rule Write the rules for adding 0 or 1 to any number, and multiplying any number by 0 or by 1.

 DESTINATION Math® **Software Support**

Course II: Module 2: Unit 2: Finding Products less than 100

Multiply and Divide with 1 and 0   **585**

③ Homework and Spiral Review

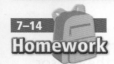

Homework Goal: Additional Practice

This Homework page provides practice multiplying and dividing with 0 and 1.

7–14	Name		Date
Homework

Study Plan

_____

_____

                                    Homework Helper

Complete.

1. $3 \times (4 \times 2) =$ `24`   2. $(5 \times 2) \times 8 =$ `80`   3. $5 \times (0 \times 9) =$ `0`

4. $25 \times 1 =$ `25`   5. $3 \times 9 = 9 \times$ `3` $=$ `27`   6. $6 \times (3 \times 2) =$ `36`

Solve each problem.

7. Paul put birthday candles on his brother's cake. He arranged them in an array with 8 rows and 1 column. How many candles did he put on the cake? _____8 candles_____

8. There are 24 people in the brass section of the marching band. They stood in an array with 4 people in each row. How many rows were there? _____6 rows_____

9. Freya doesn't like peppers, so she grew 0 peppers in her garden. She divided the peppers equally among her 4 cousins. How many peppers did each cousin get? _____0 peppers_____

10. Cal had 6 comic books. After he gave 1 comic book to each of his cousins, he had none left. How many cousins does Cal have? _____6 cousins_____

UNIT 7 LESSON 14   Multiply and Divide with 1 and 0 **193**

Homework and Remembering page 193

Remembering Goal: Spiral Review

This Remembering page would be appropriate anytime after today's lesson.

7–14	Name		Date
Remembering

Solve each problem.   *Show your work.*

1. Dakota had some money. Then she earned $6.84 at her family's garage sale. Now she has $9.75. How much money did she start with? _____$2.91_____

2. Frankie's dog weighs 82 pounds. His cat weighs 17 pounds. How much less does his cat weigh than his dog? _____65 pounds_____

3. Ghita had 9 trophies. 4 were tennis trophies, and the rest were soccer trophies. Then she won 3 more soccer trophies. How many soccer trophies does Ghita have now? _____8 soccer trophies_____

Draw three different coin combinations for each amount.
Answers will vary. Possible answers are given.

4. 73¢	5. $0.32	6. 57¢
DDDDDDD PPP	Q N PP	QQ N PP
QQ DD PPP	NNNNNN PP	DDDDD N PP
Q DDD NNN PPP	DDD PP	NNNNNNNNNNN PP

Add or subtract.

7. $500 - 327 =$ `173`   8. $87 + 264 =$ `351`   9. $902 - 209 =$ `693`

194 UNIT 7 LESSON 14   Multiply and Divide with 1 and 0

Homework and Remembering page 194

Home and School Activity

Multicultural Connection

Math Haikus Haikus are a traditional form of Japanese poetry, consisting of three lines, and rarely rhyme. The first and last line of a haiku have 5 syllables and the middle line has 7 syllables. Read examples of haikus to students and have them write their own math haikus to help them remember tricks for multiplying by 0 and 1 and dividing by 1. Display students' work for others to see.

> One
>
> Multiply by 1,
> And you get the same number.
> 1 times 5 is 5.
>
> By Joey

UNIT 7 LESSON 15

Play Multiplication and Division Games

Vocabulary

organized list   divisor
dividend   quotient

Lesson Objective

● Practice with 2s, 3s, 4s, 5s, 9s, and 10s multiplications and divisions.

The Day at a Glance

Today's Goals	Materials
① Teaching the Lesson **A1:** Take Sprints for 4s multiplications and divisions. **A2:** Review count-bys, multiplications, and divisions. **A3:** Practice multiplications and divisions by playing games. **② Going Further** ▶ Differentiated Instruction **③ Homework and Spiral Review**	**Lesson Activities** Student Activity Book pp. 265–272 or Student Hardcover Book pp. 265–272 and Activity Workbook pp. 121–128 (includes Check Sheet, Game Rules, Game Grids, and Game Board) Homework and Remembering pp. 195–198 Blank Sprint Answer Sheet Check up materials Signature Sheet Study Sheet A or B Check Sheets 1-6 Dry-erase markers Sheet protectors Study Sheet Answer Strips Check Sheet Answer Strips Card stock Strategy Cards for 2s, 3s, 4s, 5s, and 9s Game pieces or other small items **Going Further** Activity Cards 7-15 Index cards Math Journals **123 Use Math Talk today!**

Keeping Skills Sharp

Quick Practice ⏱ 5 MINUTES	Daily Routines
Goal: Practice 4s count-bys, multiplications, and divisions. **Materials:** Class Multiplication Table Poster, pointer Display the Class Multiplication Table Poster. Use the number "4" for these activities. **Repeated Quick Practice** Use these Quick Practice activities from previous lessons. **4s Multiplications in Order** (See Unit 7 Lesson 4.) **Mixed 4s Multiplications** (See Unit 7 Lesson 2.) **Mixed 4s Divisions** (See Unit 7 Lesson 5.)	**Homework Review** Ask students to describe strategies they used in their homework. Students may solve the problem correctly but use an inefficient strategy. **Estimation** Use rounding to decide if the answer is reasonable. Then find the answer to see if you were correct. 1. 76 + 15 = 91 reasonable; 91 2. 82 − 36 = 66 not reasonable; 46

Teaching the Lesson

Assess 4s

 5 MINUTES

Goal: Take Sprints for 4s multiplications and divisions.

Materials: Student Activity Book p. 265 or Activity Workbook p. 121, Blank Sprint Answer Sheet (TRB M57)

✔ **NCTM Standard:**
Number and Operations

▶ **Sprints for 4s** | WHOLE CLASS |

Direct students to Student Book page 289 or Activity Workbook page 121. Read aloud the 4s sprints below, and then have students check each other's work.

× 4	÷ 4
a. $9 \times 4 = 36$	a. $40 \div 4 = 10$
b. $5 \times 4 = 20$	b. $8 \div 4 = 2$
c. $7 \times 4 = 28$	c. $16 \div 4 = 4$
d. $2 \times 4 = 8$	d. $20 \div 4 = 5$
e. $8 \times 4 = 32$	e. $28 \div 4 = 7$
f. $1 \times 4 = 4$	f. $36 \div 4 = 9$
g. $3 \times 4 = 12$	g. $4 \div 4 = 1$
h. $6 \times 4 = 24$	h. $32 \div 4 = 8$
i. $4 \times 4 = 16$	i. $12 \div 4 = 3$
j. $10 \times 4 = 40$	j. $24 \div 4 = 6$

Check Up and Independent Study

 10 MINUTES

Goal: Review count-bys, multiplications, and divisions.

Materials: Check Up materials: Signature Sheet, Study Sheets A or B Check Sheets 1–6, dry-erase markers, sheet protectors, Study Sheet Answer Strips (TRB M54), Check Sheet Answer Strips (TRB M55), cardstock; Strategy Cards, Homework and Remembering page 197

✔ **NCTM Standard:**
Number and Operations

 Ongoing Assessment

Ask students the following questions.
▶ How can you use $2 \times 4 = 8$ to help you find 4×2?
▶ How can you use $8 \div 2 = 4$ to help you find $8 \div 4$?

▶ **Check Up with 0s, 1s, 2s, 3s, 4s, 5s, 9s, and 10s**
| WHOLE CLASS |

Direct students to Check Sheets 5 and 6 on Student Book pages 267–268 or Activity Workbook pp. 123–124. Check Sheet 5 provides practice with 0s and 1s and Check Sheet 6 provides mixed practice with 3s, 4s, 0s, and 1s. There are two identical pages of these check sheets on Homework and Remembering pages.

Give **Student Pairs** a few minutes to test one another and collect signatures, using Study Sheets A or B. For students who have already collected signatures on Study Sheets A or B, have them use Check Sheets 1–6. You may want to have Study Sheet Answer Strips and Check Sheet Answer Strips (TRB M54–M55) available.

Give students a few minutes to study independently, using Check Sheets and Strategy Cards. Then have students complete the Study Plan box including any multiplications and divisions they missed during the Check Up on Homework and Remembering page 197.

Play Games to Practice Multiplications and Divisions

Organize students into pairs. Each pair will need a set of Strategy Cards (2s, 3s, 4s, 5s, and 9s), with the multiplication and division cards separated into two separate stacks.

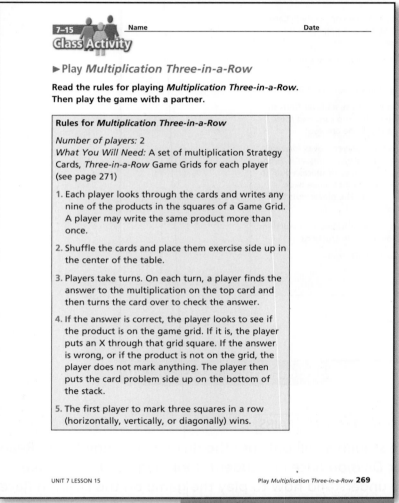

 30 MINUTES

Goal: Practice multiplications and divisions by playing games.

Materials: Strategy Cards for 2s, 3s, 4s, 5s, and 9s (1 set per student), game pieces (coins, buttons, counters, or other small items; 2 different objects per pair), Student Activity Book or Hardcover Book pp. 269–272 and Activity Workbook pp. 125–128

 NCTM Standard:
Number and Operations

Differentiated Instruction

Here are some ways to adapt *Multiplication Three-in-a-Row* to meet the needs of all your students.

Intervention: Limit the cards to certain factors. For example, have students use the cards for 2s, 5s, and 9s only, or for 3s and 4s only.

On Level: Use a 4-by-4 (or larger) grid instead of a 3-by-3 grid. Students must get four (or more) in a row to win.

Challenge: Have students use the division Strategy Cards to play *Division Three-in-a-Row*. Note that there are only eight possible factors to write in the game grid, so students will have to write some factors more than once.

English Language Learners

Review vocabulary needed to play the game: *grid, shuffle, side up, side down, diagonal, horizontal,* and *vertical.*

Student Activity Book page 269

▶ Play *Multiplication Three-in-a-Row* [PAIRS]

Tell students that they will now play a game using only the multiplication Strategy Cards. Read aloud the rules for *Three-in-a-Row* on Student Book page 269 or Activity Workbook p. 125, and make sure students understand how to play the game on the grids on Student Book page 271 or Activity Workbook p. 127. Then give students several minutes to play the game.

Activity continued ▶

1 Teaching the Lesson (continued)

Class Management

You may wish to have game materials available for students to use during down time. You might set up a game station with sets of Strategy Cards; laminated game rules, game grids, and game boards; and counters or coins to use as game pieces.

Class Management

Looking Ahead Game boards and directions for games will be needed for Lesson 16 and lessons in Unit 9. Be sure students store them in their folders or in a place where they can find them easily. If students need to replace materials for the games, use TRB M93–M96.

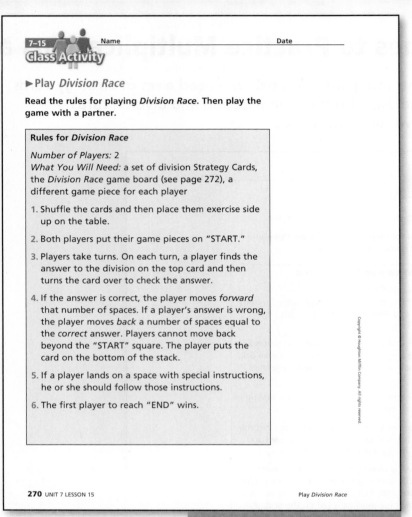

Student Activity Book page 270

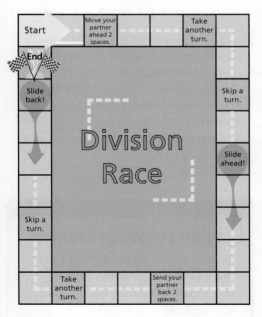

Division Race Game Board from Student Activity Book page 296.

▶ Play *Division Race* [PAIRS]

For the next game students will only use the division Strategy Cards. Read aloud the rules for *Division Race* on Student Book page 270, and make sure **Student Pairs** understand how to play the game on the Division Race game board on Student Book page 272. Emphasize these points:

● If a player gets an answer wrong, he or she moves back a number of spaces equal to the *correct* answer. So, if the problem is 12 ÷ 3 and a player incorrectly answers 6, he or she moves back 4 spaces, not 6.

● A student cannot move back beyond the first space. So, if a player is on the second space and incorrectly solves the problem 12 ÷ 3, he or she moves back only 2 spaces to "START," rather than the full 4 spaces.

Give **Student Pairs** several minutes to play the game.

Math Talk As a class, discuss how the two games they played in this lesson were similar and different. Both used the answers; One game used multiplication and the other division

②Going Further

Intervention   Activity Card 7-15

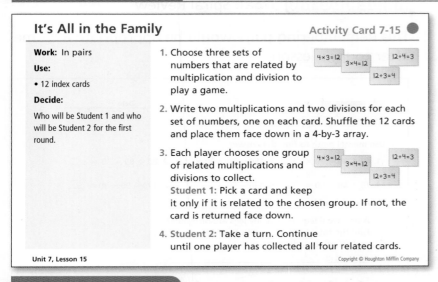

It's All in the Family   Activity Card 7-15 ●

Work: In pairs
Use:
• 12 index cards
Decide:
Who will be Student 1 and who will be Student 2 for the first round.

1. Choose three sets of numbers that are related by multiplication and division to play a game.

2. Write two multiplications and two divisions for each set of numbers, one on each card. Shuffle the 12 cards and place them face down in a 4-by-3 array.

3. Each player chooses one group of related multiplications and divisions to collect.
   Student 1: Pick a card and keep it only if it is related to the chosen group. If not, the card is returned face down.

4. Student 2: Take a turn. Continue until one player has collected all four related cards.

Unit 7, Lesson 15   Copyright © Houghton Mifflin Company

Activity Note The activity will be more challenging if students choose sets of numbers that use one or more of the same numbers in more than one set.

✏ Math Writing Prompt

Explain Your Thinking Explain why there is only one multiplication and one division in the related multiplications and divisions for 5, 5, and 25.

Soar to Success Math ★ Software Support

Warm Up 28.20

On Level   Activity Card 7-15

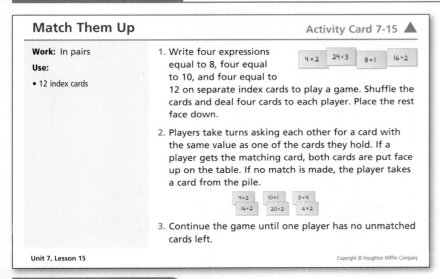

Match Them Up   Activity Card 7-15 ▲

Work: In pairs
Use:
• 12 index cards

1. Write four expressions equal to 8, four equal to 10, and four equal to 12 on separate index cards to play a game. Shuffle the cards and deal four cards to each player. Place the rest face down.

2. Players take turns asking each other for a card with the same value as one of the cards they hold. If a player gets the matching card, both cards are put face up on the table. If no match is made, the player takes a card from the pile.

3. Continue the game until one player has no unmatched cards left.

Unit 7, Lesson 15   Copyright © Houghton Mifflin Company

Activity Note Students who need help choosing expressions can refer to Study Sheets A and B. Have students check each other's matched pairs as they accumulate during the game.

✏ Math Writing Prompt

Mental Math Without dividing, how can you tell that $72 \div 8$ is greater than $64 \div 8$? Explain your thinking.

MegaMath Grades K-6 Software Support

Country Countdown, Counting Critters, Level X

Challenge   Activity Card 7-15

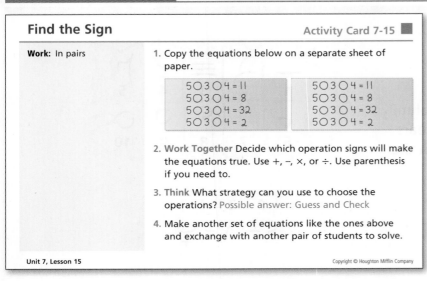

Find the Sign   Activity Card 7-15 ■

Work: In pairs

1. Copy the equations below on a separate sheet of paper.

2. **Work Together** Decide which operation signs will make the equations true. Use $+$, $-$, $\times$, or $\div$. Use parenthesis if you need to.

3. **Think** What strategy can you use to choose the operations? Possible answer: Guess and Check

4. Make another set of equations like the ones above and exchange with another pair of students to solve.

Unit 7, Lesson 15   Copyright © Houghton Mifflin Company

Activity Note Remind students to consider the order of operation and use parentheses if needed.

✏ Math Writing Prompt

Investigate Math If the dividend and divisor in a basic division are both doubled, will the answer be the same or double the original answer? Explain.

✴ DESTINATION Math· Software Support

Course II: Module 2: Unit 3: Dividing by a 1-digit Number

Play Multiplication and Division Games   **591**

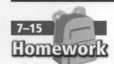 # Homework and Spiral Review

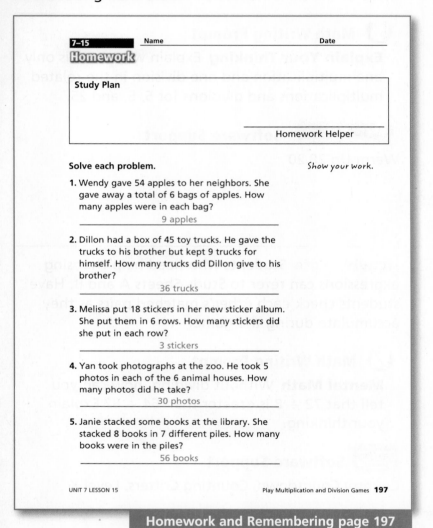

7–15
Homework **Goal:** Additional Practice

This Homework page provides practice in multiplying and dividing basic facts.

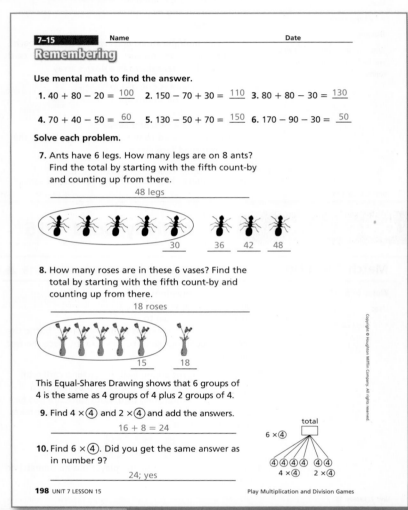

7–15
Remembering **Goal:** Spiral Review

This Remembering page would be appropriate anytime after today's lesson.

Homework and Remembering page 197

Homework and Remembering page 198

Home and School Activity

 ## Social Studies Connection

Ancient Brahmi Numbers Explain to the students that Brahmi is an ancient Indian writing system that is thousands of years old. Draw the Brahmi symbols for the numbers 1 to 10 on the board.

Demonstrate how to write the equation 8 ÷ 2 = 4 using Brahmi symbols. Have the students write three division equations using the numbers 1 to 10 and then write the same equations using the Brahmi numerals.

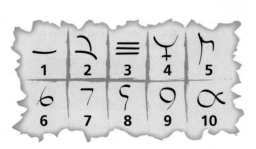

Practice with 0s, 1s, 2s, 3s, 4s, 5s, 9s, and 10s

REAL WORLD **Problem Solving**

Vocabulary

multiples
quotient
divisor

Lesson Objectives

- Practice multiplications and divisions for 0s, 1s, 2s, 3s, 4s, 5s, 9s, and 10s.

- Solve multiplication and division word problems.

The Day at a Glance

Today's Goals	Materials
1 Teaching the Lesson **A1:** Review count-bys, multiplications, and divisions for all the factors in this unit. **A2:** Practice multiplications and divisions by completing Dashes or playing games. **A3:** Solve multiplications and divisions word problems. **2 Going Further** ▶ Going Further: Divide Multiples of 10 and 100 ▶ Differentiated Instruction **3 Homework and Spiral Review**	**Lesson Activities** Student Activity Book pp. 273–280 or Student Hardcover Book pp. 273–280 and Activity Workbook pp. 129–130 (includes Check Sheet and Dashes) Homework and Remembering pp. 199–202 Blank Sprint Answer Sheet Folders Check Up materials Signature Sheet Blank Sprint Answer Sheet Study Sheet A or B Check Sheet 1, 2, 3, 4, 5, 6, or 7 Dry-erase markers Sheet protectors Study Sheet Answer Strips Check Sheet Answer Strips Card stock	Strategy Cards Multiplication and Division strategy cards Game pieces (coins, buttons, or other small items) Quick Quiz 3 **Going Further** MathBoard materials Activity Cards 7-16 Game Cards (TRB M25) Index cards Rulers and straightedges Strategy Cards (0's, 1's, 2's, 3's, 4's, 5's, 9's,10s) Math Journals 123 *Use* **Math Talk** *today!*

Keeping Skills Sharp

Quick Practice ⏱ 5 MINUTES	**Daily Routines**
Goal: Practice 1s count-bys, multiplications, and divisions. Use the Multiplication Table and the number "1" for the activities. **Repeated Quick Practice** Use these Quick Practice activities from previous lessons. **1s Multiplications in Order** (See Unit 7 Lesson 4.) **Mixed 1s Multiplications** (See Unit 7 Lesson 2.) **Mixed 1s Divisions** (See Unit 7 Lesson 5.)	**Homework Review** Ask several students to share their work. Have the class ask clarifying questions. **Nonroutine Problem** Brad has 7 coins worth $0.32. What are the coins? Explain. 1 dime, 4 nickels, 2 pennies; Add coins to find the group of 7 coins and a total of $0.32.

① Teaching the Lesson

Activity 1

Check Up and Independent Study

 15 MINUTES

Goal: Review count-bys, multiplications, and divisions for all the factors in this unit.

Materials: Folders, Check Up materials: Signature Sheet, Blank Sprint Answer Sheet (TRB M57), Study Sheet A or B, Check Sheet 1, 2, 3, 4, 5, 6, or 7, dry-erase markers (1 per student), sheet protectors (1 per student), Study Sheet Answer Strips (TRB M54), Check Sheet Answer Strips (TRB M55), cardstock; Strategy Cards, Homework and Remembering page 201

 NCTM Standard:
Number and Operations

▶ **Check Up with 0s, 1s, 2s, 3s, 4s, 5s, 9s, and 10s**

WHOLE CLASS

Direct students to Check Sheet 7 on Student Book page 297 or Activity Workbook p. 129 which contains multiplications and divisions for all the factors in this unit. Tell students that today they will have extra time to test each other from all the Study Sheets and collect signatures. For students who have signatures for the Study Sheets, have them use the Check Sheets. You may want to have Study Sheet Answer Strips and Check Sheet Answer Strips (TRB M54–M55) available.

Students who made mistakes on the Sprints for 4s in Lesson 15 (or who were absent) may take repeat or make up Sprints at this time. Students can record their answers on Blank Sprint Answer Sheet (TRB M57). Give students 10 minutes or longer to test one another and then a few minutes to study independently, using their Study Sheets, Check Sheets, or Strategy Cards. Then have students complete the Study Plan box including any multiplications and divisions they missed on Homework and Remembering page 201.

Activity 2

Practice Multiplications and Divisions

 15 MINUTES

Goal: Practice multiplications and divisions by completing Dashes or playing games.

Materials: Multiplication and Division Strategy Cards, game pieces such as coins, buttons, counters, or other small items (2 different objects per pair), Student Activity Book or Hardcover Book pp. 269–272; 275–278 and Activty Workbook pp. 125–128, 130

 NCTM Standard:
Number and Operations

▶ **Complete Dashes 1–4 and Play Games** WHOLE CLASS

Have students do one or both of the following:

● Complete the Dashes (quick self-tests) on Student Book page 275 or Activity Workbook page 130. You can have students complete one Dash at a time, or do all the Dashes at once. Time the Dashes or let students complete them at their own pace. Students can check their answers on Student Book page 277. If you do not use the Dashes as part of today's lesson, you might suggest students complete them at home in preparation for the unit test. A second Dash is included on the back for retesting if needed.

● Play *Solve the Stack, Multiplication Three-in-a-Row,* or *Division Race.* Allow students to choose the games they want to play. If students need replacements of any of the game boards or rules for the games, use TRB M90, M93–M96. Make sure to remind students to put all game materials in their folders.

Multiplications and Divisions Word Problems

► **Solve Word Problems with 2s, 3s, 4s, 5s, 6s, 7s, and 9s** WHOLE CLASS

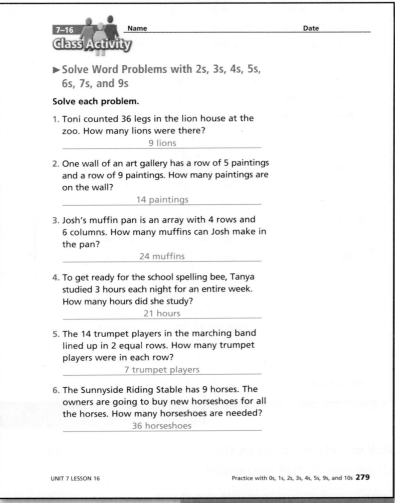

7-16
Class Activity
Name _____ Date _____

► Solve Word Problems with 2s, 3s, 4s, 5s, 6s, 7s, and 9s

Solve each problem.

1. Toni counted 36 legs in the lion house at the zoo. How many lions were there?
   _____ 9 lions _____

2. One wall of an art gallery has a row of 5 paintings and a row of 9 paintings. How many paintings are on the wall?
   _____ 14 paintings _____

3. Josh's muffin pan is an array with 4 rows and 6 columns. How many muffins can Josh make in the pan?
   _____ 24 muffins _____

4. To get ready for the school spelling bee, Tanya studied 3 hours each night for an entire week. How many hours did she study?
   _____ 21 hours _____

5. The 14 trumpet players in the marching band lined up in 2 equal rows. How many trumpet players were in each row?
   _____ 7 trumpet players _____

6. The Sunnyside Riding Stable has 9 horses. The owners are going to buy new horseshoes for all the horses. How many horseshoes are needed?
   _____ 36 horseshoes _____

UNIT 7 LESSON 16   Practice with 0s, 1s, 2s, 3s, 4s, 5s, 9s, and 10s **279**

Student Activity Book page 279

Using **Solve and Discuss,** have students complete problems 1–6 on Student Book page 279.

If students are making drawings, encourage them to use equal-shares drawings, fast array drawings, or other representations that do not show each individual item.

 15 MINUTES

Goal: Solve multiplication and division word problems.

Materials: Student Activity Book or Hardcover Book p. 279

 NCTM Standards:
Problem Solving
Communication
Representation

 Class Management

Looking Ahead Remind students to bring home their Home Check 7 on Homework and Remembering page 199.

 Ongoing Assessment

Ask students the following questions:

► How can 5 × 7 = 35, help you find 7 × 5?

► How can 4 × 9 = 36 help you find 36 ÷ 9?

► What is the product of 9 × (25 × 0)?

Where would you place the parentheses to find the product of 2 × 3 × 4? Explain your thinking.

► What is the product of 254 × 1?

 Quick Quiz

See Assessment Guide for Unit 7 Quick Quiz 3.

② Going Further

Extension: Divide Multiples of 10 and 100

Goal: Divide 2- and 3-digit multiples of 10 and 100 by 1-digit numbers.

Materials: MathBoard materials, Student Activity Book or Hardcover Book p. 280

 NCTM Standard:
Number and Operations

▶ Introduce Dividing Multiples of 10

WHOLE CLASS

Write the following on the board:

$$3 \times 2 = 6$$
$$3 \times 20 = 60$$
$$3 \times 200 = 600$$
$$3 \times 2,000 = 6,000$$

Ask a volunteer to come to the board and write related division sentences using 3 as the divisor.

$3 \times 2 = 6$	$6 \div 3 = 2$
$3 \times 20 = 60$	$60 \div 3 = 20$
$3 \times 200 = 600$	$600 \div 3 = 200$
$3 \times 2,000 = 6,000$	$6,000 \div 3 = 2,000$

● **What pattern do you see?** The answer has the same number of zeros as the number of zeros in the multiple of 10 after doing the basic division.

Write $300 \div 5$ on the board. **How can you use the pattern to find $300 \div 5$?** Write the answer to the basic division $30 \div 5$, 6. Then write 1 zero because there is 1 zero in the dividend left after using the basic division.

Explain that you can use ten-sticks, hundred boxes, and thousands bars to show why this works.

Draw the following on the board.

$60 \div 3 = 20$
6 tens ÷ 3 = 2 tens

$600 \div 3 = 200$
6 hundreds ÷ 3 = 2 hundreds

$6,000 \div 3 = 2,000$
6 thousands ÷ 3 = 2 thousands

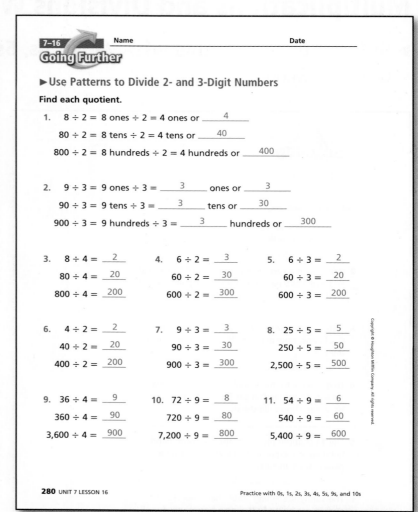

Student Activity Book page 280

Ask questions such as the following to relate the drawings to the equations:

● How many are in each of the 3 groups?

● What is the value of each group?

▶ Use Patterns to Divide 2- and 3-Digit Numbers WHOLE CLASS

Work together as a class to complete exercises 1–2 on Student Book page 280.

Then give the students a few minutes to complete exercises 3–11 independently. Once students have completed the exercises, have them come to the board and explain how they found their answers.

Differentiated Instruction

Whose Product Is Greater?   Activity Card 7-16 ●

Work: In pairs

Use:

• TRB M25 (2 sets of Game Cards)

1. Shuffle the Game Cards and place them in a stack face down. Each player draws four cards from the pile. Use two of the cards to make a multiplication.

Player 1   Player 2
4 + 7 = 28   9 + 8 = 72

2. Compare products. The greater product wins 1 point.

3. Collect and reshuffle the cards to continue the game until one player has won 5 points.

Unit 7, Lesson 16   Copyright © Houghton Mifflin Company

Activity Note Students should realize that using the two greatest factors from their four cards will give the greatest possible product.

 Math Writing Prompt

Use Strategies What strategy do you use to find the answer to basic multiplications or divisions you do not remember? Give an example.

 **Software Support**

Warm Up 12.27

Connecting Equations   Activity Card 7-16 ▲

Work: In pairs

Use:

• TRB M25 (3 sets of Game Cards)

• 30 index cards

Decide:

Who will be Student 1 and who will be Student 2 for the first round.

1. Write each of the symbols ×, ÷, and = on 10 index cards before playing a game. Place the 30 index cards face up on the table. Shuffle the Game Cards and deal all of them out.

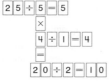

2. **Student 1:** Create a division or multiplication sentence.
Student 2: Build another number sentence onto that sentence.

3. Continue playing until one player has no more cards left or no more sentences can be made. The winner is the student with fewer cards.

Unit 7, Lesson 16   Copyright © Houghton Mifflin Company

Activity Note Caution students to align cards carefully when sentences are placed vertically, as shown in the example. Two-digit numbers such as 20 must be treated as such, not as single digits.

 Math Writing Prompt

Which Is Greater? How can you tell if 10 ÷ 2 or 16 ÷ 2 has the greater quotient without dividing?

MegaMath **Software Support**

Country Countdown, Counting Critters, Level Y

Strategy Card Sort   Activity Card 7-16 ■

Work: In pairs

Use:

• Index cards

• Strategy Cards (0s, 1s, 2s, 3s, 4s, 5s, 9s, and 10s)

• Ruler or straightedge

Decide:

Who will be Student 1 and who will be Student 2 for the first round.

1. **Student 1:** Sort at least 6 strategy cards into two separate groups, using a secret sorting rule.

Group A		Group B
3·9 9·3	3·7 7·3	2·6 6·2
		2·2
3·5 5·3		2·4 4·2

2. **Student 2:** Try to guess the sorting rule by asking questions about the groups. For example, what do you notice about the products in Groups A and B above?

3. Switch roles and repeat the activity.

Group A has odd number products; Group B has even number products.

Unit 7, Lesson 16   Copyright © Houghton Mifflin Company

Activity Note There may be more than one possible sorting rule that generates a grouping. Have students discuss whether adding additional cards to a group would allow only one rule to apply.

 Math Writing Prompt

Explain How can you use basic multiplications or divisions to find 20,000 ÷ 4 and 5 × 30,000? Explain.

DESTINATION Math **Software Support**

Course II: Module 2: Unit 2: Finding Products less than 100

③ Homework and Spiral Review

✓ Include students' completed Homework page as part of their portfolios.

This Remembering page would be appropriate anytime after today's lesson.

7–16 Name _____ Date _____
Homework

Study Plan

_____
Homework Helper

Solve each problem.

1. Maili rode her bike 10 miles every day for 5 days. How many miles did she ride?
_____ 50 miles

2. Leslie gave 72 balloons to children at the fair. After the fair, she had 9 balloons left. How many balloons did Leslie start with?
_____ 81 balloons

3. Tony hung some photographs on one wall in his room. He hung them in 3 rows, with 4 photos in each row. How many photos did Tony hang?
_____ 12 photos

4. Pepe sent 15 gifts to his family members. He sent an equal amount of gifts to 3 different addresses. How many gifts did he send to each address?
_____ 5 gifts

5. At the Shady Acres Stables, there are 5 horses in each barn. There are 4 barns. How many horses are at Shady Acres?
_____ 20 horses

6. Sixty students are in the marching band. There are 10 rows. How many students are in each row?
_____ 6 students

7. Danielle has 35 dolls in her collection. She wants to display them on 5 shelves. How many dolls should she put on each shelf?
_____ 7 dolls

8. There are 9 players on a baseball team. There are 6 teams in the league. How many baseball players are in the league?
_____ 54 players

UNIT 7 LESSON 16   Practice with 0s, 1s, 2s, 3s, 4s, 5s, 9s, and 10s **201**

Homework and Remembering page 201

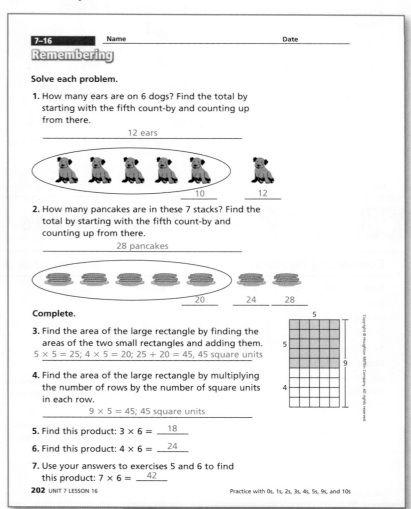

7–16 Name _____ Date _____
Remembering

Solve each problem.

1. How many ears are on 6 dogs? Find the total by starting with the fifth count-by and counting up from there.
_____ 12 ears

10   12

2. How many pancakes are in these 7 stacks? Find the total by starting with the fifth count-by and counting up from there.
_____ 28 pancakes

20   24   28

Complete.

3. Find the area of the large rectangle by finding the areas of the two small rectangles and adding them.
$5 \times 5 = 25$; $4 \times 5 = 20$; $25 + 20 = 45$, 45 square units

4. Find the area of the large rectangle by multiplying the number of rows by the number of square units in each row.
$9 \times 5 = 45$; 45 square units

5. Find this product: $3 \times 6 = $ __18__

6. Find this product: $4 \times 6 = $ __24__

7. Use your answers to exercises 5 and 6 to find this product: $7 \times 6 = $ __42__

202 UNIT 7 LESSON 16   Practice with 0s, 1s, 2s, 3s, 4s, 5s, 9s, and 10s

Homework and Remembering page 202

Home and School Activity

 Technology Connection

Calculator Count-bys Demonstrate how to use a calculator to find the count-bys for the number 3. Begin by pressing ➕ ③ 🟰 . Then continue pressing the 🟰 button. Each time you press the equals button, the calculator will add another 3 to the total. Stop when you get to 10 times the number.

Challenge students to use this method to find the count-bys for the numbers 4, 5, and 9.

Use Mathematical Processes

Lesson Objectives

- Apply mathematical concepts and skills in meaningful contexts.

- Reinforce the NCTM process skills embedded in this unit, and in previous units, with a variety of problem-solving situations.

The Day at a Glance

Today's Goals	Materials

1 Teaching the Lesson

A1: Math Connection Pose a question for a survey; give the survey to a group of people Record the results in a tally chart Answer questions about the results.

A2: Problem Solving Pose a question and answer choices for a survey; give the survey to a group of people; record the results in a tally chart and bar graph; make statements about the results.

A3: Reasoning and Proof Use reasoning to make a generalization and test it.

A4: Representation Use a drawing to show an array.

A5: Communication Tell how you know a number is even.

2 Going Further
► Differentiated Instruction

3 Homework and Spiral Review

Lesson Activities
Student Activity Book pp. 281-282 or Student Hardcover Book pp. 281-282
Activity Workbook pp. 131-132 (includes Blank Charts)
Homework and Remembering pp. 203-204
Grid paper

Going Further
Activity Cards 7-17
Square pieces of paper
Rectangular pieces of paper
Math Journals

123 Use
Math Talk
today!

Keeping Skills Sharp

Quick Practice/Daily Routines	
If you wish to include Quick Practice or a Daily Routine, choose content based on the needs of your class.	**Class Management** Select activities from this lesson that support important goals and objectives, or that help students prepare for state or district tests.

Teaching the Lesson

Math and Science

 45 MINUTES

Goals: Pose question for a survey; Give the survey to a group of people; Record the results in a tally chart; Answer questions about the results.

Materials: Student Activity Book or Hardcover Book p. 281

✔ **NCTM Standards:**
Problem Solving
Connections
Communication
Representation

7–17
Class Activity

Name _____ Date _____

▶ Math and Science

Apatosaurus   Triceratops   Stegosaurus

Take a survey. Find out which dinosaur is the favorite.

1. What question will you ask?   2. How many people will you ask?

   Sample: What is your   Answers will vary.
   favorite dinosaur?

3. Take the survey. Record your results in the tally chart below.
   Results will vary.

	Tally	Total
Apatosaurus		
Triceratops		
Stegosaurus		

4. Which dinosaur is the favorite?   5. What is the difference between
   How do you know?   the number of votes for the
                                           most popular dinosaur and the
   Answers will vary.   number of votes for the least
                                           popular dinosaur?
   _____
                                           Answers will vary.
   _____

UNIT 7 LESSON 17   Use Mathematical Processes **281**

Student Activity Book page 281

Math Talk

▶ Take a Survey on Dinosaurs

Task 1 Begin work on the survey with whole class discussion.

▶ **What is a survey?** Answers may vary. Sample: It's when you ask a group of people a question to find out what they think about something.

▶ Look at the pictures of the dinosaurs on Student book page 281. **How can we find out which dinosaur is the favorite dinosaur?** Ask a group of people which dinosaur is the favorite and record the results.

▶ Today you are going to take a survey to find out which is the favorite dinosaur. **How many people do you want to survey? Do you need answer choices?** Answers may vary. In the discussion bring out that the more people you ask the more sure you can be of predicting the favorite dinosaur in a larger sample. However, it is impractical to ask a large number of people in this activity so around 10 is a good number.

Have students take the survey and record the results in the tally chart. You might want to have students work in pairs.

▶ Discussing the Dinosaur Survey Results
Math Talk

Task 2 When students have completed the survey, discuss the results.

▶ **Which dinosaur is the favorite?** Answers may vary. If students got different results, ask them why they think their results were different. Bring out that the number surveyed was small and that they asked different people.

Teaching Note

More About Dinosaurs Have students do research to learn more about the dinosaurs pictured on their student page. You might want to have them make a graph to show something about these three dinosaurs. For example, the graph could show the number of teeth they have or their height.

Activity 2

Take a Survey

 45 MINUTES

Goals: Pose a question and answer choices for a survey; give the survey to a group of people; record the results in a tally chart and bar graph; answer questions about the results.

Materials: Student Activity Book or Hardcover Book p. 282, grid paper

✔ **NCTM Standards:**
Problem Solving
Reasoning and Proof
Connections
Communication
Representation

7-17 **Class Activity**	Name _____	Date _____

▶ Take a Survey

6. What question would you like to ask in a survey?
   Answers will vary. sample:
   Where do you like to go on
   the weekend?

7. What answer choices will you have in your survey?
   Answers will vary. sample:
   soccer game, movie, party.
   _____

8. How many people will you survey?
   Answers will vary.

9. Take the survey. Record your results in the tally chart below.

	Tally	Total

10. Show the results of the survey in a bar graph.
    Use grid paper to make the graph. Check students' graphs.

11. Make 3 statements about the results of your survey.
    Answers will vary.
    _____
    _____

282 UNIT 7 LESSON 17   Use Mathematical Processes

Student Activity Book page 282

▶ **Set Up a Survey**   **Math Talk**

Task 1 Begin with a whole class discussion.

▶ What question would you like answered in a survey? Answers may vary. Allow students to share their questions.

▶ What answer choices will you have in your survey? Answers may vary. Take one of the survey questions that students just suggested and brainstorm answer choices that might be used.

▶ How many people will you survey? Answers may vary. Talk with the students about choosing a reasonable number, 10 for example.

Tell students to take their survey and record their results in the tally chart. Tell them that there are only 3 spaces for answer choices on the tally chart in their book. If they have more than 3 choices, they will need to make a tally chart on another piece of paper. Then ask them to make a bar graph to show the results.

▶ **Discussing the Results** **Math Talk**
of the Survey

Task 2 When students have completed the survey, the tally chart, and the graph, discuss the results.

▶ What conclusion can you make from your survey? Answers will vary. Ask students to share their results.

English Language Learners

Draw three fruits on the board. Have students vote for their favorite. Record the results. Write *survey*.

- **Beginning** Say: We did a *survey*. We learned which fruit is the class favorite.
- **Intermediate and Advanced** Ask: Did we do a *survey*? yes What did we find out? favorite fruit in the class

---

Use Mathematical Processes **601**

Activity 3

When Is 2 a Factor?

 15 MINUTES

Goal: Use reasoning to make a generalization and test it.

 NCTM Standards:
Problem Solving   Communication
Reasoning and Proof

When will you know when 2 is a factor of a number? Make a generalization and test it.

sample: If the number is even, then 2 is a factor. I tested this with 5 numbers and it was true every time. The numbers I tested were 28, 24, 30, 36, 40. I also tested 5 odd numbers and 2 was not a factor of any of those numbers. The numbers I tested were 13, 23, 29, 43, 57

Hold a whole-class discussion of the problem.

▶ **What generalization did you make?** If the number is even, then 2 is a factor.

▶ **What are some examples of even numbers that support this statement?** Make a list of the numbers that students suggest.

▶ **Can anyone find an odd number that has a factor of 2?** If anyone thinks they have found an odd number that has a factor of 2, ask the class what number they could multiply by 2 to get the number. They should discover that there is no number that will work.

Activity 4

A Page of Stamps

 15 MINUTES

Goal: Use a drawing to show an array.

 NCTM Standards:
Problem Solving   Representation

Lupe has a page of stickers. There are 3 rows and 5 stickers in each row. Draw a picture of the page of stickers. The drawing should have 3 rows with 5 stickers in each row.

Can you arrange the stickers another way? Yes, 5 rows of 3 or 1 row of 15

Representation

Discuss the problem with the class.

▶ **How many rows are in your picture?** 3

▶ **How many stickers are in each row?** 5

Activity 5

Find the Even Number

 15 MINUTES

Goal: Tell how you know a number is even.

 NCTM Standards:
Problem Solving   Communication

Find the even numbers in this list: 47, 106, 357, 629, 724

Explain how you know the numbers are even. Sample answers: You can divide the numbers into 2 equal groups with no remainder. The last digit is an even number

---

Communication

Hold a whole-class discussion of the problem.

▶ **Explain how you know a number is even.** You can divide it into 2 groups with no remainder; the last digit is divisible by 2

▶ **How do you know 47, 357, and 629 are not even?** If you have 47 counters, you cannot divide the counters into 2 equal groups with no remainder. The same is true of 357 and 629. The last digits are not divisible by 2.

② Going Further

Intervention   Activity Card 7-I7

Shapes in Squares   Activity Card 7-17 ●

Work: In pairs
Use:
• Square piece of paper

1. Fold a square piece of paper along both diagonals.

2. What shapes do the folds make inside the square? triangles
3. Are the shapes congruent? Yes

Unit 7, Lesson 17   Copyright © Houghton Mifflin Company

Activity Note Students practice the process skills of representation. They also have an opportunity to apply what they learned about shapes in Unit 2 and diagonals in Unit 4.

 Math Writing Prompt

Are the Triangles Congruent? How could you show that the triangles that are formed by the diagonal of the square are congruent?

 **Software Support**

Warm Up 37.16

On Level   Activity Card 7-I7

Diagonals of Squares   Activity Card 7-17 ▲

Work: On your own
Use:
• Square pieces of paper of different sizes

1. Fold a square piece of paper along both diagonals.

2. Repeat 3 times with squares of different sizes.
3. What kind of angles do the diagonals form? right angles
4. What kind of lines are the diagonal lines? perpendicular lines

Unit 7, Lesson 17   Copyright © Houghton Mifflin Company

Activity Note Students practice the process skills of representation. They also have an opportunity to apply what they learned about perpendicular lines in Unit 2 and diagonals in Unit 4.

 Math Writing Prompt

Always Perpendicular? Do you think the diagonals of a square could ever not be perpendicular. Why or why not?

 Software Support

Shapes Ahoy: Ship Shapes, Level L

Challenge   Activity Card 7-I7

Diagonals of Rectangles   Activity Card 7-17 ■

Work: In pairs
Use:
• Rectangular pieces of paper of different sizes

1. Draw the diagonals of 3 different rectangles.

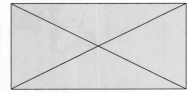

2. What kind of angles do the diagonals form? 2 acute angles and 2 obtuse angles
3. Make a generalization about what you found. The diagonals of a rectangle form two acute angles and two obtuse angles.

Unit 7, Lesson 17   Copyright © Houghton Mifflin Company

Activity Note Students practice the process skills of representation and reasoning. They also have an opportunity to apply what they learned about angles and diagonals in Unit 4.

 Math Writing Prompt

Diagonals of a Square What kind of lines do the diagonals of a square form? Why do you think the diagonals form this type of line?

 **Software Support**

Course II: Module 3: Unit 1: Area

3 Homework and Spiral Review

7–17

Homework **Goal:** Additional Practice

✓ Include student's work for Homework page 1 as part of their portfolios.

7–17

Remembering **Goal:** Spiral Review

This Remembering page would be appropriate anytime after today's lesson.

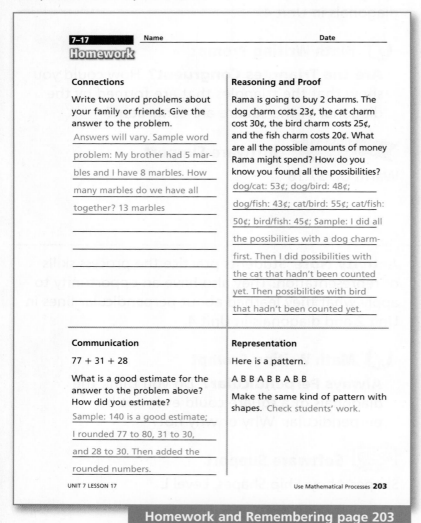

7–17 Name _____ Date _____

Homework

Connections

Write two word problems about your family or friends. Give the answer to the problem.

Answers will vary. Sample word problem: My brother had 5 marbles and I have 8 marbles. How many marbles do we have all together? 13 marbles

Communication

77 + 31 + 28

What is a good estimate for the answer to the problem above? How did you estimate?

Sample: 140 is a good estimate; I rounded 77 to 80, 31 to 30, and 28 to 30. Then added the rounded numbers.

Reasoning and Proof

Rama is going to buy 2 charms. The dog charm costs 23¢, the cat charm cost 30¢, the bird charm costs 25¢, and the fish charm costs 20¢. What are all the possible amounts of money Rama might spend? How do you know you found all the possibilities?

dog/cat: 53¢; dog/bird: 48¢; dog/fish: 43¢; cat/bird: 55¢; cat/fish: 50¢; bird/fish: 45¢; Sample: I did all the possibilities with a dog charm first. Then I did possibilities with the cat that hadn't been counted yet. Then possibilities with bird that hadn't been counted yet.

Representation

Here is a pattern.

A B B A B B A B B

Make the same kind of pattern with shapes. Check students' work.

UNIT 7 LESSON 17   Use Mathematical Processes **203**

Homework and Remembering page 203

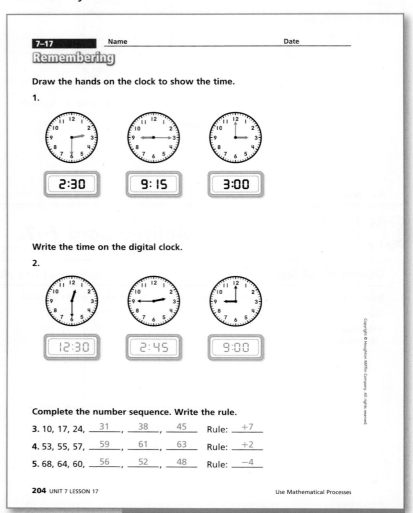

7–17 Name _____ Date _____

Remembering

Draw the hands on the clock to show the time.

1.

2:30   9:15   3:00

Write the time on the digital clock.

2.

12:30   2:45   9:00

Complete the number sequence. Write the rule.

3. 10, 17, 24, __31__, __38__, __45__   Rule: __+7__

4. 53, 55, 57, __59__, __61__, __63__   Rule: __+2__

5. 68, 64, 60, __56__, __52__, __48__   Rule: __−4__

204 UNIT 7 LESSON 17   Use Mathematical Processes

Homework and Remembering page 204

Home or School Activity

 Real-World Connection

Make a Timeline Have students think about what they would like to do if they could do anything they wanted on a weekend day. Brainstorm a list of things. Have students make a timeline showing what they would do each hour of their special day.

Unit Review and Test

Lesson Objective

● Assess student progress on unit objectives.

The Day at a Glance

Today's Goals	Materials
① Assessing the Unit ▶ Assess student progress on unit objectives. ▶ Use activities from unit lessons to reteach content. **② Extending the Assessment** ▶ Use remediation for common errors. There is no homework assignment on a test day.	Unit 7 Test, Student Activity Book or Hardcover Book pp. 283–284 Unit 7 Test, Form A or B, Assessment Guide (optional) Unit 7 Performance Assessment, Assessment Guide (optional)

Keeping Skills Sharp

Quick Practice 🕐 5 MINUTES	
Goal: Review any skills you choose to meet the needs of your class. If you are doing a unit review day, use any of the Quick Practice activities that provide support for your class. If this is a test day, omit Quick Practice.	**Review and Test Day** You may want to choose a quiet game or other activity (reading a book or working on homework for another subject) for students who finish early.

① Assessing the Unit

Assess Unit Objectives

45 MINUTES (more if schedule permits)

Goal: Assess student progress on unit objectives.

Materials: Student Activity Book or Hardcover pp. 283–284; Assessment Guide Unit 7 Test Form A or B (optional); Assessment Guide Unit 7 Performance Assessment (optional)

✕ Review and Assessment

If your students are ready for assessment on the unit objectives, you may use either the test on the Student Book pages or one of the forms of the Unit 7 Test in the Assessment Guide to assess student progress.

If you feel that students need some review first, you may use the test on the Student Book pages as a review of unit content, and then use one of the forms of the Unit 7 Test in the Assessment Guide to assess student progress.

To assign a numerical score for all of these test forms, use 5 points for each question.

You may also choose to use the Unit 7 Performance Assessment. Scoring for that assessment can be found in its rubric in the Assessment Guide.

✕ Reteaching Resources

The chart at the right lists the test items, the unit objectives they cover, and the lesson activities in which the objective is covered in this unit. You may revisit these activities with students who do not show mastery of the objectives.

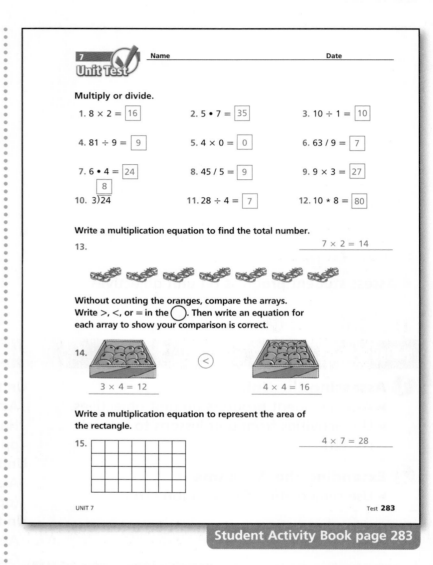

Student Activity Book page 283

Unit Test Items	Unit Objectives Tested	Activities to Use for Reteaching
1–12	**7.1** Recall basic multiplications and divisions with 0, 1, 2, 3, 4, 5, 9, and 10; use properties and rules.	Lesson 1, Activity 1 Lesson 4, Activity 3 Lesson 5, Activity 2 Lesson 6, Activity 3 Lesson 7, Activity 2 Lesson 9, Activity 3 Lesson 12, Activity 2 Lesson 14, Activity 4
13–15	**7.2** Write multiplication equations to represent repeated groups, arrays, and area models.	Lesson 2, Activity 1 Lesson 3, Activity 2 Lesson 10, Activity 3

Name _____ **Date** _____

Complete.

16. $9 + 9 + 9 + 9 + 9 + 9 + 9 + 9 = \underline{\ 8\ } \times 9 = \underline{\ 72\ }$

Write a related division equation.

17. $8 \times 5 = 40$ $40 \div 5 = 8$ or $40 \div 8 = 5$

Write a related multiplication equation.

18. $18 \div 2 = 9$ $2 \times 9 = 18$ or $9 \times 2 = 18$

Write an equation to solve each problem. Then write the answer.

19. Olivia's CD rack has 4 shelves. It holds 8 CDs on a shelf. How many CDs will fit in the rack altogether?

$4 \times 8 = 32$ CDs

*20. Extended Response Paco set up 7 tables to seat 28 children at his birthday party. The same number of children will sit at each table. How many children will sit at each table? Explain how you found your answer. Make a math drawing to help explain.

$28 \div 7 = 4$, 4 children; Possible explanation: There are 28 children altogether and they are divided up into 7 tables. So I divided $28 \div 7 = 4$. I made an equal shares drawing.

*Item 20 also assesses the Process Skills of Communication and Representation.

284 UNIT 7   Test

Student Activity Book page 284

Unit Test Items	Unit Objectives Tested	Activities to Use for Reteaching
16–18	**7.3** Write related addition and multiplication equations and related multiplication and division equations.	Lesson 1, Activity 1 Lesson 4, Activities 2, 4 Lesson 5, Activity 1 Lesson 6, Activity 3 Lesson 7, Activity 3 Lesson 9, Activity 3 Lesson 12, Activity 2
19–20	**7.4** Solve a variety of word problems involving multiplication and division.	Lesson 2, Activity 2 Lesson 3, Activity 3 Lesson 4, Activity 2 Lesson 6, Activity 5 Lesson 8, Activity 4 Lesson 11, Activity 3 Lesson 16, Activity 3

▶ Assessment Resources

Free Response Tests
Unit 7 Test, Student Activity Book pages 283–284
Unit 7 Test, Form A, Assessment Guide

Extended Response Item
The last item in the Student Activity Book test and in the Form A test will require an extended response as an answer.

Multiple Choice Test
Unit 7 Test, Form B, Assessment Guide

Performance Assessment
Unit 7 Performance Assessment, Assessment Guide
Unit 7 Performance Assessment Rubric, Assessment Guide

▶ Portfolio Assessment

Teacher-selected Items for Student Portfolios:

- Homework, Lessons 2, 8, 12, 16 and 17
- Class Activity work, Lessons 3, 9, 11, 14, and 17

Student-selected Items for Student Portfolios:

- Favorite Home or School Activity
- Best Writing Prompt

② Extending the Assessment

Unit Objective 7.1
Recall basic multiplications and divisions with 0, 1, 2, 3, 4, 5, 9, and 10; use properties and rules.

Common Error: Computation Errors

Students may have difficulty remembering basic multiplications and divisions.

Remediation Have students use the Strategy Cards to practice the 2s, 3s, 4s, 5s, 9s, or 10s they do not know. Students can also make an audio tape or CD of the basic multiplications they need to learn with a pause before saying the answer. They can then use the tape to recall those basic multiplications and divisions.

Common Error: Doesn't Distinguish × From +

Students may add instead of multiply.

Remediation Have students circle the operation symbol and name the operation they will use.

Common Error: Doesn't Recognize the Commutative Property

Students recall one arrangement of two factors but not the other.

Remediation Remind students that switching the order of the factors does not change the product. Demonstrate that the Commutative Property can be used, for example, to find 6×4 if they know 4×6.

Unit Objective 7.2
Write multiplication equations to represent repeated groups, arrays, and area models.

Common Error: Write Incorrect Numbers or Operation Signs

Students may have difficulty writing multiplication equations to represent repeated groups, arrays, and area models.

Remediation Have students label the sides of the arrays and area models, and then write the number of the repeated groups and the number of groups. They can then use these numbers to write the equations with a multiplication sign.

Unit Objective 7.3
Write related addition and multiplication equations and related multiplication and division equations.

Common Error: Add the Incorrect Number for Repeated Addition

Remediation Have students draw a box around the first factor in a multiplication to remind them that this factor stands for the number of groups. Have them ring the second factor to remind them that this factor stands for the number in each group. You might have them remember that "circle" and "size" (for *group size*) both begin with the same sound.

Common Error: Uses Incorrect Related Equations

Some students may not use the correct numbers in related multiplication and division equations.

Remediation Use examples to demonstrate that whenever related multiplications and divisions are used, each related number sentence must use the same numbers written in the correct order. The product in the multiplication becomes the dividend in the division.

Unit Objective 7.4
Solve a variety of word problems involving multiplication and division.

Common Error: Chooses an Incorrect Operation

Students may have difficulty choosing the correct operation to solve a word problem.

Remediation Have students work in pairs to analyze a variety of addition, subtraction, multiplication, and division problems. Have them summarize when each operation should be used.

- Add to find the total of both equal and unequal groups.
- Subtract to separate a group, take away, or compare groups.
- Multiply to find the total of only equal groups.
- Divide to separate a set into equal groups.

Have students create a word problem for each operation.

Student Glossary

Glossary

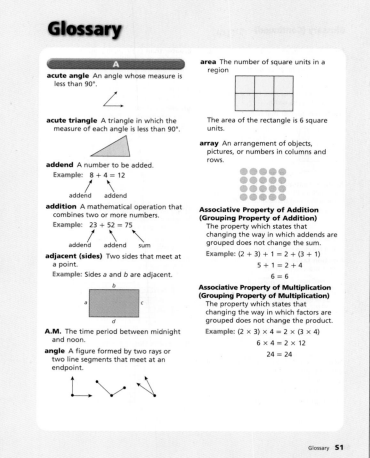

A

acute angle An angle whose measure is less than 90°.

acute triangle A triangle in which the measure of each angle is less than 90°.

addend A number to be added.
Example: 8 + 4 = 12
         addend   addend

addition A mathematical operation that combines two or more numbers.
Example: 23 + 52 = 75
         addend   addend   sum

adjacent (sides) Two sides that meet at a point.
Example: Sides a and b are adjacent.

A.M. The time period between midnight and noon.

angle A figure formed by two rays or two line segments that meet at an endpoint.

area The number of square units in a region

The area of the rectangle is 6 square units.

array An arrangement of objects, pictures, or numbers in columns and rows.

Associative Property of Addition (Grouping Property of Addition) The property which states that changing the way in which addends are grouped does not change the sum.
Example: (2 + 3) + 1 = 2 + (3 + 1)
         5 + 1 = 2 + 4
         6 = 6

Associative Property of Multiplication (Grouping Property of Multiplication) The property which states that changing the way in which factors are grouped does not change the product.
Example: (2 × 3) × 4 = 2 × (3 × 4)
         6 × 4 = 2 × 12
         24 = 24

Glossary **S1**

Glossary (Continued)

axis (plural: **axes**) A reference line for a graph. A bar graph has 2 axes; one is horizontal and the other is vertical.

Flowers in Mary's Garden

B

bar graph A graph that uses bars to show data. The bars may be horizontal or vertical.

Canned Goods at Turner's Market

base (of a geometric figure) The bottom side of a 2-D figure or the bottom face of a 3-D figure.

base

C

calculator A tool used to perform mathematical operations.

capacity The amount a container can hold.

cell A rectangle in a table where a column and row meet.

Coin Toss

	Heads	Tails	
Sam	11	6	} cell
Zoe	9	10	

centimeter (cm) A metric unit used to measure length.
100 cm = 1 m

circle A plane figure that forms a closed path so that all points on the path are the same distance from a point called the center.

circle graph A graph that represents data as parts of a whole.

Jacket Colors in Ms. Timmer's Class

circumference The distance around a circle, about $3\frac{1}{7}$ times the diameter.

column A vertical group of cells in a table.

Coin Toss

	Heads	Tails
Sam	11	6
Zoe	9	10

column

S2 Glossary

Commutative Property of Addition (Order Property of Addition) The property which states that changing the order of addends does not change the sum.
Example: 3 + 7 = 7 + 3
         10 = 10

Commutative Property of Multiplication (Order Property of Multiplication) The property which states that changing the order of factors does not change the product.
Example: 5 × 4 = 4 × 5
         20 = 20

comparison bars Bars that represent the larger amount, smaller amount, and difference in a comparison problem.

smaller amount   difference

larger amount

In Volume 2, we use comparison bars for multiplication.

7 □
56 □ □ □ □ □ □ □ □

cone A solid figure that has a circular base and comes to a point called the vertex.

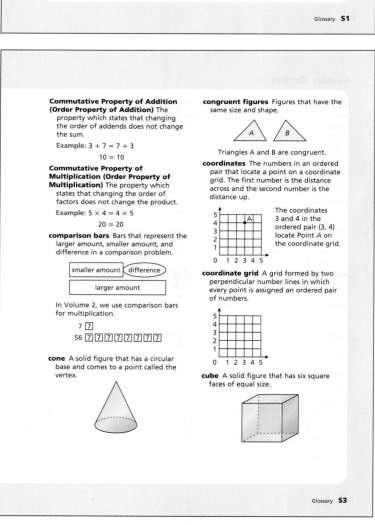

congruent figures Figures that have the same size and shape.

A   B

Triangles A and B are congruent.

coordinates The numbers in an ordered pair that locate a point on a coordinate grid. The first number is the distance across and the second number is the distance up.

The coordinates 3 and 4 in the ordered pair (3, 4) locate Point A on the coordinate grid.

coordinate grid A grid formed by two perpendicular number lines in which every point is assigned an ordered pair of numbers.

cube A solid figure that has six square faces of equal size.

Glossary **S3**

Glossary (Continued)

cup (c) A customary unit of measurement used to measure capacity.
2 cups = 1 pint
4 cups = 1 quart
16 cups = 1 gallon

cylinder A solid figure with two congruent circular or elliptical faces and one curved surface.

D

data Pieces of information.

decimal A number with one or more digits to the right of a decimal point.
Examples: 1.23 and 0.3

decimal point The dot that separates the whole number from the decimal part.
1.23
decimal point

decimeter (dm) A metric unit used to measure length
1 decimeter = 10 centimeters

degree (°) A unit for measuring angles or temperature.

degrees Celsius (°C) The metric unit for measuring temperature.

degrees Fahrenheit (°F) The customary unit of temperature.

denominator The bottom number in a fraction that shows the total number of equal parts in the whole.
Example: $\frac{1}{3}$ ← denominator

diagonal A line segment that connects two corners of a figure and is not a side of the figure.

diagonal

diameter A line segment that connects two points on a circle and also passes through the center of the circle. The term is also used to describe the length of such a line segment.

diameter

difference The result of subtraction or of comparing.

digit Any of the symbols 0, 1, 2, 3, 4, 5, 6, 7, 8, 9.

dividend The number that is divided in division.
Examples:
12 ÷ 3 = 4   4
              3)12
dividend   dividend

division The mathematical operation that separates an amount into smaller equal groups to find the number of groups or the number in each group.
Example: 12 ÷ 3 = 4 is a division number sentence.

divisor The number that you divide by in division.
Example: 12 ÷ 3 = 4   4
                       3)12
divisor   divisor

S4 Glossary

Student Glossary (Continued)

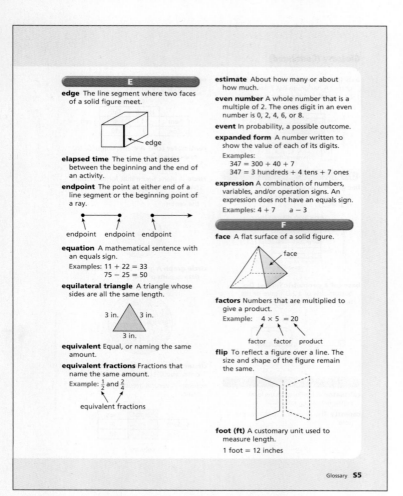

E

edge The line segment where two faces of a solid figure meet.

elapsed time The time that passes between the beginning and the end of an activity.

endpoint The point at either end of a line segment or the beginning point of a ray.

endpoint   endpoint   endpoint

equation A mathematical sentence with an equals sign.
Examples: $11 + 22 = 33$
$75 - 25 = 50$

equilateral triangle A triangle whose sides are all the same length.

3 in.   3 in.
3 in.

equivalent Equal, or naming the same amount.

equivalent fractions Fractions that name the same amount.
Example: $\frac{1}{2}$ and $\frac{2}{4}$

equivalent fractions

estimate About how many or about how much.

even number A whole number that is a multiple of 2. The ones digit in an even number is 0, 2, 4, 6, or 8.

event In probability, a possible outcome.

expanded form A number written to show the value of each of its digits.
Examples:
$347 = 300 + 40 + 7$
$347 = 3$ hundreds $+ 4$ tens $+ 7$ ones

expression A combination of numbers, variables, and/or operation signs. An expression does not have an equals sign.
Examples: $4 + 7$ $a - 3$

F

face A flat surface of a solid figure.

face

factors Numbers that are multiplied to give a product.
Example: $4 \times 5 = 20$
factor   factor   product

flip To reflect a figure over a line. The size and shape of the figure remain the same.

foot (ft) A customary unit used to measure length.
1 foot = 12 inches

Glossary (Continued)

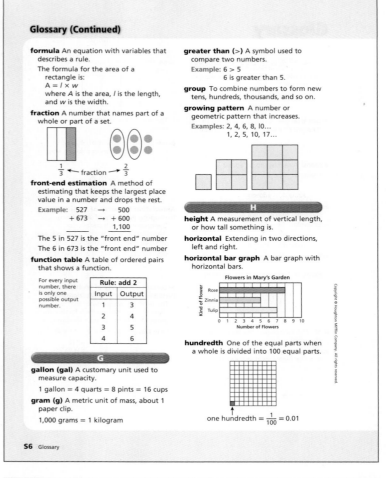

formula An equation with variables that describes a rule.
The formula for the area of a rectangle is:
$A = l \times w$
where A is the area, l is the length, and w is the width.

fraction A number that names part of a whole or part of a set.

$\frac{1}{3}$ ← fraction → $\frac{2}{3}$

front-end estimation A method of estimating that keeps the largest place value in a number and drops the rest.
Example:
$527 \rightarrow 500$
$+ 673 \rightarrow + 600$
$\overline{ 1,100}$
The 5 in 527 is the "front end" number
The 6 in 673 is the "front end" number

function table A table of ordered pairs that shows a function.

For every input number, there is only one possible output number.

Rule: add 2	
Input	Output
1	3
2	4
3	5
4	6

G

gallon (gal) A customary unit used to measure capacity.
1 gallon = 4 quarts = 8 pints = 16 cups

gram (g) A metric unit of mass, about 1 paper clip.
1,000 grams = 1 kilogram

greater than (>) A symbol used to compare two numbers.
Example: $6 > 5$
6 is greater than 5.

group To combine numbers to form new tens, hundreds, thousands, and so on.

growing pattern A number or geometric pattern that increases.
Examples: 2, 4, 6, 8, 10…
1, 2, 5, 10, 17…

H

height A measurement of vertical length, or how tall something is.

horizontal Extending in two directions, left and right.

horizontal bar graph A bar graph with horizontal bars.

Flowers in Mary's Garden

hundredth One of the equal parts when a whole is divided into 100 equal parts.

one hundredth $= \frac{1}{100} = 0.01$

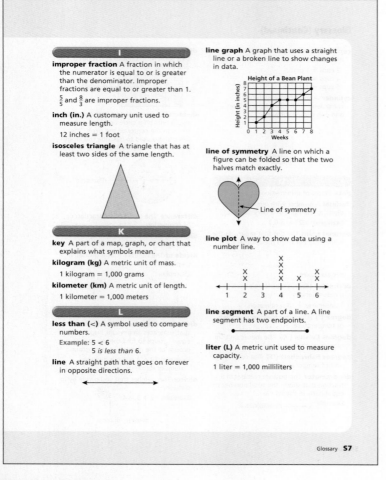

I

improper fraction A fraction in which the numerator is equal to or is greater than the denominator. Improper fractions are equal to or greater than 1.
$\frac{5}{5}$ and $\frac{8}{3}$ are improper fractions.

inch (in.) A customary unit used to measure length.
12 inches = 1 foot

isosceles triangle A triangle that has at least two sides of the same length.

K

key A part of a map, graph, or chart that explains what symbols mean.

kilogram (kg) A metric unit of mass.
1 kilogram = 1,000 grams

kilometer (km) A metric unit of length.
1 kilometer = 1,000 meters

L

less than (<) A symbol used to compare numbers.
Example: $5 < 6$
5 is less than 6.

line A straight path that goes on forever in opposite directions.

line graph A graph that uses a straight line or a broken line to show changes in data.

Height of a Bean Plant

line of symmetry A line on which a figure can be folded so that the two halves match exactly.

Line of symmetry

line plot A way to show data using a number line.

line segment A part of a line. A line segment has two endpoints.

liter (L) A metric unit used to measure capacity.
1 liter = 1,000 milliliters

Glossary (Continued)

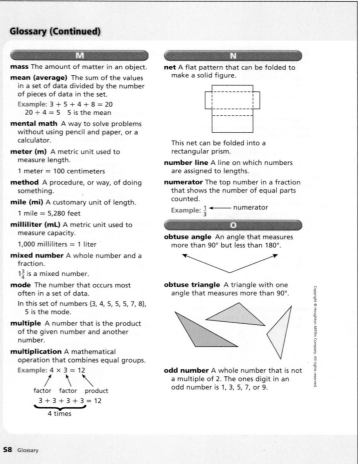

M

mass The amount of matter in an object.

mean (average) The sum of the values in a set of data divided by the number of pieces of data in the set.
Example: $3 + 5 + 4 + 8 = 20$
$20 \div 4 = 5$ 5 is the mean

mental math A way to solve problems without using pencil and paper, or a calculator.

meter (m) A metric unit used to measure length.
1 meter = 100 centimeters

method A procedure, or way, of doing something.

mile (mi) A customary unit of length.
1 mile = 5,280 feet

milliliter (mL) A metric unit used to measure capacity.
1,000 milliliters = 1 liter

mixed number A whole number and a fraction.
$1\frac{3}{4}$ is a mixed number.

mode The number that occurs most often in a set of data.
In this set of numbers {3, 4, 5, 5, 5, 7, 8}, 5 is the mode.

multiple A number that is the product of the given number and another number.

multiplication A mathematical operation that combines equal groups.
Example: $4 \times 3 = 12$
factor   factor   product
$3 + 3 + 3 + 3 = 12$
4 times

net A flat pattern that can be folded to make a solid figure.

This net can be folded into a rectangular prism.

number line A line on which numbers are assigned to lengths.

numerator The top number in a fraction that shows the number of equal parts counted.
Example: $\frac{1}{3}$ ← numerator

O

obtuse angle An angle that measures more than 90° but less than 180°.

obtuse triangle A triangle with one angle that measures more than 90°.

odd number A whole number that is not a multiple of 2. The ones digit in an odd number is 1, 3, 5, 7, or 9.

T2   Student Glossary

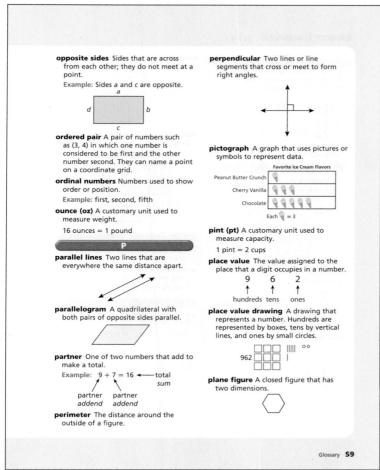

opposite sides Sides that are across from each other; they do not meet at a point.

Example: Sides *a* and *c* are opposite.

ordered pair A pair of numbers such as (3, 4) in which one number is considered to be first and the other number second. They can name a point on a coordinate grid.

ordinal numbers Numbers used to show order or position.

Example: first, second, fifth

ounce (oz) A customary unit used to measure weight.

16 ounces = 1 pound

P

parallel lines Two lines that are everywhere the same distance apart.

parallelogram A quadrilateral with both pairs of opposite sides parallel.

partner One of two numbers that add to make a total.

Example: 9 + 7 = 16 ←— total
sum
partner   partner
addend   addend

perimeter The distance around the outside of a figure.

perpendicular Two lines or line segments that cross or meet to form right angles.

pictograph A graph that uses pictures or symbols to represent data.

Favorite Ice Cream Flavors

Peanut Butter Crunch
Cherry Vanilla
Chocolate

Each 🍦 = 3

pint (pt) A customary unit used to measure capacity.

1 pint = 2 cups

place value The value assigned to the place that a digit occupies in a number.

9   6   2
hundreds tens ones

place value drawing A drawing that represents a number. Hundreds are represented by boxes, tens by vertical lines, and ones by small circles.

962

plane figure A closed figure that has two dimensions.

Glossary **S9**

Glossary (Continued)

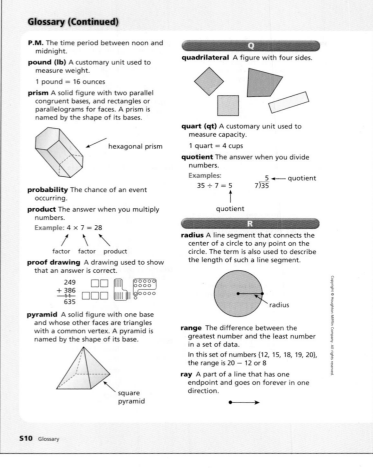

P.M. The time period between noon and midnight.

pound (lb) A customary unit used to measure weight.

1 pound = 16 ounces

prism A solid figure with two parallel congruent bases, and rectangles or parallelograms for faces. A prism is named by the shape of its bases.

hexagonal prism

probability The chance of an event occurring.

product The answer when you multiply numbers.

Example: 4 × 7 = 28

factor factor product

proof drawing A drawing used to show that an answer is correct.

249
+ 386
11
635

pyramid A solid figure with one base and whose other faces are triangles with a common vertex. A pyramid is named by the shape of its base.

square pyramid

Q

quadrilateral A figure with four sides.

quart (qt) A customary unit used to measure capacity.

1 quart = 4 cups

quotient The answer when you divide numbers.

Examples:
35 ÷ 7 = 5   5 ←— quotient
7)35

quotient

R

radius A line segment that connects the center of a circle to any point on the circle. The term is also used to describe the length of such a line segment.

radius

range The difference between the greatest number and the least number in a set of data.

In this set of numbers {12, 15, 18, 19, 20}, the range is 20 − 12 or 8

ray A part of a line that has one endpoint and goes on forever in one direction.

S10 Glossary

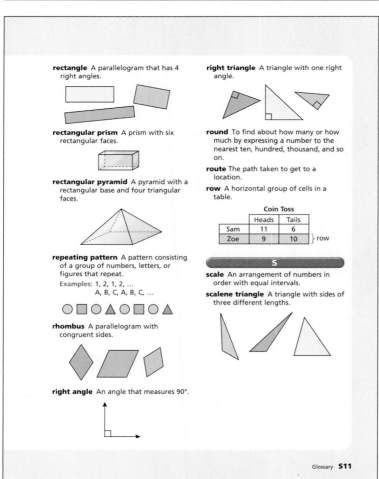

rectangle A parallelogram that has 4 right angles.

rectangular prism A prism with six rectangular faces.

rectangular pyramid A pyramid with a rectangular base and four triangular faces.

repeating pattern A pattern consisting of a group of numbers, letters, or figures that repeat.

Examples: 1, 2, 1, 2, …
A, B, C, A, B, C, …

rhombus A parallelogram with congruent sides.

right angle An angle that measures 90°.

right triangle A triangle with one right angle.

round To find about how many or how much by expressing a number to the nearest ten, hundred, thousand, and so on.

route The path taken to get to a location.

row A horizontal group of cells in a table.

Coin Toss

	Heads	Tails
Sam	11	6
Zoe	9	10	} row

S

scale An arrangement of numbers in order with equal intervals.

scalene triangle A triangle with sides of three different lengths.

Glossary **S11**

Glossary (Continued)

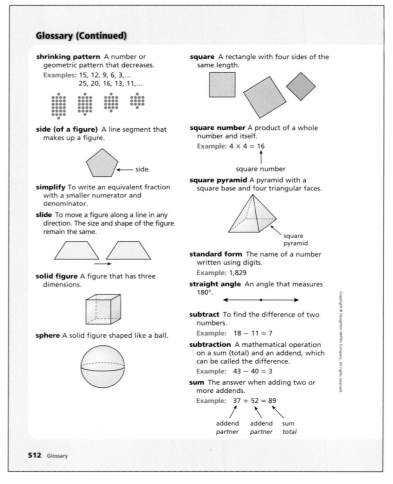

shrinking pattern A number or geometric pattern that decreases.

Examples: 15, 12, 9, 6, 3,…
25, 20, 16, 13, 11,…

side (of a figure) A line segment that makes up a figure.

side

simplify To write an equivalent fraction with a smaller numerator and denominator.

slide To move a figure along a line in any direction. The size and shape of the figure remain the same.

solid figure A figure that has three dimensions.

sphere A solid figure shaped like a ball.

square A rectangle with four sides of the same length.

square number A product of a whole number and itself.

Example: 4 × 4 = 16

square number

square pyramid A pyramid with a square base and four triangular faces.

square pyramid

standard form The name of a number written using digits.

Example: 1,829

straight angle An angle that measures 180°.

subtract To find the difference of two numbers.

Example: 18 − 11 = 7

subtraction A mathematical operation on a sum (total) and an addend, which can be called the difference.

Example: 43 − 40 = 3

sum The answer when adding two or more addends.

Example: 37 + 52 = 89

addend   addend   sum
partner partner total

S12 Glossary

Student Glossary (Continued)

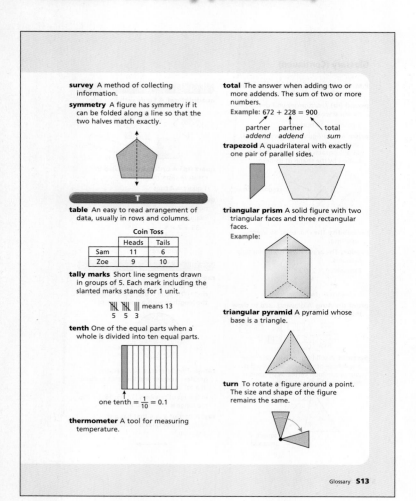

survey A method of collecting information.

symmetry A figure has symmetry if it can be folded along a line so that the two halves match exactly.

T

table An easy to read arrangement of data, usually in rows and columns.

Coin Toss

	Heads	Tails
Sam	11	6
Zoe	9	10

tally marks Short line segments drawn in groups of 5. Each mark including the slanted marks stands for 1 unit.

|||| ||| ||| means 13
  5   5   3

tenth One of the equal parts when a whole is divided into ten equal parts.

one tenth = $\frac{1}{10}$ = 0.1

thermometer A tool for measuring temperature.

total The answer when adding two or more addends. The sum of two or more numbers.

Example: 672 + 228 = 900

partner addend partner addend total sum

trapezoid A quadrilateral with exactly one pair of parallel sides.

triangular prism A solid figure with two triangular faces and three rectangular faces.

Example:

triangular pyramid A pyramid whose base is a triangle.

turn To rotate a figure around a point. The size and shape of the figure remains the same.

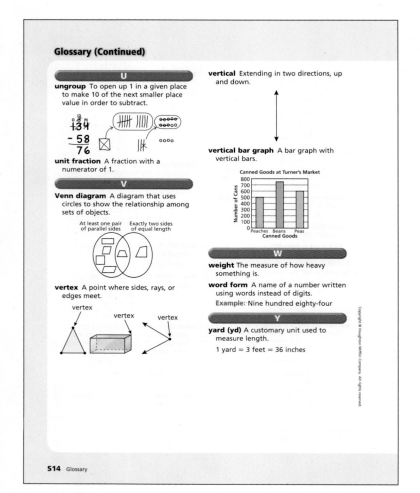

U

ungroup To open up 1 in a given place to make 10 of the next smaller place value in order to subtract.

$$\begin{array}{r} {}^{12}13\overset{14}{4} \\ -\ 58 \\ \hline 76 \end{array}$$

unit fraction A fraction with a numerator of 1.

V

Venn diagram A diagram that uses circles to show the relationship among sets of objects.

At least one pair of parallel sides   Exactly two sides of equal length

vertex A point where sides, rays, or edges meet.

vertex   vertex   vertex

vertical Extending in two directions, up and down.

vertical bar graph A bar graph with vertical bars.

Canned Goods at Turner's Market

W

weight The measure of how heavy something is.

word form A name of a number written using words instead of digits.

Example: Nine hundred eighty-four

Y

yard (yd) A customary unit used to measure length.

1 yard = 3 feet = 36 inches

Teacher Glossary

5s shortcut A strategy for multiplying by numbers larger than 5. For example, to multiply 7 × 3, students think of the 5 count-by of 3, 15. They then think of the additional count-bys of 3, 18, 21. Therefore, 7 × 3 = 21.

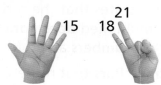

7 times 3 equals 21

A

acute angle An angle whose measure is less than 90°.

acute triangle A triangle in which the measure of each angle is less than 90°.

addend A number to be added. In the equation 8 + 4 = 12, 8 and 4 are addends.

adjacent (sides) Two sides that meet at a point. In this example, sides *a* and *b* are adjacent.

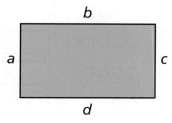

A.M. The abbreviation for *ante meridiem*, Latin for "before noon". Used to indicate a time between midnight and noon.

analog clock A clock with a face, a shorter hand, and a longer hand.

angle A figure formed by two rays or two line segments that meet at an endpoint.

area The number of square units in a region.

area model A model that uses square units to show a multiplication.

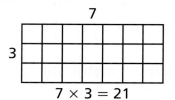

7 × 3 = 21

array An arrangement of objects, pictures, or numbers in columns and rows.

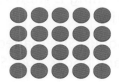

Associative Property of Addition Property which states that changing the grouping of addends does not change their sum. For all numbers *a*, *b*, and *c*, $a + (b + c) = (a + b) + c$.

Associative Property of Multiplication Property which states that changing the grouping of factors does not change their product. For all numbers *a*, *b* and *c*, $a \times (b \times c) = (a \times b) \times c$.

axis (plural: axes) A reference line for a graph. A bar graph has 2 axes; one is horizontal and the other is vertical.

B

bar graph A graph that uses bars to show data. The bars may be horizontal or vertical.

base (of a geometric figure) The bottom side of a 2-D figure or the bottom face of a 3-D figure.

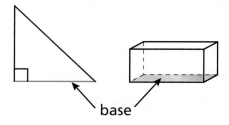

base

benchmark A reference whose size is familiar to students and approximately equal to a unit of measure. A benchmark helps students visualize the size of the unit. Comparing a known benchmark to an item of unknown size helps students to make a reasonable estimate.

Teacher Glossary (Continued)

C

capacity The amount a container can hold.

cell A rectangle in a table where a column and row meet.

centimeter (cm) A metric unit used to measure length. 100 cm = 1 m

change minus problem A problem that begins with a given quantity which is then modified by a change—something is subtracted—that results in a new quantity.

Sarah had 12 books. She loaned her friend 9 books. How many books does Sarah have now?

change plus problem A problem that begins with a given quantity which is then modified by a change—something is added—that results in a new quantity.
Alvin had 9 toy cars. He received 3 more for his birthday. How many toy cars does Alvin have now?

circle A plane figure that forms a closed path so that all points on the path are the same distance from a point called the center.

circle graph A graph that represents data as parts of a whole. (Also called a pie graph or pie chart.)

circumference The distance around a circle.

Class Multiplication Table A poster in table form that displays the multiplications for 1–9. Columns of the table are labeled 1–9 and rows are labeled 1–10. The product of the labels is found in the cells where the row and column meet.

clockwise A turn in the same direction as the hands of a clock move.

column A vertical group of cells in a table.

combinations Arrangements of elements

common denominator Any common multiple of the denominators of two or more fractions.

common multiplier The same number that multiplies the numerator and denominator of a fraction so that the resulting fraction is equivalent.

Commutative Property of Addition Property which states that the order in which numbers are added does not change the sum. For all numbers a and b, $a + b = b + a$.

Commutative Property of Multiplication Property which states that the order in which numbers are multiplied does not change the product. For all numbers a and b, $a \times b = b \times a$.

comparison bars Bars that represent the larger amount, smaller amount, and difference in a comparison problem.

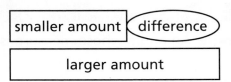

comparison language

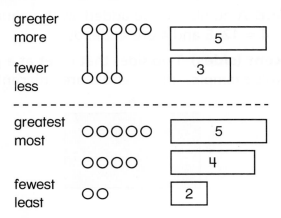

comparison situation A situation in which two amounts are compared by addition or by multiplication. An additive comparison situation compares by asking or telling how much more (how much less) one amount is than another A multiplicative comparison situation compares by asking or telling how many times as many one amount is as another. The multiplicative comparison may also be made using fraction language. For example, you can say, "Sally has one fourth as much as Tom has," instead of saying "Tom has 4 times as much as Sally has."

compatible numbers Numbers that are close to the original numbers and are easy to compute with. The numbers 35 and 80 are compatible numbers for estimating 36 plus 82.

cone A solid figure that has a circular base and comes to a point called the vertex.

congruent figures Figures that have the same size and shape. In this example triangles A and B are congruent.

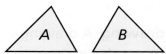

coordinate grid A grid formed by two perpendicular number lines in which every point is assigned an ordered pair of numbers.

coordinates The numbers in an ordered pair that locate a point on a coordinate grid. The first number is the distance across and the second number is the distance up. The coordinates 3 and 4 in the ordered pair (3, 4) locate Point A on the coordinate grid.

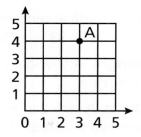

count-bys Products that are found by skip-counting a particular number; 5s count-bys would be 5, 10, 15, 20, 25, and so on; 3s count-bys would be 3, 6, 9, 12, and so on.

counter clockwise A turn in the opposite direction as the hands of a clock move.

count on An addition or subtraction strategy in which children begin with one partner and count on to the total. This strategy can be used to find an unknown partner or an unknown total.

$$5 + 3 = \boxed{8}$$
$$5 + \boxed{3} = 8$$
$$8 - 5 = \boxed{3} \quad \text{Already } 5$$

cube A solid figure that has six square faces of equal size.

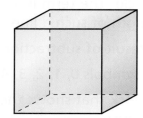

cubic unit A unit for measuring volume such as a cubic inch or cubic centimeter.

cup (c) A customary unit of measurement used to measure capacity. 2 cups = 1 pint
4 cups = 1 quart   16 cups = 1 gallon

cylinder A solid figure with two congruent circular faces and one curved surface.

D

data A set of information.

decimal A number with one or more digits to the right of a decimal point. 1.23 and 0.3

decimeter (dm) A metric unit used to measure length. 1 decimeter = 10 centimeters

degree (°) A unit for measuring angles or temperature.

degrees Celsius (°C) The metric unit of temperature.

degrees Fahrenheit (°F) The customary unit of temperature.

Demonstration Secret Code Cards A larger version of the Secret Code Cards for classroom use. (See **Secret Code Cards**.)

denominator The bottom number in a fraction that shows the total number of parts in a whole. In the fraction $\frac{1}{3}$, 3 is the denominator.

diagonal A line segment that connects two corners of a figure and is not a side of the figure.

Teacher Glossary (Continued)

diameter A line segment that connects two points on a circle and also passes through the center of the circle. The term is also used to describe the length of such a line segment.

difference The result of subtraction.

digit Any of the symbols 0, 1, 2, 3, 4, 5, 6, 7, 8, 9.

digital clock A clock that shows the hour and minutes with digits.

dimension A way to describe how a figure can be measured. A line segment has only length, so it has *one* dimension. A rectangle has length and width, so it has *two* dimensions. A cube has length, width, and height, so it has *three* dimensions.

dimensions The measurements of sides of geometric figures.

dimes place In dollar notation, the first place to the right of the decimal point. In the amount $3.47, 4 is in the dimes place.

Distributive Property of Multiplication The product of a factor and a sum (or difference) equals the sum (or difference) of the products. For all numbers *a*, *b* and *c*, $a \times (b + c) = (a \times b) + (a \times c)$

dividend The number that is divided in division. In the equation $12 \div 3 = 4$, 12 is the dividend.

divisible A number is divisible by another number if the quotient is a whole number with no remainder. The number 6 is divisible by 3, but not 4.

divisor The number that you divide by in division. In the equation $12 \div 3 = 4$, 3 is the divisor.

dollars place In dollar notation, the first place to the left of the decimal point. In the amount $3.47, 3 is in the dollars place.

Dot Array An arrangement of dots in rows and columns.

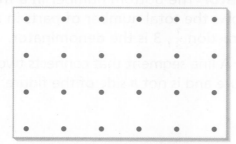

edge The line segment where two faces of a solid figure meet.

elapsed time The time that passes between the beginning and end of an event.

equal (=) Having the same value as that of another quantity or expression. $3 + 1 = 4$ is read as 3 plus 1 is equal to 4.

equal groups Concept used in multiplication and division situations. $5 \times 6 = 30$. There are 5 equal groups of 6 items.

Equal Shares drawing A drawing which children create that represents factors and products. It is a numerical form of a Repeated Groups drawing.

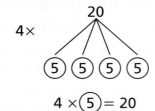

$$4 \times \boxed{5} = 20$$

equally likely outcomes In probability, events that have the same chance of occurring.

equation A mathematical sentence with an equals sign. $11 + 22 = 33$ $75 - 25 = 50$

equilateral triangle A triangle whose sides are all the same length.

equivalence chain A series of equivalent fractions connected with equal signs.
$$\frac{1}{2} = \frac{2}{4} = \frac{4}{8} = \frac{8}{16}$$

equivalent fractions Fractions that name the same amount. $\frac{1}{2}$ and $\frac{2}{4}$ are equivalent fractions.

estimate A number close to an exact amount. About how many or about how much.

evaluate To find the value of a mathematical expression.

even number A whole number that is a multiple of 2. The ones digit in an even number is 0, 2, 4, 6, or 8.

event In probability, a possible outcome.

expanded form A number written to show the value of each of its digits.
Examples: 347 = 300 + 40 + 7
347 = 3 hundreds + 4 tens + 7 ones

expression A combination of numbers and operation signs. 4 + 7

F

face A flat surface of a solid figure.

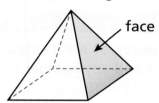

face

factors Numbers that are multiplied to give a product. In the equation 4 × 5 = 20, 4 and 5 are factors.

Fast-Area drawing A representation of an area model that students can sketch quickly to label the units appropriately on a rectangle.

	6 ft			6 ft
7 ft	?		7 ft	42 sq ft

Fast-Array drawing A representation of an array that shows a missing factor or missing product.

```
        10
     ooooooooooo
     o
  5  o   ┌────┐
     o   │ 50 │
     o   └────┘
     o
```

fewer Fewer is used to compare two quantities that can be counted. There are fewer red books than blue books. Less is used to compare two quantities that can be measured. There is less water than juice. *See comparison language.*

flip To reflect a figure over a line. The size and shape of the figure remain the same.

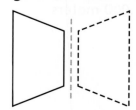

fluid ounce (fl oz) A customary unit of capacity equal to 2 tablespoons.

foot (ft) A customary unit used to measure length. 1 foot = 12 inches

formula An equation with variables that describes a rule. The formula for the area of a rectangle is: $A = l \times w$, where A is the area, l is the length, and w is the width.

fraction A number that names part of a whole or part of a set.

fraction bar A visual representation of a whole divided into equal parts. The fraction bar shown here represents one-third.

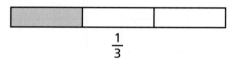

$\frac{1}{3}$

fraction strip Strips of paper divided into equal unit fractional parts that students can fold to explore equivalent fractions.

fracture To divide into smaller equal parts.

front-end estimation A method of estimating that uses the largest place value in a number. In the equation 527 + 673 = ☐, you would round 527 to 500 and 673 to 600 for a total of 1,100.

function A set of ordered pairs such that no two ordered pairs have the same first member.

function table A table of ordered pairs that shows a function.

Rule: add 2	
Input	Output
1	3
2	4
3	5
4	6

G

gallon (gal) A customary unit used to measure capacity. 1 gallon = 4 quarts = 16 cups

Teacher Glossary (Continued)

gram (g) A metric unit of mass.
1,000 grams = 1 kilogram

greater than (>) Having a value that is more than that of another quantity or expression. 6 > 5 is read as 6 is greater than 5.

group To combine numbers to form new tens, hundreds, thousands, and so on.

growing pattern A number or geometric pattern that increases.
Examples: 2, 4, 6, 8, 10 ...
1, 2, 5, 10, 17 ...

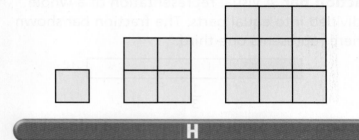

H

half turn A 180° rotation.

height In geometry, the length of a perpendicular line segment from a vertex to the opposite side of a plane figure.

hexagon A six-sided polygon.

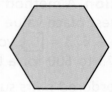

horizontal Extending in two directions, left and right parallel to the horizon.

hundred box In a place value drawing, a square box representing that 10 ten-sticks equal one hundred. A hundred box is a quick way of drawing 100.

hundred
boxes

hundredth One of the equal parts when a whole is divided into 100 equal parts.

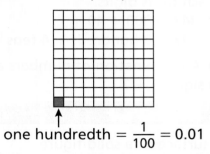

one hundredth = $\frac{1}{100}$ = 0.01

I

Identity Property of Multiplication The product of 1 and any number equals that number. $1 \times 10 = 10$

improper fraction A fraction in which the numerator is equal to or is greater than the denominator. Improper fractions are equal to or greater than 1. $\frac{8}{8}$ and $\frac{8}{3}$ are improper fractions.

inch (in.) A customary unit used to measure length. 12 inches = 1 foot

inequality A statement that two expressions are not equal.

input In a function or rule, the value that is entered into the function or rule to produce an output.

inverse operations Opposite or reverse operations that undo each other. Addition and subtraction are inverse operations. Multiplication and division are inverse operations.

isosceles triangle A triangle that has at least two sides of the same length.

K

key A part of a map, graph, or chart that explains what symbols mean.

kilogram (kg) A metric unit of mass.
1 kilogram = 1,000 grams

kilometer (km) A metric unit of length.
1 kilometer = 1,000 meters

L

less than (<) Having a value that is less than that of another quantity or expression. 5 < 6 is read as 5 is less than 6.

line A straight path that goes on forever in opposite directions.

line graph A graph that uses a straight line or a broken line to show changes in data.

line of reflection A line around or over which a figure is flipped to produce a mirror image of the figure. Each point of the original figure and flipped figure is the same distance from the line.

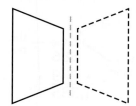

line of symmetry A line on which a figure can be folded so that the two halves match exactly.

line plot A way to show data using a number line.

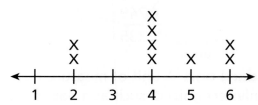

line segment A part of a line. A line segment has two endpoints.

line symmetry A figure has line symmetry if it can be folded along a line so the two halves match exactly.

liter (L) A metric unit used to measure capacity. 1 liter = 1,000 milliliters

M

Make a Hundred Strategy An addition or subtraction strategy in which the student finds the 100-partner of the larger addend and then breaks apart the other addend into that 100-partner and the rest to find the total.
To add 80 + 70 using the Make a Hundred strategy, the student finds the 100-partner for 80 which is 20, breaks apart 70, the other addend, into 20 + 50 and then adds the rest, 50, to 100. Thus, 100 + 50 = 150 so 80 + 70 = 150.

Make a Ten Strategy An addition strategy in which students find the 10-partner. To add 7 + 9, the student finds the 10-partner for 9 which is 1, breaks apart 7, the other addend, into 1 + 6 and then adds the rest, 6, to 10. Thus, 10 + 6 = 16, so 7 + 9 = 16.

Make a Thousand Strategy An addition strategy in which the student finds the 1,000-partner of the larger addend and then breaks apart the other addend into that 1,000-partner and the rest to find the total.
To add 800 + 700 using the Make a Thousand strategy, the student finds the 1,000-partner for 800 which is 200, breaks apart 700, the other addend, into 200 + 500 and then adds the rest, 500, to 1,000. Thus, 1,000 + 500 = 1,500 so 800 + 700 = 1500.

mass The amount of matter in an object. (Mass is constant; weight varies because weight is the effect of gravity on matter.)

Math Mountain A visual representation of the partners and totals of a number. The total (*sum*) appears at the top and the two partners (*addends*) that are added to produce the total are below to the left and right.

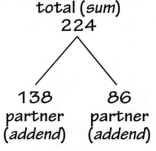

mean (average) The number found by dividing the sum of a group of numbers by the number of addends. For the set of numbers 3, 5, 4, 8: 3 + 5 + 4 + 8 = 20, 20 ÷ 4 = 5, 5 is the mean.

median The middle number when a set of numbers is arranged in order from least to greatest. For an even number of numbers, the median is the average of the two middle numbers.

Teacher Glossary (Continued)

mental math A way to solve problems without using pencil and paper, or a calculator.

meter (m) A metric unit used to measure length. 1 meter = 100 centimeters

method A procedure, or way of doing something.

mile (mi) A customary unit of length. 1 mile = 5,280 feet

milliliter (mL) A metric unit used to measure capacity. 1,000 milliliters = 1 liter

mixed number A whole number and a fraction. $1\frac{3}{4}$ is a mixed number.

mode The number that occurs most often in a set of data. In this set of numbers {3, 4, 5, 5, 5, 7, 8}, 5 is the mode.

multiple A number that is the product of the given number and another number.

Multiplication Table An array of numbers with rows and columns labeled from 1 through 12. The product of the labels is found in the cell where the row and column intersect.

multiplier One of the factors in a multiplication equation. In the 9s count-bys or multiplications, each of the numbers that 9 is multiplied by, is the multiplier.

multiplier finger Used with the multiplication strategy Quick 9s strategy, the bent finger that indicates the number that 9 is being multiplied by.

3 tens   6 ones

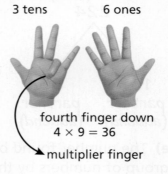

fourth finger down
4 × 9 = 36

multiplier finger

---

net A flat pattern that can be folded to make a solid figure. This net is for a rectangular prism.

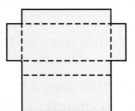

New Groups Above Method A strategy for multi-digit addition. The new groups are placed above the existing groups. This is the current, common method of addition.

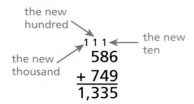

the new hundred

the new ten

the new thousand

$$\begin{array}{r} {\scriptstyle 1\ 1\ 1} \\ 586 \\ +\ 749 \\ \hline 1{,}335 \end{array}$$

New Groups Below Method A strategy for multi-digit addition. The new groups are placed below the existing groups on the line waiting to be added.

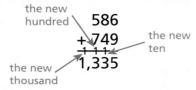

the new hundred

the new ten

the new thousand

$$\begin{array}{r} 586 \\ +\ 749 \\ {\scriptstyle 1\ 1\ 1} \\ \hline 1{,}335 \end{array}$$

non-standard unit A unit of measure not commonly recognized, such as a paper clip. An inch and a centimeter are standard units of measure.

non-unit fraction A fraction that is built from unit fractions. $\frac{2}{3}$ is a non-unit fraction. It is built from the unit fractions $\frac{1}{3} + \frac{1}{3}$.

number sentence Numbers and expressions related to each other using one of these symbols: =, <, or >.

numerator The top number in a fraction that shows the number of equal parts counted. In the fraction $\frac{1}{3}$, 1 is the numerator.

---

obtuse angle An angle that measures more than 90° but less than 180°.

obtuse triangle A triangle with one angle that measures more than 90°.

octagon An eight-sided figure

odd number A whole number that is not a multiple of 2. The ones digit in an odd number is 1, 3, 5, 7, or 9.

operation A mathematical process. Addition, subtraction, multiplication, division, and raising a number to a power are operations.

opposite sides Sides that are across from each other; they do not meet at a point. In this example, sides *a* and *c* are opposite.

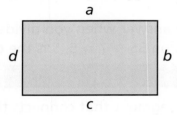

ordered pair A pair of numbers such as (3, 4) in which one number is considered to be first and the other number second. They can name a point on a coordinate grid.

Order of Operations A set of rules that state in which order operations should be performed.
• Compute inside parentheses first
• Multiply and divide in order from left to right
• Add and subtract in order from left to right

ordinal numbers Numbers used to show order or position. For example, first, second, fifth.

ounce (oz) A customary unit used to measure weight. 16 ounces = 1 pound

output In a function table, the value resulting from a specific input and rule.

parallel The same distance apart everywhere. This can describe lines, line segments, or faces of a solid figure.

parallelogram A quadrilateral with both pairs of opposite sides parallel.

partner One of two numbers that add to make a total. In the equation 9 + 7 = 16, 9 and 7 are the partners.

pennies place In dollar notation, the second place to the right of the decimal point. In the amount $3.47, the 7 is in the pennies place.

pentagon A five-sided figure.

perimeter The distance around the outside of a figure.

perpendicular Two lines, line segments, or rays that cross or meet to form right angles.

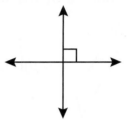

pictograph A graph that uses pictures or symbols to represent data.

pint (pt) A customary unit used to measure capacity. 1 pint = 2 cups

place value The value assigned to the place that a digit occupies in a number.

place value drawing A drawing that represents a number. Thousands are represented by a bar, hundreds are represented by boxes, tens by vertical lines, and ones by small circles.

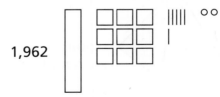

plane A flat surface that extends without end in all directions. It has no thickness.

plane figure A geometric figure that lies entirely in one plane.

P.M. The abbreviation for post meridiem, Latin for after noon. Used to indicate a time after noon.

Teacher Glossary (Continued)

polygon A closed plane figure make up of line segments.

pound (lb) A customary unit used to measure weight. 1 pound = 16 ounces

prism A solid figure with two parallel congruent bases, and rectangles or parallelograms for faces. A prism is named by the shape of its bases.

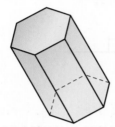

hexagonal prism

probability The chance of an event occurring.

product The answer when you multiply numbers. In the equation $4 \times 7 = 28$, 28 is the product.

proof drawing A drawing used to show that an answer is correct.

$$
\begin{array}{r}
249 \\
+ 386 \\
\underline{11} \\
635
\end{array}
$$

put together problem A problem that involves putting together (combining, joining) groups of things to form a total.

pyramid A solid figure with one base and whose other faces are triangles with a common vertex. A pyramid is named by the shape of its base.

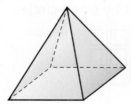

square pyramid

Q

quadrilateral A figure with four sides.

quart (qt) A customary unit used to measure capacity. 1 quart = 4 cups

quarter turn A 90° rotation.

Quick 9s A short-cut for multiplying by 9 in which students bend down one finger to represent the multiplier. The remaining fingers to the left of the bent finger represent the tens digit of the product and the fingers to the right of the bent finger represent the ones digit of the product.

3 tens   6 ones

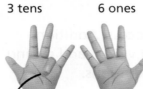

This method works because
$3 \times 9 = 3 \times (10 - 1) = 30 - 3 = 27$

fourth finger down
$4 \times 9 = 36$

multiplier finger

quotient The answer when you divide numbers. In the equation $35 \div 7 = 5$, 5 is the quotient.

R

radius A line segment that connects the center of a circle to any point on the circle. The term is also used to describe the length of such a line segment.

range The difference between the greatest number and the least number in a set of data. In this set of numbers {12, 15, 18, 19, 20}, the range is $20 - 12$ or 8.

ray A part of a line that has one endpoint and goes on forever in one direction.

rectangle A parallelogram that has 4 right angles.

reflection (flip) A transformation that involves flipping a figure over a line. The size and shape of the figure remain the same.

reflectional symmetry See **line symmetry**.

remainder In division, the quantity that is left over which is not large enough to make another whole group. In the division example, 32 divided by 6, the quotient is 5 with a remainder of 2. There are 5 groups of 6 and one more group that has only 2 items (the remainder).

repeated addition An introduction to multiplication in which students add the same number (3) several times (4) to show that $3 + 3 + 3 + 3$ produces the same result as 4×3.

Repeated Groups drawing A drawing which children create that represents factors and products.

4 × 5 = 20

repeated groups problem A type of multiplication word problem that involves multiple groups with the same number of items in each group.

repeating pattern A pattern consisting of a group of numbers, letters, or figures that repeat. Examples: 1, 2, 1, 2, …
A, B, C, A, B, C, …

rhombus A parallelogram with congruent sides.

right angle An angle that measures 90°.

right triangle A triangle with one right angle.

rotation (turn) A transformation that involves a turn of a figure about a point. The size and shape of the figure remain the same.

round To find *about* how many or how much by expressing a number to the nearest ten, hundred, thousand, and so on.

route The path taken to get to a location.

row A horizontal group of cells in table.

rule In a pattern such as a function table or number sequence, what is done to the first number to get to the second number and so on. The rule *Add 3* is shown in the function table.

Add 3.	
0	3
1	4
2	5
3	6

The rule $n + 7$ is shown in the number sequence: 2, 9, 16, 23 . . . .

S

scale An arrangement of numbers in order with equal intervals.

scalene triangle A triangle with sides of three different lengths.

Secret Code Cards Cards printed with the digits 0 through 9, multiples of 10 from 10 through 90 and multiples of 100 from 100 through 1,000. The number is represented on the back of the card by dots, sticks, or boxes. The cards are used to teach place value.

1 0 0 0	9 0 0	8 0	3
Thousands Card	Hundreds Card	Tens Card	Ones Card

Assembled Cards

set A group of numbers or other things.

Show All Totals Method A method for finding a total of multi-digit numbers.

```
                   586
the new
thousand  ——→  + 749
the new        1,200
hundred  ——→    120
the new  ——→     15
ten           ———————
              1,335
```

Teacher Glossary (Continued)

shrinking pattern A number or geometric pattern that decreases.
Example: 15, 12, 9, 6, 3,...
25, 20, 16, 13, 11,...

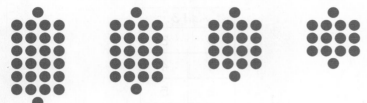

side (of a plane figure) A line segment that makes up a plane figure.

simplify To write an equivalent fraction with a smaller numerator and denominator.

situation equation An equation children write to show a story problem situation. It may or may not have the unknown isolated on one side of the equals sign.

slide To move a figure along a line. The size and shape of the figure remain the same.

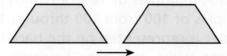

solid figure A figure that has three dimensions.

solution equation A situation equation that has been rewritten so that the unknown is alone on one side of the equals sign. It is related to the operation needed to solve the problem rather than to the actions in the story problem.

sphere A solid figure shaped like a ball.

square A rectangle with four sides of the same length.

square number A product of a whole number and itself. 4 × 4 = 16, so 16 is a square number.

square unit Unit used to measure area that is 1 unit on each side. A square foot, for example, is a unit that is 1 foot on each side.

standard form The name of a number written using digits. For example, 1,829.

standard unit A recognized unit of measure, such as an inch or centimeter.

straight angle An angle that measures 180°.

strategy cards Cards that display a multiplication or division exercise on one side. The other side shows the answer to the exercise, the count-bys (up to the product) for both factors, and a Fast-Array drawing that shows the product and the two factors.

sum The answer when adding two or more addends. In the equation 37 + 52 = 89, 89 is the sum.

survey A method of collecting information.

symmetry A figure has symmetry if it can be folded along a line so that the two halves match exactly.

T

table An easy to read arrangement of data, organized in rows and columns.

take apart problem A problem that involves separating a group of objects.

tally marks A group of lines drawn in order to count. Each mark stands for 1 unit.

 means 13
5 5 3

ten stick In a place value drawing a vertical line used to represent 10.

ten stick

tenth One of the equal parts when a whole is divided into ten equal parts.

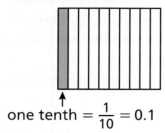

one tenth $= \frac{1}{10} = 0.1$

thousand bar In a place value drawing, a bar used to represent 1,000. A thousand bar is a quick way of drawing 1,000.

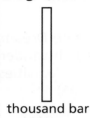

thousand bar

three-dimensional figure A figure with three dimensions.

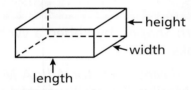

total The sum of two or more numbers. In the equation 672 + 228 = 900, 900 is the total.

transformation One of three basic motions: reflection (flip), rotation (turn), and translation (slide).

translation (slide) A transformation that involves sliding a figure along a line. The size and shape of the figure remain the same.

trapezoid A quadrilateral with exactly one pair of parallel sides.

turn To rotate a figure around a point. The size and shape of the figure remain the same.

two-dimensional figure A figure with two dimensions.

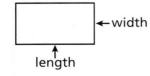

---

ungroup To break into a new group in order to be able to subtract.

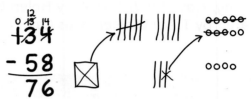

unit fraction A fraction with a numerator of 1.

Venn diagram A diagram that uses circles to show the relationship among sets of objects.

At least one pair   Exactly two sides
of parallel sides   of equal length

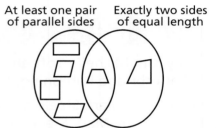

vertex A point where sides, rays, or edges meet.

vertex   vertex   vertex

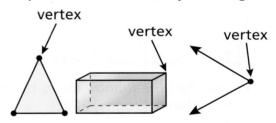

vertical Extending in two directions, up and down.

volume The measure of the amount of space occupied by an object.

weight The measure of how heavy something is. (Weight varies because weight is the effect of gravity on matter; mass is constant.)

word form A name of a number written using words instead of digits. For example, nine hundred eighty-four.

yard (yd) A customary unit used to measure length. 1 yard = 3 feet

Recommended Books

Unit 1

How Much, How Many, How Far, How Heavy, How Long, How Tall Is 1000?, by Helen Nolan, illustrated by Tracy Walker (Kids Can Press, 1995)

Unit 2

Grandfather Tang's Story: A Tale Told with Tangrams, by Ann Tompert, illustrated by Robert Andrew Parker (Bantam Doubleday Dell Books for Young Readers, 1997)

Unit 3

One Less Fish, by Kim Michelle Toft and Allen Sheather (Charlesbridge Publishing, 1998)

A Bundle of Beasts, by Mark Steele and Patricia Hooper, illustrated by Mark Steele (Houghton Mifflin, 1987)

Unit 4

Sam Johnson and the Blue Ribbon Quilt, by Lisa Campbell Ernst (HarperTrophy, 2002)

Unit 5

Amanda Bean's Amazing Dream: A Mathematical Story, by Cindy Neuschwander, illustrated by Liza Woodruff, Math Activities by Marilyn Burns (Scholastic Press, 1998)

The Greatest Gymnast of All, by Stuart J. Murphy, illustrated by Cynthia Jabar (HarperTrophy, 1998)

Unit 6

One Hundred Hungry Ants, by Elinor J. Pinczes, illustrated by Bonnie Mackain (Houghton Mifflin Company, 1993)

One Grain of Rice, by Demi (Scholastic Press, 1997)

Unit 7

A Grain of Rice, by Helena Clare Pittman (Yearling, 1995)

Amanda Bean's Amazing Dream: A Mathematical Story, by Cindy Neuschwander, illustrated by Liza Woodruff, Math Activities by Marilyn Burns (Scholastic Press, 1998)

Unit 8

Building with Shapes, by Rebecca Weber (Compass Point Books, 2005)

Spaghetti and Meatballs for All!: A Mathematical Story, by Marilyn Burns, illustrated by Debbie Tilley (Scholastic Press, 1997)

Unit 9

The Doorbell Rang, by Pat Hutchins (Greenwillow Books, 1986)

Sea Squares, by Joy N. Hulme, illustrated by Carol Schwartz (Hyperion Books, 1993)

Unit 10

Jumanji, by Chris Van Allsburg (Houghton Mifflin Company, 1981)

Secret Treasures and Magical Measures: Adventures in Measurement: Temperature, Time, Length, Weight, Volume, Angles, Shapes, and Money, by Chris Kensler (Simon & Schuster, 2003)

Recommended Books (Continued)

Unit 11

Fraction Fun, by David A. Adler, illustrated by Nancy Tobin (Holiday House, 1996)

The Big Orange Splot, by Daniel Manus Pinkwater (Rebound by Sagebrush, 1999)

Jump, Kangaroo, Jump!, by Stuart J. Murphy, illustrated by Kevin O'Malley (HarperTrophy, 1999)

Mega-Fun Fractions, by Martin Lee and Marcia Miller (Teaching Resources, 2002)

The Fraction Family Heads West, by Marti Dryk, Ph.D., illustrated by Trevor Romain, D.M. (Bookaloppy Press, 1997)

Piece = Part = Portion: Fractions = Decimals = Percents, by Scott Gifford, photographs by Shmuel Thaler (Tricycle Press, 2003)

A Remainder of One, by Elinor J. Pinczes, illustrated by Bonnie Mackain (Houghton Mifflin, 1995)

The Great Divide, by Dayle Ann Dodds, illustrated by Tracy Mitchell (Candlewick Press, 2005)

Unit 12

Building with Shapes, by Rebecca Weber (Compass Point Books, 2005)

Unit 13

Penguins at Home: Gentoos of Antartica, by Bruce McMillan (Houghton Mifflin Company, 1993)

Room for Ripley, by Stuart J. Murphy, illustrated by Sylvie Wickstrom (HarperTrophy, 1999)

How Tall, How Short, How Faraway?, by David A. Adler, illustrated by Nancy Tobin (Holiday House, 2000)

Unit 14

Alice Ramsey's Grand Adventure, by Don Brown (Houghton Mifflin Company, 1997)

Index

D

Index (Continued)

Index (Continued)

M

Index (Continued)

Index (Continued)

Multicultural Connection
  Chinese Multiplication Table, 744
  Egyptian Fractions, 892
  Foods from Around the World, 76
  International Coins, 28
  Math Haikus, 586

Multiplication
  algebraic notation method,
    1128–1130, 1141–1143
  Associative Property, 581–583
  by 0, 578–580, 582–584
  by 1, 483, 576–578, 582–584
  by 2, 500–503, 507, 535
  by 3, 537–538, 535
  by 4, 560–561
  by 5, 458–465, 476–477, 490, 497,
    500, 507
  by 6, 535, 639–641
  by 7, 674–676
  by 8, 656–659
  by 9, 518–522, 529, 535, 554
  by 10, 511–514
  common multiples, 690, 823
  Commutative Property, 483–486, 538,
    561, 581–583
  Distributive Property, 565, 663, 678
  doubles, 562
  equations, 490–496, 554–556,
    582–584, 638–644, 648, 656–661
  estimate products, 1121, 1158–1159,
    1161
  Expanded Notation method,
    1128–1130, 1141–1143
  models
      area, 510–511, 548–551,
        563–565, 644, 659, 667–668,
        1108–1113, 1122, 1125,
        1140–1141
      arrays, 475–488, 525, 533,
        569, 585, 667–668, 671,
        1108–1113
      base ten blocks, *See* Base
        ten blocks.
      connecting cubes, 479, 503, 519
      counters, 585
      Equal Groups, 935, 1164
      equal shares drawings, 471, 482,
        564
      fast-area drawings, 651, 659
      fast-array drawings, 531,
        569–570, 661–662, 679
      math drawing, 470
      number line, 502
      Rectangle Sections method,
        1128–1130, 1140–1143
  multi-digit
      1-digit by 2-digit, 730,
        1109–1110, 1122–1124,
        1128–1131, 1134–1136

  1-digit by 3-digit, 730,
    1140–1142, 1146–1148
  2-digit by 2-digit, 1111
  multiplicative identity, 483, 576–578,
    582–584
  relate 9s and 10s, 519–520, 525
  relate to addition, 460–461
  relate to division, 490–496
  repeated addition, 460, 640–641,
    645, 667–668, 1125, 1164
  repeated groups, 468–470, 473, 479,
    484, 659, 667–668
  Shortcut method, 1135
  square numbers, 703–707
  using factors and multiples to divide,
    1152–1155
  using multiples, 556, 823, 1116–1119
  using patterns, 458, 461, 465,
    501–502, 511–512, 518–520, 529,
    537–538, 556, 560–561, 576–579,
    639–640, 656–658, 674–675,
    704–705, 1116–1119, 1133
  word problems, 505, 514, 530, 555,
    595, 667–671

Music Connection
  Bottle Xylophone, 1038
  Count the Beats, 566
  Multiplication Rap, 526
  Musical Notes, 884
  Rap a Round, 306

N

NCTM correlations
  Curriculum Focal Points and
    Connections, xl–xlii, 9D–9E,
    137D–137E, 175D–175E,
    251D–251E, 291D–291F, 433C,
    457D–457F, 609B, 637D–637E,
    755B, 781D–781G,
    951D–951E, 989D–989E, 1079B
  Standards and Expectations, xliii–li,
    9D–9E, 137D–137E, 175D–175E,
    251D–251E, 291D–291F, 433C,
    457D–457F, 609B, 637D–637E,
    755B, 781D–781G, 951D–951E,
    989D–989E, 1079B

Nets, 952–954, 968–971, 974, 976–977

New Groups Above method, 44, 47–48

New Groups Below method, 44, 47

Number line, 294, 422, 460, 502
  find the distance between two
    points on a, 894
  identify and locate fractions on a,
    894–898, 918, 1042
  identify and locate mixed numbers
    on a, 895, 918

  identify and locate whole numbers
    on, 894

Number sentence, 182–183, 220, 230,
  581–584

Numbers. *See* Whole numbers.

O

Octagons, 275–276, 995, 1019

Odd numbers, 57, 113, 197, 505, 602, 748
  resulting sums of, 748

Ongoing Assessment, in every lesson

Open–Ended problems, solve, 333, 722

Order
  decimals, 909–910
  fractions, 888, 895
  whole numbers 310, 313, 1103

Order of operations, 726–727

Ordered pair, 1086–1089, 1092–1095

Organized lists, 41, 327, 532

P

Parallel
  lines, 147–148, 252
  line segments, 147–148, 252,
    1093–1094

Parallelogram, 148, 152–155, 157,
  160–163, 166–169, 252, 275–276
  rectangle, 142, 148, 153–155, 157,
    160–163, 166–169, 252
  rhombus, 153, 163, 166–169, 252
  square, 142, 153–154, 157, 160–163,
    166–169, 252

Partner, 107, 113, 122
  unknown partner, 189–191, 194

Patterns, analyzing, creating,
  extending, describing, recognizing
  calculator, 441, 446, 598, 645
  calendar, 59, 682
  count-bys and multiplication, 458,
    461, 465, 501–502, 511–512,
    518–519, 529, 537–538, 560–561,
    576–578, 639–640, 656–658,
    674–675, 704–705
  functions and function tables. *See*
    Functions.
  growing, 29, 223, 446–447, 619, 665,
    803, 1031
  in tables, 349–350
  money, 75, 223, 321, 665
  non-numeric, 151, 435, 437, 442–443,
    447, 451, 619, 815

Index (Continued)

Index (Continued)

189, 201, 202–204, 216, 217–218, 219, 220, 224–226, 227–228, 229, 234–237, 257, 302, 312, 320, 324, 331, 338–339, 340, 349, 354–355, 370, 379, 384–388, 392–394, 470, 471, 481, 482, 493, 495–496, 514, 530, 541, 542, 555, 584, 595, 615, 616, 651, 667, 680, 687, 688, 698, 741, 922, 930, 931, 999, 1036, 1124, 1136, 1147, 1160

Special Needs, 220, 504, 842, 1124

Spheres, 982–983

Sports Connection
Baseball Ticket Prices, 120
Lines Around You, 150
Numbers in Sports, 544
Sports Problems, 198
What Figure Is It?, 984

Square Numbers, 703–707

Step-by-Step at the Board, 56, 74, 82–84

Strategy Cards, 547–548, 569–573, 589, 597, 711

Student Leaders
In Activities, 20, 218, 486, 1105, 1147
Quick Practice, 19, 29, 37, 43, 51, 59, 65, 71, 77, 87, 97, 105, 115, 121, 175, 187, 193, 199, 209, 215, 223, 233, 291, 299, 307, 315, 323, 329, 335, 343, 353, 363, 369, 375, 383, 391, 399, 409, 417, 467, 475, 489, 499, 701, 709, 715, 725, 733, 739, 781, 791, 797, 803, 809, 823, 829, 841, 849, 855, 863, 869, 875, 885, 893, 901, 913, 921, 927, 935, 989, 997, 1003, 1013, 1021, 1031, 1039, 1045, 1063
The Learning Classroom. *See* Learning Classroom, The.

Student Pairs, 62, 73, 102, 112, 118, 123, 128, 140, 154, 205–206, 230, 238, 271, 275, 283, 284, 303, 312, 326, 350, 402, 406, 435, 447, 476–477, 490, 500, 510, 518, 528, 532, 536, 546, 554, 555, 560, 568, 576, 584, 588, 589, 590, 648, 656, 666, 674, 684, 694, 702, 716, 726, 734, 736, 740, 742, 760, 767, 820, 834, 835, 836, 838, 931, 953, 958, 961, 962, 1023, 1025, 1026, 1081, 1086, 1087, 1093, 1118, 1135

Helping Pairs, 38, 53, 61, 102, 117, 139, 228, 282, 332, 348, 378, 404, 472, 494, 531, 555, 613, 729, 736, 757, 760, 768, 819, 961, 1026, 1036, 1082, 1093, 1123

Subtraction, 4–7, 54–55, 78–85, 128
across zeros, 88–90, 93, 115
basic subtractions, 4–5, 7, 72–75, 78–85
common U.S. method, 80
counting on by hundreds strategy, 55
counting on by ones strategy, 1B, 5–6
counting on by tens strategy, 54
estimate differences, 292–297, 302, 304, 417, 587, 701, 829, 1104–1105
equations, 176–180, 217–218, 234–237
Expanded Method, 80
fractions, 886–887, 889–891, 897–898
in other countries, 80
larger numbers
4-digit number subtracted from 4-digit number, 94, 112, 117, 119, 122, 125
5-digit number subtracted from 5-digit number, 124, 1103–1104
5-digit number subtracted from 6-digit number, 1104
make a hundred strategy, 55
make a ten strategy, 6, 643, 660, 678
make a thousand strategy, 55
money, 65, 91–92, 101–103, 118, 123, 233, 323, 391, 439, 457, 575, 1091
multi-digit
2-digit number subtracted from 3-digit number, 55, 106–110
3-digit number subtracted from 3-digit number, 88–95, 98–100, 103
3-digit number subtracted from 4-digit number, 94
relate addition and subtraction, 106–111, 122, 188
Ungroup First method, 80, 88–90
ungrouping, 78–84, 88–90, 98–100, 110–111, 117
using proof drawings, 78–79, 81–83, 88–93, 98–100, 102, 106, 108, 112
vertical format, 93–94
whole dollar amounts, 91–92
with base ten blocks, 85, 103, 106
word problems, 78–80, 88–90, 116–117, 849, 1103

Sum, 176–177
See also Addition.

Survey, 406, 600
conducting, 406, 416, 600–601
resulting data, 367, 406, 499, 600–601, 733, 841, 1101
using data from, 367, 406, 1101

Symbols
cent sign, 23
division, 492
dollar sign, 23

equals sign, 16, 182–183, 220, 308–312
is greater than, 16, 220, 308–312
is less than, 16, 220, 308–312
is not equal to, 182–183
multiplication, 462
right angle, 268

Symmetry, 253–255, 257, 264, 475, 951

T

Tables, 344–351
analyze data from, 344–351, 354–357, 420, 1170
cell, 344
column, 344
compare data from, 354–357, 1170
complete missing cells, 347–348, 356–357, 367
finding and writing patterns for data in, 349–350
frequency tables, 418–421
function tables, 350, 472, 565, 585, 642–643, 645, 660, 677–678, 681, 1170
making, 351, 361, 364–365, 367, 467, 673, 863
row, 344–345
solve problems using, 346–348, 354–355, 358–359, 467, 673, 863
using data from, 347–348

Tally chart, 406, 499, 600–601, 913, 1101

Tally mark, 406

Teaching Note
Another Common Method, 80
Algebraic Expressions, 660
A Statue Where You Live, 242
Benchmarks and Comparing Fractions, 896
Common Error, 903, 906
Commutativity, 538 561
Creating Collections, 128
Critical Thinking, 227, 512, 785
Faster Ten-Sticks, 10
Fractions, 686
Help the Teacher, 72
Home Practice Charts, 539
Homework, 14
Language and Vocabulary, 11, 45, 52, 79, 110, 138, 146, 152, 177, 190, 200, 203, 210, 216, 254, 268, 317, 330, 336, 344, 364, 377, 401, 410, 436, 458, 463, 496, 519, 650, 687, 768, 782, 824, 830, 870, 871, 877, 915, 931, 993, 1040, 1052, 1152
Make a Tens-Number Strategy, 643
Making Drawings, 530

Index (Continued)

Z